PRAISE FOR *A SORROW IN OUR HEART*

"One of those rare books pulling the reader so effectively into another world that the realities of life in the here and now appear alien when one emerges reluctantly from the pages."
—*The Washington Post Book World*

"It is hard to imagine an author better qualified to write a definitive biography of Tecumseh than Allan W. Eckert. . . . Eckert's astounding breadth of knowledge is on full display."
—*The Plain Dealer,* Cleveland

"Only someone with Eckert's skill and background could have reached back through two centuries of tangled historical records to give us such an intimate account of Tecumseh's life. . . . [A] rich and probing epic."
—*Detroit Free Press*

"If by some magic Tecumseh could have chosen his own biographer, he surely would have named Allan Eckert."
—Dee Brown, author of *Bury My Heart at Wounded Knee*

THE *NARRATIVES OF AMERICA* SERIES

"Vigorous, engrossing."
—*Chicago Tribune*

"Swiftly paced with a dramatic flair."
—*Kirkus Reviews*

"Crackling . . . vibrant."
—*Detroit Free Press*

Chronicles of the Ohio River Valley

That DARK *and* BLOODY RIVER

Allan W. Eckert

BANTAM BOOKS

New York   Toronto   London   Sydney   Auckland

THAT DARK AND BLOODY RIVER

PUBLISHING HISTORY

Bantam hardcover edition / December 1995
Bantam trade paperback edition / October 1996

ISBN 0-553-37865-1

Published simultaneously in the United States and Canada

Bantam Books are published by Bantam Books, a division of Bantam Doubleday Dell Publishing Group,
Inc. Its trademark, consisting of the words "Bantam Books" and the portrayal of a rooster, is Registered in
U.S. Patent and Trademark Office and in other countries. Marca Registrada. Bantam Books, 1540 Broad-
way, New York, New York 10036.

PRINTED IN THE UNITED STATES OF AMERICA

FFG   20   19   18   17   16   15   14

To my friend and blood-brother,
fellow historian, screenwriter, and
knifemaker extraordinaire,
PHILLIP W. HOFFMAN—*Walking Hawk*
of Westlake Village, California,
this book is dedicated
with
appreciation and affection

Our system is to live in perpetual peace with the Indians, to cultivate an affectionate attachment for them by everything just and liberal which we can do for them within the bounds of reason and by giving them effectual protection against the wrongs from our own people. When they withdraw themselves to the culture of a small piece of land, they will perceive how useless to them are the extensive forests and will be willing to pare them off in exchange for necessaries for their farms and families. To promote this, we shall push our trading houses, and be glad to see the good and influential individuals among them in debt, because we observe when these debts go beyond what the individual can pay, they become willing to lop them off by a cession of lands. But should any tribe refuse the proffered hand and take up the hatchet, it will be driven across the Mississippi and the whole of its lands confiscated.

        — PRESIDENT THOMAS JEFFERSON
          Excerpt from a letter written to
          Indiana Territory governor
          William Henry Harrison

Maps

Author's Note

In writing a history of the Ohio River and the struggle for dominance in the great Ohio River Valley, it has been the author's aim to present as much fresh material as possible: accounts of the people and events heretofore bypassed or only lightly touched upon in his other historical works in which the Ohio River played a significant role. As a result, in this work much more will be found about the lives of the Wetzel family, the Zanes and the Bradys, among others, than was possible in earlier works. The same holds true of much of the anecdotal material that has been tapped from early documentation—the letters, diaries, journals, reports and similar data.

By the same token, however, there are important events that could not be overlooked in this book simply because the author discussed them in a previous work. Thus, events that were critical in the shaping of the history of the Ohio River have been touched upon again here, such as the Battle of Point Pleasant, the expeditions of Henry Bouquet, Edward Hand, George Rogers Clark, Josiah Harmar, Arthur St. Clair, Anthony Wayne and others. Where this occurs, an effort has been made to depict the event from another viewpoint than previously done, incorporating new, expanded, or corrective material where possible. If not possible, then the event, in some cases, is portrayed with less detail than before and reference is made in the Amplification Notes to a more detailed account that appears in one of the author's previous works. The goal in all cases has been to present the events, if at all possible, from the perspective of characters who were previously less fully developed.

Quite often there are several—or even many—accounts of the same event in the historical record, and with dismaying frequency those accounts differ considerably one from another. Deciding which to select, of such accounts, as the most accurate portrayal of the event involved is often very difficult; the actual participants who wrote about it then or later not infrequently had their own personal biases that may have led them to incorrectly or unfairly state what occurred. Where discrepancies do occur in the historical record, greater reliance has been placed upon those written by observers or participants who have established a reputation for accuracy, though sometimes a divergent account will be interesting or intriguing enough that it is discussed in the Amplification Notes section.

This book is written in the form that the author chooses to call *narrative history,* in which the reader may, as with a good novel, feel himself drawn into the current of events and identify closely with the characters. It is designed to utilize all the better elements of the novel form, for excitement, pace and continuity, yet at the same time strives to remain a reliable, accurate depiction of the history it embraces. In this respect the author uses considerably more dialogue than one normally associates with strictly historical works. Such dialogue is a form of painstakingly *reconstituted* dialogue that lies hidden in abundance in historical material. It is normally written as straight historical commentary, without direct quotes, but in it are couched the keywords that legitimately allow such information, if the effort is made, to be returned to vibrant and meaningful dialogue that remains accurate to the intent and direction of what is occurring at any given time.

That the reader may better understand what is meant by keywords that point to hidden dialogue, it is necessary to show here only a brief paragraph as it actually appears in an original account. The following paragraph appears in the great body of work (close to five hundred volumes of material) called the Draper Papers, housed in the Archives of the Wisconsin Historical Society Library at Madison. The paragraph, dealing with the frontiersman Capt. Samuel Brady, appears on pages 298–99 of volume 2 of the thirty-three-volume series designated S, under the general title of Draper's Notes. By paying close attention to those phrases the author has *specifically* italicized, the reader can easily see how the keywords show a hidden conversation that virtually cries out to be brought back from straight text to lively and accurate dialogue.

> Brady, Francis McQuire, & their party went to the block house. Thomas Wells & another went ahead a short distance, to see. They discovered two young Indians, nearly grown, climbing trees. — these discovered the whites & made their escape. The Indian camp altogether numbered 10 Indians, the two young fellows, & two squaws. At the first alarm both of the squaws ran off, but one soon came back & surrendered herself. Joseph Edgington shot her — *for which Brady blamed him; thought it unkind · & discreditable to make war upon women. Someone volunteered the remark that Edgington, when he shot, supposed he was shooting a warrior.* The thing was dropped, *that being deemed a good excuse.* This was after the affair or attack was over; but *Edgington privately declared he would kill any & every thing in the shape of an Indian whenever he could get the chance, from the size of his fist to any old gray-headed Indian, be they he or she.*

Obviously there is not only hidden dialogue in such a passage, but hidden emotions, thoughts and physical actions as well. These, of course, are the bits and pieces that, when properly and accurately reconstituted, form the flesh and blood that bring to life the bare bones of history.

The many Amplification Notes keyed to the text become quite important to the reader in helping to better understand motivations, geographical locations pinpointed to modern sites, character expansion and enlarged explanation of data touched upon. It is for this reason that the author recommends the reading of the notes where they are numerically indicated in the text; they are not *vital* to understanding, but they are a definite help.

—Allan W. Eckert
Bellefontaine, Ohio
May 1995

Prologue

[Setting the Stage: 700 B.C.—June 1768]

Among the major eastern rivers of the United States, from the great Mississippi eastward, none resisted discovery and exploration longer than the Ohio; nor did any other become the scene of such prolonged violence and bloodshed in its conquest as that which occurred along the Ohio's thousand-mile course before emptying into the midsection of the Mississippi.

The Ohio is a stream that has been known by many names over the years. The Shawnees called it Spaylaywitheepi, while the Miami tribe's designation for it was Causisseppione. The Iroquois referred to it as Oligensipen, meaning "the beautiful river," and the Delawares called it Kitonosipi. The Spanish had two names for it, alternately—the Dono and the Albacha—and the Dutch, on their map of 1708, called it Cubach. One distant tribe, possibly the Cherokee, called it Saboqungo; others referred to it as the Alliwegisipi or the Ouabouskigou. The French, from their very first contact, designated it as the Iroquois had, as "the beautiful river"—La Belle Rivière. The present name, Ohio, most likely derives from the Wyandot name for it —Oheeza; along this same line, a map published in 1710 rather mysteriously listed it as the O-o. Finally, the following year another map came very close to today's usage, calling it the Ochio. In whatever language, it was—by literal translation of most of the names—a river of great beauty.

It was also a river of death.

The first humans known to have existed in the Ohio River Valley were the Adena and Hopewell cultures, the Adenas preceding the Hopewells by a few centuries or more (perhaps as early as 700 B.C.) and erecting their distinctive conical burial mounds along the entire course of the river and its tributaries from the present Wheeling, West Virginia, area down into and including the Mississippi River Valley.

The Hopewells followed in about 400 B.C. with mysterious effigy mounds extending throughout the same region, perhaps most pronounced in present southern Ohio and southern Wisconsin. The two cultures appear to have coexisted for about 800 years, until around A.D. 400. Some accounts claim the Adena Culture continued perhaps 100 years or more after the Hopewells mysteriously vanished, but by the end of the sixth century, both cultures had disappeared, leaving behind only tantalizing remnants of their tenure buried in the amazing mounds they had created.

Exactly when the more modern tribes began inhabiting the Ohio Valley is unknown, but the first of whom we have definite knowledge is the Cahokia Culture in the southern Illinois country, whose realm extended from the Mississippi River eastward to the Vermilion and Embarras rivers, perhaps including the lower Wabash down to the Ohio. This culture reached its peak in A.D. 1045 and then began a slow decline until by 1565 it had ended, although a few remnant branches remained and regrouped into tribes and subtribes called Illinois, Peoria, Mascouten, Vermilion and Kickapoo.

At this time, living on one of the major Ohio River tributaries, the Great Kanawha River, was a little-known and little-understood culture called the Xualae. These were apparently a relatively docile people whose culture peaked in 1526 and remained at that level for a century and a half until 1671, when they were exterminated by war parties of Cherokees from the south.

By this time the Miami tribe—along with their subtribes called Weas, Piankeshaws, Eel Rivers, Ouiatenons and Mississinewas—had risen in power and influence, filling the area from the mouth of the Chicago River southward and eastward throughout the northeastern portion of Illinois, southern Michigan and most of present Indiana and Ohio.

It was a time of flux, with various tribes almost constantly warring with one another. What were loose territorial boundaries one year might be altogether changed the next. Among the only northern tribes strong enough to establish reasonable permanency in location were the Miamis and the five principal tribes of present upper New York State: Seneca, Cayuga, Onondaga, Oneida and Mohawk. Strong though they were, the Miamis were essentially nonbelligerent, unlike their New York counterparts, who lusted for battle, conquest and new territory. For a long while the two fought each other, with neither side gaining an advantage until they finally lapsed into an uneasy neutrality. At length, however, the New York tribes resumed making raids into Miami territory, this time so successfully that they established a few villages along the Iroquois and Kankakee rivers of the Illinois country and in the valley of the Great Kanawha River of present West Virginia. These villages were basically advance posts for their incursions against enemy tribes—particularly the Miamis and Cherokees, using the Ohio River as their launching site and highway. It seemed only a matter of time before a huge onslaught by these tribes from the east would engage the Miamis, if not the Cherokees as well, in a life-or-death struggle.

Enter then, at some early indeterminate date, the Shawnees—a nomadic tribe of absolutely ferocious mercenary Indians who, according to their own traditions, migrated an incalculable time before from their original Asian homeland; a tribe that purportedly crossed the Bering Strait to Alaska in skin boats (and on the backs of turtles and whales, so tradition goes) and then gradually moved southeastward across the continent. They eagerly attacked, fought and—evidently without exception—defeated every tribe they encountered that offered the least resistance. At length they arrived in the country of the Miami Indians, who were then still the most powerful stationary tribe east of the Mississippi and north of the Ohio, but who were still fighting off incursions of the Five Nations of upper New York State.

Methodically, mercilessly, the loose coalition of New York tribes had not only defeated many surrounding tribes and subjected their people to the most diabolical tortures, they also deliberately exterminated some, such as the Erie tribe in 1648 and the Neutrals during the following year. Other tribes were simply defeated and driven out, including the heretofore powerful Hurons. That tribe, longtime inhabitants of the Niagara area and greatly revered by the other tribes, under the duress imposed upon them by the Five Nations, meekly migrated to the Michigan country in 1650. Soon afterward those same Hurons divided themselves to form yet another tribe, the Wyandots. The parent Hurons remained in Michigan, but the newly formed Wyandots planted fresh roots in the soil of the Ohio country just south of Lake Erie.

Recognizing the power of the Shawnees, the Miamis made peace with them and offered them Ohio country land to live upon temporarily in the largely uninhabited valleys of such major Ohio River tributaries as the Scioto and Muskingum rivers. This was to be in exchange for the Shawnees using their fierce skills against the New York tribes if and when they attempted further invasion of the Ohio country or navigated the Ohio River en route to strike the southern tribes. The Shawnees agreed with alacrity, and the result was a series of pitched battles with individual war parties of one or another of the New York tribes. Without exception the Shawnees emerged victorious, which encouraged the Miamis to evict the New York bands that had rooted themselves along the Iroquois and Kankakee. The Five Nations of New York, unaccustomed to being thwarted, much less defeated, dubbed the Shawnees with the disparaging name Ontoagannha, meaning People of Unintelligible Speech, but name-calling did not alter the fact that they had more than met their match. Within only a few short years, the tribes, in their own languages, had begun calling the beautiful Ohio River by another name: the River of Blood.

To combat this new menace, the Five Nations of New York met in a great council at a centrally located village called Onondaga and, after considerable discussion, formally established themselves into a highly democratic and tightly knit confederation in which the good of one was the good of all. Now, an attack against any band of the Five Nations would be taken as an act of war against the entire confederation. They named their strong new alliance the Mengwe, or Iroquois League.[1] It did indeed make them all the more powerful in respect to neighboring (and even distant) tribes, but the Shawnees were neither awed nor overcome by their formally confederated foes. They continued to emerge victorious in virtually all encounters, including an intense war in the valley of the Susquehanna River in 1607.

The struggle might have continued to escalate but for an unexpected intervention. The Iroquois suddenly found themselves busy fighting off a new threat—the incursion of a persistent group of whites who had ascended the St. Lawrence River. They called themselves Frenchmen, and most unfortunately for them, before they fully understood the implications of what they were doing, these whites made the mistake of allying themselves to several tribes who were mortal enemies of the

Iroquois. They provided these enemies of the Iroquois with goods and weaponry that nearly enabled them to demolish their great and powerful enemy—until the Iroquois themselves were able to become similarly armed and the pendulum swung back even more in favor of the Iroquois League.[2] The result was that the Iroquois now considered the French as adversaries.

So far as the mercenary Shawnees were concerned, however, once again with a challenge more or less overcome, their nomadic instincts came to the fore, and gradually the tribe split apart into its five basic septs or clans and migrated elsewhere.[3] The larger faction moved southward, fighting and defeating the southern tribes they encountered, including even the proud Cherokees and Creeks. Part of that faction settled in Cherokee territory along a broad, winding river in present Tennessee that the Cherokees called Pelisipi but that was soon being called the Shawanoe River, in honor of the nomadic warrior tribe.

The other portion of this Shawnee contingent continued southeastward, finally settling down again at the mouth of a great black river that emptied into the Gulf of Mexico and that they promptly named after themselves—calling it the Shawanee, which, over the years, evolved to be called the Suwannee River.[4] It was here, at the village located practically on the broad Gulf beach at the mouth of the Suwannee that a boy was born and named Chiungalla—Black Fish. He was destined to become the principal chief of the Shawnee tribe's Chalahgawtha sept.

Back in the Ohio country, a smaller but still significant faction of the tribe moved eastward and took up residence among a docile tribe, the Susquehannocks, who lived along a major Pennsylvania river named after themselves, the Susquehanna. Here this faction of Shawnees lived in peace, not only with the Susquehannocks but with a neighboring tribe far to the east along the Delaware River. That tribe was the Lenni Lenape who, in a vain effort to try to live in harmony with the growing number of white colonists called the British, even changed their tribal name in honor of the Virginia colonial governor, Lord De La Warr, and were henceforth called the Delaware tribe. These Delawares were a powerful tribe—so strong that in precolumbian times they had evicted the Cherokees from the Pennsylvania area as punishment for their treacherous attack on an ally of the Delawares—but even the Delawares had been cowed by the much more powerful Iroquois League. Now, however, with their fierce new Shawnee friends to back them up, some of their erstwhile courage returned, and they became much less deferential to the Five Nations. This infuriated the League, but it was a matter that, for the time being, they ignored as they concentrated on their problems with the French.

The final contingent of Shawnees still in the Ohio country left there under their war chief, Opeththa, in 1683 and journeyed to the Illinois River. Here they established themselves not far from present Starved Rock, where La Salle had only the previous year erected Fort St. Louis. They had no trouble with him and his men but were not comfortable with his presence there. All too soon, with the Ohio River Valley clear of Shawnees, the Iroquois once again began to use the river as a principal route for incursions against other tribes and for bringing the spoils of their raids back to their own villages, though in a more limited manner than before.

All the tribes were having troubles to some degree with this new breed of pale-faced humans that had entered their country. Their problems were aggravated by the fact that the whites were themselves divided into factions called French, English, Spanish, Dutch, Portuguese and Swedes and that they constantly bickered and fought over what they seemingly wanted and valued more than anything else, territory to claim as their own. America's easternmost tribes had initially welcomed the new-comers and aided them where possible, but they had soon discovered that if they aided one white group, this would place them in opposition to another, and some-how, no matter which side they chose, it was always Indian land that was lost and passed into possession of the whites.

War between Indians and whites had broken out on several occasions, but the primitive weaponry of the tribes deeper in the interior could not withstand the onslaught of modern weaponry. What Indians were not killed in the resultant warfare were quickly whittled away or sometimes even exterminated by epidemics of the dreadful diseases that the whites brought with them and for which the tribes had built up no immunity—measles, whooping cough, smallpox, chicken pox, typhoid fever and cholera. The worst of the earlier plagues to hit the tribes occurred during 1616–17 and wiped out tens of thousands of Indians all along the Atlantic coast.[5]

In spite of these disasters, some of the tribesmen continued to fight for their territory, but they were quickly overwhelmed and taken into captivity, placed aboard ships and sold as slaves in the West Indies. At the same time the whites were bringing to America their own slaves whose skins were black. The first shipments of these unfortunates were brought to Jamestown for sale by the Dutch in 1619. Within two decades the British realized what a lucrative trade slavery was, so they ousted the Dutch slave traders and, in 1639, established their own Royal African Company to make massive raids on the native villages of the Dark Continent and bring the chained captives to America to satisfy the ever-growing demand for slave labor.[6] In all such matters, the human cruelty inflicted on people of either red skin or black was of precious little concern to the imperious British.

By the middle of the seventeenth century, virtually all major rivers flowing into the Atlantic and the Gulf of Mexico had become reasonably well explored, if not settled. Yet with the exception of the St. Lawrence and the Mississippi, all these streams had their origins *east* of the Alleghenies, that mountain chain extending from southern Canada and New England all the way down to northern Georgia, Alabama and Mississippi.

The Spanish, having established themselves in Florida shortly after its discovery by Juan Ponce de León in 1513, went on to explore, conquer and colonize Latin America, but an offshoot expedition under Hernando de Soto landed at Tampa Bay in 1540 and began to explore to the north and west. The following year he discov-ered the Mississippi River and ascended it to Arkansas. Some biographers have claimed he went as far upstream as the mouth of the Ohio; if true, this would make him the first white man to view that great stream.

Within 50 years of their first landing in America, the adventurous French had explored and established themselves to conquer, claim and proselytize not only in the St. Lawrence Valley but in the farthest reaches of all five of the Great Lakes and beyond. By 1632 the black-robed Jesuits were already winning converts among tribes well west of Lake Superior, more than a century before most British colonists were even aware of the existence of the Ohio River, apart from vague, unconfirmed rumors of a great stream system existing somewhere beyond the crest of the Alleghenies—a mysterious river that was said to flow through a land inhabited by savage tribes. In 1658 Pierre Radisson found the upper Mississippi River in the wilderness of present Minnesota and Wisconsin, almost a century before the British colonists began plying the waters of the Ohio.

Louis Joliet and Jacques Marquette noted the mouth of the Ohio in 1673 as they passed down the Mississippi from Wisconsin to Arkansas—and again as they returned upstream—but they paid it scant heed and went up the Illinois River instead, leaving their paddle marks on history's pages in the area of Chicago, Milwaukee, Green Bay and other Lake Michigan locales. Inconclusive evidence indicates that Robert Cavalier de La Salle may have briefly touched upon the Ohio River in the vicinity of the low rapids called the Falls of the Ohio in late 1669, but if he did see the Ohio, he did not linger.[7]

French explorers and traders undoubtedly traversed the Ohio in increasing numbers during the next half-century, since they established trading posts on such major Ohio River tributaries as the Beaver, Kanawha, Scioto, Great Miami and Wabash rivers, yet they made extraordinarily little mention of the Ohio itself, until the first map depicting its location was drawn by the French geographer Franquelin in 1688. It was a fairly accurate map, considering what little was known about the Ohio River, and it was better, in fact, than a few maps that were published some years later.[8]

The most signal accomplishment of the Franquelin map was to bring the English colonists to the uncomfortable realization that while they had been occupied with their own concerns in the relatively narrow strip of land between the Atlantic and the Alleghenies, the French were energetically—and with alarming rapidity—laying claim to a vast empire beyond those mountains: everything north and west of the St. Lawrence to the Great Lakes, as well as the entire Mississippi River Valley. Already they were establishing a line of forts and posts to protect these claims from Quebec to the mouth of the Mississippi. Fort Frontenac was situated at the mouth of Lake Ontario, Fort Niagara at the mouth of the Niagara River, Fort Pontchartrain on the Detroit River, Fort Michilimackinac at the Straits of Mackinac, Fort La Baye at the head of Green Bay and, on the Mississippi, Fort de Chartres. These six forts encompassed a vast territory about which almost nothing was known, but all of which the French felt was in their possession.[9] It was a territory the French were determined to exploit to the utmost, and to this end they gradually bisected the region and established subsidiary trading posts on five major portage routes leading southwestward from the Great Lakes to the Mississippi.

The first, easiest and by far most frequently used route started at Green Bay, ascended the Fox River of Wisconsin, passed through Lake Winnebago and continued up the Fox to a three-mile portage at its headwaters that connected to the Wisconsin River, which in turn flowed into the Mississippi.[10] The second was at the head of Lake Michigan, at the marshy area the Indians called Checagou, up the river of the same name to its difficult portage through the shallow, extensive Mud Lake, connecting with the Fox River of the Illinois country; that river in turn merges with the Kankakee River to form the Illinois River and subsequently empties into the Mississippi.[11] The third route was also at the head of Lake Michigan but some 30

The Five Major Portages
Great Lakes to Mississippi River, 1688

miles farther southeast, up Salt Creek some 14 miles to a tough portage over four or five miles of sandy ground to the headwaters of Crooked Creek and down that winding stream to the Kankakee, encountering it some 100 miles upstream from the Illinois.[12] The fourth route was a passage used by La Salle and the Franciscan priest Louis Hennepin, encountered some 40 miles northeast of the Indiana route, on the eastern side of Lake Michigan—from the mouth of the St. Joseph River upstream about 50 miles and then on a somewhat easier portage southwestward over hard ground for five miles to the headwaters of the Kankakee and thence downstream some 150 miles to the Illinois and, eventually, the Mississippi.[13]

The fifth route was accessible from the western end of Lake Erie, where an ascent of about 100 miles up the Maumee was made extremely difficult by the 15-mile-long Maumee Rapids, involving an arduous portage that discouraged all but the most hardy, to where the river is formed by the confluence of the St. Marys River and another river called St. Joseph, then continuing up the St. Marys about five miles to the start of a portage path that went westward across a moderate portage to the headwaters of Lost Creek, down that stream to the Little River, and then downstream to where it joins the upper Wabash River; then westward on the Wabash to the French post of Ouiatenon, where the stream turns southward, flows past the French trading center called Post St. Vincent, and reaches the Ohio River some 140 miles upstream from its mouth at the Mississippi.[14]

As part of the program of building a string of forts to guard its communication between Quebec and New Orleans, the French, in 1711, built a small fort on the

Illinois bank of the Ohio River 40 miles upstream from the Mississippi, ostensibly as a headquarters for missionaries and to protect river-traveling French traders from raiding Cherokees descending the Shawanoe River. This was the first military installation ever built on the Ohio River.[15]

Now there were murmurings that a much easier (though far more dangerous) route was being investigated by these enterprising Frenchmen. This passage would take them from the eastern end of Lake Erie to a direct connection with the Allegheny, and from that point some 150 miles downstream to where it merges with the Monongahela River to form the Ohio River, 1,000 miles above its mouth at the Mississippi.[16]

The French were claiming all this encompassed territory and cared not at all that their claim included lands granted through charter by the British Crown to English colonists. That the territory involved was inhabited by native tribes of dangerous warriors—Shawnee, Delaware, Wyandot, Miami, Seneca, Potawatomi, Ottawa, Chippewa, Menominee, Sac, Fox, Winnebago, Illinois, Kickapoo and their various subsidiary tribes—was largely considered little more than an annoyance that would be attended to in due time.

Because of their propensity for close intermingling with the natives and often for intermarrying with their women, the French by and large got along well with the tribes, except for the Five Nations of the Iroquois League. There were occasional flare-ups between them, but these rarely lasted long, mainly because the Indians realized that, having been suddenly projected out of the Stone Age and into an era of modern weaponry that included steel knives, tomahawks, firearms, fabrics, paints, blankets, liquor and other desirable commodities, they had quickly become dependent upon the trade goods brought to them by the French.

Suddenly, to the consternation of the French, competition for the incredibly lucrative Indian trade reared its head as some of the more enterprising British traders made their way to the tribes with goods that were both better in quality and far less expensive for the Indians to obtain in trade. The French realized at once that it was time to establish in more definite terms their claims to the trans-Allegheny west.

The search by English colonists for access to the Ohio River basin was haphazard and lackadaisical at first. Among the first of the British to embark on the quest was Ralph Lane, governor of Walter Raleigh's ill-fated Roanoke Colony. He followed the Roanoke River upstream in 1586 in the belief that it would lead him to the great Western Sea, which was believed to lie just beyond the mountains, but the river played out as a navigable stream within 100 miles, and Lane and his party turned back.[17] The next attempt was by Capts. Christopher Newport and John Smith who, in 1606, explored up the James River to the falls, but they too were disheartened by the labors involved in portaging and turned back hardly before beginning to ascend the eastern slope of the Alleghenies.[18] The following year, Newport tried the James River ascent again and managed to get 40 miles farther upstream than before, but once again the difficulties discouraged him and he returned. Several other exploring parties later followed both the James and the Roanoke rivers practically to their headwaters, but none passed over the crest of the Alleghenies. That feat was not accomplished until nearly half a century after Newport's trip, when, in 1654, a hardy pioneer named Abraham Wood, resident near the Falls of the Appomattox, ascended the Roanoke with a party of men under commission from Gov. Sir William Berkeley and succeeded where Lane, Newport, Smith and others before him had failed.[19] He crossed the Blue Ridge and Allegheny divide into the Ohio drainage and discovered a river that was first named Wood's River after him but soon became known as the New River; this is the same stream as the Great Kanawha but is still known by the name of New River above the mouth of the Gauley River. Wood hadn't followed it very far downstream when he encountered hostile Indians—most likely a Cherokee war party on a raid against the Xualaes—and fled for his life.

Twelve years later, in 1666, another party under Henry Batte, also commissioned by Sir William Berkeley, followed the route Wood had taken and got much farther downstream on the New and Kanawha River, past the low Falls of the Kanawha to the mouth of a creek where there was a large salt spring only about 60 miles upstream from where the Kanawha empties into the Ohio River.[20] They found some vacant Indian shelters at the spring, in which they left a number of trinkets as gifts. However, unnerved by such abundance of Indian sign, they made an immediate about-face and hastily retreated to their own side of the mountains.

Three years later another explorer commissioned by Berkeley, Dr. John Lederer, a German physician, followed the Rapidan River upstream and reached the crest of the Blue Ridge in northern Virginia.[21] He did not go far beyond that crest, and though he was not actually in the Ohio River drainage as he supposed, he encountered no streams and soon turned back toward home. Berkeley, disappointed at the failure, sent him on the same route the following year, this time with a larger party including Indian guides, but once again, having achieved the Blue Ridge summit, Lederer simply turned around and went home.

It was during the following year, 1671, that the Cherokees wiped out the Xualae tribe and took possession of the Kanawha, only to be ousted themselves the ensuing year by an Iroquois war party. That same year, 1672, may have been when Robert Sieur de Cavalier de La Salle ascended the Maumee from Lake Erie, portaged to the Wabash and followed it down to the Ohio River. There he traveled upstream on the Ohio some 240 miles to the Falls of the Ohio before retracing his canoe route back up the Wabash.

The Franciscan priest Louis Hennepin reported that in 1677 he was on the headwaters of the Allegheny about 150 miles above where that stream joins the Monongahela to form the Ohio River, but the statement is in doubt because of Hennepin's propensity for self-aggrandizement by falsifying his reports.

During the next decade, certain bold British traders made their way to the Monongahela and followed it to where it merges with the Allegheny. No record has been found that any of them descended the Ohio, although logic indicates that some of them must have. It is known that a large party of these traders did ascend the Allegheny, portaged up to Lake Erie and greatly alarmed the French when they were sighted in their ten canoes filled with trade goods on that lake in 1686. The French trade agent Denonville wrote about it to Seignelay in Quebec, saying:

> *I consider it a matter of importance to preclude the English from this trade, as they doubtless would entirely ruin ours . . . by the cheaper bargains they would give the Indians.*

In 1690 an emissary from the upper Susquehanna Delawares visited the Shawnees living on the Illinois under war chief Opeththa and invited them to come to the Pennsylvania country to help discourage the rapidly encroaching British colonists. Weary of living on the Illinois, Opeththa agreed, but on the way he and his people stopped for a time with the Miamis at their principal village of Pickawillany on the upper Great Miami River.[22] Here they were invited by the Miami principal chief, Unemakemi, to return to the Scioto Valley and make their home there again, and to encourage others of their tribe to do so as well. Opeththa said he would consider it and perhaps in a few years take him up on it. In the meanwhile he would stay in the Scioto Valley only a short time before continuing to the Susquehanna to aid the Delawares, as he had promised.

Arriving at the Susquehanna in 1692, Opeththa was appalled at the number of whites that were flooding into the fertile valleys from the east, and he realized at once that if they were not stopped and turned back quickly, there might be no turning them back at all. He immediately sent word to his fellow Shawnees in the south, still living on the rivers that bore their tribal name, both in the Tennessee country and Florida, asking them to come to the Susquehanna as soon as they could to participate in the looming struggle. It took a while, but by 1694 many of the southern Shawnees had abandoned their villages and were again on their way north.

This migration suited the southern tribes very well, as they had never entirely overcome their fear of the Shawnees. To hurry the warriors on their way and resume dominance in their own lands, they had formed a confederation much as the Iroquois had done years before and demanded that the Shawnees leave. The confederation included a number of tribes that had previously warred savagely against one another —the Cherokee, Creek, Chickasaw, Natchez, Choctaw and others. Had these southern tribes not done this, the no-longer-welcome Shawnees would probably have left the south sooner in response to Opeththa's call, but wishing to avoid any semblance of fleeing before an enemy, they lingered for almost two years longer and only then began leaving at their leisure.

Despite the added strength their arrival gave to the Indians in the valley of the Susquehanna, the influx of whites continued. Farther south, in northern Virginia, more and more traders were making their way up the Potomac to a major trading point that had been established at the mouth of Will's Creek, less than 25 miles east of the Allegheny divide.[23] By following an Indian path known as the Nemacolin Trail, they soon crossed that divide and continued following the trail as it angled to the northwest and finally terminated at an ancient earthworks studded with reddish rocks. The place was promptly dubbed Redstone Old Fort. Here they found themselves on the shore of a very substantial river—the Monongahela—flowing northward toward its confluence with the Allegheny to form the Ohio, only a bit over 50 miles downstream. At that point, the entire Ohio River Valley was open to them.[24]

In March 1700, William Murray encouraged westward expansion, and his urgings undoubtedly had effect: A brief, tantalizing tidbit in the historical record, annoyingly without names or details, indicates that British traders in that same year began plying the waters of the Ohio—the first authentically recorded instance.

Among those hardy souls who took Murray's advice was an individual named Ebenezer Zane, who had come to Pennsylvania with William Penn in 1681 when the Colony of Pennsylvania was established by charter from King Charles II. The following year he had been with Penn when the site of Philadelphia was purchased from the Indians. Ebenezer Zane, like Penn, was a Quaker, but he did not entirely agree with his fellow Quakers' strong contention that Europeans were only guests of the native inhabitants and, as such, should in all matters treat them gently and with kindness, regardless of what provocation there might be to do otherwise.

The Quaker elders had forbidden all their followers from participating in any act that would separate the Indians from anything that was rightfully theirs or from engaging in acts that might injure the Indians in any way. Zane did not endear himself to the Quaker elders when he attended, with Penn, the Kensington Treaty— or Great Elm Treaty, as some called it—on April 23, 1701, to purchase a tract of the great forested lands stretching north and west from the site of Philadelphia—a treaty that years later, because of an ambiguity, greatly defrauded the Delawares. Were that not enough, Ebenezer Zane was finally ostracized by his Quaker brethren when he married without the sanction of the Society of Friends. Infuriated and wanting nothing more to do with them, he moved out of the land now called Penn's Woods —Pennsylvania—and into Virginia, following the South Branch of the Potomac upstream to the site of present Moorefield, where he started carving a new settlement out of the wilderness. It was there, several years later, that his son was born and named William Andrew.

In 1699 and 1700 another notable Frenchman passed the mouth of the Ohio River with very little comment about it. This was Pierre LeSeuer, who had been exploring on the upper Mississippi in the Minnesota country for more than a decade. He left there in 1699, floated down to the mouth of the Mississippi where he remained for some months and then paddled all the way back to Minnesota. Though he noted in his journal passing the mouth of the Ohio in mid-July, he seemed singularly unimpressed.

In 1710 the Tuscarora tribe in the Carolinas, harassed by the Shawnees and southern tribes, appealed to the Iroquois League to be allowed to move to their country and be taken in as a member of the League. The Five Nations met and discussed the matter for nearly two years. At the end of that time, as much because it would irritate the Shawnees as for any other reason, they agreed to accept them—but with provisos: The Tuscaroras would be on a ten-year probation in the League and could be ejected during that period at any time, with or without cause; even after full and final acceptance in 1722, they would bear the status of "children" of (and therefore subservient to) the Oneidas, who sponsored them; finally, while they would be allowed to send delegates to the tribal councils and express their views just as any other delegates could, they would have no power to vote in any League matters until and after their full acceptance. The Tuscaroras agreed to the terms without hesitation, and henceforth the Iroquois League was known as the Six Nations rather than the Five Nations.

Meanwhile, British traders continued penetrating deeper into the unknown territory that would eventually become Ohio, Indiana and Illinois. In 1715 a hardy group of them paddled up the Wabash and convinced the Ouiatenons that it would be to their advantage to allow a small British trading post to be built in their village on the Wabash. Dazzled by the array of goods the traders brought, the Ouiatenons were delighted. Not so the French traders already on hand who, only a few months earlier, had built their own trading post at the village under the direction of Jean Baptiste Bissot, variously calling it Gatanois, the Miami Post and the Ouiatenon Post. The intrusion of these British traders greatly angered the French traders, and they endeavored to convince the Ouiatenons to leave and resettle on the St. Joseph River of the Maumee, which would effectively take them out of reach of the British traders. The Ouiatenons adamantly refused, and the frustrated French traders found themselves helpless to do anything except send runners with reports of all this to Detroit, Niagara and Montreal.

In 1716, 46 years after the failure of the last expedition sent by Gov. Berkeley to explore beyond the crest of the Blue Ridge, the new Virginia governor, Alexander Spotswood, became determined to succeed in a like endeavor and planned to insure that success by personally leading the exploratory party up the Rapidan. He did so, reached the crest and went through a gap and well into a great valley beyond, coming to the shore of a large northward-flowing river.[25] Convinced that he had discovered a major tributary of the Ohio River if not the actual headwaters of that fabled stream, he nevertheless solemnly named it the Euphrates.

The explorers killed and roasted an elk and a buffalo, feasted well, fired a salute with their muskets and drank a toast to the King. Then, leaving a party of rangers behind to explore, Spotswood returned home. The name Euphrates did not stick, however, because the name the Indians had already given that stream was too well entrenched and more euphonious. They called it the Shenandoah, and instead of being a tributary of the Ohio, it angles northeastward and eventually empties into the upper Potomac, which itself runs into Chesapeake Bay, an arm of the Atlantic.[26]

By 1723, even the staid Governor of Pennsylvania, John Keith, had joined Gov. Spotswood in his sharp concern occasioned by the French presence and claims west of the Alleghenies. Both governors wanted increased expansion westward and advocated giving every individual the right to claim as much as 400 acres on the frontier, provided he lived upon it. Settlers immediately began flocking into the land.

All this became too much for the long-beleaguered Delawares. Even with the help of the Shawnees and some bands of Wyandots, they were unable to check the white tide moving in on them, and so in 1724 they began moving away and settling considerably farther west upon the Allegheny and Beaver rivers in far western Pennsylvania and on the Muskingum River in the Ohio country. The Shawnees went with them, some settling with them, others in different places. With warm Miami approval, they reestablished their numerous former villages on the Muskingum, Scioto, Little Miami, Great Miami and Mad rivers and some new ones as well. In 1725 they established a substantial village French traders named Chiniqué, located on a broad bottom of the right bank of the Ohio 22 miles below the Forks.[27] Here for the first time they used skills learned from the whites and built substantial log cabins instead of the usual flimsy wegiwas, constructed of interwoven branches covered with skins. Almost at once, ignoring the name presently being used, the British traders dubbed the place Logstown, and the name stuck.[28]

Moving farther down the Ohio, the Shawnees established a new village on the Ohio side of the river several miles above the mouth of the Kanawha, calling the place Conedogwinit, which the traders called the Upper Shawnee Town. The Lower Shawnee Town—a much larger and more substantial village built by the Chalahgawtha sept of the Shawnees, was located on a broad flat bottom on the downstream side of the mouth of the Scioto River. They named the village after themselves—Chalahgawtha—although it was more familiarly known by the name of Sinioto. Nevertheless, the traders persisted in calling it the Lower Shawnee Town. The principal village of the tribe, however, called Wapatomica, was established at the Forks of the Muskingum, where that river is formed by the confluence of the Walhonding from the west and the Tuscarawas from the east. Wapatomica was situated on the point of land formed at the downstream side of the mouth of the Walhonding. Directly across the Muskingum from it, on the point of land formed at the downstream side of the Tuscarawas, was the new principal village of the Delawares, Goschachgunk.[29]

Slowly but surely the British settlers inched westward. In 1726 a Welshman named Morgan Morgan crossed over the Blue Ridge in Virginia and gained the distinction of being the first British colonist to erect a permanent residence west of the Allegheny Divide and in the Ohio River drainage.

In 1727 some of the Shawnees returning from the south found, in the valley of the Greenbrier tributary of the Kanawha, a Shawnee village that had been established here some 20 years earlier, and they were met by the villagers with great joy. Among those greeting the Shawnees arriving from the south was a young man of about 18 who had been born in the Greenbrier village less than two years after its establishment; a young man who was destined to become the tribe's principal chief. He was named Hokolesqua—Cornstalk. The Greenbrier location was not, however, quite to the liking of the newly arrived group of Shawnees, and they soon prepared to leave and continue their journey to the Ohio country. They had company: The long-established village there was abandoned, and its inhabitants—including Hokolesqua—went with them and reestablished themselves in Sinioto, at the mouth of the Scioto.

The British fears that the French would soon open their proposed new route from the eastern Great Lakes to New Orleans became a fact in 1729, when a party in canoes, commanded by the military surveyor, Capt. Chaussegros de Léry, opened a portage route from Lake Erie via Lake Chautauqua to the upper Allegheny River, which was at that time considered to be the upper Ohio River.[30]

Carefully surveying as they traveled, de Léry and his party followed the Allegheny 150 miles to where the Ohio River actually begins at the mouth of the Monongahela—called the Forks of the Ohio—then continued down the Ohio another 490 miles to the mouth of the Great Miami River. They then followed this waterway upstream some 200 river miles to Pickawillany, where they were met coolly by the Miami principal chief, Unemakemi, and discourteously hurried on their way, but not before they had seen the encampment of the British traders. De Léry warned the traders to leave before the next visit of the French or bear the consequences, but they only sneered and ignored the warning. The de Léry party then followed a tributary of the Great Miami to near its headwaters, portaged to the St. Marys River, floated down to its mouth at the Maumee and followed that latter stream down to Lake Erie. They then followed the south shore of Lake Erie back to the Niagara Portage and continued east on Lake Ontario to the head of the St. Lawrence. Their journey ended at Montreal, culminating an absence of more than five months.

It was only two and a half years after the conclusion of de Léry's journey that a baby was born in Westmoreland County, Virginia, who was to develop keen interest in and have a great impact upon the Ohio River Valley. His parents, Augustine and Mary Ball Washington, named him George.[31]

The following year, in Reading, Pennsylvania, another individual was born who was destined to have as much influence on the opening of the western frontier as anyone: Daniel Boone. About this same time tangible evidence of the expansionist inclinations of Virginia came as the colony divided its huge Spotsylvania county and created a new county named Orange—a county that encompassed more than the whole of present West Virginia. Its white population was virtually nil, its permanent Indian population rapidly diminishing, and it seemed temptingly poised to accept any new settlers who might be courageous—or perhaps foolhardy—enough to risk staking a claim. There were plenty of takers, and the tempo of settlement picked up markedly from this time onward.

During 1737 those Delawares still in Pennsylvania were learning a bitter lesson about just how dishonorable the whites could be in their treaty making. The treaty William Penn had made with them half a century earlier had a clause in it that had never been acted upon. Now, 19 years after his death, the Proprietary of Pennsylvania took advantage of it in a way that would never have occurred to Penn himself. The treaty signed by the Delawares stated that the Proprietary of Pennsylvania was given title to lands west and north of the Delaware at Philadelphia *"as far as a man can go in a day and a half."* In that remark the Delawares had meant this to be nothing more than a good brisk walk of perhaps 30 miles. The distance had never actually been measured out, and now with good land availability diminishing in the Philadelphia area, the proprietors elected to interpret the nebulous remark in their own way. With considerable care, beginning at the farthest inward bend of the Delaware River within Philadelphia, they cleared a very straight path angling only slightly north of due west. Then they carefully selected a man noted for his athletic abilities and stamina, and one minute after midnight on the appointed day, April 9, 1737, they set him running as fast and as steadily as he could on that path. At the end of 36 hours he collapsed, having accomplished the feat of running a full 150 miles. This was the spot from which the Proprietary of Pennsylvania established the western boundary. The Pennsylvanians laughingly referred to it thereafter as the "Walking Treaty." The Indians were justifiably angry, but they had made a bargain and reluctantly adhered to it. Whatever Delaware and Shawnee villages remained within the new limits of Pennsylvania were abandoned, and their native inhabitants moved to the valleys of the Wyoming and Shamokin or farther west—many all the way to the Muskingum in Ohio.

It is perhaps ironic that Penn's former companion, Ebenezer Zane, died that very year, and Zane's son, William Andrew, now 25, happily married and still living in Moorefield on the South Branch of the Potomac, sired a son. In honor of his own newly deceased father, William named the infant Ebenezer. It was this Ebenezer

Zane—and his brothers and sister yet to be born—who would, in time to come, make a lasting mark on the upper Ohio River Valley.[32]

The so-called "Walking Treaty" and numerous other encroachments on lands the Indians considered their own, plus trade abuses perpetrated by the very British traders the Indians had allowed to establish posts in their lands, finally reached such a point of aggravation to the tribes that the Indians decided it was no longer wise to step back meekly or turn aside when injured. This was becoming evident by the fact that throughout the Indian territories a greater amity was growing between the various tribes who heretofore had been enemies. At long last they were beginning to realize the need to put aside their own differences and concentrate both individually and together on the greater potential danger threatening them all, a danger heralded by this burgeoning encroachment by the British colonists. With this growing realization, even the intermittent squabbling between the French and the Indians abated to a marked degree. Over the past few years a sort of quasi-alliance was developing between the frontier Frenchmen and the westernmost Iroquois League nations—the Senecas, Cayugas, Onondagas, Oneidas and Tuscaroras. Only the Mohawks—closest to British contact—retained their alliance with the British.

For a long while the French had been urging the Indians not to let the British continue insidiously to take their lands through illegal settlement. For equally as long the French had promised to support the Indians with supplies, arms and ammunition should they decide to thrust these intruders back. So now, with just such covert assistance, the Indians finally began to retaliate, and clashes broke out all the way from the Kanawha Valley to western New York, with the preponderance of attacks being made upon new British settlers in the Indian lands. Cabins were burned, cattle were butchered and a number of individuals were captured or slain.

In Virginia a whole new series of settlements were forming near the Blue Ridge crest of the Alleghenies. Orange County, formed only four years before, was divided into Frederick and Augusta counties, with the latter embracing all of Virginia west of the Blue Ridge. Very quickly a number of settlements were laid out, such as Pattonsburg and Staunton, and soon other parties, using these frontier villages as launching points, were starting new and more daringly extensive expeditions into the unknown lands west of the Allegheny crest.

In 1740 a party led by John Howard and James Salling moved down the Kanawha with the idea of claiming lands. Unlike the John Van Bibber party seven years earlier, however, they did not find the valley empty. Unexpectedly encountering a party of Indians, Negroes and French, the pair were taken captive and carried all the way down the Ohio and Mississippi to New Orleans, where they were thrown into prison. Here they remained for some 18 months before finally escaping and, by land and sea, gradually making their way back to their homes in Virginia, where everyone thought them dead. They had been gone for a total of 27 months.

In May 1743, far to the north, a French-Seneca half-breed named Peter Chartier led a party of Indians down the Allegheny from his village on that stream. Just below the mouth of the Kiskiminetas River and some 20 miles upstream from the Forks of the Ohio—called Duendaga by the Indians—they encountered a group of English traders ascending the river. He caught them by surprise, confiscated their goods and took them captive to Montreal. Within two years, however, Chartier, disgruntled with the number of British—traders and settlers alike—still moving into this Allegheny River frontier area, abandoned his village and moved with his followers to reside among the Kickapoos on the Vermilion River in the Illinois country. It was in this same year that King George's War—also called the War of Jenkins' Ear—began between the French and Spanish.[33] It had little effect on the western frontier in America except to heighten the tensions already existing between the traders.

The year 1744 brought the first British trader far down the Ohio and into the Kentucky country. Oddly, there were no Indian villages in the land they called Kan-tuck-kee. It was a well-established neutral ground for the various tribes, and with good reason: There were an abundance of salt springs there, such as those that became known as the Blue Licks, Upper Blue Licks, Boone Lick, Big Bone Lick and many others. These salt licks were great attractions for the huge herds of woods bison that roamed the eastern forests, as well as for elk, deer and other animals that craved the salt there. The Kentucky country was therefore a favorite hunting ground of the Indians, and through a long-established tradition honored by all, no tribe could build permanent villages or wage war against one another there. In this wonderful neutral land they could establish their temporary camps and move about in peace to hunt, sometimes even within sight of enemy tribesmen whom, had they met them anywhere else, they would have instantly attacked.

Having traded with the Shawnees for several years, learned their language and customs and endeared himself to them with his honesty in trade, John Findlay learned of the Kentucky country and yearned to see it. He felt it would be an ideal place to establish a trading post for the various visiting tribesmen. The Shawnees granted him permission to do so, and in 1744 he became the first American colonist to visit Kentucky and build a structure there. His little log cabin trading post was erected on North Elkhorn Creek.[34] Neither he nor the Shawnees had any idea that in the not-too-distant future, this idyllic hunting paradise would become part of what would be fearfully known as "that dark and bloody land."

That same year of 1744 saw a treaty made between the British and the Iroquois League that opened the door for the disastrous times to follow. The Iroquois had long proclaimed themselves, by right of conquest, masters of all this land west of the Alleghenies. Other tribes simply smiled and shook their heads at the ridiculousness of the claim; the Shawnees openly scoffed and challenged the Iroquois to fight it out to see who would emerge master by conquest. The Iroquois wisely declined but continued their boasting to such extent that the British colonial government accepted the claim as fact. Thus, when they met the Iroquois leaders in grand council at Lancaster, Pennsylvania, in this year, the British treaty officials believed—or at least *chose* to believe—that the Iroquois had the right to sell or otherwise dispose of any land they wished that fell under their "right of conquest" claim. For the sum of £600, the British colonists "bought" a vast territory of undefined extent from the Iroquois—a territory that extended to the Ohio River and downstream from there, including the entire Ohio River drainage. That, of course, took in lands inhabited by the Shawnees, Delawares, Kickapoos, Miamis and other tribes, none of whom had even been invited to the Lancaster treaty council. That such a treaty would, without doubt, generate great contention between the British and those tribes did not cause the Iroquois League the slightest discomfiture.

Even more British traders now streamed into the country, but these were of a different temperament from the traders who had moved about among the tribes for years, established their honesty and gained the trust of the tribes. The newer arrivals seemed to go out of their way to cheat the trading Indians in any manner possible; the goods they sold were no longer of the quality they had once been and wore out or fell apart very quickly. Food goods were tainted or diluted. The traders bullied the Indians wherever possible, made unwelcome advances to their women and, perhaps worst of all, brought cheap liquor—primarily rum from the West Indies—which the Indians could hardly resist and which fired them into uncontrollable acts; liquor that was soon gone, with nothing to show for it except a headache and economic loss. Complaints by the Indians to authorities had virtually no effect, and so the cheated Indians began attacking the new traders entering their country, confiscating their goods and usually releasing the men to wander back where they came from, though in some cases taking them captive or killing them. Ever more, due to the trade abuses, the tribes were swinging their allegiance back to the French. Yet the French traders were not themselves without peril. A delegation of Iroquois visited the Wyandots on the Sandusky River and presented Chief Orontony with war belts and urgings to strike the French as well as the English. In June 1747 five French traders returning to Detroit were struck by a band of Hurons, and all five were killed. Later, a few more French traders were slain in other areas from western Lake Erie to the Mackinac Strait.

The Treaty of Aix-la-Chapelle in October of that year ended King George's War, and even though it did not resolve the overlapping territorial disputes on the frontier, the tensions eased somewhat. Attacks by the Indians against the traders—even the more unscrupulous ones—diminished, but the ill feelings remained. Competition remained keen between English and French traders but now with a small degree of mutual tolerance.

The following year John Findlay, back in Virginia from Kentucky, met with a group of men eager to hear an account of his adventures in the wilds. The leader of this group was a physician named Dr. Thomas Walker, who was far more interested in surveying, hunting and otherwise adventuring than in doctoring. He and his group, which included James Patton, John Buchanan, Charles Campbell and James Wood, became highly inspired by tales Findlay told them of a land called Kentucky where there was incredibly fertile soil, vast fields of rich grasses and cane, immense herds of buffalo and untold numbers of elk, deer, wild turkey, grouse, waterfowl and other game. They listened spellbound to his accounts of how the buffalo milled about by the thousands at the salt licks and of the beauty of the gently rolling Kentucky hills.

When Findlay finished, Walker and his party hired him as guide, along with a number of other men as hunters, and set out from the Blue Ridge settlements to explore west and north of the Allegheny crest. The only reasonable access to that country had been down the New and Kanawha rivers, but Findlay advised against it since that route had become so dangerous in recent years. Instead, they struck out toward the south and west, following the Blue Ridge and hoping to find, as Findlay was sure they would, a passage through the mountains and into the lands beyond. They did find it when they encountered a mountain range the Indians called Warioto but that no one in the party had ever heard of before. In the midst of this impressive range was a very significant gap with a major stream running through it in a north-westerly direction. The stream was the headwaters of the river already called the Shawanoe, but the Walker party had no knowledge of this, and it would not have made much difference if they had. With the full approval of his party, Walker named the mountain range, the broad gap through it and the stream that flowed through the gap all by the same name—Cumberland—in honor of the current prime minister of England, the Duke of Cumberland.

The party filed through the newly named Cumberland Gap, followed the Cumberland River downstream and explored a good portion of the Tennessee and Kentucky country, dallied for a while in the impressive valley of the Kentucky River and then, not having encountered any Indians at all, elected to return home via the Kanawha and New rivers. They had seen enough to convince them where the colonial future of America lay. Immediately on their return late in the fall they organized the Loyal Land Company and soon received a grant from King George II of 800,000 acres lying north of the North Carolina border and west of the Alleghenies.

It was not the only land grant King George authorized in this year of 1748. Thomas Lee, a member of His Majesty's council in Virginia, organized the Ohio Land Company, its backers comprising a dozen wealthy land owners in Maryland and Virginia, including Lawrence and Augustine Washington, elder brothers of George, as well as a prosperous merchant of London named James Hanbury. The company, formed with the stated objective of settling lands and engaging in large-scale trade with the Indians, was given a grant of 500,000 acres within the Dominion of Virginia but west of the mountains, all the way to the Ohio River and the Kanawha, with the stipulation that the company establish 100 families on that land within seven years.

One of the Ohio Company's first acts was to hire a well-known trader and frontiersman, Christopher Gist, to survey both the Ohio and Kanawha for them in the area included under the terms of the grant. He was to keep a journal of his journey, draw accurate maps, explore the country inland from the river for some distance to assess its value for projected settlement and farming and make a full report to the company. He was also advised that if he thought it practicable to do so, he might carry that survey all the way down to the Falls of the Ohio—a distance of just over 600 miles. Merchant Hanbury's contribution to the plan was to send to America two full cargoes of trade goods valued at £2,000 sterling.

Another appointment by the Ohio Company was to make the experienced interpreter and guide Conrad Weiser their agent to the Iroquois and dispatch him at once to meet delegates of that confederation at Logstown and get permission—deemed desirable, though not essential—to go on with their plan. In the 23 years since the Shawnees had first established Logstown, it had undergone a considerable change. Disenchanted with all the unaccustomed activity, they had moved out and returned to the Scioto Valley, but other tribes—and traders—had continued using the place as a rendezvous point and trading center.

Logstown had grown considerably, now having upward of 40 log cabins and numerous wegiwas erected by more transitory Indians. The population now was more Mingo than anything else. The Mingoes were not a tribe but rather a very loose confederation of Indians from a variety of tribes—Senecas, Cayugas, Delawares, Wyandots and even a few Shawnees—who, disgruntled with the politics of their individual tribe or simply expatriates for one reason or another, had banded together. There was to be no argument about who would be chief of their unusual confederation. Their spokesman was Talgayeeta—better known to the English traders as Chief Logan. As he put it, "We are all warriors and we are all chiefs. Among the tribes to the south, a chief is called a Mingo, so we now call ourselves Mingoes, as we are all chiefs."[35] Conrad Weiser, when he visited Logstown that year, was astounded at the town's growth and at the amazing amount of trading that was going on—mostly between the Indians and British traders, but even with a few French traders on hand.

News of the successfully completed Walker expedition through the Cumberland Gap and of the wondrous land they had found called Kentucky swept through the colonies, instigating a resurgence of interest in establishing new settlements. One group so inspired to "go west and grow up with the country" included John Draper, along with his wife, Bettie, and their two nearly grown children, John Jr. and Mary.[36] Adam Harmon and his son, Jacob, were part of that group, as were Henry Lenard, James Burke and Thomas Ingles, along with Ingles's three sons, William, George and John. Moving southwestward from the Pattonsburg settlement, where they had been staying for some time, they followed the Blue Ridge, gradually angling westward until they crossed the Allegheny Divide. At length they came to a beautiful grassy meadow with a stream running through it to the northwest. This was the New River—or Wood's River, as some were still calling it—and it was here that they decided to establish their settlement. With everyone working to help each other, in a short time all the families had their own cabins, and the settlement was proudly named Draper's Meadows—the first Virginia settlement on the Kanawha River drainage.[37] In a very short time this most remote settlement in Virginia became a rendezvous for adventurers and new settlers bound for the forbidding interior beyond.

That matters on the frontier would eventually cause a confrontation between the French and the British was considered a possibility by many. But the vague possibility became a strong likelihood in 1749. With both factions claiming territorial rights to the vast unknown lands between the Alleghenies and the Mississippi, France decided it was time to establish those claims in a more concrete manner. In Montreal, the Marquis de la Galissonière, governor-general of New France—which was what the French were terming their claims in the New World—commissioned a young officer, Capt. Pierre Joseph de Céloron de Blainville, to lead an expedition to the Ohio Valley.[38] At various major streams he was to pause and bury an engraved lead plate that reaffirmed French ownership of the entire Ohio River drainage. Each plate had blank spaces in the inscription, those blanks to be engraved in the field, when the time came, with a knife blade as to date and location.[39]

On June 15, 1749, Céloron left Montreal with a total force of 272 men.[40] Using the rude map made by de Léry 20 years earlier, they ascended the St. Lawrence River to Lake Ontario and followed its southern shore westward to the lake's head at the mouth of the Niagara Portage, where on Thursday, July 6, they reached the French post called Fort Niagara, the predecessor of which had been erected by La Salle more than 70 years earlier. Here they paused only briefly to exchange news with the post commander, Capt. Daniel Joncaire, brother of the Canadian commander with the expedition, Chabert Joncaire.[41]

Early the following morning they began the long and arduous Niagara Portage past the falls, the Great Whirlpool and Niagara Rapids and in record time relaunched their canoes just above the mouth of Buffalo Creek.[42] They followed the south shore of Lake Erie some 60 miles and, on Sunday, July 16, spotted a cairnlike Seneca rock structure that marked the mouth of a stream identified on their map as Rivière aux Pommes—Apple River. Here they headed upstream but quickly had to portage.[43] It turned out to be the most arduous portage most had ever encountered. The path moved rather sharply uphill, rising almost 1,000 feet above the level of Lake Erie to the divide that separates the Great Lakes drainage from the Ohio drainage. The portage was a mere five miles long, but hampered by rains every day, it required a full week of unbelievable effort to traverse it with their boats and baggage, an effort that severely sapped the stamina of the men. At the end of the portage path they came at last, on Saturday, July 22, to the head of Lake Chautauqua, marked on Céloron's map as Lac Tjadakion.[44]

After an overnight stop to rest and allow the men time to prepare decent meals for themselves, the journey was resumed in the morning, moving southward down the 16-mile length of Lake Chautauqua. It is a lake of peculiar shape, squeezed together to a relatively narrow passage at about the midpoint and resembling an elongated hourglass. It was from this configuration that the lake had been named by the Indians, the term *Chautauqua* signifying a sack tied in the middle. It was at this narrow point that they camped for the night. The next day they reached the southern end of the lake and found its outlet, Chautauqua Creek. Disappointment was great when they discovered the stream was at first little more than an extensive shallow swamp area.[45] Despite all their efforts, the day's progress had amounted to just a mile. The next day the swamp was left behind, but the stream became very shallow and rocky, and an entire day was required just to move the canoes a couple of miles. The boats were badly damaged in the process. As Céloron that evening wrote in his journal:

We proceeded about a league with great difficulty. In many places I was obliged to assign forty men to each canoe to facilitate their passage.

Eventually their tortuous movement down Chautauqua Creek led them to where it flows into Cassadega Creek.[46] It was a little larger but not much better, and the difficulties continued until they reached that stream's mouth at Conewango Creek where, with little ceremony, the first of the lead plates was correctly inscribed with the proper location and date and then buried.[47] At noon the following day— July 29—the creek they were following at last emptied into the broad, smoothly flowing expanse of the river they sought. It was the Allegheny River, but so far as they were concerned, it was the Ohio.[48] Opposite the creek mouth, on the south bank of the river, a hole was prepared, the engraved lead plate carefully marked with place and date, and this second plate buried directly beneath a huge red oak.[49] To that tree was also tacked a shiny sheet of tin embossed with the coat-of-arms of France. At that point Céloron addressed his assembled men in a loud voice.

"In the name of France and to her benefit," he intoned, "I, Pierre Joseph de Céloron de Blainville, do this day and time, take and renew possession of all this country and proclaim King Louis the Fifteenth undisputed lord and protector over all these territories. Beneath this great tree to which I have had attached the insignia of France, I have now buried the leaden plate which substantiates this claim for all time and for all men. *Vive le Roi!*"

In a rising thunder of voices, the final homage was repeated by his assembled men three times in succession: *"Vive le Roi!"*

Oddly enough, at almost the precise time this ceremony by the French was being enacted, a claim equally grandiose was being made at Williamsburg. An official proclamation had just been issued by Thomas Lee, president of the Virginia Council and Governor of the Dominion of Virginia. It was publicly posted first in Williamsburg and later elsewhere throughout the colony. The proclamation read:

> *The boundaries of Virginia are the Atlantic on the east, North Carolina on the south, the Potomac on the north, and, on the west, the Great South Sea, including California.*[50]

The problem with the claims of both these major colonial powers was not only that they included the same territory, but that the land they were so grandly claiming was occupied by scores of Indian tribes and subtribes who didn't feel required to make claims; they *knew* the land belonged to no one; it was a gift of their god Moneto to His red children, but not as a possession. Rather, it was a treasure in trust, given to them only to use wisely and well and then to pass on to future generations in as natural a state as when they received it. They could not comprehend the ownership of land as the whites owned things. They were merely the guardians of a deeply revered trust, and they had no intention of meekly turning away from it.

The process of burying lead plates was continued by Céloron and his men as the expedition floated downstream. They encountered numerous Indian villages—many of which had been abandoned at their approach—and to the Indians they did find, the commander gave assurances that their mission was friendly and they had come to protect the interests of those Indians. The Indians were not pleased with Céloron's presence, but his force was large enough that they did not risk attacking.[51] Now and again they came across English traders and bluntly told them that they were trespassing in French territory and ordered them to leave, taking their goods with them. Whatever they did not take was placed inside any structures the English had erected as camps or trading posts, and these structures were then burned.

The third lead plate was interred at the base of a large emergent rock on a small bottom along the left bank nine miles below French Creek.[52] The reason Céloron chose this place instead of the mouth of a major stream was because on this bottom the isolated emergent rock inclined upward from the soil. The exposed portion of the rock was 22 feet in length and 14 in breadth, but the remarkable thing was that its inclined surface was inscribed with what appeared to be some sort of ancient pictographic writing. All in the party were greatly moved by the sight, but none could translate the glyphs. Joncaire said the Indians regarded the rock and its writings with great reverence.[53] The tin plate with the coat-of-arms was tacked to a nearby oak tree.

A short distance downstream from there, a few miles below the mouth of the Kiskeminetas, Céloron landed his force at a long-deserted Shawnee village at the mouth of a creek where some English traders from Pennsylvania had gathered. He evicted them, burned their trading post and gave them a letter he hurriedly wrote, to be carried to their governor, Alexander Hamilton:

To the Governor of the Pennsylvania from Captain Pierre Joseph de Céloron de Blainville. From our camp on La Belle Rivière, at an ancient village of the Chouanons, 6th of August, 1749.

Sir, — Having been sent with a detachment into these quarters by M. the Marquis de la Galissonière, Commandant-General of New France, to reconcile among themselves certain savage nations, who are ever at variance on account of the war just terminated, I have been much surprised to find some traders of your government in a country to which England never had any pretensions. It even appears that the same opinion is entertained in New England, since in many of the villages I have passed through, the English who were trading there, have mostly taken flight.

Those I have fallen in with, and by whom I wrote you, were treated with all the mildness possible, although I would have been justified in treating them as interlopers, and men without design, their enterprise being contrary to the preliminaries of peace, signed five months ago.

I hope, sir, you will carefully prohibit for the future this trade, which is contrary to treaties; and I give notice to your traders that they will expose themselves to great risks in returning to these countries, and they must impute only to themselves the misfortunes they may meet with.

I know that our Commandant-General would be very sorry to resort to violence; but he has orders not to permit foreign traders in his government.

I have the honor to be, with great respect, sir, your humble servant,

Céloron

Shortly after this incident they were once again afloat. On the point of land at the junction of the two major streams, they found a village that was the finest they had yet encountered, but like so many others it was abandoned except for three Seneca warriors and an old woman whom they learned from Joncaire was named Aliquippa. She was chief of the village—though Joncaire called her *Queen* Aliquippa, and the term stuck.[54] She informed Céloron through Joncaire that nearly all of the villagers had fled to Chiniqué—Logstown—because they had been warned by the

English traders evicted by Céloron, who passed this way and then disappeared up the Monongahela, that a French army was coming to destroy them. If she were to die, she told him defiantly, it would be in her own village, facing the enemy, not in flight from a party of whites, be they French or English.

Admiring her courage, Céloron told her through Joncaire that they were not here to harm any Indians and she would be left in peace. He presented her with gifts and immediately set off for the village his map designated as Chiniqué, 22 miles below on the right bank.[55] On their arrival at Logstown, they visited briefly with the Indians gathered there, but the atmosphere was suspicious and hostile. It was at that stop that most of their own Indian escorts abandoned them, and because they were pointedly made unwelcome, the French party quickly moved on without burying a plate.[56]

The fourth plate was buried on August 13 when they came to a fine bottom on the left side of the river where the stream split around a large island. At the foot of the bottom, a considerable stream entered, which their map drawn by de Léry indicated was the Kanououara, although the eight uninvited Indians who had accompanied them from Logstown referred to it as Wheeling Creek.[57]

Some 75 river miles farther downstream, after seeing great numbers of deer, bear, bison, elk and a wide variety of other wildlife, they arrived at the mouth of the Muskingum River, a stream shown on Céloron's map as the Yenanguakonan. Here, where there were the ruins of an old Wyandot town, they established camp on the downstream point of land formed at the river's mouth, and the fifth of his plates was prepared. Céloron noted in his journal that this plate was:

> *buried at the foot of a maple, which forms a triangle with a red oak and elm, at the mouth of the river Yenanguakonan, and on its western bank.*[58]

Just short of another 100 miles downstream, having passed occasional small abandoned Indian villages, the party came ashore at the mouth of a major river, the Kanawha, entering from the south—a stream de Léry's map identified as the river Chinodaista but that Father Bonnecamps—the Jesuit priest with the expedition—termed the Chinodahichetha.[59] With the usual ceremony the sixth plate was buried at the foot of a large elm tree, to which was tacked the identifying coat-of-arms. The date was August 18, and here the party camped for the night.[60]

Céloron had fully planned to bury another lead plate at the mouth of the Scioto River, site of the major Shawnee village of Sinioto—which his map showed as St. Yotoc. That plan was abandoned, however, as the Shawnees there were very un-friendly and allowed them to pass only after extensive talks over four days. As Céloron remarked in his journal:

> *My instructions enjoin me to summon the English traders in Sinhioto and instruct them to withdraw on pain of what might ensue, and even to pillage the English should their response be antagonistic; but I am not strong enough; and as these traders are established in a village and well supported by the Indians, the*

attempt would have failed and put the French to shame. I have therefore withdrawn with what pride such encounter as we have suffered has permitted us to retain.

They were quite glad enough to depart with their scalps still attached and wasted no time in paddling rapidly downstream. It was at noon on August 30 when they reached the mouth of the river indicated on Céloron's map as Rivière à la Roche—Rock River—but better known to the English as the Great Miami River, named after the powerful tribe living on its headwaters.[61] It was here that the seventh and final lead plate was buried and a well-guarded camp made for the remainder of the day and night.[62]

The following morning they started their upstream journey on this tributary river, heading for Pickawillany, principal village of the Miamis or, as the tribe was more often referred to by the early French and English traders, the Twigtwees; the chief—called Demoiselle by the French traders, Old Britain by the English traders and Unemakemi by his own people—was the foremost chief of the Miamis and was known to be strongly pro-British.[63]

Even as the Céloron expedition started up the Great Miami, concern in the British colonies of North America was running high. Word had gradually filtered through them of the daring French expedition under a commander named Céloron, and of the engraved lead plates he was burying that claimed all territory west of the Alleghenies to the Mississippi as part of the French empire.

First had come the startling news from Sir William Johnson on the Mohawk River, who had been informed of the expedition by some Senecas. Their word alone might not have been taken seriously had they not brought along one of the actual engraved leaden plates that they had stolen from the French before it could be buried.

Then Pennsylvania's governor, Alexander Hamilton, had received an imperious letter from the French commander and quickly dispatched Sir William Johnson's most skilled and trusted field agent, trader George Croghan, to Logstown to see what he could discover. A better choice could not have been made; of all the English traders, none was held in such great respect and esteem among the northwestern tribes as Croghan, nor was any other white man so influential among them. He had long been one of the very select number of traders, English or French, who could move about at will and with impunity throughout the Ohio country. For many years he had traded with the tribes, helped them in every way possible—not infrequently to his own detriment or financial loss—and because of this he was honored, deeply trusted and unequivocally the most influential white man among the tribes inhabiting western Pennsylvania, the Ohio country and the far lands beyond. Only the influence Sir William enjoyed with the Iroquois League was comparable to Croghan's.

In a matter of weeks Croghan had accomplished his mission, and the intelligence he brought back to Gov. Hamilton was most alarming. He reported that he had arrived at Logstown only days after the force under Capt. Céloron—whom he referred to as "Monsieur Calaroon"—had passed through. From the Wyandot chief, Monakaduto—called Half King by most of the traders—he had learned of the threats these French were making against the British traders and the staggering territorial claims they were bolstering by planting engraved lead plates at the mouths of major tributaries of the Ohio.[64] To British colonial officials, all this was tantamount to a declaration of war, and carefully detailed reports were written and sent at once to His Royal Majesty, George II.

Disturbing as all this was, it did not discourage the British from taking steps to extend their colonial influence and possession west of the Alleghenies. More British traders than ever were crossing the mountains and engaging in trade with the Indians, and even those traders who had actually been ousted by the Céloron party were making their way back and rebuilding their trading posts.

To the south in Virginia two surveyors, Col. Joshua Fry and Peter Jefferson, were busy at work under a commission to establish the boundary line between North Carolina and Virginia. One of these two, while engaged in the appointed task, remarked with amusement to his partner that he had experienced difficulty in convincing his son that the trip was too dangerous and too strenuous for him to come along. The boy was only six, and his name was Thomas Jefferson.

About this same time the group of wealthy Virginians who had formed the Ohio Company with the goal of extending and populating Virginia's domain, as well as her trade with the northwestern Indians, erected at the mouth of Will's Creek on the upper Potomac, at the eastern terminus of the Nemacolin Trail and just south of the Pennsylvania border, a large, well-built and handsomely supplied trading house that was being called Will's Creek Station.[65]

So despite the disturbing news about the Céloron expedition, those who had been pushing for continued and even increased expansion in the beautiful but forbidding lands to the west were not overly concerned.

It was September 12 when the Céloron party reached Pickawillany. Although they knew in advance that it was a good-size village, they had not been quite prepared for what they found. The English traders there, of whom fewer than a dozen were on hand at any given time, had firmly established themselves and were even planning to construct a trading post that would be more like a fort than a store. Coming by canoe along the route Céloron had followed or by packhorse train along the sinuous forest trails, the traders arrived in an almost constant procession, bringing bounteous amounts of all those wondrous goods so coveted by the tribes. As a result, the fame of Pickawillany had spread widely among the Indians. The original village had by this time expanded to upward of 400 permanent dwellings—reasonably substantial log buildings—but there were, in addition, transient villages all along the perimeter where wegiwas, quonsets, hogans, tepees, trade tents and other temporary abodes had been set up. As a moderate estimate, Céloron set the population at not less than 4,000, including women and children as well as transients.

Obviously, since this was the principal village of the Miamis—or Twigtwees—there were far more of them than of any other single tribe or faction, but there were also healthy representations of Delawares under chiefs Pimoacan—whom the whites called Pipe—and Wingenund; Shawnees under the chief of their Maykujay sept, Moluntha; Hurons under Orontony; and Wyandots under Tarhe.[66] In addition, there were small factions of Kickapoos and Potawatomies, Sacs and Foxes, Mascoutens, Ottawas, Cahokias and Winnebagoes, and even a scattering of such distant tribes as Mandan Sioux, Menominees and Chippewas. Over them all, so long as they were at his village, Unemakemi reigned as principal chief.

Some of the tribes congregated here were hereditary enemies, and others were barely on speaking terms; but over the years Pickawillany had evolved into a neutral site where all, by unstated agreement, observed peace and could come and go for trade purposes without fear of attack.

A flame of envy flickered in Céloron's breast. This should be a village where trade was dominated by the French, not the British. More than ever he was determined that, if he had his way, that was how it would soon be. He counciled at length with the chiefs gathered here and distributed virtually all of the gifts he had remaining. The greater preponderance of those goods were given to Unemakemi, but Céloron's efforts to bribe or threaten him away from British influence failed, and it was Céloron and his men themselves who were threatened and left hastily before misfortune could befall them.

They continued following the river upstream, portaged to the St. Marys River and followed that to its confluence with the St. Joseph River, where they form the Maumee.[67] Now the party breathed a little easier because here was located a tiny French installation called Fort Miamis, commanded by Lt. Paul de Raimond.[68] They had anticipated a warm reception, good food and rest upon reaching the fort but were hugely disappointed to learn that the entire 22-man garrison was suffering under an epidemic of influenza. Unwilling to expose his men to it, Céloron ordered camp made outside the fort, breathing a sigh of relief that it was not his lot to be assigned to such an isolated post. Lt. Raimond, too miserable from the ravages of the flu to show much interest in Céloron's visit or hear an account of his journey, was short on rations himself and had no food to give them, but he was glad enough to let the expedition members select what watercraft they needed from the large number of bark canoes and French-style piroques stored at the fort and send them on their way.

The trip down the Maumee was uneventful, and on October 2 they arrived at the mouth of the river, with Maumee Bay and Lake Erie stretching out before them. Skimming along the western edge of Lake Erie, they ascended the Detroit River and arrived at Fort Pontchartrain on October 6. The French settlement of Detroit beyond its walls was quaint but decidedly rustic, with many Indians—mainly Ottawas and Hurons—walking the streets swathed in trade blankets despite the heat. The fort itself was a huge disappointment—dilapidated, unkempt and much smaller than Céloron anticipated. He pitied the officers and men stationed there and considered their being ordered to serve at such a post little short of a punishment and a certain road to obscurity without likelihood of advancement. With his letters of authorization from Galissonière, he acquired from the fort's store what further supplies they would need, gathered up dispatches and mail to be delivered at Fort Niagara, Fort Frontenac and Montreal; then his party was on its way once again on October 8.

Following the northern shoreline of Lake Erie, they once again reached the Niagara River, traversed the portage without problem and barely paused in passing Fort Niagara. They finally reached Fort Frontenac at the mouth of Lake Ontario on the third day of November. Seven days later, on November 10, they arrived back in Montreal, after being absent a total of 148 days and having traveled some 2,400 miles.

As Céloron had anticipated would be the case, the Marquis de la Galissonière had been recalled to France and the Marquis de la Jonquière was the new governor-general. It was to him that Céloron reported, presenting him with a fully detailed written report of the expedition, which he concluded with the notation:

All I can say is, that the nations of these countries are very ill disposed towards the French, and devoted entirely to the English.

"An excellent report, Captain," the governor-general said, looking up at the officer as he finished, "despite its negative conclusions. I commend you. If I have any questions as I study it further, I will contact you. Excused."

Perplexed at his rather cavalier treatment after so arduous an expedition, Céloron saluted smartly, turned and strode toward the door. As he opened it, the governor-general's voice halted him.

"Oh, Captain." Jonquière paused until Céloron turned and faced him. "I almost forgot. You have a new assignment. You will be leaving here a week from today to take command of Fort Pontchartrain at the Detroit."

Despite his treatment of Céloron, the Marquis de la Jonquière realized at once the seriousness of the situation and made an instant determination that something had to be done quickly to oust all English from the entire Ohio Valley drainage region—not just the traders but the settlers and land speculators—and make even more concerted efforts to win back the affections of the tribes for the French. He sent an immediate plea to the colonial minister in Paris, requesting that 10,000 French peasants be sent to New France at once, to be relayed as settlers to the Ohio River Valley, where their very presence would help solidify the French claims.

Some five months later—late in April 1750—at the Forks of the Muskingum, an Indian named Pucksinwah stood in the dimness of the large council house in Wapatomica, the capital village of his tribe, and let his gaze pass across the large assemblage of Shawnee chiefs and warriors before him. A very distinguished-looking man in his thirties, he was second war chief—under Kishkalwa—of the Shawnees and chief of the Kispokotha sept. More than that, he was a highly skilled negotiator who, in past years, had been one of the principals representing the Shawnees at important treaty negotiations. In addition to a number of Indian tongues, he spoke both English and French flawlessly, which was why he had been chosen to head the dual mission from which he had just returned.

He had not been pleased to learn, on his return, that the English trader George Croghan had only a short time before convinced the Indians at Logstown, after providing them with a large number of gifts, to permit the erection of a British fort at the Forks of the Ohio. While he liked Croghan personally—held the man in considerable esteem, actually—he felt the Indians at Logstown had acted hastily and unwisely.

Pucksinwah had been speaking to the assembly for nearly two hours, clearly and concisely recounting the occurrences of two separate missions he had just completed. The first had taken him to Philadelphia, the second to both Quebec and Montreal. At these places he had met in council with high governmental figures for penetrating discussions as to the intentions of the French and English in the territory occupied by northwestern tribes. It had been no easy matter to sift through the promises, half-truths and outright lies that had abounded in the talks, but the task was made easier because the whites on both sides underestimated the intelligence of the Indians. As a result, many of their flagrant falsehoods became painfully apparent.

The object of the crucial mission was to determine what stance the Shawnees would take in future events. It was clear to the tribe that in the not-too-distant future the French and English would be involved in a war over possession of the vast interior. Would the wisest course for the Shawnees be to support the French against the English, or the English against the French, or merely to remain neutral?

Pucksinwah had explained his findings carefully. To take a neutral stance was not advisable because not only would the trade upon which the Shawnees relied so heavily for their very survival be cut off by both sides, but sooner or later they would be drawn into the forthcoming conflict whether they wished it or not; their bargaining advantage would be lost, and they might well find themselves in the unenviable position of fighting both white factions simultaneously and possibly even neighboring tribes who were allied to them, yet without the resources to properly carry on such a conflict.

The whites themselves were fairly evenly matched in respect to waging war against one another without tribal alliances. Therefore whites on both sides were endeavoring to form balance-tipping alliances with tribes, and the French seemed to be having the greater success. Grudgingly or not, most tribes had to admit that although relationships had become strained in recent years, the French were easier to get along with than the British.

At the moment, Pucksinwah had gone on, the Shawnees were, as this assemblage knew, more closely tied to the British, largely due to trade; supporting them would be an easier matter than supporting the French. Their coolness toward the French was evident in the less-than-cordial reception given so recently to the expedition that had passed through their country under the man named Céloron. But they could not afford to lose sight of the fact that the British clearly aspired to expand westward beyond the mountains far more than they had already done.

The decision the Shawnees were ultimately to make had to be the result of close consideration of the consequences, Pucksinwah said. If these British happened to win a war against the French and forced them off the continent, how then could the Shawnees fend off the British bent on acquisition of their lands? From whom could they get the weapons, ammunition, gunpowder, supplies and all the other things necessary to fight and defeat so powerful an enemy? If, on the other hand, they were to support the French, they would lose the valuable trade of the British, which was far better in quality and much less costly than the French could provide, despite the rampant trade abuses of late. Yet if the French should win the conflict, the possibility of the Shawnees losing their lands was much reduced because, to their favor, the French clearly did not have the colonizing ambitions exhibited by the British and were more interested in continuing and expanding the fur trade among the tribes than in claiming and settling lands.

Both white factions had made similar offers to Pucksinwah's delegation in order to secure an alliance with the powerful warrior tribe, but no commitments were made. Now it was up to this body of Shawnees to decide what course would be followed: neutrality, support for the British, or support for the French. When Pucksinwah was asked what his own recommendation would be, since he was most familiar with all aspects of the problem, he considered this for a long moment before replying.

"What we decide," he said at length, speaking slowly, "will undoubtedly influence many of our neighboring tribes, and that is good, because in such a struggle the Indian should not be fighting the Indian. I have always believed that it is a mistake for Indians to take sides in any struggle between the whites. Yet in this case I think it best to stray from that position. Our thought must be not only whom we should support but, of perhaps greater importance, whom best could we live with *after* such a war if the side we support is the victor. Consider: If we join the British, there is but little doubt that they will win. If they do, we will then be faced with forcing them out of our lands—a struggle it is only too possible we could lose. If we join the French, there is a fair chance that they will win, and if so, we will then have them in our lands, but we have been able to live with them in friendship and peace before. Should we then someday have to force them out, the task in that case would be easier than against the British. For myself, I would say our best course—though bearing more risk—would be to support the French."

Discussions continued for many hours, and when at last they were finished, a decision had been made: Until such time as war broke out between the French and English, they would continue relations with the British as usual, especially in matters of trade. However, if a war of that nature did break out, the Shawnees would declare themselves allies of the French.

While all these matters of grave portent were occurring, there were some lighter moments. In late May 1750, well up the Kanawha, where it was known as the New River, what was being touted as the first white wedding west of the Allegheny crest was occurring at Draper's Meadows. Because there was not room enough in the Draper cabin for all who attended, the ceremony took place in the barn. The groom was the handsome, dark-haired, 21-year-old William Ingles, who had been accompanied to the Draper place by his father, Thomas, and two brothers, 19-year-old George and 15-year-old John.

Mary Draper was the bride, and at 18, she was said to be the prettiest girl on either side of the Blue Ridge. Her parents, Bettie and John, were there, of course, along with her brother, Johnny, who was now 20. Guests included the neighboring Burke, Lenard and Harmon families, as well as nearly a dozen others who had come from more distant settlements, such as Pattonsburg.

The ceremony was performed without problem, followed by an abundance of good food for everyone present. The barn soon reverberated with laughter, music and dancing. Without any doubt, the most indefatigable dancer was none other than the bride herself. She was not only an uncommonly beautiful young woman, she was also extremely athletic. Having no sisters, she had been raised with her brother, who was devoted to sports and outdoor activities of all kinds. In order to be included in what he did, she had to be able not only to keep up with him but to excel. At first she had a tough time, but eventually she was able to outrun, outjump and even outshoot him, much to her delight and his chagrin. Her athletic prowess, in fact, made her something of a celebrity. From a standing position beside her horse she could, with a single bound, leap full into the saddle. She could run, without misstep or fall, along the top of a split-rail fence and had no trouble crossing creeks and ravines on tree trunks or heavy branches that had fallen across them. One of her favorite exploits was to stand on the floor and suddenly leap like a gazelle completely over the back of a chair.

Occasionally she would be mildly chided for such unladylike acts, but she would simply toss her head and laugh, and her eyes would glint as she replied, "Well, one never can tell when it might come in handy to be able to do things like this."

The wedding festivities lasted well into the night, and when virtually everyone else—including her new husband—had petered out from exhaustion, Mary Draper Ingles was still ready and willing to dance.

Draper's Meadows, long the most isolated settlement on the frontier, could no longer boast that dubious honor. Settlers had filtered through in growing numbers, and by midsummer 1750 they had moved farther down the New River onto some of its tributaries. One such stream, called Onepakesipi by the Delawares, was surveyed by Col. John Lewis and his son Andrew.[69] Father and son were both badly scratched by the long, fierce green briers through which they had to push their way in order to make the survey. When Andrew, who was doing the survey notations, asked what name he should put down for the river, his father grimaced, held up a hand made bloody by the thorns and said, "Just call it the Greenbrier."

The Greenbrier Valley, despite its thorny vegetation in some places, was very beautiful and quickly became an area especially favored by settlers. Two of the new-comers, who decided to be partners, Stephen Sewell and Jacob Marlin, together built a little cabin near the mouth of Stony Creek.[70] This pair had formed a close friend-ship that lasted until the day they began to discuss religion. Marlin was Catholic, Sewell a Protestant, and the discussion degenerated into a dispute, then a heated argument and finally into a fistfight, which Marlin won. The upshot was that Sewell moved out, crossed to the other side of Stony Creek within sight and hearing of the cabin and set up housekeeping inside an enormous hollow sycamore tree. They never resolved their dispute, but for their mutual protection, each morning whoever was first to rise would call out to the other to see if he was all right and continue calling at intervals until he got a response. Once it was heard, that was their last vocal contact for the day.

Others were more inclined to roam than to settle. Far to the north on the western Pennsylvania frontier, one such individual was a hunter who would often spend long periods away from his family in their cabin on the Juniata River, his only companion being a large, yellow dog. They were on just such an outing in late October 1750, moving along at a steady mile-eating pace through the dense wood-lands not far from the Allegheny—the hunter with his Pennsylvania rifle held ready for instant use and the dog with tail held at a jaunty angle, close at his heels. Once they paused briefly when a large turkey gobbler burst from cover before them, rocketed upward in a steep climb over the treetops and in an instant disappeared from view beyond bright fall foliage. The dog looked at his master and gave the faintest little whine, and the hunter grinned, reached out and patted his head.

"No birds for us today, Kicker. We're heading for home, and we want some more substantial meat than that to take along."

Kicker tilted his head as he listened, and his tail waved back and forth twice. The hunter chuckled and resumed his pace, and the dog fell in beside him. They had walked for nearly an hour more when suddenly the hunter stopped in a half-crouch, holding out a hand palm down. Kicker immediately dropped to his belly and remained still, though keenly alert. No more than 40 yards ahead, a fine fat doe stood beside a fallen tree. It was a tribute to the hunter's abilities that he had seen her at all, so well was she camouflaged. Without undue movement he checked and readied his gun and slowly brought it to bear. The sharp crack of the rifle was followed instantly by the deer flopping to the ground, where she lay motionless. The well-aimed ball had broken her spine high on her neck.

Kicker issued a small whimper of eagerness but remained in place, as did the hunter. He rapidly reloaded and then for fully a quarter-hour remained crouched where he was, watching and listening for anyone who might have been attracted by the shot.

At length he straightened and held out a hand again. "Kicker, you stay put for now, hear?" He moved away, cautiously approaching his prey, the dog watching him intently. At the fallen deer the hunter took one last careful look around and, satisfied there was no one about, leaned his gun against the fallen tree, unsheathed his knife and began skinning his kill. He worked swiftly and was nearly finished when a tremendous blow on his back sent him sprawling, his knife spinning out of his hand. At the same moment a terrifying squalling filled the air.

It was a mountain lion, undoubtedly attracted by the scent of the deer's blood and willing to risk making this unusual attack to steal the carcass. The hunter yelled and grappled with the big cat, intuitively wrapping his arms tightly around the large head and his legs around the animal's middle, frantically endeavoring to avoid the powerful teeth and slashing claws. Locked together, they rolled over and over in the leaf litter on the forest floor. An instant later Kicker plunged onto the scene and flung himself upon the cat, clamping his powerful jaws on the most vital spot he could reach—the big animal's testicles.

The cat screamed in pain and fury and turned upon its new attacker. Hit by a blow from a muscular paw, Kicker released his grip and leaped away a dozen feet, then circled, growling savagely. The cat crouched and turned with the movements as the big dog looked for an opening. By this time the hunter had recovered his gun, and a single quick shot to the brain solved the problem. Kicker dashed in and worried the carcass a moment, then moved off a short distance and lay down. His left rear haunch had been laid open by two of the animal's claws, and he began licking the wounds.

The hunter, breathing heavily, was unhurt save for a single claw slash on his left forearm and quickly reloaded. Then he walked over and checked his dog's wounds. The two gouges were ugly but not dangerous, and he grinned as he ruffled the dog's ears.

"You're a right good pal to have along, Kicker," he said. The dog raised his head, thumped his tail against the ground a few times and then resumed licking. "Well, now," the hunter said as he straightened and looked back toward the dead cat, "won't little Simon's eyes open wide when he sees that painter's skin!"

The "little Simon" he referred to was the eldest of his four sons, a very self-assured eight-year-old who could already be relied upon to help his mother take good care of his younger brothers, George, James and the toddler, Thomas. Chuckling at the thought, the hunter turned away, recovered his knife and bent to finish skinning and quartering the deer. Skinning the big cat would be next. It would make a heavier load for him to carry than anticipated, but he'd manage. He always had. This was the man who had once carried the heart, liver and hindquarters of an elk he had killed some ten miles in order to bring the meat back to his family.

This was the well-known hunter Simon Girty.

About this same time, another experienced frontiersman, Christopher Gist, left Will's Creek Station on the Potomac on behalf of the Ohio Company to inspect possible settlement areas in the tract the company had received as a grant from King George. He stopped first to visit the Indians at Logstown, where he was received with pleasure by the Wyandots, Delawares and Mingoes on hand and spent many hours counciling and smoking with them. While there he also visited with resident trader Barney Curran, who had traded there longer than anyone else.

Curran readily admitted to Gist that he was worried. Though the tribes were treating them well enough, he had a "feeling" that all was not as it seemed and there were some big troubles ahead. Yet when Gist tried to pin him down to specifics, Curran simply shook his head and shrugged. He said trader George Croghan, who might know more, had passed through with his Seneca half-breed friend, Andrew Montour, and a dozen other traders only a few days before en route to Goschachgunk. Gist set off at once, descended the Ohio to the Muskingum and then paddled upstream to the principal Delaware village. There he met Croghan, who had stopped by Goschachgunk to pay his respects, drop off some trade goods and gather up some of the traders there to journey with him to Pickawillany. Croghan said he knew nothing more than Barney Curran had already told him but that he himself had been experiencing the same sense of disquiet. He also said he was thoroughly disgusted that, despite the fact the Indians had—through Croghan's own efforts—granted permission for the erection of a British fort at the Forks of the Ohio, governmental decision had now been made against doing so: by Virginia on the grounds that the post would be too distant and too exposed to be properly maintained, by Pennsylvania on the grounds that it did not have funds enough to do so. Both the Pennsylvania Assembly and the Virginia Council had even condemned Croghan for placing them in a position where they had to refuse.[71] Croghan was bitter, considering it a very serious mistake that he was sure they would eventually come to regret.

While Gist conferred with the tribal leaders at Goschachgunk for three days, Croghan and some of his traders left, Montour accompanying them, and went to the little Indian town called Whitewoman's Creek Village on the stream of that name, a tributary of the Tuscarawas a short distance above Goschachgunk. The village, though small, was one of the oldest established Wyandot villages. There, as they had done on numerous past occasions, the traders paid their respects to the medicine woman, who had great influence in the tribe. There was always a sense of wonderment in such visits; wonderment that came from the fact that she was the white woman for whom the tributary had been named. Some 40 years previously she had been captured in New England as a young woman named Mary Harris. After being shunted from tribe to tribe for several years, she came into possession of the Wyandots, who admired her courage and were more than impressed with her knowledge of herbs and folk medicine. Before long she had become established in her own village, and the place became a focal point for those who were suffering from maladies or injuries. She had married a Wyandot and bore him children but had outlived them all and now was content to live out the rest of her days practicing her lore. She dearly loved rum, and even though Croghan never traded in any form of whiskey, he always made sure to bring along a small bottle for her. They visited with her for a day, and when they returned to Goschachgunk, they found Gist had finished his counciling and was ready to leave.

As soon as Croghan proposed that Gist accompany them to Pickawillany, he accepted, and the long journey together was made safely. They arrived at Pickawillany on January 18, 1751, and found close to 20 British traders already present— English, Scots and Irish. All pitched in and by the end of March had erected, under the approval of Unemakemi, a spacious log trading post that could almost pass as a fort; the large main building was enclosed within a wall of split logs that had three gates. They had even dug a well within the walls.

Early in April an extended council was held with the Miamis, Weas and Piankeshaws under Pickawillany and representatives of the Shawnees, Delawares, Wyandots and Mingoes who were on hand. Some were glumly predicting bad things to come from the French because of the treatment the party under Céloron had experienced here the previous year. Unemakemi merely laughed and sloughed off the concerns, saying the French would not be fools enough to come here and attempt to make trouble. Almost as if on cue, a party of four Ottawas arrived bearing a French flag and gifts from the Marquis de la Jonquière. Unemakemi, with no vestige of tact, gravely insulted the Ottawa deputation, threw some of the gifts into the fire and told them to take the rest of the gifts and get out and tell the governor-general that so long as he was alive, Pickawillany would never again trade with the French. Then, as if nothing had happened, he gave an order, and a large, quite impressive feather dance was put on by some 40 Indian men and women.

Gist was not at all sure they'd heard the last of this matter, and when he reported back to officials at the Ohio Company the following June, bringing good information respecting where settlements could best be established along the south bank of the Ohio, he also warned that there might be trouble afoot stemming from the French. Pickawillany he described to them as the largest and strongest Indian town in America, and he added that George Croghan had announced to all the Indians there that a major council, to which all the northwestern tribes were invited, was to be held in early June the following year at Logstown. At that time, Croghan had said, representatives of the Colony of Virginia would make a strong effort to effect a formal alliance with all the tribes.

Taking advantage of this upswing of fortune for the British trade on the frontier, John Fraser, who had established himself well at the villages from Logstown up to the mouth of the Kiskeminetas on the Allegheny, now built a very good trading post at the Seneca village of Venango, located at the mouth of the stream the Céloron party had named Rivière aux Boeufs.[72]

The fury of the Marquis de la Jonquière was great when he learned not only of Fraser's new post but also of how his Ottawa emissaries had been treated by Unemakemi. Immediately he sent an express to Detroit with orders for Céloron to attack and destroy Pickawillany. With it he dispatched a strong body of Canadian militia under a wild-tempered Canadian-Ottawa half-breed, Charles Michel de Lan-glade, to aid the Fort Pontchartrain regulars.

In July 1751, Mary Draper Ingles and her husband, William, the first couple to get married west of the Allegheny crest, now became the parents of the first white child born to that distinction—a fine healthy boy they named Thomas, after William's father. But there were a growing number of stories of Indians prowling about in the area, and all the settlers were becoming nervous. Up the Greenbrier, at the mouth of Stony Creek, Dr. Thomas Walker passed through with his party, just completing his second exploratory trip, which had taken him west of the New River to the Holston River, Clinch River, Cumberland Gap and other locations. He had intended to go farther, but his party became so unnerved at all the Indian sign being discovered that they turned back. They followed the Bluestone River down to the New River, descended that as far as the mouth of the Greenbrier and then went up that latter stream to Stony Creek. There they encountered Stephen Sewell and Jacob Marlin, still living within sight of one another but still estranged. The Walker party continued toward home but not before warning the two whites about the Indians. Soon Marlin packed up and returned to the eastern settlements. Sewell, however, decided he'd explore on his own a bit. He followed the Greenbrier down to the New River and started down that stream, but he had traveled only about ten miles when he encountered a party of Indians, who promptly killed and scalped him.[73]

In Quebec, where the ailing governor-general Jonquière had gone for treatment, he received word from the colonial minister in Paris that his request for 10,000 peasants to settle in the Ohio Valley had been denied. No news had come in respect to his order that Pickawillany be destroyed, and somehow he just didn't care anymore. His health continued to degenerate, and on a bright Sunday morning—May 17, 1752—he quietly died. The Baron de Longueuil immediately assumed control until the favor of His Majesty could be known.

Had Jonquière lived only a little longer, he would have been gratified with what occurred at Pickawillany. Exactly five weeks later, on June 21, the force he had sent utterly destroyed the Miami principal village. Langlade, who had led the Canadians—and a party of Chippewas and Ottawas under Chief Pontiac—in their attack, had personally slain Unemakemi, cutting out his heart while he was still alive, eating a portion of it and then beheading the chief's dead body. Many other Indians had been killed, along with some of the traders on hand, and those who were not killed were taken captive, to be executed later.[74]

Immediately following the death of Unemakemi and the destruction of Pickawillany, Unemakemi's second, Michikiniqua—Little Turtle—became principal chief of the Miamis, and in a very short time he had established a new capital village of the tribe, called Kekionga, at the head of the Maumee River, where it is formed by the confluence of the St. Marys and St. Josephs rivers.[75]

The major council of the tribes that had been scheduled by George Croghan was held at Logstown on June 9, 1752, and it ended up satisfying no one. Croghan was there, of course, as was Gist, along with Commissioners William Patton, Joshua Fry and others. For many of the Indians on hand, it was the first time they truly learned the details of the Lancaster Treaty of 1744, in which the Iroquois had blandly sold to the British for £600 the entire Ohio River drainage. They were furious and absolutely repudiated that treaty on the grounds that the Iroquois had had no right to sell lands not belonging to them—and the British had had no right to buy. When they learned that the Ohio Company, acting on the surveys Gist had made, was already preparing to establish settlements in the Ohio Valley—the first to be at the mouth of Chartier's Creek, two miles below the Forks of the Ohio, where the company also intended to erect a fort—they warned against it in the most serious manner. The talks continued, and the Indians again offered the British the right to build a fort at the Forks of the Ohio, and though they signed the Logstown Treaty on June 13, they continued to maintain that the British had no right to settle on the Ohio.

Because his fortunes seemed to be swinging toward the Ohio River as a result of his connection with the Ohio Company, Christopher Gist, in July 1752, abandoned his settlement on the Yadkin River and, along with 11 other families, established a settlement that included his own combined cabin and trading post 12 miles west of Laurel Hill, at the foot of the west slope of Chestnut Hill, only a short distance northeast of the Nemacolin Trail.[76]

At the same time the Ohio Company erected a strong storage house at the mouth of Redstone Creek. Called a hangard, the storage house was constructed of stone and notched logs, 20 feet wide and 30 feet long, and was to be used to house trade goods at the western terminus of the Nemacolin Trail. It was situated on the slope just above the Monongahela and adjacent to the prehistoric Indian ruins called Redstone Old Fort.

For the Shawnees, it all seemed to emphasize the assessment that Pucksinwah had made: The British meant to continue their encroachment, and with ever more settlers sinking roots on the frontier, the Ohio would be next. So despite what the French force had done at Pickawillany, the Shawnees still considered the British to be the more dangerous potential enemy and remained convinced that, as Pucksinwah had warned, the British had "very bad designs" against all the Indians, including the Shawnees; thus they maintained their resolve to side with the French when the rapidly looming war between the two finally broke out. While biding time for that to occur, they had other problems. On May 23, 1753, excessive rains caused heavy flooding on the Scioto River, and the Shawnees at Sinioto had to scramble to safety on higher ground and watch stoically as the water rose nine feet high in their expansive village and the powerful current swept it all away except for three or four cabins. George Croghan was visiting at the time and sympathized deeply with them, giving them what stores he could out of his own supplies to help make up for their loss. He expected they would now relocate the village far up the Scioto, perhaps at the Pickaway Plains, where other Shawnee villages were located, but such was not the case. Within a few days a new Sinioto was being established, still close to the mouth of the Scioto, but this time to the east of the river on the much higher terrace overlooking the Ohio.[77]

Although the Baron de Longueuil had hoped he would be permanently appointed to the position of governor-general, which he had temporarily filled on Jonquière's death, it was not to be. That top post was quickly filled by a particularly distinguished soldier and statesman who arrived from France, the Marquis de Duquesne de Menneville.[78] The new governor-general quickly familiarized himself with the situation on the frontier and ordered Capt. Henri Marin to take a force of 1,000 men and build three new French forts to protect a better portage route that had been discovered from Lake Erie to the upper Ohio—a route that avoided the difficult Lake Chautauqua Portage. By the time they reached there, the force had been augmented by other detachments to a total number of about 1,500. The new route began at the peninsula called Presque Isle—which Duquesne termed "the finest harbor in nature"—on Pennsylvania's Lake Erie frontage, where Marin's men built Fort Presque Isle. They then constructed a good portage road some 15 miles south to the headwaters of the Rivière aux Boeufs, where Fort Le Boeuf was built. It was too late in the season by then to start construction of the third post—Fort Machault—but they nevertheless followed the stream nearly 60 miles down to its mouth at the Allegheny, where Venango was located and where the new English trading post had been erected by John Fraser. The Indians had fled from the village on the approach of the French, but the trading post was captured and all its goods confiscated. Fraser was not there at the time—he was occupied with building a new log cabin as his residence on the Monongahela at the mouth of Turtle Creek, ten miles above the Forks of the Ohio—but two of his men were taken captive.[79]

One of the more experienced and reliable of the English traders, John Fraser, built a cabin of his own the following year far closer to the Forks than anyone previously—on the right bank of the Monongahela, only ten miles distant from where the Ohio River forms.[80] A French flag was raised over the trading post, and Capt. Daniel Joncaire, who had accompanied the force, was given a small detachment and ordered to hold the place until Fort Machault could be erected there. Seneca Indians had watched the whole tableau from hiding, and they immediately sent runners to inform the Indians and British at Logstown of what had happened.

When Robert Dinwiddie, Governor of Virginia, learned of the unprecedented French action at Venango, he saw the danger signs clearly and was more than ever convinced of the necessity for the British to get a fort erected at the Forks of the Ohio without delay; if they did not, he warned, the toehold the French were presently establishing would quickly become an iron grasp on the entire Ohio Valley. When the Virginia Assembly continued to ignore his plea for funds to build the fort that the Indians had given them the right to erect, determined Scot that he was, Dinwiddie appealed directly to the King, and the response was exactly what he wanted: the authority to supersede the Assembly in this matter. As His Majesty George instructed:

> *Your plan for the construction of forts, in particular a strong fort at the Forks of the Ohio, is approved for the security and protection of our subjects and of the Indians in alliance with us. You are directed to procure funds from the Colonial Government that a sufficient number of cannon may be shipped for emplacement in the forts. Our will and pleasure is that you use your utmost endeavors to erect the said forts as soon as the nature of the service will admit. Our further will and pleasure is that you should bring forth with cause the whole or part of our militia of the Province of Virginia now under your government, to be drawn forth and armored as you may judge necessary for our service. In case any of the Indians not in alliance*

with us or dependent upon our Crown, or any Europeans under pretense of alliance with the said Indians, should presume to interrupt you in the execution of these our orders, you are first to represent our undoubted right and to require the peaceable departure of any such Europeans or Indians. But if they should still persist, our will and pleasure is that you should repel by force. Since the Crown has received infor-mation that a number of Europeans not our subjects are appearing in a hostile manner in the area, you are instructed to inquire into the truth of the report. If you shall find that any number of persons shall presume to erect any fort or forts within the limits of our Province of Virginia, you are first to require of them peaceably to depart; and if, notwithstanding your admonitions, they do still endeavor to carry out any such unlawful and unjustifiable designs, we do hereby strictly charge you and command you to drive them off by force of arms, in execution of which, all our officers, civil and military, within the limits of your government, are to be aiding and assisting to the utmost of their abilities.

Dinwiddie set wheels in motion on October 13, 1753. The man he selected to carry the eviction order to the French commander on the Allegheny was a promising individual only 21 years old whom he had recently appointed adjutant of Virginia's Southern Military District—a tall, intelligent young major named George Washing-ton.[81]

Overcoming a great many difficulties and distinct hazards on his way, young Washington performed his mission well, aided by Christopher Gist as his guide. In a brief visit at Logstown, he was able to acquire Chief Monakaduto and some of his warriors as escorts; Monakaduto was far more in favor of the British than the French, especially since some of his own men had been among those injured in the French destruction of Pickawillany.[82] In a very dangerous winter trek through 500 miles of wilderness, Washington delivered the message to the French officer holding the Fraser Trading Post at Venango, Capt. Daniel Joncaire. That officer sent him farther up the Rivière aux Boeufs to address himself to Joncaire's superior, Capt. Jacques Legardeur de St. Pierre, and it was to him that Washington presented the letter from Gov. Dinwiddie, who had written:

To the Commander of the Western
Forts of the French
Sir:

As Governor of the Province of Virginia, it has come to me to my astonish-ment that French troops have built forts upon lands so notoriously known to be the property of the Crown of Great Britain. I must desire you to acquaint me by whose authority and instructions you have lately marched from Canada with an armed force, and invaded the King of Great Britain's territories. It becomes my duty to require your peaceable departure; and that you would forbear prosecuting a purpose so disruptive and interruptive of the harmony and good understanding which His Majesty is desirous to continue and cultivate with the Most Christian King. I persuade myself you will receive and entertain Major Washington with the candor and politeness natural to your nation; and it will give me the greatest satisfaction if you return him with an answer suitable to my wishes for a very long and lasting peace between us.

Robert Dinwiddie

St. Pierre conferred with fellow officers for three days before handing Washington a written reply for Dinwiddie, which was short and disappointing:

It is not for me to set forth the Evidence and Reality of the Rights of the King [of France] and to contest the pretensions of the King of Great Britain there. I would have preferred to have Major Washington proceed to the main French headquarters in Montreal, but since his instructions are to go no farther than here, I will transmit your letter to the Marquis Duquesne, Governor of New France, for his orders. Meanwhile, I will remain at my post, according to the commands of my general.

Washington and his party accepted the message and returned at once to Venango. There, because of the urgency Dinwiddie stressed in regard to the mission, he proposed that he and Gist continue the journey overland on foot while the other members of the party made their own way back, following the river at a slower pace. Gist thought it a bad idea and said so, but Washington was adamant. Monakaduto was very upset, as there were chiefs waiting back at Logstown to hear the results of the mission.

On January 6, 1754, Washington and Gist arrived back at Will's Creek Station on the Potomac, after much difficulty and suffering. Here they encountered a number of families on their way to settle in the Monongahela Valley. It was at Will's Creek Station that Washington left Gist, continued to Williamsburg and delivered the written French response into the hands of the much-impressed Gov. Dinwiddie at Williamsburg, who soon had Washington's journal published.[83] Word of the young major's rather incredible feat spread throughout the colony, and quite soon his name was on everyone's tongue. As for Washington himself, his brief taste of the upper Ohio had inspired an appetite for much more. Already connected with the Ohio Land Company, he was now determined to involve himself deeply and personally in the claiming, settlement and development of the Ohio River Valley, quite well aware that fortunes in both land and money awaited those astute enough to take advantage of the opportunity just beginning to open there. He also, in the strongest possible terms, advocated construction of a fort at the Forks of the Ohio.

Gov. Dinwiddie was not slow in reacting to the French response. He wrote out instructions for young Washington, giving him another task of considerable responsibility:

I am giving you a new command. You are to go to Frederick city and take command of the militia of that county. I am also appointing the trader, William

Trent, as your lieutenant, with the rank of captain. I have already sent him to Augusta County to recruit fifty more and to go with them at once to the Forks of the Ohio to build a strong fort. I don't think it is necessary for me to tell you the urgency of this step and how essential it is that no one is permitted to stand in the way of its execution. The remainder of the force is to assemble at Alexandria, where it will be equipped. There, you are to train and discipline them in the best manner possible. Having all things in readiness there, you are to use all expedition in proceeding to the Forks of the Ohio with the men under your command, and there you are to finish and complete in the best manner and as soon as you possibly can, the fort which I expect will already be begun by then by Captain Trent. You are to act on the defensive, but in case any attempts are made to obstruct the work or interrupt our settlements by any persons whatsoever, to make prisoners of, or kill and destroy them.

With these matters in motion, Dinwiddie's task then became one of convincing the other colonies—and their respective Assemblies—to help quash the French claims and secure the Ohio for Britain. It was difficult in the extreme and occupied his entire time during February and March 1754. Often he had to exhort them in passionate terms to get even the least compliance. "Think!" he cried in his address to the Virginia House of Burgesses. "You see the infant torn from the unavailing struggles of the distracted mother, the daughters ravished before the eyes of their wretched parents and then, with cruelty and insult, butchered and scalped. We must prevent this. We must vote funds enough to raise troops and clear the French from the area and safeguard British interests!"

Gradually he got some of the help he sought, both in manpower and funds, though nowhere near what he considered the minimum needed.[84] Yet he forged ahead, still working on that problem while endeavoring to attend to others no less pressing. Among these was selecting a commander to go to Alexandria and lead the varied force that would gradually come together. He considered Washington for that post but realized in the same thought that, capable though he had proven himself to be, he was still too young and inexperienced for the job. Eventually he decided upon an old friend, Col. Joshua Fry, who had formerly been professor of mathematics at William and Mary College. Washington was named second-in-command and, on March 2, 1754, only a short time after his twenty-second birthday, was promoted to the rank of lieutenant colonel in the Virginia militia.[85]

Col. Fry arrived at Alexandria and began to mold into military shape the 300 men already assembled who were being called the Virginia Regiment. Soon half of these men were placed under Washington's command, and he marched them to Will's Creek Station, which was to form their base of operations. It was discovered that the French were preparing their own force to secure the Forks of the Ohio, and so it now became a race to see who would arrive first and with the best. Will's Creek Station was 140 miles away from the Forks, and there were now two chief concerns: whether Capt. Trent would be able to fortify himself at the Forks before the French arrived, and whether Washington and Fry would arrive in time with their force to secure the position.

At Fort Le Boeuf, Capt. St. Pierre had been stricken with fever, and the Marquis Duquesne had no recourse but to regretfully replace him with a new commander. He selected for that post his own aide-de-camp, Capt. Pierre de Contrecoeur, who, though younger and less experienced than St. Pierre, was nonetheless a good soldier who combined imagination and daring with solid dependability. With 1,100 combined regulars and Canadian volunteers, he moved at once to Venango—dropping off reinforcements at both Fort Presque Isle and Fort Le Boeuf —and began construction of a substantial fort there. By April 12 it was nearly completed and had already been named Fort Machault.[86]

Impressed with the number of French soldiers flooding into the country and knowing that a great confrontation between the French and the British was now very close, most of the tribes had elected to support the French, and great numbers of warriors hovered nearby, waiting and very ready. The wait was not long. Informed by the Indians that a small British force had already begun constructing a fort at the Forks of the Ohio, Contrecoeur left a small body of men behind to complete the works and led 500 men down the Allegheny in 60 bateaux and 300 canoes.

On April 17 they took the incomplete works at the Forks of the Ohio without firing a shot. Capt. William Trent was away with a small detachment at the time, having gone back toward Will's Creek Station to get food, as supplies were all but gone. He had left Ens. Edward Ward in command of the 41 men still at the Forks, but when they saw the size of Contrecoeur's force they capitulated without resistance. They were treated well and allowed to leave but were given orders never to return. Within moments after their departure, the poor works they had already completed were being torn down and construction had begun on a much larger and better fort that Contrecoeur was already calling Fort Duquesne.

Pucksinwah was among the Indians who had witnessed the bloodless taking of the Forks of the Ohio by the French, and had there been any doubt in his mind of his decision to back the French instead of the British, it was now dispelled. Indian runners had raced off to spread the word at various villages, and Pucksinwah knew what the general reaction would be: The French are men, and the British are weaker than women!

Washington, heading for the Forks of the Ohio, had led an advance detachment of two infantry companies out of Alexandria on April 2. Three weeks later he arrived at Will's Creek Station and learned of the French capture of the unfinished works at the Forks of the Ohio. He decided to move his small force to the mouth of Redstone Creek and build a fort there, then await further orders. Just after crossing the upper Youghiogheny, Washington was joined by Chief Monakaduto and 150 warriors. The chief informed him that a French detachment of 32 men was on a spying mission in the area under command of Ens. Coulon de Jumonville. The Indians having tracked the French detachment to where they had camped in a well-hidden place at Great Meadows, about six miles distant, Washington took a detachment of 40 men and set out to strike them under cover of darkness. The surprise was complete, and a fierce attack was made about dawn on April 28. Ten of the French soldiers were slain, including Ens. Jumonville, who was killed by Monakaduto with a tomahawk blow. Another 21 of the French were captured, and only one escaped. Washington had one man killed and three wounded. All the French dead were scalped, and Washington gave Jumonville's scalp to Monakaduto to take to the Delawares as an encouragement for them to side with the British.

The following day, Col. Fry, who had advanced with his force to Will's Creek Station, was killed when he was thrown from his horse. Washington was building an entrenchment at Great Meadows when Christopher Gist brought word of it, and Washington immediately assumed command. It was on June 5 that Fry's army reached him, raising his total force to 360, exclusive of Indians.[87]

Just about this same time, Pucksinwah was a member of Kishkalwa's deputation representing the Shawnees in the council of tribes called by Contrecoeur at the Forks. Fort Duquesne was almost completed, and it was an imposing structure. There was little doubt in the minds of the Indians attending, despite the defeat of the Jumonville detachment, that the French were here to stay. Pierre de Contrecoeur had given a rousing address, pausing every few moments to let the various interpreters catch up in relaying his message. He told them that the French and English were now at war and, with the force of his speech, his logic and his directness, convinced them all—Shawnees, Delawares, Mingoes, Wyandots, Senecas—to take up the hatchet against the English.[88] Since the Shawnees were already predisposed to do exactly that, their agreement came quickly; the other chiefs, impressed that the ferocious Shawnees should so swiftly make alliance with the French, fell in line with alacrity.

Washington had decided to improve the road leading to Redstone Old Fort. He pushed on in that effort on June 16 and reached Gist's settlement at the west foot of Chestnut Hill on June 26. The following day he learned that a force of 500 French, under the command of Coulon de Villiers, half-brother of the slain Coulon de Jumonville, were on the march to attack him. He at once ordered a retreat to the Great Meadows entrenchment and dug in, naming the rude defensive works Fort Necessity. It was here, on July 3, that the French attacked, and the nine-hour Battle of Fort Necessity was fought. When Washington's casualties numbered about 100, he surrendered, signed the capitulation and was allowed to lead his battered survivors back to Virginia.[89] Capt. Villiers, leading his force back to Fort Duquesne, burned Gist's settlement, the Ohio Company's storehouse and whatever other cabins could be found.

The French and Indian War had begun, and the Indians—with the exception of Monakaduto and his followers—were jubilant with the first results. With Contrecoeur's blessing they dispersed, some back to their villages but the majority on raids against outlying settlements. All were ready in an instant to return when he should issue a call.

Those Indians who set out on raids had ample targets, especially in the valley of the upper New River. In addition to the Draper's Meadows settlement, a new one called Ingles' Ferry was established right on the New River, and the ensuing settlement was scattered on both sides of the stream. Close to Ingles' Ferry a Dunkard family named McCorkle settled on a fine bottom, and their community immediately became known as Dunkard Bottom. Just a little over five miles west of the New River, the James Reed family established a settlement and named it after their former home in Ireland, calling it Dublin. Perhaps the boldest of the new settlers in this area of southwestern Virginia, however, was James Burke. He struck out westward from the Dublin settlement and finally stopped 35 miles later to sink his roots on the west bank of the headwaters of a sparkling-clear little stream that he named after the first animal he saw on its bank as he approached—a large gray wolf. Wolf Creek flowed somewhat north of east and emptied into the New River some 40 miles below Draper's Meadows.[90] Burke poetically called his new settlement Burke's Garden, and soon half a dozen others who had heard of it came, saw and settled. It did not take too long, however, for Burke to pay the ultimate price for tempting fate. In October, while riding his horse on a little exploratory trip down Wolf Creek, he had not traveled more than a mile when he suddenly felt a thud on his chest and looked down to see a feathered shaft protruding, already stained scarlet from his blood. He wheeled his horse around and galloped back to his cabin. When his horse stopped, he tried to dismount but found he could not move. A moment later he tilted to one side and fell heavily, dead before he struck the ground at his doorstep.

Far to the north and slightly east, the families of David Tygart and Thomas Files, unlike other families that turned downstream when they came to the Monongahela, made their way upstream. They felt they would be much safer from Indian incursions there than would those who were settling farther downstream. They followed the river until they came to a fine stream emptying into the Monongahela from an exceptionally pretty valley. Tygart promptly named it Tygart Valley and, not terribly imaginative, named the stream Tygart Valley River.[91] The two families paddled up the lovely tributary, and soon Files saw the place he liked, a fine meadow area at the mouth of a small creek, and decided he would make his claim there. He put ashore at once with his wife and four children. Tygart continued a few miles more and settled in a place he thought even prettier than the selection Files had made. Both families built their cabins and were doing quite well, but being so isolated, they began to get nervous. They finally decided to leave and settle somewhat closer to other border settlements. Before they could get their goods together and packed, however, Indians ascended the creek and struck the Files place. The 12-year-old son, William, was some distance away from the cabin when the attack came, but he was close enough to witness everything. He ran all the way to the Tygart cabin to get help. Heavily armed, the Tygarts came to the still-burning cabin and found Tom Files, his wife and three children close to the house, all five dead and scalped. They buried them quickly, and that same day, bringing William Files with them, they departed for good, leaving behind only an empty cabin and a stream and valley that were named.

In early November 1754, troops bivouacked high up the Potomac at Will's Creek Station and began to build a fort that would be the launching post for the new army that would move against the French the following summer—an army that would have as its commander a seasoned officer of high repute from England. King George, in appointing him, was certain that he was the man who would bring the French in America to their knees. He was a 65-year-old major general who sailed from England on January 15 with 1,000 top-quality regulars—the 44th and 48th regiments. His name was Edward Braddock. He would rendezvous his army at Alexandria and then follow the Potomac upstream to Will's Creek Station for final preparations at the fort there, assuming its construction was completed by then. In fact, it was only 16 days after Braddock's departure from England that the fort in question was completed. It was named Fort Cumberland.

During the following month Christopher Gist visited old friends and neighbors in the area where he had previously lived along the Yadkin River. He held his listeners enthralled as he regaled them with the tale of his exploits with George Washington, both in the journey to Fort Le Boeuf and in the disaster that had occurred at Great Meadows. When he told them about Braddock's impending arrival and that the famed general would be building an army to strike the French at Fort Duquesne, a young man of 21 years seated among his listeners asked if he thought Braddock was going to need good wagon men. Gist replied that he undoubtedly would, and the young man, Daniel Boone, said he was as good a man as there was with horses and wagons, and he reckoned he'd mosey on back to Fort Cumberland with Gist when he left and join up. He did so, separating from Gist and heading for Alexandria with Gist's son, Nathaniel, when the elder Gist himself veered off on another path to return to his burned-out place at Chestnut Hill and continue the rebuilding he had begun.

In April young Boone was actively at work as a wagoner for Braddock's army in Alexandria and was becoming very friendly with another wagoner who had not only journeyed down the Ohio and visited with the Shawnees in their villages but had even built a small trading post in their Kan-tuck-kee hunting grounds south of the Ohio River. John Findlay, former trader, explorer and adventurer, without half-trying had ignited a spark in the imagination of Daniel Boone and an absolute determination to one day see for himself that marvelous land.

Early in May 1755 the long-anticipated call came to the various tribes from Contrecoeur, a note of desperation in his summons. The new British army—larger, stronger and commanded by Maj. Gen. Edward Braddock—was advancing on Fort Duquesne, where there were now only 300 soldiers. Braddock had 2,500 men, and the French, without the help of their Indian allies, would be annihilated. The British Army was approaching by way of the Nemacolin Trail, now being called Braddock's Road.

Some of the Indians were on raids so far distant that they were unable to get news of the summons in time to respond. One of these was a 40-man war party led by the Shawnee subchief Black Wolf. For weeks he had been leading his warriors in fierce attacks against isolated cabins on the frontier. On July 8, 1755, they found themselves farther up the New River than any of them had been before, and abruptly they discovered the settlement known as Draper's Meadows.

The attack they launched that bright Tuesday morning was so wholly unexpected that scarcely a hand was raised in defense. The first to see them coming was Bettie Draper, who was a little distance from her cabin. She shrieked a warning and ran back to the house, snatched up her baby and bolted through the back door, running as she had never run before. A shot sounded, and the lead ball broke her right arm, causing her to drop the infant. She stumbled, caught herself, snatched up the baby with her left hand and resumed running. In a moment she was overtaken, captured and brought back to the cabins, where a general massacre was occurring. Her baby was crying, and the warrior finally snatched it away from her, swung it around by an ankle and crushed the child's head against one of the cabin logs.

Col. James Patton, 63, who had arrived only the day before with a supply of gunpowder and lead for the settlement, was inside one of the cabins writing, his sword on the table beside him. He snatched up the weapon and ran to the door, almost colliding with a cluster of Shawnees entering. He managed to cut down two of them before he was killed.

Elsewhere in the little community similar events were occurring. Early that morning Col. Patton had sent his 16-year-old nephew, Tom Preston, to the cabin of Philip Lybrook on Sinking Creek, three miles distant, to ask him to come and help with some heavy work. Grateful that the lad was gone, Patton was reaching for his rifle over the fireplace when he fell with Black Wolf's tomahawk buried in his skull. Hannah Schmidt, a visiting German woman from Pennsylvania, cowered in a corner, then was captured without resistance by the ferocious subchief.

Ruth Draper, trying to escape from her cabin through an open window, was tomahawked from inside and from outside simultaneously and died draped over the sill. Henry Lenard, realizing the futility of any resistance, simply raised his hands and surrendered. Casper Barrier grappled with two Indians but was no match for them, and a knife plunged into his heart ended his struggles. Mary Draper Ingles, athletic though she was, might have been able to outrun the attackers and escape but for two things: she was greatly pregnant, and her two sons, four-year-old Thomas and two-year-old George, were terrified and clung to her legs. All three were easily captured.

Her husband, William, was cultivating a small cornfield beyond a rise some distance away, out of sight and hearing of the settlement. He was unaware that anything was occurring until he happened to see a plume of smoke rising from that direction. Instantly he dropped his hoe and ran as fast as he could toward the cabins. Topping the rise 100 yards or so distant, he saw the buildings in flames, Indians loading goods onto the settlement's own horses and captives being led away. Even at this distance he could make out his wife and sons among them. At the same instant he saw two tomahawk-wielding Indians running in his direction, and he realized he had been seen. He turned and raced away but was about to be overtaken by the time he reached the nearby woodland. No sooner had he entered it than, in attempting to leap over a fallen tree, he caught his foot in the branches and fell. Immediately he rolled into the heaviest of the cover and lay still. Moments later the two Indians, silent and deadly, raced past without seeing him. After a moment or two he came to his feet and slipped away hastily in another direction.

Ingles encountered John Draper who, like himself, had been working in a distant field, had seen what was happening and had escaped unobserved. Together they headed in the direction of Pattonsburg to spread the word and get help in attempting a rescue.

The Indians had wasted no time in heading away with their stolen horses, loot and prisoners, following the path that led to the mile-distant cabin of an old man named Philip Barger. When they encountered it, a handful of the Indians rushed ahead and burst in, found Barger alone and beheaded him with Col. Patton's sword. They took his gun and whatever other goods they wanted, set the place afire and moved on. Fortunately for young Preston and Philip Lybrook, that moment on their way over the mountain heading toward Draper's Meadows, they were not seen by the Indians, who quickly vanished as they followed the New River downstream. Because of her greatly advanced pregnancy and her attempts to carry both her little sons, Mary Ingles was finally allowed to ride one of the horses, holding two-year-old

George before her and four-year-old Thomas astraddle behind and clinging to her waist.[92]

Not too far from there an even worse massacre occurred when the Shawnee principal chief himself, Hokolesqua, leading a war party of 80, struck on Muddy Creek and wiped out the Filty Yolkum and Frederick Lea families, then followed the creek to its mouth at the Greenbrier, where some 50 settlers had gathered at the house of Archibald Clendenin, and wiped out all the men and many of the women and children. From there they went to the settlements on Jackson Creek and struck them equally hard.

Simultaneously, far to the north, the Indians responded in droves to Contrecoeur's summons, coming overland from the northwest and in flotillas of canoes up the Ohio and down the Allegheny.[93] With only a modicum of French assistance, the Indians ambushed the British force on July 9 along the right bank of the Monongahela, just ten miles from Fort Duquesne, and inflicted a devastating defeat on them, killing 456 and wounding an additional 421.

In the midst of the battle, the Shawnee subchief Red Hawk recognized George Washington, whom he had first seen at Logstown. Though priding himself on being an excellent shot, the Shawnee did not realize that his rifle barrel had become slightly bent in the affray. He took a bead on Washington, fired and was amazed when he missed. Angry with himself, he reloaded and fired again, with the same result. A third effort was no different. Now it became a matter of honor and pride to bring the officer down with his shot, and so he kept his eye on Washington, following him and shooting whenever the opportunity afforded itself. Eleven times he shot, and 11 times he missed. At that point, believing Washington to be under the protection of the Great Spirit, he ceased his attempts and soon lost sight of Washington in the tumult.[94]

Even Gen. Braddock was dead, but he had been shot by one of his own men rather than the enemy. An advocate of the traditional British method of battle—standing in fully exposed formation and firing at an army similarly arrayed against him—he simply could not adjust to a foe who fought from behind protective cover, as the Indians and Canadians did; nor would he tolerate such "ungentlemanly" conduct in his own troops. When he spied one of his militia soldiers, Pvt. Edward Faucett, firing from behind the cover afforded by a large tree, he ordered the man to fight in the open as a proper soldier should. Pvt. Faucett refused, whereupon Braddock instantly struck him down with his sword. The militiaman's younger brother, Thomas, crouched behind another tree nearby, saw what Braddock had done and, in retaliation, promptly shot him in the back. Severely wounded, Braddock finally died on July 13. The remaining provincial soldiers nearby continued fighting from under cover, and as a result, many survived who would otherwise have been killed.[95] The scope of the victory was enhanced when the statistics involving the French and Indians were considered: three French officers had been killed and two wounded, plus a total of 27 soldiers and Indians killed and about the same number wounded. Late on the night of the battle, numerous British prisoners were brought back to Fort Duquesne and tortured to death on the banks of the Allegheny opposite the fort.[96]

Despite the victory, the Shawnees feared that the British would mount another

The Shawnee Village of
Chalahgawtha

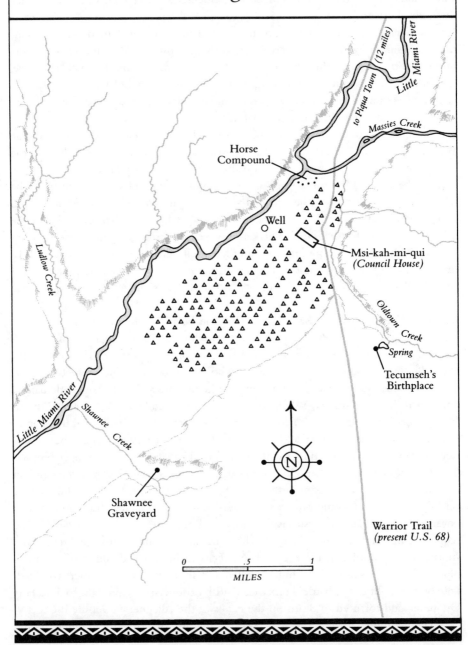

Little Miami River

to Piqua Town (12 miles)

Massies Creek

Horse
Compound

Ludlow Creek

Well

Msi-kah-mi-qui
(Council House)

Oldtown Creek

Spring

Tecumseh's
Birthplace

Little Miami River

Shawnee Creek

N

Shawnee
Graveyard

Warrior Trail
(present U.S. 68)

0   .5   1
MILES

offensive that was even stronger, that they would overwhelm the French at Fort Duquesne and then stream down the Ohio. With this fearful thought in mind, the Shawnees soon abandoned their upper and lower towns on the Ohio— Conedogwinit and Sinioto. The majority of those inhabitants moved up the Scioto River to the Pickaway Plains or beyond, as far as the upper Little Miami and the remote headwaters of the Mad River. Even the huge village of Chalahgawtha on the Scioto near the mouth of Paint Creek was felt to be too exposed, and it was reestablished, after several temporary placements, on the Little Miami River, fully 70 river miles above its mouth on the Ohio.

By now the frontier from New York to South Carolina was afire with burning settlers' cabins and littered with the bodies of horses, cows, hogs, poultry—and people. Many hundreds of people were taken into captivity by the Indians, among them the three Girty brothers, Simon, James and George. Their father, also named Simon, had died some time ago, and the three were living with their mother and stepfather, John Turner, when they were captured in July 1756 by Delawares and Shawnees on the Juniata River and taken to the large village of Kittanning on the Allegheny. Turner was executed in grisly manner. Kittanning was destroyed the following September by an army under Col. John Armstrong, but the Girty boys were not recovered. Simon had been taken away and adopted by the Senecas, James by the Shawnees and George by the Delawares.

The war raged everywhere on the frontier and kept the greater majority of men, red and white alike, away from their homes for long periods. Gradually the British forces took the upper hand, and the initial jubilation among the French and Indians diminished as the fortunes of war turned against them.

In September 1758 the British under Gen. Thomas Forbes moved again against Fort Duquesne. There the unnerved French, to the dismay of their Indian allies, spiked their only cannon, dumped it into the river, packed up what they could carry, set the fort afire and fled—half ascending the Allegheny to their forts and beyond, the other half descending the Ohio to Fort Massac, only 60 river miles above the Mississippi. The fire they had set did little damage, and the British took it over, made repairs and improvements and renamed it Fort Pitt.[97]

It marked the end of the French presence in the Ohio River Valley, and as if a switch had been thrown, a marked influx of settlers from Virginia and Pennsylvania spilled into the area between the crest of the Alleghenies and the two large rivers that formed the Ohio. Undaunted by the terrible dangers that might well befall them, all wanted land as their share of the spoils of war, and though the colonial governments inveighed against such precipitate actions, they came anyway. Thomas Decker established the Decker's Creek Settlement where the stream he named emptied into the Monongahela; within six months the Indians had slain the inhabitants and destroyed it. The three Eckerly brothers, who were Dunkards, settled on and named Dunkard Creek close to where it entered the Monongahela. Dr. Thomas Eckerly took some furs they trapped to a trading post on the Shenandoah, and when he returned, the settlement had been destroyed and his two brothers killed and scalped. Other settlements were similarly formed and destroyed, but some managed to hang on to their precarious existence. Among the many new settlements that were so quickly formed was the first one to actually be in sight of the Ohio River. It sprang up as a scattering of shacks and lean-tos and half-face camps, then rapidly gave way to more substantial cabins. It was outside the walls of Fort Pitt and was given its own name—Pittsburgh.

By 1759, new forts were springing up all over the frontier—some built by the government, others by private individuals or groups. Fort Redstone was built by Col. William Byrd near the ruins of the Ohio Company storage post at the mouth of Redstone Creek. Cassino's Fort and Westfall's Fort were built on the Tygart Valley River, and Jackson's Fort and Prickett's Fort on the Monongahela tributary creeks for which they had been named.

It was this same year when Col. John Gibson left Fort Pitt under the command of Lt. David Williamson and led a detachment in pursuit of a party of Indians that had struck another new settlement at the mouth of Decker's Creek. The Indians had fled down the Ohio and, feeling safe, made camp. Gibson came up on them before they were aware anyone was nearby. They were a party of ten Mingoes, under the temporary chief, Kiskepila—Little Eagle.[98] Gibson and his men approached stealthily and then unexpectedly burst upon the campsite. Kiskepila shrieked a war whoop and sent a shot at Gibson. The ball passed through the edge of his shirt without harming him and wounded the soldier directly behind him. Gibson, with a mighty swing of his sword, lopped off the chief's head, and the other Indians immediately fled. Later, at their village, the Mingoes held a war dance and filled the air with shrieks for revenge on "the long knife" and his "long knife nation," meaning the Virginians. The name stuck, and from that time forward the Virginians were referred to as the *Shemanese*—the Long Knives.

When the British under Sir William Johnson took Fort Niagara in July 1759, the French quickly abandoned Forts Machault, Le Boeuf and Presque Isle. Quebec fell to the British the following September, and a year later Montreal fell as well, and the French capitulated. All French posts in the region of the Great Lakes were to be given up, making Canada and all its dependencies British Crown possessions. By the terms of the treaty, however, this did not include the French in Louisiana, who were morally bound to continue the war still in progress elsewhere between England and France; they did all they could to promulgate bad feelings in the Indians toward the British until informed that an official French-English treaty had been signed. As a result, many of the western posts, instead of being formally surrendered, were simply abandoned, and their garrisons fled to the Mississippi Valley to join the French garrisons in southwestern Illinois and farther downstream on the Mississippi. The French installation closest to the new British holdings in Canada and the Northwest was now Fort de Chartres.

British trade boomed in the Great Lakes region, but the new British commander was Sir Jeffrey Amherst, who not only did not understand Indians but actively and intensely disliked them. So, too, evidently, did the new British sovereign, George III, who was crowned on October 25, 1760, following the death of George II. The Shawnees, Delawares and other northwestern tribes had agreed they would cease attacks on settlers coming over the Alleghenies, but the British had to agree as well to prohibit further settlement. George Croghan had become Sir William Johnson's new first deputy Indian superintendent in the west, and to salve relationships with the tribes, he scheduled a huge council with them at Pittsburgh. He arrived from the east with an extensive packhorse train of goods to distribute to the tribes as a measure of goodwill, following the customary protocol of gift-giving in the interest of a strong Indian trade. For this measure Amherst soundly castigated both Johnson and Croghan, considering this to be extravagant and unnecessary.

The Shawnees were among the tribes who attended at Pittsburgh and agreed to a new peace with the British. Along with the gifts they were given there, however, they also came away with smallpox. The disease ravaged the tribe—and other tribes as well—and among those who died was the Shawnee war chief, Kishkalwa. Pucksinwah now became the new war chief of the tribe and head of its Kispokotha sept, with the ugly, powerful Shemeneto—Black Snake—as his second.

The trade restrictions promulgated by Amherst soon reduced the majority of the tribes to a degree of poverty they had never before known. The permission given to the British to build a fort at the Forks of the Ohio was understood to have been a temporary grant, and that as soon as it was no longer needed in order to fight the French, it would be dismantled, and all the whites, except for traders, were expected to withdraw east of the mountains. When this did not occur and, instead, forts all over the frontier were strengthened and regarrisoned with seasoned soldiers, and when settlers continued to move west of the Susquehanna and Shenandoah and into the valleys of the Youghiogheny, Cheat and Monongahela, the anger of the tribes rose.[99] That anger finally spilled over in the person of the war chief of the Ottawas—a fiery individual named Pontiac—who, encouraged by promises of support by French agents still secretly moving through their country, united the tribes in a confederation and in May 1763 directed a simultaneous attack against all northwestern installations under British control.[100] In one fell swoop, virtually all of the western posts were overthrown and destroyed by surprise attacks, their garrisons killed or captured. This included Forts Sandusky, St. Joseph, Miamis, Ouiatenon, Michilimackinac, Presque Isle, Machault, Le Boeuf, and Edward Augustus (formerly Fort La Baye). Detroit—that name now supplanted the French designation of Fort Pontchartrain—was put under siege by Pontiac and his allies from May to October but managed to hold its own.

At the same time the Shawnees, Wyandots, Delawares and Mingoes struck with unparalleled fury in raids against settlers all along the frontiers of Pennsylvania, Maryland and Virginia; the raids were led by such chiefs as Hokolesqua, Pucksinwah, Shemeneto, Black Wolf, Monakaduto, Wingenund, Wolf, Pimoacan and others. Eighty Shawnees under Hokolesqua and Black Wolf swept up the Kanawha and devastated new settlements in the valleys of Muddy Creek, the Greenbrier River, the Jackson Valley River, the New River, and the Shenandoah River. A similar Delaware party under Chief Wolf struck in the valleys of the Youghiogheny and Monongahela. His 20 warriors struck the little settlement established by Col. William Clapham, 25 miles southeast of Fort Pitt, and killed five, including Clapham himself, one of his men, two women and a child. Similar raids were occurring elsewhere, many with combined parties of Shawnees and Delawares, leaving a bloody swath through the valleys of the Susquehanna, Juniata, Sherman and Tuscarawas Creek, while combined Senecas and Susquehannocks fell upon Connecticut settlers in the Wyoming Valley of northeastern Pennsylvania.

Pucksinwah's Shawnees and some Delawares under Chief Wolf placed Fort Pitt under a brief siege, but they broke it off when word came that Col. Henry Bouquet with 460 soldiers was on the march against them. Pucksinwah immediately led his 95 warriors to Edge Hill, 26 miles east of Fort Pitt, and set up an ambush. Striking Bouquet's force from under cover, rarely exposing themselves and making their shots count, they quickly killed and wounded eight British officers and 116 men. Bouquet was able to save his force from sure disaster only by effecting a clever counterambush, at which the Indians retreated after losing 22 men, including chiefs Kittiskung and Wolf. This was the Battle of Bushy Run on August 5, which Bouquet declared a victory for the whites, then continued his march to Fort Pitt without further loss.

At last, to the intense relief of everyone, Sir Jeffrey Amherst was recalled on November 17, 1763, and his place as commander in America was taken over by Gen. Thomas Gage.[101] Even more gratifying, the British Board of Trade finally took the advice of Sir William Johnson and issued the Royal Proclamation of 1763, negating the boundaries of the Lancaster Treaty of 1744 insofar as settlement by whites was concerned and creating a hard and fast boundary between the whites and Indians. The proclamation made the crest of the Alleghenies the dividing line, with the words

> *everything west of the heads of the streams that ultimately empty into the Atlantic are to be, for the present and until our further pleasure be known, reserved for the tribes.*

While it helped, this did not entirely end the frontier conflicts, which continued until October 1764, when Bouquet gathered up his force and marched on an expedition into the Ohio country, determined to bring the Indians to their knees. The upshot was that the tribes sued for peace and met with Bouquet at the Forks of the Muskingum. There, at Goschachgunk, they surrendered all their prisoners—eventually a total of 310.[102] Among the surrendered prisoners were the three Girty brothers, Simon, James and George, who soon became interpreters at Fort Pitt.

An official treaty was to be drawn up the following summer, based on the Proclamation of 1763, but now, with the prisoners released and Bouquet prepared to return to Fort Pitt, it was Hokolesqua who expressed to Bouquet the stance of the combined tribes, saying: "When you first came among us, you came with hatchet raised to strike us. We now take it from your hand and throw it to Moneto, that He may now do with it that which shall seem good in His sight. We hope that you, who are a brave warrior, will take hold of the chain of friendship we now extend to you. We, who are also brave warriors, will take hold as you do, and in pity for our women and children and our old people, we will think no more of war."

The formal peace treaty was concluded with Sir William Johnson during the summer of 1764, and for the first time in many years, the frontiers were safe, but this was a situation that did not last. Almost as if it had never been drawn up, the Royal Proclamation of 1763 was ignored. Thousands of immigrants were coming to America from England, Scotland, Wales and Ireland, and there was an even greater need than before to extend westward expansion. Would-be settlers flowed over the Alleghenies in alarming numbers, spilling into the fertile valleys beyond, each seeking the place that particularly appealed to him and then making his mark on boundary trees—called tomahawk improvements—and claiming the land as his own.[103]

Even though trade was still tightly controlled and only licensed fur agents were able to pursue the practice without fear of imprisonment, the unorganized settlers had only their own needs and desires to consider, and it was virtually impossible to keep them from settling ever deeper in the interior. In essence, this situation, after all these many years of travail, was right back where it had been, with the Indians once again seeing their lands encroached upon and stolen, their game herds slaughtered, their fields and forests burned and the great beauty of their pristine lands horribly desecrated. So when continued appeals to British authorities failed to curtail the invasion and oust the intruders, the Indians took matters into their own hands, and small parties again launched raids against the least protected settlers and settlements, especially in the valleys of the Monongahela and Kanawha, whose tributaries funneled the growing flow of settlers toward the Ohio Valley. These attacks quickly escalated, yet ever more settlers came, and with good reason.

The Ohio River Valley, still devoid of white settlement, was beckoning like a ripe plum ready for the picking—but there were nests of red hornets close to that plum, and their stings were deadly; whatever plum was plucked would not be taken without utmost peril. The country bordering the long serpentine course of the Ohio River was a land fraught with almost unimaginable danger.

The stage was now set. It was a territory very soon to be termed "that dark and bloody land," and the principal highway into that region was the 1,000-mile-long stream called the Ohio—*that dark and bloody river*.

Chapter 1

[July 16, 1768 — Saturday]

Simon Girty stood silently in the dense cover fringing the area of the hunting camp, his garb blending so well with the underbrush about him that it would have required a keenly trained eye to pick him out and, even then, the eye would have to know exactly where to focus. His head turned slowly from side to side, cocking now and again as he listened intently for anything that might indicate the danger still existed.

A man of slightly less than average height, Girty was of a chunky, muscular build. His hair was black and flowed free to his shoulders, his features were well formed, and many of the women he encountered considered him quite handsome. But those features could harden into fierce, harsh lines at times, and now was one of those occasions. His expression was set in grim lines, making him look rather older than his 27 years, and his dark gray eyes probed deeply into the dappled foliage, searching as intently as his ears were listening. A jay scolded briefly from a nearby tree and his gaze flicked instantly to the source, then moved away and his head swiveled slightly when a trio of crows cawed raucously from the uppermost bare branches of a dead tree some 300 yards upriver.

To the west, the distant opposite shore of the Shawanoe showed no signs of movement. The river itself issued only a faint hissing gurgle as it slid past, heading for its junction with the Tennessee some 20 miles downstream and then, ultimately, with the Ohio another 25 miles below that.[104] Girty let his gaze move back to the scene before him, and a muscle in his jaw twitched as he studied the jumbled bodies more closely. He could not decide from this distance whether anyone of the party was missing, but he knew he would find out soon enough.

He had known from the beginning that it was a mistake coming here; Shawnees did not take lightly to white hunters trespassing on their Kan-tuck-kee hunting grounds. The others had not listened to his warnings, however, and despite the presentiment that had risen in him, he had allowed himself to be talked into it.

They had left Kaskaskia on this hunt just two weeks earlier in two large canoes, each towing a sturdy piroque behind for transporting their take. All 19 in the party were traders or hunters associated with the Baynton, Wharton and Morgan Company. Not one of them had ever met either John Baynton or Samuel Wharton—those two, in recent years, rarely left the firm's headquarters in Philadelphia—but all were fiercely devoted to George Morgan, field superintendent for the company. Morgan, some years ago, had become a partner in the firm, not because he had married the beautiful Molley, Baynton's daughter, but because he was a man of consummate ability in his position, a man whose diminutive size belied his toughness and sagacity, and who somehow had the knack of extracting the utmost in loyalty from his men. It was that very devotion, in fact, that now drove Girty to make the extra effort to go back to Kaskaskia and tell Morgan what had happened here, rather than move on to Fort Pitt, as he would have much preferred doing.

Remaining in place in the underbrush, Girty felt a welling of mixed anger and pity for these men who had been slain. How short a time ago they had been filled with life; laughing, joking and raising a purse among them as a prize to go to the best hunter. They had paddled down the Mississippi from Kaskaskia to the mouth of the Ohio and then upstream on the latter, not doing any real hunting until reaching the Shawanoe. And what hunting they had discovered here! They had found this secluded little bottom along the riverbank and made their camp, and over the succeeding ten days of actual hunting, they had delightedly competed and bagged nearly 100 deer and 39 bears, along with a number of wolves, a few buffalo and three elk. Their evenings in camp had been busy, relating their tales of the hunt as they skinned the animals, bundled the hides, quartered and salted down the meat and rendered the bear fat to oil. One of the piroques was already two-thirds full of bear oil, and the other one was half full with the meat and hides.

The hunting had been markedly less fruitful yesterday, and last night, working about the camp and discussing whether to continue the hunt or return, they had decided to ascend the river perhaps another 20 miles to hunt a few more days and fill the boats to capacity before starting back. Then, just as they were starting to load their gear into the boats at dawn this morning, a barrage of 30 or more shots had come, and most of Girty's companions had fallen where they stood. Two besides himself had managed to leap away, rifles in hand, but one of these was downed in a few steps. Girty had no idea what happened to the other since he was himself being pursued by four. He raced away downriver through the woodland at all the speed he could muster. Two of the Shawnees had quickly been outdistanced, but one had followed him at an equal pace until at last Girty dodged behind a tree, waited a moment while swiftly checking his gun, then emerged from the other side and put a ball through the leading Shawnee's heart at close range. He raced off again at an angle, heading toward a huge rock he had seen while hunting and, reaching it, crouched behind cover at its base, swiftly reloading.

The fallen Indian's two companions came into sight, cried *"Waugh!"* at seeing their dead companion and halted. They looked about fearfully but, seeing nothing, picked up the dead man and carried him back toward the camp. Girty had then quickly scaled the rock and thrown himself prone on top. Though the river was barely visible through the foliage, he could not see the campsite. The yells of the Indians reached him faintly, but after a while the sounds diminished. A short time later the two large canoes floated past, aimlessly adrift on the current, and then there was only silence. Nevertheless, he remained on the rock for over an hour longer. At last, ready to flee in an instant, he descended and stealthily approached the camp to this place in hiding where he now stood.

Still there was no sound or movement, and so with infinite care he made a wide semicircle around the camp, studying the ground for what he was sure he would find and soon did: traces that the Indians had left, moving toward the southeast. He also found, at the treelined edge of the bottom, the body of the man he hoped might have escaped, his gun, powderhorn, shirt, and shoes gone, along with his scalp. Girty shook his head and walked boldly into camp and surveyed the carnage. Seventeen bodies were there, all scalped, many mutilated with tomahawk blows or knife thrusts. All their guns, powder and lead were gone, along with their pouches and selected articles of clothing. The two piroques had been scuttled, the bear oil loosed into the water and the salted meat and bundles of furs thrown into the river, all of which convinced Girty that his surmise was correct: The attackers were a war party traveling light, possibly marching against the Cherokees and not wishing to be encumbered with plunder. That they had encountered the white hunting party had evidently been sheer happenstance.

Girty looked around a final time and grimaced. "Reckon I'd'a won our bet, boys," he murmured. Then he turned and left without a backward glance.

[July 20, 1768 — Wednesday]

In the headquarters of the Baynton, Wharton and Morgan trade building at Kaskaskia, George Morgan watched the door of his office close and the latch click into place. For a long while he sat quietly, mulling over the report he'd just received and considering its ramifications. At length he sighed and reached for the quill pen he'd been using to write a letter to his partners in Philadelphia when the interruption occurred. Now he shook the excess ink free into the pot and continued the missive:

> *I was going on with the foregoing When Simon Girty one of our Hunters came in from the Shawana River & informed me that about thirty Indians had attacked our Boats & that no body had made their escape but himself that he knew of. He is a Lad Who is particularly attach'd to me otherwise he would not have come here to give me this Intelligence but would have immediately proceeded to Fort Pitt. Mr. Hollingshead will give you his Character. The inclosed Letter which I write to Mr. Rumsey, will give you a short but plain Relation of this Tragical Affair, that I need not have the Trouble of again recollecting every Part & writing it over. I therefore refer you to it. . . .*
>
> *Had not this Disaster happened, we should have collected more Skins from*

that Quarter by Dec'. next than we trade for here in twelve Months. There was a generous Strife between the Hunters, who should do most for me — & pleased themselves very greatly with reckoning up every Night how much Money We shoul[d] make by their Industry — Which each of them daily declared should not be Wanting — for that Mr. Morgan had used them so well that they could not do too much for him.

Besides the Skins, they would have renderd about 20 M W'. of Tallow & brought in Meat sufficient for the Garrison all next Year.[105] They had agreed to move about 15 or twenty miles higher up the River that very Day. . . .

[September 3, 1768 — Saturday]

The penetration of new settlers westward of the Allegheny Divide continued sporadically all along the frontier, from the New York border in the north to the North Carolina border in the south. Individuals, families, groups of families and even whole companies of people were filtering over that crest and tentatively sinking their roots along streams that flowed west or north or northwest; waters that gradually found their way into the mighty Ohio.

For many, it was an opportunity to have, for the first time in their lives, a piece of land to call their own. These were the people who had worked for years as indentured workers paying off the price of their passage to America and who had dreamed of one day establishing their own farms. They were willing to undergo whatever rigors or hazards it took to make the dream come true.[106] These were also the people who were restless, adventurous, energetic and, often enough, fugitives from justice who were eager to leave behind a criminal past.

In the earlier years they had come by foot or, if lucky enough, on horseback, threading their way through unknown territory in a trackless wilderness or along faintly visible game trails or Indian paths. Now even that was changing. Their very passage was creating better trails and better roads with fewer hardships along the way. The most direct and least difficult route was what had once been the old Nemacolin Trail but was now better known as Braddock's Road, though until this year it was still little more than a wider trail than most. Recently, however, the Virginia colonial government had authorized the creation of a national road, suitable for the passage of large wagons, following the Braddock's Road route not only from Will's Creek on the upper waters of the Potomac to the Monongahela at the mouth of Redstone Creek, but even beyond, following the Monongahela all the way to the town of Pittsburgh, which had sprung up in the shadow of Fort Pitt. Toward this end— though more for the establishment of better trade with the Indians than to ease the passage of pioneers—the government had just appropriated the sum of £200 and empowered such enterprising individuals as Dr. Thomas Walker, Abraham Kite, Thomas Rutherford and James Wood to proceed with the creation of this first National Road.[107] Many, especially those in Pennsylvania, who did not have ready access to the new road were continuing to follow the old military road from Philadelphia to Lancaster and Harris Ferry, then beyond the Susquehanna to the newer towns of Carlisle and Chambersburg and past even them to the military posts called Fort Bedford, where a little village called Raystown was growing, and Fort Ligonier.[108] In other areas, however, the trails remained difficult at best and continued to be negotiated on foot or on packsaddles. They could not carry much with them, but then they most often had little to carry. The important thing was to get there, find the land that was most appealing or best suited for settlement and dig in. Anyone could take up land if he had the hardihood to build a cabin and raise a small crop, coupled with the fortitude to face hardship or even extreme jeopardy. For such physical and mental expenditure, the individual could lay claim to 400 acres and stake out preemption rights to an additional 1,000 acres that could eventually be secured through a land office warrant. When certificates of settlement right were properly filled out and submitted to the land commissioners, they then lay in trust for six months, and if no one had already claimed the land or there were no overlappings or counterclaims, at the end of six months a patent was issued and the land was then theirs free and clear.

Making so-called tomahawk improvements was the most popular form of marking the land being claimed, and such claims were then called tomahawk rights. The process was simple enough: The individual stepped off the bounds of his claim and at the corners used a tomahawk to chop his initials or mark into a large tree.

During the summer the families of Jacob Vanmetre, Thomas Hughes and John Swan toiled their way to the mouth of Redstone Creek. Here they crossed over the big Monongahela River, turned upstream, followed the shoreline for 15 miles and came to the mouth of a roily stream they promptly named Muddy Creek. They then followed the creek upstream for five miles until coming to a lovely bottomland at the outward bow of a large bend. Here they made their claims, sank their roots, built their cabins and planted grain, and they called the place Vanmetre's Settlement.[109]

Arriving soon after the Vanmetre party and traveling even farther upstream on the Monongahela but along the east bank, two brothers named David and Zackwell Morgan came to the Cheat River, which they crossed and continued up the east side of the Monongahela another dozen miles until they came at length to the mouth of the stream called Decker's Creek. There they found the ruins of the old Decker's Creek Settlement, where the first settlers, under Thomas Decker, had been slain in an Indian attack four years ago last May. Undaunted at possibly tempting fate, the Morgans made their own tomahawk improvements and left, determined to return with their families the following spring; determined as well that their settlement would survive and they would call it Morgantown.[110]

They were not the only ones undaunted by what disasters may have befallen others who had arrived before them. Fourteen years ago David Tygart and Thomas Files had settled on the Tygart Valley River, where shortly afterward the Files family was massacred and Tygart moved away, leaving only his name. Ten years later a new settlement had been made by the Pringle brothers, John and Samuel, in that same valley. They had held on for four years, and now, leaving Samuel to hold the place, John went east and returned in a couple of months with the families of George, Edward and John Jackson, Edgar Hughes, Philip Hacker, William Radcliffe and others. They spread out in the valley and made their own settlements on such Tygart tributaries as the Buckhannon River, Hacker's Creek, Bushy Fork, Turkey Run and others . . . and they, too, hung on.[111] The Solomon Burkham family, seeking more security, settled on the Youghiogheny River not very far above its mouth at the Monongahela, close to the little blockhouse built by Jacob Beeson and being called Beeson's Fort, adjacent to the claim recently made by a well-known young soldier, Capt. William Crawford.

Among those who came to the Redstone area was a 21-year-old man from the settlement his own grandfather had daringly established on the South Branch Potomac River 67 years ago. Accompanying him were his two younger brothers, Silas and Jonathan, a few Negro slaves, several other young men and his own new wife. This young man had wooed and won a lovely girl a year younger than he, Elizabeth McCulloch, and they had been married last February. Now the newlyweds were establishing themselves near the mouth of Redstone Creek, but it was, he warned, a temporary place for them only. Despite the potentially extreme danger involved, he was intent upon settling on the very shore of the Ohio River far below Fort Pitt. That was no place to take his young wife until he had at least staked his claims and built a cabin. But come next spring, he and his brothers—and perhaps a few hardy volunteers with them—would head for the area in question and make his dream a reality. Then, he promised, he would come back for her. He was a very determined young man who never made promises lightly and who was every bit as hardy a pioneer as his grandfather had been, after whom he had been named.

He was Ebenezer Zane.

[N o v e m b e r   2 2 ,   1 7 6 8 — T u e s d a y]

Few things in the past had stirred such excitement in the colonies as the treaty just consummated by Sir William Johnson on behalf of the British with the Iroquois. It was one of the largest and best-attended councils ever held. In addition to commissioners from Virginia, Pennsylvania, New Jersey and New York, more than 3,000 Indians had attended, by far the great majority being representatives of the Six Nations comprising the Iroquois League, but also a scattering of others—Caughnawagas, Abnakis and Algonkins, a few Hurons and their splinter tribe, the Wyandots, a few Ottawas and Delawares and, uninvited and coldly treated, some Shawnees.

The treaty council had been held at Fort Stanwix, on the Mohawk River headwaters.[112] It began on October 24 and ended just last week, and its ramifications were staggering for Indians and whites alike. For one thing, the restrictive policies established by the Royal Board of Trade were rescinded, and control of trade was placed back into the hands of the individual colonies, meaning that a great swell of traders would undoubtedly flock into Indian lands, and without the previous regulations being enforced, there would be a huge increase in the trade of weapons and liquor. As serious as that was, it was as nothing compared with the foremost goal the treaty accomplished for the colonists: abolition of the Indian-white boundary line set by the Proclamation of 1763—the wavering line following the Allegheny crest from deep in the South to upper New York. A new boundary was agreed upon—the Ohio

River; everything to the north and west of that stream would be Indian territory, proclaimed inviolate. South and east of the Ohio, including the whole of the Kentucky lands south to Tennessee and east to the Allegheny crest, would now be open for settlement. No longer was there a ban—even nominally—on prospective settlers crossing the summit of those mountains. Now they could legally migrate into this vast area, and far more significantly, speculators in large landholdings, such as the Ohio Land Company, were free to advertise their western lands for sale. Almost immediately George Washington, Arthur Lee and others set themselves up as the Mississippi Land Company and petitioned King George for a grant of 2.5 million acres in the Kanawha River Valley, where they planned to establish a new British colony to be called Kanawha. Benjamin Franklin—one of the treaty commissioners —along with Thomas Walpole, George Mercer, Thomas Pownall and the firm of Baynton, Wharton and Morgan were not far behind, setting up the Walpole Land Company, hoping to get a similar grant in the Illinois country and establish a new British colony named Vandalia.

The great tract of land involved was not, of course, the property of the Iroquois League by any stretch of the imagination, and for them to sell it was tantamount to a farmer blandly selling the fields belonging to another farmer some distance away. Yet as they had done in the past, the Iroquois grandly proclaimed that all those lands were theirs "by right of conquest," and the British, as they had in the past, chose to accept and honor the preposterous claim. For goods to the value of £10,000, the fraudulent land sale called the Fort Stanwix Treaty was consummated.[113]

Sir William Johnson, superintendent of Indian Affairs and closely allied to the Iroquois through marriage into the tribe and adoption by the Mohawks, was fully aware that the Iroquois claim to the western lands was fanciful, but he went along with it, even to the extent of not inviting delegates from the tribes living on or using those lands—the Shawnees and Cherokees in particular—to attend the council. When they showed up in small numbers anyway, he was very upset, spoke to them curtly, treated them coldly and grudgingly allowed them to sit in on the council, but without voice or vote.

Pucksinwah, who was head of the Shawnee delegation, was positively outraged at what was occurring and angrily confronted Sir William. The Indian superintendent listened impatiently to the harangue that declared him guilty of cheating the Indians of the Northwest, then shook his head with unbudging finality.

"It is you Shawnees," he told Pucksinwah, "who should feel guilty, considering the way you have previously treated Englishmen. You should go home and pay due regard to the boundary line now made." He then added insult to this injury by giving the Shawnee delegation £27 worth of goods as a sop, with the order that they give half of it to the Delawares.

Pucksinwah, nostrils flaring, was silent for a moment, bridling the temper that encouraged him to jerk out his tomahawk and strike down this friend of the Iroquois, this enemy of the Shawnees. When at last he spoke, the words were steely, cold:

"At the close of the last war," he said, "we and you buried our hatchets deep that they might never again be seen, but now the wind that has issued from your mouth these past days has blown away the dirt and exposed them. They now wait only our picking them up. By what you have done, you have already picked up yours. When my chiefs learn of this, we shall soon see whether we pick up ours. I have nothing further to say to you, Warraghiyagey!"

[December 30, 1768 — Friday]

Pucksinwah stood before the chiefs in the great *msi-kah-mi-qui*—council house —at the Shawnee capital village of Wapatomica at the Forks of the Muskingum River. He was finished speaking now, and as war chief of the tribe, he would be bound to follow their decision, whatever it might be.

For the past two hours he had spoken, recalling to them what he had heard and witnessed at the great council held at Fort Stanwix. He had reminded them of how, when he had returned here following the conclusion of that council and reported to them, they at first did not believe him, saying the report was so incomprehensible that he must have misunderstood those things said and done. It was well known, they said, that the Iroquois despised them and would not hesitate to hurt them if such were in their power, but they would do so in an honorable way. There was no iota of honor in what Pucksinwah had told them the Iroquois had done.

He reminded them that at that point they had selected another delegation led by him, to return to the Iroquois and speak to their head men and clear away the fogs misting the view of what was real. And, he reminded them, he and his delegation had returned, and spoken to the chiefs, and their own ears had heard the response: The Iroquois chiefs had refused to recant the stance they had taken at Fort Stanwix; refused to return the goods they had accepted for fraudulently selling land that was not theirs to sell; refused to admit that Shawnees, Delawares, Wyandots, Miamis or other northwestern tribes had any right whatsoever to any of the lands they had sold.

"The bargain has been made," they had told Pucksinwah, "and now you must accept it and you must not again pick up your hatchets, which you run about with doing great mischief. If you do so, then a great party of our warriors will strike out into Ohio against you and the consequences will be fatal."

"Many summers ago," Pucksinwah had responded coldly, "we drove the Iroquois out of our lands on the Susquehanna River. Fewer years ago we drove them out of the valley of the Spaylaywitheepi—the Ohio River. Be warned. Should you again show your faces in our land, it will be for the Iroquois, not the Shawnee, that the consequences will be fatal."[114]

Having heard and considered all these matters, the Shawnee chiefs came to their decision. They held nothing but contempt for the hollow threat of the Iroquois, knowing they had nothing to fear from that direction. Where the Long Knives were concerned, however, they had no recourse but this: They would maintain peace so long as they were not themselves injured, but they refused to acknowledge the Spaylaywitheepi as the border between white man and red—and they would not allow the *Shemanese* to take the game or the lands south of the river.

[June 28, 1769—Wednesday]

Of the five men who made up the party of hunters led by John Findlay, none was so skilled in hunting, tracking and stalking, nor so totally enthralled with the Kentucky country, as the man with whom he had served as a wagoner under General Braddock in that disastrous campaign 15 years earlier—Daniel Boone.

Boone, at 35, was steady and dependable, a man one could count on when things got tough. Ever since Findlay had first told him of the incredible richness of Kentucky and its boundless herds of buffalo, elk, deer and other game, Boone had been burning to go there, but it hadn't been until earlier this year that they had finally made the long-considered trip an actuality. The other four who accompanied them were good hunters, but they had eyes only for the game they were seeking. Only Boone, of them all, appreciated the country to its fullest—the great fertile valleys watered by fine clear streams, the vast stretches of forest wilderness and the rolling hills cloaked in lush buffalo grass and towering cane, the many intriguing caves and, most compelling to him, the numerous excellent salt licks that attracted unbelievable congregations of game animals.

They had left the valley of the Yadkin River in North Carolina the first of May, and Findlay had guided them through the Cumberland Gap into a land that surpassed even the glories that Boone had imagined from the stories Findlay had told him. For weeks they had moved along at their leisure, hunting in the beautiful valleys of unnamed streams that they called Red River, Green, Kentucky, Elkhorn and Licking, among others. In all their miles of traveling thus far, they had seen no other humans. They had established a base camp on a particularly pretty little tributary of the Kentucky River, calling the spot Station Camp and the stream Station Camp Creek.[115] From here they spread out individually or in pairs, drinking in the wonders of the land as if it were the sweetest of nectars.

The men had told their families they would be gone for about a month, yet here it was almost the end of June, and even if they started home immediately, it would probably be another month before they got back, and they would have been gone three times longer than planned.[116] Though some of the men were itching to start back, Findlay and Boone would gladly have stayed on indefinitely had not Findlay been taken ill and then given in to the majority opinion to return. Boone, however, reckoned he would remain and continue to hunt and explore. Findlay was not surprised and, promising to tell Boone's kin he was all right, set off with the others.

Boone watched them go without regret; he had always preferred being in the woods alone, where he was responsible only for himself. And now, spread out before him was a land that continued to enthrall him as none other had before—a land, he was now convinced, where his destiny lay.

[June 27, 1769—Tuesday]

Ebenezer Zane, at 22, was a man with a vision and the determination to make that vision become reality, despite whatever difficulties the fates might thrust into his path. He was also, befitting his Scots Presbyterian heritage, a young man who planned ahead.

Over the winter he had talked with several traders who had been down the Ohio for considerable distances, and when specifically questioned, all gave the same answer: The Ohio River below Fort Pitt angled northwestward for 25 miles to the mouth of the Beaver River, then turned and angled southwestward for a similar distance to where Yellow Creek entered from the Ohio country. At that point the big river turned again until it was running only a little west of due south, and maintained that course, excluding a few major bends, for at least 200 miles more, before angling north and west again.

Sketching this out in his mind's eye, Zane had come to the rather exciting conclusion that if he crossed the Monongahela at the mouth of Redstone Creek and headed due west, eventually he would find a stream flowing westward and emptying into the Ohio instead of the Monongahela. Or even if he didn't hit such a tributary stream, sooner or later, by continuing to follow that westward course, he would encounter the Ohio River itself.

Another fascinating and equally exciting bit of information had reached him in midwinter: details of the Fort Stanwix Treaty last fall and the momentous news that the Ohio Valley—at least the land south and east of the river—was opened for settlement. Though he had planned on claiming Ohio Valley land anyway, as many others had been doing despite prohibition, this wonderful news of the Proclamation of 1763 being negated only served to strengthen his resolve, because now the land-claiming he envisioned would be perfectly legal.

Young Zane was quite sure that with such news sweeping across the land, there would undoubtedly be a rush of would-be settlers coming in to make claims as soon as the weather warmed sufficiently in the spring; he knew as well that the over-whelming majority would take the course of least resistance and simply float down the Monongahela to Pittsburgh and then down the Ohio from there. He aimed to get first choice of the lands that would be available. So during late winter he got everything into readiness and waited. It was not until early April, however, that those bent on claiming Ohio lands began reaching Redstone and setting off downriver toward Pittsburgh. At once he and his brothers, Silas and Jonathan, together with a friend named Isaac Williams, four of the Zane dogs and two of their Negro slaves, loaded up their mounts and packhorses, kept their flintlocks at ready and set out on their great adventure.

They had swum their horses across the Monongahela just above Redstone Creek and struck out on a due-west course. Isaac Williams, who loved to hunt more than anything, had been this way before on short hunting trips, and easily recognized Tenmile Creek when they encountered it less than two hours later. However, the party then did what he had never done before: They turned upstream and followed its winding course to the headwaters.

Although reason told Zane that on the other side of the divide lay streams eventually draining into the Ohio, he was hardly prepared to encounter one so quickly. Only three miles after leaving the head of Tenmile Creek, they came to a lovely clear little stream running southwest.[117] There was always the possibility that it might curve around and wind up heading eastward again to empty into the Monongahela, but they took the chance. In a short time, to their great joy, the stream swung west and then even somewhat northwest. They had taken their time following it, noting approvingly each time another spring-fed stream emptied into it, camping beside it at night and refreshing themselves with its sparkling clean waters. By the end of the third day they found that this stream was no longer a little brook running through the hills but a substantial creek, deep and strong.

At length they came to a major fork where another creek entered from the east, not much smaller than the one they were following.[118] Below this point the principal creek was considerably enlarged, and there were some quite impressive bottomlands. It was here, quite unexpectedly, they encountered an old Delaware Indian in his small camp, holding a lengthwise spitted fish over his fire. He was apprehensive at first, but they made it clear he had nothing to fear from them, and he relaxed. They gave him some tobacco and jerky and discovered he could speak a smattering of English.

"What is this stream?" Zane asked, indicating the creek with a turn of his thumb. The Delaware, confused, shook his head. Zane tried again: "Name. Name of creek. Name of . . . of—*sepe.*" He was pleased to have remembered the Delaware word for river.

The old Indian nodded and grinned. *"Weiling,"* he said, then nodded again and repeated himself: *"Weiling."*

"Wheeling, eh?" Zane automatically spoke the word in a phonetic sense. "All right, then, Wheeling it is. Jonathan, Si"—he smiled at his brothers—"this is Wheeling Creek."

They had left the old Indian in peace and continued downstream. Silas was frowning, and soon put his thoughts into words. "Supposing," he said, "he tells some of his friends about seeing us?"

Ebenezer, expressionless, reined up and looked back at his brothers as they, too, stopped. "Did you want to kill him?"

"No," said Silas at once.

"Good. Me neither. So then, you want to turn back?"

"No!" both younger brothers answered in unison.

"Then let's get on with it. I can't imagine there's much farther to go. Keep alert, though, and keep your guns ready."

They encountered no one else, and just short of eight miles farther downstream, they came to the mouth of the creek, where it emptied into what could be nothing but the great Ohio River. The immense bottom they found here overjoyed them, and they made camp at once. The first claim made was by Ebenezer who, as leader of the party, got first choice. He selected the fine level terrace on the upstream side of the creek's mouth, some 16 feet above the water. Jonathan also paced off a claim near the creek mouth. Then, for the next month, the brothers spent their waking hours exploring, pacing off claims, and carefully marking them, eventually claiming all the way upstream to the Forks of the Wheeling, where Silas finally chose his own special claim.[119] Wherever possible, they or their servants climbed high into trees to make tomahawk improvements, sometimes 30 to 40 feet above the ground, where they couldn't easily be reached and defaced. When there were no trees where markers were needed, they erected cairns of flat rocks with their initials carefully chipped into them.

Isaac Williams was not so driven to claim as were the Zanes, preferring to hunt and provide the party with meat while they made their claims. However, on one of his outings upstream on the Ohio, he encountered a sizable creek 16 miles above Wheeling Creek. He followed it a considerable distance upstream to a pleasant little bottom where he spied a small herd of woods bison feeding on lush grasses. Selecting a fine yearling for the best meat, he brought the animal down with a well-placed shot and, even before approaching his kill, decided the stream should be named Buffalo Creek. He expertly dressed out his quarry, taking the tongue and other select cuts to share with the Zanes. Before starting back, however, he made tomahawk improvements on a 400-acre tract that he found especially appealing, including the bottom.[120]

As the Zane party worked, occasional boats passed with individuals or teams of men bent on locating and claiming good lands. Invariably they stopped to talk, sharing news of the moment, looking with envy at the wonderful bottom these boys had discovered and claimed, wishing they had gotten there first. For his own part, Williams envied their downstream adventure on the Ohio and several times remarked that if he had a canoe, he'd head downstream, too. He was more than pleased when one of the parties that stopped agreed to give him, in exchange for a good supply of fresh meat, a small canoe they were towing that was interfering with their travel by continually overtaking them.

As soon as they finished claiming, they engaged in a final, considerably harder labor—clearing a good-size area and erecting a good cabin. This was done on a ten-acre tract of Ebenezer's claim at the creek mouth. When it was finished, Isaac Williams gave his horse into the keeping of the brothers, shook hands and cheerfully set off downstream into the unknown with only his gun, knife, tomahawk and a pouch containing jerky and some essentials.

"You'll see me when I get back, boys," he said, tossing them a wave, "and I do intend on getting back."[121]

Now it was time to go home. The brothers had agreed among themselves that Silas would remain behind in the cabin, holding the claims from possible interlopers and await the return next spring of Ebenezer and Jonathan, who this time would be coming with all their goods and the family. While Silas lent a hand with the packing, Ebenezer told them to keep at it, he'd be back before long. He strode off then, heading toward the large bluff overlooking the bottom from the north.

It took him the better part of an hour to climb the heavily forested slopes of the hill and reach its summit.[122] Now at last, it was all spread out well over 300 feet below him. A quarter-mile to the west, the Ohio was a silvery ribbon that split itself into two channels as it swept around the large island opposite the Wheeling bottom. A half-mile wide at its thickest, the island tapered to a sharp point at either end and was about two miles long. It was heavily overgrown with trees and shrubbery, indicating that it was not an island prone to being washed away by seasonal flooding and Ebenezer reckoned that at some future time he would claim the island, too, and perhaps plant crops there.

Directly below was the Wheeling bottom itself, a half-mile-square area of rich lush growth, where one day, perhaps, there would be a sizable town to offer welcome haven to river travelers.[123] Far across the bottom, at the mouth of Wheeling Creek, the cabin stood isolated in the midst of the wilderness. He could see the tiny stick figures that were Silas and Jonathan, busily loading the three packhorses, and knew he must get back down to them. Still, he took one last lingering look.

"I'm coming home now, Elizabeth," he spoke aloud, "to get you and bring you back here, because all this is yours."

And many miles away, in the Zane cabin on Redstone Creek, Elizabeth Zane was at this very moment giving birth to their first child—a daughter who would be named Catherine.[124]

[September 30, 1773 — Thursday]

It had taken a while for the word to spread that the Fort Stanwix Treaty had abolished the Proclamation of 1763 and suddenly opened to legal settlement everything west of the Alleghenies and east and south of the Ohio River.

Among the very first to act on the incredible occurrence were the large land companies—the Mississippi Land Company, Ohio Land Company, Illinois Land Company, the Walpole Company and others—who swiftly dispatched numerous teams of skilled surveyors down the Ohio to seek out and claim the very best lands.

Along with these were many individual land-jobbers and surveyors who saw this as an opportunity not to sink roots into a new land, but to get very rich very quickly by claiming lands far beyond the limitations prescribed, mapping these locations and then quickly returning to the frontier areas and selling these claims to the eager would-be settlers streaming to the frontier. And there were those surveyors and claimers who did the same but who also retained for themselves the very best of the land they encountered.

George Washington, already with considerable frontier experience under his belt and trained as a surveyor, was among the first. In 1770, he set out down the Ohio with a strong party of men, including his friend Capt. William Crawford, who had already claimed 1,600 acres for Washington in the valley of the Youghiogheny. They inspected lands at the mouths of all the major streams but missed seeing Wheeling because they passed it on the channel that flowed on the west side of Wheeling Island. They claimed at Round Bottom, on a sharp bend of the river, where a surveyor named Michael Cresap was already busily claiming, and they stopped and explored at the Hockhocking and Muskingum and Little Kanawha.[125] Because they had been told by traders that there was a small Delaware village a short distance up the Little Kanawha—a village they called Bulltown, under a surly chief named Captain Bull—they did not explore up that stream but continued downriver some 70 miles farther to the mouth of the Great Kanawha.[126] There they turned upstream, and just above its mouth, Washington personally claimed 10,000 acres on both sides of the river. They followed the stream up to the fine salt licks at Campbell's Creek, where Washington and another friend, Andrew Lewis, jointly claimed 250 acres.[127]

At the same time his helpers were claiming additional lands for him, for themselves and others. In effect, they and the other land-jobbers and surveyors now on the Ohio were like little children loosed in a candy store, snatching and grabbing the best of everything that caught their eye.

Finished in the Kanawha Valley, the Washington party returned to the Ohio, floated down to the Big Sandy and ascended it.[128] Twenty-five miles up that river, they came to where a good-size stream entered from the southwest. Washington turned up that creek and stopped in about a mile at a good bottomland and marked out a considerably oversize claim, in excess of 2,000 acres, for his friend John Fry.[129] Finally, exhausted with their efforts, they returned up the Ohio to Fort Pitt, finding the river peppered with boatloads of settlers hurrying to find land and numerous camps of claiming parties on the shores. Washington finally got home on December 1, having been absent for over nine weeks.

Among the many surveying parties on the Ohio was one led by Dr. John Wood and Hancock Lee, who had been commissioned by the new Governor of Virginia, Lord Dunmore, in the name of King George III, to survey for possible future development by the colony. They, too, had been busy claiming down as far as Big Sandy.

The Thomas Bullitt party of surveyors went much farther. Instead of descending the Ohio from Pittsburgh, they had descended the New and Kanawha rivers, claiming well over 1,000 acres as they went, entered the Ohio River at the Kanawha mouth and joined briefly with other surveying parties they met, such as that under Wood and Lee, as well as the rough group of frontiersmen-cum-surveyors led by Joel Reese and Jacob Greathouse, including the Mahon brothers, John and Rafe, and the party led by Hancock Taylor and the McAfee brothers—James, George and Robert.

It was Bullitt's party and that under Taylor and the McAfees that were the most daring. These two parties descended past the stream one of their surveyors, Thomas Hedges, named Limestone Creek, continued well below the mouth of the Licking and stopped to survey the Big Bone Lick area, where they, as others had before them, used the huge individual fossilized vertebrae of woolly mammoths as camp stools. At the mouth of the Kentucky River the Taylor-McAfee party went up the tributary and did extensive surveying some 80 miles above.[130] The Bullitt party continued down the Ohio even farther, to the Falls of the Ohio, where they ascended a stream they called Beargrass Creek, penetrating many miles into the Kentucky country.[131]

At the same time, much farther down the Ohio, in the Illinois country, William Murray, acting on behalf of the Illinois Land Company, made illegal purchases from Indians of two large land tracts, one on the Illinois River and the other south of Kaskaskia, fronting on the lower Ohio just above its mouth at the Mississippi.

Wolf Creek Fort, a small log blockhouse, was built in 1772 on the west side of the New River at the mouth of Wolf Creek to protect the scattered settlers of that area. Shortly after its erection, a party of four men left there and descended the New and Kanawha rivers, to explore and claim. They were led by John Van Bibber and included his brother, Peter, as well as Matthew Arbuckle and Joseph Alderson. These four reached the Falls of the Kanawha, and luckily for them, saw a war party of Shawnees without themselves being seen. They quickly went into hiding beneath a large shelving rock and stayed throughout the night to escape detection. After the Indians were well away, John Van Bibber chipped out his name with the poll end of his tomahawk, and then they continued downstream.[132] At length they came to the salt lick at Campbell's Creek, followed it upstream several miles and came to a most remarkable sight: a spring that was afire with a peculiar blue and orange smokeless flame that constantly covered its surface. They named it Burning Spring.[133] So prevalent was Indian sign in the area that they gave up the idea of claiming lands at this time and returned home in haste.

While the skilled surveying teams were among the first to descend the Ohio and Kanawha when these lands were opened for settlement, they were only the vanguard. Ordinary citizens inclined to make their own tomahawk improvements throughout the entire frontier took longer to prepare to emigrate into these forbidding, unknown lands, but what began as a scattering of people acting on unprecedented opportunity quickly evolved from a trickle to a flow to a flood of humanity spilling over the Allegheny crest.

They came on foot, rifles in hand, possessions in backpacks. They came by horseback, singly, in small family groups, among friends and neighbors, in trains of mounted people leading scores of heavily laden packhorses. They came in wagons where they could, though with only two wagon roads open and jammed with traffic, progress was slow, especially when inclemencies turned those roads into mires. Still they came.

Where Braddock's Road ended at the mouth of Redstone Creek on the Monongahela, there was great congestion, and people who had boat-building skills were abruptly deluged with orders for canoes, piroques, bateaux, flatboats, broadhorns, even ordinary rafts—anything that would enable prospective settlers means for getting to and down the Ohio River. Where the Military Road terminated at Pittsburgh, the community swelled out of all proportion, and people erected tents, half-face camps, lean-tos, shacks, cabins, anything for shelter, and they, too, needed water transportation. Wagons that did reach a terminus became objects for barter, to be torn apart and the planking used to build shelter or boats.

Entrepreneurs flourished. Boatyards were established, taverns and wayhouses built, sawmills and gristmills sprang up, supply houses and stores were erected, and still the demand by far exceeded the supply. Pittsburgh swiftly changed from a community of scattered camps and cabins to a town that couldn't grow quickly enough, and new communities named Braddock and Elizabethtown were being established along the Monongahela, the latter already becoming noted as a boat-building center.

There was surprisingly little concern for safety in these terminal areas; the very numbers of people who congregated engendered a false sense of safety. Everyone able to continue down the Ohio, however, understood the peril, knew that around any given bend or behind any given bush or tree or rock, death might lurk, but it did little to deter them, the desire to possess land overshadowing the risk. Friendly Indians who visited were regarded with fear and suspicion, while those even glimpsed along the river shores immediately became targets and many were killed. It wasn't a war—not yet—but the river was becoming known as a deadly place to be, for whites and Indians alike, where all too often the waters became stained with blood.

Everywhere, *everywhere* on the frontier, people fearing to penetrate deeper into the unknown interior to the west elected to find a suitable place along this nebulous frontier fringe to sink their roots, either temporarily or permanently. New settle-

ments were established in the most isolated places as the human overflow spread up
the valleys to the remote reaches of every creek or run that emptied into the Monongahela and Allegheny, the West Branch Susquehanna, the Cheat and Tygart Valley
rivers, the Youghiogheny, the Kiskeminetas, Conemaugh and Loyalhannon, the West
Fork Monongahela, the Buffalo, Chartier's, Dunkard and Tenmile—and the upper
Ohio River.

Alarmed by the number of Indian attacks occurring against the flurry of settlers
establishing themselves in the Greenbrier Valley, the Virginia government, late in
1769, had erected a strong little fortification some 35 miles up the Greenbrier from
its mouth at New River and called it Camp Union.[134] Now, when danger threatened, at least the outlying settlers might be able to make it to the refuge the fort
provided. Comfortable in this knowledge, John Stewart, Robert McClennahan,
Thomas Renix and William Hamilton all settled close together nine miles north of
the new fort.[135]

True to his word, Ebenezer Zane moved his wife and new daughter and all their
goods from Redstone to the Wheeling Creek claims as soon as the season opened in
1770. As he anticipated, Elizabeth was quite as taken with the beauty of the area as he
had been, and they agreed they had at last found the place to permanently sink roots.

Lewis Bonnett, formerly a captain in Braddock's army, and his friend John
Wetzel, a powerful middle-aged German of renowned courage, had settled close
together on Dunkard Creek early in 1769. Now they joined forces with nine other
family heads at Redstone and were among the first to strike out, as the Zanes had
before them, overland to the west.[136] These 11 men found the headwaters of Wheeling Creek and eagerly followed it downstream, only to be deeply disappointed when
they reached the Forks of the Wheeling and found the land from that point to its
mouth already taken up with claims being protected by Ebenezer Zane and his
brothers. So they settled on Wheeling above the Forks, Bonnett, as party leader,
getting first choice and the others drawing lots to make their tomahawk improvements on the remaining choice locations.[137] The parcels of land adjoined one another for several miles above the Forks. Wetzel, with poor luck in the drawing of lots,
wound up with the claim farthest up from the mouth of the creek, 14 miles upstream
and seven miles above the Forks.[138] Claiming his land, he followed a rill to its source
at a beautiful spring. Close at hand was a dead hollow tree, and in its branches some
distance up was a young black bear that had climbed the tree to take refuge at
Wetzel's approach. Wetzel easily brought the rotted tree down with hefty strokes of
his ax. When the bear tumbled out, somewhat dazed by its fall, Wetzel leaped on its
back, encircled its throat with one arm and quickly killed it with a few well-aimed
tomahawk blows, amidst the laughter and hooting of his companions.[139]

A short time later a new settlement was started by the Abraham Earlywine and
William Sivert families, who had followed Wheeling Creek three miles above Wetzel's claim and found a beautiful little stream entering from the north. They followed
it upstream another mile and then climbed a hill to where there was a fine level
ground with a clear bubbling spring 250 feet above the stream. With such isolation as
this, they felt reasonably safe from Indian attack, and so they made their settlement
here, and from the nature of the soil, they named it Sand Hill.[140]

Soon afterward an Irishman named William Boggs settled with his family at the mouth of a run that entered the Ohio only two miles below Wheeling Creek. Directly across from the creek mouth, almost on the Ohio shore, was an island not quite half a mile long but only 70 yards wide. Establishing his own little bit of immortality, he named the stream Boggs Run and the isle Boggs Island. And of course, he called his cabin and the immediate surroundings Boggs Settlement.[141]

Not terribly far from these settlements on Wheeling Creek and its tributaries, the McDonnell brothers—Bartholomew and James—who had come all the way from Connecticut, claimed on a fine little bottomland that they named Yankee Bottom. And at very nearly the same time seven members of the same family established their claim at the mouth of a creek only nine miles above the mouth of Wheeling Creek. The father was named Samuel McCulloch and his wife was Rachel. Only one of their two daughters, Nancy, was with them. The other was named Elizabeth and she was already well settled at the Wheeling site as the wife of Ebenezer Zane. The eldest son was named Samuel, after his father, and the other three were John, Abraham and George. All were well grown, and shortly after the McCulloch Settlement was made, the parents, fearful of Indians, returned to their home on the South Branch Potomac. Their daughter and four sons refused to accompany them; this was their new home and they meant to stay.[142]

Another family group settled at the mouth of a major creek entering the Ohio 12 miles below Wheeling Creek. These were the Tomlinson brothers, Joseph, James and Samuel, and their sister, Rebecca Tomlinson Martin, whose husband, a trader, had been killed by Shawnees on the Hockhocking River earlier the same year. In their initial explorations in the area, Joseph discovered, on a level terrace some 75 feet above the normal level of the Ohio River, an enormous cone-shaped mound, 70 feet high and more than 900 feet in circumference at the base. There were also seven smaller mounds within a few miles, all rising from very level bottomland. Huge, fully grown trees grew from the sides of a cone-shaped mound leveled off at the top to a circular plateau some 50 feet in diameter, upon which in the midst of a peculiar declivity grew two enormous trees—a white oak and a beech. Strange markings scored the latter's smooth bark, obviously carved into the wood at various times over a long period, most of which were indecipherable, although there was one, newer than most, that bore the date 1734—39 years earlier.[143] Curious, he did some preliminary digging into them and found artifacts of a prehistoric culture along with great numbers of human bones. He surmised that these were ancient burial mounds, and he promptly and appropriately named the stream here Grave Creek, and the expansive level bottomland he called Grave Creek Flats.[144] Before long Joseph left to return briefly to their previous home at Will's Creek Station on the upper Potomac, and when he came back he had with him a new young bride, the former Elizabeth Harkness.[145]

Late in the summer of 1770, William Houston arrived in his well-loaded canoe at Pittsburgh, fully prepared to settle there, but he was repulsed by the vulgarity and debauchery he found so prevalent. Leery of going too far down the Ohio lest he run into Indians, of whom he was very fearful, he decided to head upstream on the first creek of good size encountered, but ascend it far enough to be well beyond the vices of Pittsburgh and the likelihood of anyone else settling near him for a good while. It hadn't taken him long to find a creek that suited him, and it turned out to be

Chartier's Creek.[146] He turned in here and paddled upstream for more than 40 miles before coming to a particularly attractive creek entering from the southeast. Putting ashore at its mouth to rest, he rigged up a fishline and hook, baited with some beetle grubs he found by kicking apart a rotted log, and tossed it out into the water. He packed his pipe with tobacco while he waited but had no chance to spark some tinder to light it before the line began moving, heading up the smaller creek. He set the hook with a sharp tug and was dumbfounded at the strength of the pull from the other end. For some 15 minutes he fought the fish and finally pulled it up on shore—and discovered he had caught a large yellow catfish that he estimated would weigh 30 pounds. Very pleased with his catch, he knocked it in the head and tossed it into the canoe to prepare later for his dinner. Then he picked up a fist-size rock along the shoreline and lobbed it into the smaller stream.

"I christen you Catfish Creek," he said aloud, then laughed at his own silly little ceremony. But Catfish Creek it was, and when he ascended it about a mile, he found a fine high clearing about 30 yards in diameter, surrounded by forest that would provide timbers for a cabin and wood for fuel; he knew he had found the place he was seeking. He pulled his canoe up on shore, unloaded some of his things and built a fire to cook his catfish. Then, looking around, he grinned to himself and spoke aloud again. "Reckon if I could name the creek," he said, "I can name this place, too. From now on, this is Catfish Camp." And Catfish Camp it was.[147]

Shortly after, other settlers ascended Chartier's and, liking Houston's choice of location, took up claims and settled in rapidly growing numbers around him. Some claimed considerably more than legally permitted. One of these was Andrew Van Swearingen, who took out claims in both his wife's name and his own and, according to some, under some fictitious names as well.[148] Thomas Edgington was one of the earlier settlers at Catfish Camp, but he didn't get his land by claiming it. Born and raised in Hampshire County, Virginia, he was an adventurous man, and life on the frontier appealed to him. In 1771 he left home for good and settled at Redstone, but within a year tired of the constant transient activity there and sought a new place. Far up Chartier's Creek he found Catfish Camp. The most desirable land there was already taken, but he learned that Andrew Van Swearingen had enough land that he might sell him some. They negotiated, and Van Swearingen, for the sum of $160, sold him a 700-acre tract of his holdings. By the following spring, Edgington had built his own cabin there and settled in with his family. The following year, Van Swearingen, having sold off the remainder of his claims at Catfish Camp to half a dozen new settlers, moved with his family down the Ohio to the large bottom that began at the mouth of Buffalo Creek and extended northward along the east side of the river for two and a half miles. Well up from the river level, he claimed a 400-acre location and built a new cabin.[149]

About that same time, another party that went far upstream before stopping was led by the Bane brothers—Isaac, Jesse and Nathan—who turned their large canoe up Tenmile Creek from the Monongahela, ascended for 16 miles, then turned into a stream coming from the north and followed it another three miles until, just above the mouth of a fine clear run, they found a good, level, lightly wooded terrace 20 feet above the creek waters. Here they established Bane Settlement. Soon afterward they were joined by two more of their brothers, Joseph and Ellis.[150]

Paddling far up the Monongahela in mid-April 1770, James Booth and John Thomas passed the mouth of Tygart Valley River and in three miles came to another stream, considerably smaller, entering from the southeast. They followed the tributary upstream for five miles and discovered an extensive rolling meadow rimmed by forest that was so appealing, they immediately made their claims and called the place Booth's Settlement and the stream Booth's Creek.[151] Later that same month, a settlement was established by the Prickett-Hall-Ice party on the Monongahela River, five miles below the mouth of the Tygart Valley River at the mouth of the stream they named Prickett's Creek. Fearful of being attacked, they petitioned for government protection and, later in the summer, a small fortification called Prickett's Fort was established adjacent to the settlement by David Morgan, built under direction of Col. William Byrd on the Monongahela adjacent to the settlement.[152]

It was in 1770 that hardy explorers moving about in the Greenbrier Valley discovered animals congregating in an area eight miles east of Camp Union, where a series of springs bubbled from the earth, issuing a strong sulfurous odor. The rocks at the edges of the springs were coated with a white mineral crust, and the area was named White Sulphur Springs. Soon the medicinal value of these waters was recognized and a new flurry of settlement occurred in the area.

As soon as weather permitted reasonable travel down the Ohio in 1770, surveyors—individually and in teams—started the descent. Many were looking for any places along the left bank where there were good bottoms that could be claimed for themselves or their employers. Quite a few of them ascended the major streams they encountered and made tomahawk improvements along the way. One of the very first parties was led by the Taylor brothers, Richard and Hancock, who followed the Ohio all the way to its mouth at the Mississippi before turning back.

In May 1771 a settlement called Holliday's Cove was established 66 miles down the Ohio from Fort Pitt and 25 miles above Wheeling Creek. It was located a couple of miles up Harmon's Creek and among its earliest settlers were John Doddridge, Benjamin Biggs, George Lefler and Harmon Greathouse, the latter having two huge loutish sons named Jacob and Daniel.[153]

Later that same year a young giant of a man paddled down the Ohio with two companions bent on locating what were reported to be the most fabulous hunting lands imaginable—a mysterious area called the canelands far down the river in the Kan-tuck-kee country. They searched for a long while and didn't find them at first, so they gave up for the time being and paddled up the Kanawha. At the Elk River they turned upstream and stopped two miles later at the mouth of a small stream. The young man followed a well-used game trail some five miles to where another creek emptied into the Kanawha, near which there was a fine salt lick and evidence of many animals having been attracted. He returned to where they had put in with their canoe and here they made a semipermanent camp to spend the winter, perhaps longer. The companions of the young man were named George Strader and John Yeager. The big young man himself was named Simon Kenton.[154]

In 1772 Richard Wells searched widely for good stream bottoms that were unclaimed and finally, in exasperation, claimed his 400 acres, plus a thousand-acre preemption right on the high level ground of the divide separating Harmon's Creek from Cross Creek.[155]

The Abb's Valley Settlement was established in 1771 on the headwaters of the Bluestone River by Absalom Looney and quickly attracted new settlers, such as the families of James Moore and John Pogue. About the same time the Simpson's Creek Settlement, begun five years earlier on the West Fork of the Monongahela, was enlarged by the arrival of a number of families, including those of John Powers, Jonas Webb and James Anderson.

Walter Kelly brought his family down the New River to the Kanawha and, on the upper reaches of that river, at the mouth of a stream he named Kelly Creek after himself, he established the Kelly's Creek Settlement.[156]

With great courage—or perhaps foolhardiness—a pair of surveyors named Thomas Hedges and Thomas Young descended the Ohio over 430 miles and, on a narrow bottomland along the left bank, pressed their luck by building the first "improver's cabin," as they called it.[157]

While numerous forts were being erected during this period, a major one was deliberately destroyed. Fort de Chartres, a bastion for the French since 1720 and under British control since late 1765, was finally deemed to be a strategic liability rather than an asset and was ordered by Gen. Thomas Gage to be destroyed. This was done by its final commanding officer, Capt. Hugh Lord, in April 1773.[158]

All the northwestern tribes were at first dumbfounded and then deeply concerned by this sudden overwhelming movement of whites into the lands where they lived or hunted. Yet despite the ominous portent it posed to their way of life, they showed remarkable restraint. Though absolute war against the whites was prohibited in general tribal councils, it was agreed that everything possible should be done to force these people back to their own side of the Alleghenies. They began doing so by the only legal means open to them: They attended council after council with the whites and lodged official complaints to the Indian agents—men such as Sir William Johnson, George Croghan, Conrad Weiser, Alexander McKee and others—as well as to governmental authorities, who were usually sympathetic to a degree but invariably professed helplessness in controlling the situation. Though such counciling with white authorities continued, the Indians then took to confronting interlopers and politely asking them to leave. When these requests consistently had little effect, they demanded the whites leave and laced those demands with threats. When even that had little or no effect, greater degrees of harassment occurred—the killing of cattle and other livestock, theft of horses, burning of outbuildings and cabins. True, some killings had occurred from the beginning, but these were most often the actions of hot-headed braves who believed such action was necessary, not only to definitely put the point across to the whites that they risked their lives by coming into Indian lands but, equally, in retaliation for the murders of Indians that were being committed, murders that not only went unpunished but were applauded by other whites. Nevertheless, the actions of these young warriors were not condoned by the tribes in general.

When a party of Shawnees under a subchief called Captain Will discovered Daniel Boone and five others of his party wandering about Kentucky and hunting there, a fight broke out and one of Boone's men was killed. Boone and the other four were captured and held for a week, yet treated with surprising courtesy and concern.

Amazingly, the Indians even apologized for the death and, though they confiscated the furs the whites had collected in Kentucky, along with their horses and some of their weapons and supplies, they left them enough to get them safely back home. Captain Will, who could speak English surprisingly well, released Boone and his four men, saying:

"Now, Brothers, go home and stay there. Do not come here anymore. This is the Indians' hunting grounds, where we must hunt to provide for our families over the winter. All the animals, skins and furs were given as a gift by Moneto for our support, without which we could not survive. You must go. Consider us to be the stinging bugs who guard their nests: if you are so foolish as to come here again, you may be sure the wasps and yellow jackets will sting you severely."

The Boone party started away, all except Boone and his companion, John Stewart.[159] Instead of taking the good advice, these two followed the Indians, crept into their camp by night and managed to take back a few of their horses. Then it was they who were followed and recaptured. Amazingly, they were not killed and, in fact, as before, were treated quite well. Two days later they escaped again and this time overtook their companions. It was during this period that Boone spied a Shawnee boy fishing in a stream and took a bead on him with his rifle, then decided against killing him and lowered the gun, only to find that a warrior he hadn't even seen, the boy's father, had similarly taken a bead on him and would have fired instantly had he hurt the boy in any way. They talked together politely and then each went his own way. Boone was going home, but he knew that he would soon be back.

The worst incident at this time of Indian attack against whites actually had nothing to do with the northwestern tribes except for its aftermath. In the spring of 1772, Adam Stroud, a Dutchman formerly of the Philadelphia area, along with his wife and five children, had descended the New River to the mouth of the Gauley River, then ascended that stream to a lovely area they called The Glades, and here they established themselves. Hardly had they planted their roots, however, when they were discovered by a roving war party of Cherokees, who massacred all seven. When the deed was discovered, a great fear shot through the other settlers establishing themselves farther down the Kanawha and along the Ohio. A party of men was assembled by William White and William Hacker on the upper New River and descended the stream searching for the perpetrators. The Cherokees had long departed by that time, but the party heard from a trader of the existence of the Delaware village of Bulltown on the Little Kanawha and decided those were the Indians who must have done it. They fell on the town by surprise, killed the chief, Captain Bull, and five families of Delawares before the remainder made their escape. About 20 Indians were killed, and when the survivors eventually returned and found the dreadful remains, they immediately abandoned the village and paddled down the Ohio to the Wabash, up that stream to the mouth of the White River, then up the White for 18 miles before stopping to establish a new village.[160]

Oddly, little attention was paid to this incident, the whites generally feeling that the Stroud massacre had been avenged and the Indians more or less accepting it as an unfortunate occurrence but one that did not require retaliation, lest a general war break out. The most direct result seemed to be that Indians living in their proximity made another general movement away from the intruders and reestablished their villages deep in the Ohio country or even farther west, in the Indiana country. Four other Delaware villages were abandoned—one near the mouth of the Loyalhannon not far from Fort Bedford, another on the upper Allegheny near the mouth of Conewango Creek, the third at the mouth of the Kiskeminetas, also on the Allegheny, and, most significantly, the largest village still existing on the Allegheny, Kittanning.[161] Also, the village called Mingo Town, long situated on the right bank of the Ohio 70 miles below Fort Pitt, was abandoned.

Not all the whites who descended the Ohio were bent on claiming lands. Some came for what they believed to be altruistic purposes. One of these was a Welshman named David Jones, who was a Baptist minister from New Jersey and self-styled "missionary to the heathens." Escorted by a young land-claimer named George Rogers Clark, he had stopped briefly at Wheeling where, to the Zane family and some others, he proudly preached what he called the first sermon ever delivered in the Ohio River Valley. Continuing downstream, he went where even the boldest of adventurers feared to tread, ascending the Scioto River and boldly entering one of the largest Shawnee villages, Chalahgawtha, at the mouth of Paint Creek. There he found English trader Richard Conner in residence. Conner was not at all pleased to see him, but the Shawnee villagers welcomed him, fed him, gave him hot chocolate to drink and otherwise treated him cordially enough until he explained that his mission was to bring the heathen Shawnees into the embrace of God.[162] At that point the Indians became cool, and Jones was approached by one of the leading men of the village, Outhowwa Shokka—Yellow Hawk—who spoke to him sternly.

"Our Great Father, Moneto, the Maker of Life, long long ago explained to His children, the Shawnees, how they should live and how they should honor Him. It is by His rules alone that we have always lived. We do not need or want the white man's religion here and if you speak one further word of your God or your religion in this place or anywhere else among our people, you will not find pleasant what happens next."

The Rev. Jones wisely held his tongue, which undoubtedly helped him to retain his scalp as well. After staying awhile longer, he meekly floated back down to the Ohio and, not stopping to preach at Wheeling or anywhere else on the return trip, returned to Fort Pitt far more subdued than when he left.

Soon afterward another missionary, this time a Moravian named David Zeisberger, also visited the Shawnees on the Scioto and spoke with their principal chief, Hokolesqua—Cornstalk. The chief listened to what he had to say, then launched into a harangue against the whites that continued for some time. When he finally ran down, he told the Lutheran missionary, "I cannot permit you to preach here, but if you are still determined to do so among others of the Shawnee villages, you may go to them. In which case," he added grimly, "you must rely on having your brains beat out very quickly." Not a fool in any sense, Zeisberger returned home at once.

On the whole, the Shawnees and some of the other tribes were showing remarkable tolerance, in light of the fact that the country they considered their own was being invaded by an unprecedented number of whites. Some of the tribes were not so forbearing. Here and there British traders were slain, but usually as much for reprehensible trading practices as anything else. John Findlay, returning to the Kentucky country to rejoin Boone and claim land, was one of those who disappeared, never to be heard of again, and it was generally assumed he had been killed by Indians. And far down the Ohio near its mouth, some Kickapoos began attacking traders traveling on the river, but this lasted only a little while, as a new intertribal war broke out between them and the Osages, and the Kickapoos forgot about the Ohio River attacks in order to concentrate on their enemy in the Missouri country. Farther to the north, however, English traders were still occasionally being killed or taken into captivity by Potawatomies.[163]

Isolated cabins on the frontier, especially on the East Fork Monongahela and Tygart Valley River, were still attacked on occasion, with goods taken, and now and then an individual—usually a youngster—was carried away into captivity to be adopted into the tribe, but there was remarkably little bloodshed except in instant retaliation to Indians being unjustly killed.[164]

That was what happened with the Thomas Bullitt surveying party. Some of Bullitt's men, against orders, camped on the Ohio side of the river and were observed by a party of Shawnees. While the remainder of the Indian party remained hidden, one warrior approached to tell them they were on Indian lands and must leave, but Bullitt's men panicked and shot him dead. They in turn were killed, and then the remainder of Bullitt's party, on the Kentucky side of the river, was also attacked and either killed or, as occurred with Bullitt himself, captured.

Proposals were made to the Lords of Trade in England that at least two new forts be established—one at the mouth of the Ohio and another at the mouth of the Illinois—to protect the British trade in this remote region, but the idea was quashed by Lord Hillsborough, president of that board, who wrote:

> *Forts and military establishments at the mouths of the Ohio and Illinois Rivers, admitting that they would be effectual to the attainment of the objects in view, would yet, I fear, be attended with an expence to this Kingdom greatly disproportionate to the advantages proposed to be gained.*

It was while all this frontier activity was taking place that one of the more significant events in Virginia government occurred. In 1770 the colonial governor of Virginia, Norborne Berkeley—Baron de Botetourt—died in office and the colonial governor of New York, John Murray—Earl of Dunmore—was transferred to the Virginia governorship. At age 40, Lord Dunmore was an overweight, rather pompous man of fiery temperament. He had taken his seat in the House of Lords in 1761 and was named Governor of New York Colony only two years ago, in 1767. Now, in his new role, he was an outspoken believer in strengthening Virginia's hold on its western lands, with little regard to its native inhabitants. In a letter to the colonial minister in England he wrote:

> *The Americans acquire no attachment to Place: but wandering about seems engrafted in their Nature. . . . In this colony Proclamations have been issued from time to time that restrain them. But . . . they do not conceive that Government has any right to forbid their taking possession of a Vast tract of Country, either*

uninhabited, or which serves only as a Shelter for a few scattered Tribes of Indians. Nor can they easily be brought to entertain any belief of the permanent obligation of Treaties made with those People, whom they consider but little removed from the brute Creation.

To this end he not only issued a proclamation encouraging citizens to emigrate beyond the Allegheny crest to settle and make tomahawk improvements, for which they would receive clear title to their claims, but he also named Dr. John Wood and Hancock Lee as official colony surveyors and dispatched them at the head of about 150 men to survey Ohio Valley lands with an eye to future development for the colony.

Lord Dunmore had met and was particularly taken with an enterprising young doctor in Pittsburgh named John Connolly, who had been a medical officer with the militia during Bouquet's campaign. A nephew of the renowned Indian agent George Croghan, he had gone to Kaskaskia after that campaign, where he traded and studied Indian languages for three years, until 1770. He was keenly interested in the development of the Ohio Valley and was a very literate man with a knack for writing reports and letters that were descriptive and accurate. And even better, in Dunmore's opinion, this young man held neither high regard of—nor sympathy for—the Indians that was manifested by his illustrious uncle. As Dunmore himself felt, he believed the Indians were merely creatures of inconvenience; minor aggravations to be thrust out of the way to make room for more civilized people. Dr. Connolly was also a man well experienced in moving about on the frontier, having for some years been an employee of the trading firm of Baynton, Wharton and Morgan at its western headquarters in Kaskaskia. He was one of the few men who had traversed the entire length of the Ohio River by boat not just once but on a number of occasions.

Only last year, on March 14, 1772, the 29-year-old John Connolly had passed the Falls of the Ohio with Maj. Henry Hamilton's Royal Irish Regiment on its return to Fort Pitt from the Illinois country. The company was traveling in nine large bateaux and, because the river was swollen by spring rains, they had been able to pass the Falls without portaging. Connolly conceived the notion of having a new colony established in this area, with a great town built as its capital on the shores of the Falls of the Ohio. The regiment camped overnight here, and Connolly had taken that opportunity to explore about on the shoreline adjacent to the rapids. He was very taken by the large number of fossils he found, especially coprolites, and during the evening at the campfire he wrote of them:

Various petrifications are to be found upon the shores and upon the rocks at this place; even buffalo excrement with the small vegetable substances discoverable therein, curiously turned into stone, yet so nicely retaining the original appearance as to be immediately known.

In recent months Connolly had made it clear to all who would listen that he was in full accord with Lord Dunmore and did not in the least sympathize with the recent rise in revolutionary sentiment that was sweeping the colonies. Party strife was currently rampant among all the colonies and the idea, however fancifully bandied about, that these colonies ought to disengage themselves from home rule and establish themselves independently as Americans was as repugnant to him as it was to the Virginia governor.

Whatever early approbation Lord Dunmore had won among the Virginians was quickly being undermined by his tyrannical actions. Having returned to Fort Pitt, John Connolly was delighted to find Lord Dunmore there, publicly on a pleasure jaunt but privately with other business in mind. Connolly hastened to laud the governor for the decisive action he had just taken that arbitrarily dissolved the right of assembly in Virginia because of the revolutionary sentiment being expressed. Few among the Virginians—especially those on the frontier—shared the admiration.

There was another problem developing and rapidly escalating in this particular area of the frontier. With the rapid growth of Pittsburgh's population and strategic location, it was clear to everyone that the town was destined to become possibly the greatest city in the west. Suddenly, both Virginia and Pennsylvania were claiming jurisdiction over Pittsburgh and Fort Pitt, as well as the entire valley of the Monongahela. The border dispute heated rapidly and, since the population in the area was almost evenly divided between citizens of both colonies, tensions were running high and battle lines beginning to be drawn.[165]

The more important business that had brought Lord Dunmore to Fort Pitt was the fact that he had received notification from the King that Fort Pitt was, effective immediately, abandoned by the British government and that he was now taking possession of the installation on behalf of the Dominion of Virginia. Further, he was appointing Connolly as both land agent here for Virginia and also its Indian agent. Even more unexpectedly, he appointed Connolly a major of the Virginia militia and placed him in command of the fort.[166]

Connolly was greatly delighted with his appointments and immediately announced that henceforth Fort Pitt was to be called Fort Dunmore. At this the frontier people balked; the name Fort Pitt was too deeply ingrained to be cast aside in such cavalier manner, and they continued to call it Fort Pitt. Connolly did not really care that much; Lord Dunmore knew he had proposed the name change, and that was what counted. All in all, Connolly was very much satisfied with the turn of events. Presently basking in the favor of Lord Dunmore, as he most assuredly was, he saw his own future prospects escalating with the future of Virginia. A decidedly ambitious man, he was suddenly even harboring the notion that if, in fact, a new colony could be established with its capital at the Falls of the Ohio as he proposed—a proposal that even appealed to George Washington—who might be in a better position to be named its governor than himself?

[October 10, 1773—Sunday]

At age 42, Talgayeeta—more familiar to the whites as Chief Logan—was a very tall man with fine strong features and kind eyes. He had been born in the village of Shamokin, where the great Forks of the Susquehanna were located.[167] His father, the renowned Cayuga chief Shikellimus, was himself born on the shore of Cayuga Lake, far to the north in the New York Colony, but had removed to Shamokin to be closer to the English, for whom he harbored a great affection. He was noted for his unfailing hospitality to whatever whites visited the village, treating one and all with a generosity far beyond anything anticipated.

It was through this kind nature of his that Shikellimus had come to know and admire William Penn and, through him, John Logan, who was an intimate of Penn's and also provincial secretary for Pennsylvania Colony. A close friendship had developed between Shikellimus and John Logan, so it was not too surprising that when the son of Shikellimus was born in 1731 and named Talgayeeta, the Cayuga chief bestowed an alternate name on the baby boy—Logan—in honor of his friend.[168]

Much of this same generous nature became apparent in Talgayeeta as he matured. When, to his overwhelming sorrow, his father finally died, he established his own village, called Talgayeeta's Town, at a beautiful spring in the valley of Kishacoquillas Creek. The health of his wife, Mellana, was ruined by smallpox when his sister, Koonay, was still a young girl, and it was at his town at the spring that he and Mellana raised Koonay to young womanhood.[169] His home there became just as noted for hospitality as his father's had been, and Talgayeeta became well known as "the friend of the white man."

Prior to the French and Indian War, he announced he would remain neutral and not join the French in alliance against the British, as the rest of the Cayugas were planning to do. For this he was castigated to such extent by his own people that he permanently disavowed any connection with the tribe and thereafter considered his own little community autonomous, welcoming any Indians who felt as he did and cared to join him. A considerable number did so, and he gave this group a new name: Mingo—chiefs, all, and warriors, all. He was their spokesman, but none among them had greater rank than anyone else. He was particularly pleased when his elder brother, Taylaynee, was one of those who joined him.

Talgayeeta's ethics and integrity remained at a high level and, though he had become noted as a fearsome fighter in his younger years, he had a remarkable capacity for keeping his temper in check and avoiding conflict wherever possible. In 1766 he was visited at the spring by William Brown, James Reed and Richard McClay, who were among the earliest of settlers in the Kishacoquillas Creek Valley. Talgayeeta fancied himself a good shot and challenged the best shot of the three to compete against him, shooting at a mark with the wager of a dollar per shot. McClay accepted the bet and he was very good. Talgayeeta lost five times in succession and sheepishly admitted he had been fairly defeated. He then went to his house and returned with five tanned deer hides—the hide of a deer called a "buck" and worth a dollar—which he handed to McClay.

"I can't take these," McClay protested, attempting to give them back. "We're your guests, and we didn't come here to rob you. What we did was just a little contest of skill."

Shaking his head, Talgayeeta refused to take the skins back. "We bet to make us shoot our best," he said. "You did and I did. If I won, I would have accepted your dollars. You won, so you must accept these five bucks." He then even refused to accept a hornful of gunpowder in return.

A year later Talgayeeta paid a visit to the cabin of William Brown, several miles from the spring. Brown was absent, but his wife and daughter were home, the little one running and jumping about in bare feet. Mrs. Brown remarked sadly that she could not buy her daughter a pair of shoes small enough to fit. After visiting for an hour, Talgayeeta prepared to leave and asked her to let him take the child for a visit to his cabin for the rest of the day. Mrs. Brown was uneasy about it but, knowing her husband's respect for Talgayeeta, she agreed. She was becoming extremely uneasy when they had not returned by late afternoon, but then, just at sunset, Talgayeeta and the child came into sight. The little girl ran to her mother's arms and proudly showed off the beautiful pair of moccasins Talgayeeta had spent the day making for her, refusing even the help of Mellana or Koonay. Instead, while he worked on the moccasins, his wife and sister had spent the afternoon entertaining the little girl.

Three years later, in 1770, with white settlement closing in and game disappearing, making life difficult for all Indians in that area of Pennsylvania, including the Mingoes, Talgayeeta regretfully abandoned the village on Kishacoquillas Creek. The Mingoes broke up into little groups of their own and many moved to the Ohio country. Talgayeeta, Mellana and Koonay, along with other relatives, did so, too, taking up residence in the Indian village located on the Ohio at the mouth of Indian Cross Creek, 70 miles below Pittsburgh.[170] While it was a Delaware village initially, so many Mingoes from Talgayeeta's Town had taken up residence there over the years that the place had come to be called Mingo Town and was frequently visited by the early traders. However, less than two years after Talgayeeta's arrival, the Delawares—as the result of the destruction of Bulltown—moved out, and then the Mingoes, too, began drifting away into the interior and either joined established villages or set up small villages of their own.

Talgayeeta moved with his family again, this time adjacent to a fine bubbling spring up on a terrace well above the Ohio River shore, just above the mouth of Beaver River and 25 miles below Pittsburgh.[171] It was here that Talgayeeta and his family met the trader John Gibson. Very soon Gibson and Koonay fell in love and were married. The new location, despite its excellent spring, was in an area where there was little game, and the hunters of the village became discontent. In council they discussed moving again, this time to Yellow Creek, another 25 miles farther down the Ohio, not so much because the hunting was better in that area, but because, while still providing them access to the Ohio River, there was also an excellent Indian trail leading westward to the Forks of the Muskingum and the excellent hunting lands that lay beyond there in the valley of the Walhonding.

Now he had just finished telling Koonay that they would be moving again, expecting her to be downcast at the news, but she was not. She smiled and admitted that, except for meeting and marrying her husband here and bearing his daughter less than a year ago, she had never really been fond of the location and was looking forward to the new site at Yellow Creek. It might make things a little more difficult for John Gibson when he was able to come back to her and their daughter, which he did as frequently as possible, since they would be double the distance from Fort Pitt, where he had to spend so much of his time, but it was not a problem of special concern.

Besides, she confided, her smile widening, there was now another reason for him to make extra effort to come to her: a new little life was stirring within her and she was sure their second child would be born during the next Planting Moon.

[October 14, 1773 — Thursday]

Five miles below the mouth of the Muskingum, on the high bank of the Ohio River at Briscoe's Settlement, Dr. John Briscoe stood and looked downstream.[172] No boats were in sight, but he was sure more would be passing before winter closed in. For the past six months, since early May, when he had led a party of 15 men in five canoes to this location, he had been developing this little settlement almost 90 miles below Zane's Wheeling settlement. He felt a certain pride in having established the most remote settlement down the Ohio, yet there was also a prevailing sense of apprehension. Five cabins stood here now, built by men he had hired for that purpose, and next year, God willing, they would build more—perhaps even a blockhouse for everyone's protection.

Over these months a multitude of boat parties had passed on their way downstream, some of them traders laden with goods en route to the tribes, traveling with or without Indian escorts, but by far the greater majority were parties of men who had never seen the Ohio before: men bent on surveying and claiming lands. All had stopped off here to rest and visit, some for an hour or so, some for several days, but most for an overnight stay where they could enjoy the relative security of an established settlement.

Briscoe's present apprehension stemmed from the recent alarming increase in the number of stories told of attacks by Indians. The large surveying party led by Capt. Thomas Bullitt, for example, had disappeared. Several of his men had been found dead on the shore, but the remainder were simply gone, and everyone feared the worst. A similarly large surveying party under Hancock Taylor and the McAfee brothers had simply vanished.[173] Then word had been brought by the Joel Reese party that the hunting camp established up the Kanawha by the big young frontiersman named Simon Kenton had been hit by Indians and that one of his two companions, John Yeager, had been killed. Kenton and George Strader had narrowly escaped death themselves and had been saved only by accidentally stumbling into Reese's camp on the Ohio shore. Another party brought word that two men named Richards had been killed farther up the Kanawha. There were rumors of other attacks as well and an aura of growing tension in everyone. It was the consensus that these attacks were only a bare taste of what lay in store for whatever land-seeking parties descended the river next spring.

That was when Briscoe came up with the idea almost everyone was commending: Instead of all these various parties descending the river next year as individuals or small groups, there should be a general rendezvous held at his settlement. From here, for mutual safety, they would all descend the river together in a force so strong, the Indians would not dare attack.

For the past two months, everyone who came by, going upstream or down, was informed of the planned rendezvous and urged to pass the word along to everyone else encountered on the river who might not have heard about it. Since most of those intent on surveying and claiming lands were planning to be afloat on the Ohio as soon as the river was relatively clear of ice, the date set for the rendezvous was March fifteenth. They would gather at Briscoe's for a period of two weeks and then, on the first of April, begin the great odyssey, with individuals or groups gradually splitting off up tributaries or at other areas that appealed to them as they were reached.

Briscoe had already passed word of the rendezvous to a score of boat parties working their way back upstream toward Fort Pitt, and now, even though no more were immediately in sight, he knew others would be coming. He would remain here for a final two weeks and then, leaving behind a few men to guard the claims and cabins, would return to Pittsburgh himself. Optimist that he was, he truly believed that the spring rendezvous here would have only good results.

[January 20, 1774—Thursday]

At Fort Pitt—which he was still vainly trying to get everyone to call Fort Dunmore—Maj. John Connolly issued a statement calling up the militia and ordering the men to appear with their rifles at the fort in five days. Pittsburgh and nearby settlements dutifully brought up their required numbers and dispatched them to the fort, though all were perplexed over why such a call had been issued, as no further Indian disturbances had been reported since the beginning of winter.

At just about the same time, in Williamsburg, Lord Dunmore, having already dissolved the right of assembly in the colony, now went one step further. As much as anywhere else and quite likely even more, revolutionary sentiments were regularly being voiced in the august halls of the Virginia Assembly itself. Legislators such as the fiery Patrick Henry, Richard Henry Lee and Thomas Jefferson were continually making speeches maligning King George and introducing resolutions to oppose his restrictive royal decrees. It was Patrick Henry, in fact, who had evoked applause, cheers and foot-stamping when he stood before the Assembly and thundered: "Caesar has his Brutus; Charles the First, his Cromwell; and George the Third—may profit by their example!" Now they had even had the effrontery to initiate what was being called the Intercolonial Committee of Correspondence in an effort to rile up citizens elsewhere as they had been riling their fellow Virginians. So unexpectedly and to the intense anger of practically everyone, Lord Dunmore now issued by proclamation a peremptory executive order dissolving the Virginia Assembly.

[January 25, 1774—Tuesday]

The Shawnees camped near the mouth of Saw Mill Run were pleased that they had been summoned to Pittsburgh by George Croghan because at last he might have good news for them in reply to their complaints about whites flooding into their lands. They were a bit apprehensive, however, when they saw a large number of white men assemble at the fort, listen to one who spoke for a long while and then form themselves into ranks and practice marching. The drilling men were not wearing uniforms, but they all carried guns and it was evident they were soldiers. Why should so many soldiers be gathered here at a time when the Shawnees had been summoned to speak of peace? It was all very strange.

They continued to watch the exercises, until at last the man who had been speaking to them earlier halted them, said something else, the formation broke up and the men started away. The largest cluster moved toward the watching Shawnees, came within 100 yards or less, raised their weapons and abruptly fired in ragged chorus. Suddenly bullets were making little spurts in the creek water nearby, clipping twigs off low-hanging branches and ricocheting off nearby rocks with menacing whines.

The Indians dived for cover behind trees and rocks or even in the tall grasses along the stream. They peered out fearfully, only to see the soldiers in frontier clothes running off, laughing and yelling.

The Shawnees were not pleased.

[January 28, 1774—Friday]

When George Croghan's deputy Indian agent, Alexander McKee, had confronted Maj. Connolly inside Fort Pitt yesterday, it was only with the greatest of difficulty that both had held their temper.

"No," Connolly had replied to the question McKee posed, "my militia did not fire on those damned Indians on my orders. They were just having fun. No one was hurt. So why are you coming to me?"

"The Shawnee delegation came here in peace, Major," McKee said, eyes glinting angrily. "Whether or not anyone was hurt makes no difference. They have a right not to expect to be treated in such a manner. They're human beings, you know."

"They're *animals*! They're a mob of thieving beggars who are always asking for favors and presents. They deserve nothing from us. *Nothing!*"

"So you're not going to do anything about what happened?"

"Yes, I'll do something. I will, by God, give my militia orders to improve their marksmanship. Get out!"

That was yesterday. Now McKee was addressing the group of Shawnees before him, speaking slowly and seriously in the Shawnee tongue. "You have told me," he said, "of your reasons for coming here; that more than ever white men are coming into your lands and you wish them stopped and turned back. You have told me that you came here in peace, to talk peace, and that three days ago you were fired upon by soldiers who were not wearing soldier clothes. I am happy that none of you were hurt, but saddened that this thing should have happened. I have talked with Major Connolly in the fort, and he says he knows nothing of this affair. I do not know if he tells the truth or not. But for myself and your friend Croghan, who could not be here, I apologize that this bad thing happened. As to the first"—he raised his arms in a helpless gesture and then let them fall to his sides—"I deeply sympathize with you, as I, too, have seen the white men entering your lands. We have asked Lord Dunmore to stop them from doing this, but he does not know if he can. He has said he will ask our King, but that will take time, and I can only ask you to have patience. I am sorry I cannot do more."

Pucksinwah nodded. "I, too, am sorry. The Shawnees have already shown much patience. It has solved nothing. What has been happening continues to happen, and now there is little patience left to give. If the whites do not stop coming into our lands, who is to say what will happen next?" He paused for a long while and then added, "We were sent by Hokolesqua to council with Croghan. Yet he is not here. He has always helped us before. We will wait nearby for his return. We will harm no one, but let no one attempt again to harm us."

[February 16, 1774 — Wednesday]

Throughout this past fall and winter word had spread of the great rendezvous that was to take place far down the Ohio at Briscoe's Settlement on March 15. Now, in the valleys of the Cheat, Youghiogheny and Monongahela, settlers, land-jobbers, surveyors, hired claimers and others had begun a general movement back toward the Ohio Valley. They moved confidently, with little fear. Since early fall almost no Indian attacks had been reported, the first time in years that it had been so quiet. There were hardly even any reports of Indian movement, and that, too, was highly unusual. Was it possible that the large numbers of whites flooding the Ohio River Valley last year had made them realize the futility of trying to resist? In the past, hadn't the Indians given up and moved away to other areas as the whites moved in? Certainly it wasn't so far-fetched to believe they might have done so again. Everyone knew from the talk of the traders that one of the recurrent themes of their councils was consideration of moving west of the Mississippi to get far out of harm's way. Perhaps at last they had done so.

The optimism drained away, however, when they reached Pittsburgh. There they found stories rampant of attacks, murders, scalpings, barbarities. Here were reports of robberies and of two deaths having been perpetrated by Indians in the area of Wheeling. Here was the report of a large party of land-jobbers that had gone downriver only a few weeks ago and been robbed by Indians near Grave Creek, their canoes and all their goods stolen, their own lives hanging in the balance as they overcame terrible hardships to get back to safety. Here was the story of the party of emissaries sent by Virginia to council for peace with the Shawnees, who were fired upon and barely managed to escape with their lives. Here was the story of the isolated cabin "somewhere downriver a ways" that was attacked and burned with a man, his wife and three children roasted to death inside.

No one seemed to question the fact that the stories were always about a "party" or a "family" or "some surveyors" or "messengers" or "traders" or "emissaries" or "hunters." Yet unfailingly no names were provided; no verification of any kind. They were simply accepted as having truly occurred, and in each telling and retelling, the stories became more frightening, the peril waiting down the Ohio more deadly.

The stories were rumors, of course. More than that, they were outright lies. In a deliberate campaign to create fear and unrest and, most desirably, to provoke actual attacks by the prospective settlers on whatever Indians they might encounter, Maj. John Connolly had been making up these tales out of whole cloth or, wherever possible, lending an aspect of authenticity by embellishing ordinary events with bloody, horrible trimmings.

So as the land-jobbers and surveyors and prospective settlers headed downriver from Pittsburgh for the rendezvous, it was with their guns close at hand and constant glances over their shoulders for whatever hazard might be approaching.

Despite the word-of-mouth broadcasting of the rendezvous over the fall and winter, some had not heard of it, while others had enough men that they felt themselves sufficiently protected. Among these were two especially large parties, each with more than 50 men and both with the particular interest and sanction of Lord Dunmore. Oddly enough, though several hundred miles apart, these two parties set out on the same day for the Kentucky country. The party being led by John Floyd and Hancock Taylor had been poised for weeks to head for the Ohio River Valley from southwestern Virginia by way of the New and Kanawha rivers. Now they set out in a whole flotilla of canoes and small bateaux. They knew nothing of the planned rendezvous.[174] The other party was led by James Harrod, who had surveyed in Kentucky last year and who now had assembled his men at Redstone Old Fort. The party included the young Hite brothers, Abraham, 16, and Isaac, a year younger. They, in turn, invited a neighbor lad, John Cuppy, to accompany them, saying by way of inducement that they would pay for his land warrants and even survey for him 1,000 acres of the best canelands in Kentucky. Cuppy was eager to go, but his father said no; not only was it a distant and dangerous trip, he wasn't all that convinced the Kentucky lands were worth the effort and risk. Besides, John Cuppy, though big for his age, was only 12 years old.

The Harrod party set off in a small fleet of canoes from the mouth of Redstone Creek, pausing only briefly at Pittsburgh. Though the rumors of Indian attacks reached them, they simply sloughed them off and went on their way, convinced they were strong enough to ward off any trouble. They decided not to wait for the rendezvous because they wanted to get the long journey to Kentucky behind them, and they didn't really believe the Indians were going to be that much of a problem. Harrod had made plenty of claims there last year, and this time he meant to return up the Kentucky River to the area he liked best and there establish a strong, permanent settlement.

[F e b r u a r y   2 7 ,   1 7 7 4 — S u n d a y]

Michael Cresap was surprised to see the small group of Indians standing on the shore at the mouth of Yellow Creek. Fifty miles below Pittsburgh, he had camped at this very place last fall on his way back to the settlements, and there hadn't been a trace of these Indians in the area. Now there were a temporary dwelling and two campfires at the creek mouth, and he caught a glimpse of a couple of canoes just disappearing around a bend upstream on the creek.

Not wishing to push his luck, he had been tempted to merely skim past without stopping and put to shore at Baker's Bottom on the Virginia side a few hundred yards below, where Joshua Baker had claimed last summer and built a little cabin.[175] But then he saw that one of the Indians at the mouth of the creek was waving, and he recognized him at once. It was Chief Logan, whom he had met on several occasions before, both at Pittsburgh and at his village near the mouth of Beaver River, the chief who was noted for his hospitality to travelers and whose daughter John Gibson had married. It would be impolite not to stop, so he swung his canoe toward shore.

Cresap had been an officer on Col. Bouquet's expedition to Goschachgunk in October of '64.[176] Shortly after that, he had entered the Indian trade but failed at it because of his inherent dislike of Indians, which, while not manifest, became evident in his actions and speech. He had then made some fairly extensive claims over the past five years on the Monongahela in the Redstone Creek area. He was one of the individual settlers there who did not put much credence in the rumors floating about of increased Indian attacks down the Ohio. It was possible, he knew, but he had long ago learned to be suspicious of the "I heered tell of . . ." stories that didn't give names and places. They rarely had much foundation in truth.

In recent months he had grown disenchanted with the Redstone Creek area; it had become rowdy and congested, filled with transients tramping all over one's property. So when a pair of brothers named Brown showed up one day and offered to buy all his claims fronting on the Monongahela just south of Redstone Creek, he sold out to them. The Brown brothers immediately began laying out a town on the land and called it Brownsville, while Cresap used the money he got to equip himself well for the claiming he meant to do down the Ohio this spring.[177] In addition he had formed a loose association with George Rogers Clark and William Crawford, who were actively employed by the Ohio Land Company and looking to the establishment of a new colony beginning at the mouth of the Kanawha. Even more exciting—and dangerous—was the fact that George Washington, one of the founding members of the company, was not only intent on claiming some 200,000 acres along the Ohio but had hired John Floyd to locate lands right in the midst of the Shawnee territory in Ohio. His orders to Floyd were to claim for him some 10,000 acres of prime bottomlands in the valley of the Scioto River.[178]

Now, painfully aware that his canoe was packed with camping gear, axes and shovels and all the other accoutrements requisite for such claiming, Michael Cresap nosed his little craft onto the shore and stepped out, immediately shaking hands with Chief Logan, who had stepped forward to greet him.

"How," Talgayeeta said, smiling. "You are Captain Cresap. I remember you. Welcome."[179]

"How. Wondered where you folks'd gone when I saw you weren't up at Beaver anymore," Cresap replied. He nodded at the few warriors standing together a short distance away. They gravely returned the nod but made no move to approach.

"Too many people," Talgayeeta replied. "Here there are not so many. None where we make the new village, there a little way." He pointed upstream on Yellow Creek, where the canoes had passed from sight. Then he indicated the temporary shelter nearby. "Come. Smoke with me. We will talk."

Cresap followed him inside the half-face stick structure, and they squatted by the fire. They shared a pipe, talking casually, touching on such matters as the easy winter now ending, the health of their respective families, the recent incident at Pittsburgh when the rowdy militia soldiers had fired on the camped Shawnees, the increased white settlement on the Virginia side of the Ohio River, the growing irritation of the tribes about it and the rumors currently circulating about recent Indian attacks.

Talgayeeta shook his head sadly. "The stories," he said, "must be tales carried by bad birds, for I have heard nothing of them, and I would know if such things had happened. What the soldiers did near Fort Pitt was a foolish thing to do, even though no harm came of it, as it causes bad feelings. It would be well if both my friends, the Indians and the whites, could learn to live together in peace."

They talked a little more, finished their smoking, left the shelter and walked back to Cresap's beached canoe. Talgayeeta looked at Cresap and smiled. He tilted his head toward Yellow Creek. "You are welcome to come see our new village. Come, eat with us, stay with us tonight."

The settler hesitated, then shook his head regretfully. "I appreciate your hospitality, Chief Logan, but there is still a good bit of the day remaining, and," he added untruthfully, "I have urgent messages I must deliver at Wheeling."

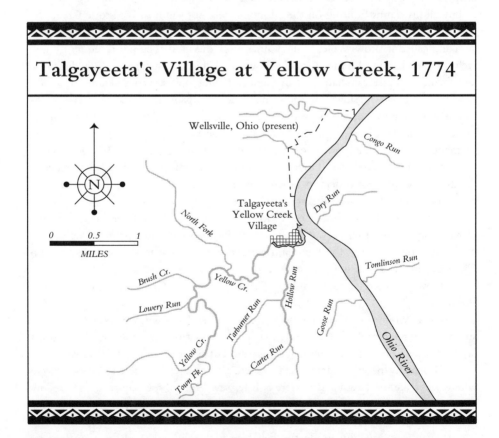

Talgayeeta's Village at Yellow Creek, 1774

Talgayeeta did not take offense. He simply shrugged and shook hands with Cresap again, inviting him to stop back when he had more time. He watched the white man paddle downstream for a time, then turned toward the new village where the Shawnee ·delegation had gone, the one that had arrived by canoe just before Cresap. These were some of the same Shawnees that had been fired upon a month ago in Pittsburgh.

Within minutes Talgayeeta reached the village site where already half a dozen cabins had been built, as well as a small longhouse for councils.[180] He moved directly to that latter structure and, now accompanied by his older brother, Taylaynee, joined the delegation waiting inside. The visitors had just finished eating bowls of savory venison stew brought to them by Koonay, and now, as she gathered up the empty bowls and carried them away, the Cayuga brothers took their place on a mat by the fire beside the deputation's chief and spokesman, Pucksinwah. They smoked their pipes quietly, and then Pucksinwah spoke respectfully.

"We have come to ask your help, Talgayeeta, as chief of the Mingoes."

"You give me more strength than is mine, Pucksinwah," Talgayeeta replied. "I am but one man. Among the Mingoes there are no chiefs and there are no warriors, yet we are all warriors and we are all chiefs."

Pucksinwah nodded. "I understand that," he said, "yet I also know that you are highly respected. The Mingoes go where you go, follow your lead in what you do. You know well of the great many whites who are coming into our lands. The Shawnees can fight their own battles against the *Shemanese*, but your word, Talgayeeta, is needed to encourage other tribes and the Mingoes to stand fast and to stop —by battle, if necessary!—any whites crossing into the Ohio country. We Shawnees cannot and should not be expected to stand alone and guard the entire frontier against the flood of whites, when it is for the benefit of all the tribes that this be done. *All* tribes must help stem the Shemanese. The word of Logan would sway many who would otherwise hold themselves apart from it."

Talgayeeta was moved by the Shawnee leader's words, but he shook his head regretfully. "Pucksinwah, you do me great honor coming here. The Shawnees are now and always have been my friends." He paused and shook his head again. "But never has Logan raised his hand against the whites; not even when some members of my own family fell in battles against them. There is no future in warring with a nation that has unlimited resources and more men by far than all the tribes together."

He smiled to take the sting out of what he was going to say and continued gently. "Are not you Shawnees yourselves guilty of stealing horses and equipment from the whites on the border? Have you not, when occasion has prompted it, slain the whites? Consider your defiance of the whites: Will it make their armies wither and die? Or will it instead cause immediate violent retribution against which no tribe can stand? You Shawnees are very proud and equally brave, and your complaints against the whites are certainly justified. But can you not see how much better it would be to be guided by clear thought rather than blind emotion? Somehow, Pucksinwah, there must be a way in which white men and red men can live in harmony and peace. But such a goal can never be achieved without thoughtful restraint on both sides. No, Pucksinwah, return to your fellow chiefs and tell them that Logan will not raise either his hand or voice against the whites, but that I will send emissaries to them and ask of them the same restraint that I ask of the Indians."

Pucksinwah sighed and motioned to his men, who came to their feet as he did, preparing to leave. Before stepping away, however, the Shawnee war chief looked down at Talgayeeta, and there was bitterness and frustration in his voice as he spoke again:

"We must return to Fort Pitt for a final talk with our friend Croghan, but I would say one final thing to you." He paused, choosing his words carefully as he continued. "You are a wise man, Talgayeeta, but beware lest the Bad Spirit, Matchemenetoo, blind you to the inevitable and you one day find yourself in grave danger from the very white man you like so much. You, who call yourself Logan, heed this: There is not now, nor can there ever be, a true and equitable peace between Indian and white."

[M a r c h 1 5 , 1 7 7 4 — T u e s d a y]

Joseph and Samuel Tomlinson, who had spent the winter making tomahawk improvements up the Kanawha and New rivers and their tributaries, as far as the Greenbrier Valley, were very eager to claim down the Ohio in the Kentucky country. They had expected that because of trouble they had experienced with floodwaters on the Kanawha, they would be late for the rendezvous, but their concerted efforts had paid off, and close to noon today they came to shore at Briscoe's Settlement.

Half a hundred men or more were already on hand, some of whom they knew, and there were dozens of individual campfires burning with men crouched about them. On the whole they were a rather unkempt lot, all well armed and clad in motley garb of furs, heavy leathers, greatcoats and boots or knee-high heavily greased moccasins. They clustered about the new arrivals asking where they had come from and what news they had heard, at the same time telling them of the alarming reports so prevalent of attacks occurring on trading parties and land-claimers.

The Tomlinsons had little to contribute. There had been some talk among settlers up the Kanawha of Indians prowling about but, except for a few horses having been stolen, no real problems. On their way up the Kanawha last fall, they had stopped off for a day at the new little Kelly's Creek Settlement some 20 miles above the mouth of Elk River, and again on their way down, just days ago, but everything seemed all right there. Twice over the winter Indian parties had passed, but they had been left undisturbed.

The brothers were pleased that Dr. Briscoe and his party had not yet arrived, nor had the big party expected under Dr. John Wood, of West Chester, and his partners, Hancock Lee and Angus McDonald. Those two groups would swell their numbers considerably and add greatly to their sense of security during the trip to Kentucky.

[March 24, 1774—Thursday]

William Butler, long a trader with the Shawnees, had arrived at Pittsburgh several weeks ago to find the Shawnee delegation still encamped at Saw Mill Run under Pucksinwah. He had gone to them at once and told them he had just come from their Scioto villages where he had conferred with the principal Shawnee chief. Hokolesqua had given him a message instructing Pucksinwah to return to the villages with his party as soon as possible following the talks with George Croghan and Alexander McKee. The young warriors in the village were working their way up to a pitch of war fever and talking of striking the whites streaming down the Ohio. The steadying influence of their war chief, Pucksinwah, was necessary to hold them in check. Hokolesqua also hoped that the talks with Croghan that had been going on since late fall were having some good results and also that Pucksinwah had managed to get a promise of support from Talgayeeta—Chief Logan—should matters with the whites further degenerate.

Soon after delivering his messages to the Shawnees, Butler had gone to the Baynton, Wharton and Morgan cabin, where he learned of John Connolly's reports of increased Indian attacks, blamed primarily on the Shawnees. Butler said he had no idea where the Fort Pitt commander could be getting such reports, since he knew absolutely that the Shawnees had been sending out no raiding parties, and in fact when he left them, they had been preparing for a late winter hunt, which certainly would not have been the case if they considered war in the offing. Butler neither liked nor trusted Connolly and suggested, as the firm and numerous Pittsburgh residents had already concluded, that perhaps the Fort Pitt commander was just making up these stories to create unrest, though to what end was a mystery.

Putting aside these speculations, Butler accepted a commission from the fur-trading firm to carry a load of goods downriver and back to the villages located up the Scioto. The days since then had been spent in preparation. Other traders were readying, too, and Baynton, Wharton and Morgan planned to be first this year to get their man into the field and to the tribes. Two Indians and another white were hired by the firm to accompany Butler as helpers, and today he was instructed to rest and be prepared to leave as soon as an expected shipment of goods arrived from Philadelphia.

[April 2, 1774—Saturday]

Dr. John Briscoe, himself somewhat late in arriving at his settlement for the rendezvous, was disappointed at the turnout. He had expected somewhere between 200 and 300 men to be on hand; instead there were only about 90.

He had been delayed in starting downstream because a shipment of goods—primarily new axes, saws and other tools—on its way to him from Philadelphia had become mired in the muck of an early thaw. The supplies had finally reached Pittsburgh a fortnight late, and as soon as the goods were transferred into the boats, he had set off downstream.

He was pleased to see the increased settlement along the Virginia shore as he traveled. Joshua Baker's little trading store at Baker's Bottom had obviously been strengthened, and Baker himself had smugly observed that he had been doing a good business with the Mingoes in their new town right across the river on Yellow Creek. In a matter of only a few weeks they had just about depleted his supply of rum that he had thought would last into midsummer.

The Strain brothers—William and Samuel—were already claiming in the area of Cross Creek when he passed there, and they said they probably wouldn't attend the rendezvous because they didn't really plan on claiming any farther downriver for the time being. Maybe next year. Ten miles farther downstream he found the McCulloch family continuing to build and strengthen their settlement at Short Creek.

Wheeling Settlement, nine miles farther downstream, was the biggest surprise. It had quickly become the regular stopping place for virtually all river travelers. Many who passed discovered that Ebenezer Zane, who was becoming quite an entrepreneur, was quite willing to sell lots and decided to join the little community. Now there were upward of 40 people in residence and a lot of building occurring. Silas Zane was living there, too, having sold his holdings at the Forks of Wheeling Creek to David Shepherd, who had only days before married his sweetheart, Rachel Teague, and they were already building their own cabin at the Forks. Silas and Jonathan Zane had then explored down the Ohio somewhat and had even penetrated the Ohio country for little distances on the Muskingum and Hockhocking. They had returned safely without encountering Indians. John Caldwell, newly arrived from Baltimore and another of those who had purchased a plot of ground from Ebenezer Zane, was busy putting the roof on his new little cabin when Briscoe stopped briefly at the settlement.

Sam Meason was also here, just as loudmouthed and trouble-making as he had always been on the Monongahela, freeloading on whomever he could and talking about settling a few miles below Wheeling, on the bottom where a man named William McMechen had just begun the new McMechen's Settlement.[181] Generally disliked, Meason was a large, rough-and-tumble man without social graces and minimal human compassion. It was commonly known that he had come to this frontier to escape criminal prosecution in eastern Pennsylvania. Several years ago, upon stealing some horses from a Capt. William Hite, he had been pursued, overtaken and shot. The wound was not severe and, with the horses recovered, Meason had been thrown in jail to await trial. He escaped and simply disappeared for a long while before eventually turning up here and settling on Buffalo Creek. Although most grudgingly admitted he was a good frontiersman, few liked him and nobody trusted him.

Ebenezer Zane himself had recently been busy claiming on Wheeling Island, clearing a tract of more than 300 acres, on which he planned to plant crops as soon as the danger of frost was past.[182] Less than a year after Zane had brought his wife, Elizabeth, and year-old daughter Catherine to Wheeling, another daughter had been born, whom they named Ann. Now, only a month ago—on February 28—Elizabeth had presented Ebenezer with a third daughter, whom they had named Sarah.[183] Seeing that she was comfortable and well cared for by the slaves under direction of their younger brother, Jonathan, Ebenezer and Silas Zane set off down the Ohio to do some claiming about 100 miles farther down.

Dr. Briscoe had stayed overnight at Wheeling, leaving early the next morning, and, against his better judgment, giving Sam Meason a lift for the five miles down to McMechen's Settlement, where there was a camp area and several tents but no cabins had yet been constructed. William McMechen greeted Briscoe warmly but did not seem particularly pleased to see Meason, and his disposition soured markedly when he learned the big frontiersman meant to stay there a while. The two were soon embroiled in an argument, and Briscoe had quietly shoved off, leaving them behind before he might become saddled with Meason even longer.

Four miles farther downstream he reached the Tomlinson Settlement at the mouth of Grave Creek. Here there was a half-faced camp but no cabins, the camp itself occupied only by young James Tomlinson and his 21-year-old sister, Rebecca Martin. James told Briscoe that he expected by now his brothers, Joe and Sam, were probably waiting at the doctor's own settlement; they had left here last fall with the idea of first clearing a piece of land they had given to Rebecca on the claim they had made opposite the mouth of the Muskingum. From there they had planned to continue down to the Kanawha and up that stream to New River and the Greenbrier to claim lands over the winter. Both brothers had, however, planned on being back in time for the rendezvous.

Briscoe had set off again, but now there were no more settlements. With nothing more than hesitant waves of his hand, he passed two different small parties of Indians, one in canoes, the other on shore. They waved back but did not approach him, and he was glad enough to pass them by without difficulty.

Some four miles below the mouth of Captina Creek, which entered from the Ohio country, he came to the large bottom along the Virginia shoreline where Michael Cresap was busy establishing himself on the claim he was making and already calling the place Cresap's Bottom.[184] With him were half a dozen men he had hired at Pittsburgh, who had followed a day or two after he left there; unimaginative men who had no interest in claiming lands themselves, enticed by the high wage he offered of £2.10s per month. For that amount they would have tackled almost any job, and the clearing they did in a few days was more than Cresap could do in a month. They talked for a while, and Cresap said he had planned on attending the rendezvous but had got caught up in his work here and had evidently missed it.

"As a matter of fact, Captain Cresap," Briscoe assured him, "you have not missed the rendezvous. I am myself on my way there at this moment, and you are welcome to accompany me."

Cresap grunted a negative. "Can't right now. I have to get these men started on a new area before I can leave. Tell you what, though—I'll finish up soon as possible and then come on down."

Grateful for that, Briscoe had pushed on. Three miles below he came to the mouth of Fish Creek, and on the Fish Creek Flats he found a little settlement he hadn't even heard about. There was a finished cabin and one being erected. He had stopped briefly and introduced himself to the two men who came out to greet him. The older man was named Yates Cornwell, an acquaintance of George Washington, for whom he had been claiming land. The second man, young, personable, and also a correspondent of Washington's, had stopped by here and stayed, claiming land for himself and helping Cornwell finish building the cabin. His name was George Rogers Clark, and he had been sharing Cornwell's cabin and teaching the Cornwell children their lessons even while he and Yates were in the process of building Clark's cabin. They were calling their little settlement Cornwell's.[185] Clark had heard about the rendezvous and expressed an interest in going, so Briscoe invited him to travel the remainder of the way with him. From this point it was only about 65 miles to Briscoe's Settlement. If they started first thing in the morning, they should be able to get there by late afternoon.

Clark had agreed, and shortly after dawn they were on their way. As Dr. Briscoe had predicted, they put to shore at Briscoe's Settlement, six miles above the mouth of the Little Kanawha, just as the sun was setting behind the hills rimming the Ohio to the west. Dr. Briscoe was recognized as they approached, and a cheer erupted from the men on hand. But the cheers came from the throats of about 90 men rather than upward of 300 that Briscoe had expected. He quickly discovered that a number of parties that had stopped by here in the middle of March were disappointed at the meager turnout and, after waiting a day or two, had gone on downstream. Even worse, as the men gathered around, it became evident that those who had remained here were markedly apprehensive. Every new arrival, it seemed, brought new stories of Indian attacks occurring all around. Messages had been received from Maj. Connolly at Fort Pitt of reports of considerable unrest and a possible major Indian attack in the offing. Everyone was looking now to Dr. Briscoe to tell them what to do, but he wasn't at all sure himself.

"I still think there'll be more parties showing up," he said, "that have been detained for one reason or another. Let's give them a chance to get here. We'll wait a week or so more, and then we'll head for Kentucky."

[*A p r i l   4 ,   1 7 7 4 — M o n d a y*]

The tall, self-possessed man who had stopped at Cornwell's Settlement an hour ago, accompanied by the trader Barney Curran and the Seneca half-breed Andrew Montour, was already preparing to leave, and Yates Cornwell was disappointed, wishing they would stay longer.

The small party had come to the Ohio Valley to inspect lands the tall man had claimed earlier, as well as other parcels that agents of his had been claiming for him over the past few years. When that inspection was completed, they were in close enough proximity that the tall man had decided to come this much farther downstream to see George Rogers Clark, whom he had never met but with whom he had been in correspondence for some time. He was very sorry to learn that Clark had left here two days earlier with Dr. John Briscoe, heading for the rendezvous some 65 miles below. There wasn't much point in heading down there, if he were so inclined, Cornwell told his visitor, since chances were the party wasn't even there any longer but was afloat and heading for Kentucky.

The tall man stepped into the canoe and sat down in the center as Curran shoved them off, and then he and Montour began paddling upstream. Yates

Cornwell, standing on the shoreline with his wife beside him, called after them, "If George comes back, I'll tell him you were here to see him, Colonel."

The tall man raised his hand in farewell toward Yates and smiled. "Thank you, Mr. Cornwell. Mrs. Cornwell."

The couple watched in silence for a little longer, and then Cornwell spoke wonderingly: "Who would ever have thought that we would be visited here by George Washington?"[186]

[April 9, 1774 — Saturday]

Ebenezer Zane and his brother, Silas, had been claiming at the mouth of Sandy Creek, seven miles below the mouth of the Little Kanawha, when the rumors of Indian troubles first reached them.[187] They had tended to ignore the first story, related to them two days ago by a land-jobber who passed, because he was obviously a very timid man whose fears had become magnified in his own mind. He had been able to give them no specifics, only that some of his fellow land-jobbers had been robbed, before he hastened on his way.

The Zane brothers were more watchful after that but continued making their tomahawk improvements. Then today, before noon, another report came that was similar to the first, this one from a party of three men who didn't even stop as they passed but merely called out to them to get away while they could.

Ebenezer and Silas, still not convinced the rumors were true, were nevertheless prudent men. They had both already made good claims here, so common sense dictated departure; they could always come back a little later when, as they believed would occur, the stories proved to be nothing more than the product of fearful imaginations.

They packed up their gear and soon were on their way upstream, hugging the Virginia shoreline. They saw no sign of Indian activity, and the mouth of the Little Kanawha was devoid of anyone, red or white, as they passed. Six miles above that point they came to Briscoe's Settlement and found a large number of men camped, all of them extremely nervous. It was late in the day when they arrived at the rendezvous, and so, to take advantage of the safety in numbers, they decided to camp there for the night and continue paddling back toward Wheeling in the morning.

Many of the men clustered about them, seeking any news they might have brought, but they could only shrug and say that, apart from some frightened passersby, they had seen nothing to indicate danger. The men drifted back to their own campfires but were unconvinced. Ebenezer and Silas Zane were known to be steady men, and the fact that they were heading for the relative safety of Wheeling was construed as being, at the very least, ominous.

[*April 14, 1774 — Thursday*]

The undercurrent of fear prevailing among the men gathered at the Briscoe's Settlement rendezvous increased sharply with the arrival of the Jacob Greathouse party. Those men had spent much of the winter at and near the mouth of the Big Sandy River, 140 miles downstream from here. Everyone crowded around, eager for whatever information Greathouse could impart, and he didn't disappoint them.

A huge man, brutish in appearance and speech, Jake Greathouse positively loathed Indians and, according to those who knew him, had murdered several in the past. He immediately recognized the unsettling mood among the men gathered here and delighted in adding fuel to the fire of their fears. Though he knew nothing of the alleged raiding parties of Shawnees stealing horses on the frontier, nor had he seen any such raiders, he gravely agreed that, yes, that was likely the case since he personally had seen war parties on the move. He told them that his men, fearful for their own lives, had left three of their number—Simon Kenton, Sam Cartwright and Jim Lock—at their cabins and had come upstream to warn those gathered for the rendezvous. None of his listeners thought to question why, if such was the case, they had left three of their men at the isolated cabins. Actually, their party had finished the winter's hunting and trapping, and Greathouse and his men were merely on their way to Fort Pitt with their peltry to trade for goods and new equipment, leaving the three behind to claim more land during their absence.

Still, they clung to every word he uttered as he told them that some time ago James Harrod's party had passed, heading for Kentucky to claim lands, and had reported seeing small war parties on the move but had not themselves been molested because of their numbers. Then, just after that, a lone canoeist had come upstream and stopped by their camp. He told them his name was Davis and that he'd been trading at Horsehead Bottom, a short way up the Little Scioto.[188] There, Davis had said, he saw Shawnees preparing for war. He added that those Indians had roughed him up and stolen his goods but that he had managed to escape in his canoe. Since Greathouse knew very well that the village at Horsehead Bottom was Mingo, not Shawnee, he believed nothing the man said, yet he now relayed the story as truth to these men gathered here under Dr. Briscoe. He went on to say that this trader named Davis, in his own canoe, had accompanied them upriver to the mouth of the Kanawha and then separated from them to ascend the Kanawha and New rivers to return to the Greenbrier area, where he lived.[189]

When asked if he knew about the party of land-claimers who killed and plundered a party of Shawnee hunters—one of the stories going the rounds—Greathouse nodded gravely, but then added, "Dunno nothin' 'bout it firsthand, though," making his previous tales that much more believable.

The men at the rendezvous were greatly agitated by all this news. They immediately began arguing among themselves about what they should do. Many were drinking heavily and becoming increasingly rowdy. They decided they should mount an expedition and head out to attack the Indian village at Horsehead Bottom.

Several groups of the men, more alarmed than ever now, announced they wanted no part of what they considered suicide, and began loading up their canoes. Despite Briscoe's efforts to make them stay, they shoved off to return to Wheeling or even to Pittsburgh. Briscoe, angry, disgusted and fearful, announced that the rendezvous was officially canceled, and he and his party soon left as well.

Those who remained to look for Indians to fight began discussing who should be their leader. None of those on hand, including Greathouse, wanted the responsibility, and, after several hours of discussion, they finally decided to try to get the nearest man around who knew anything about leading a fighting force and who heartily disliked Indians to boot—Capt. Michael Cresap. Though by now it was late in the day, they dispatched two messengers to him in a canoe and were amazed when this pair returned some 20 minutes later with Cresap in his own canoe behind them. They had met him only a mile or so away and escorted him back here. He had left his own crew early in the morning to join the rendezvous and perhaps continue down to Kentucky with them. When he encountered deserting land-jobbers and even Briscoe's party coming upstream, he learned from them what had occurred and decided to continue to Briscoe's Settlement and see for himself what was going on.

Cheers erupted as he stepped ashore, and then a great knot of men swelled about him, thumping his back and everyone talking at once. It took a considerable while to calm them down so they could discuss the matter fully. At last it was Cresap's turn to speak, and they were sure he would begin by laying out a strategy for attacking the Indians at Horsehead Bottom.

"Boys," he said, "from all you've told me, there seems to be plenty of reason to believe the Indians are up to something, but who can say what? I think it would be a big mistake to move against them. Even with all we've heard, you've got to admit there's none among us that've actually seen the Indians doing anything wrong. There's not been any war declared that I've heard about, and if we attack those Indians, you can bet on it, there'll be a war, and we'll be blamed. You boys want to have that on your heads?"

There was a disappointed uproar, and when he finally quieted them, he went on. "Now listen to me a minute! See if what I'm going to say doesn't make sense. I suggest we go—all of us—on up to Wheeling. I saw Eb and Silas Zane heading up, and they've got lots of folks up there and shelter, too. From there it'll be a simple enough matter in a few weeks to get intelligence of what's going on. If there's a war, then I will, by God, lead you against 'em. If there isn't, then there'll still be plenty of time to get down to the Kentucky country, and I'll go with you. What do you say?"

There were a few disagreeing voices, but a vote was taken and the overwhelming majority voted to adopt Cresap's proposal. It was about that time that an express arrived with a circular letter from Fort Pitt, dated April 12 and signed by Dr. John Connolly, Major Commandant. It warned all settlers along the Ohio to be aware that some serious incidents with the Indians had been reported, that they would be wise to curtail plans for going farther downriver and, instead, to gather together and fort up for their own protection until it could be officially determined exactly what the problem was. He therefore required and commanded them to hold themselves in readiness to repel any insults that might be offered by the Indian.

Even the dissenting voices at the rendezvous were stilled now, and another vote was unnecessary. Cresap said he was well pleased with it and vowed on the spot to put to death every Indian he met on the river. Within two hours the remaining body of men were paddling upstream toward Wheeling. Not all of them went there directly, however; Cresap announced that he wanted several parties to move slowly and check for fresh Indian sign at the mouth of every stream—from rivulet to large creek —on both sides of the river as they ascended. They were to meet again at Wheeling. The first to volunteer for this duty was a group of about two dozen men under George Rogers Clark and Jacob Greathouse.[190]

[April 13, 1774—Wednesday]

It was when the large, downriver-floating fleet of boats was 42 miles below Wheeling that they came to the stretch of the Ohio River called the Long Reach, a term derived from the fact that for a distance of about 17 miles, the course of the great waterway was uncommonly straight in a southwestwardly direction.[191] By far the largest single group heading downstream this season, the boats belonged to the party of 150 surveyors and laborers being led by Hancock Lee, John Wood and Angus McDonald. Their fleet consisted of a dozen ten-man canoes, two large bateaux and eight piroques—the latter loaded with baggage and other gear and being towed. They were running late for the big rendezvous but hoped to arrive before everyone left for Kentucky.

As they were in the midst of the Long Reach, they received disturbing news. Several canoes heading upstream were encountered and, as they passed, men called out that they had come from Briscoe's Settlement, where news had come in of Indian attacks occurring downriver. They said land-jobbers had been attacked and robbed and some, perhaps, even killed.

Dr. Wood and his companions at first put little credence in the rumors, although they admitted having seen two parties of Indians camped upstream about five miles apart, near the mouths of Pipe Creek and Captina Creek. Just to be safe, however, they put ashore on the Virginia side and decided they would do some claiming in this area while they waited for more definite news about what was really going on.

The first boat to approach after that, several hours later, was heading downstream—three traders in a canoe. They hailed it and asked the men to come ashore, which they did. The traders turned out to be John Gibson, Matthew Elliott and Alexander Blaine. They said they had come from Pittsburgh and the same rumors were prevalent there—rumors that seemed to be stemming from none other than the Fort Pitt commander, Maj. John Connolly—and that they didn't believe a word of them. Only two days ago, they went on, they had encountered trader John Anderson returning to Pittsburgh from a long stint in the Delaware and Mingo villages on the Muskingum, and he had assured them everything there was peaceful.

All three of these traders knew the Shawnees well and were, in fact, on a trading mission to that tribe right now. They admitted that while the stories were almost certainly false, the Wood party had been wise not to continue downstream until getting more definite word.

The most disturbing rumor at the moment, related to them now by Dr. Wood, was rather involved: A party of land-claimers—no one seemed to know exactly who they were—who had been improving near the mouth of the Kanawha had seen another party of whites who informed them that they and some others had fallen in with a party of Shawnees who had been hunting on the southwest side of the Ohio River; that they had argued with these Indians and, when a fight broke out, had killed all the Shawnees; that they had then taken all the Indian horses and goods, and then, anticipating an Indian war would result, the land-claimers had, with the exception of a few who went upriver by boat, fled overland eastward.

"When was all this supposed to have happened?" Gibson queried.

When Dr. Wood told him, Matthew Elliott burst into laughter. "That's ridiculous," he said. "I was with the Shawnees then, and that was long before I left them. There's not the smallest chance that could have occurred. All hunting parties that were out had come in before I left them. But tell you what—there's a Shawnee party making canoes up the Hockhocking right now. We're headed that way anyway, so we can check with them and find out if they know anything."

That was when one of the hired laborers in the Wood party spoke up. "Wait a minute," he said, pointing at Elliott, "I know him. And him, too." His pointing finger swung to Gibson. "The both of 'em got Injen wives. They're squaw men. You fellers ain't gonna believe squaw men, are you?"

There was an ugly rumbling from the other men, and one in particular called out, "Damned traders are worse'n Injens. They oughta be killed!"

The workers had quickly become a mob and now began moving forward. They jerked to a halt when Angus McDonald shot his rifle into the air over them. Dr. Wood nodded gratefully to his companion and turned back to the traders. "I expect," he said softly, "it might be wise for you gentlemen to leave. We'll keep them calmed down here. And we'll wait here for a while. Thanks for your help."

The traders returned to their canoe and shoved off, quickly putting distance between themselves and the men on shore.

[April 15, 1774—Friday]

At his Pittsburgh headquarters, George Croghan pointed out to William Butler the bundles, boxes and kegs that made up the material promised to the Shawnees during the recent lengthy council with the delegation under Pucksinwah.

"The goods arrived yesterday, Mr. Butler," he said. "I checked out the entire shipment, and everything's here. You can check them again and sign the lading bill. Now, how soon can you start down to the Scioto with them?"

Butler shook his head. "As a matter of fact, I won't be able to start at all—other business to see to—but one of my better traders just came in. John Anderson. He's going to need two or three days to rest up in, then a day to get some help and get the boat packed. And I've got an apprentice trader named Stevens who'll go along to help with the paddling."

Croghan nodded. "All right. There are a couple of Delawares here who will go along as escorts. They'll also be carrying messages to Hokolesqua. I want them on their way by the morning of the twentieth."

[*April 16, 1774—Saturday*]

The three traders nosed their canoe into the mouth of the Hockhocking River, paddled about 400 yards upstream, and then put to shore in a sheltered indentation of the left bank and came ashore at the level bottom where they had often camped before.[192] It was not yet midday, and they were weary from having paddled throughout the night. All three were deeply disturbed at the amount of activity occurring on the Ohio this spring. Even worse was the mood of the boat parties they had encountered, as it was only too apparent that most of the whites were convinced the rumors were true. But it was the incident with the big party under Dr. Wood at Long Reach that had been the most unsettling.

"Guess we were lucky to get away as we did," said Alexander Blaine as he grunted and pulled the canoe farther up on shore for the others to step out. "They keep on with that kind of foolishness, an' all hell's like as not to bust loose."

John Gibson nodded as he moved past some of the bundles stacked in the canoe and stepped lightly ashore. "Hate to admit it, but you're probably right, Alex. Sure would like to know who's feeding all these tall tales to Connolly. He's mad enough as it is to do something stupid and get the whole country in an uproar."

Matthew Elliott shook his head and grimaced. "Damn fools, all of them," he said. "Probably not many on this whole river know more of what's going on than us three, so you'd think they'd believe us when we tell them the stories have got to be damn lies and nothing's being planned against them."

"They believe what they want to believe," Blaine said.

"They're scared," Gibson put in, "and people who are scared are dangerous."

Blaine nodded and, without needing directions, set off along the river edge to gather up dry driftwood for the fire. They were all looking forward to an hour's rest and some good hot tea before continuing. Youngest of the three and newest to the Indian trade, Blaine was a friend of Elliott's from years past. He was apprenticing with him for the second season and learning a great deal, as well he should; he had a good teacher. Matthew Elliott had traded with the Shawnees for over a decade and for half that time had been married to a Shawnee woman. He was highly respected in the tribe as an honest trader and a courageous man. Not having seen his wife for a year, he was glad to be heading back to her village on the Scioto once again.

Elliott stepped from the canoe, and he and Gibson fell silent as they began digging out the pewter cups, pot and tin of tea. Gibson took the pot and moved automatically to the nearby spring for water, his mind elsewhere. He was distinctly concerned for Koonay, not only because of the nervous mood prevailing in the Ohio Valley but because now she was pregnant with their second child. After an absence that had been too prolonged for his liking, he had managed to spend a fortnight with her at the new village on Yellow Creek but had missed seeing her brother; Talgayeeta and a party of his men had gone off to hunt deep in the Ohio country on the Walhonding.

The visit with Koonay was restful and pleasant, but all too soon Gibson had to get back to Pittsburgh on trading business. That was where he had rejoined Elliott and Blaine, who had all the goods ready and were awaiting him. Elliott had quickly filled him in on the rumors that had been circulating and also about the talks

Croghan had been having there with the Shawnee delegation for the past three months or more. Those talks were wrapping up, and the Shawnees were very disgruntled over the fact that hardly anything had been accomplished in respect to keeping the whites from coming down the Ohio and spilling onto their lands.

The three men had set off downstream shortly after Gibson's arrival and were amazed at the number of canoes, piroques and bateaux on the river, the majority of them staying close to the Ohio shore. More often than not the traders, bent on their business and in midstream or closer to the Ohio shore, merely waved at those they passed and continued on their way.

The second day after leaving Pittsburgh they encountered and talked with an old trader friend, John Anderson. He was on his way up to Pittsburgh, his pelt-laden canoe paddled by a Delaware and a disreputable-appearing white man, neither of whom they knew. Anderson had just come from a long stint of trading at the villages up the Muskingum and Tuscarawas and assured them he knew of no mischief afoot where the Delawares or Mingoes were concerned, but he, too, was apprehensive over what he'd heard was occurring on the Ohio. After talking a short while, the two parties set off again on their separate ways.

The three traders had made their big mistake when, against their better judgment, they had put ashore at the hailing of the Wood party. Gibson's party had been told, of course, about the big rendezvous of claimers and land-jobbers at Briscoe's Settlement, but they had no desire to put in there. They had, in fact, deliberately passed it by unseen, under cover of darkness, nervous at its proximity across the river and wholly unaware that the men who had rendezvoused there were already well on their way back to Wheeling.

Worry was uncharacteristic for John Gibson, yet today he was experiencing it. He was also not a man given to presentiment, but now he had a bad feeling about what might lie ahead in the weeks and months to come.

[April 17, 1774—Sunday]

The party of Shawnees under Pucksinwah had swum their horses across the Ohio River to the mouth of Yellow Creek and again, as they had done two months earlier, stopped by Talgayeeta's Town to tell him, as a matter of courtesy, about the disappointing results culminating the long period of counciling with George Croghan at Pittsburgh. They discovered that Talgayeeta had been gone for some time on a hunting trip with a large number of his young men from the village. A few men had remained behind, including Talgayeeta's older brother, Taylaynee, and they spoke to him briefly.

"Our friend, George Croghan, is very sympathetic to our problem," Pucksinwah told him, "and would like to help us, but his hands are tied. He can only pass along our complaints, as he has done numerous times before, to those who rank over him. What will come of it will no doubt be as before—nothing. You have heard that we were shot at in our camp at Pittsburgh three moons ago for no good reason. No one was hurt, but it is only one example of how little regard the whites have for us.

Croghan gave us presents to take to our people, which they can use, but presents are not our great need. We must protect our lands and everything on them from those who are coming into them."

Taylaynee nodded gravely. "We, too," he said, "are aware of how whites move into Indian lands and take them as their own. More than once we have moved away, that we may be beyond their reach. Perhaps the Shawnees should do the same."

"No!" The vehemence of Pucksinwah's reply startled even his own men. "No," he repeated, "we will *not* move away. You yourself say that more than once you have moved away from them to where you think you are beyond their reach. Has that stopped them? Are they not again at your doorstep? Will you again meekly move away? No, Taylaynee, the Shawnees will not do this. We are where we are, and we will protect with our life's blood these lands that are ours."

Taylaynee lifted his hands in a helpless gesture. "I will give your words to my brother when he returns. It is all I can do."

Pucksinwah nodded curtly, features grim and mouth set in a thin line, and led his party away on the trail heading westward into Ohio's interior. For more than a mile he said nothing but then abruptly reined his horse to a stop and turned to face the men who made up his deputation.

"The *Shemanese* are very active on the Spaylaywitheepi this spring. We must be aware at all times of what they are doing. We must especially be aware of any who come across the river to hunt or take the lands."

His eyes passed across the men and settled on a heavily built individual who bore a large scar at his right temple where, as an infant some 25 years before, he had been mauled by a bear. As a result, he had been named after the animal.

"Muga," Pucksinwah said, "you will lead a small party. Two others. Aquewa Apetotha will be one." His eyes flicked briefly to a thin, horsey-featured 17-year-old who was the youngest member of the party, his name meaning Child in a Blanket. "My son, Wehyehpihehrsehnwah, will be the other." Not his son by birth, Wehy-ehpihehrsehnwah—Blue Jacket—was a 20-year-old white who had been captured in Virginia three years before and adopted into Pucksinwah's family. So well had he adapted to the new way of life that he had become as much an Indian as any about him, and Pucksinwah was as proud of him as he was of his two eldest children, Chiksika and Tecumapese.

"You three," the war chief went on, "will not return directly to the Scioto with us. It is Hokolesqua's wish that you follow the shoreline of the Spaylaywitheepi, hunting as you go, if you like, but keeping ever watchful for any whites on our shores. You will do this all the way to the Scioto. Should you encounter any whites on our shores, you will, if circumstances are appropriate, advance to them in peace and speak with them, but not in anger. You will address them politely and inform them that they are on our lands and must leave. Avoid conflict. If any threatens, withdraw. We will then see to it in a manner to our advantage. Be careful. Be brave. Moneto go with you."

Pucksinwah reined away and set off on the trail, the remainder of the party following. The three young men watched them, and then Muga, pleased that he had been named to lead, grinned in his usual happy-go-lucky manner.

"Well, we've been given our task. Let's do it."

[April 20, 1774 — Wednesday]

Muga, Aquewa Apetotha and Blue Jacket had painstakingly followed the shore-line of the Spaylaywitheepi according to the orders given them by Pucksinwah. At times it was difficult in the extreme, due to the craggy nature of the terrain, but they were determined to obey completely. When they came to streams entering the Ohio, they made a point of following each upstream a fair distance to make sure no one had ascended a little way before camping.

It was as they were following a game trail along Pipe Creek today that Blue Jacket, who happened to be 100 yards or so ahead of his companions, smelled smoke and then heard the faint clink of metal from far ahead. He turned and held up a hand, stopping his companions where they were. Then, tying his horse to a sapling, he crept forward and at length found himself peering through a screen of bushes at a group of some two dozen rather rough-looking men, their canoes drawn up on the shore of Pipe Creek and most of them gathered around a campfire.[193]

Unseen, Blue Jacket quickly backed away and silently returned to his companions. He told them what he had seen and suggested they avoid the men and simply report their presence to Pucksinwah when they reached their home village of Kispokotha.

Muga shook his head. "I think we should advance on the camp as Pucksinwah told us Hokolesqua has advised, showing we intend them no harm. Who knows what good might come of just such a simple meeting as this?"

Aquewa Apetotha agreed and despite his better judgment, Blue Jacket nodded. They tied their horses out of sight in a wooded copse and crept forward carefully until they came to where Blue Jacket had observed the camp. Blue Jacket again slipped into hiding behind the bushes and motioned the others to follow, but Muga and Aquewa Apetotha continued walking openly toward the whites, smiling, their right hands raised in the sign of peace. They walked another dozen yards or more before anyone in the camp saw them, and then abruptly there were hoarse yells and the whites scrambled for their guns.

Muga and Aquewa Apetotha stopped, still with hands upraised, and Muga opened his mouth to speak but never had the chance. Several rifles fired, and both Shawnees flopped to the ground, dead as they fell. At the same instant, Blue Jacket plunged back toward the heavier cover as more shots came and the lead balls buzzed about him, ripping through bushes and smacking into trees. Remembering Pucksinwah's advice to do the unexpected when surprised, he raced in a half-circle around the camp, slipped into hiding in heavy brush and watched what was occurring, his heart hammering. One man already held Aquewa Apetotha's scalp in his hand and was shaking it free of blood. Another man—big, heavily bearded and rough in appearance—was at that moment scalping Muga. He straightened and held the scalp high with a triumphant cry, then broke into a wild, prancing series of steps, accompanied by hootings—evidently his interpretation of a war dance.

Two other men, whom Blue Jacket had not previously seen, raced into the camp, and an argument ensued. Blue Jacket listened intently but could only make out scattered words. Someone mentioned the names Cresap and Clark and Greathouse and then "Logan . . . Yeller Creek . . . kill 'em all!"[194]

It was enough for Blue Jacket. He slipped away, made another wide circle keeping to cover and returned to the horses. In moments, riding his own mount and leading the other two, his heart heavy with grief for his companions, he was heading back toward Talgayeeta's Town to warn them that they were in great danger.

[A p r i l   2 1 ,   1 7 7 4 — T h u r s d a y]

It was late in the day, and the large gathering of people at Wheeling were in an ugly mood. Settlers had come in from everywhere in the region, and upward of 400 people were now on hand. The Wheeling residents were alarmed at so many people arriving to congregate at their settlement. Busily engaged in turning one of the cabins into a makeshift fort, they had halted their labors to listen to what was being said. Michael Cresap was making it clear that he was for falling upon any body of Indians they could find and wiping them out, but he was being strongly opposed by Ebenezer Zane.

"By God," Zane thundered, momentarily stilling the general rumble of voices, "what you men are contemplating is insane! Don't you see that if you do this, you'll bring on an all-out war? Our women and children are here, and a lot of innocent people are going to wind up getting killed. You just can't do this!"

The debate went on for a long while, and Zane seemed to be making headway when an express arrived by canoe from Fort Pitt. He bore another circular letter from Maj. Connolly, this one much stronger than the first. Cresap read it aloud to the assembled crowd. Connolly had written that messengers sent to the Indians had returned to Fort Pitt bearing news that the tribes considered war inevitable and that as soon as they were fully prepared, they would strike. The Fort Pitt commander urged that those settlers who were not already doing so fortify themselves at once or leave the country. He also urged that parties of scouts be formed to patrol the frontier and intercept any approaching bodies of Indians.[195]

It was all Cresap needed. Climbing upon a barrel and standing high for all to see and hear, he formally declared war on the Indians, asked for a response and received a roar of approbation. Moments later the enthusiasm became more focused, when the messenger who had brought the missive from Connolly reported that some nine or ten miles above Wheeling he had passed two traders and two Indians camped onshore at the mouth of Indian Short Creek.[196] At once Cresap proposed that they move against the party first thing in the morning. Once again Zane objected strenuously, warning that if they did so, it would be plain and simple murder, and they would disgrace their own names forever. This time few listened.

[A p r i l   2 2 ,   1 7 7 4 — F r i d a y   m o r n i n g]

John Anderson nudged his helper with his elbow and grinned. "C'mon, Stevens, finish off your coffee, and let's go. Sun'll be up pretty quick, and our pals are waiting." He inclined his head toward the two Delawares, Compass and Shemadota, crouched on their heels near the beached canoe.

Stevens, a lanky young man, nodded, gulped the remaining swallow in his cup and dumped what remained in the pot over the dying coals of their campfire. He and Anderson gathered up the remaining gear and stowed it in the canoe, shoved the craft out until it was afloat and then took their places. The younger of the two Delawares, Shemadota, took his place in the bow. Three separate stackings of goods were in the boat, and Stevens took his place between the first two, behind Shemadota. Anderson got between the two behind him, and Compass, a well-built middle-aged man, shoved the canoe out into the current and skillfully hopped into the stern. Both Indians began paddling at once, fairly close to the Ohio shore.

Well ahead, near midstream, three canoes loaded with men were angling toward them. Up to now on the trip down from Pittsburgh, the boats they had seen were hugging the Virginia shore, and they had talked to no one. As the three boats drew nearer, they could see that all the men who were not paddling were holding rifles, and Compass said something to Shemadota in the Delaware tongue. Shemadota ceased paddling and held the dripping paddle athwart the bow. Compass angled his own trailing paddle and turned the canoe more directly toward those approaching.

"You figure there's been some kind'a trouble downriver, John?" Stevens asked.

Anderson did not reply. He suddenly did not like the looks of things here at all. His own rifle was leaning against the bundles directly ahead of him, and he thought about picking it up, then decided that wouldn't be too wise.

They were within about 30 yards of the approaching boats when there was a sudden harsh command, followed by a burst of gunfire. Shemadota was slammed backward against the bundles behind him, blood spurting from several wounds in his chest and head. In the rear Compass had been struck and had risen high on his knees, clutching his bleeding stomach with one hand, the other arm hanging limply from a shattered shoulder. More shots came, and he was struck in the face and chest, knocked backward and sprawled across the thwarts.

Stevens had been grazed by a ball on the right side of his neck and had clamped his hand to it to staunch the bleeding. He was crying and trembling so terribly that his whole body shook. Anderson was unharmed but stunned and speechless at the devastation.

The leading canoe of the three held seven men, including Michael Cresap, and it drew up beside the drifting trader's canoe. Compass and Shemadota were scalped and their bodies shoved overboard, where they disappeared beneath the surface. At that point Anderson finally found his voice.

"Why have you done this?" he asked hoarsely.

Cresap eyed him with distaste. He didn't know Anderson, but he had never much liked any of the traders he had been associated with. "We're at war with the tribes again," he said, adding bluntly, "and any Indian we see is a dead one."[197]

About an hour later, the canoe bearing the two traders in tow, the Cresap party returned to Wheeling and beached their boats. An immediate division of all the confiscated trading goods was made among those who had participated in the attack, while those who had remained at Wheeling gathered around and looked on. The

Zane brothers were among them. They saw two fresh scalps and the canoe with bullet holes in it fore and aft, along with a great deal of blood.

"What happened to the Indians who were with this party?" Ebenezer Zane asked.

Cresap stared at him a moment, and then his lips spread in a humorless grin. "Seems they fell overboard and never came up," he said. A roar of laughter erupted from the crowd, and Zane grimly turned and walked away, followed by his brothers.

[A p r i l   2 2 ,   1 7 7 4 — F r i d a y   n o o n]

When Blue Jacket arrived at Talgayeeta's Town on Yellow Creek, he expected to find Talgayeeta still absent with his hunting party but was gratified that he had just returned. The hunt had been very successful, and a number of bison were killed. Talgayeeta had returned merely to get another party of his people to help jerk the meat and bring it back to the village. On seeing the urgency in the young Shawnee, however, he put everything aside, and they went to his lodge to talk. He called for food to be brought to his young guest, but Blue Jacket shook his head, apologized for his rudeness and said there was no time for that. The words then spilled from his mouth in a steady stream as he told Talgayeeta what had happened, concluding with what seemed to be a threat to Talgayeeta himself. He was stunned at the Mingo's response.

"I am sorry, Wehyehpihehrsehnwah, for what you have gone through and about the death of your companions, but I think you must have misunderstood what those men said. You must realize, my young friend, that the whites have been the friends of Logan for many many years, just as the Shawnees have been. They have often been welcomed in my village and would have no reason to attack me or my people. I am sure you must be mistaken, but I will prepare myself in any event. I am indebted to you for coming to tell me. My home is yours. Food and bed will be prepared for you."

Blue Jacket's reply was laced with poorly disguised anger. "I cannot stay," he said tightly, coming to his feet. "Pucksinwah must be told what has happened, as must the families of Muga and Aquewa Apetotha, so they may begin to mourn their loss and prepare for revenge. My own people," he added bitterly, "will believe what I have to say."

[A p r i l   2 3 ,   1 7 7 4 — S a t u r d a y]

The party under Jacob Greathouse and George Rogers Clark arrived at Wheeling just before noon. Once again a crowd gathered, and the men proudly displayed the two scalps they had taken at Pipe Creek. Cresap was more interested in what Greathouse had to say: After having shot the two and taken their scalps, they had searched for a third Indian that was seen, but he had gotten away. Fearful that he was part of a war party and would bring others swooping down upon them, they had taken to their boats a short while later.

Greathouse went on to say that on emerging from the mouth of Pipe Creek, they had spied a lone man in a canoe along the Virginia shore and had intercepted him. The man, a settler who had been downriver to make tomahawk improvements, told them he was quitting the country for now because there were too many Indians about, that only three or four miles below he had passed a hunting party of Mingoes setting up a camp at the mouth of Captina Creek. Immediately the Greathouse party had left the settler behind to come along as best he could and themselves paddled at top speed back here to Wheeling.

Cresap at once, much to the disgust and opposition of the Zanes, gathered together a new party of 30 men and left within minutes to hit the Mingoes.

[April 24, 1774—Sunday]

John Gibson, Alexander Blaine and Matthew Elliott were very relieved that the Shawnee party building canoes here, well up the Hockhocking, knew nothing of any attacks being made against the white surveyors, land-jobbers or settlers. They, in fact, had laughed, just as Elliott had laughed, when the rumors were repeated to them.

"Well," Gibson said, "it was something we really had to check on, and I'm glad it's turned out to be wild stories. I've seen it happen before; tales get started, and things get all twisted around. Connolly, if he didn't start all this himself, ought to have his neck wrung for becoming a part of it. Stories like that can sometimes cause big problems."

Trading their canoe and some goods for three horses to ride and two packhorses to carry the remainder of their merchandise, the three now set off overland, heading due west for the Shawnee villages in the Scioto Valley. It was a beautiful spring morning, and they felt much better now as they left the canoe-making party behind, reasonably sure the current scare along the Ohio River would quickly die away.

[April 25, 1774—Monday]

The Cresap party, on its return to Wheeling, was far more subdued than when it left. They had descended the Ohio swiftly to the mouth of Captina Creek and found the Indian camp, but they lost the element of surprise when one of their party inadvertently shot his rifle before the signal could be given. It gave the Indians a chance to snatch up their own weapons and return the withering fire that was suddenly pouring in on them. There were somewhere around 20 Indians in the party, and the Cresap party managed to kill three and wound a couple of others, but the remainder escaped. In the brief firing the Indians returned, three whites had been shot, two of these only slightly wounded, but a huge bull of a man known only as Big Tarrener had taken a ball through the stomach. He was in bad shape, and a horse litter was rigged to carry him overland to Catfish Camp and from there on the rough wagon trail to Pittsburgh.

The enormity of what they had done began penetrating, along with consideration of what the repercussions would be. Quite a large number of the men at Wheeling, as well as many of the residents, now decided that very soon this whole Ohio Valley was going to become a very dangerous place for whites. Their fear became contagious and a mass exodus began, the people avoiding river travel and heading eastward by land on the main trail to Catfish Camp, the Monongahela, Redstone and beyond. By the end of this day, except for the corps of men still with Cresap, Wheeling was virtually abandoned. Cresap, however, at the urging of Jacob Greathouse, had decided that one final attack was in order before they vacated: Talgayeeta's Town on Yellow Creek.

[April 27, 1774 — Wednesday]

It was just after the 11 canoes passed Upper Twin Island that Michael Cresap, in the leading canoe, raised a hand and pointed to the Virginia shore, where there was a narrow bottom, and angled in that direction. The others followed and beached their boats close to his, wondering what was going on. Wheeling lay five miles down-stream, and since Yellow Creek was still some 35 miles upstream, the sudden put-in to shore confused them.

Cresap waited until they had all gathered around him and then held up his hands for silence and spoke. "Boys," he said, "I've been doing some hard thinking ever since we left Wheeling. What's been done so far this past week can maybe still be smoothed over by some counciling with the tribes and some payments from us. But if we go on with this attack on Logan's camp, there's nothing in the world that'll prevent all-out war. Is that what we really want?"

"Dammit, Cresap," someone called, "you're the one who's been doing all the talking an' leading. You gettin' cold feet now?"

Michael Cresap did not even try to see who spoke. He merely shook his head and continued as if there had been no interruption. "I expect most of us here, if we haven't personally met Logan, have heard about him. He's a damned fine man, and he's always been a friend to the whites. Whenever there's been trouble between the Indians and us, he's stayed neutral. So I've been asking myself, why are we heading up to his village to attack him? It just doesn't make good sense. He's up there with a handful of men but a lot more women and children. They haven't harmed us, and they don't show any signs of doing so, so I propose we call off this whole thing and follow the others back to the Monongahela for a spell till all this cools down. So what do you think?"

He expected, having brought them this far, that they were going to be irate over his suggestion, but he was pleasantly surprised to find that he was not the only one having second thoughts. By far the great majority of the men had been growing ever less inclined to continue with this ridiculous and dangerous expedition, yet none had had courage enough to bring it up.

They loaded up their pipes and smoked while discussing it further, and though there were some among them who were all for going on, more by far held the opinion that their best course was to do as Cresap suggested. At last they put it to a vote, and the majority agreed to turn back.

One group, somewhat apart from the rest, was disgruntled. They murmured among themselves for a while and then seemed to come to an agreement. Their spokesman, Jacob Greathouse, came to his feet, tapped out his pipe bowl against the stock of his rifle and then spoke in a scathing voice.

"I see a bunch o' cowards here," he said, "an' I guess it's a good thing we found out now 'stead of up at Yeller Crik. Us'ns here"—he indicated the 30 men of his clique—"we're for going on with the whole thing. Well, fact is, we ain't got enough to do it, so I reckon it's off. But we ain't got much good feelin' 'bout headin' back t'Wheeling with the likes of you and then goin' cross-country with our tails 'twixt our legs, so I reckon you'ns can go on 'thout us. We'll head on upriver for Pittsburgh in our boats, and t'hell with the Injens an' you an' ever'thing else!"

They separated then. The Greathouse party remained on shore and watched with disgust as the others returned to their canoes and paddled back toward Wheeling. Then Jake turned to his men.

"Good riddance, I say. Aw'right now, let's talk more 'bout what I mentioned afore. We ain't got too many left, but they's enough for the plan I got in mind. I still aim to get us a passel of scalps off them red niggers up at Yeller Crik. Anybody wants to back out, now's the time."

No one left.[198]

[April 30, 1774—Saturday]

Jacob Greathouse had been crouched behind the big rock on Baker's Bottom for about an hour when his vigil finally paid off. Four Indian canoes came into view from upstream on Yellow Creek and pulled ashore at the point formed where the stream empties into the Ohio. The river was about 500 yards wide at this point, and they were a few hundred yards above where Greathouse was hidden, so he couldn't make out much detail, but at least a couple dozen individuals came ashore at the point.

Jake remained hidden, watching intently as the Indian party evidently discussed something. Then nine of them reentered two of the canoes, shoved off and began heading across. A crooked grin spread the big man's lips as he backed away, then strode to where his men were gathered about the small campfire in a broad clearing well up from the shore and mostly hidden from the river. They were a disreputable-looking crew, dirty, unkempt, half with scruffy beards, and all 31 of them had rifles in hand and tomahawks and knives in their belts.

"Okay, boys," Jake said, "it's workin', jus' like planned. They're comin' acrost. 'Bout eight or ten of 'em in two boats. More stayin' over on the point, waitin'."

He looked over the group, and his gaze settled on his brother, Daniel, squatted beside Joe Tomlinson. He nodded and pointed at them. "Dan'l, Joe, you two get your guns ready an' stay with me." He indicated some men close to them. "Same with you four. All the rest, get your guns ready, too, and get hid where I tol' you. An' don't make no noise! Damn Injens got ears like wolves. Ever'body watch me. When I yell *'Now!'* that's when you give it to 'em. Now get hid. Joe, Dan'l, come with me. You four stay by the fire here. Act normal, frien'ly."

He strode back toward the shore, his brother and Tomlinson following. They passed the rock where Greathouse had hidden before and moved down to the edge of the beach area and waited. Greathouse's grin returned when he saw that the two canoes were nearly halfway across and still coming steadily, being watched by the group of Indians still on the point.

Greathouse mentally congratulated himself on how well everything was working and thought about how he'd set it up. Yesterday morning, still coming upstream after Cresap's group had returned to Wheeling, they had stopped at the cabin of Charles Polk, located on the bottom near the mouth of Cross Creek, some 18 miles downstream from here. They tried to get Polk to join them but, on hearing what they had in mind, the settler refused to take part.

The party had then, early in the afternoon, reached Baker's Bottom about a mile below here and stopped off at a cabin that had been erected earlier this year by James Chambers and Edward King. Greathouse had solicited this pair to join them and, though Chambers refused, King agreed and came along. Next, at Tomlinson's insistence, they had stopped at Joshua Baker's little cabin store a half-mile below here. Tomlinson's sister, Sarah, was Baker's wife and, after making sure she was all right, they had talked with her husband. When they finished explaining what was planned, Baker gave them two kegs of whiskey and a gallon jug of rum to aid in the deception and, leaving Sarah to watch over the store, joined them.

They had then come to this spot and set up the little camp. Later in the afternoon, taking along the jug, the Greathouse brothers had crossed the river alone and ascended Yellow Creek to Talgayeeta's Town. Chief Logan, they soon discovered, was absent with a large party, bringing in meat from a hunting trip, but his brother, Taylaynee, greeted them cordially enough and gratefully accepted the jug Jake presented to him. Greathouse told him that he and his brother and four others were camped on the bottom across the river and that they had a couple of kegs of whiskey they'd gladly share with the Mingoes if they came across tomorrow. Knowing well their predilection not only for liquor but for gambling, he suggested they bring some of their beaver skins along, and he'd figure out some kind of a sporting contest. The Indians would get a fresh keg of whiskey all their own to take away with them if they won, but Greathouse's party would get the beaver skins if the Indians lost. The idea appealed to Taylaynee, and he agreed in his broken English to come over with some of his people in the morning soon after the sun had cleared the hills to the east.

Now, as the two canoes coasted to shore and the Indians began getting out, Greathouse stepped forward and extended his hand to Taylaynee, welcoming him. He and the six warriors with him all had flintlock rifles. There were also two women —one middle-aged, the other a younger woman whose stomach was well swollen with her advanced pregnancy and who carried a little girl, about a year old, on her back in a cradleboard attached to her by a harness affair called a *hoppase*. The older woman helped her to shore.

Greathouse smiled at the younger woman in a friendly manner. "Reckon I know you, don't I? Ain't you Chief Logan's sister?"

She nodded. "Yes, Talgayeeta is my brother." She indicated the other woman. "This is Mellana, who is his wife. You know my other brother"—she indicated Taylaynee, then turned to a young warrior, about 20—"and this is his son, Molnah. The others are our friends."

Greathouse dipped his head to them and indicated the two who were with him. "Well, this here's my brother, Dan'l, an' our frien', Joe Tomlinson. C'mon up t'the camp an' have a drink." He turned and strode away, his two men following, and in a moment the Indians also followed.

Taylaynee's gaze flicked across the campsite as they came in view of it. The four men squatted near the fire smiled and nodded to them, and Taylaynee saw that their rifles were carelessly leaning against a rock, clearly out of arm's reach. He also saw the two kegs of whiskey, one open with battered pewter cups hanging on the rim.

"Well," Greathouse said jovially, "there's the whiskey, just like I promised. He'p yourselves."

Suspicions allayed by the normalcy of the camp and the evident friendliness of the whites, Taylaynee nodded. He rattled off a string of words in his own tongue, and the seven warriors converged on the keg, dipped the cups and drank greedily. The women stayed to one side.

Greathouse continued speaking in a pleasant, conversational tone. "Reckon your Chief Logan ain't got back yet, eh?"

Taylaynee swallowed his mouthful of rum and shook his head. "Logan back soon. Two suns. Maybe three." He eyed Greathouse with a flicker of suspicion and said, "Other braves, 'cross river there"—he pointed—"come here soon."

Jake pretended surprise. "That right? Well, they's sure 'nuff whiskey for them fellers, too." He paused and then added as an aside, "Heered tell you boys're damn good hunters. Ain't likely, though, you k'n shoot a mark nowhere near as good as us'ns."

Swallowing more rum, Taylaynee replied boastfully. "Cayuga shoot straight. Shoot good."

Greathouse chuckled. "Reckon my boys're better, though. We k'n sure 'nuff find out. Tol' you we'd have a sportin' match. Look over yonder, an' you k'n see a couple targets we hung on that big ol' beech tree." The tree he indicated was some 40 yards distant, where two squares of a torn white kerchief had been pegged to the smooth bark one above the other, about four inches apart. Jake continued without pause, "You fellers shoot at that bottom one all at the same time. Then me an' my boys'll shoot at the top one all at onct. Then we'll go see how many hits in each. Iffen you win, we give you that whole keg of whiskey. Iffen we win, we get seven beaver skins. How's that sound? You bring along them skins?"

Taylaynee nodded. "Skins in canoe." He looked at Greathouse directly, his suspicions not entirely allayed. "Cayugas not shoot first. White men shoot first."

"Reckon that's fair 'nuff," Greathouse replied. "Boys, get your guns. We're gonna show 'em how it's done."

Greathouse gouged a long line in the dirt with his heel, and all seven of the whites took their places side by side and primed their weapons. The Indians, separating from one another somewhat and gripping their rifles, watched closely.

"Aw'right, boys," Greathouse ordered, "top target when I count three. Ready? One . . . two . . . three!"

All seven guns barked almost simultaneously, and a large cloud of blue-white smoke rose. As it cleared, it could be seen that the top target had been hit by at least three or four of the balls. Greathouse and his men, grinning, stepped away from the line with their empty rifles, and Jake spoke jeeringly but good-naturedly.

"Now, let's see what the great Injen hunters k'n do."

Taylaynee nodded and smiled briefly at his sister-in-law and sister watching with interest from one side. With the weapons of the whites empty, his suspicions evaporated, and he gestured to his men. All stepped up to the line as the whites had done and aimed at the lower target. Taylaynee counted.

"Negote . . . neshwa . . . nithese!"

All seven guns fired at once, but this time, before the cloud of smoke could dissipate or the clustered warriors move apart, the whites leaped off to the side and the roar of Jake's voice filled the air. "Now!"

Even as the somewhat tipsy Indians dropped their rifles and clawed for their tomahawks, the 26 hidden men rose and fired in a great barrage. All seven of the warriors were killed instantly. Off to the side, Mellana was screaming as an attacker ran up to her with flintlock pistol in hand and pointed it at her head. She put up a hand, palm outward, in front of her face, but the ball passed through her hand and into her forehead, and she fell dead.[199]

Koonay, the child still in the cradleboard on her back, had broken into a run toward the canoes, but one of the shooters lunged out of hiding and tackled her. The infant girl rolled free, crying, and another man ran up, grabbed the baby and covered her mouth. Koonay was struggling hard to get away from the man who had tackled her, but he was too strong and, as she began to scream, he clamped his hand fiercely over her mouth.

By this time the others had emerged from hiding and run up to the fallen warriors and were already getting their weapons and scalping them. A short distance away, closer to the river, one of the ambushers called out.

"Jake! Two more canoes comin'. 'Bout fifteen Injens and some young'uns."

"Take cover an' reload," Greathouse ordered, setting his rifle aside. "We ain't done yet. An' keep that goddamn squaw quiet! Joe, Dan'l, put your guns down an' come with me."

The men scattered and took cover behind underbrush close to the river's edge. Koonay, still struggling, was dragged behind a rocky ledge, pulled to the ground and held down. Tomlinson and Daniel Greathouse fell in with Jake and walked toward the beached canoes. The rapidly approaching canoes were well within rifle range now, but the three men continued to saunter casually to the shoreline. Their lack of guns obvious, they waved to the Indians in a friendly manner as the canoes coasted in toward shore near them. The Indians were looking about anxiously for their fellows, and one cupped his mouth and called out, "Taylaynee! Taylaynee!"

Behind the ledge, still pinned to the ground by the man astraddle her, Koonay heard the voices. She brought her knee up savagely into the man's groin. He grunted with pain and jerked his hand away from her mouth to protect himself. Instantly she shrieked a warning, cut off in midscream as her captor struck her in the face with his fist, stunning her.

The Greathouse brothers and Tomlinson dropped flat to the ground, Jake shouting "Now!" as he went down. Again a ragged barrage of shots broke out from the hidden men. Some Indians in both canoes crumpled. Several men and boys leaped out and tried to surge away in waist-deep water. All but two were cut down by more shots. The remaining two, by alternately diving and surfacing until out of range, managed to escape to the other side of the river.[200]

Tomlinson came to his feet, a strained expression on his face. The Greathouse brothers grinned at one another as they stood up. Jake looked at Tomlinson and pulled his tomahawk from his belt. "Joe," he said, "you wanted some o' them scalps, so he'p yourself. Me, I got a 'pointment with a squaw."

He strode away and came up to where Koonay lay on the ground at the feet of her captor, who was still groaning from the pain she'd caused him. The woman, on her back, was just beginning to stir, a large ugly bruise already forming on her temple close to her left eye. Greathouse nudged her roughly with the toe of his boot, and she moaned.

"What'cha gonna do, Jake?" the other man asked.

Greathouse looked at him and snorted, then raised one foot and planted it firmly on Koonay's distended abdomen. The expression on his face was one of pure malevolence. He reached to the sheath on his belt and pulled out his scalping knife.

"I aim," he said, "t'get the smallest Injen scalp ever been took."

Chapter 2

Talgayeeta's expression was frozen in mingled grief and disbelief as he moved slowly from one to another among the bodies of his family and friends at Baker's Bottom. His warriors had gently gathered them up and placed them side by side. Here lay the scalped and otherwise mutilated bodies of his friends. Here, in similar condition, lay the bodies of his wife Mellana, his brother Taylaynee, and his nephew Molnah.[201] But worst of all was the discovery of the body of his sister Koonay, a short distance away.[202] His men had tried to take her down before Talgayeeta saw her, but he came upon them too quickly. Her face was battered almost beyond recognition, and then she had been hung by her outstretched wrists from two saplings. Evidently while still alive, she was then scalped and disemboweled, and her nearly full-term unborn son removed from her body. This child had also been scalped and stabbed and then tossed aside.

The piercing, wailing death cry abruptly burst from Talgayeeta and after a moment was picked up by the warriors in his party. Soon the bottom resounded with the eerie chorus. Gradually it died away, and though the grief remained in Talgayeeta's expression, now his features became contorted with demonic rage as he lifted his tomahawk and spoke, his words frightening with their cold and terrible intensity.

"I, Talgayeeta, give my vow. . . . For every life taken here, ten of the *Shemanese* will die under my hand. . . . And I, Talgayeeta, vow it: By my hand alone, *twenty* lives for my unborn nephew!"[203]

[May 2, 1774 — Monday]

The Greathouse party largely remained together until they reached Catfish Camp, where no one yet knew of the massacre of Talgayeeta's family. Most of the residents there were still on hand, though they were packing up their goods preparatory to leaving, fearing the retribution that the Indians would launch against the settlements in response to Cresap's attacks on the trading party at the mouth of Indian Short Creek and that on the Mingo hunting party in their camp at the mouth of Captina Creek.

Big Tarrener had been brought in by litter from Wheeling, but he was obviously slipping fast, and the consensus was that he could not possibly survive the journey remaining to get him to medical care at Pittsburgh. They were correct. Though they took him to the cabin of William Houston, where James Chambers had come after refusing to participate in the Greathouse plan, and Houston attempted to treat Big Tarrener's wound, it was to no avail; within two hours of their arrival, Tarrener had died. The two men slightly wounded from that attack had quickly pressed on to the east.

As more of Greathouse's men showed up and assembled at Houston's cabin, one of them carrying an infant Indian girl, Houston himself had a difficult time believing the enormity of what had been done by the Cresap and Greathouse parties on the Ohio River.[204]

Chambers was positively furious about the Baker's Bottom affair and decidedly more vocal, verbally castigating his friend Edward King for participating.

"I can't believe," he said, "that you actually took part in this thing, Ed. I had considered you as my friend, but no longer. I won't have as a friend a man who could do something like this. What you've done"—he turned and let his gaze swing across the entire Greathouse group, and his tone was contemptuous—"what *all* you men have done is the grossest, most atrocious murder!"

Joseph Smith, a one-armed man who had participated in the massacre, jerked his tomahawk from his belt and advanced on Chambers, his eyes burning dangerously. "You sanctimonious son of a bitch!" he growled. "Make one more remark like that, and I'll bury this 'hawk in your head."

Chambers stood his ground a moment, ready to grapple with the man if it came to that, but then he simply shook his head and turned away.[205]

Almost as fearful of Greathouse and his men as they were of the Indians, the people at Catfish Camp avoided them when they first showed up, though looking upon the ruffian group with undisguised loathing. Gradually, however, as word spread among the residents of the atrocity that had occurred at Baker's Bottom, quite suddenly the fears of the settlers turned to panic, and the majority fled precipitately.

The Greathouse party itself soon split into smaller groups or individuals and dispersed, heading eastward. The account of the destruction of Talgayeeta's people spread even more rapidly.

[*M a y   3 ,   1 7 7 4 — T u e s d a y*]

The first fearful whispers of the tragedy at Baker's Bottom reached Pittsburgh as some of the Greathouse party came through and hardly paused long enough to impart the news. There were shock and recriminations from among the listeners, but the Greathouse men did not linger. Within mere minutes of their arrival, they disappeared eastward on foot along the Military Road.

Alexander McKee, deputy Indian agent under George Croghan, was on hand to hear what had been said, and nearly beside himself with rage, he ran to the fort immediately and confronted Maj. Connolly without any trace of tact.

"This is all your doing, Connolly! You, with your stories about attacks that never occurred, danger that never existed, robberies that were never committed. You spread those lies and then promoted white retaliation with those damned circular letters of yours. You ought to be—"

John Connolly cut him off with a savage jerk of his hand. "How dare you come in here talking like that, McKee? You Pennsylvanians are all the same—loudmouthed and stupid. Get the hell out of here or, by God, I will damned well have you shot!"

Still seething, McKee left, sought out the half-breed Andrew Montour and told him to get ready to carry an express to the tribes. Then he returned to his quarters, wishing George Croghan were here now to do what he was going to do, even though it was probably already too late. He knew what he had in mind might cost him his job, but somebody had to try to do something to stop an all-out war.

Swiftly he wrote out the brief message:

from Alexʳ McKee, Pittsburgh

Brothers—We are under the necessity, from some disagreeable intelligence we have just received, of calling upon your immediate attendance at this place, where we shall have some things of importance to communicate to you, which intimately concerns the welfare of us both: This will be sufficient, we expect, to induce your speedy appearance here, as delays upon those occasions may be attended with the most dangerous consequences.

He folded the letter and thrust it into a flat leather pouch. Then, snatching a string of white wampum from where it hung on a nail near the fireplace, he strode to the door and threw it open. Montour was waiting, and he handed him the wampum and pouch. "Take this to Hokolesqua," he directed, "then to White Eyes, Monakaduto and Pimoacan. And to Talgayeeta."

[*A p r i l   4 ,   1 7 7 4 — M o n d a y*]

Incredibly, in the midst of all this havoc he was creating with his deliberate instigation of an Indian war, Maj. John Connolly was also waging a war of sorts for Lord Dunmore on behalf of Virginia against the Pennsylvanians at Pittsburgh. Connolly meant to make certain this whole portion of the frontier was locked up solidly at

as part of Virginia's domain, and he didn't care one iota what steps he had to take to do so.

Already having embodied close to 100 men in his militia at Fort Pitt, Connolly now gave them orders to go out in squads and gather all the provisions they could from the inhabitants, especially Pennsylvanians. Acting on these orders, the squads went out and confiscated any horses they found, to be used by the military. They also shot cattle and hogs belonging to the inhabitants and transported the carcasses to the fort to be butchered for meat for the military. When residents strenuously objected, he had them arrested and thrown in the Fort Pitt guardhouse and then also, in their absence, conscripted their property.

One of Maj. Connolly's particular Pennsylvania enemies in Pittsburgh was Devereaux Smith, formerly of Philadelphia, who was prominent in politics as well as in other areas. Smith was just as adamant that Pittsburgh and the Monongahela and Allegheny valleys belonged to Pennsylvania. Yesterday, Smith was arrested by Connolly's militia for disobedience of government orders in wartime and was put in irons to be taken away for incarceration in the blockhouse at Wheeling. Before he could be led off, he gave instructions to trader William Butler, who was residing with him, to protect his wife and property in his absence.

Now Connolly, wasting no time, sent an armed guard of six men to Smith's house to confiscate all the blankets stored there for the Indian trade and all the parcels of goods that had been set aside to be distributed at Indian councils. Butler, himself armed, barred their access to the house, and a certain amount of pushing and shoving, with threats of greater violence, were exchanged before the guards returned to the fort to tell the commander of their being balked. Furious, Connolly immediately led a larger armed squad—12 men—to the Smith house. A fierce argument broke out between himself on the one side and Butler and Mrs. Smith on the other.

"Butler," Connolly warned, "stand clear, or I will, by God, have you shackled and marched to Williamsburg and take every particle of your trading goods from you."

"Major Connolly!" The words, like rifle shots, burst from Mrs. Smith. "Mr. Butler is protecting this house and home and everything in it at the orders of Mr. Smith and myself. What you are doing is illegal, and if you do not desist and leave here at once, I promise you, I will have Mr. Butler shoot you. And should you manage to get past him, then I, sir,"—and here she drew out a large flintlock pistol from beneath her apron—"will shoot you dead in your tracks. Do not," she warned, "think I will hesitate an instant to do so."

"You goddamned bitch!" Connolly stormed. "I'm in command here, and my orders are to be followed!"

"Not at *my* house, you're not in command." She cocked the flintlock with a loud click, and it was echoed by the heavier click of Butler's rifle. "Now," she added coldly, "you get the hell off my property before I count three, or I swear to God, sir, you will die where you now stand. One . . . two . . ."

Connolly wheeled, cursing bitterly, and started away, his squad following. While stalking off, the major called bitterly over his shoulder, "Goddamn you, Mrs. Smith, you've not heard the end of this!"

"Nor have you, Major Connolly," she replied, "I assure you of that."

[*May 5, 1774 — Thursday*]

On the Jacob's Creek tributary of the Youghiogheny, Valentine Crawford was very nearly finished with the letter he had been writing to Col. George Washington, advising him of the peril now afoot in the frontier districts.

The letter was already long and detailed and largely contained information that had been brought to him yesterday. He wrote that his brother, Capt. William Crawford, traveling with a friend, Edgar Neville, had left his Youghiogheny settlement in the forenoon yesterday, heading on horseback for Neville's home in Pittsburgh. They had left William Crawford's place under the watchful eye of his friend and indentured servant, John Knight, who for the past year had been working off the cost of his passage from his native Scotland by tutoring William Crawford's children. Less than an hour after the two men started, they encountered a group of men who were obviously very nervous. These men had admitted to being part of the Greathouse party until reaching Catfish Camp, where they had broken away on their own. They had with them some fresh Indian scalps and, in a cradleboard basket, an infant almost continuously crying. On being questioned rather sternly by Crawford, they soon admitted everything that had occurred at Baker's Bottom.

Crawford and Neville were horrified at the news. The baby, since being taken four days earlier, had been fed only a few mouthfuls of gruel and had been given a chunk of jerky to suck upon and was obviously crying from hunger. Neville questioned the man who had her and learned that she was the daughter of trader John Gibson and an Indian squaw and that her mother had been butchered in the attack. The man who was carrying the baby said he had taken no part in that, although he admitted to giving thought to knocking the infant's brains out, but he said that he had been prevented from doing so by a welling of pity at her helplessness. He added that "all hell was bustin' loose" and reckoned that all the settlers in the whole upper Ohio Valley were on the move to the east and probably reaching Redstone about now.

Crawford had demanded the child, and the man gave her to him, obviously thankful at being relieved of the unwanted responsibility. Chiding the men for their part in the incident—though they themselves heaped all the blame on Cresap, Greathouse, Tomlinson, Baker and a few others—Crawford had sent them on their way, and then he and Neville immediately retraced their own steps to his settlement on the Youghiogheny.[206] There he had placed the infant in the care of a wet-nurse— one of his slaves who was nursing her own baby—and in moments the baby girl was sucking greedily at her breast.

Aware that what the Cresap and Greathouse parties had perpetrated would certainly result in a general Indian war, Crawford and Neville separated and set out to warn all the settlers they could of the impending danger and advise them to get east of the mountains as soon as possible.[207] Crawford's route took him as far distant as Brownsville and the other Redstone area settlements, after which he had finally stopped by briefly to see Valentine and tell him the bad news.

Valentine went on to explain to Washington that by the time his brother arrived, he was already aware of the amazing exodus in progress but had no certain knowledge of the cause. William's visit had filled in the gaps, and while the information being relayed to Washington was thirdhand, it was being related as received. Now, wanting to get the letter off by express as quickly as possible, Valentine Crawford bent to finish what he was writing, penning the words swiftly:

> . . . *and, on Saturday last, about 12 o'clock, there was one Greathouse and about 20 men fell on a party of Indians at the mouth of Yellow Creek, and killed 10 of them, and brought away one child a prisoner, which is now at my brother William Crawford's. This alarm has made the people move from over the Monongahela, off Shirtee [Chartier's Creek] and Raccoon as fast as you ever saw them in the year 1756 or '57 in Frederick County, Virginia. There were more than one thousand people crossed the Monongahela in one day at three ferries not one mile apart.*

On the Youghiogheny, only a few miles distant, settler Gilbert Simpson was also writing a letter to George Washington, who had hired him to construct a mill. Though unnerved by all that was occurring, his inherent tenacity came to the forefront. After relating some of what he had heard, he added:

> *The country at this time is in great confusion, the Indians declaring war against us. I suppose there have been broken up and gone off at least 500 families within one week past, but I am determined to stand to the last or lose my life with what I have. There have been two or three skirmishes with whites and Indians. There have been 19 Indians killed and one white man killed and one wounded—all between the Mingo Town and Pittsburgh, & I believe it has been the white people's fault altogether.*

Finally, William Crawford, back home again after his marathon round of warning settlers, also wrote to George Washington:

> *Our inhabitants are much alarmed, many hundreds having gone over the mountains. In short, a war is every moment expected; we have a council now with them. What will be the event I do not know. I am now setting out for Fort Pitt at the head of 100 men; many others are to meet me there and at Wheeling, where we shall wait the motions of the Indians, and shall act accordingly. We are in great want of some proper person to direct us, who may command—Mr. Connolly, who now commands, having incurred the displeasure of the people. He is unable to take command for two reasons; one is the contradiction between us and the Pennsylvanians, and the other that he rather carries matters too much in a military way and is not able to go through with it. I have some hopes that we may still have matters settled with the Indians upon a method properly adopted for that purpose.*

However much Capt. Crawford and others hoped to conciliate the Indians, their efforts continued to be undermined by individual acts of barbarity. A fiery-tempered little Irishman, John Ryan, called Jack by his friends, having stowed all his gear in his saddle packs, was ready to leave the area where he was claiming just below the mouth of Grave Creek when he saw a lone individual approaching in a canoe from well upstream. He slipped into hiding, took a position behind some rocks and carefully checked the load and priming of his flintlock. In a few minutes the canoe was beginning to pass at a distance of about 60 yards, its occupant an Indian, apparently a Delaware. With great care Ryan took aim and fired. The large lead ball struck the Indian in the left temple and slammed him out of the canoe, which rocked violently but somehow managed to stay upright and float off empty. The Indian had disappeared beneath the surface, and Jack Ryan experienced a pang of regret that he was unable to get the scalp.

[May 8, 1774 — Sunday]

George Croghan, with Alexander McKee, watched despairingly as the Indians departed from his council. A smaller number of chiefs than had been hoped for— only a few Delaware and Iroquois delegates—attended the meeting, which had been held at Croghan Hall rather than Fort Pitt, due to Connolly's antagonism. Croghan had warmly approved of McKee setting up the council in his absence, but it had done little good. Croghan had done all he could to placate them but, though they had listened politely, they said it was too late; Talgayeeta had sworn vengeance, and they understood his wrath and supported him in it.

[May 11, 1774 — Wednesday]

Little John Ryan, who six days ago shot the Indian out of his canoe on the Ohio, was now on the Monongahela not far below the mouth of Dunkard Creek and found himself with an opportunity to repeat his recent history.[208] A short while before, riding up the path on the east side of the river, he had detected smoke and hastily left the path, tied his horse and then advanced on foot toward the source. He soon spied a lone Indian sitting by his campfire, his back against a tree, his small canoe wedged on shore only a few yards away.

This Indian was the ancient Delaware chief who had been pointed out to Ryan a year before at Redstone as a harmless, solitary old man named Bald Eagle who was humorously eccentric and who often visited the settlements to trade fur skins or deer meat. His command of English was fair, and the settlers had grown to like him and welcome his visits. Ryan did not share their views, and now, from his hiding place no more than 50 feet away, he took careful aim. Just as the frail and skinny old Delaware was lighting his pipe, he coldly sent a lead ball the size of the end of his thumb through his heart, killing him.

Ryan waited a few minutes to see if anyone else might show up, and when no one did, he approached the camp. The old Indian had tumbled forward but now lay on his back, sightless eyes open wide and already glazing, his pipe beside an outstretched hand and floppy hat lying a short distance away. Ryan checked the Indian's pack and found nothing of any real value—a few cakes of dense cornbread, a tin of pipe tobacco, some jerky, an extra pair of moccasins, well worn. His musket, leaning against the tree, was in such bad shape, it was not worth bothering with, but there was a skinning knife and tomahawk that Ryan set aside to take, along with a small amount of powder and lead.

Ryan scalped the old man and then easily picked up the body and carried it to the canoe. There he used the old musket to help prop it up into a sitting position in the stern and positioned the floppy hat to cover the wound where the scalp had been lifted. He also tried to wedge the battered pipe in the old man's mouth, but the jaw was slack and it kept falling out. Returning to Bald Eagle's pack, Ryan got the corn cakes, moistened them slightly with river water and crammed them into the mouth until there was room for no more. Then he stuck the pipestem in it and stepped back to survey his handiwork. The old man looked remarkably alive, as if half-dozing while he smoked, and Ryan laughed aloud.

"Have a nice trip," he murmured, freeing the canoe from shore and thrusting it smoothly into the current. It quickly floated out of sight beyond a bend, and within minutes Ryan, with the scalp and meager plunder in his own pouch, was again on his horse, heading for the Cheat Valley.

The floating canoe stayed fairly close to the right bank as it drifted downstream. As it approached the mouth of George's Creek a mile and a half below where it was launched, the canoe passed several settlers on shore who thought old Bald Eagle was returning from a friendly hunt with the settlers still at Dunkard Creek, and they waved and called hello.[209] They were surprised when he did not put in to see them and even more when he didn't even return their greetings.

The current entering the river from the mouth of George's Creek pushed the canoe farther out toward the middle, and it continued the downstream drift for nearly another six miles, before being caught by an eddy and propelled toward shore. There it wedged itself in a willow overhang within sight of the Provance Settlement.[210] Frederick and Martha Provance, cautiously hunting mushrooms while also keeping a sharp eye out for danger, saw the craft skim into the branches and stop. Recognizing Bald Eagle, they wondered why he didn't come ashore and soon came to investigate. They were sickened by what they found and later that same day gave the old Delaware a decent burial.

[May 12, 1774—Thursday]

Now, all over the frontier, settlers who had not fled very far to the east began to wonder if they had not been too precipitous in leaving as they had. It was nearly two weeks since the attack at Baker's Bottom and three weeks since the attacks farther downriver. Yet despite these provocations, there was no real evidence that the Indians were retaliating. Many of the settlers began coming back to their cabins, especially those of the Wheeling area. As William Crawford put it in another of his letters to George Washington:

> *Several of the inhabitants of that part are gone back and are planting their corn. David Shepherd, who lives down at Wheeling, moved his family up to my house, but he has gone back himself and is planting his corn.*

Some, of course, even in the face of the supposed danger looming, had refused to leave, determined to face up to whatever came their way in order to protect their interests. Among these were the Tomlinson boys—Joseph, Samuel and James—and their widowed sister, Rebecca Martin, who kept house for them. Joe, the eldest and clearly the leader, had spoken little about his participation in the Greathouse affair up at Baker's Bottom. He and Sam often went out alone for several days at a stretch, saying they were going hunting, and occasionally young Jim went with them. Rebecca was convinced that what they were hunting was definitely not meat for the table. This was one of those times. The three had offhandedly remarked to her that they were "going a little farther this time," and she was not to be concerned if they didn't get back for five or six days. As for her, she was to stay inside the cabin with door and window shutters barred until their return.

Soon after their departure, however, she had grown concerned for their sister, Sarah Baker, who, so far as she knew, was still up at Baker's Bottom with her husband. Putting aside the final admonition of her brothers, she decided to visit her and make sure she was all right. She knew that her brothers, had they been home, would never have allowed her to do so, but if Rebecca Tomlinson Martin was anything, she was a very determined and self-possessed young woman.

Three days ago, making sure her flintlock was loaded and taking along a shot pouch and powderhorn as well as a packet of food, she climbed into her own light canoe and set off on the 52-mile upstream journey. Twenty-one miles upstream she stopped at the McCulloch Settlement at the mouth of Short Creek but found the cabins deserted. She made herself comfortable in one of them and spent the night, completing her journey to Baker's Bottom by noon the day before yesterday. She found Sarah and Joshua there, still all right but, having observed increased Indian activity over the last few days, preparing to head for Catfish Camp, where they would be less exposed to danger and be with other settlers if it became necessary to defend themselves. They invited her to come along, but she refused, saying she had to get back to Grave Creek and protect the Tomlinson interests there until her brothers returned.

Rebecca had started her journey back downstream yesterday afternoon and made it to a few miles above Wheeling Creek by nightfall. Leery about traveling without some light to guide her along the shoreline, she nosed her canoe to the Virginia bank, tied it to some willows with a rawhide tug and leaped lightly to shore. She made a little cold camp, had a bite to eat and stretched out to wait for the moon to rise and provide enough light for her to continue. Close to midnight the half-moon cleared the trees in a cloudless sky and transformed the black river into a silvery ribbon. She returned to where her canoe was and found that her leap to shore earlier had thrust the light craft out a little from shore, and for a frightening moment she thought it was gone. Then in the pale moonlight, she saw that it was still held by the line attached to the willows, although it was out so far that she had to wade through the shin-deep shallows to reach it.

As she reached her little boat, her foot encountered a loose mass that she took to be a clump of floating debris, and she stepped upon it to get back into the canoe, thrusting it against the bottom. Once settled aboard, she glanced down to the water to see what she had stepped upon and discovered, as it rose back to the surface, that it was the bloated face-up body of an Indian. She gasped and for a long moment sat dead still, staring at the gruesome sight. Gradually recovering her composure, she moved to the bow and untied the line, shoved the boat out and drifted away from the sight she knew would return in nightmares the rest of her life.

Closely following the shoreline, she paddled throughout the remainder of the night and just after daybreak this morning reached the mouth of Grave Creek. She guided the canoe into the safe little mooring where her journey had begun, pulled it well up on shore and walked up to the cabin, finding everything as she had left it.

Now, hardly an hour later, with the new sunlight bright and cheerful in the clearing, she heard her brothers coming and met them at the cabin door. They were obviously relieved at finding her all right, and Samuel picked her up in a big hug and kissed her cheek.

"Glad to see you stayed inside where it's safe, sis," he said. "You weren't skeered, were you?"

"Well," she replied, smiling, "I'm glad you're back. It's lonesome and I have to admit I did get a little scared once, but it was nothing."[211]

[May 14, 1774 — Saturday]

The atmosphere on the frontier these days was a decidedly unhealthy one for Indians. Early this morning, while crusty old Sam Meason was visiting Pittsburgh to buy supplies, he saw an Indian emerge from the woods and approach the bustling village with his hand upraised in the peace sign. Before any of the townspeople nearby realized Meason's intent, the frontiersman snatched up his rifle and shot the Indian dead.

The dead man proved to be a Wyandot youth barely past puberty who was carrying a small string of white wampum, a sign that he had a message to deliver, evidently one of peace or conciliation. George Croghan was summoned and became furious at what had occurred. The dead youth was unfamiliar to him, but the fact that he had been killed while bearing such a message—now never to be delivered—had ominous portent.

The Indian agent went to Fort Pitt at once and demanded that Meason be arrested. With so many witnesses to the killing, Connolly had no choice but to comply, and, though most of his militia were presently off on patrol, he sent a small squad and had Meason arrested, placed in irons and locked in the guardhouse. Word of it spread throughout Pittsburgh and, even though no one had any great love for the uncouth and loudmouthed frontiersman, a sense of outrage bloomed that a white man had actually been jailed for killing an Indian.

A mob quickly formed and, while Connolly restrained his own men from making what he termed "futile resistance," forced their way into Fort Pitt, broke the guardhouse lock and knocked off the irons that shackled Meason. The fugitive immediately left Pittsburgh and returned to his claim on Buffalo Creek, six miles from Catfish Camp.[212]

This very same day, more than 100 miles to the southeast, in the vicinity of

Moorefield on the South Branch Potomac, four other friendly Indians—three men and a boy—who were well known in the area, were coldly gunned down by Nicholas Harpold and Henry Judah who, instead of being punished for the murders, were elevated by their fellow settlers to near heroic status.

[May 17, 1774 — Tuesday]

In the dimness of the council house at Wapatomica, close to 30 chiefs and subchiefs had assembled, representing the Shawnees and Delawares, Wyandots and Mingoes. Pucksinwah was there, as was Talgayeeta and a number of his followers. For several hours various chiefs had spoken, each relating his own experience with the current rash of outrages being perpetrated against them by the *Shemanese*. All had been hurt in one way or another, though none so severely as Talgayeeta, who had not yet risen to speak.

Though the individual stories varied, the litanies were similar: They had been injured through unprovoked attacks that had also taken many lives; yet they had also received messages from their friends Croghan, McKee, Elliott, Gibson and others among the whites, begging them please not to make war against the whites, assuring them that the recent acts of violence had been undertaken by irresponsible individuals, not the government, and that those individuals would be punished. Would they please come to Fort Pitt under the mantle of peace, their safety guaranteed, and try to reach an accommodation rather than dash their nations into war with a very deadly foe?

This was the question they asked themselves now, and the answer seemed to lie in the enormously influential Talgayeeta. It was to him that Pucksinwah directed the last of the general remarks of the chiefs.

"We have all been provoked beyond what any of us should bear. We Shawnees have lost good people, as have the Wyandots and Lenni Lenape, and certainly the followers of Talgayeeta. Now we have been asked to come to Fort Pitt to try to settle all this. The Shawnees and our neighbors have agreed to try, and we are on our way there now. Talgayeeta," he directed his gaze to him, "not long ago I came to you and asked you to help us make war on the *Shemanese,* to drive them back from our lands. Now we have turned around and wish to try for the peace that is offered, and we ask you to lay aside the harm that has been done to you and join us. What has occurred may yet be repaired. Certain bad *Shemanese* have killed our people, and, in retaliation, some of the Mingoes apart from Talgayeeta have killed some of the white traders and forced the others into hiding. These are bad things, but the harm can be undone if there is goodwill in the hearts on both sides. The harm that will be done to our tribes by a full war with these whites could well become a blow from which we may never recover. Talgayeeta, tell us what is in your heart."

As Talgayeeta rose, his face etched with recent suffering, a deep hush fell over the assemblage. He stood silently for a time and then spoke softly, yet with utter implacability. "My heart grieves for the losses that have been inflicted upon you here. I would not lead you into a war that would do you even greater harm. But I and those Mingoes who look to me tell you now that the injury that has been done us is beyond accommodation; it cries upon me and upon the Mingoes for vengeance. I have vowed to take that vengeance and will do so before ever again my hatchet is grounded. A few of the Mingoes, as you have said, have already killed some of the traders and badly frightened others, but the *Shemanese* have not yet begun to feel the vengeance of Talgayeeta. I have for a time put it off, promising to listen in this council before acting. I have listened. What I have heard only makes me the more certain that the vow must be carried out. I have said. I will say no more."

Pucksinwah's reply was level, firm: "We here respect what Talgayeeta has said, and from the injury done him, we cannot find fault in his vow. But we have given our promise to talk with Croghan at Fort Pitt. If accommodation can be reached, we will lend ourselves to it, but not to the detriment of our Mingo friends. And if accommodation cannot be reached, then we, too, will raise our hatchets in war."

[May 18, 1774 — Wednesday]

John Gibson was not a particularly large man, but he was tough, smart and well experienced, having made a very good living in the hazardous Indian trade for the past 15 years. He rarely became angry, but when he did, he was a particularly dangerous man because his anger was well controlled.

Today, on Redstone Creek, the unrelenting fury that had seethed within him for nearly three weeks had finally become focused. Having tied the reins of his horse to the rail nailed to a pair of posts, he stepped up to the cabin door and knocked loudly. It was opened by a man he did not recognize, who gazed at him inquiringly.

"I'm looking for Michael Cresap," Gibson said. "I was told I'd find him here."

"Who're you?" the man asked suspiciously. He seemed ready to say more, but another man, shorter, more stockily built and with sandy red hair, appeared at the doorway, and the first man stepped back a little to give him room.

"I'm Michael Cresap," he said. "You look familiar, but if we've met, I've forgotten your name."

"You'll never forget it again, you son of a bitch!" Gibson reached forward before Cresap could react, bunched the front of the Irishman's blouse in his fist and jerked him out into the clearing before the cabin. Cresap whirled, off balance, and fell heavily but immediately came to his feet in a half crouch, hands clenched.

The trader stepped closer and scowled at him. "The name's Gibson," he said. "John Gibson. And you're the bastard who killed my wife and baby." His fist shot out and caught Cresap on the right side of his forehead, sending him tumbling, and once again the stocky man came to his feet, shaking his head to clear his vision, then started to circle as he looked for an opening, realizing now what this was all about.

"Yeah. I know you—you're the trader whose squaw got killed," he said. "Well, dammit, I had nothing to do with that. It was Greathouse and his boys."

"They did the killing," Gibson agreed. "*You* lighted their fires." He launched himself at Cresap and for the third time bowled him over, the two of them grappling and rolling in the dirt, punching one another. Cresap had been in brawls before and usually held his own rather well, but this time he was no match for his adversary; if any of his own blows landed, they had little effect. Gibson pummeled him unmercifully, and when at last Cresap could no longer stagger to his feet, the trader squatted beside him, gripped his hair and jerked his head around so they were face to face.

"I'll say this only once, Cresap." Gibson's voice was deadly with menace. "Get the hell out of this country and don't come back. If I see you again, I'll kill you."

He shoved the man from him and rose, stared down at him a moment and then walked to his horse. The first man was still at the cabin door but was now holding a rifle. Gibson stared at him, and after a few seconds the man shook his head faintly and set the gun aside. Without another word, the trader mounted his horse and rode away.

Cresap came slowly to his senses, his face bloodied and one eye already swollen to a mere slit. He realized full well how close he had come to death. Within an hour he was on his own horse, heading southeast on Braddock's Road toward Fort Cumberland and beyond.

[*M a y   2 0 ,   1 7 7 4 — F r i d a y*]

Jack Ryan's luck was still holding; he saw the Indians before they saw him. A pair of warriors traveling one behind the other on the faint path along the Cheat River began crossing a forest clearing moments before he would have entered that same clearing from the other direction. He quickly moved his horse behind a screen of brush and tied it, then ran with his rifle to a gnarled old oak beside the path. Peering out cautiously, he had a clear view of the two men approaching. The Indians were walking rapidly, talking as they did so and occasionally laughing. Ryan took careful aim at the center of the first man's chest, hoping the bullet would pass through him and hit the second man as well. It didn't happen. The ball smashed into the first man's chest and tore through his heart, then struck his spine and broke it but lodged there. The second Indian leaped away, raced back into the woods from which they had emerged and disappeared before Ryan could reload. The white man remained in place, even after reloading, until, some five minutes later he saw the fleeing Indian swimming rapidly across the Cheat River far upstream and well out of range. He watched until the man emerged from the river and ran into the woods on the opposite side. Then, congratulating himself as being some fine Injen hunter, he went to the body, took all the dead man had that was worthwhile, scalped him and continued on his way.

[*M a y   2 1 ,   1 7 7 4 — S a t u r d a y*]

The delegation of eight Shawnees led into Pittsburgh by Hokolesqua and Pucksinwah were an impressive sight as they boldly rode their horses through the frontier town.

In addition to the Shawnee principal chief and its war chief, the party included Silverheels, younger brother of Hokolesqua. He could speak English quite as well as Pucksinwah and had long been employed as guide by the trading firm of Baynton, Wharton and Morgan, but he was also frequently named to attend councils such as the one they were heading for now. With them as well was Nonhelema, the sister of Hokolesqua and Silverheels. Well over six feet tall and quite well proportioned, she was an impressive woman who had often accompanied war parties in the past and fought with the strength and ability of the most seasoned warrior. Because of her great size and skill in battle, she had long ago been dubbed by the whites as The Grenadier Squaw. Silverheels and Nonhelema were flanking Pucksinwah as they rode.

The remaining four members of the Shawnee party included Outhowwa Shokka—Yellow Hawk—who was chief of the village of Chalahgawtha, where Paint Creek empties into the Scioto River, and his wife, a sturdy woman named Sheshepukwawala—Duck Eggs—rode beside him.[213] The final two members of the delegation were young men. One was Elinipsico, son of Hokolesqua and nephew of Silverheels and Nonhelema; the other was Blue Jacket, adopted son of Pucksinwah.[214]

An aura of hatred emanated from the scores of men who lined the wide dirt road leading to Fort Pitt, all of them armed and made all the more dangerous by the fear resident in their minds, but the delegation paid little attention to them. The Indians were preceded by five traders and followed by five others. Pucksinwah found it ironic that his delegation, having rescued William Butler and these other traders on the Muskingum, should here be finding the situation reversed and their safety in the hands of those they had helped.

They knew William Butler well and respected him as a trader who had always dealt fairly with the Shawnees. When word had reached them at Wapatomica from Delaware Chief White Eyes that this trader and a number of his friends were in jeopardy and he was hiding them from the Mingoes, they at once detoured the short distance to White Eyes' Town, hardly a mile from the Forks of the Muskingum, and met with the chief. White Eyes told them several traders had already been killed and others were presently hiding in the Moravian missions that had been established on the Tuscarawas River.[215]

The situation was very tense, White Eyes had told them, adding that even he had been threatened if he interfered further—a warning that stemmed from the most recent incident. It had begun several days ago when the trader Richard Jones and two of his men, unaware of what had occurred at Baker's Bottom, were trading among the smaller Muskingum villages near Goschachgunk. Those three had been warned by a Delaware woman that the Mingoes had gone on the warpath and were killing every trader they encountered and they would die as well if they ran into those Mingoes. She had then pointed out a little-used path that, if followed, would perhaps allow them to reach Fort Pitt safely.

The Jones party, White Eyes went on, had started out on that path, but it was difficult traveling, and as they passed a trail in much better condition, one of his men decided to go that way. He had traveled only a short distance before he walked into a party of 15 ranging Mingoes, who instantly killed and scalped him and then chopped his body into pieces. White Eyes said that shortly afterward he had come by and found the gruesome scene and had gathered up the body pieces and buried them. The next day, however, the Mingoes had returned that way and, finding the body buried, dug it up and again scattered the pieces. White Eyes had watched this from hiding, and when they left, he gathered up the pieces a second time and reburied them. He, in turn, was observed, and later the Mingo party came to his town and threatened him, saying they would treat in like manner every trader they encountered, and if White Eyes interfered again in any way, his lot would be the same.

It was then, White Eyes told them, that he had quickly sent out parties to locate whatever traders they could and bring them in safety to his town, where he would hide them until they could be escorted to Pittsburgh. Though they did not find Jones and his remaining man, they did locate traders William Butler, William Wood and eight of their men and brought them to White Eyes' Town. Now an opportunity was at hand, if Hokolesqua's delegation would act as escort, to get them away safely.

Hokolesqua had readily agreed, and they had reached Pittsburgh, only to find that the men they had rescued had now themselves become the protectors and were escorting the Shawnees toward Fort Pitt, where the council was to be held. Butler sent a rider ahead to seek out George Croghan or Alexander McKee and get their assistance, and McKee, as soon as the situation was explained, hastened to Maj. Connolly and requested a body of militia be sent out to protect the delegation. Connolly refused to do so, called McKee an Indian lover, threatened him and his family and ordered him away.[216]

Now, as the delegation approached the main gate of the fort, the body of horsemen paused. Butler shook hands with Hokolesqua and Pucksinwah and, on behalf of the traders, thanked the Shawnees for their help. Then he led his traders away toward the Baynton, Wharton and Morgan post on the other side of town. Their departure was a bit premature. The delegation continued its short ride to the gate, keeping a close eye on the large cluster of ugly-tempered men who were gathered near the portal. No sooner had the riders stopped and dismounted at Hokolesqua's command than someone among the whites yelled an order, and the mob rushed upon them. A wild melee broke out that ceased only when George Croghan rushed up, brandishing a pistol in each hand and firing one into the air.

"Dammit, stop!" he shouted, white with anger. "Get away from these people. I'll shoot the next man who makes any move to harm them."

No one doubted the seriousness of his threat, and the whites fell back, muttering, but the damage had been done. Silverheels lay on the ground gasping past frothy red bubbles. Blood was flowing profusely from two knife wounds, one in his right shoulder, the other in his chest. Sheshepukwawala was on her knees beside him, already stuffing the chest wound with buzzard down from her pouch to staunch the bleeding. Nonhelema, Elinipsico and Blue Jacket, tomahawks in hand, crouched beside them, ready to fend off further attack. Pucksinwah and Outhowwa Shokka, also with drawn tomahawks, stood ready to protect Hokolesqua.

Now, too late, a squad of militia ran up and dispersed the crowd. Croghan ordered that Silverheels be carried to the post surgeon for treatment and apologized profusely to Hokolesqua as this was done. The surgeon dug out the blood-saturated buzzard down from the chest wound, cleansed and bandaged both wounds and announced that though the chest injury was serious, it would not likely be fatal provided the man was well cared for. McKee offered to take the delegation to the quarters that had been prepared for them, but Hokolesqua refused. His expression set in grim lines, he said they would not stay and that now there could be no further talk of peace.

Croghan and McKee immediately confronted Connolly and demanded that he order a company of militia to escort the delegation back to the mouth of Cross Creek, where they would cross the Ohio to Mingo Bottom on their way home. The canny Connolly readily agreed, knowing others would see it as a humanitarian gesture that would help absolve him of any complicity in what had occurred. It mollified Croghan but did not in the least reduce his apprehension for what now lay ahead: The final hope of averting a general war had just been lost.

[May 23, 1774—Monday]

The express messengers to the Virginia governor from Maj. John Connolly and Capt. William Crawford reached Williamsburg within hours of each other and informed Lord Dunmore what had occurred on the Ohio—the attacks by Cresap's party, the massacre perpetrated by the Greathouse party and the ensuing mass exodus of the majority of the settlers.

Other messengers dispatched from the frontier eastward to Philadelphia, Baltimore and New York were also arriving at their destinations about this same time. When the word spread, both in Virginia and elsewhere, a mantle of shock settled over the populace at the enormity of the barbaric acts perpetrated by the whites against the Indians on the basis of unfounded rumors. A wave of revulsion grew in particular over the brutal massacre that had occurred at Baker's Bottom, and recriminations were immediately raised. Thomas Jefferson labeled the deed inhuman and indecent; Benjamin Franklin portrayed it as uncivilized butchery without precedent, even among the savage tribes. Charles Lee called it a black, impious piece of work, and even Lord Dunmore admitted that the affair at Baker's Bottom was marked with an extraordinary degree of cruelty and inhumanity.[217]

Within hours after the arrival of the messengers in Williamsburg, all of the Virginia capital was abuzz with the news, and by day's end, an emergency session of the Virginia Assembly called by Dunmore had approved a war plan that he placed before them. There were those who remarked that Dunmore had not seemed surprised by the news from the frontier and, in fact, had seemed almost to be holding himself in readiness for it; yet no one thought to question how the governor could have so swiftly devised such a detailed war plan against the Indians.

The war plan called for Dunmore's surveyor friend, Angus McDonald, who had been a major during the French and Indian War, to be immediately given a brevet commission as colonel and empowered to repair at once to Fort Pitt, there expeditiously to raise a force of 400 militia and immediately lead them into Ohio against the Delaware and Wyandot towns at the Forks of the Muskingum River and particularly against the adjacent Shawnee capital, Wapatomica.

In the meanwhile, the plan continued, throughout the remainder of the summer, a much larger army of 3,000 men would be formed in two wings of 1,500 each. The southern wing, to be led by Gen. Andrew Lewis, would assemble by late August at Camp Union in the Greenbrier Valley and descend that river, the New River and the Kanawha to the rendezvous site at the point where the Kanawha empties into the Ohio, arriving there about October 1. The northern wing would be raised by Dunmore himself in the tidewater and piedmont areas of Virginia and be marched to Fort Pitt. There, Maj. Connolly—who was now being elevated to the temporary rank of colonel—would turn over to Dunmore the men he had raised on the frontier. From that place they would descend the Ohio in boats to Wheeling and, subsequently, to the mouth of the Kanawha, to rendezvous there with the Lewis force about the first of October. At that point Gov. Dunmore, now as general and commander-in-chief, would lead the combined force across the Ohio in the boats he had brought down. They would then march overland to the Shawnee villages on the Scioto, the object being to destroy them all and engage in combat any and all forces of Indians directed against them.

Proclamations and announcements were issued immediately and posted in every public place throughout Pennsylvania and Virginia, ordering all able-bodied men to assemble as soon as possible at Fort Pitt or Camp Union to become part of the armies being formed. There was little doubt that the multitude of frontiersmen, settlers, surveyors, farmers and ordinary citizens who had longed for the opportunity to finally drive the Indians back and open those lands for settlement and development in safety would flock by the hundreds in response to this call.

Dunmore also put other projects into motion. The large teams of surveyors he had sent to Kentucky very early in the year—those under James Harrod, Hancock Taylor, John Floyd and others—were presently surveying and claiming lands at the Falls of the Ohio and in the Kentucky interior from there. These parties had to be warned to clear out before the armies started their march. Two men of proven woodland ability were asked to undertake the dangerous assignment of carrying the warning to them, and they accepted without hesitation. One was a large German man from Richmond named Michael Stoner, who had a reputation for successfully accomplishing any task assigned to him. He would descend the Ohio on his mission. The other was the man who probably knew Kentucky better than any other white man at this time and who would head for the same area overland from southern Virginia, through the Cumberland Gap—Daniel Boone.[218]

[J u l y   1 1 ,   1 7 7 4 — M o n d a y]

Sir William Johnson, undoubtedly the white man most influential with the Indians in America, gazed at the nearly 3,000 tribesmen who had assembled here at his home in the Mohawk Valley of New York. These delegates represented some 130,000 Indians, and what went on here would affect them all. Soon the Grand Council would begin, and he was discouraged, expecting it would not go well.

For the past 37 of his 59 years, Johnson had been closely associated with the

Planned March of Dunmore and Lewis
Against the Scioto Villages,
Autumn 1774

Indians—especially with the Iroquois League—and had worked hard against tremendous odds to try to protect their rights. Yet even now, with revolutionary talk rampant among the colonies, he still had no sure idea what would happen to them if war broke out between England and her colonies. He was gloomily convinced that whichever side might win such a contest, it boded no good for the native inhabitants. He was unalterably opposed to the rebellious fever rising in this country, and his job —and the reason why all these tribal representatives were here today—was to convince the Indians that it would be in their own best interests to support the King if war became reality.

He ordered that refreshments be provided to the Indians on hand, along with a small quantity of liquor to warm their bellies and pipe tobacco to soothe their minds. He was very tired, and that would give him time to rest a bit before the council began. He drank a small cup of wine and, with a long sigh, sat down in a comfortable elbow chair. He looked around at the gathering of Indians for a moment and smiled faintly, then leaned his head back and closed his eyes.

And then he quietly died.

[July 20, 1774 — Wednesday]

There was no longer any need for John Connolly or anyone else to concoct stories of Indian attacks upon whites. Since shortly after the attack on the Shawnee delegation at Pittsburgh, raiding parties had spread throughout the frontier and were fiercely descending upon settlements and isolated cabins, burning, killing and scalping. Most of the raids were being carried out by the Mingoes, and many of these by Talgayeeta himself, accompanied by a cordon of eight of his most skilled warriors.

The exodus of so many settlers to the Monongahela and Cheat river valleys had not availed them much, since quite a few of the attacks were occurring in areas well away from the Ohio River itself. Walter Kelly and his family of five, who thought themselves safe in their little settlement far up the Kanawha at the mouth of Kelly's Creek, were attacked and wiped out, and their slave girl and an indentured Scots boy were taken captive, causing William Morris shortly afterward to build Fort Morris on the site to protect other settlers in the area; another family of nine was destroyed on the Monongahela a short distance from the mouth of Dunkard Creek; a Redstone man who went out in the morning to find the horses he had hobbled the evening before had had his head cut off and all the horses taken; yet another was killed and scalped within sight of Redstone Old Fort; two other men east of Laurel Hill, where it was believed no attacks would occur, were similarly shot down and scalped, and when a small force was raised to pursue them, the Indians had melted away into the forest without trace; the John Flinn family of four was slain in their cabin at the mouth of Cabin Creek, and then, after the scalps were taken and the place plundered, the house was burned over their bodies.

Experience in woodsmanship seemed to serve but little. One of the most experienced of fur traders, David Connor, fell beneath the tomahawk of Talgayeeta himself, as did Coleman Brown at Simpson Creek. The McKinzie cabin on the Kanawha was hit while Moredock McKinzie and his eldest son were away; his younger son and wife were killed, and his two daughters, Margaret and Elizabeth, aged 12 and 10 respectively, were captured.[219]

Daniel Boone and Michael Stoner had been successful in reaching and warning the surveying parties under Hancock Taylor at the Falls of the Ohio and James Harrod well in the Kentucky interior, where he was establishing the first permanent white settlement, Harrodsburg.[220] Those parties immediately began their return, but both groups were attacked; Hancock Taylor was killed and scalped near the Falls, and one of the surveyors laying out Harrodsburg, Jared Cowan, was similarly killed and scalped near that place.

A flurry of fort-building was now occurring everywhere on the frontier but most particularly east of the Monongahela. On June 8, after fortifying his cabin at Spring Garden on the Youghiogheny, William Shepherd wrote to Col. Washington:

> *Our whole country is in forts, what is left; but the major part is gone over the mountain. With much ado I have prevailed on about a dozen families to join me in building a fort over against my house, which has been accomplished with much difficulty and a considerable expense to me. Valentine Crawford has built another at the same rate. It was with great difficulty that any could be prevailed upon to stay, such was the panic that seized the people. If something is not done, I am much afraid the whole country must fall into the hands of the enemy. The Delawares seem to be on our side as yet, but on them there is not much dependence. I believe an Indian war is unavoidable. I have been on a scouting party as low as Grave Creek . . . but could see no signs of any parties. However, as soon as I returned, a party crossed the river that did mischief. Fort Pitt is blockaded, and the inhabitants of the town are picketing it in. They have about one hundred men fit for arms in town and fort, which I do not think sufficient to protect those places.*

Shortly after this, David Shepherd, who had moved to the crossings of the Youghiogheny, built a small fortification there and called it Shepherd's Fort.[221] Connolly was still calling for men to assemble at Fort Pitt, and many had answered; enough that, in preparation for the campaign into Ohio ready to be launched by Col. Angus McDonald, he dispatched William Crawford at the head of 200 men to Wheeling to build a fort there and name it Fort Fincastle.

Oddly enough, in the midst of the exodus of settlers, there were not only a large number who doggedly stayed on their claims but others who incredibly continued to come into the frontier area and establish themselves. Not only did William Morris build his fort where the Kelly family had been killed, two of his brothers settled on tributaries of the Gauley River—Leonard at the mouth of Slaughter Creek, Henry on Peters' Creek. Even in the high danger area of Wheeling, William Linn was undaunted and set about building a cabin on the claim he had bought from Ebenezer Zane, just over two miles up from the mouth of Wheeling Creek.

The intrepid Rebecca Martin, sister of the Tomlinson brothers, refused to leave their cabin on the Grave Creek Flats. Today, only two months after the frightening experience of stepping on the body of the dead Indian in the river, she had another experience no less harrowing and infinitely more dangerous. Joe and Jim had gone to

Fort Pitt to join in the McDonald campaign, and Sam would have gone as well, had he not been temporarily lamed in a fall down a ravine.

This morning at sunrise, Sam had hobbled out to the cornfield a few hundred yards distant to do some hoeing, taking one of his rifles with him and leaving the other, loaded and primed, hanging on its hooks over the fireplace for Rebecca, should she need it. No more than a half-hour later, she was busy building a fire in that fireplace and was on her hands and knees, blowing at the coals to get the flames going better. Hearing a creaking of the floorboards behind her, she thought it was Samuel and turned, but her smile vanished. A tall Shawnee warrior clad only in moccasins and breechclout, with raised tomahawk in hand, stood within arm's length. She stifled a gasp as he made a sign with his free hand for her to remain silent. She remained outwardly calm, her eyes fixed on the threatening tomahawk and ready to lunge to the side if it started to descend. They stood this way for a long moment, and then the Shawnee, obviously nervous and fearing someone would enter, let his eyes flick around the cabin. When he saw the rifle over the mantel, he took a step away from her and lifted it from its hooks, backed to the cabin door, took a quick look outside for danger and then leaped out and was gone.

A deep shudder ran through Rebecca, and she came unsteadily to her feet. She glanced at the empty hooks over the fireplace and shook her head in exasperation; with the gun gone, she would have no choice but to tell Samuel what had happened.

[A u g u s t   2 2 ,   1 7 7 4 — M o n d a y]

The expedition led by Col. Angus McDonald against the Shawnees at Wapatomica turned out to be a great disappointment to all the whites on the frontier.

For many weeks during the early summer, men had gathered at Fort Pitt to take part in the campaign, their hopes high that they would resoundingly defeat the Indians and force them so far away into the northwestern wilderness that the Ohio River Valley would become safe for their continued claiming and development. It hadn't turned out quite that way.

In early July, McDonald had arrived at Fort Pitt with a few hundred men and found enough others gathered there to swell his force to nearly 400. Among the men on hand were Simon Kenton, George Rogers Clark, William Linn, Jake Drennon, John Hardin, the Greathouse brothers, the Tomlinsons and McCullochs and Zanes. Simon Girty was there as well, with the rank of ensign, and he and Kenton met and got along so well together that they made an oath between themselves of perpetual friendship. Girty had only shortly before been released from the guardhouse in Fort Pitt, where he had been temporarily incarcerated by newly promoted brevet Col. Connolly for voicing sentiments that were in sympathy to the plight of the Indians.

Cols. McDonald and Connolly quickly got the men organized into companies, after which McDonald left Connolly in charge of a small garrison at Fort Pitt and marched the majority to Wheeling, arriving there on July 24. Capt. William Crawford's advance force of 200 men was at that time just putting the finishing touches to Fort Fincastle, which enclosed about three-quarters of an acre, and there were about

30 settlers' cabins in the cleared land between the fort and the forested bluffs to the east. Jonathan Zane, Thomas and Joseph Nicholson and Tady Kelly were commissioned to guide the army through 90 miles of wilderness to Wapatomica. A majority of Crawford's force joined McDonald for the march into the Ohio country, with Crawford and the remainder left behind as a garrison for the new fort.[222]

A variety of boats had been brought down from Pittsburgh, and the army, having marched down to the mouth of Fish Creek, 23 miles below Wheeling, was ferried across the Ohio River. Forming on the other side near Captina Creek, they moved overland toward the Shawnee capital village of Wapatomica at the Forks of the Muskingum. They encountered no Indians until within just a couple of miles of the Forks, when they were ambushed by 50 warriors. Col. McDonald, instead of taking the lead with his force, had appointed Capt. George Rogers Clark to that position, while he remained well toward the rear and, much to the discomfiture of his troops, grew increasingly unsure of himself. When the ambush broke out at the head of the line, Angus McDonald had literally dived to safety behind a log and cowered there until the attackers were driven off. The fight was very brief; two militia men had been killed in the first firing and eight others slightly wounded, including Capt. John Hardin, who was nicked by a ball in the knee, and William Linn, who took a ball in the left shoulder.[223] Simon Girty became the object of cheers when he pulled off a spectacular long shot of well over 150 yards, badly wounding one of the Shawnees who had imprudently shown himself, the only known casualty among the attackers. Within minutes the skirmish was all over.

When the army arrived at the Forks of the Muskingum a short time later, they found Wapatomica abandoned and most of the wegiwas and cabins on fire. Those not already burning were set afire at McDonald's orders. The Shawnees had moved their capital much deeper into the interior, and no one was quite sure where, but it was rumored that it would be reestablished on the headwaters of the Mad River, 100 miles due west. Announcing this to be a great victory, McDonald quickly turned his army around and now, eager to be in front, led them back to Wheeling. Respect for the commander had disintegrated, however, and he seethed with fury when, in their camps, a voice would call out of the darkness on one side, "Who hid behind the log?" and 100 voices or more would immediately thunder in chorus, "The colonel!" It was about that time when Capt. George Rogers Clark won the respect of the men by soundly thrashing a burly hare-lipped private named Strother Crawford, who was advocating outright rebellion and mass desertion in the face of Col. McDonald's cowardice.

Nothing else untoward occurred on the march back to Wheeling and, with a full company of men left behind to garrison Fort Fincastle at Wheeling, McDonald continued the march to Fort Pitt, arriving here today. Everyone was relieved to find that Lord Dunmore was on the march with his force and should be arriving soon to begin his campaign against the Shawnee villages on the Scioto. Similarly, Gen. Andrew Lewis was ready to begin his march down the New and Kanawha rivers to the rendezvous at the mouth of the Kanawha. When these two forces met, they would merge into a powerful army of some 3,000 men. With that in the offing, the militia bivouacked at Fort Pitt to wait and join the expedition.

[*A u g u s t   2 8 ,   1 7 7 4 — S u n d a y*]

The Shawnees had long been considering a new site for their capital village of Wapatomica—one that would be well removed from any likelihood of attack from the whites. For several years they had been considering an isolated site on the upper Mad River some four miles above the village of Mackachack, principal village of the Maykujay sept of the tribe under Chief Moluntha, and just over two miles downstream from the Wyandot village called Tarhe's Town. Now, having been forced by McDonald's army to abandon Wapatomica at the Forks of the Muskingum—the town of Kikusgowlowa, chief of the Thawegila sept—they had wasted no time coming to this new site and getting themselves established. Wegiwas were quickly erected, and a large log council house was begun. With over 100 warriors working at the task, plus twice that many women and children, the work went swiftly. Though construction was not yet completed, today Kikusgowlowa opened the first council held in the new *msi-kah-mi-qui*—council house.[224]

The meeting was brief. Their little victory over the McDonald force had not left them with any illusions that their trouble with the whites was over. Spies were watching the two armies—under Dunmore and Lewis—now being readied to come against the Scioto towns, and for this reason Wapatomica had not been reestablished in their vicinity. McDonald's invasion had clearly shown just how vulnerable the villages on the Muskingum and Scioto were to attack from the *Shemanese*. For that reason, a large section of the Thawegila sept had decided they wanted no more war and, despite the scorn of Kikusgowlowa and the rest of the tribe for such weakness, left their Ohio friends and kin and went south to live again among the Creeks.[225]

The main item of business at today's council was to select and dispatch runners to the various allied tribes. Within an hour they were on their way to inform those allies of the relocation of Wapatomica and that the time was now at hand for them to live up to their promises previously made: They were to raise parties of warriors and send them to join with the Shawnees as soon as possible at Chalahgawtha on the Scioto. There the battle plans would be decided upon and a march made against the threatening armies of *Shemanese,* who were soon to assemble at the mouth of the Kanawha.

And nearby, in the new wegiwas that had been set up, Shawnee mothers, who used to quiet their children by invoking the traditional superstition that owls would come to carry noisy children away, were now employing a new phrase to silence crying babies and rowdy toddlers: "Hush now, or Cresap and Greathouse will come to get you, for they both have ears like wolves!"

[*S e p t e m b e r   5 ,   1 7 7 4 — M o n d a y*]

Today the potential revolution moved a large step closer to reality. The First Continental Congress assembled in Philadelphia, with all the American colonies represented except Georgia. They elected Peyton Randolph of Virginia as president and set forth the framework of a Declaration of Rights and Grievances to present to George III. Part of their resolutions included plans to import nothing further from Great Britain after December 1 and to export nothing to them unless their grievances were redressed. They agreed to resist restrictive taxation and other obnoxious measures employed by the King against them and to raise forces of minutemen to actively resist coercion. They also resolved to cease all official intercourse with England.

George Washington was among the Virginia delegates but not entirely in line with their desire for independence from the Crown.[226] He described as repugnant the idea of a revolutionary war and added: "I abhor the idea of American independence. . . . No thinking man in all of North America desires independence."

He couldn't have been more wrong.

[S e p t e m b e r   3 0 ,   1 7 7 4 — F r i d a y]

A rousing cheer erupted from more than 800 throats as the army of Gen. Andrew Lewis emerged from the trees and saw, stretched out before them, the broad expanse of the Ohio River. For 19 days they had been on the move, and all were exhausted from the toil of marching 165 miles through the wilderness to this point. Where possible, and to avoid the deep ravines and difficult creek crossings near the main rivers, they had followed the old Indian paths along the base of the hills, traveling by way of Muddy Creek, Keenys Knobs, Rich Creek, the Gauley Valley, Twentymile Creek, Bell Creek, Kelly's Creek and then finally the Kanawha itself. That latter stream, as they had followed it, seemed very large and yet now, only a short distance ahead to the left of the large triangular bottom being called Point Pleasant, the glistening clear waters merged with the slightly murkier waters of a river easily three times larger.

For by far the majority of these men, this was their first view of the great Ohio, the river called Spaylaywitheepi by the people they were prepared to destroy. Some 400 yards across its smoothly rolling surface loomed the Ohio shoreline, stretched out in a wide bottom there but, beyond, rising into hills 300 feet above the river level.

They had hoped, all of them, that Dunmore's army would be there awaiting them, but it was immediately apparent that they had arrived first. Once again a sense of apprehension rose in many; was this, perhaps, confirmation of the rumors that Dunmore was deliberately setting them up for disaster?

The stories had been prevalent among the men as they first began assembling at Camp Union on the Greenbrier during the final days of August. It was clear to all that Lord Dunmore, both as Governor of Virginia Colony and as a private citizen devoted to the King, deplored the rising revolutionary sentiment, and his previous unprecedented actions of arbitrarily abolishing the right of assembly, of curbing free speech and of even dissolving the Virginia Assembly clearly indicated he would go to almost any length to harass and humiliate the colonists. Would it not be the ultimate humiliation to put them into the position of suffering a defeat at the hands of half-naked savages armed with knives and bows and war clubs? And if that occurred, would not other colonists who might have been leaning toward the revolutionary sentiment be inclined to draw back and lean instead toward continued colonialism?[227]

The army of men drawn largely from Botetourt, Fincastle and Augusta counties had grown quickly at Camp Union under the overall command of Gen. Andrew Lewis, who had commanded regular army troops under Gen. Braddock during the French and Indian War but who had never before commanded an army of militia. By the end of the first week of September, the full complement of 1,100 men had assembled and the army was formed into its various regiments and companies. Nearly all the young volunteers were good hunters and woodsmen but without experience in warfare.

The commander's brother, Col. Charles Lewis, headed the Augusta Regiment, consisting of eight companies whose captains were Benjamin Harrison, Samuel Wilson, John Dickinson, Joseph Haynes, Alexander McClannahan, William Paul, George Mathews and John Lewis, the latter a nephew of Andrew and Charles Lewis. Capt. Mathews's company boasted of having no man under six feet in height and most of them at least two inches taller than that.

The Botetourt Regiment was under command of Col. William Fleming and consisted of seven companies under Capts. Robert McClannahan, Matthew Arbuckle, James Ward, John Murray, James Robertson, John Stewart and another John Lewis, the latter being the son of the commanding general.[228]

Col. William Christian was named to command the division made up of three independent Fincastle County companies under Capts. John Herbert of New River, Evan Shelby of Holston River and William Russell of Clinch River, plus another independent company from Bedford County under Capt. Thomas Buford and a company of scouts and spies under Capt. John Draper of Draper's Valley. Still trying to bring his own command up to regimental strength, Christian took leave to return to Fincastle County to recruit more men.

Finally, as something of a fly in the ointment, an independent company of 70 men had been raised in Culpeper County by Col. John Field, who was miffed that he had not only been passed over for full command of this southern army but had not even received a regimental command, which he felt he deserved more than any of the other field officers.

Lt. Daniel Boone was on hand also, having returned from warning the Kentucky surveyors. He and Michael Stoner had been gone 61 days and covered more than 800 miles on the dangerous mission. He was promoted to captain, and though it was thought he would certainly be placed in command of a company, he was instead ordered to stay behind in command of three garrisons on this frontier—Camp Union and Donnelly's Fort on the Greenbrier and Jarrett's Fort where Wolf Creek empties into the New River. Boone was soon also given command of Moore's Fort, located at Castle's Woods in the Clinch Valley, a remote post where three of his men had already been killed and scalped by Talgayeeta within sight of the fort.

The march began on Sunday, September 11, guided by Capt. Matthew Arbuckle, who had been to the Ohio several times on claiming expeditions. Despite a certain military bearing to the force, it had a ragtag appearance at best. No man in the entire army was wearing a uniform, although Col. Charles Lewis had brought along his scarlet coat to wear on special occasions. All others were clad in linsey-woolsey and leathers of wide variation and little distinction. No wagons could be used, so everything was being carried either in backpacks or on packhorses. The independent regiment commanded by Col. William Christian did not start with the main army. He had not yet returned with the additional men he had set out to raise in Fincastle County, and so orders were left for him to immediately follow with his full force upon his return. In the meanwhile, Lewis's army had marched 12 miles on the first day, which was respectable, considering the terrain. Many days followed when they marched far less. Every step of the way the path had to be improved to allow passage not only for the packhorses but also for the small herd of beef cattle being herded as their meat supply. There were also many small difficulties, and one major tragedy right at the start.

Col. Field, still irked at being passed over for a substantial command, decided he would march his company of 70 men by a different route from that taken by the main army. Having twice before been downriver as far as the Kelly's Creek Settlement, he felt the route he was taking would be faster and safer. Faster it may have been; safer it was not.

On the third day two privates named Edward Clay and John Coward strayed from the main body of troops to hunt deer at a creek bottom called the Little Meadows. Unbeknownst to them, a pair of Mingoes had been spying on the detachment's movements, and the privates accidentally stumbled into them. Clay was somewhat ahead when one of the Indians rose from behind a log and shot him dead. When the warrior raced out to scalp his victim, he was himself shot and killed by Pvt. Coward. The second Mingo fled, leaving behind a bundle of ropes, which led the commander to conclude that their intent had been to steal some of the packhorses. This incident prompted Col. Field to rejoin the main army, and the full force traveled the remainder of the way together.

Nothing else untoward occurred during the rest of the march. When they reached the mouth of Elk River, they paused to build canoes with which to float the heavier supplies the remaining distance to Point Pleasant.[229] The boats were quickly built and loaded, and the remainder of the army continued down the east shoreline of the Kanawha.

So now, arriving at Point Pleasant and finding abundant Indian sign but no indication of Dunmore's army, Gen. Lewis dispatched messengers up the Ohio to discover where Dunmore was and when he would arrive. Meanwhile he ordered his army to set up camp while they waited. He also assumed that the size of his army was such that there was simply no danger of attack and therefore neglected to order temporary fortifications erected.

It was a very serious error.

[*O c t o b e r   1 ,   1 7 7 4 — S a t u r d a y*]

On the day that Lord Dunmore had established as the rendezvous date with Gen. Lewis's army at Point Pleasant, he was still 175 miles away—a greater distance than the Lewis force had marched in order to reach the Ohio.

It was only yesterday that the crusty, chunky, grizzled old Scot governor had reached Wheeling, and he appeared in no particular hurry to move on. His arrival with so huge a force—1,200 men, of whom 700 had come by water from Fort Pitt and the remaining 500 under Capt. William Crawford by land, driving the beeves with them—was a festive affair unprecedented on the upper Ohio. The handful of regulars with his force were arrayed in their scarlet coats, white trousers and black boots, accompanied by fifes and drums, and the governor's own personal guard of Scottish Highlanders in kilts and ceremonial bonnets disembarked to the wailing strains of bagpipes and the rattle of drums. The vast majority of troops, however, were clad simply in the same type of hunting shirts, leathers and linsey-woolsey worn by the army of Gen. Lewis.

Dunmore left Williamsburg on July 10 and had begun collecting men as he moved from post to post. The majority of his force, exclusive of those who had previously assembled at Fort Pitt under Col. Connolly, had been raised in Frederick, Rockbridge, Dunmore and adjacent counties and assembled first at Fort Frederick and then at Fort Cumberland.[230] The march from that latter post along the Braddock Road to Fort Pitt was begun on September 8, and they arrived at Pittsburgh on September 18. Dunmore immediately began a series of secret conferences with Col. Connolly, along with a private council attended by a number of Indian delegates.[231] It was believed by the assembled men that they would set off downriver from Fort Pitt immediately in the large number of boats that had been assembled and prepared by Col. Connolly, but that did not occur. Ten days passed with Dunmore always giving the impression of being very busily engaged in details, but precious little of significance was accomplished. On the eighth day—September 26—he started Capt. Crawford off with the land detachment of 500 men and the herd of beef cattle and two days later embarked in boats with his remaining 700 men, leaving behind only a small garrison at Fort Pitt. The Dunmore force camped overnight at Logstown and arrived at Wheeling almost simultaneously with Crawford's detachment.

Dunmore immediately selected George Rogers Clark, Simon Girty, Simon Kenton and Peter Parchment as his personal spies and couriers, and he also named Ebenezer Zane as his disbursement officer and John Gibson as aide and chief interpreter. Michael Cresap, despite Gibson's threat to him, was part of Dunmore's party, having gathered a party of men for the campaign, but he kept a close watch for Gibson and studiously avoided him so they never came face to face.

Instead of immediately putting his troops into motion again to reach the rendezvous with Lewis as speedily as possible, Dunmore dispatched Crawford with his land force of 500 men, 50 packhorses and 200 head of cattle with orders to continue descending the left bank of the Ohio for 100 miles until opposite the mouth of the Hockhocking. There he was to swim his detachment across the Ohio and erect a fortification for the deposit of supplies at the Hockhocking River mouth. Dunmore promised that he and the army would follow in a few days in the boats.[232] The general also sent dispatches, carried by Kenton, Girty and Parchment, to Gen. Lewis with a change in orders that was not immediately made known to Dunmore's own men: Lewis was not to wait for the northern army but was to ascend the Ohio to a new rendezvous point some 80 miles above Point Pleasant, at the mouth of the Little Kanawha.[233]

Now, the day following Crawford's departure, word was beginning to circulate that Dunmore had no intention of making the rendezvous with Lewis's army at Point Pleasant because he was concerned lest his flotilla of boats be attacked on the river. Instead, he had decided to ascend the Hockhocking and follow the Indian trail overland to the Pickaway Plains, where Hokolesqua's Town was located, along with several other villages.

It was all very confusing and worrisome, and once again rumors began circulating that Dunmore was maliciously exposing the southern wing of the army to extreme jeopardy.

[October 2, 1774 — Sunday]

Despite the presence of the Dunmore and Lewis armies on the Ohio, attacks did not cease against the various small settlements. At Draper's Meadows the Philie Lybrook family living on Sinking Creek was attacked. Philie, working in a nearby field, managed to escape and hide himself in a cave, but when he returned to the cabin after the attackers were gone, he found the scalped bodies of his five children. At a cabin not too far distant from Lybrook's, Jacob, John and Joshua Snidow were captured by the same party of Indians. Jacob and John, older boys and more fleet of foot, managed to sprint away from their captors and escape, but Joshua was taken away.[234]

On Tenmile Creek, not terribly far from Redstone, two settlers were killed and two captured, and a family of four on Dunkard Creek, after putting up a valiant fight, were roasted alive in their cabin.

As if flaunting the very presence of Dunmore's force, last night, only 24 miles above Wheeling at Harmon's Creek, a large party of Mingoes had attacked the Harmon Greathouse cabin just after dark. Harmon's grown sons, Jacob and Daniel, were away, but he and his second wife, Mary, and their three small children were there, as was his sister, Jane Muncy and a visiting neighbor, Benjamin Davis. Fortunately, they had barred the door from the inside, and as the Indians chopped at it with their tomahawks, Greathouse gave instructions to his wife and sister and then climbed up into the loft. The women immediately began shouting and tossing furniture about and making a great commotion, calling out various names of men to come down and help fight, that they were being attacked. At once Davis shot through the door, and Greathouse shot from a tiny window in the loft, both shouting hoarsely. The Indians, convinced the house was filled with men, quickly dispersed into the darkness.

Once sure the Indians were gone, everyone in the cabin fled to the mile-distant cabin of Thomas Edgington, which was much better fortified and had a dozen men on hand. They spent the remainder of the night there and all day today, planning to return to their own cabin tomorrow. Now, however, just after dark, as a light drizzle began falling, the Indians attacked the Edgington cabin and fired upon it at intervals until nearly midnight before finally leaving. All inside were very relieved and thanked God for the rain that had prevented the attackers from setting the place afire.

[October 9, 1774—Sunday afternoon]

Gen. Andrew Lewis was not in a very good humor. For some time he had been speaking to the subordinate officers that had been summoned to his tent, and now he shook his head in exasperation.

"I do not pretend to know just what the devil is going on," he said, "but I don't like any of it."

For the past nine days his army had been camped here at Point Pleasant, awaiting the arrival of Dunmore's army, their patience becoming very thin and morale disintegrating as the men groused about their limited rations and the poor quality of the beef from the animals they had herded with them. Four days after their arrival, the party of 42 surveyors from Kentucky, under James Harrod, appeared in their sturdy boats. They were on their way home after Dunmore's warning had been delivered to them by Boone. Now, however, finding the army camped here, all volunteered to stay and help.

When messengers came to Lewis, bearing orders for him to lead his force upstream to a new rendezvous point at the mouth of the Little Kanawha, the general had absolutely refused, considering the order stupid and a reckless endangerment of his troops, to say nothing of the fact that it would also leave the southern Virginia frontier open and vulnerable to massive invasion and assault by Indians moving up the Kanawha. He immediately sent the messengers back with his refusal and with word of his determination to await Dunmore's arrival.

Then, today, had come Sam McCulloch, Simon Kenton and Simon Girty with another dispatch from Dunmore, who was furious at the disobedience of the earlier order and who now told Lewis in no uncertain terms that he absolutely must obey the present order: Plans had been changed, Dunmore was now going to lead his force up the Hockhocking and then directly overland to the Scioto towns, and it was there that the two armies would finally merge.[235] Gen. Lewis was to begin marching his men to that location at once.

Although he disliked that order nearly as much as the first, Andrew Lewis realized he could not disobey again. He told the messengers he would comply, and they left at once to return to Dunmore. That was when he had called these officers in to explain the situation. It was Capt. John Stuart who put into words what all of them felt.

"None of this makes any sense!" he growled. "Lord Dunmore is placing both armies in jeopardy. Who ever heard of an attacking force going into enemy territory and not joining until they were in the midst of their enemy's stronghold?"

No one had an answer, of course, but Gen. Lewis sighed and gave the order.

"We will break camp first thing in the morning and utilize the canoes we built, as well as Captain Harrod's boats, to ferry the men across as quickly as possible. Then," he added grimly, "we will march to join the governor as he has directed."

At practically this same moment, Lord Dunmore and his army, in more than 100 canoes, piroques and a few large keelboats, had just landed at the mouth of the Hockhocking and made camp, with orders for the march to begin first thing in the morning. Dunmore then inspected the small fort that had been built by Capt. Crawford and approved of the good job that had been done. He named the place Fort Gower and promoted William Crawford to the rank of major.

[O c t o b e r   9 ,   1 7 7 4 — S u n d a y   n i g h t]

In the pale light of a three-quarters moon, Hokolesqua, as commander of the allied Indians, assembled his force of more than 900 warriors at the mouth of the creek that enters the Ohio three miles upstream from Point Pleasant.[236] His expression was set in grim lines as he watched the warriors preparing their weapons and painting their faces. What was in the offing this night would undoubtedly result in many lost lives, but there was no turning back now.

He thought of the inexorable chain of events that had brought them to this point and concluded that what was happening now must be the will of Moneto. All the high hopes had gone awry, beginning with the mission they had made to Fort Pitt in an effort to bring about a peace before all-out war could descend upon them. But instead of hearing their words of peace, the whites had set upon them, and Silverheels had been stabbed and nearly died. Yet Moneto had smiled upon them, and the younger brother of Hokolesqua had survived his wounds and was among the warriors gathered here this night.

The reaction of the tribe to this insult to a peace delegation led by their principal chief was, however, one of consummate outrage far greater than that evinced by Hokolesqua himself. He told them that he was grieved that his brother had been stabbed and that he shared their anger that such could have occurred, but that he was strongly opposed to their cries for immediate retaliation. War with the *Shemanese,* he believed, would be a grave error. Far better, he advised, to suffer the sting of that insult than to sacrifice the lives of many fine warriors, a certain outcome if they went to war.

"You know me well," he had told the assembled council. "I have not become your chief by avoiding battle. But this time you must take a long, close look at what embarking into warfare against the whites can do to you. Destruction of our tribe is entirely possible. Heed my words! In this instance, would it not be better to swallow the insult, put aside our pride for once and resume peaceful negotiations with the whites? In the end result, far more would almost surely be accomplished in this way than by bloodshed."

But then, for the first time in the years they had been close friends, Hokolesqua found Pucksinwah openly opposed to him. Addressing the assembled warriors, the war chief had spoken forcefully. "Hokolesqua is my revered chief and also my friend.

Yet, as war chief of the Shawnees, I believe we have moved beyond the realm of negotiation and can only suffer by attempting more. There will be time enough to resume negotiations after we have confronted and bested the whites and can then negotiate from a position of strength rather than from a position of weakness and fear."

It had been enough. By vote of the chiefs of all the septs, the Shawnees accepted the counsel of Pucksinwah and overruled that of Hokolesqua. Deputations carrying war belts had immediately been sent to neighboring tribes, this time not asking but demanding that they ally themselves to the Shawnees in the coming war and delivering the same message to each: "We Shawnees stand between you and the whites and we mean to oppose them, which is to your benefit as well as our own. But you must send warriors to aid us. We will not fight the *Shemanese* alone while you sit in the comfort of your lodges and watch our blood being spilled for your benefit. Your choice is this: Either send warriors to fight at our side, or we will simply not fight at all, but pack our goods and move well beyond the grandmother of rivers, leaving you then to face the white enemy on your own when he comes, which there is no doubt he will."

The truth of this had become clear to the Wyandots, Miamis and Delawares as increased expeditions of whites moved down the Spaylaywitheepi to mark out territory in the Kan-tuck-kee lands; even more when the army of 400 whites had penetrated into the very heartland of the Ohio country, causing abandonment and destruction of Wapatomica; finally more than clear when the huge armies of whites began moving toward them, to invade their country and crush them. So they had sent warriors to help, but the Shawnees had been greatly disappointed in the small number those neighboring tribes committed to the effort—only 100 apiece, a paltry 300, plus somewhat fewer than 100 Mingoes under Talgayeeta. Added to the 600 supplied by the Shawnees themselves, they had fewer than 1,000 warriors—hardly the force desirable to fight an enemy that had much finer weapons and odds of better than two to one in their favor.

Now they had come to this point where they would launch their canoes and cross the great river to attack, and to the assembled Indians Hokolesqua had made a final appeal. "I ask you one last time to think not of the glory of battle but of the future of our race. Give me your answer and I will abide by your wish: Do we sue for peace or do we fight them?"

The cries of "Fight them!" were overwhelming.

[O c t o b e r   1 0 ,   1 7 7 4 — M o n d a y]

The combined force of Indians under Hokolesqua moved into position for their attack with no more noise than the wisps of fog enshrouding the woodland in the first gray glimmer of dawn. They had come across the Spaylaywitheepi during the darkness just as silently as they moved now, crossing in relays that brought them to the mouth of the creek where long ago an old town had been, two and a half miles above the camp of Gen. Andrew Lewis.[237] Armed with bows and spears, knives and

The Battle of Point Pleasant

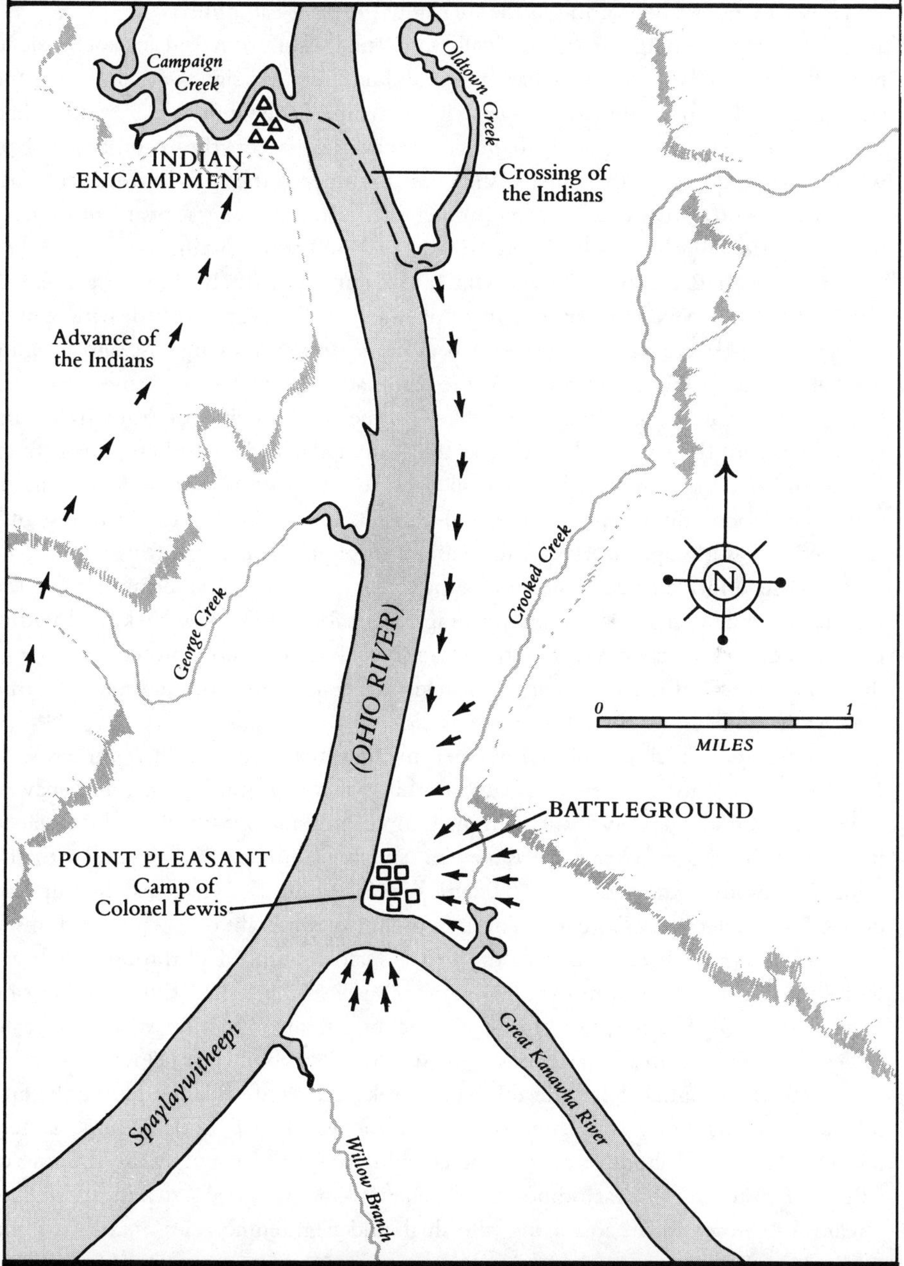

Campaign Creek

Oldtown Creek

△ △ △

INDIAN
ENCAMPMENT

Crossing of
the Indians

Advance of
the Indians

George Creek

Crooked Creek

(OHIO RIVER)

N

0   1
MILES

BATTLEGROUND

POINT PLEASANT
Camp of
Colonel Lewis

Spaylaywitheepi

Willow Branch

Great Kanawha River

tomahawks, rifles and pistols, they spread themselves only a few yards apart in a long line that formed the base of a triangle stretching from the Ohio on their right to the Kanawha on their left. A number swam across the Kanawha and took post on the other side lest an attempt be made to escape in that direction. The woodland ahead of their principal line gradually thinned and then dwindled away altogether to knee-deep weeds as the ground narrowed to the point where the rivers converged—the spot called Point Pleasant—where at this moment the blanket-enshrouded forms of some 800 men lay about a multitude of barely glowing campfires.

The early morning fog that gradually thickened was both friend and foe; it aided by muffling any sound they may have made and masking any sight of them, yet at the same time it hid their ultimate targets. It also ruined their initial plan, which had been to creep up close enough to pour a withering fire on the recumbent forms when Hokolesqua gave the signal. With the thinning of the trees and the fact that there were sentries patrolling the perimeter of the camp, their forward movement slowed considerably when they were still about 1,500 yards distant.

The actual Battle of Point Pleasant broke out prematurely through a fluke of circumstance. Two young privates, in disobedience of orders against leaving camp, arose early and set out in the hope of bagging a turkey, moving eastward roughly parallel with the Ohio River shore. As the pair reached a small rivulet, the fog in this area abruptly lifted and exposed to their stunned eyes a line of painted Indians extending from the river's edge as far as they could see in the enfolding mists. Even before the hunters could react and rush back to camp with a warning, a warrior named Epinoosa flung up his rifle and shot. One of the hunters was instantly knocked flat as a grape-size lead ball smashed through the center of his chest.[238]

The second man fled, quickly disappearing in the again-gathering fog. To the Indians it seemed he screeched his warnings every foot of the way back, and within moments the whole camp was in motion. Taking advantage of the protective cover of the most forward of the trees, and with many warriors squirming through the dense grasses, the Indians continued to move as close as they could.

Gen. Lewis quickly deployed his men in three wings, placing his brother, Col. Charles Lewis, and his men to hold one-third of the ground from the Kanawha toward the Ohio, Col. William Fleming's force holding one-third of the distance from the Ohio shore toward the Kanawha, and the commanding general with the remainder holding the center. Col. Lewis, when first aroused, had snatched up and donned his scarlet officer's coat and even in the misty dim light of dawn made himself a prime target. He became one of the first casualties with a ball through his head. Col. John Field was killed in the same manner early in the action. On the other side of the line, Col. Fleming was almost as quickly put out of action when two balls passed through his arm and another slammed through his body just below the ribs.[239]

With these initial shots, the full battle broke out, and with the gunsmoke and fog mingling, visibility was reduced to mere inches. The fighting became largely hand-to-hand for an hour or more, the general uproar punctuated by the crashing of rifles and pistols, the meaty thuds of tomahawks and war clubs striking flesh, the screams of the wounded and dying, the shrill and frightening cries of warriors and soldiers alike.

The Shawnee war chief, Pucksinwah, took a ball in the chest and died in the arms of his 18-year-old son, Chiksika.[240] His daughter's husband, Chaquiweshe, was also killed only a short distance away.[241] Throughout the duration of the battle the stentorian voice of Hokolesqua could be heard encouraging his warriors with the repeated shout *"Oui-shi-cat-to-oui!"*—Be strong![242]

Hour after hour the seesaw battle raged until at last, late in the afternoon, word reached Hokolesqua that another large force of whites was rapidly approaching from upstream on the Kanawha—upward of 500 men less than three hours away; a force strong enough and fresh enough to turn the tide of battle in favor of the whites.[243] Hokolesqua raised a new call that was relayed back and forth among the Indians, and slowly the warriors began to fall back to the mouth of the creek where they had initially landed. Gen. Lewis, considering this a ruse to lure them into ambush— which was exactly what Hokolesqua figured his reaction would be—pulled his men back closer to the camp and set them to work throwing up hasty fortifications.

The withdrawal of the Indians was no precipitate retreat; it was deliberate, methodical, well-defended, and very gradual, with the warriors picking up their dead and wounded as they went. Hokolesqua himself walked backward, continuing to face the enemy, and even when he was in the final boat heading for the Ohio shore, he stood facing toward the battleground so that it could never be said that he had turned his back in a contest against the *Shemanese*.

The Battle of Point Pleasant was over.[244]

[*December 31, 1774—Saturday*]

The eventful year of 1774 drew to a close with a tenuous peace once more prevailing in the Ohio River Valley. Dunmore's War, so called, had been brief in the extreme—a single skirmish near Wapatomica in the McDonald Campaign, the fiercely fought Battle of Point Pleasant and then the agreement that had been reached between the whites and the Indians at Dunmore's Camp Charlotte.[245] Immediately following the battle and the return to the Scioto Valley, all of Hokolesqua's allies had abandoned him, save some of the Mingoes. Talgayeeta and a small number of his men had stayed with the Shawnees, but the majority of the Mingoes had retreated to a tributary of the upper Scioto, the Olentangy River. There was no doubt in Hokolesqua's mind, nor anyone else's, that the army they had just fought, its strength rejuvenated by the arrival of the large reinforcement, would soon be coming against them, and a strong fear rose in the warriors. That was when Hokolesqua called them all to council at Yellow Hawk's Town—the former Chalahgawtha—at the place where Paint Creek empties into the Scioto River. When he spoke, he began gently, but his voice had quickly hardened, his expression stern and cold.

"You fought well, my children," he had said, "and my heart sings the songs of praise for your strength in battle, just as it sings the song of mourning for our brave warriors and chiefs who fell. Now I must ask you, was this all in vain? Many among you have already said to me, 'Let us now seek peace with the *Shemanese*, lest they come against us even more strongly.' My heart is filled with shame that my ears have heard these words. If it was peace you wanted, why did you not say so when I begged you to do so five days ago?

"What do we do now?" The words were spoken angrily. "The *Shemanese* are coming upon us by two routes, far stronger than those we met alone, while we are weaker in the return of our brothers to their homes, where they will be safe." His words had become scathing, filled with contempt, and he repeated: "What do we do now? Shall we turn out and fight them?" Dead silence followed his query, and after a moment he continued, eyes flashing. "Shall we now kill all our women and children and then fight the *Shemanese* ourselves until we are all dead?"

Still no one responded and, in the silence, the fire of anger and resolve in Hokolesqua drained away. He drew out his bloodstained tomahawk and held it high for all to see, then threw it to the ground with such strength that the head of the weapon was all but buried in the earth. He shouted loudly: "Since you are not inclined to fight, we will go and make peace!"

The trader Matthew Elliott, who was in the village with his Shawnee wife, was summoned, and a message was dictated to him to be carried to Lord Dunmore—a message asking for peace talks and a promise to accommodate any reasonable request from the whites. If, however, the offer was refused, the Shawnees and Mingoes would creep up under cover of night and hit Dunmore's army hard, then fall back across the Scioto and go into ambush to strike them again if they followed. Finally, if still pressed, they would fall back again to Chalahgawtha on the Little Miami, where they would stand their ground and fight to the end.

The contingency plan had been unnecessary; Dunmore had accepted the request for peace with good grace and had reached the Pickaway Plains on October 17 and established his nonfortified camp, which he named Camp Charlotte in honor of his wife. A series of messages summoned all the chiefs to meet there at a specified time, and this was agreed to, but a potentially devastating problem still remained.

Gen. Lewis, his army reinforced by the arrival of Col. Christian's force, had left the wounded at Point Pleasant under the care of Capt. Matthew Arbuckle, quickly crossed the Ohio with the remainder and spearheaded toward the Scioto Valley Shawnee villages, bent on retaliatory attack.[246] Nonhelema's Town, directly in his path, had already been abandoned and was on fire. Hokolesqua's Town was next in line, and Dunmore immediately sent a message to Lewis, telling him to desist and return to Point Pleasant. Lewis ignored the order and continued his advance. A second message was no more successful. Finally, Dunmore himself mounted a horse and, escorted by a few of his trusted aides and some Indians, intercepted the Virginians, demanded Gen. Lewis turn his force back and even threatened to strike him down with his sword if he did not obey. It was an extremely fragile situation for a little while, but then Lewis finally backed down, much to the dismay of his men, and started his return to Point Pleasant, with orders from Dunmore to build a fortification there.

A minor difficulty had occurred when Talgayeeta refused to attend the peace council at Camp Charlotte. Hokolesqua said that without this influential chief's participation, there would be no real peace. Although Talgayeeta's vengeance had been fully assuaged over these months, he nevertheless now hated and distrusted the whites and wished nothing more to do with them. To resolve the dilemma, Dunmore sent three men—Simon Girty and Joseph Nicholson, who were both skilled interpreters, and Simon Kenton—to Talgayeeta's camp beneath a huge elm tree on the banks of Congo Creek.[247] Talgayeeta shook his head and said, "Logan is no councillor; Logan is a warrior," and he still refused to enter into council with Dunmore and the other chiefs at Camp Charlotte. He did, however, agree to dictate a message to Dunmore. He handed Girty a wampum belt, which signified the message was official, and then spoke strongly and with deep emotion:

"I appeal to any white man to say if ever he entered Logan's cabin hungry and I gave him not meat; if he ever came cold or naked and I gave him not clothing. During the course of the last long and bloody war, Logan remained idle in his tent, an advocate for peace. Nay, such was my love for the whites that those of my own country pointed at me as I passed and said, 'Logan is the friend of the white man.' I had even thought to have lived with you, but for the injuries of one man. Colonel Cresap, the last spring, in cold blood and unprovoked, murdered all the relatives of Logan, not sparing even my women and children. There runs not a drop of my blood in the veins of any living creature.[248] This called on me for revenge. I have sought it. I have killed many. I have fully glutted my vengeance. For my country, I rejoice at the beams of peace; but do not harbor the thought that mine is the joy of fear. Logan never felt fear. He will not turn on his heel to save his life. Who is there to mourn for Logan? Not one."

Talgayeeta then accompanied the messengers back to the vicinity of Camp Charlotte, where he left them to carry his message to Dunmore. He himself went to where his son-in-law, John Gibson, was sitting and talking with Hokolesqua and some other Shawnee chiefs. Talgayeeta asked Gibson to walk out into the nearby woods with him to talk, and it was not until then that Talgayeeta was finally informed by Gibson that while Cresap had been involved in the killing of the Shawnees at Pipe Creek and the Indians in the John Anderson trading party, as well as the Mingoes at the mouth of Captina Creek, he had not been personally involved in the murder of Talgayeeta's family at Baker's Bottom; that it was Greathouse who had planned and led that attack. By this time, however, the speech had been delivered to Dunmore and it was not changed.[249]

While Dunmore had now been assured of Talgayeeta ending his war, it was clear he spoke for himself alone, not for the other Mingoes. Word had come that a large number of these confederated warriors had gathered and were war dancing some 40 miles to the north at Seekonk—also known as the Salt Lick Town—on the upper Scioto tributary called the Olentangy River.[250] Dunmore had immediately sent a force of 240 men under Maj. William Crawford to cut them off, but he masked the intent of the mission from the tribal peace delegates at Camp Charlotte by announcing that they were going back to the mouth of the Hockhocking for supplies.[251]

The talks at Camp Charlotte lasted for several days, and those who witnessed Hokolesqua speak agreed they had never seen nor heard anyone so majestic and powerful in delivery.[252]

The agreement was concluded and, by its terms, Hokolesqua, on behalf of the Shawnees, agreed that the Spaylaywitheepi—Ohio River—was hereafter to be the boundary between whites and Shawnees and that the Shawnees would desist in their attacks against white boats traveling on the Ohio, but that there should be no further settlement of whites in the Kan-tuck-kee hunting grounds of the Indians and that whites were strictly prohibited from setting foot north of the Ohio River to hunt, claim land, settle or for any other reason, except that some white traders would still be allowed to come among them.[253] In addition, the Shawnees turned over the plunder they had taken on some of their raids, along with several white captives that were at their villages.[254] Finally, the chiefs promised to appear for a major council at Pittsburgh the following spring to formally incorporate the items of this agreement into an official peace treaty. As a guarantee to this end, they gave Dunmore four Shawnee subchiefs to hold as hostages till the faithful consummation of their promise.[255] Then Dunmore withdrew his force by the route he came, escorted by Hokolesqua and Nonhelema as far as the upper Hockhocking River.

The Dunmore Army reached the mouth of the Hockhocking on November 5 and stopped at Fort Gower. There, in opposition to Lord Dunmore's wishes, the colonial militia held council among themselves and on that day passed a "resolution of liberty," which said:

> *Resolved, that we will bear the most faithful allegiance to His Majesty, King George the Third, whilst His Majesty delights to reign over a brave and free people; that we will, at the expense of life, and everything dear and valuable, exert ourselves in support of his crown, and the dignity of the British Empire. But as the love of liberty, and attachment to the real interests and just rights of America outweigh every consideration, we resolve that we will exert every power within us for the defense of American liberty, and for the support of her just rights and privileges; not in any precipitous, riotous or tumultuous manner, but when regularly called forth by the unanimous voice of our countrymen. Resolved, that we entertain the greatest respect for his excellency, the Right Honourable Lord Dunmore, who commanded an expedition against the Shawanese, and who, we are confident, underwent the great fatigue of this singular campaign from no other motive than the true interests of the country.*
>
> *Signed by order and in behalf of the whole corps.*
> *Benjamin Ashby, Clerk.*

Despite the conciliatory final sentence, the resolution was a distinct slap in the face to Lord Dunmore, and he could barely restrain his wrath when he heard it read, but he was powerless to do anything about it. The army then recrossed the Ohio, returned to Wheeling and was disbanded. Far to the south, the Lewis army returned up the Kanawha to Camp Union, and there it, too, disbanded.

Lord Dunmore's War had ended, and now, with relative peace restored to the Ohio Valley, once again the Americans were turning their thoughts to where they had by and large left off early last spring—to the claiming and settling of more Indian lands.

[*April 19, 1775 — Wednesday*]

Twenty-seven days ago at the Virginia Convention in Richmond, Patrick Henry had thundered out seven words that had touched the American colonials to the core; seven words that had echoed and reechoed ever since and undoubtedly would continue to do so for a long time to come:

". . . give me liberty or give me death!"[256]

Today those fateful words became reality when Lt. Col. Francis Smith and Marine Maj. John Pitcairn arrived with a force of Redcoats at Lexington, Massachusetts near dawn and encountered a group of minutemen under John Parker. When the British began advancing upon them, Parker called to his men: "Stand your ground. Don't fire unless fired upon. But if they mean to have a war, let it begin here."

And so it did. Eight of the minutemen dropped under the blast of musket fire from Smith's force, and the remainder were forced to retreat at bayonet point. The British then cut down a liberty pole at Concord and skirmished with the militia at Concord bridge.

Reinforcements arrived at Lexington for the British under command of Brig. Gen. Sir Hugh Percy, bringing with them a six-pounder cannon and raising the British strength to 1,800 men. But the militia were reinforced as well and quickly became a force of 4,000 men. Percy was forced to retreat after the American marksmen struck with devastating accuracy, and the Redcoats returned to Boston with 65 of their men having been killed, including 15 officers, 173 others wounded and 26 missing.

Come what may, today the American Revolution had begun.

[*July 25, 1775 — Tuesday*]

As everyone had anticipated—the Indians as well as the Americans—no one paid much attention to the accords reached between Lord Dunmore and the Indians at Camp Charlotte. As soon as the weather permitted this past spring, a new flood of land-claimers, surveyors, settlers and adventurers poured into the Ohio Valley.

The upper Ohio Valley was experiencing the greatest influx of settlers. George Washington, already holding some of the most extensive land claims in that area, only ten days ago had received from Lord Dunmore a patent for another 3,000 acres of land at the mouth of Beaver River, but he suspected he wouldn't be doing anything much in that area for quite a while, as the war was keeping him very busy. Wheeling, though still not laid out as such, could now almost be described as a town on its own, and settlements such as Catfish Camp, Baker's Bottom, McMechen's Settlement and others were also growing rapidly. Some that had been temporarily abandoned during the war, such as McMechen's, had been burned by the Indians and had to be rebuilt. The Tomlinsons, having returned to their Grave Creek Flats settlement after briefly taking refuge at Redstone, now found many other settlers coming in to sink roots near them, Maj. William Crawford among that number. So much had the population of the area increased over the past months—by several thousand, in fact—that a second Augusta County court was established by Virginia at Pittsburgh, and court sessions would now be held alternately at Staunton and Fort Pitt.

The second greatest surge of settlement was aimed at Kentucky. Far to the south on the Watauga tributary of the South Holston River, Daniel Boone, having been discharged from the militia, had accepted employment from a big-time land promoter named Richard Henderson, who, with a group of other men, established the Transylvania Land Company with the view of founding a new republic to be called Transylvania.[257] Boone, leading a force of 30 workmen, had been commissioned to enter that land, create a Wilderness Road leading into it, bring prospective settlers there and establish the new government and its settlements.

With the war in progress and America endeavoring to separate itself from British rule and become established as a union of independent states, Henderson dealt directly with the Indians for the purchase of 20 million acres of land, that land being in the Kentucky country. He had heard that the Cherokees claimed this land as their own, and so it was to them he made his offer to buy. Though the Cherokees had no real title to the land, either by habitation or conquest, in a treaty council with Henderson's representatives at Sycamore Shoals on the Watauga on March 17, they nevertheless agreed to the sale. For the sum of $10,000 in guns and goods, the deal was consummated on April 20. Henderson immediately advertised these lands for sale and was getting many buyers, as well as much opposition from governmental officials on grounds that his whole operation, including the purchase from the Cherokees, was illegal. Meanwhile Boone had already traveled overland to the Kentucky River on his Wilderness Road and was busily laying out the settlement of Boonesboro at a salt lick some 60 yards from the left bank of the river. There were some scattered Indian attacks and a few men were killed, but the rest remained undaunted and the settlement progressed. Boone intended to have his entire family relocated here by September.

George Rogers Clark was intrigued by the Kentucky country and made his move in that direction, too. In March he had paddled down to the Kentucky River and there became associated with the party already surveying for the Ohio Land Company. A week or so later, on April 1, he wrote to his brother:

> *I have engaged as deputy surveyor under Captain Hancock Lee for to lay out lands on ye Kentuck, for ye Ohio company, at ye rate of £80 year and ye privilege of taking what land I want.*

Nine weeks later, on June 6, he wrote again, this time from the new settlement of Leestown. His enthusiasm for what was occurring in Kentucky was apparent. He wrote:

> *Colonel Henderson is here and claims all ye land below Kentucke. If his claim should be good, land may be got reasonable enough, and as good as any in ye world. . . . We have laid out a town 75 miles up ye Kentucke, where I intend to live, and I don't doubt but there will be 50 families living in it by Christmas.*

Clark, however, quickly became disenchanted with Henderson and his grandiose schemes. Siding with the Virginia government, he considered it an illegal purchase, especially since it included lands that were part of Virginia's own western lands
in the extensive Fincastle County. Clark was also honest enough to admit to himself
that the Kentucky settlers were giving the Indians considerable provocation, and he
marveled that the red men had been so restrained in retaliating. There had been some
isolated killings, true, along with some destruction of cattle and theft of horses, but
these were without exception the work of bands of young bucks evidently out to
make their marks as warriors, not the well-organized attacks that would have occurred had they been tribally sanctioned. With the Kickapoos far to the west, however, it was another matter. They had been crossing the lower Ohio from the Illinois
country in ever increasing numbers, ascending the Cumberland River and making
raids on the Kentucky settlements from the west. With that growing problem and the
certainty in his own mind that it was only a matter of time before the Shawnees
started retaliating in earnest, Clark felt strongly that the settlers here in central Kentucky were going to need government protection.

With this in mind he set out for Williamsburg to ask Virginia officials not only
to send troops to protect Kentucky settlements but to vigorously oppose Henderson's
agents, who were already applying to the Continental Congress to validate Henderson's treaty and the vast purchase he had made from the Cherokees. Clark believed it
was imperative that Virginia create a new county out of the westernmost Fincastle
lands, a great tract to be called Kentucky County, from which the settlers would have
the right to elect their own delegates to the Assembly.

Certainly there would very soon be quite enough people for a county govern-
ment such as he proposed. James Harrod and his people had returned to the so-called
Buffalo Wallow of Kentucky to reestablish his Harrodsburg Settlement, still better
known as St. Asaph's, and another new settlement was under way at nearby Boiling
Springs. John Floyd was busy with his crew, claiming and settling large tracts of
Kentucky lands, and Simon Kenton, after wintering with his new partner, Thomas
Williams, at the mouth of Cabin Creek, finally landed at the mouth of Limestone
Creek, went inland and discovered the fabled Kentucky canelands and the great Blue
Licks. Already they had set up camp there and were considering establishing a real
settlement. George McClelland was erecting a station for his little party on North
Elkhorn Creek, and Robert Patterson had ascended the South Elkhorn and was busy
making tomahawk improvements in that area when Simon Kenton arrived and vis-
ited just as word was brought of the Battle of Lexington in Massachusetts. Patterson
immediately named his new settlement Lexington in honor of that first victory of the
Revolution.[258]

Thomas Hinkson, too, was one of those visiting Kentucky for the first time. He
ascended the Licking River and, enthralled with what he found, established a new
settlement in an area dubbed The Cedars. By March 15, his party had built a small
fortification and raised a cabin for each of the 15 men, and he named this settlement
Hinkson's Station. It was about this time that on several occasions he observed a
Shawnee following him—a warrior named Wipey. Deciding in his own mind that
the Indian meant eventually to kill him, the next time he caught sight of him, he
turned and approached. Wipey smiled and held out his hand, but Hinkson simply

raised his rifle and coldly shot the Indian dead, then hid his body in a clump of brush well off the trail.

That sort of unprovoked Indian killing had become something of a game for many of the settlers, who considered the Indians as nothing more than vermin. Any Indian who showed himself on the Ohio shore, as would-be settlers were passing downstream, ran the risk of being shot just for the fun of it. Alexander Scott, heading downriver to make claims, spied a young Indian man hunting near the mouth of the Muskingum. The Indian quickly ducked into cover, but Scott knew he was still there watching and so he paddled his canoe close to shore and, smiling, called in a friendly way, "Hey, c'mon out. Let's you'n me talk. I got some t'bacca here I'll share with you."

The canoe coasted to shore and lodged itself. Scott set aside his paddle and, still smiling in a pleasant manner, began loading his pipe. The Indian pushed his way out of the bushes and slowly approached, holding his rifle at an angle before him but not in a particularly threatening manner. Scott lifted a hand as if to wave to him and seemed to inadvertently knock the pipe out of his own mouth. It fell into the canoe, and he immediately bent over and reached down for it. When he straightened, however, it was with a cocked flintlock pistol in his hand, and before the young hunter could react, a bullet smashed through his chest, killing him. Scott, continuing to smile, stepped ashore, took the man's gun, powderhorn, knife and tomahawk, along with his necessaries pouch and moccasins, then rolled the body into the river and watched the current carry it a dozen feet or so before it sank. He then continued his journey. He was still smiling.

Peter Parchment, noted for his hatred of Indians, was only a mile or so above Pittsburgh on April 23, walking along the bank of the Allegheny, when he spied, sitting on the shore ahead of him, a Delaware Indian drinking from a jug and so intoxicated he had difficulty bringing the container up to his mouth without spilling it. Parchment, unseen, unheard, crept up behind and slammed his tomahawk into the man's head. The jug fell from his hands and rolled into the river, where it sank. Parchment scalped the Indian and rolled him into the river, where he sank.

Three days later, on April 26, less than a half-mile from that spot, Parchment encountered another Delaware, this one coming toward him on a faint trail. They nodded to one another and muttered a greeting as they passed. One step beyond, Parchment whirled and buried his tomahawk in the man's nape, severing the spinal cord. Glancing around, Parchment spied a huge sycamore with a large hollow about four feet off the ground. He dragged the body there and, with some difficulty, crammed it into the hollow until it fell from sight. He was breathing heavily when he finished and cursed the fact that he had to hide bodies like this, just because this was a period of nominal peace. So far as he was concerned, there would never be peace between the Indians and whites.

Thus far the insurrection in the east had been having relatively little effect on the frontier, except for the fact that there were more new faces here now, many of them men who had decided it was safer and more profitable to claim land here than to be drafted into war service. George Washington, who usually tried to get here each spring for at least a little while, had been absent this year. Not quite six weeks ago—on June 17—he had been elected by the Second Continental Congress at

Philadelphia as commander-in-chief of the American forces. His reaction was that he thought the appointment really should have gone to Gen. Andrew Lewis.

On that same day the Battle of Bunker Hill had been fought, and this time the Americans were the losers, but the British paid a stiff price for their victory, losing 1,150 men. The Americans themselves lost 411. Washington headed for Massachusetts as soon as possible, arriving there and taking command on July 3.

One significant effect the young revolution was having on the frontier was that it caused the planned council with the Indians at Fort Pitt to be canceled. A few Delawares and Mingoes had shown up and met in a cold, unfriendly council with John Connolly, but none of the Shawnees or delegates of other tribes had come. Nevertheless, Hokolesqua had given his word that attacks against whites descending the Ohio in boats would cease, and he didn't require a formal treaty to make every effort to live up to that promise. Galled though they were that this new influx of whites was in contravention to those agreements, the Shawnees largely restrained themselves in deference to their chief. But little by little the feeling grew, especially among the hot-headed young braves, that if the whites were not being bound by those agreements, then why should the Shawnees?

The very fact that two forces of whites had last fall penetrated deeply into their country had instilled a deep uneasiness within them all, and gradually they began abandoning their villages in the Scioto River drainage and moving to the far less accessible areas of the upper Mad River, Great Miami and Little Miami, some even as far as the Auglaize River and other streams that eventually flowed into the Maumee River and Lake Erie. The new Wapatomica on the upper Mad River remained their capital village, but the Chalahgawtha located on the upper Little Miami, near the mouth of Massies Creek, was now by far their largest and most populous village.[259]

As part of this general movement, the surviving family of Pucksinwah moved to Chalahgawtha. In line with tribal tradition, the family of a fallen war chief became the responsibility of the tribe's peace chief. Pucksinwah's entire family of seven—his widow, Methotasa, eldest son Chiksika, 20, daughter Tecumapese, 18, middle son Tecumseh, 8, and the three youngest sons, an unprecedented set of five-year-old triplets named Sauwaseekau, Elkskwatawa and Lowawluwaysica—all became wards of Chiungalla, called Black Fish by the whites, who was principal chief of the Chalahgawtha sept of the Shawnees. And the new Shawnee war chief, succeeding Pucksinwah, was Shemeneto—Black Snake.

This early in the Revolution, most of the tribes tried to remain neutral, considering the war between the whites as a struggle between father and son, a family matter in which they had no business participating. But this did not last long. The young Mohawk war chief Thayendanegea—Chief Joseph Brant—only recently named war chief of the entire Six Nations, prevailed not only upon his fellow Mohawk tribesmen but upon the entire Iroquois League to side with the British. This came as a direct result of the new Indian superintendent, Guy Johnson, nephew of Sir William, appealing to them toward this end.

"Think!" he told them in the first general Iroquois council after the Revolution began. "Are the Americans able to give you anything more than a piece of bread and glass of rum? Are you willing to go with them and suffer them to make horses and oxen of you, to put you into wheelbarrows and bring us all into slavery?"

The remarks struck home with his listeners, and they leaned toward British support. The leaning quickly became commitment when it came Thayendanegea's turn to address them.

"We long ago made a covenant with the King," he told them, "and now is not the time to break it. We must remain under the King's protection and stand forward and help him in his difficulties in this war that has begun between him and his American children. Go now! Fight for your possessions. Whatever you lose as a result, the King will make it up to you."

Of the six Indian nations in the Iroquois League, only the Oneidas and some of their Tuscarora wards were determined to stay neutral.

The same decision faced the Shawnees at a great council held at Chalahgawtha and attended by 350 chiefs and subchiefs of the five Shawnee septs. For many days the council droned on, with chief after chief expressing his own feelings—and those of his own constituency—in respect to whether they should take sides in this war or remain neutral. It was much the same problem that had faced them before the French and Indian War, when they had to decide whether to remain neutral or support the French or British. They had finally chosen support of the French, and all eventually realized this was a mistake. Now a new decision had to be made, with many new considerations involved, and it worried them considerably.

The general discussion evolved, however, to the problem most directly affecting them: the whites swarming into the Ohio Valley. Many of the chiefs were demanding freer rein to repay like with like against the settlers, who all too often shot at them on sight, who wasted so much of what Moneto had provided for His Indian children and who left such great devastation in their path. The agreements made with the white chief Dunmore at Camp Charlotte had resulted this year in the *Shemanese* floating down the Spaylaywitheepi in great numbers of craft, from small canoes and piroques to huge high-sided boats and great rafts upon which houses were built and small herds of cattle and horses transported.[260] They came like locusts, these *Shemanese,* and where they stopped, they cut down the trees and burned the prairies. Worse yet, in the sacred hunting grounds of the Kan-tuck-kee, they wantonly slaughtered buffalo and elk by the hundreds, often only for the tongue or the liver or the hide, leaving the rest to rot, which was an insult to the beneficence of Moneto. Equally destructive, the horses and cattle they brought with them consumed the lush pastures that the wild herds depended upon for their own subsistence. Already the buffalo herds were fewer, their numbers smaller, and the elk had become solitary, always on the alert and far more difficult to hunt.

Bad as those matters were, they were not the most terrible. The worst was the *Shemanese* themselves who, while floating down the great river, would shoot to kill whenever any Indian appeared on the Ohio shore. Nine Shawnee warriors had been slain in this way since the Hunger Moon—February—and four Shawnee hunters who had crossed into the Kan-tuck-kee lands to get meat for their families had never returned. *Shemanese* were landing on the Shawnees' own Ohio shore and attempting to build cabins and then growing angry when told they could not do so. As Chief Outhowwa Shokka put it:

"They insult us and our wives and our children and our way of life. We are losing our dignity, our self-respect. Why must it be we who must turn our backs and walk away when it is we who are injured? Why may we not, as we always have, repay in kind for what we receive at the hands of our enemies?"

Hokolesqua was next-to-last speaker, and as principal chief of the tribe, his words would carry great weight among those present. The honor of speaking last, however, would go to the chief whose village was hosting this council, Chiungalla. Now, at last, it was Hokolesqua's time to speak. He knew many of his people placed the blame for these problems at his feet, since he had been the one most responsible for the Camp Charlotte agreement with Dunmore. His voice was heavy with sadness as it filled the huge council house.

"It is a bad time for us, yes, and as your chief, the fire in my breast wishes to burst forth in vengeance for those injuries that have been committed against us. I hold back in this desire for I have given my word," he looked around sternly, "as have many of you here, that we will remain at peace. Do not think now, or *ever!* that Hokolesqua so advises through fear, except that it is fear that our nation will perish. If once again we war with the *Shemanese,* it will be the beginning of our end. The white man is like the worm who, when cut in half, does not die but merely becomes two. For each one that is killed, two or three or even four rise to take his place. As the treaty last autumn opened the dam to let the whites down the river in a flood, so warfare against them will be opening the dam to permit them to flood into our country here and take it from us."

He sighed and shook his head. "It is no easy matter to bear the injuries being turned upon us. Yet it may be that if these injuries can be borne for a while more, a better relationship will come and we will be able to live with the whites as neighbors."

Older chiefs of the Maykujay, Peckuwe and Thawegila septs nodded in approval of these words, but an undertone of exasperation and anger arose from the younger chiefs and warriors, particularly those of the Kispokotha and Chalahgawtha septs. Hokolesqua waited patiently until the disturbance abated and then continued:

"My young men are hard to hold and want to strike back when struck and it is not in my heart to tell them they are wrong. They are not wrong! But look deep into your hearts, each of you, and ask if any personal insult or injury is worth the destruction of our nation, which retaliation must surely bring."

He returned to his place beside Chiungalla and sat down as the host chief rose to speak. Because Chiungalla was peace chief of the tribe, it was expected that this burly, barrel-chested, middle-aged chief would concur with Hokolesqua's sentiments, but he surprised them. There was a large roseate scar on his right breast, and he tapped it with his forefinger.

"This is my memory," he said slowly. "It tells me that no white man can be trusted at any time, any place. It tells me that when I accepted injury and insult from the white man, believing it would not happen again, it became worse than before. The Shawnee must live in dignity; he must not only demand respect of others, white or Indian, but even more important, he must retain his self-respect and he can never do this by turning his back on injury and insult." He tapped the scar again and added, "My memory tells me this."

A loud murmuring of approval arose, and he waited until it faded away before continuing. "I do not say we should make war unless war is visited upon us, but I do say we must protect ourselves. If *our* men are killed, *we* must kill. If our buffalo and elk are destroyed, then so must the cattle of the whites be destroyed and their horses taken away. If our woods are cut and our fields burned, then so must the cabins of the whites be burned. Only in this way will the *Shemanese* know that we will not allow our country to be ravished and they will think well on it before giving us further injury."

There was general approval for what Chiungalla said, but there was equally a recognition of the logic in what Hokolesqua had said and, even more, a strong and sobering memory of the words spoken earlier in this council by the principal chief of the Thawegilas, Kikusgowlowa, who was also oldest of the Shawnee chiefs. His long white hair flowed over his shoulders and framed his incredibly wrinkled face as he had spoken in a strong and passionate voice:

"The septs have always been joined together closely in all important phases of Shawnee life; yet, I tell you now, the Thawegilas have seen their last war with the *Shemanese*. If once more the tomahawk is struck into the war post, the Thawegilas will leave the Shawnee nation and cross the great-grandmother of rivers to the west, never to return."

The council ended as so many others had in the past: with nothing truly resolved and the whole situation in a delicate balance.

The problems the Virginians were having with their governor and his henchman at Fort Pitt, John Connolly, had finally reached a conclusion that was allowing everyone to draw breaths of relief. Lord Dunmore, shortly after his return to Williamsburg, was given a perfunctory vote of thanks from the House of Burgesses for his "valuable services" in the campaign just ended. But Dunmore, still rankled over the Fort Gower resolution—and according to many, over the fact that the army of Gen. Lewis had not been annihilated at Point Pleasant—quickly ordered the cessation of all work on the under-construction fortification at Point Pleasant and the disbanding of the garrison there under Capt. Matthew Arbuckle. The order was not obeyed.

As spring approached and matters further degenerated between the colonists and the King, Dunmore began taking steps that caused Virginians to seethe with fury. Immediately following the Battle of Lexington, he initiated proceedings against Thomas Jefferson on charges of treason and secretly had all the gunpowder stored in the Williamsburg magazine taken to a British vessel lying at anchor off Yorktown. He then announced that if any sign of insurrection became apparent in the colony, he would set Williamsburg afire and reduce it to a pile of ashes. Patrick Henry raised a force of volunteers and confronted Dunmore, demanding he return the powder. Lord Dunmore refused to do so, but he did pay for it, then turned right around and issued a proclamation declaring that Patrick Henry and his followers were rebels.

Within another week he had sent his own family to safety aboard one of the British vessels. He then issued another proclamation granting protection to all Tories and freedom to all slaves who would support himself and the King of England. He sent a message to John Connolly, including a full commission to him as colonel instead of the brevet rank, and instructed him to enlist the aid of whatever militia commanders he could, through the use of large rewards. Connolly was also instructed to form an alliance with the Indians, assemble his forces at Fort Pitt and march them through Virginia to Williamsburg to assist him in the establishment of martial law.

Before Connolly could do so, however, he was arrested by officials of Pennsylvania and taken in irons to Fort Ligonier. In retaliation, three Pennsylvania magistrates in Pittsburgh were arrested and taken in irons to Wheeling. It was a stand-off, and before long the prisoners on both sides were released. Connolly returned to Fort Pitt.

In Williamsburg, Dunmore finally realized the growing momentum of the revolutionaries was more than he could withstand; he abdicated his office and then had the British man-of-war H.M.S. *Fowey* transport him to Norfolk, Virginia's largest town and most important port. Upon his arrival he burned the entire town.

As soon as it became known that Lord Dunmore had fled, the Assembly reformed, declared the office of governor vacant and gave themselves, for the first time, absolute home rule.[261] The Virginians, furious at Dunmore's actions, petitioned that the name of Dunmore County be abolished. This was done immediately, and the name was changed to Shenandoah County. The Virginia Convention then raised nine regiments, called the Virginia Line, and sent two companies of 100 men each to garrison Fort Pitt and a company of 25 men to Fort Fincastle at Wheeling. Now a colonel, William Crawford was given command of the Thirteenth Regiment, and his friend, John Knight, enlisted in that unit. Knight, having by this time worked off his indenture to Crawford, was now calling himself Dr. John Knight because he had studied medicine at the University of Aberdeen before coming to America as a stowaway.

A strong force was mounted under Gen. Andrew Lewis and advanced against Dunmore, who had taken refuge with the fleet at Gwynn Island in Chesapeake Bay. When they found him, Lewis himself fired the first gun. The fight was short but harsh, and the British fleet quickly fled with heavy losses. Lord Dunmore decided he would not return to Virginia.

By this time John Connolly, having failed to raise the force Dunmore had requested, left Fort Pitt for the east, and he, to the great joy of virtually everyone on the frontier, would not be returning to Fort Pitt.[262]

[October 26, 1775—Thursday]

Capt. Michael Cresap had been living in New York City since shortly after Dunmore's War. A year ago, when Dunmore's army had been disbanded after returning across the Ohio River, Cresap had wasted no time leaving the frontier again, convinced that if he remained, he would eventually encounter John Gibson, who would live up to his threat and kill him. But though Cresap escaped death at the hands of Gibson, he didn't escape it in another way. Just over a week ago, at age 32, he contracted smallpox and four days ago he died. Yesterday he was buried with military honors.

And today, in a cabin on Harmon's Creek, 24 miles above Wheeling, another man died—this one of measles—but there was no military funeral for him. His name was Daniel Greathouse, brother of Jacob.

[*J u l y   4 ,   1 7 7 6 — T h u r s d a y*]

Even though everyone in America knew that a war of revolution had been going on for over 14 months, it was still simply a war being carried on by colonists against their British government. It was time for them to unshackle themselves from this connection, and a major step in that direction had occurred during the June session of the Continental Congress, when Richard Henry Lee presented a momentous resolution:

"Resolved: that these United Colonies are, and of right ought to be, free and independent states." John Adams immediately seconded it, and a committee of five delegates was chosen to draw up a declaration embodying that resolution. Those five were Robert R. Livingston of New York, Roger Sherman of Connecticut, Benjamin Franklin of Pennsylvania, John Adams of Massachusetts and Thomas Jefferson of Virginia, but it was Jefferson who did the greatest amount of work.

Today that Declaration of Independence was read, and immediately John Hancock, president of the Continental Congress, signed his name in a very bold hand that, as Hancock put it, "the King of England can read without spectacles." In rapid succession the other delegates signed their names, and the document became official. The 13 colonies had now become independent states—assuming they could successfully defend this declaration.

America went wild with joy at throwing off the ties that had bound them to mother England. At the Pennsylvania Statehouse in Philadelphia, the great bell was pealed with such vigor that it cracked, and in New York City patriots gleefully pulled down the gilded lead statue of George III and melted it into bullets. On the upper Ohio, Fort Fincastle at Wheeling was immediately renamed Fort Henry, after Patrick Henry.

Without delay, a call was issued to enlarge George Washington's Continental Army as well as the various state militias. As an inducement to enlistment in their states, Connecticut, Massachusetts and Virginia promised to those who would volunteer and serve, bounties of land in the northwestern wilderness included in their original charters—land situated in the Ohio country. They did not dwell on the fact that the land in question was presently occupied by Shawnees, Delawares, Wyandots, Miamis, Potawatomies and Ottawas.

There was an immediate outcry from the remaining ten states; they protested, not that the land to be doled out through bounties belonged to these tribes, but rather that their own charters did not include large chunks of the unappropriated western lands. They insisted that if they were to give their services and shed their blood in this revolution, those western lands should be appropriated by the Congress for the benefit of all the states, according to population.

Congress agreed and urged those states owning these unappropriated western lands to make liberal concessions of them for the common benefit. It was the only fair thing to do, and Virginia led the field by initiating action to cede her lands north of the Ohio—on condition that if her lands south of that river proved insufficient to satisfy bounties for her own troops, the deficiency was to be made up from her lands north of the Ohio, situated between the Little Miami and Scioto rivers—territory that was the homeland of the Shawnees.

[May 31, 1777—Saturday]

In the 11 months that had passed since the colonies declared their independence, the Revolutionary War had become very hot in the east, but those Americans on the Ohio River frontier were faced with matters of more immediate concern. Ever more parties of Mingoes and Wyandots were making hit-and-run raids against the settlers, and each such attack was worse than the one preceding it. Now even the Delawares, who had for so long adamantly remained neutral, began sending out raiders, no longer willing to turn away when their people were insulted or physically abused or even murdered along the shores of the great river. But what had begun as raids by small groups were lately escalating into full-scale war parties, and suddenly more whites than Indians were being killed from well up the Allegheny and Monongahela rivers all the way down to the mouth of the Ohio.

During the preceding late summer, commissioners had been sent to Fort Pitt in an effort to bring the Indians to council and work out a new peace, but they were signally unsuccessful. British agents headquartered at Detroit had begun actively moving about among the tribes, instigating retaliation against the Americans for the injuries suffered. The Potawatomies, Ottawas and Wyandots, in council with Detroit's commander, Col. Henry Hamilton, who was also lieutenant governor of Canada, had already pledged alliance with the British. The Delawares seemed on the verge of doing so as the council continued and a large number of Chippewas were on their way down to Detroit from the upper regions of the Michigan country. All these tribesmen gathered in council were disturbed that the Shawnees were not represented here beyond a small handful of delegates. Runners were sent to Wapatomica, Mackachack, Chalahgawtha, Kispoko Town and Hokolesqua's Town, besieging the Shawnees with pleas to forget the Camp Charlotte agreement, since it had never been formalized into a treaty and the whites had never paid the slightest attention to it anyway. Still, Hokolesqua refused: He had given his word on behalf of the Shawnees, and until it was no longer even remotely possible for him to honor that word, he would not commit his tribe to war.

The chain of events that transpired, however, finally overruled him. In January, the number-two war chief of the Shawnees, Plukkemehnotee—called Pluggy by the whites—led a sizable party from Kispoko Town down the Scioto River and across the Ohio River and quickly killed two settlers they encountered, then moved on to attack McClelland's Station. George McClelland was killed in that attack, but so, too, was Plukkemehnotee, at which the Shawnee party withdrew.

Plukkemehnotee had been a lifelong friend of Chiungalla, and when the latter learned of the death, he could no longer restrain his anger. Hokolesqua was still at his village on Scippo Creek at this time, and without his knowledge or approval, Chiungalla called a council at Chalahgawtha.

"The death of Plukkemehnotee," he told the large assemblage, "is an unspeakable affront to our tribe and, to me, an act that cries in my heart for vengeance. I wish for two hundred brave and experienced warriors to join me. I will lead them from this village and intend to destroy every white settlement in our Kan-tuck-kee hunting grounds."

Winter was not normally the season to launch a war party, but what Chiungalla asked was exactly what the young warriors had yearned for, and he had no trouble assembling his force. Accompanied by some British from Detroit and a number of warriors who joined them from other tribes, he led them to Kentucky, where they made a series of fierce assaults against the settlements. Surviving whites abandoned their weak stations and fled to Harrodsburg, Boonesboro or Benjamin Logan's sturdy little St. Asaph's Station, and soon these three were the only settlements remaining in Kentucky. Chiungalla struck these final three places repeatedly, placing Harrodsburg and St. Asaph's under a prolonged siege and putting Boonesboro under siege three different times over a period of several months. Numerous men were killed on both sides, especially among the whites, but it would have been much worse for the settlers had nature not taken a hand. After months of being hampered by severe cold weather and storms, Chiungalla finally called off the major attacks and, leaving a large number of warriors behind to continue harassing the *Shemanese* in Kentucky, led a portion of his men back across the Ohio.[263]

Everyone on the frontier seemed to realize that the troubles that had beset them thus far were only a prelude of what was to come. In the upper reaches of the Ohio rumors were again rampant of large war parties of Wyandots and Mingoes preparing to move against them, and there was a flurry of activity as new blockhouses sprang up all over and existing cabins were fortified. These became places where threatened settlers could take refuge and from which parties of men could range outward to intercept the raiding Indians.

At his settlement near the mouth of Short Creek, John Vanmetre spent weeks fortifying his cabin, and the place soon became known as Fort Vanmetre. Similar cabins were fortified or new little blockhouses erected at Beech Bottom and at the mouths of Cross Creek and Grave Creek. They helped a little, but everyone knew that, apart from Fort Pitt, only Fort Henry at Wheeling had any chance of withstanding a major assault.

The Kentucky country was gaining the reputation of being a dark and bloody land, but attacks were increasing throughout the entire thousand-mile length of the Ohio Valley. And the Ohio River itself, known by so many different names in the past, was being given a new and menacing designation that was destined to last for decades to come: It was being called that dark and bloody river.

[J u n e   1 7 ,   1 7 7 7 — T u e s d a y]

The new Grand Council at Detroit, being held by the lieutenant governor of Canada, Col. Henry Hamilton, had by now attracted somewhat more than 3,000 tribesmen from hundreds of miles distant: Kickapoos from the southern Illinois country, Potawatomies from the lower Lake Michigan country, Winnebagoes and Menominees from the Wisconsin country, Chippewas and Mississaugi from the upper Michigan country and Iroquois delegates from upper New York and adjacent Canada. Hundreds were also on hand from the closer tribes: the Wyandots and Miamis, the Mingoes and Delawares and Shawnees. Speaker after speaker had risen to pledge support to the British, and many more raids were promised by the Wyandots and Delawares.

Hamilton had issued a proclamation that was now posted not only at Detroit but at every frontier station and fur-trading post where it might be read by any who were still wavering in their loyalties:

> *By virtue of the power and authority to me given by his Excellency, Sir Guy Carleton, Knight of the Bath, Governor of the Province of Quebec, General and Commander-in-Chief, &c., &c., &c.*
>
> *I do assure all such as are inclined to withdraw themselves from the tyranny and oppression of the rebel committees, and take refuge in this settlement, or any of the posts commanded by His Majesty's officers, shall be humanely treated, shall be lodged and victualled, and such as come off in arms and use them in defence of His Majesty against rebels and traitors till the extinction of this rebellion, shall receive pay adequate to their former stations in the rebel service, and all common men who shall serve during that period shall receive His Majesty's bounty of two hundred acres of land.*
>
> *Given under my hand and seal.*

God Save the King   *Henry Hamilton*
                                                      Lt. Gov. & Superintendent

Last Sunday, Hamilton, still having received no specific instructions from Quebec in respect to what was expected of the Indians on this frontier, had written to Gov. Carleton about the pending council:

> *Detroit 15th June 1777.*
>
> *I have the honor to inform your Excellency, that the Ottawas, Chippewas, Pouteowattamis, Hurons, Miamis, are come to this place and are to meet in Council on Tuesday next. There are also some Shawnees, Delawares, Quashtanows, but a few in Number.*
>
> *I shall keep them together as long as possible in expectation of your Excellency's orders. Tho' the Majority should return home I make no doubt of being able to assemble a Thousand Warriors in three weeks, should your Excellency have occasion for their services.*
>
> *I have the honor to be most respectfully Your Excellency's most devoted & most humble servant.*
>
> *Henry Hamilton*

Now council was in progress, and it had begun on an encouraging note. War belts had been ceremonially presented to Col. Hamilton by delegates from the Iroquois in New York, advocating attacks against the whites who had risen up against their father across the great waters. Hamilton, in turn, passed the war belts on to the Great Lakes tribes assembled, and he addressed them in strong terms.

"Turn your strength and fighting skill against those whites who are the enemies of the King and, therefore, your enemies as well," he told them. "Do not dip your hands in the blood of their women and children, but concentrate on the men, the warriors who will rise up against you, because it is they who consider all Indians their enemies." Despite Hamilton's words, the Indians knew that they would be rewarded for bringing in prisoners as well as for all scalps taken, including those of women and children, even though the word *bounty* had been studiously avoided.

With a lavish hand Hamilton provided great feasts, distributed weapons and bestowed gifts on the assembled Indians, and all of these were gratefully accepted. He especially commended the Iroquois delegates for the attacks being made in the Mohawk Valley and other places against the American settlers on that frontier. Though the Iroquois maintained little affection for the western splinter group of Cayugas and Senecas who had long called themselves Mingoes, the Six Nations delegates now publicly applauded those very Mingoes, as well as the Wyandots, for the vigor with which they were opposing the whites in the upper Ohio Valley and urged more of the same.

"In what has already passed," responded Pimoacan—Captain Pipe—of the Delawares, "they have felt but the tips of our spears and arrows and have smelled only the first faint whiffs of our gunpowder. Now they will come to know the full thrust of the blades of our knives and tomahawks, and the smell of our gunsmoke will choke them."

[J u l y   2 6 ,   1 7 7 7 — S a t u r d a y]

The appeals for help made to Virginia by the Kentuckians in the three remaining fortified settlements—St. Asaph's, Harrodsburg and Boonesboro—had finally had an effect: Col. John Bowman arrived with a mounted company of 100 men. A young officer highly impressed with his own importance, Bowman was disgruntled at having been sent to this remote frontier instead of to the British-American battlefront, where great recognition and subsequent advancement could be gained by enterprising officers, such as was presently occurring with Anthony Wayne and Arthur St. Clair. He disdained the rude living conditions here and the scraggly militia drawn up in his honor by Maj. George Rogers Clark and became incensed over the fact that no barracks were available for his men, nor stables for the horses.

Most galling was the fact that, so far as Bowman could see, there was little problem here requiring military attention. A few marauding Indians were still out causing some annoyances, but they hardly constituted the invasion that had been reported. Ignoring Clark's friendly greeting, Bowman informed him that he was taking over his militia command.

Clark, presently in the midst of planning an attempt to capture the British posts at Kaskaskia and Cahokia in the Illinois country, had only a few weeks ago sent out two men—Benjamin Moore and Samuel Linn—to spy there. He had hoped the reinforcement under Bowman would help in this endeavor. Instead, he was coldly rebuffed. Stung by such treatment, he refused to serve under Bowman. Instead, he began at once to recruit new men for his endeavor. He did not have a wide selection; even though Boone's friend, Bailey Smith, had recently arrived with 40 men from North Carolina, there were only 102 men left at the three stations—65 at Harrods-burg, 22 at Boonesboro and 15 at St. Asaph's.

Bowman had been in Kentucky but a few weeks when, without orders to do so, he returned with his men to eastern Virginia, leaving Kentucky once again virtually defenseless.

[J u l y   3 1 ,   1 7 7 7 — T h u r s d a y]

The new Ohio County in Virginia, which included Wheeling, had established its militia almost two months ago during its first court session. Col. David Shepherd, now living in a cabin he had fortified on Wheeling Creek, was named its com-mander. Samuel McCulloch, who had been active in Dunmore's War and was then promoted to major, was named second-in-command of Fort Henry, with that rank. John Mitchell, Samuel Peters, Joseph Ogle, Jacob Lefler, John Vanmetre and Sam Meason were all named captains, while the lieutenants appointed were Sam Tomlin-son, Thomas Gilleland, John Biggs and Derick Hoaglin. William Sparks was commis-sioned as ensign. All of the captains had at once begun recruiting men for their companies, most of which were by now up to full strength. It was none too soon, as the Indian raids had increased considerably almost everywhere on this upper Ohio River frontier, usually involving bands of Indian raiders of ten or fewer warriors who moved with great speed, struck with terrible ferocity and then quickly vanished, only to strike again soon somewhere else.

Today one such band of Chippewas, unleashed by Henry Hamilton and led by a renegade white named Thomas McCarty, who had been with the tribe for many years, struck at the cabin of George Baker, situated at the mouth of Raccoon Creek, just 30 miles downstream from Fort Pitt.[264] Baker, his wife and five sons—the eldest of whom was 11 years old, and the youngest, only four—had settled at this site in mid-May and erected a small but secure cabin.

Yesterday afternoon one of the younger boys reported that he thought he had glimpsed some Indians lurking about and, since the dogs had been barking more than usual, George Baker checked around a little. Finding nothing, he discounted it as a too-vivid imagination on the part of his son. Then at dawn today, the door was abruptly broken open, and in instants the entire family of seven was taken prisoner and the cabin burned.[265]

The news of the capture of the entire Baker family spread quickly, and Col. Edward Hand, commanding at Fort Pitt, immediately increased patrols and strength-ened security. Outlying settlers were warned to move to the nearest secure fort at once. Among those who took this advice was the Tomlinson family at Grave Creek. Rebecca Tomlinson Martin, sister of the Tomlinson boys and their housekeeper since the death of her husband, trader John Martin, in 1770, was now living in her own cabin nearby on the Grave Creek Flats and had a new name. Not quite two years ago —in October 1775—she had married a new settler to the area, Isaac Williams.[266]

They had fallen in love soon after his arrival there, and when a traveling preacher happened to pass through, they were married without much ceremony, he in his hunting garb and she in her everyday homespun dress.

Now, however, with Indian raids increasing so alarmingly, the men at Grave Creek Flats were ordered upriver to Wheeling to help protect it against a large force of Indians rumored to be preparing to launch a massive attack against that settlement. Joseph and James Tomlinson, along with Isaac and Rebecca Williams, abandoned the Grave Creek Settlement and moved back to the Monongahela, but Samuel, now fully recovered from his lameness, elected to go to Wheeling and aid in its defense.[267]

[A u g u s t   8 ,   1 7 7 7 — F r i d a y]

Old John Wetzel, as the other settlers on Wheeling Creek called him, looked considerably older than his 46 years. His face was deeply lined and craggy and his hair prematurely gray, which gave rise to the sobriquet, but he was a strong and very active man. He loved farming and already had well over 100 acres in crops in the fertile land he had claimed 14 miles above the creek's mouth and seven miles above the Forks of Wheeling Creek. Seven years ago when he had claimed here, he was not terribly pleased at being so far upstream on the creek. Now, however, with the Indian troubles having increased so, this very remoteness was an added measure of protection. If the Indians did take a notion to raid this way, there were plenty of other settlers farther downstream between here and Wheeling they could hit first. Maybe not a charitable view, he admitted to himself, but that was the fact of it.

Family protection was his primary concern. His wife was a good woman, and he was inordinately proud of the six children she had borne him during those years they had lived at the Moorefield Settlement on South Branch Potomac and the seventh while they were living on Dunkard Creek, near the Monongahela. The two girls were learning all the skills of homemaking and self-defense from their mother and would make good frontier wives; Christina, now 21, was the eldest of the seven, while Susan, who was next to youngest, had just turned nine.

Where his five sons were concerned, John Wetzel was determined that they would learn wilderness skills that would stand them in good stead on the frontier. Martin, eldest of the boys, had been born in 1757, followed by George in 1760. Lewis was presently 13; Jacob, 11. John Jr., whom the family called Johnny and who had been born on Dunkard Creek, had celebrated his seventh birthday just a few weeks ago.

With painstaking care, Old John had taught the boys well; most of all, how to stay calm and use their heads in the most trying of circumstances. He also taught them important physical skills: how to run at full tilt through woodland without running into a low-hanging branch or a tree trunk; how to fight with knives and tomahawks, or even a club; how to make and use a bow effectively; how to shoot a gun accurately; and how to load a flintlock rifle while at full run. It was a skill some of the best of the frontiersmen had not mastered, yet Martin and George could do it almost as well as their father, Lewis was getting pretty good at it and even Jacob had begun to learn. Soon it would be Johnny's turn to begin practicing.

Their father also taught them the all-important elements of survival in the woods in any season, with or without weapons: tracking and outthinking the animal, or man, they were trailing; fire-building without flint and steel; building snares, traps and deadfalls. All these and more were part of the routine every time they went anywhere. Only a few weeks ago, in fact, Old John had taken Lewis and Jacob out into the woods along Fish Creek many miles from home, set up a camp and proceeded to prepare his own dinner but none for them.

"You boys want to eat," he told them, handing Lewis his flintlock, powderhorn and bullet pouch, "it's up to you to find it, kill it, clean it and bring it in."

The boys looked long and hard for deer or turkey, grouse or squirrels or rabbits, but game was uncommonly scarce at this time, and for two days their gun went unfired. In camp at the end of the second day's hunt, they watched, ravenously hungry, as their father ate his evening meal and then lit up his pipe and chuckled.

"Reckon you young'uns ain't hungry enough yet to realize they's plenty out there can be et iffen ye k'n git over bein' too dang picky."

The third day's hunt was no more successful than the previous two, but still their father gave them nothing to eat. On the fourth morning they left camp at dawn and hardly ten minutes had passed before Old John heard a distant shot and set about rebuilding the fire they would need to cook whatever game had been killed. Half an hour later they came in, grinning, with two haunches of a fairly large animal. They cut the meat into chunks, spitted it on sharpened saplings, cooked it and ate it with gusto.

"I ain't never seen no bird with meat like that," observed their father when they were finished, "an' it surely didn't look like deer meat to me, nor bear nor elk, neither. So what'd you boys eat that you liked so much?"

Lewis and Jacob looked at each other and burst out laughing. It was Lewis who replied: "Wolf, Paw. A big ol' wolf, an' I reckon we never ate nothin' that tasted so blamed good!"

The rigorous training Old John Wetzel put his boys through was soon put to the test. Despite the fact that he felt they were reasonably safe so far up Wheeling, the recent Indian attacks and the call for men to come to help defend Wheeling had convinced him to take the family there. After a week, however, with no further threat materializing, Old John and three of his sons—George, Lewis and Jacob—returned to their place to do some work with the crops. They were almost there when Old John shot a fine buck, and they brought it to their cabin with them. The three plow horses were still grazing in the fenced pasture, and the bitch who had borne four pups a couple of months ago was still caring for them by herself and everything seemed fine. The weather was warm, so to preserve the meat they cut it into strips for jerking and hung the pieces over the chimney fire to cure.[268]

In the morning, anticipating no problems, Old John and 17-year-old George left their guns in the cabin, and the four of them took their hoes and headed out to the turnip patch to do some cultivating.[269] They worked hard together, and about midmorning Old John paused and leaned on his hoe. The boys paused as well and looked at him. He nodded as if he had reached some decision in his own mind.

"Lew, you an' Jake take a walk down to the cabin an' put some more wood on the fire an' check on how that meat's curin'. Make sure that dawg ain't stealin' none of it. Also, it might not have been a good idea, me an' George leavin' our guns at the house. Bring 'em along when you come back."

Lewis and Jacob left immediately, glad to be relieved of the hoeing for a while. When they got to the cabin, they found the venison strips curing well but the fire considerably burned down. There were a few pieces of wood in the cabin and, while Jacob put them on the coals, Lewis went outside to get some more wood. He was just stooping to pick up a piece when he heard a sound that caused him to straighten and begin turning around. As he did so, there was the crash of a gun, and he felt a searing pain as a ball slammed into the right side of his chest and scored a deep gash before exiting on the left side. He was knocked off his feet and rolled over on the ground but almost instantly rose again to run. He had no chance. Two Indians close by shrieked wildly and grabbed him by the arms. Jacob came running out of the cabin to see what was happening and, taking it in at a glance, turned and tried to run off, but he, too, was caught by more Indians who dashed out of the nearby woods.

They were a party of seven Wyandots who gathered around the boys, and from what Lewis and Jacob could understand of what they said, the Indians had decided to take them along and make good Wyandot warriors out of them. Four of the warriors went into the cabin and brought out the two rifles and some other goods that were there and used the blankets they found inside to tie the goods into bundles.[270] Even in his pain, Lewis thought it strange that they didn't take the meat that was curing. Three of the Wyandots, however, caught the three plow horses in the pasture, brought them to the cabin and tied the bundles on them.[271]

Old John and George, hearing the shot and shrieks, knew in one horrible instant what was occurring. Cursing himself for leaving his gun at the cabin— something he had never done before and vowed savagely never to do again—John told George to follow him, and they plunged across the creek to the east side and raced up a steep hill. There, from a clearing through the trees, they had a good view of the cabin. Father and son were relieved when they saw both boys were still alive and the Indians busy loading bundles of plunder on the plow horses. Without weapons, however, Old John and George were helpless to do anything but watch and stay out of sight.

At the cabin one of the Indians discovered the dog and her litter. Selecting the largest of the pups to take along, he handed it to Jacob to carry. Jacob shook his head and shoved the puppy aside. The Indian snatched it up and handed it back to him, and again Jacob turned it loose. The Indian caught it once again and this time gave Jacob a fierce swat on the head and threatened more of the same if he didn't carry the puppy, so Jacob accepted it.[272]

Lewis's shirt was heavily stained with blood, but the Indians looked at his wound and nodded in agreement that it was not serious and he could survive.[273] Then, with Lewis and Jacob forced to walk in their midst and three of the Indians now riding the plow horses, they moved off into the woods. The entire episode had taken no more than 15 minutes.

Well above on the hill, Old John and George watched them go and then immediately set out at top speed by a different route to reach Wheeling and try to get a rescue party on the move. Staying clear of the creekside path lest they be ambushed, they didn't reach Fort Henry until evening. Capt. Sam Meason was now in temporary command and there was considerable concern over what had occurred and a rejuvenation of fears that had been abating. Night was approaching and, still expecting the rumored attack to occur, Capt. Meason refused to mount a rescue party, saying they all sympathized with the Wetzels, but the safety of the people now gathered at Wheeling took precedence.[274]

The party of Wyandots marched the Wetzel boys through the woods until midafternoon, when they finally came to a small stream and followed it down to its mouth at the Ohio. Neither boy had been here before, and so they had no good idea where the crossing would be made, although Lewis told Jacob they were probably well downstream from Wheeling. In whispers, the boys agreed that neither of them would try to escape unless they could do so together.

Some 25 yards upstream on the creek from its mouth, the Indians had hidden two canoes under brush. They loaded the goods and their captives aboard and crossed the Ohio, one of the Indians riding one of the horses and swimming it across while leading the other two behind.

On the Ohio side, the canoes were pulled into another creek mouth and there weighted with rocks and sunk for use another time. Then the party began marching again to the northwest along a dim winding trail. At twilight the Indians stopped and made camp, and Lewis estimated they were by then four or five miles from the Ohio. The Indians came to where a deerskin pouch was hanging from a tree out of the reach of animals, and they took it down. Inside were cracklings—strips of deer skin from which the fat had been rendered—and they began eating it. They offered some to the boys, who refused when they saw it was infested with maggots, and so the Indians gave them some wild lettuce, which Jacob called squaw salad, and then tethered them for the night. Each of the boys had a rawhide cord passed around his waist through his belt loops and his shoes taken away. Each boy was then forced to lie down between two Indians, with one end of the cord tied around his wrists to alert them if he attempted escape. Lewis's wound was beginning to fester and was very painful, but he made no complaint, and the approval of the Indians was apparent as they nodded and murmured, "Make good warrior."

The next day they traveled again all day and by late afternoon had reached Will's Creek.[275] Once again they camped as before, and one of the Indians attempted to talk to Lewis, using sign language and a scattering of English words. He pointed at an angle toward the eastern sky and repeated the word *Goschachgunk* several times. From this Lewis deduced that they would reach Goschachgunk about ten o'clock the next morning. He also knew that when they did, they would be forced to run the gauntlet. Fearing they would not survive the ordeal, the boys, speaking in undertones, agreed to make an escape attempt this night.

When evening came, the boys were unshod and tethered as they had been the night before. All the Indians went to sleep except one who remained on guard. Soon, however, he became sleepy and drifted off. Jacob then carefully began squirming out of his pants, careful not to jerk the cords and awaken either of the Indians to whom he was tethered. He was successful and was just getting to his feet when the sentinel started to awaken. Lewis pretended to be asleep, and Jacob, thinking quickly, snatched up a small kettle and started walking with it. The guard stopped him with a cry, and Jacob pantomimed that he was thirsty and going down the creek bank to get water in the kettle.

By this time the other Indians had awakened, and Jacob was soon tied again the same way, but this time more securely. Once more the boys had a long wait before all the Indians, including the guard, again fell asleep. Then both Lewis and Jacob once more began trying to hitch and inch themselves out of their pants. Jacob's tether was now too tight and he could not get free, but Lewis did. Very silently he crept to one of the Indians and gradually, carefully, slid his knife out of its sheath. He then went to Jacob and cut his tether away, returned and cut the tether off his own pants and put them back on.

Their shoes were nowhere to be seen, but the Indians had hung their own damp moccasins on sticks by the fire to dry them out overnight, and the boys crept there and each took a pair. The footwear was stiff and shrunken, so they slipped down to the creek and soaked them enough to stretch them over their feet.

Jacob was all for getting away in a hurry then, but Lewis stayed him. "We got to go back to the camp," he whispered. "We got to get the guns, Paw's and George's." Jacob didn't much care for the idea, but he agreed, and they crept back into the camp.[276] George's rifle was leaning against a tree with powderhorn and shot pouch and was easy to get. Lewis gave it to Jacob and turned to get the other one. This was more of a problem: The stock was partially under the head of one of the warriors, and he had to work it out very slowly and with great care. At last it came free, and he and Jacob slipped away.

They began following the trail back the way they had come but had gone no more than 100 yards or so when they heard an outcry raised behind them; the Indians had discovered their escape. Dawn was still about an hour away, and Lewis was sure they would not attempt to follow until then, but they would surely do so at that time, so they continued on the trail and the easier passage it provided until day began to break. At this point they left the trail and struck out roughly parallel with it, but several hundred yards distant. The going was much more difficult this way, and by late morning they were exhausted.

"Let's go back to the trail, Lew," Jacob suggested. "We can tell easy enough if they came past hunting for us."

Lewis agreed, and they swung back to intercept the trail. In a short while they encountered it and saw at once the hoofmarks of two horses heading toward the river on the trail. The hoofprints were broad and showed the marks of horseshoes and were obviously two of their own plow horses being ridden by Indians in pursuit of them. Instantly they turned away from the path again and took a due east course overland.

They traveled almost constantly, pausing only occasionally to rest and briefly nap before moving on. At one point they stopped long enough to cut off some slippery elm bark and chew it to make a poultice to put on Lewis's wound, which was giving him more pain than at any time previously.

It was close to noon the following day when they came to the Ohio, and they nearly wept with joy when they saw Wheeling Island and, beyond it, Wheeling itself and Fort Henry. They found chunks of wood on the shore and lashed their guns to them with willow withes, then entered the water and pushed the logs ahead of them as they swam to the island. Lewis was so weak by this time that without Jacob's help, he would not have made it across to the island.

On the island they found a small party of boys from Wheeling who had come over by canoe to pick some of the succulent wild summer grapes that grew in abundance here. The party gave up their quest for grapes and quickly ferried the two exhausted Wetzel boys across to Wheeling.

Word of their return spread quickly, and a crowd gathered around them, shouting congratulations at their escape and demanding details. Then the crowd parted and let Old John Wetzel through, followed by George and Martin. There was a very joyous reunion, and Lewis grinned and handed the two rifles to his father.

"I'm sorry we got them wet, Paw," he said.

Chapter 3

[August 22, 1777—Friday]

Martin Wetzel and John Baker were the closest of friends and about as inseparable as two adventurous young men of 20 could be. Usually they tried to arrange things so they were together, whether it was going out on a hunt, trailing marauding Indians or defending the settlement forts. They were equally skilled in woods lore, and Martin was as proud of John having recently been made a captain in the militia as he would have been had the appointment been his own.

Ever since the capture of Martin's two young brothers, Lewis and Jacob, and their subsequent escape, the rumors of an impending Indian attack of major proportions had increased, and many more upper Ohio River settlements and isolated cabins were abandoned, their inhabitants taking refuge at Wheeling. Regular militia patrols were now going up and down the river, watching closely for Indians or for any sign of their crossing to the Virginia side. Capt. John Baker was put in command of one such patrol yesterday, and no one was surprised when he selected Martin as one of his squad, as well as Martin's brother, George, and their father, Old John.

Their first assigned task on this patrol today was to paddle five miles downstream from Wheeling and check around the ruins of McMechen's Settlement to see if there was any fresh sign of Indians having been there, since the McMechen cabin and outbuildings had been burned by Indian raiders on August 12. Fortunately, it had happened just after the McMechens had left it to take refuge at Wheeling, but this was the second time the settlement had been burned, and William McMechen, while thankful that his family was safe, was very depressed and considering leaving the frontier.

Baker's squad paddled their canoe very near the Virginia shoreline, closely studying the banks for any indication that Indians had come ashore. They found no fresh sign along those banks or at the burned-out settlement and so continued their patrol downstream, studying the shoreline, for another nine miles to Round Bottom. Several families had taken refuge in the small unnamed blockhouse that had been erected there, and Baker's squad stopped briefly to check on them. The half-dozen men and several women and children were all right, but they reported something of a scare a few days earlier, when a small party of Indians had been spotted on the opposite shore. However, the Indians had quickly vanished, and there had been no trouble.

Still paying close attention to the banks, the squad then continued down the Ohio the remaining distance of its patrol, which was to the small blockhouse that had been built at the head of Cresap's Bottom, six miles below Round Bottom and 20 miles below Wheeling.[277] They landed here and were inside the blockhouse when a party of eight Indians emerged from the woodland across the river and moved close to shore.

"Watch this," Baker said. He leveled his rifle and pointed it toward them.

"Hell, John," Martin chuckled, "that's more'n three hundred yards. You don't really figger you k'n hit one, do you?"

"Mebbe not," Baker murmured, "but I'm sure gonna scare hell out of 'em." He took a careful bead on one, then raised his aim a foot or so over the Indian's head. The rifle crashed, and the four men ducked low to avoid the cloud of gunsmoke and watch the reaction. To their amazement, the warrior Baker had aimed at clutched at his chest, staggered and then fell. The rest of his party instantly took to their heels and disappeared into the woodland.

"Well, I'll be damned!" said Old John Wetzel. "By God, John," he thumped Baker on the back, "that's sure 'nuff the finest shot ever I seen!"

The rest of the squad congratulated him as well, and Martin shook his friend's hand warmly. "You'll go the rest of your life and never make another shot like that, John," he said.

Baker was grinning and obviously very pleased with himself. "C'mon, boys," he said, "let's go across. I want that scalp, and I want to see if I plugged him clean through the heart like I aimed."

"Now hol' on," Old John warned. "Them other red niggers're apt t'be waitin' fer someone to show up. Reckon we oughta wait a mite 'fore goin' over."

They all recognized the wisdom of this and so remained where they were, talking casually and keeping their eyes on the opposite shore. At the end of an hour, Baker spoke up.

"I 'spect if they was still around, we'd'a seen 'em by now. I'm goin' over. Anyone comin' along?"

Keeping sharply alert, the four returned to the canoe and paddled across, beaching their craft within a dozen feet of where the fallen warrior lay. As they had agreed to do on the way across, they didn't approach the body immediately but instead spread out quickly and began checking the woodland fringe to make certain the Indians were gone.

They weren't. Several shots shattered the silence, and Baker fell, writhing in pain. As the three Wetzels leaped into hiding among the trees, two Indians jumped out close to where Baker lay, grasped him by the wrists and just as quickly dragged him out of sight. There was momentary quiet, and then from well into the woods came a terrible scream. Hardly had the first begun dwindling away than there was another, equally agonizing.

Slowly the three Wetzels came together and crouched, quietly intent as they watched and listened. At last Old John slowly straightened, and George and Martin did the same.

"Reckon they're really gone this time," the elder Wetzel said. "Let's go find John. Careful, boys."

They moved from tree to tree in sequence until they reached the place where Baker had fallen and then been dragged into the woods. There was a good bit of blood and, still keeping to cover, they followed the trail. They found him 50 yards or so into the woods. He was scalped but still alive and had dragged himself a short distance on his stomach until he was partially under a log, but he was unconscious now. They pulled him out and turned him over, then gasped at what they saw. His shirtfront was soaked with blood from two bullet wounds, one low in the right chest, the other in his stomach. Both eyeballs had been gouged out and torn away.

With careful haste, they carried him back to the canoe and paddled swiftly across the river, where they moved him gently into the blockhouse and laid him on the earthen floor. He had not regained consciousness and his breathing was erratic. There was nothing they could do for him, and they merely squatted beside him and watched. Martin put his hand to his friend's cheek and simply held it there.

Ten minutes later, without having regained consciousness, Capt. John Baker died.[278]

[*A u g u s t   3 1 ,   1 7 7 7 — S u n d a y   e v e n i n g*]

Fort Henry at Wheeling was not a terribly large fort—its spear-sharpened, eight-foot-high pickets enclosed less than an acre of ground—but it was far more a haven for the settlers than most of the little fortified cabins and local blockhouses at many of the settlements. As always, it was a welcome sight to Capt. Thomas Ogle and his squad of a dozen mounted men when they reached it at twilight this evening at the end of their latest three-day patrol. He dismissed the squad, and nine of the men went immediately to their quarters. The remaining three—Joseph Biggs, Abraham Rogers and Robert Lemon—accompanied him as he reported immediately to Col. David Shepherd.

Shepherd himself had arrived here at Wheeling just before noon today. Concerned for his family, he felt they would be more secure here than at his own little Shepherd's Fort at the Forks of Wheeling Creek, seven miles above, even though a number of settlers were still there. Accompanying him today was his 19-year-old son, William, with his wife, Rebecca, and their infant daughter. Col. Shepherd also felt he should be on hand at Wheeling in case the Indians should attack, and immediately upon his arrival, he had assumed command of Fort Henry from Capt. Samuel Meason, which made no one particularly unhappy except perhaps Meason himself.

There was now a distinct possibility that an Indian attack might materialize. A dispatch had recently been received from Fort Pitt that was more than a little unnerving. A pair of converted Delawares from the Tuscarawas had come to Gen. Hand bearing secret intelligence from the Moravian missionary, John Heckewelder, to the effect that close to 400 confederated Indians had assembled at Half King's Town, the principal Wyandot town on the upper Sandusky River. Heckewelder had initially been led to believe the big war party was preparing to strike at the Kentucky settlements. However, they had unexpectedly appeared at the Forks of the Muskingum instead, and it was now evident they were aiming to attack somewhere on the upper Ohio. Wheeling, with its 30 permanent houses and a score or more temporary dwellings, plus herds of cows and other livestock, a multitude of horses and without a regular army garrison on hand to protect it, seemed the most likely target.

At this time, with the return of the patrol squad, there were only 35 men on hand to protect Wheeling, and the commander listened closely to Tom Ogle's report. He said that on the entire patrol up the principal river path, all the way to the mouth of Raccoon Creek and back, they had watched the ground carefully for any sign of Indians, especially in the vicinity of the trails, but had found none.

"I believe I can say with assurance, sir," Ogle concluded, "that no parties have come across the river above here." He appeared about to say more but then did not.

"I seem to detect there's something else, Captain," Shepherd prompted.

"Well, nothing really definite, sir, except that while we were between Beech Bottom and here about half an hour ago, we noticed something peculiar."

Beech Bottom was 12 miles upstream, and the colonel nodded, a faint edge of impatience in his voice. "All right, let's have it. What?"

"The air became hazy, sir. More downstream than anywhere else. We"—he looked at his companions as if for confirmation— "all of us thought it looked sort of like smoke. Couldn't smell any smoke, but it looked like it."

"From where, do you suppose?"

"Well, I don't know, Colonel, but if I were to make a guess, I'd say there's a possibility the blockhouse at Grave Creek has been burned."

"That's it?" Col. Shepherd asked. The little Grave Creek Blockhouse was a dozen miles below Wheeling, and it seemed to him that that was a long distance to detect any smoke in the atmosphere.

"Yes, sir, that's it."

"All right. Thank you, Captain Ogle. You and your men get some food and rest now."

"Yes, sir. Thank you, sir."

Saluting, the four men turned and left, and Col. Shepherd walked to the small window and looked out. It was almost dark now, and the temptation was to forget about it until tomorrow morning, but he shook his head. This was not the time to be careless about anything that seemed even remotely suspicious.

Thirty minutes later, two men slid their canoe away from shore near the Wheeling wharf and headed downstream in the early darkness.[279] Their instructions from Col. Shepherd were to reconnoiter as far as the mouth of Grave Creek, ascertain if there were any Indians in the area and return as quickly as possible. He expected to see them back before dawn.

[August 31, 1777—Sunday night]

It was well after eleven P.M. when the Indian force began its swift and silent crossing of the Ohio River, in canoes brought along or hastily constructed for this purpose. The little boats, each carrying six to ten warriors on the way over and one or two on the way back, repeatedly crossed the big stream. First, the Indians went across the west channel to Wheeling Island, then quickly moved on foot to the east shore of the near half-mile-wide island, then crossed the east channel just as silently and swiftly to the Virginia shore to a point about a quarter-mile above Fort Henry.[280] Within three hours the entire war party of 389 Wyandots, Ottawas, Chippewas and Mingoes had completed the crossing.

The gates of Fort Henry were closed, and numerous lanterns glowed from within, but most of the houses, cabins, shacks and outbuildings beyond its perimeter were dark. The broad trail running north from the fort toward small, seven-mile-distant Vanmetre's Fort at the mouth of Short Creek was flanked by fields of tall standing corn, and it was in these fields that half the Indians secreted themselves in two separated lines. The other half spread out in a broad arc beyond the dwellings, stretching their line all the way to Wheeling Creek. A small group of six Indians remained apart from the others, prepared to show themselves when daylight came to any group or party that emerged from the fort and to serve as a decoy to lead an attacking force from the fort into ambush.

Within an hour of their crossing, there was no visible sign of an Indian in the area. Tense and excited about what lay ahead, they had settled down in hiding to wait for daylight.

[September 1, 1777—Monday, 3 A.M.]

The two men in the canoe, returning in the darkness from their mission to Grave Creek, angled their slim little craft into the mouth of Wheeling Creek, paddled upstream about 30 yards and put to shore just below Fort Henry. They quickly pulled the boat well up from the water's edge and then turned to climb the steep bank to the level where the fort was located. As they passed the bulk of a large log barely visible in the darkness, two figures rose from hiding and stepped quickly up behind them. The men heard a slight sound and began to turn, but never completed the movement. Two tomahawks simultaneously plunged through their skulls, and both men dropped without uttering a sound. They were quickly and silently scalped, their weapons taken and the bodies shoved into a cavity beside the log.

[September 1, 1777—Monday, 6 A.M.]

Dr. David McMahan was thoroughly disillusioned about living on the frontier.[281]

Last spring, when he was back in Baltimore, the idea of coming to the western wilderness and claiming fine tracts of land as his own had seemed like a glamorous adventure. So had serving in the army under Gen. Washington. A permanently shriveled left hand from a bullet wound received at Braddock's defeat 22 years earlier had made him unacceptable for further military service, but he could not be disqualified from a western adventure, and the idea, once conceived, consumed him. An impulsive man at times, within a week he had turned his medical practice over to a colleague and set off on horseback with his two Negro slaves, Sam and Ezra, on their own horses, each leading two packhorses laden with baggage and tools. They had made their way to Fort Cumberland and followed the Braddock Road to Brownsville, then crossed the Monongahela and followed the trail that led to Catfish Camp and, finally, Wheeling.

He was disappointed when he found worthwhile land in that vicinity all taken up, and he didn't much like the idea of striking out into the wilderness on his own to find land still available. A bit late, he discovered, as well, that he very much missed the medical life and the comforts of a more civilized existence. And though he did not care to admit it, he was morbidly fearful of being attacked by Indians, even to the point of having nightmares where he saw his own scalp hanging from the belt of a half-naked savage.

Here at Wheeling he had treated some of the most fearsome wounds and mutilations he had ever seen, not only among the men, where they might be expected as an occupational hazard of being an Indian fighter, but among women and children as well. Less than a month ago he had treated that nasty, infected chest wound the Wetzel boy had suffered from the Indians, and he had not been entirely convinced the lad would recover, though he had; there were too many others who had not.

Last night he had lain awake most of the night thinking about the situation here and at last he had come to a conclusion: This was not the way he wanted to spend the rest of his days. He would leave Wheeling and return to Baltimore, where he belonged. With Dr. David McMahan, a decision made was a decision acted upon. He dressed himself and then roused his slaves in the first gray light of dawn.

"Sam, Ezra," he said, "I want you to get two or three other men—tell them I'll pay them a dollar each—and go out to where the horses are grazing and bring them in. We're leaving for Baltimore this morning."

The expression on the faces of the two black men brightened. Sam, who had been taken into slavery in Guinea when a boy, grinned broadly. "For sure, Massa?" he asked. "For good?"

Dr. McMahan nodded. "For sure and for good. Now get to it. If possible, I want to be on our way by sunrise."

[*September 1, 1777 — Monday, 6:30 A.M.*]

The two men hired by Sam and Ezra to help round up and bring in Dr. McMahan's seven horses were a young Irishman named John Boyd and the huge down-on-his-luck German named Jacob Greathouse. Both were militiamen but off duty at the moment.[282]

The horses had been put to pasture along Wheeling Creek in a small bottom a bit more than a mile above Fort Henry. The four men had little difficulty in rounding them up and getting them haltered. They had no sooner started leading them back toward the settlement, however, than Sam drew up sharply and pointed. "Who's that?" he asked.

Four men were emerging from the nearby brush along the riverbank, and as Sam's companions turned to see, a single shot was fired. The ball struck John Boyd in the throat, severing his spine, and he fell dead. Instantly, Sam, Ezra and Greathouse dropped the ropes and scattered at top speed. Ezra had not gone more than a dozen yards, trying to reach cover in some trees, when two more Indians lunged out and grabbed him, pulling him shrieking with fear into the brush. Both Greathouse and Sam got away and were not pursued.[283]

[September 1, 1777 — 6:45 A.M.]

The alarm raised in Wheeling spread quickly throughout the settlement. Most of those not already within the walls of Fort Henry fled there at once, all with nothing more than the clothing they wore and perhaps a hastily snatched gun. Silas and Jonathan Zane, along with some other men and their wives and a few children, decided to remain in the Zane blockhouse some 60 yards from the fort, but they quickly closed the shutters and manned the rifle ports.[284] Elizabeth Zane immediately set about checking the loads on every gun not in hand and, when finished, took post at one of the portholes herself.

Betsy Wheat, one of the women who had just taken refuge there from a nearby cabin, was settling the children securely in the loft with orders to remain there and keep quiet, when she abruptly realized that her baby was still asleep in her cradle back at the cabin. Quickly climbing down, she strode to the door, unbarred it and ran out, calling over her shoulder, "Don't lock it. I'll be back in a minute." It didn't take quite that long. She returned with the blanket-wrapped baby, still sound asleep, cuddled in her arms.[285]

Inside Fort Henry, Col. Shepherd calmed the settlers, gave orders for defenses and quickly learned the details of the attack from Greathouse. Before the big frontiersman had finished spilling out his words, Sam came in, gasping for breath and repeating over and over again, "I thought I was dead! I really did. I thought I was dead!"

Col. Shepherd, deciding it was a small hit-and-run raiding party, ordered Capts. Meason and Ogle to take a couple dozen men to investigate the scene and bring in the bodies of Boyd and Ezra, if they could be found. They left at once.[286] Col. Shepherd put every remaining man in the fort on active alert. Old John Wetzel was assigned to post as lookout in one of the four blockhouses; his eldest son, Martin, had marched off with Capt. Meason's company.

Ten minutes after the departure of the party, three of Capt. Ogle's men in the fort decided they wanted to join their company commander. They were Pvts. Joseph Biggs, Robert Lemon and Abraham Rogers.[287] They asked permission of Col. Shepherd to do so, and he let them go. The trio, rifles in hand and grinning at the prospect of an Indian hunt, trotted out after the company.

There were now, left within the fort, a total of only 33 able men.[288]

[September 1, 1777 — Monday, 7:30 A.M.]

"By God, Sam, they're still there!"

The company led by Capt. Meason was not yet to the spot where the attack had occurred, but Sgt. Jacob Ogle—brother of Capt. Tom Ogle, who was bringing up the rear—pointed to where, several hundred yards ahead of them, six Indians had leaped up from hiding and started loping away toward the dense paw-paw growth rimming the Wheeling Creek bottoms.

Capt. Meason immediately ordered double time, putting his 24 men into a hard run after them. He was gratified to see that they were quickly closing the gap. The pursuit led them into an area where the thicker cover was close on both sides, the Indians just managing to keep ahead of them by about 100 yards.

Then, horrifyingly, there were scores of Indians all around Capt. Meason's company, leaping out from where they had been hidden, their decoy ambush having worked perfectly. The air was rent by the crashing of guns, and in that first burst of gunfire practically all of the whites were hit, many of them fatally.[289] Among them, marching beside Capt. Meason, was Lt. Samuel Tomlinson, who took a bullet through the head. And just behind Tomlinson, at the edge of the column, Pvt. Martin Wetzel had his hat brim neatly clipped off by another ball that then smashed into the temple of the man beside him and killed him—Pvt. Jacob Eindstaff.

The 17-year-old Wetzel instinctively dropped as if he, too, had been shot and rolled into the heavier cover beside the road. There, with the multitude of shots still crashing behind him and the shrieking of the Indians a horrible accompaniment, he scrambled through the tall weeds, slithered down into an erosion ravine and, with the cover it provided him, raced as fast as he could in the direction it ran, which was toward the extensive cornfield to the north. The ravine diminished rapidly in size and all but disappeared before reaching the corn, but he slipped among the tall stalks without having been noticed, the cries of the Indians far behind now very faint.

Three privates toward the rear of the column managed to escape the first burst of fire and broke away, running back toward the fort. One was 19-year-old William Shepherd, eldest son of Col. Shepherd; the other two were his brother-in-law, Hugh McConnell, and the third was Thomas Glenn. These three were pursued by seven or eight howling warriors brandishing tomahawks, who gradually closed the gap separating them.

"Split up!" Glenn shouted, and angled toward the creek. McConnell and Shepherd separated somewhat from one another, both still heading for the fort. Young Shepherd got his foot caught in a grapevine and tumbled. As he tried to scramble back to his feet, the Indians overtook him and a tomahawk smashed into his head, killing him. Others continued to pursue Glenn and McConnell. The former was overtaken just before reaching the creek, and he fell when a thrown tomahawk buried itself in his back. Before he could rise, another tomahawk blow killed him. McConnell alone, of the three, reached the fort and sped inside as the gates were opened slightly for him.

Two privates near the head of the line—John Caldwell and Robert Harkness—somehow missed being hurt, and both plunged into the underbrush, but not together. Caldwell managed to get across Wheeling Creek, though several shots struck the water near him as he swam, and a couple more smacked into the bank as he emerged on the other side. It was densely brushy there, and he was able to disappear from sight quickly, but not before he saw one of the warriors plunge into the stream in pursuit of him. It lent speed to his flight, and he continued to run as fast as he could, heading upstream toward the Forks where Shepherd's Fort was located.

Harkness had tumbled into deep grasses bordered by trees and evidently was thought to have been hit, since no one came after him. He squirmed through the grasses until reaching the trees and then regained his feet and raced away, heading for the only haven he thought he could find, Catfish Camp, some 24 miles to the east.

Capt. Meason, his gun having been shot out of his hands, and his sergeant, Jacob Ogle, raced through a gap in the Indian lines and plunged up the overgrown hill in front of them, Ogle about ten yards ahead of his captain and still gripping his rifle. Both men were slowed by wounds they had taken and were running erratically to avoid the shots kicking up tufts of ground about them. One of the balls took Ogle low in the back, and he fell with a cry, struggled back to his knees but was unable to regain his feet. As Meason passed, Ogle tossed him his weapon and shook his head.

"Go on, Cap'n," he gasped. "I'm done for. They'll stop when they get to me. Go on!"[290]

Meason ran on, angling now toward the mile-distant fort, but his speed was considerably diminished by the uphill run and his wounds. A ball had passed through the fleshy part of his left shoulder, and another had lodged in his right buttock, causing him to already feel light-headed from loss of blood and his exertions.[291] Behind him he could hear a pursuing Indian drawing closer, and he expected any moment to feel a tomahawk blow. Abruptly, he whirled and began raising the rifle to fire, but the warrior was already too close, rushing at him with tomahawk upraised, and he could do no more than thrust out a hand. The higher ground he was on gave him a slight advantage, and the heel of his hand caught the Indian in the forehead and caused him to stumble backward. As the warrior scrambled to regain his balance, Meason managed to bring the rifle to bear and snapped off a shot. The ball caught the Indian in the left side of his forehead and killed him.

Meason pressed on, but he knew now he would never make it to the fort. His flight had carried him quite a distance north when he came to a split-rail fence, well grown up with weeds about it and a pile of poles lying parallel to it. With the last of his strength he staggered into the space between fence and poles and collapsed, rolling into the weeds and partially under the pole pile.

Capt. Thomas Ogle and Pvt. Matthias Hedges had leaped into dense cover together, both wounded, Hedges the more seriously. Ogle, still gripping his rifle, had taken a ball through his right side; Hedges had been shot high in the right chest, and blood was running down the corner of his mouth. His rifle was gone, and he was holding his right hand over the chest wound. The two, keeping to heavy cover, gradually worked their way back to the fence line where there was a heavy growth of tall horseweed and tangled briars. Despite the savage thorns that tore at them, they thrust their way deep into the tangle at the fence corner and hid themselves in the densest portion.

Far to the other side of Wheeling, almost two miles distant, a rider had appeared on the road from Vanmetre's Fort several minutes before the ambush. He was Francis Duke, son-in-law of Col. Shepherd and a deputy commissioner at Wheeling, who was returning from the little Beech Bottom Settlement, three miles above Vanmetre's, where he had spent the night in an abandoned cabin. Now, approaching Wheeling, he began passing between the flanking cornfields when, far in the distance to the southeast, he heard the firing of many guns. He hesitated, looked back and saw Indians emerging from the corn well behind him. He spurred his horse into a gallop toward Fort Henry, but he was still some 75 yards from the walls when he was killed by a barrage of gunfire and fell from his horse onto the road. The horse itself was captured.[292]

The initial outbreak of gunfire stopped Pvts. Biggs, Lemon and Rogers, who had been trying to overtake and join the detachment. Ahead, there was more gunfire accompanied by shrill shrieks, and the three didn't have to discuss what was happening. Instantly they took to their heels, heading back to the fort. As they came into the clear, they heard a smaller burst of gunfire to the north and west, and within moments they saw numbers of Indians spilling out of the cornfields and running to cut them off. They sprinted even harder, and as they neared the fort, several shots were fired at them. At this a whoop was raised at one end of the line of Indians and was picked up all the way down the line in a tremendous cry. Immediately, a ragged volley came from the lower blockhouses of the fort. The Indians stopped whooping and fell back a little to keep out of range.

At the point of the cornfield closest to the Wheeling Settlement cabins, Martin Wetzel burst into view at a dead run. He wove past the cabins and outbuildings and was shouting "Open the gate!" long before he reached the fort. The main gate in the east wall came ajar as he reached it, and he dashed inside and heard it closed and barred as he fell to the earth, gasping for breath.

[September 1, 1777 — Monday, 8 A.M.]

There was a gasp from the onlookers peering out of the fort at the distant Indians when their lines parted and an individual in scarlet coat, gold epaulets, white trousers and black boots strode into view from the cornfield, accompanied by a man in frontier garb who was holding upright a flintlock, to the muzzle of which a white cloth had been attached.

With military bearing and no trace of fear, the British officer strode to within 30 yards of the fort and called out for the commander of Fort Henry to come to one of the ports and speak to him. The man in leathers with him said nothing but merely stopped behind him and slightly to one side.

Inside the fort, Ebenezer Zane sought out Col. Shepherd, whom he found, along with Hugh McConnell, consoling his daughter-in-law, Rebecca. McConnell, Rebecca's brother, had reported the news of the ambush and her husband's death. Now he was awkwardly patting her shoulder as she wept, and Shepherd was holding her hand, though the pain in his own heart at losing his son was all but unbearable. Zane apologized for interrupting and asked that he be allowed to make the response to the British officer.

"I don't trust that feller with the flag on his gun," he said. "You go to the window, Colonel, he could pick you off 'fore you knew it. Reckon I'm a mite more expendable than you. Let me answer." Shepherd was reluctant to do so but finally agreed, and Zane went to the porthole.

"All right," he called out, "I'm Colonel Zane. Who are you, and what do you want?"

"I," said the officer, apparently a captain, "am the representative of His Britannic Majesty, George III.[293] In his name I call upon you to surrender this fort and garrison. You see before you a small part of a large army that has come to escort to Detroit in assured safety all who will accept the terms of Governor Hamilton and renounce the cause of those rebelling against His Majesty. I call upon you to remember your fealty to your sovereign. His Majesty wishes to avoid the effusion of blood, which will certainly be the result if you refuse or if one gun is fired to the annoyance of my army, as then there will be no curbing the savage vengeance of the Indians here gathered."

He paused and withdrew from his tunic a paper that he then read aloud to them: a copy of the proclamation issued by Henry Hamilton the previous June. Finishing, he folded and replaced the paper, then returned his attention to Zane. "You have but fifteen minutes to consider this proposition," he said. "I will wait."

Zane disappeared from view, and a quick meeting was held. Everyone in the fort was painfully aware of just how limited were their supplies of food and, more important, ammunition. Lead balls could be dug out of the wood where they had struck and lodged, and these could be melted and poured into the bullet molds to make new balls, but gunpowder was very scarce, and it was obvious that even with the most conservative use of it, the supply would soon be gone. Once that fact was ascertained by the Indians, they would swarm over the walls, and that would be the beginning of a great massacre. Yet despite this awful knowledge, their response to the surrender demand was a foregone conclusion. Within five minutes Ebenezer Zane had returned to the porthole below which the British officer and frontiersman were waiting.

"We have consulted with our wives and children," he said coldly, "and we are of the opinion that this is a choice between slavery and death. We are unanimously resolved to perish before we will voluntarily place ourselves under the supposed protection of an army of savages like this with you at its head. Nor would we, for that matter," he concluded, "even consider turning our backs on the cause of liberty and the welfare of the states."

"I beg that you reconsider," the British captain responded. "There is before you a great force of Indians and not the least possibility that your fort can withstand their concerted assault. I again assure you: The offer of protection, if you accede to His

Majesty's wishes, is not an idle one; and I assure you likewise that if you continue to refuse or resist in any way, I will be entirely unable to restrain this army of savages, as you call them, and all inside the fort will be destroyed without mercy."

The only response to this was a shot that rang out from another part of the fort, and a ball plowed into the earth near the officer's feet. He and his companion immediately turned and withdrew, and as soon as they disappeared back into the cornfield, a loud cry was raised, and the Indians poured a furious fire at every aperture of the fort. With frightening swiftness they quickly occupied most of the houses and half-face cabins in Wheeling that in any way commanded a view of the fort and were within 50 yards. At the same time they endeavored not to expose themselves to the crossfire that came from Ebenezer Zane's residence blockhouse, where Jonathan and Silas Zane and a few other men were ensconced. A number even took cover behind the paling fence between Zane's blockhouse and the fort.

And now the firing began in earnest.

[*S e p t e m b e r   1 ,   1 7 7 7 — M o n d a y ,   8 : 3 0   A . M .*]

Pvt. John Caldwell, who had escaped across Wheeling Creek from the ambush of the company of soldiers under Capt. Meason, had finally reached Shepherd's Fort at the Forks of Wheeling Creek a few minutes ago. He'd had no easy time of it. His clothing was shredded from the briars through which he had plunged, and his flesh was scored and bleeding in a multitude of places from the cruel thorns. He was exhausted, still teetering on the edge of panic and nearly incoherent, but gradually those in the fort pieced together from his inchoate phrases what had occurred. They needed to know; there was not a person here at Shepherd's who did not have family or friends in Wheeling.

Caldwell related that the Wyandot warrior who had followed him across Wheeling Creek had been tenacious in his pursuit and gradually closed the gap until they were only about 30 yards apart. In leaping over a fallen tree, Caldwell didn't fully clear it and sprawled headlong, becoming momentarily wedged between the far side of the tree trunk and a sapling growing beside it. He struggled frantically to get loose, and by the time he did so and began running again, the warrior was within a few yards, tomahawk upraised and shrieking in anticipated triumph. That was when the Wyandot made a mistake: Instead of rushing up and tomahawking Caldwell, as he certainly could have done, he threw his weapon at him . . . and missed. Caldwell continued running, and when he glanced back, the Indian had picked up his tomahawk and was turning back.

Apart from Caldwell's statement that "the damned Injens were everywhere," the men at Shepherd's Fort had no clear idea how many warriors were involved in the ambush of Capt. Meason's company or how many others might at this moment be investing Wheeling; nor had Caldwell been able to tell them how many men had been killed in the ambush, but the number was evidently large. What it all came down to was that the strength of Wheeling itself had been greatly diminished, and unless relief could be sent there at once, the whole settlement might fall. Yet here at Shepherd's Fort there were only a few men, none of whom could be spared without jeopardizing the women and children on hand.

With the absence of Col. Shepherd at Wheeling, Lewis Bonnett was in temporary command here, and at once he dispatched a rider to follow a circuitous route well away from Wheeling and go to Fort Vanmetre and Holliday's Cove. Apart from Wheeling itself, more fighting men were gathered at those two places than anywhere else, especially at Fort Vanmetre, where Capt. Samuel McCulloch was in command of upward of 30 militiamen. Another dozen, perhaps, were at Holliday's Cove, 17 miles above Vanmetre's.

But Bonnett admitted glumly that it was dubious whether anything could be done to save Wheeling.

[September 1, 1777 — Monday, 10:45 A.M.]

Maj. Samuel McCulloch was facing the worst predicament of his entire life and had only instants in which to make a decision that could well result in a terrible death no matter which way he chose.

The whole situation that had brought him to this point had begun just a little over an hour ago, when the express messenger from Shepherd's Fort had arrived at Fort Vanmetre, where McCulloch was in command. The rider had covered the circuitous route of some 18 miles to Fort Vanmetre in record time, arriving just after nine-thirty. As soon as he blurted out to them what had transpired at Wheeling and then spurred his horse on toward Holliday's Cove, Sam McCulloch had ordered his men into a flurry of activity, preparing their weapons and mounts for departure. Within a quarter-hour they were on their way.

With Sam in the lead on his big white gelding and his brother John, also a major, close behind, the 30 men of the company galloped on the river bottom road to Wheeling, seven miles distant. With the fort finally in sight, they thundered past the flanking cornfields and abruptly found themselves in the midst of an attack by scores of Indians emerging from among the tall stalks.

"Take 'em in, John," Sam yelled, spinning his mount around and heading toward the rear to see that everyone got through. As he galloped, he repeatedly shouted, "To the fort!" and not until he had thundered past the rear did he wheel his own mount and attempt to follow. It was too late: A horde of Indians had burst from cover between him and his company, and he had no choice but to try to get away on the road he had just traveled. But it was too late for that too, for as he wheeled and started back, more Indians flooded into view in that direction. With all these Indians shrieking hideously and running toward him as fast as they could, he reined to the right and spurred his horse through the corn, heading toward the base of Wheeling Hill and the trail that led to its summit.

In Fort Henry the defenders had witnessed what was occurring, and as the riders approached through the hail of gunfire, the main gate was momentarily thrown open enough to let John McCulloch and his men plunge in. The instant they did, the gate was slammed shut and barred. Several of the arriving militia had received superficial wounds, and several of the horses had taken bullets, but no one had been killed. At least not yet; Sam McCulloch's fate still hung in the balance.

His horse emerged from the cornfield near the southernmost base of the hill and close to the trail that led to the crest. Having already run well over seven miles, the big gelding was beginning to strain badly and slowed despite his urgings. Behind, the swarm of following Indians burst from the cornfield and continued their pursuit, less than a minute behind him and running fast. They followed him onto the trail.

The grade of the trail was steep, and it was 250 feet to the summit. By the time McCulloch reached it, his weakened horse gasping for breath, the Indians behind him had closed the gap to about 50 yards and were coming on hard. That was when more warriors appeared on the trail well ahead to the north and others began emerging in numbers from the woods to the west.[294]

The shrieking Indians approaching at a run were now on three sides of him, while to his right there was nothing but a veritable precipice plunging downward in a series of benches or narrow levels until it reached the base where Wheeling Creek makes its sharp horseshoe bend: a drop so steep that only a dozen feet or so from the edge were the tops of tall trees projecting from below.

It was an extremely desperate situation, and there was no time for lengthy deliberation. Sam McCulloch knew full well what lay in store if he surrendered, and he had no intention of doing so. Instead, he spun the big white gelding around and spurred him over the edge. The horse whinnied in terror as he dropped and, virtually sliding on his haunches, plunged down the precipitous slope, straining to avoid the trees growing in the few precarious toeholds.

There was a great clatter of rocks jarred loose, adding to the crackle and snapping of branches and saplings struck as the horse scrambled and slid down the slope. A wild thought struck McCulloch as he clung fiercely: He and his mount would undoubtedly reach the bottom, but whether they would be alive when they got there was doubtful.

Above, the Indians gathered, panting, at the clifftop and looked down in wonder and admiration for the courage of the man they had been pursuing, an admiration that even overcame their disappointment at losing their quarry. And a few moments later, when the white horse and its rider emerged from the woods at the bottom and continued riding upstream on the narrow right bank bottom of Wheeling Creek, their admiration became vocal as they actually cheered the incredible feat. There were few things the Indians admired more than great daring and courage.

McCulloch, as battered and bruised as the gelding he rode, having emerged on the creek bottom, reined the horse down to a panting, snorting trot upstream toward the mouth of Wood's Run, somewhat over a mile distant.[295] There he planned to head up the smaller stream and follow it northward to where he would encounter a trail that would take him to Fort Vanmetre and Holliday's Cove.

Now, shortly after safely reaching the bottom of the great slope, he leaned forward and patted the big gelding's sweat-soaked neck with soft slaps.

"You did good, boy," he said. "*Real* good!"[296]

[S e p t e m b e r   1 ,   1 7 7 7 — M o n d a y ,   1   *P.M.*]

For some six hours the assault against Wheeling had raged virtually without pause. The Indians fired at every gap in the upright pickets that enclosed the fort, at the gate, at every porthole and at every conceivable spot behind which someone might have been taking cover; at the same time, another body of the Indians were firing at the fortified Ebenezer Zane house. They wasted a great deal of ammunition with little real effect.

A very serious situation arose at the Zane Blockhouse. There were four men there and three women, all of whom had been firing continuously from the rifle ports ever since the fighting first broke out. Up in the loft space, where they had been taken to get them out of the way and give them greater safety, seven small children were huddled, four of them the Zane girls.[297] Now the defenders discovered that a keg of gunpowder that was supposed to be on hand was empty, and the remaining supply in their powderhorns was nearly exhausted. Their only hope was to try to get some from the fort, where there was believed to be an ample supply. But Fort Henry was fully 60 yards away. The men began discussing who among them should attempt to pass through the gauntlet of gunfire twice to get it and bring it back here.

"I'll go get it." The words were spoken by Elizabeth Zane, and the others were shocked.

"You can't do that, Betsy!" exclaimed Jonathan. "It's too dangerous. One of us will go."

Elizabeth shook her head. "No, it'll be safer for me than for one of you. We all know that any man leaving here will be killed before he can get ten feet away. No," she repeated, "they'll see I'm a woman, and I'm betting they won't shoot."

They argued for a while, but Elizabeth was adamant, and everyone knew that once her mind was made up, there was no changing it. Silas gave in with an exasperated groan. "All right, do it, but try not to get killed. If you don't get through, it won't be the Indians who'll kill me, it'll be Ebenezer." He was only half-joking.

Gathering up her skirts so they would not impede her, Elizabeth nodded for the door to be opened, and as soon as it was, she raced outside and headed for the nearest portal of the fort, which in this case was the small sally port in the south picket wall. She knew lookouts in the fort would see her coming and have the doorway open for her when she arrived.

The Indians were stunned when she ran out, and at once the cry was raised, "Squaw! Squaw!"

As she anticipated, no shots were fired as she ran the 60 yards, and she was able to get into the fort safely. She was met by her husband, who scolded her for taking such a chance, but she merely shrugged it off. "I thought I would get through all right, Eb," she said, "and I did. I'll get back just as safely, I promise. Now there's no time to waste. We've got to have gunpowder there, or we're going under. And the girls are there, Eb."

Col. Zane nodded grimly and, though their own supply was low, called for a keg to be brought. However, when they tried to lift it to her shoulder, it was simply too heavy for her to manage, especially since she would be running. The top of the keg was removed, and while Elizabeth held the ends of her apron to make a pouch, the gunpowder was poured in. She was able to handle about two-thirds of it, and she pulled the apron ends to her chest, the large bulge of the apron in front now making her look as if she were pregnant. She smiled at Ebenezer and kissed him and then nodded her head for the sally port to be opened.

Once again she raced out, going a little slower now because of the weight she was carrying. She covered a third of the distance back before being discovered, and once again the cry of "Squaw" was raised, but this time there were shots as well. Little spurts of dirt flew up as bullets struck the ground near her, and she began running a zigzag course. More shots were fired, and several balls passed through her skirts without striking her. Amazingly, she reached the blockhouse and plunged inside as the door was momentarily opened. Their own gunpowder was now completely gone, and that which she brought back was their salvation.[298]

Within the fort no one had been idle since the assault was first initiated. As many women as men were firing from the rifle ports—Mrs. Henry Glum was particularly outstanding in this respect—and those among the women who could not shoot well were kept busy molding bullets or loading empty weapons and carrying the newly charged flintlocks and additional powder and bullets back to the shooters. Some of the women cooked and carried food and water to the defenders, with the heavy-set 42-year-old mulatto slave called Aunt Rachel—Rachel Johnson—leading in this effort.[299] Even the youngsters who could handle tasks were put to work. Lewis Wetzel, largely recovered from the bullet wound across his chest, was positioned near the south wall sally port and was cautioned to be alert and ready to open the door to any who escaped the ambush or who might otherwise reach the fort, and he had done just that when Elizabeth Zane had dashed across. Jacob Wetzel had been given the same charge at the river wall sally port.

Ebenezer Zane seemed to be everywhere at once, moving from rifle port to rifle port and shooting from any from which he saw an Indian. He was usually accompanied by Pvt. Nicholas Rogers, who carried messages or ran errands for him whenever needed. By this time, Zane was credited with downing seven Indians, including an exceptionally good shot when he gave his rifle an extralarge charge of gunpowder and knocked down an Indian who had perched on the top rail of a fence on Wheeling Island—a shot probably in excess of 300 yards.

Meanwhile, Capt. Ogle and Pvt. Hedges were still lying in the briars and horseweeds at the corner of the fence row, where they had remained hidden all this time. Hedges had slipped in and out of consciousness all morning, and the officer thought his companion would die if he didn't get assistance. His own wound was very painful, but he didn't think it was terribly serious so long as infection didn't set in.

As if their troubles were not enough already, two hours ago, during one of the periods when Hedges was unconscious, Ogle had detected a movement near his head, then sucked in his breath when he saw what it was. A large timber rattlesnake had poked its wedge-shaped head into view no more than eight inches away. The head lifted and the forked tongue slithered in and out as the snake tested the air. After a moment the head lowered and came toward him another few inches, then turned away. Ogle continued to hold his breath as the four-foot length of the thick, squat body slid past in front of his eyes, the scaly sides blotched with yellowish markings separated by broad black splotches. As the body narrowed toward the tail, it became almost black, and the half-dozen rattles at the tip were equally dark. And then, as if it had never been there, the snake was gone, and a wave of trembling that Ogle could not control shuddered through him for a time.

About an hour ago Hedges had come more aware, and they had talked in faint whispers. Ogle said nothing about the snake, not wanting to alarm the private even more, but he did say he was going to try to get to the fort and bring back some help. Hedges had nodded and then, with some difficulty, had pulled a silver button off his sleeve and handed it to the captain.

"Give this," he whispered, "to my brother, Joe. Tell him I was thinking of him kindly at the end."

Capt. Tom Ogle slipped the button into his pocket but shook his head. "You're not going to die," he said. "As soon as it looks safe enough, I'll head out."

Hedges lapsed back into unconsciousness, and Ogle was just on the verge of creeping out when he heard Indian voices approaching in the distance. He cocked his gun and remained still and tense. He was prepared, if discovered, to kill at least one of the Indians before losing his own life.

There were two Indians, one old and one young, the latter suffering from a wound high on his left side and groaning with the pain it was causing him. The pair stopped at the fence no more than a dozen feet from where Ogle lay. He could not understand what they were saying, but the young man perched himself on the top rail, and the older one looked at his wound, then reached into the pouch at his waist and took out a clump of downy feathers and carefully shoved them into the wound, where they checked the bleeding. Then the older man climbed up and sat beside him, and they talked for a long while. At last, after what seemed an eternity to Ogle, who was terrified lest Hedges regain consciousness and make a noise, the pair got down and ambled away in the direction of the fort. Ogle slowly relaxed and uncocked his gun, deciding it would not be safe to leave this hiding place until dark.

Quite some time ago, a body of the more daring warriors had rushed to the outer walls of the fort and begun firing through any small gap that could be found. It was extremely dangerous to those inside, and so from the overhangs of the blockhouses at each corner of the fort, the men and women returned fire so briskly and with such effect that within the space of a few minutes the Indians had retreated from the walls, some hobbling away or being half-carried, but only four known to have been killed. After that the firing became more scattered and erratic.

Now even that firing was dying away somewhat, and the majority of the Indians gradually began drawing away to the base of the high, steep hills to the east and north of Wheeling. A number scaled the slopes, some to the tops, where they posted themselves advantageously, others taking position on the slopes themselves.

It looked as if the Indians were digging in for a very long siege indeed.

[September 1, 1777—Monday, 3:45 P.M.]

At Holliday's Cove near the mouth of Harmon's Creek, Col. Andrew Van Swearingen gave an order, and his 14 men began getting into a large, bulky canoe of the type called a continental.[300] It was the only means of transportation on hand that would accommodate them all, but he wished again that they had had enough horses to go by land, since they would be able to reach Wheeling faster and undoubtedly safer than by water, but there had not been that option. He wished, as well, that the messenger had not almost killed his horse by pushing it so hard and, in the end, delaying his arrival by far more than if he'd traveled at a more reasonable pace.

The express, having galloped all the way from Shepherd's Fort to Fort Vanmetre with word of the attack at Wheeling, immediately continued northward at the same punishing gallop, heading for Holliday's Cove, still 17 miles distant. The horse simply couldn't take it, especially over such terrain, and played out before half the distance was covered. As a result, the rider had been forced to dismount and lead the animal on foot for a long while. Even when he finally mounted again, the animal refused to be coaxed into more than a walk. Thus instead of arriving here at Holliday's Cove by noon or shortly after, he had not arrived until about an hour ago.

Col. Van Swearingen had 18 men on hand, but he left four, along with the messenger, to remain at the little blockhouse and protect the women and children. There were half a dozen horses at the settlement, but that was not enough to carry his party, and so he had reluctantly settled on going downstream the 24 miles to Wheeling in the big unwieldy continental canoe.

Now the time had come to set off on the hazardous mission. Col. Van Swearingen was last to enter the canoe, and, as he thrust it out from shore into the current and took his position in the stern, he wondered uneasily if they would see the Indians first or vice versa.

[September 1, 1777—Monday, 5:30 P.M.]

The private who escaped the ambush and headed eastward through the forested hills toward Catfish Camp finally reached his destination. As he staggered into view, faint with exhaustion, several men rushed out to help him, and within minutes he had told them all he could.

As luck would have it, this was muster day at Catfish Camp, and two companies of militia were on hand, under Capts. Reasin Virgin and John Boggs. In another half-hour they would have been dispersing to their homes, but they had not yet been dismissed. A hurried council was held, and they decided to prepare their gear and move out as quickly as possible toward Wheeling. Night marches were difficult at best, but with luck, they felt, they should be able to reach Wheeling by dawn or shortly after.

Twilight was gathering when, their shot pouches and powderhorns full, rations in their packs and rifles on their shoulders, the companies of Capt. Virgin and Capt. Boggs marched westward out of Catfish Camp on the road leading to Wheeling.

[*S e p t e m b e r   1 ,   1 7 7 7 — M o n d a y ,   6 : 3 0   P.M.*]

After more or less withdrawing for an hour and a half, the Indians had renewed their assault on Fort Henry at about half past two in the afternoon, with even more fury than before. They had poured a sustained fire at the walls, gates, portholes and every conceivable aperture. Some had returned to their previous protected positions in the nearest cabins eastward of the fort; others had congregated in and behind the blacksmith shop and stable just to the north. The greater number, however, had taken new positions south of the fort under cover of a split-rail worm fence and behind several large trees that had recently been felled. Under cover of the fire from their comrades, a number of the Indians had moved closer, taking cover as they advanced behind the stumps of trees in this previously cleared area. So hot was the firing here that most of the defenders inside the fort had moved to the two lower blockhouses at the south end. It was exactly what the Indians had planned, and while the bulk of the fighting was going on here, a group of others dashed out of Zane's yard with long heavy logs and began battering the east gate in an attempt to smash it open.

Defenders on that side of the fort, quickly joined by others from the south end, opened fire from the blockhouse overhangs. The women who were not actively shooting aided by bringing scalding water and hot stones from the fires and tossing them down from the parapets at the attackers. Unwilling to give up at first, the Indians continued the battering until five of their number had been killed and a few others wounded. Then, screaming in anger and frustration, they had withdrawn to the cabins again. From there they continued their general firing, most hotly on the fort's north and east sides, having decided the ground to the south side, because of the slope, favored the garrison more than themselves.

At one point the Indians had worked in relays and with exceptional speed, using their tomahawks to split a six-foot section of maple log and then hollow out a smooth half-round groove three inches across and to a depth of three inches for the whole length of the log except for the final foot at one end. When these two log sections were finished and a wick hole made in one end, they were fitted together and formed a cannon barrel with a bore in the center six inches in diameter. The two halves were tightly lashed together with soaked and stretched rawhide straps that, as they dried, contracted and tightly sealed the sections. When finished, they carried their makeshift artillery to the cabin nearest to the main gate and carefully positioned it to be aimed at the closed portal. A thin piece of rope into which gunpowder had been pounded was put into the wick hole, and then a large amount of gunpowder was poured into the barrel and forced to the closed end by wadding made of clothing found in the cabins. Then a similar large quantity of lead balls, nails, bits of metal and other items were inserted; they, too, were rammed solidly with cloth wadding. Then the wick was lighted, and a large number of Indians gathered around with childlike anticipation, tomahawks in hand and ready to rush the gate as soon as it was blown apart.

The explosion, when it came, was horrendous. The maple log burst into thousands of pieces, with very little of the charge ever reaching the gate. Upward of 20 Indians suffered injuries ranging from superficial to serious from the flying splinters and debris. Three were killed.

The cheer that erupted from those in the fort who were watching was an explosion in and of itself.

Thwarted by this setback, some of the Indians moved about among the buildings, plundering them of anything worthwhile and setting several afire. Others moved to where livestock were corralled or pastured and began shooting them down, killing scores of cows and hogs as well as numerous geese and chickens. All horses they found were taken.

By late afternoon, most of the rifles in the fort had been rendered useless because their barrels were so hot from continuous firing. Fortunately, a stock of muskets was on hand in a storehouse, allowing many of the defenders to switch to those weapons for a while. And now, with evening coming on, the firing of the Indians was beginning to dwindle, bringing hope to many inside the fort that they were going to give up and leave, but making the more experienced fighters wonder what the Indians would do next.

Col. Shepherd estimated that thus far somewhere around 20 Indians had been killed and perhaps twice that many or more were wounded. In the fort not a single person had yet suffered a scratch, but Shepherd knew the score could quickly change. It all depended on what the Indians had in mind for after nightfall.

[S e p t e m b e r   1 ,   1 7 7 7 — M o n d a y ,   9   P . M .]

Capt. Thomas Ogle, wincing with pain from the wound in his right side, had begun inching his way out of the horseweed and briars at the fence corner as soon as darkness had fallen. Pvt. Hedges, again conscious when he left, wished him luck and reminded him to give the button to his brother.[301]

Ogle was thankful for the fog that had come in at nightfall, as it would help mask and muffle his movements. In a half crouch and still gripping his rifle, he slowly followed the fence row to its closest approach to the fort, some 400 yards from the bastion's southeast corner. At that point he knew the only cover remaining now between himself and the fort was a single half-face cabin and a number of stumps and logs. He crept toward where the cabin should be but almost ran into it before its bulk loomed before him. He froze when he heard the murmur of voices and caught the scent of smoke and food cooking. The voices were definitely Indian, and so he quietly backed off and made a wide detour past the cabin, the movement carrying him to the creek bank.

The fog lay even heavier near the water, and he followed the stream's edge until he estimated he was directly below the south end of the fort, where there was a sally port. When he almost stumbled over a canoe pulled well up onshore, he considered launching it and floating downstream but, fearful that there would be Indians at the mouth of the creek some 30 yards below, he decided against it.

Still moving silently and with the utmost care, Ogle ascended the bank and saw, looming in the darkness before him, the shape of a large log. He moved to it to take momentary advantage of the cover. Abruptly he slid down into the cavity beside it and had a tremendous scare when he landed on someone. The person was stiff and cold, and he realized at once it was a body. At first he thought it was an Indian who had been killed by fire from the fort, but then his outstretched hand encountered a second one, and they were both clad in white man's clothing. As he moved his hands across them, he touched their heads and found both had been scalped. He realized suddenly that these had to be the two men that Col. Shepherd had sent downriver the previous night to check on the suspected burning of the Grave Creek Block-house, and the canoe beached on the shore behind and below was evidently theirs.

Moving stealthily out of the cavity, he continued up the slope to the fort's south wall and felt his way along it until he encountered the sally port. Fearful of the slight noise he had to make now, he tapped on the door. There was no immediate response, and he tapped again, slightly harder. This time a whispery, boyish-sounding voice came from above him, over the pickets.

"Who's out there?"

"Ogle," he whispered.

"What's your first name?"

"Tom. Thomas. Open the port, I'm wounded."

The door remained closed. "What's your rank?"

"Captain. Dammit, open the door!"

"What's your brother's name?"

"Jacob. And he's a sergeant. Now, for God's sake, open the damned door!"

There was no reply, but in a moment Ogle heard the bar sliding, and then the portal opened and he moved inside. Immediately the door was closed, and in the dim light of a lantern turned low, a boy slid the heavy beam bar back into place. The youth turned and grinned.

"Sorry, Captain Ogle," Lewis Wetzel said. "I had to make sure it was you."

[*S e p t e m b e r   1 ,   1 7 7 7 — M o n d a y ,   9 : 1 5   P . M .*]

Capt. Samuel Meason had remained hidden, partially under the pile of fence poles, throughout the day. He was in great pain but had managed to nap off and on and regain some of the strength that he had lost during his ordeal.

The noise that had come to him during the day—plus the fact that several groups of Indians had walked past within mere yards of his hiding place—had convinced him that Wheeling had been attacked by a very large force of Indians. Besides, looking in that direction, even though now it was fully dark, he could see a ruddy glow, indicating that structures were on fire, perhaps even Fort Henry itself. It would clearly be suicidal for him to try to make it back to the fort.

Stiff and aching, he eased himself out of his hiding place. The air was calm and somewhat foggy here, though not so densely misted as down closer to the river. Earlier in the day, when the noise of the attack on McCulloch's party had reached him, he realized the unlikelihood of finding any sanctuary at Vanmetre's, even if he could get there. Shepherd's Fort was closest, but that would mean heading back in the direction where his company had been ambushed, and he rejected that idea. The only reasonable alternative seemed to be to get to the road and head for Catfish Camp.[302]

[September 2, 1777—Tuesday, dawn]

"I want two volunteers to go with me," said Col. Andrew Van Swearingen. "We have got to determine whether they're gone or if it's a ruse."

In the large continental canoe, the 14 men whom he addressed did not immediately respond. In the gray first light of dawn, they looked at one another, and each man knew that the sense of mortality he was witnessing on the other faces was reflected on his own. It was a disconcerting possibility, but a very real one, that this was the last dawn any of them would experience.

The journey downriver from Holliday's Cove had not been ideal. They had paddled vigorously at first and made fairly good time for a while. Then the daylight had dwindled away, and as evening turned into night and a heavy fog formed over the river, visibility had dwindled to no more than a few feet. A dozen times or more, they had bumped harshly into banks or wedged themselves on mud or gravel bars, requiring them to step out of the ungainly craft to free it. At last Col. Van Swearingen came to a reluctant decision: They would have to let the current do their work for them and simply float with the flow where it took them. The great problem, of course, was that without visibility, the current might well carry them past Wheeling without their even knowing it.

Van Swearingen did some rapid calculations, trying to figure how far they had traveled and at what speed during the time they had been paddling, how much time had been lost in contact with the banks and becoming grounded on bars, and then, how fast the current alone was carrying them as they floated at its whim.

Now, with the cold gray light of dawn beginning to filter through the fog, they had clearly lost the advantage they had anticipated having by arriving under cover of night: an opportunity to land on the riverbank adjacent to the fort and, in the darkness, gain admission to the fort before the Indians were aware they had arrived.

Moments ago they had detected a pinkish glow through the fog to the east, and they all knew at once that it was not the sunrise but the reflection of fire on the mist particles. Col. Van Swearingen had immediately ordered the men to paddle to the east shore and beach the canoe. That was where they were now, and Van Swearingen, who had stepped into the shallows, made an irritated sound.

"Come on, men, I called for volunteers. I need two to go with me to reconnoiter. That way, if we run into something bad, there might be a chance of at least one of us getting back here to warn the others."

"I'll go with you, Colonel." It was Capt. Charles Bilderback who volunteered. Pvt. William Boshears spoke up to become the second. They, too, stepped over the gunwales and into the shallows, then pulled the bow of the big canoe farther up onshore as the colonel addressed those remaining.

"You men wait here," he said. "If you hear a triple whistle, come arunning. Otherwise, stay put till someone comes back."

Beckoning to his two volunteers and admonishing them to stay close, he moved up the bank, and the three quickly lost sight of the others in the gray gloom. As they rose cautiously above the river level up the steep bank, the low-hanging fog thinned and visibility improved until they could see perhaps 100 yards ahead. The glow of the fires was close, and in the dim light, as they crept forward, the bulk of Fort Henry became visible, and they began to breathe more easily.

They moved to the north wall sally port and called out softly. Almost at once there was a response from a port in the nearby blockhouse: "Who's down there?"

"Colonel Van Swearingen. We've come with relief from Holliday's Cove."

The head of Old John Wetzel appeared at the port, and they heard the click of his gun being uncocked. "God Almighty!" There was relief in his voice. "I damned near shot when I first saw you. Just a minute."

He disappeared, and they could hear him calling aloud, and a moment later the beam bar scraped and the portal opened. Other people were gathering and, with the door shut and barred behind them, they were taken by Wetzel to the fort headquarters, where they were heartily welcomed by David Shepherd, Ebenezer Zane, John McCulloch and Dr. McMahan, then quickly briefed on what had transpired here in the past 24 hours.

"I wouldn't whistle for the rest of your men to come in yet," Shepherd warned. "The fact that you men have made it here is no guarantee the Indians are not still there. They may be lying in the cornfield just waiting for us to relax our guard and come out so they can make a drive at us. If they're still out there, they may not even realize you've come in, but they would if they heard your signal. I suggest you send your two men back to lead them in quietly. Then we'll have to devise some way of determining whether the Indians are gone."

[September 2, 1777—Tuesday, noon]

The Indians were gone.

It had taken a while to ascertain that fact to everyone's satisfaction, and it involved some rather frightening examinations of places where they might be hidden, but then it had become clear that they truly were gone.

Shortly after the remainder of Col. Van Swearingen's men were brought to the fort, a two-man party consisting of Old John Wetzel and Hugh McConnell was sent out to examine the cornfield at its nearest approach to the fort. The consensus was that it would be here, if anywhere, that the Indians were hidden. As the morning brightened and the fog began to dissipate, Wetzel and McConnell walked from the fort with extreme caution, their weapons at ready, and entered the cornfield. There were plenty of tracks and other indications where Indians had been, but no sign of any lingering in the area. Within half an hour they had returned to the fort and reported.

Col. Zane was encouraged but not entirely convinced. Assembling a squad of 20 men, he personally led them out and scoured the entire cornfield and the ambush site. They discovered no Indians—not even dead ones—but they did find more than 300 head of cattle and hogs that had been killed, along with many chickens and geese. They also found and brought in the numerous bodies of the militiamen, as well as Matthias Hedges, who was still alive. And just now, as if to emphasize the fact that the Indians were gone and were not lying in ambush somewhere along the road leading east, two forces arrived after marching all night, grimly determined to fight it out with the Indians who were attacking Wheeling—the two companies of men under Capts. Virgin and Boggs from Catfish Camp and a smaller force of 30 men under Col. Joseph Hedges and Capt. Andrew Fouts from Ramsey's Fort on Buffalo Creek, six miles up from its mouth. Though they had arrived too late, they were of great help in burying the dead and dragging the dead animals to the river and throwing them in to be swept away by the current.

More than anything else, it was a comfort to all at Wheeling to know that the relief forces had come as swiftly as possible.[303]

[September 20, 1777—Saturday]

"The two men I sent down to Grave Creek on the night before we were attacked here at Wheeling," said Col. David Shepherd, "were killed just below the fort here on their return, before they were able to report. So we still have no idea whether or not Mr. Tomlinson's buildings have been burned there or whether or not the blockhouse is still standing. That's something we need to know, and it's your assignment to find out."

The militia captain standing before him in Fort Henry's headquarters nodded. "I'm sure we can do that without any real difficulty, sir."

Col. Shepherd studied the officer and hoped he was not making a mistake. Capt. William Foreman had come highly recommended as a gallant officer, but the man also exuded a sense of invulnerability that Shepherd had seen too often before and that he always found a little disconcerting. Foreman was a man without previous experience in Indian warfare, and that was decidedly a liability, but with manpower here so limited, Shepherd did not have much choice.

Capt. Foreman had arrived at Wheeling with his company of 30 men the day before yesterday, having raised the force and marched them all the way from the South Branch Potomac in Hampshire County as soon as word had reached there of Wheeling being under attack. He had exhibited some degree of disappointment at discovering that, even though some Indians had been spotted at a distance, it had been reasonably calm here since that attack three weeks earlier.

"Since you are not familiar with this area, Captain Foreman," Col. Shepherd went on, "I am assigning Captain William Linn as scout and guide for your detachment. He's a good man with considerable Indian fighting experience, and you would be wise to heed whatever counsel he has to offer."

"Yes, sir." Foreman paused and then added, "He's a captain, you say?"

Shepherd recognized the symptoms and managed not to smile. "It's an honorary title, not official rank. You will be in sole charge of the detachment. Now, you have only thirty men, and I'd prefer it if your company were a little stronger. I'm going to issue a call for volunteers, and we'll see how many we can spare to go along with you."

[September 21, 1777—Sunday]

The company of 45 riflemen under Capt. William Foreman was ferried in relays by canoe across Wheeling Creek, just up from its mouth a short distance, and was drawn into formation on the path that led southward along the east shore of the Ohio to the Grave Creek Settlement, 12 miles distant.

Foreman's force had been augmented by 20 volunteers from among the men at Wheeling—the maximum number Col. Shepherd thought he could spare. The majority of those remaining behind, some 60 in number, would guard the Wheeling Settlement and continue with the work of rebuilding the cabins and outbuildings burned during the attack three weeks ago.

Along with Bill Linn as guide, the Wheeling volunteers going with Foreman included Robert Harkness who, after his harrowing run to Shepherd's Fort, had returned a couple of days later. Jacob Greathouse was another of those who volunteered, along with Jim Tomlinson, much against the wishes of his older brother, Joe. Fifteen-year-old John Miller went along, despite mutterings that he was too young, and Lewis Wetzel wanted to go but was rejected, not only because of his age but because his chest wound was not entirely healed. Moses Shepherd, ten-year-old son of the colonel, was allowed to accompany them and beat the marching drum, but only for the first half-mile, after which he would return to the fort. Included in the volunteers Foreman had brought from Hampshire County were his son and two of his nephews.[304]

The majority of the Wheeling settlers had assembled on the north bank of the creek to see them off, and the eyes of many of the women were wet as they watched the proud little band march southward to the tapping of Moses Shepherd's drum. True to his promise, the drummer boy turned back in half a mile.

Bill Linn marched in the lead beside Capt. Foreman, watching for fresh Indian sign. In five miles they forded McMechen's Creek and came to the burned-out ruins of William McMechen's settlement. There were some tracks of Indians there that Linn figured had been made four or five days earlier. Nothing else of significance was noted until they began passing through The Narrows. Here, beginning about six miles south of Wheeling and extending for some two and a half miles, the trail became squeezed between the riverbank on their right, sharply inclined to the water, and a very steep hill rising more than 100 feet immediately on their left, a trail so narrow it could accommodate no more than two abreast. Linn was particularly alert here, especially in view of the fact that he found a sizable number of Indian tracks that didn't look to be more than a day old. His concern grew when, as they neared the end of The Narrows and were still about four miles above the mouth of Grave

Creek, they spied a number of Indians passing through a clearing on the opposite side of the Ohio.

At Linn's suggestion, Capt. Foreman called a halt, and the whole company hunkered down to avoid detection. The Indians on the other side continued moving without pause and soon disappeared from sight in the trees. Foreman was quite sure his company had not been seen and ordered the march resumed.

A few hundred yards later, they had left The Narrows behind and were moving more easily across the large bottom called Grave Creek Flats. Some 40 minutes later they arrived at the mouth of Grave Creek. The families of Joseph Tomlinson and Isaac Williams had moved to the Monongahela above Redstone for greater safety some time ago, but Foreman's company found the abandoned cabins still standing, as well as the little blockhouse. Pleased that he would be returning to Col. Shepherd with a favorable report, Foreman ordered the company to make camp for the night, and they would start their return in the morning. At Linn's urging, however, he did double the number of sentries he would normally have posted.

[S e p t e m b e r   2 2 ,   1 7 7 7 — M o n d a y]

"Captain," said Bill Linn as they prepared to leave Grave Creek Flats and enter The Narrows, "I got me a bad feelin' somethin' ain't right. I don't think we oughta be marchin' up The Narrows. Ain't no place I know better for an ambush than here."

Capt. Foreman raised a hand and halted the line behind him. "Have you seen some fresh Indian sign I may have missed, Mr. Linn?"

Linn shook his head. "Nope. But we did see them Injens on t'other side yesterday, and I 'spect they seen us, too."

"There was no indication that they saw us, Mr. Linn," Foreman said. "But even if they did, what's your point?"

"My point is," Linn said, trying to keep his temper, "if they seen us, they've had plenty of time to cross over an' set up an ambush. Seems to me, we'd be a whole lot smarter and safer to climb up there and follow the ridge." He indicated the steep hill now rising to their right.

"I think not," Foreman responded, drawing himself up somewhat. "I see no justification for doing so. It would be a difficult climb at best and would add considerably to the time it will take us to get back to Wheeling." He shook his head. "No, we'll follow the trail."

"Mebbe *you* will. *I* sure as hell won't."

"I would remind you, Mr. Linn, I'm in command here."

"An' I'll remind you, Captain, sir," Linn shot back, "you got orders from Colonel Shepherd to take my advice."

"Actually, Mr. Linn," Foreman said archly, "I received no such orders. Colonel Shepherd merely suggested I consider your recommendations. I, for one, am not afraid of your Indians. However," he added, smiling faintly and unbending a little, "if you're insistent on going through with this added difficulty without any just reason apart from a 'feeling' you're having, I won't prevent you from doing so. And I'll put it to the men; any who wish to go with you are welcome to do so. I doubt you'll have many takers."

Foreman was right. Of the 44 other men in the column, only three elected to go with Linn—one of Foreman's original volunteers named James Clark, a cousin of Linn's, Daniel McLane, and 15-year-old John Miller, who knew Linn well and trusted his judgment. Robert Harkness, one of the few who escaped the ambush three weeks earlier and who had sat on a log nearby and listened to Foreman and Linn argue their points, was tempted to go with Linn but, in the end, he stayed with Foreman because of his sore eyes.

As these three began scaling the steep, rather treacherous slope, Foreman started his men on the move again. They marched casually, ambling along in pairs, with a lot of talking, horseplay, and laughter. Partway up the slope, Linn paused and looked down. Through a gap in the trees he saw one of the soldiers swat off the hat of another and, in the midst of the faint whoops of laughter that followed, the two men had a brief pretend-sparring match. When they took up the march again, the rich baritone voice of Pvt. Tom Brazier, a noted singer of Foreman's company, broke into song, just as he had sung yesterday on the march. Several other voices joined in, but his carried the best and most melodiously.

"Nothin' like advertisin' they're acomin'," Linn said sourly, spitting a stream of tobacco juice to one side. "C'mon, boys, let's go."

They continued the climb and soon reached the summit, along which they moved parallel to the company somewhat over 100 feet below. Very faintly, the sound of the singing, laughter, and talking continued drifting up to them.[305]

It was close to ten A.M., as the ragged column of men on the trail was approaching the upper end of The Narrows, when those in the lead saw some items glinting on the trail ahead. They were scattered pieces of jewelry—trinkets, silver armbands, small beaded bags, strings of beads. They rushed forward and snatched them up, and others came up and crowded around to see what they had found.

That was when the ambush was sprung.

Twoscore or more Indians rose from their hiding places before and behind the company and fired their guns. The multitude of blasts reverberated in the river valley. A large number of the militia fell where they had been standing, and the rest scrambled for cover like frightened quail.[306]

Thomas Brazier, the singer, died instantly with a ball through his heart. Capt. Foreman was killed in the first fire, as were his son and two nephews. John Cullen took a ball in the brain and was dead as he fell. William Engle, an uncommonly athletic young man near the rear of the line, dropped his rifle and scurried monkeylike up the slope and was swiftly out of sight. The man who had been beside him, James Tomlinson, lay dead on the trail. Not far from where Engle was making his escape, Robert Harkness and Jacob Greathouse scrambled away close together. Harkness, with every step, kept berating himself for not having gone with Linn, as he'd had a notion to do, sore eyes or not. He scaled the slope swiftly, pulling himself up by gripping saplings. A ball narrowly missed his head, struck one of these saplings, and painfully sprayed splinters into his face, yet he managed to get out of sight of the attackers. Beside him, Jake Greathouse, glancing back down the slope to see if he was being pursued, ran the back of his neck into a low-hanging limb and fell, momentarily stunned. In a few seconds he recovered his senses, thought for a short time that he had been shot, then realized what had occurred and pressed on and quickly reached the summit. Pvt. John Wilson had almost gotten out of sight up the slope when a ball plowed through the fleshy part of his left forearm, but he still managed to get away. Several others were not so lucky and were killed by shots or thrown tomahawks before ascending more than a dozen feet, among them Bill Sheno, the half-breed. Kinzie Dickerson, the initial shots having missed him, shot his rifle point-blank into the stomach of an Indian rushing him with upraised tomahawk, then whirled and broke the gun in half by slamming it over the head of another. Tossing aside the stock section he was still holding, he vaulted up the slope and in several huge jumps had disappeared from sight. Jonathan Pugh, on the trail, was trying to take aim at one of the many Wyandots that had burst out of hiding when another warrior knocked his gun away with a tomahawk blow and captured him.

Above, Linn, Miller, Clark and McLane, realizing at once what was happening, plunged down the slope to help, yelling loudly as they did so to make the Indians think a reinforcement was arriving. The ruse didn't work. They were not halfway down when balls began whizzing past them and smacking into trees or buzzing off rocks in vicious ricochets.[307] To continue was to be killed for certain, and Linn bawled at his three companions to split up and get away, back to Wheeling. He was turning to do so himself when he heard someone scrambling up the slope toward him and saw Pvt. William Cullen, one of Foreman's Hampshire County men, weaponless, struggling upward as fast as he could, leaning forward and using his hands as much as his feet.[308] He abruptly screamed as a ball tore through his right leg six inches above the ankle, shattering the bone and sending him rolling. He wedged against a tree, moaning and sobbing. An Indian scrambled into view behind him, wielding a tomahawk, and Linn put a bullet through his chest, sending him tumbling back down the slope.

Linn rushed to Cullen and immediately saw there was no possibility of the man being able to walk, even with help. He propped him up and thrust his own rifle into the private's hands. "Here, take this. Don't drop it!" He put his arms under Cullen's legs and back and lifted him. With great difficulty, he struggled back up the slope, carrying him. He did not pause until they reached the top and by then was so exhausted he could scarcely breathe. Nevertheless he moved along the ridge with him another 40 feet before suddenly moving off to the east. In a few more steps he came to a rocky ledge, beneath which there was a considerable hollow, almost a cave. He lay the groaning Cullen inside against the back wall near where a small spring dribbled out of a crack in the rocks and trickled through a little gully out the entry. Linn took his rifle back and, still gasping for breath, reached into his pouch and extracted three hard biscuits.

"Take these," he said. "They's water there for you to drink. I'm going for help. Keep quiet, and don't try to crawl off. I'll be back as soon as I can. Do you understand?"

Cullen, still groaning but trying to stifle the sound, nodded. Without another glance at him, Linn set off running in a northeast direction, determined to make a wide arc away from the river to try to reach Fort Henry.

[September 23, 1777 — Tuesday]

Once again a strong sense of panic was gripping Wheeling. It was late yesterday afternoon when the first survivor, a hatless and bramble-torn Pvt. Robert Harkness, plunged into Wheeling Creek and swam across, bearing news of the ambush of Capt. William Foreman's company.

The news spread quickly, and once again those in the settlement outside the fort dropped their tools, snatched up their weapons and moved in haste to security within the walls of Fort Henry. Lookouts were quickly posted, and even while Harkness was being questioned, other survivors came straggling in. Everything they said led to the grim conclusion that another dreadful massacre had occurred.

Throughout the night more survivors arrived until, by early this morning, 18 had come in. One was William Linn, who told of secreting the injured William Cullen under the rock overhang. He wanted to raise a party and return immediately to rescue the man, but Col. Shepherd forbade it.

"Our first concern," the commander said, "is to see to our defenses here. We also must get runners off to the Forks and other stations and warn those who are still there, as well as all the outlying settlers we can reach. With a party of Indians like that prowling about, no one is safe. We'll get around to Mr. Cullen and start looking for other survivors as well, just as soon as possible. Now let's get busy."

[September 24, 1777 — Wednesday]

Because of the responsibility he felt for the injured Pvt. Cullen, Bill Linn finally decided he could not wait any longer to attempt his rescue. Mounting a good strong horse, he left Wheeling before dawn and headed back toward The Narrows. As he passed McMechen's, however, he angled eastward away from the river and rode his horse slowly up the manageable grade in this area to the top of the ridge. As dawn broke and visibility became better, he paused more frequently to sit quietly in the saddle for several minutes and watch for any movement that might give away the presence of Indians. He saw nothing suspicious.

A few minutes later he was peering into the cavity where he had left Cullen. The man was still there, half-asleep, faintly moaning with pain. A slight sound by Linn caused him to awaken more fully, at first fearfully and then, recognizing Linn, the joy that came into his expression filled the scout with pity and thankfulness that he had returned. "Tol' you I'd be back," he murmured cheerfully. "Now listen. I'm going to have to lift you onto this horse, and you're going to have to grit your teeth and not cry out. Think you can manage that?"

William Cullen nodded. He sucked in his breath, and a long-drawn-out, barely audible moan came from his throat as Linn lifted him and, with difficulty, raised him to the saddle. The foot on Cullen's injured leg dangled loosely, and it looked bad. When he was in place and holding on tightly, Linn mounted the horse behind him, put his arms under Cullen's to brace him, took the reins and chirped the horse into a walk. In less than an hour, with some early frost still clinging to the grasses, they arrived at Fort Henry. William Cullen was now officially a survivor.[309]

It was not until this afternoon that a strong party of mounted men left Fort Henry under Col. Silas Hedges and headed for The Narrows ambush site. Linn, again, was a member of that party, as were Martin Wetzel, Andrew Fouts and a dozen other well-mounted men. They rode carefully and with great watchfulness, prepared to wheel and thunder back to Fort Henry at the first sign of trouble. There was none, but they were heartily sickened by what they found.

The 22 bodies littering the road had been stripped of all their clothing and weapons, and each man had been scalped as well as horribly mutilated, most to the point where identification was impossible. A large hole was dug as a common grave, and all were buried in it at once. Six men were still missing.[310]

[September 25, 1777—Thursday]

The messengers sent out yesterday from Fort Henry by Col. Shepherd had ridden as swiftly as possible to all the nearby forts—Vanmetre's, Shepherd's, Holliday's Cove—as well as to all the isolated settlements where anyone might still be in residence. As a result, all the smaller forts and most of the settlements or isolated cabins were abandoned: Some residents went to Fort Henry and some to Catfish Camp, but the majority took refuge at Pittsburgh or Redstone or even returned far to the east.

Reluctantly, Maj. Sam McCulloch at Fort Vanmetre gave the order for the settlement to be temporarily abandoned and the residents to go either to Wheeling or Catfish Camp for greater safety. Four miles up Short Creek, at the Forks, was the claim where John Bendure and his wife and three young daughters lived. Fearing for their safety and for that of the Edward Morgan family a little farther upstream, McCulloch dispatched 16-year-old John Bukey to go there and warn them to leave immediately. It was a bit too late.

Even as Bukey set off upstream, a party of five Wyandot warriors struck at the cabin. John Bendure happened to be working in a field a short distance from the cabin at the time and was shot first. The bullet broke his arm but, because his dog managed to hold the Indians at bay for a short time, he was able to escape. His family was not so fortunate. The Indians rushed into the cabin and took Mrs. Bendure and her children captive. Two of the Indians took Mrs. Bendure, carrying her year-old daughter, in one direction, while the other three tied the older girls—Mary, 7, and Jane, 6—with rawhide tethers and were leading them away by a different route. Young Bukey saw them coming and, hoping he could make the Indians flee, shouted from his hiding place for an imaginary party of men to attack. It did indeed startle the Indians, and they fled, but they dragged the screaming little girls with them. Bukey returned to Vanmetre's at once, and a party went out under Maj. John McCulloch, now sheriff of Ohio County, and picked up their trail. All too soon they found the badly mangled remains of the two little girls. Mrs. Bukey and her infant daughter were never seen again.

Col. Shepherd, whose houses at Wheeling had been burned, even though his mill had come through unscathed, decided to move his family permanently to the greater safety of Catfish Camp.[311] When it was announced today at Shepherd's Fort that the danger was now deemed too great for anyone to remain there and that all should move on to Catfish Camp, the John Grist family was among those affected. They had taken refuge at Shepherd's when the Indian attacks first began, and now that they were going to have to move even farther away, they decided to stop at their cabin on the way to pick up some things they would need.

Against the advice of Lewis Bonnett, who was going to lead the exodus of the main party toward Catfish Camp, John Grist decided to leave in advance of the others, taking along his four children—a married daughter named Nancy, 14-year-old John Jr., 11-year-old Rachel, 10-year-old James—and their aunt, John Sr.'s married sister. He said they would go directly to their abandoned cabin on the Peters' Run tributary of Little Wheeling Creek, pick up their things and then intercept the Bonnett party and continue with them to Catfish Camp.

As Bonnett had pointed out, it was a foolish thing to do. They got to the cabin all right and picked up the things they needed, but as they moved along to join Bonnett's party, they were struck by a small war party of Mingoes. John Grist and his sister were simultaneously shot dead. John Jr. attempted to flee but was caught and held. Little James, also trying to run away, was killed by a savage blow from a war club.

The piercing scream of 11-year-old Rachel ripped through the woodland like a siren but was cut off sharply when she was struck with a war club and fell, her skull fractured. She was scalped, and the Mingoes, hearing the Bonnett party approaching, fled before they had an opportunity to scalp the others.

Bonnett's party had heard the shots and Rachel's scream and galloped to the scene. They checked each of the six bodies and discovered that Rachel, though badly injured, was still alive. Having no idea of the size of the war party that had done this and fearing for their own lives, they left the dead where they lay and carried Rachel with them to Catfish Camp. Here Dr. Jonathan More performed a trepanning operation to relieve the pressure of hemorrhaging and, as best he could, treated her mangled scalp. Amazingly, through it all, she remained conscious.[312]

Several miles to the south, the Stephen Spicer family living on Meadow Run, a tributary of Dunkard Creek, was warned of the troubles and told to leave if they valued their lives. They were advised to go to the new Whitaker's Blockhouse that had been built on the point of land where the Youghiogheny emptied into the Monongahela. The elder Spicer scoffed at the idea that any Indians were even aware of the existence of his isolated cabin and refused to leave. Less than three hours after they were warned, Indians struck and killed Spicer and his wife and took prisoner their 12-year-old son, William, and his friend, Francis McClure.

Once again raw fear spread throughout this frontier, and there was little doubt that within the next few days, virtually all of the isolated settlements would be abandoned. Only a very small number of the settlers adamantly refused to leave their claims, determined to protect them come what may. Among this number was Old John Wetzel, who had returned with his family to his place 16 miles above Fort Henry on Wheeling Creek.

[October 10, 1777—Friday]

Hokolesqua now knew that his wish for an equitable peace between the Shawnees and the *Shemanese* could never be. Over the past year matters had so degenerated that a virtual state of war existed. Settlers had swarmed down the Spaylaywitheepi all this year. The unauthorized attack by Chief Plukkemehnotee at McClelland's Station in Kentucky that had resulted in his own death and the equally unauthorized follow-up attack against the Kentucky settlements by Chief Chiungalla had made Hokolesqua realize that his people would no longer peacefully accept the abuses to which they had been subjected.

It was for that reason that today, accompanied by his son, Elinipsico, and sub-chief Red Hawk, that Hokolesqua crossed the big river and presented himself to the commander of Fort Randolph at the mouth of the Kanawha.[313] This was the first time he had been here since the Battle of Point Pleasant, three years ago today, and it brought back many sad memories, not the least of which was the death of his dear friend, Pucksinwah.

Capt. Matthew Arbuckle looked with suspicion at the three Indians who presented themselves to him, his fear subsiding somewhat when he saw they were unarmed and that a squad of his own armed soldiers stood ready to act if necessary. He recognized Hokolesqua and vaguely dipped his head in greeting but made no attempt to shake hands.

"Why have you come here, Cornstalk?" he asked bluntly.

"I come," replied Hokolesqua in English, "with grave news. At the camp of Charlotte three years ago, I gave my word as principal chief of the Shawnees that our tribe would keep the peace, would remain on our own side of the Spaylaywitheepi and refrain from retaliation if grievances arose between my people and yours, but instead take those grievances to the white commanders and they would be smoothed. This was a talk-treaty, and papers were to be marked later at the Fort of Pitt, where the Spaylaywitheepi begins. But because of the troubles that have risen, including the war between your own people, this did not come about. We have been injured by the whites in many ways since then, and though we have brought our grievances to the Fort of Pitt and discussed them at length, they have not been smoothed and have only become worse."

Hokolesqua shook his head sadly and his voice became harder. "Now I have come here to say to you that these grievances have become too great to be borne. I can no longer restrain my young men from joining the raiding parties encouraged by our friends, the British. I no longer *wish* to restrain them. We have suffered much at the hands of the *Shemanese* who have repeatedly broken the talk-treaty. Now there is a treaty no longer. It is a matter of honor that I have come here to tell you this."

Capt. Arbuckle did not even have the courtesy to respond to Hokolesqua's comments. Instead, he ordered the guard squad to take the three Indians into custody and lock them in the isolated cabin on the drill ground that was sometimes used as a guardhouse. "Apparently," he said, "we're at war with the Shawnees again. We'll hold these three hostage."

Hokolesqua, Red Hawk and Elinipsico, dismayed at such treatment of a delegation that had come in peace, were led to the one-room cabin and put inside. Here there was a table, two chairs, a large fireplace and a ladder leading up to a partial loft. Three narrow slits in the walls served as the only windows. The door was closed behind them and bolted from without.

Only a short time later came the sounds of a disturbance outside, and through the window slits, they could see Capt. Arbuckle arguing with a large group of armed, rough-looking men, telling them the Indians were official government hostages and not to be molested. After a moment he was pushed aside, and the men surged toward the cabin. At once Elinipsico climbed up the ladder to the loft, but Hokolesqua bade him come back down, which he did.

"My son," Hokolesqua said gently, placing his arm around his son's shoulders, "the Great Spirit has seen fit that we should die together and has sent you to that end. It is Her will and She will gather us up, so let us submit."

Red Hawk was not inclined to meek submission, and he ran to the fireplace and quickly began climbing up the chimney. He had just disappeared from sight when the bolt was thrown and the door yanked open. The armed mob of soldiers and frontiersmen, led by Capt. John Hall, filled the opening.

"By God," Hall exclaimed, "it *is* Cornstalk!"

The officer brought his rifle to bear, as did Adam Barnes, Hugh Gailbreath, Malcolm McCoun, William Roan and several others, and a thunderous barrage of shooting broke out. Even after Hokolesqua and Elinipsico had fallen, others continued to crowd in the doorway to shoot at the bodies.

A search was made for Red Hawk, and when he was not found in the loft, they discovered him clinging up in the chimney. They dragged him down and shot and tomahawked him and then bludgeoned the body with rifle butts until it was battered beyond recognition.

Nothing could have more certainly ignited the fire for war in the breasts of the Shawnee people.[314]

[O c t o b e r   2 2 ,   1 7 7 7 — W e d n e s d a y]

The Shawnees did not take long to retaliate for the murder of Hokolesqua. Chiungalla—Black Fish—was named as the new Shawnee principal chief, and his first act was to send out a war party to do just that.

The ploy that the Indians had so successfully used against the whites so many times in the past worked very well once again on this occasion. Two warriors from this party made their appearance near Fort Randolph, and Capt. Matthew Arbuckle immediately sent out a squad of a dozen soldiers under Lt. Robert Moore to drive them off.

As the squad drew near, the two warriors seemed to see them for the first time and fled in apparent fear, slowed because one was limping badly and the other was helping him along. Seeing them as easy prey, Lt. Moore put his men into pursuit and followed them into a ravine a quarter-mile from the fort.

Abruptly, the two decoy Indians leaped away and into hiding with considerable speed and agility, and realizing he'd been duped, Moore ordered his men to retreat, but it was too late. In the midst of turning around, they were fired upon, and Lt. Moore and three of his men were killed. The remainder managed to flee back to the safety of the fort.

It was only the beginning.

[March 4, 1778 — Wednesday]

It was from Simon Girty, one of his principal spies, that Gen. Edward Hand at Fort Pitt had learned of the large supply and staging depot recently established on Lake Erie at the mouth of the Cuyahoga River.[315]

Girty had been sent on a spying mission up the Allegheny last fall to try to determine how the Wyandots and Mingoes were being supplied in order to support such attacks as they had made on the upper Ohio at Wheeling, Grave Creek, McMechen's and other places. Hand was the recipient of a great deal of criticism from upper Ohio settlers for his failure to do more to protect them. The fact that a proposed expedition of his from Fort Randolph into the Ohio country failed to materialize, even though he went to Point Pleasant, had not helped, and so he was looking for something that would show them his thoughts and efforts were in that direction. Then, on December 20, Girty returned and gave the report that greatly excited Gen. Hand and focused his resolve.

From what could be determined, numerous boats were making the eight-day passage between Detroit and the Cuyahoga, bringing voluminous supplies of gunpowder and weapons as well as food, clothing, trade goods and whatever else was necessary to please the Indians, keep them in the British interest and encourage them to increase their forays against the settlements on the upper Ohio, only 100 miles distant.

All captured settlers from the upper Ohio who were not killed at the villages were evidently being transported to Detroit and sold to Governor-General Henry Hamilton, where they were extensively questioned about everything occurring on the Ohio River frontier. From the information gleaned, it seemed apparent that more major assaults were planned.

Hand decided at once that a winter attack against this supply and staging area might well be successful, since it would be so unexpected at that season. Great numbers of the Indians would have put their raids on hold until spring and would be scattered at their various winter hunting camps, leaving the Cuyahoga installation relatively vulnerable. With this in mind, he began making plans. As January dwindled away into February, he was close to launching his expedition. He wrote to Maj. William Crawford at his settlement on the Youghiogheny:

Headqtrs., Ft. Pitt
February 5th, 1778

Dr Sir

As I am credibly informed that the English have lodged a quantity of arms, ammunition, provision & clothing at a small Indian town about 100 miles from Fort Pitt, to support the savages in their excursions against the inhabitants of this and adjacent counties, I ardently wish to collect as many brave active lads as are willing to turn out, to destroy this magazine. Every man must be provided with a horse, & every article necessary to equip them for the expedition, except ammunition, which, with some arms, I can furnish.

It may not be unnecessary to assure them, that everything they are able to bring away shall be sold at public venue for the sole benefit of the captors, & the money equally distributed, tho' I am certain that a sense of the service they will render to their country will operate more strongly than the expectation of gain. I therefore expect you will use your influence on this occasion, & bring all the volunteers you can raise to Fort Pitt by the 15th of this month.

I am, dear Sir, Y^r Ob^{dt} humble Servt.   *Edwd Hand*
Col. Wm. Crawford.
N.B. The horses shall be appraised, & paid for if lost.

There were an abundance of men in the upper Ohio region who were now more than eager to retaliate against the Wyandots and Mingoes for the attacks they had been suffering, and the army was quickly raised to full strength. Gen. Hand expected his move to the mouth of the Cuyahoga, attack on the supply depot and return to Fort Pitt would take less than a fortnight. With great expectations, he launched his campaign with 500 mounted men on February 15.

Gen. Hand had based his timetable calculations on the weather being cold and the ground frozen hard. Nature refused to cooperate. The weather warmed and it began to rain, thawing the ground, melting the existing snow, turning the earth into a mire and previously frozen streams into torrents. Then the temperatures fluctuated for days between freezing and thawing. The men were constantly cold and wet, many were sick and all were thoroughly discouraged. Simon Girty, guiding the expedition, recommended it be aborted, but Gen. Hand pressed on.

By the time they reached the Forks of the Beaver, where it was formed by the Mahoning from the west and the Shenango from the east, only 40 miles from Fort Pitt, half the proposed time had already been used up. If they continued, all their provisions would be gone before they even reached their target, and they would then be in serious jeopardy. Concluding that Simon Girty's earlier advice should have been followed, Gen. Hand disgustedly announced he was aborting the expedition and told the men to set up camp; they would start back in the morning.

During that night, however, one of Hand's reconnoitering detachments came in with word that they had discovered a village some three miles up the Shenango that was of a size to contain perhaps 60 Indians.[316] Gen. Hand's spirits rose at the news—here was an opportunity to keep his expedition from being a complete failure. Without even knowing what tribe he might be dealing with, he announced they were enemies, changed plans and told the army they would attack the place in the morning.

Actually, it turned out to be one of the villages of Pimoacan—better known among the whites as Captain Pipe—a very influential Delaware who had long been friendly with the Americans and had refused to enter the war against them. Pimoacan and virtually everyone else was off on a winter hunt at this time, and the village was occupied only by Pimoacan's brother, Bull, and a few women and children.

Bull was doing some work outside when the first wave of attackers arrived—of which Gen. Hand was not a part—and fired a volley at him. Everyone missed, and the Delaware snatched up his musket and fired back, his single ball breaking the arm of one of Hand's company commanders, Capt. David Scott. As Bull attempted to reload, Capt. Reasin Virgin galloped up and buried a tomahawk in his skull, killing him. From one of the wegiwas emerged Bull's elderly mother, who came out as her son was being scalped, holding her hands out toward the soldiers in a beseeching manner. She was coldly slain and then scalped by a Dutchman, who stuffed the trophy into his victuals pouch, which contained only a chunk of bread. At that point a cluster of women and children, watching from another wegiwa, ran out and headed for the nearby woods. They were fired upon but to no effect, and they scattered upon reaching their destination.

The army was more interested in the warriors they thought were hidden in the other wegiwas and cabins of the village, and they poured a hot, prolonged fire into them, which gradually dwindled away as they realized they were shooting at structures in which there were no men. Then Michikapeche, the wife of Pimoacan, emerged from a cabin and tried to flee amidst a hail of bullets. A rifle ball clipped off the tip of one of her fingers, and she was overtaken and on the verge of being tomahawked and scalped when Maj. William Crawford intervened and ordered that she be taken prisoner.[317] The village was then ransacked, but only a small amount of plunder was found and taken.

Another detachment of this brave army struck a second Delaware town up the Mahoning. It, too, was empty except for five squaws. One was taken prisoner. Nearby a young Indian boy hunting birds with his bow was spotted. He was shot and killed. Then the army set off for home.

Today they arrived at Fort Pitt, and there was little exultation over their accomplishments. Even before the day was over, the abortive expedition was being called by the derisive name it would always retain—the Squaw Campaign.

[*M a r c h   2 7 ,   1 7 7 8 — F r i d a y*]

Five weeks ago yesterday—on February 19—the Virginia Executive Council, having learned of the murder of Hokolesqua, Elinipsico and Red Hawk at Fort Randolph, issued a brief statement:

> *The Governor and Board express their strong abhorrence of the murder of Cornstalk and other Shawanese; & speak in decided disapproval of the frontier people who screen the perpetrators of that act from apprehension.*

Today, having decided that their initial statement was not strong enough, the Virginia Council issued a warrant for the arrest of five of the identified perpetrators: listed as Hugh Gailbreath, Adam Barnes, Malcolm McCoun, William Roan and their leader, James Hall, offering a reward of $200 for Hall, $150 for McCoun and $100 each for the others, charging them with being "deeply concerned and perpetrating the atrocities & barbarous murder of the Shawanese Indians on the 10th of November [October] last at Fort Randolph, as appears from sundry depositions transmitted to the governor."[318]

[*M a r c h   2 8 ,   1 7 7 8 — S a t u r d a y*]

Over the past year or so, Simon Girty had become increasingly disenchanted with the situation at Fort Pitt and on the frontier. Even though he and his brothers had been captured by the Indians as boys in 1756 and had been adopted into their tribes—Simon into the Senecas—he had come to sympathize with their plight. He could understand their anger over broken treaties, over the theft of their lands, over the frauds perpetrated upon them by governments and traders, over the brutality perpetrated upon them by the whites.

This did not preclude the fact that, after his release from captivity as a result of Col. Bouquet's invasion of Ohio in 1764, he had served as interpreter at Fort Pitt as well as express messenger and spy and eventually had become an ensign. He had served Gov. Dunmore during that brief war four years ago, and with the outbreak of the Revolution, he had separated from the British and was staunchly loyal to the Americans, serving as intermediary between the Iroquois and the new young government and winning much esteem for his skilled handling of a most difficult role. He had also been serving Gen. Hand as guide, scout and interpreter ever since that officer took command of Fort Pitt.

Simon Girty had run into certain difficulties at Fort Pitt. He strongly believed there had to be a way for Indians and whites to live in harmony, and because of his outspoken views in this respect and his anger at what was being done to the tribes by the border men and the militia, he had been passed over for promotion to the rank of captain, which had been promised to him, and at one point he was even thrown into the Fort Pitt guardhouse while an investigation went on to determine if he was colluding with the red men. His ironic sense of humor led him to escape that confinement, just to show the authorities how easily it could be done. Having escaped, that night he slept in an apple tree in the nearby orchard and then turned himself in the next day.[319] Again he was arrested while carrying expresses to the Illinois country and charged with betraying American intelligence, but the charges were untrue and he was exonerated. This did not, however, put an end to the ill treatment he received from the majority of his fellows at Fort Pitt, most of whom concluded he had just been too cunning to get caught. Few of the frontiersmen had anything but contempt for what they termed an "Injen lover."

Girty did have certain friends among the Americans who were very dear to him —Simon Kenton, for instance, with whom he had made a blood-brother pledge during Dunmore's War, and William Crawford, at whose table he had often dined in friendship, who had once intervened to get him released from jail and who had been his comrade during Hand's recent abortive Squaw Campaign. He was convinced that the Americans could never live in peace with the Indians, as the British at least attempted to do. For that reason, in combination with the abuse he had been receiving and the fact that he felt strongly that he could be of more help to the Indians with the British than with the Americans, he elected to defect.

This idea of Girty's to defect was considerably bolstered by the deputy Indian agent at Fort Pitt, Alexander McKee, who was already on the point of doing so himself.[320] McKee, with the help of the trader Matthew Elliott, who had long ago married into the Shawnee tribe, had already secretly been in the pay of Gen. Hamilton at Detroit and had a commission awaiting him there in the Indian department. In addition to Elliott, McKee's party ready to defect included his cousin, Robin Surphlet, a servant named John Higgins and two Negro slaves. Now he surreptitiously approached Girty with this long-brewing plan of defection and offered him the opportunity to become an interpreter in that department at Detroit and perhaps even part of the very important liaison between the British and Indians. It was this nudge that pushed Girty over the edge because it was a real chance to do what he personally felt was still possible: helping eventually to establish permanent harmony between Indians and whites.[321]

This afternoon he visited his half-brother, John Turner, at Squirrel Hill near Pittsburgh and signed over to him full ownership of his large Squirrel Hill Farm. A little later he dropped by Duncan's Tavern, where he had been boarding with his friend, Kate Duncan, and bade her a final farewell. "I can no longer stay and live with you," he told her gently. Then, with a low, bitter laugh, he added: "There's not much choice, since I can't work and I won't steal. I'll do all I can to save your family and kin if they should fall into my hands but, as for the rest, I'll make no promises."

It was just after darkness had fallen tonight that Girty and the other six men slipped away from McKee's Rocks just below Fort Pitt, turned their backs on the American cause and headed for Detroit.

[*M a r c h   3 0 ,   1 7 7 8 — M o n d a y*]

Gen. Edward Hand and Indian superintendent George Morgan were appalled when they were informed of the defection of the Alexander McKee party. The possible damage these men could do to American interests on the upper Ohio and among the various tribes was not lost on either. Hand quickly sent a report of it to the secretary of war, Gen. Horatio Gates, and then, aware that Col. William Crawford, a longtime friend of Girty, was at this time preparing a company of men for an intended expedition against the Indians well up the Allegheny on French Creek, immediately wrote to him of the potentially disastrous situation:

> *Ft. Pitt, March 30th, 1778*
>
> *Dr. Crawford—*
>
> *. . . You will no doubt be surprised to hear that Mr. McKee, Matthew Elliott, Simon Girty, one Surplus and Higgins, with McKee's two negroes, eloped on Saturday night. This will make it improper to proceed with the intended expedition to French Creek, which I beg you may give proper notice of to the gentlemen who are preparing for it; and as your assistance may be necessary towards preventing the evils that may arise from the information of these runaways, I beg you may return here as soon as possible.*
>
> *I am, Dr. Crawford, Sincerely yours,*
>
> *Ed^w. Hand, BG*

For his own part, Morgan was most concerned about the effect these defectors, as influential as they were among the Indians, would have on the tribes. Even as Gen. Hand was writing his letters, Morgan at once wrote to President of Congress Henry Laurens and, after a few introductory remarks, warned:

> *The elopement of Mr. McKee, late Crown Agent at Pittsburgh, who most dishonourably broke his Parole on the 28th. inst., has somewhat checked the pleasing expectation I entertain'd respecting the Delawares and Shawnese, tho' I think the former will not be altogether influenced by him. Four persons accompanied him, viz: Matthew Elliott, Simon Girty, Robin Surplis & _____ Higgins.*
>
> *Elliott had but a few weeks ago return'd from Detroit via New York on his Parole & I am told had possess'd Mr. McKee's mind with the persuasion of his being assassinated on his Road to York. Indeed, several persons had express'd the like apprehensions and perhaps had also mention'd their fears to him, which I am of opinion has occasion'd his inexcusable Flight. It is also very probable that Elliott might have been employ'd to bring letters from Canada which may have influenced Mr. McKee's conduct.*
>
> *Girty has served as Interpreter of the Six Nation Tongue at all the public Treaties here & I apprehend will influence his Brother, who is now on a Message from the Commissioners to the Shawnese, to join him.*

[*April 1, 1778 — Wednesday*]

There was a pleasant surprise awaiting Simon Girty when he reached the Delaware capital of Goschachgunk at the Forks of the Muskingum. His younger brother, James, and his Shawnee wife had arrived there only a short time before with packhorses carrying presents destined for the Shawnees. Only three days before Simon's defection with McKee's party, James had been sent by Indian superintendent George Morgan with gifts from the Indian commissioners to help appease the escalating ill feelings that that tribe harbored for the Americans and perhaps aid in preventing a full declaration of war.

James was stunned—and pleased—to learn of the defection and immediately announced he would defect as well and promptly joined them. He also confiscated the American gifts, deciding to disburse them among whatever Indians he cared to and however he saw fit: gifts that included a pair of broad armbands, a stroud, a calico shirt and pair of leggins, 18 silver rings, a large silver cross, half a dozen hair plates, six dozen brooches and a conch shell.

A council was held at Goschachgunk in order for Alexander McKee and his associates to address the tribes. These men were among the few Americans for whom the tribes had any real respect and in whom they trusted, and with good reason: Simon Girty was very influential as an intermediary between the tribes and the Americans, especially where it concerned the Iroquois and Mingoes, whose tongue he spoke fluently; his brother, James, now one of them, also had a Shawnee wife and had long lived with that tribe as a Shawnee; Matthew Elliott, too, had married into the Shawnee tribe, had traded with them for many years and had often acted as an intermediary on their behalf; and McKee, who was said to be half-Indian by birth, had also married a Shawnee woman and, as deputy Indian agent under George Croghan, had been of great assistance to the tribes and was considered a highly important man who wielded great influence.

It was McKee, in his speech now, who skillfully undermined the Americans and swayed the assembled listeners even more strongly toward the British.

"Make no mistake, brothers," he told them, "it is the avowed intention of the Americans to kill and destroy the whole Indian race, regardless of whether they are friends or foes. Why would they wish to do this? Because the very most important goal for them is this: They mean to possess themselves of this entire country. If they must do so by war, then that is what they will do, but if they can deceive you and trick you out of your lands without war, then they would prefer to do that. I tell you," he said, swinging out his arms dramatically, "that even now they are preparing fine-sounding speeches to send among you to deceive you, that they may, when the time comes and with greater ease and safety for themselves, fall upon you and murder you and your wives and children. And then they will take your country."

He paused and there was an expectant hush, every eye locked on him, every ear cocked for what he would say next. He did not disappoint them. "*Now* is the time," he thundered, "the *only* time, to turn out to a man against these intruders. Fall upon them! Do not let them place one foot on your side of the Ohio! Go and strike them wherever you find them! I say this because I know these people and I know in my heart that if you do not strike them without delay, your country will be lost to you forever!"

There was wild enthusiasm for the speech when he finished. The Delawares themselves quickly went into secret council to discuss whether to break their long neutrality and at last declare themselves at war against the Americans.

Chief Pimoacan—Captain Pipe—previously an advocate for peace, was now strongly for war because of the attack made on his villages by Gen. Hand in the unconscionable Squaw Campaign, in which Pimoacan's brother, Bull, had been killed, as well as their mother, and Pimoacan's wife wounded. It was an affront that called for revenge, and he meant to have it.

On the other hand, Chief White Eyes, who had been converted by the Moravian missionaries and was even more a friend of the Americans than Pimoacan had been, strongly advocated a continuance of their neutrality. Not until both of these chiefs, along with numerous others, had fully expressed their feelings in council—a process that would take days—would the tribe finally vote on what they would do.

And now, as the council began, Alexander McKee and the others of his party departed, with Detroit their ultimate destination.[322]

[*A p r i l   1 6 ,   1 7 7 8 — T h u r s d a y*]

Chief White Eyes had just finished giving the two runners standing before him a belt of white wampum and a crucial message to carry to the Shawnees. Now, slowly and carefully, he repeated the message aloud as the two listened and memorized verbatim what he said. He gave them a moment by themselves to get it firmly established in their minds, after which they would repeat it to him to make certain it was correct. In the interval he considered the events of these past days since the party of McKee, Girty and Elliott had visited with news of their defection and their urgings for war.

The council held here at Goschachgunk had lasted for four days following the departure of the whites, and almost every Delaware chief of significance had had his say. There had been considerable debate, with Chief Pipe leading the pro-war faction and White Eyes pleading for neutrality. In the end, however, it was Pipe who had prevailed, and the vote, when taken, showed a strong majority for war. In a desperate bid for time, White Eyes had risen then to address them again.

"Brothers," he had said, "I see with my eyes and hear with my ears your desire for war, and, though my heart is heavy with it, I accept your wish, and I, too, will fight the Americans, though I fear the outcome will be our own destruction if we do this immediately. It has come to me, however, that if we wait ten suns before we take this step, something will occur that will be of great importance to us and our future. I beg that we wait those ten days, and if nothing should occur in that time, then we may make war with greater hope for our future."

Another vote had been taken and though Pipe was opposed to delay, White Eyes was granted the ten days before active hostilities commenced. And then they had waited. Late in the evening on the eighth day, the Rev. John Heckewelder, traveling with a converted Delaware named Shabosh—who had adopted the Christian name of John—had arrived at the Moravian town and mission of Gnadenhütten, 23 miles up the Tuscarawas from Goschachgunk. They bore peace messages to the Delawares and Shawnees from both Gen. Hand and George Morgan, along with newspaper reports of the war and other documents.

It had not taken long for them to learn of the defectors' visit to Goschachgunk and how they had incited the Delawares there into a determination for war. Only two days remained before that resolve would become reality. They and their horses needed rest and so remained the remainder of the night at Gnadenhütten and then set out in the dawn light as fast as they could travel. In order to avoid war parties, they swam their horses across the river and traveled on isolated paths. It was late forenoon when they reached Goschachgunk and delivered to White Eyes the messages from Gen. Hand and Morgan.

White Eyes had felt delight at receiving the messages and the enclosures, especially the newspaper reports. He had immediately sent heralds out to run through the village calling everyone to immediate council. As soon as they had assembled, he addressed them strongly.

"My Brothers," he had said, "it is well that we waited. In doing so, we may have averted our own destruction. I have here letters that have come from Pittsburgh —from Morgan and General Hand—and I will read them to you." He did so, translating the written English into the native tongue, then went on. "I can see by your expressions that you do not believe the proposals of peace because you are saying to yourselves, 'See, this is what McKee said they would do to deceive us.' But this I say to you: The Americans have not asked us to fight our battles for them against the British, as the British have asked us to fight their battles for them against the Americans. The Americans have not done this because they know that wars are destructive to nations, and their fight is a fight between father and son, a family matter that should not involve others. From the beginning of the war these Americans advised us only to remain quiet and not take up the hatchet against either side. That is good advice.

"Now," he went on, showing them the newspaper pages, "you will see that what McKee and the others said to us has been lies. They told us the British were winning the war and that it was only a matter of a short time before the Americans would be completely defeated, but this says differently." He unfolded the newspaper so all could see and turned back and forth with it. The newspaper was explosive with notices of Gen. John Burgoyne's surrender to Gen. Horatio Gates at the second Battle of Saratoga the past October seventh, and he read to them what was printed. Then he folded the paper and put it aside.

"See, my friends and relatives," he said, "this contains great events—not the song of a bad bird, but the truth!"

The Delawares had been greatly swayed and changed their position: They would continue to maintain the neutrality they had previously held.

So now, his message-carriers ready, White Eyes listened as they spoke aloud, in unison, the words he had given them:

"Grandchildren! You Shawnees! Hear! Some days ago a flock of bad birds that had come from the east landed at Goschachgunk and sang their song to us and, upon leaving us, turned their faces toward you in order to sing to you the same song. Shawnees, do not listen to them, for they lie!"

[*A p r i l   2 3 ,   1 7 7 8 — T h u r s d a y*]

In his quarters at Detroit, Lt. Gov. Henry Hamilton had just learned from his own messenger, Edward Hazel, and Simon Girty of the defection of Alexander McKee and his party from the Americans, and he was very pleased. Now he dipped his pen and wrote swiftly, composing a letter to be carried to McKee, who was still among the Shawnees, establishing his own village, called McKee's Town, on a little creek to which he had given his name, only a few miles north of Mackachack and a lesser distance northwest of Wapatomica:[323]

Lieut. Gov. Hamilton to Capt. McKee

Detroit, April 23, 1778

Sir,

   I heartily congratulate you on your escape, and shall be happy to see you here, where you may be sure of finding friends and sincere ones.
   The sooner your convenience can admit of your coming to this place, the better, as I wish to confer with you on several points t'is impossible to touch upon in a letter. The newspapers you sent were very acceptable. They shall be forwarded to Sir Guy Carleton whom I have made acquainted with your happy release. The Council to be held at this place, and which I expect to be very full, will meet on or about the 15th of May, till when matters will remain as they are—nothing can exceed the good temper and tractable behavior of all the Indians. The bearer is a very spirited young fellow, is trusty and I hope by good behavior will deserve to be put on a good footing.
   The Six Nations are more than ever attached to the government and zealous in the cause against the rebels—considerable reinforcements expected to Canada this year.

I am, Sir, your very humble servant,
Henry Hamilton

[*A p r i l   2 7 ,   1 7 7 8 — M o n d a y*]

The sun had not been up for quite an hour this morning when Old John Wetzel, still doggedly refusing to leave his claim seven miles above the Forks of Wheeling Creek, sent his eldest son, Martin, now 21, out to get the four horses that were hobbled in the meadow a few hundred yards distant. John Wolf, Martin's 22-year-old cousin, was visiting at the time and volunteered to help bring them in. A very nervous young man without much self-confidence, Wolf had gotten married three years ago at Brownsville and had settled with his bride some 20 miles from there on Dunkard Creek. Now they had a two-year-old son and a four-month-old daughter.

"Shouldn't we have guns with us?" John asked nervously as they left the cabin.

Martin shook his head. "No real need," he said. "Horses ain't but a little way out, an' we ain't seen no Injen sign around here since we moved back from Wheeling last fall. They been hittin' more down in Kaintuck than anywhere else lately."

Martin went on to tell what he had heard of the attacks occurring in Kentucky, including the Indians having captured, a couple of months ago, a party of 25 or 30 saltmakers from Boonesboro under Daniel Boone. The party had been making salt at the Lower Blue Licks for a couple of weeks when about 100 Shawnees under Black Fish had surprised them. Whether any of them were still alive, including Boone, no one seemed to know.[324]

When Martin and John got to where the horses were supposed to be, there was no sign of them, and Martin, studying the ground with a practiced eye, pointed to the adjacent woodland. "Looks like they decided to take a stroll in the woods," he said. "Damn knotheads sure as hell ain't gonna find no good graze in there. Well, with them hobbles on, they cain't have got too far. C'mon."

Following the trail made by the four horses, they walked another 100 yards or so when Martin suddenly stopped and put up a hand, simultaneously stopping and stilling his cousin. "Listen," he said.

From far ahead came the barely audible tinkling of bells, and Martin grinned. "That's them," he chuckled. "Tol' you they wouldn't've got too far." He struck out toward the sound, and John fell in behind him.

The bells around the necks of the horses continued tinkling, and though the young men gradually closed the gap, it seemed to be taking rather longer than expected to overtake them. Following the horses by sound rather than watching their trail, Martin failed to see that there were now, here and there, imprints of moccasin-clad feet.

With the horse bells still sounding ahead, seven or eight Shawnees armed with flintlocks abruptly stepped into sight from behind trees on both sides of them. Two of the Indians had rifles. As the startled boys looked around, one of the warriors put a shot into a large beech tree near them, evidently as a warning for them to stop. John did so, instantly holding his hands high to show that he was unarmed. Martin, however, remembering his father's admonition to grasp the advantage by doing something unexpected, leaped away, successfully ducked a gun barrel swung at him by the nearest warrior and then ran and dodged around trees as fast as he could with five of the Shawnees in close pursuit.

Martin, very agile and swift, maintained his distance from them for a short while and then gradually increased it. He had run some 250 yards and was just about to pass across the crest of a small hill when the Indians opened fire. A ball grazed his hip, causing the sensation of a red-hot iron laid against him. Another grazed his left shoulder, cutting a shallow furrow in the skin. Then he was over the crest and descending to the small bottom on the other side. He raced down, leaped over the little run flowing through it and began surging up the other side when two Indians appeared in front of him, no more than 20 paces distant. Both shot at him, and remarkably, both shots missed. Ridiculously, at a time of such crisis, the thought crossed Martin's mind of what his grandfather had said at Martin's birth. Superstitious old man that he was, he had come to their cabin and performed some strange rites over the newborn infant and had then pronounced him bulletproof; that he could never be killed with powder and lead. It seemed to be holding true. So far.

Martin changed direction and redoubled his efforts. Three of the Indians stopped, but the other two dropped their rifles and continued the pursuit, some 30 yards behind. They maintained this gap over the next few hundred yards until Martin suddenly encountered a steeply sloped narrow ravine, with a small stream at the bottom. He leaped and hit the opposite slope a quarter of the distance down from the top. The surface there was thickly coated with the wet and decayed remains of last autumn's leaves and, as if he had stepped on grease, he slid and slithered all the way to the bottom.

Before he could regain his feet, the closest Shawnee plunged down the near side of the slope and landed on his back. They grappled furiously, rolling in and out of the little brook. The warrior was tall, slender and muscular; Martin was not as tall but was muscular and strongly built, outweighing his adversary by ten pounds or more, an advantage that soon had him on top of the Indian. But before he could capitalize on that advantage, the second pursuing Shawnee slid down the bank and, gripping Martin by the hair, yanked him off, throwing him on his back.

The warrior he had been grappling with sprang to his feet and pounced on Martin, his tomahawk raised menacingly. Wisely, Martin relaxed, shook his head and said, "I give up!"

The warrior abruptly grinned and looked at his companion, who also stood with tomahawk in hand, and nodded, then stretched his hand out to Martin. The young man looked at it and then at the warrior's face. Seeing no treachery there, he accepted the hand and was pulled to his feet. Still gripping his hand, the warrior spoke to his companion without looking away.

"Ahpe."

The second warrior nodded, dug in his pouch, pulled out a coiled length of rawhide cord and handed it to him. Within moments the first warrior had tied Martin's wrists, leaving a length of the cord to lead him by. They then climbed back up the bank and returned to where the other Indians were still waiting with their captive. The two Shawnees who had led the horses on to decoy the two boys were standing close by with the four horses, including Old John's fine black mare, Shine, and ten horses of their own.[325]

John Wolf was terrified, as evidenced in part by the stain down his trousers leg where he had wet himself. He was trembling badly, and his eyes were wide and frightened in a chalk-white face. Though he was not tied, the Indians seemed to be paying little attention to him.

There were ten Shawnees in the party, and they held a guttural conversation, none of which either of the boys could understand. Then six of the warriors mounted their horses and rode off toward the east without a backward glance. As soon as they were gone, the warrior who had first pounced on Martin approached him.

"Skootekitehi," he said, tapping his own chest.[326] Then he tapped Martin's chest, at the same time giving him a quizzical look.

The young man nodded. "Martin," he said.

"Mah-ten," Skootekitehi repeated. Then he tapped first Martin's chest and then his own again and said, "Mah-ten b'long Skootekitehi."

Young Wetzel began breathing a little easier. If he was going to belong to this warrior, then it was reasonable to assume he wasn't to be killed—at least not right away. He nodded and smiled wryly. "I belong to you."

Martin, still with his wrists bound, and John, still untied, were placed by the Indians on two of his father's horses, and the four remaining warriors mounted their own. With one warrior leading each of the remaining two horses—including Shine —on tethers, they all headed toward the southwest. An hour later they were swimming their horses across the Ohio River from near the mouth of Grave Creek and, for John Wolf and Martin Wetzel, into a distinctly uncertain future.

[May 3, 1778—Sunday]

Lewis Wetzel had always been big for his age, but in the past year he had grown exceptionally. Though only 14, he was as tall as most grown men, huskily built and good looking, with long black hair woven and clubbed at the nape. He was a superb hunter whose keen eyes seemed to miss nothing, and he bore himself with the assurance of someone considerably older. The wound he had received last August when captured was now completely healed, leaving behind only a broad, slightly raised scar as a permanent memento of that incident.

The Wetzel household was greatly upset over the disappearance of Martin and his cousin six days ago. Old John, George and Lewis had searched for them, of course, and found where they had been captured. The trail spoke volumes to Old John Wetzel; the two young men had at least not been immediately killed, and that was encouraging. Taken into captivity, there remained the possibility they might eventually escape. No one voiced what they all feared—that the pair would be forced to run a gauntlet, with a likelihood of being killed in the process. Or if they survived that, it might only be to face an infinitely worse death at the stake. More to the moment, however, the trail also told them that six mounted Shawnees had ridden toward the settlements, meaning the Wetzel household was in imminent danger and that their first priority must be to return and protect Old John's wife, 12-year-old Jacob, nine-year-old Susan and Little John, now seven.

Once again the family was taken to safety—this time to Catfish Camp, now ranking second in population after Wheeling, with a fort and several good fortified cabins. Leaving the family in charge of George, Old John then rode off to alert Col. Shepherd at Fort Henry. Early yesterday, Lewis volunteered to go tell John Wolf's family on Dunkard Creek about his and Martin's capture.

By midmorning, he was only a few miles from Dunkard Creek when he encountered a young man named Frazier Forrest hunting for table game. He had already bagged two rabbits and a turkey and was on the verge of heading for home

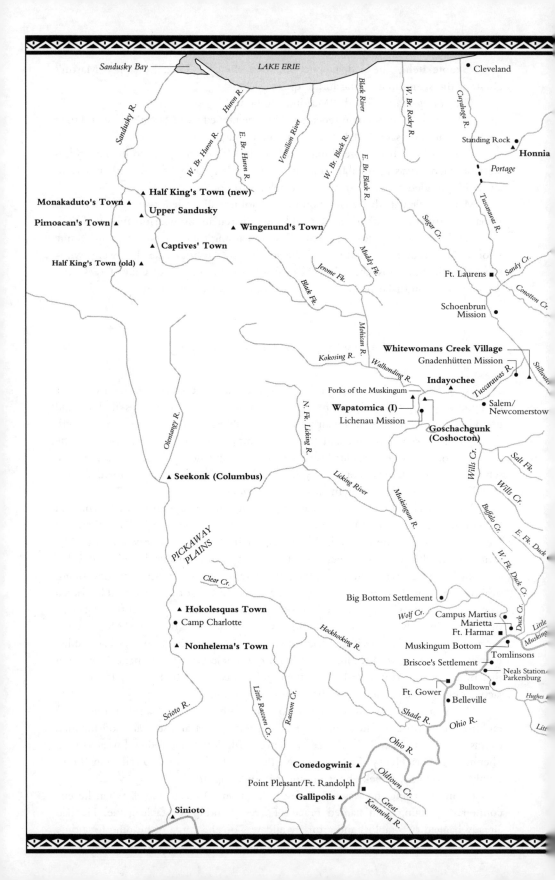

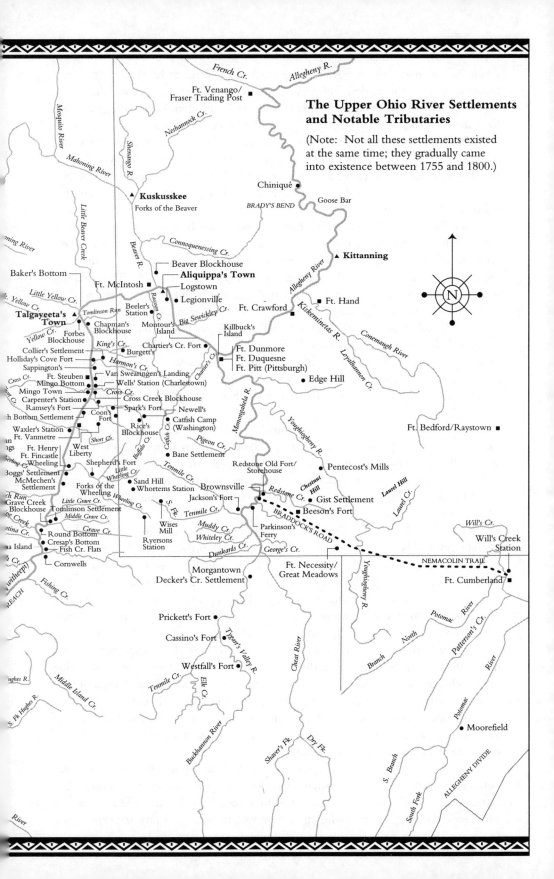

The Upper Ohio River Settlements and Notable Tributaries

(Note: Not all these settlements existed at the same time; they gradually came into existence between 1755 and 1800.)

when the two met. Forrest was newly married and referred to his wife as "the most beautiful Rose in the garden." Her name was, reasonably enough, Rose. They, too, lived on Dunkard Creek but several miles from the Wolf cabin. Forrest suggested they head that way together, and Lewis, glad for the company, agreed.

The Forrest cabin was burning fiercely when they arrived, and Rose was nowhere to be found. Frazier was wild with rage and concern. Lewis discovered tracks and deduced that four Indians, all afoot, had taken Rose away. Immediately the two young men began trailing them, traveling fast and hoping to intercept them and rescue her.

The trail led them to Cresap's Bottom, where the Indian party had evidently made a raft and crossed the Ohio. The raft-making had caused the Indians to lose a good bit of time, and the pursuers were encouraged. If they could cross the river themselves quickly, they might yet overtake the party before dark. They quickly made a floating platform of dry branches tied together with grapevines, placed their guns, powderhorns and pouches on it and swam the river, pushing it before them.

On the other side they found the abandoned raft the Indians had used, and they continued following the trail, now leading them up Captina Creek. Soon it was twilight, and they were despairing of overtaking them before it became too dark for further tracking. In another 20 minutes Lewis stopped and shook his head.

"Cain't see good," he said. "Reckon we mebbe orta' stop 'fore we lose the trail entirely."

Fearing detection themselves, they made a cold camp and huddled together at the base of a large sycamore, one on watch while the other napped. An hour or so after dark, while Lewis was on guard, there was a slight shifting of the night breeze, and he abruptly stiffened and carefully shook Frazier Forrest awake.

"I caught a whiff of smoke comin' down the crik," he whispered. "I figger it's gotta be their camp. C'mon."

They moved slowly, sliding their feet gently to avoid stepping on a twig that would crack and betray their presence. After some 500 yards they caught a glimpse of campfire coals glowing well ahead of them. They approached even more cautiously until they were within 40 yards. Three of the Indians were stretched out asleep. The fourth was hunched in a sitting position, his back against a tree, his head turning occasionally to look at Rose Forrest, who also sat cuddled up against a tree a few feet away from him. Even at this distance they could hear her occasional sobbing.

Frazier Forrest's rage returned in a surge, and he was all for firing at them and then instantly rushing up to finish them off with tomahawks. Lewis put a restraining hand on his arm and calmed him, whispering that they had to wait till daylight if they wanted to minimize the risk of getting themselves and Rose killed. They continued to watch, and after a while Rose fell asleep. The Indians changed guard and fed the fire twice during the night. It was during one such occasion when they saw that one of the men was not Indian but a white renegade.

The Indians were still asleep at dawn. Even the guard appeared to be dozing, but Lewis cautioned Frazier to be patient, and they waited for the men to rouse. They planned to shoot the first two who got to their feet, Frazier taking the man on the left, Lewis the one on the right; then they would rush the camp screeching and shouting and, with luck, the two survivors might flee, thinking a large party was coming against them.

It was fairly well daylight when the Indians began to rouse. The renegade came to his feet first, stretching hugely, and then the guard stood.

"At three, Frazier," Lewis whispered. "One . . . two . . . three."

The two shots exploded almost as one, and both men were slammed off their feet. Frazier and Lewis ran bellowing toward the campfire. The other two, who had been stirring, leaped up and ran, leaving their guns on the ground. Lewis loaded as he ran, and by the time he passed the campfire, his weapon was ready.

Frazier raced to Rose, who was screaming and crying, and gathered her into his arms. Lewis continued running and abruptly saw that the two Indians had stopped and were watching him come. Both had yanked the tomahawks from their belts and seemed ready to charge him, believing his gun to be empty. Lewis stopped, leveled his rifle and shot one of them dead. The other charged instantly, knowing now for certain the white man's gun was empty. Lewis turned and fled, and now all that practice at reloading while running at full tilt paid off. In 50 yards, with the shrieking, tomahawk-wielding Indian closing rapidly on him, he finished the reloading, stopped, whirled around, took good aim and shot that Indian dead, too.[327]

They took the four scalps and all the weapons and returned to the river, where they used the abandoned Indian raft to cross. Halfway there, Lewis paused and looked at the young woman, composure regained, sitting calmly in the center.

"Ma'am," he said, "Frazier tol' me you was the purtiest rose in the garden. You know what? Far as I k'n see, he ain't lied yet."[328]

[*May 7, 1778 — Thursday*]

Martin Wetzel stared at the fire, now all but reduced to ashes, and shook his head with dismay. The anger and frustration he was experiencing seethed inside him with no outlet, and he groaned at his own helplessness. Over the past ten days since he was captured, he had cherished the hope that somehow during the journey to the Shawnee villages, he would find a chance to escape. Now, even more than previously, he wished he had been given the opportunities for escape that had been afforded to his cousin. His initial feeling that John Wolf was a fool for not taking advantage of them had been confirmed.

Martin had been kept continually bound since his capture, and though Skootekitehi and the other three warriors had not abused him, they had watched him closely. With cousin John it was different; not only was he never tied, not even at night, but time and again he was given ample opportunity to get away.

Their pace as they headed westward through the Ohio country was easy, each day's travels not beginning until the sun was well up and ending as the night's camp was made well before sunset. Each evening the horses would be hobbled and turned loose to graze on whatever they could find, and each morning John Wolf was sent alone to fetch them, a job that sometimes took an hour or more.

On the fourth morning, after Wolf had brought the horses in and then hunkered down by the fire near his bound cousin, Martin had spoken to him earnestly in an undertone.

"John," he said, "why'n hell ain't you tryin' t'get away? You got all kinds of chances t'do it."

Wolf shook his head. "I couldn't think of getting away and leaving you alone in the hands of these Injens, Martin."

"*That's* what's keepin' you from goin'?" Martin was flabbergasted and irked. "Use your head, goddammit! I got no wife an' babies to think of, so it don't matter much what happens t'me. You, now, you got a wife an' two little ones. They need you, an' that's where your responsibility is. You got t'get back to 'em."

"You really think so, Martin?"

" 'Course I do. Now listen to me. That big black mare of Paw's—Shine—she k'n outrun and outlast any of them other horses 'thout no trouble. T'morrow when you go out t'get the horses, ketch her first an' get on her back and get the hell out'a here. You'll have half an hour, mebbe an hour, t'get clear, an' they ain't no way they could ever catch up. So do it!"

"All right, Martin," Wolf replied, nodding seriously. "I *will* do it. Tomorrow morning."

But then the next morning came and John was sent out for the horses, and nearly an hour later Martin was appalled when his cousin returned to camp leading the horses. Wolf wouldn't meet his glance, and Martin could see he was trembling, and a great contempt rose in him at John's clearly apparent fear and cowardice. They hardly spoke the remainder of the trip, and though there were more than ample opportunities for John to escape after that, he had not the courage to take them.

Skootekitehi had taken a shine to Martin, and since he could speak a little English, Martin was able to learn that his name meant Fireheart and that they were heading for the largest of the Shawnee villages, Chalahgawtha, on the Little Miami River. There, he told Martin, he and his cousin would have to run the gauntlet. It could be very bad, but because Skootekitehi had caught Martin and claimed him as his own, he would have the right, if he saw fit, to intervene and make things easier for him.

It was in midafternoon the day before yesterday when they had reached the huge sprawling village of Chalahgawtha. One of the warriors had left them an hour earlier and gone ahead to alert the village of their approach. By the time they arrived, the gauntlet line had been formed—a double line of people armed with clubs and switches and other weapons, stretching perhaps 300 yards to the large council house.

The two captives were positioned at the head of the line and stripped of all their clothing. Martin's blouse was cut away without his wrists being untied. If they reached the council house, they would then be safe. John Wolf was directed to go first. To the disgust of the Indians, he broke down and wept, pleading with them not to do this to him, but he was swatted heavily across the bare back with a stick and sent stumbling on his way. The switches, brambles and sticks that were swung at him as he passed bruised and cut him, and he was soon bleeding from the back of his head to his calves. Before covering 50 yards, he fell and was beaten repeatedly until he managed to stagger back to his feet and continue running, all the while screaming in terror and pain. Upward of a dozen times, he fell or was knocked down, and he did the last few yards to the council house on his hands and knees, but he finally did reach the big building, crossed the threshold and collapsed inside.

Then it was Martin's turn. They freed his wrists and ordered him to run. At first he refused, determined to stand and fight and, if necessary, die. Skootekitehi spoke to him earnestly, and though Martin could not understand all he said, he gathered that if he refused to run, he would indeed be killed on this spot. If, however, he ran, Skootekitehi would follow a little distance behind, and once a heavy blow had been delivered, the warrior would then have the right to step forward and protect him for the remainder of the run.

Martin nodded and, at the signal to start, began his run, Skootekitehi a few yards behind. Switches lashed across his back and buttocks, the thorns on many of the branches tearing his flesh. An older warrior in the line struck him a heavy blow across the nape that momentarily stunned him and drove him to his knees. At that, Skootekitehi ran up and, shielding Martin's back with his own body, shook his head and barked a string of words at the Indians in the line, and the blows ceased. Maintaining his position close behind Martin, Skootekitehi trotted behind him the rest of the way to the council house. John was still on the floor inside, sobbing and moaning. The cousins were taken to a wegiwa, where they were given a little to eat and their wounds soothed with a salve; there they spent the night. Chalahgawtha, Skootekitehi told Martin, aided by another warrior who spoke English somewhat better, was the village of Chiungalla—Black Fish—who was principal chief of the tribe. He was away with a war party now, turning the people at the place where Hokolesqua was killed into food for the death birds—vultures.

Yesterday, early in the morning, several warriors came to the wegiwa and took John Wolf away, motioning for Martin to remain where he was. A short while later John started to scream—first in terror and then, a little later, in agony. Throughout the day and most of the night the screaming continued, sometimes dwindling away for a time, sometimes rising to a horrifying pitch of anguish. Toward morning there were still low, choked moanings, and then these ended when a single shot was fired.

Only a few minutes ago, Martin was led outside and taken to where a ring of ashes and hot coals still encircled a post to which John Wolf had obviously been attached. He had been tied with a leather thong long enough for him to move in a circle around the post, and then a ring of wood heaped all around had been ignited. The fire was far enough away that he had not been touched by living flame, but close enough that the unbearable heat gradually blistered and then baked his skin. Evidently when only the barest vestige of life remained, after many hours of this torment, someone had finally, mercifully, sent a bullet into the brain of John Wolf.[329]

For a time Martin, sickened at the sight, was convinced that this was to be his lot as well, but now Skootekitehi came and led him to his own wegiwa and told him he was soon to be adopted into the tribe and would become Skootekitehi's younger brother. Martin was thankful he was not to be killed, but a deep hatred burned within him. Sooner or later, he knew, an opportunity would come for him to escape, and he would grasp it. If he had to kill some of these Indians in the process, so much the better.

[May 17, 1778—Sunday]

A week ago today, Chiungalla, leading more than 400 Shawnees, had placed Fort Randolph under siege. Capt. Matthew Arbuckle and his company had been relieved of duty there a few weeks earlier, and Capt. William McKee was now in command of a much smaller garrison of about 20 soldiers. The Point Pleasant Settlement outside the fort was all but deserted, as it had been since the attacks at Wheeling and Grave Creek last fall.

The first those in the fort knew anything of the coming attack was when a small party of Indians appeared some distance away and tried to lure the garrison out in pursuit, but the whites had learned their lesson in this respect last October 22, when Lt. Robert Moore's squad had been decoyed into ambush. They stayed put in the fort and were more than thankful they had. A short while later a line of Indians appeared, stretching across the entire point, from the Ohio River to the Kanawha. A messenger was sent to the fort under a white flag bearing a demand for surrender. Capt. McKee asked to have until the next morning to consider, which was granted.

In the morning Capt. McKee summoned Nonhelema—The Grenadier Squaw —who had been serving there supposedly in the capacity of an interpreter but actually as a spy—and had her carry his reply to Chiungalla that he would not comply. He also declared that neither he nor any other man in the fort had participated in any way in the murder of Cornstalk here the previous October, that it had been an act of impulsive lawlessness that was not condoned by the government and that, in fact, efforts were being made by the government to punish those who had committed the crime.

Nonhelema did not return. She delivered Capt. McKee's message, then told Chiungalla that she doubted the fort could be taken without one of the great thunder guns to blast open the gates. She was correct. The attack began at once and was maintained by about half the force while the rest ranged up the Kanawha in raiding parties, causing great havoc at many of the stations, including a harsh attack against Donnelly's Fort in the Greenbrier Valley, where four whites were killed.[330] That attack ended only when a relief detachment of 66 men under Capt. John Stewart arrived from Fort Union.

Now, ten days later, it was apparent that the Shawnees could not breach the defenses of Fort Randolph, and in a short time they withdrew, the promise lingering behind that when next they came, they would have cannons and no one in the fort would survive.

[May 31, 1778—Sunday]

The situation farther down the Ohio was serious in the extreme. Since the murder of their principal chief, the Shawnees had struck in Kentucky repeatedly, and no white person there was safe. Some settlers were shot dead while in the act of merely peeking out of their cabin door to see if it was safe to emerge. Even some of the more notable frontiersmen lost their lives, including Simon Kenton's good friend,

Jake Drennon, who had been shot out of his canoe on the Kentucky River. The capture of Daniel Boone and his saltmakers at the Blue Licks in February had been a serious blow to Kentucky generally and Boonesboro in particular.

George Rogers Clark had presented himself to Gov. Patrick Henry and convinced him that, provided with sufficient gunpowder, lead and other supplies, he would raise enough men to strike and defeat the British in their southern Illinois posts at Kaskaskia and Cahokia, from which so many strikes against Kentucky settlers —especially by the Kickapoos—were originating. When that was accomplished, Clark added, he could then move on Detroit itself. Gov. Henry liked the idea and convinced the Virginia Executive Council to go along with it. With George Washington's approval, Clark was appointed lieutenant colonel and directed to pick up the requisite supplies at Fort Pitt and proceed downriver to execute his plan. Should he succeed in the Illinois country, further supplies accumulated at Fort Pitt would be forwarded for the Detroit venture.[331]

Clark had immediately sent word ahead to Kentucky for volunteers to hold themselves in readiness to participate in the expedition and to rendezvous on Corn Island at the Falls of the Ohio with their own rifles and provisions. At Fort Pitt he got the requisitioned supplies and a few men and hurried down to Wheeling, where a few more men joined him, bringing his total force there to 100 men. He drilled them, firmly establishing himself as their commander, then set off downriver in a squadron of flatboats.

Upon reaching Corn Island, he was more than disappointed at the turnout. Kaskaskia alone, according to his spies, had a population of more than 1,000 and Clark had set the minimum number of men he needed for this enterprise at 350. All the whites in Kentucky were in sympathy with Clark's proposed expedition, but there were simply too few men to allow many to go; the Kentucky settlements would be left too vulnerable. Thus, setting off now to penetrate enemy territory and beard the British lion in his own den, Maj. George Rogers Clark had a pitiable little force of 175 men.

[August 17, 1778—Monday]

The ineptitude of Gen. Edward Hand as an Indian fighter did not go unnoticed in the east. When, shortly after the Squaw Campaign, he formally requested to be relieved of this frontier command and assigned to the fighting occurring between British regulars and the Continental Army—a type of warfare far more appealing to him—the wheels were put into motion to replace him. Gen. Washington named a proven Scots officer, Brig. Gen. Lachlan McIntosh, to take command of the Continental Army's Western Department, with headquarters at Fort Pitt. One of the principal objectives initially established for McIntosh was to prepare for and execute an expedition against Detroit.

Before the departure of Gen. McIntosh for that place, however, the Congress decided that all frontier military affairs of the west should be a federal concern. It mildly disapproved of the latitude Gov. Henry had given to George Rogers Clark.

That body then reversed itself in respect to the proposed strike against Detroit and decided that Gen. McIntosh should instead lead a punitive mission against the tribes who were harassing the upper Ohio Valley—in particular, the Wyandots operating out of their villages along the Sandusky River. It laid out orders of procedure to be followed in respect to the western frontier:

In Congress, July 25, 1778

1. Resolved, that the expedition against the fortress of Detroit for the present be deferred.

2. That Brigadier General Mackintosh be directed to assemble at Fort Pitt as many Continental troops and militia as will amount to fifteen hundred, and proceed, without delay, to destroy such towns of the hostile tribes of Indians as he in his discretion shall think will most effectually tend to chastise and terrify the savages, and to check their ravages on the frontiers of these states.

3. That such of the articles as have already been procured for the expedition against Detroit, and which are necessary for the incursion against the Indian towns, be appropriated for that purpose; and that the Board of War be directed to give the necessary orders on this point.

4. That Governor Henry be informed of the determination of Congress with respect to the intended expedition, and that he be desired to furnish General Mackintosh with such a number of militia as the General shall apply for, to make up the complement of men destined for an incursion into the towns of the hostile Indians.

Extract from the minutes.
Charles Thompson, Secretary

The Congress authorized Gen. McIntosh to call upon the county lieutenants of the specific Virginia counties of Augusta, Berkeley, Botetourt, Frederick, Greenbrier, Hampshire, Monongalia, Montgomery, Ohio, Rockbridge, Rockingham, Shenandoah, Washington, and Youghiogania, *"as he may demand to carry on an expedition against the hostile Indians, & chastise them as they deserve."*

On his arrival at Fort Pitt, Gen. McIntosh relieved Gen. Hand and, on the recommendation of George Washington, appointed militia Maj. William Crawford as his second in command with the brevet rank of colonel. McIntosh had decided that a more advanced post than Fort Pitt had to be built as a launching point for the punitive expedition against the Sandusky towns. To that end he dispatched a substantial force of soldiers, laborers and engineers—men of the Eighth Pennsylvania Regiment commanded by Col. Daniel Brodhead and the Thirteenth Virginia Regiment commanded by Col. John Gibson, plus two regiments of militia—to erect a sturdy fort farther down the Ohio. That fort was now being constructed on the downriver side of the mouth of Beaver River, on the right bank of the Ohio 25 miles below Fort Pitt, and even though unfinished, it was already being called Fort McIntosh.[332]

[September 12, 1778—Saturday]

Capt. Samuel Brady stared at the scalp he was holding. The flesh was still warm, and the blood clinging to hair and skin stained his hands as he inspected it. There was good reason why this particular scalp evoked his interest: It was the first scalp he had ever taken, the first Indian he had ever killed. He was quite certain it was far from his last, on either count.

At 22, Sam Brady was six feet tall and trimly built, tending toward the slender. A handsome young man, his hair was dark brown over a broad, smooth forehead, and his features were angular, emphasized by high cheekbones and a wide mouth in which strong, white, well-formed teeth were displayed when he grinned or laughed, which was frequently. But his most arresting characteristic was his eyes: Wide set, large and very expressive, they seemed almost to change color with his mood, usually pale, cool blue when he was in a jocular frame of mind but turning hard gray and unnervingly penetrating when he became angry or intent.

There had been little distinctive about Sam when he was born to John and Mary Brady in 1756 at Shippensburg, Pennsylvania, 20 miles southwest of the frontier town of Carlisle.[333] He was firstborn of ten children and named after his uncle, who was a husky, large-framed man topping two inches over six feet, a captain who had served under Gen. Braddock.[334] Pleased at having a namesake, he had come to see this new offspring of his younger brother, and after staring down into the cradle for several minutes, he had straightened and shaken his head at the proud parents.

"John, Mary," he said half-seriously, "I think you ought to knock so ordinary-looking a child in the head."

Refusing to take offense, both parents had laughed and then Mary shook her finger at him. "Never mind, Samuel Brady," she retorted. "He may yet become a great warrior."

Young Sam had indeed become a warrior, though thus far greatness had eluded him. In 1775, shortly after the Revolution broke out, his father had joined the Continental Army as a private and was sent to Boston. Only a few weeks later, on August 5, Sam, then 19, working in a field with his brother James, who was a year younger, abruptly threw down his mattock and said he was done grubbing in the dirt and was going to war. That very day he joined a volunteer company, and they, too, were marched to Boston.

So highly patriotic and conscientious was Sam as a soldier that he had quickly caught the eye of his commanding officer, who offered him a commission. Sam was on the verge of taking it when his father heard about it, intervened and forbade it. "First," said the elder Brady, "let him learn the duties of a soldier, and then he will better know how to act as an officer."

Sam served the full year as an enlisted man that his father had insisted upon, fighting in the battles around Boston. Then in August 1776 during the Battle of Long Island, he so distinguished himself that he was commissioned first lieutenant. The following October he participated in the Battle of White Plains, New York, where the 20,000 American troops were forced into retreat by 34,000 Redcoats. He was with George Washington in New Jersey during the dreadful winter of 1776 and crossed the Delaware with him on December 26 to capture 1,000 Hessian troops.

Eight days later, on January 3, 1777, he was nearly captured in the Battle of Princeton and was hailed for what his commander called "impetuous gallantry." That gallantry continued in the Battle of Brandywine a year ago yesterday; in that same battle his father, now a captain, was badly wounded and sent home. Col. William Crawford, still commanding the Virginia Thirteenth Regiment, had fought at Brandywine as well.

Less than a month later, last October 4, Brady—and Col. Crawford, too—fought in the Battle of Germantown, six miles from Philadelphia. Even though the Americans lost and had 1,000 men killed, Sam Brady was again conspicuous for his bravery and received a brevet promotion to captain. For the first time he came to an impressed Col. William Crawford's attention. The courageous young man seemed to be leading a charmed life and was obviously approaching that status of "great warrior" that his mother had predicted.

Brady's good luck continued at the massacre at the Battle of Paoli, Pennsylvania, when he and some others had been cut off by the Redcoats and surrounded. So close was the fighting that at one point he was pursued by British soldiers who thrust bayonets at him as he leaped a fence. They missed him but impaled his greatcoat to the fence. He slipped out of the coat and raced away, only to be overtaken by a British cavalryman who ordered him to surrender. Instead, he killed the horseman and escaped into a nearby swamp. Other American soldiers had also taken refuge there, and he gathered together 55 of them and led them to safety in the American lines. For one who was then only 21, it was quite a list of achievements.

By now, his character had been well established. In warfare he was a fierce, intelligent fighter who never gave way to panic, irrespective of the circumstances. His temperament at other times was mild and his personality captivating. He was pleasant company and would have an occasional drink with friends, but he never indulged to excess and had never been observed drunk.

He was in Col. Daniel Brodhead's Eighth Pennsylvania Regiment when Brodhead was ordered to take his command to Pittsburgh to serve under Gen. McIntosh. On the march west he asked and received permission to take a slight detour and visit his parents during a brief furlough, with instructions to rejoin his unit at Fort Pitt.

When he got to Shippensburg, there was good news and bad. The good news was that his father was recovering well from his wound. The bad news was that his family was just then preparing to bury his younger brother, James, to whom he was deeply devoted, who had been killed by Indians. It had happened on August 9 while James and a few other men were harvesting oats. Because there had been a few Indian attacks in the area in recent weeks, they had posted one of their number as a sentinel, stacked their own guns against a lone tree in the center of the field and set to work.

The sentinel's attention was distracted by the men who were harvesting, and he had watched them for a while. When he looked back, a group of Indians was already crossing the nearby fence and racing toward them with guns and tomahawks. James Brady had seen them at about the same time as the sentinel, and he dropped his scythe, sprinted toward the tree and shouted, "Every man to his gun!"

Instead of following him, the others had dropped their implements and fled precipitately in the opposite direction. Brady had nearly reached the tree when one of the advancing warriors stopped, aimed and shot at him. The ball went through both of Brady's arms, but despite this, he was able to snatch up his rifle and kill the Indian who had shot him.[335] By then, the rest of the war party were upon him. Even wounded as he was, he managed to grapple with one and throw him down, but then he was himself struck down with a tomahawk blow to the temple. A young warrior on his first raid was called forward and given the opportunity of taking his first scalp, but he botched the job and wound up not only cutting off more of the scalp than was necessary but taking one of James's ears along with it. The Indians considered this a huge joke and laughed uproariously. Then they gathered up the weapons and their fallen comrade and departed the way they had come.

Sometime later James had recovered consciousness. With no one left to aid him, he crawled inch by torturous inch to the nearby river, where he was able to drink. He passed in and out of consciousness but eventually saw a canoe passing and hailed it. He had then been taken to the fort, where he lingered for nine days before finally dying a day and a half before Sam's arrival home.[336]

Samuel Brady had blamed those who abandoned his brother almost as much as he blamed the Indians who had attacked. Only with great difficulty was he restrained from taking them to account for their cowardice. But it was for the Indians that an even greater rage had been ignited within him.

"I swear," he told his parents grimly, "I will hunt and kill these damned hostile Indians until either I'm dead or they're all dead or we finally bring them to their knees. I swear it!"[337]

Brady saw an opportunity for living up to that oath when he reported for duty at Fort Pitt. Most of the regiment had already gone down to Beaver River, where they were helping build the new Fort McIntosh, but Col. Brodhead asked Brady if he would like to lead a small mission against a party of Indians reportedly terrorizing settlers some 30 miles up the Allegheny, near the mouth of the Kiskeminetas. He would be given a trustworthy guide and could pick his own squad of five men from among any of the soldiers left here.

Accepting the assignment with alacrity, Brady selected five experienced Indian fighters. As his second in command he chose Capt. Samuel Murphy, a tough little red-headed Irishman who had been fighting Indians for years. At first, however, Brady was not overly pleased when he discovered that the trustworthy guide Col. Brodhead mentioned turned out to be a 50-year-old Delaware Indian who went by the name of John Thompson. Brady quickly ascertained that the man had proven his abilities and loyalty to the Americans on numerous missions in the past as spy, guide and warrior, and though he had been prepared to detest him, instead he found himself liking the man considerably.

It was John Thompson who suggested that instead of wearing uniforms or the garb of frontier people, he dress his men as Indians, even to the use of war paint, saying that if they encountered the raiders, it might give them a slight edge that could become all-important. Brady thought it a good idea and cleared it with the colonel, who suggested that the Indian-clad rangers tie strips of bright cloth around their left upper arms to distinguish them from the real Indians, lest on their return they be mistaken for the latter and shot.

Today, as they neared the mouth of the Kiskeminetas, John Thompson spied an Indian in a canoe coming toward them far upstream. Since none of the men in the squad could speak the Indian tongue fluently, he suggested that Brady and his rangers go into hiding, and he would endeavor to lure the man ashore. Brady thought it a good idea, and the squad quickly hid themselves in the underbrush.

Fifteen minutes ago, when the approaching Indian was still some 40 or 50 yards upstream from them, John Thompson showed himself and hailed him. The Indian— a Mingo—was suspicious, but John Thompson convinced him that he was a member of a party that had captured some whites and were taking them to their villages when they were attacked by a party of whites who had followed on horseback and over-taken them. The rest of his party had tomahawked the prisoners and then scattered, so now he was on his own but nonetheless determined to continue attacking the whites by himself until his ammunition gave out. The Mingo seemed pleased to hear this and said that he, too, was out hunting whites, and it might be a good idea if the two of them joined forces. He put in toward shore, approaching with some lingering traces of wariness.

As the little craft glided to shore, John Thompson abruptly jerked up his gun and shot. The ball caught the Mingo high on the inside of his right arm and knocked him off his feet and into the bottom of the canoe. As he struggled to regain his feet and take aim at his attacker, John Thompson called for Brady to come help. Sam rushed out of hiding and placed a well-aimed ball at the base of the Mingo's throat, killing him.

Now Samuel Brady stood with this Indian's scalp in his hands. He felt no remorse or anything else for this first Indian he had killed—only a sense of satisfac-tion that he was gone and an unwavering determination that this was far from the last Indian scalp he would lift.

They took the dead man's gear, set his canoe adrift and left his body lying on the shore as a warning to others. Then they continued their patrol and less than three hours later spied a war party of 15 garishly painted Mingoes moving in single file along the Allegheny shoreline. At Brady's signal his men slipped into hiding and readied themselves.

Brady had previously given orders that no firing was to be done until he gave the signal, and so though all guns were aimed at the approaching Indians, they held off. Not until the party was less than 50 yards distant did Brady shout "Now!" and the rifles crashed. Four of the Indians were killed instantly. Brady and his men burst from cover with terrifying yells. The remaining Indians dropped their packs and other gear and fled.

For Sam Brady, it was an auspicious beginning for his personal war against the Indians.

[*D e c e m b e r   1 0 ,   1 7 7 8 — T h u r s d a y*]

The force under Gen. Lachlan McIntosh had arrived back at Fort McIntosh yesterday. They were hungry and exhausted men, but their commander was well pleased with the results of the expedition into the Ohio country. For the first time the Americans had built a permanent fort to the north and west of the Ohio River, and now, well garrisoned, it stood on its own some 80 miles from here on the banks of the Tuscarawas River—an installation that had been named Fort Laurens.

The construction was part of the frontier war plan outlined by George Washington, who said, "The only certain way of preventing Indian ravages is to carry the war vigorously into their own country." To this end he had already named Maj. Gen. John Sullivan to lead an invasion of "destruction and punishment" against the Iroquois as soon as the weather permitted; an expedition designed to penetrate into the very heart of their territory in upper New York State, engage them wherever possible and destroy every village encountered.

The McIntosh expedition, on the other hand, which was originally intended to march against Detroit, had been altered. Direct attack against Detroit was deferred, and instead, an advanced fort deep in Indian territory was to be built as a haven and a launching point for attacks against the Wyandot towns on the Sandusky River—the stream originally named Sahunduskee by the Wyandots, meaning Clear Water.

The force of 2,000 men—1,500 of them militia—rendezvoused at Fort Pitt and then, guided by Col. William Crawford, who had followed the same Indian trail with Col. Bouquet, moved downriver to Fort McIntosh, which was now finished and boasted four strong blockhouses and a six-pounder cannon.[338] McIntosh sent emissaries to the Delaware chiefs, asking permission to pass through their country, and considering the affronts the Delawares had recently suffered at the hands of the Americans, no one felt that any good would come of it. The Delawares, however, still thought it possible for whites and Indians to live in peace, and permission was granted. Delighted, McIntosh left Col. Brodhead in command of Fort McIntosh and led his force out on September 11, taking a northwestward course. They arrived at the Tuscarawas 14 days later. The more hostile tribes were aware of the movement, of course, and believing this to be the long-feared attack against their stronghold, they had fallen back to meet the assault in their villages. As a result, during the nearly four months of its absence, the McIntosh expedition never had any engagement with the Indians.

The expedition's greatest enemy turned out to be hunger. The expected supplies had not arrived, and the beeves herded along with them, poor-quality animals to begin with, were insufficient to sustain them for long. The hides of those killed for food on the march out were stretched over the branches of trees and bushes to dry in the sun and air, to be collected on the return trip, taken back and tanned into leather.

An engineer from Virginia, Col. William Campbell—better known among the troops as "Swearing" Campbell due to his foul language—was put in charge of construction on the site selected for the new fort, on the west side of the Tuscarawas River two and three-quarters miles downstream from the mouth of Sandy Creek.[339] A little over 100 yards from the river itself, the fort was laid out on a level treeless bench of high ground—the highest anywhere in the area, some 40 feet above the normal river level—as protection from the periodical seasonal flooding. The nearest substantial growth of trees was about a half-mile distant, preventing any kind of attacking force from having access to cover close to the fort. This meant that the men had to carry cut timber some distance, but it was considered worth the effort for the added protection. Several good springs some 40 feet from the fort bubbled out of the base of the eminence and drained across a narrow bottom to the river. The north, west and south perimeter walls were built of strong, six-inch-thick hardwood pickets sunk three feet deep and extending straight up 15 feet above ground level. Those walls, on the inside, were lined with cabins and soldiers' barracks. The longest side of the fort, unpicketed, was along the river, and there was one gate, situated on the west side of the fort. To the right of that gate was a blockhouse, about 20 feet square, that formed a part of the outside wall in place of picketing. The blockhouse was the principal fortification and was constructed to jut beyond the line of the walls, with floor openings so that if Indians approached closely, the garrison could shoot down through these openings directly upon the enemy below. There were portholes all around the blockhouse, about five feet from the floor and three feet apart, through which to fire in case of attack; the roof was sloped toward the interior of the fort. There were two cabins built on each end of the fort in which to store baggage and provisions. These cabins, not quite together, were in a line with the picketing and helped to form the enclosure; these too had overjutting and portholes similar to those at the blockhouse.

While construction was in progress, a party of some 50 Indians, including women and children, approached under a white flag and requested a council to talk peace. Gen. McIntosh met with them and told them that so long as their intentions were friendly, they had nothing to fear from the fort or the soldiers gathered here.

Through his interpreter, Gen. McIntosh asked them the significance of a small mound within sight of the fort. They related that a fearful fight between the Senecas and Wyandots had occurred here in 1755, immediately following Braddock's defeat. Though they had been allies against Braddock's army, when they reached this point on their return, an old feud between them had reignited. It promised to be a fearful and devastating battle, and to prevent that, an old chief of the Senecas named Ogista proposed that each side select its 20 best warriors and let them fight it out in a single hand-to-hand combat. It was agreed to, and each side held its war dance and sang its death songs, and the battle was begun. Thirty-nine brave warriors met their death in the carnage that followed, and at its end the only one left alive was Gahnele, the son of Ogista, who approached, congratulated him on his skill and courage and then struck him down with a tomahawk. The 40 dead were then buried in a single grave. A great feast was held to commemorate the dead—both sides participating joined— and then the hatchet was buried between the tribes, never to be raised again.

It was evident that part of the reason the Indians had come to see the Americans here was that they expected presents and provisions. There were not enough to give them either, and the Indians finally left peaceably enough but obviously disgruntled. So short were provisions, in fact, and so poor the cattle, that during the last nine weeks of construction, the entire force was placed on very limited daily rations—four ounces of not very good flour and eight ounces of poor beef per man.[340]

The fort was finished by the end of November and named Fort Laurens by Gen. McIntosh in honor of his close friend, Henry Laurens, who was the first president of the Continental Congress.[341] Col. John Gibson was placed in command of the new fort, and 150 men of his own regiment made up the garrison. They were ordered to remain six months, at the end of which time they would be relieved by others.

The remaining men started back toward Fort McIntosh. So critically short were supplies at Fort Laurens that each of those departing was provided with only one day's rations for the march back. By the third day they were ravenous—so hungry, in fact, that when they passed the cowhides they had spread over branches to dry on their way out, they cut the hides into strips, then roasted and ate them for what little sustenance they could provide. Sam Brady was one of the lucky ones: He rescued an Indian squaw along the way who was being ill treated by some of the militia, ordered the soldiers away and escorted her a short distance until she was out of danger of further molestation. She could speak a little English and told Brady her name was Hannah. In gratitude, she presented him with three small bags of parched corn, which helped sustain him on the return march.

On arrival at Fort McIntosh, it was discovered that a few supplies had arrived, and each man was allowed to draw two days' provisions and a half-pint of whiskey, both of which were disposed of in record time. More supplies were reported on the way, and as soon as they arrived, a pack train of provisions would be made up and dispatched to Fort Laurens. Nevertheless, there was hardly enough food to keep that garrison going for more than a few weeks and considerable doubt that the outpost garrison could survive very long after that.

The news awaiting them from elsewhere on the Ohio River frontier was not encouraging except that from the Illinois country. Everywhere, it seemed, the Indians had stepped up their attacks. Simon Kenton had been captured by the Shawnees while returning from a spying mission to Chalahgawtha, and his companion, Alexander Montgomery, had been slain.[342] Daniel Boone—who had been given the Indian name of Sheltowee—had finally escaped from his captivity among the Shawnees and warned the remaining Kentucky settlements to brace for a major assault presently in the making.[343] That attack had come—a tough, long-lasting siege that resulted in many deaths on both sides. Raids against isolated settlers and small forts in the Kanawha Valley had increased considerably, and in most places everywhere on the frontier it was an extremely perilous time.

The only really good news was that George Rogers Clark, with his little band of 175 men, had actually captured both Kaskaskia and Cahokia and had taken possession of the Illinois country from the British. Whether he could hold it was another matter, since word had also come that Gen. Hamilton had led a force out of Detroit and was heading for Vincennes on the lower Wabash, from which point he would undoubtedly, aided by numerous Indians, launch a major counterattack against Clark next spring.

[January 30, 1779—Saturday]

The situation at Fort Laurens had gone from bad to worse, and there was every indication this was only the beginning.

The small amount of provisions left by Gen. McIntosh when he returned with the majority of his force to Fort McIntosh was quickly depleted, despite the strict rations imposed by Col. Gibson. The specter of starvation haunted them all, eased only when an express arrived from the general saying that a shipment of supplies was being readied and would soon be transported to Fort Laurens in a packhorse convoy escorted by a small detachment under Capt. John Clarke of Col. Brodhead's Eighth Pennsylvania.

Several times Capts. Samuel Brady and Peter Parchment had slipped out of the fort in an effort to kill some deer or other game animals to augment the meager amount of food remaining. Not only had game been very scarce, but they had been fired upon by Indians and driven back to the fort without bagging anything for their efforts. Before long, just one barrel of largely spoiled flour was the only food remaining for the entire garrison of 150. At about that time a large party of Indians assembled and began ineffectually firing at the fort from a distance; some of them rolled logs before them to provide cover closer to the walls. The firing went on sporadically for a week or more, some days fairly heavily, other days without any.

On one bitterly cold day, the number of Indians beyond the walls of Fort Laurens increased substantially. They seemed as hungry as the men inside and, calling loudly from a distance, demanded food. At first the response was that they would be given nothing, but when ever more showed themselves until their numbers reached near 500, Col. Gibson, knowing the Indian temperament very well, decided it would be worth the gamble to give them that last remaining barrel of flour in the belief it might make them disperse, at least temporarily. He read them correctly. As the garrison watched with dismay, late in the afternoon that final barrel of flour was rolled out 100 yards or so and left there. Gibson issued strict orders that no one was to shoot any Indians who approached it, but none of the warriors did before nightfall. In the morning the barrel was gone, but hundreds of Indians were still hovering about. That was when Sam Brady's Delaware friend, John Thompson, told Col. Gibson he thought, if given a chance, he could make them go away. Gibson, who had known John Thompson for many years and trusted him implicitly, gave him permission to try.

The gate was briefly opened, and John Thompson walked boldly out to near where the Indians were congregated and mounted a stump. "Listen!" he shouted. "You are fools to go out and fight against the American Congress! Go home! You stand out here cold and hungry, while inside the fort we have plenty of provisions, plenty of men, plenty of ammunition—enough to kill you all if you continue this way. Fools! Go home!" He looked back and forth across them imperiously for a moment and then repeated, "Go home!"

Then he hopped down from the stump and returned to the fort. Incredibly, by the time he got there most of the Indians had disappeared from sight. A few minutes later a lookout in the blockhouse reported he could see them moving off, and within minutes after that they were gone.

John Thompson could not have been prouder of himself. He strutted about within the fort, tittering with his peculiar laughter that so amused the men and boasting extravagantly of how he had frightened off the savage horde. "Five hundred warriors!" he chortled. "*Five hundred!* With all my words, I scare them. I tell them all 'Go home!' and they all go! My name no longer John Thompson. My name now Scare the World!" To show that he meant it, he no longer responded when addressed as John Thompson, only when the new name he had chosen was used.

Whether it was because of what Scare the World had said or not, the Indians did seem to have disappeared, but the hunger of the men inside the fort had not, and now matters were becoming desperate. On January 21 Brady and Parchment were grimly preparing to go out again to try to bring in some deer when word spread swiftly through the garrison that the small, long-expected supply convoy under Capt. Clarke and his escort of a sergeant and 14 men had finally come into view. A great exultation arose in the garrison as the convoy neared and, despite the colonel's order for them to hold their places, they threw open the gates and tumultuously rushed out to meet the packhorse train, yelling in delight and firing their guns as they did so. Their actions panicked the packhorses, which reared, bucked and bolted; the majority threw off their packs, scattering and losing much of what had been brought.

The men, subdued by what they had done, picked up what they could recover and carried it into the fort. Though the sum amount was not as much as they had anticipated, there was enough to sustain them for perhaps a month to six weeks longer. Angered by such behavior, Col. Gibson had the supplies locked in storage cabins and doled out only enough for each man to have a good meal. After that, he told them, they would again be on strict rations, and if ever again they disobeyed orders in such a manner, he would have every perpetrator placed in irons and court-martialed.

The following day, armed squads were sent out to try to locate and recover the packhorses that had run off. All but two were found and brought in, and it was believed that the missing ones might have been caught by Indians who were still hovering about.

The next day—January 23—Capt. Clarke and his 15 men, packhorses in tow, set off on the return trip to Fort McIntosh, carrying dispatches to Gen. McIntosh telling of the recent attacks and of the need for reinforcement as well as more food and ammunition. They had traveled only three miles when they were attacked by a mixed party of 17 Wyandots and Mingoes, this group accompanied by Simon Girty, dressed in Indian garb but recognized by one of the soldiers.[344] Two soldiers were killed in the first firing, and the remainder fought their way back to the fort, with one packhorse killed on the way. A new general attack against the fort was commenced as more and more Indians made their appearance.

Col. Gibson, under cover of darkness two nights later, sent an express to Gen. McIntosh with news of what had happened and a plea for help. Just over a mile away, the messenger was taken prisoner by Girty and his party and was immediately taken to Detroit, along with the dispatches he was carrying.

[February 9, 1779 — Tuesday]

Maj. James Lernoult, acting commander of Detroit, listened carefully to the report of Simon Girty. The three American prisoners the Indian agent had brought with him to Detroit had been incarcerated and would be questioned later. At the moment, having already read the captured dispatches and letters, Lernoult was far more interested in what Girty had to say.

"As you can see, Major," Girty said, indicating the dispatches the officer had just placed to one side on his desk, "the garrison at Fort Laurens is small and weak. They have few provisions and no artillery. The Wyandots on the Sandusky are ready to hit them, but they need ammunition, food, coats, what-all. You let me take some to them and send along one of your officers to observe, and he can tell you how they behave. They're damn wicked fighters, Major. Support 'em, and they'll take the whole damn upper Ohio for you."

They discussed it further, and Lernoult made his decision. He would send the necessary supplies and Capt. Henry Bird as observer.[345] If Bird's report was favorable, it was altogether possible greater British support would be forthcoming, not only in supplies and ammunition but in regular troops and artillery.

[F e b r u a r y   2 3 ,   1 7 7 9 — T u e s d a y]

A general impression prevailed among the garrison in Fort Laurens that the majority of the Indians had moved off. The siege had been maintained against them for over a month now, and the supply of firewood in the fort was almost depleted. Late yesterday afternoon Col. Gibson ordered a fatigue party to go out after some— four of the 18 men to lead packhorses and cut and gather wood to be carried in, the remaining 14 riflemen to guard them. When finished, they were to take the packhorses and go to Fort McIntosh for supplies, then return with them. Capt. Benjamin Biggs was officer of the day, and as soon as he learned of the assignment— and hoping to have the opportunity of returning, however briefly, to Fort McIntosh —he presented himself to the commander.

"Sir," he said, "I would like your permission to accompany the fatigue party in the morning and lead them to Fort McIntosh and return."

"Permission denied," Col. Gibson replied, shaking his head. "When I have occasion for a captain's command, I will thank you to command them. At present you will attend to your duty in the fort."

Just after sunrise this morning, the lookouts having ascertained that there was no sign of Indians about, the fatigue party, led by a sergeant, left the fort by the west gate and headed for the half-mile-distant woods to the southwest. They had hardly entered it, however, when a large party of Wyandots, Chippewas and Mingoes poured a devastating fire at them from ambush. In a few moments, 16 of the 18 men were killed and the remaining two captured. The bodies of the dead were quickly scalped and their weapons and all valuables taken, along with the four packhorses.

Immediately following this, some 200 more Indians, largely Wyandots, appeared and once again commenced a general firing at Fort Laurens. The siege was obviously not yet over, and now the men inside were beginning to believe they would never leave this godforsaken outpost alive.

[*February 25, 1779 — Thursday*]

Once again George Rogers Clark had pulled off a coup that stunned the entire frontier.

Informed by his spies that Gen. Henry Hamilton had moved down from Detroit to Vincennes with 30 regulars and 50 French volunteers and that he had a great number of the Indian tribes aligned with him, it was only too apparent to Clark that Hamilton would launch an attack against him at Kaskaskia as soon as the season permitted, which would probably be sometime in late March or April. He had no intention of letting that happen.

On January 30 he called a council of his officers and laid out a plan that initially shocked them but that they quickly accepted with enthusiasm. In the midst of the very worst of the winter season, they would march cross-country the approximate 160 miles, take Vincennes by surprise and force Hamilton to surrender. It was a bold and dangerous plan, and Clark would not force anyone to go; he would accept only volunteers. He had no trouble getting them, and a large bateau named *Willing* was prepared to carry the heavy baggage, including two four-pounder cannons, four swivels and ammunition. Under the command of Lt. Rogers and with 46 men aboard, they would go down the Mississippi to the Ohio mouth, then upstream to the mouth of the Wabash and finally form a union with Clark's 170 cross-country volunteers.

The bateau force left Kaskaskia on February 4, and the following day Clark put his ground troops in motion. Nineteen phenomenally grueling days later—having marched in water much of the way, often to their waists or deeper in the frigid waters of streams and marshes—they arrived at Vincennes. The *Willing* had not yet arrived, and with his men so punished by the elements, Clark did not dare to wait for it to get there but pushed on with the ground force.[346] There was a brief fight as they got to the fort, but Hamilton, deserted by his Indian allies, realized he had no choice but to surrender, and he did so. His troops were allowed to take their personal baggage and leave, but Clark held Hamilton prisoner and took possession of the fort, Vincennes and the Wabash Valley. Many of the Indians in the southern Illinois and Indiana countries now sued for peace, fearful in the extreme of a small army of men that could do what Clark's force had done.

All in all, it was a remarkable military achievement.

[*March 12, 1779 — Friday*]

Brig. Gen. Lachlan McIntosh, seated behind his desk in headquarters at Fort Pitt, was heartily disgusted with this whole frontier situation. He thought of Gen. Hand, the officer he had relieved in this post, and remembered the well-masked contempt he had felt for him and his pathetic eagerness to be away from this assignment and back where war was fought in a gentlemanly manner. Now none of that contempt remained, and instead he felt a growing sympathy for what the man had gone through. The land-grabbing greediness of the border people, the methods used by the Indians to fight, the atrocities committed on both sides, the disregard of the settlers for their own safety, the difficulty of maintaining supply lines, even the lack of fundamental creature comforts—all these things combined to give any commander the desire to be almost anywhere else. McIntosh himself, at this point, was ever more often wishing he were not here and was seriously considering submitting a formal transfer request.

The general squinted and rubbed his eyes, then turned the lamp flame a little higher and looked over what he had written thus far in his letter to Gen. Washington. He shook his head in annoyance; the letter was far from finished, and if he didn't resume writing soon, he'd be sitting here half the night. With a sigh he dipped his quill pen in the ink pot and resumed writing:

The emigration down the Ohio from this quarter I fear will depopulate it altogether, unless I have orders to put a timely stop to it immediately. It is thought that near one-half of what remain here will go down to Kentucky, the Falls, or the Illinois, as they say themselves, this Spring. Their design of securing land is so great, notwithstanding the danger of this country, they will go. . . . I am sorry to inform you, that contrary to my expectations, things have taken a turn here much for the worse, since I wrote you on the 13th of January. The 30th of that month I received an express from Colonel Gibson, informing me that one Simon Girty, a renegade among many others from this place, got a small party of Mingoes—a name by which the Six Nations, or rather Seneca tribe is known among the Western Indians—and waylaid Captain Clark, of the 8th Pennsylvania Regiment, with a Sergeant and 14 Privates, about three miles this side of Fort Laurens as they were returning after escorting a few supplies to that fort and made Clark retreat to the fort again after killing two, and taking one of his men with his saddle bags and all his letters.

Upon hearing this unexpected intelligence, I immediately sent for Colonels Crawford and Brodhead to advise them upon the best method of supplying that garrison with provisions, of which it was very short, and who had barely horses enough fit for service to transport a sufficient quantity of flour over the mountains for our daily consumption, and source of forage for them, altho' they were most worn down. It was therefore thought most eligible upon that and other accounts to send a supply by water up Muskingum River by Major Taylor, who was charged with that duty. . . .

The 26th of February, a scalping party killed and carried off 18 persons, men, women and children, upon the branches of Turtle Creek, 20 miles east of this, upon the Pennsylvania Road, which was the first mischief done in the settlements since I marched for Tuscarawas, and made me apprehensive now that the savages were all inimically inclined and struck the inhabitants of Westmoreland with such a panick that a great part of them were moving away. While I was endeavoring to rouse the militia, and contriving by their assistance to retaliate and make an excursion to some Mingo towns upon the branches of Allegheny River who were supposed to have done the mischief, a messenger came to me on the 3rd of March instant, who slipt out of Fort Laurens in the night of Sunday the 28th February—

by whom Colonel Gibson would not venture to write, and informed me, that on the morning of Tuesday, 23d February, a waggoner who was sent out of the fort for the horses to draw wood, and 18 men to guard him, were fired upon, and all killed and scalped in sight of the fort, which the messenger left invested and besieged by a number of Wyandottes, Chippewas, Delawares, &c., and in the last account I had from them, which made me very unhappy, as they were so short of provision, and out of my power to supply them with any quantity, or, if I had it, with men for an escort, since Major Taylor went, who I thought now was inevitably lost; and, if I had both, there were no horses to carry it, or forage to feed them, without which they cannot subsist at this season.

In this extreme emergency and difficulty, I earnestly requested the Lieutenants of the several countys on this side of the mountains to collect all of the men, horses, provisions and forage they could at any price, and repair to Beaver Creek on Monday next, the 15th instant, in order to march on the next day to Tuscarawas; and if they would not be prevailed to turn out, I was determined with such of the Continental troops as are able to march, and all the provisions we have, at all events to go to the relief of Fort Laurens, upon the support of which I think the salvation of this part of the country depends.

I have yet no intelligence from the country that I can depend on. Some say the people will turn out on this occasion with their horses; others, that mischievous persons influenced by our disgusted staff are discouraging them as much as possible. But I am now happily relieved by the arrival of Major Taylor here, who returned with 100 men and 200 kegs of flour. He was six days going 20 miles up Muskingum River, the waters were so high and stream so rapid; and as he had above 130 miles more to go, he judged it impossible to relieve Colonel Gibson in time, and therefore returned, having lost two of his men sent to flank him upon the shore, who were killed and scalpt by some warriors coming down Muskingum River, and I have my doubts of our only pretended friends, the Delawares of Cooshoching [Goschachgunk], as none other are settled upon that water.

I have the honor to enclose you the last return from Colonel Brodhead at Beaver Creek [Fort McIntosh]. . . .

> *Lach^n. McIntosh, BG*
> *Com^g. Western Dep^t.*

His Excellency Gen. Washington

[March 19, 1779 — Friday]

For the past several years the Moravian missionary John Heckewelder had been engaging in a very dangerous sideline: acting as a spy for the Americans by reporting on the movements of the Indians and British agents in the Ohio country. He was in an ideal position to do so, since he had headquartered himself for the past several years at the principal Delaware village, Goschachgunk, at the Forks of the Muskingum.

His purpose in coming to this country had been to proselytize the heathen Indians to Christianity, and in this he had been rather successful. Between himself and another German missionary, David Zeisberger, they had established four Christian Indian villages, each with its own mission building, and they had already converted close to 350 Indians, most of them Delawares. One of these mission villages was called Lichtenau—Pasture of Light—and had been established three years ago by Zeisberger on the Muskingum only two and a half miles downstream from Goschachgunk. The other three were upstream, on the Tuscarawas tributary of the Muskingum: Salem, just 18 miles upstream from Goschachgunk, with Gnadenhütten five miles above that and Schoenbrun another eight miles above Gnadenhütten.[347]

Unfortunately, Lichtenau had just broken up this past January in the face of dire threats by Indians who suspected Zeisberger of spying. The principal threats had come from the Mohawk war chief, Thayendanegea, to whom conversion to Christianity was anathema. Heckewelder had attended the final service at Lichtenau, held on January 8, and he thought Brother Zeisberger had been particularly eloquent on that occasion.

Over 250 Indians had attended, the majority of whom were already converted, and Zeisberger had raised his hands in benediction over them and his eyes glistened with tears as he spoke.

"My children," he had said, "as most of you know by now, this is the final service here in the Pasture of Light, as we are no longer being permitted to stay. The presence of myself and the Reverend Heckewelder and other whites has been an abomination in the eyes of the Mohawk chief whom you know as Thayendanegea and we as Chief Joseph Brant. Now he has announced that we must leave, and we have agreed to do so, not for our own protection, which is as nothing, but for you assembled here who have accepted the True Belief.

"Chief Brant has said he will burn this House of God and slay all converts if we do not leave, and he shows his intention by bringing his warriors to assemble here at our very Pasture of Light and from here to sally forth and kill and plunder in the white settlements to the east. And so we go with heavy hearts, yet with our hearts singing in the knowledge that you here have come to know the true God and the true Son of God, and that you will continue to believe in Him and have faith."

Zeisberger paused to wipe his eyes and then smiled beatifically at his flock. "Now it is you who must become the missionaries among your own people, teaching them the Word of God as it has been taught to you and converting others to the doctrine of Christianity. Perhaps one day we will return. Perhaps not. But may God rest His blessings upon you now and forevermore. Amen."

After a number of voices in the congregation had repeated the "Amen," an old Delaware chief once known as Netawatwees, but now called Abraham, stood and responded to Zeisberger.

"We are grateful to you and the other missionary fathers for directing our paths. You have shown us the True Light, and we will carry it in our hearts wherever we go. We will continue here as before, working our fields and bearing no malice toward any man and continuing in the worship of our Lord Jesus Christ. Thayendanegea does not understand Christianity; will not *permit* himself to understand. He is more content in the field of war than in the field of peace. He is angry that we have not joined the confederacy of Wyandots and Mingoes and Delawares, but we will not. We will continue here at peace with all men for all time. Our hearts, too, are heavy at your leaving, but you will be in our prayers and, when our time here is finished, we will be reunited in great joy in Heaven."

The missionaries had not gone back east, of course, but by moving among their many Delaware friends in Goschachgunk—not the least of whom was Killbuck, long a friend of the Americans—they had at least spared their flock being further jeopardized by Chief Brant or other hostile Indians. Here Heckewelder had continued his spying operations, often hiding his messages under the saddle blankets of horses being ridden to the destination he wished, sometimes carried with the knowledge of the rider but frequently without. Two of the principals to whom Heckewelder sent his very secret letter reports were Col. Brodhead, now commanding at Fort McIntosh, and Col. Gibson at Fort Laurens, both of whom had sworn not to divulge the identity of their spy at Goschachgunk. He also wrote letters for them to forward to Gen. Washington, Col. Crawford and others.

Obviously, it was extremely advantageous to the Americans to have such a spy, since he could observe and report so much of what was going on among the enemy. But it was a very dangerous game for John Heckewelder to play.

[*March 21, 1779—Sunday*]

Over the past three days two events had occurred, the ramifications of which were apt to aid the Americans in their continuing war—not only against the British King but against the Shawnees.

On Friday, after literally years of discussing the matter of what to do in regard to the whites encroaching on their lands, part of the Shawnees reached a momentous decision in a full tribal council at Chalahgawtha. The eldest of the Shawnee leaders— and one of the most revered—was Kikusgowlowa, chief of the Thawegila sept. He rose and stated unequivocally that if once more the Shawnees voted, as a tribe, to go against the whites in war, he would leave the tribe and take his sept with him and all those from other septs who would follow him. He was seconded in his stand by Outhowwa Shokka—Yellow Hawk.

Opposing Kikusgowlowa—called Black Stump by the traders—was Chiungalla, principal chief of the tribe as well as chief of the Chalahgawtha sept, and he was seconded by the tribe's war chief, Shemeneto—Black Snake—who was also chief of the Kispokotha sept.

The arguments went on for hours, and at last the vote was taken, and the Chalahgawthas and Maykujays were adamant for war; the Thawegilas, Peckuwes and Kispokothas, despite Shemeneto's stand, for peace. And with this the Shawnee tribe today split irrevocably. The three latter septs, comprising upward of two-thirds of the warrior strength of the tribe, immediately packed up and headed west to settle in the area of Cape Girardeau in the Missouri region of the Louisiana Territory, west of the Mississippi. The Chalahgawthas and Maykujays, joined by a small number of the more bellicose chiefs and warriors of the other septs, stayed behind to direct their full strength against the Americans—but that strength was now greatly diminished.[348]

The second event that would be of aid to the Americans was that today, far across the Atlantic Ocean, Spain declared war on the British—a matter that could not help but effectively divide the British King's attention from the American Revolution.

Chapter 4

There was only one principal reason why the garrison at Fort Laurens did not starve to death during this prolonged siege by the Indians: a reason named Samuel Brady.

Time after time, armed with rifle, powderhorn and bullet pouch, with knife and tomahawk in belt, Capt. Brady would steal out of the fort well after nightfall and carefully, stealthily slip away. Normally he went upstream on the Tuscarawas, keeping well away from the Indian trails and never stopping to hunt until he was at least several miles distant from the fort, well beyond the sound of a gunshot reaching the Indians.

Sometimes, when game was scarce, he would be gone for two or three days, even longer. Normally he was back sometime during the night. Returning, however, was even riskier than leaving. He could not simply hoist the deer or other game animal on his shoulders and return. The method he devised was ingenious but required tremendous stamina and self-control.

Having downed his game, he would skin and butcher it, cutting it into manageable pieces and tying each piece tightly with long, narrow strips of hide to a dry dead branch. When all the pieces—hams, loins, shoulders, rump, neck, liver and heart—were well secured, he gathered other branches and constructed them into a sort of raft with a hole on the center. He would float it on the river close to shore, and the pieces of wood to which the meat was tied were distributed levelly on the surface. Close to the hole would go his rifle and powderhorn. Then he would cover the whole with a formless jumble of branches, vines and brambles, mounding it to leave a sort of spacious hollow over the center hole. With the raft ready, Brady would wait until nightfall, then enter the frigid water, duck beneath it and poke his head and shoulders and arms through the hole, well masked by the covering branches.

In the darkness, even under full moonlight, the raft then had the appearance of nothing more than a mass of driftwood that had broken free from somewhere upstream. Alternately swimming in deep water and squirming through shallows, Brady would gradually move down the Tuscarawas, often passing Indians camped along the shores or passing in canoes. At length he would reach the fort and guide the raft to shore directly below it. There, soldiers of the garrison would bring everything up to the fort, even the branches, which would be used as firewood.

It was a very risky business, repeated time and again during this time of famine in the fort, and because of it the Fort Laurens garrison had thus far survived . . . and Brady's reputation as an incredibly skilled and heroic woodsman grew.

[M a r c h   2 8 ,   1 7 7 9 — S u n d a y]

Gen. Lachlan McIntosh's relief of Fort Laurens had finally arrived and was warmly welcomed, but an unspoken accusation hovered over the garrison that had he arrived but a few hours earlier, two fine young men would not have died.

This whole situation had come about as a result of the arrival of a party of Moravian Delawares at the mouth of Beaver River with intelligence from John Heckewelder to Col. Brodhead, to be relayed to Gen. McIntosh at Fort Pitt. Using the method he had so successfully used in the past, Heckewelder hid his letters in the folds of the saddle blanket beneath the saddle of one of the least significant members of the Delaware party. The Indians were known to be friendly, and standing orders declared that they were not in any way to be molested. They were admitted into Fort McIntosh, held a council with Col. Brodhead and delivered both their verbal and written messages. Within a few minutes, Brodhead was writing to Gen. McIntosh:

Rec^d. several letters from Killbuck and others at Cooshocking [Coshocton] that Mr. Heckewelder sent me in the pad of a Moravian Indian's saddle. The Mingoes, Wyandottes, Muncies, Shawanese, and a few Delawares who live with the Wyandottes, have lately made two attempts on Fort Laurens. Unfortunately, in the first, on February 23rd, a sergeant and seventeen men were killed, except two, who are prisoners. . . .

The Delaware chiefs informed me that four British officers and sixteen privates in an armed vessel arrived at Sandusky a few days ago, and brought with them a great quantity of liquor and goods to engage the Indians to go with them to Fort Laurens. They are to proceed to Kyahoga, then up that river to a carrying place about five miles from the head of Tuscarawas, and make a road that distance for some artillery, thence down the Tuscarawas to Fort Laurens and besiege it. The Indians say this is practicable, and have offered me two of their best young men to go and watch the enemy, and bring me intelligence of their approaches. The loss or evacuation of Fort Laurens would greatly encourage the enemy, at the same time it would discourage our inhabitants. . . . I am informed that the Mingoes living up the Allegheny, at a place called Conewango, are much reduced by the smallpox. Should the intelligence respecting the designs of the enemy against Fort Laurens prove groundless, I have thought of taking some circuitous route to attack a small town of the River LeBoeuf, because the Indians there have been remarkably hostile.

The letter was dispatched by express to Gen. McIntosh and reached him while he was in the midst of writing a letter asking that he be recalled from his frontier post. On receiving Brodhead's letter, he immediately set aside the request and sent out messengers to the county lieutenants asking them to supply men and horses to go to the relief of Fort Laurens. It took precious days, and even then he did not get what he felt was necessary. Among the 200 militia who had joined him were the companies of Capts. Nathan Ellis, Andrew Van Swearingen, John Crow, James Brenton and John White. Fearing to delay any longer, he marched these men and some of the regulars from Fort Pitt to Fort McIntosh, where he hastily scribbled a letter to Gen. Washington:

Fort McIntosh, 19th March 1779

Sir:

I am just setting off to Fort Laurens with about two hundred men I have collected of the militia, and better than 300 Continental troops from this garrison and Fort Pitt, but unfortunately have not collected horses enough . . . the time will not admit of an hour's delay to wait for any more. I consulted the principal men from each County, with all the field officers, who are unanimously of opinion that Fort Laurens is a post of such consequence that it should not be evacuated by any means, if it can possibly be kept, and that it may be defended by 100 men, if provision cannot be carried for more. And indeed, we are scarce enough of it here— not above one month's provisions this side of the mountains. The difficulty of getting it over, and the distance of carriage, is the grand objection to every enterprise from this quarter.

I have thought it necessary to leave Colonel Brodhead on that account here, and use every exertion in getting further supplies soon. Major Taylor also is ordered down the country for the same purpose, and to hurry the staff departments, lest they disappoint us, and nothing can be had on this side.

I had some intelligence last night from Coshocking, which I have desired the Colonel to give you the particulars of, as I have not time. It appears the Savages are all combined against us.

I have the honor, &c.,
Lach^n. McIntosh, B. G.

But though McIntosh headed his 500 unmounted men toward Fort Laurens as quickly as he could under the circumstances, they arrived just a little too late. The new commander of Fort Laurens, Maj. Frederick Vernon of the Eighth Pennsylvania Regiment, was not having an easy time of it. Hunger among the 106 men at the fort was still a serious problem but had been alleviated somewhat, not only by the daring hunting activities of Sam Brady and Peter Parchment but because a shipment of corn had just arrived, brought to them by some friendly Indians who had been sent by the Reverend Heckewelder. Though he could ill spare it himself, he understood only too well the desperation of their need. Nevertheless, while food was not at this moment an absolute imperative, the garrison was desperately in need of firewood, and Maj. Vernon, unaware that help was on the way, early this morning had sent out a strong detachment for that purpose: 40 men commanded by Enss. Thomas Wyatt and Philip Clark, to be broken into several well-guarded wood-gathering parties to cut and bring in their loads as swiftly as possible. The first few parties were at work within moments of being placed and sentinels posted.

Clark had already set three parties under his command to work and now moved with the final sentinel, Pvt. William Adkins, to the outermost point to show him the area of his watch. They had only arrived at that point when a group of ten Wyandots fired from ambush and killed both Clark and his sentinel instantly.

Behind them, the first groups of men already had loads cut and were taking them to the fort while others continued cutting. At the shots, all of them raced for the fort and reached it safely, Ens. Wyatt bringing up the rear. Maj. Vernon immediately sent out three of the Moravian Indians to assess the size of the party that had struck, then began a letter to Gen. McIntosh. The party returned and reported before he was finished, and he incorporated their intelligence in the letter and swiftly finished what he was writing. Then he entrusted the letter to two of the Indians who had brought the corn, promising to pay them for their efforts, and sent them off to Fort McIntosh.

Less than an hour away from Fort Laurens, they encountered McIntosh's relief force and gave the general the letter they were carrying. McIntosh broke the seal and read it quickly.

Fort Laurens 28th March, 1779

Dear General,

   This morning I sent out a party of about forty men commanded by Ensigns Wiatt and Clark to bring in wood for the garrison. As Ensign Clark was placing the last centinel, he was fired on by a party of Indians (that lay concealed some small distance beyond where the centinel was placed); they killed him and the centinel, and scalped them before the party could come to their assistance, as the greatest part of the men had got their loads and were on their way to the fort. What few men had not got their loads up ran towards the fort, expecting there was a large party of Indians. When this happened, Mr. Wiatt had not got up with his party as far as Mr. Clark was. I immediately sent out three Indians to make a discovery how large the party was. They returned in a short time, and told me the party was not large, but they had discovered a number of tracks on the point of a ridge some small distance from where the Indians were that did the mischief. From their accounts, I think there were more parties than one. I got two Indians to go express to Beaver Creek with the intelligence to you as soon as possible.

I then sent out a party with Captain Brady and Ensign Wyatt to bring in the dead bodies. They went to the place where the Indians sat and found four blankets, two green covers and a long knife lying on top of a lying tree. There appeared to be about 10 Indians in that party.

Mr. Heckewelder, one of the Moravian Missionaries, was here two days ago, and told me we may depend there will be a large party of Indians and some English, with several pieces of artillery, will pay us a visit in a short time. I would be glad to have two pieces of cannon to exchange a shot with them. Please send me your opinion of it, as I am determined to defend this post while I have one man alive and able to fight.

I have received a gratuity of corn from Cooshocking [Goschachgunk], but I have not goods that will suit the Indians to satisfy them for bringing it up. I have given a certificate to them for twenty bucks, which they expect to be paid to them at Beaver Creek. The bearers of this letter are not paid for their trouble, nor have I set any price with them; they expect pay there also. I am informed that there are several Indian parties out—some are gone over the Big River [Ohio River] to murder the inhabitants; some of the parties are returned back with prisoners and scalps.

> *I am, &c.,*
> *Fred^k. Vernon*
> *Maj^r, 8th Reg^t.*

Brigd^r. Gen. Lach^n. McIntosh
P.S. The name of the soldier that was killed is Adkins, one of the new levies.

So now Gen. McIntosh and his force had arrived, and the greatest expectation was that he would order, because of its vulnerability and the difficulty of keeping it supplied, the abandonment of Fort Laurens. In this they were disappointed.

Without Fort Laurens, McIntosh informed them, the Indians—and the British —would have open access to strike the upper Ohio with irresistible force. The slaughter and destruction in that area previously would be as nothing to what would occur then. No, Fort Laurens would not be evacuated but would continue to be garrisoned and serve as a bulwark of defense.

There were a good many of the Fort Laurens garrison who, among themselves, disgustedly changed the words "bulwark of defense" to "sitting duck."

[April 1, 1779 — Thursday]

In one of the few respites he had enjoyed since the war began, Gen. George Washington was entertaining a number of gentlemen guests at a dinner party. They had finished eating about an hour before and had been conversing since then over cigars and brandy and were now on the verge of taking their leave when the express horn sounded outside, and in a few moments the butler entered bearing a dispatch upon a silver salver.

The guests were just rising from their chairs, but they stopped as Washington looked at the seal and said, "Keep your seats, gentlemen, keep your seats. Perhaps there may be some news for us."

As they sat down again and watched with mild interest, the commander of the Continental Army put on his spectacles, broke the seal and began to read the contents. Suddenly a broad grin spread his lips, and he became obviously more excited the further he read. At last he refolded the letter and took off his spectacles, still smiling.

"Gentlemen," he said, holding up the folded paper, "this is a letter from Governor Jefferson. He writes that he has just received intelligence that a Virginia colonel has conquered the Illinois country and that the Virginia flag now waves in triumph over Kaskaskia, Cahokia and Vincennes!"

A tumultuous response erupted from the guests, and Washington ordered their glasses refilled, then stood holding his glass high before them. "Gentlemen," he said, "a toast."

The others rose and held their glasses up similarly. Continuing to smile, Washington said, "To Colonel George Rogers Clark, the conqueror of the Illinois!"

At almost the same time, hundreds of miles to the west and north, the new British commandant of Detroit, Maj. Arent de Peyster, commented worriedly, "Mr. Hamilton's defeat has cooled the Indians in general."[349]

Clark's stunning accomplishment was having its effect at Redstone and Pittsburgh, too. Despite the jeopardy still prevailing for travelers on the Ohio River, scores upon scores of would-be settlers were gathering at these staging points preparatory to floating down the Ohio later this spring or during the summer to get their share of the wonderful, beautiful lands that were theirs for the taking along its shores and in the Kentucky country.

[M a y   3 ,   1 7 7 9 — M o n d a y]

Col. Daniel Brodhead, sitting at his desk in his headquarters office at Fort McIntosh, rubbed his eyes and yawned, wishing he were asleep in his bed. The days seemed always too short to accomplish what needed to be done, and crises seemed to have a way of intervening every time it looked like there might be a little break.

He glanced with distaste at the unfinished report before him that would have to go out to Gen. McIntosh in the morning. The Delawares somehow continued to maintain a stance difficult to understand: A small portion of the tribe was decidedly hostile and had been making frontier attacks in concert with the Wyandots, Mingoes and Shawnees for many months; another portion, the Moravian converts, were decidedly pro-American, doing much valuable spying for the Americans, their intelligence more than once preventing disastrous consequences. Yet the majority of the tribe did not condone either hostility or alliance and continued to hold themselves in a neutral position that, considering the provocations they had suffered from the Americans, was rather remarkable.

The most recent affront to them had come when Pvt. William Simms of Col.

William Crawford's Thirteenth Regiment shot and mortally wounded the Delaware messenger, Anacota, for no other reason than, as he put it, that he simply "saw an Injen, and they ain't no Injen better'n a dead one." Crawford's friend, Dr. John Knight, now serving at Fort Pitt as surgeon's mate, tried to save the mortally wounded Anacota but was unable to do so. Brodhead had no idea what the ramifications would be from that, and lavish presents, accompanied by a sincere apology, had already been sent to the tribe in an effort to "cover the dead," as the Indians put it.[350]

The only bright spot lately was the fact that, following intelligence received from Heckewelder of the Indians and British preparing a strong artillery-supported attack against it sometime this coming summer, orders had finally been received for the abandonment of Fort Laurens. That was scheduled to occur before the end of the month. The whole existence of the fort so deep in enemy territory, where support was almost impossible, had been a grave error in judgment, and it was now deemed untenable.

Brodhead hunched his shoulders for a moment to relieve the strain in his back and then quickly reread the portion of the report he had just finished writing:

> *One of the Privates of the 13th Virginia Regiment has maliciously killed one of the best young men of the Delaware Nation, and I fear the consequences will be bad to the innocent inhabitants. I have the fellow confined, but cannot try him for want of a field officer, &c. Several parties have been assembled to murder the Delaware chiefs now on their way to Philadelphia: Should they effect their malicious purpose, there will be an end to negotiations, and a general war with the savages will be the inevitable consequence of their barbarity.*
>
> *Great numbers of the inhabitants are daily moving down the Ohio to Kentucky and the Falls, which greatly weakens the frontier.*
>
> *Two spies are gone into the Seneca country several days ago—one of them is a white man who speaks their language very well, and the other is a Delaware Indian.*

Col. Brodhead, satisfied with what he had written so far, now dipped his quill into the inkpot and continued to write:

> *Fort Laurens will be evacuated the 25th inst., and I expect all the stores will be brought off.*
>
> *I shall be happy if we can move by the first of June. My men have worn out their shoes, and their feet, in scouting after the Indians, but with little success hitherto. I have heard where the Mingoes and Muncys have their grand rendezvous about fifteen miles above Kittanning, and hope to give a good account of them a few days hence.*

[M a y   2 8 ,   1 7 7 9 — F r i d a y]

Throughout the spring, raiding parties of Indians on the frontier increased considerably. No one could be certain where they would strike next or in what numbers, and for the settlers, just being constantly on the alert was greatly wearing on the nerves. More often than not, families would gather at the most defensible cabin in the area and stay together there for mutual protection.

The major forts on the frontier, garrisoned by regular troops, were constantly on full alert, though few were up to total strength. Fort Laurens was now, at last, in the process of being evacuated, as per Gen. McIntosh's order, and its garrison would soon be returning to Fort McIntosh and Fort Pitt. That garrison included 106 rank and file on hand under the command of Maj. Frederick Vernon, including the partial companies of Capt. John Finley, Capt. Lt. Samuel Brady, and Enss. Thomas Wyatt, John Guthrie and James Morrison. Their strength would be a welcome addition, though the entire frontier would still be greatly undermanned. Fort Randolph at the mouth of the Kanawha, now the most isolated government post, had only 28 men under Capt. Samuel Dawson; at Fort McIntosh, where Col. Daniel Brodhead was still commanding, there were 123 men in the partial companies of Capt. John Clark —a different officer from the ensign of the same name who had been killed at Fort Laurens—and Ens. John Ward, though that number would increase with a portion of the men coming back from Fort Laurens. Fort Henry at Wheeling had 28 men under Lt. Gabriel Peterson, and the Holliday's Cove Fort also had 28 men under Lt. John Hardin. The largest command was, of course, Fort Pitt, with 707 men; 392 of the Eighth Pennsylvania and 258 of the Thirteenth Virginia regiments, and Capt. Thomas Heth's company of 57 men, plus whatever would be added from the Fort Laurens contingent; but in all these forts, with 234 men ill, injured, on furlough or otherwise not on active duty, the entire present and fit for duty came to a total of 473 men. What this boiled down to was a total of only 786 men on active duty to guard a frontier of thousands of square miles against several thousand warriors in separate raiding parties of four to 100 or more men each, roaming at will and striking with horrible ferocity. By this time, Dr. John Knight had been named chief surgeon at Fort Pitt through Col. William Crawford's intercession on his behalf with Col. Brodhead.

Fort Hand, on the Kiskeminetas about eight miles upstream from its mouth on the Allegheny, was under command of Capt. Samuel Moorehead, with Lt. William Jack his second. These were militia, not regular troops, and though poorly equipped and trained, when attacked on April 26, they managed to hold out against a much superior force of more than 100 Senecas and Mingoes, aided by a company of British. During the fight, Sgt. Philip McGraw took a ball in the neck and was killed, and Sgt. Leonard McCauley was severely wounded by a ball high in his chest.[351]

At practically the same time the attack on Fort Hand was occurring, a party of hostile Delawares struck at the cabin of George Sykes on the Monongahela in the vicinity of Redstone. Sykes had made a quick trip into Brownsville for supplies that morning, and when he returned some four hours later, his cabin was in ashes and his wife, Christiana, and their six children, age nine down to a newborn infant, were all missing.[352]

Some of the attacks were occurring much farther to the east than had occurred for many years, such as the one that happened at the Sanford cabin. Abraham Sanford had built his place on Bald Eagle Creek not far southwest of Potter's Fort and fully 130 miles east of Pittsburgh.[353] He thought his family would be safe there. They were not. A band of Wyandots struck, killing seven members of his family and taking all their cattle and horses. Only Sanford himself and a young daughter managed to escape through a rear window of the cabin and into the adjacent woods. Scores of similar attacks were occurring throughout the entire frontier, and armed forces summoned to help almost always arrived too late to do anything except bury the dead.

With such incidents steadily increasing, Col. Brodhead at Fort McIntosh now took a step he had been contemplating for some time. Though he had often sent out small parties of men to scout the country and watch for Indian sign, up until now it was not an organized activity. He was aware, of course, of the remarkable bravery, ingenuity and Indian-fighting skills of such men from Fort Laurens as Samuel Brady, Peter Parchment and several others. He also remembered with satisfaction the success of Brady's scout with his Delaware guide, John Thompson, up the Allegheny last September. Thus, as soon as those men returned from Fort Laurens, he called Brady to headquarters.

"Captain Brady," Brodhead began, "I want to set up a well-organized body of men to be called Rangers—a force established to search out and attack raiding Indian parties. I want a group of good, experienced men to make regular patrols along the upper Ohio to watch for Indian sign and give warning to the settlements of any approaching danger. When a report is received of Indian attack occurring, especially when captives are taken, these Rangers are to go to the scene immediately, trail the Indian party at top speed and overtake them, the first priority being to get the prisoners back unhurt, the second to destroy the Indian raiders.

"The question, Captain," Col. Brodhead added, "is this: Would you be willing to set up this body of Rangers to undertake this dangerous type of activity and act as its commander?"

"I would be in sole command?" Brady asked.

"You would. Responsible only to me, but I want you to take the initiative. Set up the kind of force you want, with the very best and most reliable men. Volunteers only. This is an assignment that will be extremely dangerous to all who engage in it and so they must be men who have great courage and ability, men who are willing to use the Indian style of fighting against the Indians themselves, who will use judgment and discretion, yet who will kill swiftly and without emotion when the situation warrants."

"How many men?"

"I am not setting limits," Brodhead replied, "but my feeling is that you would do much better with a small force of very highly trained Rangers than with a company of less well-trained men dashing about through the woods with their rifles. The most important thing is to get the *quality* of men you want, men who are willing to be trained by you to beat the Indians at their own game. Can you do this? Let me rephrase: *Will* you do it?"

"I can, Colonel, and I will."

"Excellent. I thought you would. You can start right now."

By the end of the day, Capt. Samuel Brady had selected seven men as a foundation for his Rangers. The first selected was Samuel Murphy, the brawny, 30-year-old little Irishman who had accompanied Brady on his mission up the Allegheny last September. Peter Parchment, 34, was next; he had proven himself well during that long difficult period at Fort Laurens. The Cuppy brothers were youngest of his choices—John was 18 and Abram not yet 17, but they were tough young men with great powers of endurance, excellent marksmen and accomplished woodsmen. Then he selected the brothers Vachel and Kinzie Dickerson, who were not much older, 21 and 19 respectively, but both had proven themselves time and again in fighting Indians and were tough, level-headed, powerful young men. Finally, he chose Tom Edgington, who had come to the Pittsburgh area from Redstone and settled a short distance up Chartier's Creek. Edgington, at 35, was the eldest of this group, a serious, highly dependable man with a great deal of scouting and Indian fighting in his background. Though he was a man of about average size—five feet eight inches tall and weighing 160 pounds—he was a very swift runner and could lift objects much heavier than any of his neighbors could manage.

Brady knew these seven were ideal to form the nucleus of his elite force. Each, without reservation, was a man he would trust by his side in the wilderness. Each, when asked to volunteer, accepted instantly without question. Brady was sure that as time went on, he would be selecting others to join them, but these were enough for the present. Brady's Rangers was now an active force of eight men.

Brady first inaugurated a rigorous training program, drilling his men at all hours of day and night on how they should act in this team he had assembled. He was absolute leader, and his commands must be obeyed instantly, as lives would undoubtedly depend upon it. No one, except in case of emergency, was to fire his weapon unless Brady gave the word. They practiced different forms of ambush, different methods of approaching an enemy camp and different means of subterfuge, and Brady also devised a whole set of hand signals, so conversation would be unnecessary. A finger pointed at a man meant he was to take first shot. An outstretched hand moved back and forth, palm down, meant no one was to fire. A finger held up and twirled in a circle meant to scatter and reassemble about 100 yards behind them; two fingers so used meant 200 yards behind, and so on. An arm held straight up from the elbow, hand stiff and straight, meant to tree—that is, to instantly hide behind the nearest big tree or other available cover and fire from that position. A fist held out, wrist to the sky and the bunched fingers suddenly spread out to their widest, meant not only to scatter, but every man for himself in getting back home. There were many other such signals, all devised to give them easy and silent communication under any circumstance. Their mode of dress was not formalized, but remembering Delaware John Thompson's admonition that they would be safer clad as Indians, they wore clothing that blended well with the underbrush: buckskin leggins and blouses, their feet clad in moccasins, their hair, if long, clubbed or tied into a tail at the nape. Most elected not to wear hats or, if they wanted a head covering, wore what Brady himself always wore, virtually as his trademark—a black kerchief covering the head and tied in back.

After many hours and days of such training, they at last headed out on a scout. Sam Murphy was away, so there were only seven in their party. They headed generally eastward from Fort McIntosh, following the north bank of the Ohio toward Fort Pitt, watching for any sign of Indians prowling about the scattered settlements north of the Ohio or having crossed over to strike the settlements on the south side of the river.

It was a mile or so downstream from the mouth of Big Sewickley Creek that they encountered the trail of a large party of Indians—Brady estimated their number at about 25. The Rangers followed the trail, expecting the Indians to cross the Ohio soon, but they hadn't. Instead, at the mouth of Big Sewickley, 15 miles below Fort Pitt, the trail led them upstream along the tributary. There were several families of German settlers along that stream, and Brady feared the worst.

Brady's Rangers moved swiftly but with care. Near the headwaters of the stream, they came to the claim of Jacob Frantz, where they found the burned cabin still smoldering. Close to the ruins they found the bodies of Frantz and his 18-year-old daughter, Sophie. Jacob had been shot, and both were tomahawked and scalped. Brady's men scouted about in an ever widening circle and, where a cornfield was being planted, found another man, mortally wounded and scalped but still alive. Before he died, he was able to give them details of what had occurred.

His name, he told them, was Elmer Kribs, and he and another man, named John Sipes, had been appointed to stand sentry while others planted the corn under direction of a man named Cheny, who boarded with the Henrys. The first he knew anything was amiss was when he was struck in the stomach by a bullet and fell. He didn't completely lose consciousness, but he couldn't move and, from where he lay, he saw the other sentry and those in the field run toward the cabin. The Indians cut them off and took them prisoner. The door of the cabin had opened, and Jacob Frantz came running out, rifle in hand, only to be shot dead. Then the Indians ran into the cabin and came out with Frantz's daughters, Sophie and 16-year-old Aimy. Sophie was lame in one leg and could not walk well, so they tomahawked her and then scalped both her and her father. They plundered the cabin and set it afire and started to march the others away as captives, when one of the warriors, evidently the one who had shot Kribs, remembered him and ran back to where he lay. Kribs said he saw him coming and tried to drag himself into the underbrush but could not. The last he remembered was the warrior racing up on him with tomahawk upraised. Now Kribs tried to say more, but he failed and fell unconscious. In a few moments more his breathing stopped.

"We've got to try to get those prisoners back," Brady said. "Let's go."

They followed the trail and could see that they were gaining on the Indian party, their progress evidently slowed because of the captives. It was not long until they came to the ruins of another cabin, still ablaze but the Indians gone. John Cuppy recognized the place as the cabin of John Henry, a Dutchman, who had settled there with his wife and two children, Peter and Alma. Cuppy reckoned the two were now probably about eight and ten years old respectively. Since there were no bodies in evidence, they and their parents had evidently been taken prisoner.

The trail of the Indians headed northeast, and they continued to follow it. Within a few miles it split, the larger portion of the party angling away to the north, while the smaller party—the footprints indicating eight or ten adults and at least a couple of children—continued to the northeast on a course that would soon take them to the Allegheny. Brady decided they would follow the smaller party, not only because they would have a greater chance of success in attacking it but because the tracks made it most likely the Henry children were with them and perhaps some of the other captives as well.

The Brady party made cold camps at night, and on the third day of following the trail, the tracks became so fresh that mud still swirled in the little runs they had waded across. Brady gave orders for complete silence, and they continued with increased caution. It was just as dusk was deepening that Brady ordered his men to rest while he and Parchment scaled a nearby high hill to its summit. From this vantage they could see an extreme bend of the Allegheny River—at this point some 60 miles upstream from Fort Pitt—and, close to its edge, smoke ascending from what had to be the camp of the Indians. It was full dark by the time they returned to the other Rangers, and Brady said they would continue moving in on them, advancing warily and in single file with Brady himself in the lead.

Moving slowly and quietly, sliding their feet gently along the ground so as not to step on twigs that might snap and reveal their approach, it took them nearly two hours to get to within sight of the fire. The Indians had stopped just above the mouth of a creek entering the Allegheny from the northwest.[354] Their camp was in a clearing a dozen yards or so from a large fallen tree and about 100 yards from the west bank of the Allegheny, where the stream makes a sharp, extensive horseshoe curve to the west.[355] Brady and his men studied the situation from a distance and estimated, as the Indians moved in and out of the light of the campfire, that there were about a dozen warriors, plus a couple of youngsters who were evidently the Henry children. An Indian guard was sitting near the fire mending a moccasin. Brady and his men held a whispered council and made their plans. He directed his six men to move out and space themselves appropriately in a semicircle, while Brady himself would creep in and take a position behind the log. Because some of the Indians were far enough from the fire that they could not be seen in the darkness, the Rangers would hold off attacking until dawn. The firing of Brady's gun would be the signal for all to shoot.

The Indian guard was edgy, and several times as Brady and his men moved into position, he stopped working on his moccasin and cocked his head to listen, at which the whites, as prearranged, froze in place until he resumed his work. Brady had just reached the log when the guard rose and walked in his direction.

Brady flattened himself behind the log, lying on his back with tomahawk in hand and ready to strike if he should be discovered. The Indian stepped up onto the log directly over Brady, and though he glanced downward for a moment, the depth of the night shadows hid Brady well, and he was not discovered. But then a stream of liquid began striking Brady's chest, and he realized the warrior was urinating into the darkness from his stance atop the log. Brady continued to lie still, and after a few moments the guard stepped off the log and moved back to the fire, where he resumed his moccasin repair.

Throughout the remainder of the night Brady's men crouched in place. Finally dawn began breaking, and visibility improved. As the guard came to his feet and stretched, the crack of Brady's gun shattered the stillness. The Indian fell and then tried to rise. Shots from Brady's men broke out, and the guard warrior slumped over and remained motionless. The other Indians leaped to their feet at the same time and instantly scattered into dimly lighted woods. Two acted as if they may have been hit, but no one else fell.[356]

Closer to the fire the boy and girl, bound to each other at wrist and ankle, scrambled to their feet, and eight-year-old Peter Henry yelled, "Don't shoot! Don't shoot! I'm a white man!"

Parchment ran up to them and cut away their bonds, and the boy hugged him around the waist and tearfully thanked him for saving their lives.[357] Then he ran over to the dead Indian, pulled the warrior's tomahawk out of his waistband and struck the dead man several blows to head and body.

The Indians had left behind their rifles but, leaving nothing to chance, Thomas Edgington and three other Rangers spread out and checked to make sure they were really gone. They returned a quarter-hour later to report that the warriors had fled without pause and several of them had been seen swimming across the great bend of the Allegheny out of range of their rifles. One of them, they reported, climbed out of the water on the opposite side and yelled at them, "Damn Yankees!"[358] Thomas Edgington, grinning, then told Sam Brady, "We figured a bend in the river like this one needs to have a name, so we've named it."

"What name?" Brady asked.

"From now on," Edgington replied, "it's Brady's Bend."[359]

Brady chuckled and shook his head. "Never figured on becoming a landmark. All right, these youngsters are so tuckered out they can't walk much farther. Let's get a couple of bark canoes built and get 'em down to Pittsburgh."[360] Two large canoes were built in a few hours, and Brady and his men took the Henry children to Pittsburgh, where they were put in the care of a relative.[361] The rifles and plunder taken by the Indians from several strikes—blankets, kettles and other goods—were sold there at auction, and the proceeds went to the children.

Word spread rapidly throughout the upper Ohio region of the feat accomplished by Brady's Rangers, and there was much jubilation and approbation. And at Fort McIntosh Col. Daniel Brodhead was extremely pleased with their success and felt certain they would be at least equally successful in future forays.

[July 30, 1779—Friday]

The whites in the middle and lower Ohio River Valley were faring somewhat better than those on the upper Ohio, but there were strong fears that this was about to change. What had happened recently in the campaign led by Col. John Bowman from Kentucky into the Ohio country against the Shawnees was considered by many as an affront that would call for drastic retaliation by the Indians.

A great many whites had been killed in the continuing raids of the Shawnees against the Kentucky settlements, and a large amount of property had been destroyed, livestock killed and horses stolen. Bowman was very jealous of the fame that had come to George Rogers Clark for taking Kaskaskia and Cahokia, then capturing Gen. Henry Hamilton and his British force at Vincennes.[362] So late this past spring Bowman announced a proposed campaign against the great Shawnee village of

Chalahgawtha on the Little Miami River and called for volunteers. A total of 264 men had come forward with their own horses and weapons and the mounted operation was put into motion.

Luck was riding high on the shoulders of Bowman at this time because of two major occurrences about which he knew nothing. First, the split in the Shawnee nation last March, when more than half the tribe moved away to resettle west of the Mississippi, had greatly weakened those who remained. Second, at the precise time of his move against Chalahgawtha—the largest of all Shawnee villages, with a population of some 3,000, about a third of which were warriors—all but a small handful of males were gone from the village, attending a major council that had been called at the Shawnee capital village, Wapatomica, some 50 miles to the north. Had those warriors been at home, everyone agreed, Bowman's small force would have been annihilated.

Only 35 defenders, mainly young boys and old men, were at Chalahgawtha when Bowman's army approached, favoring the mounted force with almost eight to one odds over the Indians. They had approached the town by night but the crucial element of surprise was lost because of Bowman's failure to observe silence. His strident voice carried far and reached Chalahgawtha well before his forces. By the time they came in sight of the town, virtually all the Shawnees there had taken advantage of the darkness to abandon their dwellings and gather for mutual defense in the *msi-kah-mi-qui*—the huge council house. Many of the women were already singing the death song because all fully believed they would be destroyed in a very short time. Yet even though the sporadic firing directed at the whites from the council house indicated there were very few defenders, Bowman was afraid to make a charge to overwhelm them. Instead, seeing that the greater part of the town was empty, Bowman ordered his men to burn the houses.

Moving from wegiwa to wegiwa and cabin to cabin, the attackers not only set each of the flimsy structures afire, they also wasted a lot of time and energy in looting them—of spears, fur robes, shields, woven mats, tanned deer skins, pottery, decorative garments, silver jewelry and other goods. Very quickly the whites became far more obsessed with taking plunder than with accomplishing the mission. Their greed made them careless, and as they came very close to the almost continuous shooting coming from the council house, ten of Bowman's men were downed, while not a single Shawnee had yet been wounded.

Col. Bowman's courage, what there was of it, drained away, and incredibly, with the foe in the very palm of his hand, he ordered a withdrawal. The corral in which some 12 dozen Shawnee horses were penned was discovered, and Bowman had most of them rounded up and driven back toward Kentucky. Burdened with loot and the task of driving such a large herd of horses, the army now suddenly became very vulnerable.

Amazed at their good fortune, the few Shawnee defenders were quick to react. They managed to round up two dozen of their horses that the whites had been unable to catch, mounted and set off in pursuit. They overtook the army in about ten miles and began a harassing fire at the rear. One after another, the whites were shot off their horses until at last Bowman was forced to halt his force and form them into a square for defense, at which the Indians vanished. But as soon as the army resumed its march, the sniping began again and more were killed. That a body of only 24 warriors was pinning down a mounted army ten times larger was practically beyond belief. The soldiers desperately wanted Bowman to give an order to attack, but the colonel refused and continued the withdrawal. Five separate times, as their comrades were being killed around them, the army was forced to stop and defend, then push on again.

At last, their rage against their own commander pushed to its limits, Capt. James Harrod and two of his lieutenants acted on their own. Fully 100 of the men were ordered to throw down the loot they were carrying and charge the attackers.

With that concerted charge directed against them, the 24 warriors finally abandoned the harassment and galloped away, heading back to Chalahgawtha. Bowman, fuming at having his orders disobeyed, re-formed the army and marched them back to the Ohio River with the horses and plunder. In total, 30 men had been killed and more than 60 wounded. Upon reaching the Kentucky shore, the army was ordered to camp, and a division of the horses and loot was made. Bowman then had the unbelievable temerity to call the campaign a great success. He disbanded the army and let the men find their own way home.[363]

By this time, the large number of warriors who had been absent returned from the Wapatomica council to find two-thirds of their town burned and many of their possessions taken, along with most of the horses. There had also been two Shawnee casualties. Chief Red Pole had been killed by a ball that found its way through a small gap between the logs of the council house, and the principal chief of the Shawnees, Chiungalla—Black Fish—was severely wounded: A ball had shattered his hip socket and sent bone splinters into the surrounding flesh. He was in terrible pain and knew he would die, but he knew as well that his death would be a long time in coming.

The mortal wounding of Chiungalla and the burning of Chalahgawtha ignited a dreadful fire in the heart of every remaining Shawnee in Ohio, filling them with fearsome resolve: Their strikes would no longer be hit-and-run horse-stealing attacks. Now they would do what they as a tribe had so long refrained from doing— they would not only accept arms, ammunition and supplies from the British but would demand that a British army, with artillery, help them destroy all the *Shemanese* in the Kan-tuck-kee lands.

[August 25, 1779—Sunday]

All in all, even though he had looked forward to more direct conflict than had been experienced, Col. Daniel Brodhead was well pleased with the results of his Allegheny Campaign that was just now concluding.

In command of the Western Department of the Army, now that Gen. McIntosh had been recalled to the east, Brodhead had not been long in taking action. He was heartily tired of the recurring raids against isolated cabins and larger settlements in Pennsylvania's Westmoreland County: raids that had been carried on with almost complete impunity by the Senecas, Wyandots, Mingoes and the more hostile Delawares, the faction called Munceys. It was time, Brodhead felt, for them to be taught a lesson.

Aware that at this very moment, acting under orders from Gen. Washington himself, Maj. Gen. John Sullivan was leading a large army against the Iroquois into the very heartland of their nations and destroying all he encountered, Brodhead had reasoned that this would be a good time to do the same against the tribes on the Allegheny.[364] He had called for whatever volunteers could be spared from the various settlements, and with them and about half of his regulars—the total force close to 600 men—he started them up the Allegheny on the first of August. His field officers included Lt. Col. George Verlandigham and Majs. Frederick Vernon and Samuel McCulloch. His pilot for the main army was the half-breed John Montour. The army marched up the right bank of the Allegheny; a small herd of cattle was driven with them for beef, and the baggage and provisions were carried in canoes that paced them on the river.

As an advance unit, Brodhead sent out Capt. Samuel Brady and his Rangers, by this time increased by Brady's recruitment of 15 more very good men. At Brodhead's suggestion, Brady gladly accepted the services of Jonathan Zane and the Seneca half-breed Thomas Nicholson as his advance party's guides, since they were more familiar with the location and size of the upper Allegheny villages than Brady or any of his men. Nicholson, he knew, had long been an Iroquois interpreter at Fort Pitt and was fluent in several other Indian languages. Four friendly Delawares joined them as well, their leader a small, cheerful young man who went by the name of Captain Wilson, who said he was the nephew of John Thompson, now known as Scare the World. So the entire advance party was 30 men. Brady promised Brodhead he would hold a steady, fairly easy pace and maintain a distance of about a mile ahead of the main army.

They had encountered no one by the time they reached Brady's Bend, but a bit less than two hours beyond that point, just after having followed the Indian trail through a narrow defile and then back along the river's edge, John Cuppy, who was near the lead with Brady and Zane, said, "Hold it!" and stopped. The others stopped as well, and Brady noted with satisfaction that most of them, instead of looking at Cuppy, were scanning the area ahead, looking for whatever it was that Cuppy had seen. They saw nothing alarming.

"What?" Brady asked.

"Way up there, at the bend of the river," Cuppy said, pointing to an eastward curve in the river, "I caught a glint of something—sunlight reflecting off metal, I think."

Brady nodded. "Let's see to the tracks, then under cover. Fast."

The men cut some branches and quickly swept the trail of any footprints they had left, all the way back to the rocky defile, where the stony ground gave no clue. Then Brady held a quick conference with them and laid out what they were going to do, with Nicholson interpreting for the Indians. When they were finished, Brady sent one of his new men, Jacob Fouts, as a runner to Brodhead to tell him what was occurring and their plan. As soon as this was finished, they split in half and spread out a bit, half going into hiding on the west slope of the defile above the path, the other half on the east slope.[365]

Some ten minutes after Brady's men were situated, a war party of some 40 Indians—Senecas, Munceys and Wyandots—came into their view.[366] Most, if not all, were carrying rifles, and all had tomahawks and knives in their belts. A few also carried war clubs. Some of the warriors were painted, but most were not, signifying that while they were on their way to attack the settlements, they would wait until closer to their targets before fully applying the war paint.

The Indians strode through the pass in single file, quite close to one another, a tall, hawk-nosed and rather fierce appearing Seneca in the lead. The murmured conversation going on was low enough in tone that the whites could not make out individual words. In about five minutes the entire 40 had passed and soon disappeared from sight as the trail they were following left the defile and entered somewhat open woodland. Not a single Indian had suspected the Rangers' presence.

"Know who that was, leadin' 'em?" Nicholson asked Brady, a few moments after they had disappeared.

"No. Who?"

"That was Bald Eagle. He's the one who's been hittin' along the Kiskeminetas. Mean son of a bitch!"

Brady nodded and then held up a hand in the signal for them to stay in place and keep silent. By this time, Brady knew, Brodhead's force should be no more than five or six minutes away and were probably already hidden and ready to spring their ambush. Less than five minutes later, they heard a prolonged barrage of gunshots very faintly from the south. At once Brady stepped into view, lifted his right arm straight up, with flattened hand bent at the wrist to a 90-degree angle—the signal to get ready but to wait for his shot to fire—and then stepped back into his hiding place.

In a few minutes more, Bald Eagle's war party came into sight, running back toward them along the trail; some exhibited difficulty, as if they were wounded. Brady, near the far end of his hidden Rangers, waited until the head of the Indian formation was directly below him and then aimed at Bald Eagle and fired. The chief was knocked dead to the ground. As the Indians frantically scrambled and dodged to escape the trap, the other guns were fired amid a din of cries from Brady's men. Four more of the war party fell, and some others, who were wounded, fled with difficulty. It was a wild few moments, and by the time the guns of the Rangers were reloaded, the survivors were pretty much out of range.

They scalped the five dead men and took their weapons. One was a rather fat man who turned out to be a white renegade, identified by one of the Delawares as a brother of Simon Girty. Tom Nicholson, who knew Girty's brothers quite well, refuted the identification.[367] By this time, Fouts had returned, and at Brady's questioning look, he shook his head and spoke bitterly. "Brodhead's boys didn't kill none of 'em. Some damn fool private dropped his gun just as they was gettin' in range an' blowed his own brains out.[368] Injens took off arunnin' back this way, and there was a whole lot of shootin' for a while. Couple or three got hit, I reckon, but none of 'em fell. I see," he added, his glance flicking across the bodies, "you boys 'counted for a few."

"A few," Brady said. "Could've been more. Brodhead coming on yet?"

"Wish I could'a been here." Fouts shook his head. "No, not yet. They're buryin' that fool private. Said he'd start again in 'bout half an hour. Mebbe fifteen minutes from now."

The march upriver continued for close to a week after that without encountering any further Indians. The few villages they passed, such as Venango at the mouth of French Creek, adjacent to the old burned-out ruins of Fort Machault, were all deserted, their inhabitants evidently having been warned by the survivors of Brady's ambush. At Col. Brodhead's order these villages were burned by the main army as it passed, and the fields of corn and other vegetables near them were destroyed.

It was about ten o'clock in the morning, when the advance party under Brady was about three miles downstream from the mouth of Dagahshenodeago—called Brokenstraw Creek by the Americans—and opposite an island in the Allegheny, that they spied, far upstream, a party of Indians approaching in four canoes with upward of a dozen warriors in each. Nicholson volunteered to attempt to lure them to shore, and Brady agreed. A small stream flowing through a forested ravine entered the river near where Brady's party was waiting, and he ordered his men to get under cover.

The approaching Indians turned out to be a war party made up primarily of Senecas but with a few Munceys among them. Nicholson moved a little distance away to the shoreline and hallowed the Indians in their own tongue. They headed in toward him at once and beached their canoes, three of them close together and the last one, carrying 12 warriors, perhaps 30 yards above. All alighted with guns in hand, except for four who remained with the canoes, each standing with rifle in hand in one of the boats.

The war party was led by the Seneca chief Dehguswaygahent—The Fallen Board—and the Muncey chief named Dayoosta—It Is Light To Be Lifted.[369] As these two stood talking with Nicholson, some of the Senecas of the party spotted the head of Jonathan Zane as he incautiously peeped from behind a tree at them. Instantly they shouted an alarm and shot at Nicholson, one of the balls grazing him across the top of the thigh.

Nicholson dodged behind a tree, and the Indians of the war party tried to do the same, but there were few trees that close to the water. A deadly hail of gunfire erupted from Brady's party, and in the first few seconds a number of the Indians were downed. One of these was the Seneca subchief Dahgahgahend—White Eye—who was knocked out of the canoe he was standing in, fell into the water and did not resurface.[370] Dehguswaygahent, wounded, staggered away and reentered his canoe, but a second ball broke his spine and he fell dead in the bottom of the boat. The fight was very hot and lasted for about ten minutes. Fifteen of the Indians were killed outright, and 14 others wounded. Those wounded scattered, some into the forest and a few into the water. Dayoosta tried to reach the river and was shot just as he plunged into the water. His body sank and did not return to the surface.

The warriors of the fourth canoe managed to regain their boat—one of the men appeared to be wounded—and swiftly paddled away upstream and out of sight. The only Indian unharmed of the first three canoes was the Seneca subchief Hutgueote—The Arrow—who was known to the whites as Red Eye. He plunged into the river and by alternately diving, swimming underwater and then coming up for breath, he managed to reach the island unscathed, even though rifle balls kept sending up spurts of water as they struck close to him. He clambered ashore and raced across the island, crouching low in the weeds and brush growing on its surface. On the other side he plunged into the water again and swam to the east side of the Allegheny. As he gained the shore there, he paused and gave three loud yells, as if to notify any other Indian party within hearing, then disappeared into the underbrush.[371]

It was all over by the time Brodhead's main army arrived, even though they had broken into double time when they heard the gunfire. There were a few minor wounds and one serious one suffered by the men in Brady's party. Apart from Nicholson being creased on the thigh, young Captain Wilson had had a ball pass across the back of his left hand, and it was bleeding freely, though no bones had been broken. One of Brady's new men, David Asken, formerly a sergeant at Fort Pitt, had also been shot in the left hand, the bullet passing through the ball of his thumb—very painful but not terribly serious. Jonathan Zane, however, had taken a ball in the hollow between his collarbone and shoulder and was out of commission.

Brady's party scalped the dead Indians and stripped them of their weapons, pouches, ornaments and moccasins.[372] In the canoes were their provisions, along with seven war clubs, two more rifles and a quantity of ammunition, all of which were also taken. One of Brady's pet Delawares had seen where Chief Dahgah-gahend's rifle fell into the river when he was killed, and he dove into the river and recovered it—a much better weapon than his own, which he gave to a companion who had heretofore been armed only with tomahawk and knife.

Zane, Asken, Nicholson and Captain Wilson were ordered into one of the canoes and, with two of the pet Delawares paddling, were sent back to Fort Pitt to get their wounds treated. That night Brady's party and Brodhead's main army camped together at the mouth of Brokenstraw Creek.[373]

In the morning they pushed on together and at noon three days later reached the Muncey Towns, or Twin Towns, as they were sometimes called—sister villages located opposite each other on the shores of the Allegheny.[374] The warriors of both these towns were absent, having gone away a week or so earlier to help oppose Gen. Sullivan on his invasion into Iroquois territory. But the women, children and elderly who were still there had just abandoned both villages, obviously in great haste, with food still cooking in some of the dwellings. Provisions and other goods were abundant in the cabins and, once they had been plundered, Brodhead again ordered all the cabins destroyed, along with some 500 acres of corn in full roasting ears. All the corn was cut down—a process that took three days—and that portion close enough to the Allegheny was thrown into the river; the more distant portions were tossed into large piles to be quickly destroyed by the heat generated from their own decomposition under the hot summer sun. Thirty brass kettles that were found in the cabins were sunk in the river at Brodhead's order.[375]

The Muncey Town on the northern shore here was where Simon Girty had evidently been making his headquarters for a while, as a number of papers and other goods belonging to him were discovered and confiscated.

It was known that a few miles farther upstream there was a village named Dunosahdahgah, meaning The Burnt House. It was named after an Indian log house there that had accidentally gone up in flames some years before, just after the town

was established. This headquarters village of the famed Seneca chief Warhoytonehteh
—better known to the whites as Cornplanter—was located on the right bank, about
two miles below the mouth of Conewango Creek. Capt. Samuel Brady's party,
enlarged by some 25 volunteers from the main army, was detached to check it
out.[376] On the way they surprised two Senecas descending a tributary in a small
canoe. The warrior in the stern snatched up his rifle but was shot and killed before
he could shoot. His 16-year-old brother in the bow was shot through the lower leg
and fell into the creek. It was thought at first that he had been killed and sunk, but he
swam underwater a considerable distance downstream before surfacing beneath an
overhanging willow tree. By the time the Rangers realized it, he had swiftly scrambled to shore and escaped through some dense brush.[377]

When Brady's party arrived at Dunosahdahgah, they found the chief and most
of his warriors gone to help oppose Sullivan, but the Seneca subchief in charge,
Nantagoah—Captain Crow—and some of his men were engaged in a deer hunt
when Brady's party crept up. A number of the Indians had been positioned in hiding
in the tall grasses on a long narrow island not very far from the north shore, and a
number of others, yipping and yelping like dogs, had formed a wide semicircle and
were driving the deer toward the river. The frightened animals plunged into the
water and swam toward the island, only to have the hunters there rise from hiding
and shoot them as they came ashore.

One of the main army volunteers in Brady's force spoiled their surprise by
stumbling and falling into a ravine. He wasn't hurt, but his startled cry and the
crashing of branches alerted the Indians under Nantagoah. Hasty gunfire from
Brady's men killed a Seneca warrior named Gennehoon—Double Door—but all the
others escaped unharmed except for one Muncey warrior who was shot in the
arm.[378] Dunosahdahgah village was plundered and destroyed, and the deer that had
been killed were recovered and taken back to the main army at the Brokenstraw
Creek camp.

At that point, Col. Brodhead decided the campaign should end and started the
army back toward Pittsburgh. Only one other incident of note occurred on the trip
back, when one of his officers, young Ens. Jack Ward, while fording a small creek,
slipped on a slick rock, fell and broke his leg. Even in his pain, Ward was able to grin
and say that that gave him the right to name the creek. "From now on, boys," he
said, "this is Slippery Rock Creek." And so it was.

Now, after an absence of 25 days, they had returned to the Forks of the Ohio,
having killed 22 Indians, including four chiefs. Another 17 were known to have been
wounded, and probably more than that. For the Americans there had been only one
death—the private killed by the accidental firing of his own gun—and four
wounded, only one of whom was seriously hurt, Jonathan Zane. And one officer had
been hurt, Ens. Jack Ward, with an accidentally broken leg.

So now, in his headquarters office in Fort Pitt, smoking his pipe and sipping a
good brandy, Col. Daniel Brodhead was delighted to write in his report to Gen.
Washington that the Allegheny Campaign had been a complete success.[379]

[September 29, 1779—Wednesday]

As a result of the significant successes of Brady's Rangers on their Ohio River patrols, rescues of captives and Indian fighting, the group had already gained considerable renown. One result of this was that Sam Brady no longer had to make concerted searches to find good men to join him. He was constantly approached these days by adventurous young men for whom the elite force carried a glamour and romance that was very appealing. Only a small percentage of those who applied to become Rangers were accepted, however.

The selection was based strictly upon Sam Brady's assessment of the abilities and potential of the applicant. Age was not really much of a consideration, except that the applicant had to be able to handle himself well in almost any kind of emergency situation; his youngest Ranger at this time was 17, the eldest was 42. Formal education was not a prerequisite; to Brady it was more important that the applicant have a good knowledge of woods lore and that elusive but all-important survival instinct. He was looking for men who could load and shoot a rifle rapidly and accurately, who could throw a tomahawk and knife with reasonable skill, who were quick-witted, level-headed and in top physical condition with plenty of stamina. All his men also needed to have committed to memory the important and extensive series of hand signals that Brady had devised, by which explicit orders could be communicated between the Rangers without speech. They had to be willing to undergo regular periods of drilling, where martial arts suitable to Indian fighting were practiced exhaustively. While not required—since some simply could not master the technique involved—Brady recommended that all the Rangers try to develop the life-saving skill of reloading while running.

Sam Brady had absolutely no patience with—or a place among his Rangers for —anyone who exhibited jealousy of his companions or who was a complainer, a shirker, a braggart, squeamish, out to make a name for himself or, most important, prone to making mistakes. Errors often cost lives, and every one of his Rangers had to be fully dependable *to* the others and, equally, to place his own full trust *in* the others.

Jonathan Zane, just before the Allegheny Campaign, had been one of the applicants, and Brady had been inclined to accept him because of his woodsmanship and past experience in Indian fighting. For this reason Brady was pleased when Col. Brodhead had suggested he take Zane along on the advance party, as it would give him an opportunity to observe his behavior in dangerous situations. But then Zane had made the grave error of exposing himself to the Indians they were attempting to ambush—an act that had put Thomas Nicholson in dire jeopardy, from which he had fortunately escaped with only a slight wound, and that had resulted in Zane himself being seriously wounded. Because of that error, Brady no longer considered Zane a suitable individual for inclusion in the Rangers. Errors were not tolerated, and no one in Brady's Rangers got a second chance.

Today, on a strictly probational basis, a new applicant named Robert Bacon was being permitted to accompany the Rangers on a regular patrol. He was a big, athletic young man, 23 years old, who hailed from the Dunkard Creek settlements and had a certain amount of experience with Indian encounters. Ten other Rangers, including

Brady, were making today's patrol. Sometimes the patrols were on land, following the trails along the waterways, sometimes in canoes, skimming along close to shore. Today's outing, originating at Fort McIntosh, was designed to take them down along the left bank 25 miles to Baker's Bottom. There they would cross the river to the mouth of Yellow Creek and paddle back up the Ohio along the more dangerous right bank.

In their two canoes they had crossed the Ohio from Fort McIntosh at the mouth of Beaver River to the left bank and now, as their route carried them along the left bank of the Ohio, they were very watchful and paddled in utmost silence. Whether in canoes or moving along on shore, unnecessary conversation was strictly forbidden; more than one party of inexperienced woodsmen had been ambushed because the sound of their voices had preceded them. The Rangers' training demanded that their eyes constantly study their surroundings for tracks or traces of anything different or unusual—the broken twig on a bush, the sliver of bark newly bumped from a tree trunk, the roil of mud along the rim of a stream—anything that might indicate the passage or presence of a foe. Equally, their ears had to become attuned to the ambient sounds, so that when something inexplicable was heard—or there was a sudden cessation of normal bird songs or animal sounds—they could be on their guard for whatever was causing it. All of these practices and more very quickly became second nature to the Rangers.

Brady, in the lead canoe, abruptly raised a hand and, with fingers pointing downward, twisted it rapidly back and forth. Both boats slowed at once: This was the sign that they were approaching a tributary stream of the Ohio. Such areas were among the most dangerous because these were usually the places where war parties, crossing the big river, came ashore to take advantage of the cover afforded at the mouths of streams. With such cover they could not only screen themselves but equally hide their canoes, either by dragging them or carrying them well up from the water and camouflaging them with brush or by putting rocks into them and sinking them for recovery and use later on when returning from their raiding.

The stream they were approaching now was Raccoon Creek, its mouth 29 miles below Fort Pitt and four miles below Fort McIntosh. Because of its proximity to the latter fort, it was not generally considered a high-risk area, but Brady was not one to take things for granted or be careless. They moved up cautiously, listening carefully, watching closely, and those Rangers who were not paddling held their rifles at ready.

Brady eased his canoe into the mouth of the stream, prepared to ascend for a quarter-mile, as they always did with the larger tributaries, but then, after only 100 yards or so, his body suddenly tensed, and the Rangers behind knew he had spotted something. Brady pointed forward and to his right, and then they saw it, too—on the left bank there were fairly fresh scrape marks in the mud, where canoes had obviously put to shore. Studying the water as they moved in closer, Brady could see neither sunken canoes nor fresh roils of muddiness at the shoreline, meaning the marks had been made sometime before. With hand signals he directed the canoes to the same shore about ten yards below the marks, so their own roils would not be spotted by the raiding party returning to its canoes from inland—assuming, of course, that they had in fact hidden their canoes on shore here.

They had. Brady, allowing no more than the tip of the bow of his canoe to touch the shoreline, stepped out onto the harder ground and left the canoes to hold in place with gentle paddling while he made a quick inspection. Avoiding bare ground where he might leave a track, he stepped on leaf litter back to the canoe marks and saw at once where they had been lifted from the water and carried up the bank. He followed the trace for 20 yards and then discovered two canoes screened by a fallen tree and covered over with forest debris. Within five minutes he was back stepping into his canoe again.

He nodded at his Rangers, his expression grim, and pointed back toward the mouth of the creek; then he made a humping motion with that hand—the signal that they were to cross to the right bank of the Ohio, the north side in this instance. Halfway across, he spoke aloud for the first time as they continued paddling.

"Two canoes," he said. "Ten, twelve, maybe fourteen of 'em. Expect they've gone up to hit Beeler's." Beeler's Fort was a small blockhouse in the fairly new settlement established by big John and Sam Beeler some 18 miles up Raccoon Creek.[380] "I figure they came across here during the night. Probably so as to hit Beeler's about dawn. It's after noon now, so that gives us maybe two-three hours before they might show up back there. If they do, they won't stay on that side, and they won't chance going down the Ohio in broad daylight. They'll come right across and probably hole up till dark a little way up Four Mile Run. We'll hit 'em there." Four Mile Run, a much smaller tributary, emptied into the Ohio from the north about 1,000 feet below the mouth of Raccoon Creek.

When they completed their crossing and came to the mouth of Four Mile Run, they found little cover available for them. Brady directed the canoes upstream a dozen yards or more to where cover was available, and they pulled the canoes out at this point and carried them up the bank to where they could be effectively hidden. Then he had them cut bushes—mainly scrub willows—and carry them closer to the mouth of the run and impale them in the ground so as to look natural and provide blinds for them to hide behind. The moist soil this close to the river's edge would prevent the foliage from wilting for a long while and allow them to retain the natural appearance.

Then they settled down to wait—and this was the most difficult part. It might be an hour or two, perhaps five or six. For that matter, the Indians might not even return to their canoes until night or even tomorrow. There was no way of knowing. Contingency plans had to be made for any eventuality.

"If they don't come by nightfall, we'll clear out of here and head downstream. We'll have to chance they came out of Yellow Creek, so we'll lay a new ambush for 'em there. If they're not there by morning, we'll come back up here and start all over. They'll show up eventually."

Each man had a few hard biscuits and some jerky and parched corn in his pouch, so they wouldn't go hungry, at least not for a while, depending on how long it was before the Indians appeared. Even though all of them were watching closely, two of the Rangers were appointed special lookouts who could not vary their attention from the mouth of the Raccoon across the Ohio. Every hour they would be relieved of the responsibility by two others.

The first hour passed without incident, and the lookout was changed. The second hour a few of the Rangers dozed, and a few others did so during the third. It was toward the end of the fourth hour and late in the afternoon when the tedium was finally broken.

"There they are!" Jake Fouts's whisper was harsh and urgent and dispelled any sleepiness among the others. The men rolled into prone positions behind their blinds and peered through the leaves. The Indian canoes were just moving out of the mouth of Raccoon Creek and heading directly this way, paddling strongly and rapidly, obviously anxious to get across as quickly as possible since it was daylight and they could be seen for a long distance upstream and down.

As usual, no one was to fire until Capt. Brady did so, and then all the others were to fire as well, and swiftly reload to fire more, if necessary. By the time the canoes reached the midpoint of the Ohio, Brady could see there were 15 people in them, and in a few minutes more, it became obvious that three were captives, their arms tied behind them and a rawhide tug linking them together throat to throat.

Brady did not plan to shoot until they were actually entering the mouth of Four Mile Run because at the closer range there would be less likelihood of the prisoners being accidentally hit or being tomahawked by the Indians once the fight broke out. That plan went awry. They were still a good 40 yards from the mouth of the stream when one of the Indians in the lead canoe stood up and stared intently, then pointed in their direction and shouted a warning.

Brady shot at once and sent the warrior tumbling into the river, his canoe rocking dangerously. The guns of the other Rangers spoke in ragged bursts, and half a dozen other Indians were shot and fell into the water. Two or three leaped out of the canoes and began swimming off with the current, alternately diving and surfacing. The captives ducked low to avoid being shot. No return shots were fired, mainly because just endeavoring to keep from overturning and at the same time trying to paddle out of range was occupying the Indians' attention. One warrior jerked out a tomahawk and raised it to strike the nearest captive, but Fouts's second shot struck him before the blow descended and knocked him overboard. Another warrior, holding onto the gunwales, tried to stamp a hole in the bottom of the canoe with his heel so the canoe would sink and the bound captives drown, but he, too, was shot, slumped to one side and slid overboard.

Both canoes were now empty except for the captives and a couple of dead Indians. The heads of a few swimming Indians could be seen, quickly growing smaller with distance, but most of the Indians had disappeared beneath the Ohio's surface.

Brady shouted an order to get the canoes launched, and the whole party raced to them, jerked away the covering brush and quickly dragged them to the water's edge. In moments both were launched and being paddled furiously to emerge from the mouth of the run and then overtake the drifting canoes with their captives, who were now shouting for help.

The few swimming Indians had disappeared from sight by the time the drifting canoes were overtaken, but whether they had drowned or made it to shore, no one could tell. The captives were two men and a young boy, and one of the men and the boy were weeping with relief at being saved. The banks were so sheer here that there was no landing place, and so they towed the canoes back to the small bottom where the blinds were located. As this was being done, the captives told how Beeler's Fort had been struck by surprise by the party of Wyandots just after dawn and how they had themselves been captured as they headed out to the cornfield with their hoes to work. Four people at the fort, they said, were killed before everyone got inside to safety and the doors were barred. The Indians had continued firing at the fort at random for the better part of two hours and then had withdrawn with their captives and marched them to where the canoes were hidden.

As soon as they came ashore at the mouth of Four Mile Run, the bonds were cut away from the prisoners and a period of handshaking ensued by the grateful rescued. A certain amount of plunder and some of the Indian rifles were recovered from the bottoms of the canoes. While this was occurring, Brady walked over to the blinds and studied them for a moment before calling Robert Bacon over. The other Rangers stood where they were and watched.

"I expect," Brady asked the youth, "you saw how the Indians discovered us when they were still a good ways off?"

"Yep," Bacon replied, then shook his head, "but I cain't figger out how they knew."

Brady pointed. "This is your blind, right?"

"Uh-huh."

"I watched you when you made it, and you did just like the others, setting the bushes straight up. So how come they're tilted back the way they are now?"

Bacon blushed and stammered. "Well, . . . Cap . . . Cap'n Brady. It . . . it got kinda . . . kinda hot in that sun, and I . . . well . . . I reckon I sort'a . . . you know, . . . sort'a pulled 'em back t'get some shade over me."

"Come over here." Brady strode off toward the river's edge, and Bacon followed. The leader of the Rangers stopped about ten yards from the blinds and turned. "Take a look at the blinds from here, Mr. Bacon," he said.

Bacon looked, and the color drained from his cheeks. The other blinds were upright and green and appeared to be naturally growing bushes. At Bacon's blind, however, not only was the backward tilt of the bushes clearly apparent, but the angle had caused most of the leaves to fully or partially invert, showing the much paler light green of their undersides. The difference was like a magnet drawing the eye to it. Bacon's prominent Adam's apple bobbed as he swallowed.

"I . . . I'm sorry, Cap'n. I . . . I didn't think. . . ."

"That's right, Mr. Bacon," Brady said grimly, "you didn't think. And by not thinking, by considering your own comfort and committing an error like this, you jeopardized your fellow Rangers, the captives, this whole operation." He shook his head and his tone softened, but his gaze remained hard. "What we do on these patrols is no game. One mistake like that could kill us all. I'm sorry to have to tell you this, but you won't be going out with us anymore."

There were no second chances in Brady's Rangers.

[O c t o b e r   5 ,   1 7 7 9 — T u e s d a y]

William McMechen stared morosely at the blackened remains of some of the timbers of his burned-out settlement, still protruding above weeds that had taken root and almost hidden them. Twice he had built his settlement, and twice it had been burned by the Indians. The first time he had taken his family away for a year before returning and starting all over again. This time it had been 26 months since they had taken refuge at Wheeling, and the settlement had been burned again as soon as they had abandoned it. They had moved back to the Redstone Old Fort area and built a new home in adjacent Brownsville, and he had truly believed then that they would never return here again.

McMechen's first son, David, had refused to come west with him from Wilmington, Delaware, and was now studying law in Baltimore.[381] His second son, James, was seeking land of his own down the Ohio, five miles below Fish Creek.[382] His third son, William, Jr., showed no interest in living on the frontier or acquiring land and instead, when still a boy, went to live with his eldest brother.[383] And then, in '77, while they were living at Brownsville, his fourth son had been born and was named Benjamin.

With the birth of little Ben, William's old yearning had returned and grown, and though he had pushed it down, it kept coming back ever stronger. Now, viewing the remains, he suddenly spoke aloud: "By damn! This is *my* land, claimed by *my* toil, meant for me, for my son, for my son's children. I will not, *cannot,* give it up. This place was built by me and rebuilt by me, and now, please God, I will rebuild it again, and I vow I'll never again leave it. And when at last I die, *this* is where I will be buried, and my son, Benjamin, will continue in my place. I swear it!"[384]

[O c t o b e r   2 0 ,   1 7 7 9 — W e d n e s d a y]

Hezekiah Bukey—called 'Ki by his friends—considered himself very lucky. As short and slight as he was, he never really thought he'd have a chance to be accepted as one of Capt. Sam Brady's Rangers. His brother, John, had been accepted, but that was no surprise to anyone, since John was six feet tall—fully eight inches taller than Hezekiah—and very sturdily built. But for some reason Brady had taken a shine to Hezekiah and made him a Ranger, and now the two of them had become friends. On those rare occasions when they were not actively patrolling, they would go out hunting or fishing together or sometimes just simply walk together in the woods or along the Ohio River shore.

Now here he was, hunting again with Brady and very much hoping to prove his prowess with his rifle. Hezekiah knew he was a good shot, but he felt it important that Brady knew it as well. He had impressed Brady in target shooting, but stationary targets were not animals that could run and dodge, nor were they Indians who could fight back.

Half an hour ago, or perhaps a little more, he and Brady had separated to go around opposite sides of this hill, hoping that one or the other might flush a deer. If the one who flushed it missed his shot, the fleeing animal might run within range of the other. When he heard a crackling sound from behind some bushes ahead, he became quite alert and eased his way through them to where he could see into the clearing beyond. As he glimpsed the source of the sound, his heart raced. Twenty feet up a gnarled beech tree, crouched on a huge lower limb and beginning to tear at an oval-shaped hollow, was a medium-size she-bear. Honey bees were pouring out of the hole and buzzing madly about her, many of them alighting on her dense black fur. Except for occasionally brushing at her face with a paw, she paid no attention to them and only tore at the hole with greater vigor.

Grinning, Bukey stepped into the clearing and took a stance about 30 feet from the tree. As the black bear turned her head to look at him, the great mouth opened, exposing powerful teeth, and issued a sort of whining woof. Bukey brought up his flintlock and took careful aim at the center of her throat. He was just beginning to squeeze the trigger when a much deeper, gruffer growl filled the clearing. It took an instant for Bukey to realize the last sound had not come from her and, sensing danger, he whirled around.

Less than ten yards away, an enormous male black bear was facing him, a steady menacing growl rumbling from his chest. Bukey knew this was the breeding season for bears, and this one was evidently the mate of the much smaller female in the tree. The bear took a step toward him, and Bukey swung his rifle up, aimed quickly at the large animal's eye and squeezed the trigger. The big curved hammer snapped forward, and the flint struck the pan with a little burst of sparks. The powder in the gun's pan flashed with a puff of blue-white smoke, but there was no explosion.

The snap and plume of smoke angered the bear, and he quickly stood upright, his powerful forepaws spread and the great curved claws clearly visible. The rumbling in his chest turned into a roar as he turned his huge head to one side and snarled, then began to walk toward Bukey. On his hind legs like this, he towered over the little man and weighed about three times as much.

To his credit, Bukey didn't panic, knowing that if he turned and tried to run, the bear would be on him in an instant and he would have no chance. Keeping his eyes on the bear and prepared to leap to one side if he charged, the little frontiersman let the flintlock slide through his hands until the butt was on the ground. With his right hand he felt to his belt and touched the head of his tomahawk. Slowly he pulled it up so more of the shaft was exposed and accessible to his grip.

Behind him he heard the female stirring in the tree, and she made a low, whining sound. Bukey had the feeling she was descending the tree to strike him from behind, and he had a terrible urge to swivel around to see, but restrained himself from doing so. The male was the greater danger at this moment. He was now only 20 feet away and had paused, but the snarling continued and a strand of slobber drooled from one side of his mouth. The lips curled up and back, exposing the largest, most powerful-looking canines Bukey had ever seen. He felt his thigh muscles begin to shiver, and then abruptly he was trembling all over so badly, he thought he might collapse and inwardly he cursed himself for being a coward.

The bear began moving toward him again, tilting his head. Bukey left his tomahawk half-exposed in his belt, ready to grasp, and then slowly brought his right hand forward, gripped the end of the gun barrel with both hands and, just as slowly, raised the weapon upward and back until it was poised over his right shoulder. Then he suddenly spoke, the words coming softly, as if from someone else, surprising him.

"Back off, ol' bear. Back off, now. You come much closer, and you're gonna make me whomp you one over the snout, you hear?"

With unnerving unexpectedness, the female in the tree behind him squalled a horrendous sound, and everything seemed to happen at once, yet in a peculiarly slowed sense, as if time were ticking to a standstill. Bukey half turned and looked behind in time to see the female, still squalling, smack at her eye and muzzle with both front paws, lose her balance and fall with a heavy thump to the matted leaf litter at the tree's base. In that same slowness of time, she bounded to her feet and ran bawling into the woods and out of sight.

As Bukey turned back, the male roared again and lunged at him, mouth widely agape. The little man swung the gun a tremendous blow, catching the bear across the muzzle just in front of the eyes, striking so hard that the stock snapped in half at the grip. The momentum of the bear caused the animal to smash into him, bowling him over, but he was not clawed, the bear momentarily too stunned to grasp him.

For an instant the bear dropped to all fours, then came to his hind legs again, bellowing with pain as blood flowed from the nostrils. Time reverted to normal once more, and the furious animal charged. Bukey jerked his tomahawk free from his belt and raised it to strike, but just then there came the sharp crack of a rifle. A lead ball the size of an acorn smashed into the roof of the bear's open mouth and blasted into his brain. He toppled forward and fell so close to Bukey that he quickly had to pivot out of the way.

Tomahawk still clenched in hand and ready to defend himself, Bukey whirled to face the shooter, then suddenly relaxed and expelled a great gust of breath. It was Sam Brady, grinning broadly.

"You've got the strangest way of bear hunting I've ever seen, 'Ki," he said.

"How long were you there?" Bukey asked, uncomfortably remembering how severely he was trembling earlier.

"Long enough to see most of it," Brady replied, still grinning.

Bukey was suddenly ashamed of himself. "Then you seen how scared I was," he said bitterly.

Brady's grin faded and he stepped forward and put his hand on the little man's shoulder. "What I saw," he said seriously, "was one of the most courageous things I've ever seen. And I saw a man that I'd be proud to have at my side anytime in any kind of situation."

[N o v e m b e r   2 ,   1 7 7 9 — T u e s d a y]

The large delegation of Shawnees who came to attend the major congress of tribes being hosted by the Wyandots of Upper Sandusky were very morose. Just over two weeks ago, on October 15, their beloved principal chief, Chiungalla—Black Fish —had died. After lingering for 64 days in extreme, constantly increasing pain from the bullet wound that had shattered his thigh, he had at last slipped away, and a great state funeral had been held for him at the Shawnee burial ground two miles south of Chalahgawtha along a small stream.[385] The new principal chief of the Shawnees was the humorless man who had been second chief under Chiungalla over these past years, Catahecassa—known to the whites as Black Hoof. He was leader of the Shawnee delegation that had come here to Upper Sandusky and this delegation's pervasive anger at the suffering and death of Chiungalla was only a reflection of that felt throughout the tribe. They had sworn vengeance on the *Shemanese,* and this present council promised to help implement that vow.

Close to 3,000 Indians were assembled. In addition to the Wyandots themselves and the Shawnees, there were Hurons and Chippewas, Ottawas and Tawas, Tuscaroras, Delawares, Potawatomies and Miamis; representatives of the tribes whose chiefs had now gathered in the great council house in Half King's Town—the village of the aged but still powerful Wyandot chief, Monakaduto. There was a sense of the surreal in the dimness of this large structure as the blanket-wrapped chiefs, murmuring softly among themselves, sat upon woven mats on the hard-packed earthen floor, enshrouded in the haze of smoke from the council fire and the aromatic *kinnikinnick* smoldering in the bowls of their pipes.[386]

Among those closest to the council fire sat five white men. British Capt. Henry Bird, resplendent in his full dress uniform of scarlet, white and gold, sat in the center, flanked by Alexander McKee to his right and the three Girty brothers—Simon, James and George—to his left.[387]

Everyone present had heard, of course, of the spectacularly successful ambush that had been pulled off only 11 days ago on the Spaylaywitheepi against a convoy of five large supply-filled keelboats coming upriver on its way to Pittsburgh.[388] Many on hand here, in fact, including Simon Girty, had participated in that ambush. The boats had been attacked at the mouth of the Licking River by 130 warriors, 80 of whom had been Shawnees.[389] One of the keelboats carrying 17 men had managed to escape, but four were captured and 45 whites were killed, plus five taken prisoner. Just two warriors had been killed, and three slightly wounded.

The loot that had been taken was very impressive: a ton of gunpowder in kegs, two tons of lead in bars, two crates of new flintlock rifles, 40 bales of new clothing, numerous kegs of rum and boxes and bales of other goods, plus thousands of dollars in Spanish silver. The division of those supplies and gunpowder had provided the participants with a bounty they had not known for a considerable while. Now all the Indians, even those factions of the Delawares and Wyandots that had for so long been advocating peace, were eager for the war to be stepped up and carried out with vigor against the Kentuckians. It was what they had believed Capt. Bird was here for—to promise British support for just such endeavors. They were not disappointed.

"Brothers," Capt. Bird said, "I come bearing news of great moment to you. Our father across the eastern sea, King George, has become deeply concerned over how you have been treated by the Americans. He has wept over the burning of Chalahgawtha this past summer and the death of the great Shawnee chief, Black Fish, and he fears for the sanctity of your lands unless steps are taken to wipe out this threat.

"Brothers, my heart is glad that I am able to tell you now that Lieutenant General Frederick Haldimand, Governor of Canada, upon instructions from the

King, has authorized an invasion not only to crush the Kentucky forts but also to force the Virginia frontier back east of the Allegheny Mountains."

There were great cries of pleasure and war whoops as the three Girty brothers, each in a different tongue, interpreted the British officer's words. After a few moments Bird, smiling broadly, raised a hand and as the hubbub faded, he continued:

"Such invasion, brothers, will not only regain for you your traditional hunting grounds south of the river but will prevent the western growth of American colonies —states, as they choose to rebelliously call themselves—now threatening your lands." Another favorable murmuring arose at this, but he went on without pause, and it quickly faded. "My brothers, listen! My chief, Captain de Peyster, has empowered me to lead this invasion of the Kentucky lands, and it will be an invasion the like of which this country has not heretofore witnessed. My chief will provide an army made up of British regular soldiers and Tories, as well as officers from Detroit and green-coated rangers from Canada. The Kentucky forts are strong and have withstood attack before, but they will not be able to withstand *this* attack!"

The assembled Indians tensed, listening eagerly for the words they had so long waited to hear, and again Bird did not disappoint them. "We will march against them not only with tomahawk and knife and flintlock, but with *cannons* as well—the great brass thunder guns that can knock down the wall of a fort with a single shot. For *this,* brothers, they have no defense!"

Again a wave of cheers and war whoops swelled, now punctuated by cries of "When? *When?*"

"Brothers," Capt. Bird concluded, "the winter season is upon us now, and in the spring there is planting you must do so that your grain may grow for next winter's use. Therefore the invasion will not start until the corn and melons and vegetables have been planted. Until that time, my chief will continue to buy scalps and prisoners from you at Detroit. And when the time comes to go, your friends beside me, Agent McKee and Simon Girty and his brothers, will come to you with the news. We wish for every warrior who can, to come along. The day of reckoning will be at hand for the *Shemanese!*"

The piercing shrieks and war cries that filled the council house were testimony enough that when the time came for the British to call upon them, they would be very ready to participate in the invasion of Kentucky.

[December 14, 1779—Tuesday]

Henry Applegate, Jr., arrived in Pittsburgh just in time to hear some interesting and, to him, very pleasing news.[390] Capt. Samuel Brady's Rangers had the other day brought in two hostile Delawares they had captured on a short foray up the Allegheny. One of them was Mamatchtaga, who had been particularly troublesome in leading war parties. Because of his enormous beaklike nose, he had long been known to the frontier people as Big Nose. The other was a younger warrior known only by the name of Copper. Both had been tried and found guilty by a tribunal of officers at

Fort Pitt and sentenced to death by Col. Brodhead. The execution was to be held within the hour, along the bank of the Allegheny adjacent to the fort.

Applegate went to the fort at once and saw that a crowd had gathered on the high bank, well above the river level. Hardly 50 yards to the left, the Allegheny and Monongahela merged to form the Ohio. A few feet from the edge of the high bank were four men—the two condemned Indians and their two executioners. Those executioners, appointed by the court, turned out to be the Seneca half-breed Andrew Montour and the so-called "pet" Delaware, Captain Wilson. These two had been instructed by the court to simultaneously strike the condemned men a killing blow to the head with tomahawks. At an order from Montour, both of the condemned men kneeled to receive their death blow.

Both executioners raised their tomahawks. Montour counted aloud, the blows to be struck on the count of three. As he called out, "Three!" he swung his tomahawk a hefty blow and buried it to the shaft in the top of Copper's head, then jerked the blade free with an effort as the Indian fell.

Captain Wilson's eyes, however, locked with those of Mamatchtaga, and he was mesmerized by the condemned man's unflinching stare. This man, at one time, had been a close friend of Captain Wilson's uncle, Scare the World—John Thompson. A faint smile touched Mamatchtaga's lips, and even as Montour, only an arm's length away, was disengaging his tomahawk from his victim and preparing to roll his body into the river, Mamatchtaga sprang to his feet, roughly shoved Captain Wilson away from him and leaped down the steep bank to the river's edge and dove far out into the frigid current. There were shouts of dismay from the onlookers, and when Big Nose did not surface for a considerable while, some thought he had drowned himself in preference to being executed by one of his own tribesmen.

After about two minutes, however, Mamatchtaga surfaced well downstream and far out from shore. He gasped loudly and remained on the surface long enough to take a deep breath. As bullets began to strike the water near him, he dove again and remained under nearly as long as the first time. When he came up again he was beyond the point of the Forks of the Ohio and more than 100 feet from shore. The third dive carried him beyond accurate range of the gunfire, and this time he stayed on the surface and swam with great vigor toward the northern shoreline. A quarter-mile below the Forks, showing little effect from his exertions and the cold water, Mamatchtaga came ashore, made a wide, sweeping bow toward the distant crowd and then raced up the bank and disappeared from view.[391]

[*March 14, 1780—Tuesday*]

As always, the frontier people looked forward to maple sugar time. Late in the winter when the sap began to flow in the big stately maples, sugar camps sprouted up in many of the major groves, and it was a festive time, sort of a precursor to spring. This year 11 young people joined forces to turn the sugar-making into a wonderful outing; five of them young men in their late teens or early twenties, three young ladies of similar age and three younger boys who were there to learn how to tap the trees, boil the sap and render the sugar. Three of the party were of the Whittaker family, three of the Fulkes family, two of the Deavers family and three others named Lewis Tucker, Tom Dillow and John Sprott.

The sugar camp they set up was located on the southeast side of Rusdan's Run, a tributary of Raccoon Creek about a dozen miles upstream from the mouth of the latter.[392] For a week now the party had been busy at work rendering the valuable brown sugar and, in the evenings, singing songs, dancing about the fire and holding races, jumping contests or other games.

They had built a half-face shelter a dozen feet or so from the fire, and the girls usually slept under it. This evening of March 14 was particularly mild and pleasant, and when dinner and frolicking were finished, they turned in for the night. The girls and younger boys elected to roll up in their blankets between the fire and the shelter and let their older brothers have the shelter tonight, since they had been sitting watch in relays each night and sleeping in their bedrolls beside the fire. Everyone, the young men included, thought it would be nice if they had a good night's rest for a change.

This particular evening 12-year-old George Fulkes could not seem to get to sleep, and that was very unusual for him, since normally he fell asleep within a few brief minutes of turning in. Last night, however, he'd had a nightmare about Indians attacking them and, though the others had laughed it off, the ominous dream continued to plague him. So now, after all the others were asleep, he rose and took his blanket and crawled beneath a sugar trough that had been overturned to keep it clean and prevent water from collecting inside when it rained. Beneath its shelter he soon fell asleep.

An hour or so later he was awakened by screams and peered out from under the trough at a terrible scene: A party of about 20 painted Wyandots—a large Negro man in Indian garb with them—were tomahawking the young men in the shelter and capturing the others. George's older brother, John—one of those in the half-face shelter—had been struck a glancing blow from a tomahawk and was bleeding badly, but managed to scramble to his feet and start racing away. He might have escaped had he not been followed by Ginger, his little white dog. She was like a beacon for the pursuing Indians, and they quickly overtook John. This time when a tomahawk descended, he was killed.

The bodies of all five of the young men were scalped, and the camp plundered of its firearms and goods.[393] While this was occurring, George Fulkes slipped out from under the sugar trough and tried to run off, but he was spotted and quickly overtaken and brought back. Then he and the other two boys and three weeping young women were forced to carry the plunder and return with the war party to where they had hidden their canoes. By dawn, they had crossed the Ohio and were well on their way toward the upper Sandusky.[394]

[*May 24, 1780—Wednesday*]

Capt. Samuel Brady was on by far the most dangerous scouting expedition of his career and, from the very beginning, he expected he might have difficulty getting back with his scalp intact.

It had begun earlier this month when Col. Brodhead, having received a suggestion from Gen. Washington to send out a good spy to learn more about the Indians attacking the frontier, had called him in and asked if he wanted to volunteer for the perilous undertaking. Brady had not hesitated a moment and said he would go. Pleased, Brodhead told him he wanted explicit information about the Wyandots and other Indians gathered in the valley of the upper Sandusky River. That seemed to be the place of origin of many of the sorties against the upper Ohio settlements, and what Brodhead needed was more accurate information than he yet possessed on their numbers, the exact location of their villages, the best routes for getting there, how well they were supplied, the extent of their involvement with the British and how much support—both in supplies and manpower—they were getting from the Redcoats, plus anything else of interest he could discover. He had a few roughly sketched maps that he gave Brady but warned that they were probably not very good.

From the beginning Brady knew it would be foolish to undertake such a hazardous spying expedition with a large party of his Rangers. The more who went along, the greater their likelihood of detection. Actually, he thought he could probably do better all alone than with anyone else along, but Brodhead had prevailed upon him to take at least a few men and, though he hadn't put it into words, the implication was clear: If Brady were captured or killed, he wanted someone else along who might be able to get back with whatever intelligence the mission had gleaned.

Several of the men Brady wanted to take along—'Ki Bukey, Vach and Kinzie Dickerson, Tom Edgington—were not available at the time, so he selected four of his newer men who seemed to be competent and dependable. James Amberson was one, and Philip Cudger another. David Sprout, a tall, hawk-eyed individual who had done some spying on the Iroquois, seemed like a good choice, too. The final member was former Philadelphian John Williamson, a husky young man with great stamina and a good sense of humor.

They were going to travel light and fast, so they carried no large packs. Each man had a pouch with a 20-day supply of jerky and parched corn that would be their only source of food for the journey. No hunting would be permitted for fear of drawing attention to themselves. The men dressed as Indians, each with his flintlock, powderhorn, bullet pouch, tomahawk and a couple of knives.

Using Fort McIntosh as their jumping-off place, Brady set out with his party straight west along the trail to the site of the old abandoned Fort Laurens. The installation was still there, partially destroyed by fire and with most of the palings knocked down, but in better condition than he had anticipated, and there was even some indication the Indians themselves were using it for shelter and as a staging area.

Brady remembered that during the terrible winter and early spring when he was hunting for the garrison at Fort Laurens, he had encountered a well-used east-west Indian trail about a mile north of the fort, and he suspected that this was a main trail to the Sandusky towns. They headed for it and discovered that it was large and moderately well used, though Brady thought that for a principal war trail, it should have been bigger.

The first night after leaving the Fort Laurens area, they camped in a clearing a short distance from the trail. They built their small campfire, and Brady took first watch while the others prepared to roll up in their blankets for sleep. Abruptly Brady silenced them, and they stopped their activity and stood poised, listening. Again he heard what had first alerted him—a faint distant sound that wasn't quite right. Swiftly, he had his men arrange their blankets near the fire to appear as if they were asleep in them, and then they all took position some 30 yards away behind a fallen tree.

Within ten minutes they detected a motion, and Brady signaled for them to wait for his shot. Six Indians, tomahawks in hand, crept into the firelight, stealthily approaching the blankets. Just as they realized something was not correct, Brady fired, and one of the Indians fell. The other scouts fired, then burst out with a tremendous yelling. Two more Indians had fallen at the second firing, and the other three scattered and raced off into the woods, the sounds of their passage gradually dying away with distance. Brady and his party reloaded, scalped the dead Indians, gathered up their things and left. Thereafter, by Brady's order, they made cold camps at night, with no fire or scent of smoke to give them away.

As they continued traveling, Brady became convinced that there was another trail, one more direct than the route they had taken, and they would watch for it and take it on the way back—assuming they made it back. It would have been foolish in the extreme to march along openly on the trail and so, though it was more difficult to do so, Brady and his men stuck to the woods flanking it, keeping the westward-leading trail in sight but themselves hidden.

Their nighttime cold camps continued, with the men rotating in sitting guard near the sleepers. On the second night after the attack at their campfire, John Williamson was on guard while the others slept. Brady began to snore, and the sounds increased in volume until Williamson was convinced any Indian within a mile would be able to hear them.[395] He finally got up and awakened Brady and made him turn over, and the snoring ceased. Only a short time later Williamson heard the stealthy footfalls of someone approaching and instantly held his rifle at ready. In the dim light of the half-moon he caught sight of an Indian approaching, peering back and forth suspiciously. Williamson waited until the warrior was hardly 30 feet away, then raised his rifle, aimed and fired. The Indian leaped and then fell with a deep groan and died. The other scouts jumped up and, fearing this Indian was only one of a party, swiftly gathered up their things and, without even bothering to scalp the fallen foe, slipped away in the darkness. They did not stop again until about two miles away; then they listened intently for pursuit, but there was none.

Late on the fifth day out, both Phil Cudger and John Williamson came down with a sickness that rendered them feverish, weak and unable to continue. Regretfully, Brady put them in the care of Jim Amberson and sent them back, then continued west with Dave Sprout.

It hadn't taken Brady very long to discover that the maps were, in fact, practically worthless, and he discarded them early on, making notes of his own as they traveled so that more detailed maps could be drawn for Col. Brodhead after their return. Before long, the hills and forests were left behind, and they entered a high, level plain area where there were vast stretches of lush new buffalo grass and the trees were located in large isolated clusters like islands.[396] On their ninth day out, Brady and Sprout spied many more Indians than heretofore, and they had to take special care in order to avoid being seen, a matter made more difficult now that the extensive forests were behind them. Sighting so many warriors—and so many Indian women—made Brady fairly sure they must be close to the Sandusky towns, and that turned out to be correct. By that evening, they were lying in heavy cover along the upper Sandusky River and spying on a large Indian town. It turned out to be Half King's Town, the village of the Wyandot principal chief Monakaduto.[397] From their hiding place beneath a shelving rock on the side of a small hill, they watched the activities of the Indians, including several stirring horse races involving close to 30 warriors. In one of those races, each horse carried two riders, and there was great gaiety and excitement among the Indian spectators.

As night fell, Brady gave his maps and notes to Sprout and told him to stay put and continue to observe. Brady himself, clad much as the Indians were, was going to enter the town and walk about to see what he could discover. Should he not be back by dawn, Brady instructed, Sprout was to leave at once and get the intelligence and maps back to Col. Brodhead.

Well before dawn Brady returned, bubbling over with tales of what he had seen. Acting quite normally, he had strolled about the town, inspecting its defenses—practically nonexistent—and the number of people on hand. Able to understand scattered words of the Indian tongue, he deduced that there were several other villages downstream from here, including the large Delaware village of Captain Pipe —Pimoacan—close to where Tymochtee Creek enters the Sandusky River.[398]

Over the next three days, the two spies observed closely from their hiding place. At one point they had a scare when a warrior suddenly approached. They froze, huddling back into the deepest shadows beneath the ledge, ready with their weapons to burst into action if discovered. The warrior, however, veered to one side and then climbed atop the very ledge beneath which they were hiding and stood there for several minutes before going away.

During the succeeding nights, as before, Brady entered the town and moved about casually. He investigated every bit of the town and even eavesdropped on the conversation of some British traders who were there. He discovered that four miles down the Sandusky, about halfway between here and the mouth of the Tymochtee, were scattered Indian dwellings and two British trading stations about a mile apart, one known as John Leith's Store, the other Alexander McCormick's Trading Post. Several other Wyandot and Delaware villages were also along the Tymochtee up-stream from Pimoacan's Town. During this last penetration into the town, however, Brady noticed that some of the Indians eyed him with suspicion and, before they could investigate further, he slipped out of town and headed for the hiding place beneath the ledge. For a time he thought he was being followed but, though he stopped and listened, he heard nothing and continued back to join Sprout.

As soon as he got there, Brady and Sprout started their return; Brady deliber-ately followed the trail for the first two miles, then directed Sprout to follow his lead and left the trail to go into hiding in a nearby island of trees. There they paused and waited. In the first light of morning, a party of eight warriors showed up on the trail coming their way. The Indians were studying the ground and pointing at the tracks, evidently identifying the marks Brady and Sprout had left.

"Damn!" Sprout muttered. "We *are* being followed, Sam. How the hell did you know?" Brady simply shook his head and motioned Sprout to silence, then they moved off surreptitiously, walking along logs, avoiding bare ground and doing all they could to mask their trail. After three miles more they settled down to wait again, but no one showed up, and they breathed easier, knowing they had eluded the pursuit.

They continued to travel eastward, paralleling the trail they had followed coming here. But then, where a more traveled trail branched off to the southeast, they followed it and were amazed when it took them back directly and quite quickly to Goschachgunk and then to the Ohio River at the mouth of Indian Cross Creek, the place called Mingo Bottom.[399] Surprisingly, though the trip going out via old Fort Laurens had taken them nine days, the return trip took only five, even though they walked rougher terrain than if they had been on the trail. Little wonder the Indians could come from the Sandusky Towns and make their hit-and-run raids with such facility.[400]

Now Sam Brady was back at Fort Pitt and turning over his maps and notes to Col. Brodhead. The commander studied them with mounting excitement and congratulated Brady on his accomplishment. His confidence in Brady had been well founded: What this remarkable spy and scout had brought back was, he felt, the key to destroying the Wyandots and hostile Delawares and their allies. Now all Brodhead had to do was put together—and properly supply—the army that would undertake this operation.

[June 22, 1780—Thursday]

Capt. Sam Meason, having fully recovered from the severe wound he had received during the assault against Wheeling in September 1777, had been among the many who left the upper Ohio River to relocate much farther downstream. He was intent on making his fortune, though not in the acquisition of land, which was the draw for so many others. Instead, old horse thief that he was, he reverted to his former life of crime, this time deciding to set himself up as a river pirate and prey on other Ohio River travelers.

Assembling a gang of about a dozen rough characters, all of whom were as criminally inclined as he—including his own son, John, and two of his sons-in-law—Meason set up his hideout in an expansive cavern called Cave in Rock fronting on the Ohio River 100 miles up from its mouth.[401] For a while they were very successful, preying indiscriminately on whatever river travelers passed. From their lookout stations they could see boats approaching from either direction long before they reached this point. They would then get into their canoes and paddle along as if they, too, were ordinary travelers. Hailing the approaching party, they would wave as if in friendship and head toward them, as was the custom, to share whatever news either party had. Then coldly, methodically, they would kill everyone and take everything they had, including cargoes that were sometimes quite valuable.

Word eventually got around of Meason's nefarious activities, and a party of 20 men set out to kill him. Meason's spies, however, brought word of their intent and approach. The river pirate and his men, leaving behind the cave filled with many thousands of dollars' worth of plunder, took only the cash and escaped downriver by such a slender margin that those in the approaching boats sent several ineffective shots their way as they fled.

Meason then set himself up along the Mississippi between Natchez and New Orleans, at a place called the Walnut Hills; from here his cutthroat gang waylaid the trails and robbed passersby. It was not terribly long before he was apprehended at New Madrid on the west side of the Mississippi and sent to New Orleans for trial. However, it could not be legally proven that any of his crimes had been committed in the Spanish dominion, and so he was shackled and put into a boat to be taken upriver and turned over to United States authority at Kaskaskia. His guards were careless, however, and one night while they were at their shore camp, he seized the gun of the guard who had the key to his irons and killed him. The others ran off and escaped, and Meason, free once again, reassembled his old gang and began his old operations anew, now with a very high reward upon his head, dead or alive.

What the settlers and government could not do, however, his own men accomplished for them. Today a dispute arose among them about the equitable distribution of some loot that had been taken—Sam, as usual, demanding the lion's share—and deciding they could have all the money and the reward as well, his own men overpowered him and cut off his head.[402]

[July 16, 1780—Sunday]

Caleb Wells was one of the multitude of settlers on the upper Ohio River frontier who had responded in May to the militia muster call posted by the county lieutenant. Wheeling was now not only a very large settlement but had become something of a tent city as well, with the large number of men who had assembled for an expedition rendezvous here called by Col. Daniel Brodhead. Rumor had it that they would be crossing the Ohio River and marching against the Muskingum Valley Indian towns.

Now, two months after Caleb's arrival here, his 60-day enlistment period was just expiring—as were those of the majority of the men—and once again the planned expedition was being deferred. The first postponement had come only two days before the expedition was planned to begin, on May 22. The second starting date, June 4, also came and went. Then they were to go on June 24, but expected supplies had not arrived, and Col. Brodhead had once again postponed it, this time until June 28. Again the starting date was indefinitely postponed, and now they were asking the militia to reenlist for an additional two months. No one was very happy about it. Lately, talk was beginning that the expedition would probably not get into motion this year at all, and so all this time and effort would have been wasted.

Caleb Wells wasn't really as upset about all the delays as many of the men were, especially those who had crops that needed tending. New to the frontier, he had not had an opportunity to visit Wheeling before, and he was rather enjoying the experience. A very competitive man, Wells was intrigued with the stories that were being told about the Indian-fighting abilities and frontier skills of the 16-year-old named Lewis Wetzel.

Lewis Wetzel, he was told, when only 13, had been captured by the Indians after being shot in the chest and, along with his younger brother, Jacob, had been taken by his captors to the Ohio country. Yet wounded as he was, he had managed to escape, then even went back to the Indian camp and recovered his father's gun, which the Indians still had, after which he and his little brother got safely back to Wheeling.

Lewis Wetzel, Wells was told, had in that same year, while still recovering from his wound, taken part in the defense of Wheeling when it was attacked by a large force of Indians.

Lewis Wetzel, he was told, had developed to a fine art the ability of running and reloading at the same time. He had proven this ability when, the next year, he rescued Frazier and Rose Forrest by shooting one Indian and inducing another to chase him. The Indian saw Wetzel shoot and knew his gun was empty, so he pursued him, but Wetzel had reloaded while running and then calmly turned and shot his pursuer dead.

Lewis Wetzel, Wells was told, had last fall built a blind to hunt deer from along Wheeling Creek. Only a day or so later, his brother Jacob came to him and told him it appeared to have been tampered with. The two, with their guns, went to the site, and Lewis, in scouting around, found moccasin tracks of five Indians. With Jacob right behind him, Lewis had skillfully tracked the Indians for several miles and found them in the evening just setting up their camp. The boys crept up and Lewis shot one. The others started running off together and the brothers chased them, Lewis reloading as he ran, and they closed the gap enough that they were finally able to stop and shoot, killing two more. By then, the twilight was too deep for further tracking, and the boys returned home with the three scalps, Lewis lamenting that two had gotten away.

Lewis Wetzel, Caleb Wells was told, only a month ago, had been sent out in the morning by his father to cultivate the cornfield about a mile from their house. As he was doing so, a party of a dozen mounted men from farther up Wheeling Creek rode into view and approached him. Some of their horses, they said, had been stolen during the night and they wanted Lewis to join them to help track the Indians and try to recover the stolen animals.

"Paw said I shouldn't go nowhere 'til I got this here cultivatin' done," Lewis had responded. "An' my horse is down at the cabin."

"Hell, Lew," one of them replied, "you're cultivatin' with a horse, ain't ye? Use that one. I shore as hell know you k'n ride bareback."

Wetzel was sorely tempted. "That's Paw's favorite mare," he said, then added, "but, what the hell. Sure, let's go."

He unhitched the mare and, rifle in hand and tomahawk in his belt, leaped up on her back and was taken to where the trail of the stolen animals had been lost in a small creek. Lewis picked up the sign very easily and led the way. They followed the trail to the Ohio River, where the horses had been driven across. The party swam their own horses to the Ohio side and Lewis quickly picked up the trail again. By early afternoon they came to where the Indians were camped.

Thinking themselves safe with the Ohio behind them, the six Wyandots, having marauded all the previous night, had stopped early to rest and eat and had spanceled the horses so they could graze at will in a pasture a short distance away. The whites rushed the camp and easily put the Indians to flight, without their stolen horses. These were rounded up and preparations made to go back, but the mounts the whites had been riding were by now fairly jaded. It was decided to leave them hobbled here and ride the recovered horses back, leaving three men to watch over them for a half hour or so while they rested and grazed, then to bring them along.

They had traveled only a couple of miles, however, when the three who had been left behind overtook them on foot. The Indians, they said, had come back and surprised them, getting between them and the horses and they had had no recourse but to flee without the animals. The whites talked it over and decided it would be best not to push their luck and simply to go on back to the settlements.

Not Lewis Wetzel. He leaped off the recovered horse he had been riding and stood looking up at them. "My Paw's favorite mare is back there," he said, "which I took when I wasn't 'sposed to, an', by damn, I know what Paw's like when he's mad. I sure as hell ain't gonna go back and face him without that mare. I'd a sight rather git home without my scalp rather than without that mare! Let's go back and get them horses. Ain't that what we come t'do?"

The rest of the party, wary now that the Indians were alerted, refused to return, and Lewis, frustrated and angry, spoke tightly. "Then, by God, if just one o' you'll go with me t'back me up a little, we'll get them horses back."

Again they refused and turned their mounts and started toward home. Glaring after them, Lewis yelled, "God damned cowards! That's what you are, every last one o' you. I swear I'll get them horses back if I have t'do it all alone."

He started striding away, at which two of the party reluctantly dismounted, turned their horses over to the others and joined him. The rest rode on, leading the three riderless horses. Lewis grinned at the two and said, "Thanks, boys. I exclude you from that last remark I made. Now, let's go get them horses."

They went back on foot with care and, at the same Indian campsite they saw that the horses were still hobbled in the pasture. There were only three Indians in sight, squatting by the fire and eating, the other three having evidently gone on. Now, however, with the enemy in view, even though they were equal in number, what little courage Lewis's companions had shown evaporated, and they said they wanted to get out of there. It took several minutes for Lewis to convince them otherwise and to lay out a plan of attack that satisfied them.

Lewis's plan was to advance in single file, himself in front, until they passed two trees ahead of them, at which point the other two would take positions hidden behind them. A third tree, standing alone in the knee-high grasses and weeds, was much closer to the camp, and when Wetzel got there, it would be the signal for the attack to begin. Wetzel, however, was spotted by the Wyandots just an instant before he reached the tree and the Indians, too, leaped up and treed.

Lewis yelled for his companions to fire and, when they did not, looked around in time to see them just disappearing, running as fast as they could. It was now a very dangerous situation and Lewis thought fast. He made sure his rifle was primed and cocked and laid it on the ground beside him. He then put his hat on a stick and slowly eased it out from behind the tree, as if he were taking a peek. The range was short—no more than 50 yards—and all three Indians fired almost simultaneously. The hat spun off the stick and instantly Lewis lurched into view, gripping his chest, and then fell headlong into the weeds and tall grasses. Hidden by them, he scooted back on his stomach and recovered his rifle.

The Indians, believing him to be badly wounded if not dead, left their empty guns behind and burst from cover, tomahawks in hand, and raced toward where he had fallen. When they were 30 yards distant, he leaped up and shot the foremost Indian through the heart. With savage howls, the other two came on at full speed, knowing his gun was now empty.

Fleet as he was, Lewis was able to maintain the distance separating them, even though reloading while running. In a short while he was ready to fire again and abruptly stopped, wheeled and did so, killing the next Indian as he had the first. Then he turned and fled, the final Wyandot still approaching at full run and closing fast. Once again Lewis reloaded as he ran, but he had lost much of the gap separating them now and, as he turned to fire a third time, saw the Indian was so close that he was in the act of hurling the tomahawk at him. Lewis sidestepped the whizzing weapon, and shot from the hip a bullet into the middle of the warrior's forehead.

Lewis scalped the three dead Indians, gathered up their weapons and ammunition and tied them in a bundle. By this time twilight was gathering. He went out into the pasture, easily caught his father's mare and tied the bundle to her, then caught the hobbled horses and tethered them together in single file behind the mare. Removing her hobbles, he mounted and led the whole string of horses back the way they had come.

It had been dark for quite a while by the time he neared the Ohio River. He spied a campfire's glint and approached cautiously. As anticipated, it turned out to be the Wheeling settlers, who had decided to camp for the night rather than cross the Ohio in the dark. To avoid being mistaken for an Indian and shot, Wetzel called out, identifying himself and saying that he was coming in. The group's surprise was great and their awe and admiration boundless when they saw that he had recovered not only all the horses, but all the Indian weapons and their scalps to boot. If they hadn't considered Lewis Wetzel something of a wonder heretofore, they certainly did now, and the story of his incredible feat was still making the rounds on the frontier.

So, with all these stories being told of the amazing abilities of this remarkable 16-year-old, Caleb Wells was more than just a little jealous of Wetzel's fame. Wells, at 21, was a big man—six feet four inches in height and 215 pounds.[403] He was very muscular, a good runner, fighter and shooter—who had also long been practicing the skill of reloading as he ran. He considered himself more than a match for the young Wetzel and today he was going to prove it.

One of the more enjoyable recreations observed by the settlers at Wheeling, usually on a Sunday afternoon following services, was a competition of frontier skills. Because of the planned Muskingum expedition, the competition had at first been canceled, but now, with the expedition deferred and the assembled men very restive, it had been decided to go ahead with the event. Today's affair would be especially interesting, not only because there were a great many more men here than usual, both to participate and spectate, but because Lewis Wetzel was going to join in. Unfortunately, however, some of the more skilled men would be absent from this day's event—men such as Samuel Brady, Thomas Edgington, John and Abram Cuppy, Samuel and John McCulloch, John and Hezekiah Bukey and the Dickerson brothers, Vachel and Kinzie, all of whom were presently off on one of Brady's patrols.

The various competitions were simple yet demanding, involving speed, skill, dexterity, marksmanship and physical endurance. In each event, contestants would gradually be eliminated until only two remained, and those two would then compete on a one-to-one basis to see whose skills would prevail.

One of the highly popular events was tomahawk-throwing at different distances, both while standing still and in full run, with a series of marked barrels as targets. Knife-throwing at a number of posts planted upright in the ground to a height of six feet was yet another event, again both at a standstill and while running. Leaping was a popular and demanding event; first over two barrels beside one another, then over three with the third placed atop the other two, then over five, with three on the bottom and two on the top.

In the final event a barrel would be placed on its side, and the contestant would start off to one side with an empty gun, run about 100 yards, loading as he did so, and, as he reached a point opposite the end of the barrel some 50 yards distant, quickly wheel about and fire. The judges would then examine the barrelhead to see if the ball had struck truly and, if so, determine its nearness to the center, where there was a circle about the diameter of a walnut.

The prizes were not large—normally a quart of rum for the winner of each event and a gallon of rum to the individual judged best in all events. Of course, a certain amount of cash betting went on between individuals who had specific favorites.

Hour after hour the competition progressed and finally there were only two contestants left—Lewis Wetzel and Caleb Wells. The crowd was wild with excitement as the last round of trials began. Wetzel won the tomahawk-throw by a fair margin; Wells won the knife-throw by an even greater margin. In the barrel-jumping, Wells cleared five and so did Wetzel, so this time an unprecedented sixth was added atop the two elevated barrels. Wells couldn't clear it in three attempts and knocked the barrels—and himself—into a jumble each time. Wetzel knocked them over the first time, but on the second attempt he launched himself through the air in an upward dive, cleared the top barrel just barely and struck the ground on the other side with a rolling somersault amid the excited cheers of the onlookers.

The last test was now at hand. Two barrels were laid on end ten feet apart, 50 yards from the starting line and 50 yards apart. The two men were to begin running, loading their weapons as they did so, Wetzel firing at the first barrelhead as he passed the nearest point, Wells at the second. They were then to continue running, circle a post 50 yards farther distant and return, reloading as they ran and firing at the same barrels. At the finish line they were to turn and repeat the whole process; 400 yards and four shots. It was a test of speed, reloading ability and accuracy. A gunshot started them off, and they ran side by side, reloading, for the first 40 yards; then Wetzel took the lead by a yard or so. As he wheeled and fired at the first barrel, Wells passed him by. As Wells wheeled and fired at the second, Wetzel passed him by, and they rounded the post at the end with Wetzel having a two-yard lead. On the second pass, Wells couldn't get his gun reloaded in time and passed without shooting, but Wetzel got his shot off. On the third pass, Wetzel's foot caught on a root just before reaching the barrels and he tumbled, his gun flying and losing its prime. Wells passed him by and made his shot. Wetzel scooped up his gun and followed, not having taken his shot. The exertions were taking their toll and Wells began to flag a bit. They reached and rounded the far post with Wetzel at his heels, and they passed the barrels, wheeling and firing at almost a dead heat. At the finish line, Wetzel was fully three yards in the lead. There were wild cheers, but the winner was not yet pronounced; the barrelheads had to be checked. At the first barrel, Wetzel had placed two balls close to the center, no more than an inch apart, and a third hole was a hand's breadth away. At the Wells barrel, one bullet hole was midway between the center of the barrelhead and the rim. Another had nicked the rim. One had evidently missed.

The two contestants shook hands and then Wetzel grinned and said, "You're good. Real good. I'm better."

[J u l y   2 4 ,   1 7 8 0 — M o n d a y]

That settlers would continue to penetrate into the wilderness and establish themselves and their families there in spite of the continued Indian attacks was incredible, yet so strong was their drive to possess land that they considered the risk worthwhile. For their rashness, many paid the ultimate price.

This had been especially true of late in the valley of the Kanawha and its tributaries, where the Shawnees were ranging in a number of small- to medium-size raiding parties. Ten days ago in the Greenbrier Valley, experienced frontiersman Hugh McIver had been ambushed near his cabin and killed and his wife captured. Not far away the next day, July 15, the same or another war party spied veteran frontiersman John Pryor crossing the Kanawha River with his wife and little daughter. The Indians attacked as the boat came ashore, shooting Pryor through the chest and taking his family prisoner. Pryor, though severely wounded, managed to get away and reach the settlement, but he died that night.[404]

The next day another party of some 30 Shawnees hit three cabins about a mile upstream from the Little Levels Settlement. Creeping up unseen, they unexpectedly plunged into the three cabins simultaneously. In the first cabin they killed and scalped Thomas Drennon and captured his wife and two of their children, but his 14-year-old son, Andrew, managed to escape and ran toward the Little Levels Settlement for help. In an adjoining cabin the Indians killed Jacob Smith and took his wife and children captive. Outside the third cabin they killed Henry Baker, but his partner, Richard Hill, though wounded, managed to get inside the cabin and bar the door. Quickly plundering the two open cabins, the Indians took what they wanted and then departed with their captives. They had only gone a half-mile when they encountered Capt. Samuel McClung and his wife, along with her elderly father, William Munday, coming their way. The Indians opened fire. Munday was killed, but McClung and his wife, both slightly wounded, managed to escape into the forest.

Andrew Drennon returned from Little Levels with a party of 20 men and found the Indians gone with their prisoners and the cabins plundered. They treated Hill's wound as best they could and buried the dead. It was too late in the day and too dangerous to follow so large a Shawnee party, so they barricaded themselves in the cabins overnight. At dawn they started their return to Little Levels. Two brothers in their early twenties—John and Henry Bridges—decided to take a shortcut on a less-used trail. They were ambushed and both were tomahawked and scalped.

The following day, several miles farther down the Greenbrier, the isolated cabin of William Griffith was struck, Griffith and his daughter, Beth, were killed, and his wife, Elizabeth, and son, James, were taken captive.

The main Shawnee party broke up then and dispersed in smaller groups, most of them heading back toward the Ohio country. The trail of one of these parties was discovered by four whites who were hunting on the Kanawha. William Arbuckle, John Young, Robert Aaron and Benjamin Morris took up the trail at once, followed it across the Elk River and then upstream on that tributary to the mouth of Little Sandy Creek. Here the trail went up the west bank of the creek to an unnamed tributary entering from the west. Bob Aaron promptly named the stream Aarons Fork, after himself. This fork soon branched and they followed the raiders to near the headwaters, where they found them camped.[405] There were only two men and a boy, and they believed the latter to be a captive. They crept up close and fired on the camp, killing one of the men. The other leaped off into the dark woods and escaped. The dead man turned out to be a white renegade in Indian garb, though none knew who he was, and the boy was James Griffith, who said his mother had been taken by another group of the Indians.[406] The party named the smaller branch after the dead renegade, calling it White Man's Branch.

Yet amazingly, despite continuing attacks such as these, ever more whites were pushing into the frontier areas and making their claims, all of them believing they would be the lucky ones who would avoid detection and death.

[*August 28, 1780—Monday*]

By this time, most of the militia that had been mustered into service at Wheeling and the other forts in preparation for Col. Daniel Brodhead's proposed expedition against the Wyandots and hostile Delawares on the Muskingum and Tuscarawas rivers had been discharged, their enlistments or terms of call-up having expired.

Brodhead was angry and blamed the delays on lack of supplies, yet there were those who knew the problem ran deeper than this. Resentment was growing among Brodhead's subordinate officers for their commander in respect to rumors that had been circulating widely. Brodhead was known to be dabbling increasingly in land speculation—taking leave of his duties for extended periods to go out and explore and claim lands for himself or hiring others to do this for him. Brodhead was not a wealthy man and certain people began to question not only the propriety of the commander of the Western Department of the Continental Army doing this while he was in active service, but, equally, where he was getting the funds to hire others to do the same thing for him. Was it possible that he was appropriating funds earmarked for the procurement of supplies and that this was the reason not enough provisions had arrived? If so, was this not malfeasance, and should not charges be brought against him?

Furthermore Col. Brodhead was, in his own way, a man rather unsure of himself, who frequently blamed his subordinates for his own mistakes and who, under the protection of his rank, all too often treated his officers with contempt and rudeness virtually to the point of intolerable insult. More than once irate officers had to be restrained by their fellows from physically attacking him or challenging him to a duel.

The problem had reached such proportions that Col. John Gibson, second in command at Fort Pitt, forwarded the written complaints of other officers and himself to the War Office and requested that some sort of steps be taken to alleviate the situation. It was now clear that this problem would not soon be resolved—not soon enough, at any rate, for the Muskingum expedition to be put into operation before next spring. Therefore, no longer under the necessity of keeping themselves instantly available for such service, Capt. Samuel Brady increased and extended the number of patrols he and his Rangers were making—patrols that carried them down the Ohio as far as Grave Creek and up the Allegheny as far as Brady's Bend.

Eleven days ago—on August 17—just after Tom Edgington had moved his family from their Chartier's Creek claim to a new domicile at Holliday's Cove, another resident of the settlement, Hugh Ebbens, had arrived at Fort McIntosh, breathless from concerted paddling and bringing disturbing news. He had been out fishing along the Virginia shore of the river when, opposite the mouth of Little Beaver Creek, 14 miles downstream from Fort McIntosh, he discovered evidence of a canoe and another craft of some sort having landed. He had gone ashore himself to investigate and found, at the base of the hill and covered over with brush, an Indian canoe and a fairly substantial log raft, the latter so large that it would have taken a dozen or more strong men to carry it that far from the water's edge to hide it.

Brady immediately called his Rangers together and, in three canoes, they set off toward the site. Though Ebbens was very frightened and reluctant to go back, Brady finally managed to talk him into leaving his canoe at the fort and going along with them as their guide to show them where he had made his discovery.

The canoe and raft were still there and Brady agreed that there must be at least 20 Indians in the party. He immediately led his party to the north side of the Ohio and set up an ambush, with the usual instructions that they would strike when the Indians were close to the north bank, but no one was to shoot until Brady's gun was fired. The ambush was set up about 100 yards downstream from where the Indians would launch themselves, Brady figuring the raft would lose that much distance with the push of the current as they crossed. After several hours of waiting, the Indians appeared, laden with plunder from their raid, launched their canoe and raft and started across.

There were seven Indians—Wyandots and Mingoes, Brady reckoned—in the canoe, another 15 aboard the raft. His estimate of where they would come ashore on the north bank was quickly proving to be accurate; they would obviously make landfall about 30 yards from where the whites were hidden. Ahead of the raft by some 80 yards, the canoe had come within 100 feet of the shore when the faltering nerve of Hugh Ebbens broke. He burst from cover and ran off in the direction of Fort McIntosh as fast as he could go.

The Indians saw him, of course, and shrieked a warning. The rafters, well out of effective range, immediately began energetically paddling with their chunks of bark back toward the Virginia shore. The warriors in the canoe also tried to get away, but Brady yelled, "Fire!" and a barrage of shooting broke out. All seven of the Indians aboard were killed.

Some scattered shots were fired at the retreating rafters, but they made it back to the south shore without any being hit. Taking their weapons but leaving their plunder on the clumsy craft, they leaped away and raced into the woods—all except for one rather heavy individual who turned his back to them, bent over and defiantly slapped his behind in their direction.

"Look at that red sumbitch!" snarled Able Rankin, one of Brady's newer Rangers. He raised his gun and fired well over the warrior's head just as he was straightening. The ball caught him in the center of the back, breaking his spine, and he died instantly.

The canoe, riddled with holes, was half filled with water and drifting away with the current. All of its former occupants had sunk. Brady and his men got their own canoes out of hiding and crossed the river to the raft. Rankin collected the scalp, tomahawk, knife and gun of the Indian he had killed on shore, while Brady studied the loot and recognized enough of it to know that it had come from the small settlement a short distance up Montour's Run, some six miles below Fort Pitt. He told his men they would return it to its rightful owners—assuming they were still alive.[407]

Now, 11 days later, Brady and his Rangers, along with the old Delaware, Scare the World—who still refused to answer to the name of John Thompson—were 69 miles above Fort Pitt on the Allegheny, staring down at the bodies of the four Senecas they had just killed at Brady's Bend. Several days ago, learning that a small band of warriors had killed a few settlers and taken some prisoners on the opposite side of the Allegheny from Fort Pitt, Brady, still headquartered at Fort McIntosh, had quickly assembled a dozen of his men, including a new probationary Ranger, Pvt. Eldon Andrews of the Eighth Pennsylvania. Andrews had asked to be included on a trial basis but Brady at first refused, simply because he didn't care much for the young man. Andrews had then begged him to be allowed to come along, and when Brady started to shake his head in negation, Andrews abruptly charged that he was excluding him simply because he was a little lame from an old wound. Not even realizing before this that the young man did in fact walk with a slight limp, Brady relented and let him come along on a probationary basis, warning that he must keep up with the rest or he was out. Taking John Cuppy aside to avoid being overheard, he asked him to bring up the rear to keep an eye on the new man and give him a hand if he had any trouble.

The Rangers had then gone upriver, picked up the trail opposite Fort Pitt and followed the raiders up the Allegheny. Moving at a mile-eating pace, they were about halfway to Brady's Bend when they finally spotted the enemy—eight Indians with four prisoners—moving slowly up a steep hill some 200 yards ahead.

Keeping to cover, Brady ordered his men into quick march in order to overtake and engage them, but while the Rangers were still considerably out of range, John Cuppy saw Andrews deliberately fire his rifle into the air, then toss it to the ground. The Rangers up ahead instantly treed, thinking they had been decoyed and fallen into an ambush, but Andrews called out that it was all right, saying he had stumbled and fallen and his gun had gone off. While the others emerged, he brushed himself off, then stooped and picked up his weapon. By the time Brady was able to get a clear look ahead of them again, the Indians and their captives had vanished.

Andrews apologized profusely, ending up with, "I guess accidents will happen."

"Wa'nt no accident," Cuppy spoke up, eyeing the young man disgustedly. He turned his gaze to Brady. "You got yourself a coward here, Cap'n. This boy got skeered we was ackshully gonna get shot at. I seen 'zackly what happened." He then explained what he had seen.

A wicked fire came to life in Brady's eyes and he bunched the front of the young man's blouse in his fist and pulled him close. "You realize," he said tightly, "I could justifiably shoot you right here and now?"

Andrews, turning his head to avoid meeting Brady's steely gaze, mumbled, "I'm sorry, Captain Brady. It won't happen again."

"Damn right, it won't!" Brady thrust the private away from him. "Get the hell out of here and back to McIntosh. I won't tolerate a coward!"

Andrews stumbled away back along the trail they had come and was soon out of sight.[408] Putting that business aside, Brady put his Rangers into movement again and they resumed their trailing. Within two miles the trail ended at the shore of the Allegheny.

"They've crossed," Brady said. "Taking the trail on the east side so they can look back every now and then and see if we're crossing after them. They'll be moving fast as they can. C'mon, we'll keep to cover on this side and try to get ahead of them up at the Bend."

Again they moved swiftly, and by early the next evening, they had reached Brady's Bend. The Indian party had evidently just arrived there, too. On the flat at the river's inside curve nearly opposite them, they could see the Indians just starting to set up camp. Instructing his men to stay out of sight and telling Scare the World to come with him, Brady set out for a low, grassy-topped knoll directly opposite the warriors. On the way he explained to Scare the World what he wanted him to do.

When they reached the summit of the knoll, Scare the World hailed the warriors on the opposite side with a loud "Halloo," and both he and Brady waved their arms in greeting. Slightly over 800 feet distant, the Indians called back, their voices faint but clear enough in the still evening air.

"That one voice," Scare the World said, "I know it. That is Warhoytonehteh."

"Cornplanter himself, eh?" Brady replied. "Okay, tell him what I told you to say."

In the Seneca tongue, Scare the World called across, "Are you going down after the Americans or coming back?"

"Coming back," came the reply. "What about you?"

"Coming back, too. We are a small party and we have one prisoner. We are going to burn him. Do you have any?"

"Four. Two we are going to burn tonight."

Scare the World looked at Brady, who nodded, and the Delaware hollered back, "We also have a keg of whiskey. But we have made camp already. Come over and bring your prisoners, and we will drink the whiskey and burn the prisoners together."

"No, we are making camp, too. If you will not drink the whiskey tonight but bring it over in the morning, we can drink it then and burn the whites."

"That is good," Scare the World shouted. "We will save the whiskey for you to share and we will come over with the sun tomorrow."

Their waves were returned and Brady and Scare the World moved out of sight behind the summit. When they returned to the Rangers, Brady carefully laid out the plan. They would immediately move downriver a few miles to the easy crossing place called Goose Bar, then come up the other side in darkness and hit the Indian encampment.

The plan worked beautifully. Only minutes before dawn they were creeping in close to the camp. The four captives were tied to trees and appeared to be asleep. Six of the eight Indians were sleeping close to the fire. One was sitting upright among them, and the final one was standing guard a short distance away. At the bark of Brady's rifle, the standing guard fell. The others by the fire leaped up and, without pausing to snatch up their guns, scrambled to get away, but three more were killed before the darkness could engulf them. The one who had been sitting by the fire turned out to be Warhoytonehteh, who grabbed a broad, flat chunk of wood, raced to the river's edge close by and plunged in with it.

Brady and his Rangers bolted into sight and ran to the river's edge. In the dim gray light of first dawn, they could make out Warhoytonehteh swimming outward and away with the current, clutching the big chunk of wood. The moment they started firing at him, Warhoytonehteh positioned the wood against the back of his head and neck and held it there with one hand while he swam with the other. Several more balls struck the water close to him and at least two thunked into the wood but did him no harm. In a little while he was out of range, at which point he discarded the wood and swam with powerful strokes to the opposite side of the river. Now, with the piteously grateful prisoners released from their bonds and armed with the guns of the Senecas, Brady and his men were staring down at the bodies of the four warriors they had just killed.[409]

"Well, boys," Brady said, "get those scalps, and let's start moving back. I reckon these folks," he tilted his head toward the freed captives, "are anxious to get home."

[O c t o b e r   1 0 ,   1 7 8 0 — T u e s d a y]

In the two and a half years that he had been a captive, Martin Wetzel, now 23 years old, had come to know the Shawnees quite well, but he had never wholly adapted to their ways, and they had never wholly learned to trust him. Perhaps this was because it was always in his mind to escape and, though he did not make it obvious, somehow they seemed to sense it and they were always watchful of him and ready to pursue if he tried to get away. The fact that prisoners who attempted escape were, if recaptured, almost invariably condemned to death at the stake was a considerable deterrent. If he were going to make the effort, he would have to be convinced he stood reasonably good odds of getting away with it. Such an opportunity had not yet come along.

He had almost attempted escape earlier this year when the majority of the warriors from Chalahgawtha, including the warrior who had captured him, Skootekitehi, had gone away with the British Capt. Henry Bird and his Canadians and regulars, along with Simon Girty and others, to attack the Kentucky settlements. But those who remained were even more watchful of him than before, and when the warriors returned after going up the Licking River and capturing and destroying Ruddell's Station and Martin's Station, he was still there.[410] They had killed about 20 whites on their invasion and brought back about 450 prisoners, several of whom were burned at the stake. It was a horrible lingering death, and Martin Wetzel's hopes of escaping receded even more.

His hopes had risen when, in August, word was brought by Simon Girty and Red Snake that George Rogers Clark was advancing against Chalahgawtha with an army of Kentuckians. Martin thought the Shawnees would stand and fight but, instead, the principal chief, Catahecassa—Black Hoof—had ordered the village evacuated and burned and had retreated first to Piqua Town on the Mad River, a dozen miles to the north of Chalahgawtha.[411]

When Clark arrived at Chalahgawtha and found it burning, he continued his advance against Piqua Town. Once again the majority of the population evacuated—taking their prisoners with them—to the Shawnee villages of Mackachack and Wapatomica, much farther up the Mad River, leaving behind only a few warriors to stand and discourage Clark. The little Battle of Piqua Town resulted before the few defending warriors withdrew. Clark's army plundered the town and burned it, destroyed the crops there and at Chalahgawtha, then withdrew back to Kentucky.

Now the Shawnees had returned to the destroyed Chalahgawtha village site, Skootekitehi bringing his adopted brother, Martin Wetzel, with them, and were rebuilding the village. But a new resolve had rooted itself in Martin's mind. Somehow, some way, he was going to escape and make his way across the Ohio River to Kentucky and then back to Wheeling Creek, where he belonged.

[*D e c e m b e r   3 1 ,   1 7 8 0 — S u n d a y*]

The year 1780 was ending with the situation along the entire length of the Ohio River little changed insofar as Indian raids against the whites were concerned. Every settler lived with the disturbing knowledge that at any given moment he and his entire family might be wiped out by an unexpected attack, as had happened to so many over this past year.

The Indians themselves, especially the Shawnees, who were most exposed to attack from whites along the Ohio River, were hardly less unnerved. Most of those who had moved to the upper Mad River Shawnee towns to escape the advance of George Rogers Clark's army of Kentuckians had now moved back to the Chalahgawtha site and had rebuilt the council house and many of the residence wegiwas, but the village was only a weak reflection of what it had once been, and the majority of the Chalahgawtha Shawnees—including the principal chief, Catahecassa—knew in their hearts that it would never regain its former strength and beauty.

On the upper Ohio River, many white settlers were now reconsidering their decision to oppose the British in the Revolution. It was apparent to them that the American authorities in the east gave little thought to, and had precious little concern for, the settlers on the western frontier and the terrible attacks that were being launched against them with such undeterred frequency. Some were even beginning to mutter remarks that if George Washington and other officials did not start paying some attention to the western settlers very soon, by supporting them with supplies and protecting them with federal troops, then they just might notify the British that they were divorcing themselves from the American cause and reaffirming their British loyalty. That turn of events might already have transpired but for the fact that it was questionable whether the British government, if successful, would permit the settlers to claim more Ohio Valley lands, or even retain the lands they had already claimed.

Col. Brodhead, at Fort Pitt, was aware of the prevailing sentiment and knew it was directly traceable to his own inability to mount the long-planned expedition against the Indians on the Muskingum or even a far more dangerous campaign against the Scioto towns, now that he had detailed reports and maps as a result of Capt. Samuel Brady's expedition. As he wrote to Gen. Washington:

I learn more and more about the disaffection of many of the inhabitants on this side of the mountains. The King of Britain's health is often drunk in companies; & I believe those wish to see the Regular Troops moved from this department, & a favorable opportunity to submit to the British government.

Big Sam Beeler—Col. Beeler, as he called himself, since he was in charge of the small fortification called Beeler's Fort that he and his brother John had built up Raccoon Creek—was one of those many settlers who were becoming very discouraged, and he was preparing to do something about it. The strike by the war party of Wyandots at his settlement a year ago, when four of the residents were killed and three others captured—and fortunately rescued by Sam Brady and his Rangers at the mouth of Raccoon Creek—had demoralized everyone, but that hadn't been the end of it. There had also been numerous smaller attacks since then and the nerves of the inhabitants were drawn so tight as to be near the breaking point.

On August 2 a couple of the resident volunteers, Alexander Wright and Timothy Shane, were walking patrol through the woods about a half-mile from Beeler's Fort when they heard some shots and cautiously made their way in that direction. They separated somewhat and Wright, hearing some noise ahead, peered carefully through the bushes. He saw an Indian just raising his gun to put the finishing shot into one of the settlement's large hogs that had gotten free of its sty. As the warrior fired at the hog, Wright fired at him, and then, suspecting other Indians were nearby, shouted "Head for the fort, Tim!" and raced away through the woods.

Though not in sight of each other as they fled, the two men emerged from the woods and angled toward one another. Shane thought the Indian had shot at Wright and was relieved to discover his companion was not wounded. The two reached Beeler's Fort about the same time and gave the alarm that Indians were about. Precautions were immediately taken, but when Wright related what had happened, Sam Beeler and others in the fort ridiculed the story that he had shot at the Indian, since Wright was not a man noted for his bravery. The next day, however, a party of men went out with Shane and Wright guiding them, and where the shooting had occurred they found the carcass of the dead hog. More important, there was also a trail of blood, which they followed. Within a half-mile they found the Indian; Wright's bullet had struck him high in the stomach, just below the rib cage. He had gone as far as he could, then sat down with his back against the roots of a storm-toppled tree, facing his own backtrail and holding his rifle, ready to shoot anyone who might follow. That was how he had died, and he was stiff and cold when they found him.

Not so very far away, only a few days later, on August 6, John Slover was captured while hunting snapping turtles on Montour's Run, and nothing had been heard of him since. A lot of people feared he was dead.

Despite such continuing attacks, settlers kept coming, and some, braver—or perhaps more stupid—than most, built their cabins in areas so exposed to danger as to virtually invite disaster. One of these was Adam House, who had originally come to Wheeling early in the year and by late summer had decided he did not like to be that near so many other people, so he set off to establish his own claim in isolation. With the land he chose, he had little to fear that many—or *any*—would soon follow to settle near him. He crossed the Ohio River at Wheeling and, on the Ohio side, went up Indian Wheeling Creek about two miles, where he claimed his land and built his cabin, thereby acquiring the dubious honor of being the first American settler to sink his roots in the Ohio country.

The danger of setting foot across the Ohio was extreme, as three men who had recently settled near the mouth of Buffalo Creek quickly learned. The three—August Perrin, Lucas Schemerhorn and Jacob Frankler—fancied themselves great hunters and, despite being warned not to attempt hunting on the other side of the Ohio, they had gone over anyway. They went upstream in their canoe a couple of miles above the mouth of Buffalo to Indian Cross Creek, then up that stream five or six miles. It was late in the day by the time they got there so they made their camp for the night and Frankler, a tall, gangly man, wishing to expose himself to the least risk in case of attack, insisted on sleeping between Schemerhorn and Perrin, both of whom laughed at his fears.

During the night Frankler turned onto his back and, his feet toward the camp-fire and too warm, brought his legs up so his knees projected above the sleepers. That was a mistake. Hardly had he done so when three marauding Indians fired simulta-neously at the slumbering men from the darkness. Two balls passed through Frankler's projecting legs and a third struck Perrin low in his side and lodged near his spine. Schemerhorn, unhurt, leaped up and plunged into the dark woods without his gun.

Frankler was weeping from the pain in his legs, one of which had been broken, and Perrin lay gasping with the pain of his more serious wound. At length, when the Indians did not approach immediately, evidently making sure it was safe to do so, Frankler shouted toward the darkness.

"Dammit," he cried, "you done it to us! C'mon in, you red bastards, an' put us out of our misery with your tomahawks!"

The Indians did so.

While this was occurring, Jacob Schemerhorn, watching from hiding in the woods nearby, slipped away, managed to get back to their canoe and paddled frenziedly back to Wheeling, where once again the alarm was raised.

Prices for travelers in Wheeling and elsewhere on the upper Ohio frontier were very high for goods and accommodations and undoubtedly would have been even higher had not the county commissioners set maximum rates that could be charged by keepers of ordinaries: ten dollars for dinner, six dollars for breakfast or supper, or stabling a horse with hay for 24 hours, and even three dollars for ordinary pasturage for a day. Half a pint of whiskey was six dollars—eight dollars if sugared—and a quart of strong beer was four dollars. About the cheapest thing was a night's lodging with clean sheets for three dollars. Fresh meat was very expensive, and for this reason most of the frontier people, whether travelers, newcomers or old-time residents, did their own hunting. That was what exposed many, such as the Schemerhorn party, to such extreme dangers. The travelers and newcomers were lucky if they survived such outings. The old-time residents had learned to be very cautious at all times and to take nothing for granted.

Ezekiel Caldwell was one of those old-timers who had been on this frontier for many years. He had settled at Wheeling not long after the settlement was established by Ebenezer Zane, and had served on Dunmore's campaign six years ago. Just recently, with three other Wheeling men, he went down the Ohio on a hunt and they had very good luck, filling their canoe with skins, furs and meat in just a few days. Then they began paddling back toward Wheeling.

They were still many hours below the settlement with sunset near at hand and so decided they would make camp on the Ohio side, kill a turkey, roast it for their meal and then resume their journey in the morning. They watched the ground closely as they hunted for the turkey and were relieved when they discovered no fresh sign of Indians in the area. Had there been, they would have departed at once. Caldwell quickly brought down a nice gobbler with an excellent shot, and the big bird was taken back to their camp where it was cleaned and cooked. Then, even though there was still some lingering daylight, Caldwell took the first stint as guard while the other three rolled up in their blankets by the fire and were soon sound asleep.

The woods were not yet fully dark when Caldwell, half dozing with his back against a tree, came suddenly alert at the not-too-distant howl of a wolf. Virtually in response to the cry of the wolf came the gobbling of a turkey from the other direction. A newcomer to the frontier might have taken the sounds for granted, but

Caldwell's alertness immediately changed to alarm. One by one, first putting his hand over the mouth of each so they would make no sound, he awakened his companions and told them that while he was busy at the fire, they should leave their blankets where they were and slip away in the darkness, returning to the canoe.

Caldwell, drawing the attention of any watchers to himself, stretched and yawned loudly, then started singing as he stirred up the fire and added fresh wood. Then, with the others gone, he sauntered off toward the darkness, fumbling with the front of his pants as if he were going to relieve himself. As soon as he was away from the firelight, he broke into a run and quickly got back to the canoe, which was afloat and waiting with the other three in it. He shoved the canoe out and leaped into the stern. They had reached the middle of the Ohio before the Indians realized they had been duped. A few harmless shots were sent their way but none even came close, and Caldwell's party, laughing with contempt and relief, continued paddling in the middle of the stream until arriving safely back at Wheeling. As before, Wheeling was put on alert and the fear of the inhabitants remained at a high level for days. And, in the midst of this fear, an order came from Col. Brodhead that was devastating to them.

Still attempting to do something in respect to his long-planned, often-deferred expedition against the Indians on the Muskingum, Brodhead wrote to the commander of Fort Henry at Wheeling, Capt. John Clarke:

> *Headquarters, Pittsburgh, October 13th, 1780*
>
> *Dear Sir: As the intended expedition is put off for want of provisions to subsist the troops, and provisions cannot be collected but by parties of men employed for that purpose, you will immediately evacuate (unless relieved by a party of militia) Fort Henry, bringing from thence to Fort McIntosh all public stores, likewise those from Holliday's Cove and its garrison. When you reach Fort McIntosh you will leave the command of Capt. Biggs, two sergeants, two corporals and thirty private soldiers, the most unfit for active service, and march the residue without loss of time to this place. I have written to Col. Shepherd to send some militia to those lower posts, and expect he will act accordingly.*
>
> *Assure the inhabitants of every possible protection, and desire them to be on their guard until the expedition can be executed, and then they will have nothing to fear.*
>
> *I am, &c.,*   *D.B.*

Brodhead then immediately wrote to the county lieutenant of Ohio County, Col. David Shepherd:

> *Dear Sir: Finding that the fairest proposals to the people and the faith of the public will not procure a sufficient quantity of provisions to enable me to secure the inhabitants by acting offensively against the savages, I have determined to take provisions agreeable to recent instructions, and in order to facilitate the business have called for the garrisons of Fort Henry and Holliday's Cove. I do not mean to detain those garrisons longer than they have executed the business they are to be sent upon, and in the meantime you will please to order a captain and about twenty-five militia,*

including a subaltern, two sergeants and 15 rank and file to Holliday's Cove. Let them be supplied as the regulars were, and they shall be paid by the public.

I have received discouraging accounts from Cols. Beeler and McClerry, but all those will not deter me from doing everything I can for the good inhabitants.

I am, &c.,   *D.B.*

Directed,
Col. David Shepherd, Ohio County, Va.

At Fort Pitt, Col. Brodhead remained painfully aware of the marauders moving about so freely and with such deadly aims among the settlements but, despite what he was trying to do, his lack of suitable supplies—and lack of cooperation from his subordinate officers while charges were pending against him—rendered him powerless to do much about them.

Brodhead's fears that the worst was yet to come were bolstered by continued intelligence he was receiving from the Moravians, primarily from the Reverends Zeisberger and Heckewelder, but also from the converted Delawares themselves. Killbuck, the Delaware who had imparted so much accurate intelligence in the past, had just smuggled a letter to him in which he warned that new war belts with tomahawks worked into the design had been sent out by British agents from Detroit and were circulating among the tribes; that two forts of the Kentuckians had been captured and burned, and that more than 340 of the prisoners taken had been transported to Detroit and, imprisoned there, were being harshly questioned while awaiting shipment to Montreal; that at Sandusky a party of 60 warriors and half a dozen parties of ten warriors each had gone to watch the roads and trails and were prepared to kill all travelers, including Moravian Delawares, who they now were convinced were spying for the Americans. Should they not find enough people along these routes, the parties were planning to cross the Ohio and strike at the settlements themselves.

Brodhead had immediately written a circular letter directed to Col. David Shepherd, to be passed along to the other county lieutenants, in which he enclosed the letter that had been brought by the Delaware runners. As Brodhead told him:

I have got it translated into our language, and enclose you a copy for perusal.

The contents, if true, in our present circumstances, are alarming, and I must therefore request you will immediately upon receipt hereof, cause the whole three-fourths of the men in your country to be equipped with arms and accoutrements and as much provision as will last them 15 days, and be in readiness to march at an hour's warning; but this additional number need not furnish horses to ride, as they are intended to act defensively.

The messengers added that a party of twenty Munceys and Delawares were discovered about six days ago near the new Moravian town on their march toward our settlements, which it is expected will cross the river near to the old Mingo towns; and that they have heard that the Seneca Indians intended to come in a large body down the Allegheny to attack our settlements. . . .

Advise the inhabitants to be unanimous and I will undertake to give a good account of the enemy. The former orders tending to offensive operations we are not to lose sight of. For should the enemy fail of coming in force against us, I will, if possible, visit them.

I have the honor to be, &c. . . .

Still, despite his preparations and juggling of troops, the same problems persisted for Brodhead and caused the long-pending expedition to be further deferred. As if laughing in the face of such helplessness and frustration, Simon Girty appeared, leading a large body of Indians. They crossed the Ohio in a fleet of small canoes a mile above the mouth of Indian Short Creek, five miles below the mouth of Buffalo Creek, and began moving overland to the northeast.[412] Within a few miles they came to the cabin of Zachariah Sprigg, where they surprised him and his guest, John Stevenson, and Sprigg's slave, George. The three sprinted away and were instantly pursued. Sprigg escaped and fled to Ramsey's Fort on the Buffalo, three miles distant, but both Stevenson and George were captured. Within a short time of his capture, however, the black man escaped and he, too, fled to Ramsey's.

Prior to that event, an Indian sachem, who was not along on the trip, had spoken of a bad dream he had experienced, in which two of three men the Indians attacked had escaped and shortly returned with a powerful white force that engaged the Indians and defeated them with much loss of life. Now that the two had escaped, Girty's Indians took this as an omen and decided that before the prophesied white force could fall on them, the attack should be aborted. Nothing Girty said could make them believe otherwise and so the whole Indian force recrossed the Ohio and disappeared.[413]

Thankful for the fate that had intervened and prevented what could have been a great disaster for the settlements on the upper Ohio, Col. Brodhead now wisely decided that the season was simply too far advanced toward winter for the proposed Muskingum expedition to be put into motion. It occurred to him, however, that a brief hit-and-run expedition against the Munceys and Senecas up the Allegheny would, with its success, bolster the flagging faith in him not only among the settlers but among his own subordinates. With this in mind he ordered Col. Archibald Lochry up the Allegheny with 350 men to hit those Indians at their principal village near the site of old Fort LeBoeuf on French Creek.

Lochry's force reached French Creek without problem, but by the time they reached the Sugar Creek tributary of that stream, their provisions were depleted. Worse yet, spies Lochry had sent out returned with news that the village they were marching against was deserted, and evidence showed it had been abandoned many weeks before. Lochry immediately turned his whole force around and headed back to Fort Pitt. The weather turned bad, with heavy snows and freezing temperatures, and Lochry was forced to employ 70 of his men as hunters on the return trip. Those hunters provided enough meat for them to survive, but everyone suffered severely from frostbite and general exposure. The LeBoeuf Expedition, instead of becoming a feather in Brodhead's cap, was a complete bust and further undermined what little faith in him remained among the settlers.

With the year now rapidly dwindling to a close, Col. Samuel Beeler, greatly discouraged, decided on a desperate measure to get the help needed on this upper

Ohio River frontier. Accompanied by Joseph Tomlinson of Grave Creek Flats and William Ryerson of Ryerson's Station on the headwaters of Wheeling Creek, he had struck out in the midst of terrible early December weather for Philadelphia. Though battered and almost deranged by the elements, the three had managed to reach the City of Brotherly Love and detailed to the chief officers of Pennsylvania the deplorable conditions and increasing hazards facing the Ohio River settlers.

Moved by what they heard, those officers promised to furnish the aid that was requested. Whether they would truly come through with it—or even if they did, whether it would reach the people in time—remained yet to be seen.

Chapter 5

Martin Wetzel peered through the screen of bushes at the cluster of cabins and the small fort a few hundred yards ahead, and he knew that what he was about to do was extremely dangerous, especially in view of what had happened here last night. It would be grimly ironic, he thought, to have come this far with his plan, only to have his brains blown out by some individual who thought with his trigger finger instead of his head. Yet, considering what he had gone through in the past several days, he really had little choice but to go ahead with it.

He wondered what Skootekitehi's reaction would be when he finally put together the pieces and realized what his adopted brother had done. In a way, he felt sorry for the pain it would cause him. More than once Skootekitehi had protected him from other members of the tribe at no little risk to himself, and now Martin had betrayed him.

The whole matter had its beginning when the war party was put together at Chalahgawtha in December. Skootekitehi had planned to go and to take Martin along this time, but then, just before they were to leave, Skootekitehi was incapacitated with influenza, as were so many others of the tribe. The ill warrior, feverish though he was, placed Martin in the care of his wife's brother, Cholutha, and told them to go ahead as planned, without him. Having been with the tribe for more than two and a half years by this time, Wetzel spoke the Shawnee tongue fluently, so there would be no problem in communication.

The war party included close to 100 warriors and had been formed as much to get horses from the Kentucky settlements as it was to strike whomever they could. Wetzel had been under the impression that he would be crossing the Ohio River with them and planned that somewhere along the way he would find an opportunity to escape back to the whites. His disappointment was keen when, as they neared the Ohio River, he discovered he was not to be allowed to cross.

The large party had made its camp a few miles north of the big river and here they had broken into half a dozen or more smaller parties that were to cross the river and then spread out to strike at various settlements. A fair-size segment of the main party was to remain on the Ohio side and Cholutha, with Wetzel in tow, was assigned to that segment. Their task would be to hunt and bring in meat for the warriors who would be returning from Kentucky and bringing across the horses they had taken. Those warriors would then be fed and get some rest before being resupplied to go back across the river for more raiding. In the meanwhile another contingent of the party to which Wetzel was attached would herd the captured horses in relays to Chalahgawtha.

The hunting party to which Wetzel was attached consisted of four men including Cholutha and himself, plus a burly warrior named Kwitateh—Otter—and a younger warrior named Niewe Kilechi—Four Fingers—who walked with a slight limp from a bullet wound suffered several years ago. Each was armed with a flintlock rifle and a small amount of ammunition, as well as their tomahawks and skinning knives. They were to do their hunting somewhat to the north and east of the camp, along the waters of a tributary of the Little Miami.[414]

Knowing that, as always, he was being carefully watched, Wetzel at first performed entirely as was expected of him. Though permitted to go off by himself and hunt alone, he knew that the others were not far distant and it would be foolhardy to merely attempt to run off. His three companions were all good trackers and there was every likelihood that if he did so, they would quickly track him down, at which point they would have the right to kill him on the spot or return him to Chalahgawtha for death at the stake.

On the first day of their hunt, he managed to bring down a deer about a half-mile from their camp and carried his quarry back there. He was the first to return and he gutted and hung the deer, then gathered new wood for the fire and performed other camp duties, certain he was being watched all the while. The others came into camp one at a time over the next hour. Niewe Kilechi had been unsuccessful, but Kwitateh had bagged a turkey and Cholutha, like Wetzel, brought in a deer. Martin cleaned and cooked the turkey for their dinner, after which, sitting about the fire, each in turn related his day's activities.

By the end of the first week of their hunt, Wetzel was aware that the attitude of the others toward him had become more relaxed and he no longer felt he was under such close scrutiny as previously. He decided that he was now ready to initiate his escape plan. The next morning when they separated to hunt, Wetzel went his own way at first but then circled around quickly and began to follow Kwitateh, keeping a close watch on the big, barrel-chested hunter, while at the same time remaining out of sight and making sure that neither of the other two hunters were nearby.

Toward midday Kwitateh became more alert and crept up behind the roots of an overturned tree, from which he peered out at something ahead. As Wetzel moved in closer, he could see that what had taken the warrior's attention was a little group of seven or eight buffalo approaching from the other side of a prairie. Wetzel was now no more than 30 yards away and, as Kwitateh slowly raised his rifle and took aim, Martin brought his own gun up and sent a ball into the back of Kwitateh's skull.

The buffalo ran off together at a tangent and, after waiting a few minutes to make sure he was unobserved, Wetzel moved to the fallen tree, scalped Kwitateh and then shoved his body into the deepest part of the root hole and covered both him and his gun with dead leaves. He then covered that with branches and brush. Satisfied, he shook the scalp free of blood and stuffed it into his pouch, then hastened back to the camp, killing a raccoon on the way. As previously, he was first to return and he cleaned the animal, gathered wood, built the fire and was roasting the raccoon when Cholutha returned, having bagged nothing, and then, about half an hour later, Niewe Kilechi showed up with a yearling doe.

Twilight was gathering by the time the raccoon was fully cooked and Martin frowned. "I wonder what is keeping Kwitateh?" he asked.

Cholutha shrugged. "Maybe," he said, "he went out farther looking for a new hunting place."

"Or," added Niewe Kilechi, "he may be trailing an animal he wounded and it has gotten too late for him to get back here. We'll see him tomorrow. Let's eat."

They ate, then rolled up in their blankets before the fire and Cholutha and Niewe Kilechi went to sleep. Wetzel, however, remained awake and argued with himself over whether it would be better to try to kill the other two now or wait till the morrow and kill them one by one. He finally decided there was too much risk involved in trying to kill both at once and elected to follow the latter plan. Then he went to sleep.

In the morning Cholutha said that this day's hunt or the next should be enough and they would use the deer skins to make bundles to carry the meat back to the main camp. The three then separated to hunt and, as before, Wetzel circled and got behind Niewe Kilechi. After following him until midday, he suddenly called to the warrior and approached him as if he had just come across him by accident. The two discussed their morning's hunt and when Niewe Kilechi, completely off guard, turned to look at something, Wetzel jerked out his tomahawk and buried it in the young man's head, killing him. After taking the scalp, he dragged the body to a nearby sycamore that was hollow at its base and stuffed it inside, along with the gun, then pushed in branches and brush to hide it.

Returning to camp he waited for the return of Cholutha. Toward late afternoon he showed up carrying another deer over his shoulders and Wetzel hurried toward him as if to aid him by taking the burden from him. Cholutha bent over to let Martin get a grip on the animal and while he was in this position, Wetzel swung his tomahawk a violent blow and killed him. Relaxing now, he scalped Cholutha, taking some of the meat and whatever else he wanted from the camp and simply walked away, leaving the body where it had fallen.

He headed directly south toward the Ohio River and was just approaching it when he encountered a small raiding party of seven warriors from the main body, heading out for their second foray across the river to take horses and perhaps capture a settler from whom they could perhaps glean some important information about the present defenses of the Kentucky settlements. Familiar with him, they were not suspicious, and when he told them he had gotten lost and had been separated from his companions for two days, they told him he should come along with them. They went to where their canoes were hidden at a creek mouth and crossed the river, pulling their craft well up on the shore and covering them with brush before striking out southward.

Yesterday they had reached the vicinity of Strode's Station just a few miles southwest of the ruins of Ruddell's and Martin's stations. They carefully spied on the place from hiding during the day and that night, well after dark, moved in stealthily toward the horse corral. As they did so, Wetzel separated himself from the others in the darkness and then loped away to the south and west toward where the warriors had told him Boonesboro was located.

After a mile he slowed to a walk and continued walking for another hour or so before stopping to rest and nap. He had awakened with the sunrise this morning, inwardly exulting at having escaped his captivity, and continued in the direction he had been headed, gnawing at some of the meat he had brought along. He was now keenly aware that, clad as an Indian and with streaks of paint on his face, he was likely to be shot by any white who saw him before he had a chance to identify himself. He stopped at the next little stream he encountered. It was coated with a thin skin of ice but he broke through it easily with his tomahawk and washed away all the war paint. That still left him, however, clad in Indian garb. He considered discarding it and continuing naked, which was probably safest, but it was simply too cold for that.

A short time later he had reached the spot where he was now, peering at the cluster of buildings and the small, sturdy fortification of a settlement that he took to be Boonesboro. He could see at least two sentinels making their rounds and wondered if he would be able to make it in without being shot. At this stage of the game, there was nothing to do but try.

Setting his rifle aside and stepping boldly from his hiding place, he strode toward the station and began repeating loudly as he walked, "Don't shoot! I'm a white man! Don't shoot!"

Either they did not understand him or they believed it to be a ruse. In any case, the sentries shouted a warning and within moments armed men were appearing all over. Still, they hadn't shot and Wetzel was beginning to lose the apprehension that filled him, when, as he came within about 50 yards of the place, one of the sentries aimed at him and squeezed the trigger. There was a snap and a puff of smoke but no report; the firing, fortunately for Wetzel, had been a flash in the pan.

Wetzel immediately threw himself to the ground and bawled out even louder, "For God's sake, don't shoot! I'm white. I've just escaped from the Shawnees."

There was a confusing babble of voices and then half a dozen men began approaching carefully, their guns at ready and their gaze not only taking in the man on the ground but carefully studying the heavier cover now well behind him, more than half convinced that a large party of Indians lay in ambush somewhere out there. When it became apparent that such was not the case, they pulled him rather ungently to his feet and led him to the settlement. That was when Wetzel discovered that this was not Boonesboro but, rather, Bryan's Station, a dozen miles north of Boonesboro.[415]

Although he identified himself as Martin Wetzel and related details of his captivity, which had lasted two years and nine months, and even showed them the three scalps he had taken in effecting his escape, they did not believe him. They accused him of being a renegade spy and threatened to kill him. Part of the reason they did not believe him was because he told them that the war party he had accompanied came from Chalahgawtha, but many of the men at Bryan's Station had been on Clark's expedition last August and had found Chalahgawtha abandoned and burning when they arrived.

Wetzel had never met Daniel Boone but knew of him and asked that he be summoned to hear his story and judge for himself the truth of it. They agreed that, since Boone had himself been held captive by the Shawnees at Chalahgawtha and escaped from them, this would be a good idea and they sent a rider off to Boonesboro immediately. Slightly less than four hours later, Daniel Boone returned with the messenger and several other men. Once again Wetzel told the story of his captivity. He added, as well, that the Shawnees had rebuilt Chalahgawtha and, aided by the British, were planning to commence another major assault against the Kentucky settlements next spring.

"Well, boys," Boone said, when Wetzel finished his relation, "I don't find anything at all improbable 'bout what he says. There ain't no doubt in my mind that he's who he says he is and that things've happened the way he's told 'em. Better let 'im go."

"Still think we ort'a kill 'im," one of the settlers grumbled.

"Would you've wanted to kill me when I got away from 'em?" Boone asked reasonably. "If you're gonna kill white captives who escape from the Injens, that sure ain't gonna be much encouragement for others t'try t'get away."

Martin Wetzel was released. Impressed by Boone and the beautiful rolling hills and vast meadows of this area, and hoping to have a chance to also meet Simon Kenton, of whom he had heard a great deal, Wetzel decided he'd stay in Kentucky and serve as a scout and spy for a while before heading back to Wheeling Creek.

[A p r i l   2 0 ,   1 7 8 1 — F r i d a y]

Gov. Thomas Jefferson of Virginia sat back in his chair and gazed dejectedly at the piles of correspondence and reports stacked on his desk, material he had spent all morning and much of the afternoon going over, bringing himself up to date in matters of the war and especially the situation on the frontier in respect to the Indians. He sighed and rubbed his eyes, feeling decades older than his 38 years.

The situation in Kentucky was particularly bad, he knew, and even though the settlements there were no longer so precariously perched on the brink of extinction as they had been in recent years, yet if the planned invasion by British-supported Indians were the success the enemy anticipated, the seeming permanency of the settlements could quickly be undermined.

One factor in the Americans' favor, of course, was the large number of emigrants still streaming down the Ohio and settling along its shores all the way from

The Principal Kentucky Settlements

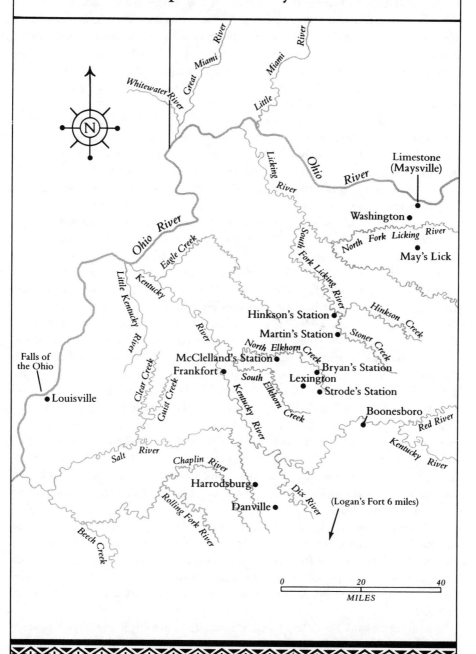

Fort Pitt down to the Falls and even lower. On the surface, things looked very good in these remote areas. Interior Kentucky, for example, now had a respectable population and many of the settlements were actually becoming real villages. Several of the older settlements, in fact, such as Harrodsburg, Danville, Lexington and Stanford—which is what Ben Logan's old fort called St. Asaph's was being called these days—had substantial populations. The initial log cabins were gradually giving way to new and better and certainly more graceful structures, including brick buildings with fine colonnades. Regular stores were being opened as well as a variety of other businesses: livery stables, blacksmiths, general merchandise establishments, marketplaces, barber shops and others. Schools were being opened and good teachers were now making their way to these distant places. And in Harrodsburg, whose population now exceeded 2,500, plans were already under way to erect a fine, large, stately courthouse, the first of any real character in that great western land.

Despite all such growth and development, Thomas Jefferson was painfully aware that numbers alone were not sufficient to provide security for the Kentucky inhabitants. They, as well as the upper Ohio settlements, needed strong backup—troops, munitions, supplies, provisions—to fend off the marauding bands of warriors constantly making incursions against them. With more massive invasions being planned by the enemy, those fragile stems of American growth sprouting in the entire Ohio River Valley could all too easily be uprooted beyond the point of recovery.

One of the bright spots in this grim prospect was embodied in the frame of the tough frontier officer who had so adroitly taken the Illinois country from British control and had recently and effectively marched his militia army against the Shawnees in their very heartland in Ohio—George Rogers Clark. Now Clark was preparing a major offensive against the northwestern tribes that was planned to be as devastating against them as Maj. Gen. John Sullivan's had been against the Iroquois in 1779. This new force was being readied under his command at the recommendation of Gen. Washington, with the states expected to pay their fair share of the cost. To that end, the Virginia Executive Council in January had issued a warrant to him for £400,000, on account. In addition, an order had been sent by that body for Capt. Quick of the Virginia War Office to immediately send to Fort Pitt, for use by Clark's officers, a total of 100 well-made grenadier swords. At the same time Clark was promoted to brigadier general over "the forces to be embodied on an expedition westward of the Ohio" and was named commander-in-chief of the Western Department of the Army of Virginia. A potential problem with all this was that, although George Washington was aware of all that was going on, he had neglected to mention any of it to Congress.

George Rogers Clark was to temporarily use Fort Pitt as a staging point, where the supplies, provisions, ammunition and some of the troops for his proposed expedition would be stored. The fact that this was a great irritation to Col. Brodhead and the residents of the upper Ohio, who had been crying for just such support for many months, could not be helped. There was not enough for all. Clark, at the moment, had priority.

Moving toward Fort Pitt, Clark stopped temporarily at the Youghiogheny, where he discovered to his dismay that much of what he expected the Continental

Congress to provide in supplies and munitions—especially respecting artillery—was not on hand. He had immediately written to Congress in something of a pique:

Yough, April 2d 1781

Gentm:

I make no doubt but that you are fully acquainted with the design of the enterprise I am ordered on to the North West, the success of which greatly depends on the stores ordered by his Excellency, Genl. Washington, to be furnished at Pittsburgh. On examination, it's found that many articles are wanting that cannot be done without, as per the indent of Capt. Craig, who commands the artillery on the campaign. As you must know, the sentiments of the Commander-in-Chief respecting those furnitures, and confident from the nature of the enterprise, you would wish to give it every aid, I flatter myself the Captain will meet with no difficulty in procuring such articles as he may want to complete him. The Captain's company at present is very weak. I would take the liberty to solicit a reinforcement to it; also nine or ten artillery artificers, and a tin plate worker. These favors I shall endeavor to acknowledge by doing all the service in my power to my country, and beg leave to subscribe myself; gentm.,

Your most obedt servt.,
G. R. Clark
Commander-in-Chief, Western Department
Virginia[416]

That the Northwest expedition being shaped up by Clark was sorely needed became clear to Gov. Jefferson as the weather warmed in spring and new droves of would-be settlers swarmed down the Ohio. There was a great and frightening increase of attacks by the Indians, especially the Shawnees, upon such boats, and the Ohio's ominous sobriquet—that dark and bloody river—had never been more accurate.

The blow dealt to the Shawnees by Clark's militia army last August had demoralized the tribe for a time, and the subsequent Indian attacks during the fall and winter had diminished. With the rebuilding and reoccupation of Chalahgawtha, however, the Shawnees seemed to have regained their confidence and now far more —and far more brutal—attacks were occurring than ever before.

It had become wise for river travelers to remain as close as possible to the Kentucky shore. Travelers in boats coming down along the Ohio side or even in the swift middle current of the river were apt to find themselves targets of Shawnee snipers who rarely showed themselves but were content with methodically picking off individuals in the boats as they floated past. And there were also times now when the seemingly peaceful river would come alive with a dozen or two warrior-filled canoes erupting from little coves or creek mouths to attack individual boats or even flotillas of craft traveling together for mutual security. More often than not there were no survivors.

Matters were little better in the interior of Kentucky and the temperament there was not improved by the fact that the Congress was calling for men to be drafted from the frontier to serve as Continental soldiers in the east. As Col. John Floyd, writing from Louisville in Jefferson County, informed Jefferson in his letter:

> *You require the Act of Assembly for recruiting this State's quota of troops to serve in the Continental Army, to be carried into execution here, but for the reasons before mentioned it must be postponed. And when your excellency is informed of the true situation of this county, I am persuaded you will think the law ought not to have extended to it. We are all obliged to live in forts in this county, and notwithstanding all the caution that we use, forty-seven of the inhabitants have been killed and taken by the savages, besides a number wounded, since the first of January last. Amongst the slain is Major William Lyn [Linn]. Whole families are destroyed without regard to age or sex. Infants are torn from their mothers' arms, and their brains dashed out against trees, as they are necessarily moving from one fort to another for safety or convenience. Not a week passes, and some weeks scarcely a day, without some of our distressed inhabitants feeling the fatal effect of the infernal rage & fury of these execrable blood-hounds. Our garrisons are dispersed over an extensive County and a large proportion of the inhabitants are helpless, indigent widows and orphans who have lost their husbands and fathers by savage hands, and left among strangers without the most common necessaries of life. Of those who have escaped, many have lost all their stocks, and some have not any land of their own, nor withal to purchase. Our dependence to support our families is upon getting wild meat, & this procured with great difficulty and danger, & should it fall to the lot of some in this County, who are thus situated, to serve as regular soldiers according to law, their families must inevitably starve.*

[A p r i l   2 7 ,   1 7 8 1 — F r i d a y]

Lewis Wetzel watched the last of the large squadron of boats beginning to disappear around the bend a mile above the Wheeling Landing and grinned, despite the pain throbbing in his swollen hands. His first participation in a regular military campaign was ended and he decided he never wanted to be part of another; if there was Indian fighting to be done, he preferred doing it on his own.

He still wasn't entirely sure what prompted him to volunteer as a militia private under Col. Daniel Brodhead for the Coshocton Campaign unless it was the possibility of simply being able to enter Ohio country and kill Indians with relative impunity. The experience had definitely cured him of any further inclination to volunteer for military service.

He and William Boggs, 17, had happened to be in Wheeling earlier this month when the notices were posted that Col. Brodhead was on his way from Fort Pitt to Fort Henry with a force of regulars. Volunteers, the notice said, were needed to accompany the force on its march to destroy the towns of the hostile Indians on the

Muskingum and Tuscarawas. At the same time, residents in surrounding areas were again urged to go to the nearest fort for safety, since word had been received that ever more parties of Wyandots were in the process of setting out from the Muskingum towns to strike the smaller settlements.

With so many men to be away on Brodhead's campaign, settlers feared they would become even more vulnerable to attack, either in their own cabins or en route from one place to another. This situation was relieved in part by the arrival at Beeler's Fort of a company of 53 volunteers—six-months men, as they were called—under Capt. Jeremiah Long. These men, for the next six months, would be parceled out to help guard the various settlements and also to guide and protect those people who had to travel. It helped, but there were still areas exposed to great danger.

Only a few days ago one of those war parties from the Muskingum, under a subchief named Mouse Knife, had struck a few miles above Wheeling, where they killed and scalped an old man and a child. That had occurred virtually on the heels of the attack everyone was now familiar with that had taken place at John Vanmetre's cabin on Stott's Run, a little tributary of Buffalo Creek.[417]

The raiding party of six Wyandots had crossed the Ohio at Short Creek, slipping out of the mouth of Indian Short Creek in their canoes and only minutes later, after crossing the Ohio, hiding their light boats only a distance up the Short Creek on the Virginia side, then striking out overland to the northeast. John Vanmetre was in Wheeling when the marauding party approached his cabin. His two daughters, Mary and Hannah, both in their early twenties, were at the nearby spring washing clothes. The sun bonnets they were wearing restricted their peripheral vision and made them wholly unaware of the Indians coming up behind them. They were simultaneously struck down by tomahawk blows and scalped. Mary was killed instantly. Hannah, though similarly tomahawked, scalped, and left for dead, regained consciousness and managed to crawl beneath the shelter of a large log.

John Vanmetre's wife, Martha, hearing a slight noise outside and thinking it was her husband returning, opened the door and was instantly shot dead on the threshold. Their three sons—Isaac, 12, Abraham, 10, and Johnny, 6, were inside the cabin and the two older boys immediately leaped out through a small window in the rear and raced away, heading toward the not-far-distant Ramsey's Fort. They were chased for a little while but managed to elude their pursuers. Johnny, who was too small to reach up to the window and pull himself through, was captured and taken away at once. The attackers immediately returned to Short Creek and crossed the river back into the Ohio country.[418] An hour or so later a party of whites from Ramsey's Fort, led by Andrew Fouts, reached the site and found Hannah unconscious but still alive. Half the whites stayed behind to bury the dead, while the others carried Hannah back to Ramsey's Fort on a makeshift litter. She did not regain consciousness and died that night.

With an opportunity at hand to avenge such border attacks, Lewis Wetzel and Billy Boggs had impulsively volunteered for a period of militia service not to exceed two months. They became part of the force of 134 volunteers under Col. David Shepherd who joined Brodhead's army when it arrived. That army, now swelled to 300 strong and—to Wetzel's disgust—guided by Brodhead's "pet" Indians, Andrew Montour and Captain Wilson, along with three friendly Delawares, crossed the Ohio the day after its arrival and took up a rapid march overland toward the principal Delaware village of Goschachgunk—called Coshocton by the whites—at the Forks of the Muskingum.

Brodhead's army met no resistance on their way and saw no Indians. They arrived at Goschachgunk just after sunset on April 19, completely surprising the 56 hostile Delaware inhabitants—31 of them warriors—in their lodges. A number of others were in a scattering of lodges across the Muskingum, on its west bank, but they escaped.[419] A brief, hot fight broke out but, with odds of about ten to one against the warriors, they had little chance. The warriors lost 15 of their number killed in the first few minutes of the fighting, and the remaining 16, along with 24 old men, women and children, surrendered. Not one soldier in Brodhead's force was wounded and his only loss was one packhorse killed.

At the commander's order, Goschachgunk was first plundered and then put to the torch. As the village burned, 40 head of cattle belonging to the Indians were killed and similarly a very large number of domestic chickens, ducks and geese. Col. Brodhead then directed the troops to hold a council of war to determine what should be done with the prisoners. It was decided that the 24 noncombatants would be marched back to Fort Pitt and held prisoner there for possible trade later on for white prisoners among the Indians. However, the 16 warriors who had surrendered were marched under heavy guard a short distance south of their camp and methodically executed and scalped, Lewis Wetzel and Billy Boggs participating in this grisly affair with great satisfaction.

The next morning an Indian called from across the Muskingum, asking for the big chief of the whites. Using Montour as interpreter, Brodhead asked what he wanted. The warrior called back saying they wanted peace and that Chief White Eyes would come over alone and talk if assured he would not be killed. Brodhead gave the promise and the warrior disappeared. Moments later old Chief White Eyes came into view, stepped into a canoe and began paddling across. The current of the Muskingum, swiftened by recent rains, swept him downstream farther than anticipated and he came ashore around a small bend several hundred yards below. As he beached the canoe and stepped out, then turned to walk to the white commander who was now out of sight behind trees and underbrush, Lewis Wetzel leaped from hiding and sank his tomahawk in the old chief's skull, killing him instantly.

Brodhead was irked by the incident but was unable to discover who had committed the murder. Putting the matter behind him, he set his army in motion and marched up the east fork of the Muskingum—the Tuscarawas River. In four miles they came to the Delaware town called Indayochee.[420] It was abandoned and Brodhead's advance force reported to the commander that a hostile they captured there had told them that 40 warriors had been in the village the previous night. They had been drinking heavily in celebration of the successful raids from which they had just returned with a number of Virginia captives and scalps but, upon learning of the surprise attack and victory of the whites at Goschachgunk, they had crossed the Tuscarawas with their prisoners and trophies.

Brodhead immediately ordered a detachment to cross the river and follow, but the heavy rains farther upstream had so swollen the river that a crossing without boats was deemed impracticable and the detachment was recalled. Indayochee was looted and burned and here, too, large numbers of poultry were destroyed.

The army then moved upstream another seven miles and camped, Brodhead deciding he would attempt to procure boats from the Moravian Indians at Salem, which some were calling Newcomerstown, or Gnadenhütten in order to transport his troops across the Tuscarawas in pursuit of the Indians who had fled, possibly up to Schoenbrun, but more likely toward the Sandusky Towns.[421] However, when Brodhead announced this plan to his troops, the volunteers were adamantly opposed, considered it nothing short of suicidal and said they were ready to head for home.

The army marched on to the Moravian village of Salem. By now the militiamen had concluded that all these Moravian villages were launching sites for many of the raids against the Virginia frontier and that they ought to destroy them and their inhabitants. Cols. Brodhead and Shepherd, however, quickly overruled such a notion and ordered that no one should in any way attempt to harm them.

There were 30 Moravian Indians on hand when they arrived at the Salem mission, and they treated the army very cordially, generously providing the men with a sufficient supply of cured meat and corn to sustain them until they reached the Ohio River again. Chief Killbuck presented himself to Brodhead, and they shook hands warmly. This was the converted Delaware who had so often in the past sent intelligence to the Americans about the activities of the hostiles.

Killbuck told Brodhead that he and another Delaware convert of Salem, Captain Luzern, having been informed of the attack on Goschachgunk and the flight of the hostile Delawares from Indayochee, had immediately pursued the latter and managed to overtake and kill a subchief named Kopechi, who had been prominent in leading many of the recent raids against the Virginia settlers. Killbuck presented Kopechi's scalp to Col. Brodhead as proof of his feat and of his continued support of the Americans. He asked and received permission to return to Fort Pitt with the army. However, noting the hard looks Killbuck was getting from many of the militia, who considered him a treacherous man, Brodhead—remembering how White Eyes had been slain—placed a protective guard of his regulars around him.

At both Newcomerstown and Gnadenhütten, Brodhead conferred with the Moravian missionaries and their converts. "I strongly advise you people," he told them, "and this goes for those upstream at Schoenbrun, to leave this valley. You are in a dangerous position between two fires and you would be very wise, for your own safety, to break up these settlements and return with us to Fort Pitt."

The offer was appreciated but declined, the missionaries stating that no matter where they were nor in what circumstances, God would protect them as faithful members of His flock. Brodhead simply shrugged and resumed the homeward march.

Yesterday—April 26—the army reached Fort Henry at Wheeling, jubilant at their own successful return. The plunder that had been taken at Goschachgunk and Indayochee was auctioned and brought in £80. The militia was discharged, the regulars bivouacked, and then, for their own protection, Brodhead ordered that Killbuck and the Indian prisoners be placed in the guardhouse for the night.

Lewis Wetzel and Billy Boggs watched closely and then put their heads together. Fifteen-year-old Jacob Wetzel joined them. Lewis declared that he had been watch-

ing Killbuck closely ever since the Indian had joined them at Newcomerstown and
had become convinced Killbuck was one of the party of Indians who had shot him
and then captured him and Jacob four years ago. He proposed that they kill him.
Boggs, who had also been a captive of the Indians some years ago, thought it a great
idea. Jacob, however, objected, pointing out that the Indians who had captured Lewis
and himself had been Wyandots and Killbuck was a Delaware, but this reasoning was
wasted on his older brother.

Late in the evening, when the militia guard opened the guardhouse door to
carry in food, Lew Wetzel and Billy Boggs slipped inside behind him, tomahawks
concealed under their hunting shirts. Lewis quickly located Killbuck, who was sharing a room with his namesake nephew, Young Killbuck. The two lads walked in and,
before the Delawares were even aware they were in any danger, Lewis buried his
tomahawk to its shaft in Killbuck's skull. Young Killbuck, convinced he was to share
the same fate, began crooning the ululating tones of the death song and bent his head
down to receive the death blow. Lewis, however, was unable to free his tomahawk
from Killbuck's skull and, after a few moments of trying to pull it free, left it embedded and both he and Billy ran out.

It was about nine P.M. when Col. Brodhead was presented with the murder
weapon and informed of what had occurred. He was furious and immediately made
extensive inquiries but no one could—or would—identify the tomahawk's owner
and, though several people admitted Lewis Wetzel was the most likely candidate to
have committed such an act, no one came forth as an actual witness. Nevertheless,
Brodhead sent out a squad of soldiers to bring Wetzel to him for questioning.

From midnight until about two o'clock this morning, the 17-year-old Wetzel
was questioned but denied any involvement in the matter. From two A.M. until dawn,
the questioning continued with sterner measures. A thumbscrew was brought into
use and screwed down first on his thumbs and then his fingers, one by one, causing
excruciating pain and considerable tissue damage, yet through it all, young Wetzel
maintained his stance of knowing nothing about the murder of Killbuck.

In the end, muttering a few dire threats, Col. Brodhead finally released Wetzel,
turned the tomahawk over to Col. Ebenezer Zane with instructions to continue
trying to find the owner, then gave his troops orders to prepare to leave for Fort Pitt.
Lewis Wetzel walked down toward the Wheeling Landing and watched expression-
lessly as the blanket-wrapped body of Killbuck was sunk in the Ohio River. He
remained there, continuing to watch as the troops got the boats ready and then finally
placed the Delaware prisoners aboard and embarked upstream.

Now, watching the last of those boats disappear around the bend to the north,
the tall, dark-haired young man lifted his badly swollen hands and looked at them. He
grinned crookedly and shook his head.

"Reckon it'll be a little while," he muttered, " 'fore I do any reloadin' on the
run."

[*June 17, 1781 — Sunday*]

Talgayeeta—Chief Logan—approached his cabin on the headwaters of the Scioto with no suspicion that anything was amiss. This was the cabin that Simon Kenton and Simon Girty had helped him build two years ago during that brief time when Girty had temporarily rescued Kenton from captivity.[422]

Talgayeeta was very tired, having walked all the way from Detroit. He was considerably disgruntled, as well. He had gone to Detroit to get liquor, to which he had become very addicted in the past couple of years. When he was scorned and his wheedling requests refused, he became angry and showed some of the spirit that most thought had been burned out of him.

"If the British won't give me what I want," he threatened, "maybe the Americans will. I'll go see General Clark."

What concerned British officials was whether or not Talgayeeta still carried enough influence with the Mingoes, as well as with his own Cayugas and other tribes, that in going to the Americans, he would pull those other Indians away from British influence. It was not a matter that could be left to chance.

So now, just as Talgayeeta was approaching his cabin, an unknown assassin slipped up behind him and slammed a tomahawk deep into his brain.

[*July 20, 1781 — Friday*]

It was during his regular patrol begun today from his post at Holliday's Cove Fort that Capt. Sam Brady detoured out of his way to the Catfish Camp area to visit briefly with the commander, Capt. Andrew Van Swearingen. Actually, that was not entirely true; though there *were* matters of frontier defense to discuss, what Brady had really come to see was Van Swearingen's daughter, Drusilla—better known to everyone as Dusy.

She had seemed just a little girl when Brady first saw her three years ago, when Van Swearingen was commanding at Holliday's Cove Fort, but something had definitely changed. From a gangly, tomboyish 13-year-old, she had blossomed over this past year into a very attractive 16-year-old young lady with a shape that was decidedly more womanly than girlish. Her large blue eyes looked into his own with disconcerting boldness, and her shoulder-length flaxen hair framed well-sculpted features; a young lady who carried herself with self-confidence and little, if any, of the coyness that other young ladies affected, bearing the trademark strength of her Holland Dutch heritage.

Since this remarkable change had occurred in Dusy Van Swearingen, Brady found himself making it a point to just happen to stop by their place a couple of miles from Catfish Camp more often than previously, although until today he would probably have denied that such was the case. Today there was a difference because Dusy was not here, and Brady was surprised at the intensity of disappointment that arose in him.

"Sort of quiet around here these days," Van Swearingen remarked, as if sensing Brady's state of mind, "with Dusy gone."

"Gone? Gone where?"

"Philadelphia. Sent her there for a year to get some of the ashes off. Expect she'll be ready for some of the young fellows one of these days."

"When she is, I'll claim her." Brady surprised himself with the remark.

"You?" Van Swearingen said. "You're too old for her, Sam. What are you now, thirty?"

"Twenty-five."

Andrew Van Swearingen shook his head and chuckled. "Old man. Nine years' difference. She's going to want a younger man, closer to her own age, like that boy David Bradford who's been flitting about lately."

Bradford was not quite so young as Van Swearingen implied, but his prospects, so far as Van Swearingen was concerned, were certainly better than Brady's. He was 22, came from a wealthy, stable family in Carlisle, Pennsylvania, and was now quite successfully embarked on his new career as a frontier lawyer. Obviously, Van Swearingen preferred Bradford over Brady for his daughter. Just as obviously, Brady was not particularly concerned about what Capt. Van Swearingen's preferences were.

"When she comes back," Brady reiterated, "I'll claim her."

[July 30, 1781 — Monday]

Billy Boggs, who had just turned 18, was still worried that there would be repercussions for the murder of Killbuck. No one had any proof that he and Lew Wetzel had done it, yet it seemed to be common knowledge, and there were a lot of people on this frontier who, while not having any love for Indians, felt that Killbuck had been useful to them. Certainly, by providing timely intelligence about the movements of the hostile Indians, he had helped the whites on a number of occasions. Unlike Wetzel, who seemed to have no trace of a guilty conscience over what they had done, Billy pondered about it often.

Only once had his father brought it up, simply stating his feelings about the matter and not asking questions. Capt. John Boggs was a stern and straightforward man and, shortly after the incident he had taken Billy aside near their cabin at the Buffalo Creek settlement and spoken to him seriously.

"Folks are saying you and Lewis Wetzel are the ones who tomahawked Killbuck, son," he said. "Whether he deserved to live or die is a matter of opinion, but no man deserves being killed the *way* he was killed. That was out-and-out murder and it was wrong. I don't know whether you had any part in it or not—I don't *want* to know, and I'll not bring it up again. But if you did, then I want you to think about it."

Billy Boggs did think about it and was feeling progressively more guilty, not only about the murder but over the recent rash of attacks in this area that had left the settlers stunned and, in many cases, grieving over the death or disappearance of loved ones. Several weeks ago Joseph McNulty and James Chambers were captured by a party of nine Indians on the Youghiogheny, and just a few days ago, when Andrew

Zane and James Lewis were passing through The Narrows above Grave Creek Flats, some Indians had fired on them from behind the rocks. Zane had been wounded and escaped, but James Lewis had been killed.

Now, having been sent by his father on this foggy morning to drive out the calves that had gotten into the field where they had newly shocked some of the early wheat, Billy wondered as he walked along if maybe those attacks wouldn't have happened had Killbuck remained alive to perhaps warn the settlements of marauders approaching. He was so steeped in these thoughts that he wasn't really paying much attention to what was around and didn't even see the Indians rise from hiding behind the shocks until they had their weapons trained on him and were quickly advancing. He had no choice but to drop his gun and surrender.

The party of a dozen Wyandots, led by the half-breed Sam Gray, relieved him of the knife and tomahawk in his belt and treated him rather roughly, which made Billy fearful that they knew of his complicity in Killbuck's death. Five of them hustled him off into the woods, while Sam Gray and the other seven headed for the Boggs cabin.[423]

Inside the cabin were Capt. Boggs and his wife, the other three Boggs youngsters and a visiting 15-year-old neighbor boy, William Cruger, whose left leg was still considerably swollen from having been bitten by a copperhead just after his arrival there three days ago. He had only this morning begun hobbling around, though apparently with great difficulty.

Capt. Boggs happened to glance out of the open cabin door and caught a glimpse of the Indians approaching, dodging from cover to cover. Instantly he slammed the cabin door shut and barred it, then directed his wife and children and Bill Cruger to go out through the back window and run to Newell's cabin a half-mile distant, where there were half a dozen men. Finally, using all three rifles in the house alternately, he began laying down a covering fire toward the attackers while the family escaped.

The Indians shot at the cabin several times but kept their distance, evidently believing there were several defenders in the cabin. Continuing to reload and fire as rapidly as he could, Boggs held them at bay for about ten minutes, after which he squeezed through the back window also and raced into the woods, heading for Newell's. The attackers did not follow and, when Boggs reached Newell's, he discovered that all those who had fled the cabin at his order had made it there all right—but the one who ran the fastest and got there first was the snakebitten William Cruger.[424]

[A u g u s t   6 ,   1 7 8 1 — M o n d a y]

Capt. John Bailey, commanding officer of the post at Vincennes on the Wabash River, was irked with the way his hand was trembling as he dipped his pen to write. He shook the excess ink into the pot and closed his eyes for a moment, willing himself into a calmer state. When he opened them again and held the quill pen before his eyes, there was no tremor, and a faint smile touched his lips. He bent to the blank page on the desk before him and began to write to his immediate superior, Col. George Slaughter, commander of Fort Nelson at the Falls of the Ohio—Louisville:

Post St. Vincennes, Augt 6th, 1781

Dear Sir:

I am sorry to inform you of the following news. The boat commanded by Captain Coulson started from this [post] *the 11th July, was defeated within 75 miles of the Falls of the Ohio; the Captain was killed and three of his men; several others were wounded. The remainder of the company came back & gave me the unhappy news. They retreated to the mouth of the Wabache* [Wabash]*, left the boat, & came by land, the enemy close in the rear of them.*

Four days ago I received news from Detroit that they were much annoyed of the Americans coming against them; also that they [the British garrison at Detroit] *were weak, about 100 men, provisions scarce and dear, & goods plenty, the Indians greatly exasperated against them, not meeting with the treatment as they had formerly done.*

Sir, I must inform you once more, that I cannot keep garrison any longer without some speedy relief from you. My men have been 15 days upon half allowance. There are plenty of provisions here, but no credit. I cannot press, being the weaker party. Some of the gentlemen would help us, but their credit is as bad as ours. Therefore, if you have not provisions, send whiskey, which will answer as good an end.

I hope, if my express gets in, you will not detain him. Pray use the Indian well, having no other to send. I expect his return in twelve days from this date and for some one man to come with him to this post. It appears that the communication is stopt between Canada and Detroit from the commencement of this year, by account from thence.

Jno Bailey, Captain

[A u g u s t   9 ,   1 7 8 1 — T h u r s d a y]

The commander of Fort Nelson at Louisville, Col. George Slaughter, took a healthy swig of brandy from the flask on his desk and felt the warmth expand within him. It was comforting—one of the last comforting things still extant at what he considered one of the world's most godforsaken military posts. He could not remember ever before having plunged so deeply into a state of depression. He was clearheaded enough to realize that in his state of mind he should not write the letter he was about to pen to the new Governor of Virginia, Thomas Nelson, but in this state of mind he also didn't give a damn. He hoped some of that feeling would get through to the governor and, with that thought, he began to write:

Falls of the Ohio, August 9th, 1781

Sir:

> *By the bearer, Major Quirk, you will receive information of public affairs in this country, and as the miscarriage and interception of letters are so frequent, I shall forbear to trouble your excellency much on that head.*
>
> *The situation of my little corps at this place is truly deplorable, destitute of clothing, victuals & money. The commissaries have furnished them with little or no provisions these three months past, nor give themselves the least concern about it, & unless unexpected & immediate supplies of clothing & provisions are obtained, I shall evacuate this post. We are neglected in every respect. No dispatches from Government or Gen. Clark for such a length of time, that patience is almost at an end. In short, Sir, the service here must be painful and disagreeable to any man of sensibility since I have had the honor to command.*

I am, Sir, Your Most Obdt Svt

George Slaughter

[A u g u s t   1 8 ,   1 7 8 1 — S a t u r d a y]

The more than 300 warriors under the Wyandot chief Monakaduto—Half King —were in the Moravian village of Gnadenhütten on the Tuscarawas and now preparing to use force, since reason had been unavailing.

The old chief, while he had no proof of it, had finally and reluctantly come to the conclusion that Simon Girty was correct and that the Moravian Delawares—or at least their missionaries—must be spying for the Americans and reporting the movements of the hostile Indians, which was the reason so many of the forays had been ambushed or had to be aborted because of the unexpected preparedness of the settlers for the approach of the attacking forces. It was time, Monakaduto felt, that the situation was resolved once and for all; force was now the only recourse.

This present determination had its genesis two months earlier when the confederated northwestern tribes had met in a major council at Chief Coon's village called Lower Sandusky.[425] Here some 800 Indians had assembled to listen to the words of the British agents Alexander McKee, Matthew Elliott and Simon Girty. Two large oxen had been butchered and roasted and a large quantity of liquor had been distributed.

A special honor was paid at that time to Thayendanegea—Chief Joseph Brant of the Mohawks—who had unexpectedly arrived with a contingent of 14 of his warriors. The war in the east had been going badly for them and, ever since the destruction of the Iroquois villages and crops in the very heartland of their country by the army of Maj. Gen. John Sullivan two years ago, they had suffered famine and reversals that had left them diminished and frustrated. But when it was learned that he intended to come to this council, plans had been made to honor him and encourage him to stay in the Ohio country and throw his own warriors and the weight of his influence against the Americans in the continued fighting on the Ohio.

At that council great praise had been heaped upon Thayendanegea, increasing his already substantial prestige, and he was formally presented with a fine green coat decorated with 700 silver brooches. He was also presented with a fine British sword in a scabbard, which he buckled to his waistband with great satisfaction. The lavish praise and honoring of the Mohawk war chief did not sit at all well with Simon Girty, who had long known of him during his own extensive captivity as a youth. He had often seen how Thayendanegea boasted well beyond his prowess. Girty considered him little more than a conceited individual who was singularly successful in convincing others that he was a great fighter and leader.

The great concern of the council revolved about the fact that their spies had reported Brig. Gen. George Rogers Clark was presently at Fort Pitt, having come there from eastern Virginia with a small army and now gathering more men at the head of the Ohio River. He was also preparing a great number of boats eventually to float down the Ohio River to the Falls, there to recruit more men and launch a major invasion into the Ohio and Indiana countries. Everyone was in agreement that all possible steps should be taken to hamper or entirely thwart his intentions.

Simon Girty was passionate in his diatribes against the Moravian Indians in general and the two principal Moravian missionaries, John Heckewelder and David Zeisberger, who, he declared, were constantly sending intelligence to the Americans about the movements and activities of the Indians. Chiefs Monakaduto, Pachgan-shehilas, Coon, Pimoacan, Wingenund and others were inclined to be of the same mind, and it was at this council that it was decided to do something about that situation without any further delay.

Leaving the Lower Sandusky council, the Indians had repaired to Half King's Town on the upper Sandusky to prepare to resolve the problem with the Moravians on the Tuscarawas. A number of spying parties were sent out to penetrate both the Kentucky country and the area around the upper Ohio and it was not long before those sent to the upper Ohio brought back the intelligence that Gen. Clark's force at Fort Pitt had finished its preparations and was on the verge of embarking downriver to the Falls of the Ohio.

At once, Simon Girty, Alexander McKee and Thayendanegea left for Chalah-gawtha with a force of about 200 warriors. There they planned to collect another 100 warriors—Shawnees—that James Girty had been priming for an attack on the Kentucky settlements. With the full force of 300, they might be able to intercept Clark on the river and launch a successful attack against him.

Monakaduto's remaining force of 440 warriors at Half King's Town split and 140 left with him and Matthew Elliott, heading directly for the Moravian towns. The remaining 300 stayed on the upper Sandusky for the time being, preparing to strike out, when the time was right, under Pimoacan—Pipe—and Wingenund on a slightly different route, perhaps to launch an attack against Wheeling or, if it was too well supported by troops, to spread out in raids against the Virginia and Pennsylvania settlements.

It was while the force heading for Chalahgawtha was in a temporary camp that Thayendanegea took to strutting about and boasting about his great prowess as a warrior, of the number of men he had personally killed and the large number of prisoners he had taken. Simon Girty had never cared much for Thayendanegea and had enough of the pompous posturings of this war chief who called himself Joseph Brant. Abruptly, he stood up and looked at Thayendanegea. "You lie!" he said. He stared contemptuously for a moment at the Mohawk and then turned disdainfully and strode from the tent.

Thayendanegea, furious at the insult, followed Girty out into the darkness. Unsheathing his new presentation sword, he crept up on him where he was standing near the fire and, without warning, slashed him across the right side of his head, cutting a gash more than three inches long from behind the right ear to the top of his head, the blade fracturing Girty's skull. Simon fell and lay motionless, bleeding profusely.

Alexander McKee came rushing over and bent down over his deputy agent, who was still alive but in bad shape. McKee turned and snarled at Thayendanegea, "If Girty dies, I will have you hung!" He then ordered the injured Girty to be left to the ministering of an Indian healer.[426]

Monakaduto, meanwhile, with his 140 warriors, had arrived on August 10 at the Moravian village of Salem. They took the Rev. David Zeisberger captive and intimidated his converts into submission. The following day 40 Muncey Delawares arrived, joined with Monakaduto, and the whole force moved up the Tuscarawas toward Gnadenhütten, the intimidated Moravian Indians with them. The Moravians from Schoenbrun mission were forced to move downstream, and the whole party converged at Gnadenhütten, where they took the Rev. John Heckewelder prisoner.

All of the Moravian Indians, headed by the Delaware convert who was originally named Netawatwees but who now called himself Abraham, went into a series of councils with the hostiles. Abraham argued that the Moravian Indians were not spies for the Americans or anyone else. Monakaduto, in turn, declared that, as Indians, they should support their fellows and take up weapons and join them in the continuing fight against the Americans. Abraham disagreed, saying they were now Christians and did not intend to take up the hatchet against anyone, American or otherwise; that they were, in fact, neutral, had always been so and meant to stay that way. Monakaduto was becoming irritated and he now warned them that, being in the path of war between the Indians and whites, they were in great danger and that they should have sense enough to see this and move away voluntarily. Once more Abraham respectfully declined on behalf of the Moravians.

On August 15, leading the 300 warriors that had remained behind at Half King's Town on the upper Sandusky, Pimoacan, Coon, Pachganshehilas and Wingenund arrived at Gnadenhütten. The force included a contingent of Delawares from Lower Sandusky, another of Shawnees under Shemeneto and a final group of 40 Munceys from the upper Allegheny.

Monakaduto related to them that he had been counciling here with the Moravians almost daily since their arrival but that none of the talking had brought the Christian Indians closer to voluntarily leaving this area. At that juncture the elderly Delaware chief Pachganshehilas—Hailstone—said that perhaps the converts might be convinced more readily by a fellow Delaware than by a Wyandot of the danger they were in and that he would endeavor to make them see it would be to their benefit to leave here. Calling all the Moravian Indians to assemble, he spoke to them for a long while, alternately wheedling and haranguing, and finally ending with the warning: "Think on what I have now said to you and believe this: If you stay where you are now, one day or another the *Shemanese* will speak fine words to you and, at the same time, murder you!"

The Moravian Indians deliberated among themselves and, after more discussions with Pachganshehilas, their spokesman, Abraham, declined the offer of an allegedly safer place to live, far away from here on the Tuscarawas where they already had their villages, their chapels, their crops and livestock, their homes. "As for the danger we are supposedly in," Abraham concluded, "God has protected us in the past and we trust Him to do so in the future."

At this, the patience of Matthew Elliott reached the breaking point. He stepped forward with an angry wave of his hand. "What do *you* know of God?" he railed condescendingly. "Can you really be so ignorant as to believe that because you have been, as they say, 'converted' and changed your name from Netawatwees to Abraham, that this provides you protection of God? I tell you that God will not help you here once we begin to attack these Americans in earnest. The whites will try to retaliate and you will be killed. Can't you understand that it is for your own protection that we have requested you to leave? We hoped you would be wise enough to do so without being forced. Instead, we find you a stupid, stubborn old man."

After more hours of discussion with Monakaduto and the other chiefs, Elliott became convinced that all had finally reached the limit of their patience in trying to deal with these stubborn Moravians. Assured by Monakaduto that the problem would now be taken care of without further ado, Elliott nodded and turned his attention to preparing his few English and French assistants, along with 250 warriors, to march for the upper Ohio.

David Zeisberger was unaware of what decisions had been reached in the council with the chiefs, but the fact that Elliott was now readying a large war party alarmed him. A few days ago he had written a letter to Col. Gibson at Fort Pitt that he had been unable yet to smuggle out to him. Now, though he knew full well his life was jeopardized by doing so, he retired to a secluded spot and hastily penned a second, more urgent letter to Gibson, warning him of the force under Monakaduto and Elliott that was preparing to strike somewhere on the upper Ohio, though whether in numerous small raiding parties or in a mass assault, he did not know. However, he was certain Wheeling would be a priority target.

Moments after finishing the letter, Zeisberger had handed it, along with that earlier letter, to a trusted Moravian youth who, having received his instructions, slipped away into the forest with them, heading for Fort Pitt. With luck, those letters would be in the hands of Col. Gibson within a week. Zeisberger, watching him go, had the feeling that it might be the last intelligence he would be able to get off to the Americans.

True to his word, Monakaduto had no further patience with the Moravians. Less than an hour later, in a peremptory manner, he ordered them to gather up what few personal belongings they had. They were to be escorted to Upper Sandusky, where a plot of ground would be allotted for them to build their own village. When the dismayed Moravians asked what about their corn and other crops that were ripening in the fields, and their cattle, hogs and poultry, Monakaduto told them all those must be left behind for use of the various war parties as they needed them. As for the German missionaries, Heckewelder and Zeisberger, they would be taken along as captives and sent to Detroit to be tried on charges of treason and spying for the Americans.

Now the Moravians, in the custody of Pimoacan and Wingenund and some 60 of their warriors, resignedly began gathering up some of their things preparatory to the long walk to the upper Sandusky via the trail leading up the Walhonding. With Matthew Elliott still at his side, Monakaduto ordered a large force of the warriors, including his three sons, Scotach, Scoleh and Dakadulah, to remain here at Gnadenhütten with him to organize new raids against Wheeling and the other white settlements, those assaults to be initiated as quickly as possible.[427]

[August 19, 1781—Sunday]

The friction between Col. Daniel Brodhead and his officers had continued to grow over these past months, though it was not so pronounced as the anger that was exhibited toward him by the citizenry, who were now convinced that in their own need and danger, he had betrayed them; that Brodhead had usurped, for his own personal gain in land acquisition, funds that should have rightfully gone to the relief of the people.

The fact that an investigation ordered by Gen. Washington into the allegations lodged against Col. Brodhead was now under way left little room for confidence among his subordinates. Torn in their allegiance and confused as to how they should proceed, they found themselves in a state of limbo that Col. John Gibson knew was detrimental not only to themselves but to the entire frontier. With the Indian threat as great as it was, there was no room for continued dissension among the officers.

Taking it upon himself to bring some order out of this chaos, Gibson discussed the matter with Col. Brodhead, then assembled the officers and suggested a course of action to which, after some further discussion, all agreed. With that and with the unanimous concurrence of the subordinate officers, Gibson officially announced himself in command of Fort Pitt and wrote a letter to Brodhead that stated for the record the decision reached, under which the officers of Fort Pitt had already been acting unofficially for some time:

> *Head Quarters, Fort Pitt*
> *August 19th, 1781.*

To Colonel Brodhead:

> *Agreeable to your request, we now inform you that, from the letters of his Excellency, the Commander-in-Chief, to you, which have been shewn us by Captain John Finley, that it is our opinion we cannot, with propriety, be commanded by you, until you have cleared yourself of the charges which have been exhibited against you and which are now depending.*
>
> *At the same time we wish to assure you that we entertain the greatest respect*

for you, and was it not for the present situation of affairs, there is not one of us but would wish to serve under you.

We are, Sir, your most obedt. hble. servants,

John Gibson, Colonel, Commanding Fort Pitt

In succession the remaining 13 officers stepped to the desk and signed below Gibson's bold signature, their own names and stations:

Fredk. Vernon, Major, 8th Pennsylvania Regiment
Uriah Springer, Captain, 7th Virginia Regiment
Benjn. Biggs, Captain, 7th Virginia Regiment
Saml. Brady, Captain, 8th Pennsylvania Regiment
William Martin, Captain Lieutenant of Proctor's Artillery
Lewis Thomas, Lieutenant, 7th Virginia Regiment
John Harrison, Lieutenant, 7th Virginia Regiment
Archibald Read, Lieutenant, 8th Pennsylvania Regiment
John Ward, Lieutenant, 8th Pennsylvania Regiment
Jacob Springer, Lieutenant, Virginia Regiment
Jacob Coleman, Engineer, Virginia Regiment
Joseph Wrinlock, Ensign, Virginia Regiment
John Beck, Ensign, 8th Virginia Regiment

[A u g u s t   2 4 ,   1 7 8 1 — F r i d a y]

Undeterred by the fractious behavior of his officers and the growing antipathy toward him among the settlers, Col. Daniel Brodhead still thought of himself as commander of Fort Pitt and only momentarily indisposed. Knowing he had long been a favorite of Gen. Washington, he now wrote to him in a manner that he hoped would subtly portray himself as having been taken advantage of and just as subtly hinting for intervention by the commander-in-chief as to reinstatement:

An Expedition against the Sandusky Towns is in contemplation. The troops will be rendezvoused at Fort McIntosh on the 4th and 5th of next month. The country appears to be desirous to promote it, and I intend to command it, if the militia and volunteers do not suffer themselves to be induced into a belief that I have no right to command. If they should, I shall be at a loss how to act, being unwilling to give up my command and as unwilling to prevent the expedition taking place. I will attempt to be governed by prudence.

And mere yards away, in his own quarters in Fort Pitt, Col. Gibson was also writing to the commanding general, though he was more concerned with the condition and safety of the frontier than with his personal station:

General Clark is gone down the river with about 400 men, composed of Colonel Crockett's Regiment of Virginia State Troops, Captain Craig's Company of Artillery, except one Captain Lieutenant, one Sergeant, and six matrosses who remain here, the rest volunteers and militia.

I delivered to him all the articles he demanded of me, agreeably to your Excellency's instructions, and which I thought could, consistently with the safety of the garrison, be spared. As many of the troops in this Department were quite naked, and all of them thro' want of clothing rendered unfit for a long campaign, the General concluded it would be best for them to remain here, and proposed that I should endeavor to call out as many militia or volunteers as would enable me, with the regular troops, to make a short excursion against the Wyandotte Towns, at the same time that he should begin his march from the mouth of the Miami River against the Shawanese, and which was to be about the 4th of September, and would of course attract the attention of the greatest part of the Indians.

Colonel Brodhead returned the 11th instant to this place. He informed me that your Excellency had ordered him to return to this post, and that after the depositions were taken relative to the charges exhibited against him, and it would suit his own conveniency, that then he was to repair to Head Quarters to take his trial. I then informed him of General Clark's proposal and, after some time, shewed him a letter which I had received from Colonel Cannon, a principal gentleman of Youghiogheny County, requesting my attendance on the 14th instant at Pentecost's Mills, as there was to be a general meeting of the County, and that it would be a very proper time to engage the people to turn out, or at least to know their opinion. Previous to this, General Clark had informed Colonel Cannon something of this kind would be attempted.

Colonel Brodhead approved much of the plan, and informed me that we would both go, and try what could be done. On the evening preceding the meeting, I asked Colonel Brodhead if we should set off the next morning. He then shewed me a letter from Mr. Fowler to him, requiring his attendance next day to be present at the taking of depositions in support of the charges exhibited against him, and said, "You see, my friend, these fellows are determined to give me no respite, and that I must go down the country soon. I would therefore advise you to go and try to engage them to turn out with you. I shall give you every assistance in my power and, as so many reports have been spread to my disadvantage thro' the country, my going might possibly retard the people in turning out. Besides, I might see a number of the damned rascals who signed the remonstrance and their presence would be disagreeable to me—in particular that rascal, Colonel Cannon, should I meet him, I would spit in his face."

The next morning I went to Pentecost's Mills where a number of people were collected, the principal of whom I informed my intention. They asked me if Colonel Brodhead was to command. I told them the present situation of his affairs prevented his commanding, that he was obliged to go down the country, but that he had assured me he would give every assistance in his power in furthering the intended excursion. They then asked me to commit my proposals to writing, which I did. The purport of which was that the 4th day of September should be fixed on as a day of general rendezvous at Fort McIntosh; that from the unsettled dispute respecting

*territory, they should consider themselves as volunteers, and choose their own of-
ficers; that each man should be well mounted on horseback and bring with him 30
days' provision, and that the whole should bring as many spare horses as would
mount 150 regular troops, for which number I engaged they should be paid a
generous hire and, if killed or taken by the enemy, that they should also be paid.*

*They unanimously approved of my proposals and requested me to go to an-
other meeting the next day, which was to be held a few miles from thence. I went
there and found near 600 collected, and everyone present most heartily agreed to my
former proposals, and those fit for service promised to go. . . .*

*The only thing I dread is that the expedition will fall through, which must
engender the loss of General Clark and his army, should Colonel Brodhead persist
in re-assuming the command, as the people in general are prejudiced against him and
are determined not to serve under him, tho' with what propriety, time must discover.*

*We have been much distressed for provision, owing to the change of the
Executive of the State of Pennsylvania in their commissioners of purchase, and the
rapid depreciation of the State money; and had it not been for a supply of twenty-
seven thousand weight drawn from General Clark's magazine, and for some salt in
store which we exchanged for beef, we could not possibly have maintained this post.*

Gibson broke off writing at a tapping on his door, and an ensign entered with
two separate folded documents, which he extended to the commander.

"Sir," he said, "these have just arrived by a Moravian runner. They, uh . . ."
he hesitated, evidently discomfited, ". . . they were handed to Colonel Brodhead
first." Gibson's gaze narrowed, but he said nothing and the ensign continued. "As
soon as he read them, sir, he returned them to the runner and relayed him on to this
office. I'm sorry, sir. I knew nothing about it until they were handed to me. The
runner says they are from Zeisberger and to tell you they are urgent."

"Thank you," Gibson said, accepting the letters. "Please ask him to wait, that
I'd like to talk with him in a few minutes. In the meanwhile, provide him with some
food and coffee."

"Yes, sir." The ensign saluted and left the room, closing the door behind him.

Gibson unfolded the letters, noted the dates and read the earliest one first, then
the other. Finishing, he sighed and set them aside on the edge of his desk, planning
to enclose them with his own letter he was presently writing. He then strode to the
door, opened it and spoke briefly to the ensign, who nodded, saluted and left at
quick speed. Gibson then returned to his desk to hastily finish the letter to George
Washington:

*I have received, since writing the above, two letters from Rev. Mr. Zeisberger
at the Moravian Towns on the Muskingum. The intelligence contained therein is
very alarming. I have sent to alarm the country, and hope they will turn out. . . .*

Even as Col. Gibson put the finishing touches on his letter to Gen. Washington,
Col. Brodhead, in his own quarters, had summoned an express rider, who was now

standing ready and waiting to carry the dispatch the colonel was swiftly writing, addressed to Col. David Shepherd at Fort Henry in Wheeling:

Fort Pitt, August 24th, 1781

Sir:

> *I have this moment received certain intelligence that the enemy are coming in great force against us and particularly against Wheeling.*
>
> *You will immediately put your garrison in the best posture of defence and lay in as great a quantity of water as circumstances will admit, and receive them coolly; they intend to decoy your garrison, but you are to guard against stratagem, and defend the post to the last extremity.*
>
> *You may rely on every aid in my power to frustrate the designs of the enemy, but you must not fail to give the alarm to the inhabitants in your reach and make it as general as possible, in order that every man may be prepared at this crisis.*

> *D.B.*
> *Col. commanding W.D.*
> *To the commanding officer at*
> *Ft. Henry (Wheeling.)*

[August 25, 1781 — Saturday]

The large bison that had been killed the evening before had been butchered during the night and the soldiers were looking forward to their morning repast of the considerable quantity of meat that would soon be cooking over several fires. For many, it would be the first time they had ever tasted buffalo meat and, having heard how good it was, they were looking forward to it.

Four or five miles below the mouth of the Great Miami, some 500 miles below Pittsburgh and still 100 miles above the Falls of the Ohio, Col. Archibald Lochry's lead boat had just scraped ashore, and he stepped out at once. He had decided he would let his detachment of 106 men have three full hours in which to eat and rest before continuing downstream. Perhaps by that time Maj. Craycraft would have returned with dispatches from Gen. Clark.

It had been almost exactly a month ago that Lochry, on his arrival at Fort Pitt, discovered that boats were waiting for his detachment but that Gen. Clark had already departed for Wheeling and had left orders for Lochry and his force to meet him there. Col. Lochry, as county lieutenant of Westmoreland County, had experienced considerable difficulty in recruiting men in his home region and those he did raise had been late in arriving at Pittsburgh. By the time they assembled, Clark's force had had several days' head start on them.

Lochry and his men had finally left Pittsburgh but, on arriving at Wheeling on July 29, they found that Clark, with his force augmented by some Wheeling militiamen, had also left there; his orders were for Lochry to follow immediately with his detachment. Clark had also changed the place of rendezvous from the mouth of the Great Miami River to the Falls of the Ohio at the new settlement of Louisville.

Clark had been having his own troubles on the descent. A few days after leaving Wheeling he had reached a huge island three miles long and half a mile wide in the Ohio a mile below the mouth of the Little Kanawha River, and here he had ordered his troops to camp overnight.[428] During that night two officers—Lieutenants Samuel Craig and Paddy Hunter—led 50 men in a mass desertion. Some of them struck out overland for the east, while others stole boats and began returning upstream. The latter were intercepted by Lochry and put under arrest, to be returned to Clark and brought up for courts-martial.

When Clark and his force continued down the Ohio, the commander left behind Maj. Craycraft and Q.M. Richard Wallace with a squad of five men to wait with dispatches to give to Col. Lochry when he arrived.[429] With this done, the Lochry force continued downstream. At the Three Islands, some 400 miles below Pittsburgh, Lochry's force encamped and Maj. Craycraft and his squad, with Lochry's approval, continued in a single canoe to attempt to overtake Clark and inform him about Lochry coming behind with the deserters he had managed to capture.

Less than 100 miles downstream, the main party of Indians under McKee, George Girty, a renegade named Brice Reagen, who had deserted from the Thirteenth Virginia Regiment, and Thayendanegea, reached the Ohio and were heading down toward the Falls when some of Shemeneto's spies had overtaken them with the news that a single canoe with seven men was coming downstream.[430] Using canoes brought along on packhorses, the Indians took positions on both sides of the Ohio and waited. When the canoe bearing Maj. Craycraft and his squad appeared, the soldiers suddenly found a horde of Indians in canoes on all sides and, with resistance futile, were easily captured without a shot being fired.

Jim Girty and Reagen questioned the captives, and though both Craycraft and Wallace refused to talk, the other men broke when threatened with death and told of the Lochry force coming along behind them to join Clark. McKee confronted Craycraft and detailed the excruciating tortures awaiting him if he did not cooperate and lure Col. Lochry's force ashore. He also assured Craycraft that it was the only way to save Lochry and his men, as otherwise they would be attacked and killed down to the last man. Maj. Craycraft agreed to call them ashore when they neared and the Indians took up posts in hiding on both sides of the river. McKee ordered that Craycraft and Q.M. Wallace, along with the other five men, be tied to trees and a close watch be maintained over them throughout the night.

Meanwhile, late yesterday afternoon Col. Lochry's force had come ashore again and camped on the wide bar at the mouth of the Great Miami. It was there, after they had messed and were preparing their blankets for the night, that the lone buffalo had blundered out of the woods and was shot before it had a chance to wheel and gallop out of sight. Since the men had already eaten and were preparing to turn in, Col. Lochry promised that after an early start in the morning, they would come ashore in order to cook and eat the buffalo meat, so several of the men had stayed up late to finish cleaning the animal.

This morning they had proceeded four or five miles downstream when Col. Lochry, spying the broad pleasant bottom along the right bank, ordered the boats ashore for the buffalo feast. By a quirk of happenstance, it was only a few dozen yards above the place where the proposed ambush of Lochry's force had been set up. Lochry, of course, was wholly unaware that Maj. Craycraft and his squad, prisoners of the Indians, were behind a screen of brush there and had been on the point of stepping out and hailing the boats to shore. Now, with the Lochry boats already coming ashore, it hadn't been necessary to use Craycraft as a decoy.

As Lochry's boat scraped to a stop and he stepped ashore and other boats of the flotilla were beginning to do the same, McKee's horde of Indians burst from cover and McKee shouted for the soldiers to surrender instantly or be killed. Those still in their boats and coasting to shore tried desperately to get away but a barrage of gunfire broke out at them. More than 30 of Lochry's men were killed and others were wounded. Only one gun was fired in defense—that by Pvt. Ephraim Relfe, who was quickly cut down by several shots.

The captive force was made to sit down and their wrists were bound behind them by some of the Indians, while others retrieved the boats still drifting on the inshore eddy, scalped the dead and collected guns and other supplies. Capt. Robert Orr, wounded in the shoulder, was led with Col. Lochry to a driftwood log and directed to sit. They had not been there more than a minute when a Shawnee warrior walked up and methodically killed Lochry with a single tomahawk blow and scalped him.[431] Orr was certain he would be killed, too, but the warrior simply walked off with his bloody trophy.[432]

Not far away, the heavy-set Capt. Thomas Shannon was seated on the ground beside Capt. William Campbell. They were similarly approached and, before either suspected what was going to happen, Campbell was tomahawked and scalped.[433] The same thing happened to a number of the privates. These, however, were isolated cases and it did not turn into a wholesale slaughter as the captives feared.[434]

And now, having been so successful in their attack on the Lochry force, the Indians sent the prisoners north toward Detroit under strong guard and turned their steps toward Gen. George Rogers Clark at the Falls of the Ohio.

[September 13, 1781—Thursday]

Col. David Shepherd, commanding at Fort Henry in Wheeling, was flushed with anger as he ran toward the open gate of the fort where the men were racing out. Those who saw him coming hesitated in their rush and he thrust past them and planted himself in the center of the main portal.

"Back!" he ordered furiously, jerking his pistol out of his belt. "Back! Dammit, are you men completely crazy? Where the hell are your brains? Get back! I promise you, I'll shoot the next man who tries to leave!"

He couldn't believe, after all the warnings that had been given, what these fools were doing. It wasn't as if their exodus were coming as a surprise. Everyone was aware of the danger; notices had been posted for over a fortnight now, ever since the warnings had been received from both Col. Brodhead and Col. Gibson. Had none of it sunk in? Had they learned nothing from past experience?

These past couple of weeks had been a hectic, fearful time. Even before the warnings were received, troubles had broken out. The planned rendezvous at Fort McIntosh for the Sandusky Expedition was, of course, put in abeyance. There was a sharp increase in the number of small raiding parties of Indians ranging over the frontier and, though every effort had been made to alert even the inhabitants of the most isolated cabins and settlements, for some the warnings had not come in time.

On the very next day after the warnings were written at Fort Pitt and well before they had been transmitted to the more distant settlements, about 100 Indians appeared in the vicinity of Wheeling in the afternoon. Two youngsters named David Glenn and Johnny Ryan were, at the time, playing near the spring at the foot of Wheeling Hill. They saw the Indians and ran. Both were closely pursued, and ten-year-old Ryan tried to get away by racing along a log spanning the swampy ground below the spring. The Wyandot chasing him overtook him halfway across and slammed a tomahawk into him, sending him sprawling dead in the mud. Twelve-year-old Glenn was captured a short distance away.

By this time, those in Wheeling, alerted by Glenn's cries, were racing for cover. George Reagan was only about five yards from the gate of Fort Henry when a ball passed through his wrist, and though it spun him around, he managed to retain his feet and get safely inside the fort. A few shots were fired by the inhabitants in the direction the Indian shots had come from, but there was no response. There was good reason: Under questioning, David Glenn told his Wyandot captors that Wheeling and the entire frontier in general had been alerted to the approach of the Indians, and that everyone was alarmed and on guard, especially at Wheeling.

They believed him and, deciding it would be wise to avoid Wheeling for the moment, the Indians moved on to range through the hills eastward. On Middle Wheeling Creek, 14 miles above Fort Henry, they came to the cabin of Jacob Link. Link's wife and daughter were absent, visiting friends in Wheeling, but Adam Miller had spent last night in Link's cabin, and this morning they had been visited by two young men they knew, Moses Shepherd and Jacob Wetzel. Those two had been engaging in some target practice with Link and Miller and had just left there only a short time before the party of Indians arrived. Link and Miller, hearing someone outside, thought it was Shepherd and Wetzel returning and swung the cabin door open. They were taken by surprise by the Indians and both killed and scalped.

The following day the Indians appeared on the Dutch Fork of Buffalo Creek and attacked the Jacob Peek cabin. Two or three men were killed in an exchange of gunfire, and then the Indians captured Peek's son, Presley, along with John Blackburn and William Hawkins. The latter, a rotund, red-headed little Irishman, was all but hysterical in his fright. He begged the Indians to spare his life and said that, if they would, he would lead them to where his wife and children were, hardly a quarter-mile away, convince them to go with him and they would all go and live with the Indians. They started for the place, but the distant gunfire had been heard in the other cabin, and the inhabitants had attempted to escape. Hawkins's wife and three of her children, one an infant only two weeks old, fled into a large thicket of hazel bushes and managed to get away. Her eldest daughter, Rebecca, was ill, but she and a man who had been in the cabin with them, John Hill, whose leg was badly swollen from a copperhead bite, raced into the nearby cornfield. The pair, because of their respective ailments, could not go far and so they tried to hide themselves among the cornstalks. The Indians followed their tracks, however, and caught them. They killed Hill and took Rebecca captive.[435]

Sam Gray, the half-breed who had captured Billy Boggs on July 30, was leading one of the small war parties of Wyandots sent out by Monakaduto, and he was definitely making his mark. In the forenoon on September 9, his party killed William Huston while he was working in his cornfield. Huston had ignored his brother's entreaty, only ten minutes earlier, to get to the fort for safety.[436] A short distance away, less than two hours later, Jesse Cochran was similarly killed by them and, the same afternoon, Benjamin Rogers took Sam Gray's bullet through the heart while hoeing in his little corn patch adjacent to his cabin. Hardly an hour after that, William Ayres, fleeing to the protection of Rice's Settlement on the upper Buffalo, at the new blockhouse called Rice's Fort, was shot from his horse in a hasty ambush set up by Sam Gray. And before sunset on that same busy day, Sam Gray capped his party's activities by killing Capt. Sam Leter and a settler he was riding with at the head of Buffalo Creek.

By now most of the frontier was alerted to the new attacks and most of the residents had taken refuge at Fort Henry, Ramsey's Fort, Shepherd's Fort and Catfish Camp. The fact that the Holliday's Cove Fort had burned to the ground a month ago hadn't helped matters. The fire had been accidental and no one was hurt, but an imperative link in the frontier defense structure had been broken.[437] Reconstruction had already been undertaken by Thomas Edgington and others, but it would be a very long time before a fully functional fort was reestablished. A fairly substantial fort was presently being erected on the Ohio side of the river at Mingo Bottom by Jacob White and his company, but it was much too exposed and not yet completed enough to be of any real use. A small fortified cabin had also been erected, just a few weeks before the Holliday's Cove fire, on the George Sparks claim at the mouth of Short Creek. It was being called Sparks' Fort, but it certainly didn't answer the needs that Holliday's Cove Fort had. As a result, the majority of the residents from Holliday's Cove had come to Wheeling for protection.

That settlement, with its own large population and now the center for those fleeing to safety from miles around, was bulging at the seams. In addition to the scores of women and children, somewhat over 100 men were at Wheeling, all of whom were longtime members of the militia or had just been inducted into temporary service. Duties had been outlined, regular around-the-clock sentry patrols were inaugurated and longer spying scouts undertaken. All this was done by Col. Shepherd in response to the warnings from Brodhead and Gibson at Fort Pitt, but the urgency was augmented by the receipt late on September 9 of a letter written by Brodhead two days earlier:

Headquarters, Fort Pitt, September 7th, 1781

Gentlemen: By the inclosed extract of a letter just come to hand by express, you will learn the fate of the Moravians on the Muskingum and the dangers to which our dependent posts and the settlements are exposed.

I think it is probable that this large party of Indians would not have remained so long at the Moravian town had they not expected a greater force from another quarter down the Allegheny river to cooperate with them. It will therefore be highly expedient for the militia immediately to assemble in bodies consisting of at least one hundred men, and step to the frontiers to cover them to keep out spies and small scouts at least for a few days, or until we can ascertain what the principal object of the enemy is.

You will therefore immediately appoint such places of rendezvous as may be best calculated for the purpose I have mentioned, and give me notice thereof that in case of extreme necessity they may be collected to a general rendezvous, in order to raise a siege, or otherwise act according to circumstances.

County lieutenants who have not and cannot otherwise procure a supply of ammunition are immediately to apply to me to have a suitable quantity deposited in their respective county to enable the militia to act in conjunction with the regular troops, and this application, with the means of transportation, must not be delayed. I am, &c.,

D.B.

Circular to the County Lieutenants

The earlier attacks in the isolated areas were, Col. Shepherd believed, only preliminaries to a major assault to be leveled against Wheeling itself. Under his orders, this principal settlement braced itself for whatever was to come. For three full days they were on utmost alert, and only this morning, believing the attack had been aborted for one reason or another, Shepherd reduced the full alert by one-half.

Now, only moments before, distant shots had been fired and an orderly had run to Shepherd's headquarters room with the excited announcement that a small group of Indians—one of them believed to be Sam Gray—had appeared halfway up Wheeling Hill. They had fired several random shots at the fort, then gone off in a manner that could only be described as casual, pausing now and then to bend over and slap their behinds toward the fort in an insulting manner. It was more than some of the newly inducted settlers could tolerate and they snatched up their guns, opened the gate and began streaming out in pursuit, led by John Caldwell.

By the time Col. Shepherd reached the gate and stopped others from following by threatening to shoot the next man who tried, Caldwell and nine other men were already at the base of Wheeling Hill and starting their ascent. Above them, Sam Gray and the few Wyandots were still climbing uphill casually and just reaching the top. There they paused and pointed at the men scrambling upward after them at top speed and laughed lustily. Then they turned and walked out of sight over the crest.

Caldwell and his nine men were gasping for breath when they reached the summit, some 250 feet above the fort, arriving there hardly half a minute after the small party of Wyandots left. They rushed over the crest, prepared to stop and shoot the instant they saw the departing Indians ahead of them. What they found, instead, was a great horde of Indians in a semicircle before them and another group appearing behind, all of them leveling their own weapons and beginning to fire. Several of the whites fell in the first barrage, and more were killed as they raced to the only avenue of possible escape open to them—the precipitous slope to the northeast, plunging down to Wheeling Creek.

Two of the men who made it to the lip of that steep dropoff were David Herbert in the lead and his friend, John Caldwell, in the rear. Scrambling and sliding, they started down, each losing his rifle almost immediately. Within mere yards a ball struck Herbert in the back and he tumbled down 30 feet or more before wedging against a tree. As Caldwell passed, Herbert called out, "John, don't leave me," but Caldwell didn't pause.

Hearing a clattering of rocks behind him, Caldwell glanced back and saw two Wyandots scrambling after them, one wielding a tomahawk, the other, Sam Gray, a spear. The former stopped at the motionless form of David Herbert and struck him with his tomahawk, but Sam Gray kept coming. Two-thirds of the way down, with Sam Gray virtually at his heels, Caldwell tripped over an exposed root, fell and rolled up against a log wedged between a couple of saplings.

Gray was very quickly upon him and thrust his spear with a powerful jab. The point barely grazed Caldwell's hip, hit the top of the log and glanced upward, burying itself deeply in the sapling on the down side of the log. While Sam Gray struggled to pull the embedded spearhead free, Caldwell regained his feet and plunged on. At the bottom he turned sharply right and raced along the narrow bottom back to the level ground of the Wheeling bottom. Fifteen minutes later, almost dead from exhaustion, he staggered to the gate of Fort Henry and was let in. Some 20 minutes later another of the party came in with one of his arms broken and dangling. All eight others had been killed.

In the meanwhile, what Matthew Elliott and Monakaduto had been able to observe of Wheeling and Fort Henry convinced them that the place was teeming with soldiers and settlers and what the captive boy had told them was evidently true; the populace was in arms and ready, and whatever element of surprise the Indians had hoped to have had evidently been lost. Monakaduto was convinced the only way the American frontier could have been brought to this state of readiness in anticipation of his arrival was by the Moravian missionaries, or their converts, relaying intelligence from the Tuscarawas and Muskingum to the *Shemanese* leaders. Now he was more pleased than ever that he had uprooted them and sent them to the Sandusky. This present attack was finished, but next time, he was sure, the Americans would be receiving no early warning.

[September 13, 1781 — Thursday]

Matters had not gone at all well for Brig. Gen. George Rogers Clark and his little army since his arrival at the Falls of the Ohio. Fort Nelson was found in a state of disrepair, its commander, Col. George Slaughter, despondent almost to the point of suicide, its garrison destitute, with clothing falling off their bodies in rags, the men themselves thin and weak from the starvation diet of quarter-rations for the past week and half-rations for the six weeks preceding that. And, in the face of this, the merchants of the little Louisville community outside Fort Nelson, with ample provisions on hand, continued to refuse to give any to the suffering garrison; they dealt strictly in cash, Clark was told, and considered extending credit to an American military establishment a total waste, as they were never repaid.

Obviously, the supplies Clark had brought downriver with him from Fort Pitt, while not abundant, were certainly worthy of the cheers with which the men of the Fort Nelson garrison greeted them. Anger swirled in Clark's breast as he wrote to Gen. Washington, the Continental Congress and Gov. Nelson about the situation here, but he had little hope that anything would be done very soon to alleviate the situation. Worst of all, there was a strong likelihood that his call for Kentucky volunteers to accompany the planned invasion against the Shawnees and the upper Wabash tribes would largely go unanswered.

Things went from bad to worse. Shortly after their arrival, word was brought of the destruction of Col. Archibald Lochry's force, the colonel himself killed along with 41 of his men and the remaining 55 captured, including the deserters he was returning to Clark.

On September 7, Gen. Clark was informed that a large commercial flatboat with a cargo of 250 barrels of flour had anchored at the foot of an island just below the Falls of the Ohio, quite near the Kentucky shore.[438] The captain of the flatboat was an entrepreneurial riverman, Capt. Robert Elliott, who, with a crew of six, was transporting his cargo from Pittsburgh to New Orleans.[439] In the morning Clark sent Lt. Jerry Johnson, an officer from the Monongahela, with a squad of ten men to see if any of the flour might be procured for the garrison.[440]

Lt. Johnson and his men marched down the shoreline to the crossing place just below the smaller island, where a small barge was tied up, a craft frequently used by scouts when they crossed the Ohio River on spying missions. Capt. Elliott's barge was moored some 70 yards distant when, as Johnson's men were boarding the little barge and Pvts. Aquilla Whittaker and Jim Armstrong were having a playful dispute about who was going to sit where, a party of Shawnees lying in ambush opened fire.[441] Pvt. Benjamin Wright was shot through the forehead and fell dead in the barge. His brother, Pvt. William Wright, was shot through the right wrist. Pvt. Adam Keller was struck in the nose by a ball that then tore through his cheek and exited from the side of his head, but he was not killed. Pvt. Michael Humble took a ball high in the hip and fell, unable to rise. James Armstrong was struck in the side, but was still functioning. Their commander, Lt. Johnson, was shot through the shoulder and either fell or leaped into the water to escape. As he was swept downstream with the swift current, James Lindley, a seaman on Capt. Elliott's flatboat, quickly launched a canoe and paddled to his aid. Johnson, however, unable to swim because of his wound, sank from sight just as Lindley was nearing him.[442] The other privates, Whittaker and the wounded Armstrong among them, leaped into the water and turned the boat on its side to act as a shield from the second round of bullets just then coming from the Indians. By this time, a few ineffectual shots were coming toward the Indians from Capt. Elliott's flatboat, and the Indians immediately fled into the woods and disappeared.[443]

A party was sent out by Gen. Clark to follow the Indians and engage them, but the trail ended a mile or so downstream where the Indians had hidden a canoe in a small inlet and it was evident that they had escaped to the north side of the river.

Shortly after their arrival here at Louisville, Gen. Clark had assigned squads of his men at the neighboring stations up Beargrass Creek to aid in their protection. One of these squads was commanded by Lt. William Crawford, son of Valentine Crawford, whose second in command was Ens. Thomas Ravenscroft. Among the privates were the brothers Thomas and Joseph Mason and the tough little Irishman, Samuel Murphy, late of Brady's Rangers. They were assigned to Wells' Station, nine miles above Louisville on Beargrass Creek.[444] This little company, on September 9, went out hunting for buffalo with some of the resident Kentuckians and were having a wonderful time when a large party of Indians under Shemeneto, Thayendanegea and Alexander McKee showed up and chased them for many miles. They finally reached refuge of sorts at Squire Boone's Station, established by Daniel Boone's brother. Here they discovered that two men had just been killed while working in one of the adjacent cornfields and the residents were very fearful of venturing out.

Two days ago, on September 11, Lt. Crawford's party escorted a group from here to Lexington. A scout around that settlement resulted in the discovery of a new pair of moccasins and other signs of Indians and it was decided that the rather weak settlement, consisting of 28 families, should be evacuated. Yesterday, half of these people, taking many of their goods with them and escorted by Crawford's squad, set out for Linn's Station, the idea being that another escort would be sent to guard the remainder when they followed. Young Isaiah Boone, Squire's son, was along, proudly wearing a broad-brim beaver hat of Quaker style and carrying a rifle that seemed bigger than himself.

They had traveled only a few miles when a Kentucky militia officer with them, Lt. John Welch, was abruptly taken so violently ill that he was unable to continue. It was decided the rest of the party should go on while a dozen men under Lt. Crawford, including Sam Murphy and the Mason brothers, stayed as a guard for Welch, to bring him in when he felt better.

The larger portion of the party continued to be escorted by Ens. Ravenscroft and Sgt. Philip Muckano and, in a mile or so, they were abruptly ambushed by that large body of Indians, mainly Shawnees, under Shemeneto, McKee and Thayendanegea. Sgt. Muckano managed to get a shot off, and his bullet broke a warrior's neck, but before he could even reload, he was himself shot dead and tumbled from his horse. After that, all was chaos. Little Isaiah Boone managed to escape but lost his beaver hat in the process, and Isham Floyd tossed away his empty gun and galloped off.

By this time, beyond earshot, with Lt. Welch feeling a little better, the Crawford party had begun following the others. Abruptly, they encountered a riderless horse coming toward them with a traveling bag attached to the saddle and recognized it as belonging to the party who had left them. Moments later a young woman and a little boy were observed coming in their direction, obviously captives of the two Indians with them, one of whom was mounted. Seeing Crawford's squad, the Indians were startled and fled, although one swung his tomahawk at the young woman as he dashed away, which fortunately missed, and she told them of the attack during which many had been killed, including her mother. The little boy was her brother. A few others, she said, might also have been taken prisoner.

Taking her and the little boy with them, Crawford's party went on by a circuitous route and reached Linn's Station after dark last night. There they found others of the defeated party who had managed to escape, including militia Col. John Floyd, who was in the process of berating his younger brother, Isham, for having discarded his gun. Murphy was pleased to find at Linn's an old schoolmate of his, Sam Wells, Jr., from back on Jacobs' Creek near Pittsburgh. Wells and his father had emigrated to Kentucky several years earlier.

Col. Floyd assembled 27 mounted men to leave under his leadership at three o'clock in the morning in an effort to rescue any survivors or wounded who might be found and to bury the dead. About 15 others, without horses, wanted to come along. Col. Floyd advised against it, but when they insisted, he agreed.

Well before dawn this morning they started out, Floyd riding his fine black gelding named Shawnee. He was flanked by his brother Isham and Pvt. Aquilla Whittaker, with Sam Wells, senior and junior, riding directly behind.[445] Only a few days before, young Sam Wells had so infuriated Col. Floyd by some sort of prank that Floyd had literally thrown him out of his house. After traveling a few miles, the party encountered an elderly couple who had been in the attacked party and had managed to escape. Traveling slowly and carefully during the night, they had seen a number of Indians but had avoided detection. The couple told them where these Indians were and then, escorted by two of the unmounted men in the party, hurried on toward the safety of the fortified Linn's Station.

It was early daylight as Col. Floyd's party approached the point where the Indians were supposed to be. He split his force into three columns, himself leading the center, Capt. Sturgus on his right and Ens. Ravenscroft, Sam Murphy with him, on the left. They crossed Floyd's Creek and advanced up a hollow, directly into an ambush set up by Alexander McKee, James Girty and Thayendanegea. Capt. Sturgus, glimpsing the enemy first, was the only man to get a shot off before the Indians opened up with a tremendous volley and quickly moved to surround the columns. Sturgus was mortally wounded, as was Samuel Wells, Sr. Some of the men, especially those afoot, took cover, but the majority began retreating.

Floyd's horse, Shawnee, panicked by the explosion of shots, became unmanageable, reared and screamed and then plunged away, with the colonel trying to bring the animal under control. In a few hundred yards the horse passed beneath a lowhanging branch that swept Floyd from the saddle and slammed him to the ground. The horse ran off. With Indians approaching at a run, Floyd turned and fled on foot, having lost his gun in the fall.

Toward the rear of the retreaters, Sam Wells, Jr., occasionally wheeled his horse and presented his rifle at the pursuers, helping to keep the Indians at bay while the whites, both mounted and afoot, continued to race away. Finally, having helped the others get a good lead on the Indians, he wheeled his horse and galloped forward. Off to one side he saw Col. Floyd running with Indians pursuing not far behind. He galloped to him and, seeing the colonel was so spent that he was nearly falling, he leaped off his horse and tried to help Floyd into the saddle. So exhausted he could not at first swing his legs up, Floyd rode for 30 yards or so on his stomach across the saddle, young Wells running beside. Even in this distress, Floyd recalled with chagrin that this was the young man he had thrown out of his house only a few days ago because of a silly prank. At last he was able to swing a leg over the horse's back and settle himself in the saddle.

Sam Murphy got one shot off and, while trying to reload, dropped the lead ball. While fumbling for another, Indians started rushing toward him and he retreated. He was chased a considerable distance and every once in a while he would whirl and point his rifle at his pursuers. They would immediately dodge behind trees and he would run on. A ball struck him in the hip but he continued to flee. Then he spotted an Indian angling in ahead of him on an interception course. They aimed their rifles at one another, but the Indian's gun snapped in a misfire and Murphy jumped behind a tree.

Hearing a sound at his rear, Murphy whirled and found a warrior ready to pounce on him. He brought his gun up and the Indian, trying to dodge away, tripped and fell. He was abruptly slammed into by the Indian who, moments ago, had snapped his gun at him, and the two rolled around on the ground, but then the other Indian joined in the tussle and they soon had him pinned. Murphy reached for his knife but discovered that the handle had been shot off by the ball that entered his hip and the blade was wedged in the sheath.

Close by, Valentine King, wounded below the shoulder blade, was captured, as were Ens. Ravenscroft, Daniel Whittaker and Nicholas Soap.[446] Murphy was led past the latter two and Whittaker smiled at him. The pair were the subject of a dispute between two rival clusters of Indians over who should have them as captives. At that point Thayendanegea walked up and methodically killed both of them with his sword. Then, in attempting to wipe the blood off the weapon on his leg, he inadvertently turned the blade and severely sliced open his own flesh.[447] Ripping up the dead Whittaker's shirt into strips, Thayendanegea bound up his badly bleeding wound and then approached Murphy.

"What did your party come here for?" he asked in perfectly good English.

"To bury the dead," Murphy replied, expecting to be killed any second.

"Why don't you do it then?"

"I will if you'll let me."

"Aye, damn you!" Thayendanegea snarled, seeming on the verge of striking him down, but then he turned and strode off.

Murphy was then approached by another man who he thought at first was an Indian but then recognized as James Girty. The little Irishman held out his hand to shake, but Girty refused to take it, though he said, "You're safe enough now."

When the Indians led the captives away, they passed the place where the party from Squire Boone's Station had been ambushed, and Murphy counted ten dead and scalped men, women and children still lying on the ground.[448]

This incredible day's tragedies were not yet over. At Louisville three of Gen. Clark's officers, Capts. Charles Tipton and John Chapman, along with Ens. Thomas McGaughey, asked his permission to take an excursion up the Lower Road to the Beargrass settlements. Clark granted them leave to do so and even let Tipton borrow his sword, the captain's own sword having been broken in an affray some days earlier.

The three, with a slave along to attend them, set off on the road and hardly an hour later were ambushed by a small party of Shawnees under a subchief named Gushawa. Chapman and Tipton were killed instantly, but McGaughey and the slave managed to escape and get back to Fort Nelson with the news.

Gushawa, taking the sword Capt. Tipton had been wearing, saw engraved in script upon it, the name *George Rogers Clark,* and for some time believed he had actually killed the great white chief, especially since Tipton and Clark were of approximately the same build and both had reddish-sandy hair.

But Gen. George Rogers Clark was still very much alive—as he was determined to prove to them in the weeks and months ahead.

[S e p t e m b e r   1 9 ,   1 7 8 1 — W e d n e s d a y]

Monakaduto and his Wyandots had reached the headwaters of the Walhonding when they overtook the Moravian Indians and captive missionaries still being herded toward Sandusky by the mixed Indian party under Chiefs Pimoacan and Wingenund. They halted and the chiefs conferred for some time, Monakaduto sourly telling them of having the planned attack against Wheeling aborted, because of the high degree of preparedness among the settlers and soldiers. That the roving Indian parties had enjoyed considerable success in striking outlying cabins and killing numerous whites as well as taking quite a few prisoners did little to mollify the keen disappointment Monakaduto felt over failure of the principal objective.

"The *Shemanese* had been warned we were coming and were very ready to receive us," he told them, his hard gaze moving toward missionaries Zeisberger and Heckewelder, who sat a little distance away with their wrists bound behind them, "and that warning must have come from those two. Our British friends in Detroit will get the truth out of them, and then we shall see what kind of punishment they will receive."

"You have come back to us," Pimoacan observed, "with half of the warriors who went with you. The others have returned to the Muskingum and Tuscarawas?"

"Some," Monakaduto said, nodding. "Most have stayed behind in small parties to continue striking the places where the *Shemanese* are most unprotected. My son, Scotach," he added proudly, "leads one of these parties. It includes six other warriors, including his two younger brothers, Dakadulah and Scoleh. They have vowed not to return without many scalps."

"Are we not to attack Wheeling at all then?" Wingenund asked.

"For this season, no. As I have said, they are strong and ready and protected in their fort. Without the thunder guns of our British friends to crack open those walls, we cannot root them out. The winter is too close to organize any further attempt on Wheeling this season, but next year we will strike them hard, and they will not be able to withstand us. You will see."

[September 23, 1781 — Sunday]

Lt. Matthew Neely, stationed at Fort Pitt, decided that since this was such a gloriously beautiful warm day—perhaps the very last of the season that would permit such activity—he would take a refreshing swim in the river adjacent to the fort. Clad only in an old pair of trousers, the legs torn off at the knees where they had worn through, he plunged into the cool water. After the first momentary shock, he quickly became accustomed to it and paddled about, gleefully kicking water into the air.

Originally from the coast, Neely very much enjoyed fresh seafood, especially shellfish. Clam chowder was one of his favorite foods and, though in his estimation freshwater clams could not compare with those from saltwater, he decided he'd gather some from the river bottom. For half an hour he repeatedly dove and searched, finding almost two dozen in that interval. Deciding to make one last dive, he slid beneath the surface to the bottom and all but collided with a large hard object. At first he thought it was a log, but then he became excited when he realized it was a cannon.

Five hours later, having used heavy ropes and a team of horses and a good deal of trial and error, the three-inch brass swivel, complete with mountings, lay dripping on the shore. A large crowd had gathered and an old Frenchman, who had traded with the Indians for many years, first under the French and then under the British, identified it as of French manufacture and guessed it was from the time when his countrymen had occupied Fort Duquesne, where Fort Pitt was now.[449]

Neely claimed the big gun as his own. It was heavily coated with river muck and corrosion and had obviously been spiked, but he was determined to clean it up, remove the spiking and get it back into top-notch condition, no matter how long it took.

But first, he decided, he was going to celebrate his discovery with an absolutely wonderful batch of clam chowder.

[September 30, 1781 — Sunday]

Col. John Gibson had become convinced that Col. Daniel Brodhead had lost his mind. He had seen men go insane before, when under torture or in battle or under such duress that they could no longer tolerate a situation, but in those cases it had been a sudden snapping. In Brodhead's case, it had been very gradual, subtle and insidious, but Gibson no longer had any doubt about it—Col. Brodhead was totally, hopelessly mad.

Now, writing to Gen. Washington, Gibson considered how he should report this to the commander-in-chief. To flatly assert that such was the case was perhaps too bold and might give rise to suspicion that he was simply impugning the character and abilities of his superior. To hint vaguely at it might not put the point across strongly enough or perhaps make it appear he was merely whining. In the end, he decided all purposes could best be served by simply stating the facts of what had occurred as best he could honestly express them.

He quickly read through the first paragraph of the letter, in which he told Gen. Washington what he had been able to discover in regard to the hostile northwestern tribes forcing the Moravians out of their towns on the Tuscarawas. He had also informed the general that he had sent spies up the Allegheny to French Creek, checking on the report of a major British force advancing from Presque Isle by way of Le Boeuf. He was pleased to state that they had uncovered no evidence to support the story. Now he focused his thoughts, dipped his pen and continued with the writing:

> *A large party* [of Indians] *has since done some mischief in the County of Ohio, and on Ten Mile Creek they have killed and taken 16 persons, and have effected this with the loss of only two of their party.*
>
> *In my last, I informed your Excellency that I had fixed on ye 4th of September as a day of general rendezvous for the troops to assemble at Fort McIntosh, to make an excursion against the Wyandot Towns. On receiving the intelligence contained in the minister's letter, with the advice of the principal officers, I postponed it until the 12th day of September, as by that time we might be able to obtain certain intelligence of the enemy.*
>
> *Colonel Brodhead, though for what reason I am at a loss to determine, wrote circular letters informing the country that he had fixed on the 15th of September as a day of general rendezvous on Montour's Run for the militia to assemble. This, and the Indians striking near Wheeling, threw the country into confusion. However, at the day I had appointed, upwards of 100 assembled, but the number was too small to attempt anything; while Colonel Brodhead had the mortification to find that not a single man appeared on the day fixed on for his general rendezvous. A day or two after, the officers wrote Colonel Brodhead a letter, informing him it was their opinion he could not, with propriety, in the present situation of affairs, re-assume the command, a copy of which I did myself the honor of enclosing in my last letter to your Excellency. He sent me an arrest by the Brigade Major, informing me that I was arrested for assuming the chief command at this post, thereby exciting mutiny and sedition amongst a number of the officers in this Department, and also for neglect of duty and disobedience of orders, and I was to confine myself to the range of the garrison; on receipt of which I desired the Brigade Major to inform him that I should pay no attention to his arrest, as it was evident to me as well from the letters of your Excellency, as also from the charge that had been exhibited against him, that he could not with any degree of propriety re-assume the command.*
>
> *He continued attempting to command until the return of the express with letters from your Excellency at the Head of Elk. This put an end to the dispute, though Colonel Brodhead, even after the receipt of those letters, sent to inform me that he intended to publish it in General Orders that I was to take command of the Western Department, and wished to know whether it would be agreeable to me. I returned him for answer, that I thought there was no necessity for doing so, as the letters from your Excellency had been made known to the officers.*
>
> *The express returned here on the 17th instant, and the depositions against Colonel Brodhead were not begun being taken until yesterday, owing to a difference*

between Colonel Brodhead and Captain Fowler respecting the appointment of the Deputy Judge Advocate; however, the matter is now settled, and I hope the business will go on without any interruption.

I hope your Excellency will pardon my intrusion on your patience with the length of this letter, as I do it in justification of my conduct in this dispute, lest any reports may prejudice me in your Excellency's esteem.

I have, with the advice of Colonel William Crawford and other principal gentlemen of this country, fixed on the 15th day of October for the militia to assemble at Fort McIntosh, in order, if possible, to make an excursion against the Wyandotte Towns; and from the accounts which I have from the different parts of the country, the people will turn out, and I expect to be able to collect 700 men at least for that purpose. Colonel Crawford goes with me, and most of the principal gentlemen of this country.

Inclosed are the returns of the troops of this department. This will be handed your Excellency by Major William Croghan, who has spent some time in this department; he will be able to give your Excellency a full account of every transaction in this country. Permit me, therefore, to refer your Excellency to him.

I have the honor to be, with perfect respect,

> *Your Excellency's most ob't. humble Servant,*
> *John Gibson, Col.*
> *Comdg. W. D.*

His Excellency Genl Washington

Gibson put his pen aside, pushed his chair back and rubbed his eyes. He hoped that what he had written would give Gen. Washington a firm enough nudge to at least make him consider removing Col. Brodhead from this country, where his erratic interference was creating so much unrest and disruption.

Col. John Gibson need not have concerned himself; only six days ago—on September 24—Gen. George Washington had issued a recall for Col. Daniel Brodhead and had appointed a new commander of the Western Department of the Army —Gen. William Irvine.

[S e p t e m b e r   3 0 ,   1 7 8 1 — S u n d a y]

Capt. Andrew Poe had taken his turn on the guard watch 15 minutes ago and, from the small woodpile close at hand, he had added the last remaining piece to the campfire coals.[450] The unexpected drop in temperature from yesterday had resulted in a fitful night's sleep for him and for the dozen others in his little company. Now he huddled near the new bloom of warmth emanating from the combusting fresh wood. It was still quite dark, though he knew that dawn would be breaking in another half-hour. That was when he would awaken the others, so they could all be in their saddles and on their way as soon as there was sufficient light to see the ground.

He thought about what had brought them to this place and wondered if they would be successful in today's search. It had been near noon yesterday when young William Jackson had reached the small fort at Collier's, where Andrew Poe was commander. The 17-year-old was disheveled, exhausted and very upset. It had taken some while for Capt. Poe to sort out the fragmented pieces of Jackson's story.

William and his father, Philip Jackson, who was in his early sixties, had spent the previous night at tiny Burgett's Fort, a fortified cabin on the North Fork of King's Creek, where they had been staying for safety's sake during the recent rash of Indian raids. Two other families had been there with them, but only two other men besides themselves. In the early morning his father had risen and, taking his rifle with him, said he was going to their cabin, a mile and a half distant, to get something but that he would be back for breakfast. When he hadn't returned by the appointed time, William became worried and went to the cabin. He found it plundered and his father gone.

William told Capt. Poe that he then carefully checked the ground outside the cabin and found tracks of both his father and a number of Indians, and it was evident he had been captured. The tracks, William said, headed north. He knew it would be useless to go back to Burgett's, since they did not have horses, manpower or firearms enough to mount a pursuit. Holliday's Cove Fort, three and a half miles distant to the southwest, had only recently burned down, and most of the people from that settlement were still at Wheeling. His only alternative had seemed to go to Collier's Settlement on Harmon's Creek, where he knew Capt. Poe commanded a small militia company.[451] He had alternately run and walked up and down the hills for six miles south and had finally reached the little fort.

As soon as he got the details, Andrew Poe raised the dozen men of the militia that were on hand, including his 33-year-old brother, Adam, who was six years his junior, as well as John Jack, David Marks, Thomas Cherry and seven others. William Jackson said he would go, too, if someone would let him borrow a horse.

The 13 mounted men left Collier's about noon and, rather than going back to the Jackson cabin, which Capt. Poe said would accomplish nothing but make them lose valuable time, he led them on a direct northwestern course, figuring the party would be heading for the river and hoping to cross their trail or intercept them. The ground was well cluttered with autumn leaves, so they had to travel slowly and study the surface closely for any signs of passage. They found none and, by the time it was too dark to see trails any longer, they had traveled about ten miles. Beside a cornfield they found an old corncrib with some corn still in it, which would provide food for their horses, so this was where they had made camp last night, the men taking turns sitting guard-watch.[452]

Now, in the predawn darkness, Andrew Poe came to his feet and stretched hugely. He was a large man with dark hair and hazel eyes, two inches over six feet in height and powerfully built, weighing 225 pounds. Feeling the urge to relieve himself, he walked several yards away from the fire and was momentarily puzzled at the crunching sound under his feet. He bent to look but could see little in the darkness, so he stretched his hand down and felt. The whole surface of the ground, as well as the weeds and grasses above it, were coated with a hoary rime of heavy frost, first of the season. It could not have come at a more appropriate time.

A surge of energy and exultation flooded him and he spun back to the campfire, shaking each of the men in turn and saying, "C'mon, c'mon, get up! We've got a heavy frost! Let's use it while we can. C'mon, get up!"

The men rose, quickly wolfed down some of the food they had brought and saddled their horses. As soon as it was light enough to see the ground sufficiently, they set off to the north, following a ridge. Knowing the frost would disappear quickly when the sun struck it, they moved as rapidly as possible. The day grew brighter and the frost glistened like a fairyland icing over everything on the ground. They studied the surface carefully as they rode and then, hardly over a mile from where they started, found the tracks they were seeking. The marks of Philip Jackson's shoes were clearly evident and, though he couldn't be sure, Andrew Poe estimated that there were six or seven Indians and the party was probably no more than a quarter-hour ahead.

The footprints led northwest, and the pursuers moved more rapidly now that they were on the trail. In another two miles they reached the summit of a hill overlooking the Ohio River. The tracks went down that hill, heading toward the mouth of a stream that Andrew Poe immediately recognized as Tomlinson Run. He believed the Indians had canoes hidden there and that it would be their intention to cross the Ohio and paddle upstream two miles to the mouth of Yellow Creek on the Ohio side.

"We'll leave the horses here and move down on foot," he whispered. "Check your loads. And no talking now, we don't want 'em to hear us or they're likely to kill Mr. Jackson and scatter."

They descended the wooded hill as silently as possible, although John Jack seemed incapable of moving without making some sort of noise, either with his feet or his mouth. At the base of the hill they crossed a little rill where the water was still swirling with mud from the passage of the Indians and their captive. The noise made by Jack as he plodded through the water exasperated Poe, and he decided to separate from the others. With hand signals he indicated they should follow the tracks to the stream's mouth, now no more than 100 yards ahead, though still not visible because of the screen of riverine bushes. Andrew set off to the left, directly toward the Ohio, about 50 yards distant.

In a few moments Capt. Poe reached the high bank. He approached it cautiously and peered over its edge and downward. Some 15 feet below were two Wyandots shoulder to shoulder, both crouched and with rifles leveled, cocked and ready to shoot. They were listening intently and looking toward the mouth of Tomlinson Run, wholly unaware of Poe above them. Glancing at the mouth of the creek, Poe saw four more warriors tugging a fairly large raft out of hiding in the bushes and hard at work trying to get it launched. Farther up on shore sat Philip Jackson, watching the Wyandots and guarded by another warrior standing a few yards away.

From the intentness of the pair below him, Poe was fairly sure they had heard the noise John Jack was making in the approach, and that though not sure what the sound signified, they were nevertheless ready to fire as soon as anyone came into view. One of the Indians below was very large and muscular, the other of medium size and build. These two were Monakaduto's sons, Dakadulah and Scoleh.[453] Poe knew immediately what he had to do: He would shoot the big Indian and then leap down onto the smaller one and kill him with his sheath knife.

Silently bringing his rifle to bear, Poe took dead aim at Dakadulah's head and squeezed the trigger. The hammer of his rifle leaped forward, but only snapped; it was a total misfire, without even a flash in the pan. Instantly the two Indians below spun around, uttering "Waugh!" in their surprise. Just as instantly, Poe dropped his gun and launched himself off the bank and dived onto the pair. He struck them heavily, locking his left arm around the neck of the big one, throwing him down onto his back with Poe fully on his chest, while the captain's right arm simultaneously tightly locked around the neck of the smaller one. Dakadulah and Scoleh dropped their rifles, screeched mightily and began struggling. Scoleh's cocked rifle fired when it struck the ground, the ball going harmlessly into the nearby bank.

The five Wyandots at the mouth of the stream jerked into alertness, and the four by the water—including the war party's leader, Scotach—snatched up their rifles, which they had laid on the raft's surface. The warrior guarding Jackson immediately swung his tomahawk at the captive's head. Jackson tried to lunge away, and the blade embedded itself in his shoulder. As the warrior jerked it loose for another attempt, Adam Poe shot him dead. The four raft-launching Indians exchanged shots with the whites charging out of the underbrush, but only two balls found their targets, one passing through the left hand of Scotach, another mortally wounding Thomas Cherry as it entered his side and tore through the lower part of his lungs. Scotach barked a command, and he and another warrior, dropping their empty guns, broke into a frantic run up the shoreline of Tomlinson Run; the other two, still standing in the shallows, discarded their guns, pulled out their tomahawks and crouched low to the water, attempting to hide behind the short weeds along the shore.

In his precipitous leap upon the Wyandot brothers, Andrew Poe had not had time to draw his knife and now he had gotten himself into quite a predicament. Dakadulah was as large and strong as Poe himself, and he bucked and struggled against Poe's grasp around his neck and the white man's weight on his chest. At the same time, Scoleh squirmed and kicked as he attempted to escape from the iron grip Poe had around his neck with the other arm. Poe's knife was in its sheath and pinned for half its length between his own body and Dakadulah's. Nevertheless he tried to inch himself up enough to where, with his left hand, without removing his grip around Dakadulah's neck, he could reach the haft. But the Wyandot realized what he was trying to do and grasped Poe's left wrist in a powerful grip.

Acting more intuitively than anything else, Poe then tried to force the frantically struggling Scoleh downward so that without loosening that grip around the warrior's neck, he might be able to grip his own knife and pull it free from the sheath. He managed to grasp the end with thumb and forefinger and took a desperate chance: He relaxed his grip around the smaller Indian's neck, knowing the Wyandot would instantly pull free but hoping that at the same moment he could jerk the knife out and stab him before he could move out of reach.

Scoleh did duck out from the loosened grip, and at the same moment, Dakadulah released his grip on Poe's wrist and bucked Poe upward. The captain's knife was momentarily no longer pinned between the two bodies, and the jerk Poe gave to the hasp with thumb and forefinger pulled the knife out of the sheath so easily that it flipped from his grasp, spun through the air and landed on the shore several feet away.

As all this was going on in a matter of seconds, more shots broke out from Poe's men, and the two Wyandots who crouched with tomahawks in hand by the raft were both killed in the shallows. The two who had raced up Tomlinson Run—Scotach and the warrior with him—split at the leader's command. The warrior continued running upstream and Scotach, cradling his wounded hand against his stomach, broke off into a tight turn and angled back through the trees and weeds toward the Ohio well below where his brothers were struggling with the big white man.

David Marks and three or four others had pursued the two running up the stream, while young William Jackson ran to his father to guard him. Marks and another of the whites, both good runners, outdistanced the others. They did not see Scotach angle away from the stream and race through the woods, but continued to close on the fleeing warrior until the man with Marks suddenly stopped, threw up his rifle and snapped off a shot that took the warrior through his upper leg and tumbled him into the leaves. Before he could rise, Marks was upon him, and his own shot, at point-blank range, smashed into the warrior's brain, killing him.

Back at the river, having lost his grip on Scoleh, Andrew Poe tightened his arm even more firmly around Dakadulah's neck, but the big warrior got his own arms around Poe's middle in a fierce grip that all but cracked the captain's lower ribs and severely limited his ability to breathe. Scoleh, free of the struggle, jerked the tomahawk out from his waistband and swung a blow with it at the white man's head. Poe saw it coming and kicked out savagely, his right foot catching Scoleh's wrist and sending the tomahawk spinning into the river.

Scoleh recovered, scrambled to Dakadulah and pulled his brother's tomahawk from the waistband and began circling with it, feinting blows and looking for an opportunity to strike Poe without hitting his brother. He saw his chance and swung, but Poe again saw it coming and held up his right arm to ward it off. The tomahawk plunged deeply into his lower arm, making a gash over seven inches long, severing one of the wrist bones and the tendons to three of his fingers. Jerking with the pain, Poe pulled the embedded tomahawk free from Scoleh's grasp. The weapon stuck to his wrist a moment more and then fell to the ground beneath the struggling combatants.

Scoleh, having lost the second tomahawk, snatched up his rifle. Adam Poe was by now running down the shoreline toward them and, knowing his gun was empty, stopped some 40 yards away and began swiftly reloading. Scoleh also began reloading, and it became a race as to who would finish first. Scoleh, in his haste, dropped his ramrod and instantly scooped it up again, but he had lost a precious second or two. Adam Poe finished first and, just as Scoleh began raising his gun, Poe sent a shot into the center of his chest and killed him.[454]

Dakadulah and Andrew Poe had by this time, in their continuing struggle, rolled into the river. There were no shallows along this stretch of shoreline, and both men went under. Poe managed to grasp Dakadulah's hair with his uninjured left hand and attempted to keep the warrior's head under the surface. Their struggling carried them farther out into the river until they were some forty feet from shore. Poe had managed to get a gasping breath of air or two as they rolled, and he was sure he had prevented the big Indian from doing so. When his adversary suddenly went limp, he thought he had drowned and, unable to swim with his injured arm, he released his grip on the hair and struck out for shore.

Immediately, Dakadulah came to the surface just below him, gasping and choking, and he, too, swam for shore. Uninjured, Dakadulah got there first and scrambled back to where his rifle lay on the bank, snatched it up and leveled it at Andrew, who ducked down and began kicking farther out into the river. Dakadulah aimed at Poe's exposed head and shot, but the gun only snapped, having lost its prime when dropped. By this time, Adam Poe had again reloaded and, in order to save Andrew, shot too hastily. His bullet struck Dakadulah high in the hip, slamming him back into the water some 20 feet from Andrew.

Capt. Poe surged back toward where Dakadulah had gone below the surface and was practically on him before he rose. Again he was able to grasp the big Indian's hair with his left hand and force his head under water. They rolled and thrashed in the water and Poe brought up his knee, catching Dakadulah in the groin. The Indian went limp, and Poe kicked again and then again. He got his own head above the surface and sucked in a breath, then planted a foot in Dakadulah's stomach and kicked him outward and downward, at the same time releasing his grip on the hair.

Adam Poe, gun reloaded and pointed at the water, was ready to shoot again as soon as the big Indian's head should reappear on the surface, but Dakadulah had drowned and sunk. Several hundred yards downstream, Scotach peered from hiding at what was occurring. Wounded, weaponless and greatly outnumbered, he realized there was nothing he could do. Staying to cover, he continued down the shoreline another quarter-mile, then entered the water and swam across to the Ohio side.

Andrew Poe had defeated his adversary, but now his own strength was all but gone, and he struggled feebly to get back to shore. At this moment John Jack and another of Poe's men came running along the high bank above to assist Adam and, seeing the man in the river and taking him to be an Indian, loosed shots at him. Jack's companion shot first, and his ball struck the water a foot or so from Andrew's head. Jack's ball, however, struck Andrew in the rear of his right shoulder close to his neck and inside the collarbone, passed through his body and exited at the top of his ribs on the left side. Andrew was now so disabled, he could not swim and began to sink. Adam tossed his own gun aside, leaped into the water, just managed to catch hold of Andrew's shirt before the current swept him away and, with some difficulty, hauled him back to shore.

Andrew Poe was carried to where the rescued Philip Jackson was sitting beside the dying Tom Cherry. The tomahawk wound in Jackson's shoulder was painful but not serious. The whole little company gathered at this spot, and Andrew's numerous wounds were treated as best could be done, but it was obvious that he needed competent medical treatment as quickly as possible. There was no time to scalp the dead Indians or do anything more than collect what weapons could be quickly found. While some of the men moved speedily up to the ridge to get the horses and bring them here, others constructed a horse litter out of a blanket and poles cut from saplings. By the time they finished, Tom Cherry had died. They draped his body over his saddle and fastened it securely. Then they tied the litter between two of their horses and put Capt. Poe into it and immediately headed for the nearest place where there was a doctor—Wheeling.[455]

[October 8, 1781 — Monday]

Scotach, approaching his father's village—Half King's Town on the upper Sandusky—knew it was time to stop and prepare for his arrival. Though he had long since steeled himself to ignore the pain in his wounded hand, his movements were nevertheless clumsy as he gathered some twigs and dry grasses. Using flint, steel and tinder from his pouch, he soon had a small fire going and continued to feed it with pieces of bark, seeking especially bark from the white oak, which would leave a residue of black ashes. With the small fire fueled enough, he crouched beside it, settling back on his heels, and once again let the grief he was bringing home to Monakaduto fill his own mind and heart as he thought of what had occurred over these past few days.

Having swum to the Ohio side of the river following the attack, he had cautiously made his way back to a point opposite the mouth of Tomlinson Run. From a high point of ground, he was able to see the *Shemanese* tying a dead man stomach down over the back of one of their horses and another on a litter between two other horses. In a few minutes they had mounted their own horses and were quickly swallowed up by the woods as they followed a trail up into the hills to the south.

Though certain it was no ruse, Scotach nevertheless decided he would not leave this place until late in the day. As he waited, he searched for and found several of the herbs—now wilted from the frost—that would ease the pain throbbing up his left arm from his wounded hand. These he mashed between two rocks into a pulpy mass, which he then stuffed into the wound, followed by a wadding of buzzard down from his pouch packed into both sides of the wound to curtail bleeding and promote coagulation. Locating some mandrake plants, he broke off a few of the large wilted leaves and wrapped them around his entire hand and then tied them in place with a long rawhide thong carried in his pouch.

Just before sunset Scotach moved farther up the bank of the river, estimating how far the current would carry him downstream as he crossed so he would come ashore near where the action had occurred. In the twilight, pushing a large chunk of dry wood before him, he waded into the river and, clinging to the floating wood, struck out swimming as best he could to the other side. Despite his calculations, he still came ashore somewhat below where he had intended. He walked back upstream and, in the gathering gloom of nightfall, came to the body of his brother Scoleh close to the river's edge. Though he searched the vicinity closely, he could not find his other brother, Dakadulah, and somehow he knew the Great Spirit had lifted him home in Her net from beneath the river's surface. Grateful that Scoleh had not been scalped, he picked him up with some difficulty and carried him in his arms to where the raft had been and was gratified to find it still wedged in the reeds and weeds along the shore. The bodies of the two warriors that had been killed there were still in the weedy shallows close by. He laid Scoleh's body on its surface and then waded out and loosened the raft enough that he could easily pull it free when the time came. The other two dead warriors he placed beside Scoleh, and then he began to search for the others.

He easily found the body of the warrior who had been guarding the captive and carried him the short distance to the raft and laid him beside the other three. That left only two missing—Dakadulah and the warrior who had run up the smaller stream with Scotach. Dakadulah, he was sure, had been swallowed by the river, and, remembering the two shots that had been fired behind him moments after he and the warrior split, Scotach assumed his companion had been killed. But since there would be no way of finding his body in the darkness, he reluctantly dismissed any idea of searching for him.

He waded into the stream again and, as he struggled to free the raft, he stepped upon something hard. He reached down to the bottom and was more than a little pleased when his hand closed around a tomahawk that had been dropped by one of the warriors who was killed here. He put the weapon securely in his waistband, continued to tug at the raft until it was free. He tied the raft to his waist with a short cord and pulled it along behind him as he swam, pacing himself so as not to become exhausted. It was very difficult with the current tugging at them, and as a result, he was fully three miles downstream from the point where he started when he finally staggered to shore at a broad bottom.[456]

One by one he carried the bodies well up on the shore to a point above the normal spring high-water level. Using the only tool he had—the recovered tomahawk—he dug a grave more than three feet deep, wide enough and long enough to accommodate the four bodies lying side by side, their heads toward the east. By this time it was sunrise and Scotach had very little strength left, yet he searched farther up the shoreline and into the woodlands to find the appropriate herbs, which he gathered and scattered over the bodies. From his pouch he removed the last of his kinnikinnick, saturated and useless now for smoking, and scattered it over the bodies. Then slowly, tiredly, he began refilling the grave with the soil he had removed. By noon he had finished and he searched for a large rock. He found one too big to be carried but managed, with difficulty, to roll it to the foot of the grave—a marker that he and others of his tribe, when he described it to them, would be able to find again. Eventually, he knew, they would come back here and disinter the remains, scrape away what remained of the flesh and carry the bones back to their own burial ground close to the village for proper final ceremonies.

It was by then early afternoon, the first day of October, and he walked wearily away into the woods. Well into the hills, he discovered a large fallen tree with a large, cavelike hollow in its bole. Making sure it was not occupied by *muga* or *peshewa* or *meshepeshe*—bear or wildcat or panther—he backed into the opening and lay on his stomach, tomahawk in hand, and went to sleep. He slept without interruption the remainder of the day, through the night and well into the following morning.

When he awoke, Scotach was stiff and sore and hungry. His left forearm and hand were swollen from his injury, and a deep, pervasive throbbing emanated from the wound. He had some pieces of food in his pouch, watersoaked but still edible—jerky intermingled in a mass of now glutinous parched corn—but he ate none of it. This was a day of mourning, a day to grieve for his lost brothers and companions. He built a little fire and kept it so by adding only minimal quantities of wood at relatively short intervals. For a long while he crouched by the fire, more often than not simply staring at its flames but, on occasion, muttering sing-song incantations or tossing his head back and giving vent to mournful howls. Several times he wept, his shoulders heaving spasmodically. Twice, after stoking the little blaze, he circled the fire in a strange shuffling dance, punctuated by high leaps in which he arched himself backward and then bent far forward at the waist, issuing more of the melancholy cries. Finally, at nightfall, he allowed the fire to die away and crept back into the log and slept again.

On the third day of October, he started his walk home, eating the distasteful mess of jerky and parched corn as he walked, moving to the west and eventually coming to a path he recognized. He began to follow it but soon camped for the night. By evening the next day, after crossing the Tuscarawas not far above the remains of Fort Laurens, he was fortunate enough to bring down a cottontail rabbit with a good throw of the tomahawk. He roasted it for his dinner over a somewhat larger campfire and slept close by it for the warmth it generated. For three more days he walked, making his little camp each night, usually going hungry but one time climbing a tree to dispatch a raccoon he spied in the upper branches and that he ate with great enjoyment.

By nightfall yesterday, he knew he was close to his father's village and would arrive on the morrow about the time the sun was at its highest. Twice he saw other Indians at a distance, but he did not approach them or make himself known. He ate nothing and made his camp beside a stream, where he bathed himself, scrubbing every inch of his body with coarse gravelly sand. He slept this night sitting with his back to a large tree.

This morning he had walked until within a mile of the village, keeping off the trail so he would not meet anyone else, as it would not be seemly to explain what had occurred before the village as a whole had been alerted. Then he had stopped and built his little fire and fed it the chips of white oak bark until all the wood was consumed and only ash remained. Now, at last, coming out of his reverie, he poked and scattered the ashes somewhat so they would cool more swiftly. As soon as it was possible for him to do so, he scooped up handsful of the ash and rubbed it into his chest and onto his face until his skin was stained a dark gray. Then he straightened and began walking the final mile to Half King's Town.

Half a mile from the village he began chanting the death song and issuing the death howls that would alert the villagers that he was arriving with news of defeat and death. They began coming out to meet him, and seeing who he was and his ash-coated appearance, they picked up the cry and fell in behind him. The eerie sound, rising and falling from ever more throats in unison, was picked up now by those still in the village, a deeply melancholy sound.

Scotach stopped in the center of the village, and they formed a wide circle about him. His father, Chief Monakaduto, appeared and stood with the villagers and, when Scotach raised both arms high overhead and then let them slowly lower straight out from his shoulders, the howls and chanting began dying away. By the time his arms were at his sides, silence had fallen over the assemblage.

Scotach again raised his arms, his right hand straight up and spread to show five fingers, his injured left hand similarly raised, the fingers clenched as best he could close them, except for his index finger, which pointed straight up. There was a gasp, and a low moaning sound began among some. They now knew that six warriors had been killed. Scotach lowered his arms again and slowly pivoted in place, letting his eyes sweep across the people. When he saw the mother of the warrior who had been killed while guarding the captive, he pointed at her, and she immediately began to weep and raise the death cry. He turned further and pointed at the father of one of the warriors who had been killed at the raft, and he, too, broke into the death cry and tears began coursing down his cheeks. For the relatives of each in turn he pointed, and the cries were raised. Finally he faced his own father. Toward him he pointed with both hands. Monakaduto's expression darkened, and he wept and raised his plaintive cry with the others.

The larger circle broke up and smaller circles formed around those who had been designated, and they comforted them and raised their voices with them in the death song. Scotach moved to his father and he and Monakaduto embraced, and then they wept more together over the loss of sons and brothers.

The grieving in the various circles lasted for a long time. Then finally, as they became still, Scotach again became the center of attention as he related the details of what had occurred—the capture of the white man, the unexpected attack by the whites who followed, the deaths, the flight across the river and then back to recover the dead, the burial, the mourning, the long journey home.

Gradually Monakaduto's grief was overshadowed by a growing anger. Were the Moravian missionaries, Heckewelder and Zeisberger, still in the new village called Captives' Town, three-quarters of a mile upstream from Half King's Town, where the converted Indians were now staying, he would have ordered their death at the stake as appeasement for their loss, but the German missionaries had already been sent to Detroit.[457] There were, however, eight American prisoners in the town. Monakaduto ordered them executed but then spared one. The seven who were killed were not burned at the stake, but simply tomahawked and scalped.

The reprieved one was a 15-year-old youth who had been captured at age 12 during an attack on a sugar camp on the Rusdan's Run tributary of Raccoon Creek 31 months before. Several young men, including his older brother, had been killed in that incident, and he and several others captured. Though never adopted into a family, he was kept at the village as a slave and had learned their language well and made himself useful. It had been thought that eventually he would be adopted. What saved his life now was the fact that a young Wyandot maiden his own age, chunky and not particularly pretty by his standards, had fallen in love with him. She intervened and begged Monakaduto to spare this one, and Monakaduto had agreed.[458]

The young captive's name was George Fulkes.

[*O c t o b e r   1 2 ,   1 7 8 1 — F r i d a y*]

Few men on the frontier ever became so expert in the dangerous pursuit of Indian fighting that the Indians knew them by name and reputation and greatly feared and respected them. Capturing one of these elite few was a very high priority among them, and usually a very special death by prolonged torture was in store for that individual; assuming, of course, that they could continue to hold him once he had been caught.

Daniel Boone was of this ilk. He had been captured by the Shawnees, even adopted by them, and remained with them long enough to discover their plans and then neatly escaped and thwarted those plans that had been so long in development. Simon Kenton was another. He, too, had been captured and condemned to death at the stake. Yet he had escaped the death sentence, eventually made his way back to Kentucky, and he remained a grave threat to the tribes. There were others: Martin Wetzel had been captured and ultimately escaped; his younger brothers, Lewis and Jacob, had been captured when mere little boys, yet had escaped, and Lewis, since then, had become a terror to the Indians, widely known and feared for his survival skills and remorselessness in killing Indians. Then, too, there was Sam Brady, who ranked as perhaps among the most feared and respected of all.

While Capt. Samuel Brady ordinarily did not like to have his scouting parties exceed two dozen men, his incredible successes in beating the Indians at their own game had made him so popular that his scout and spy force, now known to all as Brady's Rangers, had grown to more than 50. Usually he would divide this force in separate ranging parties under different, well-proven members of his command and send them on patrols in different areas. Their principal goals were to watch for Indian sign heading toward the settlements and to give timely warning. If they encountered small parties, they were to use their discretion as to whether they should attack.

Once in a while, however, Brady was ordered to take more men than customarily, when the Indians he had been sent to spy upon constituted an especially large force. His present mission was one of those times. A particularly large war party—comprising, it was believed, primarily Mingoes, Senecas and Wyandots—had been moving about some distance up Beaver River, and Brady was ordered to take 40 of his Rangers and discover where they were and what they were about.

They had been gone on this mission for nearly a fortnight now, initially striking out up the Beaver. Close to where that river is formed by the confluence of the Shenango and Mahoning, they had picked up the trail of the large Indian war party and followed it up the Mahoning River. Some 20 miles upstream, the Indians left the river and followed a well-used trail heading west.[459]

Late in the afternoon the day before yesterday, they had come within sight of where the Indians, some 60 of them, were camped and had observed them from a distance. It was an area Brady had scouted several times in the past and he was familiar with the terrain. The camp was located on the east side of a substantial creek where the trail crossed at a fording place, just south of an oval-shaped swamp about 1,000 feet long lying between the fording place and the southern tip of a lake 1,500 feet to the north.[460] Brady knew that a smaller Indian trail angled northward from where his party was now hidden and followed a narrow ridge that separated the lake from the swamp, that trail passing through a narrow defile of wooded slopes that would be ideal for an ambush.[461]

As soon as it became dark enough to mask their movements, they eased into the defile. Brady gathered his Rangers and, in whispers, laid out the plan. It would

Brady's Ambush and
Leap Over the Cuyahoga River

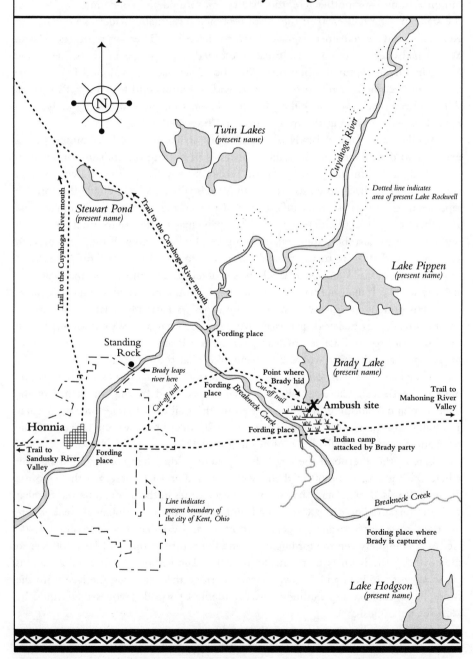

Twin Lakes
(present name)

Stewart Pond
(present name)

Cuyahoga River

Trail to the Cuyahoga River mouth

Trail to the Cuyahoga River mouth

Dotted line indicates area of present Lake Rockwell

Lake Pippen
(present name)

Fording place

Standing Rock

← Brady leaps river here

Point where Brady hid

Brady Lake
(present name)

Fording place

Cut-off trail

Cut-off trail

Breakneck Creek

Ambush site

Trail to Mahoning River Valley →

Honnia

← Trail to Sandusky River Valley

Fording place

Fording place

Indian camp attacked by Brady party

Line indicates present boundary of the city of Kent, Ohio

Breakneck Creek

↑
Fording place where Brady is captured

Lake Hodgson
(present name)

involve the same kind of ruse the Indians had so often—and so successfully—used against the whites. Fourteen men were to take their places, well spaced and hidden, on the forest slope north of the defile, another 14 on the south slope.

The remaining 12 men, led by Brady, would move around the west end of the swamp to approach the Indian encampment from the north and get themselves into position to fire into the Indian camp as soon after daylight as the Indians were up and gathered at their breakfast. The Indian force was large and, no matter how many they killed or disabled, they knew they would be pursued at once. Immediately upon firing, Brady and his dozen men would flee back the way they had come, around the west end of the swamp and then eastward along the ridge trail that led through the defile, with Brady himself bringing up the rear. Utilizing the long hours of practice they had expended in learning how to do it, they would reload as they ran. Passing through the defile where the remaining 28 Rangers were hidden, the runners would listen for Brady's call, which he would give as they reached the eastern end of the passage. As soon as that call was given, the men would spread out in a line across the trail, kneel, aim and prepare to fire. When Brady, in the rear, reached that line, he too would stop, spin about, kneel and take aim. The 28 on the slopes, meanwhile, were to select specific individuals of the pursuing Indians as their targets, take careful aim and attempt to make killing shots when the signal for firing was given. However, the orders were to be observed very strictly: Not until Brady fired were any of the men on the slopes to reveal their presence or fire any guns. Once Brady's signal shot was made, then all the Rangers were to fire simultaneously. It was Brady's hope that they would kill or wound a good many, but undoubtedly many more of the enemy would be unhurt. The instant their rifles were fired, the Rangers were to scatter and head back for Fort McIntosh, every man on his own and no more than two men traveling together. They were to reload as they ran and be prepared to defend themselves if selected for pursuit.

Having approached to within 60 yards of the Indian encampment under cover of darkness, Brady and his dozen men crouched in the tall dry weeds and awaited the dawn. When it came, there began to be activity in the Indian camp, and within half an hour the majority of the Indians were up and about, had gone to the stream to drink, had relieved themselves and had gathered about their several campfires to breakfast. It was then that, at Brady's signal, the Rangers rose from hiding and fired.

The surprise was complete, and about ten of the warriors fell where they stood. The remainder, some 50, seeing the 13 men racing away on foot, snatched up their weapons and were immediately in pursuit, shrieking and howling in their fury. Around the west end of the swamp the pursuit was maintained, the Rangers about 100 yards ahead of the Indians. On reaching the northwestern edge of the swamp, they turned to the east on the trail and followed it through the defile, loading as they ran. At the eastern end Brady barked his command and they stopped, wheeled about and formed their line, dropped to one knee and presented their weapons. Brady, last to do so, took a bead on the warrior who had moved into the lead among the pursuers. Effective range was about 70 yards, but, murmuring "Steady, boys, steady!" he waited until the man was no more than 50 yards distant before he fired.

Instantly a barrage of 39 other rifle shots came, and a large number of the Indians tumbled, many dead, others writhing in the agony of their wounds.[462] Those unhurt halted and fled back the way they had come until out of range and then took to cover. By that time the Rangers themselves were well on the move, scattering as instructed, no one pausing to take a scalp, collect a weapon or do anything else but get out of the area as quickly as possible.

Only one of the Rangers was caught. Ironically, it turned out to be Samuel Brady.

Having skirted the eastern edge of the swamp and knowing that the majority of his men would be traveling generally eastward first before swinging to a more southerly direction, he struck out almost directly south, reloading as he ran. A few minutes later, as he approached the main Mahoning Trail, he stopped and peered from cover toward the Indian camp a quarter-mile to the west. A few Indians were moving about but not many and, as soon as he thought it safe, he ran across the trail and into the woodland on the opposite side. Then, settling down to the steady, mile-eating pace he could maintain for hours, he continued to run, angling slightly eastward.

In less than a mile he approached a fording place higher up the same stream the Indians had camped along, now coming from the east.[463] He plunged into the creek and started surging across the waist-deep water. He was about at the midpoint when a party of five Wyandot hunters, one of them carrying a dead spike-point buck draped over the back of his neck, stepped out of the woodland ahead.

Any attempt to flee would have drawn shots at once, and he knew he would be killed before he got back to the bank he had just left, so Brady tried to brazen it out. He stopped and grinned broadly, held his rifle pointing skyward to the rear and raised his hand in the peace greeting.

"How'd'ya do," he said in a friendly manner.

The leader of the party, a man of about 40, wasn't fooled. He recognized Brady and barked a command, and he and another brought their rifles to bear on him. The one carrying the young buck remained in place, but the other two waded into the stream and relieved Brady of his rifle, tomahawk and knife. Then, motioning him ahead of them, they all moved to the north bank and began following a dim foot trail that roughly followed the course of the creek, leading directly back to the Indian camp.

Brady was sure these five were not part of the war party he and his men had attacked and that they knew nothing of the ambush. He was equally sure that the war party was not yet gone from that encampment, and he was correct. It was still there, and more Indians had returned from the ambush site, some carrying dead, some helping wounded. Had he not been recognized, the Ranger commander would very likely have been executed—as he expected he would be the moment he was led into the camp. But the very recognition of him saved his life. Brady was a very important prisoner, and his execution must be a national event, witnessed and participated in by as many as possible.

So, though he was considerably jostled and abused, he was not immediately killed. A hemp rope was used to bind his wrists behind him, and a long rawhide tug was fastened snugly around his neck. He was led across the fording place of the stream at the camp and then westward on the trail another two miles to another fording place, this one crossing the 100-foot-wide Cuyahoga River, on the opposite side of which was a small Mingo village called Honnia. Here the trailing end of the tether around his neck was attached to a post in the midst of the village. There he sat throughout the remainder of the day, as numerous bodies were brought in from the ambush. There was great grief for the number who had been killed, and runners were sent in different directions to various villages with news of the ambush, the capture of their notorious foe and the plans for his execution to be held at Half King's Town on the upper Sandusky. From what he could understand of their conversation, Brady gathered he was going to be forced to run the gauntlet here the following morning, then be marched on toward Half King's Town, slightly more than 100 miles west.

Late last evening a bowl of stew was brought to him by an overweight middle-aged squaw who spooned it into his mouth. He ate it eagerly, knowing he would need the strength it would restore; knowing as well that in order to escape he must be as rested as possible. Having had virtually no sleep the night before, he paid no attention to the three guards positioned to watch him throughout the night and simply curled up on his side and slept, though he awakened in discomfort several times because of the cold night air.

This morning, remarkably refreshed by the food and sleep, he was again fed a bowl of food, this time a sort of porridge in which there were small pieces of meat. Obviously they were intending to keep him healthy so that his death by torture, when it came, could be extended for as long as possible.

Shortly afterward they began assembling and stretched themselves out in a long double line to the west, armed with switches, briars, clubs, sticks and other weapons with which to strike him as he passed. At the starting point, beside the principal campfire, a ring of Indians who would not be participating in the gauntlet—mainly small children, the elderly and women holding babies—had gathered to watch Brady go through his ordeal. But seeing them, a plan bloomed in Brady's mind. It would be a desperate gamble, but it was his only hope. Just a few moments ago the snug rawhide thong was loosened and removed, the rope binding his wrists behind him was cut away and he was led to the starting point amidst a babble of voices, laughter and derisive shouts.

Now, as he stood beside the fire at the beginning of the gauntlet line, Brady was told by word and sign language to remove his clothing. He shook his head and, as a warrior stepped up and stretched out his hands to grab his hunting shirt and rip it off, he struck the Wyandot a solid blow between the eyes, sending him sprawling. In the same movement he leaped to the nearest part of the circle of onlookers, snatched a blanket-swathed baby away from a squaw and pitched it onto the coals of the campfire. The screams of the baby, the shriek of the mother and the cries of concern from the onlookers intermingled. There was a scramble of bodies as many of the people leaped instantly to rescue the infant, and in that instant Brady was off and running. Pursuit was immediate as a horde of warriors fell in behind in the race to overtake and recapture him.

As fast as he had ever traveled on foot, Brady ran northward, keeping the Cuyahoga River to his right. The village was at a broad stretch of the river and the fast current splashed across the wide shallows that formed the fording place they had crossed yesterday. Now, however, he was upstream from that place and the river here narrowed, was even more swift and very deep. From previous patrols when he had studied this area, Brady remembered the big stone called Standing Rock that projected from the swirling water upstream from here.[464] About 100 yards above that landmark, the Cuyahoga passed in wild turbulence through a narrow gap in the great rocks of the shore. It was toward that spot Brady headed.

Certain he could not outdistance them and wanting to take him alive, the pursuing Indians close behind Brady did not fire any shots but merely put all their effort into overtaking him. Just about a mile from where he began his run, Brady passed The Standing Rock, and when he reached The Narrows in another 300 feet, the closest of his pursuers was no more than 60 feet behind him. Without pause and gathering all his strength into one huge effort, Brady reached the rim of the ledge and projected himself out over the deep swirling river in a gigantic leap.

The shore from which he jumped was on the same level as the shore on the opposite side 22 feet away, but on the east bank there was a ledge about four feet wide and perhaps five feet lower. Brady landed on this ledge, his momentum carrying him into the bank and nearly rebounding him into the river.[465] Not pausing to exult over his accomplishment, Brady scrambled to his feet and immediately climbed the remaining five feet to the level ground above.

Completely dumbfounded by this feat, which none of the pursuers would even have considered attempting, the Indians halted at the edge. Now, seeing their incredible foe on the verge of escape, one of them fired his gun. The ball dug a deep trench through the outside of Brady's right thigh and tumbled him, but he regained his feet and hobbled into the protective cover of some nearby trees.

For the Indians, there was no possibility of crossing the Cuyahoga here—the turbulent water was about 20 feet deep—and they had no recourse but to rush to the nearest crossing places. About half of them returned to the fording place at the village, a mile below, the other half to a place about half a mile upstream where, just below a small island, a crossing could be made with difficulty. The head start it would give Brady was not much, but it was something.

Favoring his injured leg, which was bleeding profusely and, to his dismay, leaving a trail of blood a child could follow, Brady ran to the east. In three-quarters of a mile he came to the west bank of the same creek upon which he had been captured, but now considerably larger and only half a mile above where it emptied into the Cuyahoga. Here he encountered another Indian trail that, within mere yards, went to a fording place.[466] He crossed here and, emerging on the other side, found that he was leaving a blood trail even more apparent than before, but he also realized that this was the same trail that skirted between the lake and the swamp, where he and his men some 30 hours earlier had effected their successful ambush.

He hastened along that trail toward the lake but, before reaching there, heard the sound of voices coming in the distance behind and knew they would overtake him in minutes. He redoubled his efforts and reached the southern extremity of the lake shore. There were a few lily pads here and some patches of flagweed but not enough that he could hide among them and escape detection. But just before him was the trunk of a huge chestnut tree on the bank that must have fallen into the lake a year or so before. It angled into water that was 12 feet deep here and he raced down its length to the water and plunged in. He returned to the surface in the little space under the angled log but knew that this was exactly the place the Indians would look first. Deciding that however little protection the lily pads offered, they were probably his only hope, he raised his left foot to thrust himself away from the tree trunk. Instead of wood, however, his leg went into a cavity and as quickly as he realized it, he submerged and found the opening. The cavity was large enough only for him to squirm inside to about his knees before it narrowed sharply. But in the space where it narrowed, his head broke free of the water and, in the dimness, he could see a faint bit of daylight entering from a branch hole along the side of the log a few feet above him and no larger than the diameter of his arm.

Drawing himself up as much as he could, he pressed his wounded thigh against the inside of the cavity in an effort to curtail the flow of blood that would be a giveaway in the water. Half a minute later he heard voices again and, immediately on the heels of that, footfalls on the log. There was a lot of talk from the Indians, and they stayed a long while. What little he could make out of their muted conversation, they had followed his blood right down the log to the water and, after waiting a long period, keeping a close watch on the scant lily pads, flagweeds and the open water, and closely studying the gap between the angled log and the water, they came to the conclusion that, in keeping with the courage expected of a brave warrior, he had chosen to drown rather than to allow his enemies to take his scalp.

It was perhaps an hour after their arrival at the log that the sounds of the Indian voices disappeared and silence fell. Brady, not ready to trust anything to chance at this point, remained huddled and cramped in the small hollow, even dozing now and then, until the little amount of light entering the branch hole dimmed in the twilight, and finally all was dark as night settled in.

When at last he wriggled out of the cavity, he came to the surface cautiously and eased himself with scarcely a ripple to the shoreline.[467] There he lay in the shallows for another quarter-hour or more, simply listening. Finally, he pulled himself up on shore and began moving away. His wounded leg was very stiff, but gradually it limbered up as he walked. A light rain began to fall, and, despite the discomfort it caused him, he knew it was washing away traces of his escape.

He also knew that the Indians, who were undoubtedly rejoicing in his demise, had not seen the last of Capt. Samuel Brady.

Chapter 6

Martin Wetzel, having become acclimated once again to living among his own kind these past nine months following his long captivity, was still in Kentucky. His skills as an Indian hunter and his first-hand knowledge of the Shawnees—their language, strength and disposition—were invaluable to the Kentuckians in their continuing struggle against them. Lately, however, Wetzel had been thinking of home, and he had just about decided it was time for him to return to Wheeling Creek, from which he had been absent for three and a half years.

One of the things that had kept him here in Kentucky was his desire to meet and perhaps go on a hunt with the 26-year-old young giant of a man who had become legendary in his feats as a frontiersman—Simon Kenton. Now that time had come. He and Kenton had met at Boonesboro just a few weeks ago and Wetzel, prepared to be impressed, was not disappointed. Few men on the entire Ohio River Valley frontier impressed Martin Wetzel, but Daniel Boone was one and Kenton was definitely another.

Six and a half feet tall and very muscularly built, Simon Kenton had packed more experiences into his young years than most men on the frontier acquired in a lifetime. Here was a man who was a hunter among hunters, a man who had led innumerable expeditions against the Shawnees, who had spied for Clark in the Illinois and Indiana country, who had been captured by the Shawnees, run their harsh gauntlets seven times, had his arm and his skull broken by them, escaped and been recaptured, been twice condemned to death at the stake and yet managed to get away; who had spied on the British in Detroit during his captivity and somehow managed to get back to Kentucky to continue protecting the settlers here. Little wonder that he had become so legendary.[468]

Kenton had heard of Martin Wetzel, too, and, though he normally hunted alone, was amenable to going out on a hunt with this young man two years his junior. Apart from Boone and a select few others, there were not many he had hunted with who were not only truly self-reliant but dependable in case of emergency. Wetzel had a look about him of both. Kenton was very impressed, as well, with the new double-barreled rifle Wetzel had recently acquired, and curious about its accuracy.

Together they headed into the rolling hill country near the mouth of the Kentucky River for their hunt. While there were no longer the great herds of buffalo that had been in this area some years ago, there were occasional small groups of them and the area also still had a small population of elk and bear and quite a large number of deer.

Kenton and Wetzel hunted for a few days and each man was impressed with the abilities of the other. Then, the day before they were ready to call it quits and head for home, they discovered the tracks of an Indian party. Sign of Indians in the area didn't come as a complete surprise; the evening before they had faintly heard some distant shots. Though it might have been other Kentuckians hunting, Kenton was not one to risk his life on such a presumption. They made a cold camp for the night and took turns sitting watch, but the darkness passed uneventfully. In the morning, just after dawn, they heard a single shot in the same general direction. Unlike most whites, who would have speedily headed in the opposite direction, Wetzel and Kenton immediately moved cautiously toward where the distant gunfire had been heard and, before long, came across day-old moccasin tracks.

"How many you figure, Martin?" Kenton asked.

Wetzel, without having to glance at the tracks again, promptly answered, "Five. Mebbe six. More likely five."

"That's what I figure, too. You want to leave?"

"Hell no," Wetzel replied. "Let's get us some Injens."

Kenton grinned and nodded. The pair began tracking at once, moving slowly, keeping well to cover and leaving virtually no sign of their own passage, not only studying the tracks they were following, but just as often watching well ahead for that telltale movement or glint of metal or any other sign that might indicate they were themselves discovered and moving into an ambush. In a bit over two hours they came to a small run, along which the Indians had camped the previous night, but had now moved off.

"They killed a deer," Wetzel murmured, finding traces of where the animal had been butchered and the offal carefully buried to avoid detection. "Yesterday, looks like. Reckon they jerked the meat during the night, what they ain't et of it."

"An' a 'coon, too. This mornin'. Had 'im for breakfast, I 'spect. Not hunters, though. War party."

Wetzel, who hadn't put that together yet, was surprised. "How you figger that?"

"Mixed up paint powders here an' put 'em on." Kenton indicated a spot near the still-warm ashes of the fire where a little smudge of yellow ocher had smeared the edge of a rock and a barely visible drop or two of vermilion was on the dry grass. "Reckon they're huntin' two-legged game today. Let's go."

They continued following the trail, still using great caution but moving faster now. The trail ranged far, and the little war party was obviously moving rapidly, too. It was early in the evening when they crept up near to where the Shawnees were establishing their night's camp. As they had figured, there were five warriors in the party. The camp was in a broad clearing along a small creek, the surrounding area comprised of low, dry grasses and not much cover except for a long-decayed log on the ground some 40 yards from their campfire on the stream bank.

The main concern now was to make certain that this party was not making a rendezvous here with another party thus far undetected by Kenton and Wetzel. To preclude such a possibility, they used what remained of the daylight to back off about 1,000 yards and make a complete circle around the camp, studying the ground closely. They found no tracks other than their own and those of the Indian party. Returning in the last of the daylight to where they had first spotted the enemy, they took up a position to watch them from cover.

"You want to get a couple of 'em or all five?" Kenton whispered.

"All five," Martin whispered back. "What you got in mind?"

"If we fire on 'em during the night, we'll get two, mebbe three, 'fore the rest get off in the dark. We want all five, we're gonna have t'crawl up to that log in the dark an' wait there till daylight."

"Let's do it," Wetzel murmured.

They discussed their mode of planned attack and then waited until well after dark, when all but one of the Indians had fallen asleep by the fire. Then they slowly and silently squirmed forward through the low grasses to a position behind the moldering log. Here they remained, watching the little camp until dawn. A short time later the Indians arose and moved about a little, relieved themselves and drank from the stream, then settled by the fire to eat some of their jerked meat.

At a nod from Kenton, the two whites took careful bead on their targets, fired simultaneously and killed two of the Indians. Wetzel immediately fired his second load and brought down a third one. Then he and Kenton, leaving their guns behind, leaped over the log, tomahawks in hand and, shrieking at the tops of their voices, charged at the remaining two warriors. That pair, having no time to snatch up their guns leaning against a nearby rock, took to their heels in different directions as fast as they could run. Kenton followed one, Wetzel the other. Ten minutes later Kenton returned to the camp with a bloody scalp in his hand, and, five minutes after that, Wetzel returned with the scalp of the fifth Indian.

They then discovered that one of the Indians, though mortally wounded, was still alive, lying on his stomach and moaning. Wetzel turned him over and saw to his shock that it was his former captor, Skootekitehi. The Shawnee, though in great pain, recognized him as well.

"Mah-ten," he gasped. "Shoot me. Kill me."

Wetzel refused to do so and, when he explained his connection with the man, neither would Kenton. They gathered up the Indians' guns, which they decided should go to settlers who needed them, and then hunkered down by the fire and ate some of the jerky from the pouches of their dead foes. Skootekitehi's breathing became more labored and it was evident the end was near. At last he asked for water. Wetzel formed a cone of a broad weed leaf and brought him a few swallows, which he drank, then groaned pitiably for a moment and died. Though they had scalped the other four, they did not, by unspoken agreement, scalp Skootekitehi.

The two young frontiersmen talked a while longer at the fire. Finally, Wetzel shook his head. "Reckon since I'm this close to the Ohio," he said, "I'll head on back to Wheeling. It's about time."

Kenton nodded and held out his hand, and the two men shook warmly. "Watch your scalp, Martin," the big frontiersman said. "You're a good man to be out with."

Martin Wetzel nodded, picked up his double-barreled rifle and moved off. After 30 feet or so he stopped and turned. He dipped his head at Kenton again, smiled, then walked away, filled with pride at what he considered to be the greatest compliment he'd ever received.[469]

[October 18, 1781—Thursday]

Scare the World, despite his being a Delaware, had become one of the men whom Capt. Samuel Brady most depended upon in his forays. Though he was getting "a mite long in the tooth," as Brady put it, Scare the World could still keep up quite well with the younger men and, in fact, outlast many of them. He was now about 70 years old, but his abilities in reading sign, in outthinking hostile Indians and in providing good advice during their expeditions against them had not faltered in the least with his increasing years.

Scare the World's only real failing, so far as Brady could determine, was his passionate fondness for liquor. He never drank in moderation, only in excess— whenever and wherever liquor was available. He had a great capacity for alcohol and did not care the least in what form it came. Neither did he concern himself unduly about who was the owner; he watched for it constantly, and if he encountered it, he would drink it. Whether a pint or a gallon jug, a keg or a barrel, he would drink until either the liquor was gone or he sprawled unconscious from its effects.

Today, having gone five days without his favorite beverage, Scare the World prowled about Fort McIntosh as he was wont to do, peering into every nook and cranny, every traveler's bag, every cabinet or box he encountered. It was in the hospital room of the fort that he came upon a small box of medical supplies just received from the east and rummaged through it.

The pint bottle he found had a label on it, but since he could not read, it meant nothing to him. He uncorked it and smelled alcohol, and that was all he cared about. The taste of the stuff was not good, but he was sure it would have an effect. It did. This was a bottle of medication that had been ordered for use in treating the somewhat promiscuous Fanny, daughter of the present Shawnee interpreter at Fort McIntosh, Nonhelema—The Grenadier Squaw. Fanny was suffering from a particularly virulent venereal disease, and the label on the bottle warned that it must be used in small, carefully measured doses, since it was poisonous.

Scare the World was correct in believing the alcohol-smelling liquid would have an effect. It killed him in less than half an hour.

[O c t o b e r   2 2 ,   1 7 8 1 — M o n d a y]

The Seneca half-breed Andrew Montour was now convinced that suggesting this fall hunt to Rousch and Danagh had been a mistake. Their sneaking off in the middle of the night had placed him in a very ticklish situation with these Munceys now gripping his arms and eyeing him in a most unfriendly manner.

This whole business had begun about a week ago when two Pittsburgh trading partners, a Dutchman named George Rousch and a red-headed Irishman named Neil Danagh, stopped their canoe at Montour's Island five miles below Fort Pitt to visit with him.[470] As they sat having a drink and talking, Montour had mentioned that he was planning to go on his fall hunt soon, this year to Connoquenessing Creek, a tributary entering Beaver River from the east 11 miles above Fort McIntosh.[471] He planned to hunt for deer and turkey on the headwaters of the Connoquenessing. When Danagh and Rousch showed an interest, Montour invited them to come along, and they accepted.

They had gone some 35 miles upstream on the Connoquenessing and made a nice camp and had been enjoying a fairly successful hunt until late this afternoon when the party of seven Muncey Delaware warriors showed up under a subchief named Shingwelah.[472] They greeted Montour in a cordial enough manner but the looks they gave his companions were decidedly unfriendly, and they neither greeted nor conversed with the Americans and, when they spoke at all, it was in the Delaware tongue.

Montour, though his expression did not change, recognized one of the warriors in the party as none other than Mamatchtaga, one of the two warriors who last year had been condemned to death at Pittsburgh; one of the two who were to be executed by tomahawks in the hands of Montour and Captain Wilson. Montour had successfully executed the Delaware named Copper, but that had been the occasion when Mamatchtaga had leaped into the river and escaped amid a rain of shots. Since it was Captain Wilson who had been in charge of Mamatchtaga and was supposed to deliver the lethal blow, it seemed possible that Mamatchtaga did not recognize Montour; certainly he showed no indication of it.

The war party decided to spend the night in their camp and Mamatchtaga, without looking at the whites, made an offhand remark to one of his companions: "I intend to have a red-haired scalp by morning." Having spoken in his own tongue, he did not think either of the whites could understand, but Rousch understood enough to get the gist of what had been said.

"I think," Rousch murmured to Danagh, "they mean to kill us tomorrow morning."

"Never did trust that half-breed Montour," Danagh muttered back. "What d'ya think we should do?"

"We got that jug of rum," Rousch replied. "I think our only hope is to get 'em drunk and then kill 'em all while they're asleep tonight."

Danagh agreed and they brought out the big brown glazed crockery jug and offered it to the leader of the war party. Shingwelah accepted it without thanks and took a large swallow, then handed it to the warrior beside him with a guttural comment. The warrior took a swallow and passed it on. When it had made the rounds and came back to Shingwelah, he extended it toward Rousch.

"No, no," Rousch said, "you keep. For you to drink. All of it. For you."

Shingwelah grunted a negative and continued holding the heavy jug out to Rousch until he took it back. The Dutchman looked toward Montour, who shook his head.

"They will drink no more," he told the whites. "Shingwelah told them one swallow only, no more."

Thwarted in their plan, Danagh and Rousch made another. They built their own campfire a short distance from the Indians and, without telling Montour about it, agreed they would lie down and pretend to go to sleep, but in the midst of the night they would slip away and head for Pittsburgh. This they had done and Montour had no knowledge of it until, just a short time ago, as dawn was breaking, he was roughly awakened by a warrior on each side gripping his wrist and yanking him up to a sitting position. Now Shingwelah, the heavy liquor jug in his hand, confronted him with narrowed eyes.

"You warned the two *Shemanese* to get away in the darkness," he accused.

"No," Montour replied, shaking his head, "I did not. I said nothing to them."

Shingwelah's voice became harder. "You and another, one year ago, tried to tomahawk Mamatchtaga at Pittsburgh."

Montour swallowed. "I did nothing to Mamatchtaga," he said. "Another man had him. I was told to execute a different Indian. I did so, but I did not try to harm Mamatchtaga."

The expression on Shingwelah's face was set in cold, harsh lines. "You killed the Indian who was with Mamatchtaga," he said. "That man's name was Copper. He was my brother."

Montour saw him draw back the heavy jug and knew what was to happen now. There was no hope of escape, so he simply shut his eyes and did not see Shingwelah swing the jug in a powerful arc. The tremendous blow caught him full in the center of his forehead, and the thick crockery smashed into pieces. It also caved in the whole front of his skull and left jagged shards of the crockery sticking in his head.

Andrew Montour was dead.[473]

[*D e c e m b e r   3 1 ,   1 7 8 1 — M o n d a y*]

The year 1781 closed in relative quiet, yet with the sense that things were afoot that would cause significant change and, perhaps, wreak great havoc. The electrifying news of the surrender of Gen. Cornwallis at Yorktown on October 19 seemed to signify that the war of the Revolution was nearing an end and the Americans had won. Even though there had been no official cessation of British-American hostilities and no peace conferences yet called, the feeling was strong that the war was all but over in the east. The situation in the west, however, was not so encouraging.

Kentucky was still in grave jeopardy from the attacks of the Shawnees, and the apprehension of the Kentuckians—as these far western Virginians were now calling themselves—grew considerably when all the plans for a major government-backed offensive by Gen. George Rogers Clark seemed to be curtailed. Clark, still at Louisville, had just received the devastating news in a letter from Col. William Davies of the Virginia War Office:

> *Sir:*
>
> *I have the honor to correspond with you by the direction of the Governor in Council, on the subject of your present and future military prospects. It is peculiarly unfortunate for the public interests, and it must be painful to your feelings, that the exhausted, debilitated state of the country is unable to support the smallest attempt upon the plan of offence. What were the sentiments of the Legislature, you will be able to judge more fully by the enclosed resolution. I wish it was in my power to promise you any proportion of that assistance, which the Assembly seem willing to supply for the purposes of defence, but the want of money puts every design upon the footing of uncertainty; and indeed I am utterly at a loss to know how we shall be able to forward to you the few supplies we are able to furnish. To possess you more fully of what you may expect, I promise you a probability of your being supplied with 200 suits of clothing for your men, & six brass four-pounders for your forts or gunboats, or any other preferable purpose. You shall have the whole of my influence to have the whole of the State infantry annexed to your command. They amount to about 150 men for the war under Col. Dabney. How to send the men, the cannon or clothing to you, I know not; at all events there appears no probability of getting them forwarded to you before next Spring. In addition to your regular force, you are vested by Government with unlimited powers to call from the militia of Jefferson, Fayette & Lincoln Counties, what numbers you please.*

Gov. Benjamin Harrison, writing to Clark on that same day, confirmed the grim news from the War Office but at least extended some hope that by spring the situation might change. As Harrison put it:

> *The delay of an answer to your several favors has been occasioned by a variety of causes which Major Crittenden will explain to you.*
> *Soon after his arrival they were referred to the consideration of the Assembly. The deranged situation of the finances of the State, and the reduced value of the*

paper currency made this step necessary. Their determination on the subject you have enclosed, by which you will find that an offensive war cannot at this time be carried on. We must therefore turn our attention to defensive measures, and make use of every means in our power, that this be done in the most effectual manner. On your exertions this must rest. The Executive have the most entire confidence in, and reliance on your abilities & integrity and therefor will leave much to your discretion.

The news of the surrender of Cornwallis and its promise of a near end to the Revolution had the effect of sending a new wave of land claimers to the Ohio Valley, and many of them, not finding land available to claim, rented properties from the owners, disregarding the hazards that still prevailed on this frontier. George Washington had already leased quite a few of his land claims to others and, in fact, had just written to a prospective renter:

I have a small tract called the Round Bottom, containing about 600 Acres, which would also let. It lyes on the Ohio, opposite to Pipe Creek and a little above Capteening [sic].

The bordermen on the upper Ohio were inordinately proud that George Washington, whom they considered one of their own, if not the first of the true bordermen in this area, had achieved such recognition as both a military and political leader. There was considerable discussion that, when the time came that the Revolution was over and the colonists won their independence from the British Crown, it should be he who was proclaimed King of America. An early demonstration of their appreciation of him and his accomplishments became apparent at Catfish Camp. That settlement had grown so much of late, that the brothers John and William Hoge formally laid it out as a village, and, by almost unanimous vote of the residents, the name was changed from Catfish Camp to the village of Washington, Washington County, Pennsylvania.

Prospective land renters were encouraged to take their chances in this volatile region because over these past few months the theater of conflict on the upper Ohio River frontier had subtly shifted. While incursions of the Indians were still occurring on the American side of the Ohio, ever more parties of Americans were carrying the warfare across the river into the country of the Indians, though not always too successfully.

On October 18, Lt. Matthew Neely at Fort Pitt was ordered to take command of Fort Henry at Wheeling. He took with him 15 privates and the old French swivel he had recovered from the river at Fort Pitt a month before, now unspiked and reconditioned and in fairly good condition. So pleased were the residents of Wheeling to at last get a piece of artillery, however small, that they formed a volunteer work party and quickly constructed a platform for it in the middle of Fort Henry—a raised log pen high enough that the "little big gun" could overshoot the pickets.

In mid-November a party of 15 men under Capt. Joseph Biggs pursued a party of eight Wyandots that had stolen five horses in the Wheeling area. Jacob Wetzel, now 15, was a member of the party—his first real venture into the Ohio country since he and his brother, Lewis, had been captured and briefly taken there by the Indians over four years earlier, in August of '77. Brady Rangers John Bukey and Alexander Mitchell were also members of the party.

When they reached the Muskingum Bottom, Capt. Biggs felt they were close to where the Indians were camped. He split his party into small groups to spy about and see what they could find, keeping especially alert for the smell or sight of smoke from an Indian camp or any noise that might be coming from one. Young Wetzel thought he saw a movement and took cover behind a large tree. An Indian carrying a deer draped over his shoulders passed very close and Jacob could have killed him easily, but he held off firing because he was afraid his shot would alert the Indians in their camp, wherever it was, and they would escape. As soon as the Indian was out of sight, Wetzel went back to the others and reported and a search was made in that area throughout the night without the Indian camp being discovered. When daylight came, they discovered where the Indians had been camped, very close to where the principal part of the Biggs party had repeatedly passed during the night without discovering it; but the Indians, becoming aware of the whites, had quietly slipped away. Jacob Wetzel then regretted that he had not killed the Indian when he had the opportunity.

Two nights later—on November 19—Indians crept into the camp of a detached party of scouts comprising Kinzie Dickerson, Joseph Hedges, John Hough, Jacob Linn and Thomas Biggs. They fired into the sleeping men. Young Biggs sat straight up, cried, "God have mercy on me!" and fell over dead. Hedges, shot through the heart, leaped up and ran almost 100 yards before he, too, fell dead. Jacob Linn never moved, having been shot through the head. Dickerson and Hough escaped in bare feet, though a tomahawk was thrown at the latter as he climbed a bank and stuck in the earth only inches from his head. When a larger party of the whites came to the scene to bury the dead, they found all three dead had been scalped but not otherwise mutilated, the Indians having evidently hastened on in fear of the larger party.

Everyone knew by now of the forcible removal of the Moravians to the Sandusky Valley by the hostile Wyandots and Delawares, and it was rumored that their evacuated towns were now being used as staging sites by the hostiles for their raids against the frontier. Everyone felt that important things were in the offing, partly because of tentative plans soon to send a large force of whites over the Ohio to march on those Moravian towns in the valley of the Tuscarawas and find out if the rumors were true.

The Moravian Indians themselves and their missionaries were not doing well at all. The promise by Monakaduto that they would be given a tract upon which to build a village was fulfilled, but the tract was a poor piece of land, subject to flooding and exposed to the elements. The Moravian Indians built some mean shelters and the place was dubbed the Captives' Town, but without adequate food, cover or shelter, the Indians were suffering badly and their pleas for help fell mainly on deaf ears. Even when their chief, Abraham—the former Delaware chief Netawatwees—asked several times for permission to lead a party of his people back to the area of their towns to try to gather what remained of their corn and other unharvested crops in the fields, they were put off with the remark, "Perhaps later, not now." Their missionaries,

John Heckewelder and David Zeisberger, along with other missionary teachers and their families, suffered even more than they, being held prisoner in abominable conditions with never enough warmth or food and with excessively bad treatment, especially from Simon Girty, who seemed to bear a particular hatred for the missionaries. The plan was eventually to take them to Detroit for trial as spies against the Crown, but as yet no one had found the time to convey them there.

One spot of bright news was that Gen. William Irvine had finally arrived at Fort Pitt to take command, and Col. Daniel Brodhead returned east, no longer to be a thorn in the side of the settlers on the upper Ohio. And in the last significant change this year on the upper Ohio, Irvine ordered the Continental regulars at Fort Henry— Lt. Matthew Neely and his 15 privates—back to Fort Pitt. Relieved today by Washington County Militia Lt. John Hay, who brought with him a sergeant and 15 privates, Lt. Neely generously left his French swivel at Fort Henry.

"I rather suspect," Neely commented to Ebenezer Zane, "you folks here are going to need it a lot more than I."

[January 3, 1782 — Thursday]

Frederick Haldimand, British Governor of Canada, had been justifiably upset with last October's surrender of Maj. Gen. Charles Cornwallis to George Washington at Yorktown. There was no doubt that the war was going badly for the British in the east, and he felt that it behooved him to prove to His Majesty George III that the Americans did not hold the upper hand everywhere. That proof, he felt, lay in the triumphs the Indians had been having on the frontier, all the way from North Carolina to the Great Lakes, particularly in the remote regions of New York and down the Allegheny and Ohio rivers for their entire lengths. The Indians had shown themselves to be excellent allies who hated their American foes with boundless intensity. If King George could be convinced to throw even more strength of arms, munitions and supplies to these Indians, there was little doubt in Haldimand's mind that in a very short time the Americans could be ousted everywhere west of the Alleghenies.

One way the Canadian governor hoped to show what great effect the Indian warfare was having on the frontier was to ship to England the substantial lots of scalps that the Indians had taken, which they had turned in at Detroit and other frontier British posts. For these, of course, they had been paid handsomely. With that in mind, shortly after the defeat of Cornwallis, Haldimand dispatched orders to these posts to send in their lots of scalps without delay. He was especially interested in those that would be forthcoming from the Iroquois, who were still carrying the war forward in the valleys of the Mohawk and Allegheny, because they would represent tangible proof of the falsity of the American claim that Gen. John Sullivan's 1779 campaign against the Iroquois had utterly destroyed the Six Nations—especially the Senecas.

Detroit, beyond doubt, had the greatest accumulation of these grisly trophies of frontier war—bales and boxes of them, in fact—but similar quantities had been building at other posts and collection points, such as Presque Isle and Fort Niagara.

Now, in accordance with those orders, the first of these scalp shipments—eight large oilskin-wrapped bundles—had just been prepared by one of the Royal Indian agents for transport to Gov. Haldimand with the following letter:

January 3d, 1782

May it please Your Excellency,

At the request of the Seneca Chiefs, I herewith send to Your Excellency, under the care of James Boyd, eight packages of scalps, cured, dried, hooped and painted with the Indian triumphal marks, of which the following is invoice and explanation:

No. 1. Containing 43 scalps of Congress soldiers, killed in different skirmishes; these are stretched on black hoops 4 inches in diameter; the inside of the skin painted red, with a small black spot to note their being killed by bullets. Also, 62 of farmers killed in their homes; the hoops painted red, the skin painted brown, and marked with a hoe, a dark circle all around to indicate their being surprised at night, and a black hatchet in the middle, signifying their being killed with that weapon.

No. 2. Containing 98 of farmers killed in their houses; hoops red, figure of a hoe to mark their profession, great white circle and sun to show they were surprised in the daytime; a little red foot to show they stood upon their defence, and died fighting for their lives and families.

No. 3. Containing 97 of farmers; hoops green, to show they were killed in the fields; a large white circle with a little round mark on it for the sun, to show it was in the daytime, black bullet mark on some, and hatchet on others.

No. 4. Containing 102 of farmers, mixed of several of the marks above, only 18 marked with a little yellow flame, to denote their being prisoners burned alive after being scalped, their nails pulled out by the roots, and other torments; one of these latter was supposed to be an American clergyman, his band being fixed to the hoop of his scalp. Most of the farmers appear, by the hair, to be young or middle-aged men, there being but 67 very grey heads among them all; which made the service more essential.

No. 5. Containing 88 scalps of women, hair braided in the Indian fashion to show they were mothers, hoops blue, skin yellow ground with little red tadpoles to represent, by way of triumph, the tears of grief occasioned to their relations; a black scalping knife or hatchet at the bottom, to mark their being killed by those instruments; 17 others, very grey, black hoops, plain brown color, no marks by the short club or casse-tete, to show they were knocked down dead, or had their brains beat out.

No. 6. Containing 193 boy's [sic] scalps of various ages, small green hoops, whitish ground on the skin, with red tears in the middle, and black marks, knife, hatchet, or club as their death happened.

No. 7. Containing 211 girls [sic] scalps of various ages, small green hoops, white ground, tears, hatchet, club, scalping knife, &c.

No. 8. This package is a mixture of all the varieties above mentioned, to the number of 122, with a box of birch bark containing 29 little infant's [sic] scalps of various sizes, small white hoops, white ground, no tears, and only a little black knife in the middle, to show they were ripped out of their mother's [sic] bellies.[474]

[March 2, 1782 — Saturday]

Col. David Williamson listened closely as Col. Ebenezer Zane and Majs. John and Samuel McCulloch filled him in on the details of what had been occurring here in Wheeling and the upper Ohio River area over the past couple of months; details of incidents that had led him and his men to make this the rendezvous point for the expedition now forming.[475]

"Things've not been good around here lately," Zane told him. "Usually we can count on a respite from the attacks during January and February because then the weather's so bad, the Indians have a tough enough time just surviving without making raids. Not this time. This past winter has been the warmest I've ever experienced here, and it's played havoc with us. They've been crossing over around Yellow Creek, Cross Creek, Mingo Bottom, Pipe, Captina, all over. They hit places on Chartier's, King's and Raccoon, killed some and captured more. Been one attack after another, and they've even been seen watching us from a distance here in Wheeling. Unnerving."

"Same thing at Vanmetre's," Sam McCulloch put in, wincing a little as he shifted position. He was still troubled with pain in the stump of his upper left arm from the amputation, though no one had heard him complain about it. Somehow he seemed to take it in stride, and he hadn't even let it prevent his wedding here in Wheeling a month after the accident. He and Mary Mitchell, sister of Sam's good friend, Alex Mitchell, had gone on with their planned wedding on January 30, though Mary had been agreeable to putting it off if he had wanted to do so. He hadn't.

The accident had occurred while Sam McCulloch and David Fouts were out hunting together and had stopped to rest. McCulloch had leaned his gun against the log he was sitting on and a few moments later accidentally jostled it. The gun discharged, sending a ball into his upper left arm, shattering the bone. So severe was the injury that by the time they got back to Wheeling, nothing could be done except amputate the arm just below the shoulder.

What bothered Sam McCulloch most of all about losing his arm was the continual inconvenience it caused him. He could mount a horse and ride and even shoot his rifle when it came to that—though he still had quite a tough time reloading—but the multiplicity of things that really required two good arms and hands sorely aggravated him. It was bad enough to lose a limb as the result of an Indian fight, but to shoot yourself accidentally and lose an arm as a result was so completely unnecessary and frustrating. Now, even though he had proven to everyone he could still function well enough, he had lost command of Vanmetre's Fort, that position having been taken by his brother, John. Nor would he be able to participate, as he undoubtedly would have chosen to do, in this present expedition forming up under Col. Williamson. John had already announced that he was going along.

"I'm sure," John McCulloch spoke up, "you've heard about John Carpenter being caught and then getting away, haven't you?"

Col. Williamson shrugged. "Just a mention of it, John," he said. "No details. What happened?"

McCulloch shook his head. "Case of pure bad luck turning into pure good luck. Happened a couple of weeks ago—February sixteenth, I think it was. Carpenter's got a little place on Buffalo just below Ramsey's. Party of six Delawares surprised 'im. Said two of 'em spoke good Dutch and claimed they were Moravians. Anyway, they took him and his two horses and swam over the Ohio. Carpenter said the horses had never been in big water and he thought they were going to lose 'em before they got across. The Indians roughed him up a lot when they got to the other side. Saw a number of other war parties heading down Tuscarawas toward the Moravian towns. His party made camp eventually on Tuscarawas and hobbled the horses. Guess he could hardly walk by that time, but they sent him out to get the horses anyway. He followed their tracks and found the horses had circled around the camp and got back to the trail they'd come on. He found 'em headin' back for the Ohio. Figured the Indians were probably going to kill him when they got to their village, so decided to take a chance on escaping. Took the hobbles off and lit out with the two horses. Came back by way of Fort Laurens and Pittsburgh and got in all right."

"He said war parties were heading down the Tuscarawas?" Williamson asked.

"That's what he said."

"To the Moravian towns?"

McCulloch shrugged. "Presumably. Don't know if he knew for sure."

"Well, we'll soon find out," Williamson said grimly. "What else?"

Zane spoke up. "Worst one recently was the hit on Wallace's place up Raccoon." He went on to explain that last week a fairly large war party of Wyandots crossed over near the mouth of Little Beaver and struck the cabin of Robert Wallace on Raccoon Creek. Wallace himself had gone off early in the morning to Washington village, formerly Catfish Camp. When he got home that evening, he found his wife, Jane, and their three children gone. Two of the children were boys; James, 10, and Bob, only two and a half, while the third child was Sarah Jane, a nursing infant. The cabin had been plundered of everything of value, the furniture destroyed, the cabin itself broken up and his cattle all shot to death. Wallace raised a party of men and they started to follow, but a snowfall quickly obliterated the tracks and they had to return. Wallace, aflame with desire for vengeance, swore he would make himself part of the first force to be raised to cross the Ohio and crush the Indians.

The closest attack to Wheeling recently, Zane had gone on, occurred three days ago, only three miles below Fort Henry, at the sugar camp established by Sam Boggs a few weeks ago on Boggs' Run. The camp consisted of a new cabin, a half-face cabin, and a number of troughs for sap collection. When Boggs had requested a couple of the militia soldiers from Fort Henry to serve as guards, two privates—Hugh Cameron and Richard Davids—were assigned to the duty. Boggs had hardly begun his operation, however, when he discovered the tracks of a pair of Indians close by, so he immediately moved his family to Wheeling. Cameron and Davids, however, did not think the tracks of two Indians constituted much of a threat and decided to remain at the camp for a while to make some syrup. They had been at work only a few hours when the Indians crept up and fired on them. Davids was not hit, but Cameron was shot through the hand. It was not a serious wound, but he was so terrified that when Davids shouted "To the fort!" and raced off, Cameron simply stood where he was, quaking with fear, and allowed the Indians to rush up and capture him. They started taking him away, but then one of the Indians, fancying the new hat Cameron was wearing—a black wool cap bound with white linen—drove his tomahawk into the back of Cameron's neck, severing his spine and killing him. They then scalped him and took his gun, as well as his hunting shirt and new hat, and fled.

The very boldness of such attacks so close to the largest and strongest settlement on the Ohio River had led the settlers to appeal to Gen. William Irvine to mount an expedition to punish the hostile Indians. The general said he approved of the idea but could not commit Continental troops to such an operation without higher approval. However, he notified the county lieutenant of Westmoreland County, Col. James Marshall, that if he wished to raise a militia force to march against the hostiles, believed now to be operating out of the former Moravian towns on the Tuscarawas, he could certainly do so. Col. Marshall issued a call and raised 100 men for such an expedition, then assigned his second in command, Col. David Williamson, to lead it. They were to rendezvous at Wheeling with their own food and weapons and horses and march on the Moravian towns from there.

So now they had assembled in Wheeling, and Col. Williamson, having met with Col. Zane and the McCulloch brothers, was more than ever determined to punish the offenders. Without further delay, he issued an order for the expedition to begin.

[March 5, 1782—Tuesday]

The Moravian Indians were in a very pitiable state. Though the winter had been exceptionally mild, they had nevertheless suffered terribly in their makeshift quarters at the Captives' Town on the upper Sandusky River. Hunger continued to be the greatest menace to their survival. The leader of these Delaware converts, Abraham—Chief Netawatwees—had been unflagging in continuing his pleas to Chief Monakaduto to allow a party of the Moravians, led by himself, to return to their towns to salvage whatever small amount of unharvested corn might have weathered the winter. At last Monakaduto had given in.

A party of 150 of the Moravian men, women and children had made the difficult march back to the Tuscarawas, where they split into three groups of 50 each. One, under Abraham, would work in the Gnadenhütten area, gathering what could be found of the crops still in the fields. A second group at the Salem Village, some 12 miles downstream from Gnadenhütten, would do the same, as would the final group at Schoenbrun, a like distance upstream.

As it turned out, more of the crops remained, especially corn, than they had dared to hope for, and they worked diligently to gather it up, clean and dry it and store it in old cloth and skins sewn into sacks. They were still busily engaged in this work today when a large party of warriors arrived at Gnadenhütten, returning from their raids across the upper Ohio. They had prisoners with them, along with a considerable amount of plunder from the American settlements, and they boasted loudly of the success of their raids and of the people they had killed without the loss of a single warrior.

"You should not have come here," Abraham chided them. "We have troubles enough already. You are not welcome, and we wish you to go."

The warriors laughed and said they would leave only when they were ready to go, but it was obvious that some among them were anxious to push on. For a little while the warriors mingled with the Moravians and even traded a few items for corn to fill their pouches. But before long they did leave, heading for the Sandusky Valley.

Shortly after their departure, Abraham held a meeting with the elders of all three Moravian villages to discuss what they should do at this point. There was a distinct fear that the Americans might be following the war party and would show up here, but Abraham calmed them.

"Even should that happen," he said reassuringly, "we have nothing to fear. The Americans know we are not hostile; they know we are Christians and have taken the hand of God and wish harm for no one. They have long known of our peaceable ways and of our innocence in any of those bad things that may have occurred."

The discussion continued for a long time and, in the end, they accepted what Abraham proposed: that they would begin at once to gather up the small residue of corn remaining in the fields now, clean and pack it. That would take only one more day and as soon as the task was finished, they would head for the Captives' Town with the desperately needed grain.

[March 8, 1782—Friday]

Col. David Williamson's little army of 100 militiamen had been sickened by what they found shortly after leaving Wheeling and crossing the Ohio River. They had not traveled more than six or eight miles along the path leading toward the Tuscarawas when they encountered two bodies that had obviously been deliberately left for them to find. The bodies had been impaled on two saplings trimmed of branches, cut off at a height of about five feet and the standing ends sharpened. The victims, tomahawked, scalped and nude, had been thrust down over these stakes and wedged there, face up; a warning to any who might be following.

One of the bodies was that of Jane Wallace; the other, her infant daughter, Sarah Jane.[476]

Robert Wallace was a private in Williamson's force, and his grief and rage at the hideous discovery of his wife and daughter communicated itself with remarkable intensity to the others. They wept along with Wallace as the bodies were gently removed, wrapped together in a blanket and buried, and they resolved among themselves to "make the savages pay" for this unconscionable outrage.

Two days later, as evening approached, they were within a mile of Gnadenhüt-ten, mere hours after the war party had passed through. The horses and men had been pushed hard, and Col. Williamson ordered his men to make a cold camp for the night, establish a strong sentry patrol, eat some food, and get as much sleep as they could in order to start off fresh in the morning for the village. During the evening, as they ate, they discussed their plan of approach for the morning.

In the morning Williamson sent out a detachment under Capt. Charles Bilder-back, a greatly overweight man with the reputation of being the type of individual who shoots first and asks questions later.[477] A cooper by trade, Bilderback had settled near the mouth of Short Creek four or five years earlier. His instructions were to circle around along the Tuscarawas and then approach from the north while the main force approached from the southeast. The detachment moved away quickly, and just before reaching the river it came upon one of the Moravian converts, a young Delaware named Kemah, who had taken the Christian name of Jacob. He had been sent out early from the village to catch a horse that had wandered off, and the detachment had intercepted him before he realized they were near. One look at the expressions of the men convinced Kemah that they meant to kill him. He dropped to his knees and clasped his hands together in front of him, addressing his comments to Bilderback, who was in the front of the squad.

"Please," he begged, "don't kill me. I have done nothing. I am a Christian. My name is Jacob. Don't kill me. I am not your enemy. I am—"

His words were cut off as Bilderback jerked out a tomahawk and swung a vicious blow that struck Kemah in the temple, the narrow blade penetrating into his brain. He tumbled onto his side and his body was still twitching when they scalped him. With scarcely another look at him, the detachment continued toward the river-bank. Before reaching it, however, they passed a fairly large field of weatherbeaten corn.

In that cornfield, squatting down while tearing cobs of dried corn from their husks and stuffing them into a sack, was another of the Delaware converts, Shabosh, or Joseph, brother of the wife of Kemah. He saw the squad of men coming before they saw him. He paused in what he was doing, largely hidden in the corn, and watched them closely, not sure at first who they were.

The detachment would undoubtedly have seen him in a moment or so more had not their attention been distracted by a movement on the river ahead of them. It turned out to be yet another Delaware convert, paddling his canoe downstream, apparently arriving from Schoenbrun.

As the squad passed at their closest point to him, Joseph abruptly recognized one soldier as a man he knew from Fort Pitt. He was just on the point of hailing him when one of the soldiers brought his rifle to his shoulder and it cracked crisply in the morning air. The man in the canoe half rose, flinging out his hands and losing his paddle, then toppled into the bottom of the canoe. The men in the squad yelped with glee and congratulated the shooter.

Shabosh was stunned and uttered no sound, only crouched lower to avoid detection. As the soldiers moved farther away, he scrambled off on all fours in the other direction until safely out of their range, then leaped to his feet and ran through the remainder of the cornfield and into the woodland beyond. He continued to run, even there, and did not stop until he was a few miles away, at which point he crept into hiding and remained there, determined not to budge again until the following morning.

In the meanwhile, Col. Williamson and the main party reached the Tuscarawas just below Gnadenhütten and saw a number of Indians in a cornfield on the opposite side of the river. The stream was running high and fast, risky for a horse crossing, so Williamson detached 15 men to go across with him in a large, boatlike sugar trough they found lying on the bank. It could carry a paddler and two men at a time, so it took the better part of half an hour for all 16 to get across. As soon as they were all on the other side, Williamson reassembled them and they moved toward the workers in the cornfield.

The main part of the army, having waited until the colonel and his detachment had safely crossed, now moved into the village proper, expecting to find a large number of Indians there, but they discovered only two, a man and his wife, both of whom they killed instantly with their tomahawks to prevent their raising an alarm. When the men spread out to find others, John McCulloch went down near the riverbank and found two young boys there. Looking around and seeing no one else nearby, McCulloch spoke to them hurriedly. "You're in danger. Go hide yourselves. Quickly!" The pair raced off at once.[478]

As the detachment under Col. Williamson approached the cornfield across the river, the Indians saw them coming and rose up from their work. There were considerably more of them than Williamson at first realized: 48 men, women and youngsters, nearly all of whom had weapons. The colonel had the men of the detachment wave and hail them as friends and warmly shake hands when they came up to them. The leader, an elderly Indian with very long gray hair, introduced himself as Abraham Netawatwees, Delaware by birth and Christian by choice. He seemed very glad to see the Americans and was anxious to learn what had brought them here.

Williamson introduced himself and then added blandly, "I come with good news. We have been sent here to take you back with us to the neighborhood of Fort Pitt where, in the future, you will be protected from all harm. You may quit your work here now; there is no need. Soon you will be given good food in abundance, warm clothing and sturdy shelter."

Abraham smiled broadly and enthusiastically shook the colonel's hand again. For those of his followers who had not understood, he interpreted, and there were cries of joy and relief. They all remembered how last year some of their people had been taken to Fort Pitt in a similar manner and had been well treated by the commander of the fort and at length dismissed with fine gifts and tokens of lasting friendship. Because of that, the Moravian leader had no objection when Williamson smoothly added that as a show of good faith, Abraham's people should surrender their weapons, then all go back across the river immediately to rejoin the soldiers already in town. At Abraham's order, his people turned their weapons over to the detachment and he then led the way to where they had beached their canoes. The trip back across was much more easily made with the canoes.

On a high point of ground some distance west of the river, two of the Moravian Delawares, John Martin and his son, Little John Martin, watched curiously and with a faint stirring of concern over what was happening. They saw the detachment cross the river and greet the Moravians in the cornfield in what seemed to be a very friendly manner, complete with handshakes. Still not sure exactly what was going on, Martin directed his son to go over to the town, while he would himself go downstream to Salem to tell his Moravian brothers there what was happening at Gnadenhütten.

By the time the river crossing was completed again, Col. Williamson had discovered from Abraham that 50 more of his people were at the Salem Mission, a dozen miles downstream. Before the Moravian leader had a chance to remark that another 50 were upstream at the Schoenbrun Mission, Williamson interrupted and suggested that he send at once for those at Salem to come to Gnadenhütten. Abraham dispatched a pair of runners for this purpose at once. Those runners, approaching Salem, encountered John Martin and two of the men from Salem coming toward Gnadenhütten to see what was happening. When it was explained, all five returned to Salem, announced the good news to the remainder there, and the whole group started the walk back to Gnadenhütten.

Back at that village, all the Moravians on hand had assembled with the soldiers, and perhaps Col. Williamson might really have taken them back to Fort Pitt, but then something occurred that changed everything. Pvt. Robert Wallace abruptly uttered a cry of outrage and pointed at a young Delaware woman.

"By damn!" he cried. "That's Jane's dress. She's wearing my wife's dress!"

It was true. The young woman had gotten the somewhat bloodstained dress early yesterday from the hostile Indians that had passed through, giving one of them a pouchful of the dried corn in exchange for it. There was an immediate echoing cry of outrage from the soldiers. Were that not enough, the atmosphere quickly became even more tense when a volunteer pointed at a Moravian man who was wearing a hunting shirt and a black wool cap bound with white linen. He identified both as having belonged to Hugh Cameron, the soldier who had been slain at the Boggs' Sugar Camp.

At once the volunteers all brought their weapons to bear on the Indians. Greatly frightened, the Moravians tried to explain that they had just gotten those items of clothing in trade for corn from the party of Indians that had passed through the previous day. The militiamen were by this time in no mood to listen to any explanations; the clothing was, to them, clear proof that these Moravians, only suspected till now, were actually confederates of the hostiles.

At Col. Williamson's order, a further search of the village was made. All sorts of pewter tableware, clothing, guns, cookpots, basins and other goods were discovered and declared to be items stolen from settlers. They also found some horses with brands on them and said this proved them to be horses that had been taken from the settlements.

Abraham desperately tried to refute the charges. The Moravians, he said, had their own branding irons that they had always used to mark their horses, and as for the goods, those were items that had either been acquired from traders over the years or that their own missionaries had brought to them from the Pennsylvania missions. By this time, however, the volunteers were in an absolute rage, and demanded all the Moravians be put to death.

At a harsh command from Col. Williamson, all the Christian converts, even the

women and children, had their wrists bound behind them. The only exceptions were
the women with babies, who were allowed to carry them. The mission and the
largest structure in the village—a cooper's shed—were side by side, and the prisoners
were segregated and marched into the two buildings, men and older boys into the
former, women, girls, smaller children and babies into the latter. Once inside, they
were ordered to sit on the floor, and then their ankles were similarly bound.

Col. Williamson assembled his men outside and discussed what should be done
with the prisoners. The majority by far were clamoring for them to be executed and
Williamson at last put it to a vote. All those in favor of taking the Moravians captive
to Fort Pitt were invited to step forward. Of the 100 volunteers, only 18, including
John McCulloch, took that step. These men were ordered to move off to one side.
Then another vote was called for from those who remained as to what manner of
execution it should be. After considerable discussion it was agreed they should be
struck dead in the buildings where they were, their scalps taken, and then the structures set afire. When the question arose as to what weapons should be used in the
execution, Col. Williamson's opinion was asked, but he simply shrugged and said,
"Do as you please about the prisoners."[479]

By this time the party of 50 more Moravians from Salem had come in sight and
Col. Williamson, with a detachment, went out to meet them, greeting them with
smiles and handshakes and telling them that their brothers and sisters were awaiting
them in the mission. He added that Abraham had directed them to turn their arms
over to him. Without suspicion of anything amiss, they did so and were escorted the
remainder of the way into Gnadenhütten. There, to their dismay, they were peremptorily taken prisoner, bound and led into the buildings. Williamson then put John
McCulloch in charge of the 18 who voted against execution and sent them as a
detachment to Salem to burn the town and then return here.

Abraham shook his head sadly as the new prisoners from Salem were brought in,
wondering how all this could have happened and what it meant. Unaware of the vote
that had been taken outside, he could only assume that they were all to be taken to
Fort Pitt and held there as hostages for some purpose. He was thankful that he had
not had time to tell Col. Williamson about the remaining 50 Moravians upstream at
the Schoenbrun Mission.

The Moravian leader's confusion ended when Col. Williamson entered the
mission and told him that a vote had been taken and the decision was that all of the
Moravians should be executed. Shocked and unbelieving, Abraham finally recovered
enough to speak.

"I call upon God as witness that my people are perfectly innocent of any crime
against you. We are prepared and willing to suffer this death. Yet, this much I ask of
you: When we were converted from our heathen ways and baptized, we made a
solemn promise to the Lord that we would live unto Him and endeavor to please
Him alone in this world. But we know, too, that we have been wayward in many
respects, and therefore we wish to have the right granted to us to pour out our hearts
before Him in prayer and beg His mercy and pardon."

Williamson saw no reason why the request should not be granted and said the
execution would be put off until the next morning, giving the Moravians the remainder of this day and through the night to make their peace with God. He then

left them to themselves. As he passed by the cooper's shed next door, one of the women captives, a widow named Christiana who could speak English well, cried out to him through the open door, asking him not to imprison them like this and to help her. Williamson paused and looked inside, shook his head and said, "I have no power to help you." He then walked off.

As soon as Abraham explained what was to occur and this horrible news jumped the gap to the female prisoners next door, a great wailing of terror arose that only slowly subsided into a prolonged weeping of the women and smaller children. Many questioned among themselves why God was allowing this awful thing to happen to His children, and Abraham reassured them by saying that God worked in mysterious ways and if it was His will that His children should be brought home to Him at this point, then they should accept it and rejoice in the knowledge that they would soon be with their Heavenly Father. He managed to get his back against a wall of the mission and, with difficulty, slid himself up against it until he was on his feet.

"My children," he said, "hear me. Our sentence is fixed, and we shall soon all depart unto our Savior. This I say now: I have sinned in many ways and have grieved the Lord with my disobedience, not always walking the path I ought to have walked. But still I will cleave to my Savior, with my last breath, and hold Him fast, though I am so great a sinner. He will forgive me all my sins and not cast me out."

Together, then, they prayed long into the night until only he and a few others remained awake. Among those few were Thomas and Abel, two young boys who, back to back, worked throughout the night at loosening each other's bonds. By daylight they had succeeded in freeing themselves and positioned themselves so that when an opportunity came, they might be able to escape.

Shortly after dawn this morning, squads of volunteers were assigned to carry out the executions. Twenty men, led by the fat Capt. Charles Bilderback, approached the mission building. By the drawing of lots, he had been given the dubious honor of starting off the executions. At that time someone had remarked that Abraham's long flowing gray hair would make a fine scalp, and Bilderback had decided that this scalp would be the first one he would collect. In his hands he carried a heavy cooper's mallet that he had brought along on the expedition in his saddlebag.

As the door opened and the volunteers filed in, Abraham gave a loud call, awakening those of his followers who were asleep and telling them to come to their knees and sing with him the Twenty-third Psalm. They did so, and their voices, many quavering with the fear that filled them, rose in the dim daylight filtering into the interior. The leading voice of Abraham did not last long. Bilderback, without a word, stepped up behind him and swung his mallet in a heavy blow that caved in the entire back of the chief's skull. Even as his bound arms and legs jerked spasmodically, Bilderback cut away the scalp and held it aloft triumphantly while his men cheered.

The psalm-singing faltered but then continued as Capt. Bilderback moved along from Abraham, almost methodically felling and scalping others in succession, each blow making a hideous smacking sound in the gloomy, dim interior of the mission. Then he came to the boy named Abel, who was kneeling beside Thomas. The hoped-for opportunity to escape had not yet come for the two boys, who held their arms behind them as if they were still tied. Bilderback's mallet struck and glanced somewhat, and Abel fell face forward onto the floor. Bilderback turned, holding the bloody mallet before him and made some comment about it to his fellows, who laughed and engaged in a brief repartee with him. While they were thus distracted, Thomas, with amazing presence of mind, put his hand forward into the puddling blood from his friend and smeared the back of his own head with it, then lay down beside Abel, his movements scarcely visible in the minimal light. When Bilderback turned back to finish his job, it was at the prone form of Thomas he stopped with his knife in hand and scalped him. Steeling himself against the pain, Thomas made no sound or movement. Bilderback moved on to his next victim and struck and scalped him, then moved on again. Following the fourteenth execution, the fat officer blew out a great gust of air and handed his mallet to Pvt. George Bellar.

"My arm's failing me," he said. "You go on in the same way. I think I've done pretty well."

Bellar answered with a grin and, as Bilderback left, carried on, using both hands to bring the mallet down with such heavy blows that often bits of skull and gray matter splattered his clothing. He played out quickly and managed to murder only 11 before he handed the mallet to the next man.

In the cooper's shed next door, a small boy named Adam Stroud, only ten years old, had managed to free his wrists and ankles of their bonds. He slipped over to where he knew there was a trapdoor that led down into a small fruit cellar, which had a narrow door in the foundation of the shed leading to the outside. An even smaller window opening was there, covered with the stretched, oilsoaked skin of a rabbit that allowed light to enter but kept moisture out. A slender girl named Esther, a year or two older than he, was lying on the trapdoor without knowing of its presence, and he pushed her to the right in order to open it. To the left was a boy named Peter, a pudgy youngster about Stroud's age. Working as quickly as he could, young Stroud whispered to Esther that he would drop her down into the cellar, and as soon as she hit the ground below, she was to roll out of the way. She nodded, and he pulled her to the opening and dropped her down feet first. Then he turned to Peter and did the same. A woman of about 30 was next closest, and he began pulling her to the hole, she helping as best she could, but at that moment the executioners entered. Stroud instantly slipped down into the opening, pulling the trapdoor closed above him, and the young woman rolled herself atop it.

The squad of executioners who entered were led by Capt. William Welch. Without any preliminary discussion, he pulled a tomahawk from his belt and killed seven women and children in succession with blows to the head and then scalped them. Other men, not awaiting specific turns, began to do the same, moving about among the women, girls, small children and babies and striking whomever they found still alive. As a private with a bloody tomahawk approached one of the women holding a baby, she held the infant out toward him beseechingly, silently willing him to take it and perhaps protect it. Instead, he instantly tomahawked it, knocking the baby out of her grip. The woman gasped but then meekly bowed her head for the death blow, which the private delivered just as methodically.[480] Nathan Rollins, among the tomahawk-wielders, had previously had his father and uncle killed by marauding Indians; he now took his vengeance by successively tomahawking 19 of the women and children, but when he finished he sat down and wept because what he had done gave him no degree of satisfaction for the deaths of his kin.

Back in the mission, the low singing was continuing among those still alive. There had been no cries, no pleas for mercy. Incredibly, Thomas felt Abel stir beside him. His friend, not dead from the blow, had come back to consciousness and was struggling to get to his feet. The effort was detected, and the individual presently doing the executing came back and swung a blow so hard that Abel's head virtually exploded, and this time when he fell, no doubt remained that he was dead. It was too much for Pvt. Otho Johnston, who abruptly vomited and then fled out the door with the laughter of his companions following him.

In his flight from the building, Johnston had left the door open. This was the opportunity Thomas had been hoping for. As the men moved back along the line and the executions resumed, Thomas waited until a blow was descending and then scrambled to his feet and dashed out of the open door. Blood still streaming from his scalped head, he dashed around the building and was just entering the woods before the cry was raised of his escape. No attempt was made to pursue him. His bloody head made them sure his skull was broken and he would soon die anyway. But Thomas knew he was not going to die; he knew he must get to Sandusky and relate what had happened here. He found a good hiding place and pulled himself into it, then curled into a ball, moaning faintly for the first time with the pain from his head. He planned to remain here until dark and then head for that destination with his grim news.

In both of the buildings the executions continued until all those inside—save for the three children in the fruit cellar of the house—were dead and scalped. Williamson then ordered his men to search every structure for anything of value and take it, after which they were to burn the town, cabin by cabin, until only the two execution buildings remained—the Gnadenhütten Mission and the large cooper's shed next to it.

By early evening the entire town save for those two buildings lay in smoldering ashes. Williamson then ordered those buildings put to the torch, with all the bodies to be left inside. In the encroaching darkness, the blaze caused by the two buildings lighted the sky, reflecting off the low overhanging clouds. Two miles away Thomas, already on his trek to the Sandusky, paused and looked back. The blood coating his skull had coagulated, but his head ached terribly and he winced as he squinted toward the ominous glow on the clouds. He knew what it meant, and now, for the first time since all this began, tears flooded his eyes and dribbled down his cheeks. A barely audible crooning of the death song issued from his lips, and then he turned and continued his journey.

The three children still in the fruit cellar of the cooper's shed, Adam Stroud, Esther and Peter, had hoped to remain hidden there until late at night. Adam had removed the cords binding the wrists and ankles of his companions shortly after the three had made their escape into the cellar. Now, with the structure crackling in flames above them, what had at first been a haven might soon become a crematory. They had long before discovered that the single narrow door in the foundation that led to freedom was evidently barred from the outside, as all their efforts to open it had failed. The only hope was to squeeze through the window opening. They ripped away the rabbit skin and were dismayed at how truly small the opening was.

Adam Stroud volunteered to go through first. With the help of the others behind him, he got his head through and then, with considerable difficulty, his shoulders. With a lot of squirming, as the other two shoved from behind, he finally slid through all the way and fell to the ground outside. He peered around quickly, but the only people he could see were some of the volunteers standing in the clearing in front of the mission and house. He also discovered that the door was not merely barred; it was buried more than knee deep in dense mud that had slid into the cavity due to heavy rains over the winter.

Adam whispered to them that the door couldn't be opened, and he told Esther to come through the window next. She started through at once, arms outstretched and hands clasped before her. Adam grabbed her wrists and pulled, and though the framing of the window gouged her flesh deeply, she made no outcry. It was even more difficult for her to get through than it had been for him, but she finally slid free and was out. Then it was Peter's turn, but his pudginess betrayed him. He managed to get his head and shoulders through as Adam and Esther pulled on his wrists, but then he wedged solidly, able to move neither forward nor back. The floor above the cellar abruptly caved in and filled the little space with burning debris, and only an instant later the burning walls began tumbling down about them. Terrified, Adam and Esther turned and scrambled up out of the inclined hole. They were just in time; the remainder of the wall above them fell, burying the hole—and Peter—beneath fiercely burning timbers.

The boy and girl fled to the woods only a short distance away and watched a moment longer as the remainder of the burning buildings collapsed into themselves amid the faint cheering of Col. Williamson's volunteers. The bodies of the 92 men, women and children inside were incinerated.[481]

Adam Stroud and Esther, both weeping, turned then and began their run toward Schoenbrun, to warn their Moravian brethren still there.[482]

[March 9, 1782 — Saturday]

Great consternation erupted among the 50 remaining Moravians at the Schoenbrun Mission at the arrival of the children, Adam Stroud and Esther, just before one o'clock in the morning. Expecting the whites to come here soon after daybreak, they gathered and loaded up their things, along with the meager amount of corn they had gathered, on their horses and struck out well before dawn, heading directly west for the Sandusky.

Less than three hours later, Col. David Williamson arrived with his force and found the place abandoned. They put it to the torch and then, satisfied with the success of the expedition, headed for home. Williamson was confident that what they had done would be very gratifying to the settlers on the upper Ohio and would now make the hostile Indians curtail their raids on the frontier.

He was wrong on both counts.

[April 1, 1782 — Monday]

Thomas Edgington was very glad the work of rebuilding Holliday's Cove Fort was nearly completed. Already the William Thomas family had returned, and it was apparent they would soon be followed by the others who had gone to Wheeling when the fort had accidentally burned, although such returns might be slowed in view of the retaliation expected for Williamson's massacre of the Moravians three weeks ago.

Yesterday was Easter, and they had observed a simple ceremony at the fort and then spent the rest of the day in conversation, although the weather was so beautiful that Edgington would really rather have been out plowing his ground to prepare it for spring planting. To do that he would need his singletree, which he had loaned to the Sappington family at the little fort they were erecting a mile and a half up Harmon's Creek at the mouth of Sappington's Run.

Now on his way there, he felt uncomfortable without his rifle. He had deliberately refrained from taking it when he left his house, simply because if he had, his wife would have thought he was slipping off on another expedition without telling her, as he had done in the past. Knowing she wouldn't believe he was just going to Sappington's, he did not want to have to listen to another of her tirades. Besides, the likelihood he would encounter a raiding party between here and there was, he felt, very remote.

Just about a mile up Harmon's Creek from home, however, Edgington abruptly found his way barred by a small party of Wyandots who had stepped out into the path ahead of him. He wheeled to flee back the way he had come and discovered others behind him. He leaped into a run through the brush and heard a voice he thought he recognized as Simon Girty's calling to him to surrender. He paid it no heed and ran, with the Indians in pursuit.

Encountering a small run, he leaped over it but slipped on the muddy bank on the far side, lost his balance and tumbled into the stream. By the time he came to his feet, the Indians were upon him, and the voice was still calling for him to surrender. He knew he now had little choice but to do precisely that.

"No kill!" he cried, raising his hands. "No kill!"

The Indians took him, immediately relieved him of his tomahawk and hunting knife, and returned with him to the path. The voice really had belonged to Girty, who now stepped forward and shook his hand.

"It's a good thing I recognized you, Edgington," Girty said. "Otherwise these boys would've kilt you on the spot. You're lucky they didn't do it when you ran."

The leader of the Indians, a well-built young man with a large new scar on his left hand, was eyeing Edgington in a speculative manner, and the frontiersman said to Girty, "Is he planning to kill me?"

"Don't think so," Girty said. "You remember that big fight the Poe brothers had last fall?" At Edgington's nod he went on, "Well, this here is Scotach. He was in that fight, an' his hand got shot plum' through. Two of his brothers were kilt. Saw you comin', an' soon as I tol' him I knew you, he said they would catch you and take you back to his daddy, Monakaduto—the one you know of as Half King—to adopt as his son to take the place of one o'them that was kilt. Reckon you're safe for now. Let's go."

They tied his hands behind his back and marched him back toward Holliday's Cove Fort. When the party arrived, they kept under cover and studied it from a distance. "Don't you make no sounds now, hear?" Girty said. "You do, an' Scotach'll fergit all 'bout adoption and jest take your hair back."

At the fort, Thomas Williams emerged with a halter in his hand and headed for the lot where his horse was hobbled. A few of Scotach's warriors slipped through cover, moving closer to where the horse was and, though Edgington yearned to shout a warning to Williams, the Wyandot guarding him with upraised tomahawk made him realize the truth of what Girty had said, and he reluctantly kept still.

Just as Williams neared the horse, a single shot rang out and the settler crumpled to the ground and did not move. The horse neighed sharply and galloped back toward the little stable adjacent to the fort. Shrieking loudly, the Indians burst from cover and ran up to the dead man, cut off his scalp and returned, shaking the blood from it.

"How many men inside, Edgington?" Girty asked. His voice became threatening as he added, "An' don't you lie t'try an' git us kilt. We seen men going in an' out all day yesterday."

The men that had been seen, Edgington knew, were just himself and Williams, who had gone out and in at intervals throughout the day for various reasons, with no suspicion they were observed. With only his own family and that of Williams inside, this party could take the place easily, but Girty had opened the door for him to possibly prevent that from happening.

"Nine," he replied. "Well, eight men and a boy. Reckon they'll be able to hold you off for a while."

Girty shook his head and said what Edgington had hoped to hear. "Ain't worth it to us right now. We ain't tradin' lives if we don't have to." He turned and spoke to the Indians rapidly in their own tongue, and the one named Scotach nodded.

In moments they were on their way again, heading now, Girty told him, toward Half King's Town on the Sandusky and, for Edgington, into a very uncertain future.[483]

[*A p r i l   2 ,   1 7 8 2 — T u e s d a y*]

News of the Moravian Massacre, as it was being called, spread rapidly, and the reactions were greatly varied, though in most cases disapproving at best.

The settlers on the upper Ohio, with but few exceptions, tended to support the elimination of the Moravian towns. However, they were uneasy about the wholesale execution of the Christian Indians and feared a swift and massive retaliation in which they, being closest, would suffer most from the wrath of the hostile tribes. Some felt that the best way to thwart this possibility would be to quickly mount a follow-up expedition and similarly destroy the Sandusky towns. It was evident that Gen. Irvine at Fort Pitt was leaning in this direction as well, as was reflected in his letter to Col. David Shepherd, in which he wrote:

> You are already acquainted with the resolution of Congress, and orders of the President and Council of Pennsylvania, respecting my command in this quarter; in addition to which, I have received instructions from his Excellency, General Washington. As making arrangements to cover and protect the country is the main object, and as it is to be done by a combination of regulars and militia, the business will be complicated. And, further, as there will be a diversity of interests, I think it of the utmost importance that, whatever plan may be adopted, it should be as generally understood as the nature of the service will admit. You will conceive that I stand in need of the counsels and assistance, on this occasion, of some of the principal people of the country. I wish, therefore, to see you and at least one field officer of every battalion in your county; for which purpose I request you will be pleased to warn such as you may think proper, to attend this post, on Friday, the 5th of April next. Punctual to the day will be necessary, as I have written to Colonel Marshall, and others, in Washington County also, to attend on the same day. Whatever difference local situations may make in sentiments respecting territory, a combination of forces to repel the enemy is clearly, I think, a duty we owe ourselves and our country.

The settlers in Kentucky, despite the prolonged suffering they had endured at the hands of the Indians, particularly the Shawnees, were shocked and dismayed by the barbarism of the Moravian Massacre and fearful in their belief that retaliation, when it came, would be directed at them as much as against the upper Ohio frontier. Yet some among them felt that, with the Indians decidedly off balance, a follow-up expedition should quickly be mounted to again strike at the Shawnee towns.

The settlers more distant from the frontier in both Pennsylvania and Virginia were awed that such a deed had been committed. A few were very outspoken in denouncing the inhumanity of the massacre, but the majority by far felt the Indians "got what they deserved." Losing no time, they made highly premature plans to rush to the frontier and claim lands, perhaps even in the Ohio country itself, "now that it was safe" to do so.

The leaders in the east were, on the whole, deeply disturbed by the news of the Moravian Massacre and publicly denounced it, while privately pleased that at last it was the Indians who had been on the receiving end. For the most part, however, they had greater and more immediate concerns: The peace negotiations with the British in Paris were bogging down, political problems were besieging the new states and the problems of establishing an effective federal government were complex and vexing. Gen. Irvine, in the east at the time, was immediately ordered by Washington to return to his command at Fort Pitt and investigate. Appalled at the ghastliness of the deed and at the confusion and recrimination that was weakening Fort Pitt's garrison, Irvine privately felt that the perpetrators ought to be hanged. He expressed these views in a letter to his wife and then, fearful of what might occur should those views become known, he added:

Whatever your private opinion of these matters may be, I conjure you by all the ties of affection, and as you value my reputation, that you keep your mind to your-self . . .

The Moravian Indians still at the Captives' Town on the Sandusky were devastated by news of the massacre. Word of it had first been brought by the party of Wyandots and Delawares who had stopped by the Moravian towns just before the attack, then lingered in the area long enough to see Williamson's force begin the destruction. The extent of the killings was not at first known, however, until Shabosh arrived with a few more details, and then the boy named Thomas, his scalp gone, came with his more detailed and horrifying account of the full extent of the massacre. Every one of these surviving Moravians had lost kin or friends.

The Moravian missionaries, headed by John Heckewelder and David Zeisberger, were overwhelmed with guilt, realizing that in a way it was their own spying activities for the Americans that had started the chain of events that ultimately brought this terrible conclusion. They felt, with certain justification, that they had failed their flock of converts and were deserving of the cruel treatment they had been receiving from Simon Girty and others. The missionaries and their families had been taken to Lower Sandusky to be transported to Detroit for trial on espionage charges and, while awaiting that transportation, had been severely mistreated by Girty and even threatened with death. They had finally gotten away from him through the humanity of a Frenchman named Francis Levallie, who refused to treat them as brutally as Girty had ordered and instead escorted them safely to Detroit.[484] In Detroit the missionaries underwent grueling questioning and a trial and, while everyone suspected them of being spies for the Americans, no proof was presented. They were exonerated and returned to their despondent flock, whom they moved to a slightly better area near the mouth of the Auglaize River where it empties into the Maumee.[485]

The British in Detroit were appalled by the Moravian Massacre, yet were not laggardly in putting it to their advantage, using it to light even hotter fires of unrest among the tribes and promote increased raids on the frontier from Fort Pitt to Kentucky.

The hostile Indians—in particular the Delawares, kin to the Moravians despite their persuasion—were infuriated beyond expression. They considered the Moravian Massacre to be a wanton outrage of the blackest nature, clearly depicting the real character of the *Shemanese.* Yet at just this bleak moment, word was circulating among the Indians that the British were pulling back, curtailing their support of the Indians because of peace negotiations going on with the Americans across the big water. On hearing this, Pimoacan—Captain Pipe, chief of the Delawares—angrily confronted the Detroit commander, Maj. Arent de Peyster. Holding in his hand a short stick, to the end of which was tied a human scalp, he spoke in a steely manner, his eyes never wavering from those of the commandant.

"Father! Some time ago you put a war-hatchet in my hands, saying, 'Take this weapon and try it upon the heads of my enemies, the Long Knives, and let me know afterward if it was sharp and good.' Father, at the time when you gave me this weapon, I had neither cause nor inclination to go to war against a people who had done me no injury; yet, in obedience to you, who say you are my father and call me your child, I received the hatchet, well knowing that if I did not obey, you would withhold from me the necessaries of life, without which I could not subsist, and which are not elsewhere to be procured but at the house of my father.

"Father! Many lives have already been lost on *your* account. Nations have suffered and been weakened. Children have lost parents, brothers have lost brothers and relatives have lost relatives. Wives have lost husbands. It is not known how many more may perish before *your* war will be at an end. Father! You say you love your children, the Indians. This you have often told them; and, indeed, it is for your interest to say so to them that you may have them at your service. But, Father, who of us can believe that you can love a people of a different color from your own, better than those who have a white skin like yourselves?

"Father!" Pimoacan's eyes narrowed and his voice became harder. "Pay attention to what I am going to say! While you are setting me on your enemy, much in the same manner as a hunter sets his dog on the game, while I am in the act of rushing on that enemy of yours with the bloody destructive weapon you gave me, I may happen to look back to the place from whence you started me, and what shall I see? Perhaps I shall see my father shaking hands with the Long Knives; yes, with those very people whom he now calls his enemies. I may then see him laugh at my folly for having obeyed his orders, and yet I am now risking my life at his command.

"Now, Father," he went on, after pausing to hand the scalp-stick to de Peyster, "*this* is what has been done with the hatchet you gave me. I have done with the hatchet what you ordered me to do, and have found it sharp. Nevertheless, I did not do *all* that I might have done. No, I did not; my heart failed within me. I felt compassion for *your* enemy. *Innocence* had no part in your quarrels, therefore I distinguished—I spared; I took some live flesh, which, while I was bringing them to you, I spied one of your large canoes, on which I put them for you. In a few days you will receive them and will find that the skin is the same color as your own. Father, I hope you will not destroy what I have saved."

Some of the fire in Pimoacan's voice faded and was replaced by a more beseeching note as he concluded: "You, Father, have the means of preserving what, with me, would perish for want. The warrior is poor and his cabin is always empty, but *your* house, Father, is always full."

It was clear now that, in view of what the Williamson expedition had done, the total annihilation of these detested enemies had become paramount in the minds of the Delawares, Wyandots and other tribes. No one could deny that they had the determination, courage and fighting ability for the task. All they lacked were horses, firearms, gunpowder, cannons, food, supplies and manpower.

And now, at last, the British at Detroit committed themselves to providing their Indian allies what they lacked.

[*April 5, 1782 — Friday*]

Gen. William Irvine was in something of a quandary. It was clear that the settlers of the upper Ohio were strongly in favor of forming a more powerful expedition to march against the Sandusky villages, and the general thought this a splendid idea. At the same time they expected the regulars at Fort Pitt to participate in the campaign and this was something he would not be able to permit without specific orders from the War Department.

Three days ago he had received a letter from the Washington County lieutenant, Col. James Marshall, that distilled the feelings of the upper Ohio River settlers to a single sentence:

This is most certain, that unless an expedition be carried against the principal Indian towns early this summer, this country must unavoidably suffer.

Part of what made Marshall so definite in his conclusion was the extremely important intelligence that had just been obtained in respect to the plans of the British and Indians. That intelligence was brought by a man long since believed to be dead—John Slover.

Slover knew the northwestern Indians very well, especially the Shawnees, Miamis and Wyandots. In 1761, when only eight years old, he had been captured by a party of Miami Indians on the bank of Montour's Run, within a stone's throw of his parents' cabin. Taken by them to their principal village of Kekionga at the head of the Maumee River, he lived among them for six years, at which time he had been traded to the Shawnees and lived with that tribe for another six years.

In 1773, at age 20, Slover had gone to Pittsburgh with a party of the Shawnees and, while there, was recognized by white relatives and convinced to return home with them. He did so, but reluctantly, because by then he had become much attached to the Indian way of life. Serving off and on as a guide to the military at Fort Pitt and Fort McIntosh, he gradually became accustomed to living with the whites again and became popular among them.

Then, on August 6, 1780, Slover was again captured by Indians, this time by Wyandots, while he was hunting snapping turtles. Ironically, his second capture was again on Montour's Run. His neighbors thought he had probably been killed, but that was not the case. He had been taken to Half King's Town, where he successfully ran the gauntlet and later was adopted into an Indian family. A quick study, he learned their language rapidly and could soon converse fluently with them. Thanks to this ability he was able to listen with great interest to their councils and, in so doing, learned their plans in respect to the settlers on the upper Ohio. He acquired a great many minor bits of information, but the most important thing was that the Indians had, in their war councils, determined upon two expeditions with British assistance—one to go against the Kentucky settlements; the other a major assault against Wheeling.

Today, the meeting called for by Gen. Irvine with the various county lieutenants and principal field officers of those counties was brought to order. Col. David

Shepherd, accompanied by one-armed Maj. Samuel McCulloch, represented Ohio County, Virginia.[486] In turn, each of the officers from the different posts reported on their manpower, defenses, supplies and preparedness, as well as the projected number of militia and volunteers that could be raised. It was a huge disappointment to these officers when Gen. Irvine informed them that, while he would aid them in any way possible in the defense of their forts, settlements and people, these counties could not expect much, if any, material assistance from the government for an offensive measure against the Indians and that they would have to depend upon the valor and skill of their own county residents. Any plan of offensive nature, however, would nonetheless be under his control and military direction.

Though the Pennsylvania county lieutenants had received instructions from their state's executive, none had been received by the lieutenants of Monongalia and Ohio counties from the executive of Virginia, so it was agreed among the officers present that those counties would act on a voluntary basis until such authority was obtained.

The regulars presently stationed at both Fort Pitt and Fort McIntosh, Gen. Irvine told them, must remain at their posts, making it the full responsibility of the militia to regularly patrol, as they had been doing, the entire frontier from Pittsburgh downstream 90 miles to Wheeling. New and extended patrol schedules were laid out, and among the assignments made were those that appointed Thomas Younkins and Martin Wetzel as spies for Beeler's Station and Wheeling respectively. Their duties involved scouting through the woods and along the Ohio River shoreline in the vicinity of these forts, ever watchful for sign of Indian incursions. If and when such sign was discovered, they were to follow to its source and ascertain, if at all possible, the strength of the Indian force and where it might be heading next to make an attack.

The most immediately important business under discussion was the projected expedition against the Indians in the Sandusky Valley. Even though it had now been clarified that regulars could have no part in such an offensive and that there would be many obstacles to overcome, it was the consensus that a volunteer force could be assembled of a magnitude great enough to insure success in carrying the war to the heart of the Indian country. Then came the task of firming up the details of organization as well as when the expedition would begin and where it would rendezvous.

The number of volunteers to participate was the first consideration and it was essential that the force be large enough to handle any and all contingencies. A first tentative figure was set at 500 men. Every volunteer was required to provide his own rifle, bedroll, provisions and horse. It was also deemed necessary that the expedition be set into motion as soon as possible and that the line of march and destination be kept secret. The rendezvous was to be held on May 20, and it was assumed that three or four days would be required for all the troops to arrive, cross the river, assemble there and elect their officers for the expedition. Selected as the site for the rendezvous was the east shore of the Ohio directly opposite Mingo Bottom. Once all assembled, the men would cross the river to make their base camp on Mingo Bottom proper. Named after the Mingo village that had existed there prior to 1772, Mingo Bottom was a broad elevated bottomland of some 250 acres. It was situated three-fourths of a mile above the mouth of Indian Cross Creek, 20 miles above Wheeling and 70 miles below Pittsburgh, and was selected not only because it was most centrally located for their designs but because it was one of the easiest crossing places.[487] The 20-acre Mingo Island was in the Ohio at this point, and just above the head of it, where crossings were usually made, the river was shallow enough that in especially dry years it could be forded on horseback without the animal ever being forced to swim. In more normal conditions the portion that required swimming was quite limited.[488]

So at last the wheels were in motion to end, once and for all, the Indian threat on the upper Ohio River frontier.

Or so it seemed.

[April 28, 1782 — Sunday]

Joseph Parkinson felt very lucky. He was certain he was going to succeed where others before him had failed. Thus far all previous efforts to establish a regular Ohio River commerce between Pittsburgh and New Orleans had failed. But Joe Parkinson had the strong feeling that his star was in the ascendancy and that this was only the maiden voyage of the first boat of a fleet that would establish him as the pioneer founder of commercial cargo transport on the Ohio.

The fact that they had experienced a temporary delay yesterday when they ran aground on a bar was only a minor inconvenience. Now, allowing himself the luxury of just lying still in his bunk for a little while before the others began rousing, he considered their journey so far.

A ferryman by trade, he had established Parkinson's Ferry on the Monongahela a few years ago and had done very well with it, but ambition for bigger and better endeavors gripped him. Selling out his ferry business and pooling all his resources, plus those of a few daring investors, he had this large broadhorn built, with a good dry hold for cargo storage and an excellent cabin capable of sleeping a dozen in individual bunks lined with cornhusk mattresses.

With just about all that remained of his capital, he had purchased a full cargo of flour in sacks, kegs and barrels, hired ten good shooters as guards and crew and set off for the far-distant bayou country. His initial plan had been to make no stops whatever but to maintain a daily 24-hour drift down the main current.

All had gone well, and yesterday about noon, some 40 miles below Wheeling, they had entered the Long Reach, that 17-mile stretch of river that was practically free of the sinuous bends that marked most of the giant river's course. They were within a few miles of the foot of that stretch when they noticed a derelict canoe wedged along the Virginia shore. Hardly more than half a mile beyond that, there was a sudden heavy scraping sound and then a jolt as the big broadhorn slid through the skin of mud cloaking a sand bar and wedged itself tightly.[489]

Irked at the inconvenience, Parkinson first ordered four men overboard, then four more and finally all ten of his men in an attempt to free the craft. It was all to no avail, and after working at it for a couple of hours, he sent two men back to recover the derelict canoe. He hoped that by putting as much as possible of the cargo into the canoe, he would lighten the load in the larger boat enough that the crew would be able to pry it free.

The two men soon returned with the canoe, paddling it with pieces of bark located on shore. It took a great deal of work but it finally had the desired effect and the broadhorn floated free. They nudged the big boat very gently back onto the bar to facilitate the reloading of the flour, and by the time that was finished it was growing dark and the men were exhausted. That was when Parkinson broke his 24-hour drifting plan and decided to let the boat remain lightly wedged here for the night and allow the crew a solid night's rest.

Now, with the dawn growing brighter, Joe Parkinson swung his legs off the bunk, stretched hugely and said, "All right, boys, the holiday's over. Let's get drifting."

With low groans and some grumbling, the men came awake and began to stir. After a little while one of them scuffed sleepily toward the doorway and stepped outside. A moment after he disappeared from sight came the sharp crack of a rifle nearby. Another of the guards, close to the door, snatched up his rifle and raced outside. Instantly there was another shot.

"Men inside!" came a call. "Two of your people are already dead. All will die if you do not come out now and surrender. You will not be killed if you surrender. If you try to fight, you die. No guns! You must come out now or die. *Now!*"[490]

They had no choice and knew it, so Parkinson glumly gave the order and the remaining eight crewmen filed out. Parkinson followed them, his expression set in grim lines as he saw the two dead crewmen on the deck. Indians were already swarming over the gunwales and quickly searching the survivors for weapons. Others raced into the cabin to see if there were more men who had not emerged, and three removed the hatch over the hold and stared into the dimness below. Parkinson counted 15 warriors, but there may have been more out of sight. The tracks on the bar showed that they had crossed to it from shore during the night and had evidently hidden beneath the bow of the broadhorn until daylight.

Within 20 minutes the dead men had been scalped and their bodies thrown into the river, while the captives were led ashore. Parkinson glanced back just before the trees cut off his view and saw the Indians already beginning to unload the cargo.

Joe Parkinson no longer felt at all lucky.

[April 28, 1782 — Sunday]

It had been a long time since Old John Wetzel had gone out hunting with his sons and, when Martin, now 25, remarked that he had seen a lot of game along the Ohio River on the Indian side of the stream during his captivity, plans were made to do some hunting in the bottoms there. Two of Old John's younger sons, George, 22, and Lewis, 18, decided they would go along, too, as did two of their Wheeling Creek neighbors, Thomas Mills and Hamilton Carr, both 18. The Wetzel dog, a medium-size brown-and-white mongrel, also came along and sat with Old John in the bow.

George took the stern. This was an unusual outing for him, as he had never become the skilled woodsman and Indian fighter that his four brothers were. George was of a gentler nature, a good-looking, serious-minded, studious young man.

Now, having paddled down the Ohio in their canoe close to the right bank, they continued studying the muddy banks and bars and the closer cover for signs of game. It was noon when they came to a good-looking stretch of bottomland with some deer tracks visible near the water. Tom Mills suggested he go ashore and move along slowly on foot through the bottoms, while the Wetzels continued down another mile or so before putting in. By walking toward one another, they might be able to corner some deer between them.

They let him out and resumed paddling along the Ohio shore but had not paddled much over a mile when, just as they were nearing a small willow-grown island closer to the Virginia shore, they caught sight of a large broadhorn well ahead that appeared to be wedged on a bar. Men were unloading sacks and kegs and carrying them to shore, and Old John, shading his eyes and staring intently, suddenly hissed a warning.

"By damn, they're Injens!"

The words had barely left his lips when a flurry of shots broke out from the dense undergrowth on the nearby shore. George Wetzel grunted and fell partially forward as a ball struck him in the chest, but then he caught himself and straightened. The Wetzel dog let out a brief yelp and fell dead in the bottom of the canoe.

"Down, everybody!" George cried. Blood was drooling from the corner of his mouth. "Stay down. I'll get us over t'that island. Don't show yourselves. I'm dead anyway."

The others dropped and lay down in the bottom of the big canoe as George, gasping with the effort, paddled on an angle away from the Ohio shore and toward the willow-covered island. More shots were coming and, though none struck George a second time, a number punched through the sides of the canoe and had some effect. Martin felt a pain as if a hot iron had been laid against his skin, and he saw that a ball had creased his right shoulder, gouging a shallow two-inch trench. Hamilton Carr cried out as a ball caught him more solidly, entering high in the right arm, breaking the bone and exiting from the back of his shoulder.[491]

With commendable effort, considering the seriousness of his chest wound, George managed to paddle the big canoe out of effective range and slip behind the cover provided by the little willow-cloaked isle.[492] A few shots were still being fired at random by the Indians, but when Lewis and his father began a return fire, the Indian shots died away. It soon became evident that they were gone.[493] A glimpse downstream revealed the big broadhorn floating aimlessly, evidently having been set adrift after the cargo, or at least a good portion of it, had been offloaded and taken away.

George Wetzel was in bad shape. Frothy red bubbles kept forming at his lips, and his color had gone, leaving him waxen and only semiconscious. It was essential to get him to medical care as soon as possible, and that meant Wheeling. Carr, in considerable pain, needed treatment, too. They had no idea what had happened to Tom Mills, though they hoped he had made his escape up the Ohio shore.[494] They started upstream, staying close to the Virginia shore, but for all the effort they put in their strokes, it was to no avail.

They were still about 20 miles below Wheeling and just passing Captina Island when George Wetzel died. They buried him at the head of the island.[495]

[May 6, 1782 — Monday]

As more reports of the Moravian Massacre filtered through the country, each retelling magnified and even more atrocious than the original brutal act, the sense of outrage swelled and caused extraordinary reactions.

Hundreds of miles to the south, the Cherokees, while never great friends of the Delawares, sympathized with them to the point where a chief named Rattlesnake in the village of Toque gathered 30 of his best warriors and led them toward the Ohio River to aid the northern tribes—the Delawares and Shawnees in particular—against the settlers in the Kan-tuck-kee hunting grounds. They were not the only ones to decide that Kentucky should bear the brunt of retaliation. Well to the north, at Detroit, British Capt. William Caldwell began concerting plans with Girty and the Shawnees for a major assault against those settlements during the forthcoming summer.

Today, in Richmond, Virginia Gov. Benjamin Harrison was writing his message to the House of Delegates, and he relayed to them a compilation of the news he had thus far received in dispatches from the west. Two weeks ago the first of the reports had arrived, and the ripple of shock that spread in its wake quickly became a large wave of anger that such an act of inhumanity could have occurred. A week ago, having received additional details, many of them unnecessarily exaggerated, Gov. Harrison sent outraged circular letters to the county lieutenants and leading officials on his state's frontier:

In Council, April 30th, 1782

Gentlemen—

The Executive, having received information by the enclosed papers of the most shocking and cruel murder being committed on some friendly tribes of Indians, are called on by every tie of humanity and justice to use their utmost endeavors to bring to condign punishment all those concerned in it, who live within their jurisdiction, and as there is no certain way of coming at the truth of this massacre but by the assistance of some persons of known honor and integrity who live near the place from whence these murderers went, I most earnestly request the favor of you to make the strictest enquiry into the matter, and when you find guilt that you punish it with all the rigor of the law, and that you give me a particular account of your proceeding and the discoveries you make as soon as possible. Any reasonable expenses you may incur in the prosecution of this business, shall be repaid you. The honor and justice of the country will be so materially wounded if the culprits escape punishment, that I am sure if you had no other inducements to exert yourself but their preservation, you would not leave anything in your power undone to investigate the truth of this cruel affair; but if these were out of the question, your sentiments of humanity and the duties you owe to society and to heaven, would call on you in too powerful a manner to be resisted. If force should appear necessary to you to answer the purposes of your appointment, you'll please to apply for it to the commanding officers of Hampshire & Monongahela.

    I am, &c.   *Benjamin Harrison*

In addition to reports of the Moravian Massacre, Gov. Harrison had been receiving an abundance of disturbing reports on the sharply increased attacks being made on the settlers in retaliation for that act, along with disturbing intelligence about enemy plans in the making for launching large-scale attacks. In one attack a few weeks ago, a few of Capt. Sam Meason's Negroes were captured by the Indians. Peter Stalnaker, Henry Baker and Henry Yoho immediately headed for Wheeling to give the alarm. They were ambushed by Indians hiding behind a large rock at The Narrows of Wheeling Creek. Stalnaker shot the Indian closest to him, and both he and his horse were instantly killed in return fire. Yoho's horse was also shot and fell but scrambled back to its feet and carried him to safety. Henry Baker's horse took a bullet in the side just behind the foreleg but ran about 100 yards before falling dead and pinning Baker beneath it. Baker extricated himself and tried to flee, but was overtaken and captured.[496]

Now, continuing the writing of his message to the House of Delegates, Harrison added:

General Clark, by his last letter, expects a powerful attack this spring on Kentucky from Detroit; his information comes from Illinois, and he thinks it may be depended on. We have sent him artillery and stores down the Ohio. I hope they will get to them in time, but in this, as in every thing else, we have been greatly obstructed by poverty.

The inhabitants of Monongahela, Montgomery and Greenbrier are in great distress. Many families have been either killed or carried off. The earliness of the attacks gives them reason to apprehend it is only a prelude to what they have to expect, and that though mischief has been done, it was rather by reconnoitering parties coming before a much more powerful invasion, than intended as any thing serious. A sufficient number of men have been ordered out to protect the country for the present, and more will be sent if there should be occasion. The expense attending these various parties when brought into an aggregate sum amount to something serious, and when the losses of our people are taken into the account, probably to more than would have been sufficient to have set on foot two or three expeditions against the restless savages and have answered the purposes of protecting the country much more effectually. I do not think a just idea of the expense of carrying on such a war can be formed from what has hitherto been done, where parade and ostentatious show seem to have prevailed, all which should be discontinued. Provisions might be laid up in different parts of the frontier this fall which could be procured in commutation for money taxes. When this was done, a sufficient number of militia could be marched to either or all of those posts in a very short time, to make a sudden attack on such nations of Indians as were the most troublesome, which, repeated two or three times, would bring them to reason, or force them to quit their country altogether, and settle at so great a distance from us as to put it out of their power to annoy us much. I give this opinion with diffidence, yet think it worthy of consideration.

Whatever would eventually occur, this was shaping up to be a most eventful year on the western frontier.

[May 1, 1782 — Wednesday]

Monakaduto had listened in grim silence as his spies, fresh from the upper Ohio frontier, related their disturbing news. They had discovered that the Americans were organizing a large invasion into the Ohio country by the end of the month, this one aimed directly at the Wyandot and Delaware villages on the upper Sandusky River. The army was expected to be 500 men or more, and their principal target, apparently, was to be Monakaduto's own large home village, which the Americans called Half King's Town. Highest up the Sandusky River, it was also the first village the whites would reach if and when they did come.

Monakaduto wasted no time. Runners were dispatched at once to Detroit, requesting help from the British in terms of food, ammunition, troops and artillery. Others were sent to the chiefs of the Delawares, Shawnees, Miamis, Potawatomies and Chippewas, urging them to send war parties to the upper Sandusky at once to strike the Americans when they arrived.

Then he gave orders for his large village to be abandoned and two new villages to be established by the inhabitants. Most of the women, children and elderly would be moved farther out of reach and protected by a buffer of other villages inhabited by warriors. That more distant village, to be called Monakaduto's Town, would be some 15 miles down the left bank of the Sandusky River, on a piece of good high ground just above the mouth of Tymochtee Creek.[497] The second village, the New Half King's Town, where the majority of the warriors would stay until this crisis ended, would be established eight miles below this village being abandoned and seven miles above Monakaduto's Town. It would be on both sides of the Sandusky River at a fording place adjacent to the long-established British trading post called McCormick's Store and close to a small settlement of Delawares. Another store was also close by—John Leith's Trading Post, where British provisions and annuities were doled out to the Indians.[498]

Most important, the New Half King's Town was so situated that if, in fact, the Americans did show up, a nearby blind ravine some 30 feet in depth would prove ideal for staging an ambush.

Monakaduto's eyes glittered at the thought.

[*M a y   2 4 ,   1 7 8 2 — F r i d a y*]

Although the rendezvous of volunteer troops to march against the Sandusky Towns was scheduled for May 20 and many men had shown up that day, it had taken until today for everyone to arrive and for the army to form itself into an organized unit of close to 500 men. Everyone participating had brought his own horse, gun and supplies for a month. Even Col. Crawford had to buy a new, sturdier horse.[499] That more men would continue to show up, even after the army began its 150-mile march, and follow the force in an effort to overtake and join it, was a foregone conclusion.[500]

The initial groups of mounted men arrived and rendezvoused on the left bank —the east, or Virginia side—of the Ohio River and crossed over the fording place individually and in small clusters to the expansive Mingo Bottom where the Indian trail led westward.[501]

The army that formed was not made up largely of border ruffian types. To the contrary, though none were in any kind of uniform and most wore long hunting shirts belted at the waist and soft-brimmed hats and some, such as Pvt. John Hays, looked almost Indian in their breechclouts and leggings, quite a significant number of the volunteers had ample experience as frontline veterans of the regulars who had served at the battles of Quebec, Germantown, Brandywine, Saratoga, Trenton, Monmouth, Princeton and Yorktown. Some had served in Clark's campaign against Kaskaskia, Cahokia and Vincennes and others had suffered the terrible winter at Valley Forge under Washington. Quite a few had served as scouts and spies in the border patrols of the upper Ohio to protect the settlers and had helped defend the settlements when necessary.

A certain number of the militiamen, especially those of means, who as bona fide members of the militia were required to answer the call to accompany the expedition had, instead, hired stand-ins to march and fight in their place—a practice entirely legal, provided one had the means for doing so and could locate an uncommitted individual avaricious enough to become a stand-in for a fee. Among those who availed themselves of this practice were William Rowe, whose substitute was William Orr, and John McCaddon who hired Aaron Longstreet.[502] Richard Elson sent his Negro slave, Sam, to fight in his stead. Elson was not the only one to take this permissible way out of risking his own life, even though it was generally looked upon askance. Most of the men, however, felt honor-bound to answer their militia call to duty without attempts at evasion because it was a matter of personal pride and integrity to do so.

A number of the notable border men were not on hand for the rendezvous. Among them were Capt. Samuel Brady and most of his Rangers. Realizing the necessity of continuing to protect the frontier in case bands of Indians should attempt to make raids while the majority of the men were gone on the expedition, Brady and his men were exempted from serving on the campaign, although Peter Parchment elected to go anyway. Other upper Ohio residents simply chose not to go, among them the Tomlinson boys and the Wetzels. Lewis Wetzel scoffed when asked if he was going along. "Me?" he snorted. "Reckon when it comes t'killin' Injens, I'll do it in my own way an' in my own time."

So, with the majority of the men assembled, the election of officers was begun. Two men were especially favored for the top command spot—Col. David Williamson and Col. William Crawford. Williamson was undeniably the popular choice for the command, but Gen. Irvine wanted no repetition of the rashness, poor leadership and insensitivity that Williamson had exhibited in the Moravian campaign. Thus, for the past several weeks Gen. Irvine, in a more or less clandestine manner, had brought to bear considerable influence among the more prominent men who would accompany the expedition, that when it came time to elect the officers for the campaign, William Crawford would be named to the top command. By the time of the rendezvous, Irvine had little lingering doubt that the selection for leadership would ultimately fall to the man of his own choice. Nevertheless Gen. Irvine's letter of instructions for the design and comportment of the campaign was addressed *To the Officer who will be appointed to command a detachment of Volunteer Militia on an expedition against the Indian town at or near Sandusky,* and it said, among the variety of details covered:

> *The object of your command is to destroy with fire and sword (if practicable), then you will doubtless perform such other services in your power as will, in their consequences, have a tendency to answer this great end.*

Knowing and respecting Crawford as a seasoned veteran officer of the Continental line, Irvine was prepared to give him written instructions in regard to the comportment of the troops and to leave no question this time as to whether the campaign had official authorization.[503] Yet, despite his confidence in the man, Irvine also meant to have a close watch kept on Crawford and to be provided with a full and very accurate report of his activities and those of the army at the close of the campaign. To this end, Gen. Irvine magnanimously loaned his own aide, Maj. John Rose, to Crawford to act as Crawford's aide-de-camp. He also honored Crawford's request to have his old friend, Dr. John Knight, as surgeon for the campaign.

Maj. Rose, 29, who was actually a Russian fugitive and soldier of fortune named Gustavus Heinrich de Rosenthal, was instructed by Gen. Irvine to record surreptitiously everything about the campaign. He elected to do so by the expedient of innocently keeping a comprehensive daily journal, which would later provide him a fitting resource for filing the full report that Gen. Irvine wished. Accompanying Rose was a Negro slave named Henry, who belonged to Gen. Irvine and worked for him at Fort Pitt as a vegetable gardener, tending the commander's prized little plot of peas and asparagus. Irvine loaned Henry to Rose as valet and servant during the campaign.[504] The prominent men who had been influenced by Gen. Irvine in turn swayed many of the men who had gathered at the rendezvous. As it was, the election was very close, and despite Irvine's influence, Crawford was elected as colonel commanding by only five votes over Williamson; the latter was elected to the rank of major and named second-in-command.[505]

The force was to be divided into four battalions, each commanded by a field major. Williamson—though still addressed by most of the men by his militia rank of colonel—was one of those, along with Thomas Gaddis, John McClelland and John Brinton, the latter three named third, fourth and fifth in command of the army respectively. Crawford's aide-de-camp, John Rose, was elected adjutant with rank of major, while Daniel Leet, a chunky man of medium height but weighing more than 200 pounds, was elected brigade major.[506] The brigade surgeon was Dr. John Knight, who carried his array of surgical instruments in saddlebags. The three guides for the expedition were Jonathan Zane, John Slover and Thomas Nicholson.[507]

Now came the matter of troop organization. The nearly 500 men on hand distributed themselves into 18 companies.[508] There were a great many among the volunteers who had two or three or even more relatives in this army. Even Col. Crawford had three, including his son John; a namesake nephew, William Crawford, who was son of his brother, Valentine; and a son-in-law named William Harrison.[509] All immediate family members—fathers and sons and brothers—as well as other kinsmen and even neighbors, by general agreement, were divided into separate units, the reasoning being that if any single company was hit hard by the enemy and suffered great loss, no single family would be wiped out or their home neighborhood left defenseless by the loss of all its able men. Each of the 18 companies thereupon voted again, and each elected a company commander with the rank of captain, plus a second and third in command ranked, respectively, as lieutenant and ensign. There was one exception to the process of separation of kinsmen: Capt. John Hardin, Sr., a bullheaded miller, elected as one of the company commanders, refused to let his family be separated from him, and so they all stayed together in a company of only 12 men. Because of his dictatorial nature among his employees at his mill and his notorious rashness on past expeditions, few of the other men assembled would agree to join Hardin's company, certain he would lead them into the worst possible danger.[510]

With the army now well formed, the commander issued orders for it to begin its march at ten o'clock on the morrow.

[M a y   2 5 ,   1 7 8 2 — S a t u r d a y]

Col. Crawford, at 60 years of age, was still a very active man, despite the fact that he had put on so much weight in recent years that people politely described him as heavy-set. With his light complexion, dense dark gray hair and piercing steel-blue eyes, he presented a military bearing and commanding appearance that elicited respect. He had been closely involved in the opening of the west for most of his life and had come to epitomize a frontier leader in matters military and civil. He was proud of being chosen commander of this expedition against the Wyandots and Delawares on the upper Sandusky River, and he had no doubt that it would be the crowning role of his long career in the west.

It was at ten this morning that he set his army into motion and began moving out from Mingo Bottom on a campaign he knew was destined to make history. Though he would have preferred to be at the head of a fine corps of smartly uniformed regulars, he nevertheless set out with confidence in the fighting abilities of the volunteers, despite their ragtag aspect.

While a small number of these volunteers were, like himself, well mounted on fine saddles, the majority were not. His principal aide, Maj. John Rose, shook his head at the disreputable appearance of the army and privately considered them a collection of clodhoppers. Most rode scrawny, poorly fed farm horses that only with difficulty carried the maximum allotted weight of 150 pounds of equipment and provisions in addition to the weight of their riders. The majority of these riders did not have saddles for their horses, and they perched themselves on sacks of meal slung across the horse's back, their feet precariously wedged in rope stirrups, their guidance of the horse limited to a single rein attached to a hair-rope halter. One exception to this general situation was young Pvt. Thomas Mills, who had borrowed his father's fine gray gelding and excellent saddle, and he was very proud of both. To aid him in recovering the horse should it wander off while hobbled or be stolen by Indians, he had carefully cut a broad V in the gelding's hoof. Tom Mills had grown up considerably in the past month since going out hunting with the Wetzels, when George Wetzel was killed.

Three advance columns of horsemen took the lead, preceding the main column of the army, which rode four abreast as they headed westward through the wilderness. The whole force, moving at a much slower pace than Col. Crawford had hoped to establish, stretched out for miles. They followed a tolerably good Indian trail out of Mingo Bottom only briefly and then, to avoid detection, left the trail and proceeded westward through unbroken forest.

Not unexpectedly, there were a few problems right from the beginning. Pvt. John Shannon, for example, was in exquisite pain because of several painful boils that had formed—perhaps psychosomatically—on his behind, so he was sent home. Before they had gone five miles, Pvt. John Smith, a neighbor of Col. Crawford, experienced difficulty controlling his unruly mare. When the horse unexpectedly lunged off the trail, Smith's foot was smashed against a tree, the resultant injury so severe that he was unable to go on. He, too, was ordered home by Col. Crawford.[511]

Col. David Williamson brought up the rear late in the afternoon, detained not only by the slowness of the column but by the want of a horse for the third pilot. His portion of the militia traveled only ten miles this first day, despite the ease of the ride over the better-than-average woodland trail at the beginning.

It was hardly an auspicious start.[512]

[M a y   2 6 ,   1 7 8 2 — S u n d a y]

Col. Crawford was irked by the slowness of the first day's march yesterday and the loud, careless conversation that the men engaged in as they rode. Their four-abreast columns had been ragged and disorderly, their behavior more like a group of youngsters out on a lark than an army marching to surprise an enemy. Now, as camp was struck and the army prepared to mount for its second day's ride, he ordered a sign to be made and posted on a tree for all to read as they passed:

> *Every Man ought to be convinced that the success of our enterprize depends in great measure upon a rapid & secret march.*

[*M a y   2 8 ,   1 7 8 2 — T u e s d a y*]

The route of Crawford's army carried them past several good springs before reaching the valley of the Tuscarawas, so there was no want for water. Tension heightened as the force approached the Moravian town of Schoenbrun. Three times yesterday and once earlier today, individual Indians had been spotted at considerable distances ahead, evidently spying on the army's movements. Thus far, however, nothing of significance had occurred except that on the morning of the second day of the march, three volunteers could not find their horses which had been hobbled the night before. There was some speculation that they may have been stolen by the spying Indians, but no proof to back it up. However, not wishing to have any of his men afoot, who would only become a burden on others, Crawford ordered the three to return home, and the march progressed. Pvt. Thomas Mills, fearful that his father's fine horse would be stolen or wander off, decided that henceforth he would not let the gelding get much more than an arm's length away from him.

The commander continued to be disappointed at the army's slow progress—averaging only 15 miles per day, when he had hoped for 25—but he knew the hills ahead would gradually become less severe and was confident the speed of their march would increase as the difficulty of travel eased.

Though its sister villages, Salem and Gnadenhütten, had been destroyed by Col. Williamson on his infamous expedition a few months earlier, Schoenbrun had been only partially destroyed and rumor was rampant among the volunteers—bolstered by the sightings of the distant Indians—that the hostiles had reoccupied it and were waiting there to ambush them.

As they came in view of the place, the three advance columns, ignoring the orders, curses and threats of their officers, abandoned caution and put their sweating steeds into an unruly headlong charge. The left and right columns galloped to opposite sides of the town, and the center headed directly for the three partially burned log structures in the midst of the village. Had Indians in fact been lying in ambush there, these unauthorized advance columns would have been devastated, but fortunately no one was there.

As soon as the realization came that Schoenbrun was devoid of life, the lust for plunder took over and the men spread out everywhere to search for anything of value. Fully a third of the advance plunged across the Tuscarawas to hunt for horses they thought might be pastured there. Another large cluster jumped off their mounts and leaped into a nearby pond, surging about in water armpit deep and feeling with their feet for any goods that might have been tossed into the water in an effort to hide them. The majority tore through the buildings still standing or only partially destroyed. All the efforts were in vain. With the exception of an old, rusted and totally useless flintlock and a broken tomahawk, nothing was found.

When finally some sort of order had been restored, Col. William Crawford, obviously exasperated, addressed the men in strong terms, berating them for their foolhardiness and refusal to obey orders and threatening severe punishment for any further lapses in discipline. But even as he spoke, the commander had the distinct foreboding that they could well find themselves in truly serious trouble if attacked by the Indians in force.

As they set up camp for the night, Maj. John Brinton and Capt. Joseph Bane set off to reconnoiter the area and saw, only a quarter-mile away, two Indians. They immediately fired at the pair—the first shots fired in the campaign—but the Indians were not hit and quickly disappeared. Col. Crawford was disheartened when he learned of the incident, as he had still been hoping to maintain secrecy and take the Sandusky Towns by surprise. Now, quite obviously, the Indians were well aware of their presence, and all the army could do was press forward at the best speed possible.[513]

And now, as well, Crawford's sense of foreboding increased.

[June 1, 1782—Saturday]

The Delaware and Wyandot spies who were carefully watching the progress of the army marching against them, saw the large force reach the headwaters of the Sandusky River and begin following its left bank along the trail that led to their villages. They immediately sent runners to those villages to alert them, and now preparations began in earnest for the confrontation that would doubtless occur sometime in the next three or four days.

At the orders of their chiefs, Pimoacan and Wingenund, the majority of the Delaware women, children and elderly in the villages and settlements near McCormick's Trading Post gathered up their goods and trudged northward. Seven miles later, just west of the new Monakaduto's Town at the mouth of Tymochtee Creek, they entered a deep, well-hidden and expansive ravine.[514] Here they set up a temporary camp, where they would remain for their own safety until the confrontation was concluded.

Wingenund and Pimoacan then conferred with Monakaduto and made plans for a surprise attack upon the Americans. Encouraging word had reached them that a force of close to 100 British Rangers was en route to help, and, behind them some miles, under Maj. Butler, was the promised British artillery—two cannon and a coehorn.[515] Traveling with the Rangers, under command of the British deputy Indian agent, Capt. Matthew Elliott, was a fair-size war party of Chippewas and a few Potawatomies, Ottawas and Miamis. Word had also come that upward of 200 Shawnees under their war chief Shemeneto—Black Snake—would be arriving from their villages along the Mad River, some 40 miles to the southwest.

The Indian spies informed the Wyandot and Delaware chiefs on the upper Sandusky that the advance column of Americans had regularly been traveling no more than a few hundred yards ahead of the main force. This made the planning of their ambush easy. In the area the Indians chose to spring their trap, they would simply let the advance pass by unharmed and then strike the main body on all sides simultaneously. They harbored no doubt as to what the outcome of the struggle would be, but it was Pimoacan—the feared Captain Pipe—who put it into words.

"We will destroy them all," he said simply.

[*J u n e   4 ,   1 7 8 2 — T u e s d a y*]

For those of the army who had never before seen the Sandusky Plains, their first view of it yesterday was breathtaking. The heavily forested hills through which they had been riding for the better part of a week had abruptly leveled out into high plains, with vast fields of grass as far as the eye could see. Their guides told them this type of terrain would continue all the way to the Sandusky towns, still some 30 miles distant: deep, thick grasses that were emerald green in their lush new growth and so high that the early morning dew soaked their horses and bathed the riders themselves to their waists. There was a deceptive sense of peace to the vista and a strong illusion that they had entered upon an expansive green sea where the surface was calm and smooth except where breezes touched down and rippled the grass in pleasant waving swaths all the way to the western horizon. The illusion of a sea was further enhanced by, here and there in the distance, great isolated groves of trees projecting above the grasses, appearing to be a series of lovely islands. So strong was this sense, in fact, that almost immediately the men referred to these groves as islands and dubbed them with colorful names based on their size or shape or color.[516] Smaller groves, hazy and indistinct in the distance, loomed above the grasses like ships traversing the sea from one of the larger islands to another.

Some of the men, however, viewed the deep grass with a rise of fear; in this sort of cover, a whole great army of Indians could lie hidden beyond detection, abruptly to rise at any given moment and pour a devastating fire into the troops. Their fear became infectious, and soon the initial serenity of the scene was replaced in the men's minds with uneasy expectation.

Their route since leaving the deserted ruins of Schoenbrun behind had been gradually to the northwest for some 15 miles before their guides turned them on a more directly westward course, a course they had more or less followed over the days since then. Having seen scattered individual Indians at intervals and occasional small parties of them, everyone realized that any hope of reaching the Sandusky villages and attacking by surprise had been lost. When they finally encountered one of the main Indian trails leading toward the Sandusky, they directed their course along it and the traveling became easier.

The first casualty to the army had occurred when one of the privates who complained of not feeling well abruptly leaned sideways and flopped loosely to the ground. When his companions stopped to assist him, they found he was dead and attributed it to exhaustion. He was buried and his grave ridden over by the column of horses so it would not be found by the Indians and the body perhaps disinterred for the scalp.[517]

At length the trail crossed a small stream that was meandering generally northward. Their guides, John Slover, Jonathan Zane and Thomas Nicholson, reputed to be very familiar with this country, said it was the headwaters flow of the Sandusky River. In only a few miles they encountered it again, the stream having swung back to the south and now beginning to take a more generally westward flow. From this point on, the trail they rode followed the left bank of the stream as it gradually increased in size by tributary creeks and the outflow of numerous good springs in the region. Visions of farming such a lush, richly soiled and well-watered land were strong in the minds of many of the volunteers; a seed planted and already germinating that one day, when the Indians had been driven out or destroyed, they would return here to claim land and establish their own prosperous farms.

Just after sunset yesterday they had come to a fine spring where the water was cool and fresh and sweet. It was here that Col. Crawford ordered the army to halt and make camp for the night, warning the men to see to their weapons because the likelihood was strong that they would engage the Indians the following day; not only had glimpses of Indians been seen on their flanks, but the guides had informed him that they were, at this point, only seven or eight miles from Half King's Town.[518]

As dawn broke this morning, the army roused to find itself in the midst of a dense fog, which made the soldiers very nervous, for fear the Indians would take advantage of it to creep up close and attack them. An order to maintain silence was softly relayed through the companies, and the men squatted at their cookfires and ate their breakfasts with freshly loaded and primed rifles close at hand. Sunrise, when it came, did little more at first than brighten the fog, though they knew that as the sun climbed higher, its rays would quickly burn away the mist. But the sunrise brought something else that was chilling in its implication.

Barely audible in the far distance to the north came the deep dull booming of cannon being fired. Maj. John Rose noted it in his journal, as did Pvt. Michael Walters, the latter writing that he heard the sound of six cannons fired.[519] Hurriedly checking their rifles again, saddling their mounts and reloading their gear, the army started its march again in three columns, each with four riders abreast, while a company of light horse under Capt. William Leet, acting as an advance unit, rode a quarter-mile ahead. Shortly after this morning's movement began, the trail they were following rounded a wide bend in the Sandusky River, and now the army moved in a more northwestward direction over the gently rolling sea of grasses. Very quickly the sense of tension among the men increased, as word was passed that they were approaching the principal target of their expedition, Half King's Town, believed to be the major stronghold of the Wyandots.

Soon they came to the place to which guide Thomas Nicholson said the Moravian Indians had been relocated the previous fall when forced by the Wyandots and hostile Delawares to move. He said it was called Captives' Town. He also had heard, he said, that the Moravians, soon after learning of the massacre of their kin at Gnadenhütten, had moved to the mouth of the Auglaize River on the Maumee. They expected to find no one at Captives' Town and were not disappointed. The level ground overlooking the Sandusky River where the Moravians had stayed throughout much of the winter was plain enough to see, but scant trace of their temporary residence remained; nothing more than a number of places where fires had been built and a few jumbles of sticks where makeshift shelters had collapsed.

Soon afterward Col. Crawford brought the troops to a state of full-alert readiness as they approached the place where guide John Slover said the principal Wyandot village, Half King's Town, was located. Slover said he had been there many times during the six years he had spent in captivity with the Miamis and occasionally after that, during the succeeding six years he had spent as a captive of the Shawnees. Then he had actually lived there for a considerable while after being captured by the Wyandots. No one, Col. Crawford was certain, was better qualified to guide them at this point than John Slover, and the commander was thankful to see that the grasses were less dense here, most of them only knee high or less and thus affording little cover for any kind for ambush. Nevertheless, a strong aura of apprehension overhung the whole army.

Now, when the village itself came into sight, they saw no signs of life, apart from a single dog that quickly slunk out of sight with its tail between its legs. They advanced with care and saw there was something very strange about the place. The doors to the cabins were open or missing, the wegiwas were caving in on themselves and the whole village was unkempt, uncared for, unlived in. It was apparent to Col. Crawford that not only had this major Wyandot village been abandoned, it had been so for a considerable while. This, for many of the men in his force, confirmed their worst fears: They were expected. The commander immediately summoned the guides and asked for an explanation.

"Colonel," said John Slover, "I have no idea what's happened here. This place was bustin' out with Wyandots last February. I can't imagine they're really gone."

"Been a month, mebbe, since they were here, from the looks of things," Jonathan Zane put in. "Where you figger they went, Tom?"

Nicholson, who had spent a great deal of time among the Wyandots, shook his head and shrugged. "Dunno. Mebbe down to Lower Sandusky. Mebbe only to McCormick's." Lower Sandusky was in excess of 40 miles farther down the Sandusky River, just above its mouth at Sandusky Bay, and Alexander McCormick's Trading Post was on the Sandusky about eight miles downstream from this abandoned village.

Col. Crawford gave orders for the army to rest and drink at the fine spring here, fill their canteens and let their horses graze on the lush grasses, but he warned that all should keep themselves at the ready for instant action. He then called his officers to council.

Immediately heated arguments erupted among the officers. Some felt that the Indians, fearful of the approaching Americans, were in flight ahead of them and should be pursued all the way to Lower Sandusky if necessary; others believed all indications underlined the fact that the Indians were aware of their approach and had now positioned themselves somewhere ahead, where the terrain was most advantageous to themselves, to ambush the American army. This latter group favored returning home immediately.

The guides were asked for their opinion, and those three men briefly discussed the matter among themselves as the officers waited. Then both Thomas Nicholson and John Slover deferred to Jonathan Zane as their spokesman, and he turned his attention to the commander, slowly shaking his head.

"Colonel," he said, "I got me a bad feeling. We all do. We don't like the looks of this at all. I don't know what's goin' on, but the three of us"—he indicated Slover and Nicholson—"know there's some more Indian towns—Wyandot and Delaware both—just a few miles ahead. The fact that we haven't seen *any* Indians at all might mean they could be waiting for us in force, that all of 'em are gathering someplace ahead to hit us with maybe two, three, four times as many men as we've got. I—all three of us, in fact—think we ought to get the hell out of here quick-like."

"You mean turn back?" Col. Williamson blurted incredulously. "Without firing a gun?"

"I mean turn back and get ourselves back to where we came from just as soon as we can," Zane said firmly.

Capt. John Hoagland snorted and then laughed without humor.[520] "Oh, sure," he said derisively. "We've just marched ten days through the wilderness to engage the Indians, and because we find an abandoned village, we simply turn around and go back. Makes sense to me." He snorted again and then spat to one side. "For God's sake, Colonel, let's get on with what we came here to do."

"Give me fifty men of my choice," Col. Williamson spoke up, "and let me go ahead to the town that's supposed to be there, and I'll burn 'em out."

Col. Crawford shook his head. "Permission denied. We are not going to weaken this force by sending out detachments on a whim."

Crawford was personally inclined to take Zane's advice. Nevertheless, considering that the majority of the other officers seemed to agree with Hoagland, the consensus was to continue forward on the trail following the Sandusky River downstream. Col. Crawford decided that they would go onward at least until this evening and, when camp was made, the matter would be discussed again in light of what they had discovered between now and then. Allowing the troops and horses to have a little more rest, Crawford at length gave the order for the march to resume, now with Capt. William Leet's advance light horse company hardly 300 yards ahead.

Three miles later, still not having encountered any opposing Indians, the army paused again when it came to several more fine large springs bubbling from the earth at a slight bluff. Here Crawford, more nervous than he cared to admit, called a halt and gave the order to dismount and break ranks for the noon meal, despite the fact that they had rested only a short time before.[521] As the men did so, some of the more outwardly apprehensive began murmuring that, since many of them now had only five days' provisions remaining in reserve, maybe the advice of their guides ought to be followed.

Crawford held another council with his officers. Ever more suspicious of possible ambush, he directed his adjutant and aide, Maj. John Rose, to take a detachment of two dozen men and reconnoiter the country ahead. The main army would follow as soon as they had finished eating. Maj. Rose selected his men and set out at once.

Through the prairie grasses the advance detachment now rode, heading directly northward toward a large island of trees looming in the distance. Their passage through the grasses on both sides of the narrow path left a clear trail for the main army to follow. The grove, three miles north of where the army had paused, turned out to be a relatively dense woodland, somewhat oval shaped, with the southeastern end squeezed together and then flaring out again, almost like the neck of a flower vase. The trail they were following passed through this grove for a quarter-mile close to its northwestern edge, where it flowed over a small knoll. Maj. Rose made a mental note that because of the timber's elevation on this small hill, it could prove to be a vantage point from which to fight, should the Indians attack.[522] Though the trees were close together and there was abundant fallen timber in various stages of decomposition, there was not a great deal of undergrowth. A short distance into the island of trees, Maj. Rose discovered a pleasant glen less densely filled with trees. Here he ordered his men to leave most of their excess baggage and continue forward as a light unit traveling fast, ready to engage a small force of Indians or to flee in the face of a larger one.

Leaving their excess gear in the care of a four-man guard, who would await the arrival of the main army, Maj. Rose and his men rode on, soon leaving the grove and continuing through the prairie along the Indian trail now angling to the northeast. In less than a mile the trail forked, one portion turning more to the north and the other somewhat more easterly. Rose elected to follow the branching left path—the road that the guides had said led northward to Lower Sandusky and, eventually, Detroit.

They traveled another mile and a half, with the way ahead appearing to be nothing more than a continuation of the unbroken undulating prairie to the left and a line of trees three-quarters of a mile distant to the right, which Rose correctly assumed was the growth along the Sandusky River.

Abruptly, three Indian horsemen were sighted, who apparently saw Rose's detachment simultaneously. They fled, and the detachment pursued. The Indians maintained a steady distance ahead of them and Rose, after a few minutes, suspecting the three were leading them into an ambush, called a halt. It was wise that he did. With startling suddenness, a huge horde of Wyandots and Delawares, led by Monakaduto, Pimoacan and Wingenund, war-painted and wearing little more than breechclouts, boiled up and out of a hidden ravine and engaged them with musket fire. The attackers split into a V-shape in an effort to encircle the detachment.[523]

The Indians in the forefront of the attack were Delawares under Pimoacan and Wingenund, and Simon Girty was with them. Close on their heels were the Wyandots led by Monakaduto, accompanied by the newly arrived British force of Rangers, most of them clad as Indians, along with a number of Frenchmen and slaves, plus the Indians brought along under Capt. Matthew Elliott—Chippewas, primarily, with a scattering of Ottawas and Miamis.[524]

Most fortunately for the American advance detachment, Maj. Rose had stopped them just in time. The Indians had been forced to spring their ambush prematurely, when most of the volunteers were still out of range of the Indian bows and muskets. Rose instantly sent Pvts. William Meetkirk and Cornelius Peterson galloping back to warn the main army and, with the remaining force, fought off the attack while gradually falling back through the prairie from rise to rise, pausing every so often to fire at the Indians and temporarily halt them, all the while returning toward the island of trees where they had left their baggage. Rose consistently kept himself closest to the Indians during the retreat—so close, in fact, that on one occasion some of the few Indians who were mounted came close enough to hurl tomahawks at him, which he coolly dodged in a rather remarkable display of horsemanship.

As the riders sent back to warn the army passed through the grove, they alerted the baggage guards to prepare to fight. Without pause they continued back on their own trail and in five miles met the main army, which was just beginning to come toward them from the area of the springs. Crawford listened grimly to the report Meetkirk and Peterson brought.

Fearing for the safety both of Rose's advance detachment and of his own men here—knowing how fatal it could become to be surrounded by the approaching enemy in this open prairie terrain—Col. Crawford immediately ordered his entire force forward at a gallop to the grove, where if necessary a more protected defensive stand could be made in the cover the timber would provide.

Rose and his men, in the meantime, with their retreats and pauses, had finally reached the grove of trees again, an hour after the ambush had first been sprung. Taking cover behind trees and logs, they sent a more effective fire at the enemy, causing them to swing wide to the southeast and begin to enter the woods there to similarly afford themselves of cover.

Crawford's force neared the grove on the other side, and the commander and his men could hear the distant gunfire coming from the northern fringe of the island of trees. Following the trail, they thundered up the low wooded hill to the glen where Rose had deposited his baggage. Recognizing the advantage the elevation on this slight hill would play as a defensive position, the commander selected its crest as a core for their stand. He ordered a number of the companies to spread out on the perimeter of the entire woodland, drive out any enemy encountered and hold the ground. Immediately, then, he led the remainder of his troops down the northern slope of the wooded knoll to the relief of Rose's detachment.

None of Rose's men had been killed, either in the ambush or during the three-mile retreat, although a couple were slightly wounded. Rose reported, however, that he believed that at least a couple of the attacking Indians had been killed, despite the advantage their ambush afforded. It was difficult to be certain, however, because of the shoulder-high grasses.

Even though all this initial fighting had occurred on the northern and eastern perimeters of the woodland, a rumor soon circulated that, under cover provided by the tall grasses, the Indians had spread out around the entire grove. Whether true or not, those on the northern side provided little target for the Americans as they popped up into sight only long enough to aim and fire, then squatted again, hidden, to reload.

The Battle of Sandusky was on.

Capt. John Hoagland, who had so brashly advocated going on, against the advice of Jonathan Zane, soon became one of the first casualties. A ball struck him in the forehead and knocked him lifeless to the ground.[525] A short time later Pvt. James Little also fell dead, when he momentarily stepped from behind his protective tree and took a bullet in the center of his throat that broke his neck.

Crawford was informed that the Indians had penetrated the southeastern end of the grove, and he ordered several companies to drive them out, which they did after a brief hot fight, during which Capt. James Munn pursued several warriors into the grass, only to be sent sprawling when a bullet passed through his right leg just above the ankle.[526] A Wyandot with upraised tomahawk raced past screaming and Munn tried to scramble out of the way, but his leg was broken and he was unable to lunge as much to the side as he intended. It was enough to save his life, but the tomahawk grazed him and laid open the side of his face. Before other warriors could rush up and finish the job, one of Munn's privates, William Brady, hoisted him onto a horse and plunged back into the woodland with him.[527] The private brought him to the knoll where the wounded were being treated, and Dr. John Knight skillfully set Munn's leg and bandaged his face.

At the same time, Indians all along the woodland's northern perimeter continued firing from the grasses. If there were Indians on the south side of the grove, they were keeping well hidden and the way seemed open for retreat, but, though Crawford seriously considered such a move, he decided against it, figuring it to be a trap where his force, strung out in a retreat march, could be successfully ambushed by unseen Indians already in hiding in the tall grasses.[528]

Pvt. Jonas Sams had taken a position behind a huge, relatively isolated black oak standing at the very edge of the northern flank of the woods. Unlike so many of his fellow volunteers, who were firing at every movement of the grass, real or imagined, he chose his targets with care. At age 26, he was an experienced hunter and woodsman, and well knew the value of waiting to let the quarry betray itself.[529] When the call had been raised for this campaign against the Sandusky towns, he had ridden with other militia members from Thorn's Tavern—located on the road from Redstone to Washington village—to the rendezvous at Mingo Bottom.

Using a Pennsylvania rifle that shot a .69 caliber ball, Jonas Sams methodically selected his targets and fired with considerable success throughout the day. Specializing in long shots, by the end of a few hours he had fired his rifle 18 times and knocked down at least half of the Indians at whom he had aimed, with little doubt in his mind that he had killed the majority of those who fell. At one point he spotted a British officer a considerable distance away, clad all in white except for his hat and boots. Jonas took a bead on him and fired. The range was even greater than he thought, and the ball ripped through the grasses short of his target. Jonas reloaded and, revising his aim, shot again. As he later wrote to his father:

> the second time I fetcht him to the ground. He was a great way off but I had a gun
> that carried almost an ounce ball and I raised the hind sight the second time and he
> fell off his white horse.[530]

A short while later Sams again shot an Indian, and, spotting another within range, he got in too much of a hurry and dropped a fresh ball into the barrel of his gun before putting in the gunpowder. Because of this, he was forced to run back into the woods to get the jammed ball out by on-briching it.[531] While doing so, he was disgusted to see a number of the volunteers hiding from the Indian gunfire, cowering behind fallen trees or in root holes, either not firing their rifles at all or occasionally shooting at random, without aiming and without the least possibility of hitting an enemy.[532] Once he got the ball out and properly reloaded his weapon, he raced back to the isolated oak tree and continued to fire at the Indians until it got too dark to see them.

Casualties were fairly light during the first few hours and, in the middle of the afternoon, convinced that the Indian force attacking them was not as strong as at first believed, Col. David Williamson sought out Col. Crawford and requested permission to take a detachment of 200 men and make a sudden charge out of the woods to engage them. Crawford, however, continued to believe it would be ill advised to divide his force and, much to Williamson's dismay, rejected the plan. Crawford was correct in his refusal because, as the day wore on, it became evident that the Indian force ranged in numbers from 600 warriors to as many as 1,000, perhaps more. Pvt. Hugh Workman of Leet's light horse had been paying close attention to how many Indians were arrayed against them and he was appalled by the odds, concluding that there were no fewer than 1,000 warriors on hand, plus the British Rangers, making the odds greater than two to one against the Americans.[533]

Not long after the battle first broke out, the rifle of Pvt. John Sherrard of Capt. Biggs's company became jammed and useless. Looking for some way to continue helping, he approached Dr. Knight at the knoll, who was having a tough time keeping up in his care for the wounded. The surgeon, in the process of treating Pvt. John McDonald, whose right thigh had been broken by a ball, suggested that since Sherrard had no weapon, he scout around in the woods and try to find a spring or some other source of water for the men, wounded or otherwise, who were suffering from thirst because of the acrid smoke that so severely burned their throats.

Sherrard methodically searched the woods for the better part of an hour before he finally located a deep pool of stagnant water in the root hole of a large storm-toppled tree. From that point on, while the battle continued raging about him, he made frequent trips to the pool, filling canteens and other containers and bringing the water to the wounded and to the soldiers still actively fighting. The water was warm and distasteful, but it was wet and the soldiers accepted it gratefully. Unfortunately, it was also contaminated and, within just a few hours, the men who drank it began getting very sick, weak and feverish and were wracked by vomiting.

By four in the afternoon, the noise of the gunfire was deafening and the fighting had become quite general all along the grove's northern perimeter. A pall of murky bluish-white smoke drifted wraithlike through the trees and hung like an evil mist over the prairie. Several of the horses of the volunteers had been killed or injured early in the fighting, and by this time all that could be reached and moved had been taken well into the woods.

While directing the defense amid the trees, Col. Crawford reached for the powderhorn on his hip, but it was shattered and carried away by a ball only an instant before he would have grasped it. A nearby private who had two powderhorns stepped up and, grinning, handed the extra one to his commander. "Try to take better care of this one, sir," he said jokingly. An instant later that soldier's grinning was ended for a long time, or perhaps permanently, as his upper lip was shot away.[534]

In the midst of all the thunder of gunfire, shrieks, yells and cries of pain, there came the wholly unexpected sound of singing. It was Pvt. John Gunsaula. His rifle had misfired and, in checking it for the reason, he found that he had fired so much that a charred residue of gunpowder was coating the underside of his flint, preventing it from creating a spark when it struck the pan. So now, seated on a log with his hunting knife in hand, he unconcernedly sang a Dutch melody of his youth while he picked his flint with the tip of his knife, bit by bit cleaning off the black debris.

"Mighty nice singin', John." The voice of Pvt. Daniel Canon drifted down to him from above, and Gunsaula looked up and waved, continuing to sing through his smile. High overhead in the treetop, Canon and a few other men had found a far more advantageous and successful location than ground level for spotting their attackers. Their gaze moved back and forth continuously as they watched the grasses beyond the trees, anticipating that telltale movement of the foliage that would indicate the hiding place of a warrior who would sooner or later rise to shoot and would instead meet a bullet from one of these sharpshooting snipers.

By late afternoon, a number of squaws had come forward and joined in the affray in their own way. Beating on kettles with sticks and screeching in shrill, harsh voices, they added significantly to the din in an effort to further intimidate and demoralize the Americans. When they happened across dead Americans, most of them already scalped, they took their weapons and goods and stripped them of their clothing. If the dead they encountered were Indians, they quickly carried them off. Mortally wounded prisoners they encountered were dispatched with tomahawks or knives, scalped and similarly stripped of anything worthwhile. Any soldiers not mortally wounded were carried off as prisoners to the villages to be questioned and most likely tortured to death.

It was from one such prisoner that the Indians learned that Col. David Williamson, perpetrator of the Moravian Massacre, was with the Americans as second in command. At once plans were discussed about how they might be able to kill him.

Later in the afternoon, Simon Girty, riding a large gray horse, appeared alone at a distance, a white cloth of truce hanging from the end of a pole tilted over his shoulder. So far as could be seen, he was unarmed. When a slight lull came in the firing, he cupped his mouth and called out loudly:

"I want to talk to Colonel Williamson. The Indians are agreeable to talking peace if he will come out to meet me and discuss terms."

Someone among the defenders yelled back for Girty to wait while the colonel was summoned. Girty, responding with a wave, remained sitting quietly astride his horse. At the end of some ten minutes, Col. Williamson, on foot, appeared at the fringe of the woods, accompanied by several volunteers and Dr. Knight. The latter had known Girty well at Fort Pitt, and there had been a degree of friendship between them at one time. Col. Williamson had known Girty, too, but he viewed the distant horseman with distaste; no love had ever been lost between himself and Girty at Fort Pitt. In fact, eight years ago, just before Dunmore's War, he and Girty had been engaged in a brawl, until Girty, who was getting the worst of it, was unexpectedly rescued by a huge young frontiersman who turned out to be Simon Kenton. Now the officer motioned those with him to stay where they were among the trees, and he took several steps out into the open.

"Girty!" he called. "This is Dave Williamson. What do you want?"

"Peace talk," Girty shouted in return. "Just you'n me to start. Let's end this damn fight right now. C'mon out here, an' you an' me'll talk it out."

"So you can kill me when I get close?" Williamson replied scornfully.

"I ain't got no weapons," Girty replied. "Tell you what. You come seven steps forward an' stop, an' I'll do the same."

Williamson considered this a moment and then stepped forward seven paces and stopped. Girty kneed his horse forward even more than that and stopped, the movement carrying him within range of a good shot. Immediately one of the volunteers at the fringe of the woodland leveled his rifle and took a bead on Girty, and was in the process of squeezing the trigger when Dr. Knight's hand closed across the cocked hammer and thwarted the shooting.

"What's the matter with you, man?" he growled. "You don't shoot a man under a flag of truce."

Almost on the heels of this little tableau, an Indian suddenly rose from hiding in the grasses, hardly 30 yards from Williamson, and snapped off a shot at him. The ball missed, and the colonel wheeled and raced back behind the closest tree, a large sugar maple slightly apart from the grove. As he spun into cover behind the broad trunk, five or six other shots came from the grasses and slammed into the tree but did not harm the officer. Immediately the volunteers returned the fire, but neither Girty nor any of the Indians appeared to be hit. Girty, cursing loudly, wheeled his big gray horse around and galloped off in the deep grass.

Once again the pitch of battle rose and continued as the day dwindled away. The Indians found a certain degree of both satisfaction and frustration in the prolonged fighting: satisfaction in the knowledge that their bullets were gradually taking a toll on the Americans boxed in within the island of trees, and frustration from the failure of the attempt to kill Col. Williamson and from the fact that these Americans had managed to get themselves ensconced in a defensive posture considerably to their advantage. Already too many Indians had been killed or wounded in the effort to draw them out of the timber and onto a more equal footing. Many of the younger, brasher warriors, overconfident in their fighting abilities, wanted merely to plunge into the woods and meet the Americans in hand-to-hand combat, but Pimoacan, Wingenund and Monakaduto dissuaded them of such a notion; it was not the Indian way to engage in a war of attrition. Nevertheless, not even the chiefs themselves were pleased with the results of the battle thus far.

"Patience, my brothers," Matthew Elliott told them. "You have them where you want them. They cannot go anywhere and they have no water, so they will very soon begin to suffer from the lack of it. It will drive them to do desperate acts, and men who are desperate make mistakes. You have only to hold them here until the artillery arrives, and then the woods will no longer protect them."

It was reassuring, but only because they were as yet unaware that the British artillery was bogged down in a marsh some seven or eight miles to the north; the exhausted horses were no longer able to budge the heavy guns.[535]

Just before sunset a number of individual American soldiers, their eyes reddened and smarting from the searing mist of gunsmoke in which they had been fighting for so many hours, began making daring dashes out of the protective timber and into the prairie in search of the enemy. One of these was Pvt. Michael Myers, who took refuge behind a single large black walnut tree some distance from the grove. As he stood leaning against the tree and looking for an Indian to shoot, the bark of the tree exploded close to his head as it was struck by a ball, showering splinters painfully into his cheeks and forehead but luckily missing his eyes. Carefully peeking around the trunk in the direction from which the shot had come, Myers saw a warrior ducking down below his own cover, an oak that was the only other isolated tree in this area. The oak tree forked into two main trunks three feet above the ground, and Myers aimed his rifle steadily at the base of the V. A few moments later there was a movement, and the head of the hidden warrior came into view. The ball from Myers's rifle struck him in the center of the forehead and carried away the whole back of his skull.

A short while later, Myers detected a movement in the grass that he assumed was several Indians crawling along. Instead of shooting at the moving grass as so many others were doing, he waited, watching closely. Eventually the crawlers reached an area where the grasses were thinner and Myers saw one of them rise to shoot. He shot first, sending the Indian tumbling with a broken thigh and scattering his companions. Two of the army's sentinels rushed out into the grass and one, who had a sword, cut off the wounded Indian's head with a single hard slash.

The other volunteers who had left the cover of the woods moved about in a stooped manner below the tops of the deep grasses, emulating the mode of fighting of their attackers, bobbing up to aim and fire, then ducking down again to reload before continuing their crouching search. But it was a very hazardous pursuit and so many were being wounded—Pvts. Joseph Edgington and James Bane among them— that Col. Crawford quickly sent out an order curtailing the practice.

Pvt. Angus McCoy, while remaining in the fringe of timber, did not take advantage of the available cover but chose to stand fully exposed to the Indians as he fired. Remarkably, after several hours he remained unwounded, but his clothing had been riddled with holes from the balls that had so narrowly missed him.

As evening came on and the twilight deepened, the heavy gunfire gradually diminished until it became only isolated and momentary exchanges. The question of whether the Americans were truly surrounded by the foe was more or less resolved when, in the growing darkness, fires sprang into life in a wide arc out of effective rifle range. Both to contain the Americans and to prevent their making a surprise night attack, the Indians built 50 or more individual fires, mainly along the northern rim of the woodland and around its eastern end, closest to the Sandusky River, but there were also scattered blazes on the southern flank and the western end. They kept the fires burning brightly all night. About the only areas that remained dark were those where the trail to the south passed through, and toward the southwest where an expansive cranberry bog was close to the grove.

The day-long battle had left the Americans exhausted and victims of growing demoralization. They were all suffering from thirst, and those who had drunk the contaminated water from the root pool were miserable in their sickness and could no longer be considered effective fighting men. Worse yet, their supply of ammunition was precariously low; the hours of shooting had gravely diminished their powder and lead. As the soldiers refilled their powderhorns and shot pouches from the dwindling reserves, they were cautioned about excessive shooting and advised to choose their targets carefully and fire only when reasonably sure of hitting an enemy.

Col. Crawford ordered double-strength sentries for the night's guard: two men at each assigned post along the perimeter of the woods, so that the weary guards could help keep each other awake and fire alarm shots if, under cover of the darkness, the Indians attempted to infiltrate the woods.

The Upper Sandusky Villages
and Battle of Sandusky,
June 1782

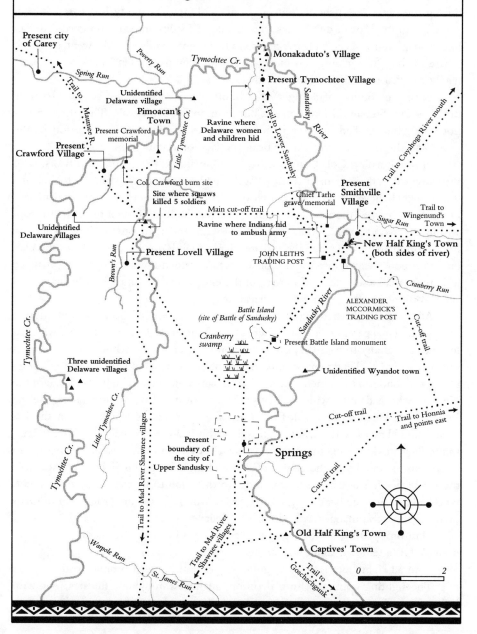

Present city
of Carey

Poverty Run

Spring Run

Trail to Maumee R.

Tymochtee Cr.

Monakaduto's Village

Present Tymochtee Village

Unidentified
Delaware village

Pimoacan's
Town

Present Crawford
memorial

Ravine where
Delaware women
and children hid

Little Tymochtee Cr.

Sandusky River

Trail to Lower Sandusky

Trail to Cuyahoga River mouth

Present
Crawford Village

Col. Crawford burn site

Site where squaws
killed 5 soldiers

Main cut-off trail

Chief Tarhe
grave/memorial

Present
Smithville
Village

Sugar Run

Trail to
Wingenund's
Town

Unidentified
Delaware villages

Ravine where Indians hid
to ambush army

New Half King's Town
(both sides of river)

Brown's Run

Present Lovell Village

JOHN LEITH'S
TRADING POST

Cranberry Run

Tymochtee Cr.

Battle Island
(site of Battle of Sandusky)

Cranberry
swamp

Present Battle Island monument

ALEXANDER
McCORMICK'S
TRADING POST

Sandusky River

Cut-off trail

Three unidentified
Delaware villages

Unidentified Wyandot town

Little Tymochtee Cr.

Trail to Mad River Shawnee villages

Present
boundary of
the city of
Upper Sandusky

Springs

Cut-off trail

Trail to Honnia
and points east

Cut-off trail

N

Warpole Run

Trail to Mad River
Shawnee villages

Old Half King's Town

Captives' Town

St. James Run

Trail to Goschachgunk

0   2

[*J u n e   5 ,   1 7 8 2 — W e d n e s d a y*]

As the first light of dawn filtered through the island of woods, Col. Crawford's army was not in good shape. Three of their wounded had died during the night, and three of the 19 remaining wounded were close to death. The men were haggard and hollow-eyed, few of them having gotten any sleep at all because of the sporadic whooping and shooting from the Indians during the night, each time causing the Americans to brace themselves for a full-scale attack that never developed. Morale had sunk to a low ebb and was not helped when it was discovered that sometime during the night 15 of the volunteers from Washington County had deserted and, evidently through plain dumb luck, had managed to slip unseen through the Indian lines and gotten away.[536] Hearing this, Pvt. Thomas Mills quickly went to check where his big gray gelding was picketed, fearful they had stolen it, and was inordinately relieved to find the horse still there.

With the coming of daylight, the shooting picked up again, at first "by little flirts," as Pvt. Stephen Burkarn put it, but soon on full battle scale. The situation was not good; Indians had once again infiltrated into the southeastern portion of the grove and the lack of water was critical, the lack of ammunition serious.

In midmorning Col. Crawford held a council with his principal officers, who were divided in their opinions as to what should be done at this point. Col. Williamson strongly believed that the first order of business should be to drive the Indians out of the lower end of the woods. He suggested that he lead 50 men to hit them from within the woods, while Maj. John Rose, with 150 men on the best remaining horses, simultaneously charge the Indians' flank. Maj. Rose was agreeable to the plan but, after considerable discussion Col. Crawford vetoed the idea, declaring it to be little more than a suicide mission that, in the end, would accomplish little and would result in the loss of many good American lives.

All the while the fighting continued on the perimeter of the woodland, though without much apparent effect on either side. Volunteers hidden behind trees watched for and shot at any Indians they could pinpoint in the grasses, while return fire from the dense growth kept them constantly pinned down behind their trees. Though most of the shooting was ineffective, a few Indians were seen to be hit, and one of the Negroes who had come with the British from Detroit and was fighting alongside the Indians, was killed when a ball from one of the volunteers struck him in the left temple and blew away the whole right side of his head. A few balls from the Indians found their marks among the volunteers as well. Pvt. John Orr was one of the first to be hit this second day of the battle, a ball slamming through his right side just below the rib cage. He was carried by comrades to the knoll to be treated by Dr. Knight, who had just finished bandaging a fairly severe wound in the upper left arm of Orr's own battalion commander, Maj. John McClelland.

"Just dropped by, Major," gasped Orr through his pain, "to see how you were doing." His attempted smile was largely a failure.

"I'm all right, son, and we're going to get you home, I promise you."

The fighting continued in a desultory manner throughout the day, but with little effect. Along about midafternoon the Indians began hurling verbal threats toward the woods. After a while the threats tapered off and the Indians, acting almost as if they were drunk, began exposing themselves to view rather recklessly, at the same time actually beginning to parley, telling the Americans that if they gave up, they would not be harmed. The volunteers scoffed at this, of course, and shouted back that they would never give themselves up to an army of Indians and slaves.

The shooting having tapered off to a large extent, many of the soldiers retired deeper into the woods and were either catching naps or baking stick bread and roasting chunks of bacon over campfires and stuffing food into their saddlebags. Many of them talked about running off during the night, as the group from Washington County had done the previous night.

The battle seemed to have become a stalemate, but that did not last long. Throughout the day small groups of Indians arrived from different quarters to aid in fighting the Americans, and along about sunset the Shawnees showed up under their war chief, Shemeneto. Some 200 strong, they were garishly painted with whirls and stripes of red, blue, white and ocher on their faces and bare chests.[537] The Wyandots and Delawares greeted them with evident enthusiasm and the groups intermingled at a distance. Soon the Shawnees, trailed by some of their allies, approached the grove, waving a solid red flag and giving vent to exuberant whoopings. They aligned themselves for a considerable distance along the north flank and then began an odd ritual. One of the warriors at the far end of the line raised his gun and shot it skyward, and then others did the same in succession, with only about a second or two between shots, the firing becoming a ripple effect that went clear down the line to the other end. The volunteers had no idea what was going on, and Pvt. Angus McCoy thought it was a superstitious act—that they were firing at the sun to put it out so they could attack the Americans in the dark. Maj. Rose, however, knew that was not the case; he had seen this sort of thing before and explained:

"It is," he said, "what the French call a *feu de joie*—a fire of joy—actually, something of an act of defiance. The Shawnees must have seen Frenchmen doing this at some time or another. In doing this, they are flaunting their strength, showing us they have gunpowder and lead to waste and that there is no escape for us. It is, in effect, a celebration of our impending death."

Immediately upon its conclusion, the firing at the grove broke out again from all the loudly shrieking Indians, as strongly as it had been since the beginning of the battle, and volunteers near the perimeter had to dive for cover behind trees and logs to avoid being shot as bullets smashed bark off the trees and clipped branches in showers around them. This time the grove seemed more completely encircled by the attackers, with shots coming from the grasses all around the grove except in the area of the trail to the south and in the adjacent cranberry bog quadrant to the southwest.

Pvt. William Davies's rifle was put out of commission when a large ball struck it in the lock area and carried away much of the breech, and Davies looked in disbelief at the barrel and stock still gripped in his stinging hands. There was amazement among many of the men, as well, when 19-year-old Ben Newland abruptly appeared among them. Newland, a popular young man on the frontier, had been captured by Indians ten months earlier and was thought to have been killed by his captors long ago. Now here he was in their camp, having escaped from the Shawnee warriors who had just arrived. He brought word that those Shawnees were determined to torture to death in the worst possible ways any of the Americans who fell into their hands.[538]

Col. Crawford, having ascertained that the guards were still all in place and watchful for any advance of the Indians toward the woods, called a council of the officers and announced that they would continue returning the fire until dark, at which time they would kindle their fires as they had the night before. This time, however, they would gather their forces and make a sudden concerted break out of the woods and back along the trail upon which they had arrived.

"Excuse me, sir," interrupted Brigade Maj. Daniel Leet, "but I think that is a serious mistake. The Indians are too alert. There has to be a reason why they haven't fired from that direction. They evidently want us to make some kind of an attempt in that direction. The southern trail *has* to be some kind of a trap."

"That's possible, Major Leet," Crawford conceded, "but it doesn't appear we have much of a choice. Unless, of course, you have a better idea."

"I think so, Colonel," Leet replied. "I've been studying the firing. There's been practically nothing coming from the southwest, but that's all marsh country and it's not likely we could get through there. But, other than that, directly to the west of the woods there hasn't been much firing at all, and it's high ground. I would suggest we launch a surprise attack in that direction and break through the Indian line."

"That's stupid!" David Williamson spoke up bluntly. "God Almighty, that would put us even deeper into their country and in an area we're not familiar with. That's a lot riskier than going south, where at least we know the lay of the land to some extent."

"I'd have to agree with Colonel Williamson in that regard," Crawford said. "The break will be made toward the south, not the west."

Maj. Leet shook his head, obviously not in agreement. "Our maps tell us there's a trail west of us about a mile called the Oak Creek Trail. We could hit that, circle around these damned prairies and bogs and go south, then cut eastward to hit Bouquet's old war trail at the Muskingum and follow it home."[539]

"I said we will go south, Major," Crawford said sharply, "and we will. Now let's start getting things ready."

Disgruntled, Leet shrugged but said nothing more. Then the miller, Capt. John Hardin, spoke up brashly.

"There have got to be at least twelve hundred Indians out there!" he exclaimed. "For all we know, most of 'em are lining that road just waiting for us to walk into their trap. I think we would stand a much greater chance if the individual companies separated and each went off on its own, and made its own way back to safety."

Col. Crawford gave Capt. Hardin a scornful look and immediately quashed that idea, then issued the direct order that the entire army would stay together as a complete unit and that absolute discipline must be maintained.

A definite sense of foreboding permeated the Americans in the grove as the twilight deepened into night and the men began making preparations for the retreat; though they were relieved that at last they would be leaving this place, they feared what lay ahead. Were the Indians, as so many suspected, lying in wait for them in great numbers along the trail by which they had arrived here? Were they at this moment silently slipping into the woods under cover of night to fall upon them as they packed their gear and readied their horses? It was 150 miles of wilderness between here and the Ohio River, in every mile of which they could be struck with a devastating force that they would not be able to counteract. Would that occur?

As Col. Crawford had directed, a large number of small fires were built to give the illusion that the army was settling into its camp for the night. Some of these fires were built on the graves of their fallen comrades to disguise the freshly turned earth and prevent the Indians from digging up dead to scalp them. Among the 23 wounded were seven who were so severely injured they could not ride; litters were made that could be suspended between two horses to carry them. Pvt. John McDonald, in severe pain from his broken thigh, was one of these. The whole body of the army was to form in four divisions, keeping the wounded in the center.

While these preparations were under way, the hard-headed Capt. John Hardin gathered together his own men and drew them off to the side. All four Hardins were together—Capt. John Hardin Sr., and his son John, Jr., as well as his illegitimate son John, called Jack, and his nephew Thomas. He whispered to his men that he was sure the army was going to ride straight into an ambush, and he had no intention of becoming a part of it. In direct disobedience of Col. Crawford's orders, he told them he would lead his own company to safety his own way, and any among them who did not wish to accompany him was free to leave now and be cut to pieces with the main army. Only a few refused to go along, and within a few minutes Hardin and his men were quietly leading their horses toward the western fringe of the woodland, close to half a mile west of the south trail. Here the fires of the Indians were farther apart, and it seemed the men would be able to slip through the enemy lines.

The full movement of the retreat was scheduled to begin at nine o'clock, and by sunset just about all were in readiness. Gradually the main army, under guidance of its various commanders, moved into a marching order, with Maj. John McClelland's battalion in the lead position, ready to move the instant the order was passed in whispers through the line. McClelland glimpsed Pvt. John Orr, horseless, arms clasped snug against his bandaged side, standing ready, with several other men who had lost their horses, to move on foot with the retreat when it began. Despite the waves of pain emanating from his bandaged upper left arm, the major remembered his earlier promise to this severely injured soldier, and now he dismounted and gave Orr his own horse, helping the grateful private into the saddle.[540]

It was at about this juncture when word reached Col. Crawford that Capt. John Hardin was slipping off with his company, intent on finding his own way to safety. Infuriated at such flagrant insubordination bordering on desertion, Crawford placed the army in temporary command of the only officer near him, Brigade Maj. Daniel Leet, and galloped off westward from the trail to overtake Capt. Hardin's company and order the men back to the army. Almost immediately angry murmurings rose from the men who saw him depart but did not understand his intention and presumed he was deserting them to save his own life. And because their surgeon, Dr. Knight, and their guide, John Slover, were also missing, they thought all three had fled on their own.[541]

Col. Crawford had traveled away from the main force on Hardin's trail for only a few minutes when everything fell apart. Hardin's company, several hundred yards ahead of Crawford, in the prairie darkness near the western perimeter of the woods, had spotted an extensive dark area between the fires in one location, which Capt. Hardin took to be the dividing line between the newly arrived Shawnees, whose fires arced southward and eastward, toward the marsh and the road, and the Delawares and Wyandots, whose fires arced northward and then eastward flanking the northern perimeter of the woods. Selecting that darkest spot between the Indian fires as the area where they were most likely to succeed in breaking through the Indian line, he led his men quietly in that direction. It didn't work out; midway in its passage, the small company was detected and, in moments, a whole barrage of shooting broke the silence of the night. Only one of the volunteers was hit, and that just a minor graze across the shoulder. Hardin instantly put his force into a gallop and surged ahead, making for the darkness beyond and putting distance between themselves and their pursuers.

The burst of gunfire, however, had far-reaching ramifications. In one brief instant the men in the main army formation concluded they were being attacked by the whole Indian force, and their fear turned into abject panic. Men yelled in terrified voices, and horses screamed as they were suddenly kicked into a milling, confused welter of hooves and bodies. The Indians on the north line instantly added their voices and gunfire to the confusion and plunged headlong into the woods.

The greater part of the army was abruptly in chaotic motion, thundering madly through the darkness to the south, generally along the trail but with splinter groups breaking off here and there, their horses rearing and shrieking and filled with unbridled terror. Among those behind Maj. McClelland's advance party but in the van of the main army was Pvt. Thomas Mills, who had vaulted into his saddle the instant panic broke out and kicked his gray gelding into a gallop at the very forefront of the tumultuous rush.

The men on foot in the advance division, including Maj. McClelland, were simply ridden over by the mass of horses behind them, and a good many were badly injured and left behind to their fate. Abandoned as well were the many volunteers still on sentry duty, especially along the northern perimeter of the woods, who had not yet even been informed that a retreat was planned. These sentries—some patrolling and others taking their turns at getting some sleep—were simply overrun by the many fiercely shrieking Indians charging into the woodland from the north. The sentries had little chance and were killed or captured at their posts, some never even awakening before tomahawks ended their lives.[542]

The initial pandemonium of the troops in the main army continued, and McClelland's advance mounted battalion, fearing to be overridden by those behind, plunged ahead even more furiously, distancing themselves from the followers and, as had been feared, surging directly into a mass of Indians, largely Shawnees and Delawares, positioned for just such an eventuality. Both McClelland's precipitous advance and the Hardin company's flight were providential acts that, though horribly disconcerting at first, aided the bulk of the main army immeasurably.

The Indians were not quite sure what was occurring. The chiefs were at first under the impression—bolstered by the initial breakthrough of the Hardin company —that the movements were feints to decoy them into an exposed position. That impression did not last. Their hesitation evaporated as the realization dawned that this was a panic-inspired full-scale retreat, and they immediately surged to attack in the darkness.

With Col. Crawford still gone and likely by this time either to be dead or captured, Col. David Williamson now relieved Brigade Maj. Leet and took over command of the army, assisted by Maj. John Rose. Their portion of the army was no longer so panic-stricken as before, and they were, for the most part, still together as a unit. Fortunately, Jonathan Zane was with them, and when he suggested a way he might be able to lead them through the Indian lines, the new commander listened closely. It was a reasonable plan and now, at Williamson's orders, they veered southwest, away from the road. While the Indians were diverted into concentrating on Hardin's company at the western prairie front and on McClelland's advance force on the road south, the main army skirted the northern arc of the expansive cranberry bog and began moving down its western side, fortuitously getting the bog between themselves and the Indians.[543] Zane, riding beside Col. Williamson, continued to guide them through the darkness.[544]

As the panic had broken out and the troops thrashed away in the darkness, Francis Dunlavy, at the northeastern edge of the occupied portion of the grove, found himself left suddenly crouching behind a log with another soldier and wondering what was happening. Dunlavy had a horse, but the young soldier with him, his panic rising, had none. Dunlavy urged that they both get on the horse and rush after the others as swiftly as possible, but the young volunteer was frozen with fear.

"Come on, man!" Dunlavy urged. "Get on the horse. There's no time to waste." Still the youth remained locked in place, wailing in his terror, and now Indians, attracted by the noise he was making, shrieked triumphantly as they burst into the far end of the glen on foot. One charged with uplifted tomahawk and Dunlavy instantly leaped into the saddle and kicked his horse into a gallop to the south. The young soldier fell dead with a tomahawk in his brain just as Dunlavy plunged into the deeper darkness of the woods beyond.[545]

Back on the road close to the woods, Maj. John McClelland, still afoot and dazed from having been overridden and passed by his troops, suddenly heard Indians coming toward him, and he broke into a run. Wounded as he was, he could not run fast and tired quickly. Within 100 yards he was overtaken and felt his arms gripped on both sides by warriors—Shawnees—and his weapons ripped away from him. He braced himself for the tomahawk blow that would end his life, but it did not fall. Instead, he was hustled off in the darkness by the Indians toward one of their watchfires.[546]

Col. Crawford, upon hearing the outbreak of firing at Hardin's company, wheeled his horse around and retraced his path back toward the south trail where it emerged from the woods and where the main army had been. He arrived there just as the rear of that force, mostly afoot, was leaving the woods, and he mingled with the men, calling out for his son, son-in-law and nephew, who, last he knew, should be among these men. They did not answer, and none of the passing men had any idea where they were. Fearing they were still deeper in the woods, Crawford reined his mount back into the grove to search for them.

The chaos continued and, as balls whistled among the rear divisions under Majs. John Brinton and Daniel Leet, the woods were rapidly emptying of the volunteers, except for those who were confusedly moving in circles or who were wounded and horseless. Among the latter was Capt. Ezekiel Rose, who had taken a ball that passed through his chest and out his back. Though conscious, he was in shock and certain he was dying. He considered it most important that he say The Lord's Prayer before he died. In his confused state he kept making mistakes in the wording, and upon realizing he had done so, he would immediately break off and begin the prayer again. Men of his own company and others tried to help him onto a horse, but he struggled against them, deeming it necessary that he complete the prayer before attempting escape. Maj. Leet happened by, saw what was occurring and, exasperated, picked him up and practically dumped him into the saddle, then ordered a private up behind him to hold him on as they rode.

Maj. Brinton abruptly took a ball and, badly wounded, was himself helped away, while Maj. Leet took over his command, and with some 90 men in tow, including Col. Crawford's son John, he led them directly west through the woods, heading for the Oak Creek Trail he had earlier advocated using, taking a chance on breaking through the Indian line in that direction. He succeeded, not only in bursting past the Indians but in reaching the trail running west of the cranberry bog. The Indians fired in wild abandon as the whites charged through, but they did not follow so large a body of men in the darkness, fearing that they would themselves be slain.

Pvt. Michael Myers, one of the sentries on the northern perimeter, heard the gunfire and assumed the Indians were attacking from the west. He leaped up onto the broad trunk of a fallen tree and looked into the woods toward the southwest, trying to ascertain more accurately the origin of the firing. He heard a noise behind and spun around to see the shadowy forms of Indians emerging from the deep grasses and rushing toward him. He snapped off a shot but missed and, almost in the same instant, an arrow buried itself in his leg just above the knee, tumbling him to the ground. He scrambled to his feet, gripping his empty rifle now by the barrel to swing as a club. The warriors were swarming to him by then, and he managed to hit several with the gun, but then a tomahawk blow knocked the rifle out of his grip, cut his hand badly and dislocated his thumb. Driven to his knees by warriors swarming over him, he still managed to shake them off and get to his feet again. He yanked out the arrow projecting from his leg and raced off toward the darkest part of the woods. Despite the wound, he eluded his pursuers and emerged from the grove just above the marsh, into which he plunged without pause.

As Col. Crawford penetrated deeper into the woods searching for his three relatives, another horseman, hearing him calling their names, rode up to him. It turned out to be Dr. John Knight, coming from the direction of the knoll, and they joined. Knight evinced concern about a couple of men still on the knoll who were dying and whom he had been loath to leave as the retreat formed up. He had decided to stay with them as long as possible. Then had come the pandemonium from the panicked troops on the south and the howls and shrieks of the Indians entering the woods on the north approaching the knoll. He'd had no other choice then but to leave his trunkful of surgical tools and medical supplies behind and the dying men to their fate, snatch up a rifle, powderhorn and lead pouch belonging to one of the dying men, and try to overtake the army. That was when he encountered his commander.

Now Col. Crawford and Dr. Knight tried to decide what their best move might be. Knight assured his commander that by this time all the men were well ahead of them with the retreating army. Crawford was, of course, unaware that his son was already breaking through the Indian line to the west under Maj. Leet, while his nephew, William Crawford, and his son-in-law, William Harrison, were together with Maj. McClelland's advance force, now under heavy attack and scattering like flushed quail. The two young men, for the moment, having become separated from others, rode southeastward until they were well away from the road, then turned south again, expecting to intersect the trail once more in a mile or so and rejoin their unit.

Col. Crawford grimly concluded that if Dr. Knight was incorrect, his three relatives had already been taken prisoner or killed, and so he terminated his search. But now the question was what to do. He was furious at the disorder of the premature retreat and complained bitterly about the disobedience of the troops. From the sounds to the south, the screams of the Indians dominating, it seemed evident that the Indians were now in force in that direction. The cries of the Indians approaching through the woods from the north cut off that avenue of escape, so with a few murmured words Crawford led the way toward the northwest. They picked their way carefully through the dark woodland, pausing now and then as they heard nearby Indians approach and then pass them unseen. At length they came to the far northwestern edge of the grove and found the prairie silent before them, a few untended watchfires dimming. Logic dictated that they turn southward and pass west of the bog, as Maj. Leet had earlier suggested, but, still convinced the Indians lay in wait there, Crawford took a different tack.

"I think our best chance," he told Knight, "is to head straight north for a while until we've cleared the Indian lines and then head east for the river, get across and continue in that direction for a good way before swinging to the south, then east again, and then south again to confuse any of the Indians that might be trying to follow us. That way maybe we can avoid them, and we should be able to hit the trail again by daylight and perhaps intercept the army." Having no better suggestion, Knight agreed, and they moved off at once.

While the height of the panic prevailed, the rear guard of the army was all confusion. Many of the men, hearing the crash of guns and seeing muzzle flashes in the dark woods behind them, struck out in whichever direction happened to lead away from the assumed danger. A good number, emerging from the woodland, immediately galloped to the southwest and almost at once encountered the northern swell of the expansive cranberry marsh. Into it they plunged with reckless abandon. Very quickly their horses mired and they abandoned them and continued on foot, slogging waist deep, sometimes neck deep, in water and muck, losing weapons, provisions and footwear in the process. All the while they were pressed by those behind, who were hastened by the hail of balls following them and ripping through the tangle of bushes and other marsh growth. For six volunteers who hesitated or fell, including Pvt. Benjamin McQueen, the Indians were almost instantly upon them with tomahawks and scalping knives.

Back at the rear of the main army, McQueen's brother, Thomas, also a private, got separated from his company during the retreat and linked up with a Frenchman and a lieutenant in similar straits. All three were still mounted, but their horses were in bad condition, and concluding they could not catch up, the three struck out overland in an effort to get home on their own.[547]

Pvt. John Sherrard of Capt. Biggs's company, who had supplied men with water from the root-hole pool in the woods during the battle there, found himself separated in the wild retreat from his unit and riding beside a longtime friend, Pvt. Conrad Harbaugh of Capt. John Beeson's company. Sherrard's horse was in better condition than Harbaugh's, which was wheezing and groaning from exertion, but Harbaugh had a good saddle while Sherrard was uncomfortably seated on a packsaddle. The two young men discussed whether it would be wisest to trot their horses after their units and conserve the strength of the animals, or put them into a gallop at once to overtake them. At that juncture Sherrard glimpsed a shadowy figure nearby and correctly guessed it was an Indian.

"Take cover!" he hissed, and leaped down, pulling his horse toward a big tree behind which he might find cover. Harbaugh's reaction was slower and, as he dismounted, a lead ball whined out of the darkness and drilled straight through the right side of his chest. He dropped to the ground, struggled a moment to get up and then sank back into a sitting position.

"Lord have mercy on me," he said aloud. "I'm a dead man!"

The Indian, evidently expecting the second man to return fire, raced away on foot in the darkness. Sherrard ran to Harbaugh to assist and was dismayed to find his companion dead, still in a sitting posture. He sadly lowered the body into a supine position and, unwilling to be burdened with carrying two guns, lay the dead man's rifle beside him. The death was a great blow to him, but this was no time for indecision, so he swiftly removed saddle and bridle from Harbaugh's horse and turned the animal loose. Jerking his own uncomfortable packsaddle and pack off his horse and tossing them aside, then removing the makeshift rope rein, he replaced them with Harbaugh's bridle and saddle and in moments was mounted and moving off. No shots came and no one pursued him, but he had traveled fewer than 100 yards when he suddenly realized he had left behind his bedroll attached to the packsaddle and that all his provisions were inside the rolled-up blanket. He turned back.

He found Harbaugh's body where he had left it but was amazed to find that in the short time he had been gone, the Indian had returned and taken Harbaugh's scalp and gun. The horse he had turned loose was also gone. Searching about quickly, Sherrard fortunately located his packsaddle with the bedroll still attached, overlooked by the Indian, and he swiftly tied it behind the saddle on his own horse. Then he remounted and slapped the horse into a gallop. Within three miles he managed to catch up to the rear of the retreating army.

Pvt. Michael Walters was another of those soldiers afoot at the rear of the main army and, as he trotted along trying to keep up with the horsemen, he was joined by two other privates afoot, Christopher Coffman and James Collins, all three of Capt. Beeson's scattered company. They concluded, as Thomas McQueen had, that they would never be able to overtake the mounted men ahead of them, and they quickly made a pact to remain together through whatever might occur and to do their utmost to protect one another.

Before the panic occurred, John Slover, knowing his horse would need all its strength on the retreat, had taken his mount to a nearby glade and was feeding the animal there. On the outbreak of panic, he instantly realized what was occurring and leaped into the saddle and headed for the southern edge of the woodland, emerging a little distance west of the road. He reined his horse toward it but traveled only a short way when he discovered that the main part of the force had veered to the southwest. He headed his mount that way and put it into a gallop in an effort to overtake them. In doing so, he overshot their path and wound up in the extensive marshland.

Slover forced his mount through the water and muck for a time, but the horse eventually bogged down badly and was quickly losing its strength. Not far behind he could hear some warriors closing in, so he dropped off the saddle, smacked the horse on its rump to send it floundering away with a splashing racket for the Indians to follow and himself waded silently straight ahead toward the western edge of the marsh a mile distant.

Slover had continued wading through the marsh without pause and at last, only a short time ago, the ground became firmer under his feet. In a few more minutes he left the mire behind, and now, after continuing westward for a time, he had finally come to the Oak Creek Trail. There he encountered five volunteers who had become separated in the darkness from the group under Maj. Daniel Leet. They included Col. Crawford's nephew, Ens. William Crawford, and the colonel's son-in-law, William Harrison, along with Pvts. William Nemins, James Paull and Thomas Heady.[548] The six immediately joined forces and began angling toward the southeast, hoping to link up again with their units but, failing that, to reach the Ohio River on their own. With Slover, one of the expedition's guides, now with them, their chances of doing so were greatly improved.

Hardly half a mile away, Pvt. James Collins, having become separated in the panic from his brother Joshua and several others, had been struck by a vagrant ball that entered his hip at a sharp angle and passed through the muscle tissue without striking any bones, exiting close to his backbone. It had knocked him off his horse, and the animal raced away. Dazed, a few moments later Collins tried to rise and was surprised at being able to do so successfully. The wound hurt considerably, but he found he could still walk, albeit with difficulty.

"Helluva thing," he muttered, "to go out on my first real Injen hunt and get shot in the ass!"

Continuing to limp along carefully in the darkness, he soon connected with three other privates on foot who had become separated from their company. In whispers they discussed their present dangerous situation and, convinced they could not catch up to the army, decided to strike out eastward on their own and head for home as best they could.[549]

Less than a mile farther south on the trail, Collins's brother, Joshua, was also afoot, his horse having given out. In the darkness he linked up with two other privates, Michael Walters and Christopher Coffman, whose horses had also failed beneath them—the penalty of having set out on this campaign with horses that were essentially worthless in the beginning. As his brother James had done only a short time before, Joshua Collins suggested they strike out overland, away from the trails, and try to get back to the Ohio. Coffman and Walters agreed, and they set off, determined to travel as rapidly as they could through the remainder of this night to put as much distance as possible between themselves and the Sandusky towns.

Meanwhile, in water, muck and mire to his armpits, Michael Myers had bulled his way through snaggly brush and stumbled over unseen submerged logs to the middle of the marsh. At that point, some 15 minutes ago, he had had a severe scare when there was a thrashing in the mucky cover to his right. He reached for his belt sheath to free his hunting knife and defend himself, but the approaching person turned out to be a friend and neighbor, Martin Swigart. They had almost wept with the relief of encountering each other. Together they floundered through the remainder of the muck to the west side of the marsh.

Emerging and quickly encountering the Oak Creek Trail just as John Slover had done a short time before them, they found a soldier who had dropped out of Leet's movement with a ball lodged in his ankle. Unable to walk farther with the ball still inside and seeing that Myers had his knife in the belt sheath, he begged them to cut the ball out.

"It'll hurt like hell," Myers warned, "but you'll have to keep quiet, or you'll bring the Injens down on us."

"For God's sake, do it!" the soldier moaned. "I won't make a sound."

Myers removed his knife from its sheath, leaned over the man's foot and began probing with the tip of the blade. Despite his effort to remain silent, the man screamed at the pain. Myers clapped his hand over the man's mouth, and his words came out in a hiss.

"No more crying out, you hear?" The man nodded, and Myers added, "You holler again, we'll have to leave you on your own."

The man moaned an assent and Myers again bent over him and touched his blade to the wound. Once more the man's scream rent the air, and Myers desisted. "We're not gonna let you get us killed," he said with finality, and he and Swigart left the man lying where he was and moved on.

A short while later Myers and Swigart, hearing Indians nearby, separated and, both fearing to call out and reveal their presence, each moved on by himself. Myers came to where some Indian horses were picketed together. He slipped quietly among them, selected the one that appeared to be most powerful and secured it by forming a bridle out of willow withes, which he put around the horse's lower jaw. He quietly led the horse out of hearing of anyone who might be nearby, then mounted and rode through the remainder of the night.[550]

Well ahead of where Myers and Swigart became separated, a group of ten men south of the marsh had also become separated in the darkness from Maj. Leet's retreat as it passed through a region of thick brush. Their horses, already jaded, could barely push their way through, and finally the ten, including Pvt. Jonas Sams, dismounted and left their mounts, continuing on foot. In the pale moonlight they eventually managed to make their way back to the prairie grass. Using the moon to get their bearings, they moved off slightly east of south and soon came to a dimly perceived trail heading in a more easterly direction. Some of the men declared it was the trail they were seeking, but Sams and others argued the point.

"Ain't no way," Sams said, "our boys could've passed 'long this here trail 'thout leavin' a bigger swath than this. I'm fer goin' on the way we been headin'."

Split in their opinions, the group split in their action, half following the small trail just encountered, while Sams and the other four continued moving just east of south.[551]

The Sams group were not the only men to get separated from their comrades in the darkness. The unit under Maj. John Rose fell back from that under Col. Williamson and took a wrong trail in the dark, angling toward the west. They increased their speed to catch up to the others, and were wondering why they had not done so when the moon rose and they discovered their error. By the dim moonlight, they could see that no body of horsemen had ridden this trail just before them and that they were riding southwest.

"Well," remarked Pvt. Angus McCoy philosophically, "one thing you can say for takin' a wrong trail—we ain't been bothered by the Injens lately. 'Course, in the direction we're headin', we'll wind up in the Shawnee towns, an' I reckon they'll have a warm welcome for us."

Without further ado, Maj. Rose turned the column to the left and, cutting straight through untrammeled prairie grass, rode rapidly for over two miles before finding the correct trail again, which, at that point was running nearly parallel to the less used trail they had mistakenly taken.

Having intercepted the principal trail, Maj. Rose discovered they were at this point about three miles south of the old Half King's Town that they had found abandoned on their approach here. He also found that the main force under Col. Williamson had not yet passed here, but in only a matter of minutes that portion of the army arrived, the big gray gelding with Pvt. Thomas Mills perched on its back clearly visible in the moonlight. The two units quickly merged, swelling the number of the whole to around 250 men.

Williamson's force had not had an easy time of it. Its delay in arriving at that point had been due to a couple of unfortunate circumstances. First, their mounts had initially been pushed too hard when the panic broke out and had played out to the point that a fair number had to be abandoned and their riders forced to accompany the remainder afoot; only a small number of the horses seemed capable of going on with a hard ride—Pvt. Mills's gray being one of them. Second, the following Indians and British Rangers had quickly overtaken them and inaugurated an annoying rear action, sniping at the retreaters from under cover and quickly killing or capturing any stragglers. About a dozen men were missing and presumed killed or captured.

Now, with the two principal forces of the main army rejoined, Col. Williamson placed Capt. John Biggs's company as a strong rear guard and resumed the march through the darkness, intent on getting as far away from the Sandusky towns as possible before the break of day.

[*June 6, 1 7 8 2 — T h u r s d a y*]

As the first light of day came to the grove where for the past two days the Americans had holed up and fought, there was no longer any gunfire. Though many of the Indians were gone in pursuit of the broken army—the majority dogging the main force, but other parties now beginning to follow the trails of smaller scattered groups or individuals—a substantial number of Wyandots and Delawares had stayed behind and now began scouring the woods for any dead or wounded soldiers not yet found. Throughout the night exultant Indians had turned up at the various villages along the Sandusky River and Tymochtee Creek with fresh scalps, with prisoners in tow, some of them wounded, and with militia horses that they had found wandering loose and captured.[552] Groups of Indian women and children scoured the battle areas as well, gathering up any items the volunteers had lost that might be of value—rifles, tomahawks and knives primarily, but also cooking gear, pouches containing food or ammunition, pieces of rope, wallets, shovels, shoes, items of clothing, saddles and saddlebags. They also scalped any of the unscalped dead they found and stripped the bodies of anything worthwhile. Many of them looked for places where balls had struck trees in the woods and used their knives or tomahawks to dig out the chunks of embedded lead to be melted down and reused. Finally, some of the younger warriors gleefully chopped at the bodies of dead Americans, dismembering them, tying the pieces to lengths of rope and triumphantly dragging them behind their horses through the various villages.

But though the Indians searched meticulously in the first light of morning for any trace of two particular Americans on whom to exact their vengeance, they did not find either Col. Crawford or Col. Williamson. They had escaped.

That same first light of the dawn found Col. William Crawford and Dr. John Knight only about ten miles east in a straight line away from the site of the Battle of Sandusky, though they had traveled perhaps double that distance. Throughout the night they had traveled, constantly on the alert for ambush or pursuers, guiding themselves by frequently taking bearings on the North Star.

After leaving the island of trees last night, with the sound of gunfire and frightening yells still resounding behind them, they struck a course north and traveled in that direction for six or seven miles before turning due east. It had been about midnight when, by the light of the moon, they had crossed the Sandusky River a few miles above the mouth of Tymochtee Creek without seeing any Indians at all. They had continued eastward for a mile or so and then turned south and traveled another mile or more in that direction. With the pattern thus set, they continued alternating their passage, east a mile and then south another, east and then south.

Now, in the wan light of dawn, they had begun to lose the apprehension that had dogged their steps all night. They had seen no Indians and, though they were still in the Sandusky Plains, there were more trees now, the islands of woodland closer together and often connected for miles. On the horizon far ahead, a barely visible dark line seemed to indicate unbroken forest.

"I do believe, Doctor Knight," Crawford observed, "we have a good chance of making it."

"I trust you're right, Colonel," Dr. Knight replied, "but I won't be convinced until I see the Ohio."

The regimental surgeon's pessimism took on the aspect of a presentiment when, less than an hour later, both horses gave out from exhaustion, came to a stop and stood spraddle-legged, their heads drooping nearly to the ground. Unsaddling them and hiding the riding gear in the tall grass where it was unlikely to be found by passing Indians, the two abandoned their mounts and set off on foot, taking their guns and carrying what they could from the saddlebags: a meager supply of food and all the ammunition they had, which was precious little.

After traveling eastward another hour and spotting Indians at a distance on three occasions, they decided that traveling farther in the daylight was simply too risky. Besides, they too were very weary, having had practically no sleep over the past two days and nights. Crossing Broken Sword Creek, they entered a small, oval-shaped island of trees, made a cold camp and stretched out on the ground to rest.[553]

Ten miles away from them as the crow flies, almost due south, the main army being led by Col. Williamson was straggling along on the road by which they had arrived at the Sandusky Plains. The colonel was holding the unit together, but only with considerable effort. More splinter groups had broken away during the night in the belief they could fend for themselves in smaller parties better than in the main body. In the first light of day, Col. Williamson stood high in his stirrups and looked back over the fatigued men still following his lead.

"Listen to me!" he shouted, his voice tight with controlled anger. "Not a man of you will ever reach home if anyone attempts to shift for himself. Your only salvation is keeping in line. If our ranks are once broken, all is lost. We *must* keep together!"

The march along the trail continued, and only a little over an hour ago they had reached and briefly paused at the fine springs where they had camped two nights before, though to many of the men it seemed like a lifetime ago. It was here, as they took their brief rest, that the army was increased in size again by the arrival of the almost 100 men led by Maj. Daniel Leet. Though the unit had traveled farther, swinging widely to the west and then arcing back to the southeast, they were in better shape than the others, not having pushed their mounts to the point of uselessness. The respite at the springs, while appreciated by the men, had a drawback: It allowed more time for the pursuing enemy to overtake them. When, in the new light of this day, the army went into motion again, the soldiers were more seriously annoyed by sniper fire from hidden Indians as they passed small islands of trees. Several of the shots found their mark, wounding soldiers.

One of those who abruptly cried out in pain and crumpled to the ground near the end of the straggling line was the already-wounded Pvt. Thomas Ogle. During the panicky retreat last night, he had taken a bullet in the arm. The bullet that just now felled him had taken him full in the spine, and he knew the wound was mortal. He shook his head and waved off the men who stooped to help him.

"I'm done," he gasped. "Tell my brother that you left me here lord of the trail. I'll keep my tomahawk, pretend I'm dead, an' when them red devils comes t'take my scalp, I'll fix one of 'em."

There was nothing to do but leave him, and when they glanced back, his eyes were closed and he appeared dead, though his right hand was clasped around the handle of his tomahawk, which lay all but hidden against his leg.

By noon the attacks at the front of the column had increased as well. Col. Williamson had sent Maj. Rose and some of his men somewhat ahead as an advance, which was at first one of the safer places to be, but the security did not last. Rose and four of his men, including his slave, Henry, and Pvt. John Hays, still in his breech-clout and leggins and looking much like an Indian, were riding slightly ahead of the main part of the advance and just passing a small woods at about eleven o'clock when a force of mounted enemy—Indians and British Rangers alike—broke from hiding in the woods and attempted to get between them and the main body of the advance. Rose, however, quickly perceived the jeopardy and barked an order, turning his party into an about-face and galloping back toward the others. It was a close race, but Rose managed to pull away from the Indians bent on intercepting him and reached the advance unscathed. His Negro servant, Henry, was briefly boxed in by some of the British Rangers but extricated himself and also reached the advance safely.

Pvt. Hays, however, found his return cut off and tried to gallop away, but his horse was too weary. Before a hurriedly mounted squad of light horse could effect a rescue, he was overtaken by a mixed group of Rangers and Wyandots. The first Ranger to reach him slashed at Hays with his sword, inflicting a terrible head wound and knocking him from his horse. As he struggled to get to his feet, a Wyandot warrior rushed up and hurriedly tried to scalp him, but botched the job so badly that he only got half of it, leaving one side of the private's bare skull exposed. Then the assailants rushed off. By the time the American light horse reached him, John Hays was soaked with his own blood and a ghastly spectacle, but still alive. He was carried back and a makeshift litter rigged to transport him with the other wounded.

Immediately following the attack on Maj. Rose and his party, Col. Williamson curtailed having an advance party and the retreat continued. With storm clouds gathering and rain imminent, they approached a small stream that was a branch of the headwaters of the Olentangy River. Here Williamson called a halt, and Maj. Rose rode up to him at once.[554]

"Sir," he said, pointing toward a long grove of trees about a mile ahead, "I don't think we should delay here. There's some protective timber ahead, and I think we ought to get there as quickly as possible and not take the risk of being surprised again in the open."

Williamson shook his head. "The horses need to be watered, Major Rose, and they need it now. We won't be here for long."

However short the time, it was too long. As stragglers caught up to the main body and dismounted to rest the horses and let them drink, companies intermingled and the milling men became separated from their officers. It was at this juncture that a party of pursuing Indians and Rangers once again burst from the deep grasses in full gallop and attacked the rear. As if they were ants in a disrupted nest, the volunteers on foot raced about in dismay, fearful, but this time not giving way to panic.

Several groups of volunteers ran off the trail and away from the creek, plunged into the tall grasses and vanished from sight. At first they were merely searching for a hiding place, but then two separate small groups formed and decided on the spur of the moment to desert. One group consisted of 17 men, the other 12. They struck off on their own, weakening the army in the process but also providing it with an unexpected benefit. Their departure had been observed by the enemy, and two parties of Wyandots and Delawares broke off from the fighting and immediately began trailing them, effectively weakening the attack on the main army. Within the hour both groups of deserters were overtaken, and every man among them was killed.[555]

The skirmish was on, and for a time the men held their ground and fought back determinedly at rather close range.[556] The fighting raged for the better part of an hour, and thus far there were eight Americans wounded and three dead. Pvt. John Walker was wounded in the shin, his leg the only part of him still exposed when he tried to take cover behind a tree, while one of those killed was Sam, the slave who had been sent to fight in the stead of his master, Richard Elson. When a lull developed in the battle and the attackers pulled back somewhat, though continuing their firing, Col. Williamson decided the retreat should recommence at once.

Fearing a possible ambush where the trail they were following went through the woods, the commander ordered Capt. Timothy Downing to select three of his men who, in a short while, were to precede the army through the long grove and watch for Indian sign. The three privates chosen by Capt. Downing for the dangerous assignment were John Clark, Robert McBride and James Allen, all three from the same neighborhood on the Virginia side of the Ohio. Williamson then ordered Leet's light horse to take the van and be prepared to prevent the enemy from blocking the trail's entrance to the forest.[557] Capt. John Biggs's company had acted as rear guard throughout the entire retreat and, now reduced to only nine men of the original 32, asked to be relieved. The whereabouts of Capt. Biggs himself was still unknown since his separation from his troops in the wild flight at the beginning of the retreat.[558] Williamson, sympathetic to the request of Biggs's men, appointed other companies to take that hazardous duty in rotation for the remainder of the retreat. The formation of the continued retreat now established, only one final distasteful chore remained to be done before starting: The bodies of those killed in this little Battle of the Olentangy were gathered together and a shallow grave, large enough to accommodate them all, was ordered quickly dug.

To the north of them, Col. Crawford and Dr. Knight, ensconced in their well-hidden little camp, remained alert for the approach of any enemies. Now that alertness paid off. In the distance they heard the sound of voices approaching and secreted themselves, ready to ambush an enemy party and then escape in the resultant confusion. It turned out not to be necessary. As the group whose voices they heard came into view, Crawford and Knight saw that they were four fleeing Americans on foot. Their leader was Capt. John Biggs.

The newcomers had a terrible start when Col. Crawford and Dr. Knight hailed them from hiding, revealed their identity and cautioned them not to shoot as the pair stepped out of hiding. There was an enthusiastic reunion. Biggs's three men turned out to be Lt. Hankerson Ashby of Capt. John Dean's company, Pvt. James Mitchell of Biggs's own company and another private who did not identify himself. Ashby was badly wounded with a ball in his side but was still ambulatory.[559] Crawford immediately apprised them of his plan to continue their flight by night, at least for a day or two more, to help avoid detection, and the newcomers thought it wise and fell in with it. The whole group now settled down to rest and await nightfall to resume their flight.

To the south of them at this moment, the dead of the Battle of the Olentangy had been gently laid side by side in the shallow ground and then covered over with soil. Atop this grave a fire was built, using plenty of dried prairie grass as kindling, to create a fast, hot fire that would quickly consume the extensive arrangement of twigs and branches placed upon it. It was a race of time against the impending rainfall, and the army won. Within minutes of being ignited, the fire had done its job, effectively hiding the grave beneath a circle of smoldering ash. Now it was unlikely that the Indians would find the grave in order to disinter and scalp the dead Americans.

While this was occurring and before the order could be given to move out, Maj. Rose spoke to the commander briefly and sketched out a plan suggested to him by Pvt. John Gunsaula that might aid them. Convinced the enemy would attempt a rush on them from the rear as soon as they resumed the retreat, Rose asked and received permission to stage a small ambush with a select group of his men. Secreting himself and his hand-picked men in the tall grass and fringe of trees and brush lining the creek, Rose cautioned the men to cup their gunlocks to protect them from the rain that had just begun to fall, and there they waited.

The three privates now selected as an advance squad by Capt. Downing were given the order to start out, and they did so at once. When they were some 200 yards out, the remainder of the force was put into motion. In accordance with the plan of Pvt. Gunsaula and Maj. Rose, a handful of seemingly wounded stragglers were allowed to linger in sight as decoys. The ruse worked perfectly. As soon as the army cleared the creek, the British Rangers and Indians rode up, intent on taking the stragglers. They were met by a barrage of accurate gunfire from Rose and his men that swept about a dozen of the attackers from their horses and caused the others to hesitate and fall back out of effective range.

Rose and his men immediately remounted, brought horses to the men who had been the decoys and, gloating with their triumph, galloped after the main army and quickly overtook them. The Rangers and Indians followed but continued to stay just out of rifle range, not only from fear of running into another ambush but because the rain was now falling harder and shooting had become very difficult.

The army continued heading for the distant grove of trees, towing along with them the horses in tandem that bore litters carrying the wounded. Other individuals were double-mounted with newly wounded men in an effort to carry them to safety.

Maintaining their lead of about 200 yards ahead of the main body, the trio of privates in the advance entered the quarter-mile-wide grove with some apprehension, expecting at any moment to find themselves in the midst of a hail of bullets. No shots came and they reached the far side unscathed. They were very lucky: A party of some 60 Indians and British Rangers had circled unseen around the Americans during the battle and concealed themselves among the trees flanking the trail. Now they deliberately let the three privates pass by unmolested. Thus far their hastily conceived plan was working perfectly: The attack by their fellows at the stream had been designed not as a major engagement—though it had very nearly assumed that proportion—but for the purpose of driving the main army into the woodland and directly into the jaws of their ambush. The element of surprise, they hoped, would compensate for their fewer numbers—less than a third that of the Americans—and they knew they would be bolstered by the other portion of their force presently harrying the army's rear. The plan was to pin the army between themselves and their pursuing fellows in a fatal pincer maneuver.

Col. Williamson's force, now more tightly bunched than before, entered the grove at a rapid pace, and that probably more than anything else was the Americans' saving grace. Williamson himself had moved up near the front with Leet's light horse. At the midpoint of the woodland, the roar of gunfire angling in from ahead sent a barrage of balls whistling among the volunteers, but surprisingly few found their targets, and many of the enemy's guns, with powder now damp from the steady rain, misfired and greatly diminished the effectiveness of the ambush. A few men fell, including a private riding beside Thomas Mills on his gray gelding, and Capt. Downing snapped off a shot that found its mark and tumbled a Shawnee subchief who had stepped out of concealment. Capt. James Munn, from his litter between two horses, fired at the same time and was convinced he was the one who brought the subchief down.[560]

Realizing that all could well be lost at this point, Col. Williamson, instead of stopping his force to disperse among the trees and fight a standing battle, as his attackers anticipated he would do, wisely put the army into a gallop and continued past the Indians and Rangers before they could reload, thundering through the woods and out the other side. The volunteers fully expected to be pursued, but the enemy, disgruntled that their ruse had failed, followed only to the edge of the woods.

Well ahead of the army, Pvts. Clark, McBride and Allen had been prevented from rejoining the force by a small party of Indians that cut them off just after they had emerged from the woods. That party began chasing the privates, but when the main army emerged from the woods behind the Indians at a full gallop moments later, they broke off the pursuit and scattered in the tall grass. The three advance privates halted in their flight and waited until the army reached them and rejoined it. Then the whole force continued generally eastward on the trail.[561]

At this moment, hardly two miles northeast of them, the three privates whose horses had given out early in the retreat and who had traveled all night and through-out the day thus far—Joshua Collins, Michael Walters and Christopher Coffman—were now fully 25 miles east of the battle scene. Pleased at having gotten away, they were following a small path through a 20-acre grove of trees when they abruptly jerked to a halt at the sight of four Chippewa Indians standing 50 feet ahead with rifles leveled at them—part of the contingent of lake Indians brought down from Detroit by Matthew Elliott to help fight the Americans. The three privates instantly spun around to flee, only to see four more Chippewas with rifles step into the path behind them.

Walters and Coffman immediately dropped their own guns and held up their hands, but Joshua Collins leaped from the path and into the woods, racing through the trees as swiftly as he had ever run. He expected at least some of the Chippewa warriors to pursue him, but they did not, content with the two captives who had surrendered.

Leaving nothing to chance, Joshua Collins continued running for over a mile before pausing on a little grassy knoll on the west side of a small island of trees. There he looked back to see if he was being followed. He was not. As he watched his back trail, however, four Wyandots silently emerged from the woods and crept close. As he turned to continue the escape alone, his arms were pinned and his rifle snatched away. For a moment he was sure they were going to tomahawk him, but they merely tied his wrists behind him and started him back toward the Sandusky, arriving just before nightfall at the new Monakaduto's Town at the mouth of Tymochtee Creek.

About that same time, Col. Williamson, having led the remains of the army eastward after the Battle of the Olentangy and marched throughout the remainder of the day, found they were entering an area where the trees were becoming more numerous around them and the dense prairie grasses diminishing. He called a halt in a broad clearing in a woods they were passing through and issued the order that, since the Indians obviously knew exactly where they were and there would be no point in making a cold camp, small cookfires could be built on which to prepare some food. He further ordered, however, that the troops eat sparingly of what few provisions they had remaining.

A larger than normal number of sentinels were placed to remain alert for the enemy and to be relieved every hour. As night closed over them, the groans of the wounded, no longer muted by the sounds of travel, had a very depressing effect on the men. Capt. Charles Bilderback allowed Pvt. Angus McCoy, at his own request, to stay close to the wounded and give what comfort he could. The injury in John McDonald's thigh had become much worse, and Bilderback was sure the man would not make it back home. At the same time, since Dr. Knight was not on hand to care for any of the wounded, Bilderback asked Angus McDonald to also make some of the other injured men as comfortable as possible.[562] Those men, with wounds of varying degrees of severity, lay nearby untended on blankets in the continuing drizzle. Among them was the half-scalped John Hays, whose blood had caked and dried into such a hideous mess on his head and chest that he looked as if he had just crawled from a grave. Now, in the rain, the old blood had become runny and dirty red, making him look, if possible, worse than ever. Amazingly, however, he was more alert this evening than previously, and seemed to be on the mend, since he remarked on how hungry he was and announced his intention of riding a horse when the march resumed on the morrow, rather than be carried in a litter. Angus McCoy, putting aside his own weariness and hunger and holding his gunlock under his armpit to keep it dry, trudged about among the wounded all night, trying to provide them some comfort, but he was himself extremely depressed.[563]

[*J u n e   7 ,   1 7 8 2 — F r i d a y*]

With a start, Col. Crawford awoke in the darkness. A glance at the moon and stars showed him that dawn was not far off. So exhausted had he and the five others been from the battle, the flight and the lack of sleep that, shortly after settling down to await nightfall yesterday, they had all fallen into a deep slumber. Now, mentally cursing himself over the loss of valuable travel time under the cover of darkness, the commander quickly awakened the others and, cautioning them to silence—especially the four who had joined them, since their voices had announced their approach before they were seen—he now led them eastward.

As they strode along single file in the predawn darkness, they crossed a stream running southwest, which Crawford accurately assumed was the headwaters of the Sandusky River.[564] Immediately after the crossing they came to a well-traveled trail that, in the poor light, they mistook for the trail they had followed on the way to reach the Sandusky villages. Convinced that the army they were endeavoring to rejoin could not be very far ahead, they followed it at increased speed, congratulating themselves on their success thus far in their escape.

They were a bit premature. The trail was not, in fact, the one that they had followed on the way out but was, instead, the main Indian trail from the upper Sandusky villages to the village of the powerful Delaware chief who had been so prominent at the battle, Wingenund. However, so convinced were they that they could only be a short distance behind the army that, as dawn lightened the eastern horizon, they put aside their plan to go into hiding during the daylight hours and continued following the trail. The morning grew brighter, and the air soon was vibrant with the cheerful sound of meadowlarks and robins and other songbirds greeting the new day with their territorial warblings. For over half an hour the men followed the trail as the day gradually became brighter.

It was close to sunrise when Crawford, becoming progressively more concerned, came to the conclusion that the trail they were following was not, in fact, the one by which they had arrived. It was not quite so broad as that one, and, equally disconcerting now that they could see the ground clearly, there was no evidence that the main army had passed this way. In a low voice Col. Crawford made known his growing fears to the others, cautioned them to be especially on the alert and began looking for a place where they could go into hiding for the day.

It was already too late for that. A dozen of Wingenund's warriors, themselves unseen, had glimpsed the six men approaching and instantly realized they were Americans, even though they were walking in single file as the Indians habitually traveled. The Delawares quickly took up a position in hiding near the edge of a fairly open woodland to waylay and capture them.

Crawford and his men had already decided to hole up for the day in that very woods, and they came to it without pause, wholly unsuspecting of any trouble until the Delawares leaped into view with leveled guns and ordered them to throw down their weapons and surrender. Instantly assessing the situation, the colonel, who was in the lead and most vulnerable, obeyed the command, but behind him the reaction was different.

"Scatter!" Capt. Biggs shouted, and the five men behind Crawford plunged off the trail and into the woods like startled deer. Dr. Knight treed behind a large oak nearby, but the other four kept going, running at top speed and staying fairly close together. The surgeon snapped off a shot at the leader of the Indians but missed in his haste.

"Stop shooting!" Crawford called. "It's no good. Throw down your gun and surrender, or they'll kill you."

Dr. Knight, on the verge of being killed by the Indians, tossed his weapon to the ground and emerged from behind the tree with his hands raised. The leader of the Indians, a tall, well-built young man, gave an order and the gun was snatched up at once. The surgeon was brought back to the trail. At the same time half the warriors raced off in pursuit of the four whites who had escaped.[565]

The leader of the six remaining Delawares recognized Col. Crawford and stepped forward and took his hand. The colonel breathed a little easier, taking this as a demonstration of friendship. It was not; rather, it was a public avowal to the other warriors that, as the leader, this warrior was claiming the capture of Col. William Crawford, knowing that when word of it spread, he would receive much acclaim as the captor of their dreaded enemy.

Crawford and Knight, with two warriors ahead of them and four behind, were now taken the remaining short distance to Wingenund's Village and confined with nine other soldiers already being held prisoner there, all of whom were greatly heartened at seeing their commander.[566] Crawford immediately asked to see Wingenund, whom he knew well from that chief's numerous visits to Fort Pitt in the past. They had become more than mere acquaintances, and once, in fact, Wingenund had even stayed overnight as a guest in Crawford's house.

In a short while Wingenund appeared and shook hands with Crawford, but his expression was grim, his demeanor cold.

"Don't you remember me, Wingenund?" Crawford asked.

"I remember you well, Crawford."

"Do you remember that we were friends?"

"Yes, I remember all this and that we have often drunk together and that you have been kind to me."

"Then I would hope," Crawford said earnestly, "the same friendship still continues."

"We would still be friends if you were in your proper place and not here."

"What do you mean by that, Wingenund? I hope you would not desert a friend in time of need. Now is the time for you to exert yourself in my behalf, as I would do for you if you were in my place."

Wingenund shook his head and made a slashing gesture with one hand. "No! You have placed yourself in a position where your former friends cannot help you."

"And how have I done that? Friends are friends, and they should always help one another."

"There is the matter," Wingenund said slowly, "of the cruel murder of some of my people who had become Moravians, who would not fight and whose only business was praying. The Delawares—and the Wyandots and Shawnees, too—are very angry for what happened and are crying aloud for revenge."

Crawford nodded. "Your anger and theirs is justified. I myself thought those murders were despicable, and I spoke out strongly against those who committed them. I had no part in them. I, and other friends of yours and all other good men, oppose such acts."

"That may be. I believe it. I have always felt that you are a good man, Colonel Crawford. Yet you and these friends and other good men did not prevent him from going out again to kill the remainder of those inoffensive yet foolish Moravian Indians. I say foolish," Wingenund added, "because they believed the whites in preference to us. We had often told them that they would one day be so treated by those people who called themselves their friends. We told them there was no faith to be placed in what the white men said; that their fair promises were only intended to allure, in order that they might more easily kill us, as they have done many Indians before they killed those Moravians."

His surge of optimism oozing away, Crawford shook his head. "I am sorry to hear you say that, Wingenund. As for Williamson's going out again, when it was known he was determined on it, I went out with him to prevent his committing fresh murders."

Wingenund snorted in derision. "This," he said, a note of irritation in his voice, "the Indians would not believe, even were I to tell them so."

"And why wouldn't they believe it?"

"Because it would have been out of your power to prevent his doing what he pleased."

"Out of my power?" Crawford protested. "Have any Moravians been killed or hurt since he came out?"

"None. But you went first to their town and finding it empty and deserted, you turned on the path toward us. If you had been in search of warriors only, you would not have done so. Our spies watched you closely. They saw you while you were gathering on the other side of the Ohio. They saw you cross that river. They saw you when you camped at night. They saw you turn off from the path to the Moravian town. They knew you were going out of your way. Your steps were constantly watched and you were allowed to proceed until you reached the spot where you were attacked."

Crawford started to interject something, but Wingenund cut him off with another slashing gesture of his hand. "No! What you did, Colonel Crawford, was wrong. You departed from where you should be. You not only made no effort to punish that bad man, Colonel Williamson, now you have gone to war with him against us. Williamson was the man we wanted but unfortunately he ran off with others in the night at the whistling of our warriors' balls, being satisfied that now he had not Moravians to deal with, but men who could fight and with such he did not want to have anything to do. Now," he said, and here a tone of regret crept into Wingenund's voice, "*you* must pay for Williamson's crime because you have not attended to the Indian principle that as good and evil cannot dwell together in the same heart, so a good man ought not to go into evil company."

"What will they do with me now?" Crawford asked, his voice barely a whisper.

"I say, as Williamson has escaped and they have taken you, they will take revenge on you in his stead."

"And is there no possibility of preventing this? Can't you somehow get me off? I promise you, Wingenund, if you can save my life, you'll be well rewarded."

Wingenund shook his head emphatically. "Had Williamson been taken with you, I and some friends, by making use of what you have told me might, perhaps, have succeeded in saving you. But as the matter now stands, no man would dare to interfere in your behalf. The King of England himself, were he to come to this spot with all his wealth and treasure, could not do so. The blood of innocent Moravians, more than half of them women and children, cruelly and wantonly murdered, calls out for revenge. The relatives of the slain, who are among us, cry out and stand ready for revenge. The Shawnees, our grandchildren, have asked for your fellow prisoner," he pointed at Dr. Knight, "and on him they will take revenge." His voice rose with wrath. "All the nations connected with us cry out, revenge! *Revenge!* The Moravians, whom you went to destroy, having fled instead of avenging their brethren, the offense has become national and the nation itself is bound to take revenge."

With nothing left to say, Wingenund sadly shook his head and walked away, leaving Crawford crestfallen and without hope.

Less than an hour later, the Delawares who had set out after Capt. John Biggs and his four men returned bearing five bloody scalps, two of which Crawford recognized as the hair of Biggs and Lt. Hankerson Ashby.[567]

It was just after sunset this same day that Thomas McQueen and the lieutenant and Frenchman accompanying him stopped in their flight, this time planning to get a full night's rest, as much for their horses as for themselves. Since the beginning of the wild retreat, when they had become separated from the main army, they had moved along at a steady pace day and night, pausing only four times, for an hour each time, to give their jaded horses a much-needed rest. Now, only a short distance from the old Fort Laurens area—as McQueen put it, "within spittin' distance of home"—they hobbled their horses in a meadow clearing in the woods and stretched out nearby.

Having had nothing to eat these past two days except a handful of parched corn apiece, they were ravenous. The Frenchman suggested they hunt some game, but McQueen said he thought it would not be a good idea, as a gunshot might be heard by Indians. A few minutes later, however, the lieutenant, turning his head as he lay supine in the grass, saw a raccoon climbing about in the upper branches of a tree.

"By God," he exclaimed, "there's dinner!"

He snatched up his rifle and, over McQueen's protests, ran over to the tree and brought down the raccoon with a single shot through the head. He carried it back to the other men, grinning broadly, told McQueen to gather up some firewood and started to skin the dead animal. McQueen reluctantly got to his feet, and the lieutenant had no more than inserted his knife blade under the raccoon's skin when a party of ten Wyandots emerged from the trees with their guns trained on the three volunteers. They had no choice but to surrender.[568]

As nightfall approached, the eight Chippewa captors of Pvts. Michael Walters and Christopher Coffman stopped at their temporary camp a few miles to the east of Wingenund's Town. Now, however, instead of having just the two captives, they had three.

After the Indians had ambushed them and Joshua Collins managed to escape, the Chippewas had started with their captives back to their own little camp a mile or so from where Walters and Coffman had been captured.

Shortly after the Chippewas began marching the two prisoners toward their camp, they came across a wounded volunteer sitting on the edge of the trail—Pvt. James Guffee. He had taken a bullet through his shoulder during the retreat but had not been knocked out of the saddle, and he managed to get this far through the prairie before he collapsed, weak and exhausted, and fell to the ground. When he finally came back to awareness, his horse was nowhere in sight. He had walked until he had come across this trail, where he had sat down to rest and where the Chippewa party found him. Knowing he was not strong enough to flee from the approaching Chippewas, he simply drew his hunting knife from its sheath, threw it in the trail and made no resistance to being taken captive.

Michael Walters gave Pvt. Guffee some jerky to eat, and within minutes it seemed to have a decidedly recuperative effect upon him. This was perhaps in part inspired by Walters whispering to him that if he was unable to walk along with them as a captive, he would be tomahawked. In a few minutes they were on their way again. It was deep twilight before they finally arrived at the camp of the Chippewas in a secluded glen within a small grove of trees. The instant they stopped, Pvt. James Guffee slumped to the ground. He did not look at all well, and both Walters and Coffman noticed that his shirt was showing fresh blood from his shoulder wound.

"I hope," Walters murmured to his companion, "the rest he'll get tonight will help him."

Christopher Coffman nodded, but he seriously doubted it.

[June 8, 1782 — Saturday]

In the early morning light the residue of the main army of the Americans, on orders relayed from Col. Williamson, began its movement. The travel yesterday had been without major incident, though throughout the day the Indians, following at a safe distance, occasionally rode up close enough to fire random shots at the troops. Only one man had been hit, and that was a mere graze of the flesh on his forearm.

They were a dispirited group this morning, however, riding horses so weary from the exertions of the preceding day that most could do nothing more than maintain a slow walk. The commander knew that if the Indians hit them again today, there would be no possibility of putting the horses into a gallop to get away. Fortunately, they saw no sign of Indians this morning, but although they seemed to have withdrawn, Col. Williamson harbored no illusions that his army was out of danger.

As the army moved off from the little open grove where they had spent the night, the half-scalped Pvt. John Hays lingered behind. Yesterday, riding in the litter, he had become increasingly more uncomfortable and had announced, when they stopped to camp last night, that he was feeling well enough to ride by himself. Glad to have one less wounded to care for, Angus McCoy had provided him with a horse belonging to one of the men killed in the battle on the upper Olentangy. Hays, not having eaten anything during the past two days, was now ravenously hungry and was in the midst of baking some stick-bread over a campfire when the order was given to start the day's march.

"You go on, Angus," Hays told Pvt. McCoy. "I'll follow in a few minutes, soon as this bread is cooked."

McCoy nodded and, aided by several other men, got the wounded reloaded in their horse litters and set off with the main body of troops. None of the wounded had died during the night, but several were in extremely bad shape and all were in great pain.

Squatting beside the small cookfire, Hays finished making his bread, stuffed two warm pieces of it into his pouch and kept one in his hand to munch upon as he rode. He mounted his horse without further delay and set off to overtake the others, who were now about ten minutes ahead of him. Hardly a minute after he started out, eating his bread as he rode, he passed near a cluster of brush and small trees. He did not even hear the approach of the whizzing arrow that buried itself in his back. He stiffened sharply and began leaning toward one side when a rifle cracked. The ball struck a handsbreadth from where the arrow was lodged, ripping through his heart. He was dead when he hit the ground, and a few moments later the remaining portion of his scalp was taken, along with his gun, his horse and his pouch containing the remaining still-warm stick-bread.

Miles to the north and west, the party of Chippewas, with their three captives, roused and prepared to continue their march. Both Christopher Coffman and Michael Walters were in good shape, but the wounded private the party had found yesterday, James Guffee, was not. He had considerable difficulty getting to his feet and, in fact, had to be helped by Walters.

The Chippewa warriors, squatting by their own little fire a few yards away, muttered among themselves and seemed to be paying little attention to the captives. After a few minutes, however, three of them came to their feet and strode to the captives. Without a word or sign of warning, one of them jerked his tomahawk from his belt and buried it in the back of Pvt. Guffee's head, killing him. The other five warriors at the campfire murmured in approval and came to the scene.

As Walters and Coffman stared aghast, the warriors scalped the downed man and then ripped open his shirt, plunged a knife into his chest and cut out his heart. From one to another they passed the bloody organ, each in turn lifting it to his mouth and biting out a chunk of the muscle, which they chewed and swallowed. It was not an uncommon practice among the Chippewa to do this—a ceremonial act that they believed imbued them with the strength and courage of the enemy they had slain— but to Pvts. Walters and Coffman, it was the most horrifying sight they had ever witnessed. A short time later, as the Chippewas broke camp and set off westward along the trail toward Wingenund's Town with their two remaining captives, both were silently wondering which of them might be next in line for similar treatment.[569]

After a mile or so, a fine white-tailed deer flushed from cover and bounded away in front of them, untouched by the several bullets shot by the Chippewas. To Michael Walters's amazement, one of the warriors approached and handed him his own rifle, which had been taken from him the day before. It was empty of powder and lead but, through a mixture of signs and scattered English words, the Indians gave him to understand that he was hereafter expected to help them hunt game for provisions. When another deer, or perhaps a buffalo, was sighted, hopefully in time for them to plan some hunting strategy, they would load his gun and he would have one shot with which to help bring down the quarry.

There was a second reason the gun was restored to Walters, though this one the Chippewas kept to themselves: Prisoners were less obvious if they were carrying rifles, and the Chippewas, knowing they would be passing through Wingenund's Town soon, feared their prisoners would be taken from them or killed.

Less than an hour later, they came to Wingenund's Town, where the Delawares welcomed the Chippewa war party with restrained cordiality. The residents looked at the two white men appraisingly. They paid little attention to Michael Walters, assuming, as the Chippewas had hoped they would, that since he had a rifle, he was an ally of the Chippewas and helping to guard a single prisoner. They gave much closer study to Christopher Coffman, and a minor argument arose between them and the Chippewas. The Delawares evidently wanted to form a gauntlet line for Coffman to run through, but the Chippewas refused to go along with the idea, making it clear that they were saving him in good health to run gauntlets at their own villages, which was their right as the captors. The Delawares reluctantly gave up on their idea and the Chippewas, relieved, stayed only a little while to exchange news and relate battle experiences with Wingenund's people.

While there, Walters and Coffman were shocked to see, being held in a little compound under heavy guard, their army's commander, Col. William Crawford, along with Dr. John Knight and nine other soldiers, including a couple from their own company. Walters wished he could talk to his colonel, but he was not close enough, and before an opportunity could present itself, five Delawares arrived triumphantly with scalps, and the Chippewas, motioning to Walters and Coffman to come along, left the village abruptly, lest their captives be stolen from them by the excited Delawares. They headed in the direction of Monakaduto's Town, on the Sandusky near the mouth of Tymochtee Creek.

Some 80 miles east of the Sandusky battleground, John Slover was still leading the little group of men with whom he had linked up on the Oak Creek Trail. Having pushed farther south than the rest of the army, they had followed a well-used trail for many miles until it came to the headwaters of a southeastward-flowing stream that seemed familiar to Slover. After following it for a few miles, he finally realized it was the Walhonding and that they were on the trail that led directly to where the great village of Goschachgunk had once stood, at the point where the Walhonding and Tuscarawas meet to form the Muskingum River. Not wanting to raise their hopes too soon, Slover kept the knowledge to himself until they were much farther downstream.

When his companions—William Nemins, James Paull, Thomas Heady and Col. Crawford's nephew, William Crawford, and son-in-law, William Harrison—realized that they were now only seven or eight miles from that confluence, they were jubilant and congratulated Slover and themselves on getting this far. Escape seemed firmly in their grasp at this point. Their exultation, however, just as Slover had feared, was premature.

The six men had not gone another mile when, wholly unexpectedly, a party of Indians—a dozen Shawnees and four Wyandots—leaped into the trail before and behind them with weapons leveled. Harrison, Heady and Crawford froze in place, but Slover, Paull and Nemins plunged off toward the underbrush. William Nemins was shot dead before he got there. Slover was pursued a few yards by three Shawnees who overtook him and pounced, bringing him to the ground. James Paull, more fortunate than the others, got into the heavy cover and, through fast running and adroit maneuvering, eluded his pursuers and got away.[570]

Back on the trail, several of the Shawnees had disarmed and were holding young Crawford and William Harrison. The four Wyandots had similarly taken Thomas

Heady who, though by far the largest and most muscular of the party, had suffered a shallow tomahawk gash across his thigh and so had made no attempt to flee, submitting without struggle.[571] John Slover, still rolling about on the ground with the three Shawnees who had caught him, abruptly cried out to them in the Shawnee tongue as they pinned him, hoping to confuse them enough that he might be able to break away. His impromptu plan backfired.

The Shawnees immediately recognized Slover as their former captive and chortled in glee. Swiftly tying his wrists behind him, they took him back onto the trail. Another of their number had scalped the dead Nemins and joined them with his trophy and the private's gun and knife.

The Wyandots held a brief exchange with their Shawnee allies and, on completion of the discussion, led Pvt. Thomas Heady to where their horses were hidden to take him back to the Sandusky. The dozen Shawnees conversed more after the Wyandots were gone and then took the captives to their horses. At once they mounted and began driving the three toward the west.

"God Almighty, John," Harrison gasped, "where are they taking us?"

Slover, with sinking heart, did not respond. He had understood most of what he could catch of their conversation, and he was aware that they were taking them directly to the Shawnee capital village of Wapatomica on the upper Mad River. He also knew only too well what their fate would be when they got there: death at the stake.

[June 9, 1782—Sunday]

The Chippewa war party with Michael Walters and Christopher Coffman in tow reached the Sandusky River in the late afternoon today, crossed to the west side at a fording place and moved downstream from there on the main trail. The earlier fears of the captives that they were eventually to be executed had been diminished by their stop at Wingenund's Town, and by the Ottawas refusal to let the two men run the gauntlet there because they wanted the captives in good shape to run the gauntlet when they reached the Chippewa Towns. That, Walters reasoned, had been only a ploy to get them away from the Delawares quickly. Since then, during this day's journey toward Monakaduto's Town, he had been able to gather that the Chippewas planned to take them to Detroit and turn them over to the British for the ransom they would receive.

Having crossed the Sandusky River, it was only a matter of a few more miles downstream to the mouth of Tymochtee Creek and the Wyandot village. Before sunset they arrived there, and the residents of Monakaduto's Town greeted the Chippewas with greater warmth than had the Delawares. Nevertheless, they too were disappointed when the Chippewas would not permit their captives to run the gauntlet. The Wyandots fed their guests, including the captives, and they exchanged news and experiences of the recent battle into the evening.

Coffman and Walters were more than surprised to see, among the prisoners on hand here, their earlier companion, Joshua Collins. As with Col. Crawford in

Wingenund's Town, however, they did not get close enough to speak to Collins and ask how he had come to be captured after making his escape from the Chippewa party. The bruises and swellings on his head and upper body were clear evidence he had been forced to run a gauntlet upon arriving here. They were glad to see that he had survived it.[572]

While the Chippewas were being entertained, Coffman and Walters, tied to a post nearby, were approached by several British Rangers who stared at them with such loathing that Walters was sure they would have killed them had they thought they could get away with it. Despite this, Coffman asked the men if they would help them escape.

"Help you escape?" said one of them incredulously. He spat on the ground at their feet. "You two ought to be hanged for fighting against King George."

Even though the Chippewas were being treated cordially, they remained apprehensive that their hosts might try to confiscate the two captives and, at last, with the twilight deepening, the Chippewas returned to Walters and Coffman and led them northward out of the town to an isolated hut that had been offered them for the night. Here, with the two whites tied back to back, they settled down to await the morning, leaving one of their number on guard should the Wyandots come during the darkness to steal their prisoners.[573]

[June 10, 1782—Monday]

Early this morning, Col. William Crawford, Dr. John Knight and the nine other American prisoners being held at Wingenund's Town for the past three days were led away from the village, heading westward, guarded by a strong party of 17 Delaware warriors. The captives were greatly dejected, having just been told they were being taken to Pimoacan's Town on Tymochtee Creek. They would be marched first to the old Half King's Town, where they would spend the night, and tomorrow they would complete the journey.

The procession soon passed the place where Crawford and Knight had been captured and not long afterward began following the trail by which the army had made its initial approach to the old Half King's Village. When that trail moved toward the southwest, however, the party continued straight west on another, smaller trail that was a more direct route than the one following the left bank of the Sandusky River.

Now, as they continued traveling, Crawford learned that his companion of many years ago, Simon Girty, was presently staying at Monakaduto's house in the New Half King's Town, not far from where the battle was fought. Seeing a possible ray of hope there for getting himself out of this present predicament, Crawford managed to convince his captors to take him there to talk with Girty instead of with the others to the old Half King's Town.

When they came to where the trail split, 15 of the warriors led all the prisoners, except for Crawford, to the left fork, heading west and slightly south toward the old village, still about another seven miles distant. The other two warriors directed

Crawford to follow the northwest fork and said they would reach Monakaduto's new town in about an hour.[574]

Almost at this very moment, someone else was entering that New Half King's Town who was not at all happy to be there—Pvt. Thomas Heady, under guard of the small party of Wyandot warriors who had been involved in his capture. The muscular young volunteer was in fairly good shape, considering he had been forced to run along with the horses much of the distance from where he had been captured toward this principal town. Only when his wounded leg began bothering him more and he became so exhausted that he slowed them considerably had he been permitted to ride double with one of the warriors for the remainder of the journey.

Now, having arrived at the town, they were greeted by a large number of Wyandots, including many women and children, who streamed out of their dwellings with loud cries, cheers and whoopings. With hardly a pause in the main part of the village, on the east side of the river, they crossed at the fording place to the west side and continued westward, passing McCormick's Trading Post, where a number of other warriors emerged, along with half a dozen or more British Rangers.

With Heady's captors leading the way, the entire group moved gradually west a short distance to where, close to the John Leith Trading Post, they formed a double gauntlet line some 200 yards in length. At the far southern edge of the line, Heady was stripped of all clothing and his face and body smeared with black paint—the mark of the condemned man. He was made to understand he was to run to the painted post at the north end of the line, adjacent to Leith's store. If he made it there, his life would supposedly be spared. Blackened as he was for death, however, Heady didn't believe that for a moment. Despite the tomahawk wound on his thigh, now somewhat inflamed and causing him to limp a little, he thought he could reach the far northern end of the gauntlet, and he resolved that if he got close enough, he would burst through the line and dart into the store, hoping to find refuge there. If nothing else, he might at least be able to snatch up a weapon and die fighting.

Most of the women and children who took their places in the line were wielding switches and larger sticks with which to strike the captive as he passed. Younger boys readied themselves with tomahawks and small bows and arrows with sharpened but not barbed points. Some of the men also had clubs, and a few had tomahawks, but the majority were armed with rifles heavily charged with gunpowder but not lead. There was little delay in starting Heady on his way. One of the warriors cried "Go!" and, at the same moment, he was whacked savagely across the small of his back with a club; the blow caused him to stagger, though he managed not to fall. At once he began running as strongly through the double line as he could. A roar of shrieks and screams rose all the way down the length of the gauntlet, and participants positioned themselves to strike most effectively.

The rules of the gauntlet run, such as they were, required that no one could strike or shoot at him as he approached and thereby check his forward progress, but they were free to inflict whatever injury they could to his sides and back as he passed. The result was that a multitude of blows rained upon him as he ran past the screaming Wyandots, and soon the skin of his back and buttocks, arms and legs, was badly bruised and lacerated, and a number of arrows were stuck shallowly in his flesh.

Worse yet was the intense stinging and burning pain inflicted upon him by powder burns, as warriors thrust their guns within inches of him and fired as he passed.

Despite the injuries, Heady's constitution was such that he was holding up well as he approached the northern end of the line and the nearest point to Leith's Trading Post. Abruptly he turned and smashed into the line, bowling over several people, and continued running right into the store.

John Leith was inside and Heady ran up to him and stopped, unable at first to talk as he gasped for breath but looking at the trader imploringly.[575] Tempted though he was to thrust a weapon into the young man's hands so he could defend himself, Leith did not do so, knowing it would place his own life in jeopardy. An instant later an Indian who had pursued him from the gauntlet line appeared in the doorway and threw his tomahawk. It struck Heady in the right side of his back, causing him to leap into the air with a cry of pain. He spun around and, with the weapon still embedded in his back, raced toward the door and bowled over the approaching Indian. The instant he plunged through the open doorway, however, he was struck by another tomahawk. The blade smashed into his brain and killed him.

As John Leith watched in horror, the shrieking Indians scalped Thomas Heady and then severed his head and stuck it on the end of a sharpened pole a dozen feet in length. They planted the butt end of the pole in the ground close to where he fell and left the body lying near the doorway to the trading post. As the excitement diminished, Leith approached a small group of the Wyandot leaders and asked permission to take down the head and bury it, along with the body, away from his store some distance. At first they refused to let him do so.

"Your people," one of the chiefs told him, "do not bury our dead, and we will not bury yours."

Leith was not so easily dissuaded, knowing that if he did not press the issue, the head and body might well remain where they were until they rotted. He shook his head angrily and resorted to the only form of pressure he could exert. "If you don't let me bury those remains, I promise you I will move my trading post from here to Chief Pipe's Village on the Tymochtee."

The village of Pipe—Pimoacan's Town—was about five miles to the west, and if Leith reestablished himself there, it would cause a considerable inconvenience for the Wyandots here at the New Half King's Town. So, with poor grace, they gave in and told Leith he could do with the body as he wished. After a short while, when the Indians dispersed and returned to the village, Leith took down the head and returned it to the body. He washed the blood off both, wrapped them together in a clean blanket and buried them. A short time later some of the warriors returned and, seeing what he had done, took several sharpened stakes and drove them deeply into the fresh grave and through the buried body as a final act of triumph.

The villagers were still keyed up over it all when, hardly a quarter-hour later, a party of Delawares arrived with the American commander, Col. William Crawford, in tow. Another stir of excitement rippled through Half King's Town. The Delawares were on their way to Pimoacan's Village with Crawford but stopped by here to show him off and to see if Simon Girty would consent to seeing him, assuming that such a meeting would be all right with Monakaduto.

Permission was granted by Monakaduto himself, who led Crawford and his two guards to his own house where Girty was temporarily lodging. Despite the fact that it was now nearing midday, Girty was still asleep, having drunk himself into a stupor the preceding night. Monakaduto roused Girty and then let the captive and the British agent talk privately.

"Heard you was took, Colonel," Girty said, regarding him through bloodshot eyes. "I get no pleasure seeing you here. Guess you know you've got yourself into bad trouble."

"I know that, Girty," Crawford replied. "That's why I asked to see you. I was hoping you'd somehow be able to help get me out of this. I'll see that you're well rewarded."[576]

Girty shook his head. "I ain't got much hope of that. Trouble is, it's the Delawares got you, not Wyandots. Them Delawares are plenty damn mad over what happened at Gnadenhütten."

"I had no part in that," Crawford protested. "That was Dave Williamson's work."

"Figgered as much. But you led this one, an' they'll just figger you done both. Reckon you boys didn't come here for no friendly visit, so they ain't gonna be no kind feelin' toward you."

"The point is, can you get me off? You can tell them I'll divulge military information in exchange for my freedom, but for nothing less. Can you ransom me?"

Girty shrugged. "Dunno. Doubt it. But I got me some friends aroun' an' I'll talk to 'em an' see what mebbe we can do. You wait here and I'll do some checkin' an' see. Might take a few hours."

Then he was gone. Crawford settled back to wait, still apprehensive but also with more optimism than previously, knowing the influence Girty carried with many of the Indians. Crawford's optimism was not at this moment being experienced by his namesake nephew, his son-in-law and one of the expedition's guides. Those three, Ens. William Crawford, Pvt. William Harrison and Guide John Slover, were at this very instant approaching the Shawnee capital village of Wapatomica, some 40 miles to the southwest.

As these men were led into the town, they passed the still smoldering remains of a fire and the body of a man who had been tortured to death at the stake. As they came closer, they recognized the freshly burned remains of Maj. John McClelland. Grateful to leave the scene behind, they moved on to the center of town, where they were surrounded by a noisy swarm of Shawnees. Slover was well known here, of course, having been a Shawnee prisoner for six years, and many of the Indians called to him and made remarks, most of which were not complimentary. Surprisingly, however, several approached and shook his hand and seemed delighted when he addressed them by name.

A group of warriors were on hand from the village of Mackachack, some six and a half miles southwest of here, down the Mad River. After some discussion between them and the others, the leader of the Mackachack Shawnees pointed at Ens. William Crawford, who was immediately turned over to them and led off toward their village to be burned at the stake.[577]

More discussions were begun and dragged on and on, and gradually verbal disputes broke out among them. After two hours or more, they seemed no closer to agreement than when they began. The conflict seemed to arise from what they should do with John Slover. Ordinarily, an escaped captive who was recaptured was condemned to death as a matter of course. Slover, however, had been well liked during his tenure here, and there were those in the crowd who apparently thought his life should be spared. At last, after two hours of squabbling, it was decided that a formal council would have to be held where all who wished to have their say in the matter could be heard, a vote taken and the matter resolved. A young woman with whom Slover had been more than friendly, Pahcotai Sisqui—Autumn Leaf—requested and was given the responsibility of keeping him—and preventing his escape —until the council was held in three or four days.

Where Pvt. William Harrison was concerned, however, there was no debate. As Slover was now taken off to one side, the private was stripped of all clothing and taken out 100 yards or more from the village. A double gauntlet line quickly formed, extending all the way from where Harrison was positioned to the huge *msi-kah-mi-qui,* or council house. If he managed to make it through the gauntlet and into the structure, he would be safe, at least for a while.

Harrison was started down the gauntlet by a savage blow with a club across his buttocks. It lifted him off his feet and knocked him flat, and he was struck numerous times more with switches and clubs before he was able to regain his feet and commence running. Once started, however, he amazed everyone with his fleetness and ability to dodge the blows aimed at him.

As he approached the council house, still relatively unharmed, one of the Indian women ran up with a panful of hot coals, stepped directly in his path and threw them full in his face. Many struck him and bounced away, doing little harm, but one hit his open eye and he screamed with the pain. At the same time, using the momentum he had built up, he leaped and kicked her in the stomach with such force that it killed her. Immediately pummeled by the weapons of those nearby, he tried to break free and get to the council house, now only mere yards away. It was not to be. The husband of the woman he had killed rushed up brandishing a rifle and put a bullet through Harrison's head.

Harrison was scalped and his body dumped beside the burned remains of Maj. McClelland. Then both were beheaded, their bodies dragged outside the town for the dogs to feed on and their heads impaled on tall poles, which were then stuck in the ground in the center of the village near the council house.

Back at Half King's Town in the late afternoon, Col. William Crawford, awaiting the return of Simon Girty, had begun to think that his former companion would not return at all. As the hours passed, he had become progressively more depressed. Now, with sunset approaching, his depression became overwhelming as Simon Girty finally returned to him, his expression grim. What the British Indian agent had to say did nothing to elevate Crawford's spirits.

"I have tried with all those I know who might have helped," he told the colonel. "All but a few refused even to listen. They don't have much fondness for Americans. Most said you deserve whatever may be in store for you, which most hoped was death. Those few who might have helped can do nothing to get you released."

Crawford said nothing, but he shook his head slightly. Girty continued: "You will be staying in this village tonight, and in the morning the Delawares will take you to Pimoacan's Village, which will almost surely be the beginning of the end for you. There is only one possible hope left. Escape. Tonight will be your only opportunity, and I strongly urge you to take it. Only one Indian will be guarding you tonight, and he is almost certain to go to sleep, at which time you can slip away. I have told you where my camp is. Come there, and you will find my horse already saddled and ready for you. My Negro will also be waiting to go with you, and he will guide you on the road toward Detroit, as far as he can go and still get back to my camp by morning. At Detroit you can give yourself up at the garrison and you will be taken into custody, but at least you will be safe with the British officers there. This, my friend, is all I can do for you. You can easily get away, if you will. If not, tomorrow they will kill you."

Crawford continued shaking his head and replied in a voice so soft it was barely audible, "I am too weak and tired to try that."

"You may come to wish you had, my friend," Girty murmured sadly. "Don't give up hope yet. I will still be tryin' t'save you somehow."[578]

A short while later Crawford's Delaware guards led him away to the hut that had been provided for them for the night. The colonel went with them meekly, as if sleepwalking in the midst of a worsening nightmare.

[June 11, 1782 — Tuesday]

It was sunrise when Col. Crawford was roused by his two Delaware guards. He had slept little during the night, dozing fitfully and occasionally moaning as if in pain. He refused to accept any of the food the guards offered him and when they left the New Half King's Town for the abandoned town, just over eight miles distant up the Sandusky River trail, his movements were so lethargic at first that they had to prod him along with growing impatience.

As they passed the island of trees that had been the battleground, he barely took note of it and simply plodded on. Not until they reached the springs where the army had stopped to rest and drink before heading north into battle did he seem to come out of his torpor somewhat. He drank deeply at the springs and even wondered if Dr. Knight would still be at the abandoned Half King's Town when they arrived. When they moved on, continuing south, he vaguely noted that they passed several bodies beside the road. He took them to be volunteers, but he could not recognize any, since their heads were missing.

John Knight was, in fact, at the old town when they arrived, as were four of the nine soldiers who had arrived there with him. He and those four had been stripped to the waist, and their faces and chests had been painted black shortly after their arrival at the town. Crawford knew what that meant.

To Dr. Knight's query about whether he had received any encouraging news from Girty, Crawford shrugged. "Girty has promised to do all in his power for me but is doubtful he can succeed. The Indians are very much inflamed against us."

Pathetically glad to see their commander again, the men crowded about him, asking for any news that might be encouraging. The other five soldiers who had arrived with them, Dr. Knight told him, including the good-natured Pvt. John McKinley, had been similarly painted, but they had been taken away shortly before dark.

Within minutes of his arrival, Col. Crawford was similarly painted on his face and chest. Then the two Delaware chiefs, Wingenund and Pimoacan, approached him. In an oddly cordial manner they greeted him and shook his hand. Then all 19 of the Delawares herded the six prisoners before them northward on the trail by which Crawford had just arrived.

As they neared the spring area again, the five bodies were still sprawled along the road where Crawford had vaguely noted them earlier. Now a number of Indian boys moved among them, occasionally pausing to plunge knives or tomahawks into the carcasses. Two of the boys were kicking a round object in the road and, as the prisoners passed close by, the youngsters paused and stared at them malevolently. The object they were kicking turned out to be a severed head that had been scalped. Disfigured and battered though it was, the captives recognized it as the popular Pvt. John McKinley, and the horrifying realization dawned on them that these bodies being abused were those of the five volunteers that had been taken away from the old town the evening before.

The procession, augmented by several other warriors who had joined them along the way, paused briefly at the springs again to drink, then continued northward on the trail leading back to the island of trees where the battle had been fought. In less than a mile and a half, however, they turned left on a smaller trail that angled to the northwest, just south of the extensive cranberry bog.[579]

At this point they were joined by a substantial party of Shawnees led by their war chief, Shemeneto. The two Indian parties paused while Pimoacan, Wingenund and Shemeneto talked animatedly for a time, gesturing occasionally toward the captives. When their conversation was concluded, Pimoacan spoke a few words to his men, and at once two of the Shawnee warriors came to the prisoners and separated Dr. Knight from the others, taking him into the midst of their group. It was obvious that the regimental surgeon was now their captive. The combined groups immediately resumed the journey toward the northwest.

Within four miles they came to a small Delaware village where there were perhaps a dozen warriors and easily four times that many women and children, the latter mainly boys.[580] They paused here briefly as the villagers clustered around Pimoacan and Wingenund, chattering excitedly, and the word *Gnadenhütten* was frequently voiced. After a few minutes Pimoacan issued an order and the warriors escorting Col. Crawford and the four privates took those latter four and turned them over to the villagers.

What happened then was horrifying in the extreme. The four soldiers were at first pushed and shoved about violently, struck with fists and clawed at by the grasping hands of the frenziedly shrieking women. The four began screaming in terror and crying for help, and then one of them was struck a vicious blow in the back of the neck with a tomahawk and killed. He was immediately scalped. In succession the other three were similarly tomahawked and scalped by the shrieking horde of women and boys. Some, bearing the freshly taken scalps, rushed up to Col. Crawford and Dr. Knight and slapped them across the face repeatedly with their bloody trophies. The tormentors continued to slash at the bodies with tomahawks until there seemed no area of those four bodies that was not mutilated.

A short gauntlet line was formed then, the women and children arming themselves with switches and sticks cut from a nearby clump of brush. Col. Crawford and Dr. Knight were led to the head of the line. First the colonel, then the surgeon ran through, both men taking a pelting and suffering a number of painful welts but no severe injury. At a command from Wingenund, the gauntlet lines broke up and the march was resumed.

Now, as they progressed on the trail due north, followed by a number of the villagers who maintained a short distance behind, mistreatment of both surviving Americans by their guards began. They were shoved, struck with fists, sticks and clubs and occasionally kicked as the march continued. In about another mile the trail they were on was intersected by a trail from the east; approaching them on this trail was a small mounted party of Wyandots, half a dozen British Rangers, a few traders and Simon Girty, who was riding his fine gray horse.[581]

This new group gathered about the chiefs and an animated discussion followed in the native tongue, which neither Crawford nor Knight could follow. Girty was especially urgent in his remarks to Pimoacan as he offered his horse and saddle, his Negro slave, his rifle and all the money he had with him—$1,000—in an effort to purchase Crawford, but Pimoacan shook his head and gruffly refused. Girty's considerable influence with the Wyandots did not extend to the Delawares.

The newcomers joined the ever growing procession to the northwest, and Girty spoke briefly to Crawford, saying that although he would continue trying to save him, he doubted if anything could be done.

"The Indians are very bitter against you," he said, "so much that I doubt I could save you if you were my own father."[582] In another mile and a quarter the trail turned just slightly north of due east and they followed it another three-quarters of a mile to the principal village of the Delawares, Pimoacan's Town.

Crawford and Knight were fearful that there would be another gauntlet to run here but, instead, they were taken directly to a council ring, where a fire was already burning and the majority of Delaware chiefs and subchiefs were on hand, along with many warriors. Two of the most notable on hand were Chief Tarhe—The Crane—and Chief Buckangehela, their villages closest to those of their allies, the Shawnees.[583]

Within a short time the council was in full session, with Simon Girty acting as interpreter and also making a strong plea for Col. Crawford not to be sentenced to death. A barrage of recriminations was raised against the officer, foremost among which was the accusation that he participated in the massacre of the converted Moravians at Gnadenhütten just a little over three moons previously.

"That's not true," Crawford protested. "I was not there and did not participate in that expedition in any way. Col. David Williamson was in charge. I would never have done something like that."

Girty interpreted and Pimoacan frowned. "Then how is it," he asked through

Girty, "that you have just led an army against the Indians—Delawares and Wyandots alike—with the intention of killing all you encountered, even women and children?"

Crawford had no response for this, but he attempted to veer the matter off course by taking a different tack. "I do not personally hold any enmity against the Indians," he said sincerely. "Four years ago when everyone was for killing them, I very much favored the Delawares at the salt licks on the river you call Mahoning."

When Girty interpreted, there were immediate gasps and a loud outbreak of angry accusation and denunciation. When it faded away, Pimoacan summoned his wife, Michikapeche, and she soon appeared before him. As they conversed, she became very agitated, stared at Crawford and nodded. She pointed at him and, as she broke into a tirade, Crawford could see that one of her fingers was missing to the first joint. Gradually her outburst died in its intensity and, when Pimoacan gestured, she left immediately.

"You were with the white chief general called Hand when he destroyed the villages of my people," he said coldly, addressing the colonel. "And not only on Mahoning, where you killed little boys who were innocently hunting. You also helped to destroy Kuskusskee, where my brother and mother were murdered and where part of my wife's finger was shot off. Where our women were murdered."

When Girty finished interpreting, Crawford responded, "If the one with the end of her finger gone is your wife, then ask her about the soldier who was going to tomahawk her and the chief soldier who saved her life. I am the one who saved her. I had nothing to do with the death of your brother, Captain Bull."

"She would not have been hurt," Pimoacan replied coldly, "if your soldiers had not gone there. Our women would not have been killed. Our boys. My brother, who was their chief. You have brought death to the Delaware people many times, and now you have tried to do so again, but we were too much for you, and now it is your soldiers who have paid for your foolishness. And now it is you who must pay for it."

Girty himself had been a part of Gen. Hand's bungled Squaw Campaign but had wisely hidden the fact from these Indians. Now Crawford, by his own admission, had placed himself there and could not have more surely sealed his own fate. The assemblage clamored for Crawford to be executed and, one by one, Pimoacan called for the views of the chiefs. Not one spoke in his favor and, when they were finished, he passed the final judgment—death at the stake.

In a desperate effort Girty launched a fresh plea for the life of his friend, offering more and more ransom, until the chief silenced him with a slashing motion of his hand.

"We will free him," Pimoacan told him, "only if you are willing to take his place for the burning."

The Indian agent shook his head and looked away.

There was a flurry of activity as Pimoacan issued a series of orders and a large segment of the population of the village quickly moved off. The black charcoal paint on the face and upper body of both Dr. Knight and Col. Crawford had thinned and run due to their perspiration, and now they were taken to one of the huts, where fresh paint was applied. Both were given some food, but neither touched it. They simply waited in silence for what was to come. As they waited, Crawford remembered his refusal the night before, in Monakaduto's Town, to accept Girty's help in escaping; remembered as well Girty's warning that he might come to wish he had accepted the offer.

It was beyond midafternoon when the two captives were taken from the hut and marched back three-quarters of a mile along the road by which they had arrived, to the point where the trail turned from the north to the northeast. Now, at that point, they turned to the north again and followed a much narrower path toward the line of trees that grew along the banks of Tymochtee Creek. Within 300 yards they came to the edge of a bluff overlooking the stream bottom 20 feet below. On the level surface of this bluff, a fire was burning in a clearing among white oak trees, and several hundred people had already gathered. Most of those already assembled were warriors, but there were also about 70 women and boys, plus a small number of British Rangers and traders. Even some other longtime captives, some of them adopted into the tribe, were on hand.[584]

Standing in an isolated area 20 feet or so from the fire was a sturdy young tree that now resembled a post. Though still firmly rooted in the soil, it had been cut off 15 feet above the ground and all its branches stripped away. Less than a foot below where it had been topped, a rope had been firmly tied and trailed down to the ground, where it ended in a little coil. The two captives were led past it and, a short distance from the fire, they were made to sit on the ground. Here they were verbally abused by the spectators and subjected to a spate of mild blows with fists and sticks until Chief Pimoacan put a stop to it.

Several chiefs in succession spoke to those assembled, but neither Crawford nor Knight had any idea what was being said. Simon Girty, who would have been able to tell them, was at this time seated on the ground quite a distance from them, close to Pimoacan and Wingenund. The talking lasted for upward of an hour, concluding late in the afternoon.

At a motion from Pimoacan, several warriors went directly to Col. Crawford, pulled him to his feet and stripped him. His wrists were bound behind him with a length of rawhide. Then he was led to the tree post by Scotach, son of Monakaduto, and the end of the rope trailing down from the top of the tree post was firmly tied around the short length of rawhide ligature between Crawford's wrists. When completed, there was enough leeway in the tether for the condemned man to move straight out from the tree a few feet or to circle it two or three times before being forced to more or less unwind in the other direction.

Pale and drawn, Crawford watched as Scotach finished his task, and then his gaze moved across the assemblage, paused for a moment on Pimoacan and Wingenund and then fixed on the Indian agent seated on the ground near them.

"Girty," he called, shaking his head as if this were all a bad dream, "do they really intend to burn me?"

"Yes," Girty replied.

"Then," Crawford responded, straightening in resolve, "I will try to take it all patiently."

As Scotach continued to stand nearby, the colonel lifted his head and looked skyward. "Lord God Almighty," he prayed in a soft voice, "have mercy on my soul. Dear God, help me to conquer my fear and bear with strength what is going to be done to me here and now. In God's name, I ask this." Crawford remained looking upward and his lips continued moving, but now his voice became inaudible, even to Scotach standing close by.

Pimoacan now took a stance a short distance away and addressed the assemblage in a strong, hard voice, telling them that this was the man who had brought so much grief to the Indians; the man who had been involved in the destruction of the Delaware villages on the Mahoning four years earlier, and who, at that time, at the destruction of Kuskusskee, had been involved in the murder of Pimoacan's brother, Captain Bull, and their mother, and in the wounding of Pimoacan's wife, Michikapeche, as well as others; the man held responsible for the massacre only a few months ago of nearly 100 of their Christianized brethren at the Moravian town of Gnadenhütten; the man who had now marched an army of men into the very homeland of the Delawares and Wyandots with the avowed intention of killing all they met and showing mercy to none, not even women and children. This, then, was the man who was condemned to death for these crimes, and that death should begin now.

The assemblage broke into whoops and screams as he finished and, as Scotach withdrew a short distance and sat on the ground, one warrior broke from the crowd and, drawing his knife from his belt as he ran, rushed to Crawford. He jerked the colonel's head down and swiftly used the blade to slice off both the officer's ears. Crawford gasped but did not cry out. The warrior stuffed the trophies into his belt pouch and withdrew.

A few moments later a large number of warriors approached Crawford, whose neck and shoulders were brightly stained with his blood. All were armed with flint-lock rifles heavily charged with gunpowder only. One after another, as Crawford moaned and vainly tried to jerk out of the way, the muzzles of the weapons were held close to him and the guns fired, the resultant blasts scorching and charring his flesh and sending burning bits of the powder through his skin, where it continued to burn and sting with a fury far worse than any swarm of hornets. A total of about 70 shots were fired until his entire body from neck to knees was peppered and burned with shallow, extremely painful wounds, including even his genitals, from which smoke from the burning gunpowder continued to rise well after they were finished shooting.

Simon Girty appealed to Pimoacan to end this torture and free Crawford and once more offered, in exchange for this favor, his horse, his possessions, his rifle, the $1,000 he carried and $2,000 more he could get. But Pimoacan continued to shake his head and, as the pleas continued, the chief finally became so aggravated that he whirled toward Girty with a savage expression, his words filled with malevolence.

"Silence! You keep begging—*say one more word!*—and I will make another stake to burn you!"

Girty fell silent and watched as a new torment was begun for Crawford. The Indians, men and women alike, gathered at the fire where slender hickory poles, each a dozen feet in length, had been laid across it and burned through in the middle, leaving six-foot lengths with one end still burning around a white-hot core. These were thrust at Crawford everywhere from neck to feet, sizzling as they poked into skin and flesh and blood. It seemed almost to be a contest among the tormentors to see where they could poke the burning end to cause the utmost pain, again his genitals being a favored target as well as his rectum, his nipples, navel, armpits. He circled in an attempt to get away, stumbling and falling as he went around the tree post as far as he could in one direction and then again in the other, but each time he scrambled back to his feet and moved on. He bore the torture with great fortitude, yet time and again he would moan in agony as a burning pole poked a previously untouched spot, and at length there were no more undamaged spots. His skin, first reddened and blistered, became blackened and curled into little charred crisps, exposing raw red flesh beneath.

Several squaws went to the fire with broad pieces of bark and scooped up quantities of the hot coals. These they carried up close to Crawford and heaved at him. Those that struck his body did little additional damage to him as they simply bounced off and fell to the ground. But on the ground they caused a new torment for him, as he soon was unable to step anywhere within his bounds without putting his bare feet down on glowing embers and hot ashes.

While this was occurring a small group of British traders showed up—men who dealt almost exclusively with the Delawares and who were held in high esteem by Pimoacan, Tarhe, Wingenund and other Delaware chiefs. Girty, the evening Crawford came to see him, had sent messages to these men at their posts at Lower Sandusky and on Mohican Creek, begging them to come and use their influence with the chiefs to save Crawford's life. Now they had come, as quickly as they had been able, but they saw at a glance that it was too late, and they shook their heads and did nothing to intervene; Col. Crawford was beyond help.

The torture continued past sunset and into the twilight, and at one point Col. Crawford glimpsed Simon Girty sitting close to Pimoacan and Wingenund, his features frozen in grim lines. He called loudly to him then.

"Girty! Girty! For God's sake, Girty, shoot me through the heart!"

Girty turned his head and saw Pimoacan and Wingenund staring at him, and then he looked back toward the colonel and called out, "I dare not, Crawford. They would burn me as well."

There was no response from the man being tortured, and it appeared he had not heard the reply. A moment later, unable to witness any more of this, Girty got to his feet and walked off without looking back.[585] Staring straight ahead, he paid no attention to the man he passed who was approaching the fire—a white man dressed like an Indian. It was his own brother James, who, after a curious glance after his older brother, continued forward and sat on the ground near where Simon had been seated.

The torture continued, but it was obvious now that Crawford was growing weaker. He tottered and shuffled, all the while still being poked with the burning poles, and finally he called out again.

"Girty, *please,* shoot me—kill me!"

James Girty looked at him with disgust for a moment and then grinned. "I can't, Crawford," he said. "Don't you see I ain't got my gun?" Then he turned and made some comment to the Indians seated behind him, and they all laughed loudly.[586]

Finally, after some two hours of intense agony, Crawford fell to the ground at the base of the tree post and lay still, only semiconscious. At this, Shabosh—Joseph—who had escaped the Moravian Massacre, leaped up from where he had been sitting as a spectator, rushed to the pole and scalped him. That, as well as the long moan that issued from the colonel's lips, delighted the spectators, who hooted and howled their approval, a sound that grew in volume when Joseph took the scalp over to Dr. Knight and held it before his eyes.

"This is your great captain!" he said, then slapped Knight repeatedly with it until the surgeon's own face was stained with the blood.

When Crawford continued lying there, face down in the deepening twilight, an old Cherokee woman who had lived many years with the Delawares picked up one of the broad pieces of bark and scooped up a mound of hot coals from the fire. These she carried to the recumbent colonel and heaped on both his back and his bare skull where his scalp had been. Again a deep prolonged moan rose from Crawford, and he struggled back to his feet and once more began shuffling around the tree post as the prodding with fire poles was resumed.

It was then that Knight's Shawnee guards forced him to his feet and led him away to Pimoacan's Town, where they were planning to stay the night at the Delaware chief's invitation. But as John Knight walked away, the grisly scene behind him remained all too clear in his mind, and he knew he would never entirely be free of that image.

Out of sight behind him, the same woman who had piled coals on the colonel now scooped up another heap of them and, returning to the tree post, scattered them thickly all over the ground to which he was confined. Amazingly, Crawford walked across them, his shuffling forcing some of the coals up onto his toes and arch, others under the soles of his feet, yet he showed no reaction. The prodding and poking with burning poles continued and, at last, just before nightfall, the shuffling stopped and the tortured man teetered in place for a moment, then fell heavily and did not move again, his ordeal ended.

Col. William Crawford was dead.[587]

At a gesture and some words from Wingenund, two warriors came forward and cut the bonds away. Then they grasped him by the ankles and dragged him to the fire, which had just been replenished with numerous sticks, branches and logs. Two other warriors came to help, and they pitched the body into the hottest part of the blaze. At this, a prolonged wild cheering erupted from the crowd.[588] The Indians then piled fresh firewood over the body until it was completely covered. Within minutes the fire had become a roaring conflagration. A dance began around the blaze, the dancers and spectators alike raising their voices in the repetitive, hypnotic chant of the scalp song that lasted far into the night:

"Aw-oh . . . Aw-oh . . . Aw-oh . . . Aw-oh . . ."

[June 12, 1782 — Wednesday]

Shortly after dawn Dr. Knight, who had finally fallen into a fitful sleep, was awakened by his Shawnee captors and told by one who could speak some English that he was to march with them today for the Shawnee capital, Wapatomica. The Shawnee who spoke to him was a husky man of about 30 named Tutelu, whose very expression told Knight that when they arrived there he would have to run the gauntlet and, if he survived that, soon after he would be burned at the stake.[589]

Before setting out, the Shawnees went to Pimoacan to thank him for his hospitality, but then the Delaware chief told them that their strength was still needed; other parties of Delawares, Shawnees and Wyandots were still ranging to the south and east as far as the Ohio River as they attempted to overtake and kill or capture whatever members of Crawford's army were still eluding them.[590] The Shawnees agreed to help. It was decided, however, to send the captive on without delay. Since Dr. Knight gave every appearance of being a weak man—neither a big man nor one who gave the least indication of being able to fight, much less attempt to escape—it was decided that Tutelu should be the one to take him back to Wapatomica.

Knight's hands were bound behind his back, and soon Tutelu was nudging the captive ahead of him along the trail. The warrior, however, unable to resist the opportunity, first took Knight back to the site of last night's prolonged execution. Forcing the captive to look at the ashes and pointing at the small residue of charred flesh and bone, Tutelu spoke in an ominous voice.

"That your captain," he said. "Big captain no more." He laughed and added, "Soon that be you."

[June 13, 1782 — Thursday]

It was in the forenoon today, 19 days since leaving Mingo Bottom, that the residue of Crawford's army arrived back at that initial rendezvous point under Col. David Williamson. They were overjoyed to find that a number of men, thought to have been lost, had arrived there the day before.

Carrying their most seriously wounded in horse litters and many of the men afoot, Williamson's force was a haggard, fear-ridden group who had been harried practically every step of the way by Indians in pursuit. The retreat had been very slow, and on some days they had not put more than ten miles behind them. The knowledge was always foremost in their minds that any who lagged behind would almost certainly be killed and scalped or captured and then tortured to death. This was emphasized when, hardly half a mile before reaching the river, two of the men in the rear guard had been shot at by Indians and one of them slightly grazed across the back of his hand by a ball. Worse yet, among those who were suddenly missing was Pvt. Thomas Mills, whose big gray gelding that had served him so well on this campaign had gone lame. He had paused to rest the animal and see what he could do for it, promising he would follow shortly and overtake them. He hadn't, and now he was feared dead or captured.

A strong body of sentries was ordered on patrol by Williamson as soon as the army stopped here on the banks of the Ohio. At the same time, the wounded were made as comfortable as possible, and as their wounds were carefully bathed with water from the river and clothing torn into strips to make fresh bandaging, Maj. John Rose swiftly wrote in his report to Gen. Irvine:

> *Those volunteers who marched from here under the command of Col. William Crawford, are this moment returned and re-crossing the Ohio with Col. William-son. . . . Several of them are in a dangerous condition, and want immediate assistance of which they have been deprived since the loss of Dr. Knight. . . . I am sorry to observe they did not meet with that success which so spirited an enterprise, and the heroic bravery of the great part deserved.*[591]

His concern over the absence of Dr. Knight to treat the wounded was eased somewhat, however, when a boat that put out from the Virginia shore arrived on the Ohio side and Dr. John Donathy stepped out. Word had already swept through the frontier about the disastrous defeat of Crawford's army, and when it reached Dr. Donathy, he had immediately taken his medical supplies downriver and waited on the Virginia side opposite Mingo Bottom for the return of the army.

Now, having crossed the river, his first concern was those in most desperate need of attention. Capt. Ezekiel Rose was one of them. Despite his pessimism about surviving his serious chest wound, he was still alive and convinced, during his lucid moments, that it was his recitation of The Lord's Prayer without an error that had pulled him through. A new trauma was in store for him now, however. The wound was dirty, clotted with old blood and gummy with debris that had stuck to it. With the evidence suggesting that more debris had been carried into the flesh, it was necessary to cleanse it at once to prevent infection.

Dr. Donathy called for a ramrod, and one was brought to him at once. From his kit he removed a fresh yard-square silk cloth and put the end of the ramrod to the middle of it, draping the remainder down its length. Then, with two men propping Capt. Rose up in a sitting position, he pushed the cloth into the bullet hole in the chest. Capt. Rose gasped but endured the new pain. The doctor pushed on the rod gently, gradually increasing pressure. Little by little the cloth-draped rod passed through the chest cavity until it began protruding from the hole in Rose's back. Gripping that end of the cloth firmly, Donathy now ordered a militiaman to carefully withdraw the ramrod. Again an extended gasp wheezed from Rose's mouth as the instrument was removed.

Gently, then, Dr. Donathy began pulling the fabric through. Rose groaned loudly, but the sound quickly died away. The first part of the cloth emerged dark with old clotted blood and some debris, but as more of it emerged, it became soaked with the bright red of new blood, which was precisely what the physician wanted. By the time the cloth was fully pulled through the hole, the wound was reasonably cleansed of foreign matter, and there was much less likelihood of complications. With compresses pressed against the wounds front and back, the doctor snugly wrapped the torso in bandaging. Then he squeezed the man's arm and grinned.

"You did very good, Captain Rose."

Rose did not reply. He had passed out from the pain.

The physician then moved on to treat others of the wounded, including Maj. James Brinton, Capts. James Munn, Joseph Bean and George Brown, Ens. James Collins, and Pvts. John Orr, John Walker and Joe Edgington. He assured all of them that they would survive their injuries.[592] There were some, however, he knew could not possibly recover.

Among the most seriously wounded was Pvt. John McDonald, who was in extreme pain from his broken thigh. When Pvt. Angus McCoy fetched Dr. Donathy to his side, the physician shook his head almost immediately upon seeing the wound, realizing at once that nothing could be done. The bullet had shattered his thigh bone very high, and the damage was massive. Worse yet, he had now developed gangrene and amputation was impossible.

Dr. Donathy shook his head again, murmured a few words of comfort and then moved on to tend others. Angus McCoy took McDonald's hand and squeezed it.

"Can you hear me, John? . . . John?"

"I . . . hear."

"Listen to me. I promise you, John, I'm going to get you home, and you're going to be alive when we get there. I swear it!"[593]

As soon as all the wounded were attended as best as was possible and the men and horses had rested somewhat, Col. Williamson called in the sentinels in preparation for the crossing of the Ohio River.[594] Within minutes the entire remainder of the defeated army was fording the great river.

The Crawford Campaign was over.[595]

Chapter 7

Now began the lying and the maneuvering for position in an uncertain future. Capt. John Hardin, having returned earlier with his men in an escape unheralded by any Indian attacks, let it be known in his official letter to Col. William Davies of the Virginia Board of War that it was through his own great skill as an officer and strategist that his company had survived the campaign. Subtly, very subtly, he planted the seed for himself to command any future undertaking against the tribes, writing in part:

> . . . *There seems to be a great spirit in general amongst the people for another campaign, which I am in hopes will have the desired effect.*

Col. David Williamson, too, began feathering his own nest by claiming victory snatched from the jaws of defeat. In his report of the campaign, undertaken today, he made it clear that Crawford had disappeared and that he, Williamson, had assumed command of the army, bringing it to safety. As he wrote to the commander of the Western Department:

> *I take this opportunity to make you acquainted with our retreat from San-dusky Plains, June 6th. We were reduced to the necessity of making a forced march through the enemy's lines in the night, much in disorder; but the main body marched round the Shawanese camp, and were lucky enough to escape their fire. They marched the whole night, and the next morning were reinforced by some companies, of which I can not give a particular account, as they were so irregular and so confused. . . .*

I must acknowledge myself ever obliged to Major Rose for his assistance, both in the field of action and in the camp. His character in our camp is estimable. . . .

During the twenty days of the campaign, each one, with a single exception, was a day of marching. Two battles were fought in the meantime and two victories won. The extrication of the army from the toils woven around it by a foe so much superior in numbers may be considered remarkable.

[June 14, 1782—Friday noon]

Lewis Wetzel had not been in favor of this present project from the beginning, and that feeling had grown in him throughout this entire morning. In all the years he had traveled these trails, he had never seen Indian sign so prevalent as it was now. He keenly regretted letting himself be swayed into taking on this fool's errand, and he regretted even more that he had decided to let the boy, Joshua Davis, come along with Tom Mills and himself.

It had all begun late last night, when Davis and Mills had shown up at his cabin and the latter had launched into his story. Though Wetzel had heard hearsay regarding the failure of Col. Crawford's Sandusky Campaign, he had talked to no one yet who had actually survived it, and so—mentally congratulating himself on having had sense enough not to have participated in it—he listened carefully as Mills briefly went over the details of the march, the battle near the Sandusky Towns, the panic that had swept through the army as the retreat began and the follow-up battle on the upper Olentangy.

Mills referred frequently to his big gray gelding, belonging to his father, that had served him so well in the campaign and that he had taken such pains to care for. When they were some 35 miles from the Ohio, he said, the gelding began going lame. He had checked the hoof on the leg being favored but could see nothing wrong with it. Nevertheless he was beginning to lag back from the main army, and apprehension had risen in him that both he and his horse would be taken. He had left the trail and stopped, well hidden in a glen to one side, to rest the horse for half an hour and then remount and catch up.

During that interval a party of some 60 Indians trailing the army passed by, and Thomas Mills had stood fearfully, his hand cupped over the gelding's nose so he would not snort and give away their presence. They hadn't been seen, and after the Indians passed, there was no further thought in Mills's mind about overtaking the army.[596]

He remounted and found the horse was no longer limping, and so he headed southwest and soon found a trail he had heard about heading southeast—the Wheeling Road, some of the border scouts had laughingly called it—that eventually hit the Ohio River opposite Wheeling. He followed that trail at a fast pace, faster than he should have, he admitted, in view of the gelding's recent lameness. Some 18 miles from Wheeling, approaching well-known Indian Springs, the jaded horse began limping again badly and simply gave out.[597]

Mills then made the decision that had ultimately brought him to see Lewis

Wetzel. He unsaddled the gelding and turned him loose to graze and wander, tying a small bell to the animal's neck to aid in recovering him. Then, hiding the saddle and gear he could not carry, he set out the remaining distance on foot, arriving at the Ohio at sunset and swimming across to Wheeling.

There he had rested at the Davis cabin, lamenting the loss of his father's horse and expressing his determination to go back and recover him. Fifteen-year-old Joshua Davis had volunteered to go along, and it was decided they needed someone more experienced than themselves in woods lore and Indian fighting to lead them. Lewis Wetzel was the natural choice, so, taking their rifles along, they went to his cabin at once.

Wetzel had at first rejected the idea, saying it was crazy, with all the Indians skulking about, to go into their territory to search for a horse, but Mills was insistent and gave Lewis a French crown as preliminary payment and the promise of three more when they returned, whether they had the gelding with them or not, and Wetzel gave in and agreed. He was dubious about Joshua Davis going with them, but Davis, a strongly built young man, was insistent, claiming he meant to join Brady's Rangers in a few years and needed the experience.

"Okay, you're in," Wetzel had said, grinning. Then he added to Mills, quite seriously, "Josh'll make a scout yet. He's got mettle."

Davis had long harbored a hero worship for Wetzel, so the praise pleased him more than any compliment he had ever before received, and he seemed to swell with pride.

This morning, then, they had left at first light, and Wetzel gave them one last chance to quit. "This is a dangerous thing we're settin' out on," he warned. "Iffen you boys don't back out now and call this off, be prepared to fight, 'cause chances are you're gonna have to."

They had elected to go on, and Wetzel had finally shrugged and led the way, crossing the Ohio by canoe at the point of Wheeling Island and striking up the so-called Wheeling Road trail as it moved westward along the ridge south of Indian Wheeling Creek. Depending on his companions to keep up—which they did, though with difficulty—Wetzel had moved rapidly but also listened carefully and studied the ground closely as they traveled.

Throughout the morning they progressed, and now, late in the forenoon, as the day was growing hot, they were approaching the spot where Thomas Mills had abandoned his horse. They came to Indian Springs, and young Mills was elated when Wetzel pointed out a fresh hoofprint, hardly an hour old, with a distinct V-cut apparent.

"That's him!" he chortled. "We oughta hear the bell pretty quick."

They followed at a swifter pace, and within about two miles more they heard the tinkle of the bell in the woods just off the trail ahead. At the same moment, Wetzel grunted in alarm as he encountered fresh Indian moccasin tracks atop those of the horse, obviously made only minutes before. Homing in on the sound of the bell, Mills abruptly broke into a run past Wetzel, ignoring his hissed warning to stop.

Instants later, a burst of gunfire came from ahead. Mills screamed, dropped his rifle and collapsed, holding his left leg, the femur broken by a heavy lead ball.[598] Wetzel himself felt searing pain as a ball creased his hip. Ahead of them some 50 yards, a dozen Delawares under a tall, lean warrior named Long Pine burst from cover and rushed toward them.[599]

Wetzel threw his rifle to his shoulder and fired, killing a Delaware running close to Long Pine. Behind him, Davis fired but no Indians fell. Mills had by now recovered his own rifle, and Wetzel yelled at him to shoot at them, his words garbled because of the extra lead balls he made a habit of carrying in his mouth, but Mills seemed paralyzed with fear and made no attempt to shoot.

"Go!" Wetzel shouted at Davis, standing ten yards behind, and instantly the boy, empty rifle still in hand, turned and fled. Wetzel, close at his heels, was already spilling gunpowder from his horn into the rifle barrel as he ran.[600] He glanced behind and saw the Indians reach Mills and instantly fell him with a tomahawk blow to the head. Four of the Delawares, including Long Pine, dropped their empty guns and continued to run, taking up the pursuit of Wetzel and Davis, confident the guns of the two fleeing whites were empty.

Wetzel, easily as swift a runner as Davis, lagged behind as he reloaded, letting Davis increase his lead and the Indians close the gap. When they got within a dozen yards, the Delawares screeching in anticipated triumph, Wetzel whirled and sent a ball through the chest of one, dropping him, then immediately rushed on, reloading.

The Indians paused momentarily at their companion, saw he was dead and shrieked in anguish and anger. Deciding the two guns that the whites had initially shot included the gun of the white they had tomahawked, they were now certain the enemy guns were empty and resumed pursuit with even greater vigor, rapidly closing the gap again between themselves and Wetzel.

With the powder and ball loaded, Wetzel turned the gun around, muzzle pointing back, to pour a charge in the pan. The Indians closed faster than he anticipated and he had no sooner finished than the rifle was nearly torn from his grasp by one of his pursuers, who overtook him with a burst of speed. They wrestled briefly for control of the gun, and with the two remaining Indians almost upon them, Wetzel jerked the gun toward himself so that the warrior's arms holding the barrel were stretched out in front, and in that instant Wetzel cocked the gun and pulled the trigger.

The blast of the gun drove the warrior back into Long Pine, who caught him as he fell, a hole spouting a fountain of blood at the base of his throat.[601] The other warrior leaped to the side to avoid them and briefly stumbled. Again Wetzel raced off, getting a 20-yard advantage before Long Pine and his fellow warrior resumed pursuit.

Wetzel was closing in on Davis, now only 40 yards ahead of him. The youth was tiring and Wetzel knew he couldn't last much longer. Rounding a bend in the trail and seeing another 100 yards ahead, Wetzel yelled at Davis.

"Josh! Soon as you clear that bend ahead, dive into cover and lie still. I'll come back."

Davis raised a hand without replying and a few moments later sped around the bend. A steep hill on the right offered no cover, but on the left was a drop-off densely grown with weeds and brush. Without pause he dove into it, clearing the weeds next to the trail so as to leave no trace and rolling downhill some 20 feet before stopping.

Even as he stopped, he heard Wetzel coming and then glimpsed him, again reloading, as he raced past.

A few moments later the two following Indians came up and, as they rounded the bend, Wetzel's rifle fired again and the warrior with Long Pine went down, a ball in his thigh. Long Pine stopped and shrieked in rage, shaking his fist after the rapidly disappearing Wetzel. He pursued no farther, fearful now of the man whose gun was never empty. Picking up his companion in his arms, he carried him back toward their fellows.[602]

Davis remained hidden for some ten minutes until, from the trail above, he heard Wetzel softly calling for him. He replied, telling Wetzel where he was hidden.

"C'mon out, Josh," Lewis said, "an' let's get the hell outta here 'fore they show up agin."[603]

[June 14, 1782 — Friday noon]

One hundred fifty miles due west of Mingo Bottom, just as the sun reached its highest, the Shawnee warrior Tutelu stopped abruptly as he spied a young tom turkey high in a nearby tree. Dr. Knight, a few paces behind, also stopped and watched as Tutelu raised his rifle, took careful aim and shot. The bird dropped and fell to the ground with a thump. The warrior gave a triumphant grunt, quickly reloaded, then ran to get the bird and brought it back. He had held up the bird and proudly pointed to where most of its head had been shot away.

"Good shot, me," he said. "Make fire. Cook. Eat."

Knight, who had eaten nothing but a single small piece of jerky at their camp last night, was very hungry, and he nodded, glad for the break. They were just over 25 miles from Wapatomica, and he followed the Shawnee as Tutelu moved on a short distance to a pretty glen in the woods on the edge of the Scioto River.[604] Here Tutelu dropped the bird, leaned his rifle against a tree and then turned and removed the pack from Knight's back. The surgeon gratefully sank to the ground.

Yesterday the Shawnee and his captive had traveled at an easy pace, walking only 15 miles from Pimoacan's Town before camping. The doctor had hoped to escape during the night, but Tutelu had remained much too watchful, and there had been no opportunity. So far today they had already covered ten miles, and Knight was exhausted. Though his hands were still bound behind him, Tutelu had forced him to carry the heavy backpack containing the Shawnee warrior's own meager food supplies as well as considerable loot taken from Americans killed at the battle and on the retreat. Tutelu himself had carried only his weapons—tomahawk, knife and a flintlock rifle, along with powderhorn and bullet pouch.

Now Tutelu, ordering Knight to stay where he was, set about gathering dry wood and tinder to make a cookfire. In a short while he came back close to his captive and dumped the wood on the ground. He made a little pile of the small handful of dry grasses and moss he had gathered and then squatted down with flint and steel to light the cookfire. Time and again he struck, and time and again the sparks flew, but the tinder stubbornly refused to ignite. Tutelu became progressively more exasperated.

"You people still don't know the first thing about fire-making with flint and steel, do you?" Dr. Knight said scornfully.

"Grass no good," Tutelu growled. "White man no do better."

"Of course I can do better," Knight said. He added, with a short laugh, "A little white boy could do better. Untie my hands, and I'll show you."

"If turn loose, you run," Tutelu said suspiciously.

"No, I promise I won't try to escape. Untie me, and I'll show you how to use flint and steel the right way."

"White man no do better," the warrior repeated, but he nodded, moved behind Knight and removed the cord that bound him. Knight came to his feet, rubbing his wrists and flexing his hands, but no sooner did Tutelu turn his back to return to the tinder pile than the surgeon stooped, snatched up a length of hard dry branch and slammed it hard across the side of the Shawnee's head. Tutelu staggered and almost went down, then turned to confront his attacker, one hand clasped to his temple, which was bleeding profusely. Knight, however, had scooped up the rifle and now had it pointed at the Shawnee's chest. Tutelu, still with one hand pressed against his temple and squalling loudly, raced off and vanished in the woods.

It was fortunate for Knight that he did. The surgeon, in his haste to cock the weapon, had broken the lock spring, and the flintlock was now worthless. Not yet realizing this, he grabbed up the pack and, still with the rifle in hand, plunged off into the woods in the opposite direction. He moved deviously for the first mile and then raced with all the speed he could muster straight away to the east. Finally, his strength failing, he found an advantageous spot from which to watch his back trail and sat gasping, a tree at his back and the gun in his lap, ready to pick off Tutelu if he should be following.

Some 25 miles away to the southwest, John Slover was still surviving, but his future remained uncertain. The fact that he knew many of the Shawnees personally and had been very popular with them during his six-year captivity had worked in his favor to some degree. He had been spared the gauntlet in Wapatomica, for which he was very grateful, especially after having witnessed the death of his companion, William Harrison, in his gauntlet run shortly after their arrival.

For the past three days Slover had been kept in the wegiwa of the Shawnee woman named Pahcotai Sisqui, whose husband had been killed the previous year in Kentucky. She had been attracted to Slover when he was a captive here and had mourned in her own private way when he had escaped. The following year she had married, and now, the widowed mother of a small son, she thought perhaps Slover might receive leniency and be reinstated in the tribe. If such were the case, it was possible that he could take the place of her husband.

That Pahcotai Sisqui was very concerned for John Slover's welfare was obvious. Aware that a passionate anger rode high in many of the young men of the tribe, she feared that a few of them might get together and take him from her and kill him before the council could even be held. Thus, whenever any of the men came near her wegiwa, she hid Slover under a pile of furs and was prepared to defend him, if necessary.

It had not been necessary and, at noon today, shortly after George Girty and a party of 40 Shawnees returned from the upper Sandusky, a crier ran through the village announcing that the council was being called and that the prisoner should be brought to the council house. Slover, unable to predict what was going to happen now, was brought to the big building by Pahcotai Sisqui, who was allowed to sit in on the proceedings.

As the council began and individuals spoke one after another, Slover's spirits sank. While a number of them spoke favorably in his behalf, by far the greater majority were speaking against him and calling for him to be condemned to death at the stake. For several hours the talks continued, and it was while they were still in progress that there was a disturbance outside. A boy rushed in and announced that the warrior Tutelu had returned and that the prisoner he had been escorting here had escaped. Deliberations were put in temporary abeyance, and Tutelu was summoned.

In a few minutes the warrior was standing before them. The back of his head, neck and back were stained with dried blood from his wound, and he was shame-faced and nervous over having lost his prisoner. As the assemblage listened carefully, he told them of escorting Dr. Knight to the point where he escaped.

"I shot a *peleo* out of a tree," he said truthfully, "and then gathered tinder and wood to build a fire and cook him. But the tinder was damp and would not catch fire when I sent sparks into it. The white doctor made fun of me for not being able to start it and said even a little white child could start it easily. I told him he could not do any better, but he said he could, and so I untied him to let him try, so I could laugh at him when he, too, failed."

The assemblage murmured in an approving manner, considering this to have been a reasonable thing to do. But now, as they turned their attention back to the speaker and the big room stilled, Tutelu continued, this time not quite so truthfully as before.

"Before I knew what was happening," he went on, "he grabbed up my gun and struck me over the head with it. I was knocked down, and he leaped on me and we fought. But he was a big man, strong and powerful and, because I was still dazed from where he hit me, he was getting the best of me. I managed to pull out my knife, and I stabbed him in the back and the stomach. He pulled away from me and ran off. He was a very tall man and could run like a deer, and I was still too dizzy to overtake him, so he got away."

Again the assemblage murmured their understanding, accepting the loss philo-sophically, but then a voice cried out, "He lies!" and all eyes turned to the speaker. It was John Slover.

"He lies!" Slover repeated, coming to his feet. "I know Doctor Knight. He is a little man, a weak man, and he could not have done the things that this man says."

Tutelu seemed about to argue the point, but then he shrugged and admitted that he had made a mistake and was ashamed to admit he had been outwitted by a tired little man.

The humor of such a situation struck the Indians, and a ripple of laughter grew into whoops and howls of merriment. After a few moments even Tutelu abashedly joined in and sat down to participate in the council.[605] Gradually the laughter died away, and the assemblage returned to the matter at hand.

There was little humor in what followed. Those who were in favor of leniency for Slover were overruled; had it just been a matter of Slover having once been their captive who had escaped, he might have gotten off, but he had compounded his crime by helping to lead an army of whites against the Indians for the avowed purpose of destroying them, and that was unforgivable. When the speeches were concluded and the vote taken, the overwhelming majority had agreed to death at the stake. The execution was to take place tonight at Mackachack, which had been rebuilt since its destruction by Benjamin Logan's army of Kentuckians three years before, but the march to Mackachack would take a detour en route to McKee's Town, where Slover would be forced to run a gauntlet. He was stripped naked, painted black as the mark of the *cutahotha*—condemned man—and escorted in this condition by George Girty and a strong guard of Shawnee warriors the two and a half miles northwest to McKee's Town.

The gauntlet run there, under skies that had become threatening with heavy clouds, was short, even though most of those escorting the captive participated in the line. Slover, somewhat bruised and bloodied, managed to get through without serious injury. Anxious to reach Mackachack before a storm could break out, the party immediately headed for that place, six miles south and a mile east.

Runners from Wapatomica had already reached Mackachack, and by the time the party with Slover arrived, in the early dusk amid the heavy rumbling of thunder, they found the painted stake erected and the fire burning nearby. The captive was immediately tethered to the post, but before the torture could begin, the skies opened up and a deluge of rain fell, extinguishing the fire and washing off most of the black with which he had been painted.

Slover was untied and led back to a wegiwa where he was to spend the night, the execution rescheduled for the morrow. He moved in a totally dejected manner, head hanging and limbs seeming to fail him so badly, he could hardly walk, and he had to be aided to the wegiwa. None of his captors, however, noticed that his eyes remained alert, and his gaze took in every aspect of the quarters to which he had been taken. He moved mechanically to the mat where he was told he would spend the night and dropped to it with a pitiable groan and lay there on his back, making no protest when his ankles were bound. When told to hold his hands out so they, too, could be tied, he held them out, palms together, but he braced the heels of his hands against each other to allow a gap as the rope was snugged.

John Slover had escaped from the Shawnees once before and, if there was any humanly possible way to do it again, he was prepared to snatch whatever final opportunity this night might offer.

[*J u n e   1 5 ,   1 7 8 2 — S a t u r d a y*]

The storm lasted until almost midnight, with great searing bursts of lightning and tremendous cracks of thunder. When it finally passed, John Slover, who had been feigning sleep for several hours, continued to work at loosening his bonds. His heart had sunk when two warriors were posted inside the wegiwa, one on each side of him, to keep watch and prevent any escape attempt. They talked in undertones, but Slover heard them agree to take turns napping, and his spirits rose.

One of the guards fell asleep quickly, and the other sat near the small fire, watching the prisoner. It was probably more than an hour after midnight before Slover saw, through slitted eyes, the remaining guard's head nodding as he fought to stay awake. At last that guard, too, dozed off, and Slover concentrated all his energies on getting loose. The gap he had held between his wrists, now that he closed it, relaxed the bonds somewhat—enough that when he brought his hands up to his face, he was able to get his teeth substantially on the cord. The knot was drawn too tight for him to hope to pull it free, so he set about gnawing on the cord.

He nipped and chewed at the rope until his jaws ached, but he gradually made progress as, fiber by fiber, it slowly frayed. Some four hours later the rope was finally bitten through and fell free. Drawing up his knees, he worked on the ankle cord with greater facility and in only a few minutes had it untied. With considerable care and maintaining utter silence, he came to his feet. He briefly considered snatching up the guard's gun and braining him with it, but he feared the other guard would awaken and call out to alert others. In the end, one careful step at a time, he eased his way to the portal and slipped out into the night.

Dawn, he knew, could only be a short time off. Keeping to the darkest shadows, he slipped from wegiwa to wegiwa until at last he encountered what he sought—a tethered horse. His hands, moving gently over the rump and flanks, told him it was bony and probably in bad shape, but he had no other choice. He swiftly untied it and then leaped to its back, but the horse snorted loudly. Discarding further silence and caution, he kneed the mount into a run and galloped through the remainder of the town, heading toward the lightening sky to the east.

Behind him he heard voices calling loudly, and knew he would soon be pursued. He headed through the prairie toward a distant grove silhouetted against the dawn-streaked horizon, kicking the horse into the fastest possible pace. In a short time, however, he felt the animal weakening, and he knew it could not last much longer. As he entered the woodland, he glanced back and saw several riders coming hard after him.

The horse stumbled a time or two going through the narrow grove, but emerged from the opposite side still running. Slover had gone only a few hundred yards in this particular prairie when two riders emerged from the woodland behind and two more appeared rounding the far end of the grove and angling to cut him off. His heart sank as he now saw they had dogs running with them to trail him. He urged his rapidly flagging horse to greater exertion, and the animal was gasping and panting as it came to a deep erosion cut through the prairie, a gap some 20 feet across and with sheer sides seven or eight feet high.

Leaping from the horse's back, he jumped down into the cut, thankful for the soft earth he alighted on with his bare feet. Now in the erosion channel, however, he found that the opposite side offered no foothold for scaling it, and he began running up its crooked course. At last he came to where a large bush at the lip of the ravine had toppled over into it but was still anchored above by a few roots. He got a handhold on it and scrambled up the far side, just as the four pursuers leaped from their own horses and into the ravine some 50 yards distant.

Two emerged from the erosion cut behind him but no more, and Slover could only assume that the bush had pulled free as the third tried to use it and toppled him back to the bottom. So far as he could tell, none of the dogs had been able to make it across the erosion cut, but he decided he would not count on it. The two warriors who had emerged from the deep ditch raced after him through the prairie grass, and now they had a distinct advantage. Their feet were clad in moccasins, while his own were bare. But fear added strength to Slover's run, and he gradually increased the gap between them. He headed for another distant grove and was an eighth of a mile ahead of them by the time he reached it.

Now his wilderness abilities came to the fore, and he used a variety of wiles to make it difficult for them to follow, backtracking short distances and leaping off in another direction, running atop the surface of fallen trees, changing direction often. A small stream ran through the woods and, just in case the dogs were still after him, he ran upstream in the water for a considerable distance. When he emerged at the edge of the woodland, he ran to one of three smaller groves nearby and vanished into it before the pursuers emerged from the one he had just left, and without further elusive tactics, he raced through it and out the eastern side.

He encountered another erosion cut, only four or five feet deep, and he entered it and raced along its course in a bent-over position for some 600 yards before coming to a stop and cautiously peering over the rim. Far behind he saw the two emerge from the trees and then stop, looking about in apparent confusion. No dogs were with them and, after a few minutes, obviously exasperated, they turned around and headed back.

It was still a long way back to the settlements for a man naked and unarmed, but he knew the wilderness well, and was quite confident he would survive and make it home eventually. John Slover had won.[606]

[*June 23, 1782 — Sunday*]

Michael Myers, having successfully escaped the Indians and arrived back at the settlements, considered the present state of unrest in the border country to be a blessing in disguise. Yesterday, not much more than a week after returning from the campaign, he and his brother, George, decided that with the Indians still busy chasing down stragglers of the campaign and gloating in their villages over their victory, this would be an ideal time to claim some land across the river in the Ohio country. It wasn't.

[*July 5, 1782 — Friday*]

An electric tension gripped Pittsburgh today, its nucleus at Fort Pitt in the form of the man carried into the installation just before noon. He had arrived by boat from Fort McIntosh under the protection of a squad of soldiers, and his identity—and bits and pieces of his story—was quickly known to everyone.

He was Dr. John Knight.

Early yesterday, so the news was passed, he had been discovered in the woods by a party of hunters west of the Ohio River above Wheeling and below Indian Cross Creek. His clothing—or what was left of it—was in tatters, his shoes gone, his feet badly cut and bruised, his chest laced with a latticework of deep scratches from brambles through which he had fought his way, his skin a multitude of insect bites, his general condition deplorable. In a state of near starvation, emaciated and utterly exhausted both physically and mentally, he was barely coherent when found. It took him some while to comprehend that the men who had found him were settlers and that, after three weeks of walking through the wilderness following his escape, beset by the demons of his imagination, he had finally reached safety. When the full realization came to him at last, he collapsed and wept.

He was taken to Fort McIntosh and there was bathed, fed and given clothing, and in little bursts of conversation his story unfolded. He had been captured after the Battle of Sandusky. Sentenced to death at the stake, he was being taken to the Shawnee capital of Wapatomica when he managed to escape from his warrior guard. The guard's flintlock, which he had managed to take, had proven worthless, and he had finally thrown it away. Without a gun to bring down game, without a tomahawk or even a knife, he was able to find precious little to eat; a few green gooseberries here and there, a few unrolled fern fronds, the tender tops of nettles, some green May apples, a terrapin he caught in a creek and broke open on a rock and devoured raw. He had caught a newt and several crawfish when he turned over rocks in the edge of a stream; those he had eaten raw as well. His big meal during those three weeks was when he found the nest of a catbird with three hatchlings in it. He had taken them all, but, at the frantic behavior of the mother bird, he had put one back, which seemed to satisfy her, and he had eaten the other two, again raw.

All these elements of the Knight story were fascinating and evoked wonder and sympathy and praise. What overshadowed everything else by far, however, creating a great depth of sorrow and fever of passionate anger, was his relation of the gruesome, prolonged death of Col. William Crawford; all on the frontier knew him, all respected him and most were genuinely fond of him.

One who heard fragments of Knight's tale through hearsay was a lawyer relatively new to Pittsburgh, having arrived here only the year before. A Scot by birth, he had immigrated to North America in 1753 and lived in Philadelphia for a time, working as a schoolteacher. At intervals he wrote plays that never gained much recognition, satires that fell flat and essays that were essentially either pointless or displayed an unmitigated hatred for Indians. Though he had never met any Indians personally, he considered them loathsome creatures and seemed incapable of writing about them without abundant use of the word *savage*. Not having gained his expected renown in any of these fields, he finally became a magazine publisher, guaranteeing that at least some of his writings would be seen by eyes other than his own.

His background, according to an ungenerous few in his circle of acquaintances, was an apt foundation for his next career step—studying law in Maryland. It was shortly after becoming a lawyer that he came to Pittsburgh, a town that in recent years had become a very litigious place, due to the many land disputes being filed. It was a place, perhaps, where a smart—or crafty—lawyer might make his fortune. He had not yet made that fortune in the year since coming here, but he had more deeply established a virulent dislike for Indians generally, for the British who used them against the Americans and, most pertinently, for the renegade Simon Girty, who had long lived in the Pittsburgh area; the man who had turned his back on his own people and gone over to the British and Indians.

Now, as he heard the stories going the rounds and saw the reaction of the border people to what they conceived as the heroism of Dr. Knight and the anger and depression caused by the news of the execution of their beloved Col. Crawford, he quickly realized that there was probably no better way to become more noted here and elsewhere than by becoming actively involved in the matter. He meant to show the Indians in the worst possible manner, highlighting their savagery and ignoring anything that might mitigate what they had done—such as the unspeakable massacre of the Moravian Indians, for which they sought vengeance—or anything that might display honestly, if not sympathetically, their motives for opposing the encroachment of the whites. And as a focal point toward which the reader might direct his rage, he meant to ignore anything showing Simon Girty as possessing any degree of compassion—such as the multitude of times he had saved captives from death and befriended them in many ways, or the manner in which he had tried to assist Crawford during that ordeal, even to the point of putting his own life in jeopardy on the colonel's behalf. He was determined to portray Simon Girty, deliberately and with calculated maliciousness, as the most despicable and detestable renegade who ever existed on the American frontier.

It was with this idea in mind that the lawyer acted swiftly to present to the American people the story of Dr. Knight and Col. Crawford . . . and Simon Girty. He now presented himself at the bedside of Dr. John Knight, armed with paper and pens and ink, and introduced himself with a disarming smile.

"Doctor Knight," he said, "I am a writer and publisher, and I would like to have you dictate to me, so I can prepare it for publication under your name, your narrative of the fullest possible details of the ordeal suffered by you and Colonel Crawford. My name, incidentally, is Hugh Henry Brackenridge."[607]

[J u l y   2 2,   1 7 8 2 — M o n d a y]

As a result of the disastrous Sandusky Campaign, 34-year-old Col. Ebenezer Zane, now commanding Fort Henry in Wheeling, had become very apprehensive about the safety of Wheeling in general and his own family in particular.[608]

The sharp increase in attacks by the Indians since the campaign, along with the sighting of several Indians moving about stealthily across the Ohio, had convinced him that the Indians, perhaps the British as well, were preparing to make another major strike against Wheeling, similar to the one they had made five years ago, and he felt it imperative to be as prepared as possible for that eventuality. If such an attack did occur, it could well wipe them out, as the settlement was now very weak. Gen. Irvine had recalled all the regulars from Fort Henry, and only a small handful of militia remained under Zane's command to defend this largest settlement beyond Pittsburgh.

Fortunately, they still had the old French swivel that Lt. Matthew Neely had left behind when he was recently reassigned from his command here at Fort Henry. But what was so distressing at the moment was the great lack of gunpowder. Soon after the return of the defeated Crawford army, Col. Zane had sent a requisition to Gen. Irvine at Fort Pitt to replenish his stock, and Irvine returned a dispatch directing him to draw the quantity he desired from the supply that had just been forwarded to Col. Marshall opposite Mingo Bottom. Zane had immediately gone there for it, only to find that the gunpowder Marshall had received was already spoken for.

Now Col. Zane sat down at his small desk and wrote to Gen. Irvine once again in swift, sure strokes:

Wheeling, July 22, 1782

Sir: I applied to Colonel Marshall for powder to furnish this garrison of that you have sent to Mingo bottom. He tells me it is already issued to the militia, which lays us under the necessity of applying once more to you for 30–40 pounds. Any powder you may now furnish for the use of this garrison I will undertake to account for and replace if not burnt at the enemy.

Five militia are all the strength we have at present, excepting the inhabitants of the place. A few Indians have been viewing our garrison yesterday and have returned on their backtrack, in consequence of which, we may shortly expect an attack. If any aid can be afforded, it will be very acceptable; if it cannot, we mean to support the place or perish in the attempt.

I am, with due respect, your obedient, humble servant,

Ebenezer Zane
William Irvine, Brigadier General, Commanding Western Department,
Fort Pitt.

[July 30, 1782 — Tuesday]

Tom Mills, Sr., father of the young man who had been killed by the Indians just 16 days ago, was having a difficult time shaking off the depression that had settled over him then. While his son's determination to recover the big gray gelding that belonged to his father was understandable and something the senior Mills admitted he would probably have done too, it had not been worth sacrificing his life. But Thomas Mills, Jr., like his father, had been a bullheaded young man who often acted on impulse and ignored the possible consequences. As a result, he had paid the price. Now the elder Tom Mills, having lost his son, his horse and his fine saddle, remained plagued by a depression that wouldn't let go.

Realizing that he needed to do something to get his mind off the tragedy, Mills turned to his favorite pastime, fishing. An inveterate angler, he fished the Ohio River and its tributaries with great frequency, usually did very well and often sold his catch of bass, pike, muskellunge and catfish to other residents of the Wheeling area. Lately he had been pitting himself against a huge catfish that on three occasions had thwarted him over the past few months.

Mills had first become aware of the big yellow catfish—a shovelhead, he called it —last April, when he paddled his canoe into the mouth of Glen's Run, four miles above Wheeling on the Ohio side of the river. The water was clear, and he had baited his hook with a walnut-size hunk of rancid deer liver and flipped it with his cane fishing pole into the water beside a large submerged log just a short distance up from the stream's mouth.[609] He had watched, amazed, as what seemed to be a section of the log disengaged itself from the shadows and swam to the bait. Though Mills had caught many shovelheads up to 30 pounds and two that had tipped the scale in Wheeling at 40 pounds, this fish appeared to be at least twice that large. Nonchalantly, the catfish had opened its mouth and virtually inhaled the bait.

Tom Mills had jerked on his pole to set the hook and momentarily felt the awesome power of the fish before the pole shattered at midpoint. Then the strong line had broken close to the hook. A week or so later Mills had gone back with a sturdier line and pole, and virtually the same scenario was repeated. About a month ago, while his son was off on the Sandusky Campaign, he had tried again, this time relinquishing the use of a pole and tying the line to his canoe, but he lost the fish again when, after being hooked, it thrashed and fought so hard against the weight of the boat that the hook straightened and jerked free.

So now, just after dawn on this beautifully clear day, Tom Mills was heading for Glen's Run again, this time confident that, with changed tactics, he was going to get the fish that had become something of a personal challenge. Instead of hook, line and pole, he was armed this time with a gig he had fashioned from a three-tined pitchfork, the tines straightened and strong sharp barbs forged at their tips.

The whole Wheeling community knew by now of Mills's contest with the big fish, and while all were hoping he would be successful this time, a few were concerned about his setting out on the river when so many Indians were still hovering about. Tom Mills, a big, self-confident man, was not overly concerned, but he did agree to take a couple of young men along with him, though more to help in getting the big catfish than as defenders. The mouth of Glen's Run was off the beaten path, and he doubted that Indians would trouble him there. The two young men, both 18, were Henry Smith and Hamilton Carr, the latter still not fully recovered from the broken right arm he had suffered when shot by Indians on the hunt with the Wetzels at the end of April, when George Wetzel had been killed. All three had their flint-locks with them.[610]

Arriving just after sunrise at the mouth of Glen's Run, Mills outlined his strategy to his two companions. While Carr, in the stern, poled the broad oversize canoe quietly toward the spot where the big catfish lurked in water five feet deep, Mills would stand in the bow, arm cocked to thrust the gig as soon as they were near enough to their quarry. Smith, close behind him, would hold the rope attached to the butt end of the spear, to contain the fish if the gig were jerked out of Mills's grasp. Even if that didn't happen, it would take the combined efforts of the two to haul the huge fish into the boat.

The plan worked well. With Mills standing in the bow and Smith crouched close behind, the canoe slid quietly toward the submerged log. Abruptly Mills lunged, thrusting the gig with all his strength and making a perfect strike, all three barbs penetrating deeply into the fish just behind its head. The water erupted in violent splashing, and the three men shouted triumphantly and yelled advice to one another as the fight was waged.

The struggles of the fish carried them back to the creek's mouth and into the Ohio some 20 feet from shore, the canoe twice taking on water as the shifting weight of the men nearly capsized it. The barbs, however, had penetrated deeply, severely wounding the fish, and it soon weakened. In a few moments more, chortling with glee, Mills and Smith got their quarry to the side of the boat and, with combined effort, slid the huge brownish-yellow fish over the gunwale and into the bottom of the canoe, where it continued to flop and slosh about weakly in the accumulated two or three inches of water. All three of their rifles, now useless, were also in that water.

The men were still laughing and congratulating one another when the shots broke out. A party of about 30 Wyandots, attracted by the splashing and excited yelling, had crept up and fired from hiding at a distance of about 40 yards. Both Mills and Smith were hit. The latter, bleeding from multiple wounds, fell into the bottom of the canoe, groaning and trying to keep his nose and mouth out of the water. Smith had been struck by a single ball that creased his groin and, squalling with pain and fear, he leaped into the river away from the Indians and quickly grasped the side of the canoe.

The Indians burst out of cover shrieking, throwing down their guns and jerking out their tomahawks as they raced to the shore. Unharmed in the stern, Hamilton Carr shoved with his pole to get them away from the shore, though hampered by the weight of Smith hanging on. He shouted at Smith to get back in or let go, and Smith hoisted himself back aboard, the canoe nearly capsizing and shipping more water as he did so. But now, with another thrust of the pole, Carr managed to get them out into deeper water and swifter current. Mills, bleeding badly, struggled to his knees with his hands braced on the opposing gunwales.

By this time the Indians had surged back to shore, snatched up their guns and were reloading. The moment they resumed shooting, Smith once again jumped out of the boat and, as before, grasped the side. Mills grunted, struck by more bullets, and again fell into the bottom of the canoe. Carr, miraculously still unscathed, now dropped the pole into the boat, snatched up a paddle and began using it.

"Head for the other side!" Smith screamed. "Tom's done for. We'll leave him there. We'll have a better chance on shore."

"We're not leavin' anybody!" Carr snapped. "Either get in or let go."

Once more Smith clambered aboard, again nearly capsizing them. Scattered shots were still being fired but were going wide of their mark as the current and paddling moved the boat farther away. Sixteen more Wyandots appeared on the Virginia shore where Smith had wanted to land, and they began taking long shots, but none had effect. They also fired, at even longer range, at a canoe being paddled by Andrew Zane and James Fulton. Those two, heading upstream to fish, had been attracted by the struggles with the big catfish and had headed in that direction, but had turned back when the firing broke out. Now, with shots coming at them from both the Ohio and Virginia shores, they paddled furiously downstream to warn the residents of Wheeling. Those settlers who were presently on Wheeling Island, alerted to the imminent danger, immediately crossed back to Wheeling and took refuge in Fort Henry.

Crying, moaning and holding his crotch, Smith made far more of a fuss over his slight flesh wound than Mills was making over his many wounds, some of which appeared serious. The canoe was a quarter filled with water now and very sluggish in the water, but Smith refused to help with the paddling, claiming his side hurt too much.

"Then for God's sakes, Henry," Carr said disgustedly, "at least hold Tom's head up out of the water so he won't drown in the bottom of the damn boat!"

Wheeling was undergoing a flurry of activity when they got there: People were running to the fort carrying guns, food and cherished possessions while other men climbed into the two blockhouses and onto the swivel platform. The canoe was seen approaching, and a crowd met them on shore and carried the semiconscious Tom Mills, nearly dead as much from drowning as from loss of blood, to the quarters of Elizabeth Zane. Shooing out everyone except two women to help her, she ordered Mills stripped and then, one by one, tended his bullet wounds—17 of them, plus two slight grazes. That he was alive at all was nothing short of a small miracle. Bullets had pierced both arms at different places and broken one of them below the elbow. Both legs had been hit several times, the right one most seriously, as one ball had entered above the knee and shattered the bone. He had been struck in the fleshy part of both hips, and a single ball had passed through both buttocks as he kneeled in the canoe. He had also been wounded in the right side, the right shoulder twice and the inner thigh.

Had he been taken to a military surgeon, Tom Mills would almost certainly have had both his arm and leg amputated, but Elizabeth Zane could only treat him as best she knew how. Fortunately for him, he fell unconscious as she probed and cleansed the wounds, used a straight razor to remove the misshapen lead balls that had lodged in him, applied medicated salves and poultices of pulverized slippery elm bark and jimpson weed and then bandaged each wound. Mills did not regain his senses until an hour after she was finished. She thought his first question when he aroused would be whether he was going to live. It was not. Neither did he inquire if his companions were all right, or if the Indians were attacking Wheeling.

"Mrs. Zane," he asked, "how much did that damned catfish weigh?"

Elizabeth burst into a hearty peal of laughter and admitted that she didn't know but would certainly find out. She left and returned ten minutes later, smiling broadly.

"Eighty-seven pounds."

"Almost makes it worth it all," he murmured, lapsing again into unconsciousness.[611]

At this moment, about 12 miles upstream from Wheeling and nearly two miles above Vanmetre's Fort at the mouth of Short Creek, Elizabeth Zane's brothers, Samuel and John McCulloch, having spent the previous night at Holliday's Cove Fort, were coming back to Vanmetre's, where Samuel had commanded before losing his left arm last November and where John McCulloch commanded now. Unaware that any trouble had occurred a few miles downstream, they rode casually, alert for Indian sign, as always, but in no way alarmed.

Maj. Sam McCulloch, riding as he always did these days, with his rifle cradled in the crook of his right arm and the reins in his right hand, was in the lead on the narrow trail, preceding John by seven or eight yards. With no warning whatever, a rifle cracked from behind, and the ball, aimed at John, missed him and his horse and slammed into Sam, ripping through his kidneys and killing him. He fell to the ground and never moved.

John immediately put his horse into a gallop, Sam's horse following close behind. After a moment he looked back and saw a warrior burst from cover, run to Sam's body and begin to scalp him. With an oath he reined up, drew a bead on the scalper and killed him with a fine shot, just as a horde of other warriors emerged from the woods. The other Indians raised their guns to fire at him, but he put his horse into a gallop again, and the balls from at least six shots merely ripped through the nearby foliage, doing him no harm.[612]

Defensive measures were instituted as soon as he reached Vanmetre's, and they waited for the attack, but it did not come. At sunset vigilance was relaxed a little, and McCulloch led a party back to the scene. They found Sam where he had fallen but, except for a quantity of blood, no sign of the Indian who had been killed by John. Not unexpectedly, Sam had been scalped, but the Indians had also paid him a gruesome tribute: They had cut his heart out and taken it away with them, no doubt to eat it and gain for themselves the courage of an enemy they had long feared and respected.

Sam McCulloch's body was taken back to Vanmetre's and, as neighbors comforted his widow, Mary, he was buried in the small graveyard there.[613]

[August 2, 1782—Friday]

Simon Girty stood before the council fire at Chalahgawtha to address the nearly 1,000 Indians who had assembled for one of the largest grand congresses of the confederated tribes of the Northwest heretofore held. Here, in what had long been the heart of the Shawnee nation and its largest and most important village, were gathered contingents of Iroquois and Mingo warriors under Thayendanegea—Joseph Brant—and Wyandots under Monakaduto and Tarhe—Half King and The Crane. Here, too, were the contingents of Miamis and their Wabash River subtribes: the Weas, Ouiatenons, Piankeshaws, Eel Rivers and Mississinewas under Michikiniqua— Little Turtle. The large party of Delawares in attendance was represented by Buckangehela, Wingenund and Pimoacan. Smaller representative groups of Chippewas, Ottawas and Potawatomies were also on hand, and even a few Kickapoos and Sacs. Most important, the Shawnees, as host tribe of this council, were represented by their finest war chiefs, Shemeneto and Wehyehpihehrsehnwah—Black Snake and Blue Jacket—as well as the 90-year-old Chief Moluntha and the present Shawnee principal chief, Catahecassa—Black Hoof.

All 950 who assembled were aware of—and many had participated in—the recent defeat of the Americans on the Sandusky Plains, and an aura of high exultation prevailed among them. Shortly after the battles near Half King's Town and on the upper Olentangy, runners had been sent to the various northwestern tribes inviting them to this congress. Simon Girty himself, aware of the contingent of 50 redcoated British regulars under Capt. William Caldwell and the many Iroquois and Mingoes under Thayendanegea and Alexander McKee, presently en route from Detroit to strike Wheeling, had ridden hard and intercepted them near the mouth of the Cuyahoga and had convinced them to divert from their course and attend this grand council.

Now, in an impassioned speech, Girty proposed a major invasion of Kentucky, targeting two of the principal Kentucky settlements within six miles of one another —Bryan's Station and Lexington. To go ahead with the planned strike against Wheeling at this time, he told them, was apt to be a mistake; Col. Williamson had returned to the upper Ohio with the residue of the American army, and now the whole frontier there was alert and in arms, prepared to meet the invasion they were convinced was coming. To attack when those forts were expecting it and were well prepared for defense, Girty argued, was simply too great a risk.

No other strategy had worked so well against the Americans in the past as the well-planned ambush, Girty went on. What he proposed now was a stronger and better-laid-out ambush than had ever before been perpetrated. Well over half the mounted force, armed with rifles and tomahawks, would secretly move into position in the most advantageous spot for an ambush at the Blue Licks. The remainder would move against Bryan's Station, which, Girty had learned from a Kentucky captive a few weeks ago, was weak in manpower and munitions.[614] They would surreptitiously observe the station until two or three people were outside the little fort's gates before attacking. They would deliberately allow those few to escape so they could alert the men at the next nearest station, Lexington, which was strongly manned at this time. There was no doubt those at Lexington would immediately mount a good-size force to come to the aid of Bryan's. If this rescue force was small enough, they could simply waylay it before it reached the beleaguered station. But if, as anticipated, it was too large for that—which they would learn from their spies as soon as the force was on the move—no early attack would be made, and the force that was striking Bryan's would retreat toward the Blue Licks. The value of the plan, Girty stressed, was that the force attacking Bryan's and then retreating would be so large that the whites would not be able to conceive that even more than that number would be waiting in ambush at Blue Licks. The retreating Indians, allowing themselves to be closely pursued, would lead the Kentuckians directly into the jaws of the ambush. At that point, Girty said, his voice rising as he jerked out his tomahawk and slashed it through the air, they would spring their trap and annihilate the Kentuckians.

The howls of approval, spontaneous war cries and breaking out of the war dance were confirmation of the acceptance of Girty's plan. Capt. William Caldwell was both surprised and disgruntled that the Indians now selected Girty as leader of the proposed Kentucky invasion, the role Caldwell had intended for himself.

There was but one significant amendment to the plan: Not all the Indians here assembled would be used in the Kentucky invasion. Six hundred would proceed with

Girty and Caldwell to accomplish the strategy the Indian agent had outlined; the remaining 360, under McKee and Thayendanegea, along with 40 Queen's Rangers under Capt. John Pratt and accompanied by George Girty, would lead a strike against Wheeling.

[September 10, 1782—Tuesday]

It was this evening, as the force of Indians that had massed near the Ohio River were in their camp preparing for the strike against Wheeling, when a pair of runners arrived from Chalahgawtha with word of the smashing success of Simon Girty's invasion into Kentucky and the subsequent ambush at Blue Licks.

They listened closely and became increasingly excited as the runners related the details. The force of 600 Indians had crossed the Ohio and reached the Blue Licks on the Licking River undetected. There the majority of the force, 350 warriors, had positioned themselves for the ambush while the remaining 250, including Capt. William Caldwell and his 50 redcoats, went on and fiercely attacked Bryan's Station. The presence of the British with the attackers, as Girty had anticipated, helped convince the Kentuckians that this was the whole attacking force. Indian spies watched as the two whites they allowed to escape fled to Lexington and raised the alarm. First a party of 50 men, including ten who had arrived from Boonesboro, galloped to Bryan's in an attempt to provide relief for the besieged station, but they

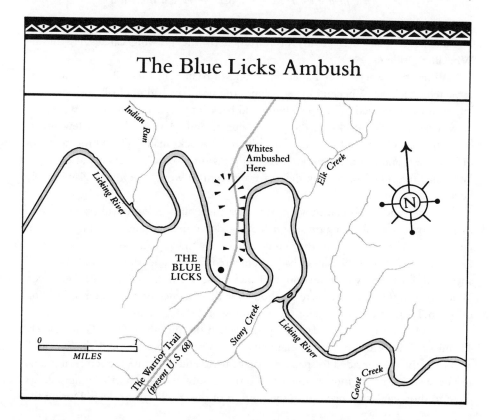

The Blue Licks Ambush

were quickly beaten off and retreated to Lexington with word that a greater force would be necessary to drive off the Indians.

The Indian spies who followed them quickly brought back word that reinforcements had arrived at Lexington, and a mounted force of some 200 had quickly formed and were on the way. At this intelligence, Girty ordered the attackers to mount up, and they headed directly for the Blue Licks, making no effort to hide their trail. The pursuing whites were not far behind and, when the trail of the party they were following crossed the Licking and continued past the Blue Licks and up a ravine on the other side, they followed. Girty's ambush was sprung with devastating success. Seventy-two of the Kentuckians were killed, and the rest fled in panic. Only three Indians were killed and four others slightly wounded. Taking scalps, weapons, horses and other plunder, Girty's force then returned in triumph to Chalahgawtha.[615]

All this was electrifying news, adding to the exhilaration that already existed among them at the successes recently achieved by the 100 warriors from this party who had broken into smaller war parties since their arrival here to maraud among the settlements. Now these remaining 260 Indians under Alexander McKee and Thayendanegea set about painting their faces, preparing their weapons and vowing among themselves to make their assault against Wheeling as successful as Simon Girty's had been against the Kentuckians.

[S e p t e m b e r   1 1 ,   1 7 8 2 — W e d n e s d a y]

Ebenezer Zane was greatly disheartened by the growing carelessness of the Wheeling residents.

When two weeks passed after the killing of Maj. Sam McCulloch without the expected attack on Wheeling materializing, the residents had gradually begun moving out of the protection of Fort Henry and back into their houses. They were now convinced that the attacks on the catfish giggers and McCulloch and a few others since then, had been nothing more than the usual attacks made by small roving bands of marauders and did not signify that a major assault against Wheeling was pending. What had transpired since then did not even seem to worry them, and Zane firmly believed it should.

As the residents began moving back into their houses, Zane had asked for two men to go on a small spying mission in a canoe down the Virginia side of the Ohio as far as Grave Creek and see if they could detect any unusual sign of Indian presence. Jacob Hefler and John Neisinger had volunteered for the undertaking, and Zane had suggested, for their own protection, that they dress like Indians and paint their faces. When they returned, they were to shout out their names first, so the sentinels on duty would not think they were the real thing and shoot them.

Starting out late in the day, the pair reached the mouth of Little Grave Creek, 11 miles below Wheeling, just at nightfall. Since it was becoming too dark to see well anymore, the pair decided to spend the night there and continue the remaining mile to Grave Creek in the morning. They tied their canoe to some overhanging willows close to shore and stretched out in the bottom of the small craft to sleep. During the night Hefler was awakened by a noise and a jostling of the canoe, just in time to see Neisinger killed with a tomahawk blow. Four or five Indians had silently waded out to the canoe, and now they turned their attention to Hefler, who in the darkness, snatched for his gun and grabbed a paddle instead. Using it as a club, he swung it wildly to and fro, knocking three or four of the Indians away, but then one warrior swung his tomahawk and knocked the paddle out of Hefler's grip, cutting off two fingers of one hand in the process.

Hefler, unable to swim, nevertheless leaped into the water and crawled along the bottom until he was close to shore before slowly rising. He was underneath the willows, unseen in the darkness. The Indians, believing he was swimming underwater and would soon rise some distance out and start swimming away, waited and listened, prepared to pursue him. Hefler eased away close to shore some distance before stopping, well hidden. The Indians hovered about for the better part of an hour before leaving, but Hefler remained in place until morning, thankful for the fog cloaking the river. At that point, staying in the water, he continued sliding and wading upstream for the better part of a mile before coming back on shore. It was close to noon before he reached Wheeling. He reported to Col. Zane what had occurred, and then, his hand in bad shape, was taken to Pittsburgh for medical treatment. Still, the Wheeling residents again considered it just another attack by an isolated raiding party.[616]

Then, on August 22, one of Col. Zane's younger brothers, Jonathan, had been returning home after hunting his horses when, ahead, just on the outskirts of the Wheeling Settlement and not more than 100 yards or so from his own house, he saw five Indians leap into the Ohio and begin to swim toward the big island. He immediately stopped, tied his horses, took careful aim at one of the swimmers and fired. The Indian thrashed and disappeared. The others swam more frantically to get away, but in rapid succession he loaded and fired, killing three more. The fifth, nearing the island, managed to reach a sawyer—a tree bobbing and swaying in the current, but its roots wedged on the bottom—and hid among the branches. Zane, rifle ready, waited for several minutes, then caught a glimpse of the Indian's head just barely visible above the surface, next to a large branch. Again he took careful aim and fired. The man splashed, clung a moment more, then floated free for a while before he disappeared beneath the surface and was seen no more. Still the Wheeling residents considered the swimmers no more than another isolated party of marauders.

Then, only four days after that, Michael Myers had been on spying patrol up Yellow Creek on the Ohio side of the river with his younger brother, Christopher, when they found the trail of a war party heading downstream toward the creek's mouth. That was where Capt. William Forbes had only recently established the little two-story fortification called Forbes' Blockhouse. The pair, knowing Forbes and four other men were there, moved quickly downstream to warn them, but they arrived too late; the war party of Wyandots had hit them the day before. Forbes and two of his men were still all right, but a young man named George Tinkey had been taken by surprise on the riverbank and captured. Two other men with him escaped into the little blockhouse, but the Indians followed and managed to break in the door. They caught one of the men as he was climbing the ladder to the second floor, pulled him down, tomahawked and scalped him. They were driven out by gunfire from the floor above and, for the rest of the day, until nightfall, the Indians kept the place under siege before they finally moved off in the darkness. When word of this reached Wheeling, the residents became a little more cautious and some even moved back into Fort Henry, but the majority remained unconvinced that any of these scattered incidents presaged an assault on Wheeling itself.

Yesterday, having learned from a spy that a party of Indians with horses had established a longtime camp on Stillwater Creek in the Ohio country, Ebenezer and Jonathan Zane, with Stephen Burkham along, set out on horseback to spy on the encampment themselves and try to steal some of the horses. They followed Indian Wheeling Creek to its headwaters, then crossed the dividing ridge to Stillwater Creek, a tributary of the Tuscarawas. Following it downstream, by late in the day they had found the camp and, watching it from under cover at a considerable distance, estimated there were about 30 Wyandots. By careful circling, they discovered where the horses were being contained in a rope corral for the night some 20 yards or so from the camp. They decided to wait until the warriors were all asleep before making the attempt.

It was not until sometime after midnight that the last few warriors lay down near the fire to sleep, leaving one of their number on guard. That individual sat with his back to the trunk of a tree and was very watchful at first. After a few hours, however, he seemed to be getting sleepy. Still he held on, shaking off his drowsiness until the very first gray of dawn streaked the eastern sky. At that point, just when they were on the verge of giving up, his head drooped three or four times in succession and then finally sagged and did not come up. After a few minutes the three white men slipped quietly to the horses and were about to cut the rope when a loud shriek erupted from behind them, and they wheeled to find the guard had roused, come toward the horses and discovered them. He was already breaking into a sprint back toward the others.

The three wheeled and raced away, heading for where their horses were tied, knowing with certainty that the Indians would be after them in a moment. They reached their horses and had no more than mounted when they heard some of the Wyandots, themselves on horses, coming toward them. The pursuit was on and they managed to hold their lead, but it was a long chase and their horses were very nearly done in by the time they reached the Ohio and swam across, at which point the Indians gave up and disappeared the way they had come.

That narrow escape somewhat changed the lackadaisical attitude prevailing among the Wheeling area settlers, as did the fact that early this morning, heading for what used to be Catfish Camp and was now Washington village, Stephen Burkham and Edward Wright had gotten only three or four miles away when they encountered an abundance of Indian sign and thought they heard Indians picking flints in the woods nearby.[617] They had turned about at once and returned to Wheeling with the alarming intelligence. Apprehension rose even more when, at three o'clock this afternoon, John Linn arrived, his horse also nearly collapsing from being overridden. Going at once to Col. Zane, he reported that while ranging on his patrol on the Ohio side of the river he encountered a huge party of war-painted Indians that he estimated to number upward of 400, accompanied by British Rangers, heading directly and quite rapidly for Wheeling. He had been seen, fired at and hotly pursued, but had managed to escape, swim his horse across the Ohio and reach here. There was no doubt in his mind whatever that an attack on Wheeling was imminent.

Without losing an instant, Col. Zane had the alarm sharply sounded and residents, at last genuinely fearful, began flocking to the two most secure places in the settlement—Fort Henry and Zane's own fortified residence some 60 yards distant.[618] Only ten able-bodied militia were on hand, plus ten other men and, though he knew he would need every one of them, Zane also realized that without reinforcements they could not hold off such an enemy force for long. He dispatched Capt. William Boggs to ride at once to the nearest strong settlement—Washington, 25 miles distant —and inform Col. David Williamson, who was in command there, what was occurring and urgently request he raise the strongest force possible and come to Wheeling in quick order. Boggs was to pause only briefly en route to warn any of the smaller settlements he passed to send their women and children to relative safety at Washington village and their men, if possible, to join the reinforcement that would be coming to Wheeling.[619] Thankful that his wife, Elizabeth, was away at the time visiting her father, Abraham McCulloch, near Washington village, he then ordered everyone to cooperate in bringing water from the river to the fortified house and Fort Henry. He elected to get the water from the nearby river rather than farther away at the usual place, the springs near the base of Wheeling Hill, for fear that the Indians might already be lurking in the heavier cover there. While the women and children aided the men in bringing up buckets of water from the river, the Indians and British appeared some distance away amidst beating drums and piping fifes.

Below Wheeling Island, a body of warriors crossed the Ohio at Boggs' Island, then circled to the north through the woods and crossed Wheeling Creek, spreading themselves out east of the settlement. At the same time a body of some 60 Indians was observed moving into position on Wheeling Island and, with that, Wheeling was effectively surrounded. Some of the enemy, on hill and island alike, began firing random long shots at those carrying water, and Zane quickly ordered everyone into the fort. At this point, as prearranged by Zane, everyone in the fort, including women and children, raised a deafening yell, tossed hats and brooms into the air, beat on kettles and made all the noise possible for a prolonged time, all designed to convey to the enemy the impression of a very large number of people on hand for defense. Then Zane turned over command of Fort Henry to his brother Silas, also a militia colonel, and placed himself in his own fortified house in order to establish a crossfire zone between his place and the fort for any attackers trying to gain entry.

Ebenezer Zane's house, resembling a blockhouse more than a residence, had regularly spaced loopholes for rifle fire and contained much of the military stores that had been accumulated from the Virginia government for the defense of Wheeling. With Ebenezer Zane in the house were eight others—Andrew and Molly Scott and Andrew's younger brother, Bob. George Greer was there, too, along with Miss McCulloch and, in the adjoining kitchen structure, Rachel Johnson, the Negro slave who had also gone through the first siege of Wheeling with the Zanes, plus Ebenezer Zane's other two slaves, Old Daddy Sam and Kate, a married couple.[620] Within the fort there were a total of 23 men, counting militia and civilians alike, plus 14 wives.[621]

About this time, a more concentrated shooting broke out from the approaching

Indians, who quickly separated and took cover wherever possible around the fort as they opened their offensive. Within short minutes almost continuous rifle fire was being directed at both Fort Henry and the settlement.

Boggs, hardly a mile and a half distant, heard the firing and urged his mount to even greater exertions. In another half-mile he encountered Ebenezer McCulloch heading for Wheeling and warned him that the Indians were attacking.[622] McCulloch, unconvinced, rode on, only to hear the firing himself before riding another half-mile. At once he turned around and overtook Capt. Boggs and continued with him toward Washington.

The initial firing lasted for a quarter-hour, harming no one but causing consternation among the majority of the Wheeling residents. Then, as the initial spate of firing dwindled away, British Capt. John Pratt, accompanied by Ens. John McGillen and George Girty, plus a pair of uniformed soldiers, approached the fort under two flags—one the British standard, the other a white flag. When they stopped within 20 yards of the gate, Silas Zane called loudly from inside the fort, telling them to state their business. British Capt. Pratt cupped his mouth with both hands and shouted loudly in response:

"I wish to speak to the officer in command here."

Zane approached one of the portholes and shouted back, "I am Colonel Silas Zane, in temporary command of this post, sir, and again I demand to know what you wish."

"I am Captain John Pratt," the officer replied, "of the Queen's Rangers, and I wish no harm to come to you and your people here. I wish to give you an opportunity to avoid the profusion of blood which will surely flow if the fort and the entire Wheeling Settlement are not immediately surrendered to us. We know you have only a few men and are defended mainly by women and children. I promise you in the name of King George, if you give up, everyone will be treated with humanity, but I also warn you that if you do not capitulate, we are a large force and prepared to attack with a strength you cannot withstand and, in that circumstance all here will most certainly be killed, as no quarter will be given."

McGillen then spoke up, telling them he was a Scot and a man of Christian heart who, like Capt. Pratt, would hate to see them and their women and children massacred by the Indians, which would surely occur if they did not surrender at once.

Not to be outdone, George Girty then spoke up. "You ought'a know," he told them, "that the other part of us jus' whipped hell out'a the Kentuckians at Blue Licks an' kilt most of 'em, jest like we whipped Crawford an' jest like we'll whip you iffen you don't give up. Artillery'll be here tomorry, 'long with fifteen hunnerd more Injens. Give it up, Zane—you ain't got no chance."

"You can go straight to hell!" Zane responded. "All of you. We're not surrendering. McGillen, you say you're from Scotland. Have you come all this way to butcher women and children? How heroic! Girty, you always were a liar, and I don't figure you've changed now. As for you, Pratt, we don't believe your promises for an instant."

He gave a signal, and Stephen Burkham immediately fired a shot that tore through their standard. Pratt and McGillen, along with their soldiers, took to their heels and quickly vanished in nearby cover. Girty momentarily cursed them, but

Burkham had reloaded and sent another shot that kicked up the ground at the renegade's feet, and he followed the others. Burkham reloaded a second time and sent his third shot whistling past Girty's head just as he plunged into the cover afforded by the cornfield.

Almost immediately a brisk firing was raised by the enemy, and a great many Indians charged out of the cornfields and into the settlement, dodging from house to house as they fired at the defenders; this fire was returned by everyone in both Fort Henry and Zane's fortified house who was capable of handling a rifle. The brisk return fire from these places—especially the unexpected hot enfilading fire from Zane's house—drove the attackers back momentarily, but they quickly recovered and charged again with even greater fervor. They were repulsed a second time as the grapeshot-loaded French swivel on the platform within the fort—which the attackers had initially thought to be merely a dummy gun made of wood—was fired into their midst time and again by Conrad Stoup and John Tate. The small cannon's fire created consternation among the Indian attackers, scattering them, and Capt. Pratt, who recognized at the first explosion of the big gun that this was no fake artillery piece, immediately ordered his Queen's Rangers to fall back and stand clear. They and the Indians retired back into the cornfield as well as to the cover of the woodland at the base of Wheeling Hill, from which they continued their assault with rifle fire.

Just after five in the evening, a settler galloped into Shepherd's Fort at the forks of Wheeling Creek, urgently told them to evacuate to Washington village on instructions received from Capt. Boggs and for the men to either go directly to the aid of Wheeling or to join the relief force that would be mounted at Washington village. Eight men were on hand at the fort under Col. William Shepherd, two of whom were ordered to escort the women and children to Washington, the remainder heading at once under their commander toward Wheeling to try to break through the enemy force, gain admission to Fort Henry and aid in Wheeling's defense.

By six-thirty this first relief party arrived within sight of Wheeling, and Col. Shepherd, assessing the strength of the attacking enemy, determined that such an effort would almost certainly fail and result in unnecessary casualties. He ordered his men to head for Washington village to intercept and join the force supposedly being mounted there.[623]

At nightfall the firing by the enemy dwindled away and died, replaced by an ominous quiet. Thus far, with no one killed or even injured, the Wheeling defenders were encouraged and their morale remained high, but both Silas and Ebenezer Zane warned them not to become too confident as, at this stage of the assault, anything could still happen.

A little later George Girty's voice came out of the darkness: "Hey! You got any whiskey there in the fort?"

Betsy Wheat, a bold young Dutch woman serving as one of the sentinels at that point, shouted back, "Sure, we've got plenty of it."

"How'd you make it?" Girty asked.

"In a lead melting ladle," the young woman called back. "Come on in closer, and we'll give you a belly full of it."

"If that's 'sposed to scare me off, it ain't workin'," Girty snarled. "I'll have this fort before runnin', or go t'hell!"

"Then it's hell for you," she laughed, "because you're surely not getting into this fort."

Girty snorted scornfully but said nothing more, and things quieted for a while. Then, at ten P.M., a broadhorn approached on the river laden with dispatches and a cargo of cannonballs from Fort Pitt destined for George Rogers Clark in Louisville at the Falls of the Ohio. It was commanded by boat Capt. Cobus Sullivan, who had a two-man crew. They had no inkling that Wheeling was under siege and, as they put to shore at the Wheeling wharf below the fort, Indians who had crept up unseen in the darkness and gathering fog, aided by others who came over from the island, attacked. Sullivan and his mates raced up the embankment in a hail of bullets and managed to reach the safety of Fort Henry. They immediately joined in the fighting alongside the others.

The Indians lost no time carrying away the cargo of cannonballs. Though they had no cannon, they found a hickory log with a hollow through it approximately the size of the cannonballs and decided to make one. They remembered only too well the similar attempt during the first Wheeling siege five years earlier, at which time a hollowed maple log bound with stretched rawhide had burst when fired, killing and injuring quite a number. They were determined to avoid that mistake this time and carried the log to the vacant blacksmith's shop. There they sawed it in half and reamed out the hollow for its entire length to sufficiently accommodate the ball. This time when they sealed the halves together, they used the smithy's equipment to forge a secure binding with chains and metal bands. When finished, they carried it to point-blank range of Fort Henry's main gate, poured in a heavy charge of gunpowder, rammed home one of the balls and ignited the powder-impregnated wick. They really believed that this time it would work for them, but the back end of the makeshift gun blew out with a squishing sound that made even the Indians themselves laugh. They left it where it lay and returned to reliance on their rifles.

Soon the Indians again charged the fort, firing their guns and lofting fire arrows over the walls, but the defense returned fire so hotly and steadily that once again the attackers were thwarted and retired, filled with frustration. Then they tried a new tactic. Indians with armloads of flax gathered in the nearby fields piled it against the palings and set it afire, but the flax was still too wet and smoldered more than burned, doing little damage.

Cobus Sullivan—Cobe to his friends—took his turn at firing from the north blockhouse above the pickets. He was injured in the foot when a bullet entered at an angle from below, penetrated his big toe and exited out the arch. Painful though it was, he remained at his post and continued firing.

The galling fire that kept coming from Zane's house as the Indians made their attempts on the fort finally convinced them that they should attempt to seize or destroy the place. Molly Scott was doing as much firing through the loopholes as the men, as well as helping to load guns. Late into the night they made the effort. An Indian crept close with a glowing, though not burning, firebrand in his grasp and, when he made it successfully to the kitchen adjoining Zane's house, he waved it rapidly back and forth to rekindle the flame so as to set the place afire. In a few moments the glowing end, receiving more oxygen, rekindled itself and burst into flame.

Zane's slave, Old Daddy Sam, detected the effort.[624] Though his forehead had been grazed by a ball and his face was bloody, it was not a serious wound, and he rushed up yelling, "Take care! Sambo is here," and just as the warrior began applying the burning torch to the kitchen wall, the Negro sent a shot at him, wounding him so badly that he screamed in pain, dropped the torch and was barely able to hobble away into the darkness. They did not try that tactic again.

At about eleven-fifteen the Indians managed to temporarily occupy the house of Jacob Reagan, but the French swivel was brought to bear upon it, and two shots with one-pound balls managed to cut the joists and cause the loft to collapse, which was enough to make them evacuate the place in great haste. Fifteen other times during the night the swivel boomed and sent grapeshot whirring through the darkness, keeping the enemy largely at bay.

During the night other efforts by the Indians to scale the walls or undermine them to gain entry—especially a massive all-out assault that occurred about midnight —failed, due to the strength of the wall pickets, as well as the constant watchfulness of the sentries and the firing their alarms evoked from the defenders, men and women alike. The vibrations from the swivel did, however, cause two of the pickets that had become rotten at their base to fall inward, but before the enemy had a chance to notice and take advantage of the gap, those pickets were quickly set upright again and a board firmly nailed across them on the inside. Had the attack on the walls become more threatening, kettles of water maintained at the boiling point were ready to be splashed over them, but thus far it hadn't become necessary. On the orders of Silas Zane, tomahawks had been stuck in the pickets at intervals, and the women were instructed, should the enemy actually begin scaling the walls, to chop off their fingers.

Tom Mills, still in his hospital bed in Fort Henry, was visited briefly by his friend Stephen Burkham when the latter was finally relieved from his post by one of the women so he could get some sleep. After a little discussion about how things were going in the fight, Mills looked at his friend intently and spoke seriously.

"I want you to make me a promise, Steve."

"Sure, Tom," Burkham replied. "Anything."

"If the Indians manage to break in, I want you to promise to come here and tomahawk me. I aim to deprive those red bastards of the fun of doing that."

Burkham promised.

[S e p t e m b e r   1 2 ,   1 7 8 2 — T h u r s d a y]

There were two more strong attacks by the Indians and British to breach the walls of Fort Henry after midnight and before dawn, but both failed, with ever more of the attackers becoming casualties.

Shortly after daybreak, with a lull in the shooting continuing but no one daring to hope the siege had been lifted, Molly Scott abruptly raced out of Ebenezer Zane's house and ran to the fort without any shots being fired at her. Panting somewhat on her arrival, she announced with a grin that she was preparing breakfast for the defenders at the house and had run out of bacon and needed more. Dumbfounded at her boldness, Silas Zane cautioned her about making what could be the dangerous run back, but she was determined to do so. Having encountered her stubbornness and determination before, he gave her what she needed and assigned several men to cover her run back to the house. Again she traversed the distance without a shot being fired, and those in the house enjoyed a very good breakfast.

At Washington village a lot of activity was occurring, but little being accomplished. Capt. William Boggs and Abraham McCulloch had arrived well after dark last night on horses wheezing and panting from exhaustion, and Boggs's horse was somewhat lame in the right foreleg. Col. David Williamson had listened grim-faced to Boggs's report and cursed the fact that the militia that had paraded here only yesterday had been dismissed and that the men had gone to their individual homes, some of them miles away. As quickly as possible those on hand in the settlement were summoned, but they amounted to only nine men. By dawn another three had arrived, but Williamson knew a mere dozen men were not enough, and so, in the early morning light he sent them out in pairs to ride to the more distant cabins and settlements and recruit more men to come to the aid of Wheeling.

At eight A.M. a Negro man clad in Indian garb and carrying a white flag emerged from cover at the base of Wheeling Hill and came rather apprehensively toward Fort Henry. He stopped some 50 yards distant and called for the commander. This time it was Col. Ebenezer Zane who opened the door to his fortified house and called out to him, asking him what he wanted.

"I been tol' t'come an' tell you folks," he said, "that y'all got one las' chance to surrender. An', suh, I thinks may be you ought'a do it. They got two hunnerd an' sixty warriors an' a British cap'n with 40 Rangers that're gonna' kill ever' las' one o'you, you don't give up."

"You tell that damned British officer and the chiefs," Zane said in a deceptively mild tone, "that as long as even one person in Wheeling has strength enough to pull a trigger, we'll keep right on fighting. Tell them as well that the next time you or anyone else comes walking in here, flag or no flag, he'll be shot dead in his tracks. Now get the hell out of here!"

The man licked his lips nervously and then nodded, turned and started walking away, but his nerve gave way, and he broke into a run and was quickly gone. Shortly after that the firing resumed from the Indian force, coming mainly from those under cover on the sides and at the base of Wheeling Hill.

Throughout the day there was sporadic firing from both sides with little accomplished, but small parties of the Indians began driving off the settlement's cattle and killing the hogs, sheep and poultry. By late afternoon most of the livestock was either gone or dead except for the dozen cows and 11 horses within the fort.

At ten P.M. another major assault against the walls was mounted with as much fury as any that had preceded it but, as before, it was unsuccessful, and the enemy finally pulled away, nursing its wounds.

Meanwhile, at Washington, the men who had been summoned from their outlying cabins were still coming in, but with agonizing slowness. A total of 30 had gathered by nightfall, but there were others yet to show up, and Col. Williamson, frustrated and angry with the delay, could maintain his patience only with great effort. He filled the time by having all who had thus far assembled check and double-check their weapons, their horses and all their gear.

Finally, close to midnight, it seemed that all had arrived who were going to show up. Forty men were on hand, and the question now was, should they wait until daylight, when they could ride at good speed and arrive at Wheeling in a few hours, or should they start out at once in darkness, when the going would be much slower and take them about twice as long? Concerns were raised, as well, about the strong possibility that the attacking Indians, no doubt expecting some kind of militia reinforcement to arrive, might have set up an ambush on the main road.

Time was of the essence and took priority and so, with the fog making the night even blacker than normal, Col. Williamson put them into motion, hoping to arrive at Wheeling just as dawn was breaking.

[September 13, 1782 — Friday]

Throughout the night sporadic firing from the Indians had continued at Fort Henry but with little real effect. In the first light of morning, however, an unexpected quiet fell. The Indians on Wheeling Hill and in the cornfields seemed to have withdrawn. Only a few were still visible moving about on Wheeling Island, and some of the defenders now emerged from the fort, cautiously at first but then with greater boldness when no shots were directed their way. They advanced to the edge of the embankment over the Ohio and began pouring a hot fire at the warriors still on the island. Those Indians quickly left and, though it took a little while to fully realize it, the fact finally became clear that the Indians and British had actually terminated their efforts and the second siege of Wheeling was over.

Hardly had the enemy pulled out than the 40-man reinforcement from Washington under Col. David Williamson came into sight on the main road, weary from lack of sleep and nerves raw from anticipating being ambushed at every step of the way. Williamson, in the lead, was flanked by Capts. Andrew Van Swearingen and Eleazar Williamson, with Capt. William Boggs and William Shepherd's son, Moses, close behind. Finding the action all over, squads of men were sent out to scout around and make sure the enemy was gone, while the remainder helped the Wheeling men drag the already bloated carcasses of the dead livestock to the river and throw them in so the current could carry them off. Hardly more than two hours after its arrival, the force from Washington was on its way home.

Though no Indian bodies were found, it was certain the defenders had killed a number of them and wounded many others. As for casualties in Wheeling, there had been only two: the slight graze on the forehead of Old Daddy Sam, and the foot wound suffered by Cobus Sullivan. Considering that the odds against them had been at least five to one, the Wheeling defenders were justified in the pride that welled among them.[625]

[September 14, 1782 — Saturday]

Col. Ebenezer Zane detested writing out official reports, so the one he was preparing for Gen. William Irvine was brief in the extreme:

Wheeling, 14th September, 1782

Sir: On the evening of the 11th instant a body of the enemy appeared in sight of our garrison. They immediately formed their lines around the garrison, paraded British colors, and demanded the fort to be surrendered, which was refused. About twelve o'clock at night they rushed hard on the pickets, in order to storm, but were repulsed. They made two other attempts to storm, before day, to no purpose.

About eight o'clock next morning, there came a negro from them to us, and informed us that their force consisted of a British Captain and forty regular soldiers, and two hundred and sixty Indians. The enemy kept a continual fire the whole day. About ten o'clock at night they made a fourth attempt to storm, to no better purpose than the former. The enemy continued around the garrison till the morning of the 13th instant, when they disappeared. Our loss is none. Daniel [Cobus] Sullivan, who arrived here in the first of the action is wounded in the foot.

I believe they have driven the greatest part of our stock away and might, I think, be soon overtaken.

I am, with due respect, your obedient servant,

Ebenezer Zane.

[September 16, 1782 — Monday]

When Lewis Wetzel stopped by Wheeling last evening after a weeklong hunting trip down the Ohio, Col. Ebenezer Zane told him about the siege the settlement had weathered and his regret, when it began, that Lewis had not been on hand to aid them.

"We're still having one problem, though," he added, "that you might be able to help us with, Lewis."

"Which is?" Wetzel asked.

"Three of our men have been wounded since then, one pretty badly, evidently by one of the Indians still hanging around and taking pot-shots at them. Took us a while to figure out what was happening. Seems this Indian's got himself into hiding in the rocks up the creek. Anyone comes near, he gobbles like a turkey, and when they come looking for the bird, he shoots."

Wetzel grinned. It was exactly the kind of challenge he relished. "I'll take care of it," he said.

After questioning the men still recovering from their wounds about exactly where the attacks had taken place, he slipped off into the woods after nightfall and climbed well up into an elm tree close to the rocks and waited. Dawn came and went, and there was no trace of the Indian. By sunrise, Wetzel was beginning to believe the Indian was gone, and he was just about ready to descend when a movement in the rocks caught his eye, and he saw the warrior cautiously moving about in a well-hidden cleft in the rocks behind some bushes. Very quietly he reached into his pouch and extracted a fist-size rock he had picked up on the creek bank the preceding evening. He pitched it well away through a gap in the foliage, and it hit the ground a little distance away, bounded and rolled some distance through the dry leaves before stopping.

Instantly the Indian came alert and then stealthily crept from behind the brush. He crouched behind a rock, rifle ready, looking intently in the direction from which he had heard the rustling of the leaves. Cupping his mouth with one hand, he sounded a short gobble that was a very credible imitation of a tom turkey.

Less than an hour later Lewis Wetzel strode up to Ebenezer Zane, pulled a bloody scalp from his pouch and, grinning broadly, showed it to him.

"Your boys here oughtn't have no more problems," he said. "Here's your redskin turkey."

[O c t o b e r   4 ,   1 7 8 2 — F r i d a y]

As soon as Capt. Samuel Brady heard that the daughter of Capt. Andrew Van Swearingen had returned from Philadelphia to her father's home near Washington village, he had left Holliday's Cove and come to pay court, as he had told her father he meant to do.

Brady had thought Dusy—Drusilla—was beautiful before she left 15 months earlier, but she had returned even more lovely, with an added measure of maturity and poise in her bearing. At 17, she had changed from a girl to a young woman; the whole upper Ohio Valley took note of it, and Sam Brady was not the only man attracted.

Most of the smitten young men who came to pay their respects evoked no reaction in her, but there were two exceptions. One was David Bradford, the young man with whom she had shared a mutual attraction before leaving for Philadelphia. Now he had become quite a handsome, serious, 24-year-old young man, cultured and intelligent, if a bit stodgy, and she experienced the same stirring of attraction she had known before. Furthermore, he had become a lawyer now, had opened his own office in Washington village and was becoming quite successful. He would definitely be a good catch.

The other was Sam Brady, who was three years older than Bradford. Brady was strong, capable, self-confident, good-looking and bold, though considerably rougher around the edges than his rival. He was not a particularly good businessman, and his prospects for the future were decidedly uncertain, yet he was an exciting man, and he stirred her as none other ever had before.

She saw a good deal of both of them in these first few weeks after her return and, while she appreciated young Bradford's almost fawning attention, the wildflowers he plucked to bring to her, the poetry he read to her and the esoteric thoughts he put to words, in the end the more down-to-earth, solid character of the self-assured Sam Brady attracted her more. There was a sense of aliveness about him, of barely controlled wildness. This was the man who, she had learned, only a few days before her return, had visited Nathan Ellis and, as the two men walked to the spring behind his cabin without their rifles, they had encountered a very large black bear that immediately advanced toward them, snarling. Ellis was ready to flee to the safety of the nearby cabin, but Brady had simply reached to his belt and said, "Suppose I tomahawk that bear?" Incredibly, he had charged at the big dangerous animal and done exactly that, killing it with just one well-placed blow. Yes, there was no doubt he was quite a man and, perhaps most important, she thought she might be in love with him.

Yesterday, when Sam Brady asked her to marry him, she had said yes, and just that simply they were engaged. But that was yesterday, and today was another matter. Today, now, at this moment, Samuel Brady had casually announced he was heading for Kentucky to claim lands there and that he would be gone for a while.

"A while?" Dusy said, frowning. "And just exactly how long is a while?"

Brady shrugged. "Just a few months. Maybe a little more. Depends on how things go."

"Sam!" Points of anger flickered in her eyes. "How can you even contemplate leaving me like that? We just got engaged!"

"That has nothing to do with it," he said, shaking his head. "Listen, Dusy, Captain Lodge and Captain Carnahan have formed a partnership, and they want me in on it. I'd be a fool not to join them. Can't you understand? This is a once-in-a-lifetime chance. Before long there's going to be nothing left to claim in that country, and I aim to get there before that happens, and get my share."

"But it's so dangerous," she said. "Please, Sam, don't do this. You could be killed."

"Oh now, Dusy, don't get dramatic. You know I can take care of myself, and I don't have any intention of getting killed, either."

"I doubt," she flared, "that any one of those near hundred men who got killed at Blue Licks a few weeks ago had any intention of getting killed. No, I won't have it, Sam. You can't go!"

"I can," he told her firmly, "and I will. I'm leaving tomorrow. Listen to me, Drusilla. I love you and I know you love me, and when you get right down to it, that's all that really matters. I'm doing this for you as well as for myself, and I expect you to support me in this. I also expect you to be here waiting for me when I get back."

"Don't count on it, Sam Brady!" she snapped. "Just don't you count on it!"

[December 31, 1782 — Tuesday]

The final months of 1782 had dwindled away no less eventfully than the earlier months had, making this year one of the most tragic and portentous the Ohio Valley had ever known. It had been the year of many attacks by the Indians on the tributaries of the upper Ohio and the unspeakable horror of the Moravian Massacre at Gnadenhütten; the year of the capture of Thomas Edgington at Holliday's Cove and Joseph Parkinson's cargo of flour intended for New Orleans; the killing of George Wetzel and Samuel McCulloch; the rendezvous of Crawford's army at Mingo Bottom and the disastrous Sandusky Campaign that followed; the awful execution of Col. Crawford and the miraculous escapes of Dr. John Knight and John Slover; the terrible disaster that had befallen the Kentuckians at the Blue Licks.

The good fortune that had marked the activities of the hostile Indians throughout the first eight months of the year, however, finally took a downturn with the failure of the second siege of Wheeling, and in the four months that had passed since then, matters had not improved for them. A terrible blow had been struck against them when, in retaliation for the Blue Licks defeat, George Rogers Clark had mounted a second expedition of more than 1,000 Kentuckians and marched them against the Shawnee towns, utterly destroying Chalahgawtha and Piqua Town and forcing the tribe to once again move deeper into the Ohio country.[626]

The worst blow of all to the tribes, however, had come early in November, when a provisional treaty of peace had been signed between the British and Americans. The British relinquished to the Americans all their claims to the territory north and west of the Ohio River, effectively turning their backs on their red allies and not even mentioning them in the negotiations. With sweeping prisoner exchanges already in the offing between British and Americans, the Indians occupying this vast territory were left on their own to face the onslaught of encroaching settlers that was sure to follow. Part of the territory ceded to the Americans was the territory of the Iroquois tribes in upper New York—in direct violation of the promises made to them by the Canadian governor, Sir Guy Carleton, when those tribes had agreed to leave their homes and support the British cause. Carleton was no longer there, and Gov. Frederick Haldimand, through his agents, blandly said the Great King had directed him to tell his red children that his American subjects were sorry for what they had done and begged his forgiveness, and that he was now going to pardon them, and that he desired that his red children would no longer kill the Americans. Not in the least fooled, the Iroquois retorted that the Great King was lying and that he was going to forgive the Americans only because he had no choice but to do so, since they had defeated his armies. Their anger was great, and they said they would no longer be allies of the British. In an effort to mollify them, Haldimand set aside a parcel of land for them in Canada, which they accepted, but it was not their homeland and they remained deeply disgruntled.

The northwestern tribes got no such concession, and their appeals to Maj. Arent de Peyster in Detroit for continued support in arms, ammunition, supplies and manpower were thwarted. Haldimand had instructed him to tell the Wyandots, Shawnees, Miamis, Delawares and other Great Lakes tribes that, regrettably, he could not aid them as he had in the past and asked that they curtail, at least temporarily, their attacks against the settlements on the Ohio River and in Kentucky.[627] Baffled and frustrated, the northwestern tribes vowed that with or without British help, they would not give up their struggle for survival against the Americans. But now their prospects looked bleak indeed.

The attacks had continued, as had retaliation by the whites. Only five days ago, a party of bordermen, perhaps still under the influence of Christmas spirits drunk the day before, descended upon the camp of the longtime friendly Delaware Indian, Captain Wilson, on Killbuck's Island, in the mouth of the Allegheny opposite Pittsburgh.[628] They did not care that Captain Wilson had so often guided American troops and parties of Brady's Rangers up the Allegheny against the hostile Indians, nor that he had once been selected by the whites, along with Andrew Montour, to execute a pair of hostile Munceys within sight of the island. Their only concern was that he and those with him were Indians and, so far as they were concerned, all Indians were enemies.

The party of whites crossed to Killbuck's Island and crept up to the camp under cover of darkness. At a given signal they shot all the Indians in Captain Wilson's party, including him. Then, as if realizing there might be repercussions, they fled without even taking the scalps. All the Indians had been killed instantly except Captain Wilson, and he was mortally wounded. He managed to get up after the attackers left, stagger to the river and, with great effort, swim to the shoreline at Fort Pitt. There, as he used the last of his strength to drag himself out of the water, a sentry saw him. Recognized, he was taken inside the fort for medical treatment, but it was too late. He smiled weakly at the doctor trying to treat him and said, "I know they would not have killed me if they had known it was little Wilson." And then he died.

To allow time for Captain Wilson's friends among the whites to gather to pay their last respects, the burial was postponed until today, and now, in the final hours of this eventful year, a goodly number of those friends came to pay last respects, along with many others who were simply curious onlookers.

Among the latter was David Morgan, a settler from Whitely Creek. He was clad in leather trousers and vest, both of an unusual nature, very smooth grained, soft and supple and sewn with meticulous care. When questioned about them by another onlooker, he grinned broadly.

"Best wearing clothes I've ever had," he boasted, "vest and pants alike. Made 'em from the hides of two Injens I killed a couple months ago. Best job of tanning I ever did, too. Everybody ought to have some. And I'll tell you something else, there's nothing better for honing a razor than a strop made from Injen hide."

[A u g u s t   2 2 ,   1 7 8 3 — F r i d a y]

After the unprecedented turbulence of 1782, the year that followed was thus far very mild. Weary of the war that had prevailed between them for so long, both the whites and the Indians were relieved to pull back their bloody tomahawks and, though not yet ready to bury them, at least only hold them in reserve until a more binding peace could be established between them.

This did not mean that the valley of the Ohio River was suddenly free of conflict; only that the incidents were less numerous and, for the most part, less brutal, with attacks more often resulting in captures than in killings. That a definitive peace treaty was in the offing was all the more evident as numerous prisoner exchanges occurred between the British and the Americans.

Among those exchanged was Thomas Edgington who, after 11 months of captivity, had finally been set free in March. His captivity, while fraught with dangers, had been a valuable experience for him and had taught him a new respect for the Indians. This was especially true with regard to the warrior who had captured him, Scotach, son of Monakaduto.

Had it not been for Scotach, Edgington was certain his lot would have been much worse, if not fatal. Scotach had treated him as if they were brothers, patting him on the back and encouraging him to stand and fight for his rights when imposed upon by other Indians and protecting him when it became necessary. More than once Scotach had engaged in brief scuffles with other warriors, slashing and feinting with knives, war clubs or tomahawks, avoiding giving or receiving fatal stabbings, blows or hackings. The arguments were always settled when Scotach unfailingly drew first blood. In addition, Scotach had shared with Edgington his blanket, his buffalo skin robe and his food, seeming always to give him the greater or better part. Those months with Scotach made a lasting impression, and Edgington, after finally being turned over to the British and exchanged by them, repeatedly declared to all that "Scotach has the highest principles and is the noblest and best man I ever met, be he white, black or red." And when he finally was exchanged, Edgington did not leave his captors without a certain degree of respect and a greater understanding of why some whites who had been taken captive refused to return to their own culture when opportunity arose.

Having been released, along with Daniel Kinney and John Fitch, who had been captured while map-making on the Ohio near the mouth of the Muskingum, Edgington was finally reunited with his family at their old place on Chartier's Creek and, not long after that, returned to Holliday's Cove on Harmon's Creek.

There were still many widely scattered incidents occurring on the frontier that made it clear that Indian and white relations remained far from settled, but life along the Ohio was, for the Americans, settling down to a greater degree of normalcy. Isaac and Rebecca Williams returned at last from Redstone on the Monongahela to their abandoned claims at the mouth of Grave Creek, as did Rebecca's brother, Joseph Tomlinson, and soon their cabins had been rebuilt and their frontier lives resumed. Downstream from them some 82 miles, at the mouth of the Little Kanawha River, Alexander Parker had bought the tomahawk claims of Robert Thornton and hired Capt. James Neal to survey the site for him. It was the genesis of a town he planned to name after himself—Parkersburg.[629]

As if in testimony to the changes that were occurring along the river, with the Indian problems abating, settlers now began having troubles with their own kind. Six miles below the mouth of Yellow Creek but on the Virginia side of the river, a wealthy new settler named George Chapman, who hailed from near the Potomac River, had now claimed 1,000 acres of land.[630] His first step, wisely enough, was to build a small fortified structure called Chapman's Blockhouse for the safety of his wife and children. As soon as it was completed, he headed back east to get some money that was due him, leaving his wife and children in the care of a man named Bowler Skyles, whom he had hired to help with construction.

Skyles planned to murder Chapman on his return with the money. He waited until just before he was due to arrive home and then, pretending alarm, rushed into the residence blockhouse.

"Better take your kids an' hightail it to the nearest neighbor, ma'am," he said. "I seen Injens acomin' this way from up Yellow Crik way and reckon they're fixin' t'hit this place."

Mary Chapman, however, was no man's fool. She had not liked Skyles from the beginning, and now, instantly suspecting his design, she nodded and said, "I'd better get the gun to protect the children." She took it down from its wooden pegs over the fireplace and turned with it leveled at the center of Skyles's chest. "Now, Mr. Skyles," she said menacingly, "if there are any Indians about, you're the one. You've got ten seconds to get out of sight before I start shooting."

Skyles knew immediately that she was not bluffing, and he leaped away and fled into the nearby woods.[631]

An incident perhaps most indicative of the change in attitude between the Indians and whites had just occurred. Yesterday a lone Wyandot Indian appeared at the door of the house where Andrew Poe was now living with his wife, whom he had married about a year earlier. The Indian said his name was Ronyeness and that he was hungry and would appreciate some food. Actually, he was the brother of one of the Indians killed in the big fight that Andrew Poe's party had had with Scotach's party in September, two years earlier, and his sole purpose in coming here was to kill Poe to avenge his brother's death.

Poe and his wife welcomed him. Poe used his left hand to shake hands with him, since the right hand was now useless and atrophied as the result of the injury he had received in that fight. The Poes not only invited him in and asked him to share their meal with them, they invited him to stay overnight. Deciding this would give him an ideal opportunity to kill them both while they slept, Ronyeness accepted.

The Poes were very friendly to him, fed him well at their table and showed a genuine interest in him and his people as they conversed over dinner. Afterward they used some of their best bedding to make a pallet for him on the floor before the fireplace. When they all retired for the night, Ronyeness feigned sleep until the heavy breathing of the Poes convinced him they were asleep. Yet Ronyeness hesitated, thinking of the kindness with which they had treated him. At last he arose and, tomahawk in hand, crept stealthily to their bedside. A shaft of moonlight entering the window illuminated their faces in peaceful repose. He raised the tomahawk over Andrew's head and then hesitated again, abruptly stricken by the thought of the awful deed he was about to commit upon these people who had treated him so cordially. For a long moment he stood that way and then gradually lowered the weapon and returned to his pallet, where he quickly went to sleep.

The next morning, as they finished the good breakfast Mrs. Poe had prepared, Ronyeness hesitantly admitted that he had come well over 100 miles just to find Andrew Poe and kill him, and he told them how he had stood over them in the night. "But you were so kind to me, so caring," he said, rising and moving toward the door, "that my heart would not let my hand have its way. I will go away now and never trouble you again."

Though Mrs. Poe had become a little pale, Andrew rose as well and walked to the door, where he shook the Indian's hand again. "My people are presently digging the hole to bury the hatchet that has so long been raised between us and your people," he said. "We must now learn to live in friendship with each other. And we hope that you, Ronyeness, will return and visit us again in peace."

[August 30, 1783 — Saturday]

Samuel Brady had returned from Kentucky to the upper Ohio after somewhat longer than the "few months" he had initially anticipated. Having been headquartered in the Louisville area, he and his two partners had found it necessary to go considerably deeper into Kentucky than anticipated to find land not yet claimed by others. Yet the three had wound up doing very well—Brady alone had claimed more than 10,000 acres of good land—and they considered the whole journey a success.[632] There was also the matter of a group of Kentuckians who had decided to cross the Ohio and penetrate deep into the Ohio country to steal horses from the Shawnees; horses, they said, that had originally been taken from the Kentucky settlements. Brady and his companions had been urged to go along but had refused and even recommended against it because of the efforts being made by the American government to end the Indian war and effect a lasting peace between the red men and the whites. When they returned, they learned the Kentucky party had been successful in stealing the horses, but the furious Shawnees had pursued and overtaken them before they reached the Ohio again and attacked. Two of the Kentuckians had been killed along with one of the Shawnees, while the Indians recovered most of their horses.

At last, after many months in Kentucky, Brady and his companions headed back to the upper Ohio. Never much of a letter writer, he had not written to Drusilla Van Swearingen at all since his departure. Now he was regretting not having done so and thought she would probably be irked. Actually, it turned out to be a lot worse than that. When he arrived at Washington on a hot Sunday afternoon in mid-August, he found that the absence of letters from him during the whole period he was gone had led her to conclude that he had been killed, or that he was not planning to return, or that he had simply forgotten about her. In any case, he learned, she was now engaged to Brady's former rival, David Bradford, who had become quite a prominent lawyer. The match evidently pleased her father considerably. Not only was the 18-year-old belle of the Ohio frontier engaged, but the wedding arrangements had been made, as had the wedding gown, and the ceremony was set for the following Thursday, four days distant.

Brady immediately wrote her a note telling her of his return, apologizing for his long absence and for not writing and saying that he had learned of her pending wedding to Bradford. In view of his own failings, he wrote, he did not blame her for this unexpected development, and she was certainly free to do as she felt best. However, he wished to see her face to face and have her tell him that she actually preferred Bradford over him. If she could do that, then he would step out of the way, but if she wavered and inclined toward him, he was ready and willing to fulfill his previous pledges to her and marry her at once. To this end he would immediately pay a visit to her father to ask for her hand. Then he dispatched the note to her by way of a friend riding in that direction.

True to his word, Brady spruced himself up and rode to the Van Swearingen place. As he approached, he saw Capt. Andrew Van Swearingen working in his rye field and immediately rode to him. They greeted one another and shook hands, and then Brady wasted no time getting to the point.

"I've heard Dusy plans to marry Lawyer Bradford next Thursday," he said. "Expect she's doing that because she figured I'd gotten killed or something in Kentucky. Well, I didn't and I'm back. I aim to have her if she'll have me, and I'm asking your consent."

Van Swearingen picked up a long rye stem and chewed on the end for a moment. Then he pointed at a nearby shock of rye and shook his head. "Those rascals that stacked my rye there put the butt ends in and the heads out, and it'll have to be done over again."

The evasion did not balk Brady. "I asked your consent to marry Dusy," he said, a slight edge to his voice.

"Can't imagine why they would've stacked grain with the heads sticking out," Van Swearingen went on. "Stupid thing to do, and it'll just have to be done over."

Now Brady was definitely getting heated. "Captain Swearingen, I am senior, by God! She pledged herself to me last year, and if she'll have me, I still aim to marry her. She is mine, with or without your consent, but I would thank you for an answer of some sort."

Van Swearingen looked at Brady in a speculative way for a moment and then nodded and smiled. "I would thank you to take her."

The meeting with Drusilla a few minutes later went better than Brady had let himself hope. She had been greatly excited upon receiving his note, though she didn't let it show when he reached the house and was initially cool.

"I thought you were dead, Sam. Why didn't you write to me?"

"There aren't many mailbags when you're deep in Kentucky, Dusy," he said, but then shook his head. "No, that's not the reason. I could've written those times I was in Louisville. Just that one thing or another kept coming up, and I kept putting it off." He shrugged. "Never was much of a letter writer, but that doesn't mean I didn't love you. I did. I still do. Do you love me?"

"I've promised to marry David."

"Do you love him?"

"He's a good man, Sam. He's very smart and successful and caring."

"Do you *love* him?"

She was silent for a moment and then raised her eyes to meet his. She reached out, touched his arm and shook her head. "No, Sam," she said. "It's you I love."

She melted into his arms, and after that things went much better. David Bradford was disappointed when the wedding was called off, but he accepted her decision philosophically, though his feelings for Samuel Brady were somewhat less than cordial. A new wedding date was set, nine days after the original one, to allow time for word to be circulated of the new date and the new groom.

Now the big day had arrived, a gorgeous, cloudless late summer day. Before a huge crowd, including a large number of Brady's Rangers, the bride and groom—she in her beautiful gown and he in the only presentable clothing he owned, his crisp, regular army uniform—stood before the preacher at the Van Swearingen residence and pledged their troth until death they should part . . . an eventuality that, on the upper Ohio River frontier, all too often came quickly and unexpectedly.

[September 12, 1783—Friday]

Jacob Greathouse was back, having arrived by canoe at Holliday's Cove Fort early in the morning. Though the huge, brutish frontiersman had left the upper Ohio not long after he instigated Dunmore's War by his horrible massacre of the family of Talgayeeta—Chief Logan—just over nine years earlier, no one knew where he had gone, and Greathouse himself did not elucidate.

He was traveling without the band of rough bordermen who had associated with him in those days—John and Rafe Mahon, Joe Smith, Josh Baker, Joe Tomlinson, Ed King and others. His only companion now was his wife, a rather disreputable-looking woman who was as uncouth as he and would stand up to anyone, man or woman, except to her husband, who beat her savagely at times. She always seemed to come back for more.

Few of the residents greeted him with any degree of cordiality, only too well aware of his mercurial moods and uncontrolled temper. From the doorway of their own cabin, the newlyweds, Drusilla and Samuel Brady, saw him arrive and Sam shook his head. "Can't imagine what that troublemaker wants here," he muttered. "I only hope he leaves soon."

He didn't leave soon enough. He accepted a jug from an old acquaintance who, in the course of passing news, asked him if he'd heard about the "pet" Delaware named Captain Wilson having been mortally wounded when a party of bordermen attacked his camp on the day after Christmas last year. Greathouse laughed loudly and shook his head.

"Nope," he said in his loud, irritating voice, "but I'm hellfire glad t'hear it. The sooner they kill ever' one o'them red niggers, the better. An' that goes for their damn squaws an' kids, too. Kill 'em all, is what I say, an' I'll tell y'sure. . . . I damn well done my part in hurryin' a few along t'hell."

Brady overheard, and his expression darkened. He had held a special affection for Captain Wilson and had been dismayed when he learned of the Delaware's death. Now he strode up to Greathouse and planted himself a few feet in front of him and spoke harshly.

"Greathouse, you and your kind are not wanted here. Get back in your boat and leave. *Now!*"

Taken somewhat aback, Greathouse was not one to be easily pushed around. He cocked his head, frowning, not recognizing Brady at first. His hand moved toward the tomahawk in his belt. It stopped when Brady pointed at the weapon.

"You pull that 'hawk on me, Greathouse, and I'll kill you." The words were cold, menacing.

Now Greathouse recognized who it was, and he let his hand drop to his side. His lips smiled; his eyes did not. "Now I 'member you. Ye're Brady, king o' the spies. Cain't figger you gittin' het up 'bout any Injens bein' kilt. I hear ye've kilt a few here an' there. You gittin' sof' with all this peace talk goin' 'roun'?"

"Let me tell you something, Greathouse," Brady said, his tone level but deadly. "I've lost a kind father and a loving brother at their hands, and I've gone farther in search of revenge than any man has gone—as far as any man could go, or any would *dare* to go—but I would never kill an Indian in time of peace, nor women or children in war or peace. And I won't tolerate a man who would. Now, either pull that tomahawk or get out. And if you pull it, I will kill you."

For a long chilling moment the situation hung in balance, and then Greathouse shook his head. "Ain't worth it," he growled, then strode over to where his wife was standing and cuffed her. "Git in the boat, woman," he ordered. "We ain't stayin' in no place where they's Injen lovers."

[*D e c e m b e r   3 1 ,   1 7 8 3 — W e d n e s d a y*]

The Revolutionary War was over.

During this year of talks, lengthy negotiations, and the gradual cessation of hostilities, the war had truly ended between the British and the Americans and had almost completely ended between the tribes and the whites in America who had won their freedom and independence. Everyone, Indians and whites alike, was heartily sick and tired of the fighting, which had seemed never-ending.

In May the Congress of the United States of America had resolved upon a program of sending embassies among the tribes under flags of truce and engaging in extensive talks.[633] The tribes themselves, though their strength had been greatly weakened by the years of war, nevertheless remained proud people who truly believed that the Americans, in view of the setbacks they had received, had finally given in and that, in effect, though little had really changed as a result of it all, they, the Indians, had won.

Gen. George Rogers Clark, who had so long and so meritoriously served Virginia and the United States on the western frontier, was infuriated when he was summarily dismissed and his commission rescinded. Notification of it was made to him in a terse letter written on July 2 by Virginia Gov. Benjamin Harrison:

> *The conclusion of the War, and the distressed situation of the State with respect to its finances, call on us to adopt the most prudent economy. It is for this reason alone, I have come to a determination to give over all thoughts for the present of carrying on an offensive war against the Indians, which you will easily per-*

ceive will render the services of a general officer in that quarter unnecessary and will, therefore, consider yourself as out of command. But before I take leave of you, I feel myself called on in the most forcible manner to return you my thanks, and those of my Council, for the very great and singular services you have rendered your country, in wresting so great and valuable a territory out of the hands of the British enemy, repelling the attacks of their savage allies, and carrying on successful war in the heart of their country. This tribute of Praise and Thanks so justly due, I am happy to communicate to you as the united voice of the Executive.

    I am, with respect, Sir, yours, &c.   *B.H.*

The Americans, for their part, considered themselves the victors in the war that was winding down, and, with negotiations between the United States and British nearing conclusion, they became extremely aware of the value of what they considered to be their western lands. The principal negotiators of the Paris Treaty being formulated between the British and the United States were, respectively, Richard Oswald and John Adams. It was Commissioner Adams who was the tougher of the two. Where the matter of the western boundary of the United States was concerned, the British intended for it to be—as they had promised their Indian allies—the Ohio River. Adams would have none of that, declaring it had to be the Mississippi to the west and the Great Lakes to the north, or the treaty would not be signed and the war would continue until the British lost their dominion in Canada as well. Oswald eventually acceded to the demand, with no stipulation whatever in regard to the tribes occupying those lands.

There was also little concern given in the negotiations for the Loyalists in America who, by the projected terms of the treaty, would be utterly ruined. During the war large numbers of them had fled their homes in New York, Pennsylvania and elsewhere and taken refuge close to the frontier outposts at either end of Lake Erie, Niagara in the east and Detroit in the west. With the treaty accepted by both sides, those two strongly fortified stations were expected to be surrendered peaceably to the Americans. Both, however, were crowded with British subjects—military, civilian and Loyalist—and they would, Oswald said, require time to remove their possessions and themselves. Smug in the realization he had negotiated the United States into a country half a continent wide, Adams felt he could bend a little in this respect and agreed that those posts were to be turned over to the United States *"in due time and with all convenient speed."* It was a very vexing and dangerous nebulosity to have in an all-encompassing treaty of peace.

Conveniently overlooked in all this maneuvering in Paris was the unalterable fact that the British had occupied posts in the Northwest only by permission of the tribes and, in fact, had no true ownership of it. The Americans were quite well aware of this, yet when the British in their negotiations ceded their "claims" to the territory, the United States was only too eager to construe this as meaning that they were now and forever after sole owners of the vast Northwestern Territory.

It was obvious, particularly in the case of Virginia, that there would not be sufficient lands south of the Ohio River to fulfill bounty obligations to Continental and state troops. In a carefully orchestrated move, the Legislature of Virginia empowered its delegates in Congress to *"convey, transfer, assign, and make over unto the United States in Congress assembled, for the benefit of said states, all right, title and claim, as well of soil as of jurisdiction, which this Commonwealth has to the territory or tract of country within the limits of the Virginia charter, situate, lying and being to the northwest of the River Ohio."* The fact that these claims were vague in the extreme was of little concern to the Virginians. Connecticut, realizing what was being done by Virginia, very quickly did the same with her charter lands situated within the Ohio country.

With such transference to the federal government having been accomplished, Virginia now turned right around and claimed—and was granted by Congress—the previously stipulated tract of land in the Ohio country from which to bestow land bounties upon those Virginians who had honorably served in the Continental Army. The tract in question was called the Virginia Military Lands, and it was an enormous area, taking in all the country bordered by the Ohio River to the south, the Scioto River to the east and north, where it changed course in central Ohio and headed west, and the Little Miami River to the west. The only portion not bounded by a stream was that between the headwaters of the Little Miami and the Scioto, so a diagonal connecting boundary line was drawn, moving northwest from the headwaters of the Little Miami to those of the Scioto. This tract contained a total of 4,000,200 acres of extremely rich land, which Virginia felt was adequate to satisfy the claims of her troops. Without benefit of being surveyed into townships of regular form, the land was declared open for settlement. This meant that any individual holding a Virginia Military Land Warrant could locate wherever he chose within these boundaries and take up land in any shape that he desired, providing the land had not previously been located by someone else with a similar warrant. No one paid much heed to the fact that settling on such lands would be grossly in violation of preexisting treaties with the Indians. At the same time, Connecticut reaffirmed her northwestern territory along the south shore of Lake Erie, claiming—and being granted by Congress for bounty purposes—over 3,500,000 acres called the Western Reserve Lands.

Everyone agreed that it was time the settlement of the Ohio country began in earnest; everyone, that is, except the thousands of Indians of various tribes who were living on those lands and considered them their own.

Both the Americans and the Indians, during the period of negotiations, had sent word to their respective peoples that a period of truce had been declared preparatory to the peace and that further incursions against the former enemies, by both sides, should cease at once. The Indians lived up to the agreement; the Americans did not. Against governmental edicts prohibiting such activity, a group of Kentuckians early in the summer had taken it upon themselves to cross the Ohio and invade Shawnee territory on a mission to recover horses they claimed the Indians had stolen from them throughout the past years. The mission failed, a few deaths resulted and the war very nearly flared up again as a result of it all; no doubt would have but for the quick action of a few.

Arent de Peyster, the British commander in Detroit, who was now a lieutenant colonel, having been informed of the incident, on July 17 hurriedly wrote to the British military commander, Brig. Gen. Allan Maclean, in which he said, in part:

> *Runners are just come in from the Indian country with accounts that the Kentuck people had attacked and carried off a number of horses belonging to the Indian hunters, who were hunting on their own grounds at a considerable distance on this side of the Ohio. The Indians, not willing to lose their property, pursued the Virginians, attacked them, killed two men, and had an Indian mortally wounded, who is since dead. I have made every possible inquiry, and can assure you the Kentuckers were the sole aggressors, and I have mentioned the particulars that they may be fairly related, to prevent any misfortunes that might ensue from misapprehensions of these lawless people at Kentuck. The Indians being heartily disposed for peace and friendship with the people on the frontiers of the United States.*

Immediately upon receiving the letter from de Peyster, Gen. Maclean had a portion of it carefully copied and sent to the Americans on July 31 with his own letter directed to Col. Marinus Willett:

> *I have this day received a letter from Lieutenant Colonel De Peyster, the Commanding Officer at Detroit, dated the 17th July, an extract from which letter I take the liberty of enclosing herewith, requesting that you will be pleased to transmit it, and this letter, to his Excellency, General Washington. Trifles may sometimes be the means of doing great mischief, which may be prevented by applying proper remedies in time. On the present occasion, the Virginians at Kentucky have been the aggressors, without any provocation on the part of the Indians, who are well disposed to cultivate peace and friendly intercourse with the people on the frontiers of the United States, provided they are not molested in their property or persons, by a number of people who come to settle at a considerable distance from the frontiers of the United States, that they may not be subjected to the controul of any legal law or government whatever. These lawless people would be glad to bring on an Indian war, to be an excuse for their depredations, and therefore will not scruple to misrepresent this last affair, and endeavor by that means to induce the United States to take up their quarrel. On this account I have thought it my duty to state this matter fairly and candidly, that the unlawful and improper conduct of the Kentuck people may not be a means of involving innocent people in misery and distress.*
>
> *I have the honor to be, Sir, &c.*
>
> *Allan Maclean*

Col. Marinus Willett

The missives, relayed to George Washington, were very gratifying to him and, even though the peace had not yet been finally concluded in Paris, the general began taking the steps necessary to remove the Indians from the lands that he knew the Americans would soon occupy and in which he himself had a very deep and personal interest in respect to extensive tracts of land he or his agents had already claimed and those he meant yet to claim. He cared not in the least that this was, in view of his position of power and influence in the United States government, a decided conflict of interest. George Washington had been feathering his own personal nest with Indian lands ever since his family first became involved with the Ohio Land Company in 1748, and he did not mean to curtail the activity now, even though he was reputedly the richest man in America at this point.

George Washington had already presented to Congress a written paper, which he called a plan but what was in reality no less than a monumental conspiracy, by which the western lands belonging to the Indians could now most easily, most bloodlessly and least expensively be wrested from them. He suggested, in order to *"induce them to relinquish our territories and remove to the illimitable regions of the West,"* that the Indians be maneuvered into positions where they had little choice but to sell their lands. Since the expense of a major war could not be shouldered by the young and still newly shaping United States government, he recommended that all efforts should be made to implant as many new settlers as possible on Indian lands. In order to do this, his plan went on, grants of land should be made to veterans of the Revolutionary War from such parcels in Indian territory as the Virginia Military Lands and the Western Reserve Lands—grants that were either free, as bounty for services previously performed, or priced so low that few would be able to pass up the opportunity of buying and settling. George Washington went on to make special mention of the fact that these settlers, being largely veterans of the war and experienced soldiers, might tend to awe the Indians. Even if they did not, his plan continued, and the Indians rose up in arms, these settlers would then make excellent militia to protect the United States claims in the Ohio country.

Washington's remarkably encompassing plan then pointed out a particular bonus of such settling that might otherwise have escaped the notice of Congress: the fact that in heavily populating the Northwestern Territory, the settlers would soon kill off all the game and make the land so unattractive to the Indians that *"they will be as eager to sell as we are to buy."*

He then very meticulously laid out for Congress a blueprint of negotiations for such lands. First, government agents should point out to the Indians that as allies of the British, they had become conquered when the British surrendered and, as a conquered people, they had no land rights or rights of any other kind and therefore could not make demands; yet that the United States, in its generosity, would, if the Indians gave up their alleged claims, pay them a certain amount and also provide them with new lands of their very own farther to the west. In such negotiations, the plan continued, treaty commissioners could promise them that the United States government *"will endeavor to restrain our people from hunting or settling"* on the new lands that had so generously been given to the tribes. Yet at the same time, already beginning to hedge before the agreement was even made, the plan made it clear that despite the promises made, the restrictions barring settlement on the Indian reserves would be very temporary; that, as always occurred on the frontiers, the bolder of the settlers would begin penetrating and settling the Indians' territory, and when the

Indians complained, as they obviously would, new negotiations could be undertaken and, with careful maneuvering, the tribes would again be forced farther west. Those commissioners who handled the treaties, Washington advised, should acquire the reserved Indian lands as cheaply as possible and, most important, always deal with tribes on an individual basis and reject any attempt on their part to deal with the government as a unified body. By dealing with the tribes individually, he pointed out, there would be a much greater probability of resentment arising between the tribes themselves and a reduced likelihood that they might unite to give greater strength to their demands. The commissioners, Washington added, should also remain aware that circumspection was desirable and that they should not, at any given time, *"grasp at too much"* lest some form of such unified resentment spring up and balk the westward expansion. As Washington stated it, *"There is nothing to be obtained by an Indian war but the soil they live on and this can be obtained by purchase at less expense."* It would be, Washington concluded, *"the cheapest and least distressing way of dealing with them."*

Apart from the fact that it was immoral, unethical and actually criminal, this plan placed before the Congress by George Washington was so logical and well laid out that it was immediately accepted practically without opposition and at once put into action. There might be—almost certainly *would* be—further strife with the Indians, new battles and new wars, but the end result was, with adoption of Washington's plan, inevitable: Without even realizing it had occurred, the fate of all Indians in the country was sealed. They had lost virtually everything.

A strong sense of discomfiture dawned gradually on the Indians as, in continued talks with both American and British delegates, they realized that their own allies, the British, had sold them out to save their own necks; that the British had not invited any Indian emissaries to the peace talks in Paris, nor given even the least consideration to the red people who had fought hardest, yet the Indians had suffered greatest and had the most to lose—the people whose very homelands were the principal consideration of the talks; and that the British had conceded to the Americans any rights they had to the territory to the north and west of the Ohio River.

At the same time, conceiving that new difficulties would arise between themselves and the Americans in the future, the British embarked on a strong program to convince the Indians that King George was still their greatest friend among the whites and the most concerned for their welfare. As Alexander McKee assured them at a council held at Sandusky Bay, the treaty being hammered out across the great waters in Paris was not meant "to deprive you of an extent of country, of which the right of the soil belongs to you, and is in your hands as sole proprietors. It is important that you realize that the King is still concerned for your happiness and shows this by his continued protection with his red children and our trade with one another, which is important to us both." As proof of this, he pointed out, were not the British still in their posts at Niagara and Detroit, as well as many at other smaller installations from the head of the St. Lawrence River to Lake Superior and all the way to Prairie du Chien, where the Wisconsin River enters the Mississippi? If the Americans treated the Indians badly, then the King was still in a position to come to their aid and redress the wrongs they were undergoing.

Finally, on September 3, the Treaty of Paris was signed, and the temporary truce while negotiations had been in progress now became a permanent peace. The War of the American Revolution was over, and the greatest losers were the American Indians.

There remained among the tribes, however, keenly perceptive individuals who did not believe the British were still their friends, and particularly among the Miamis, who absolutely refused to agree to any form of peace with the United States and its allies, the Iroquois. Those six tribes had split in their alliances during the war: The Mohawks, Cayugas and Senecas had largely sided with the British, while the Onondagas, Oneidas, and Tuscarawas had finally sided with the Americans. Many of those who had allied themselves to the British were already being given land to reestablish their villages in Canada, since their homelands in New York were lost. But for those who had allied themselves to the Americans, United States commissioners were already coming among them, encouraging them to sell their remaining lands to the United States and offering insulting amounts for such purchase. The Iroquois League bitterness was best expressed by the Seneca chief Sagoyewatha—Red Jacket— who said to the American commissioners:

"We first knew you a feeble plant which wanted a little earth to grow in. We gave it to you, and afterward, when we could have trodden you under our feet, we watered and protected you. Now you have grown to be a tall tree. Your top is in the clouds. Your branches spread all over the land. We were then the tall pine. Now we have become the feeble plant. When you came here, you clung to our knees. You called us father. We took your hand. We called you brother. You have grown so we cannot now reach up to your hands. We wish to cling around your knees and be called your children.

"A little while ago you lifted the war club against him who was once your and our Great Father over the water. You asked us to go with you to war. It was not our quarrel. We did not know whether you were right. We did not ask. We did not care. You are our brothers; that was enough. We went with you. We fought and bled for you. Now, when our Great Father sees blood running fresh from the wounds we received in fighting your battles, dare you tell us he has sent you to ask us to sell the birthplace of our children and the graves of our fathers?"[634]

[D e c e m b e r   3 1 ,   1 7 8 4]

This year following the end of the Revolutionary War had turned out to be even less eventful on the upper Ohio frontier than 1783 had been. Some scattered incidents of violence still occurred between diehards among both the whites and the Indians, but these were more isolated cases than the standard, as they had been for so many years previously. These days a person could even paddle his canoe on the Ohio River with reasonable assurance of getting where he was going without being shot at by someone on shore, and incursions by raiding parties from either side had become minimal.

Lest the border people became too complacent, however, there were still enough incidents to make them remain very cautious when traveling anywhere, and even isolated settlements and cabins were still hit on occasion.

That the Shawnees were truly interested in establishing a lasting harmony with the Americans and vice versa was evidenced by the fact that late last year and early this year, several attempts at peace talks had been made adjacent to the Falls of the Ohio, at Louisville. On February 7, 27-year-old Gen. James Wilkinson, after conferring at Fort Nelson with David Owens, who had been acting as liaison with the tribe, sent him among them with a written speech:

Chiefs and Brothers of the Shawanoe Nation:

> *We, the Big Knife, embrace this opportunity—by one of our great chiefs lately come from our Grand Council, your brothers—to inform you that the English and Americans have at length buried the hatchet, and concluded a firm peace. We wish you & our brothers, the Red People, to join your hands to the chain of friendship thus brightened by your brothers of America and your father, the English. We should have rejoiced to have had it in our power to send you the particulars of the Articles of the Peace, but your eldest brother has not yet forwarded them to us, though we every day expect to hear from him.*
>
> *We yesterday received the following Talk from him: "I approve the method you have taken to support your troops. Their terms of service being now expired by the happy conclusion of the war, you will please to discharge your whole corps." Thus, Brothers, we prove to you our sincerity in desiring peace and friendship—our warriors are discharged & gone home to their wives and children. We have buried the tomahawk; we have covered the blood which has been spilt, & we have gathered together the bones which were scattered on the ground, & buried them in a large grave that they may no more be seen. Now, Brothers, we wish you to do the same, to join your hands to ours, bury the hatchet, & let war come no more among us, for we desire to become one flesh & blood with you. When the peace which the Americans and British have made comes among you, you will find that the British have forgot you, their children. Nevertheless, we wish to consider you as a brother, and hold with you the chain of friendship.*
>
> *Mr. Owens informed me, that the Talks I sent you some time ago on the subject of a Treaty was not yet opened on account of your chiefs being absent. As soon as they have collected and considered the matter, it will be necessary to send a runner to let us know their sentiments, that I may inform our Great Chief, who will send persons to meet them at this place at any time they may appoint to conclude a firm peace, which we hope may continue as long as the rivers and woods shall last.*
>
> *Made at the Falls of Ohio, this 7th Day of February, 1784.*
> *To the Chief Warriors of the Shawnee Nation.*

Eight days later the garrison at Fort Nelson was discharged by their commander, Maj. George Walls, though he stayed on in the headquarters office there to handle any delegations of chiefs who might wish an audience to speak of peace. Further efforts in this direction were being made among the Miami chiefs on the Wabash by deputations from the commander at Vincennes, Lt. V. Thomas Dalton. To him, upon receiving news that the United States Congress had ratified the Paris Treaty, Maj. Walls had written nine days later:

Fort Nelson, 24th Feby 1784

Dear Sir—

 I have the pleasure to offer you my congratulations on the final ratification of the Peace, in consequence of which, by order of his Excellency, the Governor, I disbanded the troops here on the 15th instant. . . .

 As I propose setting off for the Government by the middle of April, I should be glad to see you, or some of the Ouabache [Wabash] chiefs here before that period; which, as it is an object I much desire, I hope you will endeavor to accomplish, in order that on my going down I shall be the better enabled to state the real situation of those tribes to the Assembly.

 I am, Sir, Y^r most ob^t serv^t.   *G.W.*

 Yet, with all the maneuvering going on for serious councils of peace to occur between the Indians and whites, one by one the plans fell through, and now this full year had gone by without anything definitive in that respect having occurred in the Ohio Valley. The situation was worsened by the fact that talks were being set up at Pittsburgh and Fort McIntosh with delegates of tribes to discuss the purchase of lands that did not even belong to the tribes that were summoned, the Americans not caring who signed the treaty papers, only that they were, in fact, officially transferred and that settlement could, with mollified conscience, be begun.

 Well to the east and north, the second Fort Stanwix Treaty was concluded with the Iroquois on October 22, with the humbled Iroquois ceding to the United States all of their claims—many of them imagined rather than actual—to any lands west of a line extending along the western boundary of Pennsylvania, from Lake Erie to the Ohio River.

 In keeping with the discharge of troops stationed along the Ohio River, Fort Henry at Wheeling was dismantled on the grounds that the Indians had been pushed far to the west and the danger from raiding parties was now over. Besides, the fort was a reminder of desperate times in the recent past—not a good image for a town that now, with the war ended, had become the terminus of a good wagon road that had been constructed to that point from Redstone. A new flatboat industry was sprouting at Wheeling, and it was quickly replacing Pittsburgh as the fitting-out place for travelers with the west—and western lands for the claiming—in their dreams. Wheeling was becoming, as well, a litigious society, where overlapping land claims filled the courts and suits dragged on interminably as claimants strove to prove prior ownership. George Washington himself was involved in one of these; the land he and his agents had claimed a decade or more ago was now being squatted upon by others, including members of the Cresap and Tomlinson families.[635]

 Many old-timers on the upper Ohio frontier, however, felt that everything was moving a mite too fast and that the rejoicing over reestablished peace was considerably premature. Not only had further peace negotiations not made much headway among the northwestern tribes, but a few backward steps had been taken as a result of some of the inflammatory incidents that had occurred. There were still a good many whites in this border country who, despite governmental directives to the contrary, felt Indians were legal game. One of these individuals was Lewis Wetzel.

Early in May, when returning from an illegal hunting trip in the woodlands west of the Ohio River, Wetzel took refuge from an impending storm in an unfinished cabin built along Indian Wheeling Creek, about three miles above its mouth. Deciding that he really didn't want to sleep on the damp earthen floor, he scouted about and found a few rough-sawn boards scattered about to complete the structure. He put his rifle inside a hollow log to protect it while he carried the boards into the cabin and laid them across rafter beams beneath the partially finished roof to make a pallet for the night.

While doing this work atop the rafters, Wetzel heard a noise outside and, with only his tomahawk and sheath knife for defense, froze where he was, hidden by the boards from the view of anyone below. A moment later six Shawnee Indians entered, set up kindling and twigs and struck a fire with flint and steel. They cooked their meal and talked animatedly for a time, then stretched out on the floor for sleep, rolling themselves up in their blankets as the thunderstorm struck and the rain pelted down heavily.

Wetzel waited silently above until all six were sound asleep, and then very carefully, taking advantage of the rainfall to mask any slight noise he might make, lowered himself to the cabin floor and slipped outside without awakening them. The storm continued for another hour, thoroughly drenching him as he crouched beside the log where his rifle was hidden. The wetter and colder he became, the more he blamed the Indians for his discomfort.

When the storm ended, he remained where he was with his rifle, still good and dry, now clenched in his grip as he stared intently at the cabin's entrance. He remained that way for several hours more until, in the first light of dawn, one of the warriors appeared at the open doorway, yawned and stretched hugely and inhaled deeply the invigorating, freshly washed air. It was his last breath. Wetzel's shot caught him in the V at the base of his throat, plowed through his neck and broke his spine, killing him instantly. Before the sound of the rifle blast had finished echoing among the hills, Wetzel was running away, reloading as he ran. The Shawnees did not follow, remaining hidden in the cabin for some time, not knowing how many were in the party that had attacked them. When they finally realized the enemy was gone, it was too late for pursuit, but their anger at the *Shemanese* had been rekindled.

In retaliation, these same Indians, about noon, struck Joe Tomlinson's place at the mouth of Grave Creek and, while no one was killed, they robbed him of a variety of goods. Before evening they struck again, killing two settlers in the valley of Wheeling Creek not far from the Wetzel place. And once again the anger of the whites toward the Shawnees was rekindled.

Two months later, John Hinkson's new little blockhouse far down the Ohio at the mouth of Limestone Creek in the Kentucky country was burned by a party of Shawnees, who also stole all the horses. Simon Kenton, who happened to be on hand with a party of 60 men, building his own new station on Lawrence Creek a few miles away, immediately pursued with 20 of his men and recovered the horses, killing a warrior named Leaning Tree in the process. There were now some 45,000 settlers in Kentucky, and, with choice lands daily becoming more scarce, new arrivals were spilling into the Shawnee hunting grounds north of the river; already more than 1,000 had made tomahawk improvements in these Ohio lands and were filing claims that they hoped and believed would stand up in ensuing years. What Indians they did not kill with knives or tomahawks or guns, they brought down in more subtle ways with the diseases they brought among them, against which the Indians had no defense and no immunity.

So, in view of the upsurge of encroachment into areas heretofore untouched by the whites, the cycle of strike and counterstrike continued and, in some cases, increased, keeping alive the flames of hatred that had burned so long between the Shawnees and the whites. This situation developing opposite Kentucky in the Ohio Valley was also occurring in the area to the north and west of the big river, from the mouth of the Muskingum upstream to Yellow Creek, and everyone seemed to realize that it was only a matter of time before very serious Indian troubles broke out anew, perhaps even worse than they had ever been before. At the same time, newly arriving would-be settlers found all the better bottomlands south and east of the upper Ohio laced with claims, and their only choice seemed to be the dangerous one of striking out deeper into the Ohio country and nibbling it into properties with their tomahawk claims.

In the midst of all the continuing minor skirmishes, Capt. Andrew Van Swearingen, concerned for the safety of his daughter and son-in-law, attempted to get Drusilla and Sam Brady to move away from Holliday's Cove to a safer location, preferably near his own place at Washington village. Brady, while appreciative, told his father-in-law he could not; as commander of Brady's Rangers, who were still making regular border patrols, he had to remain close to them on the Ohio. He asked Dusy if she wished to move back to Washington, and she replied stubbornly that without him, she was going nowhere. He even had difficulty overriding her insistence on accompanying him on his dangerous patrols.

Andrew Van Swearingen, still concerned for their welfare, then did what he felt was the only option left open to him: He spent a great deal of money hiring a large crew of workers to build for the Bradys a large, well-fortified home overlooking the Ohio River at the mouth of Indian Creek, centrally located to the patrol routes still regularly run by his Rangers, yet capable of being well defended in event of attack.

Peace may have come with the signing of the Paris Treaty, but very few experienced individuals along the upper Ohio, Indians or whites, were convinced of it—or believed that this lull of sorts in hostilities would last for very long. They simply kept their guard up and waited for the time when serious troubles would return. They were certain the wait would not be long.

[January 21, 1785—Friday]

The latest of the councils called by the Americans on the upper Ohio was winding down today at Fort McIntosh, at the mouth of Beaver River 25 miles downstream from Pittsburgh. Here, as a testament to the efforts of the American delegates sent among the tribes since the end of the war, had gathered the chiefs, sachems and warriors of the Ottawa, Chippewa, Delaware and Wyandot nations. Among those chiefs present were Monakaduto and Pimoacan. After their arrival they had, in turn, spoken of their desire for a lasting peace with the Americans and then had listened in stony silence as the American commissioners explained to them the elements of this newest proposed treaty.

Once again, as they had in previous treaty talks held in the Ohio Valley from Pittsburgh down to Louisville, the Americans quickly restated the situation: They had emerged victorious from their recent war with the British and were anxious to establish a permanent and lasting peace, perhaps even friendship rather than mere harmony, with these assembled Indians. But—and now came the proviso that everyone present knew was coming—in order to prevent future arguments that might eventually lead to warfare, it was necessary to establish boundaries between their peoples that were clearly defined and understood by both parties.

Unfortunately, the American commissioners went on blandly, the boundaries that had been established in the past—especially the principal one making the Ohio River the dividing line between Americans and Indians—had somehow not held up well, most likely because of vagueness in the treaty wording or lack of understanding on the part of some people. This was a situation the Americans wished to avoid in the future and why the new boundaries would be closely and clearly explained to those assembled.

"The boundary," said the American commissioner through his interpreter, "is to begin at the mouth of the river Cuyahoga and to extend up said river to the portage between that and the Tuscarawas branch of the Muskingum; then down the Tuscarawas to the crossing place above Fort Laurens, then westerly to the portage of the Great Miami River and down the southeast side of same to its mouth.[636]

"East of this line," he went on, "will be American territory and to the west and north it will belong to you tribes assembled here. The only exceptions are that we Americans reserve the right to a parcel of land six miles square at the mouth of the Great Miami and a similar amount on the portage between the Great Miami and Auglaize rivers, and the same amount on Sandusky Bay, and also a parcel of land two miles square on each side of the lower rapids of the Sandusky River; those areas being reserved so that we Americans can establish, for your benefit, trading posts thereon. Do you people gathered here clearly understand the new boundaries as now laid out before you?"

Indeed the Indians understood, far better than the American commissioner could imagine. They were uncomfortably aware that some two-thirds of the Ohio country which this new treaty gave to the Americans included very little of the land claimed by any tribes here represented. Those were lands belonging to the Shawnees and Miamis, as well as some of the Mingoes; yet no representative of those tribes had been invited to attend this treaty council. They were also painfully aware of the fact that once again, as had happened time and again, their own boundaries had been pushed back from western Pennsylvania and northwestern Virginia to central Ohio, and that as soon as this land was filled with settlers, there would come more encroachment, more fighting and more treaty talk, and once again they would be pushed farther to the west.

The conclusion was obvious to them: The treaty papers meant virtually nothing and would keep the Americans satisfied only for a while and would allow the Indians assembled here to live in peace temporarily before the next onslaught began. None of those assembled had any illusion whatever that this current uneasy peace would last, but they agreed among themselves that it would last longer than it would if here and now they refused to accept the terms.

So now they signed the treaty as the Americans wished them to, though not one person among them had any faith that it would be binding.

[M a r c h   2 0 ,   1 7 8 5 — S u n d a y]

It was early this morning that the Delaware chief Buckangehela arrived at the Shawnee capital village of Wapatomica on the upper Mad River with a young warrior of his tribe in tow. The council he had previously requested was called, the majority of the most powerful Shawnee chiefs in attendance, along with a number of Mingoes who had been invited to be on hand. Buckangehela addressed the assemblage soberly, the young warrior standing beside him.

"This, my Shawnee brothers and my Mingo friends," he said, indicating his companion, "is the warrior Weylendeweyhing, who is of my people and of my village.[637] He has just returned from attending the council that was held by the Americans at the mouth of the Beaver, in their fort called McIntosh, the council that none of us here but him attended. He will now relate to you, as he has done to me, the serious nature of what occurred there and the treaty that was signed, by which your lands and mine have now been taken."

Buckangehela nodded to Weylendeweyhing, who spoke slowly and carefully as he accurately related what had transpired at the Fort McIntosh council and the boundaries of the new claim acquired by the Americans in the treaty that resulted. A deep, ominous hush settled over the assemblage as he spoke.

"You here know very well," Weylendeweyhing continued, "that the Virginians called us to their council, and we were obliged to go. They desired us to listen to them, and these were their words: 'We have beaten the English, the Six Nations and everybody we fought against, and you Delawares with the rest. The Great Spirit is on our side, by which we have gotten all your lands. Your British father gave us all the land as far as the Mississippi and the big lakes. As we have beaten you, we have got all the country. If you had beaten us, it would have been the same case with us. We are as strong as a hickory tree that is not to be overpowered. We had no assistance in beating you, from either French or Spaniards. We have done it ourselves, as well as to all our other enemies. We are now the only people to be believed, and to us alone you must now listen. Delawares, we do not shake hands with you until you assemble all your chiefs and bring all our flesh and blood here—the American captives—that are amongst you; that then we may fix on the minute to fight if that is the choice of us both. We are going to fix a blockhouse at Lower Sandusky and another at the Big Miami River and then survey our lands and place people thereon. Then let us see who dares say anything against it.'

"This, my Shawnee brothers," Weylendeweyhing concluded, "is what the Americans told us."

As soon as the warrior had finished, Buckangehela resumed speaking to the assemblage. "Yes," he said, "what Weylendeweyhing has told you is true; it is what the Americans told us. We see now they mean to take all our lands, as we have always believed. We desire that you Shawnees, among whom the British agent McKee lives, relay to him what we have said, that he may in turn tell his father in Quebec, so that the British will tell us yes or no if they are going to help us as they have for so long told us they would. We shall be glad to know from you whether it is true or not. We have taken this earliest opportunity to inform you, and if it is true, we shall soon be obliged to listen to them. We shall be glad to hear from you, and what news you may have from Quebec, as we expect the Americans upon us very soon.

"We must now let you know," Buckangehela continued firmly, "that we are going to the Miamis. You are sensible we have been long in friendship with them, which we are now going to strengthen, after which we shall tell them what the Americans told us. We understand we are all to meet in the spring in your presence. By that time, we shall be returned from the Miamis. We listen carefully to everything you say and shall leave our head warriors here, that they may continue to do the same in our absence.

"We must now tell you," Buckangehela went on, "that the Americans intend to be soon at Detroit, being now at Beaver Creek with eight hundred soldiers, one colonel, twenty officers and some pieces of cannon. Being no longer afraid, since they say that the Detroit garrison belongs to themselves, they plan to take the English by the arm and turn them out and tell them they have no business there.

"We are glad that you recommend it to us to give up the American prisoners we have and hope, by that, you will be able to get ours away from them. This is all we heard the Americans say. We don't know what Monakaduto may have to say to you. We received from them a speech with a belt six feet long. We let you know that the Pennsylvanians spoke good on your behalf and are apt to quarrel with the other Americans, the Virginians, for being so hard with us Delawares."

Buckangehela was finished, and he and Weylendeweyhing seated themselves on the ground before the council fire to listen to the response of the Shawnees.

For a long while the Shawnee chiefs conferred quietly among themselves. At length a tall, distinguished-looking Shawnee with gray strands beginning to appear in his black hair rose from where he sat and strode to the fire to address them. He was Catahecassa—Black Hoof—principal chief of the Shawnees, and his expression was grim, his words stern.

"We are grateful to our Delaware brothers," he said, "for telling us this bad thing that has occurred, and we wonder where now it will take us. We, the Shawnees, being of a mind, as we have said to the Americans, to brighten the chain of friendship between them and us, see only that those Americans, as they always have in the past, remain greedy for our lands and will go to almost any end to take them from us."

Catahecassa stared at Buckangehela, and his words abruptly became harshly accusatory. "We see now that he has bent your heads with gifts and promises, by which you have given him rights not only to your lands but to lands that belong to us and others. This you should not have done, even though they had soldiers with them and you feel they forced you to do so.

"We Shawnees must now decide," he added, as the Delawares looked discomfited at being so reprimanded, "whether we will renew the war between us and them that has presently hesitated. It seems that it will become necessary for us to do so if we are to preserve that which is ours. But, as you ask, before we would do so, we will send our words to Col. McKee that he may relay them to his Father so that we may know what is in their heart and mind to do in this measure. That is all we have to say at this time."

As soon as the chagrined Delawares left, Catahecassa met with the other Shawnee chiefs—Chiuxca of the Peckuwes, Moluntha of the Maykujays, and Shemeneto of the Kispokothas—and they discussed the matter at length, resolving among themselves a course of action to follow. Catahecassa then retired to his wegiwa, where he dictated a letter to Alexander McKee, to be carried to him at Kispoko Town, also called McKee's Town in his honor by some, just under three miles to the northwest of Wapatomica:

Wapatomica, March 20th, 1785

Father,

> *This speech is from your children, the Shawnees, and Mingoes. You know the Wyandots and Delawares went to Council at Beaver Creek, where they met with a man appointed by the American Congress to speak to them (as he said), who told them he was glad to see them, that he had something to tell them and that what was in his breast he would declare to them directly, saying, 'What lands do you claim in this region? I ask you for a piece of ground. Take pity on me and grant it. If you say you will, I shall give you a great many thousands of dollars. And not only that, I shall give your children what they want, and will always continue giving them.' The Delawares agreed to their proposals and gave them a tract of land from the mouth of Little Beaver Creek, across the falls of Big Beaver Creek to Caughnawaga and Lake Erie. The Wyandots gave them, from Little Beaver Creek, the whole Shawnee country, the line to run through your house and the Standing Stone in the Miami River, from there to Pimoacan's line and down to the mouth of the same river. The Americans gave Monakaduto and Pimoacan each a piece of parchment and a belt, saying they might relocate their people easily to Kookhassing.[638] We shall be glad that the different Nations may not listen to anything the Wyandots or Delawares may say on behalf of the Americans, as they have sold their lands and themselves with it to them. The speeches sent to us, with one from the Six Nations, are going in three days to the southward and will be delivered by the*

Cherokees. *Our young brothers there will soon know of the treatment they received at Fort Stanwix from the Americans. The belts that the Maykujay delivered last Spring to let loose their young brothers, we beg may be given back to them, with the pipe, that they may put them to the intended use if occasion requires. We shall take it as a great favor that they will be strong and make good use of these belts. Chiuxca desires that you will write to Niagara to let them know he intends to go there as soon as the waters fall; that anything that may happen in this country, he will be able to inform them thereof. You will also please write this to your brother, Sir John Johnson, who is Thayendanegea's great friend.*

Father, you now see trouble is coming upon us fast. We think it is nearly at hand. The Virginians are settling our country and building cabins in every place. We hope you will take compassion on us, tell our young brothers, the Lake Indians, and the Six Nations, of our situation; that the Americans intend to pay us a visit early this spring when the grass is four inches high. With this letter we include the speech the Delawares this day gave to us about what happened with them and the Americans at Beaver Creek.

[March 23, 1785 — Wednesday]

The Americans continued to move apace in their steps to secure their grasp on the Northwest. They were only too mindful of the rumors circulating everywhere that the Indians, growing more cognizant of how they had been hoodwinked out of a massive section of the territory on their side of the Ohio River, were girding themselves to thwart any serious move by the Americans in that direction. With this in mind, it was essential, they felt, to establish a strong military toehold in the Ohio country as quickly as possible.

Memories were still fresh enough regarding the fate of the first white fortification built in the Ohio country, Fort Laurens. Placed too far inland to be properly supported and constantly harassed by the Indians, it finally had to be abandoned, the whole operation having cost a great deal in terms of lives and money, with no substantive return for the investment. The Americans were determined not to make that same mistake.

The place they had selected to build their first new Ohio fort since Fort Laurens was a location they could reach quickly and easily and that they could support well, and that could provide a springboard for attacks against the tribes if and when they became necessary, as everyone was convinced they soon would. The site chosen was the downstream point of land at the west side of the mouth of the Muskingum River, and the substantial fort was being constructed close to the remains of the old Wyandot town that had been there many years ago.

The troops sent to build the fort were under command of a tough United States Army engineer, Maj. John Doughty, who was himself acting under direction of Col. Josiah Harmar. The troops called themselves "dime-a-day-men," referring to the miserable pay they received as privates in the regular army—three dollars per month. They were disgruntled men who felt they were being forced to risk their necks to build a fort to protect settlers who were not yet even here, but for the most part they kept their grousing to themselves. Maj. Doughty would not tolerate complaining and was swift to punish insubordination in any form. Flogging was standard punishment for infractions and, depending upon the seriousness of the offense, a soldier might receive up to 200 lashes. The penalty for desertion, if caught, was much worse: immediate execution without benefit of court-martial.

It was expected to take nearly a year to complete the fort, which would be built in the form of a regular pentagon enclosing just under an acre of ground. The walls would be large vertical timbers buried deep in the ground and project 14 feet above it. There would be a central parade ground flanked by fine quarters for the commander and his officers, barracks for the soldiers, storage buildings, a guardhouse for prisoners and a powder magazine.

Though he had not been given instructions to do so, Maj. John Doughty, knowing only too well it was always wise to please one's superiors, had already decided to name this strong new frontier installation after his commanding officer. When finally completed, it would be called Fort Harmar.[639]

It was being erected none too soon, if the United States were to maintain its tenuous hold on the wild country now being referred to by all as the Northwest Territory.[640] Though the new government had endeavored to thwart some of the expected Indian problem by means of the Fort McIntosh Treaty, in which they had more or less coerced the Wyandots and Delawares to give up their lands involved, it was clear that they were having second thoughts about it all and were on the verge of repudiating it. The illegality of it was obvious in a more concrete manner by the fact that land purchased by the American commissioners included mainly territory that did not belong to the Indians who agreed to the sale, the Delawares and Wyandots. They had sold land that belonged to the Shawnee and Miami tribes, and no one was fool enough to think either tribe would not strongly oppose any penetration of it by illegal settlement or by the United States itself.

For the moment, during the time Fort Harmar was being built, the Indians were in a state of angry confusion, not sure exactly what they should do. In this confusion they were appealing to the British at Detroit, Michilimackinac, Niagara and other locations for help. For their own part, the British cautiously supported them, loftily reminding them that this was exactly what they had said would occur in this circumstance. For the British, too, however, the pending penetration of American settlers into the land posed a problem that affected them considerably, especially in the matter of the lucrative fur trade from this area. For that reason alone the Crown knew it was to its benefit to retain the loyalty of the tribes and their support in whatever was to come. Yet the British were in the position of maintaining a very delicate posture. They were not yet ready for another war with their former colonists and so could not promise the Indians active military support as they had in the past, though they did agree to continue providing them with the supplies they would need. They strongly urged the Shawnees to stand fast in their determination to keep the Americans south and east of the Ohio River, but at the same time they urged the tribes to restrain themselves from taking the offensive, lest they provoke the Americans into another full-scale war that might altogether too soon involve the British themselves.

Everyone seemed to be waiting for what would happen next and wondering what event would ignite the new war that everyone at this point conceded was inevitable.

Chapter 8

Lewis Wetzel had taken his time creeping up on the camp of the three Wyandots along the bank of Stillwater Creek. He had followed them most of the day without their being aware of it, knowing that sooner or later an opportunity would come for him to do what he intended. Now that opportunity was at hand.

Whether these three warriors were the ones who had committed the deed that had set him on their trail concerned him not at all. They were Indians, and that was all that mattered. His hatred of the Indians had always been strong, ever since he and his brother Jacob had been captured as young boys. It had grown stronger when his brother George had been killed by them three years ago. Now, however, it had become intense, dominating his mind, filling him with an obsessive lust to kill Indians whenever and wherever an opportunity came. There was, so far as he was concerned, ample justification.

Several weeks ago a party of Indians had killed his father, Old John Wetzel.

Ever since the Fort McIntosh Treaty, which had carved Ohio practically into two portions and given the United States ownership of the much larger southern portion—at least on paper—the Indians had fallen back in confusion as they tried to determine among themselves what to do. The changes along the Ohio River from Pittsburgh to Louisville had been remarkable.

Pittsburgh now had a permanent population well in excess of 1,000, plus nearly as many transients and military. Boats plied the waters of the Ohio in such numbers, it was almost as if a constant regatta were in progress. Wheeling, entirely recovered from its second siege, now had upward of 300 permanent residents, and its boatyards were attracting droves of people from the east. Those would-be settlers, arriving at Redstone en route to Kentucky or other places downstream, could eliminate considerable cost, difficulty and almost 150 miles of river travel that the trip via Pittsburgh entailed, by taking the continually improving wagon road westward from Redstone through Washington village to Wheeling. As a result, both Washington and Wheeling were growing with amazingly increased vigor. Wheeling itself was becoming an important river port, and along with the boatyards already existing or under construction, new wharves and landings were being built to accommodate the influx. The town was now beginning to seriously compete with Pittsburgh as a merchandise shipping center as well as the jumping-off place for journeys downriver.

Adventurous parties had begun to set their sights on claiming and settling wherever the notion took them, no longer overly concerned about landing on the Ohio side of the river to make their tomahawk improvements. Four families under Peter Patrick of Redstone, originally intending to settle in the area of Vincennes, came ashore instead near the mouth of the Scioto, sank some roots there and built a few cabins, then ascended the Scioto all the way to the mouth of Paint Creek before being driven back by irate Shawnees, though not before Patrick had made tomahawk cuts on many trees and chopped his initials into some smooth-barked beeches.[641]

The Peter Patrick party escaped disaster, but others didn't. Four hardy adventurers—Richard Wallace, Judge William Jack, Maj. James Wilson and Col. Alexander Barr—headed downstream together to claim lands, reasonably confident they would have no problem with the Indians. Wallace, who had been quartermaster with Col. Lochry's force when it was ambushed on the Ohio four years earlier, had spent a couple of years in captivity. He told the others he knew the Shawnees well, had been adopted by them and had made many friends among them. They would be pleased, he assured his companions, to see him and would tell him the best lands to claim. He couldn't have been more incorrect. They were attacked and, though Wilson and Jack escaped, both Wallace and Barr were killed. Not long after that, Andrew Zane, despite all his frontier experience, was in the process of crossing the Scioto River when he was killed by the long shot of a Shawnee he never even saw.

Other settlers were not deterred by the reports of such misfortunes, and a veritable boom of new settlements sprang up, although those south and east of the Ohio were considerably safer now from attack than those on the Ohio side. The new settlement of Limestone, where John Hinkson's Blockhouse had been burned, was attracting many settlers bound for the Kentucky interior, and a new town named Washington, seven miles inland from Limestone on the road to Blue Licks and Lexington, already had 31 cabins. Up the Great Kanawha at Campbell's Creek, Capt. John Dickinson claimed, with impunity, 502 acres that took in the old Indian Salt Springs, which he named Big Buffalo Lick. And a mile up the Little Kanawha from the Ohio, Capt. James Neal officially established his new settlement, named Neal's Station.[642] Twenty miles below the mouth of the Little Kanawha, a group of Scots families under Judge Joseph Wood established a settlement between the mouths of Lee's Creek and Pond Creek and named it Belleville.[643] Not far from the long-established Ryerson's Station, on the headwaters of Wheeling Creek, the new Wise's Mill was built among the many German settlers on Tenmile Creek, while only a few miles from there Robert Whortem built a little settlement with a blockhouse and called it Whortem's Station.[644] About this same time Youghiogheny County was divided into Brooke and Hancock counties, and experienced surveyor Ben Johnson, Jr., spent a busy week marking out and claiming some 7,000 acres in the newly formed Brooke County, not far from where the Cuppy family had just resettled and a few miles from the new Bill Logan place on King's Creek. Fifteen miles below Fort McIntosh, on the south side of the river and several miles up Mud Creek, William Langfitt established his place, but quickly abandoned it, hiding four sacks of seed corn, when some Indians were seen hovering in the area, and he moved to where the Campbells had settled on King's Creek.[645]

Two events, one on each side of the Ohio, were indicative of the sweeping changes being made. On the south side of the river, the Kentuckians gathered at Danville in a convention to discuss separating from Virginia and making Kentucky County a new state in its own right.[646] On the Ohio side of the river the Congress of the United States, immediately upon ratification of the Fort McIntosh Treaty, established what it called the Seven Ranges. These were seven ranges of townships that were to be the first public lands ever surveyed by the general government in the Ohio country. The boundaries of the tract were sharply drawn, beginning at Pennsylvania's western border on the north side of the Ohio River and extending 42 miles due west, then from there straight south to the Ohio River again, almost at the mouth of the Little Muskingum River, with the Ohio River being the southern and eastern border. With that, the official invasion of the Ohio country by the United States was begun.

With all this progress—or what some were pompously calling the "advance of civilization"—a certain carelessness had manifested itself among those traveling on the Ohio, even among those who were experienced bordermen and should have known better. Old John Wetzel was one of these. He and a neighbor, William Miller, set off on a hunting trip down the Ohio. In previous days they would have stayed close to the center of the river, keeping out of effective range of rifle shots from either shore. This time, feeling it was safe enough to do so, they paddled along close to the Ohio shore. It was a serious mistake.

As they passed near the relatively new Baker's Station on Cresap's Bottom, two miles above the mouth of Fish Creek, three Indians appeared on shore and shot at them. One of the balls struck Old John Wetzel in the side, and he half toppled, dropping his paddle. Miller, unharmed, leaped from the canoe and, by alternately diving and surfacing, quickly got out of range and then swam across the river. Wetzel, seriously wounded, stood up as the canoe drifted to the shore and leaped out onto the bank in a desperate effort to escape. Instead of hard ground, the shore here was deep mud, and he sank into it over his knees. Firmly wedged, he watched helplessly as one of the Indians appeared on the adjacent shore, deliberately reloaded and shot at him again. This time the ball went through his heart and killed him. The warrior scalped him but left the body there, projecting from the mud.

That was where Lewis Wetzel had found him the following day, after learning from the escaped Miller what had happened. With considerable difficulty and overcome with immense grief, he had managed to pull his father's body to shore and bury it. A few days later, returning to the site with Jacob and Martin, the three brothers had disinterred the body of their father, taken it back to their own place on Wheeling Creek and reburied it.[647]

Now, as he peered from hiding at the three Indians in their camp on the bank of Stillwater Creek, the hatred within Lewis Wetzel nearly choked him. It was unlikely that these Indians were the ones that had killed his father, but that was of no consequence. They were Indians, and that was all that mattered . . . or would ever matter. His only real concern now was how he could kill them all with none escaping.

The three warriors had rifles, tomahawks and knives, and so to attempt rushing them could well be suicide. Taking a shot would kill one, but two would escape. So he waited. The three Wyandots ate their meal, talked for a while and then, with their guns on the ground beside them, rolled up in their blankets and lay down. They stirred off and on for a half-hour or more and then were finally still. When he was certain they were fast asleep, Wetzel set his gun aside and moved slowly toward them as soundlessly as a cloud shadow moves across the land, knife in his left hand, tomahawk in his right.

Stopping between the first two, who lay on their backs breathing slowly and deeply, he wasted no time. With a sudden swift stroke he plunged his knife directly into the heart of one, who gave a half groan and tried to sit up but failed. At the same time he slammed his tomahawk deep into the temple of the other, who stiffened, then started kicking his legs spastically. Wetzel jerked the tomahawk free and stepped over him quickly to the third, who had grunted a query and was just rising to a sitting position, and struck him with the bloody tomahawk blade in the nape, instantly killing him.

"That don't settle the score yet," he said aloud. "Not by a long ways."[648]

[October 11, 1785 — Tuesday]

John Madison, the well-dressed man who arrived at Wheeling today, was obviously wealthy and, from what he said, just as obviously interested in claiming lands. Scion of a very wealthy family of Port Conway, Virginia, he had many very influential friends in government, not the least of whom was his own brother, James, who had been a member of the Continental Congress and who was now deeply involved in the newly forming Continental Convention.[649]

It had been from George Washington himself, via his brother, that John Madison had learned about the lands Washington had claimed 15 years earlier up the Big Sandy River, and he decided that he wanted to claim some of those same lands for himself, as well as some in his brother's name. Well informed of the dangers extant in such a pursuit, he had been for several weeks looking for the best possible man to guide him to the Big Sandy and assist him in claiming such lands. The man he wanted had to have extensive experience in fighting and outwitting the Indians and an unparalleled grasp of wilderness survival; a man who in any conceivable emergency, could keep his head. His search began in the Redstone Old Fort area, at

Brownsville, and continued as he reached Pittsburgh. With a high fee in the offing for such service, he had many applicants for the job, but he had turned all of them down after brief interviews.

While in Pittsburgh, however, Madison heard mention of a young man who seemed to have all the qualities he was seeking, and the more he inquired about him, the more convinced he was that the man in question was exactly the man he wanted. That was why he had now come to Wheeling, since the object of his search lived several miles up Wheeling Creek. The man he sought had just come back from stalking three Indians in their own camp and singlehandedly killing all three with hand weapons. That man was Lewis Wetzel.

At first Wetzel was disinclined to take the job. Looking after a novice in the woods was, he had long ago decided, a quick way to get the novice—and perhaps himself as well—killed. John Madison, however, was insistent and kept raising the amount he would pay Wetzel to undertake the project, until that payment finally became more than the frontiersman had ever earned in any one year. As an added incentive, Madison promised Wetzel that not only would he reimburse him fully for all equipment and supplies purchased for the project, he would also give him 1,000 acres of the claims they made and, if he was satisfied by Wetzel's service over the six or eight months they would be gone, a substantial bonus as well.

Wetzel had never been a mercenary individual, but all this icing added to the cake was more than he could resist. "I'll do it," he said at last—but he still wasn't looking forward to it.

[N o v e m b e r   1 0 ,   1 7 8 5 — T h u r s d a y]

In their small quarters in the new fort on the shore of the Ohio River only a short distance above the mouth of the Great Miami River, Richard Butler and George Rogers Clark, both treaty commissioners for the United States, sat on opposite sides of the small table and quietly discussed the events that had brought them to this place.[650] As Clark continued to offer helpful reminders of what needed to be said to the President of the United States Congress, Butler wrote in strong, swift strokes:

Mouth of the Big Miami—November 10th, 1785

Sir:

> *We have now the honor to inform your Excellency that after surmounting the many difficulties and disappointments attendant on so long an in-land journey, and business of this kind, we meet at this place on the 22d October ultimo, without having sustained any injury or loss.*
>
> *On our arrival we found that the Indian Nations in general had not received our invitations to treat with the cordiality which we expected; but the Miami Nation had taken away the horses of our messengers, and treated their own persons in a manner hitherto unknown among the Nations of the West. No positive answer, however, being given to our invitations, we conceived that it would not be prudent nor consistent with our duty to relinquish the business in its then doubtful state. We*

therefore concluded to stay until we should be enabled to determine fully whether the Indians were for peace or war. For this purpose we sent two of the same messengers with two Indians to inform the Nations whom we had invited, of our arrival at the place of treaty, and to demand immediate answers to our messages. We recommended it to the chiefs of the Miami Nation to make reparations for the insult that they had offered to the United States in their ill treatment of our messengers while it might be in their power, since they might assure themselves that such unmerited insult would not be passed over in silence; that the answers of the Nations who were invited would determine us either to stay and treat with them as we had proposed, or to return and make report of their Conduct to Congress.

Affairs being thus arranged, we concluded that as the time which it would necessarily take up, either to await the answers of the Indians, or to go through the business of a treaty with them, should they agree to attend, would render it impracticable for the troops to return even to the Muskingum this winter; and as this is the place to which Colonel Harmar was authorized by a resolution of Congress of June last, to extend his posts for the purpose of keeping off illegal settlers from the territory of the United States, we directed Major Finney to proceed to build a place of security and comfort for the troops and stores, which might answer all the purposes designed by that resolution, as well as protect the treaty. This work [near the mouth of the Great Miami River] *he began on the 25th day of October, and by his own industry, seconded by that of all his officers, whose exertions do them great honor, has now perfectly secured the post, and got the troops into very comfortable block-houses for the winter. The work is a quadrangle, with a strong block-house at each corner, forming a defence for each face of the work. The curtains are strong pickets, well set in the ground, and in the center of two curtains fronting each other, and forming part of the curtain, are a guard-house and provision store for the goods designed for the treaty.*

A few days since a man of the Shawanese arrived, who was sent by the chiefs of his nation to inform us that they were ready to come, and would be with us in a short time. A Wyandotte hath since arrived, who informs us that the whole of the Western tribes will attend, and that the horses, &c, taken from our messengers will be restored.

We find by the frequent robberies and murders committed on the inhabitants on the south side of the Ohio by the different Indians, that some decision is really necessary, the people being no longer able to bear such treatment. Many are deprived of every horse, and left with large families to labor out their substance with a hoe. This post, we hope, will give them some temporary safety, and very probably answer some future good purposes, should the Indians require correction.

The Miami River is found to be boatable in the Spring and the early part of the Summer about 80 miles up, to the portage between it and the Miami or Omi River, which empties itself into Lake Erie.[651] The ground at the confluence of this and the Ohio River being very low is covered by every fresh. This obliges us to fix one mile above the mouth of Miami, on the north bank of the Ohio, it being the first safe bank we could find.

Not having heard from our last messengers, we have nothing farther to communicate, but that your Excellency may assure yourself that no exertion shall be wanting on our part to bring matters to a happy and honorable issue with the Indians for the interest of the United States.

With the highest respect, we have the honor to be, Sir,

Your Excellency's most ob^t. and hb^l. sevts.

G. R. Clark
Rich^d. Butler

His Excellency
The President of Congress

[January 31, 1786 — Tuesday]

The Shawnee delegation was led by Wehyehpihehrsehnwah—Blue Jacket—who was now principal chief of the Maykujay sept of their tribe. That powerful position had been transferred to him by Chief Moluntha who, because of the frailties of his age and infirmities of his health, had recently stepped down from leadership of the sept. The others of the delegation included the warriors Chiksika, Tecumseh and Wasegoboah, along with some others. With them as well, despite his poor health, was old Chief Moluntha and his huge wife, Nonhelema.

This group of Shawnees had come here to the mouth of the Great Miami to view firsthand the negotiations that were being conducted between the American commissioners and the band of 300 pacifistic Shawnees who, without official tribal sanction, had been led here by the subchief Kekewapilethy—Tame Hawk.[652]

This newly arrived group of Shawnees under Blue Jacket, furious at Kekewapilethy for his effrontery in taking tribal matters into his own hands, observed with silent anger the fortification—being called Fort Finney—that the whites had had the temerity to build here in the Ohio country, nearly a mile above the river's mouth, under the guise that it was merely a temporary structure and would be dismantled when the treaty talks were concluded.

This Fort Finney treaty talk was the result of what had begun early last summer, when delegations of Americans had started moving through the Ohio, Indiana and Michigan countries, inviting the various chiefs and delegates of their nations to attend the important treaty that was originally scheduled by them to begin the first day of the Harvest Moon at the Great Miami's mouth.

How little the Americans understood or cared about the Indians in general was clearly apparent from the fact that they had not only selected this site for the talks, but had arranged to hold them at a time when councils simply were not held because of harvesting, hunting, and other autumn business requiring the tribes' attentions.

A number of American peace delegations had moved through the Northwest all last year, visiting Shawnees, Miamis, Delawares, Wyandots and other tribes, traveling in separate parties headed by Samuel Robertson, James Elliott, William Clark and Daniel Rinkings. Even though uninvited into their country, most of the emissaries had been received politely enough by the tribes, except for a few occasions when they had been treated contemptuously and, on occasion, their lives threatened.

The general displeasure of the tribes over the visits was voiced at one of the councils held for these delegates at Lower Sandusky last September 20, where Tarhe, now the most prominent of the Wyandot chiefs, presided.[653] He summed up the feelings of the tribes by speaking in a voice filled with constrained politeness.

"Brother Americans, we acknowledge the receipt of your messages calling us to the mouth of the Big Miami River on the Ohio, to a treaty to be held there ten days from this date. When we consider that important business already transacted with you at Forts Stanwix and McIntosh has not yet had time to be made known and determined upon by those nations concerned in it throughout this great country, we cannot help saying that you have moved too quickly. Time must be allowed for the tribes to hold council among themselves to consider your proposals carefully. Such councils are essential if we are ever to accomplish the desirable end of peace and make it permanent.

"We are equally surprised," Tarhe went on, eyes becoming hard and voice cold, "that you seem to take no notice of the ancient council fires kindled by our forefathers, at which places *only* can the good works of peace be accommodated. When our business is fully settled and *we* are ready to meet you, then such meeting should be held at the place where our ancestors formerly met to settle matters tending to their welfare and happiness."

Tarhe had then gone on to say that the place where such counciling should be held was at the great council fire at Detroit. The American delegates, however, had no wish to hold such a meeting in proximity to the British, whom they suspected would sabotage their efforts among the tribes. They insisted that the general council be held at the mouth of the Great Miami; but that, since the fort they were erecting there for that purpose was not yet completed, they would agree to postpone the opening treaty talks for three months, till the first of January.

Leaving with no firm answer from the Wyandots, the American delegation then went to Wapatomica to inform the Shawnees of this same decision. The Shawnees were considerably taken aback by the appearance of this American delegation among them, but they agreed to hold an immediate council and listen to what they had to say. It had been then, when the council convened, that the self-important Shawnee subchief named Kekewapilethy—Tame Hawk—had asked permission to speak first. When this request was granted, he rose and, to the chagrin and irritation of the other Shawnees present, made a speech altogether too conciliatory toward the Americans. He strongly urged the young Shawnee warriors to end their raiding, killing and stealing horses and to have pity upon their own women and children by not hindering the good work of peace the Americans were here for at this council.

As Kekewapilethy spoke, it became clear he was very inclined to attend the proposed treaty talks and wished to grasp the American offerings of peace irrespective of the cost. Since he was an inconsequential chief generally considered to have little of consequence between his ears, his speech astounded them and incurred such great displeasure and remonstrance among the other Shawnees in attendance that he left the council house shamed and petulant before the council was even well begun.

Next to talk was another Shawnee subchief named Piteosawa, who spoke more truly the feelings of the tribe in general.

"Brothers of the Thirteen Fires," he said coldly, "you sent speeches amongst us last year to invite us who are of one color to the council fire you kindled at Fort

Stanwix, for the peace and other good things you said you had to offer us. Soon afterward you kindled another council fire at Beaver River, at your Fort McIntosh, to which you also invited us, but to neither of which did we come because you had openly said you would keep some of our chiefs as hostages for the guarantee of our fidelity. But you ought to know this is not the way to make a good or lasting peace—to take our chiefs prisoners and come with soldiers at your backs. This cannot tend to general good between us.

"You now again," he went on, "invite us to another council fire at the mouth of the Great Miami. Your messengers have gone through several nations. But we are aware of your design to divide our councils. We are unanimous. And it is not right for you to kindle council fires among brush or nettles. Therefore, we now inform you that if you wish a council with all these many Indian nations, the proper place is at Detroit, the ancient council fire of our forefathers. When we see you there, we will take your hand—but this cannot be sooner than next spring. We must have time to hear from other nations to the westward. Nothing is to be done by us but by general consent; we, the tribes of the northwest, now act and speak like one man."

The remainder of the Wapatomica council continued and finally concluded in this vein and, disheartened, the American delegation departed. It was not until late in the year that the Shawnee chiefs found out Kekewapilethy and others had left their villages, at which time the full truth had come out. Catahecassa, Blue Jacket, and the others were thunderstruck when they discovered that before the American commissioners left Wapatomica, Kekewapilethy had secretly gone to them on his own and promised to attend the planned treaty talks in January at the mouth of the Great Miami, told them that he would treat on behalf of the Shawnee tribe and would be very agreeable to whatever terms the Americans proposed.

This was where he was now and why Blue Jacket's party had come here to the mouth of the Great Miami to discover what was happening between him and the American commissioners at Fort Finney. Now they had arrived and presented themselves to the American treaty commissioners plenipotentiary, Maj. Gen. Samuel H. Parsons, Col. Richard Butler, and George Rogers Clark. Those commissioners regarded them with dark suspicion, causing many of the whites in attendance to grip their rifles more firmly and surreptitiously check their loads.

Blue Jacket and his party were escorted to where the talks were being held and were grudgingly invited to visit and observe, but, since they were not part of the Shawnee delegation already involved here, they were told they had no right to speak. Insulted by the restriction, yet not prepared for a full confrontation with the American troops and armed frontiersmen on hand, they acquiesced. They were disconcerted to discover that there were also official deputations here from the other northwestern tribes, despite earlier refusals to attend. Included were Wyandots under Tarhe, Delawares under Buckangehela, Pimoacan, Big Cat and Awuncy, Chippewas under Wafrugahquealied, Ottawas under Nichefrewaw and Nichinesica, and Potawatomies under Nanimisea and Messquagoneke. And here, too, were the 300 Shawnee pacifists that Kekewapilethy had brought with him, most of them women and children who were bundled in skins and blankets against the January cold, but obviously suffering from it and just as obviously very hungry.

"How does Tame Hawk dare to bring those unfortunates with him and increase their misery?" Chiksika whispered angrily. "What does he hope to get out of this?"

"He wishes food and warm clothes for his people," said Moluntha mildly, "which is understandable, but better he should have applied to the rest of the tribe for them. It is a hard winter and none of us has much, but we would gladly have shared with him and them."

The talks were continuing and, in whispered discussions with chiefs and warriors who had been there from the beginning, Blue Jacket's party learned the essence of what had occurred thus far. When Kekewapilethy arrived with his 300 hungry, cold and weary followers, Col. Richard Butler had ordered the firing of a military salute to honor them, at which Kekewapilethy had puffed up with pride. Butler had then begun his talk with Kekewapilethy, and when the subchief proclaimed, "All this land is ours," and a little later, "God gave us this country," Butler had become very forceful in his remarks.

"We plainly tell you, Tame Hawk," he had retorted, "that this country belongs to the United States! Their blood has defended it and will forever protect it. Their proposals are liberal and just, and you should be thankful for the forgiveness and offers of kindness of the United States." For the subchief's acceptance of the proposals, he added, he was prepared to offer peace and immediately give his tattered followers food and blankets.

Kekewapilethy had come prepared to negotiate and had been confident of his ability to do so to his own honor in the tribe. He had brought with him a black wampum belt, signifying war, and had then withdrawn it from his pouch and placed it on the table, saying with a boldness he did not feel, "You say you have goods for our women and children. You may keep your goods and give them to other nations. We will have none of them."

At this the three commissioners had become angry and walked out. On the way George Rogers Clark deliberately knocked the black wampum belt to the floor and stamped upon it. Now, soon after the Blue Jacket party's arrival, the commissioners, having given Tame Hawk a long period of time to reconsider, returned and Butler spoke.

"Our offer," he said firmly, "remains as it was stated to you, and you can take it or leave it, but the destruction of your women and children depends on your present choice."

All of Kekewapilethy's early display of self-confidence now drained away and he meekly gave in. Butler immediately ordered food distributed to the Shawnee's followers and presented him as well with enough whiskey for Kekewapilethy and the few adult males in his party to get drunk upon, which they began to do at once.

The talks were now all but finished. With interpreters relaying their words to various factions almost simultaneously, the commissioners went over the seven articles of the treaty step by step preparatory to the signing. The first article called for three hostages to be delivered up to the commissioners, to be held until all prisoners, white or black, taken during the late war, who were in the possession of the Shawnees and who had been taken by them or any other Indians living in their towns, were restored to the Americans.

Article two stated that the Shawnees acknowledged the United States to be the sole and absolute sovereign of all the territory ceded to the Americans by the British at their treaty of peace in Paris.

Article three required that if any Indians committed murder, robbery, or injury against any citizen of the United States, the offenders were to be given up to the officer commanding the nearest American post for trial, and, in like manner, any white guilty of similar crimes against the Indians would similarly be punished according to the laws of the United States.

The fourth article called for the Shawnees to report any intelligence they gained of other tribes preparing to strike against the United States. Failure to do so would make them be considered as party to such measures, and they would be punished accordingly.

Article five stated that the United States granted peace to the Shawnees and received them into the favor and protection of the United States.

Article six was one in which the wording was so confusing that none of the Indians on hand understood it, though they were encouraged in their *misunderstanding* of it. In its entirety, the article stated:

The United States do allot to the Shawanese Nation land within their Territory to live in and hunt upon, beginning at the south line of the lands allotted to the Wiandots and Dellawares, at the place where the main branch of the Great Miami intersects with said line, thence down the River Miamis to the fork of that River next below the old Fort which was taken by the French in the year 1752, thence due west to the River de la Pansé, then down that River to the River Wabash, beyond which line none of the citizens of the United States shall settle nor disturb the Shawanese in their settlements and possessions, and the Shawanese do relinquish to the United States all title or pretence of title they ever had on the lands east, west and south of the east, west and south lines before described.

To all the Indians in attendance, this simply reaffirmed that the Shawnees would continue to live and hunt in their own Ohio territory, with the Ohio River being the border to the south and the territories of the Wyandots, Delawares and Miamis being the border to the north. To the whites, it meant that the Shawnees had ceded *all* this land east of the Great Miami River and westward to the Wabash to the United States.

Article seven simply stated that if any citizen of the United States presumed to settle on the lands allotted to the Shawnees by this treaty, he would be put out of the protection of the United States.

While the commissioners were thus going over the articles of the treaty, old Moluntha went to Kekewapilethy and sat with him for an extended period, conversing. Blue Jacket and the others were certain he was upbraiding the subchief, but they were startled when, as the commissioners finished, he came creakily to his feet and announced that he, as principal chief of the Maykujay Shawnees, along with Kekewapilethy, would be the principal treaty signer for the Shawnees.

"He has gone mad!" Wasegoboah whispered in amazed alarm to Blue Jacket, who nodded.

"Can't we stop him and Kekewapilethy?" Tecumseh asked, deeply concerned.

"We could and would, if it were necessary," Blue Jacket murmured, "but it is not. Moluntha no longer heads the Maykujays, and neither of them represents the general council of the Shawnees, so their names on the treaty will have no significance. Both will be reprimanded in council when we return, but for now we will let it be. The Americans have soldiers here who are ready for trouble, which would certainly occur if we were to try that. Our party is too small and the weather too bad to launch an attack on them. But I tell you this: I have never hated the Americans so much as I do this day. They *will* be destroyed. I will return here in the Green Moon, kill all the soldiers who remain and burn this fort which is such an insult to our dignity and intelligence."

One by one the chiefs came forward and made their marks on the copy of the treaty prepared for the specific tribes. As Moluntha prepared to do so on the American treaty with the Shawnees, he made a comment to Commissioner Richard Butler, who nodded and took out a sheet of paper, upon which he wrote something and gave it to the aged chief. Moluntha nodded, folded it and placed it in his pouch.

Why the chiefs of these other tribes were here and why they were signing their own copies of the treaty made no sense to the visiting Shawnees under Blue Jacket. The territory under discussion belonged to the Shawnees and Miamis, not them. As the signing progressed, first by the Indians, then by the attesting whites and finally by the three commissioners plenipotentiary, Col. Richard Butler became quite affable.[654] He chatted with the Indians through interpreters and never corrected their misunderstanding that the Ohio River was still the border between the Shawnees and the whites; in fact, when they remarked uneasily about the two forts the Americans had now built on their territory—this one and the one called Fort Harmar at the mouth of the Muskingum—he blandly reassured them that the purpose of those forts was not for invasion but as guard posts to turn back any whites who might attempt settling in Shawnee territory. He then remarked how delighted he was with the "new and everlasting friendship" sealed this day between the United States and the Shawnees, adding that "differences of opinion" between the two could now at last "be put aside for all time."

The paper the doddering Moluntha had received from Col. Butler, which he now showed to Blue Jacket and his party with no small measure of pride, was merely a safe-conduct pass, stating that the bearer, Moluntha, was one of the chiefs who had signed the Great Miami Treaty and that he and his people at Mackachack *"have done all in their power to keep the Shawnee from going to war and said Moluntha is included among the friends of the United States, and is therefore in no wise to be molested."* In addition to that paper, Moluntha had been presented with a written copy of the treaty. So, too, had the leaders of the other tribal delegations.

As the visiting Shawnees mounted their horses to return to the north, all were dismayed at what Kekewapilethy had taken it upon himself to do, and even more disgusted and disheartened with the actions of the lovable old Moluntha, who had for so long been held in respect by all and had become the ideal of so many young Shawnees. Now even Nonhelema, though she had said nothing against her husband, set her lips in a grim line as she helped the old man mount up and then rode close beside him, bringing up the rear of their little party.

As the ugly little bastion called Fort Finney disappeared from view behind them, Chiksika muttered aloud, "At every contact with them I understand more fully than ever before why my father, Pucksinwah, said never to make peace with the *Shemanese,* that they only mean to devour our land."

Tecumseh growled a sound of agreement, and Blue Jacket looked at them both. "My adopted father, Pucksinwah, was one of the wisest men I ever knew." He rode for a moment longer in silence and then added, "For a long time we have been making little sidesteps toward a real war with the *Shemanese.* Today we have taken a great stride in that direction."

[February 1, 1786 — Wednesday]

The United States treaty commissioners at Fort Finney breathed a collective sigh of relief that the negotiations with the tribes had finally been completed. They were grateful that George Rogers Clark had been one of their number, since his influence with the Kentuckians was considerable, and it was only through Clark's considerable exertions that extremely detrimental—if not altogether tragic—trouble had been averted. Now, as they prepared to leave Fort Finney and return up the Ohio with some of the troops in three large boats, the leader of the treaty commissioners, Maj. Gen. Samuel H. Parsons, decided that he would leave Maj. Robert Finney in command of the post, aided by Capt. David Zeigler and Lt. Ebenezer Denny, with a garrison of 200 regular troops.

There were still many details to be taken care of before they could leave but, as these were being seen to, it provided an opportunity for Parsons and his second commissioner, Brig. Gen. Richard Butler, to write their report to Richard Henry Lee, President of the United States Congress, informing him that by the treaty concluded here at Fort Finney, the United States had now acquired full ownership of not only the lands set out by the boundaries of the Fort McIntosh Treaty, but all the lands south and east of the Wabash, which included almost all of the Indian country.[655]

[February 9, 1786 — Thursday]

Because of his command of the English language, both written and verbal, Tecumseh, now nearly 18, was summoned this morning to the wegiwa of Moluntha and asked to write a letter to Alexander McKee in Detroit, which Moluntha would dictate. Tecumseh glanced at Nonhelema, and she nodded faintly, so he sat on the stool before a short table and dipped the quill pen into the inkpot. Several sheets of paper were there, and Tecumseh poised himself to write.

"I'm ready," he said quietly.

" 'To Colonel McKee,' " dictated Moluntha. " 'Father. Last fall the Americans, our brethren, called us to the Big Miami.' " He stopped, waiting for the young warrior to catch up, and when Tecumseh paused in his writing and looked up, he continued, waiting regularly to give the writer time. " 'When we arrived, in January, they told us they had something to communicate for our future welfare and that of our children after us. But, alas, we heard nothing good from them. They told us that our father, the British King, had given us to them, with our lands likewise. Father, the commissioners assured us that everything in the articles that we now send you were agreeable to our best wishes and more generous than we could have expected from them. This induced us to sign the proposals, but we find that we have been ignorant of the real purport of them till we returned here. Our hostages, however, that were detained by them, have escaped and are come home safe. We inform you how they have deceived us, by telling us that the King of Great Britain had ceded the whole country to them. We were not sensible of the error we committed till our friend Elliott explained it to us. Father, we request you will be strong and give us the best advice you are capable of in our present situation. You see, we never have been in more need of your friendship and good offices. We have been cheated by the Americans, who are still striving to work our destruction, and, without your assistance, they may be able to accomplish their end. You have too much wisdom not to be convinced of this truth as well as we are. We earnestly request you will consider, and send us a speedy answer. In the meantime, we salute you and remain your steady friends.' "

Helped by his big wife over to the table and onto the stool that Tecumseh now vacated, Moluntha sat down and, with Tecumseh's hand guiding his, laboriously signed his name at the bottom.[656]

[*April 9, 1786 — Sunday*]

The force of some 500 Shawnees under the leadership of Blue Jacket pulled up atop the high ridge and looked down at the turbulent yellowish floodwaters of the river well below them. Projecting above the surface and being battered by floating logs, branches and even whole trees were just the very tops of the pickets and the roof of the crude installation that had been Fort Finney. Of the garrison that had been in occupancy up to three days ago, according to their spies, there was no sign.[657]

"Moneto," Chiksika murmured, "has spared us the task of wiping them out."

"And deprived us the pleasure," Tecumseh added.

"There will be others to take their places," Blue Jacket said, wheeling his horse around. "There always are. There always will be. And in case you were thinking otherwise, Moneto will show us the task and provide us the pleasure—and the pain— far more than any of us really want. *That* I know!"

[*May 13, 1786 — Saturday*]

In the three and a half months that had passed since the treaty at the mouth of the Great Miami, all the expectations that this might mark the end of the Indian troubles on the upper Ohio and in Kentucky were dashed. If anything, the Indians—

especially the Shawnees—seemed more fierce in their attacks than before, as if infuriated by being led into the signing of a treaty that took from them virtually all of their
lands; a treaty they had since disavowed as being fraudulently imposed upon them and
the other tribes. The recent attacks, particularly those in Kentucky, were in the
nature of a gauntlet slapped across the face of the United States, a graphic representation of what would surely be the lot of any Americans who attempted to enter and
possess their land on the basis of that treaty.

Already, over these 14 weeks since the treaty, the Shawnees had crossed the
Ohio in Kentucky innumerable times and stolen over 500 horses, but that was by no
means the worst of it. On April 9 a party of Indians stealing horses from the settlements along Beargrass Creek near Louisville were pursued by a small company of
militia led by Col. William Christian. They followed the Indians across the Ohio and
killed three of them, but were themselves struck hard and Christian was killed, along
with Capt. Isaac Kellar. Only two days later, the Indians crossed into Kentucky again
and killed several settlers, including the well-known and very popular surveyor, Col.
John Donelson.[658]

The attacks, however, were not exclusively aimed at the Kentucky settlers in the
region of Louisville and Lexington. Renewed raids were being made up the Great
Kanawha and Little Kanawha, in the area of Fish Creek and Grave Creek, Wheeling
and Holliday's Cove, even on Raccoon Creek close to Pittsburgh and in the vicinity
of Washington village. It was not a good time to stray very far from the protection of
a strong settlement.

All the past winter and into this spring, Lewis Wetzel had been serving John
Madison as guide, hunter, camp-keeper and protector. Their journey last fall 227
miles downstream from Wheeling to the mouth of the Big Sandy had been uneventful, as had been the trip up Big Sandy for about ten miles. It was at that point that
Madison saw ground that appealed to him considerably, and he had directed Wetzel
to put to shore on the left bank.[659] In the months that had followed, they had made
tomahawk improvements on some 10,000 acres of good ground and had not once
been bothered by Indians.

Their good fortune ended today. At Madison's request, Wetzel went with him
this morning upstream on the Big Sandy two miles from their camp, located ten
miles above the Ohio. They landed on the right bank and struck off eastward a mile
to the pond where Madison had previously set some beaver traps. Just as they neared
the edge of the pond, shots rang out and Madison fell dead. Wetzel immediately shot
and killed one of the dozen Indians who burst into sight from the nearby woods, and
then he sprinted off, reloading as he ran. By the time he reached the canoe, he had
killed two more.

With the Indians continuing to chase him down the shoreline as he paddled and
with little bursts of water fountaining up close by where their shots missed, Wetzel
made no effort to try to stop at their camp to collect anything. With the aid of the
current he soon outdistanced them, but he did not begin to breathe freely again until
he reached the Ohio and turned upstream for the return to Wheeling.[660]

Difficulties of a similar nature were occurring in the Wheeling area at this same
moment, especially for another member of the Wetzel family, Lewis's youngest
brother, 16-year-old Johnny. Yesterday, four Delawares prowling about in the area

surrounding the Wetzel place managed to capture a mare that had been hobbled in the meadow. Leading her into the woods, they had removed the bell from her neck and then waited for someone to come looking for the animal.

That someone turned out to be Johnny Wetzel, who was sent out to bring the mare in. As he started away from the cabin, he saw a friend of his approaching. It was Frederick Earlywine, son of old Abraham Earlywine, who owned the adjoining property. He yelled at Fred to join him and, when the 16-year-old ran up, they moved out together to get the mare.

Many times in the past Johnny had heard his brother, Martin, relate the details of his capture by the Shawnees, when they had lured him on by ringing the bell of a horse he was seeking. Johnny had been only eight years old at that time, but he remembered very well the sadness they had suffered at Martin's disappearance and the knowledge that he had been captured and possibly killed. Yet, even though he knew the story well from Martin's own lips after his return, it never occurred to him that he might experience the same thing.

Well ahead of them, in the fringe of woodland, the boys heard the tinkling of the bell and immediately headed in that direction. As they came closer and entered the woods, however, Johnny became suspicious. Though the bell kept tinkling, as it was supposed to do when the mare was moving, the sound kept coming from the same spot, which didn't make much sense unless the horse was standing in one place continually shaking her head or else walking around in a small circle. He was just about to mention this to Fred when the Indians burst out of cover from four different directions.

Earlywine gave up immediately, but Johnny tried to run. He had gotten only a dozen or so yards distant when a rifle cracked and a ball passed through his lower arm, hitting and breaking a bone but not shattering it. The impact caused him to stumble and fall, and before he could regain his feet, he was grasped by Indians on both sides and led back to the others.

The Delawares indicated the boys should go with them, but Earlywine refused. When they shoved him, he simply spun around and replanted his feet firmly and kept shaking his head and repeating, "No! I won't go!"

"For God's sake, Fred," Johnny hissed, "don't be stupid. They'll kill you if you keep that up. Come along, and we k'n figger out how to 'scape after a while."

"No, siree!" Earlywine retorted. "I ain't goin' nowhere with these damn Injens."

Quickly tiring of the demonstration, one of the Delawares said something to another, and then the speaker and two of his companions led Johnny and the stolen horse away while the final warrior stayed with Fred. Knowing the Indians might kill him if they thought the wound he had suffered was too severe, Johnny Wetzel made light of it and went along with them with seeming cheerfulness, cradling the injured arm with his good one.

Out of sight in the distance behind, Johnny heard Fred's voice again yell "No!" and he assumed he was once again refusing to come along. A short time later, however, the warrior who had remained behind caught up with them, still shaking the blood off the fresh scalp in his grasp—Fred Earlywine's scalp.[661]

After traveling for about a mile, the Indians stopped by a small run where they washed and treated young Johnny's wound, packing it with buzzard down from a pouch and then bandaging it with strips ripped from his shirt. They rested for a while and then continued their march toward the southwest, up and down the many steep hills they encountered. They made no attempt to ride the stolen horse and simply continued leading her on a tether. Late in the afternoon they came to a run flowing to the southwest, which Johnny correctly took to be one of the tributaries of Middle Grave Creek.[662] Here they made a cold camp for the night, closely hobbling the horse in a nearby glade where she could find forage.

During the evening they gave young Wetzel some jerky to eat and reexamined his wound. One of them moved away for a short time and came back with some sassafras leaves he had gathered. These he chewed into a mass to form a poultice. Plucking away the buzzard down that had stopped the bleeding on both sides of his wounded arm, he covered the holes with the sassafras poultice and rebound it with fresh strips from the boy's shirt. Wetzel was grateful, since the daylong throbbing pain ceased almost immediately, but he was very depressed as he thought about the captivity he was being led into, wondering if he'd be killed in a gauntlet line, or if he'd be adopted into the tribe, or if, perhaps, he might manage to escape.

This morning they started downstream on the little run just after sunrise and followed it for nearly two hours before it emptied into Middle Grave Creek. Just short of three miles more, they came to where that stream emptied into the main Grave Creek. Wetzel knew the Williamses and Tomlinsons had cabins near the mouth of the creek, and he began contemplating escape, but his captors were suddenly much more alert and watched him carefully, precluding any chance of his running off in the hopes of reaching the settlers who, he knew, might not even be there to begin with.

After traveling another half-mile, the Delawares suddenly exclaimed in delight. Two of them ran ahead a short distance and took possession of a canoe, not of Indian construction, that was drawn up on shore, with two paddles lying in the bottom. They bade Johnny sit in the center with one of his captors while two others took positions in bow and stern. The fourth then mounted the horse and rode along the bank while they paced him in the canoe.

In another half-mile they came to the mouth of the creek at the Ohio River and seemed about to move directly across when the Delaware in the bow glimpsed a little group of shoats on the shore. The half-grown pigs saw them at the same time and scurried into an isolated growth of brush and did not emerge. Immediately the Delawares determined to get one and directed the canoe to shore. The one riding the horse said something to the others and then made preparations to swim the mare across the Ohio.

Two of the Indians found sticks and poked around in the brush after the shoats while one stood ready to shoot. After a moment the pigs broke out and started running off, but the armed Delaware took a bead on one and brought it down with a single shot that caused the animal to squeal loudly before it stopped kicking and lay still. They immediately slit its throat and hung it by a hind leg in the crotch of a sapling to bleed it out, then cut it open to remove the entrails.

Almost a mile away, having just crossed the mouth of Little Grave Creek, Isaac

Williams, Hamilton Carr and Jacob Hindemann heard the distant shot and paused. The three had come down on foot from Wheeling this morning to look after Isaac's cows and other livestock. When the sharp distant squeal of a pig reached their ears immediately after the shot, Williams was suddenly furious.

"God rot 'em!" he exclaimed. "Them's Kentuckian's landed at the creek an' the bastards're killin' my hogs!"

All three of the men started running toward the creek mouth, but Carr, younger and more fleet of foot, reached the embankment at the creek mouth well ahead of the others. Peering over, he saw three Indians in a canoe, along with what appeared to be a captive boy who had a bandaged arm and was sitting in front of the feet of the Indian in the middle of the boat. Just behind that Indian, also on the inside bottom, lay four flintlock rifles and a bloody dead pig. A fourth Indian, several rods from shore, was swimming a horse across. The Indian in the bow was paddling, turning the bow into the creek mouth as the one in the stern was using his paddle just then to shove them away from shore.

None of those below were aware of Carr's presence, and he quickly took a bead on the one in the stern and shot him. The Indian slumped and toppled overboard without a sound. By this time, Isaac Williams had rushed up beside Carr, taken in at a glance what was happening and raised his rifle.

In the canoe below Johnny Wetzel was shouting at the top of his lungs, "Don't shoot me! I'm white! Don't shoot me!"

Williams snapped off his shot, hitting the Delaware in the bow, who also went overboard and disappeared beneath the surface. As Wetzel was still yelling below, Hindemann, a heavy-set older Dutchman, came running up to Carr and Williams, gasping for breath. Carr snatched the Dutchman's gun and shot the Indian in the center of the boat. This Indian also fell overboard but held on to the side of the canoe away from the shooters. By this time, the canoe had reached the main river current and was a few rods below the creek mouth.

"Boy!" Carr shouted, as he quickly reloaded. "Knock that Indian's hand from the side of the boat."

Wetzel glanced around for something to use, found a tomahawk and swung it at the hand grasping the gunwale. Two fingers were cut off and the hand disappeared. The Indian sank immediately.

"Good boy!" Carr shouted. "Now grab a paddle and bring the canoe in."

"Cain't," Wetzel shouted back. "Arm's busted."

By then, however, the canoe was passing some exposed rocks close to shore, and Wetzel stood up and jumped out to them, thrusting the canoe farther out into the current. At the same time Carr shot at the warrior swimming the horse, who was now past midstream. The bullet struck the water close by, splashing him. Immediately he slipped off the horse and struck out with strong strokes back toward the Virginia shore to try to intercept the canoe. He was successful and pulled himself aboard, snatched up a paddle and headed for the Ohio shore. The horse had continued swimming across and, upon emerging from the water, simply stood there. In a few minutes the Indian beached the canoe close by. He scooped up the four rifles from the bottom of the boat, along with a length of cord. Shoving the canoe back out into the current, he went to the horse, tied the guns so there were two on each side and hung them over the mare's back, remounted and quickly disappeared into the heavier brush.[663]

[June 8, 1786 — Thursday]

It was George Rogers Clark who conceived the notion that the one great stumbling block to the settlement of the Ohio country was the Shawnees and they alone. If, he contended, that obstacle could be removed—or at least greatly weakened —the portals to the Northwest Territory would be opened wide.

What he felt was of great significance was the fact that heretofore the Shawnees, when faced with major onslaught by the Americans, had always been able to call upon their neighboring tribes well away from the Ohio River. What if those tribes could be induced—either by treaty or by force—to reject any further pleas from the Shawnees to assist them in their struggles? If such could be accomplished, then a few strong blows at the Shawnees—combined with attrition, hunger, illness, loss of territory to which retreat might be made and the discouragement these elements would engender—the Shawnees would finally be forced into either abject submission or simply wiped out of existence. The key, then, seemed to be to largely bypass the Shawnees, exclude them from further consideration for the time being and direct immediate attention to manipulating the other tribes farther to the north and west, particularly the Miamis, whose recent belligerent activities and influence with other tribes made them a primary focus for what Clark had in mind. It was with this intriguing idea in mind, therefore, that Clark was now sitting at his desk and preparing to write to the President of Congress, Richard Henry Lee.

He dipped his pen into the stained inkpot and held it poised for a moment while he considered how to begin. Then he bent to the task. He wrote swiftly and, after several pages had been filled, he mentioned the present belligerence of the Miamis and their allies and how it could be turned to the advantage of the United States:

> Since the conclusion of the treaty with the Shawnies at the Miami, the nations of Indians living on the Wabash have held a grand council at the Ouiatenon Town and other places, the result of which was a declaration of war against the United States. Their natural inclination for war, and thirst for blood and plunder, with encouragement from some of the traders from Detroit, &c, I think we may attribute the horrors of an Indian war this country seems presently involved in. Within a few weeks a number of valuable citizens have been killed in the neighborhood of this place, and I believe the war will be more shocking than both have experienced in this quarter, as it appears by their councils and conduct that they are determined to prosecute their designs with vigour. . . .
>
> If Detroit was in our possession, it might in a great measure silence the Indians; but nothing will effectually do it but dissolution, as all humanity shewn them by us is imputed to timidity. Great expenditures and numbers of lives might be

saved by now reducing them to obedience, which they so richly deserve. There is no danger of making them desperate; they are as far from that principle as any people in the world. Before they would suffer their families to perish by the sword of famine, they would become your servile subjects; this I am convinced of from long experience and observation on the disposition of various nations. The idea generally held out, that the Indians could easily be reduced to that state of desperation or even propose to murder their women, and continue at war as long as they lived, hath already cost us too much to continue under that mistake. The Indians already engaged in the confederacy against us may amount to about fifteen hundred fighting men. They are not as good soldiers as the Shawnees, and by a sufficient force marching into the heart of their country and acting with vigour, [it] might soon effect the desired purpose, and strike a damp through the different nations. Those already treated with would hold their engagements more sacred, and others at a greater distance would solicit a peace. The business of the United States on the frontiers might go on with safety, the British emissaries would be viewed by the Indians as their greatest enemies in encouraging them to gain our resentment, and a general peace, in all probability, would take place.

I have the honor to be, your Honor's most humble and obdt. svt.

G. R. Clark

[*August 12, 1786—Saturday*]

There were few things that Lewis Wetzel found more challenging or enjoyable than hunting Indians. It was rare, however, that he could make any kind of money doing so. Now had come just that sort of opportunity.

It all began when Maj. William McMahan decided he was fed up with the hit-and-run attacks of the Indians and something should be done about it. His idea of doing something about it was to announce he was going to lead an "Injen Hunt" expedition across the Ohio, and, as an incentive for bordermen to participate, he established what he called a pony purse—a reward of $100 to the first man of the expedition who should bring in an Indian scalp. Among the two dozen men attracted was Lewis Wetzel, who was determined the prize money would wind up his.

McMahan, now well established along the Ohio 13 miles above Wheeling at Beech Bottom, had earlier this year stated flatly that the treaties being made with the Indians were not worth the paper they were written on. The Indians, he knew, had been cheated out of lands and hoodwinked into those most recent treaties, especially the one at the mouth of the Great Miami, that gave the United States more than half the Ohio country and three-fourths of the Indian country—treaties made either with Indians who didn't even live in or have any interest in the land in question, or with members of the tribe who had no authority for entering into any kind of negotiations for the tribe as a whole. He had long warned that it was only a matter of time before the tribes came to a full realization of the fraud that had been perpetrated, and that when they did, the country would once again be drenched with blood. That was exactly what had happened, and now not only had the tribes come together in a closer coalition among themselves, but attacks against the settlers and settlements were once again accelerating with no end in sight. Though he could sympathize with their anger over being defrauded, he deplored the sharp increase in their attacks made since shortly after the ridiculous treaty at the mouth of the Great Miami River.

The inroads being made into Ohio, now that the United States was surging ahead with plans to shove the frontier north and west of the Ohio and populate the area with whites, had fired the Indians into numerous attacks all the way down the Ohio, from Fort McIntosh almost 850 miles to the mouth of the Wabash. There was great resentment among the Indians that not only had Fort Harmar at the mouth of the Muskingum become a very sturdy fortification that they could probably not dislodge, but the Ohio Company was establishing the first white settlement there; a town to be called Marietta, which would be protected by the fort and would soon have many hundreds of residents.⁶⁶⁴ It would also, it was assumed, establish a launching point for increased encroachment into Ohio's interior. Much the same situation was occurring with the second Fort Finney, now established in the Indiana country across the Ohio River, along with a new settlement being established there called Clarksville, after George Rogers Clark. Clark himself had been reinstated as a general and authorized to lead an expedition against the Miamis on the Wabash River, who had been harassing the Vincennes area settlers.

In the Kentucky country, attacks and counterattacks had sharply increased since spring, more often than not the result of parties of whites crossing the Ohio to hunt or explore with a mind toward future settlement. Maj. Benjamin Stites led a party across in pursuit of some Indians who stole horses and became enthralled by the beauty and richness of the land between the Little Miami and Great Miami rivers. He had told entrepreneur John Symmes about it, and now Symmes was actively planning to claim that whole area—about a third of a million acres—for settlement.

Not only were the Indian attacks becoming more frequent, they were again occurring in far-distant places where the settlers had long thought the Indian danger had ended. One of the worst of these occurred on the headwaters of the Bluestone River in southwestern Virginia. A subchief of the Kispokotha Shawnees named Pecatewah Petweowa—Black Wolf—who was a renowned leader of war parties, led his marauders in a lightning attack against the James Moore family, living in Abb's Valley. It resulted in five members of the family, including Moore himself, being killed and six others captured, three of whom were soon killed. Black Wolf, however, was himself killed when he tried to ride Moore's large black stallion, which threw him off and then proceeded to stamp him to death under his hooves.

Along the upper Ohio, attacks had been occurring on isolated cabins and tiny settlements at Grave Creek, Captina Creek, Cresap's Bottom, Fish Creek, Mingo Bottom, Short Creek, Buffalo Creek and Indian Creek. The three Crow brothers, Martin, Frederick and Jacob, were hunting on Fish Creek when they were ambushed, and all three were shot. Martin and Frederick managed to escape, but Jacob was hit by nine bullets and killed. Charley Wells was tomahawked to death while in his hunting camp on Indian Short Creek. At Grave Creek a hot little fight broke out between the settlers and a war party, in which a man, a woman and a girl were killed and a little boy wounded, but three of the attackers were killed as well. A Negro slave who was captured and bound, managed to free himself, kill his guard and escape to

Shepherd's Fort on Wheeling Creek. But the whole country was once again in turmoil and gripped by fear, and it was this that so angered Maj. William McMahan. As he put it in a letter to Capt. Thomas Hutchins at Fort Pitt:

Sir:—The difficulty of procuring hands, occasioned by the late alarms, is beyond conception; several have engaged and disappointed me. Wheeling is become a garrison. The inhabitants, as far up as Zane's, are fled, except Tomlinson and Shepherd, and a few about the Mingo Bottom, who are building blockhouses. What's to be the consequence, I know not; however, no pains shall be wanting on my part. The new blockhouse near us called Cox's Fort is about being erected by Captain [Van] Swearingen. I cannot conceive any danger as yet; however, it is prudent to be guarded. The alarm came by a certain Mr. Newland who came from the Indian Towns and made oath that a number of tribes had agreed to strike the surveyors and Wheeling settlement; that he was under promise not to inform, or spread the alarm, except to tell Zane and Shepherd to be on their guard. The former of these, Zane, has made every preparation; the latter, Shepherd, has made none and rests assured the Indians cannot spare their men in such numbers, as Clark's expedition is now in their country.[665] Newland says a number of Indians from the west of Lake Erie had joined the others.

It was five days ago when Lewis Wetzel, as part of William McMahan's force, found the tracks of some marauders. The whole party of whites crossed the Ohio where the Indians had crossed at Mingo Bottom and continued following them rapidly into the Ohio country. They searched for two more days, moving ever deeper into the Ohio country, without finding anything until late the day before yesterday, when some of the scouts who were out came back to the main party in their camp and reported that they had discovered a war party but the Indians were far too numerous to even consider making an attack. McMahan immediately held a conference with the members of his expedition, whose enthusiasm cooled considerably with this intelligence, and it was agreed among them that they should retreat and go back home.

As soon as it had been resolved to retreat, the men began packing up their gear with unseemly haste—all except Wetzel, who sat on a log calmly smoking his pipe and holding his flintlock over his knees. Maj. McMahan noted this and came up to him.

"Lew," he said, "aren't you heading for home with the rest of the party?"

Wetzel removed his pipe from his mouth and spat to one side, then shook his head. "Nope," he replied. "I come here to hunt Injens, an' now that they're found, I sure ain't gonna hightail it home like a fool with my fingers in my mouth. I aim to git an Injen scalp or lose my own in the try."

McMahan and others tried to dissuade him, but he simply sat there smoking and shaking his head, and so at length they left him there. Wetzel was pleased to see them go; he had never liked hunting Indians with a party of men; too much dependence upon others and too much likelihood that one of the party would do something stupid that would put all in jeopardy. As soon as they were gone, he rolled himself up in his blanket, setting his mind to awaken him at the slightest uncommon sound, and went to sleep. It might, he knew, be his last chance to get some rest for a few days.

In the morning, yesterday, when he arose, he rolled his supplies into his blanket and tied the roll on his shoulders, checked his weapons—knife, tomahawk and gun—and made sure his spare powder was dry and handy in its horn. He put three of his lead balls into his mouth, ready for instant use, and set off in the direction where the scouts had seen the Indian encampment. He found it by noon, but the party was gone, and he began following their trail.

Late in the afternoon he smelled smoke and cautiously followed it to its source, a dying campfire without anyone nearby. Beside the fire were two blankets and a small kettle. Wetzel was sure the two Indians were out hunting and would return. He selected a good vantage spot close by and settled down in hiding to wait. At just about sunset one of the Indians, a Shawnee warrior, returned to the camp carrying a young turkey. He searched around for new kindling and wood, which he placed on the ashes, and then blew on the coals until the flames reignited. Then he plucked and cleaned the turkey and was spitting it on a branch when the other warrior came in, just at nightfall.

Wetzel watched as they cooked their meal and ate it, then amused themselves by relating comic stories, at which they would burst into peals of laughter. After a while they sang a few songs together, and finally one of them—the one who had come in last, without game—picked up a flaming brand from the fire and, gun in hand, walked away in the darkness. Wetzel, surmising he was probably heading for a salt lick to bag a deer, was disappointed at losing one of his intended victims and decided to wait until dawn for his return. The other Shawnee soon rolled up in his blanket by the fire and went to sleep.

As the first streaks of dawn appeared in the east, Wetzel knew he could not safely wait any longer. Setting his gun aside, he slipped silently to the sleeping warrior and plunged his blade into the man's heart. The warrior convulsed and quivered for a few moments and then relaxed in death. Wetzel quickly scalped him, stuffed the trophy into his pouch and, leaving his victim lying still wrapped in his blanket, checked the Shawnee's rifle. It was very old and practically worthless. He rendered it completely so by breaking the hammer with a rock and replaced it beside the body. Snatching up a chunk of the turkey still uneaten, he recovered his own flintlock and set out for home. He moved along at a steady lope most of the day and arrived at Mingo Bottom just as McMahan's party was preparing to cross. All were glad to see him and assumed he had given up on what they considered a fool's errand. They changed their minds when he walked up to Maj. McMahan, pulled the fresh scalp out of his pouch and handed it to him.

"I'll take that hundred dollars," he said.

William McMahan, shaking his head and grinning, paid him.

[O c t o b e r   2 1 ,   1 7 8 6 — S a t u r d a y]

The latest expedition by George Rogers Clark into the heart of Indian territory had turned out to be entirely different than anyone anticipated, red or white.

Leading 1,800 mounted Kentuckians to the upper Wabash Valley in the Indiana country, Gen. Clark had been prepared to engage in fierce battle against the Indians —primarily Miamis—who were supposedly assembling to move against the settlements on the lower Wabash River and then into Kentucky. When word of the American invasion reached the Miamis and their assembled allies from among the Potawatomies, Wyandots, Kickapoos and Ottawas, they sent runners at once to the Shawnee villages on the upper Mad and Great Miami rivers urgently soliciting their help as well. At once almost all of the Shawnee warriors presently on hand at their villages formed into a large war party and set off to aid them.

As it happened, hardly had Clark started out on his expedition than word was brought from his spies of the Shawnees beginning to form a large war party. Fearing it was to be aimed at the Kentucky settlements, Clark detached Col. Benjamin Logan with orders to return to Kentucky, raise another force of Kentuckians and immediately move north against the Shawnee villages on the Mad and Miami rivers. Clark continued on his expedition, and Logan's call for men when he got back to Kentucky was enthusiastically answered; the Kentuckians were much more eager to wipe out the Shawnees, who were a greater direct threat to them than were the Miamis on the Wabash.

The large Shawnee force arrived at the Wabash fully prepared for a major battle, only to find that the Miamis and their allies who had assembled to battle the Americans, had instead engaged in peace talks. Clark had been very skillful in humoring and coddling them, promising gifts and convincing them what great foolishness it would be to fight for what they mistakenly thought were their rights, since the Americans wished no more land and no more strife from their red brothers. The Shawnees were aghast to learn that it had been the powerful and influential Michikiniqua, principal chief of the Miamis, who believed Clark, acquiesced to his proposals and was immediately supported in his decision by the chiefs of the Miami subtribes, the Weas, Salamonies, Eel Rivers, Mississinewas, Ouiatenons and Piankeshaws. The Delawares and their kin, the Munceys, were next to agree to peace and, with that, the movement became a landslide. Even the more bellicose chiefs of the Potawatomies—Mtamins, Black Partridge, Topenebe, Main Poche and Nescotnemeg—had agreed to Clark's proposals.

By the time these Shawnees arrived, bristling with weapons of war, Clark and his army had already departed in peace and headed back toward Kentucky via the Wabash Trail to Vincennes. The unstable coalition of tribes broke apart and scattered back to their own territories, so far away from the Americans that they had little to fear of attack by them, especially protected as they were by the buffer zone inhabited by the Shawnees.

The Shawnees had then dispiritedly turned around and ridden back to their own villages, only to find that Col. Logan had struck in their absence, destroying them and killing or capturing the women and children and some of the men. Among the dead was old Chief Moluntha, who had been deliberately murdered by a tomahawk blow after he surrendered and was in custody. Among the killed and scalped were ten warriors, along with 12 others, mostly women. Thirty-three women, children and a few old men had been captured. Three of the whites had been killed, three wounded. Thirteen Shawnee villages had been plundered and destroyed, including Mackachack, Wapatomica, Kispoko Town, Blue Jacket's Town, Solomon's Town, Mingo Town, Mamacomink, Kekeko, Puckshanoses, Waccachalla, Pecowick, Wapakoneta and Peckuwe. In addition, all the Shawnee crops, ready for harvesting, which were needed to sustain them over the forthcoming winter, had been destroyed.[666]

It was a devastating blow for the Shawnees, but not a fatal one.

[December 18, 1786 — Monday]

The Grand Council of Indians winding to a close today was one of the largest ever held and certainly the most all-encompassing insofar as the different tribes in attendance were concerned. It was being held in the sprawling Huron town called, after its venerable old chief, Sindathon's Village—a village so extensive that it occupied fully two square miles on the broad point of land between the mouth of the Detroit River and the mouth of the Huron River, though its center was closer to the former. More than 2,000 Indians had assembled here from a wide range of tribes; each of these tribal delegations formed its own enclave amidst the great assemblage and often viewed its neighbors with thinly masked suspicion or even hatred.

The famed Seneca orator Sagoyewatha—Red Jacket—was here, representing the residue of the Iroquois League generally, but the Senecas specifically—a rather remarkable achievement for one who was only 28 years old. Adjacent to his group sat the Mohawks of that same League, under their war chief, Thayendanegea—Joseph Brant—whose head was, as always, plucked bald of any hair except for a brushlike topknot at the crown, his lips curved in their usual, rather humorless, sneering smile and his glittering dark eyes moving constantly to and fro, missing nothing. Here, too, were the Hurons under the host chief, Sindathon, and close to them their splinter tribe, the Wyandots, who had come here under Tarhe—The Crane—and the emaciated and gravely ill Monakaduto—Half King.[667] Some 700 Potawatomies were here under chiefs Topenebe, Nanimisea and Nescotnemeg, and a smaller number of Ottawas under Nichinesica and their war chief, Oulamy. Here were the Chippewas gathered under Wafrugahquealied, along with their subtribe, the Mississaugi, under old Sekahos and Wabacumaga.[668] The Delawares and their subtribe, the Munceys, were here under Buckangehela, Pimoacan and Wingenund, and here as well were the 240 Shawnees in attendance under Catahecassa, Shemeneto and Blue Jacket.[669] And very significantly, here also were the Miamis under Michikiniqua and, under their various chiefs and subchiefs, six of the Miami subtribes—the Weas, Piankeshaws, Pepicokias, Mengakonias, Kalatikas and Ouiatenons.[670]

The Shawnees, so many of whose villages were recently destroyed by the invasion of the Kentuckians under Col. Logan, had come here from their new villages that had been built on ground given to them by the Miamis and Wyandots in the northwestern Ohio country, along such streams as the Auglaize, Little Auglaize,

Blanchard and Ottawa. The majority, however, were presently on the Maumee River, and a new village of Chalahgawtha had been established just a short distance upstream from the mouth of the Auglaize.

The present Grand Council here at Sindathon's Village was the result of a series of belts and speeches that had passed between Sagoyewatha and the western tribes via the Wyandots. Over a year ago a confederacy of sorts had been set up among the tribes at his encouragement, patterned to some extent after the old Iroquois League, in which the good of one was the good of all and mutual protection was a corner-stone. Now, even though the real power of the Iroquois League was gone, there remained a certain degree of deference and respect for individual chiefs of the Six Nations, though not so much that it let them forget the old animosities, particularly that which had existed for so long between them and the Shawnees.

All the chiefs on hand acknowledged that what Sagoyewatha had been saying over the past year or so was quite logical and very true: They really did need to form a strong confederacy among themselves for their own protection, but a major hurdle existed that virtually precluded such a formation. The simple fact was that the old intertribal hatreds seemed just too strong to wholly overcome. At the same time, however, all were uncomfortably aware that they could not really depend upon the British for help, despite some encouraging signs in this direction, including the fact that, in direct contravention to the Treaty of Paris, the British were presently begin-ning some very heavy reinforcements at the posts both at Niagara and Detroit.

It had been when this present council first began, some six weeks ago, that Sagoyewatha had addressed the assembled chiefs in a manner laced with urgency. But his words merely articulated what most of the tribes had already come to believe; that in order to survive, the tribes would have to unite and support each other in any situation involving the Americans.

Sagoyewatha leaned toward peaceful coexistence with them, and the Wyandots, among others, tended to agree and pledged themselves toward that end. Neverthe-less, it was apparent that other tribes, still more or less under the American gun, knew unequivocally that an equitable peace with the Americans was an impossibility. Prob-ably least inclined toward peace with the Americans any longer were the Shawnees.

Even though some of the more pacific Shawnee chiefs were inclined toward the premise of peace as propounded by the Grand Council, so far as the overwhelming majority of Shawnees were concerned, chiefs and warriors alike, their tribe had never been—and would never be—treated fairly by the Americans. In addition, the Shaw-nees still despised the Iroquois too much to ever believe what they said, or to enter into any kind of an agreement with them.

Thus, despite Sagoyewatha's commendable attempts to conciliate and mediate, the detested *Shemanese* would enjoy no respite from Shawnee raids. The Miamis, who were having as difficult a time as the Shawnees in putting aside their hatred for the Iroquois, also believed the Shawnees correct in their views in respect to the Americans and let it be known that they, like the Shawnees, would continue in their efforts to resist the encroaching whites and persist in their raids against them on the Wabash in the vicinity of Vincennes and in the Kentucky country. Both tribes clung to the belief that they might even find future strong support among the now waver-ing Wyandots and Delawares.

[*D e c e m b e r   3 1 ,   1 7 8 7 — M o n d a y*]

The entire year of 1787 had been one not only of gradual encroachment by the whites into the Ohio country but of strengthening their hold throughout the Ohio Valley, and resultant counterattacks by the Indians against the settlers in the Kentucky country and the upper Ohio River.

Attempts at settling things amicably always seemed to be undermined by individuals or small groups. A prisoner exchange agreed to between the Shawnees and Kentuckians took place on the Ohio shore directly across from the Limestone settlement on March 10, and for a brief time it seemed it might evolve into a more lasting peace.[671] That rosy prospect was snuffed out when, as the exchange was concluding, one of the Kentucky settlers, Luther Calvin, enlisted the aid of a number of other men and stole the Shawnee horses, swimming them across the Ohio River before the theft was discovered. Shots broke out, but no one was hit. The Shawnees, however, had just learned one more painful lesson about the perfidy of the Americans under almost any circumstance, and they accordingly retaliated.

A short time later two young men, both 18 and living in the new Washington Settlement seven miles from Limestone, set out to hunt on the North Fork Licking River. They were Nehemiah Stites and Zephaniah Wade. In the evening they made camp along the river about six miles from Washington. Early in the morning, just after they roused, the pair were fired on by a party of Indians, and young Stites was killed by bullets that struck him simultaneously in the chest and head. Wade, barefoot but uninjured, ran all the way back to the Washington Settlement. Pursuit of the Indians was made by a small party of settlers under Simon Kenton, who followed the trail as far as the Ohio River and then lost them. Back at Washington and Limestone word of the attack was quickly going the rounds, though in some tellings the dead man was confused with his friend.

At the small tavern in Limestone, where Wade dropped in after the expedition returned, he was greeted with handshakes and cheers, and one of their neighbors gripped Wade's shoulders and commented relievedly, "Why, Zeph, we heard you was killed."

"Y'know," Wade replied dryly, "I heard that, too, but decided it was a lie."

It was attacks of such nature that once again caused the Kentuckians to pass a resolution mounting another force to invade Ohio, with Benjamin Logan again their leader. Logan sent a copy of the resolution to the Virginia governor and, before the expedition could be equipped and carried into operation, he received a very strong letter by express from the state's chief executive in return:

In Council, June 5th, 1787

Colonel Benj[n] Logan.
Sir:

> *I submitted to Council the resolutions of a committe enclosed by you. They highly disapprove of the measures proposed to be adopted by these resolutions, and have advised me to direct you in no instance to give countenance to such irregular proceedings. You will, therefore, conform yourself to the wishes of the Executive by*

taking no steps which may be recommended by any self-erected body of men who may assume powers unknown to the Constitution. I have forwarded to Congress copies of all the dispatches received from your country. I have no doubt but that Honorable body will exert the Federal force in giving every relief to your present distresses.

Despite the governor's quick action in forbidding the proposed expedition, he was very worried they or another group would go ahead with it anyway and undermine the efforts being made to come to some sort of resolution of the border problem with the Indians. In this respect, he wrote to Congress on June 29:

> *Report says that the people of Kentucky are preparing for offensive operations against their savage neighbors. The Government here have used every possible means to restrain its citizens from undertaking any offensive measures whatever, although there seems to be the fullest conviction that nothing will put an end to the very cruel predatory war now carried on against the frontier of this State, but changing the scene from our settlements to the Indian towns.*

On the upper Ohio the attacks by roving bands of Mingoes, Delawares and Wyandots continued despite the edicts of the chiefs that they should cease. Many of these were merely attempts to steal horses and take them back to the Ohio country, but some were considerably more deadly. When a party of seven Mingoes came to the Wheeling area and stole five horses—three belonging to Capt. Lewis Bonnett, one of Martin Wetzel's and one of Henry Winter's—Bonnett and Wetzel raised a party of six other men and followed the Indians across the Ohio and all the way to Will's Creek before overtaking them where the Indians had stopped to repair their saddles. They fired upon them, and two of the warriors were wounded, one by Martin Wetzel and another by John McCulloch. The Indians fled and the stolen horses were recovered. Since they were not far from some of the Indian camps, the men thought it wise that they also withdraw quickly and they did so, arriving back at Wheeling without further incident.

All too often, however, attacks by maverick parties of marauders became much more deadly, such as the vicious attack on the Jacob Simms family on Fish Creek, as Col. David Shepherd reported in his letter to Virginia Gov. Edmund Randolph:

> *Ohio County, April 30th, 1787*
>
> *D*[r] *Sir:*
>
> *Three days past I rec*[d] *an express from Fish Creek that the Indians had taken a boy prisoner, & that several guns had been heard at the plantation of one Simms. Upon which I ordered a party of the militia to go down & see what was done. They returned in three days & informed me that the Indians had killed Simms, his wife & one of his children, & three more taken prisoners. They likewise saw several trails of Indians that had crossed the river with their horses, and the small tracks of a number of children & others, which we expect to be prisoners from Monongahela County. The number of Indians appeared to be about forty. This being the third time they*

have visited us this spring, I thought it my duty to inform you that unless we get some relief, the most of the County will be left desolate, as we have neither guns nor ammunition to defend ourselves, & for us to stand, in order to be a convincing proof to the Continent of an Indian War, is a situation not very agreeable.

I am, Sir, &c.   *David Shepherd*

What all this led to was the biggest news of the year: the ordinance issued by the infant United States government officially establishing the Northwest Territory. By this ordinance, all land to the north and west of the Ohio River, clear to the Canadian border and bounded on the west by the Mississippi River, was organized into a commonwealth that was the first in the world whose organic law recognized every man as free and equal. It was a unique document that became for weeks and months the principal topic of discussion, especially on the frontier, where copies were publicly posted. This Ordinance of 1787 provided, among other things, for the appointment of a governor and other territorial offices, for the establishment of both civil and criminal laws, for the laying out of counties, the setting up of a general assembly, and the authorization of a delegate to Congress who would have the right to debate but not to vote during the temporary government. The Ordinance further prohibited the molestation of any man because of his mode of worship or his religion; it provided the benefits of the writs of habeas corpus and of trial by jury; that there would not be permitted in this territory either slavery or involuntary servitude; and that with religion, morality and knowledge being necessary to good government and the happiness of mankind, schools and the means of education should forevermore be encouraged.

Article Five of the Ordinance declared that this Northwest Territory was to be separated into no less than three nor more than five divisions. The westernmost division in the Illinois Territory was to be bounded on the west by the Mississippi River, on the south by the Ohio and on the east by the Wabash River as far upstream as Vincennes and then, from there, on a line due north to the Canadian border. The middle division's southern border would also be the Ohio River and its eastern boundary a line drawn due north from the mouth of the Great Miami River to the Canadian border, the country thus enclosed to be called the Indiana Territory. The easternmost division of the Northwest Territory would take in the remainder of the land to the east of that line and to the north and west of the Ohio River and Pennsylvania border to the Canadian border as established by the Treaty of Paris and called the Ohio Territory.[672]

The portion of the Ordinance of 1787 that thoroughly outraged the people on the frontier from Pittsburgh to Louisville, however, was Article III, Section 14, which declared in part:

The utmost good faith shall always be observed towards the Indians; their lands and properties shall never be taken from them without their consent; and, in their property, rights and liberty, they shall never be invaded or disturbed, unless in just and lawful wars authorized by Congress; but laws founded in justice and humanity shall, from time to time, be made, for preventing wrongs being done to them, and for preserving peace and friendship with them.

What this amounted to, where the frontier people were concerned, was that once again it had become illegal for the whites to mount retaliatory excursions against the Indians who crossed the Ohio River to burn and steal and kill. The several county lieutenants of the Kentucky counties of Lincoln, Bourbon, Fayette, Jefferson, Mercer and Madison thereupon held a meeting at Danville on July 19 and issued a statement to the effect that:

> *the instructions of the Executive, dated the 5th day of June, 1787, prohibiting the people of Kentucky from going out of the State, unless in actual and immediate pursuit of an invading enemy, we are of opinion have placed us in so critical a situation as to oblige us to decline all offensive operations at present & can only act on the defensive.*

However much the authorities, both federal and local, prohibited it in keeping with the sweeping Ordinance of 1787, it remained the one portion of that new Ordinance that few whites on the border had any intention of obeying.

There were other immediate and far-reaching effects to the Ordinance. In New York, sales of parts of the Seven Ranges in Ohio amounting to almost $73,000 were made, and in Salem, Massachusetts, the agents for the Ohio Company, Winthrop Sargent and Manasseh Cutler, immediately made a contract with the government to buy, at the rate of no less than a dollar per acre, a section of Ohio encompassing an area of nearly one million acres—a deal consummated only ten days following enactment of the Ordinance.[673]

John Cleve Symmes, too, had lined up his backers for the Symmes purchase of the land between the two Miami rivers. Even before the sale was legally consummated, he sold to Matthias Denman of Springfield, New Jersey, a tract of 740 acres of land in Ohio directly opposite the mouth of Kentucky's Licking River. Denman paid him five shillings per acre in Continental scrip, or about 15 pence per acre in specie, which amounted to less than $125 for the entire plot. Here Denman planned to build a port settlement that he envisioned would, in the future, become one of the greatest ports on the entire Ohio River. To begin such a project he needed help, and so he journeyed to Lexington where two of his good friends, Robert Patterson and John Filson, lived, hoping to get them interested in forming a partnership with him.

Expecting a sharp increase of settlement, another land office was opened in Louisville on August 1 for the reception of locations and surveys made *north* of the Ohio River. The Virginia Legislature, now recognizing the importance of Limestone as a probable port city, also approved of the laying out of a city there on 100 acres of land that was the joint property of Simon Kenton and John May, to be incorporated as the city of Maysville. May had also recently established a new settlement 15 miles south of Limestone named May's Lick.

Fort Finney, opposite Louisville, was now well established, as was Fort Harmar at the mouth of the Muskingum, but now a new and impressive two-story walled fortification was begun on high ground on the opposite side of the Muskingum from

Partitioning of Ohio

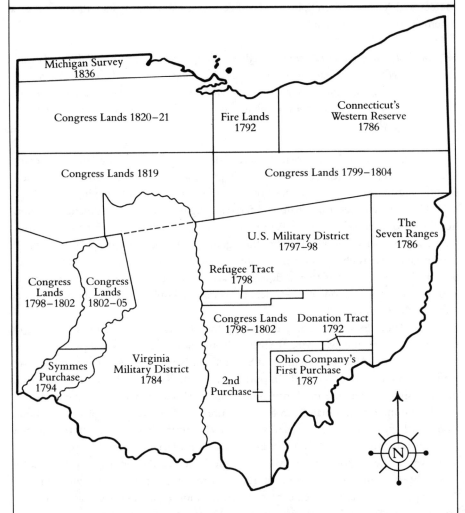

Michigan Survey 1836

Congress Lands 1820–21

Fire Lands 1792

Connecticut's Western Reserve 1786

Congress Lands 1819

Congress Lands 1799–1804

The Seven Ranges 1786

U.S. Military District 1797–98

Refugee Tract 1798

Congress Lands 1798–1802

Congress Lands 1802–05

Congress Lands 1798–1802

Donation Tract 1792

Ohio Company's First Purchase 1787

Symmes Purchase 1794

Virginia Military District 1784

2nd Purchase

N

Note: The dotted line appearing on the upper Virginia Military District and the continuing solid lines to the eastern and western borders of the state indicate the original Indian/white boundary line established by General Anthony Wayne in the Greenville Treaty of 1795.

Fort Harmar, less than a mile upstream and some 700 feet east of the Muskingum. It was being called Campus Martius.[674] On October 28 Col. Josiah Harmar at Fort Pitt received the welcome news that he had received his commission as brigadier general and, after congratulating himself with several solitary toasts of brandy, he immediately set off with the troops under his command for Fort Harmar.

In the midst of all these occurrences, the federal government finally responded to the speech made to the Americans at the Grand Council of the confederation of northwestern tribes at Sindathon's Village last December. It was the superintendent of Indian Affairs, Commissioner Richard Butler, who responded, sending his reply not to Sagoyewatha, but to the chief still believed to be heading the Wyandots, Monakaduto. It said:

> *Brothers: I received your Speech in the following effect—I am directed by Congress to inform you and all the other Indian Nations who joined the Representation made to Congress, dated 18th December 1786, that Congress, on the 18th day of the present month, July 1787, received your said Representation and have taken it into serious consideration, and in due time will send you their answer. Brothers, I advise you to mind your cornfields and hunting and to take care that your young men do no mischief to our people. I expect to have orders to call the Nations together in a short time to Council. I therefore wish you to sit still till you hear from me again.*
>
> > *Richard Butler*
> > *Sup^r. Indend^t. of Indian Affairs*
> > *To the Wyandot Half King and Chiefs*

Monakaduto, still alive but very weak, was joined by a Pimoacan in answering in a much shorter time than had the United States. His speech to the Congress by way of Richard Butler, dated September 2, said:

> *Brothers:*
>
> *You desire us to mind our cornfields and hunting and likewise to correct our young men from doing any mischief to your people. This is the second speech you sent us upon the same matter of correction to our young men. We have accordingly done as you desired us and shall do all that lies in our power to continue so. This comes from our hearts, not from our lips only, what you hear from us at present.*
>
> *Brothers, I have kept all our warriors in from doing any mischief to you. We expect you will follow our example in the same manner as we have. Be strong, and keep your people from distressing our towns in the south west quarter as they have already done. It seems very strange to us that such large bodies of men should slip off from you. It makes us doubt that you are carrying on a Confederacy with these people that strike us every now and then.*
>
> *Brothers, we repeat again, be strong! And correct your young men. It seems very strange that such large bodies of men should slip from you. Be strong, and*

prevent these bad evils. You tell us always in your speeches that you will do so. We believe that it only comes from your lips and not from your heart, as it gives us place to think so. We wish, then, that all those matters may be settled in the best terms. It is from our heart's desire that it should be so done, according to the peace made between you and us.

Brothers, as to the mischief committed on you by our people—as I may call them so, as we are all United Indians—it is those that come from a great ways, and they conceal themselves by our towns and passes, as their number is so small that we cannot discern them. Such small bodies of men we cannot look after; they are people that will not hear our speeches. But we shall do our best to prevent them.

Brothers, your people have struck ours—I mean those Wyandots that resort to the southward. We take it very hard that you allow us to be cut to pieces by your people. Call your people together and tell them not to do so anymore. Be strong and do this, as our intention is that peace shall continue between you and us as long as the world shall stand, if possible. We shew it very plain that we wish to be at peace with you.

Brothers, the United Nations of Indians do now cast our eyes daily back towards you, in waiting for your answer, which is to be held at the Great Fire, which is now already kindled.

> *Half King*
> *Captn Pipe*
> *for the United Indians*

Butler was pleased to get their message, and he reported to Congress, which in turn authorized Arthur St. Clair, an officer in the late war and a born politician now residing in western Pennsylvania, to assemble the Indians for the purpose of negotiating a peaceful solution to the land problem. Yet all this was a delicate position for the new United States, only too well aware of its own weaknesses. Further, it was nowhere near well enough informed as to the strength of the new Indian confederation.

In those messages previously received by Congress, the tribes had renounced previous treaties as having been unfairly drawn, fraudulent and illegal because of having been consummated oftentimes with mere village chiefs having no right to speak for and commit their own tribes, much less others. The Indians had indicated they did not wish war and might be willing to discuss the cession of some small areas of land north of the Ohio River, but at the same time they spoke ominously of the consequences should the government persist in failing to keep settlers and surveyors south of the river until and unless any such cessions were completed. Yet, since the United States, by reason of the Treaty of Paris, already considered itself owner of the land upon which the Indians were resident, it had no desire to reopen negotiations for the same land, but neither was it prepared, economically or in manpower, for another Indian war. As Secretary of War Henry Knox put it on behalf of Congress:

In the present embarrassed state of public affairs and entire deficiency of funds, an Indian war of any considerable extent and duration would most exceedingly distress the United States. The great distance by land which supplies and stores must be transported would render the expense intolerable.

That did not, however, prevent Congress from relaying word via Secretary Knox to Gen. Josiah Harmar to begin long-range preparations for a possible invasion he would lead as soon as feasible through the heart of the Ohio country to the Maumee Valley to chastise and humble the Indians living there. Despite the efforts for secrecy, rumors of this pending invasion were soon filling the ears of virtually everyone in the Ohio Valley—including the Indians.

Throughout the big river's valley, small but important incidents of improvement, impediment, attack and counterattack, matters of consequence and those of little significance continued to occur throughout the year. Samuel Brady and Drusilla held a happy little birthday celebration for their year-old son, Van Swearingen Brady, and began serious consideration of having another child. The impetuous, bullheaded John Hardin, much to the relief of most on the upper Ohio, left there permanently to settle in Kentucky, and Isaac Williams and his wife, Rebecca, sister of Joe Tomlinson, left their claim at Grave Creek and moved to their 400-acre tract along the left bank of the Ohio, almost directly opposite the mouth of the Muskingum, comforted by the presence of the new and formidable Fort Harmar just across the Ohio. A new wagon road was presently under construction that, when finished, would connect the settlements of the Greenbrier Valley via the Kanawha Falls to Lexington, Kentucky. And only ten miles northeast of Wheeling, a new town was laid out by Moses Chapline, Zachariah Spriggs, George McCulloch, Charles Wells, Andrew Van Swearingen, James Mitchell and Benjamin Briggs and was named West Liberty.[675] Well down the Ohio, at the mouth of the Little Miami River, a new settlement called Columbia—the first settlement by Americans in the southwestern Ohio country—was established by Benjamin Stites and others formerly from Redstone on the Monongahela and, shortly afterward, Fort Miami was constructed about a mile below the settlement.

Certain close calls and tragedies, however, intermingled with the increase of white expansion in the Ohio Valley. Samuel Brady, leading a patrol of his Rangers up Yellow Creek two miles into the Ohio country, saw an Indian appear out of the woods 100 yards ahead and yelled a warning. Though out of range, the Indian fired at the Rangers and then loped off into a dark, narrow ravine.

"Don't follow!" Brady barked. "He's a decoy. It's an ambush. Get treed, *now!*"

Instantly the Rangers leaped behind trees and prepared to fight. It was not a moment too soon. A horde of Indians burst out of the trees between themselves and where the lone warrior had been and opened fire with a hail of bullets. Bullets whined through the air and clipped off leaves and twigs, or they thumped into the trunks of the trees behind which the men had taken cover, killing one Ranger and wounding two others. The Rangers returned the fire with good effect, killing and wounding upward of 20 of the Indians. It was obvious to Brady, however, that his party was badly outnumbered, and he ordered his men to retreat. They managed to reach the Ohio, quickly launched their hidden canoes and got safely to the Virginia side without further loss or injury.

Not all incidents were so satisfactorily resolved. Silas Zane and George Green, seeing the Ordinance of 1787 as being the first major step to achieving a normal, peaceful intercourse with the Indians, decided to get in on the ground floor and establish a lucrative trade with the Shawnees, a dream they had harbored for some time. Pooling their own resources, they acquired a good supply of merchandise from the trading store that Col. George Stickney of Maryland had recently established in Wheeling. The two men filled their big canoe with the goods and paddled down the Ohio to the Scioto with them, then up that stream. The Shawnees, though startled to see them, treated them cordially enough, and the partners quickly sold out their entire stock of merchandise and started back down the Scioto with a rich load of furs. The dream, however, became a nightmare. Before they reached the Ohio River, a barrage of shots from Indians hidden on shore snuffed out the lives of both George Green and Silas Zane.

So, despite the Ordinance of 1787, the frontier situation throughout the Ohio River Valley remained in a state of flux, and ever more voices were being raised for lifting the ban on expeditions entering the Ohio country against the Indians. With this transitional year coming to a close, William McMahan and Archibald Woods, now representatives of Ohio County to the Virginia Legislature, wrote with obvious bitterness to Gov. Randolph:

> *The incursions of the savages have of late become so frequent in the County of Ohio, & their murders & depredations so alarming, as to prevent the inhabitants from following their ordinary occupations. Ohio County has a frontier on the Ohio of at least forty miles, from six to ten in breadth, forms a good barrier for the inhabitants of Pennsylvania, who appear perfectly easy in their situation. The inhabitants of Ohio County, thus dispersed, badly armed & destitute of a sufficient stock of ammunition, find it impossible to make a defense against the enemy, or to collect in time to pursue them with any provable prospect of success. Offensive operations against the hostile Indians is the only mode likely to afford peace & safety to the frontiers. But until Congress are disposed to think with the people who feel and experience the horrors of savage warfare, we beg that Virginia will employ a few confidential persons as scouts or spies, & to embody at least one company of militia, to be divided into two detachments, & be employed after the 15th of February next in constantly ranging the frontiers on both sides of the Ohio, & establish a magazine of arms & ammunition in a central part of the County with all expedition.*

In the midst of all this turmoil, this final month of 1787 had witnessed a major step for the infant United States. On December 7, Delaware was the first of the former 13 colonies to ratify the new Constitution of the United States, and it became, officially, the first state, with the city of Dover as its capital. Five days later, on December 12, Pennsylvania became the second state, with Harrisburg on the Susquehanna being named capital. And another six days afterward, on December 18, New Jersey became the third state, with Trenton its capital.

Others were working hard to follow suit shortly.

[*July 26, 1788 — Saturday*]

Arthur St. Clair was very grateful to his good friend, George Washington, for recommending to Congress that he be named governor of the newly established Northwest Territory. Thirteen days ago Congress had acted on that recommendation and appointed him to that seat. By the terms of the Ordinance of 1787, that appointment also made him military commander of the territory, with the rank of brigadier general.

There were other territorial appointments as well. Winthrop Sargent, a land speculator associated with the Ohio Company and Scioto Company, was named secretary of the territory, and nine Northwest Territory Supreme Court justices were also named: John Cleve Symmes, James M. Varnum, Samuel H. Parsons, John Armstrong, William Barton, Rufus Putnam, George Turner, Joseph Gillman and Return J. Meigs.

Today, in one of his first official acts in regard to this enormous territory, St. Clair posted a proclamation creating a huge county that embraced practically half of the Ohio country, taking in all the land westward from the Pennsylvania border and Ohio River to the Scioto River and directly northward to Lake Erie from there. No one raised objection over the fact that the new county included land that, according to the latest treaty between the United States and the Indians, belonged to the Delawares and Wyandots. Also, it came as no great surprise to anyone when St. Clair named it after his benefactor.

Thus was Washington County established.

[*October 12, 1788 — Sunday*]

Daniel Boone had finally had his fill of Kentucky. Now, with Kenton's Station still a mile or so ahead of him, he came to the decision he'd been putting off for a long while: He was going to leave Kentucky for good.

Boone had a hard time believing how rapidly this frontier was filling up and, for that matter, how swiftly the whole United States was developing. By the end of July, eight more of the original colonies—Georgia, Connecticut, Massachusetts, Maryland, South Carolina, New Hampshire, Virginia and New York—had ratified the Constitution of the United States and officially moved into statehood, leaving only North Carolina and Rhode Island yet to do so.[676] And all this while, the Ohio Valley and Kentucky continued filling with the surge of new settlers, much to the disgust of many of those now considered old-timers in these dangerous but promise-filled lands.

Daniel Boone was one of those who had quickly looked askance at the numbers of people coming into Kentucky. Knowing he was in part responsible by virtue of being one of the prime movers in opening this country for settlement did not make him feel any better about it. No one had seen Boone smile for a long time, much less explode with the great laughter that had been his trademark in bygone days. His eyes seemed now to carry a sorrowful, faraway look, as if he did not know what to do with himself. Since moving away from Boonesboro, nothing he tried satisfied him.

He had moved on to Fayette County and become sheriff there, but he didn't like the responsibilities of the job and enforcing many laws he didn't agree with himself, so he had tried his hand in the business of digging ginseng root, which had proved lucrative for others. He and his sons had dug and painstakingly dried some 15 tons of the valuable root, then loaded it into a keelboat destined for eventual market at Philadelphia, where, at the going rate of 24 cents a pound, the cargo would be worth $7,200.[677] However, after laboriously poling their load upriver 140 miles, the unwieldy boat was caught by a cross current and whirled against a pile of driftwood at the head of an island, where it sank in shallow muddy water, badly damaging the ginseng roots.[678] Though they spread the roots on shore and redried them, then repaired the damaged boat and finally reloaded the cargo, they were much delayed in getting them to market, and by then the prices had fallen. The whole effort was a great loss to Boone.

Now he had returned to Maysville and was living in a cabin Simon Kenton had helped him build, but he was still a man at loose ends, uncharacteristically unsure of himself and what he wanted to do next. He grew ever more displeased with the rapid growth of new settlements in the Kentucky country and along the Ohio and its tributaries. With the continuing arrival of so many Indian delegates from various tribes for the peace talks with Gov. Arthur St. Clair at Fort Harmar, an uneasy peace was prevailing and numerous new settlers were taking advantage of it. George Mefford, one of the many new arrivals to Kentucky, had recently established a new settlement, Mefford's Station, on a branch of Lawrence Creek not far distant from Kenton's Station. Then there was that new settlement called Columbia that had been established in the Ohio country at the mouth of the Little Miami, with Fort Miami just below it. Only a little west of there, right across from the mouth of the Licking, Matthias Denman bought 740 acres of land from Judge Symmes, who was himself beginning a settlement on the northernmost bend of the Ohio River and calling it North Bend. Denman began talking about establishing a major Ohio River port city and was looking for a couple of partners to share the cost. He found them in Lexington in the persons of Col. Robert Patterson and John Filson. The latter surveyed the entire plot for the proposed city and then gave it a name. Since the site was opposite the mouth of the Licking River, he combined the *L* for Licking with the Latin *os,* for mouth, the Greek *anti,* for opposite, and the French *ville,* for city to coin the word Losantiville—city opposite the mouth of Licking. It was not long after that when, as the three were exploring the site, Filson disappeared and was believed killed by Indians.[679] His share in the enterprise and duties of continuing to lay out the city were accepted by Israel Ludlow.

Elsewhere, there were other indications of how swiftly the frontier of the Ohio River and its tributaries was changing. The Ohio country was no longer being called Indian lands but, rather, part of the Northwest Territory. Now, at the mouth of the Muskingum, in addition to Fort Harmar, Campus Martius was being built, and new settlers were flocking into the Marietta Settlement across the mouth of the Muskingum from Fort Harmar. There was also the new Fort Clendenin being built by George Clendenin on the Kanawha at the mouth of Elk River, and a new unnamed fort a mile up the Kanawha from there.[680] And some ten miles downstream from

Fort Clendenin, Lewis Tackett had just finished building a fort at the mouth of Coal River called Coal Fort, though some were calling it Tackett's Fort.

No doubt about it, things were suddenly moving just too quickly. So far as Boone was concerned, the frontier was becoming altogether too civilized. Along with Kenton, he had increasingly been called in to testify in land dispute cases and, as was happening to Kenton, ever more of his own land was being whittled away because of overlapping and faulty claims. That was the situation he had commented upon gloomily when he visited Henry Lee a few months ago at Lee's new little station southeast of Maysville.

"Henry," he had commented bitterly, "over and over I been robbed of my lands here. I'm regular being called on t'give depositions in land claim cases an' tol' to sign papers an' then later find out I've signed away rights to my own land. These lawyers are always tryin' t'make me falsify my oath."

Lee had nodded sympathetically. Boone was far from the only one having such troubles here. The shrewd land-grabbers were making killings by preying on the ignorance and illiteracy of the frontiersmen who opened this land. He wished he could help but knew there was nothing he could do.

"By God, Henry," Boone had continued, growing angrier the more he thought about it, "it's bad enough to be stripped of my land without being abused an' accused of lyin'. From now on, no one need send to me for a deposition. All my own lands are gone, and others'll jest have to take care of their own."

He had paused reflectively a moment and then added, "I believe I'm goin' west o'the Mississippi, where it ain't so all-fired crowded. I won't live in a country where I cain't fell wood in my own dooryard." His eyes had widened and his voice registered something between surprise and consternation. "Why, at Bryan's Station they have t'haul firewood half a mile!"

"That's Spanish land west of the Mississippi, Dan'l," Lee had cautioned. "It's still all wilderness, and the Indians are moving out there. They might not take too kindly to your coming to settle."

To Lee's surprise, Boone had chuckled, and Lee could have sworn there was a note of keen eagerness in the sound.

Now, arriving at Kenton's Station and shaking hands with the huge frontiersman who emerged to greet him, Boone told Simon of his newly made decision to leave Kentucky. Kenton frowned.

"You won't be coming back at all?" he asked.

The 53-year-old frontiersman before him shook his head soberly. "Ain't nothin' t'come back to, Simon. My land's gone, most of my friends has got theirselves kilt, man can't move aroun' no more 'thout bumpin' into somebody. No, I ain't comin' back. My oldest boy, Jesse, he's got him a little place near the Salt Works, 'bout eighteen mile up Little Sandy. Reckon I'll hunker with him some, then mebbe head on t'Missouri. Hear tell it's a fine land. Wouldn't want t'come 'long, would you?"

Simon Kenton shook his head regretfully. "Not now, Dan'l. Someday, mebbe. Send back word where you're at. Someday you'll see me show up."

They shook hands awkwardly, embarrassed by the emotions that brought hot tears to their eyes. Boone abruptly turned and paced away with his characteristic stride. Kenton watched him until he disappeared into a wooded hillside to the east, then turned back toward his own station, filled with a deep sadness.

[N o v e m b e r   6 ,   1 7 8 8 — T h u r s d a y]

Lewis Wetzel was beginning to regret that he had ever made the agreement with the new settlers at Marietta to be their chief hunter the remainder of this year. He had known from the beginning, of course, that he would have no difficulty providing them with all the meat they could use and had already proved it by bringing in so many deer, bear and buffalo that half a dozen of their womenfolk were constantly at work jerking the meat. Though they admired his skill and paid him without equivocation, harsh feelings toward him were aroused when he soundly criticized them for selling guns and ammunition to the Indians.

In addition to hunting meat for the settlers, he still had the responsibility he had taken on at Fort Harmar. Word of his presence at Marietta had become generally known and, because of his reputation for woodland skills and knowledge of the Ohio country, Gen. Harmar prevailed upon him to act as a scout for the army if and when an expedition was launched into the interior. He was also to regularly patrol some distance from the fort in conjunction with his hunting, reporting on any sign of hostile Indian activity he observed, but he was definitely not to engage any Indians encountered.

There had been a considerable rise in the number of Indians seen, of course, but that was due largely to the council of peace scheduled to be held next month at the fort by Gov. St. Clair. Even though the council was not scheduled to begin until December 13, the first arrivals had reached the mouth of the Muskingum on September 9; a party of 50 Senecas from New York under Chief Cornplanter— Warhoytonehteh—who had been escorted here in boats from Fort Pitt by Gen. Richard Butler and two companies of regulars under Capts. David Zeigler and James O'Hara. They had been cordially greeted by Gen. Harmar, who immediately posted a proclamation stating that a temporary truce had been agreed upon between the Indians and Americans until the peace council was concluded, which was expected to take several weeks once it began, and ordering that none of these Indians or any others yet to come were to be molested in any way. It was an order that did not sit well with most of the frontiersmen, and the people of the Marietta Settlement, across the Muskingum from Fort Harmar, were very apprehensive.

In the weeks that had elapsed since then, additional groups of Indian delegates had shown up and joined those already on hand, who had established a common temporary campground on a broad bottom along a small unnamed stream two miles north of the fort; a stream that was since being called Indian Camp Run.[681] The delegates thus far on hand had arrived from great distances and wore their most colorful and decorative costumes. They represented all the tribes of the Iroquois League with the exception of the Mohawks, as well as the Ottawas, Chippewas, Delawares, Potawatomies, Wyandots and even the Sacs. Significantly, no Shawnees, Miamis or Kickapoos were on hand or had been invited.

Lewis Wetzel, who still harbored his abiding hatred of all Indians, had hoped he would encounter some of them on a one-to-one basis or, at most, no more than two or three at a time, but until today, that hadn't happened, though he had been spying on them regularly. Once they arrived at the camp, the Indians remained there together or traveled in sizable groups between there and the fort for conferences with Gen. Harmar while they awaited the arrival of Gov. St. Clair.

Now, however, Wetzel's luck had changed. This morning he saw a member of the Seneca delegation leave the encampment by himself, heading toward Fort Harmar. Though Wetzel had no idea who he was, this was the influential subchief Tegunteh, who had struck up a rapport with Gen. Harmar at their first meeting and who seemed particularly proud of the new name he had bestowed upon himself some time ago—George Washington. Wetzel, upon seeing which of the two paths the Indian was taking toward the fort, immediately slipped away and took a position in hiding about a quarter-mile below the encampment, on the south side of a little run flowing into the Muskingum.[682] A few minutes later Tegunteh appeared on the path. He moved down the slight north bank of the run, leaped over the rivulet easily and was coming up the south bank when Wetzel stepped out from his hiding place and shot him full in the chest. He quickly scalped the Seneca and then raced off, knowing that the report of his rifle had probably been heard in the Indian camp and that others would be coming to investigate. This time, however, Lewis Wetzel had made a serious error.

Though shot through the chest and scalped, Tegunteh—George Washington—was not dead. At least not yet.[683]

[November 9, 1788—Sunday]

It was the first time Lewis Wetzel had ever been in jail, and only the second time in his life his fate was in the hands of someone else. The first time had been when he and his brother Jacob had been captured when young boys by the Indians, from whom they had soon escaped. Wetzel was very set on escaping again now, though there was little time left before the hanging—his.

He'd made two mistakes, he told himself. The first had been in not making sure the Seneca subchief he had shot and scalped was dead, and he regretted that oversight. The second mistake had been in admitting that he was the one who killed the Indian, when, by a simple denial, he could possibly have avoided his present dilemma. Yet he did not regret having admitted it; he was proud of it then and still proud of it now.

The furor created by the shooting of the Seneca everyone was calling George Washington had been intense. Tegunteh, found by fellow Indians shortly after the shooting, had immediately been carried to Fort Harmar for medical treatment. Gen. Harmar, who had been quietly imbibing in his own quarters, was beside himself with rage when he learned of it and immediately went to the medical quarters, where the post surgeon was already trying to save the man's life. At the commander's entrance, the surgeon shook his head, signifying the wound was mortal and nothing could be done. The Seneca, however, regained consciousness and, between gasps, told what had happened and described the man who had shot him: a white man, tall, slender, dressed partly like an Indian, partly like a white man, with long black hair tied in a queue and wearing a cloth cap of three colors. The man had stepped out of the bushes before him without warning, grinned widely, raised his rifle and shot without speaking. The Seneca tried to say more but could not, and a few moments later he died.

The Indians were extremely upset, and it was only with great difficulty that Gen. Harmar prevented them from attacking the whites here. He did so by promising them that an immediate and thorough search would be undertaken to apprehend and punish the perpetrator. It hadn't taken long. The description the dying man had given, everyone agreed, fit no one but Lewis Wetzel, especially the tricolored cloth hat he had favored of late and the fact that he had grinned before killing the Indian— a Lew Wetzel trademark.

Harmer issued an arrest warrant and sent out a half-dozen different squads of men to search for Wetzel. They found him easily within minutes, at the cabin of an acquaintance. He was brought at once to the general, who asked him if he was the one who had shot and scalped the Seneca subchief known as George Washington.

"Don't recognize the name," Wetzel replied, "but I got nothin' to conceal. I sure as hell killed one o'them red buggers this mornin' at that little run to the north of here. Din't know he was any kind o'chief, though. Wouldn't've made no difference. He's the only good Injen 'round here right now that I know of."

"Damn you, Wetzel!" Gen. Harmar snapped. "Do you have any idea what you've done?"

"I surely do, Gen'ral," Wetzel replied, nodding, "an' I sure-fire don't consider it no crime. I killed one o'them sumbitches that've been killin' an' takin' our women an' chill'un for years, that've been burnin' our homes an' barns an' killin' our cows an' stealin' our horses. The same red sumbitches that killed my brother an' my paw an' a whole lot of my friends. Damn right I known what I done! I ain't never made peace with 'em and ain't never goin' to. I'll shoot 'em down like the worthless dogs they are 'long as I live."

Gen. Harmar's expression was set in harsh lines. "You are going to hang for what you have done, Wetzel, I promise you. I'm going to see to it personally."

Wetzel had thought it was just talk, that surely a white man could not possibly be executed for killing an Indian, but he had been locked up in the guardhouse, and now it was the third day he was here. A few friends and acquaintances had come to see him during this interval, but any hopes he harbored that they were bringing good news or might be able to help him were dashed. Now, with little hope remaining, he sent word to Harmar that he had something to say to him. It was about an hour before the commander arrived, and there was no glimmer of compassion in his expression or his voice.

"What do you want, Wetzel?"

"Gen'ral, I ain't never had no hankerin' t'be hung like a dog. 'Sposin' you let them Injens pick their two best fighters with whatever weapons they want—knives, clubs, 'hawks. Give me the same t'face 'em with, an' let us fight it out. They'll like it better, an' I sure t'hell will, too. If I'm goin' out, I'd 'preciate goin' as I always 'spected to someday.''

Gen. Harmar shook his head. "Can't do it. As an officer appointed by the law, it is the law by which I must be governed, and the general government has no provisions for allowing any such thing to be done. The penalty for killing an Indian in a time of peace—and this has been proclaimed as being such—is hanging. You, sir, will indeed hang. Furthermore, *I*, sir, will delight in drinking a toast over your corpse."

"Then at least, Gen'ral, grant me a request." Wetzel's voice quavered, and he seemed on the verge of breaking down.

"What request?"

"I'm a woodsman, Gen'ral, a free spirit. These three days have been—have been —God, Gen'ral, I'm going crazy in here. No fresh air, no exercise. I cain't stand it. Please, *please!* let me get out into the air and just do some exercises. That's all I ask."

"So you can escape?"

"No. If that's what you think, make it impossible. Surround me with a ring of soldiers and, outside them, a ring of Indians, so I cain't break out. Please!"

"I'll consider it," Harmar told him, then walked briskly away.

The hour that had passed since then seemed interminable, and Wetzel was beginning to think he had failed, but now a squad of soldiers came to the guardhouse and marched him in their midst to a broad clearing well away from the river or trees, where some 50 armed soldiers formed a ring. Beyond them more than twice that many Indians formed a second ring, their expressions dark as they looked at Wetzel, an air of anticipation about them, as if they assumed this was some sort of American version of the traditional Indian gauntlet.

Wetzel was now released inside the double ring and, after looking around for a moment, he let out an exuberant yelp and began leaping and twirling in a series of gyrations that caused the soldiers and some of the Indians to break into laughter. The merriment increased as he executed a series of somersaults from one side of the circle to the other, then returned doing a series of very rapid cartwheels that didn't stop in time and carried him tumbling into the line of men. He quickly regained his feet and excused himself for overshooting and then went across the circle twice more, rolling, somersaulting, twisting, leaping, cartwheeling. Each time he came close enough to the line before stopping that those surrounding him pulled back a little and broke up some to get out of the way of his feet and knees and elbows, and each time he gathered himself, came to his feet and went into a new set. The next one, however, was even more remarkable, beginning with a few full body flips in the air, several very fast somersaults and then evolving into some especially broad and rapid cartwheels.

As he neared the lines, again the men in that arc of the circle gave way and then decidedly separated as he careened directly into them. Still cartwheeling, he passed them by and continued another 30 yards. Abruptly the cartwheels ended and he was running at great speed. He was fully 60 yards past the line before the realization dawned he was actually trying to escape. The first shots were sent after him when he was 80 yards away, but they were hurriedly fired and missed. By then he was, for all intents and purposes, out of range and closing on the woodlands. More shots peppered the ground around him, but all missed widely, while the Indians behind broke into furious howls and the soldiers shouted angrily and many of the men in the line set off in pursuit.

Wetzel laughed aloud as he ran, yelled triumphantly as he plunged into the woods. Thereafter he remained silent as he ran as hard as he had ever run, taking dangerous chances in leaping over ravines and throwing himself over and beyond windfallen trees. He did nothing particularly devious in his running until he was fully a mile from the fort and the sound of pursuit behind him had faded. Then, gasping but not allowing himself respite, he went into a series of evasional maneuvers that called on all the skill he had acquired in his years as woodsman and Indian fighter. Another half-mile, and he encountered what he was looking for. He squirmed his way deep and deeper yet into the dense briars and other brush cloaking two fallen trees at angles to one another, drawing himself into the small space beneath the one that had fallen across the other and broken. Here he would wait until nightfall before resuming his flight.

Now the familiar broad grin stretched Lewis Wetzel's lips wide, and he knew he had won.

[N o v e m b e r   2 0 ,   1 7 8 8 — T h u r s d a y]

The general feeling in Wheeling over the escape of Lewis Wetzel from imprisonment in Marietta had been one of jubilation. Long having borne the brunt of Indian attacks on this frontier, the residents of the Wheeling area took little stock in the peace talks going on at Fort Harmar. To the contrary, the number of Indians coming to the talks had caused a considerable rise of apprehension among the settlers, and while some Wheeling residents thought what Wetzel had done was at least inappropriate at such a time, the majority applauded his killing of the Seneca subchief and were appalled that he had faced a sentence of death by hanging because of it.

The story had gone the rounds about how the incident took place, followed by Wetzel's apprehension and his subsequent escape; how he had waited in his hiding place until dark, then went directly to the Ohio River several miles below the mouth of the Muskingum and swam across. He had gone at once to the new cabin of Rebecca and Isaac Williams, across from Marietta, but no one was there. He'd had better luck, however, half a mile farther, when he'd come to the similarly new cabin of Hamilton Carr, who was home and welcomed him.

Carr had given Wetzel fresh clothing, fed him and, though he had no rifle to spare, given him his shotgun and ammunition. There had been no incidents as he made his way to the Wetzel homestead on Wheeling Creek, seven miles above the Forks. No one was there, and on going to the neighboring Bonnett property, he had learned that everyone was at Wheeling preparing to take shelter there should the peace talks break down and a new spate of Indian warfare break out.

On his arrival at Wheeling, there was a happy reunion with family and friends but still considerable concern for his safety. Word of his escape had preceded him and, with it, the news that Gen. Harmar had posted a reward of $500 for Lewis Wetzel, dead or alive. While he had many friends here, there was always the chance that he might be captured or killed for a reward of that size; it was almost half again as much as an ordinary soldier made in an entire year. Those closest to him suggested that he go away for a year or two, perhaps take a trip down to New Orleans, and give things a chance to cool down. Wetzel agreed to do so.

Three days ago, armed again with a new flintlock given to him by Lewis Bonnett, he bought passage on a flatboat en route to New Orleans that had stopped for the night at Wheeling. The boatmen were not informed of Wetzel's fugitive status, but it had become apparent, as they approached the Muskingum before noon today, that he did not wish to be seen. The stop at Marietta was to be brief, mainly to drop off some dispatches and supplies from Fort Pitt. During that interval Wetzel hid under a greased cloth covering sacks of beans and corn that were part of the cargo.

Not until the flatboat was shoved away from the Marietta wharf and was floating free again did Wetzel emerge, but then he let his pride cause him to make an uncharacteristic blunder. As they floated past the mouth of the Muskingum and reached their closest point to Fort Harmar, some 40 yards offshore, he saw troops parading, and he cupped his mouth and gleefully yelled, "Here's Lewis Wetzel, by God, so come and take him if you can."

The soldiers looked toward the flatboat, and Wetzel did a little impromptu jig on the deck, turned a cartwheel to eliminate any doubt and then called out again in the same vein. This time they recognized him, as they pointed excitedly and some raced off to the fort. A few minutes later Wetzel's good humor faded as a squad of eight soldiers and an officer ran to the shore and launched themselves in a sleek ten-man canoe. Though the flatboat was now several hundred yards distant as it drifted with the Ohio's strong current, it was clear that the powerfully paddled canoe would overtake them very quickly.

"They ain't takin' me," Wetzel murmured, checking the prime in his flintlock's pan and popping a few extra lead balls into his mouth.

"Surely you're not aiming to shoot United States soldiers, are you?" The boat's captain was aghast.

"They try to take me," Wetzel murmured grimly, "they damn well better start prayin'."

Intent upon the approaching boat and warning them to stay clear or pay the price, Wetzel did not see the flatboat captain signal his crew and, before he realized what was happening, he was grabbed from behind by the burliest of the six, and the captain snatched the flintlock from his grasp. Wetzel cursed and fought savagely, and it took all six crewmen and their captain to subdue him. By that time the canoe had overtaken them, and Wetzel, coldly furious with his hands tied behind him, was put aboard the smaller craft and quickly returned to Fort Harmar. None of the soldiers mentioned the reward for Wetzel's capture and the flatboat, at its captain's command, simply continued floating on its long downstream journey.

Now, hours later and cloaked by a vast depression, Lewis Wetzel sat morosely in the same guardhouse where he'd been 11 days earlier, outside the main enclosure of the pickets. But this time the military were taking no chances on his escaping again. The sentence of hanging had been reaffirmed, and immediately he had been shackled with cuffs of heavy iron attached to one another with an equally heavy two-foot length of chain. The door was strongly bolted from the outside, and a guard posted there to prohibit anyone approaching the single barred window.

A steady rain had begun falling just after sunset, and now, darkness having fallen, it continued with persistent, melancholy droning. Wetzel went to the little window and called to the guard in a low voice.

"Hey, soldier, I got to go."

"So go," the guard said, coming closer. "No one's stopping you."

"They din't leave no bucket or pot," Wetzel said, "an' I really got to go bad."

"Well, just piss on the floor."

"Pissin' ain't what a gotta do. C'mon"—he put an urgent tone to it—"have a heart. This is a small room, an' it ain't right t'make me have t'smell my own business all night. So how 'bout it? Just let me out long enough t'go, or I'm gonna' bust."

The guard gave in. He moved to the door and unbolted it, then opened it with one hand, rifle held alertly waist high and pointed at the prisoner. Wetzel emerged hesitantly, the chains clinking faintly as he walked. He paused outside the door and stood with head raised high, letting the rain wash over his face.

"God, that feels good," he murmured. Then he moved around to the backside of the small building, the guard only a couple of paces behind, gun still leveled at his prisoner's back. As soon as they were behind the building and a few paces into the weeds, Wetzel reached to his belt as if to open it and lower his pants. Instead he gripped the double length of chain in both hands and, as the guard averted his eyes to afford Wetzel some privacy, the frontiersman swung the chain in a short vicious arc that caught the guard on his temple and whipped solidly to the back of his head. With only a faint wheezing sound, the guard fell unconscious upon his own gun and, not pausing an instant, Wetzel was off and running, cupping the chain in his hands so its rattling would not betray him.

He ran to the west, occasionally stumbling in the dark, wondering how long it would be before the guard was found or regained consciousness and the alarm sounded. He did not have long to wait. Before he had gone 300 yards, he heard voices coming faintly behind him and he pushed on even faster, thankful for the rain that was masking his trail.

At Fort Harmar the alarm had indeed been raised. The guard, having regained consciousness, tried to fire his rifle to attract attention, but the powder had become wet and would not ignite. Staggering, he ran toward headquarters, and soon the whole place was in an uproar. Gen. Harmar, who was holding a private council with some of the more important chiefs, was livid with fury over Wetzel's second escape and ordered an intensive search by the whole garrison. At the same time he told the chiefs to set their warriors on the trail, and if they found Lewis Wetzel, they could do as they pleased with him and he would neither object nor interfere.

Wetzel, by this time a mile west of the fort and a few hundred yards from the banks of the Ohio, tumbled headlong over a large fallen tree. The rooted end projected into the air and was heavily overgrown with brambles. As he pulled himself back to his hands and knees, his hands encountered a large cavity on the lower side of the tree. He reached out and explored it further in the darkness and found it was large enough to hold him. He slid inside feet first and squirmed deep inside until he was all but out of sight.

Less than an hour later he heard the murmur of voices approaching that soon resolved themselves into an Indian dialect. All senses keenly alert, Wetzel thought about what he would do if he were discovered. His only chance would be to grapple with the warrior who found him and try to get his weapon from him. He braced his legs to catapult himself from his hiding place if it became necessary. The voices came closer, and he heard the scuff of feet as one or two Indians stepped up on the log that sheltered him. One came to a stop directly over his hiding place, and he hardly dared breathe, but the darkness kept his haven undetected and the warriors, after a few words to one another, moved off.

Relieved, Lewis Wetzel relaxed and considered his options. Getting across the big river was clearly his only chance. He was a strong swimmer, but he knew it would be courting disaster to attempt to swim across the Ohio with the weight of the chain and wrist irons hampering him, especially as cool as the river waters had become this late in the season. So the first order of business with the dawn would be to try to rid himself of his irons or, failing that, to locate a boat. If that were not possible, he would have to find a buoyant piece of driftwood and cling to it as he kicked his way across and hope he wouldn't become chilled beyond functioning.

Satisfied with his plan, Wetzel grinned, realizing with some amusement that his depression had lifted and he felt good again. He leaned his head against his arms and dozed.

[November 21, 1788—Friday]

Lewis Wetzel stood boldly on the shore watching the big canoe filled with Indians approaching. There was a wicked fire in his eyes, and his familiar grin had returned. When it was still 200 yards distant, he called again, repeating the words that had initially brought them toward him from the riverfront before Fort Harmar.

"C'mon, you red bastards! You're lookin' for Lew Wetzel, you've damn well found 'im. You think a bunch o'red niggers'll make me turn an' run? C'mon!"

As they shouted back at him angrily and waved their tomahawks in the air, he thought of how lucky he had been this morning, even though it hadn't started out that way. At the very first vague light of dawn, he had slipped from his hiding place in the log and carefully, watchfully, moved down to the Ohio River shore. Casting about for some way to possibly remove his irons, he had spied a large rock on shore and gone to it, then spent a half-hour pulling the chain back and forth across a jagged edge before giving up without having made the least headway.

Even more cautiously he had moved back along the shore, keeping to cover, searching, hoping to find a canoe drawn up on the shore. There was none and, as he came closer to the mouth of the Muskingum, he could hear voices of soldiers and Indians. He melted back into deeper cover and retraced his steps farther downstream. Two miles below the fort, his flagging spirits rose as he saw a small boat in the river ahead: It was a canoe with a man in it, evidently white, his hand moving up and down as he bounced a weighted and baited line along the bottom, no doubt trying to catch a catfish. Wetzel's spirits suddenly soared when, after coming closer and peering from cover, he recognized the man—his old friend Isaac Williams, whose place was across the river.[684]

"Isaac! Ike!"

The fisherman looked up, startled, reaching for his rifle. "Who is it?"

"Lew. Lew Wetzel. C'mon in, Ike. I got t'git t'the other side or I'm a goner."

Williams had come to shore then and picked him up, and together they had gone to his place, where Williams, using a file and hammer, finally freed Lewis of his irons. Then Wetzel asked if he could have back the flintlock he had sold Williams some months ago. "I'll see you get your money back for it soon's I can," he had promised.

"No, you don't have t'do that, Lew," Williams had said, shaking his head. "I'm glad t'let you have it. Jest don't tell no one where at y'got it."

Williams had furnished him not only with a gun but with shot pouch and powderhorn, knife and tomahawk, plus a blanket. Then he listened while Lewis told him what he was going to do, now that he had a rifle again. Wanting no part of it and strongly advising against it, the settler had wished him luck and quickly gone away. That was when Wetzel had returned to the riverbank and, concealing his gun in a bush close at hand, had called across to the Indians he saw on the far shore, identified himself and shouted the insults that he knew would bring them toward him.

Now, seeing him as unarmed, they approached within range. Wetzel leaned over almost casually and extracted his rifle from the bush. He methodically aimed and put a bullet through the heart of the warrior in the bow, who toppled into the river and disappeared. There was immediate consternation in the canoe as the Indians tried to shield themselves by ducking and, at the same time, paddle out of range as quickly as possible.

It was not quickly enough. With the swiftness for which he was noted, Wetzel reloaded and immediately brought down another of the warriors with a bullet through the head. He, too, fell overboard. Wetzel loaded a third time and fired, but by now the canoe was drawing out of range, and though he hit and wounded another, who fell into the boat, he doubted that the wound was mortal.

As the canoe moved back into midriver and somewhat downstream, Wetzel bowed extravagantly, waved and then loped up the bank and disappeared into the brush.

[D e c e m b e r   7 ,   1 7 8 8 — S u n d a y]

The competitive shoot in progress at the Mingo Bottom Settlement this bright Sunday had attracted bordermen from many miles up and down the river, not only because of the frontier skills competition, which they always enjoyed, but because it was known that Lewis Wetzel would be on hand.

The story of Wetzel's escape from jail at Fort Harmar, not once but twice, had been on everyone's lips, and their admiration for this indomitable 24-year-old frontiersman was boundless. Which was why, in the midst of the competition today, the jovial atmosphere suddenly turned ugly when it was learned that a detachment of soldiers from Fort Harmar were approaching to take Wetzel into custody and return him to the mouth of the Muskingum to be hanged. The bordermen quickly had a meeting, and within minutes they made an angry and all but unanimous resolve: They would ambush the detachment and kill them all.

The officer in charge of the detachment of 30 soldiers in three canoes was Capt. Jacob Kingsbury. He had been summoned by Gen. Harmar the morning after Wetzel's second escape and less than half an hour after the report was brought to headquarters that Wetzel had just killed two more Indians and wounded a third who were crossing the Ohio to capture him. Though Kingsbury had been in Harmar's command for a considerable while, he had never seen his general so infuriated. Wetzel had last been seen heading upriver on shore, presumably to return to his old haunts in the Wheeling area. Gen. Harmar had then ordered Capt. Kingsbury to take 30 men and pursue the fugitive and the sense was implicit in the order, if not spoken, that he had better not return without him . . . or at least his body.

Capt. Kingsbury's detachment had stopped first at Grave Creek, where they spent two days searching the area and questioning the Tomlinsons and other residents but with unsatisfactory results, except that one settler mentioned he had heard Wetzel was in Wheeling. That had been the detachment's next stop, but again without success. Various rumors put Wetzel at Shepherd's Fort, Vanmetre's, Holliday's Cove, Washington village, even Pittsburgh. Acting on a hunch that the fugitive might simply have gone home, the detachment ascended Wheeling Creek first to Shepherd's Fort at the Forks, then upstream another seven miles to the Wetzel place. Lew Wetzel, they learned, had been there a week ago but was gone now. At Lewis Bonnett's place, where they checked next, they were advised to try at Washington village, but again it hadn't panned out, and now it was becoming apparent that these settlers were very much pro-Wetzel and had been deliberately misdirecting the pursuers.

At last, having been gone from Fort Harmar for over a fortnight, Capt. Kingsbury finally got a reliable tip: Lewis Wetzel was going to participate in the frontier competition at Mingo Bottom. He headed there at once, cautioning his men to be prepared for anything, though he hardly expected to run into anything so drastic as an ambush directed against himself and his men.

When the three canoes touched ashore at Mingo Bottom a few minutes ago and Kingsbury stepped ashore, he saw that the targets were all set up. There were numerous on shore canoes, but no one was visible. For the first time Kingsbury felt stirrings of apprehension, and he ordered his men to stay in the boats but keep their weapons at ready. A moment later two unarmed men emerged from the woods nearby and strode toward them. One was Maj. William McMahan of Beech Bottom Settlement. The other was Lewis Wetzel.

"Sir," Kingsbury said when the pair stopped 20 feet from him, "I hope you have approached to surrender Mr. Wetzel, who is a fugitive from justice, as I have orders from the commanding general to take him into custody and return him to Fort Harmar, where he is to be executed for killing Indians."

"To attempt doing so, Captain Kingsbury," McMahan said mildly, "would be a very serious mistake. I arrived here myself only a short time ago and found that the more than one-hundred-fifty men gathered here have determined to prevent you from doing any such thing. They had planned to ambush you as your detachment stepped ashore, and I have managed to prevail upon them to hold their fire until I could inform you of the situation and give you an opportunity to peaceably withdraw."

Capt. Kingsbury lifted his hand and pointed it at Wetzel. "I'm sorry, sir, but this man is guilty of murder and has been sentenced to be hanged. I have my orders; I must take him in."

McMahan shook his head. "Perhaps you didn't fully understand me, Captain. The men here are all excellent shots. They have, all of them, at one time or another lost family members or friends to the marauding Indians, and they do not consider it a crime to kill the people who brought such tragedy into their lives. They have attached to Mr. Wetzel the stature of a hero—deservedly so, I should add—and should you and your men attempt to take him against his will, they will open fire, and you and your men will surely be killed."

Kingsbury licked his lips and glanced about nervously, then let his gaze settle on the fugitive. "Mr. Wetzel," he said, "I must ask you now if you will surrender yourself to us voluntarily."

"Hell no, I won't," Wetzel said, grinning.

"We will then," the captain said, returning his attention to the militia major, "have to take this man into custody by force. I cannot believe, sir, that your people here—assuming that they are, in fact, here—would presume to raise their weapons against a detachment of the United States Army in the performance of its legal orders."

"I commend you, Captain Kingsbury," Maj. McMahan said, an edge to his voice now, "on your intention to faithfully execute your orders, as well as on your courage, but I do not think you have yet fully comprehended the gravity of your position." He raised his right hand high and issued a shrill whistle.

Instantly just over 150 bordermen stepped into sight from the cover behind which they had been hidden, their rifles trained unwaveringly at the detachment. Capt. Kingsbury paled noticeably.

"At least five rifles are aimed at every member of your party, Captain," McMahan went on as he lowered his arm, "including yourself. If I raise my arm again, they will fire and, I assure you, marksmen that they are, few if any will miss. Nothing, at this point, will save you and your men from massacre except a very hasty return to Fort Harmar. You now have to the count of ten to return to your men and push off from shore. If you have not done so by the time I reach that number, I promise you, I *will* raise my arm. One . . . two . . . three . . . four . . ."

Grim-faced, Capt. Kingsbury turned about and strode back to his canoe, entered it and ordered his men to shove off. They did so as Maj. McMahan's count reached eight. The captain turned and regarded the fugitive as the current gripped the three canoes and sent them downstream.

"Mr. Wetzel," he called, "you have humiliated General Harmar, and he is not a man who will forgive and forget. My advice to you is to leave this country as quickly as you can."

[January 9, 1789—Friday]

The peace talks that had been going on at Fort Harmar since December 13 finally came to an end today, to the apparent satisfaction of no one except Gov. Arthur St. Clair and Gen. Josiah Harmar, both of whom deluded themselves into thinking something of significance had been accomplished. It had not.

With the Miamis—including all their subtribes—and the Shawnees and Kickapoos still maintaining an attitude of war with the United States and the other tribes still vacillating among themselves about whether to side with them, remain neutral or make peace with the Americans, the fragile unity between the tribes was rapidly disintegrating. To a large extent, that was what the United States was hoping for: By fueling the differences and magnifying the grievances developing between the tribes, they were seriously undermining the Confederacy among them. What this might mean, in the end, was exactly as George Washington had outlined in his master plan —that when the time came for the United States to take harsh measures against the tribes standing in the way, as it most assuredly would, the enemy would be only one or two tribes instead of a powerful union of them all.

The Indians had come to Fort Harmar in the belief that the United States was ready and willing to reconsider boundaries and make greater efforts toward conciliation with the tribes in this respect. In point of fact, they found St. Clair adamant in his refusal to bend one iota toward any kind of concession and doing all in his power to stir intertribal jealousies to the advantage of the United States. Further, the Indians on hand were well aware that they neither occupied nor claimed the lands in question —lands belonging to and occupied by the Shawnees and Miamis who were not in attendance—so anything they agreed to, so far as they were concerned, was simply not binding. As one of the Delaware chiefs simplified it: "I point to a horse in the meadow and say to you that I agree to sell it to you. I even sign a paper to that end. But the horse belongs to another, the meadow is not mine and the land upon which they stand belongs not to me. Can you then claim that you have legally bought the horse and the meadow and the land? No, you cannot. Yet that is what you do here today. We sign this treaty you have made, but it is meaningless. It is a treaty made of air and without substance."

Another chief complained that the treaty council was one in name only, not in action, saying, "A treaty council is where two parties negotiate to settle the differences between them, but here there is not negotiation. Though you listen to what we say, and show impatience at having to do so, when it comes your turn to speak, it is as if you have heard not one word we have spoken and instead you then tell us how things must be. You could have told us this by runners, and we would not have had to go through the expense and trouble of coming this long way for nothing."

Eventually, however, seeing there was nothing else to do, the tribes on hand gave in and signed the treaty. The Senecas in doing so merely reaffirmed the same land cessions they had agreed to with the Fort Stanwix Treaty. The Wyandots, Delawares, Potawatomies, Sacs, Chippewas and Ottawas similarly reaffirmed the previous treaties at Fort Stanwix, Fort McIntosh and Fort Finney, insofar as their own territories were considered. Their signing away the lands the United States was now claiming in the Northwest Territory was simply a case of selling a horse that belonged to another; they knew the northwestern tribes would, with justification and legality, repudiate the agreements before the ink was dry. To them all, the Fort Harmar Treaty was wholly meaningless.

That the Potawatomies, Ottawas, Chippewas and Sacs were on hand at all was ridiculous, since their lands were far away and they had no claim whatsoever to any lands here in question. Yet, they had been duped into coming by the promise that they would receive many fine presents from the Americans. They received virtually nothing and were highly disgruntled, to such an extent that they agreed among themselves to throw in their lot with the Shawnees, Kickapoos and Miamis in opposing the Americans.

Now, even the Wyandots and Delawares began to feel they had been in error by pulling away from their Shawnee and Miami allies and some of the chiefs were already advocating a full reconciliation with them and rejoining their efforts to oppose the moves the Americans were now so swiftly making into the Indian country. For decades they had contended that the Ohio River would be a barrier that would stop the American encroachment; now, finally and with great clarity, they could see the fallacy of that belief. If the Americans were to be stopped, it could only be accomplished by all the northwestern tribes uniting in that endeavor.

If that meant unconditional war with the United States, then so be it.

Chapter 9

The first session of Congress under the Federal Constitution, which replaced the Congress of the Confederation of States, had many problems to consider, many ordinances to pass.

Among these matters was one that was seen to swiftly and passed along without objection, yet it was of extreme importance insofar as the residents of the Ohio Valley were concerned, as well as the tribes north and west of the big river. It was perhaps fitting and proper that it was the First Congress of the United States that gave the Ohio Territory a permanent status among the States of the Union and thereby opened the door to statehood for Ohio in what, a great number of settlers anticipated, would be only a few short years.

[*January 22, 1789 — Thursday*]

With more and more Shawnee parties being sighted in the area of the new settlements in the southwestern Ohio country—Columbia, Fort Miami, Covalt's Station and North Bend—the residents had become apprehensive over the possibility of an attack.[685] They were singularly unprotected and appealed to Gen. Harmar for regular troops to be stationed in their vicinity.

With Judge John Cleve Symmes directly involved, and since he was a Northwest Territory Supreme Court justice and carried considerable weight politically, Harmar knew it would be wise to take action at once and that the soldiers used for this duty would undoubtedly have to come from the Falls of the Ohio—either Fort Finney or

Fort Nelson. Maj. John P. Wyllys was presently in command of the latter, and Harmar now wrote to tell him what was in the wind, to prepare him to move when the order would be given:

> *It is not improbable but that two companies will be ordered to be stationed at the mouth of the Great Miami, not only as a better cover for Kentucky but also as a protection to Judge Symmes in his intended settlement there.*

[April 30, 1789 — Thursday]

A large crowd had gathered at Federal Hall in New York, knowing they were witnesses to a remarkable occurrence. As a free and independent country, the United States of America had selected the man they thought best qualified for the job of leading the American people.

On this day 57-year-old George Washington was inaugurated as the first President of the United States—a position in which he was required, to the best of his abilities, to represent all the people of this great new republic.

All the people, that is, if one did not count the native Americans.

[December 31, 1789 — Thursday]

Two things had become increasingly clear this year: first, that no matter what the Indians did to discourage and push back the whites, their encroachments were not only continuing, they were increasing, and the Ohio River had wholly ceased to function as a boundary; second, that another full-scale Indian war was imminent.

In the first matter, the number of new settlers streaming down the Ohio and into lands on both sides of the big river far surpassed that of any previous year. More new settlements, forts, blockhouses, and individual cabins had been built than ever before, with the promise of more to come and, keeping pace with this, more formalized political boundaries were being established. A huge new county was created by Virginia on the south side of the Ohio, fronting on the big river downstream all the way from the mouth of Pond Run, five miles below the Little Kanawha, about 130 miles to the mouth of the Big Sandy, then southward to the Cumberland Mountains, encompassing some 10,000 acres; it was being called Kanawha County. Its militia was placed under command of Samuel Lewis, brother of the long-dead Gen. Andrew Lewis, who had faced the Indians in the Battle of Point Pleasant 15 years earlier. His second in command, with the rank of lieutenant colonel, was Daniel Boone, who had deferred his plan to go to Missouri and had now settled at Point Pleasant.

Farther to the west, Mason County was established in Kentucky, with Maysville —formerly Limestone—named as the county seat. The new Kennedy's Bottom Settlement was established in that county a mile from the Washington village. Twenty-five miles above Maysville at the mouth of an unnamed stream, the new little settlement of Quick's Station was established and the stream was named Quick's

Run. Just over 60 miles down the Ohio from Maysville, Clements' Station was settled in the Ohio country, three-quarters of a mile downstream from Covalt's Station on the left bank of the Little Miami River opposite the mouth of the East Fork Little Miami River.[686] And, on a somewhat larger scale, North Carolina became the twelfth of the 13 original colonies to ratify the United States Constitution and officially become part of the Union.

The aspect of the Ohio River was rapidly changing. In this year alone it was estimated that more than 20,000 new settlers had come downstream to sink roots in both Kentucky and the Ohio country and, along with this influx of people, there was a sharp increase in Indian attacks on boats all the way downstream from Fort McIntosh to the Falls of the Ohio. Since the end of the Crawford Campaign against the Sandusky towns seven years ago, a total of more than 1,500 travelers on the Ohio River had been waylaid by Indians and either killed or taken captive, but by far the greater majority of the incidents occurred this year. Sometimes the boats were simply fired upon and sunk and their occupants drowned. More often the attacks were at closer range, as parties were lured to shore by Indians dressed in the clothing of whites and then ambushed. Most of these deaths and captures involved people unfamiliar with the hazards of the Ohio River border country, but there were numerous familiar names among the casualties as well.

Charles Bilderback, who had participated in the Moravian Massacre and the Crawford Campaign, was traveling by canoe down to Kentucky with his wife, Ruhama, when they were captured near the mouth of Cabin Creek, close to the cabin he had built on land he had claimed there. He was stripped and tied to a tree, and then Ruhama was forced to watch as, in succession, they cut off his ears, nose, lips, thumbs and penis before he was struck a fatal blow between the eyes with a tomahawk and scalped. Then they took his wife off into captivity.[687]

In March the Indians had unexpectedly shown up at the mouth of Short Creek on the upper Ohio and viciously struck at Vanmetre's, killing some of the John Vanmetre family and taking others into captivity. On Dunkard Creek off the Monongahela, where no attacks had occurred for a very long time, the houses of Joseph Cambridge and William Thomas were struck; Thomas was killed, as was everyone in the entire Cambridge family, including his wife and their two children. Even farther into the Virginia country, where most Indian attacks had ended a decade ago, well upstream on the West Fork Monongahela in Harrison County, the families of John Mauck, William Johnson, Jethro Thompson, William Stalzer and John Simms were attacked, eight killed. Their cabin burned, Joseph Johnstone, his wife and three children were killed on Clinch River near Rye Cove. In Abb's Valley the Indians struck the Andrew Davidson place during his absence and took prisoner his pregnant wife, two young daughters and a two-year-old son, plus two indentured children staying with the Davidsons.[688]

At the mouth of the Kanawha, John Bruce, one of the earlier settlers at Point Pleasant, was sitting atop a fence rail at the common and was picked off as if he had been a turkey perched on a branch when a bullet shot by a distant warrior marksman passed through his head. Also at Point Pleasant, 14-year-old Jacob Van Bibber, brother-in-law of Nathan Boone, Daniel's son, was captured, and Matthias Van Bibber, his older brother, who was called Tice, was wounded as they brought in a packhorse load of bear meat.[689] Up the Kanawha, Fort Clendenin was put under siege by a large party of Indians and was saved when a frontierswoman named Anne Trotter, but called Mad Anne Bailey, rode her black horse named Liverpool through the Indian lines and all the way to Fort Union, collected a store of ammunition and brought it back in time to save the fort. A dozen miles or more upstream on the Kanawha from Fort Clendenin, at the mouth of Paint Creek, William Wyatt awoke one morning and told his wife he'd had a presentiment of himself being killed by Indians and later that same day he was. On the Carroll Branch of the Kanawha, the William Carroll family was attacked in their cabin and, though they all escaped, their cabin was burned.

In the Kentucky country Samuel Scott, the son of militia Gen. Charles Scott, was killed while fishing in the Kentucky River and, not terribly far away from there, young Johnny Hardin was killed, Jake Kelsey wounded and Jacob Cris captured by a war party under the Shawnee war chief, Shemeneto.[690] Less than a mile from Kenton's Station, Phil Skaggs was shot through the throat and scalped, while Bill Walton was hung from an oak and disemboweled within shouting distance of Lexington. Closer to the Blue Licks, William Scott, Charles Ralston and James Livingston were taking a load of cheese and whiskey from Lexington to Maysville by wagon when Indians struck. Scott and Ralston were killed and 19-year-old Livingston was taken, along with the four horses and cargo. At practically the same time, two men were shot and killed within sight of Maysville. In Jefferson County, not far from Louisville, six members of the William Chenoweth family were killed and four others wounded. In less than a month, more than 40 horses had been stolen by Indians in Mason County.

Among the new Ohio Territory settlements near the mouth of the Little Miami, nine people had been killed in separate incidents since June. A squad of soldiers escorting some civilians near North Bend was ambushed, with one soldier killed, four wounded, and two civilians also wounded. In another incident, Benjamin Stites and Nathaniel Reeder were riding together near Columbia when they were fired on by Indians in hiding. Stites was uninjured, but Reeder took a ball in the thigh and another in the arm that broke the bone. As the Indians charged out at them brandishing tomahawks, Stites grabbed the reins of Reeder's horse and led him away to safety at the fort. A short distance away, at Clements' Station, where two men had just been killed by Indians, Robert Halbers was plowing his field when he was startled by the sound of a bear thrashing through the brush nearby. Assuming it to be Indians preparing to attack, he quickly disengaged the horses from the plow, leaped upon one of the horses and galloped to the nearby station. As he entered through the gate, his head struck a crossbar of the portal and he was killed.

Perhaps the most significant construction this year on the Ohio, however, was the erection of a new fort—large, strong and impressive—within the Symmes purchase and, more specifically, adjacent to the site where the village of Losantiville was laid out. Built by a force of 70 men under Maj. John Doughty on orders from Gen. Harmar, construction had begun on June 2 and was all but completed within two months. The fort was formed of hewn timbers and was 180 feet square with an excellent two-story blockhouse at each of the four corners and with 15 acres surrounding the fort as a government reserve. It was by far the best and most impregnable military installation in the Northwest Territory and, most important, it was more centrally located than Fort Harmar for expeditions against the Indians to the north. It was named Fort Washington.[691]

Placing Fort Harmar under command of Capt. David Zeigler and leaving him with 20 men at that post, Gen. Josiah Harmar had just arrived with 300 regulars to garrison the new installation. He was pleased with what he found and sorry that President Washington could not be here to see it, certain he would not only be impressed with it and its apparent invulnerability but also delighted that it had been named Fort Washington.

One of Harmar's first acts in taking command of the new post, after first consuming a few glasses of choice brandy, was to issue a new warrant, prominently posted, for the arrest of Lewis Wetzel, charged with murder; the reward still set at $500. Wetzel, taking the advice of friends, had left the Wheeling area and was en route down the Ohio heading for Louisiana when he stopped off at Maysville. Shortly after his arrival, a boatload of soldiers under Lt. William Lawler, heading for Fort Washington, stopped there also. The soldiers were not in uniform and Lawler, learning Wetzel was there, sought him out, congratulated him on his escape from Fort Harmar and lured him toward their boat for a drink. Arriving at the riverbank, Wetzel became suspicious and was about to race off when, at a signal from Lawler, the soldiers fell upon him, took him prisoner and dragged him down the bank by his queued hair and took him aboard. There they securely bound him hand and foot and immediately set off downstream, taking him directly to Fort Washington, where they turned him over to Gen. Harmar.

Greatly pleased at once again having Lewis Wetzel in custody, Josiah Harmar, face flushed from having drunk a bit more than discretion allowed, had the frontiersman thrown into confinement under triple guard and prepared to exact his vengeance by having him hanged without delay. He was unprepared, however, for the wrath of the people.

On learning of Wetzel's capture, a party of 200 men assembled at Maysville under Simon Kenton, Benjamin Whiteman and Cornelius Washburn, advanced on Fort Washington and demanded that Gen. Harmar release him, on threat that if he did not, they would themselves overwhelm the guards, take Wetzel out and place Harmar himself in chains. Thwarted and now fearing for his own life, Gen. Harmar issued a complete pardon for Wetzel and set him at liberty. The young frontiersman returned in triumph with his liberators to Maysville, where he decided against going to Louisiana for now, or even returning to Wheeling; instead, he accepted Neil Washburn's invitation to live with him in Kentucky for as long as he wished.

Gen. Harmar might have put up a stronger opposition to the frontiersmen in their liberation of Wetzel, but he was now considerably feeling the effects of the imbibing he had done and knew well the peril of acting under the influence. Besides which, he was on the verge of something much bigger that would, he knew, very quickly be consuming all his energies. He had just received orders from President Washington and the Congress that, in view of this year's greatly increased attacks by the Indians throughout the Ohio Valley and elsewhere, he was to prepare to march against the tribes at their greatest stronghold on a punitive expedition. The recommended target was the massive village called Kekionga, the capital of the Miami tribe under Michikiniqua—Little Turtle.[692]

This was to be no minor campaign. Kekionga—meaning The Glorious Gate—was the most cosmopolitan of all the Indian villages in the Northwest and a veritable city unto itself. It had been the heart of the Miami tribe ever since the destruction of Pickawillany by Charles de Langlade and Chief Pontiac in June 1752, and it presently boasted more than 800 houses and in excess of 3,000 residents. The Maumee River was formed here and flows northeastward 132 miles to Lake Erie, providing access to Detroit and the Ottawa and Chippewa villages to the north of there, to the Wyandot villages along southern Lake Erie, and to the major routes by land or water to the ports and forts and centers of the east. Northward, up the St. Joseph, were many of the villages of the Potawatomies and Ottawas, while southward, up the St. Marys, were many of the smaller Miami villages. Like spokes radiating from a hub, several important portage routes gave direct access from Kekionga to a broad range of territory: A short portage to the north-northwest gave access to the headwaters of another, completely different river also called the St. Joseph, this one flowing northwest past the major trading center called St. Joseph that was operated by the famed and well-liked trader William Burnett.[693] Farther down that same stream, where it empties into Lake Michigan, there was access to all the tribes to the north and west of that great body of water. To the northwest from Kekionga, another relatively easy portage connected with the headwaters of the Eel River, and down that stream were the numerous villages of the Eel River Miamis. A portage leading southwest from Kekionga connected, via a tributary, to the Wabash River, which flowed westward and southward through the territory of the Wea branch of the Miami tribe, past the Tippecanoe villages and the important centers at Ouiatenon and Vincennes and finally into the Ohio River, with access at that point to the Illinois Territory and western Kentucky country as well as the entire Mississippi Valley. And, of course, a journey down the Maumee and then up the Auglaize provided portage access to the Great Miami River, the western Ohio country and, ultimately, the Ohio River and the heart of Kentucky.

While most of the residences in Kekionga were flimsy tepees or wegiwas and quonsets constructed of interwoven sticks, a substantial percentage of the structures were permanent buildings—fine, well-built cabins of good size, some of them with spacious lofts and several main-floor rooms, a few even having their own fruit cellars. There were six or seven excellent trading posts, including another of those owned by William Burnett, offering a wider variety of goods than the Indians had ever seen gathered together in one place. Regular streets had been laid out, and in front of the buildings facing the main central square, wide board sidewalks had been built so that the fine ladies from Detroit, who visited here so frequently, could pass from building to building during inclement weather and not get their flowing skirts muddied.

Many of the buildings had signs erected, identifying their purposes—some in French but the majority in English. There were stables for the horses that were ridden in by visitors, taverns for the thirsty and gambling rooms for those who wished to play at cards or dice. The wonderful trading posts were ready and able to fill the needs of any Indian man or woman who came with furs or leathers, sugar or lead, vegetables or grains to trade for the goods they wished to purchase. There was an official British government cabin where important closed-session meetings were often held with the chiefs resident here or with visiting chiefs from other villages and tribes. A huge log building with a fine floor of close-fitted planking served the dual purpose of council hall and ballroom, with a spacious dais at one end where impor-tant chiefs and prestigious delegates could sit during councils and where musicians could be situated for the frequent balls that were held. Apart from the center of the town was another large, squat log building of many small rooms where certain women—most of them French or English, but a scattering of Indian women as well —peddled their sexual favors to those who desired such services, all under the benev-olent but stern direction of the tough old Frenchman, Monsieur Louis Duchamble, and his heavy wife, Madame Josette, who was so domineering to everyone but her husband.

There were scores of residence cabins and hundreds of less permanent wegiwas and very temporary tepees, since many Indians from other tribes had also taken up residence here with the Miamis; these included a small number of Shawnees and larger numbers of Delawares, Wyandots, Potawatomies and Ottawas. There was even an enclave of Cherokees at the western edge of the town.

Among the very finest of the dwellings was the residence of the principal chief of the Miamis, the powerful Michikiniqua—Little Turtle. It was a very spacious multiroom log structure with doors on three sides and windows with actual glass panes, fine furnishings that included well-crafted tables and chairs, a sofa, feather-tick beds of such height it was necessary to step up on a small stool to climb onto the bed proper, numerous shiny brass oil lamps with glass chimneys and shades upon which were painted pastoral scenes, well-made cupboards and sideboards and dry sinks, and numerous framed pictures on the walls—artwork brought from Europe or executed by Canadian artisans. It had the largest wall mirrors most visitors had ever seen, fine china dishes and well-made glass goblets and crystal wineglasses and decanters, and, along one wall, a harpsichord that visitors, with the skill to do so, were encouraged to play. A dozen yards behind the house, with a narrow raised wooden sidewalk leading to it, was an excellent five-seater outhouse constructed of planking. All in all, Kek-ionga was by far the most important Indian target that could have been chosen, against which to direct the campaign.

Gen. Harmar was unaware, however, that at almost this same moment, Gov. St. Clair had received a very private letter from the secretary of war. Henry Knox had explained to St. Clair the elements of the expedition that was to be carried out by Gen. Harmar, but then he went on to discuss a situation not brought out in the instructions Harmar had received.

The one big problem, Knox remarked, was that there were several very large British trading posts at Kekionga and a large number of English traders, many of whom had permanently moved there with their families. Fearing that the British might construe the expedition as an attack against them and, by extension, the British Crown, Secretary of War Henry Knox ordered Gov. St. Clair to write to Maj. Patrick Murray, the British commandant at Detroit, and assure him that the pending invasion was absolutely not directed at the British but at the Miamis and their allies, and that it would be wise to immediately evacuate those British in residence at Kekionga.

Gov. St. Clair, in his quarters in Fort Washington, had spent the last hour composing his letter to Murray, in which he naively asked him to keep secret from the Indians what was afoot. Now he was just beginning the final paragraph, and he thought for a long while about how best to end the letter. He decided he should simply and succinctly restate the problem, the goal and the justification. Without further delay, he dipped his pen and completed the message in firm strokes:

> *The expedition about to be undertaken is not intended against the post you have the honor to command, nor any other place at present in possession of the troops of his Britannic Majesty; but is on foot with the sole design of humbling and chastising some of the savage tribes, whose depredations have become intolerable and whose cruelties have of late become an outrage, not only to the people of America, but on humanity.*

[January 2, 1790 — Saturday]

The meeting in Gov. St. Clair's office in Fort Washington began on time, at nine o'clock this morning, and included the three proprietors of Losantiville, Matthias Denman, Israel Ludlow and Robert Patterson. The governor wasted no time getting to the reason why he had summoned them.

"Gentlemen," he said, "you have in Losantiville the beginnings of a great American city. It will certainly be the seat of the county I will create here today. However, I must admit that I don't care too much for the name. As you may know, I am a member of the Society of Cincinnatus. I would consider it an honor and a very great favor if you would consent to renaming Losantiville and calling it, instead, Cincinnati."

The settlers had no objection, none of them particularly fond of the name John Filson had coined with rather supercilious erudition, and they unanimously agreed. St. Clair was very pleased and, though it was early morning, they gladly accepted the small glasses of wine the governor poured to toast the occasion. As they did so, Judge John Cleve Symmes and Benjamin Stites joined them and accepted glasses as well. St. Clair poured a similar measure for himself and then held up his glass. The four visitors did the same.

"Gentlemen, later today I will issue a proclamation to this end, but, for now, a toast to the new county I am establishing as of this moment: a county named after my good friend, Alexander Hamilton. And also to what will become the seat of Hamilton County—Cincinnati."[694]

[A p r i l   1 0 ,   1 7 9 0 — S a t u r d a y]

Incredibly, as the attacks by Shawnees against boats descending the Ohio increased enormously, so too did the number of boats leaving such places as Redstone, Fort Pitt and Wheeling. It was almost as if they were attempting to thwart the Indians through sheer numbers, and no matter how many reports filtered through about the ambushes, captures and terrible deaths that were occurring downstream, they had little effect; would-be settlers continued to launch their boats bravely—or perhaps foolishly—into the unknown, and commercial traffic was increasing all the time. Irregular packet boat trips had just been inaugurated by experienced rivermen between Pittsburgh and Cincinnati in both keelboats and flatboats, for which the 463-mile one-way fare, upstream or down, was five dollars, while merchandise or other cargo was normally carried at the rate of five dollars per ton.

They were a rough-and-tumble lot, these rivermen; coarse, crude, tough men who took danger as a matter of course, living hard, fighting hard and often dying young. Brownsville at Redstone had become a riotous town with wild women and wilder men, where morals were flimsy at best and where brute strength more often ruled than the law. Provance Landing, Pittsburgh and Mingo Bottom were not far behind. John Pope, upon briefly visiting Redstone, wrote in his journal:

> At this Place we were detained about a Week, experiencing every Disgust which Rooks and Harpies could excite.

Many a prospective settler's dream was lost before even begun when he drank too much and woke up the morning after lying in the mud behind a saloon or outhouse with all his goods gone, along with his horse, shoes, clothing, money and other valuables. Fighting was so commonplace as to largely be ignored by those not directly involved; duels were frequently fought, and the local graveyards filled up rapidly; often the only marker was a board into which was burned "Unknown Traveler."

The rivermen, by and large careless of life and limb and nearly always bereft of good reputation, descended on the various settlements and towns along the way in wildly unruly manner, bringing debauchery and a wide variety of mischief with them. They normally headed first to the nearest tavern to satisfy their thirst and next to common houses to satisfy their lust. Stopping at the ordinaries to buy meals and lodging was at the bottom of their list. Settlers, men and women alike, who objected to their behavior were routinely insulted or worse. In the numerous fights that broke out between such settlers and the rivermen, it was far more often the experienced, no-holds-barred fighting of the rivermen that prevailed.

As many different types of river people as there were, so too were there a multitude of boats of every manner, along with many that virtually defied description. Individuals or small groups traveling lightly preferred canoes because of their swiftness and maneuverability and the infinitely greater ease with which they could be propelled upstream on a return journey, but they were of little value in carrying payloads of goods, provisions or cargo. The next step above the canoes were the more stable but far less maneuverable skiffs and dugouts, in which somewhat more goods could be carried. Then there was the much larger piroque, an oversize dugout usually carved from the trunk of a single tree and capable of carrying up to four tons of cargo, but it was dangerously unstable; sometimes it was better stabilized by nailing two piroques of equal size together, separated by a broad thick plank that served at various times as seat, table and lookout stand.

The French had seemed to favor the more stable but cumbersome bateaux, built with high sides that kept out water while shooting rapids, afforded protection of sorts, if attack occurred, for cargo and people hidden beneath oiled skins stretched from one side to another. A single bateau could carry up to eight tons of cargo.

There were then the low-sided or no-sided rafts referred to as Allegheny flats, ferry flats or, if protected with a wooden or cloth canopy, covered sleds. Each capable of carrying up to 12 tons of goods, they were normally one-way craft, moving downstream by the power of the current, barely steerable with a broad tiller and usually dismantled at their destination so the lumber could be used for lean-tos, sheds or cabins. Now and again a small flat-roofed cabin would be built on the surface, from which the helmsman could swing the tiller or "sweep" with greater leverage for avoiding rocks, snares and other obstructions.

Among the best of the boats were the keelboats, with a cargo capacity of between 15 and 30 tons. These long, slender, rather gracefully designed boats required a downstream crew of from 6 to 20 men and were capable of sliding easily over rocky shallows. They could also be freed without much difficulty from mud or sandbars. For the upstream push, a crew of 10 to 20 rowers were employed, and they could move the big boat with remarkable speed against the current.

Generally the largest of the watercraft, highly favored for huge cargoes, were the great Kentucky flats, also called broadhorns—arklike boats 15 feet across the beam and as much as 100 feet in length, capable of carrying a cargo of 70 tons. Most often they had cabin compartments and specified cargo areas, as well as small corrals for cattle, sheep, horses, hogs and other livestock. A huge flat-roofed tillerhouse provided a surface for the helmsmen working a sweep, which was a broad-bladed rudder as long as 70 feet. On each side of these large boats was a plank walkway from bow to stern along which the 40 to 50 polemen walked as they thrust the boat forward when moving upstream along the shorelines.[695]

All these various types of boats, plus scores of others of homemade design, plied the Ohio's 1,000-mile length in remarkable abundance from Pittsburgh to the Mississippi, usually staying in midcurrent to avoid attacks from shore, but all too often being waylaid by veritable fleets of Indian canoes springing out of hidden creek mouths to overtake and overcome them by sheer numbers. The carnage and grief that resulted was frightful. It was not uncommon for bodies to be found that had floated for many miles downstream, or survivors clinging to wreckage or staggering into settlements after making it to shore from an attack, many after traveling untold miles through a disorienting and frightening wilderness.

In the recent past, in direct disobedience of the prohibitions in effect, there had been numerous crossings of the Ohio by parties of Kentuckians to pursue war parties that had raided their settlements. And lately, such parties of Kentuckians were crossing just as frequently to track down the boat-attackers and wreak vengeance on them, as well as to possibly rescue river travelers made captive. Now a great howl of frustration and anger erupted from the Kentuckians as the news just received from Richmond was relayed across the land. One month ago today, Gov. Beverley Randolph, having received a strong complaint from Gov. Arthur St. Clair, sent a circular letter-order to the county lieutenants of the various frontier counties of Virginia. It was blunt and very much to the point:

Richmond, March 10th, 1790

Sir:

The Governor of the Continental Western Territory has given the Executive information of incursions having been made by parties from this State, upon the tribes of Indians in amity with the United States. As conduct like this is highly dishonorable to our national character and will inevitably draw upon individual delinquents the punishment due such offenses, it becomes our duty to enjoin you to exert your authority to prevent any attempt of this kind in the future.

Should it be necessary, on any occasion, to order out parties to repel the attack of an enemy, within the limits of a State, you will issue the most positive orders that no such party shall, under any pretence whatever, enter the Territory either of the United States or of any Indian tribe.

I am, &c.,

Beverley Randolph[696]

[April 13, 1790—Tuesday]

"Helluva thing," Alexander McIntire grumbled, "when a man's got to have official gov'mint sanction t'go huntin' Injens that've been raidin' our places." He looked again at the fresh Shawnee scalp in his hand, shook it a final time to dislodge the remaining blood and stuffed it into his waist pouch.

Neil Washburn nodded, not looking at his companion but instead checking the trees and bushes ahead for sign of Indians. "Times're changing, Alex. Whole frontier's changin'. This may've been one of the last 'cross-river scouts. Won't be long 'fore we'll be over on this side claimin' and settlin' legal-like."

The two were with a party of 30 whites who were part of an "exercise" scout, as Gen. Harmar called it. This was the first time a true expedition against the Indians had crossed the Ohio River into the Ohio country since the latest ban had been laid down prohibiting it. The party was a detachment from the main force of 350 men that had been brought together at Fort Washington to discourage the Shawnee parties who were attacking boats so frequently of late.

The expedition was the result of an application made to Gen. Harmar by Gen. Charles Scott of the Kentucky militia, who requested permission to lead a force of 250 Kentuckians along the north shore of the Ohio, looking for Shawnee camps and routing whatever war parties they were able to find. Harmar had considered the idea and, after conferring with Gov. St. Clair and getting his approval, gave Scott the permission he sought, on the condition that Harmar would himself lead the expedition at the head of 100 regulars from Fort Washington. Both St. Clair and Harmar had agreed that this would be a good training exercise to prepare them for the very large expedition against the Miamis and Shawnees that was shaping up for next fall; an exercise that would give the regulars an opportunity to work in concert with the Kentucky militia, as they would be doing in that larger expedition to come.

The force of 350 had left Fort Washington and marched all the way eastward to the Scioto without encountering any Indians, but the situation changed a little on the way back. As they crossed Ohio Brush Creek, Alex McIntire detected sign of a small party of Indians moving toward the southwest and reported it. After conferring with Gen. Harmar, Gen. Scott gave orders for Capt. Joshua Baker to select a dozen men, follow the trail and endeavor to engage them.

The 13 men had followed the trail all day and only an hour ago, near the mouth of Eagle Creek, had discovered the camp of the Indians just a short distance above the creek mouth on its eastern side.[697] There were four Shawnees in the camp, and thus far they were wholly unaware of the whites being nearby, largely because a strong wind was blowing off of the river and causing a good deal of covering sound as it whipped through the trees that were largely still bare of leaves.

At Baker's directions, the scouts crept closer, their rifles primed and ready. Joshua Baker ordered that no one should fire until he gave the signal, causing McIntire to glance at him askance and shake his head at the effrontery, since Baker had nowhere near the Indian-fighting experience of at least half the men he was leading. As they slipped through the brush and got within 50 yards of the camp, McIntire saw one of the warriors so fairly exposed that it was a sure shot. He knew he wouldn't miss, so he fired. The warrior was slammed off his feet and fell dead to the ground. The other three leaped up, crouched and fearfully looked about in all directions. With the wind making so much noise, they could not be sure where the shot had come from and didn't want to run right into the enemy's arms.

Even while they hesitated, Baker yelled "Fire!" and a ragged chorus of shots followed. Two more of the Shawnees fell and the final one turned and jumped into a deep hole in Eagle Creek as the whites left cover and rushed toward him. Young John Williams reached the creek first and, tossing his rifle aside, jumped in after the warrior. At once his friends warned him to come back, that the warrior had a knife in his hand. Williams's sudden surge of enthusiasm considerably dampened, he returned to shore with alacrity.

The warrior stood close to shore in waist-deep water under some overhanging willows and began voicing a sing-song chant. Baker called to him to throw the knife away and surrender, telling him he would not be harmed if he did so. The Shawnee either did not understand or was prepared to die fighting. Baker quickly lost patience and put a bullet squarely between his eyes.

They scalped the four Indians, and it was McIntire who pointed out, after examining their camp, that the four had not been raiders but were simply a hunting party that had no doubt come as close as they could to their former fine hunting ground across the river. For the first time in his years of hunting Indians, he felt a surge, of pity for these people and what he and other whites had done to them. Now, as they moved to rejoin the main army, Washburn and McIntire continued their earlier conversation.

"Well," McIntire said, "I ain't never hankered to see the Injens come over and hit our folks an' steal our horses, but I'm sure as hell gonna' miss comin' acrost an' huntin' these buggers down."

"Alex," Washburn said, motioning toward his companion's belt pouch, "I don't reckon that's the last scalp you're gonna lift. Not by a long shot. They may be pullin' back, but I figger we ain't even begun t'see the worst where fightin' the Shawnees is concerned."

"Hell, Neil, it sure as hell will be by the time Harmar finishes that fall expedition he's shapin' up."

"You're aimin' t'go, ain't you, Alex?"

McIntire shook his head. "I been out with him on this one," he said, "an' I've seen enough of him t'know I ain't never goin' out on another one with him leadin'. He ain't got no real feel for Injen fightin', Neil, an' I sort'a 'speck he ain't got much backbone, either. That's the kind of man k'n lead you into a whole lot of trouble."

[September 28, 1790—Tuesday]

It seemed not to have taken the Indians very long to figure out that if, after making an attack on the Virginia side of the river, they did not linger to make follow-up attacks on other cabins or settlements but, instead, swiftly recrossed the river to the Ohio side, the usual follow-up pursuits by the Americans were not occurring. Aware that Gen. Harmar was shaping up a large force at Fort Washington to move against them in the fall, the Indians seemed intent upon inflicting as much damage as they possibly could on the south and east side of the river before it became necessary for them to draw together to meet Harmar's advance. Very soon almost all their attacks were hit-and-run, and so the late winter, spring and summer had resulted in a very bad time for the Ohio Valley settlers.

By the middle of March, close to 40 people had been killed in and around the Kentucky settlements. One of these was the much-beloved Maj. William Bailey, who had settled at Kennedy's Bottom. In the same attack, all five members of the Jason Quick family were taken captive.

Within a few days after that, three young men traveling from the Blue Licks to Maysville were fired on from ambush. Two were killed and the third, Peter Livingston, was captured. Simon Kenton managed to rescue him before he could be carried to the Shawnee towns. At the same time, on the Ohio River shoreline just below the mouth of Lee's Creek, one of the more experienced Kentucky frontiersmen and Indian fighters, Ignatius Ross, was wounded in a short fight with a small party of Shawnees, who immediately fled across the Ohio.

The well-known riverman, Cobus Sullivan—Cobe to his friends—who had so long ago inadvertently become a defender in the second siege of Wheeling, was shot and killed while delivering mail between Louisville and Vincennes.

Early in April, Stephen Carter, one of the earlier settlers at Judge Symmes's new settlement of North Bend, was shot dead and scalped in his own yard as he was splitting firewood. Later that same day a young man named Samuel Jeffers was tomahawked and scalped within calling distance of the new Ludlow's Station, which had been established by Israel Ludlow on Mill Creek, a few miles northeast of Cincinnati.

In late April, the young sisters Mary and Margaret Castleman were visiting their friends Sarah, Moses and Thomas Martin at the sugar camp their father, John Martin, had set up near the mouth of King's Creek. A party of Wyandots rushed upon them, killed the elder Martin and captured all five of the children. They immediately took them back to Half King's Town on the upper Sandusky River.[698]

In early May a party of Indians crossed the river near Wheeling during the night and approached the new cabin belonging to the Robert Purdy family. It did not yet even have a door, just a blanket hung over the door opening. They crawled under it and attacked the Purdys in their bed. Robert put up a tremendous fight, while his wife snatched up their infant son and raced outside. An Indian waiting out there struck her down with his tomahawk, scalped her and then killed the baby. Inside, Robert Purdy was finally overpowered and killed, and their two young daughters were captured. In the yard, Mrs. Purdy regained her senses but lay still until the Indians, carrying the two girls with them, hurried away. Then she crawled a half-mile to the nearest neighbor and a search was mounted, but it was too late; the Indians had gone directly back to the Ohio and recrossed to the "safe" side.[699]

Less than a week later, up the Kanawha near Clendenin's Fort, young James Hale went to a cold spring at a nearby branch to get some cool water for his fiancée, who was ill with a fever and, while dipping up the water, was shot and scalped.[700] Upon learning of his death, the young woman suddenly took a turn for the worse, her fever increased and she soon died. A few days later at another nearby branch, Charles Staten was quenching his thirst when a rifle ball shot by a Shawnee caught him at the base of his skull and blew away the whole top of his head.[701]

Hardly two weeks later, on May 29, Rebecca Van Buskirk, an extremely attractive young woman living with her husband, Lawrence, not far from the mouth of Buffalo Creek 16 miles above Wheeling, decided to go to Washington village for some weaving goods. She set off early in the morning on her horse. In less than two miles a party of Indians captured her, during which she suffered a sprained ankle when thrown from her horse. As they took her toward the river to recross to the Indian side, moving slowly because of her injury, the horse showed up back at the settlement. About the same time a settler arrived who had found some Indian canoes sunk in a creek mouth, and the men figured these were the same Indians who had taken Rebecca. Lawrence Van Buskirk, intensely concerned for his wife, who was pregnant, suggested they try to box in the Indians. He led some of the men toward where the attack had occurred, while another group posted themselves in ambush near the sunken canoes. The latter group saw them first, Rebecca among them, hobbling along painfully. One of the men in the ambush was new to the frontier and very fearful of being involved in an Indian fight. Hoping to scare them off and avoid a fight, he yelled aloud, "Here they come!" He did indeed avoid the fight. Instantly the Indians dragged Rebecca off into the brush, killed her with tomahawk blows and vanished.

In July, Joseph Tomlinson was visited at his Grave Creek home by his nephew, Robert Carpenter. Tomlinson sent him out to bring in the horses and, while he was doing so, a party of Wyandots shot him, the ball breaking his shoulder. He tried to flee but they caught him, then tried to catch the horses. The animals wouldn't let the Indians come near them, and young Carpenter, saying he'd rather ride than walk into captivity, told them the horses would let him approach and he would get the animals for them if they would let him try. They did, and he moved up slowly on the animals till he was close, and then darted away in the underbrush. He managed to get safely to the house of a neighbor, Nathan Masters. The disgruntled Wyandots, without captive or horses, immediately crossed back to the Ohio country.

The Carpenter family was at this time living at the mouth of Short Creek on the Ohio side of the river. John Carpenter and his wife were hoeing the potatoes when some Indians shot from hiding and wounded him badly, though not fatally. As they came charging out of the woods, Mrs. Carpenter ran toward the cabin, scream-ing for her grown son, George, who came running out with his gun in hand. The Indians, evidently thinking more men were in the house, broke off their pursuit of Mrs. Carpenter and turned back to scalp John, but he had by this time crawled into the cornfield and hidden, so the attackers simply fled.

The same Indians then struck the McCoy place a short distance away, also on Short Creek. They killed George McCoy and his wife and captured the two 17-year-old boys who were staying with them, Richard Tilton and David Pusley. Glimpsing the approach of William Spencer and his sons, James and John, the Indians ordered Tilton and Pusley to squat down in the tall grasses while they tried to ambush the Spencers. Pusley, however, gave a yell and alerted the three people approaching, who instantly wheeled about and escaped. Pusley was summarily tomahawked and scalped. Then, with young Tilton in tow, the party moved cross-country to Indian Cross Creek, where they came upon four men digging ginseng root—David Cox, John Fitzpatrick, William Crowley and Thomas Van Swearingen, the latter a younger brother of Drusilla Brady. The Indians fired on them, killing Van Swearingen, and charged the remaining three. Fitzpatrick and Crowley managed to get away, but Cox was cut off. Armed only with a hoe, he fought the Indians with that implement until finally downed by spear thrusts and scalped.

Next came a lightning thrust by a party of Shawnees against Tackett's Fort, at the mouth of Coal River on the Kanawha just below Fort Clendenin. John and Lewis Tackett and their mother were harvesting turnips in the field nearby when the warriors burst out and captured all three. Then the Shawnees rushed on the small fort itself, where Christopher Tackett and his 16-year-old brother, Sam, were with their sister and brother-in-law, Betsy and George McElhany, and a small boy. They were unaware that the Indians were nearby until they were almost upon them, and though Christopher leaped to get his gun, he was struck dead with a tomahawk and the others captured. McElhany continued to struggle, even after the Indians dragged him outside, and they finally tomahawked him as well. The Indians then plundered the fort and set it afire. While this was going on, John managed to sprint away and escape, but all the others were carried off into captivity.[702]

Just yesterday at Wheeling, the young Johnson brothers, Henry, 13, and John, 11, were sent out to bring in the cows. On the way, while passing through a skirt of woods, they stopped and gathered up some hickory nuts that had fallen and were cracking them open. They heard someone approaching and thought it was their father and uncle, but it turned out to be a pair of Shawnee warriors, who captured them. The two were hustled off until evening, when camp was made and a small fire built. The boys were ordered to lie down and sleep between their two captors, but were not tied. They only feigned sleep, however, and while the warriors were asleep, silently got to their feet. Henry managed to get one of the rifles of the Indians but could not get the other since the hand of the sleeping warrior was gripping it. The boys moved off a short distance and then stopped by a log. Bracing the gun firmly across the log and aiming it at the head of one of the two sleeping warriors, Henry then instructed his brother to fire when he yelled. As soon as John was ready, Henry went back to the fire and carefully pulled the tomahawk out of the belt of the other sleeping warrior and raised it high over his head in both hands.

"Fire!" he yelled, and at the same moment brought the weapon down with all his strength, burying it in the temple of the warrior. John instantly shot the rifle, but the other warrior had jerked up at the cry, and the shot, instead of catching him full in the head, exploded through his lower jaw, practically carrying it away. The Shawnee whom Henry had tomahawked flailed about for a moment and rolled over into the campfire, where he died.

The two Johnson boys then headed for Wheeling with the two Indian guns and the tomahawk and finally got back home just after sunrise today. As soon as they told their story, Jacob Wetzel raised a party of men and went where the boys directed. They found the camp with the dead Shawnee still lying across the ashes and the blood of the one who had run off. Wetzel, leaving the others at the camp, said he would follow the wounded Indian and try to collect his scalp for the Johnson boys. He followed the blood trail for half a mile but lost it in a small creek, then very nearly lost his own life in the process.[703]

Two Wyandot warriors, armed only with tomahawks, had seen Jacob Wetzel pass and followed him, determined to kill him and take his good flintlock rifle. As he gave up trailing the wounded Shawnee at the creek and turned back to retrace his steps to the others, the two Wyandots leaped out on him from opposite sides of the path. It was a wild melee for a short while. Wetzel's gun had been knocked from his grasp at the first plunge of the Indians, but he managed to jerk out his tomahawk to parry their blows. One of the warriors managed to grip Wetzel from behind, pinning his arms against his sides, and the other, seeing his opportunity, swung his tomahawk viciously at the white man's head. Wetzel, seeing the blow sweeping toward him, violently jerked and spun in the other warrior's grasp. The blade of the tomahawk, instead of striking him, buried itself in the neck hollow of the warrior holding him, who howled and released his grasp, tumbling to the ground and jerking the tomahawk out of his companion's grasp. Arms freed, Wetzel immediately swung his own tomahawk and sank it deeply into the head of the one who had swung at him, killing him. Unable to pull his tomahawk free from the Wyandot's skull, Wetzel jerked out his knife and leaped onto the other, who was writhing on the ground as he tried to pull out the tomahawk buried in his own flesh. Wetzel thrust his knife into the warrior's chest, plunging the blade directly into the man's heart. Drenched with blood from his enemies but himself uninjured, Wetzel was concerned lest these two were part of a larger party. He quickly scalped them, took their tomahawks, recovered his own gun and ran all the way back to the others. Without further delay, the party returned home with enough scalps to give one each to the Johnson boys and for Wetzel to keep one himself. He was fairly sure it would be the last Indian scalp he took on the upper Ohio, as he had decided to move to Kentucky for good and would be leaving soon.

Despite persisting Indian attacks like these occurring all down the Ohio River Valley, new white families kept pouring in to settle, and those already well settled started banding together to lay out new river towns. Typical of these was the town that had just been surveyed and platted by James Griffith on the Virginia side of the river, at the mouth of Cross Creek. Griffith had been hired to do so by the original settler of the area, Charles Prather, who registered the new village at the county court today, naming it Charlestown, and there was every indication it was a town the Indians would not be able to dislodge.[704]

[September 30, 1790 — Thursday]

Gen. Josiah Harmar stared at the letter on the desk before him in his Fort Washington quarters and reached again for the bottle of rum, almost knocking it over with his hand as his alcohol-fogged vision misjudged the distance.

"Bastard!" he murmured, looking at the signature at the end of the letter and slurring his words. "What the hell do you know about anything?"

His epithet was directed at the far-distant secretary of war and his lips curled down into a sneer as he thought about what that official had said in his letter. How did Henry Knox dare write to the first commander of the United States Army in such a manner? How did he presume to place such restrictions upon him or make such personal comments? The fact that Knox was probably parroting comments and instructions he'd received from President Washington made no difference; Washington, too, so far as Harmar was concerned, had lost the military edge and grown soft where the Indians were concerned. They should be wiped out, not mollycoddled!

Even more than earlier this year, Josiah Harmar was greatly disenchanted with the way things were shaping up on this frontier. His first impression had been that he was being given a free hand in the planned campaign against the Miamis and Shawnees. He thought he would be provided with more regulars and good artillery. He thought the use of militia would be kept to a minimum. Gradually, however, all these convictions had been undermined.

He had been very pleased, of course, when this year Congress created a genuine United States Army, though rather appalled that the total force of regulars, officers and men alike, amounted to only 1,216 individuals. He was even more disenchanted by the fact that while the majority of these men had been sent to garrison the western forts—primarily Forts Pitt, McIntosh and Washington—most of them were raw recruits. Moreover, he was authorized to raise 1,500 additional men from the militias of Kentucky and Pennsylvania on a temporary basis for the expedition to the Maumee. There were few things Harmar disliked more than trying to run a campaign with a force of combined regulars and militia. Then, even that boon, if such it could be called, was tempered by further instructions that he was not to undertake the expedition with the notion of engaging in all-out war; its principal business, rather, was simply to make a show of strength to intimidate the tribes and make them more responsive to the proposals of peace being offered—on United States terms.

In accordance with the President's instructions, both Harmar and Gov. St. Clair had spent the summer sending peace proposals to the tribes, an effort wholly wasted, Harmar thought, in view of the continued attacks occurring in the Ohio Valley. Both he and the governor had known from the beginning that there was no chance the tribes would agree to the ultimatums stated in the proposals; they were more the orders of a despot to his subjects than the sort of negotiations that should be undertaken between heads of state. So, simultaneous with the sending out of emissaries to the tribes, they also began raising their army from among the militia. Kentucky had promised 1,000 men, Pennsylvania 500. St. Clair, who was as eager as Harmar to smash the tribes, slyly noted to the general that using militia in this case might not be all that bad, since there was about them a sort of savage ferocity, fueled by the hatreds that the border attacks by the Indians had ignited, and that such a temperament for vengeance could be difficult to restrain. In fact, St. Clair had mused, perhaps it would be unnecessary, even improper, to attempt to restrain them. The Miamis and Shawnees at Kekionga, St. Clair pointed out, should be made to smart, and, of course, if the militiamen did take a harsh vengeance, the commander and his regulars could be held blameless, as these uncontrollable nonregulars would be at fault; if, St. Clair had added meaningfully, the general was not overly concerned that the militia should take the blame.

"No one," Harmar had replied at once, "can have a more contemptible opinion of the militia in general than I do."

The call for militia had been issued, and throughout the summer they had come to Fort Washington, though not quite in the numbers promised. Kentucky came through with 800 men, and the Pennsylvanians, who arrived under command of Maj. James Paull—who was anticipating his first really major action against the Indians since he had escaped in Crawford's defeat eight years ago—amounted to only 300 men. It got worse. Maj. Paull, visibly uncomfortable, was forced to admit that these militia he brought were largely poverty-stricken men who had been hired as substitutes by wealthy men who had been named to go but did not wish to do so. Not only did most of these replacements have no experience in fighting Indians, they did not own guns or even know the fundamentals of loading and firing a musket or flintlock. So now Harmar had been placed in the position of having his own regulars try to cram the basics of weaponry, marching and discipline into the inexperienced militiamen.

Then there was the matter of the secondary expedition. Harmar not only had a smaller force than he anticipated, he was notified that he might have to send some of his men as a reinforcement to Maj. John Hamtramck at Vincennes who, in concert with Harmar's move, would be leading a force of about 350 men up the Wabash to strike the Kickapoos as well as the Wea subtribe of the Miamis, and also to intercept and overpower any Indians attempting to flee Harmar's advance by descending the Wabash.

The orders went on to direct Harmar to make quick movements in order to surprise the enemy, while at the same time taking care to avoid falling into ambush. He was told to be very firm with the tribes but, similarly, to avoid antagonizing any he encountered who showed inclination toward negotiating for peace.

Now, as he sat at his desk, well in his cups, hand clenched around the long neck of the rum bottle, he reread the final paragraph from Henry Knox that he had found so insulting:

> *It has come to my attention that you are having a personal problem; that You are too apt to indulge yourself to excess with a convivial glass. Be aware that you must control yourself in this respect as, if there is any trouble in this regard, your career and reputation will be blasted forever.*

Gen. Harmar lifted the bottle to his mouth, took a healthy swig and then slammed it down atop the secretary of war's signature.

"Bastard!"

[*O c t o b e r   1 3 ,   1 7 9 0 — W e d n e s d a y*]

"The Americans are still coming, Wehyehpihehrsehnwah?" asked Michikiniqua.

"They are still coming, Michikiniqua," Blue Jacket replied. "The spies say they are very close. Tomorrow, perhaps, or the day after."

Little Turtle nodded. "Good. We will do as planned. All have been instructed. They will be very sorry they came."

The co-commanders of the Indian force stood silently for a long moment, looking out across the expanse of Kekionga. Except for a few scattered warriors moving about, everyone was gone. Weeks ago the majority of the women and children had been sent to far-distant places for safety—to the villages of their Potawatomi allies on the Elkhart and St. Joseph rivers and the Ottawa and Huron villages near Detroit.

The first information the Indians here had learned of the march planned against them by Gen. Harmar's army had come from Maj. Patrick Murray, commander at Detroit. He had received a message from none other than Gov. St. Clair. The man who the Americans now said was governor over all the Indian territories had told him of the forthcoming campaign and had then had the audacity—or stupidity—to ask him to keep it secret from the tribes. Maj. Murray had instead sent messengers galloping here at once with a warning.

Spies had been sent out immediately to watch the Harmar force and report on its progress, while at the same time urgent messages had been sent to the tribes to the north and west of them to come and aid them, as they had promised, when the danger grew near. The Potawatomies had quickly responded that they would be on hand to assist and boldly proclaimed that if and when Harmar showed up with his army, their own Potawatomi women would chase the soldiers away with switches; at the same time they told the Miamis and Shawnees to send them their women and children for their safety.

By late August the regular spy reports coming from the vicinity of Fort Washington indicated that Harmar had gathered a force of just under 1,500 men who were drilling daily and that the posted general orders said the march against Kekionga would begin in September. As soon as word came that Harmar had actually begun his march and was bringing along with him three pieces of artillery, a council of the northwestern chiefs was called at Miamitown—the place formerly known as the New French Store—adjacent to Kekionga.[705] They had not expected the Wyandots and Delawares to show up, since both tribes were inclined, for the moment, toward peace and had been listening to the messages of St. Clair. They had, however, expected a large turnout of their allies from the other tribes—Potawatomies, Kickapoos, Ottawas, Chippewas, perhaps even some Winnebagoes and Foxes and Sacs— and in that they had been sorely disappointed. Only a few more than 100 Indians had shown up, most of them the Shawnees and Miamis themselves, but with a scattering of Potawatomies. That was when the Indians themselves had become fearful at the smallness of their own number when compared with Harmar's force of nearly 1,500 coming toward them. Even the arrival of 50 Ottawas in response to the appeal for help had done little to raise their hopes.[706] That still made the odds against them virtually ten to one, but they harbored no thought of turning tail.

The assembled Indians had selected Wehyehpihehrsehnwah and Michikiniqua— Blue Jacket and Little Turtle—as co-leaders in the coming confrontation, and all the whites at Kekionga—the British, the few French, the American turncoats—were warned to leave the area until the danger was past. The greater part of Kekionga was then set afire. Many of the rebuilt Shawnee towns such as Mackachack, Wapatomica, Blue Jacket's Town, Wapakoneta and Kispoko Town—or, as some called it, McKee's Town—were similarly evacuated and burned, and all the women and children were transported to the temporary camps on the Elkhart River headwaters.

Since then, with considerable apprehension, the defenders had been waiting while the spies reported Harmar's army coming ever closer. While they waited, Little Turtle and Blue Jacket had gone over their strategy on how to best the Americans. That was when they had decided, in view of their far fewer numbers than the enemy, to remain out of sight and let Harmar think everyone had fled in the face of such danger. Then, when his defenses were lowered enough to create a vulnerability of which they could take advantage, they would attack.

[*October 15, 1790—Friday*]

The expedition led out of Vincennes and up the Wabash River by Maj. John Francis Hamtramck ended as the force returned to Vincennes today after a march of more than 200 miles.

In accordance with his orders from the secretary of war, Hamtramck had put his little army of 350 men on the move to intercept any Indians fleeing from Gen. Harmar's advance far to the east, but they had problems from the very beginning. First, the anticipated supplies for the expedition had not arrived, and there had been considerable discussion among the officers over the wisdom of beginning such a campaign without the proper provisions and ammunition. Maj. Hamtramck, however, had nipped such talk quickly and sharply; their orders were to embark on the expedition and that was what they were going to do, so long as the men were capable of marching and fighting. They would simply have to accept the fact that they would be on limited rations, and whatever shooting was to be done would be by carefully selecting targets and not wasting ammunition.

Even worse, however, was that during the first few days of the march more than half the men fell ill with a highly debilitating virus that made its appearance the very day of their departure. Only a few men were stricken at first, but it spread rapidly, and by the fourth day out, close to 200 of the men were afflicted, including Maj. Hamtramck. Fevers, vomiting and a pervasive weakness plagued them and their progress was excruciatingly slow.

At the mouth of the Vermilion they found several Indian villages that were vacant; the warriors had gone up the Wabash to aid in the impending battle with Gen. Harmar's advancing force, while the women and children had been evacuated hurriedly as soon as it was discovered that Hamtramck's force was approaching. Without opposition the army had burned the villages and destroyed the crops, but the effort of doing even that had been so exhausting in their present condition that Maj. Hamtramck finally agreed that it would be foolish, perhaps suicidal to continue, and he ordered their return to Vincennes.

It was very fortunate he did so. Awaiting them somewhat farther up the Wabash near Ouiatenon and the Tippecanoe River was a large body of Potawatomies, Kickapoos and Weas, poised to attack them ferociously when they marched into the ambush that had been prepared. When the Indians discovered the American force had turned back, some of them tried to overtake and cut off the column, but an attack was never made.

So now the army was back in the fort unharmed, having accomplished virtually nothing and, unbeknownst to them all, having avoided a great disaster only by the narrowest of margins.

[*November 3, 1790—Wednesday*]

The good fortune that the army of Maj. Hamtramck experienced was not reflected in the expedition of Gen. Josiah Harmar. Though all the odds were on his side in respect to manpower, weaponry and provisions, his campaign had become, by any yardstick other than his own, a humiliating disaster. Yet, in the first carefully worded draft of his report to the secretary of war, Harmar, if not claiming outright victory, was giving a strong impression that the expedition had been every bit the success the government had desired. As he had just put it in the conclusion of that draft:

> *No interruption whatever was offered by the enemy on our return; a convincing proof, this, of their having received a blow which they felt. I flatter myself good consequences will be the result. We have not, I conceive, lost much more than man for man with the savages. Our loss can be repaired: theirs is irreparable.*

It was a well-couched lie.

Rarely, if ever, had any army of its size made such an unnecessary and incomprehensible botch of a campaign. Supported by two troops of cavalry and fully equipped with the newest and best firearms available, bolstered by artillery, well provisioned with food and ammunition and, most significantly, outnumbering the enemy by a margin of ten to one, they faced a pitifully small number of warriors armed with less-than-adequate muskets and flintlocks and with no artillery, a meager supply of ammunition and food supplies barely reaching subsistence level. Yet for every Indian killed, at least six Americans were killed; far in excess of the man-for-man loss Gen. Harmar claimed. And though a few of the regular army officers chose to accept Harmar's evaluation of the campaign and declare it a victory, Sgt. Benjamin Whiteman of the Kentucky militia expressed the feeling of by far the majority of the men when he remarked, "If that was victory, then I pray to God that I may never see defeat!"

Most of the men could not remember any campaign that had begun more auspiciously. Among the troops, hopes had been very high, confidence unanimously strong, morale greatly elevated and prospects most encouraging. The whole strength of the army was 1,453 men, almost 80 percent of which were militia.[707] The campaign had begun when, on September 26, Harmar sent the advance force of 1,133 militia marching out of Fort Washington under Col. John Hardin with orders to proceed on Clark's trace for 25 miles and then to stop and await further orders. They drove with them the herd of beeves that would be the meat source for the troops on this campaign. Harmar and his 320 regulars left the fort at ten o'clock the morning of September 30, bringing along three pieces of artillery consisting of two brass cannon —a six-pounder and three-pounder—and a brass five-and-a-half-inch howitzer. They soon joined the militia, and the whole force moved northward.

On October 6, as the army crossed the Little Miami at the site of the still-visible remains of Chalahgawtha, Gen. Harmar studied the old Indian town site and the surrounding countryside and noted in his log:

> *All these Chillicothys are elegant situations—fine water near them and beautiful prairies. The savages know how to take a handsome position as well as any people on earth. When they leave a Chillicothy, they retire to another place and call it after the same name.*

As the army set up camp on the seventh evening of the march, the sentries caught an Indian nearby. Though he was one of the numerous spies keeping an eye on the army and reporting its progress to Michikiniqua and Blue Jacket, he convinced them he was merely trying to steal a horse. Everyone thought Harmar would question the man immediately but, when he was told about the prisoner, he called from inside his tent that he would question him in the morning. The fact of the matter was, he was well into his cups in his private source of brandy and was enjoying it too much to be interrupted.

After some rather rough questioning in the morning, the captive admitted that the Miamis and Shawnees were collecting by the New French Store next to Kekionga at the head of the Maumee River and that Simon Girty had gone across Lake Erie to collect additional forces; that if he had returned with them by now, which was likely, the Indian force would be too strong for Harmar's army to overcome. Gen. Harmar believed him and was considerably worried by the intelligence.

The army continued its march to the marsh-rimmed expanse of Indian Lake, then followed the old portage path to the upper Auglaize River and traced its course downstream to the Maumee. All this way they frequently saw Indians hovering about well out of range, but there were no skirmishes.

Simon Girty was with the Indians now, observing what the American army was doing. When his presence was seen and reported to Gen. Harmar, the commanding officer paled. From that point on he seemed very nervous and upset.

The Indians watched from hiding as the army turned upstream at the mouth of the Maumee and at length came to the newest Chalahgawtha of the Shawnees, now wholly abandoned and only a few miles downstream from Kekionga. Here the army made a more permanent camp and set about destroying crops and buildings. The Indians, biding their time, continued to watch as the army, still using Chalahgawtha as a base, entered Miamitown and burned the abandoned trading post of John Kinzie after plundering it of everything they wanted, then went on to burn all the other buildings that the Indians had not themselves burned during their evacuation. They watched with mute frustration and barely controlled anger as great portions of their cornfields were chopped down, stacked and burned and some 15,000 bushels of stored corn were destroyed, along with many other vegetables already harvested. They watched and they waited, keenly alert for the American commander to make any blunder, and at last they were rewarded.

Incomprehensibly to Michikiniqua and Blue Jacket, on the morning of October 19, the American general unnecessarily split his force and sent out a detachment of 200 of his men. The detachment was under command of Col. Hardin, but Lt. John Armstrong commanded the 30 regulars included, who were in the van of the detachment. Their orders from Gen. Harmar were to range outward to the northwest, engage any enemy encountered and destroy whatever towns they found.[708] As soon as the Indians determined what direction the detachment was heading, Blue Jacket and Michikiniqua led the Indian force swiftly around them out of sight and set up an ambush where the Indian trail passed through heavy brush in the Eel River bottom, northwest of Kekionga. Col. Hardin had not thought it necessary to send out a forward guard or flankers, and the whole detachment marched directly into the ambush. Shrieking and screaming, the Indians loosed a deafening barrage of shots, which served the planned purpose of making them seem to be a much larger force than they were. A demoralization close to abject panic took hold of the Americans, and they hastily retreated, leaving 70 men dead at the scene.[709]

Most of the Indians, remaining out of sight, paced the survivors back to the main army, where they expected the American commander would surely put his whole force into movement to return to the scene bristling for a major engagement. Gen. Harmar did indeed put them into movement, but not toward the scene of the attack; he ordered a retreat.

The soldiers were furious at the movement and their anger became intensified the farther away they marched. They could not understand why the army did not go back to the ambush scene, if for no other reason than at least to bury their own dead. Such a great outcry was made that when Harmar at last stopped to make camp for the night after a march of eight miles, he reluctantly agreed to let another detachment go out—this time a body of 360 men.[710] They started out after dark under the command, once again, of Col. Hardin, but with Maj. John P. Wyllys heading the 60 regulars.

Once again the Indians were amazed that the American general would weaken his main force in such a way, but jubilant that he had done so. This detachment, arriving at Kekionga in the early morning light of October 22, then gravely weakened itself by splitting into four bodies and moving into different quarters of the town. Again the Indians were delighted, since they could not have withstood an onslaught by the full detachment. Now it was another matter, and they did not hesitate. With Blue Jacket and Michikiniqua leading them, they struck all four sections of the detachment in an assault so devastating in its intensity that the sections of the detachment fell apart and could not fully recover. The engagement, a series of harsh skirmishes, lasted three hours, and during the fierce fighting 113 more Americans were killed. The Indians had scored a second victory more than half again as substantial as the first. What little resistance was offered was quickly beaten down, and the survivors plunged into full retreat back to the main army with the horrifying news.

Once again the troops expected Gen. Harmar would now lead the remaining 1,270 men back in a furious full-army assault against the warriors. These troops were still fresh, their weapons not yet even fired and they were extremely eager to retaliate. But Harmar, swaying under the influence of the alcohol he had consumed, once again ordered a full retreat.[711] It was begun on October 23, and this time he was determined not to stop, fearing that the wounded and sick among them, as well as their provisions and ammunition, would fall to the enemy. The artillery, brought along so laboriously, had never been used, and much of the army's equipment, provisions and ammunition—as well as the packhorses carrying the goods—were abandoned and quickly taken by the Indians.

Blue Jacket, in the Indian encampment, argued hard for the Indians to follow up their victories with assaults against the main body of troops in retreat, saying that even though the Indians were still greatly outnumbered, the army was so demoralized that they could easily throw it into a full panic that might well result in the ultimate destruction of the entire army. Besides, their own number had now more than doubled, with the arrival only hours ago of a contingent of 150 Sac and Fox Indians from the Illinois country. Michikiniqua, however, advised that they should be satisfied with what they had accomplished, that to try for more was to tempt fate and they would risk turning victory into disaster. A vote was taken and the majority sided with Michikiniqua, so no follow-up attack was made.

The campaign statistics told the story quite clearly: 183 soldiers had been killed, including 75 regulars.[712] Only 27 Indians had been killed outright and 18 wounded, of which three later died.[713] Even as Harmar's army was still making its way home, word was being carried by jubilant Indian runners throughout the Northwest: A force of only 150 Indians had attacked—and defeated!—an American army ten times its size. There was little doubt that if and when it became necessary again to mount an Indian force to strike an American army, they would have far more warriors than were with them on this occasion.

Harmar's remaining army continued the march, the dispirited and all-but-rebellious troops little resembling the eager men who had set out on the campaign, and had reached Fort Washington at Cincinnati only a few hours ago. The volunteers had been quickly discharged, and the regulars retired to their barracks. And now Gen. Josiah Harmar, in his own private quarters, drank more of his brandy and resumed working on the draft of his report to Secretary of War Henry Knox.[714]

[N o v e m b e r   1 4 ,   1 7 9 0 — S u n d a y]

Blue Jacket studied the officer seated before him at the headquarters desk in Detroit and wondered if he would be able to convince him of how much it would be in the British interest to give greater support to the Indians in their continuing struggle against the Americans. Though he had been gratified with their recent victories over Gen. Harmar, Blue Jacket was not foolish enough to think the Indian cause was won. As he had firmly told the council of chiefs that met immediately after that action, the *Shemanese* would come again, and it would be with a larger and stronger army and almost surely with a better commander.

While Blue Jacket studied him, Maj. Patrick Murray, commanding officer at Detroit, looked with interest at this tall, dark-haired man who was war chief of the Shawnees and, along with Little Turtle, one of the most imposing and influential figures among all the tribes of the Northwest. Even though the odds had been stacked against them, those two skilled Indian leaders had, to the utmost satisfaction of British agents Alexander McKee, Matthew Elliott, William Caldwell and Simon Girty, given the American army a severe drubbing and sent Gen. Harmar running back to Fort Washington with his tail between his legs. This was the first time he had ever met Blue Jacket and the very aspect of the man impressed him, as did his marvelous command of the English language. Further, what he most appreciated was the fact that, unlike the multitude of other chiefs he had spoken with in the past, Blue Jacket did not equivocate in his comments nor cloak his remarks in convoluted metaphoric phraseology. When he spoke, the words were, in fact, disconcertingly direct.

Continuing where he had left off a moment ago, Blue Jacket spoke again in a low, level voice: "Whether or not you are willing to admit it, Major, you British are dependent upon us for the continuance of the trade you enjoy in the Northwest. We, the Shawnees, are closest to the Americans and bear the brunt of every incursion into the Ohio country. The Wyandots are next, and they have helped us much in the past, though not in what has just happened on the Maumee. Because of our triumph, they have indicated they will help us again. The Miamis are next, and they are under Michikiniqua—the one you call Little Turtle—and they sometimes help us fend off the *Shemanese*. The Potawatomies are next, but they are far from the Americans. They have suffered few losses and are only halfway in their help to us. Some bands support us, such as those near here at Detroit and those on the St. Joseph, but others prefer to remain aloof. We continue to ask their help but do not know if we will get it. Whether or not we do, help from you must be given, or the British—and their trade—will be eliminated from the Northwest."

Maj. Murray was even more impressed. Virtually these same thoughts in different words had been sent to him by a committee of merchants and traders of Detroit, with the request that he relay the message to the governor-general of Canada. That message had put things in terms of economics, often the most important means to get the attention of governmental officials, including even the King. They had written:

To his Excellency . . . the memorial and petition of the merchants of Montreal trading to the Indian or upper country humbly showeth that your memorialist being ardently engaged in the Indian or upper country trade of the province are not a little alarmed for the safety of the property which they have entrusted to the Indian country by reason of the late attempt of the Americans to establish by force a post or posts on the frontiers of the province near Detroit. That should such attempt be attended by success, it is evident that the Indian trade to the south of Lake Erie must fall into their hands to the loss and prejudice of the province in the sum not short of £30,000 sterling. That from so near a vicinity to Detroit your memorialist cannot help suspecting that the views of obtaining that key to the west or the northwest are strongly entertained by our rival neighbors; and they consider with much pain that should they possess themselves of Detroit, they will have in their power the means of commanding the whole western and northwestern trade, which your memorialist esteem to produce returns for British manufactories, chiefly in furs, to the value of £150,000 sterling. Your memorialist might remark on the bad consequences which would follow in particular to the new settlement should our neighbors become masters of the post of Detroit, but knowing that your Lordship can better discern than they can point out, the political injuries which the province would sustain in such an event, they confine themselves solely to the Indian trade, of which from long expense and extensive dealings they can speak with certainty and precision. Your memorialist are aware that by the Treaty of Peace of 1783, a great part of the Indian country was ceded to the American states, but having carried on the trade of that country as was usual before and during the war under the protection and safeguard of the government; your memorialist not having since the peace encountered any difficulty from the subjects of the American states, have been led to extend the Indian trade farther west than formerly, from which circumstances their property and connections

in that country being greater and more widely extended, any sudden check to their
commercial pursuits would occasion their ruin.

Maj. Murray was only too keenly aware that already two major British trading posts—Peter Loramie's and John Kinzie's—had been destroyed, and others were in jeopardy. The recent invasion by Gen. Harmar's army—despite the fact that he had been defeated and forced back to the Ohio River—had obviously alarmed the Detroit traders tremendously. Now here was this Shawnee chief underlining the problems that lay ahead if British help were not provided.

"You have given us some guns and ammunition," Blue Jacket continued after a slight pause, "and supplies of food and blankets and fabric. But what we need most is support by men. *Armies!* Give us soldiers and officers and artillery. Support us, just as you wish us to support your interests in our territory. This I can say"—his expression had grown more stern—"if you do not help us, we will be forced to abandon our homes and withdraw beyond the Mississippi."

Maj. Murray toyed with the handle of a brass letter-seal for a moment, considering how to respond to this chief who was so unlike the others, knowing intuitively that platitudes and empty promises were not the answer. He had no authority to commit British forces to such an end, yet was quite painfully aware of the need to do so; just as he was painfully aware that if he did, it could easily provoke a new war with the Americans and, on a personally much more important level, be instrumental in the ruination of his own military career. Instructions had just come from Gov. Guy Carleton—Lord Dorchester—that he was to be effusive in his praise to the Indians for what they had accomplished but in no way to commit the British to allying themselves with the tribes in the new war that had just broken out. Should the British openly participate, there was little doubt that two of the most important targets the Americans would aim for would be His Majesty's posts at Niagara and Detroit, both of which were not only of great strategic value in the Northwest but also of tremendous commercial value. Further, while upper-echelon British governmental officials were certain they would soon have to fight another war with the Americans, they were not at this time ready to do so, since they were presently enmeshed in difficulties with France that were taking most of their energies, manpower and material. Having given these matters momentary consideration, Maj. Murray turned his attention back to the powerful Shawnee chief standing before him.

"Chief Blue Jacket," he said at last, "you must continue to protect the barrier between the white and red people, and you must not forsake the trade that links us together in amity and interest. I have the utmost sympathy for the position and needs of the Shawnees in this matter, and I commend you for the brilliant defense you have made of your country. I will give you whatever support it is in my power to give, and I will relay your words to your great father, the King, for his consideration and direction. You have stated your right to the country you are defending. You are the best judges of the rights by which you hold your lands. Your country, you say, has not been given away. You cannot then be blamable in being unanimous to defend it."

Blue Jacket frowned, not entirely sure what Maj. Murray was saying—or not saying. "Your words," he said slowly, "circle like the birds that never land. I will try to catch them and take them back to my people to hear. I will take the weapons and ammunition you have given us, and those they *will* understand. We will wait to see what *your* great father, the King, has to say. And we expect he will help his Indian children as they have helped him."

[D e c e m b e r   1 2 ,   1 7 9 0 — S u n d a y]

"I never should've gone on that damned hunt," Whittaker mumbled, just before he lost consciousness.

From the very beginning, Daniel C. Whittaker had no idea why he had agreed to go with the party from Wheeling. It had all begun with the stories that were going the rounds at Wheeling and the other settlements that the deer hunting to be had along Stillwater Creek was so phenomenally good as to be all but unbelievable. The big problem, of course, was that Stillwater Creek was a tributary of the Tuscarawas and was located across the Ohio, well into Indian territory, and the Indians had been marauding very frequently this year.

As the season had progressed toward early winter, however, the Indian attacks along the upper Ohio had diminished considerably, and it was the general belief that the Indians themselves, as was their habit, had largely gone away on their own winter hunts. Thus a group of 14 men from the Wheeling area decided that if there was ever a time to check out the fabulous hunting along Stillwater Creek, now was that time, and they invited Whittaker to go along for a week's hunt. Against his better judgment he had agreed.

Stillwater Creek was really not all that far away from Wheeling; a simple crossing of the Ohio right at Wheeling and then up Indian Wheeling Creek to its headwaters —a distance of about 18 miles, then a few miles over a ridge or two to the headwaters of the Stillwater, and down that stream another four or five miles to the prime hunting area—a good day's hike with a total distance of 25 to 30 miles.

In retrospect, Whittaker realized the Indians had doubtless been aware of their presence in the Ohio country from the moment they crossed the Ohio. They had surely watched the white hunters, biding their time and not showing themselves. How much better for them to defer a strike against these foolish whites until they were finished with their hunting and had bundled up their packs of hides and parcels of meats and were ready to start the trip back.

The hunting *had* been exceptionally good. On one day alone they had accounted for 56 deer, three bears and a good number of other game. Only twice had a day passed without at least 20 deer being taken. By the time they had hunted for six days, they had all the meat and hides it would be possible to carry on the four packhorses they had brought with them. Over the campfire the evening before last, they had congratulated themselves on their skill and chortled over the fact that what they would bring back to Wheeling the following day would feed everyone there for a long time to come.

Since they had not seen the first indication of Indians in the area during these days of hunting, they all felt quite secure and decided they did not need to post a guard as they had on previous nights. Everyone wanted to be well rested for the trip back to Wheeling.

It was at about two or three o'clock in the morning yesterday, when all the men, Whittaker included, were rolled up in their blankets and asleep around the fire, when the war party of Wyandots and Mingoes struck. There was no way of knowing for sure how many attackers there had been, but Whittaker estimated somewhere between 20 and 30. They had crept up close to the camp and then, at a signal from one of their number, had fired simultaneously at the blanket-wrapped sleepers. In that single moment, 14 men from Wheeling were killed.

The sole exception was Dan Whittaker. Miraculously, not a single shot had been directed at him. He remained dead still and, peeping out from the folds of his blanket, saw the Indians begin moving from one to another of the dead men, scalping them and taking their blankets and guns and anything else that might have any use or value.

Whittaker had always been an athletic man, very fleet of foot, and one of the feats he could still perform was being able to lie flat on his back and, in a single bound, spring up and land on his feet. He resolved that when the Indians came to scalp him, he would make such an effort, toss his blanket over the heads of the closest Indians, snatch up his flintlock—which lay on the ground beside him—and try to speed away into the darkness before they could react. The greatest impediment, he realized, was the fact that there were patches of snow on the ground and he did not have his moccasins on—they had been hung on sticks near the fire to dry out during the night.

The dead man to his right was being scalped, and two other Indians were leaning over him when he sprang up as planned. The startled warriors jerked back, and as he landed on his feet, he flicked his blanket into their faces, grabbed his rifle and plunged away toward the darkness. A furious howling erupted from the Indians and several threw hatchets or scalping knives at him, all of which missed except one tomahawk. The handle of that weapon struck his shoulder a stunning blow, causing him to drop his rifle. The tomahawk spun to the ground ahead of him and he scooped it up as he ran past and continued his desperate race.

Whittaker dodged in and out past the looming bulk of trees in the darkness, avoiding the patches of snow if he could, so he would leave no tracks. His feet were already cut and bruised, but he paid little attention to them. After running for about ten minutes, he came to the conclusion that what immediate pursuit of him there may have been had broken off. He slowed to an easier, steady run and promptly slammed his forehead into a heavy, low-hanging branch.

When he regained consciousness, it was daytime. It took him several minutes to realize where he was and what had happened. His head hurt terribly and, when he felt his forehead, it was crusted with clotted blood on an enormous swelling that was very tender to the touch. More snow had fallen while he was unconscious, and the ground was now all but covered. The overcast was breaking up, and he was shocked to see that the sun had already passed its meridian. His feet were painfully cold, though not frostbitten as he at first feared. He tore the sleeves off his woolen hunting shirt and, using the tomahawk that still lay on the ground near him, he cut strips of bark from a leatherwood tree and bound them to his feet.

Twice more before nightfall he cut more pieces off his shirt to bind his feet. Fearing he would lose his sense of direction in the night, he found a sycamore with a large hollow at its base and huddled inside, cold and hungry and miserable, sleeping fitfully until dawn this morning, when he started off again.

The course he set for himself would, he thought, bring him to the Ohio River somewhat above Wheeling. But when the great river finally became exposed before him and well below, he saw to his intense relief that he was not more than half a mile above the mouth of Indian Wheeling Creek, and the upper portion of Wheeling Island was directly in front of him.

When Whittaker reached the river's edge, he cut more strips of leatherwood and bound lengths of dead dry branches into a makeshift raft, which he leaned his upper body against in the water and kicked his way across the west channel to the island. With difficulty he dragged the raft across to the east channel and again used it as he kicked his way to the left bank of the Ohio.

Now, staggering and falling as he made his way up the bank and toward Fort Henry, his approach was seen, and several men came running to help him. His vision was fading and, as they reached him, he collapsed into their arms.

"I never should've gone on that damned hunt," Whittaker mumbled, just before he lost consciousness.

[January 2, 1791 — Sunday]

The war party of 40 Indians under Blue Jacket were largely Shawnees, but a few Ottawas, Delawares and Kickapoos had come along with them, eager to participate in the strike that would pour salt into the wound of humiliation Gen. Josiah Harmar had suffered on his recent expedition to the Maumee. What better way to do so than to attack and destroy the new settlement built so close to the large fort that bore his name? As a result, on this bright, crisp Sunday morning, they watched from cover the activity taking place among the residents of the brand-new Big Bottom Settlement and poised themselves for the moment when Blue Jacket would give the signal for the attack to commence.

Hardly a fortnight ago a party of 21 adventurous and enterprising would-be settlers had stopped briefly at Marietta and told the residents of their determination to establish a new settlement on land that had been sold to them by the Ohio Land Company at Big Bottom, 40 miles up the river from this town and Fort Harmar. When settlers at Marietta and officers at Fort Harmar warned that they would be exposing themselves to Indian attack by doing so, they were neither dismayed nor discouraged. The new settlement, they argued, was really not all that far away and, if danger threatened, they could easily flee to Fort Harmar for refuge, since by land it was only 24 miles distant.[715]

Studying the activities occurring at the Big Bottom Settlement before them,

Blue Jacket smiled coldly. A few small buildings had been erected from lumber that the settlers had brought with them, along with several half-face shelters. The men were busily engaged in cutting, trimming and shaping logs for what would probably be a strongly fortified house, but it was a long way from being finished. At the whispered instructions from the war chief, the warriors spread out in a wide semicircle around the settlement and awaited the attack signal. It was not long in coming.

As a fierce shriek erupted from Blue Jacket, the warriors sent a thunderous volley of shots at the settlers, taking them wholly by surprise and, in that first firing, killing 11 men, a woman and two children. Then they rushed the place. Three of the settlers, unharmed, managed to sprint away and escape into the nearby woods. The remaining four surrendered without firing a single shot in their own defense.[716]

Hardly twenty minutes after the three survivors reached Marietta and reported what occurred, Judge Rufus Putnam was putting the finishing words to the hurried details of the attack he was writing to his good friend, President George Washington. Now he added:

Sir, unless the government speedily sends a body of troops for our protection we are a ruined people.

[January 16, 1791 — Sunday]

In an effort to protect himself from the ramifications of his miserable showing in the recent campaign against the Shawnees and Miamis, Gen. Josiah Harmar had named Capt. David Zeigler to head a court of inquiry to investigate and determine the causes of the failure. The court had been seated and, after examination of many witnesses, exonerated the general of any fault and placed the blame entirely on the militia, describing them as an "unruly and riotous group who would not follow orders."

The Kentucky militia bellowed their fury when the results became known, and Gen. Harmar smugly retired to his own quarters to imbibe his favorite potable. His vindication, if such it was, was brief in the extreme because the Kentuckians were not mollified, nor was the federal government. The Congress felt that Gen. Harmar should be recalled in the near future and a new army commander be named to resolve this new Indian war speedily and effectively. It then gave President Washington virtually a free hand to act toward this end as he saw fit. Washington did so, calling upon Gov. Arthur St. Clair, who had served him so well during the Revolution, to once more don the mantle of generalship and punish the tribes. St. Clair, he said, would be in command of the army with the rank of major general. He ordered him to begin at once to raise an army of 2,300 men—for which Congress was appropriating over $300,000—and expeditiously prepare them to march against the Shawnees and Miamis on the Maumee and Wabash by the end of summer.

This time there was to be a different procedure. St. Clair was instructed that en route to the Maumee, he was to build a chain of intermediate forts between Fort

Washington and the head of the Maumee, with a major installation to be erected at that latter place on the site of Kekionga. Each of these posts was to be garrisoned as he left it and was to provide a place of refuge for the army should it need to fall back.

Already the wheels were in motion toward this end, though many of the Kentuckians—Simon Kenton among them—were grumbling that they would never again serve under a commander unfamiliar with Indian warfare. When the discredited and disgruntled Gen. Harmar commented that if St. Clair actually led an army against the tribes on the Maumee, he would be utterly defeated, a comment that was quickly repeated all over the frontier and did little to encourage enlistment. When Simon Kenton was asked his opinion of the governor-general, he put into words what many of the skilled frontiersmen were thinking:

"St. Clair?" he said. "Well, sir, I'll tell you. St. Clair, he's a minister-looking man. He's well disciplined, too, but he has no briar look about him, no keenness. I'll not serve under that man."

Few Kentuckians, however, would have the option to choose whether they would go, as they would be drafted from the various counties. In this respect Harry Innes, special agent of President Washington, was just beginning to write to the militia commander of each Kentucky county:

Danville, January 16, 1791

To: Henry Lee, Colonel
Commanding Officer of Mason County

 Sir:—I received a letter from Governor St. Clair on the 8th Instant dated on the 5th at the Rapids of the Ohio, by which I am informed he had come to the resolution to order out an expedition against the Indians on the Wabash and hath requested me to inform the Commanding Officers of the Militia to hold the proportions to be furnished in each County in readiness as he shall soon call for them, and that he supposes the governor of this state has made the necessary communications to you.

The residents of Cincinnati, Columbia, North Bend, Colerain and the other settlements that had been springing up so rapidly in the Symmes purchase were overjoyed with the news. Ever since Harmar's inglorious return, the boldness of the Indians in harassing this frontier was almost beyond belief. New settlement had ground to nearly a standstill and those settlers on hand were petrified with fear and felt that something *had* to be done to stop it. John Symmes himself was irate over the attacks and believed they would cause him financial ruin if not curtailed without delay, writing:

I should have had several new stations advanced further into the purchase by next spring but now I shall be very happy if we are able to maintain the three advanced stations. The settlers at them are very much alarmed. . . . I expect that the panic running through this country will reach Jersey and deter many prospective settlers.

There was more than good reason for such alarm. Recently, about a dozen miles northeast of Cincinnati, while out hunting with Abel Cook and Levi Buckingham just south of the new Covalt's Station to provide the settlers with meat, young Abraham Covalt, Jr., had been killed and scalped.[717] That was hardly the worst of it. At the larger and more populous settlement called Dunlap's Station by some and Colerain Station by others, the 75 residents were at this moment packing up and preparing to leave, even though there was a government blockhouse on the site with a cannon and a garrison of a dozen soldiers under the command of Lt. Jacob Kingsbury.[718] That was the result of an attack that had occurred less than a fortnight ago. Blue Jacket, accompanied by Simon Girty, had led upward of 300 warriors—Shawnees, Miamis, Delawares and some Potawatomies—in an attack that lasted 24 hours. The residents had managed to get into the blockhouse before the attack, and only one person—one of the privates—was wounded and the Indians were held off by fire from the cannon and rifles. Prior to arriving at the station, however, the Indians had encountered a couple of surveyors. They killed one and took the other, Abner Hunt, captive. Frustrated in their efforts to breach the defenses, the Indians tied Hunt to a tree within sight of the station, gouged out his eyes, disemboweled him with tomahawk blows and finally burned him. Withal, it took Abner Hunt a long time to die.

[March 25, 1791—Friday]

Virginia Gov. Beverley Randolph took no pleasure in the order he was writing this moment to the various county lieutenants and militia commanders throughout the state, but he had no choice. The directive he had just received from Secretary of War Henry Knox was painfully clear. By order of the Congress and President of the United States, all troops specifically embodied by the states to make expeditions against the Indians of the Northwest Territory were to be immediately discharged. Further, no man was to harm any Indians with whom the United States was presently at amity. As of the date of the order, defense of the western frontiers was now the exclusive province of the federal government, which would, at its pleasure, should volunteers and regular troops be insufficient, draft into service from the various states whatever men would be required.

Only too aware of the great increase in attacks by marauding Indians on the frontier since the failure of Harmar's campaign, Gov. Randolph sighed and began writing the orders, his only consolation being that it would take upward of a month, perhaps even longer, for the order to reach the more distant officials.

[March 26, 1791—Saturday]

At his new little station some four miles from Maysville, Col. Henry Lee, county lieutenant of Mason County, was jerked awake by the pounding on his door, accompanied by an unmistakable voice.

"Henry . . . Henry! Open up. This is Simon Kenton. No Injens here, but we gotta' talk. Open up."

"Hold on a minute," Lee called back, climbing out of bed, "and let me get a lamp lit."

He hurriedly brought up the low flame on the lamp, brightening the interior, then turned and spoke softly, calmly to his wife, who had also gotten up and stood uncertainly beside the bed. "Get your gun and hold it ready." As she moved to do so, he snatched his own rifle off the rack on the wall, checked the load and then, gun waist high, opened the door.

"You k'n put it away, Henry." Kenton's huge bulk filled the doorway, and he moved inside as Lee lowered the weapon. "Sorry 'bout the intrusion, Mrs. Lee," he added when he saw her. Three men followed him inside, two of whom Henry Lee recognized—Alex McIntire and Ben Whiteman. The third man was a stranger, a man in his early twenties with a fresh bandage around his upper left arm.

Lee motioned toward the table and invited them to sit. Without being asked to do so, Mrs. Lee put her rifle back on the rack, stirred up the fire and hung a kettle over it to heat water for tea. Kenton was speaking as she did so, and Lee joined them at the table.

"Bad news, Colonel," he said. "Shawnee war party upstream has hit hard. Harder'n ever on the river. Mebbe thirty-forty dead." He turned to the stranger seated on a hardback chair beside him. "This here's William Hubbell, cap'n of a keelboat. He'll tell you what happened."

Hubbell cleared his throat a bit self-consciously and then spoke in a low, cultured voice. "Sir," he said, "I started out at Pittsburgh, hired to bring down the families of Mr. William Plaskett, Daniel Light, Capt. John Ray, John Stoner, the Reverend Mr. Tucker, a Mr. Bagley and one other, an Irish gentleman whose name I can't recollect. Shortly after we passed Marietta, a smaller boat overtook and joined us—Capt. Francis Kirkpatrick and three passengers, a German fellow and his two daughters, and some others. Then, just after that another boat put out from shore, and the captain—he said his name was Jacob Greathouse, a big fellow—asked permission to join us for mutual protection. He had his wife, a dozen children and two young men on board. Maybe some others, too, I'm not sure. We all tied up together and continued downstream. We passed a flatboat pulled up on shore, and they waved. Mostly discharged soldiers heading for Cincinnati or Louisville. We asked if they wanted to go down with us, but the captain, he said he was Elijah Strong, said they were going to stretch their legs a little more and would follow us pretty soon."

Col. Lee interjected a question: "How many in Strong's party, Captain Hubbell?"

Hubbell shrugged and then winced from the pain in his arm. "Don't know for sure, sir, but quite a few. Twenty, twenty-five, maybe even thirty. Anyway, we kept on drifting. We took off the ropes that were holding the boats together because they were causing some difficulty in steering, but we all were still keeping within a couple hundred yards of each other. And then on Thursday morning—that was last Thursday, at dawn—when we were . . . Oh, thank you, ma'am," he interrupted himself as Mrs. Lee set a cup of steaming tea before him. She served the others as well.

Hubbell eagerly took a sip, then set his cup down and continued. "When we were about six or seven miles above the mouth of the Scioto, we sighted three big Indian canoes—fifty-footers, they looked like—paddling upstream close to the Ohio shore."

"How many Indians?" Lee asked, adding, "Shawnees?"

"Yes sir, Shawnees. About twenty or more in each one. Someone in one of the boats called and told us to put in to the Ohio shore, that we wouldn't be hurt, but we didn't believe that for a minute. Capt. Kirkpatrick stood up and hollered back at them that maybe the Devil would trust them, but we wouldn't. Then he yelled, 'Come on, we're ready for you.'

"Well, sir," Hubbell went on, "I guess maybe he shouldn't've yelled that because, right off, two of the boats started heading for my boat and the other for Mr. Greathouse's boat, which was bringing up the rear. They were a lot faster than the flatboats and we saw them catch up and scramble aboard, but we really couldn't tell what happened because we got too busy with the two that were coming at us about twenty yards apart. At Captain Plaskett's order we held our fire until they were about forty yards from us, and when he yelled, 'They're near enough!' we opened fire with seven rifles at once. I saw three of the Indians fall, and the others ducked down for cover. I guess maybe they didn't think we had much in the way of guns aboard. Those paddling started moving the canoes away fast and those who were crouched down began firing at us a lot.

"It all got pretty hot for a while," he said. "Preacher Tucker, who was kneeling on the deck and praying when they began shooting, was struck right off, and John Stoner, too. Bad hits. They were both still alive but, from the looks of it, sure to die. The German fellow took a bullet, too, pretty bad, but he pulled himself out of sight. Mr. Light caught a ball in his shoulder, and Captain Plaskett's son, who was twelve, had his forehead creased by a ball and was bleeding pretty bad. Several of the horses aboard were hit and fell down either dead or dying, and they and the others were kicking a lot and doing a lot of screaming, they were so scared.

"They got out of range of us," Hubbell continued. "At first we thought maybe they were turning back to hit some other boats that were planning to leave Marietta right after us, but they didn't. They just followed us for about half an hour before they began closing in again. We were beginning to get close to shore and there was a bar ahead and we knew if we grounded on it, we'd be lost. Captain Kirkpatrick's boat was closest in, and so he jumped up onto the roof of the big cabin and grabbed up one of the poles and began shoving out toward deeper water and better current. He got it headed right, but then he got hit by a ball in the head and fell dead off the roof and landed between two of the dead horses.

"They were on us by then, and I got up on the roof of my boat and got one shot off and knocked an Indian into the water who was just trying to get into our boat from the canoe. The canoe pulled back right away. But then I heard the women screaming below and I jumped down and went into the cabin and found a warrior with a tomahawk in his hand stuck halfway in one of the small windows. I picked up a billet of wood and beat him on the head till he was dead and then grabbed up a loaded gun and ran out on the deck again."

He shook his head and took another sip of the tea before continuing. "Both the canoes had pulled back a little again from our boats, but they were still firing pretty hard at us, and that's when I took a bullet through the arm here." He touched the bandage over his wound. "Captain Plaskett's other son, John—he's ten years old— also got hit in the arm but not so bad. I didn't think we'd get away if they closed in on us again and was beginning to think we were done, but then, I guess 'cause we'd already killed five of them, they pulled back out of range, followed us a little longer and then turned back. We then continued drifting down to Maysville, where we got to shore, and then, this morning, the boat of Captain Strong came drifting in, too, with two crewmen dead in it. Captain Strong said his boat had put into shore again close to the mouth of the Scioto, on the Ohio side, and twenty-one of the discharged soldiers had gotten out and then immediately fell into an ambush. Most, it appeared, were killed in the first firing, and Strong and his crewmen, themselves under fire, had shoved the flatboat out into the current, two being killed in the process, but they had then made it to Maysville. Not long after that," he motioned toward the other men at the table with them, "Mr. Kenton and Mr. McIntire and Mr. Whiteman came, and here we are."

Kenton now spoke up. "We buried Kirkpatrick, Stoner and the preacher, Tucker, along with the two crewmen from Strong's boat at Maysville. Whole town's in an uproar. What bothers me now, Henry, is the Greathouse boat. We've got to find out what's happened."

Henry Lee nodded. All the old-timers on the frontier, as well as the Indians, were aware that it was Greathouse who had butchered Chief Logan's family and touched off Lord Dunmore's War. That had been 17 years ago, but if the Shawnees had recognized him, the results would not be pretty, since the Indians reserved very special forms of slow death for their greatest enemies.

"All right, Simon," he said, "we'll mount an expedition. I'll write out some authorizations for you, Alex and Ben. You three separate from here and go to the nearest stations and order the militia and all the volunteers you can get to assemble at once at Maysville. I'll write dispatches for Colonel Orr"—Alexander Orr was commander of the scout system in the Kentucky district—"and place him in charge of the expedition, and also to General Scott to let him know what's happening. Have some more tea," he motioned to his wife, "while I get these things written. Then we'll leave."

[A p r i l   5 ,   1 7 9 1 — T u e s d a y]

The force of 200 men had ridden up the Kentucky shore of the Ohio River from Maysville under Col. Orr, with Col. Robert Rankin and his 100 men in three flatboats following. What they found was sickening, and it wasn't merely the Elijah Strong party, which they found first. Most of the 21 discharged soldiers had been shot to death and then scalped and savagely mutilated with tomahawk blows, their bodies now badly bloated and maggoty. A common grave was dug and the bodies buried, and all the men in Orr's party, including Simon Kenton, knew that when at last they returned home, they would have to destroy their own clothing, as the ghastly stench would never leave them.

The party had continued up the shore, looking for the Greathouse party, but that wasn't who they found. A few miles up they came to the burned ruins of another flatboat and, on the shore, the bodies of 13 men and two women, similarly killed. Kenton, Orr and many of the others recognized the leader of the party—John May, for whom Maysville had been named. It was known that he had gone up the Kanawha to bring down a number of new settlers. Now all were dead. These, too, Orr's men buried and then continued their search for the Greathouse party.

They found them, all 16 dead—making the total killed, including those already buried at Maysville, 52. These, however, were the worst, and the question that had been in the mind of Kenton and many of the others was now answered beyond doubt: The Indians had indeed recognized Jacob Greathouse and had subjected him and his wife to a very special death.

The couple had been stripped and beaten terribly with limber willow switches, though not enough to kill them. It was not difficult to deduce what had then occurred. Each had been tethered to a different sapling with a loop around the neck and the line running to the tree. Their bellies had been slit open just above the pubic hair, and a loose end of the entrails had been tied to the sapling. They had then either been dragged or prodded around in a circle so their intestines had been pulled out of their bodies to wind around the trees. Mrs. Greathouse had apparently died before getting much more than half unwound, but Jake had managed to stumble along until not only his intestines but even his stomach had been pulled out and became part of the obscene mass on the tree. They had then been scalped and hot coals stuffed into the body cavities before the Indians left.

Every man on the expedition would ever after carry the picture of this atrocity with him, and it would fill his nightmares. The message was clear: The hatred of the Shawnee was strong, his memory long and his vengeance great.

[April 21, 1791—Thursday]

Normally it was the Indians who adroitly pulled off ambushes against the whites, but on rare occasions an opportunity presented itself for the tables to be turned. This was one of those occasions, and Simon Kenton was set on pulling it off.

Five days ago Ben Whiteman and Neil Washburn had been making their appointed patrol of the Ohio River shore and were almost 30 miles below Maysville when they found four large Indian canoes hidden at the mouth of Snag Creek.[719] The first two found were 50-foot wooden canoes beached and covered with old driftwood and brush. A search turned up the other two, 20-footers made of bark, sunk in three feet of water and held down with logs angled up onto the shore. All signs indicated that a party of 50 or more Shawnees had gone inland from here to raid the settlements. Whiteman and Washburn immediately returned to Kenton's Station and reported to him. Kenton, in turn, sent out word for 30 of his scouts to meet in Maysville at dawn. He also sent young James Finley to Lee's Station to inform the county lieutenant and advise him to send warnings to the various settlements of Mason and Bourbon counties to be on special alert against attack and, if possible, mount an offensive to drive the marauders back to the Ohio River.

Kenton's party assembled at the appointed time—including Jacob Wetzel, who was now living in Kentucky—and by sunrise they had shoved off in an old keelboat carrying 20 of his men and the other 10 in a light cedar 40-foot canoe. A quarter-mile above Snag Creek, the party crossed to the Ohio shore and grounded. Kenton ordered the keelboat dragged ashore and hidden and its 20 men to move the remaining distance by land to opposite the mouth of Snag Creek and meet him and the other 10 there. Then he ordered to canoe back across to the Kentucky side, to make certain the Indian boats were still hidden there. They were, and once again they crossed directly over to the Ohio side, put into the mouth of Bear Creek 1,000 yards below, and hid the canoe there. Then they walked back and joined the others.

Kenton set up a two-man six-hour guard schedule and, with the rest, set up an ambush in a steep gap several hundred yards inland. At that point the waiting began, and it was a long one. Their rations were nearly used up and 48 hours had passed before the Indians showed up. Whiteman and Washburn spotted them first and alerted the others. Kenton came up with five men, including Jacob Boone, Joe Lemon, Bill Fowler, Alex McIntire and Jacob Wetzel. The eight men watched as three Shawnees started across, two in one of the smaller sunken canoes they had raised, the third swimming his horse across and leading six other horses tied head to tail, animals no doubt stolen from the settlements.

There was, as yet, no sign of the other Indians, and the pair in the canoe were talking animatedly and laughing as they approached. As they reached the shore, the whites fired and all three Indians were killed. The tired horses were caught easily and led into the woods. The dead Indians were scalped. One turned out to be not an Indian at all but a white renegade named Bill Frame, recognized by Joe Lemon as a boyhood friend on the Monongahela, whom he hadn't seen for ten years. All three bodies were consigned to the river and the canoe was filled with rocks and sunk.

Again they waited in hiding, hungry and tired now, throughout the remainder of the day and night, and the vigilance paid off. Shortly after dawn today virtually the same scenario occurred: This time two Indians paddled and one swam six horses across. Again they were killed as they came ashore, the horses captured and the dead scalped. Before the bodies were shoved into the river, one of the heads was severed and impaled atop a sharpened 20-foot pole and stuck in the ground at the far north end of the ambush gap as a warning to any other Indians coming south who might attempt to cross here.

With no other Indians in sight, Kenton allowed two of the men to move inland and hunt for meat. They returned in an hour or so with three turkeys, which wasn't much, but at least provided each man with a little nourishment to keep him going. Again they waited throughout the day and into the evening. At nightfall a heavy fog developed and, about midnight, one of the guards brought word that sounds had carried over the water of many men gathering on the opposite shore. Kenton immediately abandoned the plan to ambush the Indians at the gap and moved all his men into position closer to the river. Now, however, things went slightly awry. The Indians on the Kentucky shore began hallowing, obviously expecting an answer from the Ohio shore. When none came, an uneasy silence fell. Soon muttered voices were heard, and the dipping of paddles, and at just about that same moment, one of Kenton's men dropped his gun with a clatter. Immediately the sounds of the boat drew away and silence fell again, this time more ominously. Kenton ordered the shore guards to walk a 100-pace patrol each, moving apart, halting, then moving together again.

Though they heard nothing, on one of the walks a small canoe was found beached on the shore—obviously a craft Whiteman and Washburn had not discovered with the others. A daring warrior had come across, discovered the waiting whites, circled around them, climbed a high hill and, with startling abruptness suddenly yelled in a great booming voice.

"Puck-a-chee! Puck-a-chee! Shemanese!"—Danger here! Long Knives!

The element of surprise now entirely lost, Kenton ordered the big canoe to be brought up from Bear Creek. They boarded and started over, but before they were fully across, they heard gunfire from the Kentucky side. On coming to the shore, they found that a sizable group of Bourbon County men, having received Kenton's warning, had taken up the offensive and followed the Indians. Already alerted to Kenton's trap, however, and aided by the fog, the Indian party had scattered and escaped, leaving behind two dead.

While the ambush had not turned out to be quite the success Kenton had hoped, it was still a good showing—32 stolen horses recovered, eight of the enemy killed and not one person of their own number even injured.

[M a y   1 ,   1 7 9 1 — S u n d a y]

The four Crow sisters, Susan, 17, Elizabeth, 16, Christiana, 14, and Catherine, 12, were positively reveling in this beautiful spring morning. The sun was shining brightly and the new grasses were very lush and green, while many of the bushes had newly unfurled leaves or, along with most of the trees, heavily swollen leaf buds. Many of the spring flowers were in bloom, perfuming this lovely morning's air, and in the woodlands the redbud trees were in full bloom.

Only a quarter-hour ago the four had left their parents and older brothers, Martin and Peter, at their cabin on the upper waters of Dunkard Creek and had gone to bring in the cows. The two cows, each with a calf, had been pastured on the broad divide separating Dunkard Creek from the upper waters of Grave Creek, not much more than a mile from the cabin, where the grass was very lush.

As they followed the cow path up the wooded eastern slope of the divide toward the pasture, the girls were giggling and chattering as they usually did. Catherine abruptly ran ahead a few feet and then turned and walked backward facing her sisters. "Question time," she said. "How many states in the United States?"

"Thirteen," said Susan and Christiana in unison, and at the same time Elizabeth said, "That's a silly question. We all know there are thirteen."

"Wrong!" Catherine said. She giggled. "There are fourteen."

"Since when?" Susan asked.

"Since March the fourth," Catherine said, laughing aloud. "Papa told me this morning. Said he heard the news yesterday. Vermont just became the fourteenth state, and its capital is Mon—Mon—"

"Montpelier?" Elizabeth said.

"Yes, that's it. Montpelier. And Papa says—"

Her words were cut off abruptly as seven Delawares leaped out of hiding from bushes on both sides of them. The girls shrieked and bunched together for protection. The Indians, three carrying rifles and the other four with tomahawks in hand, looked fierce in their war paint, and all four of the girls were very frightened. The leader of the party looked at them with a scowl. Addressing Elizabeth, who was tallest and appeared oldest, he spoke in halting English.

"You come us," he said. "No run. Die if run."

Elizabeth nodded, and the leader nodded back. With two other warriors flanking him, he turned and began walking toward Grave Creek, and the girls, white-faced and terrified, both Christiana and Catherine crying, followed. The other four Indians brought up the rear.

"Stop crying," Susan said, speaking softly in German. "Listen to me. We've got to make a break for it right now, before we get too far away. If we scatter into the woods in different directions and run as hard as we can, maybe it'll confuse them. We'll wait till there's some heavier cover nearby, and then, when I say now, we'll do it."

The leader turned, still scowling, and said, "No talk!"

In another 30 yards or so, the path curved through a brushier area. When they were in the midst of it, Susan cried "Now!" and all four girls scattered. The plan, which had seemed reasonable to them all, did not work well.

Susan and Christiana leaped to the left, Elizabeth and Catherine toward the right. Susan got no more than a dozen steps when the leader fired and the ball caught her in the center of the back and killed her. Catherine ducked beneath the tomahawk blow aimed at her and the blade just barely skimmed across the back of her head, slicing through hair and skin but not reaching her skull. Bleeding profusely, she increased her speed and darted through bushes and around trees, running as fast as she had ever run. Elizabeth was pursued by a warrior who overtook her in several giant strides and sunk his tomahawk into the back of her neck, severing her spine and killing her. Christiana, with three of the Delawares chasing her, got a little farther but was finally also run down and grabbed. She struggled and screamed, kicked at one of the warriors and bit the hand of the one who had grabbed her arm. He howled in pain and swung his tomahawk savagely, catching her in the temple, the blade penetrating deeply into her head.

Catherine, as the smallest, had not been pursued, and in the screaming confusion that had erupted, she managed to squeeze into the hollow bole of a sycamore and squirm upward out of sight. Feet thudded past as the warriors now started searching for her, and she bit the heel of her hand to stifle her own sobs. After a while she heard the sounds of the warriors passing again as they retraced their steps. Their muffled guttural voices came to her for a moment and then faded away.

Catherine Crow remained inside the tree, very still, very frightened, for a very long time, until finally she heard the voices of her brothers and father calling as they searched for the missing girls, their voices growing louder as they neared.

Then, at last, she began to scream.

[May 19, 1791—Thursday]

For the first time in his life, Capt. Samuel Brady was a fugitive from justice—a wanted man with two rewards on his head totaling $800—one from Pennsylvania for $500, the other from Virginia for $300. He had decided that when the time was right, he would turn himself in to the authorities, but so far as he was concerned, that time was not yet.

The matter had all begun almost three months ago, on February 11, in sugarmaking time, about two miles below the mouth of Buffalo Creek but on the Ohio side of the river.[720] That was where the Francis Riley family had sunk roots last year, and this year they had set up a good sugar camp in a nice grove of maples some 300 yards from the cabin just above Riddle's Run.

On that particular day, Francis Riley and his eldest son, John, 24, had canoed the four and a half miles upstream to help build the new settlement being established on the Virginia side of the Ohio River opposite Carpenter's Station and McKim's Run. It was being established by Charles Wells, who was already calling the place Wellsburg.[721] Mrs. Riley and her son-in-law, John Schemmerhorn, were busy at the sugar camp boiling maple water, while her 16-year-old son, William, was doing chores at the cabin. Also at the cabin were William's sisters, Ruth—who was John's wife—and Abigail, 18. The two girls were watching over their younger brothers, Moses, 8, and Tom, 4. Ruth's infant daughter, Claudia, was asleep in a basket cradle that was beginning to split and fray.

Having just finished bringing in a new supply of wood for the sugar fire, John Schemmerhorn took the ax and said he would be back in a little while, as he was going out to cut a tree for some basket splints to repair Claudia's cradle. He moved off a few hundred yards looking for an appropriate tree and, when he found one, began to chop it down. He didn't hear the several warriors creep up behind him, nor the faint swish of the tomahawk that descended in a vicious blow and ended his life. The warrior who killed him took his scalp, and then they also took the inch-wide band of wampum he was wearing as a belt, the strand having been given to him by his father, who had taken it from an Indian runner he had killed.

The Indians, a mixed group of nine that included Wyandots, Mingoes and Delawares, then went to the sugar camp and very easily took Mrs. Riley captive. Seeing the fresh scalp and the strand of wampum that she recognized as John's, she knew he was dead and thought they would kill her, too, if she resisted in any way. Not knowing if they could understand her, she nevertheless told them that if they would not kill her, she would go with them peaceably. The warrior who was evidently the leader nodded and said something in his own tongue, upon which he and seven of the warriors moved off carefully toward the cabin, leaving her in the care of the one who had killed John. As soon as they were gone, her captor hurriedly tied her hands together with the wampum belt and then tied the loose ends to the low-slung branch of a beech tree. Then he loped off toward the cabin, too, in order to share in the plunder. In his haste, he had not tied Mrs. Riley well. She quickly freed herself and ran through the woods to the north, heading for the two-mile-distant Carpenter's Station.[722]

Things were very bad at the Riley cabin. Abigail and Ruth, outside, had seen the approaching Indians first, and Abbie screamed. Moses, who was hidden from view behind a little screen of brush, instantly leaped down into a ravine and scurried away in the only direction open to him, heading toward Waxler's Station, some five miles distant to the south.[723] The sisters tried to run but were grabbed before taking more than a few steps. Inside the cabin William snatched up a flintlock and started out when four-year-old Tom cried out to him. He came back, told his brother he'd protect him as long as he lived, hoisted the little boy onto his back, ordered him to hang on tight and then plunged outside and started racing away. He had covered no more than 30 yards when a rifle cracked, and he was killed. Tom was thrown from his back, bumped his head and sat up crying. A warrior ran up and tomahawked him and took both scalps and William's gun.

The warriors ran into the cabin and quickly plundered it of anything they found worthwhile. They discovered the infant Claudia in her cradle.[724] The warrior who tied Mrs. Riley to the tree, believing the baby to be hers, took the infant up in his arms and carried it back to where he had tied the woman. Discovering that she was gone, he became very angry, grabbed the baby by one ankle, swung her around his head and then dashed her brains out against the tree to which her grandmother had been tied.

Back at the cabin, the Indians ripped open the feather ticks and scattered the contents all over and set fire to the cabin. Then, obviously fearing pursuit, they started away with their plunder and the two young women. Ruth Schemmerhorn nearly fainted when she recognized her husband's scalp stuck in the belt of the warrior who had killed him. They had traveled less than a mile when Abigail turned her ankle on a root and fell. When she got back up, she was limping badly, which slowed them considerably. After a little while a few of the Indians led Abigail off into the woods and a few minutes later returned without her. When Ruth asked where her sister was, she was told by the leader, "She has gone to sleep." Deeply trauma-tized by all that had occurred in so short a time, Ruth continued with them in an enveloping aura of grief.[725]

Mrs. Riley had made it safely to Carpenter's Station, and little Moses Riley had finally gotten to Waxler's Station. Both reported the attack and the word spread swiftly, causing great alarm.[726] Immediately Maj. William McMahan raised a party of 30 men and went to the scene. They gathered up the bodies of John Schemmerhorn and the Riley children, William, Tom and Claudia, and in a melancholy ceremony buried them in a common grave. They camped for the night near the ruins of the burned cabin and in the morning began following the raiding party. The trail led them all the way to the Tuscarawas River, near the mouth of Stillwater Creek, at which point two of McMahan's scouts, who had been ranging ahead, came in and reported they had found the Indian encampment several miles downstream. The small party they had been following had merged with a much larger war party; too large, in fact, for McMahan's party to attempt to attack them. Disgruntled at not getting their revenge but thankful at not having run into the larger Indian force that could have wiped them out, the McMahan party returned home safely.

That was when the whole incident began affecting Samuel Brady. One of his scouts, a fiery-tempered Irishman named Francis McGuire, was on hand when the McMahan party returned and was outraged that, as he put it, they had turned tail and run.

"I'm going to get Captain Brady," he said, "and we'll get those damn varmints. Ain't no war party going to come here like that an' do what they did and then run off 'thout takin' their licks in return."

As soon as he could, McGuire went to Brady's place and found him there with his wife, Drusilla, and their two sons, Van, who was now five, and John, who had been born just last year. Brady had not heard of the attack and was as incensed as McGuire that the McMahan party had not struck the Indians when they had the chance. He sent for many of his scouts and then conferred with the local militia commander, Capt. Baldwin Parsons, who also put out a call for volunteers. Lewis Wetzel, who happened to be in the area of Buffalo Creek, heard about the call to arms and, though he usually preferred to do his Indian hunting on a solitary basis, volunteered to go along. So, too, unknown to his parents, did 16-year-old Solomon Hedges. Others came in from various points and, between Brady and Parsons over the next week or so, they collected a quite respectable body of about 40 men. They all crossed the Ohio at Mingo Bottom and headed up Indian Cross Creek, looking for Indian sign but not too hopeful of finding any since by now so much time had elapsed since the attack on the Rileys. The first day they followed the creek some 17 miles up to its headwaters and camped there.[727] During that night it rained very hard, a bitterly cold rain that turned into sleet, then back to rain, thoroughly drenching and chilling the men and dampening the enthusiasm of many of the volunteers as well as Capt. Parsons, who was now having second thoughts about penetrating the Indian country in disobedience of the recent governmental orders forbidding such activity. They held a meeting, and about half the force rather shamefacedly admitted they were for returning home.

"I'll have their scalps before I go back!" McGuire declared, and more than two dozen of the men sided with him. "Sam," McGuire continued, "you gonna' lead us iffen these others go back?"

"I will," Brady replied grimly.

That settled it. In the cold gray light of dawn, Capt. Parsons assembled the men who were going to return with him and directed them to give their surplus provisions and ammunition to those who were going on. They did so, and then the two groups, wishing each other well, separated.[728]

Hardly two miles away from their night's camp, Brady's party discovered the fresh remains of an Indian camp, at which several articles were found that had been discarded. One of the men in the party studied the goods and identified them as having been taken from the Riley cabin. Instantly they took up the trail and followed it to the west a half-mile, when it turned to the north, the Indians obviously traveling very rapidly. Day after day they continued following the Indians northward and then gradually arcing eastward. After about a week they were nearing Beaver River, only a little over a mile above Fort McIntosh, at its mouth. On March 8 they had come to a small run and were following it in the last light of day toward where it empties into the Beaver when they detected smoke.[729] Creeping up the low ridge separating the run from the river, they spied an Indian encampment at the east base of it, on a long narrow bottom only about 100 feet wide, close to the Beaver River shore and almost exactly opposite the blockhouse trading post called Beaver Blockhouse. That post belonged to William Wilson and John Hillman—a rather unsavory pair who, while the allegations had never been proved, were suspected of having harbored Tories and supplying the hostile Indians during the Revolution.[730] Suspicions were strong among Brady's men that the Indians were planning to cross Beaver River the next day and reprovision themselves at the trading post.

Three tents had been set up in the camp of the Indians but, with darkness coming on, Brady's party had no way of determining for certain how many warriors were on hand, so they eased back to the west side of the ridge to decide how they would attack, and then strike them at first light on the morrow. They planned to split their party and attack from two directions simultaneously. Lewis Wetzel was to lead one group, taking them over the ridge and down the east slope to attack the camp from the west, while Brady would lead the other, following the run to its mouth, a few hundred yards below, then coming up the Beaver River shoreline to attack from the south. Brady's own gunfire was to be the signal for the start of the attack. If the Indian party included any women or children, they were not to be killed but captured for possible use later in a trade for the two missing sisters, Ruth Schemmerhorn and Abigail Riley.

At the very first light of day, the two parties moved out. Brady, with McGuire, Tom Wells and others directly behind him, moved quickly down the run and then, keeping to cover, northward along the bank of the Beaver. When they were about 100 yards below the Indian encampment, they heard a peculiar whistling sound. Advancing cautiously, they spied two Indian boys about ten years old up in the branches of a young sugar maple—one about ten feet off the ground, the other five feet higher. They were giggling and blowing on willow-twig whistles. From their elevated perch the sharp-eyed boys saw Brady's party creeping up and instantly scrambled down to the ground and ran toward the camp, shouting a warning.

Brady's party followed at a run and, upon glimpsing the Indians, men and women alike, sitting or standing around their campfire, fired and dropped one of the warriors. Immediately a general firing followed, both from Brady's men and from those with Lewis Wetzel, whose party had also broken into a run downhill toward the camp. John Van Buskirk, running beside Charley Wells, tripped over a root and fell face-first into a large tree, breaking his nose. Another of the Indians killed at the camp took a ball fired by James Campbell. The rest of the Indian party, including some who were wounded, fled to the north, the warriors snatching up their rifles as they left.

Brady, with his second shot, had wounded a warrior in the shoulder. He ran to him, kicked his rifle away and pulled him to his feet. The wound was not severe, and Brady intended to take him in as a captive, perhaps to learn where the girls had been taken and plan a rescue mission.

"This one's a prisoner," he yelled. "Leave him alone."

The warrior, not understanding English but evidently misconstruing Brady's yell as a command to his men to kill him, shoved Brady hard and sprinted away. Half a dozen shots broke out and he tumbled dead to the ground no more than 50 feet away.

On the slope with Wetzel, Joe Edgington raised his rifle and took a bead on one of the runners.

"That's a squaw, Joe," Caleb Wells said.

"I know," Edgington said as he squeezed the trigger and killed her in midstride. Edgington then looked at Wells and added, "You keep quiet about me bein' the one who brought 'er down." He paused a moment and then added, "I'll tell you, Caleb, I hate these goddamn Injens an' I will kill anything and everything in the shape of an Injen whenever I get the chance, from the size of my fist to an ol' gray-head, be they he or she. An' I don't think too kindly on them as thinks I'm wrong to do so."

It wasn't an outright threat, but Caleb Wells got the message and figured he would probably live a lot longer if he kept his mouth shut.

Wetzel and several others raised their guns toward a particularly muscular warrior running full tilt, a blanket tied about his neck flapping capelike behind him. As other guns were firing around him, Wetzel aimed just below the man's shoulder and, when he fired, the warrior instantly tumbled. The Indians with him, including the two boys initially discovered, plus an older girl, a woman and an old man, continued running and quickly plunged into a dense willow thicket. As the wounded Indian tried unsuccessfully to get back to his feet, Wetzel ran up. Seated on the ground, the warrior faced him and began begging to be spared. Wetzel grinned maliciously, pulled out his tomahawk and buried it in the side of his head, killing him.

"You damn yaller sumbitch," he growled, "you make no pleas at me!"

The blanket had several bullet holes in it, but only one ball had struck him, passing through his left upper arm and into his body. Wetzel scalped the warrior, gave the blanket to the others, pulled off the bloodsoaked buckskin blouse and, grinning wickedly, donned it over his own.

As they entered the camp at a run, Jim Hoagland shot at a warrior who scrambled out of one of the tents. His ball creased the side of the warrior's neck, causing him to stumble and roll over. As he tried to rise, McGuire rushed up and shot him dead at a distance of 20 feet.

As a lull occurred in the firing, Brady shouted loudly, "Don't follow them into that cover! It's too thick. Those that've been hit will stop and cover the escape of the others. They'll kill you, and it's not worth throwing your lives away for."

Young Solomon Hedges, however, had wounded an Indian, saw him get up and limp away and meant to get his first scalp, if at all possible. He went to the spot where the warrior had fallen and found blood. At once he began following the trail of the telltale droplets. Carefully and watchfully, gun loaded and at ready, he followed the trail upriver for half a mile before it abruptly stopped. A few downy buzzard feathers on the ground told the story: The warrior had plugged up his own wound and evidently gone on. Hedges, very disappointed over the loss of the scalp, started back toward the others. Actually, the warrior, a Delaware, was very close by, and dying. He had indeed plugged his wound with buzzard down, but he had then squeezed into a hollow black oak and, with slowly fading vision, watched the youth return the way he had come.[731]

William Sherrod was another who had wounded an Indian, breaking his lower arm and causing him to drop his gun, but the warrior had kept on running. Sherrod leaped into pursuit but had to chase the wounded man for the better part of a mile before he finally overtook him and ended his life with a tomahawk blow. He scalped him, took his belt knife, powderhorn and shot pouch and went back to the others.

Tom Wells had seen one of the warriors leap down the bank of the river and crouch there behind a bush in front of a log, fairly well hidden by the bank above him. As he ran up, the Indian poked his rifle barrel through the bush and fired at him, but the gun merely flashed. Wells had ducked back out of sight as the flash occurred, and by the time he regained his footing and came down the bank, the warrior was gone. Wells stepped up on the log and looked around for him, and McGuire, a little distance away, shouted at him.

"Tom, that damn Injen is crouched down under the log, below and behind you!"

Wells turned and leaned far over. Seeing the warrior scrunched far back under the log in an effort to hide, he calmly raised his gun and put a bullet through his head.

The Indian party seemed to have been made up of Delawares and Senecas. The two dead Indians near the fire, a Seneca and a Delaware, were scalped, and nine horses hobbled nearby were easily captured. The dead woman, another Delaware, was not scalped, but her beaded moccasins and buckskin pullover dress were taken, leaving her naked body exposed. Including that woman, a total of eight Indians had been killed in the attack.[732]

There was a substantial amount of goods in the camp, including a few iron kettles, various tomahawks and knives, a couple of good flintlock rifles and a musket, a quantity of flour and about three gallons of bear oil in deerskin pouches. All these items were gathered up, later to be auctioned, along with the horses, and all members of the Brady party would share equally in the proceeds.

Brady, inspecting the dead, had no difficulty recognizing the fallen squaw, though it was over 13 years since he had seen her. She was the Seneca woman named Hannah, who had befriended him and given him several bags of corn during the McIntosh expedition late in 1778. He shook his head and said angrily, "I said no women were to be killed. Who shot her?"

"Someone," Caleb Wells spoke up, not looking at Wetzel, "probably mistook her for a warrior."

"I guess we'll just have to settle for that," Brady said. He shook his head sadly. "I'm sorry she was killed. She helped me once, long ago."

William Wilson, the trader, had emerged from his post on the other side of the river as the firing broke out. He had been followed by a few other people, including one Indian. When a few shots from the attackers came across the river toward the Indian with him, the little group ducked back into the blockhouse.[733] Now they had come out again, and Wilson crossed the river rapidly in a small canoe, berating the whites with every dip of his paddle for firing on innocent Indians. He continued to do so as he came ashore, at the same time complaining to Brady about the men who had their rifles trained on him and seemed very willing to shoot.

Brady tried to explain that they had been trailing the Indians since not long after the massacre at the Riley cabin, that the tracks had led here and that they held these Indians responsible. Wilson wouldn't accept that. He pointed at the plunder that had been piled together.

"Did you find any of the Riley items among their things?" When Brady shook his head, he went on, "That proves it. Those people had been tradin' with me, not raiding the settlements. You've taken out your bloody vengeance on innocent people and, by God, I aim to see you pay for it!"

"You think you can do that, Wilson," McGuire spoke up, "go right ahead. But let me tell you something, you no good Injen-lovin' son of a bitch, you get your ass back across the river right now, or I'll put a damn bullet betwixt *your* eyes, too!"

Wilson saw murder in the man's eyes and, seeing no sympathy in the expressions of any of the others, backed down a bit. "Well," he grumbled, pointing at the three tents, "those are my property, and I want them back."

"Take them, Mr. Wilson," Brady said tightly, "and then you better do as Mr. McGuire says, as your presence here places you in extreme jeopardy." He paused, then added, "The people on this frontier have tolerated you here for a long time under trying circumstances. It is said that you trade liquor and guns to the hostiles. I don't claim to know the facts but, whether true or not, I'm notifying you right now to get out. If you're still here a month from now, your trading post will be burned down, and your own life may be endangered. Now I suggest you get the hell out of here."

Wilson shot him a malevolent glance and then wordlessly turned and strode to the tents. He quickly broke them down and tossed them in a jumble in his canoe, got in himself and set off back to his post. Halfway across he paused in his paddling and shouted back at them.

"Brady, McGuire, all of you! You ain't heard the last of this. I promise you, you're gonna rue this day!"

The men merely laughed and hooted at him, and Brady then ordered the Indian goods loaded onto the horses and the return journey begun.

About a week after they got home, the auction was held of the plundered goods that had been stored at McGuire's place, with people attending from settlements for miles around. The total sales brought in $718.75 and, evenly split among the 26 men of Brady's party, amounted to $27.64 apiece.

Twenty days after the incident, which was now being called the Beaver Blockhouse Affair, Pennsylvania Gov. Thomas Mifflin, without mentioning any names, issued a proclamation offering a $1,000 reward for the discovery and apprehension of the person or persons who committed the March 9 murders of four friendly Indians, three men and a woman, on the west side of Beaver River, in the vicinity of the blockhouse, in the County of Allegheny—the reward to be paid upon conviction of the perpetrators.

On April 22, almost a month after the proclamation was posted, traders William Wilson and John Hillman presented themselves to Gov. Mifflin. The governor heard them out, and then, at his request, the two traders signed affidavits telling their view of what had occurred, which varied considerably from the truth. They also said that on the morning following the incident, they and some hired men crossed the river and buried the four dead Indians that they found.

Gov. Mifflin transmitted the Wilson and Hillman affidavits to the state attorney general with his recommendation that four charges of murder be lodged by the state against Samuel Brady and Francis McGuire. This was immediately done and a warrant issued for their arrest, stating that they had, without provocation, murdered four Indians in the State of Pennsylvania and then fled from justice in that state to the freedom of Virginia; that the victims of the murders were one known as Moravian Henry, a Delaware man named Chictawney, an Indian woman called Letart's Wife and a young Delaware man called The Muncey Boy.

As soon as the warrants were issued, Gov. Mifflin issued another proclamation, this one naming the accused men and calling for their arrest. He then informed Gov. Beverley Randolph of Virginia and requested that his state issue similar warrants, in line with their reciprocal criminal felony agreements and, upon capture of the fugitives, extradite them to Pennsylvania under Article 4, Section 2, of the United States Constitution. Gov. Randolph had no choice but to issue a similar proclamation and arrest warrants, which he did on May 3, offering a reward of $600 for Samuel Brady and Francis McGuire or $300 for either of them.

The result was that the whole frontier was engaged in a controversy about whether Brady and his men should be treated in such a manner. The greater majority by far were outraged that such charges had been made and staunchly supported Brady and his Rangers. One of the more outspoken of these was Col. David Shepherd, who wrote to Gov. Mifflin that he thought the governor had been badly misinformed and wished to set the record straight; that the expedition of Brady and his Rangers had been undertaken in reaction to the murder in the most cruel manner of four citizens and the taking into captivity of two others. Brady and his Rangers, Shepherd continued, had followed the trail of the perpetrators to the Indian camp on the Beaver River, where the attack was made and some of the Indians killed. He then added:

> *I have the greatest respect for Pennsylvania and lament extremely that its chief magistrate had not the true information of the situation necessary to render protection from the savages. Your Proclamation issues false information, so far as the Rangers attacking the Savages without provocation, or that the Indians were peaceable or friendly. Ohio County considers itself to be under the greatest obligations to the Rangers for their services on the occasion of the deaths of the Indians. The Settlements have enjoyed peace since those Indians were killed and I hope you, honored Sir, will destroy the effect of your Proclamation by a further one that will suffer not the men who deserve the highest credit for their conduct, to be stigmatized by having a reward offered for their persons.*

In a similar letter to Gov. Randolph in Richmond, Col. Shepherd sent him a detailed accounting of all the facts in the case, beginning with the massacre of the Riley family. He ended his letter with barely controlled temper by writing:

During the last week, 29 persons have been most cruelly murdered; yet, upon the authenticity of Wilson & Company does Governor Mifflin send out his Proclamation. His government, it appears, is not confined to Pennsylvania, & his information is from those who have feasted upon the blood of our fellow citizens by supplying the savages with every instrument necessary for our destruction. If we have erred in being avenged of our enemy, we are willing to be corrected by your Excellency, upon whom we, at this dangerous period, rely, in hopes you will if possible make provision to relieve us from distress.

I remain your Excellency's most ob^t humb^l serv^t.,

David Shepherd

Now, today, May 19, Gov. Randolph put into motion steps to rescind his previous proclamation and arrest order and reward for Brady and McGuire and to exonerate them of any wrongdoing insofar as the State of Virginia was concerned.

Gov. Mifflin of the State of Pennsylvania, however, did not.

[*M a y   2 9 ,   1 7 9 1 — S u n d a y*]

Capt. Lawrence Van Buskirk had never fully gotten over the death of his wife, Rebecca, a year ago. Ever since that terrible day, he had hoped to exact vengeance on the Indians who so brutally tomahawked her. It was the principal reason why he had volunteered to go with Brady on the expedition that had become known as the Beaver Blockhouse Affair. Yet, while they had killed Indians, Van Buskirk himself had not been one of those who brought an Indian down. Now, aware that the Indians were close by, he knew that the time had come at last, and how fitting it was that it should be on the one-year anniversary of his wife's death.

This whole thing had come about when, yesterday morning, a scout had come in with the intelligence of a body of Indians, perhaps 20 in number, hovering about Short Creek on the Ohio side, about a mile above its mouth. Lawrence Van Buskirk had immediately put out a call for volunteers, and by evening 27 men had arrived at the little blockhouse he commanded just below Wellsburg. This morning they had crossed the river and followed the trail up Short Creek. In less than a mile they found a chunk of jerky suspended by a line from a branch overhanging the trail. Van Buskirk immediately called to the men behind him to take cover, as he suspected an ambush. They did so.

His warning had come just in the nick of time . . . for the others. Before he could leap into hiding himself, however, a large number of Indians rose from behind the creek bank and poured a withering fire at the only remaining target.

Capt. Lawrence Van Buskirk was struck simultaneously by 19 lead balls, about half of which, individually, would have been fatal.

[*J u n e   1 4 ,   1 7 9 1 — T u e s d a y*]

Brig. Gen. Charles Scott, in his headquarters office at Lexington, leaned back in his chair and rubbed his eyes. Only a few moments ago the sentries had relayed their eleven P.M. call of "all's well," and now silence had once again descended. He was very tired from the exhausting campaign that had lasted over three weeks, but he felt good at what had been accomplished. By his actions it was very likely that the army of Gen. St. Clair, when it finally began its move against the hostile tribes on the Maumee, would find the tribes less consolidated against it and that, after all, had been the whole purpose of Scott's campaign. Spies sent well ahead had fed the Wabash tribes false information of an advance by the St. Clair army against the tribes on the Maumee, and the warriors of the Wabash had immediately gone in that direction in force to help repel the supposed invasion. Now it was very likely that the warriors of the Kickapoos and Weas and Ouiatenons, the Mishawakas and Mississinewas and Eel Rivers and all the other tribes of the middle and lower Wabash region would think twice before leaving their homes to aid the Shawnees and Miamis when the confrontation with St. Clair's army finally came, as come it must. The subterfuge that had drawn them away from their villages this time and left them open to destruction was something they would be unlikely to allow to occur again. Thinking of the old fable, Scott smiled; the cry of wolf had been raised and responded to. Now, when the cry was raised again and the wolf was really there . . .

Still smiling, Gen. Charles Scott picked up the campaign report he had just finished writing to Secretary of War Henry Knox. He skimmed through the preliminary data of gathering and preparing the 700 troops here at Louisville and the crossing of the Ohio and began to read where the real import of the report commenced:

> In prosecution of the enterprise, I marched four miles from the banks of the Ohio on the 23rd of May and on the 24th I resumed my march and pushed forward with the utmost industry, directing my route to Ouiattanon [Ouiatenon], in the best manner my guides and information enabled me, though I found myself greatly deficient in both.
>
> By the 31st I had marched one hundred and thirty-five miles, over a country cut by four large branches of White River and many smaller streams with steep muddy banks. During this march I traversed a country alternately interspersed with the most luxuriant soil and deep clayey bogs, from one to five miles wide, rendered almost impervious by brush and briars. Rain fell in torrents every day, with frequent blasts of wind and thunder storms. These obstacles impeded my progress, wore down my horses, and destroyed my provisions.
>
> On the morning of the 1st inst., as the army entered an extensive prairie, I perceived an Indian on horseback, a few miles to the right.[734] I immediately made a detachment to intercept him, but he escaped. Finding myself discovered, I determined to advance with all the rapidity my circumstances would permit—rather with the hope, than expectation, of reaching the object sought that day, for my guides were strangers to the country which I occupied. At 1 o'clock, having marched by computa-

tion 155 miles from the Ohio, as I penetrated a grove which bordered an extensive prairie, I discovered two small villages at my left at 2 & 4 miles distance.

My guides now recognized the ground and informed me that the main town was four or five miles in my front, behind a point of wood which jutted into the prairie. I immediately detached Colonel John Hardin with sixty mounted infantry and a troop of light-horse, under Captain McCoy, to attack the villages to the left, and moved on briskly with my main body, in order of battle, towards the town, the smoke from which was discernable. My guides were deceived with respect to the situation of the town; for instead of standing at the edge of the plain through which I marched, I found it on the low ground, bordering on the Wabash; on turning the point of woods, one house presented in my front. Captain Price was ordered to assault that with 40 men. He executed the command with great gallantry and killed two warriors. When I gained the summit of the eminence which overlooks the village on the banks of the Wabash, I discovered the enemy in great confusion, endeavoring to make their escape over the river in canoes. I instantly ordered Lieutenant Colonel Commandant Wilkinson to rush forward with the first battalion.[735] The order was executed with promptitude, and this detachment gained the bank of the river just as the rear of the enemy had embarked. And regardless of a brisk fire kept up from a Kickapoo town on the opposite bank, they, in a few minutes, by a well directed fire from their rifles, destroyed all the savages with which five canoes were crowded.

To my great mortification, the Wabash was many feet beyond fording at this place. I therefore detached Colonel Wilkinson to a ford 2 miles above, which my guides informed me was more practicable. The enemy still kept possession of the Kickapoo town. I determined to dislodge them and for the purpose ordered Captains King and Longsdon's companies to march down the river, below the town, and cross under the conduct of Major Barbee. Several of the men swam the river, and others passed in a small canoe. This movement was unobserved and my men had taken post on the bank before they were discovered by the enemy, who immediately abandoned the village. About this time word was brought me that Colonel Hardin was incumbered [sic] with prisoners and had discovered a stronger village further to my left than those I had observed, which he was proceeding to attack. I immediately detached Captain Brown with his company to support the Colonel; but, the distance being six miles, before the Captain arrived, the business was done, & Colonel Hardin joined me a little before sunset, having killed six warriors and taken 52 prisoners. Captain Bull, the warrior who discovered me in the morning, had gained the main town and given the alarm a short time before me; but the villages to my left were uninformed of my approach and had no retreat.

The next morning, June 2, I determined to detach my Lieutenant Colonel Commandant James Wilkinson with 500 men to destroy the important town of Kethlipecanunk at the mouth of Eel River, 18 miles from my camp and on the west side of the Wabash.[736] But on examination I discovered my men and horses to be crippled and worn down by a long, laborious march, and the active exertions of the preceding day; that 360 men could be found in capacity to undertake the enterprise, and they prepared to march on foot. Colonel Wilkinson marched with the detachment at half after five in the evening and returned to my camp the next day at one o'clock, having marched 36 miles in twelve hours, and destroyed the most important settlement of the enemy in this quarter of the federal Territory. In No. 3 you will find the Colonel's report respecting the enterprise.[737] Many of the inhabitants of this village were French and lived in a state of civilization. By the books, letters, and other documents found there, it is evident that place was in close connection with and dependent on Detroit. A large quantity of corn, a variety of household goods, peltry and other articles were burned with this village, which consisted of 70 houses, many of them well furnished.

Misunderstanding the object of a white flag which appeared on an eminence, opposite to me on the afternoon of the 1st, I liberated an aged squaw and sent her with a message to the savages, that if they would come in and surrender, their towns should be spared and they should receive good treatment. It was afterwards found that this white flag was not intended as a signal of parlay, but was placed there to mark the spot where a person of distinction among the Indians, who had died some time before, was interred.

On the 4th I determined to discharge 16 of the weakest and most infirm of my prisoners, with a talk to the Wabash tribes, a copy of which you will find inclosed [sic].[738] My motives to this measure were to rid the army of a heavy incumbrance [sic], to gratify the impulsions [sic] of humanity, to increase the panic my operations had produced, and, by distracting the councils of the enemy, to favor the views of government, and I flatter myself these objects will justify my conduct and secure the approbation of my country.

On the same day, after having burned the towns and adjacent villages, and destroyed the growing corn and pulse, I began my march for the Rapids of the Ohio, where I arrived the 14th Inst. without the loss of a single man by the enemy, and five only wounded, having killed 32, chiefly warriors of size and figure, and taken 58 prisoners.[739]

It is with much pride and pleasure I mention that no act of inhumanity has marked the conduct of the volunteers of Kentucky on this occasion, even the inveterate [sic] habit of scalping the dead ceased to influence.

I have delivered 41 prisoners to Captain Asheton, of the 1st United States Regiment at Fort Steuben. I sincerely regret that the weather and the consequences it produced rendered it impossible for me to carry terror and desolation to the head of the Wabash. The Corps I had the honor to command was equal to the object, but the condition of my horses and state of my provisions were insuperable obstacles to my own intentions, and the wishes of all.

It would be invidious to make distinctions in a Corps which appeared to be animated with one soul—and where a competition for danger and glory inspired all ranks. I, however, consider it my duty to mention Colonel John Hardin, who, in the character of a volunteer, without commission, had command of my advance party and the direction of my guides from the Ohio River, for the discernment, courage and activity with which he fulfilled the trust I reposed in him. And I cannot close this letter in justice to the merits of General Wilkinson, who went out my Lieutenant Colonel Commandant, without acknowledging my obligations for the faithful discharge of the several duties depending on him, and the able support he gave me in every exigency.

Gen. Scott smiled again, very pleased with his report, and leaned forward as he dipped his pen to formally sign the document before dispatching it to the War Department.

[*July 22, 1791 — Friday*]

It was not the Indians that finally brought Lewis Wetzel his comeuppance, but a man he thought was his friend.

Not long after the Beaver Blockhouse Affair, in which he had participated, Wetzel suddenly came to the conclusion that he ought to see more of this world than just the upper Ohio River Valley and, with that, he hired on to work his way down the Ohio as a flatboatsman and visit the supposedly fabulous city he had heard so much about in the Spanish Territory, New Orleans.

Nothing of an untoward nature had occurred on his way to the mouth of the Ohio or down the Mississippi from there to New Orleans. While dazzled by the grandeur of the largest and most ornate city he had ever seen and by the creature comforts available as well as the casualness of life, he did not like it. The hordes of people made him ill at ease, and the heavy air wafting off the salt marshes fringing the Gulf of Mexico was repugnant to him.

Almost on the point of heading back to his own home territory, Wetzel stopped in a tavern and happened to meet a middle-aged Spaniard whose prematurely gray hair made him look older than his years. They struck up a conversation and introduced themselves. The Spaniard said his name was Pedro Hermoso, and he intrigued Wetzel from the onset. A former trapper, guide and Indian hunter, Hermoso spoke English quite well and told marvelous stories of a western frontier enormously different in many respects from the one with which Lewis Wetzel was familiar. The man had spent considerable time not only on the Mississippi for much of its length but also far up the Red River into the land of the Comanches, which he claimed were the most ferocious Indians in America. He had also been far up the Missouri River, and the stories he had accumulated of the Indians, trapping on the western streams, hunting on the vast plains and traveling across deserts and mountains, were fascinating. Wetzel's own tales of fighting the Shawnees, Wyandots and other Indians in the Ohio River Valley were no less fascinating to Hermoso and, as one thing led to another, Wetzel found himself accepting an invitation to come and stay for a while with Hermoso, his wife Rosita and his two little daughters, Delores and Magdalena, in his small home not far from the city.

Wetzel did not suspect anything was amiss until he had been with the Hermoso family for a few weeks. When he began to notice that Pedro Hermoso spent considerable time in the woods behind his house, he followed him one morning and saw him go to a small windowless cabin in a tiny clearing. The door was locked with a heavy brass padlock. Intrigued, Wetzel watched from hiding as Hermoso went directly to a battered bucket lying on its side a few feet away. Rolling it a quarter turn, he picked up a key hidden beneath it, opened the padlock and entered the cabin, closing the door behind him. Hardly a minute later he emerged, locked the door, replaced the key where he had gotten it and rolled the old bucket back over it. Then he walked back through the woods to his house.

When Wetzel nonchalantly returned to the house a short time later, he found Hermoso preparing to leave. The old Spaniard told him he had to go into New Orleans but would be back the following day, and he hoped Wetzel would look after his family and home till he returned. Wetzel assured him he would.

Shortly after Hermoso left, Wetzel went back to the woodland cabin, got the key and went inside. It took him by surprise to see several neat stacks of Spanish silver dollars and a pile of unstacked coins on a table. He began to sense what was going on when he discovered a smelting pot and some bars of pewter. His suspicions were confirmed when he found several sets of dies for casting the silver dollars; only they weren't silver, they were pewter.

Lewis Wetzel had laughed aloud when he realized that his friend, Pedro Hermoso, was a counterfeiter.

He was still chuckling when he left the place, carefully locking the door and replacing the key in its hiding place before returning to the Hermoso house. He would not have been so amused had he seen his Spanish friend step out of the bushes as soon as he was gone and enter the cabin.

Late the following day Hermoso returned, but he was not alone. Accompanying him was a captain of the Spanish guard and several soldiers. Hermoso pointed out Wetzel and identified him as the man he said had given each of his little daughters a counterfeit Spanish dollar. As proof, he gave the two bogus coins to the Spanish captain. While the soldiers bound and held Wetzel, the captain made a search of Wetzel's small room and, in his pack, found several more of the counterfeit dollars and a pair of dies for making more. Wetzel was furious and told them about the cabin in the woods. The captain was willing to listen, and Wetzel led them there. The bucket was now standing beside the door, and the padlock was gone. Entering, they found only a chair and table. Hermoso told them this was where he skinned the animals he trapped and cleaned the fish he caught.

Wetzel was returned to New Orleans and taken before the Spanish magistrate. The trial, if such it could be called, was very brief. Counterfeiting was a very serious crime against the Spanish government itself and, with all the evidence stacked against him, Lewis Wetzel was sentenced to life imprisonment. He was taken to the prison on the outskirts of the city, and there—all his clothing but his trousers taken from him and his wrists and ankles shackled—he was confined in a damp, dim cell.

[*A u g u s t   1 ,   1 7 9 1 — M o n d a y*]

Maj. Gen. Arthur St. Clair was having a very difficult time putting together the army he had been ordered to assemble and lead this year against the hostile tribes. His trip east to recruit men and assemble them at Fort Pitt had scarcely had the result he anticipated. It had been gratifying insofar as his meetings with President Washington and Secretary Knox were concerned, but the promises and encouragement he received were not backed up by physical results. Not only were men failing to volunteer in the numbers expected, but his quartermaster corps continued to have grave difficulties getting the supplies requisite for such a campaign.

Toward the end of April, St. Clair had returned to Fort Pitt and placed the soldiers assembled there on flatboats and accompanied them to Fort Washington. The stops at Wheeling, Marietta, Point Pleasant and Maysville on the way down the Ohio had been disappointing, with only small numbers of young, inexperienced men eager for excitement and adventure coming forward and volunteering to serve in his forthcoming campaign. They had arrived at Fort Washington on May 15, and St. Clair, who had expected to find all the promised provisions and supplies awaiting him there, was sorely disappointed; there was practically nothing. He had expected to begin his campaign on August 1, but now that day had arrived and he was nowhere near ready to embark, nor did it appear he would be for some time to come, probably not until close to the end of October. His stream of letters to the east strongly stating the difficulties he was having elicited further promises but little else.

The Federal Board of War that had been created earlier this year for the defense of the Kentucky District had been the only real help, and now St. Clair was being forced to rely almost exclusively on the efforts of the members of that board, personally appointed by President Washington—Harry Innes, Benjamin Logan, John Brown and Isaac Shelby—to draft the men he needed. Most of those who were drafted, men such as Cornelius Washburn, were incensed at being forced to serve against their will, under penalty of imprisonment if they failed to comply. They felt it far more important that they remain in the border country, protecting their lands, families and neighbors from the continuing incursions of the Indians.

The fact that the campaign would be led by a general who had proven himself in battle, that the army was supposed to number 3,000 men and be well supplied with all their needs, including a dozen or more fine pieces of artillery, should have filled everyone with confidence. It did not. Instead, an uncomfortable aura of melancholy and foreboding prevailed that simply would not go away.

[September 16, 1791—Friday]

The assemblage of Indians who had gathered here on the Maumee at the mouth of the Auglaize was awe-inspiring to see. Many had come from hundreds of miles distant, and all were bristling with weapons, their medicine bags and paint pots filled and ready for application. There were the Shawnees and Miamis, of course, for whom this was home territory, but also there were Ottawas and Chippewas under chiefs Kasahda and Menetowa from as far north in the Michigan country as the great strait separating Lake Michigan from Lake Huron; Tarhe was here with his Wyandots from the Sandusky River and Tymochtee Creek, along with the Delawares under Pimoacan and Wingenund; Potawatomies in large numbers had come from villages on the Milwakee, the Checagou, Peoria Lake, the Illinois, Kankakee, St. Joseph and Elkhart rivers under chiefs Chaubenee, Siggenauk, Black Partridge, Main Poche, Gomo, Mtamins and Topenebe; Kickapoos were here from the Vermilion and Embarras rivers in the south-central Illinois country; Winnebagoes had arrived from the valley of the Wisconsin River, and there were the Sacs and Foxes from Rock River and the Mississippi; even a scattering of Iowas and Sioux were on hand from west of the Mississippi, and a few Mohawks and Senecas from near the head of Lake Ontario.

British agents from both Detroit and Niagara were present as well—men such as Alexander McKee, Matthew Elliott and the Girty brothers, Simon, James and George—who encouraged the Indians in attendance with word of a strong resurgence of interest on the part of the British in helping them.

That struggle shaping up was the reason these 3,000 Indians had come here. All knew by now of the singular victory of a relative handful of Indians against the ten-times-larger force of Americans under Gen. Harmar and how the Indians, against such terrible odds, had thoroughly humiliated the Americans and killed so many of them. And, just as they were charged with excitement over that tremendous achievement, they were angered over the recent sneaky invasions of more American forces under Gen. Scott and Col. Wilkinson, who had lured the warriors away so they could make war upon the women and children and old men left behind in the villages on the Wabash and its tributaries.

They had come to fight the Americans, all these red men, but their first order of business in this great council was to select those who should lead them against the army of Gen. St. Clair, which was now poised at Fort Washington to move against them. With all the notable chiefs on hand, it was no easy task, since many aspired to the reputation and influence that would be acquired by being named to such command.

For days the discussions had continued and, little by little, the field of those who should have the exalted role of command was narrowed. Finally it had come down to a choice between the Miami and Shawnee chiefs who had so masterfully beaten Gen. Harmar's army, Michikiniqua and Wehyehpihehrsehnwah—Little Turtle and Blue Jacket. Try as they might, they could not break the deadlock of choice between the two, and so, for the first time in the memory of any of them, they chose them both to serve equally as co-commanders. Tarhe was named as next in command, followed by Pimoacan and White Loon.

With the selections having been made, the British agents were given the opportunity to speak. Alexander McKee and Matthew Elliott orated at length on the recent division of Canada into what would hereafter be called Lower Canada and Upper Canada. Upper Canada—that area including the Great Lakes and westward, was now under command of a new white chief, Lt. Gov. John Graves Simcoe, who had already professed his interest in helping to repair the injuries the Indians had received at the hands of the Americans. In line with this, Simcoe had ordered construction of a new British post up the Maumee a little distance from Lake Erie, at the foot of the extensive Maumee Rapids. That post, in honor of the tribe that had so long lived on the Maumee, was to be called Fort Miamis—a post where there were arms and ammunition in abundance in the King's Store and a strong garrison of soldiers within its walls. It was to be built close to the ruins of the original old French fort of the same name. And though the British agents never really came out and said it in so many words, the strong impression was given that these materials and soldiers would be put to use to aid the Indians in their forthcoming struggle against the Americans.

The agents commended the Indians on their decision to join hands as brothers in the looming struggle, yet they continued to skillfully skirt the matter of active British involvement. When it came Simon Girty's turn to speak, however, he was brief in the extreme.

Standing silently before them for a moment, he suddenly reached into his pocket and withdrew an egg which he held up for all to see.

"This egg," he said loudly, holding it aloft, "will tell us where we go from here. Its whiteness represents the Americans at Fort Washington. The dark of my fingers represents the tribes gathered here. What will be the outcome when they meet?"

His grip on the egg tightened abruptly, and the egg was crushed in his grasp. The roar of approval from the assembled Indians lasted for a long time.

[November 4, 1791—Friday]

That Maj. Gen. Arthur St. Clair would have led his army out of Fort Washington at all, considering the circumstances, was little short of incredible. Everything indicated it was a huge mistake, a march that positively should not be undertaken. But the biggest mistake was the one that propelled the army into motion—the mistake of pride. Arthur St. Clair had always taken pride in carrying out the orders of his superiors, and those superiors wanted results, not excuses. Besides, in his book of conduct, it was only the most worthy of commanders who could carry out orders despite hardships.

Very little that had been promised to him, or that he had expected, had come to fruition. The force he started out with, instead of numbering 3,000 men, of which four-fifths should have been regulars, turned out to be only 1,400 men, with only 710 seasoned officers and men, the remaining 690 being volunteers with little or no experience. So few provisions had arrived that it had been necessary, on the first day of the march, to place the entire army on half-rations until an expected supply train could overtake them.

It was not unexpected that such a situation should have developed. As the summer dwindled away, week after week had passed without the expected men or provisions arriving and with the season for such a campaign to be initiated growing dangerously short. St. Clair's urgent dispatches to the east seemed to have little effect in hurrying things along, and the August 1 target date for the beginning of the campaign came and went while the army marked time. Delays continued, and St. Clair had finally decided that, come what may, he would set the army into movement on September 17. When that day came and the quartermaster had not come through, the army marched.

They had, in accordance with St. Clair's instructions from President Washington, paused first at the crossing of the Great Miami River 23 miles north of Cincinnati. Here the general ordered construction of the first of the string of forts he was to erect—this one to be named Fort Hamilton.[740] At this point, however, serious discontent had risen in the army, largely because of the near 500 camp-followers clinging to the army's coattails. Despite St. Clair's orders that they return to Cincinnati and wait there for the army's return, these wives, children and unattached women of the militiamen remained close. Since they had no real supplies of their own, they had to ask for handouts from their husbands, fathers and lovers who were already on half-rations. St. Clair's refusal to increase the rations to allow for this greatly enraged the draftees.

Building the new Fort Hamilton had consumed valuable time. It was garrisoned with a detachment of 23 men, and the northward march continued in weather growing progressively colder. Almost every day small numbers of Indians were seen observing them from a distance, but no skirmishes occurred. Nevertheless, the feeling grew among the men that if the Indians could scrape together even 500 warriors with which to engage them, this army could be in serious trouble.

After a march of 44 miles more, the army stopped at the junction of two inconspicuous little streams and, on October 21, began construction of a second fort in the string, this one to be called Fort Jefferson.[741] It was erected with greater speed than had Fort Hamilton, and the army was once again put into movement, leaving a garrison of 20 men behind. But then a major disaster struck. In a carefully concerted maneuver during the midst of the night, 300 of the militia deserted, and their absence was not reported to Gen. St. Clair until dawn, when they had been gone for six or seven hours. They had taken with them some 200 of the camp-followers. It meant that 500 very hungry people were on their own. Should they encounter the expected supply train St. Clair believed was attempting to overtake the army, it was likely they would ransack it of the goods destined for the army. Reluctantly, St. Clair ordered a detachment under Maj. Francis Hamtramck in pursuit, with instructions to arrest as many of the deserters as possible and escort the supply train to the army. Having lost 43 men in the garrisoning of the new forts, 300 in desertion and Hamtramck's pursuing detachment of 137 men, the army had been reduced to 920 men as it resumed its northward march.

At the same time, far to the north and east in their huge camp at the mouth of the Auglaize, the confederated Indians, bundled up in their blankets and heavy buffalo robes or greatcoats over their usual winter garb, awaited the command from Michikiniqua and Blue Jacket to begin their move against the Americans. Most expected they would be intercepting the army either farther up the Auglaize or just below the rebuilt Kekionga, depending upon what direction the American army chose to march. They were about to find out for sure. A council was called under threatening skies, and the 55-year-old Michikiniqua addressed them.

"My brothers," he said in a voice that rang clear in the crisp air, "our British brother, Simon Girty, told us a short while ago that he has seen many armies of brave warriors before, but never one so large and courageous as ours. To that I would add, never one so determined to crush the *Shemanese* who invade our lands and take away our women and children!"

A roar of approval erupted, and Michikiniqua let it die away before continuing. "In these weeks past," he went on, "we have sent out eyes to watch the movements of the *Shemanese* chief called St. Clair. Because of the courage and skill of the young Shawnee warrior Tecumseh, son of Pucksinwah, we have known each move of the *Shemanese* and their strengths and weaknesses. The protective hand of the Great Spirit has covered Tecumseh, for he walked among them, read their words and listened to their secret meetings without detection. He sent runners flying to us with all he learned, and we have been able to plan to meet the enemy. Now he has flown to us himself with the best words yet brought. He sits among us now, there"—he pointed toward the Shawnee contingent—"with his chiefs, Catahecassa and Wehyehpihehr-sehnwah, and I would ask him now to stand before you and tell you what he has learned and what we should now do, with which I am in full agreement."

Michikiniqua moved aside and sat down as the 23-year-old Tecumseh came to his feet and stepped to the place where Michikiniqua had stood. "Brothers," he said, "I bring news that will be short in the telling but immensely important in its mean-ing. The *Shemanese* general, St. Clair, was preparing to bring a force against us of three thousand soldiers, both Blue Coats and soldiers from across the Spay-laywitheepi. But his chiefs far to the east have failed him, and when he left Fort Washington, he had less than half the soldiers planned. His supplies failed to reach him, and so he marched with only half enough, and his men are hungry and discour-aged. He built two forts and had to leave men to guard them. Then, in the middle of the night, three hundred of his white chickens flew away, and so he sent half that many Blue Coats to chase them and bring them back and continued his own march north. He is now very weak, with just over nine hundred men—only a third part of the number of warriors assembled here."

He waited while an excited murmur rose among the assembled Indians and then died. "Brothers," he continued, "the Blue Coats he sent to chase those who fled from him may come back. The hundreds of other soldiers he expected may arrive at Fort Washington with the supplies and all these may be sent on to him. But they could not reach him as quickly as we! They move slowly, even when in haste, and if we ride against him now—this day!—we will find him still weak, still hungry and without defense in a place where the Wabash can be leaped across by a horse. We cannot afford to wait until they reach the place where Wehyehpihehrsehnwah and Michikiniqua defeated them during the last Harvest Moon. By then, his belly may be filled and his weak arms strengthened. No! Brothers, we must move to cut him off, *now!*"

War cries erupted from the Indians as they leaped to their feet in excitement over Tecumseh's words. There was a little more talk after that from the co-com-manders, but not much. Within four hours, their faces startlingly painted in red and white, yellow and black, the entire Indian force set out.

To the south and west, St. Clair's army, as weak and dejected as Tecumseh had pictured it, plodded on. The farther north it marched, the colder the weather be-came. During the first two days of November it snowed, and scouts came in with the disturbing report of greatly increased sign of Indians in the fresh snow. Finally, late in the afternoon yesterday, the army ground to a halt on the banks of the narrow headwaters of the Wabash River, 37 miles north of Fort Jefferson, only three miles east of the line separating the Ohio and Indiana territories.[742]

Only too aware of how exhausted, cold and hungry his men were, Gen. St. Clair announced they would establish a camp here and wait for the supplies to reach them before continuing, but, because of the fatigue gripping the army and the fact that it was already late in the day, they would postpone erecting any fortifications until the morrow.

The evening before, the Indians had arrived within three miles of this place and made their camp, carefully choosing a secluded spot. Their spies had reported that the path the army was traveling would lead them to the narrow headwaters of the Wabash exactly where Tecumseh had predicted and that they would arrive the next day. It was a cold camp the Indians had established, without fire, without food. The fast was upon them now, and they would not eat again until the battle had been fought.

Then the army of St. Clair had arrived, and the Indian spies had excitedly reported that something most unusual had happened. Always before, whenever the Americans had stopped overnight in dangerous territory, they had quickly raised a breastwork of logs and branches for shelter in case of attack. But this time the army was so weary and bedraggled, they had not done so. Even the wagons, which could have formed a bulwark of sorts behind which they could take cover if necessary, were simply left where they had stopped, in scattered fashion. The fatigued soldiers had all but dropped in their tracks. Some had built small fires, but most simply curled up on the ground beneath their blankets.

Word of the army's situation spread throughout the Indian camp, and a controlled excitement filled them. Many of the warriors, particularly the Winnebagoes, Kickapoos, Sacs and Foxes were eager to attack during the night, but Michikiniqua and Blue Jacket overruled them. "We must wait," Blue Jacket told them, "until the dawn. We are so many that if we try to attack them in the dark of night, we will hurt one another even as we try to hurt the enemy. Beyond this, at the dawn the *Shemanese* will be coldest and in least command of their wits, and their confusion will become our ally."

They had spent the night moving into position, stealthily forming themselves into a sort of horseshoe line a quarter-mile distant around the camp of the Americans, keeping to cover and staying out of sight, avoiding the open end of the horseshoe to the south simply because there was insufficient cover close enough for them in that direction. Even the huddled figures of the camp-followers were included within the formation.

Now, when it was yet two hours before dawn on this bleak, cold morning of November 4, with tiny stinging particles of snow still falling atop the half-foot of snow already on the ground, the Indians in the north part of the line, at the great bend of the horseshoe, became aware of an advance guard of sentries moving toward them, and they hunched down even more. Abruptly there was a brief rattle of gunfire from the whites as they shot toward a spot where no Indians were positioned. The discipline of the Indians was so well coordinated, however, that no answering fire was made. The whites clustered together for a moment, talking among themselves, and then they relaxed and turned back, convinced they had only been shooting at shadows.

An hour later, with dawn still an hour distant, a scout appeared to the general's aide and spoke briefly with him. The aide immediately entered the general's marquee tent and roused St. Clair, speaking to him in clipped sentences. At once St. Clair hurriedly dressed, pulling on his coarse capote and tricornered beaver hat. He ordered the army awakened and assembled at once and, as the runner sped away, the general nearly groaned aloud with the pain rolling in waves from his gout-afflicted feet. Then he stepped out of the tent, sword in hand, calling orders to various commanders to form their men, and the camp began to stir.

Three Ottawa spies, close in to the camp, inched back and raced to Michikiniqua and Blue Jacket with word of what was occurring—the *Shemanese* chief was moving among his men, long knife in hand, calling orders, and the men were rising. Still, it was too soon, and the Indians held their place.

In the American camp, as the very first tinges of cold, mean gray were beginning to lighten the eastern sky, the naked tree branches etching a network of crooked black lines against the ominous horizon, St. Clair was addressing his officers.

"From intelligence delivered to me during the night," he said, "I am led to believe that we will be attacked by the Indians today. Perhaps very soon. All men will see to their weapons at once. Artillerymen will position and load the cannons. Emergency fortifications to be erected beginning this moment."

The officers leaped to execute the commands, but it was already too little, too late.

"HAAAaaaaaahhh!"

The wild shriek of Michikiniqua's voice shattered the eerie stillness far to the left and was instantly echoed by a similar cry from Blue Jacket on the right. In that moment the entire Indian force erupted in a cacophony of hideous cries and plunged to the attack. Scarcely firing a shot, the forward guards on a low knoll north of the camp and on the opposite side of the Wabash abruptly panicked, threw down their rifles and ran for their lives back toward the main encampment, screaming in terror as

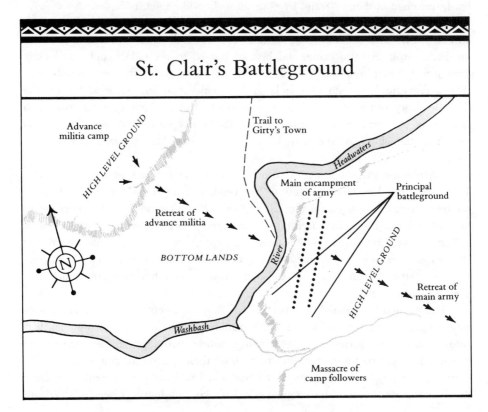

St. Clair's Battleground

Advance militia camp

HIGH LEVEL GROUND

Trail to Girty's Town

Headwaters

Main encampment of army

Principal battleground

Retreat of advance militia

BOTTOM LANDS

River

HIGH LEVEL GROUND

Retreat of main army

N

Washbash

Massacre of camp followers

they plunged across the narrow Wabash. Their panic was a contagion that swept across the entire army, and in an instant all was chaos. The white force milled about in a state of deadly confusion.

As the first of the charging Indians neared the stream, the Americans rallied enough to momentarily pour a hot fire toward them, but it was hurriedly made, ill directed and ineffective. The immediate return fire from the Indians was devastatingly accurate, and the withering blasts mowed down windrows of the soldiers.

Gen. St. Clair was screaming for the artillery to open fire, but the cannon powder was defective and packed in mislabeled kegs marked "For the Infantry." Only two of the eight pieces exploded, their charges misdirected, causing little harm to the attackers. The next moment the brunt of the Indian fire was directed at the artillerymen in a staccato din lasting a minute or two. When it was finished, all but a handful of the artillerymen were down, either dead or dying. Col. Gibson, artillery commander, was desperate in his efforts to bring the remaining few of his men together, his voice raised above the confusion: "Fight them! Fight them! Don't show fear—true Virginians never show fear. By God, I'd rather die a thousand deaths than let these damned savages take this field!" One death sufficed. At that moment a lead ball struck him between the shoulder blades and severed his spine.

The several remaining artillerymen continued to get off an occasional shot but with little effect. One by one the cannon were rendered useless by the defective powder that refused to ignite, and the frightened cannoneers fell back. Dangerously wounded, the only one of the three artillery officers remaining alive, Capt. Frederick Ford, screamed at them, "Stand by your guns! Die like men, not cowards!"

St. Clair was hobbling about painfully, calling for a horse. One was brought to him but, as he tried to mount, the animal was shot dead. Another was brought, with the same result. A third came, and he was helped to the saddle, but was luckily thrown free as that one, too, was killed. In the midst of all this, the din was unbelievable: a fantastic crescendo of shrieks and screams of anger, terror and pain, the terrible meaty thuds of war clubs against skulls, the crashing of rifles, the shrill whinnying of injured and panicked horses, the hoarse cursing of the soldiers who fought for their lives and the terrifying cries of the bloodstained warriors who took them.

Chaubenee, the young Potawatomi chief who was a close friend and admirer of Tecumseh, stayed as close to him as he could, hoping to protect him wherever possible, but it was difficult for him to keep up. The young Shawnee had become an incredible fighting machine, darting here and there, his blows with a war club rarely failing to crush the skull at which directed, leaping with amazing agility from one clash to another to engage in hand-to-hand battle. In the midst of it all, Chaubenee became separated from Tecumseh and concentrated thereafter on killing others and keeping himself alive.

Exasperated at his inability to get a horse, St. Clair hobbled off afoot. The troops were amazed and heartened to see him scrambling back and forth on his own legs among them in the hottest areas of the firing, calling encouragement and demanding perseverance, urging them to be steady, to hold their ground, to aim well, to make their shots count. He hardly noticed it when a ball whizzed past his temple so close that it took away a lock of his scraggly gray hair. He did, however, see Col. William

Darke and ordered him to lead his men in a bayonet charge at the greatest concentration of Indians. Darke instantly rallied his men and executed the order with great spirit, but the toll they paid was horrendous, and few survived the rain of war clubs and tomahawks.

Spying Col. William Oldham standing slack-jawed and wide-eyed beside a small tree, teetering on the brink of panic himself, St. Clair accosted him angrily and ordered him to lead a similar attack, but Oldham looked at him fearfully and shook his head.

"No, damn it, that's suicide. I won't do it."

"You'll do it, Colonel," St. Clair said coldly, raising his sword and leveling it at the officer's chest, "or by Christ I will run you through!"

At that instant a ball tore away the whole rear of Oldham's skull and he pitched forward, dead as he fell. St. Clair scarcely paused. Raising his sword high, he rallied Oldham's men behind himself and personally led a bayonet charge against the enemy on the left flank and momentarily repulsed them, again at a dreadful loss. Twice more he led similar attacks, himself unscathed while his men dropped in such numbers about him that there were soon not enough to mount further charges.

With prearranged calls that pierced the overriding din, Michikiniqua and Blue Jacket—the latter coated with blood but not one trace of it his own—drew a large portion of the warriors into a new assault wave, simultaneously hitting the rear and both flanks of the army, and the American dead were so numerous they fell upon one another. The attacks were parried by St. Clair's second-in-command, Maj. Gen. Richard Butler—formerly treaty commissioner for peace with the Shawnees at Fort Finney—on the right and Maj. William Clark on the left. Both counterattacks succeeded momentarily before giving way, but Clark took a tomahawk blow in the chest that pierced his heart, and Butler, four bullets in his body, leaned dying against a tree, with all but three of his men killed in the attempt to repulse the enemy. Two of these men half-dragged, half-carried him into the medical tent and left him lying on the ground. Surgeon Edward Grassen immediately began dressing his wounds, but only instants later a warrior plunged inside the tent and shot the physician. As the Indian then attempted to take Butler's scalp, the dying doctor snatched his gun and shot him. In seconds, all three men in the tent were dead.

Among the dozen British who had accompanied the Indian force, only the Girty brothers participated in the actual fighting. Clad and painted as Indians, they were unrecognizable as whites, and Simon alone had already killed six men with gun and tomahawk. The tallies of George and James were not far behind.[743]

The battle had by now been raging for the better part of three hours, and the snow underfoot had become a hideous red slush. Gen. St. Clair remained in the thick of the action, directing his troops and desperately attempting to quell the panic, his orders repeatedly being disobeyed or ignored by both regulars and militia. Encountering a group of six men clustered together weeping, he drew his pistol and ordered them back into the fight or he would kill them where they stood. Other small groups, paralyzed with fear, fell without resistance to the warriors who leaped among them. At last, however, the pain of his gout so severe that he was no longer able to walk, St. Clair was reduced to scrabbling about on hands and knees, still shouting orders and calling for someone, anyone, to get him a horse so he could direct the fighting properly. Finally, a recalcitrant, sluggish packhorse was brought, and the general was helped onto its back. Now at least he was mounted and could move about.

It was clear to the commanding general that if they were to avert an absolute massacre of the entire army, the only course remaining was to retreat—immediately. The remaining Americans who were still capable of fighting were now mainly clustered near St. Clair, attempting to find shelter behind dead horses, overturned wagons, even the bodies of their own companions.

Cupping his mouth, St. Clair shouted as loudly as he could, "Feint right! Feint right, then drive to the south—now!—retreat! *Retreat!*"

All the whites capable of doing so now rushed to the right flank, sending the Indians there reeling back, and then the troops veered sharply to the south, punching through the scattered Indians in their way and continuing as fast as they could go. But the organized retreat swiftly degenerated into a rout, with men trampling over others to gain the lead. Many dropped their weapons and even shucked off their greatcoats to make better speed, running with the breath of the devil at their heels. Some helped wounded companions along, but most of those who were hurt were left on their own to limp or hobble or crawl after them as best they could. St. Clair was among the last to leave who were capable of leaving. With no strong officer in front to control them, the rout continued unabated. St. Clair pounded the sides of his packhorse with his heels in an effort to regain the lead, but he could coax no more than a mediocre trot out of the animal. He called to those officers he saw to run to the front of the panicky men and gain control, but they ignored him.

Some of the Indians began to pursue, but a sharp, booming command from Michikiniqua stayed them, and runners passed his words to others elsewhere on the battlefield: "You must be satisfied—you have killed enough." Blue Jacket issued similar commands, and together the Indian commanders held their warriors at the scene of the battle. Sporadic shots and screams of the dying being tomahawked continued for a while but gradually diminished.

By noon it was all over, and no living Americans were left on the field. Those who had fled were no longer in sight. The scalping began in earnest then. Some of the warriors had scalped as they downed their foes, but others, such as Tecumseh and Chaubenee, had merely struck over and again. The horde of Indian women who had accompanied the warriors and had largely remained hidden in the woods during the battle emerged and joined in the business of scalping, gathering up weapons and equipment, stripping the bodies of coats, clothing and shoes, leaving them naked and bare-skulled on the stained snow. The eight cannon, too large to be taken along, were hidden for possible recovery later.

Michikiniqua and Blue Jacket ordered a careful search be made for any wounded or dead Indians. A total of 66 were found dead and gently wrapped in shrouding made from the army's abandoned tent canvas, then tied to horses to be returned to their villages or to a distant burial place. Only nine Indians had been wounded and, of these, just one seemed likely to die. By midafternoon, the whole force of Indians was moving off, the surviving packhorses staggering beneath the weight of the plunder they carried.

All the way back to Fort Jefferson, the shambles of the army ran, walked or stumbled as fast as they could go. Hardly a man among them wore clothing unstained by his own blood, and their wavering trail in the snow was that of some gigantic snake, hurt and seeking shelter. Near its tail rode Gen. St. Clair on a horse that walked slowly with its head near the ground, its body rippled with trembling, while the general himself hunched dejectedly in the saddle. His clothing and hat had been punctured by no less than eight bullets, yet he was himself uninjured.

The first pitiable remnants of the army began to arrive at Fort Jefferson about dusk, and the influx continued into the night. They were overjoyed to find that Maj. Hamtramck had returned with his regulars, but the elation was short-lived; not only had Hamtramck and his men failed to overtake the deserters, even though he had trailed them most of the way back to Fort Washington, they had not encountered the supply train or reinforcements, and so far as was known there were no supplies or relief on the way.

St. Clair called a council for his surviving field officers, Cols. Darke and Sargent, Majs. Hamtramck, Zeigler and Gaither. Both Darke and Sargent were seriously wounded but expected to recover. The six officers together concluded that the risks were simply too great to attempt to remain and try to hold on until the supplies came, if ever, and that they should leave here as soon as all the stragglers were in.

At the battlefield about this same time, as the dull gray persistent overcast deepened to the color of old lead with the approaching twilight, a new snowfall had begun that was quickly, mercifully, coating the reddened slush with fresh white and covering the ghastly, grotesquely contorted bodies of 832 dead American soldiers and camp-followers.[744]

At ten P.M., well after darkness had fallen, the army assembled in loose formation, wounded men on packhorses or carried on stretchers by companions, and started the long trek back to Fort Washington. The weight of their wounded was considerable, but not so heavy as the news they were bearing of the worst disaster ever to have befallen Americans at the hands of the Indians.[745]

Chapter 10

Maj. Gen. Arthur St. Clair's military career was finished. Much had happened during the eleven weeks that passed since his terrible defeat, not the least of which was a swift and vicious upsurge of attacks in the Ohio River Valley from above Wheeling all the way down to the mouth of the Ohio. Those who had felt that the Kanawha and its tributaries were now relatively safe to settle upon learned the error of such reasoning, and many were killed, while those who had eagerly been establishing themselves on the Ohio side of the river were paying a stiff price for the presumption that they could do so with impunity.

The Indians were taking few prisoners these days. Settlers who had come up missing were, more often than not, found a week or a fortnight or a month later in a decomposed state in some gully or ravine or creek bed within hailing distance of their own cabins. Frontier experience was no criterion for safety. Absalom Craig and Tobias Woods, for example, both were experienced and prudent woodsmen in their forties, and for five years they had run their trapline along Locust Creek, on the Kentucky side of the river 25 miles below Maysville, but late in November their scalpless bodies were discovered, and there was not a frontiersman along the river who did not shudder at the news.

The new ferry established by Thomas G. Lewis on December 9 at Point Pleasant, which crossed both the Ohio River and the mouth of the Kanawha, was kept busy for weeks bringing people and goods back across from Ohio to the Virginia side of the river, but Indians were everywhere on both sides of the river now, and those who ventured away from the forts, even in large groups, were in definite jeopardy.

The long-awaited supplies and reinforcements that were to have reached

St. Clair months earlier finally arrived much too late, and Fort Washington was continually being strengthened, as were Fort Hamilton and Fort Jefferson. A young ensign, newly commissioned by President Washington himself as a favor to his family, had arrived at Fort Washington at the head of 80 men not long after St. Clair's departure on his ill-fated campaign, and he was deeply disappointed in his misfortune at missing such an experience . . . until the battered remnants of St. Clair's army began showing up. It made him revise his sense of disappointment but only strengthened his belief that it was on this frontier that his future lay. The son of Benjamin Harrison, his name was William Henry Harrison.

He did, however, participate in the march headed by Col. James Wilkinson in January to return to the site of St. Clair's defeat and bury the dead—a grisly task that all the mounted men who participated found appalling. Hundreds of bodies and pieces of bodies were scattered all about, and it was a ghastly task to gather up what they could and bury the remains in a laboriously dug common grave. The weather was so severe that many of the men with Wilkinson's party were badly frostbitten by the time they returned to Fort Washington.

St. Clair, of course, had been generally condemned by practically everyone, not least of all by President George Washington himself, who was first informed of the terrible event early in December. When his private secretary, Tobias Lear, informed him in his office of the staggering defeat and handed him the express dispatches, Washington at first blanched at what Lear had told him and then became all but apoplectic as he hastily read the dispatches. Finished, he slammed them onto his desk and stormed about the office exhibiting an unbridled rage beyond anything Lear had ever before witnessed from the chief executive.

"Right here," Washington thundered to his secretary, "yes here, on this very spot, I took leave of him. I wished him success and honor. 'You have your instructions,' I said, 'from the secretary of war. I had a strict eye to them and will add but one word—beware of a surprise!' I repeated it— '*Beware of a surprise!* You know how the Indians fight us!' He went off with that, as my last solemn warning thrown into his ears. And yet!—to suffer that army to be cut to pieces, hacked, butchered, tomahawked, by a surprise—the very thing I guarded him against! Oh, God! Oh, God, he is worse than a murderer! How can he answer it to his country? The blood of the slain is upon him, the curse of widows and orphans, the curse of Heaven!"

Washington's tone and manner was so appallingly vehement that it actually frightened Tobias Lear, and more than once the President threw up his hands as he hurled imprecations upon the name of St. Clair. At last, however, his rage abated somewhat, and he sat down on a sofa, looked at his secretary and spoke in a more normal voice.

"This must not go beyond this room." He had then paused, steeped in thought for a long while as Lear stood waiting. When he finally spoke again, it was in a very low voice. "General St. Clair shall have justice," he said. "I looked hastily through the dispatches—saw the whole disaster, but not the particulars. I will hear him without prejudice; he shall have full justice!"[746]

Washington immediately sent orders for St. Clair to come to Philadelphia and appear before a congressional committee for a formal inquiry into the cause of the defeat. St. Clair did so, placing Fort Washington under command of David Zeigler, who had just been promoted to the rank of major. A few weeks later, however, Maj. Zeigler, too, was ordered to appear and testify, leaving Fort Washington in command of Lt. Col. James Wilkinson, the bitter foe of George Rogers Clark.

Even while the congressional committee was holding its hearings, Wilkinson took what steps he could to improve the security of the Ohio frontier. Even though his promotion to command of Fort Washington, instead of just command of the Second United States Regiment, was an upward step in his career, Wilkinson was disappointed that he had not immediately been named to command the Western Department of the Army.[747] He hoped to prove himself worthy of that post by the actions he was now taking. It was his belief that one of St. Clair's failings was that he had marched too far between each of the posts he had been erecting. Fort Hamilton and Fort Jefferson were still standing, but the two were 44 miles apart. Wilkinson now sent out Maj. John Gano, an engineer who had been with St. Clair at the defeat, with a strong force to construct a new fort at about the midway point between the two. Ens. William Henry Harrison of the Tenth Regiment was among the officers chosen to accompany Maj. Gano. The new fort was quickly erected and named Fort St. Clair.[748]

Throughout the east the public, now fully aware of the proportions of the great military disaster, was screaming for the hide of St. Clair, accusing him of cowardice, bungling and worse. George Washington, however, for all his initial rage, knew his old friend better than that and wanted the whole story of the cause of that defeat publicly told so the governor-general's name could be cleared of blame. The congressional committee's chairman was Virginia's James Giles, and he handled it fairly and well, with scores of witnesses testifying to what had occurred and impartial deliberations held in light of the testimony gathered.

Tempers flared during the hearings, and at one point Maj. David Zeigler, testifying on behalf of St. Clair, became so thoroughly disgusted and irked at the way his own character and that of Gen. St. Clair were impugned, as well as the general attitude of many congressmen toward the military, that he resigned his commission. Hardly less angry was Secretary of War Knox, who believed himself and his department severely injured by the hearing. He sent a harsh letter to Congress in which he declared the committee had done him an injustice. Endeavoring to be as fair as possible, the committee listened to Gen. Knox's statements and explanations, reconsidered the testimony accumulated and then today reaffirmed its first report, holding Knox and his War Department largely responsible for St. Clair's defeat.

The outcome of it all was a thorough report by the congressional committee stating that St. Clair had conducted his campaign with skill and great personal bravery and that the defeat was chiefly owing to the want of discipline in the militia and the negligence of the War Department, whose duty it had been to procure and forward the reinforcements, provisions and military supplies necessary for the expedition. They added that the army had been weakened by short allowances and desertion and by the fact that its finest fighting unit had been sent under Maj. Hamtramck in pursuit of the deserters. St. Clair, they added, against a force greatly superior to his own in numbers, with his own army in a state of panic, nevertheless had held the battlefield for an uninterrupted conflict of great intensity lasting over three hours, and that he had not ordered a retreat until the field was covered with the bodies of his men and further efforts were unavailing. Even then, the general had himself been last to leave the ground when the retreat was ordered. Finally, it was noted that "General Arthur Saint Clair still retains the undiminished esteem and good opinion of President Washington" and that, despite the prevailing public mood of condemnation and detestation, Gen. St. Clair "was not justly liable to much censure, if any."

It was an honorable acquittal of St. Clair but, exonerated or not, the damage had been done. Whoever again would follow into battle a man who had led his army into the worst defeat in the country's history? Though St. Clair would continue as governor of the Northwest Territory, he resigned his commission and would no longer command the military.

The question presently facing President George Washington was a knotty one: Who now should he name to take command of the United States Army and bring the savage tribes to their knees?

[June 1, 1792 — Friday]

There were few causes for joy in Kentucky since St. Clair's defeat, what with the sharp increase in attacks by the Indians and the resultant deaths, captures, burnings and horse thefts, but today was a distinct exception.

After more than seven years of effort, the news was exploding all across the Kentucky frontier: The cords that had so long bound this area to Virginia had finally been severed. Today Kentucky was admitted into the Union as the fifteenth of the United States.[749]

[June 18, 1792 — Monday]

Col. David Shepherd listened closely as Capt. Samuel Brady outlined his plan for a spying mission against the Wyandot towns deep in the Ohio country. Even under the best of circumstances, what Brady was proposing would have been highly dangerous. With the present dangerous situation that had been prevailing ever since St. Clair's defeat, it bordered on the suicidal.

Shepherd could not argue with Capt. Brady's logic that such a mission would not only provide them with extremely important intelligence, it might well light a fire under a government that was seemingly doing very little to aid settlers on the frontier; a situation on the upper Ohio, as well as everywhere else in the Ohio Valley, that had become desperate, even fairly close to Pittsburgh, Washington and Wheeling. Over recent months scores of settlers had been killed in boldly vicious hit-and-run attacks, with numerous cabins burned, dozens of horses stolen and an unprecedented number of women and children killed or taken captive. Those attacks were occurring in such profusion lately, and with such impunity, that a growing conviction had taken root among the border people that the United States government, now responsible for the protection of the settlers on the frontier, was intending to do very little to fulfill its obligations and resolve the situation.

In full sympathy with their plight and feeling much as they did, Brady had just finished telling Shepherd that unless it could reliably be shown that a major assault was actually in the offing against Fort Pitt or one of the other government installations, chances were that little was going to be done to alleviate the present situation. Brady felt strongly that the Indians were preparing for just such an offensive, and his proposal was that he go deep into their territory to seek confirmation of it.

"Even if I, personally, approved of what you have in mind, Sam," the colonel said, "I simply couldn't let you mount a big expedition when we need every man we have—and more!—to protect our people right here."

"I don't intend to mount a big expedition, Colonel," Brady objected. "Just myself and a couple of others for mutual protection and, if we're hit, for maybe one of us to get through to you with whatever intelligence we've found."

"You really think you can pull it off?" Shepherd asked.

"Dave, we both know that if anyone can, I'm the one." There was no bravado in the response, merely a statement of fact, which Shepherd acknowledged with a nod.

"Who would you take with you? And how long would you be gone?"

"Two of my Rangers—Johnny Wetzel and John Williamson. They're good men, dependable and sharp. We'll be back—at least one of us, if not all—by the end of a month."

Shepherd nodded again. "Then do it."

Brady grinned and started out, but he stopped at the door as Col. Shepherd spoke again. "Do me a favor, Sam. Try to keep your scalp intact."

[*J u n e   2 3 ,   1 7 9 2 — S a t u r d a y*]

President George Washington had no easy time of it in his efforts to appoint a successor to Arthur St. Clair as the new military commander in the west as well as commanding officer of the entire United States Army. The Congress had now appropriated funds for a new campaign to be carried out against the western tribes should the present peace overtures fail, but Washington had no desire to fit out an army of the same type that had already failed twice—an army of undisciplined militia. What was needed was an army gathered and trained in the strictest military discipline by an officer well skilled in matters military.

Washington had put a lot of thought into the list he had drawn up of 20 names of officers who might qualify for the position. This list, when presented to his Cabinet for comment, was quickly whittled away for a variety of reasons. Some, such as Maj. Gen. John Sullivan, who had so brilliantly executed the campaign against the Iroquois in 1779, were either now too old or too infirm to undertake such a huge responsibility. Others were drinkers, or they were unskilled when it came to Indian fighting, or their politics were not what was desired. Finally, there were those who simply declined. At last only one remained, and he was not considered any prize.

The individual in question had commanded a Pennsylvania battalion during the Revolution and had risen to the rank of brigadier general through his services, rendered successively at the battles of Brandywine, Paoli, Monmouth, Valley Forge, Stony Point and finally Yorktown. Though he had never been honored previously with an independent command of his own, he had proven himself to be a man of the type George Washington was actively seeking: a man who believed in strict discipline among the troops and who had shown himself to be prudent and dependable under all circumstances, as well as being somewhat of a thinker with a good grasp of military strategy. On the negative side of the ledger, he was a drinker, though not to excess, a womanizer in moderation, a man with a generally irritable disposition who did not get along particularly well with fellow officers, a man excessively vain, a man who, like St. Clair, was overweight and suffered chronically from gout.

The officer in question had retired from the military at the conclusion of the Revolutionary War, and his record as a businessman following the Revolution was not at all inspiring. He had made faulty business ventures in Pennsylvania that left him facing destitution and then had purchased a plantation in Georgia. He had moved there, only to very quickly go bankrupt. With creditors hounding him, he turned to politics and won the Georgia race for a seat in the United States House of Representatives, only to have that election overturned because of unproven charges of fraud. Yet, with the need for a commander imperative and the better choices now gone, George Washington had resignedly given in to acceptance of this individual, albeit so uncertainly that he wrote to a friend that he was "never more embarrassed making any appointment" and only hoped that "time, reflection, good advice and, above all, a due sense of the importance of the trust which is committed to him will correct his foibles, or cast a shade over them."

Bestowing upon him the rank of major general and placing him in command of the United States Army with instructions to immediately begin raising his army at Fort Pitt, President George Washington had, this past April, named as the successor to Arthur St. Clair, a man who had previously won such unflattering sobriquets as Mad Anthony and Dandy Tony—Anthony Wayne.[750]

Though President Washington had his own misgivings about naming Anthony Wayne to the top military post of the United States, some in the capital considered him the best choice the President could possibly have made. Among those—and greatly worried about the appointment—was George Hammond, British minister to the United States, who immediately wrote to the lieutenant governor of Upper Canada, Gen. John Graves Simcoe:

> *General Wayne is unquestionably the most active, vigilant, and enterprising Officer in the American Service, and will be tempted to use every exertion to justify the expectations of his countrymen and to efface the Stain which the late defeat has cast upon American Arms.*

So now the die had been cast, and the next step was for Gen. Wayne to begin gathering his army. The Congress was all too uncomfortably aware that, with the destruction of St. Clair's army, the total number of United States regulars in the west had dropped to only 750 officers and men, and the funds appropriated—$1,026,477.05—were specifically designated to raise, pay and equip a new United States Army of 5,000 regulars, of which "an adequate proportion" were to be assigned to Maj. Gen. Wayne and his second-in-command, the newly promoted Brig. Gen. James Wilkinson, for an expedition against the Indians of the Northwest. Wayne, as directed, immediately moved his headquarters to Fort Pitt to begin amassing a force of 2,500 men that Secretary of War Henry Knox had quickly dubbed the Legion of the United States. He arrived at Fort Pitt on June 14 and was saluted by a discharge of the artillery.

Wayne was given one year in which to build his army to its requisite strength and, during that interval, to mold the men into a strong, highly disciplined force. He meant to do exactly that, if at all possible. Yet already it was apparent that it was going to be difficult to raise the number of men authorized by Congress. Enlistments were very slow and practically all of the men who came were very young, hardly older than boys, seeking adventure or escaping from lives they simply didn't like.

Gen. Wayne was also informed that several different peace overtures were in progress with the western tribes and that should those efforts bear fruit—which all believed to be highly unlikely—Wayne's efforts at building the army might be largely in vain. In the meantime, however, to show the good intentions of the United States, it was imperative that during this interval of contact with the tribes, no offensive measures be launched by any force against them. It was Gen. Wayne's responsibility, therefore, to instruct all the various frontier county lieutenants of Pennsylvania, Virginia and Kentucky of this directive.

Because there were many similar letters to be written, Wayne kept the message brief and terse, beginning with the Kentucky counties in order to instantly forestall any plan the new State of Kentucky might have been harboring, now that it was no longer controlled by Virginia, to move against the Indians. His first letter was directed to Col. Henry Lee:

Head Quarters, Pittsburgh, June 23, 1792

Sir: The President of the United States has thought it proper to endeavor to come to some explanation with the hostile Indians in order to lead to such measures as will, eventually, be productive of a General Peace. In the interim, and until the effects of those overtures are known, it would be highly improper that any hostile attempts should be made against any of the Indian towns or settlements, however laudable that kind of zeal and enterprise may be in due time and season.

I am therefore ordered by the President, and I do hereby, in his name, most solemnly forbid and restrain any attempts being made against any of the Indian towns until the result of the aforesaid overtures for peace are known; but this restraint does not extend to prohibit the severest punishment against all hostile parties of Indians who may be found hovering upon the frontiers. You will, therefore, govern yourself accordingly.

[J u l y   1 5 ,   1 7 9 2 — S u n d a y]

The James Stoops cabin was on land that had originally been claimed by Brig. Gen. Edward Hand when he first came to Fort Pitt as its new commander in early 1777. Stoops had been, in fact, a private in Gen. Hand's Royal Irish Regiment and was one of several soldiers in the unit who had liked the wild beauty of the upper Ohio River area and decided to sink his roots there. Neither an adventurer nor a landclaimer himself, he had heard of Gen. Hand's extensive claims up Chartier's Creek and the fact that the general was willing to sell certain plots. When he applied to the general for this purpose, Hand told him where the lands were located from which he could choose, and Stoops had immediately gone there, liked what he saw and bought a small parcel only a few acres in size.

The land he chose was just a little less than three miles up Chartier's Creek from its mouth, on the east side of the creek and at the far end of a broad, slightly sloping bottom that angled gently upward from the creek for about a mile to the base of a steep hill. Stoops had built his cabin on that gentle rise, about three-quarters of a mile from the creek itself and some 65 feet above the stream. Directly behind the cabin a heavily forested hill rose steeply to a crest 140 feet above the cabin. It was a lovely location with a beautiful vista looking down over the sloping meadow to the creek and not really very far from Fort Pitt—six miles by water to the nearest point on Chartier's Creek and only a little over three miles by land, following the path going directly over the hills eastward.[751]

James Stoops and his wife, Jane, were among the very first settlers of the little Chartier's Creek Valley. For over 15 years they had lived in this cabin he built, gradually expanding it over the years to accommodate their steadily growing family, until now it was quite an extensive log house with six rooms and, close by, a cow barn and smaller attached milkhouse at a little spring, two smaller log sheds and a rather large outhouse. Even though, over the years, they had never been threatened by Indians, several attacks had occurred against settlers who had built their cabins close to the banks of the creek and, especially, those located closer to its mouth at the Ohio River.

Those years they had been here were generally good ones for James and Jane—Janie, as he called her.[752] When they had first come to this area and settled on the land, they had four young sons, and during the interval they had lived in this cabin, she had borne him 11 more sons and one daughter—a total of 16 children, making theirs among the largest single families in the entire Pittsburgh area. Ebenezer and Elizabeth Zane, who had thus far had 13 children, were acquainted with the Stoopses and jokingly said they kept trying to catch up to them, but the Stoopses always managed to stay ahead.[753] One of the eldest Stoops sons, who was a bit of a wag, made a remark that remained with the family through the years, saying, "There are fifteen brothers in the Stoops family, and each of the brothers has a sister."

Even in the worst of times previously, when Indian attacks had occurred with frequency and sometimes within a couple of miles or so of their place, the Stoopses had always felt themselves quite secure, and James Stoops was fond of lauding himself for having selected so safe an area in which to build a home. Yet, ever since St. Clair's disastrous defeat, a prevailing sense of apprehension had settled over the family. In the eight months since that defeat, the Indians had become extremely bold in their attacks, striking families practically in the shadow of smaller forts in some settlements and even on the very outskirts of some of the larger communities, including Wheeling, Washington and Pittsburgh. It was a very nerve-wracking time.

Yesterday, Jane Stoops was particularly nervous, as word had come early in the day that the John McCandless family, who lived along Chartier's Creek only three miles distant, had been attacked. McCandless was another of the soldiers originally of Gen. Hand's Royal Irish Regiment and a close friend of the Stoopses. Just after dawn, so the Stoopses learned, the Indians had attacked, and, while the McCandless family had been able to hold the attackers off from within their cabin and no one was hurt, their three horses had been stolen, their two cows and three pigs killed and the combined cow barn-stable burned.

For the first time since their departure, Jane Stoops was particularly grateful that all but one of her children were away. Four of the five youngest were presently in Pittsburgh, attending school, while the baby of the family, three-year-old William, was here at the cabin. The other 11 had all left here three months earlier on a very special trip that the family had discussed for many years—a trip to Mother Ireland, the origin of their parents, to stay for a year with close kin whom they might otherwise never get to meet and to experience for the first time their roots in the soil of King's County.

All through the day yesterday, after learning of the attack on the McCandless place, Jane Stoops had been very jumpy. Half a dozen times or more, while outside the cabin or when peering from the windows, she had thought she detected furtive movements in the woods or fields. Each time, she told James what she thought she had seen, and each time, when he looked, there was nothing.

"Ah, darlin'," he finally told her lightly, attempting reassurance, "t'is shadows ye're leapin' at, not Injens. The spooks have taken ye by t'hand, they have."

Despite his seeming nonchalance, James Stoops was also experiencing an uncommon case of nerves. Though he told himself it was silly and that there was nothing to fear, he had strongly barred the cabin door from the inside, as well as all the heavy wooden shutters, before they retired for the night. He had even reprimed his rifle and leaned it against the wall close to their bed, placing powderhorn and shot pouch close at hand. Jane Stoops's apprehension had lingered, and twice before midnight she had risen silently from their bed and, at different sides of the cabin, briefly opened a shutter and peered fearfully out toward the deeply shadowed woods and silvery meadow grasses beneath a ghostly three-quarters moon. Each time, although there was nothing to visibly alarm her, the fears persisted. Finally, however, she fell into a deeper, uneasy sleep.

It was three hours after midnight and two hours or more before dawn when the Stoopses were awakened by the sound of the cabin door being pushed against its bolting bar and then the heavier impact of something, no doubt a log, being smashed against it to break through. Indian voices could be heard outside, and to the din was added the cries of three-year-old William, who had awakened and was terrified. Jane snatched him up and held him close in her arms while James grabbed the flintlock and slung powderhorn and shot pouch over his shoulders. Then he shook his head and spoke grimly.

"We can't fight them off, lass. Too many. We'll have to try t'get out the back window and over the hills. C'mon. An' try t'keep William still, ye hear?"

They went to the rear window and, while the battering at the door continued, James cautiously opened the shutter, saw no one and then swung open the window. The Indian voices came more clearly now, but all from the front side of the house. James handed Jane the gun and stood on a chair that enabled him to squeeze through the small opening. He reached back in and took the gun from her, set it against the outer wall and leaned back to take little William. As Jane lifted him up, the child began to scream and she clapped her hand over his mouth, whispering to him urgently to be quiet. Again she tried to lift him, and again, as soon as her hand left his mouth, he shrieked. Once more she put her hand over his mouth, terrifying him even more, and now she shook her head.

"We cannot do it, James. They'll hear 'im, and for certain it'll be the end o'us. Go! Get away. Come back with help soon as ye can."

"No. I'll not leave without ye, Janie, nor without William. C'mon, lift 'im again."

She did so and instantly his cries erupted anew, and she stifled them. "James," she whispered urgently, "for the love o'God, *go!* Ye've got the youngun's in Pittsburgh t'think of, too, y'know. They've got to have *one* o'us, don't ye see? An' the others'll be back, too. William an' me, we'll hide in the 'tater hole an' could be they'll miss us. Come back with help if ye can. Oh, James, dammit man, *go!*"

With her free hand, she abruptly pulled the window closed and bolted it and then swung the shutter shut and locked it as well. James, with no choice remaining, groaned and snatched up his gun and raced off up the slope. In a clearing 70 feet over the house, he looked back and saw a half-dozen or more shadowy Indian figures still smashing at the cabin door with the log. He aimed and fired at them and saw them leap apart. Two instantly ran toward the hill in pursuit of him. He turned and raced away up the dark wooded slope, hearing again the battering at the door of the cabin just as he reached the crest.

Inside the cabin, Jane Stoops ran with William still in her arms to the main room and pushed aside the rocker over the two extrawide boards of the plank floor. She slipped her fingers into the slot and pulled upward, and both boards, attached to each other, came up as one, exposing the potato cellar—a cubicle compartment about four feet in each direction, empty at this time of year. The black hole yawning below frightened William as much as the window had, and try though she did to get him into the aperture with her, he fought and kicked and screamed in his terror, causing the Indians outside to redouble their efforts and making splinters fly into the room.

Realizing that even if she got into the hole with him and pulled the planks back over them, his cries would give them away, Jane ran with William to the bedroom, jumbled the coverlets together in a heap at the foot and pulled them over him.

"Darlin', darlin'," she whispered, "listen to me. Be a brave little man now and stop cryin', y'hear? Now ye've got t'lie still. Don't move, an' no sounds! Ye've *got* t'do this, William. D'ye understand, son?"

The little boy nodded and hid his face in the comforter as she covered him completely and then tossed a small pillow on the pile. Then she raced to the potato hole, lowered herself into it and pulled the pair of fitted planks over the gap just as the cabin door finally gave way and the Indians burst in. She heard the thudding of their feet as they plunged about above and the smashing of things being broken. Then came the sound she had most dreaded hearing. William suddenly screamed at the top of his lungs, and she knew they had discovered him. His cries became louder as he was carried into the main room, and she was terrified lest they kill him.

"No!" she cried. "Don't hurt him. Please, don't hurt my little boy!"

The sound of her voice stilled them as they peered about for its source. One who could speak broken English called out, "Woman! Where you are? Come out!"

Jane Stoops told them where to look, and they lifted up the floorboards and pulled her out of the hole. William, being held by one of the seven Wyandots, was whimpering, and they let her go to him and take him. Then, as one guarded her and the child, the other four plundered the house of all they felt was of value to them, gorged themselves on the food they found and then set the place afire. They led Jane, carrying William, to the milkhouse, where they drank deeply of milk from a container kept cool in the spring. Then they killed the cow, took the Stoopses' only horse and disappeared with their two captives in the darkness, the flames from the house lighting the predawn sky behind them.

[J u l y   1 8 ,   1 7 9 2 — W e d n e s d a y]

The mission to the Sandusky Towns undertaken by Capt. Sam Brady, Johnny Wetzel and John Williamson had not accomplished much, except for what one could read between the lines.

Wetzel and Williamson were both good men, and Brady was glad he had chosen them. Wetzel, at 22, had all the signs of becoming every bit as skilled a frontiersman as his brothers, Lewis and Martin, though he did not harbor quite the virulent hatred of the Indians that they held. Williamson was chosen not only because he was one of Brady's most experienced and trusted Rangers but because he had been part of Brady's party that set out to spy on the Sandusky Towns the first time, 12 years ago— a lifetime ago, it seemed.[754]

They had dressed themselves as Indians to give themselves an edge if detected, but the journey to the Sandusky Towns had been relatively uneventful. They had kept to cover as much as possible all the way and, though they had seen two small parties of Indians at a distance, they were not themselves seen. On the upper Sandusky they had spied on Half King's Town and were surprised and disappointed to find it almost devoid of men and the two trading posts on the other side of the adjacent fording place—John Leith's and Alexander McCormick's—both very quiet. Only a small number of women and children were on hand.

A similar spying effort seven miles farther downstream at Monakaduto's Town, close to the mouth of Tymochtee Creek, resulted in finding a similar situation: a good number of women, children and elderly men, but only a handful of warriors. They surmised the warriors were either off on raiding parties or attending a major council somewhere, probably the latter. In order to find out, they took a Wyandot woman captive and tried to question her.[755] Since she could not speak English and the three whites knew only a smattering of the Wyandot tongue, the questioning left much to be desired, but they gradually got the idea that a large council was being held at the mouth of the Cuyahoga. Knowing that that place had been a staging area for attacks in the past, they were half-convinced that a new strike was being organized there against the upper Ohio River settlements.

It was far out of their way to go to the mouth of the Cuyahoga and their supplies were inadequate for the journey, but they went anyway, taking the Wyandot woman along with them as a captive. Keeping to cover, they followed the trail leading to the Cuyahoga's mouth, but when they arrived there they found no one, not even any sign that a council had recently been held there. A war party of a dozen Wyandots was camped on the site, and Brady, Wetzel and Williamson observed them for a day, but they left hurriedly after their woman prisoner managed to escape during the night and disappear.[756] They were sure she had gone to the Wyandot camp and would tell them her story—including the fact that the three of them were dressed as Indians. That would instantly put the warriors on their trail. Brady decided it would be too dangerous to follow the Cuyahoga upstream to the carrying place and then to the Tuscarawas just above the ruins of old Fort Laurens, as this would be the most likely route to follow and the warriors might get ahead of them and set an ambush.[757] Instead, they headed southeast to strike the Mahoning, follow it to the Beaver and then downstream to Fort McIntosh.

Though they made it to the Mahoning, the journey had not been without problems. A party of warriors got on their trail—presumably those they had spied upon at the mouth of the Cuyahoga—and they had escaped them only after a long pursuit, in which they had plunged across numerous small streams. In the process they had lost what few provisions were left to them, along with their gunpowder, except for a single load still in Brady's gun, which he had managed to hold above the water surface.[758] Still a long way from home, they were now in desperate straits.

Without food for the past three days, Brady and his men made a small fireless camp on the Mahoning close to the Pennsylvania border, and in the morning Brady told Wetzel and Williamson to stay put in the camp while he moved out a little way to see if he could bring down something for them to eat.[759] It would use their last shot, but they would have to take the chance. However, he warned them, if anything went amiss, they were to separate at once and get back to the settlements on their own as best they could.

Brady had gone only several hundred yards when he heard a sound ahead. He crept up to peer through a screen of bushes. Five Wyandot warriors were approaching, the one in the lead riding a horse, the others following afoot. Brady took the situation in at a glance. The warrior who was riding had a small white boy in front of him, tied to him by a cord around the child's neck. He was also carrying a flintlock and had two powderhorns hung across his chest. Behind the horse walked a white woman, whose long skirt had been cut away raggedly just above the knees to facilitate better movement. Her legs were scratched and bleeding from where they had evidently walked through brambles. He recognized her as Jane Stoops, and the little boy was evidently her son.[760]

With scarcely a second thought, Brady raised his rifle and put his only shot through the riding warrior's head, tumbling him to the ground. The little boy, screaming in terror, was pulled off by the attached cord and fell on top of him. Brady instantly burst from cover, shouting loudly, "Get 'em, boys! Get 'em! C'mon, there's only four. Get 'em!"

The four warriors on foot behind Jane Stoops instantly leaped away into the woods, expecting attack.[761] The woman stood rooted in place, aghast at what had happened and at the sight of what appeared to be one Indian shooting another.

"Why have you shot your brother?" she cried.

"Mrs. Stoops," he shouted as he ran up to the dead warrior, "it's me, Sam Brady. Run! *Run!*" He reached for his belt knife as he ran to the screaming boy who was still tethered to the dead Indian, but the weapon was gone and there was no way to get the child free quickly enough. He tugged at one of the warrior's powderhorns, but a rifle cracked, and the ball sent up a spray of dirt close to his hand. He tumbled away, immediately regaining his feet. Another shot came and buzzed wickedly past his ear, and he turned and plunged away after Jane Stoops, again shouting loudly as he ran, "Fire, boys! Fire!" hoping it would be enough to encourage the warriors to stay hidden behind the trees for a while, hoping as well that his two men had fled at the sound of his shot and yells, which they were close enough to overhear.[762]

He overtook Jane Stoops quickly and grasped her hand, pulling her after him as rapidly as possible and using every stratagem he knew to throw the Indians off their trail when they took up pursuit, as he was sure they would. Brady and Jane Stoops thrashed down small streams, jumped from rock to rock, ran precariously along the trunk surface of fallen trees. Weakened as she was from having already been forced to walk so far, Jane played out quickly and began lagging. He jerked her along, coaxing, cursing, threatening, anything to keep her moving.[763]

At last, knowing she was soon going to collapse if they didn't stop, he led her into a well-hidden crevice among some rocks, and they huddled there. A little later they heard trailing Indians passing by close to where they were hidden, but they remained undiscovered and rested throughout the night. Yesterday, continuing down the Mahoning to Beaver River and down that stream to its mouth, they finally reached Fort McIntosh safely. Brady then took her by borrowed canoe to Pittsburgh, where today she was reunited with her husband, James, and her children who were there, though grieving for the loss of her little son, William.[764]

The story of the remarkable rescue of Mrs. Stoops was quickly on everyone's tongue, as was the fact that Brady, a fugitive from Pennsylvania justice, was back in Pittsburgh. The sheriff there raised a small party in an effort to arrest and hold him for trial, but he was prevented from doing so by a mob of residents who considered Brady a hero rather than a villain. Brady, for his own part, before returning to his own home near Holliday's Cove late today, sent a message to the sheriff that when he felt the time was right to do so, he would voluntarily surrender himself for trial.[765]

[*September 1, 1792—Saturday*]

Even while Maj. Gen. Anthony Wayne continued to assemble his troops at Fort Pitt and turn them into a well-disciplined fighting force, to eventually march them against the Indians, the government persisted in its efforts to bring the problem with the Indians to a conclusion through treaties of peace. Wayne was certain that any peace proposals the United States might make at this time were doomed to failure. He read the signs very well.

President George Washington was still doggedly clinging to the idea that he had presented in his plan to Congress nine years before, in which he stated that there was nothing to be obtained by an Indian war but the soil they lived on, which, he contended, could be obtained by purchase, bloodlessly and at much less expense than through war; a method that would be, as he put it, "the cheapest and least distressing way of dealing with them."

Twice now, sizable forces of the United States Army had been defeated by the Indians, and if it was possible to prevent a third tragic confrontation by the simple expedient of bringing the Indians to treaty councils, it was more than worth the effort. The fact that the emissaries who were already out had either disappeared or had been having only limited success at best was discouraging, but it was, so far as George Washington was concerned, worth continuing the effort.

The party of Iroquois that had been sent as emissaries among the northwestern tribes had come back with little of a substantive nature to report; only that the tribes were not truly inclined toward peace but had agreed that if the United States would relinquish their hold on the Ohio country and withdraw to the south and east of it, they would be willing to meet in council with an American delegation of treaty commissioners at Sandusky. That was hopeless news, of course, since there was no way Washington was going to order the settlers out of the Ohio country or agree to give back any of the Ohio Territory to the tribes and withdraw across the Ohio.

The delegation comprising William Smalley and Alexander Trueman had not been heard from since its departure and, though the worst was now feared, an element of hope still remained in the government that they were all right and would return with good news.

Seemingly the most encouraging prospect at the moment was that Gen. Rufus Putnam, at Vincennes, was meeting with Potawatomies, Kickapoos and Weas, and they seemed inclined toward peace. Further, George Washington had himself ordered Col. John Hardin of Kentucky out on a similar expedition up through the Ohio country toward Kekionga and Chalahgawtha to try to get the Miamis and Shawnees to listen to reason and stop waging a war that, despite their recent victories, they could not possibly win.

Where Col. John Hardin's efforts to get the tribes to agree to talks was concerned, he had ridden northward out of Fort Washington alone and had reached the west-central portion of Ohio, when he was met by two Indians who said they had been sent to escort him safely the remainder of his way on the journey to confer with Blue Jacket and Michikiniqua. One of the two was named Carrymaunee—Whirlwind—and the other called himself Little Blue Jacket. Promising Hardin they would reach their destination the next day, the three camped for the night. As soon as the officer was asleep, the two warriors silently rose up and buried a tomahawk to the hilt in Col. John Hardin's head.[766]

Gen. Rufus Putnam, who had been sent out under orders from Secretary of War Henry Knox, was at this moment being soundly duped. He was meeting at Vincennes, supposedly with representatives of nine western tribes, including a delegation of eight Potawatomies who represented themselves as being chiefs of their nation. In reality, none of the Indians in attendance had anything to do with tribal policy or any authority to sign any kind of agreements. They were merely common warriors and minor chiefs engaging the United States representatives in a well-executed hoax simply to get needed goods as gifts from the Americans. They eagerly signed the treaty papers Putnam presented to them and were given the supplies they wanted.[767]

Now, while continuing his army-building efforts at Pittsburgh, Gen. Wayne had learned about the brilliant spying and Indian-fighting abilities of Capt. Samuel Brady. He decided to attempt to induce him to join his army as captain of spies. Today Brady presented himself to the general and listened courteously to his proposal. When Wayne was finished, however, Brady shook his head.

"I appreciate your considering me for the job, General," he said, "but I can't accept. Not only do I not really wish to enter the regular service again, more importantly this frontier on the upper Ohio is still a long way from being safe, and this is where I am needed. However, I have an alternative suggestion: If you like, I will agree to serve as captain of your spies and train your men as best I can, strictly on a voluntary basis, as a civilian, until you leave with your army for Fort Washington or, if you stay on here longer than that, for three months—until December first. It's the best I can offer."

Gen. Wayne was perfectly aware that Brady's reason for not wanting to join this force in a regular capacity was true. That the Indians were still raiding throughout this country was well known. Six weeks ago a militia detachment at the village of Washington was fired on and, though no one was hurt, the commander there, Col. Absalom Baird, in his letter to Wayne had emphasized the distress of the inhabitants on this frontier and requested of Wayne more spies to patrol the upper Ohio as Brady's Rangers did regularly.[768]

Three weeks ago a 17-year-old named Matthias Dawson was taken while canoeing on the Monongahela above Fort Pitt. Then, only a couple of weeks ago Wayne had received a letter from Lt. R. S. Howe at the new settlement of Gallipolis, just across the river and downstream a little from Point Pleasant, relating the unpleasant news that a five-man scouting party had been waylaid by Indians and one man was captured, another shot twice and tomahawked but still living.[769] Obviously the danger Brady spoke of still existed all along the Ohio, and he truly could not be spared here.

So, while Brady's reply was less than Wayne had hoped, it was certainly more than he had any right to expect. Glad of any help his men could get from so renowned and experienced an individual, he smiled and extended his hand.

"I accept the offer, Captain Brady. Now let's get to work."

[*A p r i l   2 3 ,   1 7 9 3 — T u e s d a y*]

The pause made here at the little settlement of Wellsburg by Gen. Wayne and his army late in the afternoon of the day of their departure from Legionville was simply as an overnight bivouac before continuing the float down the Ohio River to Fort Washington. It came as an unexpected pleasure for Anthony Wayne to discover that Capt. Samuel Brady happened to be here with a several of his Rangers. The stop became even more enjoyable when Brady, with a definite twinkle in his eye, boldly stated that any two of his Rangers could outshoot a whole 100 of whatever men Wayne chose to select from his army of about 2,500. Smiling, Wayne accepted the challenge and suggested that they give the competition a little more flavor by wagering a keg of good-quality rum on the outcome.

Gen. Wayne was feeling much better now that he had his army on the move. Originally having planned to take the army down to Fort Washington late last fall, he had been irritated and exasperated when his full complement of recruits had not yet shown up, and then even the Ohio River itself had not cooperated: A hot, dry summer and lack of rainfall throughout the autumn had made the river unnavigable to the deep-drafted bateaux in which the army would descend the river, and they would have to wait for the higher waters in spring.

True to his promise to the President, Wayne had been very strict with his men from the beginning, officers and recruits alike, hammering discipline into them with an iron hand. One of his officers, Capt. Thomas T. Underwood of Petersburg, Virginia, had decided to keep a journal of his experiences and observations with the Wayne army, and among the first things he noted was Gen. Wayne's stringently enforced discipline. In his entry for October 26 he had written:

> *Pittsburg [sic]. I will name part of what took place the last few weeks. Captain Ballard Smith arrested for intemperance and tried by a General Court Martial, sentenced to be suspended for six months and then to take command of his company. Sergeant Trotter deserted Saturday night; was brought to camp Sunday one o'clock. Tried by a Court Martial and sentenced to be shot. He was shot the same evening on the grand parade. One of Captain Robert Campbell's troopers, by the name of Newman deserted. Brought back the 3d day. Tried by Court Martial and sentenced to be hanged. He was hanged the 4th day after the sentence passed on him. 8 or 9 of the infantry was tried for desertion and all condemned and shot, except for four or five deserters; these was pardoned by the Commander-in-Chief and joined their companies. We have just heard that Colonel Hardin and Major Trueman, two valuable Officers who were sent with a flag of Truce to the Indians, & both wontonly [sic] Murdered by the Indians.*

It had not been long before Gen. Wayne realized that the proximity of Fort Pitt to Pittsburgh, with its taverns, brothels and other distractions, was a very bad influence on his men and encouraged a weakening of discipline as well as an outbreak of venereal diseases. Since he could not move Fort Pitt away from Pittsburgh, he moved the men away from both. On November 1 he moved the entire army—now 1,000 men and still growing—into bivouac 17 miles down the Ohio on a high bluff with a level plateau 60 feet above the river on the right bank. Overnight the place became a sprawling tent city, the tents gradually replaced by wooden huts as quickly as lumber could be sawn. Wayne dubbed the camp Legionville, after Gen. Henry Knox's comment that his army was the Legion of the United States.[770] Here the drilling and discipline became even more stringent, and a strong guard was established that patrolled every inch of the perimeter 24 hours a day, with orders to perform as if hostile Indians might appear at any moment. Companies with meager provisions were sent out on forced marches in all kinds of weather to toughen the men and accustom them to discomfort and privation. At other times opposing forces were formed among the men to fight sham battles, with half of them dressed and behaving like Indians, the others as soldiers, the two forces alternating as the enemy. Bayonet practice and target shooting at ranges up to 50 yards were frequent, and all were required to participate. It was obvious to everyone that Anthony Wayne was molding a formidable army that would be far better than any force previously assembled to march against the Indians.

It was here that he met and accepted as his principal aide de camp an intelligent and obviously ambitious young officer who had just been promoted to lieutenant. His name was William Henry Harrison, and he had come upriver from Fort Washington with special dispatches as well as an oral report on that fort and conditions in the Cincinnati area. The fort, he said, was small and unequipped to handle a force as large as Gen. Wayne's army was growing to be. Numerous new settlements had been springing up along the Ohio River as well as along the Little Miami and the Great Miami as far upstream as Fort Hamilton. Cincinnati itself had grown remarkably and was, he regretfully reported, no less wild a town than Pittsburgh. Attacks on boats plying the Ohio, which had fallen off for a while, had increased again. And, he added, Indian attacks on the more outlying settlements and military detachments were still occurring with unnerving frequency and often devastating results. A Shawnee force had recently struck a military fatigue party out of Fort Hamilton that had been ordered by Col. Wilkinson to fell trees for logs to be used as an extension of that fort. Fourteen of the soldiers had been killed in the attack and numerous prisoners taken and tortured. Wayne shook his head, realizing only too fully how futile were the continuing attempts to come to some kind of agreement with the Indians, who were obviously now committed to fight until brought to their knees by force of arms.

Throughout the fall and winter Anthony Wayne was as hard on himself as he was on his men, pushing himself physically even more than he pushed them and then, in the evenings, staying up late in the night to read about the Indians and their culture or talk with men who had lived among or fought the Indians over the years, learning all he could about the enemy whom he would eventually engage in mortal combat.

He kept in close contact with the War Department, submitted regular progress reports to Gen. Knox and gradually imparted much of what he was learning about the inherent weaknesses of the Indians that could be exploited to the benefit of the army, such as their general disorganization and their unwillingness or inability, usually from lack of supplies, to carry out long campaigns. In this vein he wrote to Knox:

Permit me to choose the season for operations. Give me time to manoeuver and discipline the army, so as to inspire them with a confidence in their own prowess, authorize me to direct ample and proper magazines of forage, stores and provisions to be thrown into the advance posts at the most favorable and convenient periods. . . . Give me authority to make these arrangements and I will pledge my reputation as an officer to establish myself at the Miami villages, or at any other place that may be thought more proper, in the face of all the savages in the wilderness.

At Legionville, Capt. Underwood continued recording his impressions of what was occurring:

A suitable place being selected by Gen. Wayne to pass the winter, the army left Pittsburg [sic], and took up a position 22 [17] miles below Pittsburgh and on the north side of the Ohio on a high bluff, and 7 [8] miles above the mouth of Beaver Creek. The Commander-in-Chief calls this place Legionville. Our camp was fortified in a few days. The soldiers Huts was built in a few days. Then Gen. Waynes house & the Officers houses were put up. The Officers now commence drilling the Troops. They improve in decipline [sic] every day, and beyond All expectations. Gen. Wayne sent an invitation to Corn Planter [Warhoytonehteh] and New Arrow, two chiefs of the Six Nations, to meet him at Legionville. They both arrived 19th March accompanied by Big Tree and old Chief Guyasutha [Kyashuta]; during their talk with Gen. Wayne they insisted that the Ohio River should be the boundary between the White and Red People. The day the Great Chief dined with Gen. Wayne he [Kyashuta] pointed to the Ohio River and said, My heart and Mind is fixed on that River and may that Water Continue to run and remain the boundary of everlasting Peace between the White & Red People on its opposite Shores. The Quarter Master General is ordered to have flat bottom boats in readiness immediately to transport the Troops, baggage, military stores &c to Fort Washington.

Before leaving Legionville I will note several things that occurred. Captain Benj Price calling [challenging to a duel] Lt. Piercy [Percy] Pope, they met the next morning. The Captain was shot in the right breast and retired from the army. The worst duel that took place was with Lt. Daniel Jennifer and Ensign James Gapeway. The Ensign was killed and buried with Honours of War. Sergeant William Tarmir was tryed [sic] by a Court Martial for Forgery, found guilty and sentenced to run the gauntlet through the whole Legion, drummed out of camp with a labil [sic] on his forehead in large Capital letters. The Fatal effect of Forgery. Several Officers offered their resignations to The General. Every one was accepted by him. He has often been heard to say he does not want any officers with him without he had the most unbounded Confidence in him.

In the midst of all his drilling of troops and preparation for the eventual move out of Legionville and down the Ohio to Fort Washington, Wayne in no way lost sight of his obligation to protect the citizens and settlements along the Ohio. In this respect he wrote to Capt. William McMahan:

Head Quarters, Legionville, 5th January, 1793

Sir: The protection of the frontiers of Ohio County in Virginia & as far down as Muskingum is committed to your charge, for which purpose you will have under your command Captain [James] Crawford's Rifle Company & all the spies & guides of Ohio [County], & part of those of Washington County. Should those spies or guides neglect or refuse to obey your orders in patrolling or scouting, you are immediately to discharge them & appoint others in their places.

You will establish two stations, one at the Mingo Bottom, & the other at Wheeling—with patrols passing constantly between them towards Muskingum. These, together with the posts & patrols from Marietta & Gallipolis will afford effectual protection to the frontiers of Virginia, so as to preclude the necessity of State troops, which are absolutely a burden both upon the State & the Union.

You will keep me regularly informed of material information you may receive. You will clearly understand that no parties are to go into the Indian towns or settlements, or commit depredations upon them whilst the proposed treaty is pending. But should any party or parties of hostile Indians attempt to come into the settlements, or commit depredations, you are to punish them in the most exemplary manner for their temerity.

A. Wayne

Only yesterday, as his army prepared at last to embark downriver for Fort Washington, Gen. Wayne issued a proclamation that was copied and prominently displayed both at Legionville and in the various upper Ohio settlements. Though he was now certain the present efforts to come to some sort of agreement with the Indians would not bear fruit, he was nevertheless required to issue the statement:

A PROCLAMATION

By His Excellency, Anthony Wayne, Esq., Major General, and Commander in Chief of the Legion of the United States of America:

Whereas the President of the United States of America did nominate, and by and with the advice and consent of the Senate has appointed three Commissioners to hold a treaty with the hostile Indians at the Lower Sandusky on or about the 1st of June next ensuing, to endeavor to effect a permanent peace with those Indians,

And, whereas it would be highly improper that any hostile attempt should be made against any of the Indian towns or settlements whilst the aforesaid treaty is pending,

I am therefore ordered by the President, and I do hereby in his name, most solemnly forbid and restrain any attempts being made against any of the Indian Towns or Settlements until the result of the aforesaid treaty is known. Given under my hand and seal at Head Quarters, Legionville, the 22nd day of April in the Year of Our Lord One Thousand Seven hundred and ninety three, and in the 17th year of the Independence of the United States.

Anty. Wayne
By Order of the
Commander in Chief
Jn DeButts, A.D.C.

By the very first glimmering of dawn this morning, the army of 2,500 men had been afloat at last and heading toward Fort Washington. Now, late in the afternoon, Gen. Wayne came ashore for an overnight bivouac at the relatively new settlement of Wellsburg and was pleased at the growth of the settlement and the fact that Charles Prather had just established a ferry here as well as one at the mouth of Buffalo Creek. Indicative of the growth of civilization on this Ohio River frontier, Wheeling, he was informed, was no longer merely a large settlement; it had just officially become a town, with a number of streets constructed in regular fashion, and already 112 uniform lots fronting on those streets had been laid out by Ebenezer Zane. He was assured that Wellsburg would be doing the same very soon.[771] He was also delighted to discover that Capt. Sam Brady was on hand with seven of his Rangers—the brothers John and Abram Cuppy, Hezekiah Bukey, George Foulks, Thomas Dillon, James Downing and Thomas Edgington.

It had been in the course of their conversation that Brady had made his claim that any two of his Rangers could outshoot a whole 100 of whatever men Wayne chose to select from his army. Now that competition, with the keg of rum as a prize, was about to begin.

Using a tomahawk, a circular patch of bark about 20 inches in diameter was chipped off a white oak 80 yards from the firing line, and a black mark was made in the center about the size of a dollar. Brady selected, as his two shooters, Abram Cuppy and 'Ki Bukey, but he invited Gen. Wayne to have his men shoot at the target first—only one shot per man. One after another of Wayne's men fired their rifles, and observers near the target called out the result of each shot. Fully half of the soldiers did not even hit the tree. Of the roughly 50 shots that did hit the big oak tree, only a dozen managed to hit the white circular patch, not one within six inches of the black mark in the center.

Then little Hezekiah Bukey stepped up, took brief but careful aim and made his shot. The ball smacked into the tree inside the black mark but close to the edge and, when the result was called out by one of the observers, the men cheered lustily and Bukey grinned in a self-satisfied way. Gen. Wayne shook his head and remarked that it was quite a shot, but then John Cuppy stepped forward and smiled at Bukey.

"How come you was so far away from the middle of that there black mark, 'Ki?" he asked. "Reckon you're havin' a bad day."

Cuppy then raised his rifle and snapped off his shot at almost the instant the stock of the gun reached his shoulder. The observer ran to the tree and checked the mark, then called out that the ball had entered the black mark only half the diameter of the ball away from being absolutely dead center. Again a great cheer arose among the men and Brady turned to Wayne, grinning.

"Well, General Wayne, what could you do if you had a hundred men such as these two sharpshooters of mine?"[772]

"Captain Brady," the commander replied, "I'll tell you this—I wish to God I had five hundred such men, who could put a bullet in an Indian's eye at that distance. Why, with such marksmen as that, I could fight the very devil himself!"

[M a y   7 ,   1 7 9 3 — T u e s d a y]

The 2,500-man army of Maj. Gen. Anthony Wayne—the single largest body of men yet to descend the Ohio River—stepped ashore today at Cincinnati, exactly two weeks after having left Legionville. The town lay between the river and Fort Washington and, though the residents were overjoyed with the army's arrival, Wayne was not impressed with Cincinnati. It was every bit as rough and bawdy a community as Pittsburgh had been, though with fewer conveniences.

Fort Washington was much too small even to be considered as quarters for the army and, determined to keep his men as far away as possible from the brothels and taverns of the town, Wayne moved his force to the only broad, level treeless ground anywhere nearby, which was well beyond the fort, and gave orders for a permanent camp to be established. Since there was, in fact, no alternative place, Gen. Wayne, with the characteristic ironic humor he displayed in most situations, named the camp Hobson's Choice.

[M a y   3 0 ,   1 7 9 3 — T h u r s d a y]

An ugly mood had prevailed in Pittsburgh this past week, ever since Sam Brady had turned himself in to the sheriff to stand trial for murder.

The matter had all come to a head on May 18, when Allegheny County Sheriff Samuel Ewalt, acting on direct orders from Gov. Thomas Mifflin, arrived with a small posse of men at Brady's home. Unbidden, they entered the house with weapons leveled, only to find Drusilla Brady alone there with her two young sons, Van Swearingen and John.

"If you're seeking my husband," she said coldly, "you're looking in the wrong place. He's not in this house." She looked at the rifles they were holding, then back at the sheriff, adding, "However, if I'm the one you want, Sheriff Ewalt, you certainly don't need those guns. I'm unarmed and basically harmless."

Suddenly self-conscious, the sheriff lowered his rifle and set the butt on the floor, holding it by the barrel. He motioned for the others to do the same, and they obeyed. He shook his head and smiled a little sheepishly.

"Sorry, Miz Brady," he said. "You know Sam'n me are friends. It's just . . . well, I know what kind of man he is, and . . . well, ma'am, we was just keepin' ready. Man like Sam, y'know, we sort'a figgered he wouldn't let hisself be took very easy."

"You're right about that, Ewalt," said a voice at the door, and they jerked around to see Sam Brady leaning against the doorjamb, rifle held waist high and pointed in their direction. There was no levity in his voice. "Not much of a way for a man to act who calls himself my friend. You ought to know better than to come here and try to take me by force."

"Now, Sam," Ewalt protested, "I didn't have no choice. Had my orders right from Governor Mifflin."

"You had orders from the Governor of Pennsylvania to enter a man's house in Virginia and take him by force? You know I can't let that happen." Abruptly, he smiled wryly. "But I'll tell you what. I'm tired of this charge that's been hanging over me for two years, and I'd like to put it to rest. I'll let you and your boys go home in peace. You tell me when you want me in Pittsburgh, and I'll be there. I give you my word."

Ewalt nodded, relieved to let it go at that. "I want you in Pittsburgh in two days, Sam," he said. "C'mon, boys, let's go."

Word of what had happened flashed through the whole upper Ohio frontier with incredible speed. Sam Brady turned himself in to Sheriff Sam Ewalt as he had promised he would and was locked up in the combined jail and courthouse on the west side of Market Street.[773] The trial was scheduled to begin on Wednesday, May 22, and by that time more than 500 men from practically every settlement within 100 miles were on hand. Of that number some 200, led by Col. Samuel Wilson of Raccoon Creek, held a meeting on Grant's Hill in Pittsburgh and quietly passed a resolution among themselves: If Sam Brady were not honorably acquitted, they would tear down the jail and take him out, and woe betide anyone who tried to stop them. All of Brady's Rangers who were not off on patrol were on hand as well, equally determined to protect him, come what may.

Brady's father-in-law, Andrew Van Swearingen, had meanwhile scraped up $100 and sent his son, Ellzey, on horseback to Pittsburgh to hire a lawyer for Sam. The man chosen, James Ross, was a strong admirer of Brady, and he pledged to do his best to get him acquitted. In a short time another lawyer, David Reddick of Washington village, arrived to give support to Ross in court as co-counsel. Samuel Murphy stayed as close as possible to Brady and, in fact, breakfasted with him and Sheriff Ewalt on the morning the trial began.

The trial was presided over by Charles McKean as principal judge and two other associate justices. The two-story log courthouse on the west side of Market Street was so small that it could accommodate only a fraction of those who had come to attend and, as the trial progressed, there was standing room only inside and throngs of people constantly milling about outside. Judge McKean made it clear that he meant for order to be maintained. He also created quite a stir by charging the jury that if they found Brady guilty, his sentence would not be tempered with mercy, and if they did not come in with a guilty verdict, he would personally prevent the verdict from being recorded. This so angered the crowd that a riot very nearly broke out, and a voice in the crowd cried out, "You do that, McKean, and you're a dead man, by God!"

The chief witnesses for the state, John Hillman and William Wilson, maintained that the Brady party had, in an unprovoked and unwarranted manner, attacked the party of mixed Senecas and Delawares and cold-bloodedly killed them, but the testimony of the two men was contradictory, and they seemed very unsure of themselves and quite apprehensive because of both vague and direct threats from Brady supporters.

As the trial progressed, ever more men showed up on Sam Brady's behalf, and virtually every house from that of James Quigley, two miles from Pittsburgh, to the center of town was quartering armed men ready to go instantly to Brady's rescue if he were convicted. The trial itself was as much a testimonial to Brady as it was a hearing on the charge of murder. Witness after witness testified to how Brady and his Rangers had rescued their children or a wife or husband after they had been captured, of Brady's unstinting and arduous pursuits of war parties that had killed, plundered and burned and how, over these many years, he had been the prime protector on the upper Ohio frontier.

Among the many witnesses who appeared was old Kyashuta, the Seneca, who, approaching the witness chair, veered to Brady and took both of the accused's hands in his own. With John Gibson serving as interpreter for the court, Kyashuta continued to hold Brady's hands, looked earnestly at the judges and exclaimed in his own tongue, "This is a good man. He did not kill anyone who didn't deserve to be killed. They are saying the Indians killed were Senecas, but this I tell you, the Indians killed were none of my Senecas. They were bad Indians who did mischief on the frontiers wherever they could, and they deserved their fate. This"—he squeezed Brady's hands and held them up—"is a good man, and I hope you will not hurt him."

Several of Brady's Rangers also testified, among them John Cuppy, who related in a very thorough manner the events that led up to the Beaver Blockhouse Affair, beginning with the massacre at the Riley place that led to Brady's party taking up the trail after the perpetrators, following it by way of Sandy Creek to Beaver River and there discovering the camp of the Indians, which they subsequently attacked. Cuppy's testimony went far in aiding Brady.

A good bit of laughter occurred with the testimony given by a rough-hewn Irishman named James Griffith, who had actually witnessed the attack, telling the court that he happened to be at Beaver Blockhouse at the time it all happened.

"Sure, an' I was there the whole toime, don't y'know," he said, his brogue heavy and amusing to hear, "an' I seen the whole thing with one eye."

"One eye, Mr. Griffith?" interrupted Judge McKean. "Why not with both eyes?"

" 'Cause I ain't got but one eye, yer honor. Anyway, I seen it all; seen the Injens before they was attacked, an' heard the guns, an' then they began."

"Well," McKean put in again, "what was it they began?"

Griffith gave the judge a pitying look and snorted, "Bejaysus! They fired like hell and killed several of 'em, that's what."

The courtroom rocked with laughter, and there were similar outbursts as his testimony, consisting of about equal parts Irish wit and anti-Indian prejudice, described what had occurred, stating it with such hilarious descriptions that the whole court—jury, witnesses, defendant, lawyers, spectators and even Judge McKean himself—were convulsed with such laughter that McKean found it necessary to adjourn the morning session until after lunch.

Jane Stoops came forward to testify as a witness for Brady, stopping first at his chair and placing a flask of brandy and a pitcher of water beneath it for him. She touched his arm and smiled at him and then told in detail of his courage in attacking a whole party of Indians when he had but one bullet left, in order to rescue her, when he could just as easily have stayed hidden for his own safety and let the Indians pass with their captives. She had concealed a tomahawk in the folds of her dress before the trial and had announced to friends that she meant to "use it on somebody if Sam Brady's found guilty."

James Ross did the summing up for Brady and made a masterful job of it, lauding Brady's many years of service and self-sacrifice on behalf of the frontier people, his participation in a variety of dangerous campaigns, his rescue of numerous innocent victims of the Indians, his constant alertness to danger, the timely warnings he gave to the settlers, and the great and unstinting service performed by himself and his Rangers. In conclusion, Ross told the jury that for them to even consider punishing him for killing Indians shown to be hostile would be nothing short of monstrous.

The trial lasted four days, and when Judge McKean gave the jury their charge, those men did not even leave the courtroom, but simply discussed the matter quietly among themselves for less than half an hour before announcing to Judge McKean that they had reached a verdict. McKean directed Brady to stand and face the jury and called for their finding. Breaths were gathered and held, and there was barely a sound in the crowded room as the jury spokesman spoke.

"We the jury find the defendant, Captain Samuel Brady, on the charge of murder, and in view of the mitigating circumstances involved, not guilty."[774]

The courtroom went wild with cheers, and some of Brady's Rangers thumped him on the back as Brady shook hands with Ross and Reddick and thanked them for their good job of defending him. Then they all retired to the nearby Patrick Murphy's Tavern, Kyashuta accompanying them. When the old Seneca was asked why he had testified so strongly in Brady's behalf, Kyashuta said Brady was his friend, and he would have said anything, truth or not, to get him off—it was the end that justified the means—but, nevertheless, what he had said was truth.[775]

Now, at last, a whole flotilla of boats with flags waving and carrying some 300 people accompanied Brady back downriver, singing, playing music and at intervals firing a small swivel. The riverbanks at several places were lined with people who cheered lustily as they passed, and in the areas of Van Swearingen's Landing and Wellsburg, having learned of the verdict and Brady's pending return, several hundred people had come from miles around to join in the celebration of his return, playing music and firing their small arms and a booming blast of their cannon as the boats appeared. The salute was triumphantly returned by the boat party.

Drusilla Brady and her boys were on hand to greet Samuel as he stepped ashore. Brady smiled at her and said, "Well now, Dusy, I told you I'd be back." Their embrace was long and heartfelt and cheered greatly by the crowd—a gratifying close to a long ordeal.[776]

[August 9, 1793 — Friday]

Lewis Wetzel had now been incarcerated in the Spanish jail in New Orleans for just over two years. The confinement of his bold, free spirit had been very hard on him and he was gaunt, pale and haggard, a dismal shadow of his former robust, fierce and confident self. In recent months he had begun to realize that he actually might spend the rest of his life in this jail. He had not thought things could get worse, but he was wrong.

For weeks he had been working to escape, digging at the heavy three-inch-thick plank walls of his cell with a large spoon, whose handle he had laboriously sharpened on the stone floor. He had been overjoyed when he finally carved a hole all the way through, but his joy was short-lived when he discovered it opened only into an adjoining empty cell. Nevertheless, he continued to enlarge it on the chance that the door to that cell would be unlocked. Just as he had made the hole as large as his head, a new prisoner was brought in and thrown into that cell and the door locked. It was very dark in both cells, and after they had been left alone, Wetzel hailed the new inmate, who came close and put his face near the hole.

"Who is it?" the new prisoner asked. "Is there a way out of here? I have been thrown in here for making money in a way the government does not like."

Wetzel stiffened, thinking he recognized the heavily accented voice. Disguising his own, he asked, "What is your name?"

"Pedro," came the reply. "Pedro Hermoso. Who are you? How long have you been in here?"

"Two years, you son of a bitch!" Wetzel snarled and thrust the sharpened spoon through the hole with all his strength. The point caught Hermoso high in the cheek, drove through skin and tissue and emerged just in front of his ear. Hermoso screamed and reeled back, jerking the embedded spoon out of Wetzel's grasp and then lurching to his cell door, where he beat upon it with his fists and continued screaming.

The guards came quickly, took Hermoso away and then threw Wetzel, wholly naked, into a dungeon that was dank, windowless, stone-walled and less than half the size of his previous small cell. He didn't really care. His regret was not that this had happened but that his weapon had not entered the eye and penetrated the brain of the man who was responsible for his being here.

[September 15, 1793 — Sunday]

The months of treaty negotiation with the Indians had now come to a deadlock, and there was only one recourse left: Maj. Gen. Anthony Wayne should launch his campaign against the tribes at once.

It was not a decision the President and War Department had wished to make. The United States Treaty Commissioners—Timothy Pickering, Beverley Randolph and Benjamin Lincoln—had undergone many hardships and weeks of unsatisfactory meetings throughout the summer.[777] When first they had arrived at the western end of Lake Erie, escorted by British representatives, a massive council of some 2,400 confederated Indians from 16 different tribes was in progress on the lower Maumee River, at the mouth of Swan Creek.[778] The American commissioners asked to be allowed to attend that council and address the tribes, but they were not permitted to do so, the British being fearful the American emissaries would be hurt or killed if they appeared there. Instead, they were taken to the residence of Indian agent Matthew Elliott, near the mouth of the Detroit River, and kept there for over a month in relative comfort and safety while a stream of messengers passed back and forth between them and the Indians, who were counciling under the direction of Elliott's superior, Col. Alexander McKee.

The American commissioners had received instructions from the government to conclude the negotiations by the first of August, so that if no satisfactory agreement had been reached, there would still be time for Gen. Wayne to push forward his campaign against the Indians while the weather remaining in 1793—during September, October and November—would allow him to do so. However, after weeks of delays and inconclusive talks at Elliott's place, the three commissioners were finally taken by boat to the British Fort Erie, on the west side of the Niagara River, for a more formal conclusion of the talks.

Those talks and the messages preceding them had begun poorly and continually degenerated as time passed. The Indians first questioned why, if the Americans truly wanted peace, there was now an army of soldiers on the Ohio River near the mouth of the Great Miami, preparing to attack them. The commissioners replied that Gen. Wayne's army, in its encampment at Hobson's Choice, was there solely for defensive reasons and that so long as there remained any possibility of concluding a peace between the tribes and the United States, that army would take no offensive action. To that, the Indians replied that they had their own army of spies on the Ohio and knew all about what Wayne was doing there. They believed their spies far more than they trusted the words of the commissioners, who, the chiefs pointed out, made a habit of bending the truth whenever it was of benefit to them to do so.

Dropping that subject as quickly as possible, the commissioners then got into the matter of the concessions the United States was now willing to make to bring about peace. For the first time they admitted that the American government had erred in its initial belief, following the Treaty of Paris, that because they had defeated the British, they had also defeated the tribes and had thus rightfully acquired the Indian lands through conquest. The United States government now realized, they said, that the various Indian tribes were sovereign nations, undefeated and unsubdued, and that the lands north and west of the Ohio River were theirs. They confirmed the invalidity of previous land agreements made by them with the British as well as with the Indians and gave their word that any future agreements would be made with the tribes who rightfully owned the land, in which negotiations the United States would be honest in its bargaining and would be willing to pay amounts for the land that would be more than fair.

To prove their faith and good intentions, the commissioners went on, the United States was now willing to withdraw from the Ohio country and cede to the Indians all their claims of lands there except for the British posts the Americans had won, including those they were not yet occupying, such as Niagara, Detroit and Michilimackinac, as well as certain designated sites in the area of Cincinnati and along the Muskingum and Scioto rivers, where rather extensive tracts had come into possession of land developers and were already so heavily populated by Americans that it would be prohibitively expensive and inappropriate to make any effort to remove them. However, they added, the United States government was willing to compensate the tribes for these lands already occupied by paying to the tribes who had owned the lands an initial outright sum of $50,000 and an additional perpetually continuing sum of $10,000 per year. In return for this, all the Indians had to do was live in peace with the settlers already on the lands and those on the American side of the Ohio River.

Alexander McKee, continuing to act as adviser to the Indians and as translator, helped the Indians with their response to the American offer. It took another fortnight to frame the written reply in a manner agreeable to all the tribes represented. This document was presented by McKee to the United States commissioners on August 15. After a few preliminary remarks, the document continued:

> *You agreed to do us justice, after having long and injuriously withheld it. We mean in the acknowledgement you have now made that the King of England never did, nor ever had a right, to give you our Country by the Treaty of Peace, and you want to make this act of Common Justice a great part of your concessions and seem to expect that, because you have at last acknowledged our independence, we should, for such a favor, surrender to you our country. Money, to us, is of no value and, as no consideration whatever can induce us to sell the lands on which we get sustenance for our women and children, we hope we may be allowed to point out a mode by which your settlers may be easily removed, and peace thereby obtained. We know these settlers are poor or they would never have ventured to live in a country which has been in continued trouble ever since they crossed the Ohio; divide, therefore, this large sum of money which you have offered to us, among these people, and we are persuaded they would most readily accept it in lieu of the lands you sold them. If you add, also, the great sums you must expend in raising and paying Armies, with a view to force us to yield you our Country, you will certainly have more than sufficient for the purposes of repaying these settlers for their labor and improvements.*

In carefully constructed sentences, the reply went on to state that the Indians simply would not give up any of the Ohio lands, including those upon which American settlers had now already made improvements.

Although this was not the sort of response the commissioners anticipated or wanted, it gave the Americans what the President would now be able to portray as a just reason for launching Wayne's campaign to bring the Indians to their knees.[779] The commissioners, having missed the August 1 deadline for concluding the talks, finally received instructions and replied to the Indians in a terse message that chided them for their refusal to be reasonable in view of the concessions the United States was willing to make and concluded with:

> *We sincerely regret that peace is not the result; but knowing the upright and liberal views of the United States which, as far as you gave us an opportunity, we have*

explained to you, we trust that impartial judges will not attribute the continuance of the war to them.

By then it was the end of August, and the commissioners sent a coded message to the secretary of war that said they had failed to effect a peace treaty. Henry Knox immediately sent express dispatches to the governors of Pennsylvania, Virginia and Kentucky to inform and warn them. His message to Gov. Thomas Mifflin of Pennsylvania set the tone for all three letters:

War Department September 3, 1793

Sir,

> *I am intrusted by the President of the United States to state to your Excellency that information has this day been received by express that, notwithstanding the utmost efforts of the Commissioners, the pacific overtures to the hostile Indians north of the Ohio have been rendered abortive by their insisting upon the Ohio as a boundary.*
>
> *That the Commissioners arrived at the mouth of the Detroit river on the 21st of July, and waited there till the 17th Ulto. when, having received the definitive answer of the Indians, the Commissioners sailed for Fort Erie, where they arrived the 23 ulto.*
>
> *The Commissioners were not even admitted to an interview with the body of hostile Indians, but the communications were carried on by deputations from them.*
>
> *It appears that the tribes most determined for War are the Wyandottes, Delawares, Shawanese and Miamis, although it is said a considerable proportion of these were for peace.*
>
> *It is understood that the six Nations, including Captain Brandt and his Mohocks, strongly urged the hostile Indians to make peace with the United States.*
>
> *Affairs being thus circumstanced, it is probable that the sword only can afford ample protection to the frontiers.*
>
> *It is understood that the Militia embodied on the frontiers of Pennsylvania, under your orders, together with the patrols called Scouts, are deemed sufficient for their defence. But it may be proper to caution the people immediately, that every measure necessary to guard against surprise should be adopted.*

> *I am, Sir, with great respect,*
> *Your Obedient Servant,*
> *H. Knox*

News of the failed peace talks reached Gen. Wayne on September 11 but did not surprise him. He had been receiving irregular reports from a spy who had been in attendance at the Indian councils on the Maumee as they were negotiating with the commissioners through deputations, so he actually knew more about what went on in that major council than the commissioners themselves, Henry Knox or President Washington. Practically coincident with the news of the failed treaty talks, his spy reported to him, and Wayne personally took his deposition in secret. As soon as this was finished, he at once he wrote out a detailed report based on that spy's report of what had occurred in the Grand Council and sent it on September 15 to both the President and the secretary of war:

N. Western Territory

Personally appeared before me a certain ——— ———, *aged twenty-four years, born in the State of Pennsylvania on the Monongahela and employed as one of my Emissaries at the private council of the hostile Indians lately held at the Rapids of the Miami of the Lake; who deposes and saith that he arrived at the Rapids on the 10th day of July last, where he sat in Council with the hostile Indians, being adopted and considered one of them.*

That he was captured by the Weeaws [Weas] at 14 years of age and has resided with them for 9 years; and has frequently been passing from Post Vincennes into the Indian Country; that he went with a message from General Putnam last fall as far as the Rapids to invite the hostile Indians to a treaty.[780]

At his arrival on the 10th of July last at the Rapids of the Miami [Maumee] there were about 1,400 Indians assembled, and continued to arrive daily until about the 20th, when they amounted to 2,400, eighteen hundred of whom were warriors.

That they continued to council daily until they sent their Order, to the Commissioners to go home, that they would not treat with them; that they then continued to meet in Council daily for ten days after they had sent that message to the Commissioners.

That they demanded the Ohio as a boundary and in their private conversation they also said they ought to be paid for all the lands in the State of Kentucky.

That Simon Girty sat constantly with them as one of the Council—that Governor Simcoe's aide-de-camp and a Lt. Silvy of the 5th British Regiment, and one other British Officer, with Colonel McKee, remained in Colonel McKee's house at about 50 or 60 yards distant.

That every night several of the principal head chiefs—particularly the Shawanese and Delawares—used to meet in private council at McKee's house with the aforesaid aide-de-camp and British Officers.

That Colonel McKee always promised that the King, their Father, would protect them and afford them every thing they wanted in case they went to war, such as arms, ammunition and provisions at that place; but that they must come there for it—that he could not carry it any farther. That they ought not to make Peace upon any other terms than to make the Ohio the boundary line; but to defend their lands at all events, and that the King, their Father, would not suffer them to be imposed upon.

That Colonel McKee furnished the whole of the Indians with arms, ammunition, scalping knives, tomahawks, as soon as the treaty was over and promised them clothing when they wanted it. That the supply of ammunition was very abundant, even more than they could use this winter. That the arms furnished were partly rifles and partly fusees; the rifles carried an ounce ball and have three sights behind, two to lift up in proportion to the distance at which they fire: that the chiefs were furnished with horseman's swords and pistols.

That the number of warriors who would immediately operate against the

Legion would be about 1,500, provided the army moves with rapidity; but if they advance as slow as they did in the campaign of 1791, the Indians will certainly collect to at least 2,000 warriors; they appear to be confident of success.

That the Indians separated on the 28th ultimo, and were to assemble again at Auglaize twenty-five days from that time, in order to operate as circumstances may then be, i.e., to watch the motions of the Army and wait a favorable moment to strike.

Signed ———

Sworn before me this 15. Sept. 1793
Signed Ant. Wayne

Extract

It was now being left to Gen. Wayne's discretion as to whether his army was adequately prepared to undertake the campaign against the Indians on the Maumee this fall. So far as the discipline he had wrought in his force was concerned, he had no doubt they were ready for such an enterprise. The principal drawback, however, was the same one that had plagued Gen. St. Clair two years earlier: Promised supplies had not been delivered by the contractors—whom he suspected of corruption—and he had no intention of making the same mistakes St. Clair had made by pushing ahead in spite of such difficulties. So, in his communications to the President and secretary of war, he announced that he would move his army forward to an advanced post, where he would continue to drill and train his men, and it would be from there, when fully supplied as necessary, that he would launch his campaign against the Indians next year.

[December 4, 1793 — Wednesday]

The family of four remained standing at the grave for a long while after the others had gone, the dismally overcast skies and chilling rain adding to the depth of their sorrow. Samuel Brady was one of those four, and he thought again of the many years he had known this man who now lay beneath the soil at their feet and how instrumental he had been in the settlement and development of the upper Ohio country; a man who had hoped he would live to see peace come to the Ohio Valley, where boats could safely ply the waters of the great stream without having to carry men armed with rifles to protect themselves and others aboard, a time where settlers no longer had to fear being attacked in their homes and fields. Unfortunately, he had not lived to realize that dream, but Brady was determined to continue doing his part to make the dream become reality. These days, for the first time in about two decades of vicious conflict between Indians and whites in the Ohio Valley, he was becoming optimistic that such a reality was at last almost within their grasp.

Although attacks by small war parties of Shawnees, Delawares and Wyandots had continued this year all along the Ohio River, especially from just below Pittsburgh at Raccoon Creek to the Falls of the Ohio, they were much fewer in number and severity than previously. The reason, Brady believed, was that the presence of Gen.

Wayne's army in Ohio was worrying the Indians considerably, and they were spending a great deal of time and effort studying the American army commander in an effort to discover whatever weaknesses he might have that they could exploit when they finally clashed.

Where previously the attacks had numbered in the scores over the period of a year, with hundreds of people killed, wounded or captured, innumerable cabins plundered and burned and great numbers of horses stolen and livestock killed, this year the gruesome totals had diminished dramatically. That was not to say they were absent or that the problem was wholly resolved; scattered attacks still occurred. John Craig had been killed while tilling crops near Point Pleasant, and, in that same area, Joe Burwell and Andy Lewis had been shot in their canoe and both seriously wounded, Lewis with an arm so badly bullet-damaged that it had to be amputated. Peter Smith had been captured near the Falls of the Ohio, and William Fuller near North Bend in the Cincinnati area.[781] Near Maysville, just a couple of weeks ago, a party of Indians crossed the Ohio on a horse-stealing mission and got quite a few, but they had the misfortune of being pursued by a scouting patrol under Simon Kenton. The intrepid frontiersman and his men overtook the Shawnees on December 2 near the mouth of Holt's Creek, 32 miles below Maysville. In the resultant skirmish Capt. William Hardin was wounded through the body, but Kenton's party killed six of the Indians, scattered the rest and recovered all the horses.[782] In the Cincinnati area, Peter Cox was tomahawked and scalped while out looking for his horse, and at the nearby White's Station a party of Shawnees struck, killing Andrew Goble and two of Moses Pryor's children—five-year-old John and his infant brother, William. The worst attack during the year had occurred only six weeks ago, on October 17, when 250 Shawnees led by their war chief, Blue Jacket, struck a United States Army supply train of 100 mounted riflemen. That attack occurred between Fort Hamilton and Fort Jefferson, just seven miles east of Fort St. Clair, at a place that was called the Forty Foot Pitch; Lt. John Lowry and 14 regular army privates were killed.[783]

Brady and seven of his Rangers—John and Abram Cuppy, Jacob Wetzel, William Clark, Tom Deloe, Alex Mitchell and John Williamson—had, as recently as September, pursued a party of five Wyandots that had stolen a pair of fine horses from the James Caldwell place, just above the mouth of Raccoon Creek. With the news that the treaty talks had failed, the Rangers were now free to pursue the Indians across the Ohio and had done so, penetrating 100 miles into the Ohio country and finally overtaking the raiders as they camped on the headwaters of the Cuyahoga River. In their attack they killed one of the warriors, recovered the horses and also took a good bit of plunder, including a number of steel traps made in England.

Nevertheless, the overall number of attacks this year had dropped remarkably, and Brady, with far fewer fights and chases to occupy his time, finally gave in to his wife's wishes and moved away from the cabin his father-in-law, Andrew Van Swearingen, had long ago built for them on the Ohio a mile above Wellsburg. Their new residence—a much better and more spacious dwelling—was located just over two miles from the bustling new town of West Liberty, itself some five miles up Short Creek from its mouth at the Ohio, and about midway between Wellsburg and Wheeling.

They had made the move, with the help of Drusilla's father, only a month ago, and now they were very glad to have been able to spend that time with him, since just two days ago Andrew Van Swearingen had unexpectedly died. He had been one of the original pioneers on this frontier, first settling here in 1772, and, as he was known and respected by a great many in this area, his funeral had been attended by a substantial number, despite the inclement weather that prevailed.

Now, all the words of sympathy had been extended, and everyone was gone from the gravesite but the four of them, Samuel and Drusilla Brady and their two little sons—six-year-old Van Swearingen and three-year-old John. They stood beside the grave, looking down at the rain-dampened words that had been hastily chiseled into the slab of limestone that served as his marker:

> *Here Lieth the body of*
> *VAN SWEARINGEN*
> *who departed this life*
> *on the 2d day of December, 1793,*
> *in the fifty-first year of his age.*[784]

"He was a good man and a wonderful father," Drusilla murmured, her tears now gone and just a deep ache and emptiness remaining.

Brady nodded and squeezed her arm, which was linked in his. "Yes, he was, Dusy. He so much wanted peace and a safe life for his daughter and grandsons. I think before long his wish will come true."

[D e c e m b e r   3 1 ,   1 7 9 3 — T u e s d a y]

Many of the Indians who had gathered on the Maumee River, particularly Michikiniqua, had become very apprehensive about the new American war chief who was preparing his army to come against them. Though they had spied on him closely from the time he arrived at Fort Pitt, during his stay at Legionville and down the Spaylaywitheepi to Fort Washington, they had discovered he was a man of great vigilance who did not leave himself or his men open to attack.

They had watched while the white chief, Gen. Wayne, moved his army during the Harvest Moon to Fort Hamilton. He had not been content to remain there long, and he moved his force first to Fort St. Clair, then on to Fort Jefferson, where he had arrived with them on October 26. When he found that fort too small and badly placed for defensive measures, he had immediately pushed his troops on another six miles and began construction of a much better fort that he was now calling Fort Greenville.[785] That fort had been completed just two weeks ago, and it became apparent that the white chief was making it his headquarters and the winter quarters for his whole army.

Leading a large force from his army, Wayne moved on to the site where these Indians had so devastatingly defeated the army of Gen. St. Clair two years previously.[786] The next day they spread out and gathered the bones remaining above the ground, including some 600 human skulls, then buried them all in the same grave.

Their search allowed them to discover two of St. Clair's cannon hidden under a large log, and two others in a deep hole of the Wabash River headwaters. These were immediately sent to Fort Greenville. Wayne then built a fort on the site and named it Fort Recovery.[787] As soon as it was completed, the commanding general left 150 men to garrison the place and returned with the remainder to Fort Greenville where, on his return, he was saluted by the very cannon he had recovered, the artillery having been cleaned and mounted on new gun carriages.

The confederated Indians who were gathered on the Maumee discussed all these developments with great gravity. Obviously, this Gen. Wayne was preparing to lead his army against them next spring or summer, and they must prepare themselves well to meet such a dangerous foe. Once again they called for Michikiniqua and Blue Jacket to lead them against him. They were shocked, however, when Michikiniqua refused to accept the leadership. Immediately charges were made by other chiefs that he was becoming old and tired and turning into a coward. Michikiniqua listened to the charges being hurled at him in the Grand Council, and then he raised his hands. As the assembly gradually quieted, he addressed them calmly and with solemnity.

"We have beaten the enemy twice under separate commanders," he told them. "We cannot expect the same good fortune always. The Americans are now led by a chief who never sleeps. The night and day are alike to him, and during all the time that he has been marching on our villages, notwithstanding the watchfulness of our young men, we have never been able to surprise him. Think well of it. There is something whispers to me that it would be prudent to listen to his offers of peace."

Other chiefs spoke after Michikiniqua, and the decision remained to meet the Wayne army and fight it. Michikiniqua bowed to their decision and told them he would fight, if that was their desire, but that he would fight only as chief of the Miamis, not as the commander of the confederated Indians. So now they had accepted this and named as their sole commander the Shawnee war chief who had been Michikiniqua's co-commander at St. Clair's defeat, Wehyehpihehrsehnwah—Blue Jacket.

[M a y   2 7 ,   1 7 9 4 — T u e s d a y]

Despite the fact that the Ohio River had become much less dangerous for travelers and a new era of river travel had been begun, it was a serious mistake to consider it safe.

True, the Indians were deeply engrossed in watching the continual buildup of Wayne's army at Greenville and planning their strategy for how and when they would engage him, but numerous raiding parties were still moving about close to the river and occasionally striking. As a result, it did not pay to get careless, as was the case with the Mann brothers, William and Thomas.

There was good reason to think the troubles were over, principal among which were two important new ventures in regard to river travel. Though irregular commercial traffic was already moving up and down the Ohio, now a regular mail service had been inaugurated between Pittsburgh and Cincinnati by an intrepid young man named John Green, who traveled in a large piroque, sometimes alone and sometimes with a small crew, sometimes carrying freight or passengers, but always adhering closely to his schedule, which itself engendered a sort of normalcy to river travel.

Even more conducive to a false sense of security, regularly scheduled packet boat trips on four keelboats of 20 tons each had been inaugurated in January between Pittsburgh and Cincinnati, promoted as "convenient" and "with no danger to be apprehended" by passengers. The fare for the one-way trip of 463 miles was still five dollars, but the passenger had to pay extra for food and liquor. Those who had not enough money were permitted to work for their passage. Merchandise or other cargo was still being carried at the rate of five dollars per ton. The service had begun with a major advertisement that appeared in the January 11 edition of the first regular newspaper of the far west, the *Centinel*, published in Cincinnati by William Maxwell:

OHIO PACKET BOATS

Two boats for the present will start from Cincinnati to Pittsburgh and return to Cincinnati in the following manner, viz: First boat will leave Cincinnati this morning at eight o'clock, and return to Cincinnati so as to be ready to sail again in four weeks from this date. Second boat will leave Cincinnati on Saturday, the 30th inst., and return as above. And so, regularly, each boat performing the voyage to and from Cincinnati once in every four weeks. The proprietor of these boats having maturely considered the many inconveniences and dangers incident to the common method heretofore adopted of navigating the Ohio, and being influenced by a love of philanthropy, and a desire of being serviceable to the public, has taken great pains to render the accommodations on board the boats as agreeable and convenient as they could possibly be made. No danger need be apprehended from the enemy, and every person on board will be under cover made proof to rifle ball, and convenient port holes for firing out. Each of the boats is armed with six pieces, carrying a pound ball; also a good number of muskets, and amply supplied with ammunition, strongly manned with choice men, and the master of approved knowledge. A separate cabin from that designed for the men is partitioned off in each boat for accommodating the ladies on their passage. Conveniences are constructed on board each boat so as to render landing unnecessary, as it might at times be attended with dangers. Rules and regulations for maintaining order on board and for the good management of the boats, and tables accurately calculated for the rates of freightage, for passengers and carriage of letters to and from Cincinnati to Pittsburgh; also a table of the exact time of the arrival to and from the different places on the Ohio between Cincinnati and Pittsburgh, may be seen aboard each boat and at the printing office in Cincinnati. Passengers will be supplied with provisions and liquors of all kinds, of the first quality, at the most reasonable rates possible. Persons desirous of working their passage will be admitted on finding themselves subject, however, to the same order and directions from the master of the boat as the rest of the working hands of the boat's crew. An office of insurance will be kept at Cincinnati, Limestone and Pittsburgh, where persons desirous of having their property insured may apply. The rates of insurance will be moderate.

With such improvement in river travel and the lessening of Indian attacks along the great waterway of the Ohio, it was not unexpected that some people would grow overconfident. Two such were the unruly young brothers of Capt. Moses Mann, who were in his company at Point Pleasant. Lt. Col. Daniel Boone was second-in-command there now, under Col. Thomas Lewis—his plans to go to Missouri still pending—and in assigning detachments to regions of defense in the area, he named Mann's company to the defense of the nine-year-old Belleville settlement, 62 miles up the Ohio River.

The company, having arrived at Belleville, found everything calm and no report of Indians having been in the area for a considerable while. With time weighing heavily on their hands, William and Thomas Mann, having today off-duty, decided to go by canoe to a nearby salt lick along the Ohio shore to hunt deer. At the edge of Belleville, they passed the attractive young Scotswoman Mary Galrooth washing clothes at the river's edge, her husband, Thomas, asleep in their cabin a short distance up the bank. The pair veered their canoe in close to her and deliberately splashed water on her with their paddles. Bitterly berating them, she retaliated by swinging the wet clothes she was washing at the river surface and sprayed water all over them.

"Why, you bitch!" William bellowed, thrusting the canoe toward shore, Thomas helping him. Mary began running away, but they beached the canoe and ran after her, catching her in a few yards. She struggled and tried to scream, but they subdued her, covered her mouth and dragged her back to the river. Wading out waist deep with her, they repeatedly dunked her, holding her head underwater so long that she thought they were going to drown her. She was semiconscious when they finally pulled her back to the shoreline and dumped her on her back in the mud, her legs still in the water.

The Mann brothers then returned to their beached canoe and launched it as Mary Galrooth unsteadily pulled herself back to her feet, gagging and crying. They were a dozen yards from shore when Mary recovered enough to yell after them.

"You miserable devils!" she cried. "I hope to God the Indians kill you and you never return!"

Laughing and making lewd remarks about her, the two young men continued paddling toward the lick, hardly a quarter-mile distant. As they nosed their canoe in to the shore, a party of five Delawares stepped into view from behind trees at the salt lick and, before the brothers could pick up their rifles, shot both of them dead, William tumbling into the river and Thomas into the canoe.[788]

So despite the fact that the Ohio River had become much less dangerous for travelers and a new era of river travel had begun, it was a very serious mistake indeed to consider it safe.

[*July 3, 1794 — Thursday*]

It was now three years that Lewis Wetzel had been incarcerated in the prison at New Orleans. For six months after stabbing Pedro Hermoso with the sharpened spoon, he had been kept in the dark and dank solitary confinement of the tiny, stone-walled dungeon. As the cooler weather had set in last fall, he had been given a blouse and trousers to wear and a thin, tattered blanket to roll up into for sleep.

Day and night were practically the same to him in the windowless cell, and so when he was finally transferred out of the dungeon cell and into one that was similar to that which he had first occupied, he had no idea of how long he had been in the dungeon. He was sure it must have been at least a year, possibly two. The new cell, however, was more open, had a barred window overlooking the prison yard and was close enough to other cells that he was able to communicate with the men in cells on both sides and across from him. It was in talking with them that he learned the date was February 1794, which meant his stay in solitary confinement for the attack on Pedro Hermoso had been only six months. It had seemed so much longer!

Now it was July, and over these three years in prison he had been out of his cell only once. That had occurred four months ago when, during the night, there was a large fire in the city and the prison was threatened, at which all the prisoners had been led out under a strong guard, prepared to move them away if it became necessary. A shift of the wind, however, had pushed the fire away from them and, after only an hour of breathing the wonderfully fresh air, the prisoners had been herded back toward their cells.

It was then that a commotion had arisen in the prison yard some distance from where Wetzel was, and some shooting. Word spread among the inmates that a half-dozen prisoners had made a break, overpowering a guard and scaling the wall. One had been shot and killed, but five had managed to get away in the darkness. It took several days for word to filter through the inmates who the men were. The names of five, including the man who had been killed, meant nothing to him, but the sixth man was Pedro Hermoso. Wetzel gnashed his teeth at the injustice of the man responsible for his being here having gotten away. He vowed that somehow, someday, he would encounter the man again and, when he did, he would kill him.

Today, for the first time in these three years, he had a visitor. Unable to fathom who it could possibly be, he was taken from his cell to a room where the visitor waited to speak with him. He turned out to be a nice-looking man in his midthirties, clad in a good suit and a shirt with ruffled collar and cuffs, a string tie at his throat. On first glance, Wetzel thought he seemed vaguely familiar, but it was not until the man smiled and stepped forward to shake his hand that he recognized him.

"I don't know if you remember me, Mr. Wetzel," he said. "I'm David Bradford. You've been a hard man to find."

Wetzel remembered now. This was the man who had been the rival of Sam Brady for the hand of Andrew Van Swearingen's beautiful daughter, Drusilla, and who had subsequently lost her to him practically on their wedding day—a matter that had been talked about on the frontier for weeks at that time. Wetzel nodded and smiled faintly. "So why have you been looking for me in the first place?" he asked.

Bradford explained that when it became known on the upper Ohio that he, Bradford, was making a trip to New Orleans, he had been approached by Wetzel's brothers and some of their friends with the request that he ask around and see if he could discover what had happened to Lewis. No word of any kind had been heard from him since he announced he was going down the Ohio to see what New Orleans was like.

They talked for over an hour, Bradford telling him of the difficult trail he had followed in tracing Wetzel's moves and finally learning he was in prison here, then filling him in on all the frontier news, especially the fact that Gen. Wayne was preparing at this very moment to meet the Indians head-on in their own territory, and expectations were keen that he would whip them. Wetzel, in turn, told him more details of how he happened to be here, of Pedro Hermoso having framed him for counterfeiting to protect himself from the same crime, of how he had tried to kill Hermoso in the adjoining cell, his subsequent six months of solitary confinement in the dungeon, and with special bitterness, how Hermoso had escaped several months ago.

"It is tragic that you're in this place, Lewis," Bradford said at last, preparing to leave. "I'm going to see what I can do to get you out. As you know, I'm a lawyer and have some connection with certain people here in the judicial system and with a few of the higher-placed Spanish authorities. I'll try to get an audience with the governor and see if I can convince him to give you a pardon. It may take a while, but don't give up hope."

"I ain't had much of that t'give up," Wetzel said, then added after a brief pause, " 'til now."

[*J u l y   5 ,   1 7 9 4 — S a t u r d a y*]

The 1,200 confederated Indians under Blue Jacket, who had been camped at the area called Fallen Timbers, had long been chafing at the delays in attacking Gen. Wayne's army. They had been camped for a long while in this area of fallen and tangled trees—the result of a tornado that had cut a swath through the forest a quarter-mile wide and a mile and a half long, just up the Maumee from the British Fort Miamis—and had been wildly happy at last when word was passed that they were moving out to strike.[789]

Word had come to Blue Jacket that Gen. Wayne was preparing to move out of the sturdy headquarters fort at Greenville to the smaller installation called Fort Recovery, at the site of where the Indians had defeated St. Clair. How ironic and satisfying it would be, he thought, to be able to defeat a second United States army on the same spot.

However, when they arrived near Fort Recovery late on June 29, the Indians were greatly disappointed at discovering that not only was Wayne still securely in his fort at Greenville with his army, but that only a few hours before their arrival, a large supply train from Greenville carrying 1,200 barrels of flour under an escort of 140 soldiers had arrived safely at Fort Recovery.[790] The only good news brought to Blue Jacket by his spies was that the same military escort was preparing to lead the 300 load-free packhorses back to Greenville the next morning and would be vulnerable to a well-planned ambush. Those 300 horses could become a very welcome addition to the Indian force.

Studying the situation, Blue Jacket quickly called a council of the chiefs and came up with a good plan. They would make no move against Fort Recovery itself since, though small, it was too well fortified. Instead, they would wait until the packhorse train had moved far enough away from the fort to be cut off with no chance of retreating there. That attack on the military escort would be made by the Shawnees, Miamis, Delawares and some of the Potawatomies, with the object being to kill as many of the soldiers as possible in the first fire and then concentrate on catching the horses. At the same time a large contingent of Ottawas and Chippewas, other Potawatomies and a few Wyandots would remain hidden close to the fort out of firing range and wait till they heard the fighting at the packhorse train break out. At that occurrence, it was highly probable that a company of soldiers from within the fort would charge out to assist those being attacked. The force of Indians close to the fort were to wait until the reinforcement passed and then plunge in behind and cut off any attempt to retreat back into the fort.

It was a good plan that would have undoubtedly been remarkably successful had the Indian contingent near the fort not disobeyed Blue Jacket's orders. At seven in the morning the gates opened and the packhorse train emerged, and it was escorted by a good number of soldiers, but not the 140 anticipated. The Indians close to the fort expected to see the gates closed as soon as the packhorse train departed, but they were amazed when they were left open and, without informing Blue Jacket, they altered their own plans, deciding to strike the fort itself and try to gain entry.

Blue Jacket's force attacked the packhorses and escort when they were just reaching a woodland a mile from the fort. Close to half the escort fell, killed or wounded, at the first onslaught and, as the terrified horses galloped off away from the fort, Blue Jacket's force pursued, then quickly disappeared from sight of the fort.

The other Indian contingent plunged toward the fort and all but collided with 50 mounted dragoons emerging at a gallop to aid the escort. There was great turmoil as the dragoons wheeled about to thunder back through the gates and collided with 100 infantrymen also emerging at a run to help. In the great confusion four or five officers and many soldiers were killed by gunfire from the approaching Indians, and the confusion was compounded when some of the surviving packhorsemen and soldiers of the escort dodged through the melee and back toward the fort.[791] The soldiers who were not killed all got back inside the fort, and the gates were closed and barred only instants before the Indians arrived. Now the Indians became the brunt of the gunfire as rifles were fired from the blockhouses and over the walls. At least 20 of the Indians were killed, and an even larger number were wounded.[792]

As the Indians pulled back and continued firing at the fort, they expected to be reinforced immediately by Blue Jacket's force, but the latter Indians were still pursuing the horses and believed that their other contingent had successfully cut off the relief party as planned. When Blue Jacket's warriors successfully rounded up all the horses and returned with them, they were stunned to learn what had happened and that the Ottawas, Chippewas, Potawatomies and Wyandots had lost 20 men killed and at least that many wounded. A council was called and arguments broke out; the latter force blaming Blue Jacket for not coming to their aid and accusing his warriors of cowardice, while Blue Jacket angrily pointed out that none would have been killed or wounded had they not disobeyed his orders. The rupture between the two groups widened when the fort attackers demanded half the captured horses and Blue Jacket refused to give them any because their disobedience merited no reward.

Later, as they followed the Auglaize to the Maumee on their return toward Fallen Timbers, the bitterness between the two factions remained, and they spoke to each other not at all. When they finally reached the Maumee, an angry delegation of the Ottawa and Chippewa chiefs confronted Blue Jacket.

"We are no longer part of you," said their spokesman. "We return to our homes now and leave you to face the Americans, when they come, on your own. We will no longer help you."

The Indians who remained with Blue Jacket, approximately half the total force, watched grimly as the Ottawas, Chippewas and St. Joseph River Potawatomies sullenly moved off. It was a severe loss, compounded by the realization that those Indians leaving would undoubtedly turn back other parties of Indians en route from the north to join them.[793]

Blue Jacket continued staring glumly after the departing force of Indians. "What this now means," he said aloud, the bitterness clear in his voice, "is that General Wayne will strike us with two thousand of his regular soldiers and another sixteen hundred Kentucky men on horses, and we must face them with only six hundred."

Now, five days after these events, Col. Alexander McKee in Fort Miamis at the foot of the Maumee Rapids was reluctantly writing to his superior, the new commanding officer at Detroit, Col. Richard England:

Rapids, July 5th, '94

Sir—I send this by a party of Saganas [Saginaws], who returned yesterday from Fort Recovery, where the whole body of Indians, except the Delawares, who had gone another route, imprudently attacked the fort on Monday, the 30th of last month, and lost 16 or 17 men, besides a good many wounded.

Everything had been settled, prior to their leaving the Fallen Timber, and it had been agreed upon to confine themselves to taking convoys, and attacking at a distance from the forts, if they should have the address to entice the enemy out; but the impetuosity of the Mackinaw [Chippewa] Indians, and their eagerness to begin with the nearest, prevailed with the others to alter their system, the consequences of which, from the present appearance of things, may most materially injure the interests of these people; both the Mackinaw and Lake [Ottawa] Indians seeming resolved on going home again, have completed the belts they carried with scalps and prisoners, and having no provision there, or at the Glaze to subsist upon; so that his Majesty's post [Fort Miamis] will derive no security from the late great influx of Indians into this part of the country, should they persist in their resolution of returning so soon.

Captain [Matthew] Elliott writes that they are immediately to hold a council at the Glaze, in order to try if they can prevail on the Lake Indians to remain; but without provisions, ammunition, etc., being sent to that place, I conceive it will be extremely difficult to keep them together.

[August 20, 1794 — Wednesday]

This was the day.

This was the day when all the long, difficult preparations by the army of Gen. Anthony Wayne were coming to fruition. This was the day when all the prolonged waiting by the Indians under Blue Jacket was at last coming to its conclusion. This was the day when the opposing forces of Wayne and Blue Jacket would meet in battle.

And though that struggle would be occurring 275 miles away from the nearest point to the stream that the Shawnees called the Spaylaywitheepi, this was the day that would determine the future of the Ohio River Valley.

The odds were now with Wayne and even though he had heard only unconfirmed whispers of the serious rift that had occurred in the Indian force, he had long ago learned never to underestimate his enemy. The dwindling of events to this point had all come about when, at long last, he had finally, at eight A.M. on July 28, marched the army of 3,800 men northward out of Greenville, his 2,200 Legion regulars taking the lead and the 1,600 Kentuckians under Gen. Scott bringing up the rear. By August 1 they had reached the headwaters of the St. Marys River, where Wayne ordered construction begun on a post to be called Fort Randolph.[794] Here, while Wayne was resting, workers felled a huge beech tree that crashed onto his tent, dazing him with a severe head blow, multiple bruises and internal bleeding that lasted for days afterward.[795] It was here that the army was joined by another contingent of 800 mounted Kentucky militia under command of Col. Barbee, who immediately attached themselves to the 1,600 Kentucky volunteers already with Wayne's army under Gen. Charles Scott.[796]

As soon as Blue Jacket learned of this, he sent runners to the adjoining tribes, including those Chippewas, Ottawas and St. Joseph River Potawatomies who had abandoned him in such anger following their abortive attack on Fort Recovery. The runners were instructed to tell them of Wayne's advance and inform them that they, too, would be in great jeopardy if the army weren't stopped, reminding them of their stunning defeat of Gen. St. Clair's army and begging them to put aside their petty anger and send their warriors to him at once. Some, in fact, did come, but only a small portion of those who had shown up to fight against St. Clair. With their arrival, Blue Jacket's whole force amounted to only 1,000 warriors.

Michikiniqua made a hurried trip to Detroit to see Col. Richard England, telling him that the combined Indians most desperately needed help from the British now, requesting at least 20 British regulars and two pieces of field artillery. Col. England was courteous enough but evasive, and Michikiniqua was soon convinced the British would provide them with little, if any, assistance. It was hardly good news to Blue Jacket when he heard of it, but he was gratified by the arrival somewhat later of Capt. Matthew Elliott from Detroit at the head of a packhorse train well laden with food and other supplies, escorted by 200 Ottawas under Chief Kinjoino, raising his total force to 1,200.

On August 4, before the Fort Randolph construction was completed, Wayne resumed his march, leaving the place garrisoned by 40 invalid soldiers under command of Capt. Thomas Underwood, who was himself ill. When Blue Jacket's spies brought him word that the Americans had reached the Auglaize only a dozen miles above the Maumee, he ordered all the women, children and elderly in the Miami and Shawnee villages in the vicinity of the Auglaize River mouth to leave at once for the Michigan country. Once they were well away, he led his own warriors 60 miles down the Maumee, where he made a temporary camp beside the rapids at a place the old French traders had called Roche de Boeuf—an expansive clearing on shore adjacent to an outcrop of craggy rocks forming an island as they rose above the water to a considerable height and were capped by a growth of cedar.[797]

As Wayne continued marching his army down the remaining distance of the Auglaize to its mouth, they passed and destroyed great tracts of vegetables under cultivation and many hundred acres of corn just becoming fully eared. As soon as he reached the Maumee, he sent out detachments to burn all the villages in the area, as well as the Kinzie Trading Post, and immediately began erecting, in the triangular point of ground between the Maumee and the Auglaize, a new and very substantial fort. While standing with Gen. Scott looking over the continuing construction of blockhouses, pickets, fascines and ditches, Wayne had grunted in approval.

"It pleases me greatly," he commented, "to build this fort in the very midst of this grand emporium of the hostile Indians of the west. When it is finished, I defy the English, Indians and all the devils in Hell to take it!"

"Then call it Fort Defiance," Scott remarked, and Wayne did so.[798]

Wayne had then sent one final peace-talk invitation to the tribes via a squaw and an old Indian man captured in one of the villages. The chiefs held a council, but now, having become keyed up for the approaching fight with Wayne, they had voted against it for two reasons: First, only a short time ago 100 British regulars had arrived at Fort Miamis, and they took this to mean that the British there were building up their own strength for the coming battle; and second, Blue Jacket had received very encouraging news that the British Capt. William Caldwell was on his way with 53 men of the Detroit militia and 800 Chippewas newly arrived from the Saginaw area. Those militiamen had reported to Fort Miamis, and the Chippewas joined his force a day later, raising his total of warriors to 2,000. While a barrier of resentment remained between those Chippewas and Blue Jacket's force, the two sides agreed to put personal feelings in abeyance in order to face together the greater foe. And while their arrival certainly hadn't made the opposing forces equal, it helped turn the vote against any peace talks with Gen. Wayne.

Wayne had put his army on the move again on August 15, down the left bank of the Maumee, and they had moved as far downstream as the village of Chief Snake of the Wyandots, where they camped for the night under heavy guard.[799] The next day the army marched another ten miles downstream, their progress slowed by steep ravines through which it was extremely difficult to pull the wagons and gun carriages.[800] On August 17 the army had marched 14 miles and camped for the night at the head of the rapids, which put them only ten miles from the main Indian encampment at Roche de Boeuf.[801]

That was when Blue Jacket had finally decided to move his force downstream another three miles to the area of Fallen Timbers, not only for the advantage it might give them in their mode of bush fighting but for its proximity to Fort Miamis. All the Indians expected Wayne's army would march that final distance to them the next day and the battle would be on, and so on the evening of August 17, the Indians had gone into their traditional prebattle fast and waited for the army to move upon them the next morning. Wayne, however, stopped his army at the Roche de Boeuf ground the Indians had vacated and set up camp. It meant the Indians would have to continue their fast an extra day, but this was no great hardship, and there was no doubt in the minds of any of the Indians then that the battle would be fought on the morrow.

Anthony Wayne, however, was even more sagacious than they realized. Fully aware that the fast had begun and that the Indians were waiting to do battle in the area of the Fallen Timbers, the commanding general deliberately held his position at Roche de Boeuf all of yesterday, taking advantage of the delay to throw up a small bastion he named Fort Deposit, in which to store all the baggage not needed in the actual combat.

So for the Indians in their own Fallen Timbers camp, the portents were not good, and it seemed to them, as the skies opened and a veritable deluge of rain engulfed them, that both Moneto and the Great Spirit had turned their heads away from their red children. With the battle sure to take place early the next morning, not only were they facing a powerful enemy well over twice their own number, they were now light-headed and weakened from a fast that had already lasted much longer than anticipated and was not yet ended. Dejectedly, Blue Jacket and the other chiefs had discussed strategy for many hours, and though none was fully satisfied with what had been adopted as the final plan of action, there was really no alternative. If matters became desperate for them, their only remaining recourse would be to retreat downstream the three miles to Fort Miamis and take refuge there within the confines of the bastion, protected by her artillery and British troops.

Col. Alexander McKee and Capts. William Caldwell and Matthew Elliott, along with other British officers and agents, including Simon Girty, had earlier cautioned them not to expect full British aid when the battle began, pointing out that though relations were strained between them and the Americans, there had as yet been no official declaration of war and no orders giving them authority to give active support. The Indians had been told, however, that protection could not be interpreted as active support, and every intimation had been given that should the Indians have to fall back from the onslaught of the Americans, such British protection would be forthcoming, and Fort Miamis would be their haven.

So now, at last, this was the day.

The Americans, well over 4,000 strong, had risen to the reveille drum at dawn, and after a little more than an hour of preparation, they had formed their battle lines. But the rain that had ended during the night resumed again in a sudden heavy shower, and the march out of camp at Roche de Boeuf was postponed for an hour. At exactly seven o'clock, the rain having dwindled to a continuing drizzle, the army started following the Maumee portage trail downstream toward the Fallen Timbers area, which began four miles below their camp and where the 2,000 Indians under command of Blue Jacket awaited them.[802]

Those Indians were presently crouched among the jumble of fallen trees and branches, their war paint badly streaked and smeared by the morning's rain, imparting an even more frightening appearance than when first applied. Blue Jacket was in the front center of the Indians and at intervals sent runners to Fort Miamis, asking when the soldiers were going to join them behind the breastwork of fallen trees. The British replies were consistently evasive as they told the Indians to have patience and not worry, that the support was there and would become available when really necessary. Meanwhile they had already been provided with about 50 of Capt. William Caldwell's Canadians dressed and painted as Indians to assist them.

Thoroughly chilled by the persistent cold drizzle, the Indians, waiting for the American force to appear, now began to leave the Fallen Timbers area, first in small groups, then in larger numbers, to go to the temporary campground a half-mile below, where some British were serving hot soup and gills of rum and where the warriors broke their self-imposed fast. By the time word came that Wayne's army was definitely on the move toward them, the force crouched amid the fallen timbers had dwindled from 2,000 to around 1,300.

Gen. Wayne's spies had brought word of the disposition of the Indians, and now, as he approached the Fallen Timbers area at close to nine o'clock, his strategic talents became clearly apparent. Leading his army into that tract of fallen timber was apt to be suicide, and so he quickly formulated his plan. Splitting off a section of his force, he sent it to the left, out of sight of the river and the main army, with orders to advance at that point parallel to the trail and to stop and wait as soon as the Fallen Timbers area came into sight. When they had been gone for a sufficient length of time, Wayne started a battalion of the mounted riflemen straight down the portage trail, to act as a decoy to the Indians. The mounted battalion was to press forward on the trail as if they were the advance of the whole army. As soon as they were attacked, which would no doubt occur as they approached or entered the Fallen Timbers area, they were to put up a brief fight and then, in apparent fear and confusion, turn and flee back the way they had come, hopefully drawing the Indians out of the dense cover after them. When a sizable number of the attackers had boiled out of their cover in pursuit, the hidden left wing of the army, at the sound of the drum rolls, would drive to the attack and attempt to turn the right flank of the enemy and encircle it, while the main army suddenly surged ahead and engaged the enemy on ground far more advantageous to the army for a fight.

Hidden behind the downed timber, the Indians watched as what appeared to be the head of the army, a four-abreast column of mounted men with rifles, came into view at a light trot with banners waving. They slowed their horses to a walk as they neared the forward edge of the fallen timbers, as if reluctant to penetrate, but they entered it nonetheless. The first 50 of the horsemen, advancing under Lt. Harry Towles, had entered the fallen timbers area when Blue Jacket shrieked his attack cry. His warriors instantly made opening shots with bows and guns and then surged from hiding, brandishing war clubs and tomahawks. The mounted men fought back briefly, emptying their rifles toward whatever attackers they could see, milling and turning and finally, after Lt. Towles and Sgt. Eli Edmundson were killed, breaking in disorder and starting to gallop back the way they had come, the Indians in hot pursuit.

The maneuver would have worked perfectly except for one thing: The drum roll signal for the army's left wing to drive to the attack and encircle the exposed enemy could not be heard; not only was it largely drowned out by the gunfire, but it was considerably muted and muffled because of the continuing rainfall. After several moments of the Indians chasing the fleeing soldiers, the main body of the army was observed surging forward to meet the mounted battalion, and a warning was shrieked that passed down the line to Blue Jacket and the other chiefs. The Indians stopped and turned back and finally the army's left wing began to move, but by then much too late, as the Indians for the most part made it back into the tangled timberland. Several cannon shots were lobbed into the timber after the Indians from the company of Capt. John Price, which was at that moment under command of Lt. Percy Pope, on the right of the army's advance—first shells and then canister and grapeshot—but without much effect due to the density of the cover.

With the battle engaged, Wayne's army continued to surge forward. The artillery shooting ceased and the Legionnaires, on foot under Capt. Robert M. Campbell, raced into the timber with fixed bayonets and a very hot fight ensued. Campbell was killed almost immediately with a shot through the breast, and his command was taken over by Capt. John Arnold. The Indians held their ground well, at first, and both sides suffered considerable loss as the fighting moved from tree to tree, log to log. Before long, however, the sheer weight of numbers in favor of the whites began forcing the Indians back. Yard by agonizing yard they fell away, with the army pressing them hard until at last, an hour after the battle had begun, they were beginning to emerge from the other end of the Fallen Timbers area. At this point Blue Jacket issued the order for retreat to Fort Miamis.

In a rush, leaving a score or more of their number dead or dying amid the jumble of timber, the Indians sped in a disorganized mass the remaining three miles to Fort Miamis and called for the British regulars to come out and assist them as promised. The gates stayed closed. The Indians clustered in front of the gates and pounded upon them with their fists, demanding entry and protection in the fort's interior before the Americans coming behind them should arrive. The gates remained closed.

Maj. William Campbell, commander of Fort Miamis, called self-consciously to them over the walls. "My orders," he said, "instruct me to do nothing more than safeguard the integrity of this fort." Other British soldiers looked over the walls and out of the portholes at the Indians clustered below, unable to offer any support, offensive or defensive. Blue Jacket, frustrated and angry, realizing that their white allies were throwing them to the wolves, finally gave the word to disperse and the Indians fled past the fort, past the small encampment of Indians a half-mile below it and well beyond, scattering as they ran.

The Battle of Fallen Timbers was over, and the Americans were clearly the victors.

When the Americans came into view in full strength a short time later, with trumpets sounding and drums beating, Gen. Wayne assessed the scene immediately, realized the Indians were gone and then issued crisp orders. Immediately the soldiers spread out and methodically destroyed all the grain and vegetables growing around the fort and burned down all the buildings surrounding it, including the small trading post owned by Alexander McKee. The effrontery of it caused the watching British garrison to literally groan in frustration.

Wayne and his second in command, Gen. Wilkinson, along with several other officers, including Wayne's aide, Lt. William Henry Harrison, then boldly rode in plain sight to within 80 yards of the walls. So angered were the British regulars inside the fort that one officer, a captain, grabbed a torch and attempted to apply it to a cannon pointed directly at the American officers. He was restrained only when Maj. Campbell threatened to run him through with his sword if he didn't desist. The captain threw down the torch in disgust, and the commander had him placed under arrest.

Maj. Campbell himself, however, was practically as furious as the captain over Wayne's actions and sent him a note protesting the American general's near approach to a post belonging to His Majesty's troops, declaring that he knew of no war existing between Britain and America, adding that so near an approach could not again be permitted, and he would be fired on if he attempted it. Wayne, in return, immediately fired off two sharp replies, asserting that Fort Miamis had been built in contravention to the Treaty of Paris and ordering the British to get out of American territory—specifically, to leave Fort Miamis at once and retire to the next nearest British post. Maj. Campbell responded with the brief but firm note that he should certainly remain where he was until he was ordered to evacuate the place by the authority who placed him there, or the fortune of war compelled him to surrender it.

Anthony Wayne at this point very seriously considered a strike at the fort but finally decided against it. Though he possessed written authorization from President Washington via Secretary of War Henry Knox to "attack and demolish the British fort of Miami" if he so chose, he declined to expose his men to the necessary deaths it would have entailed to effect such an end.

The number of killed on both sides was not great for a conflict involving such numbers, largely because the major part of the battle had been fought among fallen timbers and far more bullets had lodged in intervening tree trunks, branches and logs than in flesh.[803] Nevertheless, the victory belonged to Gen. Wayne's army, and the Indians were more crushed and despondent than ever before.

For the first time, without any reservation, the Indians realized that the Americans were now the dominant force in their country, and the knowledge was devastating.[804]

[*J u n e   1 5 ,   1 7 9 5 — M o n d a y*]

Everyone on hand knew that this was one of the most historic days in the history of the young United States.

On this day, at Gen. Anthony Wayne's headquarters outpost of Greenville, hundreds of people had already gathered and many times that more were on their way. On this momentous day the council fire was lighted and would remain burning until all 12 of the tribes who were to participate agreed to the terms of peace outlined by Gen. Wayne on behalf of the United States government, a process that was expected to take some weeks, perhaps even months.

The very fact, however, that a true and apparently permanent peace with the tribes was in the offing was greeted by most throughout the Ohio River Valley and in the Ohio country with joy and thankfulness. Could it really be possible that after two decades of vicious, barbaric warfare, a true and definitive peace was coming at last? For the most part everyone, Indian and white alike, was optimistic at the prospects.

The defeat of the Indians at the Battle of Fallen Timbers last August had, of course, started the wheels in motion toward this end but, as was common with terminating wars, the dangers did not end with the swiftness of a candle being snuffed out. There had still been many skirmishes, many raids and a number of deaths since the battle was fought, and though now, ten months after that decisive battle, these had dwindled to near nothing, the process had been a slow and painful one for many.

As if to underline the fact that it was not all over yet, the last Indian attack ever to occur on Wheeling Creek happened on September 6, only 17 days after the defeat, and it was a devastating one for the George Tush family, who were neighbors of the Wetzels. He and his wife and their five children lived in a cabin 12 miles up Wheeling Creek at the mouth of Bruce's Run. There had been no attacks along the creek for almost a year, and residents were beginning to feel they were finally safe from further incursions. In the process, they became a little careless. On that Saturday morning, Tush, uncharacteristically weaponless, was out feeding his hogs in a sty not far from the cabin when he was fired upon by a small party of Wyandots who had been waiting for him to leave the cabin. A ball struck him across the upper chest, broke one of his ribs and lodged in his shoulder blade. He managed to stay on his feet, though the pain was intense, and raced back toward the house with the Indians in close pursuit. Oddly, however, though his wife and children were inside, he ran right past the open door and continued into the woods beyond, heading toward the Wetzel place. A few of the warriors plunged into the cabin and instantly grabbed Mrs. Tush and pinned her against the inside wall. The children were screaming and the youngest, a four-year-old girl, ran outside and tried to get away but was snatched by one of the Wyandots still outside, swung in a circle and smashed against a tree. The other four children, the eldest of which was ten, were all tomahawked inside the cabin and scalped. Fearful that the man who escaped would bring back help, the Indians snatched up a few items of plunder and started away quickly with Mrs. Tush a captive. Despite their shoving her along with them, her movements were too slow, and in just under two miles they tomahawked and scalped her as well.

Back at the cabin, the little girl who had been dashed against the tree came to her senses and crawled into the cabin, where the other children were lying in a bloody jumble. A sister was still alive, and she crawled to her and collapsed in her arms just as that older sister fell unconscious again.

Continuing away toward the southwest, the Indian party encountered the two young Beckham brothers, William, 12, and Sam, 10, leading two of their father's horses they had gone out to get. The Indians captured them and the horses. They arrived at Grave Creek in the evening and made camp and, after the boys had fallen asleep, the Indians heard a noise in the darkness and became fearful they were being followed. They instantly tomahawked and scalped the two boys and raced off into the darkness, leaving the tied horses. Though badly injured, neither boy was dead. William regained his senses and found his brother Sam still alive but unable to speak or walk. William managed to mount one of the horses and headed down toward the Tomlinson settlement at the mouth of Grave Creek, but the horse made so much noise going through the brush that he soon dismounted and left it and went a little farther himself before growing weak and creeping into hiding among some rocks.

The Indians, in the meantime, had mastered their fears and, creeping back to their own camp, saw that one of the boys was gone as well as one of the horses. They tomahawked Sam again, this time killing him, and took the remaining horse with them as they headed down Grave Creek. Before long they found the other horse and recaptured it, but they did not find William, who managed to reach a cabin after daylight came and was helped.[805]

George Tush, after being wounded and getting away, stumbled while descending a ravine, fell into a sapling that bent under his weight and then catapulted him 20 feet down onto some rocks at the bottom, further injuring him. He made it to Martin Wetzel's place, but no one was home and he collapsed there. Wetzel, returning in the morning, found him and managed to bring him around and get his story. Then he, along with Lewis Bonnett, Jr., and Moses Shepherd went to the Tush cabin and found the children. They buried the three who were dead and rescued the two still alive, taking them to Wheeling for medical treatment.[806] And once again— for the last time—the Wheeling residents made preparations to defend themselves against possible assault, but the attackers had by now disappeared.

All up and down the Ohio other scattered hit-and-run attacks of this nature were occurring in a last flurry, even as the tendrils of peace took root and strengthened. Near Ludlow's Station in the Cincinnati area, four government packhorsemen were attacked along an unnamed branch of Mill Creek, and one of them was killed instantly and fell into the stream. Another, severely wounded, was rescued and taken to the cabin of Abner Boston near Ludlow's Station, but died there in a few hours. The unnamed stream where the body of the other man was recovered was immediately named Bloody Run.

As 1794 dwindled away, settler Shaderick Harriman had the distinction, if such it could be called, of being the last person killed in the Kanawha Valley. As he emerged from his cabin door at the mouth of Lower Valuable Branch, two miles above Clendenin's Station, he was shot dead and then scalped.[807]

On December 9, a 22-year-old Kentucky settler named David Spangler was captured by the Potawatomies on the north side of the Ohio River at the Falls of the Ohio. Eight days later, 18-year-old Joseph Guy was captured along the Great Miami River in Ohio, close to Fort Hamilton, by a small party of Delawares.[808]

Capt. Sam Brady, late in December, decided to go on a deer hunt in the valley of Stillwater Creek and was accompanied by his brother-in-law, Ellzey Van Swearingen, and Benjamin Biggs. It had turned very cold while they were out, and having downed all the deer they could manage, Brady went out to get the horses where they had been hobbled so they could pack the meat on them. While crossing a small stream on a log that spanned the water, Brady slipped on ice that had formed overnight on the log's surface and fell, hitting his head on a branch and getting knocked unconscious. He narrowly missed being drowned when he fell with most of his body in the water, but his head on shore. Nevertheless, he lay in the icy water for quite a long while before regaining consciousness. With difficulty he dragged himself out of the water and got the horses, but by the time he returned to camp, his clothing was frozen and he was himself very sick. They managed to get him and the deer meat back to West Liberty, but by then he had developed a severe cold and fever and was wracked by terrible coughing. Drusilla bathed him and got him into bed, spoon-fed him with hot broth and cared for him as best she could, but, as 1794 ended and 1795 began, it was obvious that Sam Brady was a very sick man and would probably be a long time getting well. There was even talk that he might never again be able to lead his Rangers on border patrols.

Early this year of 1795, the old French post called Fort Massac, far down the Ohio on the Illinois shore, which had been in ruins for many years, was reactivated by the United States and reoccupied by a small garrison of regulars. Only a short time later, toward the end of April, settler Samuel Chew and his party of five were attacked by a party of Kickapoos and Potawatomies near Fort Massac. A survivor brought word to the fort, and a party went out and found Chew lying in the shallows of the Ohio River, scalped and severely mutilated. Another white man of his party had been scalped, dismembered and disemboweled. Near where Chew's papers and books were strewn all over the shore were also found the bodies of four of his Negro slaves.

Some of the Indians responsible were captured and taken to Kaskaskia, where officials ordered them transported to Cahokia to be jailed and tried for the murders. While on their way there, however, an angry mob of whites near Belleville took the Indian prisoners away from their guards and killed them. This caused a party of Potawatomies from Lake Peoria to band together with some Kickapoos to retaliate, and a series of attacks occurred throughout the southern Illinois country as a result, culminating just last month in the massacre of a white family and 13 Negroes living near the mouth of the Ohio River. Residents in the area, terrorized by the attacks, sent word to Gen. Wayne, begging for troops and asking that he build a new United States fort at Lake Peoria.

At about the same time on the upper Ohio, settler Mike Waxler was shot and killed on the Ohio side of the river when he happened across two Delawares, George White Eyes and his brother, Joe White Eyes, stealing some of his horses.[809]

John Decker, living in Brooke County not far from the Samuel Brady place near West Liberty, was riding to Holliday's Cove on June 4 when he was attacked by a small party of Wyandots. They shot at him and missed, but a ball broke a foreleg of his horse. Nevertheless, Decker spurred his horse on, and the animal ran on three legs until it came to a log. In attempting to jump it, the horse fell and was unable to rise. Decker tried to escape on foot but was quickly overtaken, tomahawked and scalped. He was the last white man to be killed by an Indian in Brooke County.

Eleven days after that, the last killing of whites by Indians in Pennsylvania occurred at the Samuel Hulings settlement, when a party of surveyors was attacked at the mouth of Conneaut Outlet, where it empties into French Creek.[810] Two young men of the surveying party, James Finley and Barney McCormick, were making rails when three Indians, believed to have been Senecas, crept up and tomahawked both and took their scalps. The Indians then went to the camp and found that the rest of the surveyors were out, with the exception of James Thompson, whose horse was tied near where he was working. They shot the horse and took him prisoner, terrorizing him by dangling before his eyes the scalps of Finley and McCormick.[811]

Still, while the attacks along the Ohio River Valley were disastrous for those who suffered them, there were far fewer than in previous years, and a general sense of hope rose among the border people that the Battle of Fallen Timbers had at last been the blow to end the interminable border war with the Indians.

Beginning shortly after their defeat at Fallen Timbers, numerous councils had been held by the Indians to determine what they should do now. In each of the tribes there were contingents of die-hards who wanted nothing more than to retaliate against the Americans and continue their strikes along the frontiers—which they did —but by far the greater number fully realized the hopelessness of making any further resistance against Gen. Wayne's army. Furthermore, the ingrained superstitions of the various tribesmen had now caused them to come to the conclusion that Moneto and the Great Spirit, who had turned their faces from them at the Battle of Fallen Timbers, would continue to keep them averted and let further troubles descend upon them if they did not make peace with the Americans.

In the meanwhile, swift strides were being made by whites toward developing more of the Ohio country. Simon Kenton and other Kentuckians were already busily at work claiming lands on the Mad River and the upper Scioto. Along the southern rim of Lake Erie, the three million acres of Western Reserve lands east of the Cuyahoga River were sold by the Connecticut Legislature to a syndicate of the state's citizens who had organized under the name of the Connecticut Land Company. They, in turn, were selling parcels to citizens of Connecticut and other states, who were already in the process of surveying into townships of five square miles each and establishing settlements.

Far to the south, another program was moving along at top speed for the development of an area north of the Ohio River, 18 miles wide, between the mouths of the Scioto and Big Sandy rivers. This area was being settled by a horde of Frenchmen who had been duped out of their life savings in a bogus land deal in Paris years before by a land company that had never owned any of the Ohio country land to sell. The United States Congress was sympathetic to the plight of the Frenchmen, who had lost not only the lands they had bargained for while still living in France, but equally the lands upon which they had settled in the area of Gallipolis, due to invalid titles. Now the Congress had donated a tract of just over 25,000 acres to those who had suffered in the fraud—a tract now being called the French Grant.[812]

For Gen. Anthony Wayne, the events following his victory over the Indians at Fallen Timbers well befitted a good army under a good commander. First, numerous chiefs approached him at different times under flags of truce, representing only themselves, their villages or their own tribes and with no consideration at all for the confederacy they had formed, which many had begun calling the Seven Nations, and sued for peace. Though they hadn't represented all the tribes, it was clear that they were representative of a general feeling spreading among the tribes.

Nevertheless, the hostilities were not completely ended. Even after Wayne's dead had been buried with honors and the wounded loaded on litters for transport to Fort Defiance, small parties of warriors continued dogging the army and firing on it when they could. Several Indians were killed, and the army got little rest at night as the Indians hooted and howled back and forth throughout the night like owls and wolves just beyond the perimeter of each night's camp. Occasionally, a sniper's shot found its mark. Private John O'Brian was one of a number of soldiers who were wounded or killed during the return march; a ball from an adjacent hill struck him low in the back, angled through the bottom part of his stomach and finally lodged in his penis.

During this return from Fallen Timbers up the Maumee, Wayne had sent out detachments on either side of the river with orders to destroy every village, every trading post or other structure belonging to British agents or traders and every vestige of crops in a swath 10 miles wide and 50 in length. They had done just that, and the smoke rising behind them and dissipating in the atmosphere was to many, Indians and whites alike, symbolic of the dissipation of the hopes and dreams of the red men.

Wayne's force had reached Fort Defiance on August 27, where the general detached a large portion of his force to ascend the Auglaize and return to Greenville and Fort Washington with dispatches and many of the more mobile wounded. The more seriously wounded were treated at Fort Defiance while improvements were being made on that installation and, as that was occurring, Wayne marched most of the remainder of his army up the Maumee to where it is formed by the confluence of the St. Joseph and St. Marys rivers—the site of the capital village of the Miami tribe, Kekionga. Arriving there on September 22, Wayne ordered the construction of a large, very strong fortification. Every officer and soldier participated in the construction, and the new fort was completed on October 22. Wayne named Col. John Hamtramck as its commanding officer, and Hamtramck immediately honored his commander by firing a 150-round artillery salute, led the entire force in three rousing cheers and named the place Fort Wayne.[813]

Soon after this Wayne had returned to Greenville as the army's winter quarters, and even there the Indian delegations from as far distant as the Sacs on the Mississippi had continued coming to him, asking peace. To them all his response was the same: He would grant them a temporary peace, but all were to appear at Greenville for a great treaty council next June 1 to conclude a permanent, binding and unbreakable treaty of peace between the United States government and all the northwestern tribes. In the meanwhile, to show their good faith in the petitions for peace, they were to begin, at once, to bring to Greenville and turn over to him any and all prisoners in their hands, whether they had been formally adopted into the tribes or not. Only then could and would the new boundary lines be established and forever afterward the various tribes live in peace and brotherhood with the whites.

The exchange of prisoners that forthwith occurred, and was continuing at this time, was entered into with alacrity by the tribes now anxious to please and mollify Gen. Wayne. There was not one general prisoner exchange at a specific time, but over the weeks and months that followed, prisoners were regularly brought in to Greenville.[814] It was this return of prisoners, as much as anything, that finally convinced the Kentucky settlers that peace had truly come at last and that now a man could chop his wood or pasture his cattle and horses without fear of being robbed or killed by Indians. For the very first time since settlers had begun descending the Ohio River, attacks on the boats and rafts of the immigrants entirely ceased.

If there lingered any trace of hope among the Indians that the British would finally rise and thrust the Americans out of the Northwest, it was dashed when word swept through the tribes of the new treaty of peace with the United States that the American special envoy, John Jay, had negotiated with the British in London. That treaty had been signed last November 19, and though it covered many aspects of international trade and other matters, the provision that struck home with the northwestern Indians most directly dealt with the strong British posts at Mackinac, Detroit, and Niagara.

The grave nebulosity in the Treaty of Paris over 11 years ago that had enabled the British to so disruptively retain their hold on these vital western posts in American territory had finally been resolved by the astute Mr. Jay. By the new terms to which the British had agreed, *all* British posts anywhere in the territory of the United States would be evacuated by the first day of June next year.[815] At councils held with the Indians in the Detroit area, the British quickly gave assurances that this did not mean they were actually leaving. In point of fact, they said, they were only moving across the Detroit River to Canada, where, at Amherstburg, hardly 15 miles from Detroit, they were building a very large fort, much bigger and better than the Detroit fort, and calling it Fort Malden. From here, they promised, they would continue to provide the Indians with the gifts and annuities and supplies they were accustomed to receiving. The explanations and plans did little to rejuvenate confidence in the Indians for the British.

Among the chiefs who visited with Gen. Wayne at Fort Greenville before the winter was over were Blue Jacket and Michikiniqua. After that visit, Wayne had magnanimously sent word to the displaced Shawnees under Catahecassa, as well as to other Indians, that if they wished to do so, they could resettle, at least temporarily, at their old village sites, provided they remained peaceful and quiet. As a result, Catahecassa had now returned to the site of Wapakoneta and had reestablished the principal village of the Shawnees there, reinstituting the name Wapakoneta. Blue Jacket's Town had also been reestablished when the war chief returned there, and Wapatomica was being rebuilt with a good *msi–kah–mi–qui,* but the nearby ruins of Mackachack, Mc-Kee's Town, and others remained uninhabited. Numerous other small new villages of both Shawnee and Miami Indians were springing up again in the valleys of the Maumee, Auglaize, Blanchard, Ottawa and Little Auglaize.

Another surprise came with news that Michikiniqua, accepting the commanding general's invitation, had reestablished a moderate-size village at the Kekionga site quite close to Fort Wayne. Also, though Chief Five Medals of the St. Joseph River Potawatomies had made an armistice with Wayne and had agreed to attend the Greenville council, the Milwackie and Illinois River Potawatomies were not yet committing themselves to anything.

Numerous other occurrences of interest took place throughout the Northwest prior to this day of the council fire being lighted at Greenville: Gen. Wayne's aide during the Fallen Timbers campaign, Lt. William Henry Harrison, had been promoted to captain and was now in command of Fort Washington, and young Capt. Harrison had just married a young woman named Anna Symmes, daughter of the territorial judge and land speculator, Benjamin Symmes; adjacent Cincinnati was growing rapidly, now with well over 100 cabins; 10 large brick houses; business establishments that included stores, bakeries, blacksmith and livery stables; and a population, exclusive of the garrison, exceeding 500. Similar startling growth was occurring throughout Ohio with the great new influx of whites, who were now starting construction of houses, churches, schools, even whole villages. An army colonel, John Johnston, who had struck up a rapport with Catahecassa and established a federal trading post at Wapakoneta, had since been named Indian agent to the Shawnees and would be stationed at Fort Wayne with William Wells who was now officially agent to the Miamis. John Conner, whom the Shawnees especially favored as an unusually honest trader, had established a new trading post on the Whitewater River.[816]

Due to the slowness of many of the Indian delegates in arriving at Greenville, the lighting of the Grand Council fire on June 1 had been postponed for a fortnight, and so these first two weeks of June had been filled with eating, drinking and visiting among those who were gathering, the number increasing daily. But at last today, even though many Indian delegations were still missing, Wayne had decided to wait no longer to light the council fire. The chiefs were summoned to the council house that had been prepared, and they came quickly, their followers spreading out to quietly wait outside.

Then, with fitting pomp and ceremony, Gen. Anthony Wayne ordered the council fire lighted. A great cheer erupted from whites and Indians alike as the blaze crackled to life. The hubbub continued as the chiefs seated themselves on the ground before the fire. Ceremonial pipes were lighted and passed from one to another, the chamber soon growing hazy with the blue-white smoke of the fragrant *kinnikinnick* burning in the pipe bowls. Finally, Gen. Wayne, resplendent in his dress uniform, moved to the fire and stood before them, his arms raised. Only then did the hum of voices dwindle away.

"My children," he began, his voice carrying well over the whole assemblage, "I have cleared the ground of all brush and rubbish and have opened roads to the east, the west, the north, and the south, that all your nations may come in safety and with ease to meet me. The ground on which this council house stands is unstained with blood and is as pure as the heart of Gen. Washington, the great chief of America, and of his great council; as pure as my heart, which now wishes for nothing so much as peace and brotherly love. The heavens are bright, the roads are open, we will rest in peace and love and await the arrival of our brothers. In the interim we will have a little refreshment, to wash the dust from our throats. We will, on this happy occasion, be merry without passing the bounds of temperance and sobriety. We will now cover up the council fire and keep it alive till the remainder of the different tribes assemble and form a full meeting and representation."

Teteboxti, most ancient of the Delaware chiefs, rose and responded to Wayne, saying, "All my people shall be informed of the commencement of our friendship, and they will rejoice in it, and I hope it will never end."

[*A u g u s t   7 ,   1 7 9 5 — F r i d a y*]

Even though the Indians who continued to assemble for the grand peace council at Greenville brought certain amounts of food with them, it was customary at any
such council for the host to provide for them during their stay, and they expected to
be furnished with most of their needs by Gen. Wayne. Knowing this, Wayne had
requisitioned large quantities of food and drink and was gratified when the government's quartermaster system came through promptly.

Food was distributed to the various factions on hand in equal proportions according to the number of people to be fed. In many cases this was substantial since,
along with each member of the tribal delegation, there were usually one or two
women and children to consider as well. In the case of beverages, hundreds of kegs of
rum had been received, and the liquor was doled out in very limited quantities daily
in keeping with Gen. Wayne's opening remark that they should "be merry without
passing the bounds of temperance and sobriety."

In their own enclave camps some distance away from the fort, the various tribes
played games and held sporting competitions during the day, and the air was hazed
by the rising smoke of their campfires. Many of the soldiers, at the invitation of the
Indians, were given leave to be spectators and, in some instances, invited to be
participants. Almost every evening dances of one sort or another were held to the
accompaniment of drums, rattles, flutes, ankle and wrist bells and, occasionally,
screeching fiddles—the latter usually having been acquired in the past through trade
or raid. The throbbing of the instruments, chanting, singing and clapping of hands
and stamping of feet was enjoyed by many of the regular soldiers but was greatly
annoying to some, especially when the sounds continued far into the night and were
interruptive of sleep.

Gen. Wayne and his officers enjoyed the festivities, while at the same time
keeping a close watch on everything to quell instantly any possibility of trouble.
Soldiers were instructed to always be on guard but to refrain from offending the
visitors in any way. Wayne himself was kept almost constantly busy meeting new
delegations of tribesmen as they arrived or having further private discussions with the
more important chiefs.

Day after day more delegates continued to arrive—each greeted personally by
Gen. Wayne and both giving and receiving peace belts in solemn ceremony. Many of
the arriving delegations brought American captives with them and turned them over
to Gen. Wayne, most weeping with joy or almost hysterical with relief at being freed,
others accepting the necessity of their return to white society only with the greatest
reluctance. Many of the chiefs said they would turn over additional prisoners to
Wayne as soon as they could conveniently do so.

Finally, in the middle of July—during the Heat Moon—the actual formal peace
council began.

The Delawares, at this point, constituted the largest single Indian contingent
present, numbering 381 individual delegates and led by Pimoacan, Buckangehela,
Teteboxti, Wingenund and Peketelemund. The 240 Potawatomies present were represented by a large number of chiefs that included New Corn, Asimethe, Gizes,
Topenebe, Five Medals, White Pigeon, Siggenauk, Chaubenee, Nescotnemeg and

Gomo, among others. Representing the 180 Wyandots were Chiefs Tarhe and Stiahta, called Roundhead by the whites. There were 143 Shawnee delegates under Catahecassa, Chiuxca and Blue Jacket and 73 Miamis under Michikiniqua, which included 22 Eel River Miamis under Chief LeGris and a dozen other Weas and Piankeshaws under the leadership of Chief Reyntwoco. The 46 Chippewas on hand were under Chiefs Massas and Bad Bird and the 45 Ottawas attending were led by Chief Augooshaway. Only 10 Kickapoos and Kaskaskias had arrived under Chief Keeahah, while the Sacs and Foxes, though invited to attend, had refused. A final total of 91 chiefs attended, and the full number of Indian delegates was 771. Including the women, children, elderly and other nonattendees to the council, the total number of Indians on hand well exceeded 3,000.

The Indians were all impressed with how Wayne conducted himself and the treaty, allowing plenty of time for the ritual smoking of the *calumets* and then, when discussions began, allowing ample time for each matter to be interpreted, discussed and debated, moving slowly, methodically, having prepared himself well with strings and belts of wampum, which he displayed and distributed as his points were made.[817] Once the Grand Council was begun—and with the concurrence of the various chiefs —Gen. Wayne distributed no further liquor to the Indians, to insure that all were soberly clear-minded as matters progressed.

Wayne had presented to each of the principal chiefs in attendance a large brass medallion, on one side of which was a raised profile of George Washington and the other side exhibiting a white and an Indian shaking hands. The medallions were strung on loops of brass chain or brightly colored ribbons, to be worn about the neck if the owner chose, as most did.

Blue Jacket, Chaubenee and Sauganash, along with numerous other chiefs, had all personally met the general's principal aide-de-camp, William Henry Harrison, and were impressed with him. The only incident of a troubling nature occurred early on when a British agent, John Askin, Jr., clad as an Indian, was discovered attempting to subvert the Indians and get them to insist on their sovereignty. William Wells reported this to Wayne, who immediately had the man arrested and confined until after the treaty was signed, certified and distributed.

There were points of considerable argument, of course; the greatest initial difficulty occurring with the Potawatomies. By their form of tribal politics, there was virtually no real central government, and each of the tribe's branches—and even many individual villages—acted autonomously. As a result, the chiefs of each branch or even individual village chiefs demanded separate negotiations, which in most cases was not feasible. The 240 Potawatomi delegates in attendance mainly represented those factions along the St. Joseph, Tippecanoe, Elkhart and Huron rivers and, with the exception of Siggenauk from the Milwakee villages, Nescotnemeg on the Kankakee River, Chaubenee and Gomo on the upper and middle Illinois River, most of the western factions were largely unrepresented.[818]

More Indian delegates continued straggling in even after the preliminaries had begun, and in all cases Wayne carefully went over with them what had already been discussed so they were well apprised of all things.[819] At last, however, all the Indians had arrived who were going to come—a total of 1,100 chiefs and delegates representing 12 tribes of the Northwest Territory.

Virtually without exception, the various chiefs were extremely impressed with Gen. Wayne, considering him to be the best treaty commissioner any of them had ever encountered. He was at all times gentle with the Indians in attendance, treating them with courteous firmness. He did not, as they had expected him to do, start out by reiterating the claim that the United States were the absolute owners of all the territory east of the Mississippi, in consequence of the 1783 Treaty of Paris.[820] Instead, he stated to the tribes that they were to have free and exclusive use of all lands not specifically ceded by them to the United States. At the same time, he told them that in their signing of the treaty the tribes were acknowledging they were under the sole protection of the United States, and the United States alone had exclusive right to preempt such land in subsequent treaties. He assured them as well that by the terms of the treaty, if any white man should unjustly kill an Indian, that man should be apprehended by the whites and turned over to the Indians for punishment, and vice versa. Since always before the whites had claimed the right to punish both Indians and whites—usually the former and rarely the latter—for such infractions, the chiefs were very impressed with this provision.[821]

The cession of Indian lands to the United States was the crux of the entire treaty. In trade for land, the Indians in effect purchased peace and annuities—a peace that, they now felt assured, for the first time, would be lasting—and they also, in effect, purchased the right to their own territory within the new boundaries; a right they felt assured at last would never be infringed upon.

Gen. Wayne went on to tell them that this new treaty being made at Greenville was to be based, in large measure—with some revisions, which were to be explained —on the boundary lines established by the Fort McIntosh Treaty on January 21, 1785. The biggest single land cession involved the Ohio Territory. Although the Indians would retain hunting and fishing privileges throughout the entire Ohio area, a definite dividing line between Indian and white territories was established in this treaty. Wayne read it carefully to them, explaining in detail so they would understand its significance:

"The general boundary line between the lands of the United States and the lands of the said Indian tribes shall begin at the mouth of the Cuyahoga River and run thence up the same to the Portage between that and the Tuscarawas branch of the Muskingum, thence down that branch to the crossing place above Fort Laurens, thence westerly to a fork of the branch of the Great Miami River running into the Ohio, at or near which stood Loramie's Store and where commenced the Portage between the Miami of the Ohio and St. Mary's River, which is a branch of the Miami which runs into Lake Erie; thence a westerly course to Fort Recovery, which stands on a branch of the Wabash; thence southerly in a direct line to the Ohio, so as to intersect that river opposite the mouth of the Kentucky or Cuttawa River."[822]

In addition, Gen. Wayne told them, the United States would require the cession of 16 tracts of land within the Indian territory for government reservations.[823] Each of the tracts, Wayne explained carefully, was considered important in the extreme to the United States, not only for the opening of trade by Americans to the Indians of those areas, but equally for the establishment of forts within the Indian territory from which to regulate the trade and, very important for the Indians themselves, from which to distribute annuities to the tribes so they would not have to travel so far

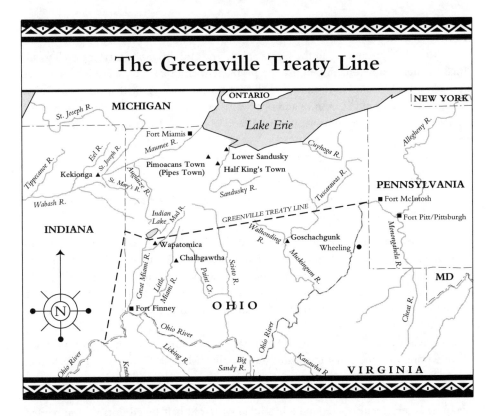

The Greenville Treaty Line

from their homelands each year to receive the payments due them.[824] At this point some of the chiefs raised objections, seeing such a penetration of their country by the Americans as only a first step to what would be subsequent American expansion in those areas and renewal of land disputes that could ultimately lead to a new war. Not enough of the chiefs felt this way, however, and it was only too clear to all in attendance—Indians and whites alike—that the Indians were tired of war, tired of disputed boundaries, tired of being caught in the pincers of two opposing white powers. And so the majority prevailed, and the land cessions were agreed to, in the belief that now they could hunt and fish in peace, enjoy a peaceful trade, and raise their crops and families in peace.[825]

With all negotiating finally finished yesterday, the 91 various chiefs made their individual marks on the treaty. Michikiniqua was final chief to sign the historic document. Before doing so, he met Gen. Wayne's gaze and spoke solemnly.

"As I am last of the chiefs to sign this peace with the Americans," he said, "so also will I be last to break the agreement."

Gen. Anthony Wayne had then formally signed the treaty, along with some of his officers and the official governmental witnesses. Throughout the night a scribe worked feverishly to reproduce an exact copy of the document and, in a final ceremony today, the signed treaties were checked by Indians and whites together for accuracy. Now Chief Tarhe of the Wyandots—the respected "grandfathers" of the other northwestern tribes—was given custodianship of the official transcript on behalf of the assembled tribes. It was a very solemn and moving moment, and an absolute silence reigned over the assemblage as the Indians listened closely to Gen. Wayne's concluding remark.

"I now fervently pray to the Great Spirit," he said, his voice carrying well to all, "that the peace now established may be permanent and that it now holds us together in the bonds of friendship until time shall be no more. I also pray that the Great Spirit above may enlighten your minds and open your eyes to your true happiness, that your children may learn to cultivate the earth and enjoy the fruits of peace and indus-try."[826]

[*September 22, 1795—Tuesday*]

The delegation of Indians who visited the 27-year-old Tecumseh today in his temporary village on the headwaters of Deer Creek was led by none other than Blue Jacket himself.[827] That the war chief of the Shawnees should pay a special visit to Tecumseh was a very real honor that underlined the level of prestige to which Tecumseh had now risen among the Indians, even though within his own tribe the chiefs still viewed him as merely a warrior.

Arriving with Blue Jacket this morning was a contingent of chiefs and warriors, all of whom were personal friends of Tecumseh, including Chiuxca, principal chief of the Peckuwe sept of the Shawnees, the burly, barrel-shaped Chaubenee, who was a Potawatomi chief, Tecumseh's own nephew Spemica Lawba, who was the son of his older sister, Tecumapese, and a bright 17-year-old half-breed Potawatomi named Sauganash, whom the English called Billy Caldwell.[828]

All were only too well aware that Tecumseh, who over the years had risen to become perhaps the foremost warrior among all the Shawnees, had voluntarily separated from the tribe in a dispute with the tribe's principal chief, Catahecassa—Black Hoof—prior to the great peace council with Gen. Wayne at Greenville. In council after council after the Battle of Fallen Timbers, as the Shawnees had discussed what they should do, Tecumseh had consistently argued against making any sort of peace treaty with the Americans. Catahecassa had just as doggedly maintained that it was his wish and demand that the other chiefs support him in making peace, on behalf of the entire tribe, with Gen. Wayne. Tempers had become short and the discussions very heated as Tecumseh, in the final Shawnee council last March, had declared he would *never* make peace with the treacherous whites and shocked those attending the councils when he openly berated Catahecassa for his willingness to do so. A number of chiefs and warriors indicated their support of Tecumseh in this matter, but the odds were against him; not only had Catahecassa been peaceably inclined all along, the disaster at Fallen Timbers had caused by far the greater majority of Shawnees to side with him.

"I cannot lend my support to such a decision!" Tecumseh had said in his concluding heated exchange with Catahecassa. "Whether or not you can see it, or will believe it, I tell you there is no doubt that the Americans continue to want—and will continue to take!—Shawnee lands and the lands of other tribes so long as they remain to be taken. I will *not* attend the treaty General Wayne has called. I will *never* make peace with the Americans. This is the land of our fathers, the land where their bones are buried and whose graves we should defend to our last breaths. That is what I intend to do."

"*No,* Tecumseh," Catahecassa had replied angrily, "you must not! You *cannot,* since the Shawnee council has now made its decision and you are bound by the decisions of this council. If you continue to make war against the whites, they will hold us responsible as a tribe and cause further trouble for us all."

Tecumseh had shaken his head, and his words had emerged as brittle and cold as chunks of ice. "If I cannot, as a Shawnee, protect the lands I love, the lands so many of our people have fought and died for, then I will do so on my own. I, and any of those who are of like mind with me, cannot stay here, which would mean that we agree and support such a decision, which we do not. We will go away from here and make our own village apart from you, and we will wait and see what shall occur. If, in fact, Catahecassa, you and the other Shawnee chiefs put your names to such a treaty of peace with the Americans, we will then forever sever ourselves from the tribe."

The assemblage had gasped at his declaration, and an angry murmuring arose. Blue Jacket was one of the chiefs who came to his feet and asked him to reconsider, but Tecumseh had remained adamant and replied, "You are my friend, Blue Jacket. You will always be so. But this is a matter that goes beyond friendships. Catahecassa and the other chiefs are wrong in their decision to make peace next summer with the Americans, and if you agree with him and them, then you, too, Blue Jacket, are wrong, and it is a decision you and they will live to regret."

Catahecassa's decision remained, however, and Blue Jacket had supported him. Immediately following that final council, Tecumseh had packed up his meager goods and left to establish his own village on the Deer Creek headwaters. With him had gone his brother-in-law, Wasegoboah, and his wife, Tecumseh's sister, Tecumapese. Tecumseh's two surviving brothers, Kumskaka and Lowawluwaysica, had gone with him, too, and a number of others who supported his beliefs and were disenchanted with Shawnee tribal leadership under Catahecassa.[829]

Now, not having seen any of these old friends since that final Shawnee council in March, Tecumseh was overjoyed to see them and warmly embraced them all. Wasegoboah and Tecumapese soon joined them, laden with pots and dishes heaped with good food, and Tecumseh's brothers, Kumskaka and Lowawluwaysica, arrived a few minutes later. All ate heartily at Tecumseh's table, smoked their pipes and spent an hour or so in pleasant reminiscences and in sharing news of less than monumental significance, saving the most important matter of discussion—the Greenville Treaty —for last.

Finally, well into the night and with all other matters laid to rest except the treaty, Blue Jacket took over and spoke steadily for a long while, relating all that had occurred at Greenville. When he finished there was a long silence, and Blue Jacket gratefully accepted the pipe handed to him by Sauganash and drew on the stem. Then, blowing out a puff of blue-white smoke, he spoke to Tecumseh with great seriousness.

"Your refusal to attend the Greenville Treaty, my friend, caused a reaction that may surprise you. Those who attended—many of them—felt coerced to come and appeared there begrudgingly, but because of the strength of General Wayne and fearing his wrath if they did not attend, they came. But what they talked about a great deal before the true negotiations began was that you, Tecumseh, had shown the courage to stay away; that you had stated you would never make peace with the whites. They see in you that piece of themselves that they had hidden away. Many of them, especially the younger chiefs and warriors, are greatly impressed with you and that you even had courage enough to temporarily pull away from your own tribe to support your view. They see you now as a champion of the rights of the Indian and one who refuses to bend under the ill wind from the whites. They see you, Tecumseh, as the one, among all, who holds true to the Indian standard of self-esteem and dignity, and you have suddenly risen greatly in prestige in their hearts and minds. Only a few were upset at your stand, most of all Chief Catahecassa, who feels you have personally insulted him."

Tecumseh's expression was grim when he replied. "I am sorry he feels that way, since an insult to him was not intended. I stated only that I could not make peace with the whites and could not live with those who did. What I had feared would happen, *has* happened: We have entirely lost, by the terms of the treaty, practically all in Ohio that was our own. Even the land of this little village where we now sit has been signed away, and we no longer have any right to be here."

The bitterness in his voice became heavier as he went on. "My people and I will remain here until we have completed the harvest we have already begun of our corn and vegetables. Then we will move away."

"But to where, Uncle?" interjected Spemica Lawba. "Catahecassa cannot allow you to return to our villages now. He says this would raise ill feelings and dissension among our people."

Tecumseh looked at his nephew. "When I left the tribe," he replied slowly, "and took these people with me, I told Catahecassa that if he and the other Shawnee chiefs should put their names to the treaty, our temporary severance from the tribe would become permanent. That has now taken place. I would not return to the villages even were I welcome, because I could not live with what is in my heart and mind and still abide by the leadership of Catahecassa. Our chief has been a satisfactory chief since the death of Chiungalla, but he is weary of war and thinks he is best serving our people by ceding lands instead of lives." He shrugged faintly. "Perhaps he is correct, but I cannot live with that. This was—*is*—our land, and it is here that the bones of our fathers and our fathers' fathers are buried, and if we cannot protect what is ours, what is left to us? No, Spemica Lawba," he went on, shaking his head sadly, "I will not return to our villages. I will go above the treaty line on the Great Miami, but in a village of my own making, and perhaps not for long.

"Wehyehpihehrsehnwah," he said, turning to Blue Jacket, "it has been good seeing you again. And you, Chiuxca. And my good friend, Chaubenee, and our new young friend, Sauganash. Though the news has been painful, I thank you for bringing it."

Tecumseh stood and walked to the doorway of the wegiwa and heard the whistling of a chilling wind beyond the buffalo-hide flap. He stood with his back to the others, but they said nothing, knowing he was not yet finished with what he had to say. When he turned back to them he looked no less grim and his voice was laced with a determination as chilling as the wind outside.

"Only this do I have left to say: My heart is a stone, heavy with sadness for my people; cold in the knowledge that no treaty will keep the whites out of our small lands that we are now left with; hard with the determination to resist for so long as I live and breathe. Now we are weak, and many of our people are afraid. But hear me: A single twig breaks easily, but the bundle of twigs is strong. Someday I will embrace our brother tribes and draw them into a bundle, and together we will win our country back from the whites."

Blue Jacket studied him with a piercing gaze and then finally nodded. "I think maybe you will," he said softly.[830]

[January 1, 1799 — Monday]

Peace!

A new decade was beginning, and at last there was peace in the land; peace in western Pennsylvania and Virginia and Kentucky; peace in the Ohio country and in the Indiana and Illinois territories to the west. And there was peace on the Ohio River. No longer would boats afloat on its never-ending current be subject to sudden and vicious attack. No longer would Indians appearing on its shores be shot merely for being there. No longer would its meandering thousand-mile length be stained with the lifeblood of those who had tried for so long to hold it and those who had finally succeeded in taking it.

No longer need this sinuous liquid highway to the west be called "that dark and bloody river."

There were people who had come along whose lives had become inextricably intertwined with the convolutions of the great river and whose names would ever-more be associated with it, whether for good or for bad; Zane, Hokolesqua, Wetzel, Shepherd, Pucksinwah, Greathouse, Monakaduto, Girty, Talgayeeta, Edgington, Pimoacan, McCulloch, Wingenund, Tomlinson, Tarhe, Crawford, Chiungalla, Kenton, Catahecassa, Clark, Shemeneto, Gibson, Bilderback, Tecumseh, Cresap, Thayendanegea, Boone, Blue Jacket, Céloron, Chiksika, Williamson, Cornplanter, Parchment, Michikiniqua, Gist, Montour, Heckewelder, Red Hawk, Plukkemehnotee, Hardin, Netawatwees, Harmar, Scare the World, Knight, Poe, Nonhelema, McKee, Moluntha, Washington, Cuppy, Sagoyewatha, McIntosh, Yellow Hawk, Bonnett, Skootekitehi, Buckangehela, Elliott, White Eyes, Zeisberger, Scotach, Wayne, Brodhead, St. Clair, Slover, White Loon, May, Baker, Croghan, Washburn, Van Swearingen and so many more, including, of course, Brady.

Samuel Brady heard about the Greenville Treaty early in September and, as so many others were doing, he rejoiced in the peace that had come to the Ohio Valley. It was, however, a quiet rejoicing, expressed in a satisfied smile and a few words of thankfulness from his rocking chair, because Capt. Sam Brady was not a well man.

The fall he had taken during the Stillwater Creek deer hunt, when he had struck his head and lain unconscious for so long in the icy waters, had left its mark on him. The cold he had developed as a result of it was very severe, and he had been feverish for a long time. Even when, for a few weeks, he seemed to be getting better, he was still so weak and achy that he could barely move about in his own house. Then, gradually, the cold had come back, and the fever with it, and he suffered badly from the effects, becoming pale and gaunt. Week after week, the cold hung on and then even worsened, eventually developing into pleurisy. By September he was more or less confined to his favorite rocking chair, swathed in blankets and able to eat little more than thin soup. By mid-October he was severely emaciated and bedridden, deeply exasperated with this illness that had hung on so long and that had now incapacitated him, making him dependent upon Drusilla for everything. In late November his fever became worse, and he lapsed frequently into delirium. In mid-December he sat up in bed and clasped his wife's hand.

"Our boys . . . ," he whispered, voice croaky and tremulous, "Dusy, our boys won't . . . won't have to go through what we did."

Her eyes overbright, Drusilla shook her head and squeezed his hand. "No, Sam, they won't. There's peace in the Ohio Valley now, thanks to you."

A faint glimmer of a smile tilted the corners of his mouth, and for a moment a little light of animation came into his eyes. He sank back onto his pillow, and his words were barely audible. "I . . . I helped, Dusy. I helped it happen."

"More than just helped, Sam," she murmured.

Brady didn't hear her, having slipped into unconsciousness as she replied. He continued to fade and had only a few periods of lucidity until Christmas Day, when he became comatose. Still, he hung on.

Then today, on this first day of a new decade, his breathing became increasingly sporadic, and late in the afternoon 43-year-old Samuel Brady exhaled a final time and died.

Epilogue

Among the major eastern rivers of the United States, from the great Mississippi eastward, none resisted discovery and exploration longer than the Ohio River; nor did any other become the scene of such prolonged violence and bloodshed in its conquest as that which occurred along the Ohio's thousand-mile course before emptying into the midsection of the Mississippi.

Now, at last, with what was occurring this day at the place where the great Ohio River is formed by the confluence of the Allegheny River from the north and the Monongahela River from the south—at the city of Pittsburgh, Pennsylvania—it could be said that a whole new era in the river's history was beginning.

No longer was this great stream the perilous ribbon of water through the wilderness it had so long been; no longer the treacherous, terror-filled river that had so long run red with the blood of red men and white alike.

There had been many changes since the Greenville Treaty 16 years ago, but they had been very gradual changes—faster than in the previous, strife-filled years but relatively slow nonetheless. Gradually the familiar faces began to disappear, the faces of those who had carved their places into the history of this great valley. The names would always be there, a reminder of times that were and the heroism and cowardice, the compassion and brutality, the desperation and perseverance that it took to mold this once-wild frontier into a tamer land and direct it into an altogether different future; not necessarily one that was better but certainly one that was enormously different.

One of the molders of the future, who had been absent for a long while, finally returned late in 1797. The hopes that had been raised in the mind and heart of Lewis

Wetzel by the visit made to him by David Bradford in the New Orleans prison had almost drained away as month after month passed with no further word from him. It had all begun to seem like a cruel trick that had been played on him by the fates to intensify his misery.

When Bradford returned to the upper Ohio, and it became known where Wetzel was, various steps were immediately made to get him freed. A petition had been sent to the Spanish governor in New Orleans asking for Wetzel's liberation, but no notice was taken of it. Philip Doddridge attempted to bribe Spanish authorities with a $1,000 offer for Wetzel's release, but he found no takers. Francis McGuire tried the same thing with an offer of $2,000 and similarly failed. Then President Washington was asked to intervene in his behalf. Whether he would have done so, none could say, because as it turned out, he didn't have to. In December 1796, after five years and five months in the prison, Lewis Wetzel had suddenly and surreptitiously been freed.

It had ultimately been the doing of David Bradford as well as the many friends and relatives Wetzel had on the upper Ohio. Bradford had returned to New Orleans with the considerable funds that he was able to collect from those who wished to aid Lewis Wetzel, and the lawyer had many meetings with the Spanish governor, winning his respect and confidence, even friendship. The governor finally agreed to help effect Wetzel's release, but he said the only way it could be done was to quietly spirit him away and see that it was reported that he was dead. For his own part, Wetzel would have to go along with the clandestine scheme and immediately, upon release from the prison, leave the Spanish Dominion forever. This was done. He was smuggled out of the prison, provided with a new set of clothing and sent on his way.[831] He walked all the way upriver to Natchez and remained there for a while and then continued all the way back to Wheeling, to the great joy of his family and friends.

But the upper Ohio that Lewis Wetzel returned to was not the upper Ohio that he had left. People moved about freely on and near the river, without fear for their lives, and Indians were rarely if ever seen—only a few who had become the hangers-on to the coattails of white civilization, doing odd jobs here and there, spending what little they earned in the taverns, where whiskey-soaked minds created a fog that smothered the memories of what had once been theirs in this great river valley.

For Wetzel, there was no danger, no excitement, no raiders to pursue, no Indians to kill. And so he drifted back down the Ohio to the Mississippi, where he worked as a hired hunter in the Indiana and Illinois country, occasionally finding a solitary Wea or Piankeshaw or Kickapoo Indian he could track down and kill. When, very soon, the Spanish secretly sold the Louisiana Territory back to the French and then France, in turn, broke their agreement with Spain to retain it themselves and sold it to the United States, Wetzel returned to New Orleans and started making quiet inquiries. It took him a long while, but he finally got information that put him on the trail of Pedro Hermoso. He found the old Spanish counterfeiter living in seclusion somewhere between New Orleans and Natchez and paid him a brief visit. No one ever saw Hermoso again.[832]

A year or so after that, Wetzel was living on two acres on the Big Black River in the Mississippi Territory, about 35 miles above its mouth at the Mississippi River and some 80 miles up the Big Black from Natchez.[833] There he lived alone in a little cabin he'd built and grew a small amount of corn and some garden vegetables for his own use. Benjamin Wells, who had been born on the Buffalo Creek tributary of the upper Ohio, paid him a visit there, and Wetzel, who had never seen him before, welcomed him, immediately recognized him as a Wells and correctly guessed he was the son of an old upper Ohio companion, Absalom Wells. Benjamin visited him numerous times after that and was fond of listening to Wetzel tell stories of his old Indian hunting days. Though only in his midforties, Wetzel looked much older, and his hair, now nearly waist length, was beginning to gray.

One day, as Wetzel was sitting in front of his cabin with Wells, reminiscing about the old days, he suddenly caught a glimpse of movement on the Big Black River. He looked back at Wells, who was watching him curiously.

"K'n you keep a secret, son?" Wetzel asked.

"I guess I can," Wells replied, "if it's necessary."

"Well, it is necessary," Wetzel said. He stood up, stepped into the cabin and got his rifle off the hooks on the wall, checked the load and then walked casually down to the riverbank and took a position behind a large tree. That was when Wells, for the first time, saw the canoe coming downriver between them and the island, being paddled by a pair of Choctaw Indians.

Wetzel very calmly raised his rifle, took a bead on the one in the stern and shot him. Slammed backward by the heavy ball, the Indian fell overboard. Then Wetzel smoothly and expertly reloaded, all the while keeping his eye on the canoe and the remaining Indian, who was paddling about in a circle, looking for his companion and wondering what was happening. His companion did not reappear and, as if suddenly realizing he was in danger himself, he began rapidly paddling toward shore, but it was too late. Wetzel leveled his rifle again and shot a second time, putting a ball through the Indian's head and dropping him into the canoe.

Young Wells, stunned and speechless, expected Wetzel would recover the canoe and scalp the Indian in the boat, but Wetzel simply reloaded while looking at the drifting boat and said, "Let them go. Somebody'll prob'ly pick 'em up downstream. Y'know, Benjamin," he said, returning his attention to the young man, "the gum'mint might do as it please an' make all the treaties it wants with th'Injens, but I ain't never made peace with 'em and ain't never goin' to, not fer as long as I live. Reckon I'll jest continue killin' all I can, ever' chanct I git, so long as there ain't too many of 'em in one bunch. Four, five's 'bout as much as I can handle at one go."

Not long after that, Wetzel paid a visit to Fort Massac on the lower Ohio. While there he saw a drunken Kickapoo Indian sleeping off the effects of his overindulgence beneath a tree not far from the fort. Mingling with the fort's soldiers for a while in the evening, Wetzel took a ramrod from one of the soldiers' guns and slipped off with it unobserved. Putting a heavy charge of powder in his own rifle, he put the stolen ramrod into the barrel and went back to where the drunken Kickapoo was still lying. Holding the point of the projecting ramrod to the sleeping Indian's rectum, Wetzel squeezed the trigger and sent the rod deep into his body, killing him. Then Wetzel disappeared in the darkness.

The shot had been heard, and soldiers came to investigate. The body was quickly found and the end of the ramrod seen projecting from his posterior. The commanding officer and his subordinate officers assembled the garrison and checked the gun of each soldier to see which had the missing ramrod. When it was found, its owner was quickly court-martialed, found guilty and sentenced to be immediately shot. A dozen soldiers were formed as a firing squad to carry out the execution, and they were on the point of doing so when Wetzel's voice called out from one side, addressing the commanding officer.

"You best not shoot that poor soldier, 'cause he ain't guilty. I stole his ramrod and kilt that damn drunken red nigger sum'bitch myself. An' iffen you want t'ketch me, you're sure as hell welcome to try."

With that he was off and running, and though they searched for him, he was never found. Nor did he ever again return to his cabin on Big Black River.[834]

Martin Wetzel was now 54 and, having married and raised his own family, was still living on Wheeling Creek, but his health had taken a downturn in the past few months, and there were those who said he'd probably be lucky to last another year.[835] Johnny Wetzel, youngest of the Wetzel brothers and now himself 41 years old, stopped by to see him fairly regularly and often brought meat he had downed in his hunting.[836] Jacob Wetzel was no longer on the upper Ohio. He had served for several years as a justice of the peace and even a two-year term as Ohio County's high sheriff, but then he fell on hard times. In 1803 he lost all his property because of faulty claims and moped about for a few years after that, usually staying with either Martin or Johnny. Then, four years ago, in 1807, he moved with his wife, two sons and three daughters to the White River in the Indiana country. Now 45, he was still there.[837]

Both Simon Kenton and Daniel Boone had moved away from the Ohio River. Boone, as long planned, had moved to Missouri and sunk new roots on the Missouri River not terribly far from St. Louis.[838] Simon Kenton moved into Ohio, settling first at Springfield, and he was now living at the town of Urbana in the heart of what had once been the Shawnee country.[839]

Simon Girty had taken up residence close to Alexander McKee and Matthew Elliott, establishing his own farm near the mouth of the Detroit River on the Canadian side, a few miles below Amherstburg and the British western headquarters, Fort Malden.

Maj. Gen. Anthony Wayne, en route to the east from Detroit, was taken ill aboard a ship and dropped off for medical treatment at Presque Isle on the southern shore of Lake Erie. His conditioned worsened and he died. Wayne was buried within the fort with little fanfare, and not even a suitable marker erected over his grave.

In Wheeling, huge crowds had turned out recently for the funeral of the very first white settler in the Ohio Valley, who had probably helped more people get settled on the upper Ohio than any other individual—Ebenezer Zane. Founder of Wheeling, Zane had just died of jaundice at the age of 64.

So, while many of the old faces were gone or going, their names continued to live on up and down the whole length of the Ohio River. And though there was peace in the Ohio Valley now, and Ohio itself had become a state in its own right in 1803, another war with the British was a very real possibility in the near future.

Equally disturbing, a new Indian war appeared to be imminent at this very moment. The Shawnee leader Tecumseh, who had never made peace with the whites and who had, for the past decade, been forming a great amalgamation of tribes as brother Indians regardless of tribal affiliations, had now formed a huge village on the Wabash River at the mouth of the Tippecanoe. There, it was rumored, he already had thousands of warriors poised and ready to strike when he gave the word, which might be any time now.[840]

There was little wonder why the Indians were again threatening war against the Americans: The United States government, despite all the fine promises in the Greenville Treaty, was still pushing forward in its aim to take ever more land from them, one way or another. New spearheads of American penetration in the west had already occurred, pointing out new lands to be taken. Capt. Zebulon Montgomery Pike had explored up the Mississippi River to its headwaters in the Minnesota country, then followed that up with an expedition up the Arkansas River all the way to its headwaters in the Colorado country. Already an expedition under Capts. Meriwether Lewis and William Clark had penetrated far west of the Mississippi, all the way to the Pacific Ocean, and wondrous tales were being told of the land "out west" available for the taking, despite the fact that it was inhabited by a multitude of native tribes. In eyeing this grand prize, the United States was simply following the guidelines established by President Thomas Jefferson, who had written to Indiana Territory Governor William Henry Harrison:

> *Our system is to live in perpetual peace with the Indians, to cultivate an affectionate attachment for them by everything just and liberal which we can do for them within the bounds of reason and by giving them effectual protection against the wrongs from our own people. When they withdraw themselves to the culture of a small piece of land, they will perceive how useless to them are the extensive forests and will be willing to pare them off in exchange for necessaries for their farms and families. To promote this, we shall push our trading houses, and be glad to see the good and influential individuals among them in debt, because we observe when these debts go beyond what the individual can pay, they become willing to lop them off by a cession of lands. But should any tribe refuse the proffered hand and take up the hatchet, it will be driven across the Mississippi and the whole of its lands confiscated.*

But such a war, if and when it did, in fact, come to be, would evidently be fought far away from the Ohio River Valley, and the event that was taking place this very day in Pittsburgh made it all seem of little consequence. Here, a giant step was being taken in the full-scale development of the Ohio River Valley.

Today, to the wild excitement of a huge crowd, a vessel that had been built in Pittsburgh was just setting off on her maiden voyage down the Ohio, bound for New Orleans.

She had been built at a cost of over $40,000.

She weighed an incredible 400 tons.

She had been designed and built under the supervision of the man who had invented the prototype, Robert Fulton.

Her name was the *New Orleans,* and she was the first steamboat on the Ohio River.[841]

A new era had begun—for the west and for the entire nation . . . and most certainly for what had once been called "that dark and bloody river."

Amplification Notes

1. The village of Onondaga, which became the seat of the Five Nations or Iroquois League, was on the site of present Rochester, N.Y.
2. Gov. William Bradford of the Plymouth Colony complained early on that the Indians were becoming more proficient in the use of firearms than the whites and that the illegal trade in firearms to the tribes *"will be the overthrow of all, if it be not looked into."*
3. The five septs of the Shawnee tribe are the Thawegila and Chalahgawtha (the peace septs, from among whom the principal chief of the tribe must be chosen); the Peckuwe (in charge of the maintenance or order or duty and matters pertaining to the Shawnee religion); the Maykujay (in charge of matters pertaining to health, medicine and food); and the Kispokotha (in charge of all matters pertaining to warfare, including the preparation and training of warriors).
4. This is the modern Suwannee River, made famous by the Stephen Foster melody; the stream rises in the Okefenokee Swamp of southern Georgia and empties in the Gulf of Mexico, some 20 miles north of Florida's famed Cedar Key.
5. The specific disease involved in this plague of 1616–17 is not known for certain. It was simply referred to as the *"pestilential sickness"* or *"the plague."* Conservative estimates suggest a mortality rate of at least one-third of the Indians east of the Alleghenies, from Canada to Florida. Existing evidence indicates that it was not yellow fever, typhoid, hepatitis or smallpox, but it may have been either measles or bubonic plague. Robert Cushman, writing of it at the time, doubted that more than one out of every 20 Indians survived; his contemporary John White firmly believed that no less than 99 out of every

100 died. All too soon the eastern tribes were either exterminated or else survived only as remnant groups that sooner or later lost their tribal identity as they became absorbed into healthier tribes to the west. In 1622, fully five years after that worst plague had abated, Thomas Morton was sickened by the skeletons he encountered in his travels in New England and wrote, after a particularly trying day of encountering untold hundreds of them, *"that as I travailed in that Forrest nere the Massachusetts, it seemed to mee a new found Golgotha."*

6. The first American slave ship, *Desire,* left from Marblehead, Mass., in this same year (1639) to collect its first cargo of slaves on the west coast of Africa.

7. The Falls of the Ohio, a low, short rapids with only a few emergent boulders, was located at the site of present Louisville, Ky.

8. The French map of the Ohio River, executed more than half a century later by Rapin Dethoyer in 1744, was much less accurate than Franquelin's map. On the Dethoyer map the Ohio River is indicated as the Hohio.

9. As historian George Bancroft wrote in 1834: *"Not a fountain bubbled west of the Allegheny but was claimed as belonging to the French Empire."*

10. The portage route from the Fox River to the Wisconsin terminated at present Portage, Wis. The Wisconsin River empties into the Mississippi at present Prairie du Chien.

11. The Illinois empties into the Mississippi 15 miles above present Alton, Ill., and 35 miles above present St. Louis, Mo.

12. The mouth of Salt Creek is at present Portage, Ind., and the start of the portage route was near the present city of Valparaiso.

13. The mouth of the St. Joseph River is at present Benton Harbor, Mich.; the portage path began in the center of present South Bend, Ind.

14. The mouth of the Maumee River on Lake Erie is at the site of present Toledo, O., and the head of that river is at present Fort Wayne, Ind. The Little River empties into the Wabash just below present Huntington, Ind., and the Ouiatenon post—named after a subtribe of the Miamis and pronounced Wy-uh-TEE-non—was located on the site of present West Lafayette, Ind. Post St. Vincent eventually became present Vincennes, Ind. The Wabash empties into the Ohio River at present Evansville, Ind.

15. This installation was later named Fort Massac and was located at present Massac State Park, at the eastern edge of present Metropolis, Ill.

16. The Allegheny and Monongahela rivers converge to form the Ohio River at present Pittsburgh, Pa. The term *"a thousand miles"* for the length of the Ohio River is a rounded-off figure. The actual river mileage, as indicated by the U.S. Geological Survey, from the junction of the Monongahela and Allegheny rivers to where it empties into the Mississippi is 981 miles.

17. This belief that the Western Sea (Pacific Ocean) lay just beyond the Alleghenies was quite prevalent among the British colonials for a considerable time. As late as 1612, Sir Dudley Digges offered what he termed *"scientific proof"* that the North American continent at its greatest expanse from east to west was not more than 360 miles.

18. The Falls of the James River are located at the site of present Richmond, Va.

19. The Falls of the Appomattox are located on the site of present Petersburg, Va.

20. The salt spring was located near the mouth of present Campbell's Creek, some six miles above present downtown Charleston, W.Va. The Kanawha itself empties into the Ohio.

21. The Blue Ridge crest was crossed in present Madison County, Va.

22. The village of Pickawillany was located at the site of present Piqua, O. The Miami tribe often referred to themselves as the Twigtwees, an onomatopoeic name derived from the call of the sandhill crane. Many of the early traders also referred to them as the Twigtwees rather than as the Miamis.

23. This trading center was located on the site of present Cumberland, Md.

24. This old Nemacolin Trail route began at present Cumberland, Md., and follows in large measure the course of U.S. Route 40, crossing the divide separating the Atlantic drainage from the Ohio drainage at present Grantsville, Md., then on to present Uniontown, Pa., and finally terminating at the Monongahela River, at present Brownsville, Pa.

25. The majority of accounts indicate that Spotswood and his party crossed the Blue Ridge crest through present Rock Fish Gap, but that is not correct. Their passage was through present Swift Run Gap.

26. Gov. Spotswood, on his return, proclaimed himself to be first to cross the Allegheny divide—wholly ignoring the several parties that had done so long before him in southern Virginia. For this alleged feat he was subsequently knighted, becoming a Knight of the Golden Horse Shoe. Despite the error of his claim, which soon became clear, his knighthood was not rescinded.

27. The site of present Ambridge, Pa. This village should not be confused with another, named Shenango but also sometimes called Chiniqué, which was located on the west bank of the Allegheny River well above Pittsburgh. The village name situation becomes a little confusing here, since there was yet another village called Shenango located at the mouth of Beaver Creek about this time.

28. At some point an early chronicler made what appears to be a typographical error and wrote the name as Loggstown. George Washington did so in his journal when he visited the place in 1753, though he may have gleaned his spelling of it from some other source. Unfortunately, this misspelling was picked up and has been used perhaps as much as the correct one, even by modern-day historians.

29. The early traders phonetically and in spelling reproduced Goschachgunk as Coshocton. It was located on the site of the present Ohio city of that name.

30. The term *Chautauqua* (pronounced Shuh-TAWK-wuh) has a great many variant spellings, none of which is exactly the one used today, but to avoid confusion, the modern spelling and pronunciation are used.

31. This was of course to be the first President of the United States.

32. The elder Ebenezer Zane had another son, Isaac, who was born the year before William Andrew. Isaac, however, was captured near their South Branch Potomac cabin in Moorefield, Va., by a band of Wyandots when he was only

nine years old. He was carried deep into the Ohio country to Tarhe's Town, on the headwaters of the Mad River, at the site of present Zanesfield, O. There he was adopted into the tribe, adapted well to Indian life and subsequently married the daughter of Chief Tarhe—The Crane. Eventually Isaac Zane became a chief in his own right, and though he never returned to live among the whites, he did return on one occasion to Wheeling and visited his grown-up nephew, Ebenezer.

33.   The War of Jenkins' Ear got its unusual name from the fact that a Spanish galleon captain named Fandino captured an English mariner, Robert Jenkins, in Havana and cut off his ear, causing an international incident that subsequently erupted into war.

34.   Findlay's camp was located on the site of present Lexington, Ky. John Findlay's surname appears in historical documents as Findly, Findley, Finlay, Findlay and Finley. The author has been unable to locate any document signed by this man so as to ascertain the correct spelling. The most reliable accounts, however, seem to favor Findlay, so that is the spelling that will be used in this account.

35.   Some accounts have erroneously assumed that the name Mingo was a corruption of the alternate term the Iroquois called themselves, the Mengwe.

36.   John Draper's wife was the former Bettie Robertson of Williamsburg.

37.   This settlement was located in present Montgomery County, Va., about ten miles northwest of the headwaters of the Roanoke River, on the east side of the New River and just east of the great Horseshoe Bend of that river. Some of the structures built were on the property later occupied by the Virginia Agricultural and Mechanical College. The closest town of note at present is Radsford.

38.   This young officer's name appears in the early documents as both Blainville and Bienville; more contemporary accounts seem to favor Bienville, yet the earlier accounts, including a report signed in his own hand, indicate that Blainville is correct.

39.   An exact copy of the inscription on one of these lead plates follows. This particular plate was stolen from Céloron by some Senecas and turned over to the British Indian supervisor, Sir William Johnson: *"L'an 1749 dv regne de Louis XV Roy de France, Novs Céloron, Commandant d'vn detachment envoie par Monsieur le Mis. de la Galissonière, Commandant General de la Nouvelle France povr retablir la tranquillite dans quelques villages sauvages de ces cantons, avons Enterre cette plaque"*—blank space for place of deposit, followed by blank space for the date —*"pres de la rivière oyo autrement belle rivière monument du nenounellement de possession que nous avons pris de la ditte rivière oyo, et de toutes celles qui y tombent, et de toutes les terres des deux cotes jvsqce avx sources des dittes rivières ainsi qv'en ont jovi ou dv jovir les precedents rois de France, et qu'ils s'y sont maintenvs par les armes et par les traittes, specialment par cevx de Riswick, d'Vtrecht et d'Aix la Chapelle."* The translation of which is: *"In the year 1749, of the reign of Louis the Fifteenth, King of France, we, Céloron, commander of a detachment sent by Monsieur the Marquis de la Galissonière, Governor General of Canada, to re-establish tranquility in*

some Indian villages of these cantons, have buried this plate of lead at"—blank space for place of deposit, followed by blank space for the date—*"near the river Ohio, otherwise Belle Rivière, as a monument of the renewal of the possession we have taken of the said river Ohio, and of all those which empty into it, and of all the lands on both sides as far as the sources of the said rivers, as enjoyed, or ought to have been enjoyed by the Kings of France preceding, as they have there maintained themselves by arms and by treaties, especially those of Ryswick, Utrecht and Aix la Chapelle."* The name of the artist who designed and engraved the lead plates, Paul de Brosse, was engraved on the reverse side of each of the plates.

40. Céloron's entire force consisted of eight junior officers, six cadets, 20 picked regular soldiers from the governor-general's own guard, 180 Canadians under command of the well-known half-breed trader Chabert Joncaire, and 55 Indians—Caughnawagas and Abnakis—plus a Jesuit priest, Father Bonnecamps, and the commander himself. Second and third in command of the expedition were Capt. C. Pierre Contrecoeur and Lt. Coulon de Villiers.

41. Daniel Joncaire has been identified incorrectly in some documents as Jean Coeur. Both of the Joncaire brothers, Chabert and Daniel, are believed to have been sired by a French trader, while their mother was Seneca.

42. Site of present Buffalo, N.Y.

43. The mouth of that stream, today known as Chautauqua Creek, is near the site of the present village of Barcelona, N.Y. The portage began about two miles upstream from the present village of Westfield and moved southward in the direction now followed by State Route 17.

44. The portage path terminated at the edge of present Lake Chautauqua near the present Chautauqua County seat, Mayville. Chautauqua is spelled on various early maps and documents in a variety of ways, but the original root in the Seneca tongue, Jahdahgwah, seems closest to the present pronunciation.

45. This swampy area lay on the site where the village of Jamestown is now situated.

46. Chautauqua Creek empties into Cassadega Creek at the present town of Levant.

47. Conewango at that time was spelled Kanaquagon. The mouth of the Cassadega is located less than a mile west of the present village of Frewsburg. The Céloron plate buried here has never been discovered.

48. Conewango Creek empties into the Allegheny River within the limits of the present city of Warren, Pa. Céloron believed, as had de Léry twenty years earlier, that the Allegheny at this point was the upper Ohio River. For that matter, the Senecas still consider the Allegheny to be the upper Ohio and refer to it as such.

49. This was another plate that has never been recovered.

50. The so-called Great South Sea meant the Pacific Ocean. California at this time was thought by the British and French alike to be an island.

51. The Indians initially encountered were largely Senecas and Loups (pronounced Loos), the latter a subtribe of the Delawares. Farther downriver the expedition encountered Shawnees, Wyandots and other tribes.

52. This bottom, not very extensive in area, was stated by Céloron to be four leagues below the site of present Franklin, Pa. (itself located at the mouth of French Creek, which the French commander referred to as Rivière aux Boeufs due to a herd of woods bison they had seen there). Close examination of his distances shows his estimation of a league is closer to two and a quarter miles than just two. The bottom where they landed is bisected by a small stream presently known as Snyder Creek, which emerges from a very steeply banked ravine. Directly across the river at this point the shore rises in a sharply angled hill to a point of land 550 feet above the river level, a hill that Céloron in his journal refers to as a bald mountain. The hill on the side of the river where they landed rises some 700 feet, on the crest of which, a mile and a half southeast of their landing site, is the present village of Coal City.

53. Unfortunately, most of this peculiar inscription has been worn away by wind, ice, debris and water, since during spring floods the entire rock becomes submerged. A reasonably accurate rendering of the inscription was made before this occurred by a Capt. William Eastman, U.S. Army, who, at the time he copied it onto paper, had to stand in waist-deep water in order to get a proper view. That rendering appears in Henry Schoolcraft's *Indian Tribes in the United States,* vol. 6, p. 172. This landmark is referred to as Harts Rock on U. S. Army cartographer Capt. Thomas Hutchins's *Topographical Map of Virginia.* Céloron wrote that the plate was buried *near* the rock, whereas Bonnecamps wrote that it was buried *under* the rock. Whichever is the case, this lead plate has never been recovered, despite the fact that its location seems more closely pinpointed than any of the others.

54. This meeting was on the site of present Point State Park—familiarly called Golden Triangle Park—within present Pittsburgh, and not at the site of present Aliquippa, 17 miles downstream on the left bank of the Ohio, where some accounts have placed it. It was evidently soon after Céloron's passage that Aliquippa moved her village to the latter site, possibly because of the periodical flooding that occurred at the *"point"* where the village was first situated, but more likely to be closer to Logstown.

55. The reason why no lead plate was buried at this important confluence of the Allegheny and Monongahela remains a matter of conjecture. The best guess seems to be that Céloron was anxious to reach Logstown, where he believed the majority of Indians who had been fleeing before him had gathered.

56. The party of Caughnawagas and Abnakis that abandoned the expedition here returned upstream on the Allegheny, pausing at each place where the territorial ceremony had been performed and ripping down the tin sheets bearing the coat-of-arms of France that had been tacked to trees. Not having the tools to do so, however, they did not unearth and carry away the lead plates.

57. This was present Wheeling Creek at the site of present Wheeling, W.Va. On what basis de Léry designated it as the Kanououara (pronounced Kan-uh-WAHR-uh) is unknown, though its pronunciation is curiously close to Kanawha. The original spelling of the Indian name was shown in the early documents as Weiling. The evolution from Weiling to Wheeling was evidently

merely a matter of a phonetic spelling that gradually supplanted the original spelling. To avoid confusion, however, today's accepted spelling of Wheeling will be used throughout. This is another of the plates that has never been recovered, though local historians at Wheeling believe—despite extensive filling that has occurred over the years—that it is still buried somewhere beneath where the old Baltimore and Ohio Railroad depot stood, not far from the present Civic Center.

58.   This is the site of present Marietta, O. The Céloron party landed and camped where, just over 40 years later, Fort Harmar would be built. Forty-nine years later that plate was discovered (on August 2, 1798) by two boys swimming and playing at the mouth of the Muskingum. Seeing it projecting from an eroded bank above them, they dislodged it with a branch. They took it home and, caring little about the letters engraved on it in a foreign language, began melting it down to make bullets. News of the find reached a local historian, who rushed to their home and rescued what remained of it, though a large portion had already been melted away. It subsequently came into the hands of historian Caleb Atwater who, recognizing its significance, sent it to the Governor of New York, DeWitt Clinton. The governor, in turn, donated it to the Antiquarian Society of Massachusetts. It is now part of the collection of the American Antiquarian Society.

59.   Whichever spelling might be correct, this is a name whose derivation has not been satisfactorily ascertained. The stream was the present Great Kanawha River, which empties into the Ohio River where the city of Point Pleasant, W.Va., is now situated.

60.   It was 97 years later, in September 1846, when a young boy who was digging worms for bait unearthed this plate and turned it over to his uncle, Col. John Beale. It created quite a sensation, and Beale showed it to Virginia legislator James M. Laidley, who borrowed it and took it with him to Richmond. There, without permission, he gave it to the Virginia Historical Society. When protests were lodged by the family of the boy who found it, two copies were made of the plate, and the original was returned to the boy. It remained with him some years until he was offered a very high payment for it. He agreed to sell; the prospective buyer took the plate with him and promised to return shortly with the money but never did. Of the two copies that were made, one is preserved in the collection of the Virginia Historical Society and the other is in the French National Archives.

61.   The designation Great Miami River exists today. The mouth of this stream presently demarks the boundary line between Ohio and Indiana. The city of Cincinnati is just a few miles to the east of this river's mouth. On a high bench directly over the river to the east is the present Shawnee Lookout County Park, which the author had the honor of naming.

62.   This was another of the lead plates deposited by Céloron that have never been recovered, so far as is known.

63.   The author has been unable to discover any literal translation of the chief's name, Unemakemi (pronounced You-nuh-MOCK-uh-mee.) The French

designation, Demoiselle, is Damselfly, which some of the English distorted to Dragonfly when they were not referring to him as Old Britain.

64. There were two Indians at this time who were known to the British as Half King. One was the Wyandot, Monakaduto, who was among the most powerful leaders in the tribe and who was also known by the name Zhausshotoh. The other was a Seneca chief named Tannacharison.

65. This trading house was established at the site of present Cumberland, Md.

66. Pronunciations of these names: Pimoacan is Pim-OH-uh-can; Moluntha is Mo-LUN-tha; Orontony is O-RON-tun-nee; Tarhe is TAR-hee.

67. The site of present Fort Wayne, Ind. The Maumee River was called by some tribes the Omee. Many of the early traders referred to it as the Miami-of-the-Lake, since it flows northeastward to empty into Lake Erie, near present Toledo, O.

68. This little fort—pronounced My-AM-mees, not My-AM-miss—should not be confused with the later Fort Miamis built by the French at the foot of the Maumee Rapids, or with the Fort Miami built by the British only a stone's throw from the ruins of the latter Fort Miamis just prior to the War of 1812.

69. The Miamis called this same river Weotowesipi.

70. Their cabin was close to present Marlinton, seat of Pocahontas Co., W.Va.

71. Gov. Clinton in New York, learning of Pennsylvania's reason for not erecting such a fort, appealed to his own Assembly for the means to help Pennsylvania but, to Clinton's anger and frustration, his appeal was rejected.

72. This stream was named Beef River by the French because of the large herd of woods bison observed there by the Céloron expedition when it passed in 1749. Later, the stream was renamed and became the present French Creek, with the present city of Franklin, Pa., now at its mouth, where Venango had been situated.

73. Stephen Sewell was slain in the area of the New River now known as the Sandstone Falls, about midway between the present towns of Brooks and Meadow Creek. The large hill rising some 3,000 feet from the east side of the river at that point today bears the name of Big Sewell Mountain.

74. A full account of the attack on Pickawillany, the death of Unemakemi and the destruction of the village will be found in the author's *Wilderness Empire* (Boston: Little, Brown, 1969; New York: Bantam, 1971).

75. Michikiniqua is pronounced Mish-ee-KIN-ee-kwa. The town of Kekionga, pronounced Keck-ee-ONG-uh, was established on the site of present Fort Wayne, Ind.

76. Gist's new post and cabin were located just a few miles northeast of present Uniontown, Pa., southeast of the old Mount Braddock Mansion. Inconclusive evidence indicates that Gist actually did start to lay out a settlement at the mouth of Chartier's Creek, site of present McKee's Rocks, but if he did, it was never finished, and Washington, when he was there the following year, made no mention of it in his journal.

77. The new Sinioto was established on the site of the present city of Portsmouth, O. Though reestablished, Sinioto never quite regained the size and importance it had enjoyed previously.

78. The grandfather of the Marquis de Duquesne, Adm. Abraham Duquesne, who died in 1688, had been one of France's greatest naval leaders.

79. John Fraser's trading post, converted to a fort, was called by many Fort Venango, after the Indian village located there, but the official designation of the fort, when it was improved, was Ft. Machault.

80. Fraser's cabin was situated at the mouth of Turtle Creek, on the site of present Braddock, Pa., just over five miles below the mouth of the Youghiogheny.

81. Gov. Dinwiddie's commission to George Washington is as follows: *"To George Washington, Esq., one of the Adjutant-Generals of the troops and forces in the Colony of Virginia: I, reposing especial trust and confidence in the ability, conduct, and fidelity of you, the said George Washington, have appointed you my express messenger; and you are hereby authorized and empowered to proceed hence, with all convenient and possible dispatch, to the post or place on the river Ohio, where the French have lately erected a fort or forts, or where the commandant of the French forces resides, in order to deliver my letter and message to him; and after waiting not exceeding one week for an answer, you are to take your leave and return immediately back. To this commission I have set my hand, and caused the great seal of this Dominion to be affixed, at the city of Williamsburg, the seat of my government, this thirteenth day of October, in the twenty-seventh year of the reign of his Majesty, George the Second, King of Great Britain, etc., etc. Annoque Domini, 1753. Robert Dinwiddie"*

82. Washington had, in addition to Gist and Monakaduto, enlisted the service of his fencing instructor, Jacob van Braam, as a French interpreter. At Will's Creek Station he hired trader John Davidson as Indian interpreter and four other men as helpers—Henry Steward, Barnaby (Barney) Curran, John McGuire and William Jenkins—plus bringing along two of his own Negro slaves.

83. Copies of Washington's journal were soon being reprinted and distributed throughout England, and many newspapers, both in England and America, carried excerpts of it or even the whole text.

84. At a meeting of the House of Burgesses on February 14, 1754, Dinwiddie was finally allocated £10,000 in Virginia currency for frontier defense. He also, on March 7, offered 20,000 acres of land in the Ohio Valley to be given out as bounties to those who enlisted to serve under Col. Fry, as soon as that area was secured from the French.

85. Washington was pleased with his promotion, but this turned to anger when he learned that his pay was only half that paid to a regular army officer of the same rank. He threatened to resign but was dissuaded by the wise counsel of the Fairfax family, who had first brought him to the attention of Gov. Dinwiddie.

86. Fort Machault (often called Fort Venango) was named after the French financial genius and statesman Jean Baptiste Machault D'Arnouville.

87. There was some friction at this time between Washington and regular army Capt. Mackay, who felt he should be in command, not a militia officer. Washington, however, prevailed.

88. Although Contrecoeur told the assembled Indians that the French and English were at war—which, in effect, they were—no formal declaration of the French and Indian War was made until May 18, 1756, when England declared

war against France. France responded with its own war declaration on the succeeding June 9.

89. The final battle statistics indicated that Washington had 12 men killed, 43 wounded, 29 missing, 25 deserted and 251 unscathed. The French had 2 killed, 70 wounded.

90. The mouth of Wolf Creek is at the site of present Narrows, Va., some eight miles south of the West Virginia border. Burke's settlement was situated on the site of present Burke's Garden, Tazewell Co., Va.

91. Tygart's Valley River empties into the upper Monongahela just above the site of present Fairmont, W.Va.

92. One rather fanciful account states that the Indian party, after putting the gray-haired head of Barger into a sack, went to the Lybrook cabin on Sinking Creek, found Mrs. Lybrook alone there, handed her the sack and told her to look in the bag and she would find someone she knew. That, of course, presupposes that the Indians knew where the Lybrook cabin was, knew that Mrs. Lybrook was there, and could speak her tongue (or she theirs) well enough to converse with her but for some unfathomable reason were not inclined to take her along with the other prisoners or loot and burn the cabin. The saga of what happened to Mary Draper Ingles after this would make a book in itself. On July 11, two days after Braddock's defeat and three days after the massacre at Draper's Meadows, Mary Draper Ingles gave birth to a daughter. Because of her fitness and strength, she came through the birth all right and refused to hand the baby over to the Indians on their demand, knowing they would certainly kill the infant. Impressed at her courage, Black Wolf let her keep the child, but the journey downstream continued. She was taken to Chalahgawtha on the Scioto, where her son Thomas was taken away to Detroit and her son George soon sickened and died. After many weeks of captivity, she and other women were taken to Big Bone Lick in Kentucky, some 20 miles southeast of present Cincinnati, to help make salt from the springs there. She put her baby daughter into the care of another woman, and then she and Hannah Schmidt escaped. Then, under great hardships, without weapons, suitable clothing or food, they headed back toward Draper's Meadows. They followed the Ohio River (often forced to make long upstream detours at the mouths of streams) up to the Kanawha River, then up the Kanawha to the New River. They were so threatened by hunger that Hannah Schmidt tried to kill Mary Draper to eat her. They fought, and Mary got away and crossed the river. The two women, then on opposite sides of the stream, continued upstream on the New River and eventually made it back to Draper's Meadows. There Mary, having traveled through the wilderness for some 1,500 miles since her capture, was reunited with her husband, William Ingles. An abbreviated account of her incredible journey and the travail she overcame may be found in *Trans-Allegheny Pioneers* by John P. Hale (Radford, Va., 1971).

93. Even Ottawas and Chippewas under Pontiac and Langlade, from as far away as middle and upper Michigan, responded to Contrecoeur's call and participated in the battle.

94. It was soon after Braddock's defeat that Dr. Daniel Craig of Winchester had occasion to meet and talk with Red Hawk, who described the peculiar circumstance to him. Red Hawk continued to believe it was through intervention of the Great Spirit that Washington escaped, but Dr. Craig surmised, most likely correctly, a defect in the gun. Years later Washington, too, met Red Hawk again and heard the same story from him. Red Hawk at that point viewed Washington with almost reverential awe.

95. Thomas Faucett was subsequently court-martialed and pled self-defense. He was discharged from the militia but not otherwise punished.

96. These tortures occurred in the area now occupied by Three Rivers Stadium. Greater details on Braddock's defeat may be found in numerous sources, including the author's own work, *Wilderness Empire.*

97. Actually, the name Fort Pitt was not officially bestowed on the installation until November 20, 1759, when it was so named after the British prime minister by Gen. John Stanwix; until then it was simply called *"the fort"* or Mercer's Fort or sometimes Fort Mercer, after the officer who was directing its reconstruction. However, to simplify matters and avoid confusion, it will be referred to as Fort Pitt from this point forward.

98. Kiskepila is pronounced Kiss-keh-PEE-luh.

99. Youghiogheny is often mispronounced YO-high-oh-GAY-nee. The correct pronunciation is YOCK-ee-oh-GAY-nee.

100. George Croghan, hearing rumors of Pontiac's plan, wrote to Amherst about them, but Amherst scoffed at the idea of the Indians being any real threat to the British, saying: *"I look upon the intelligence you receive of the French stirring up the western Indians of little consequence, as it is not in their power to hurt us."* Amherst also wrote to Sir William Johnson that if the Indians did commit any hostilities, they *"must not only expect the severest retaliation, but the destruction of all their nations, for I am firmly resolved, wherever they give me occasion, to extirpate them root and branch."* A little later, becoming somewhat more aware of the seriousness of the situation, Amherst recommended to his field commanders that they attempt to spread smallpox among the Indians by giving them infected blankets as gifts; he also advocated hunting *"the vermin"* with dogs. Pontiac's siege against Detroit failed, and though for several years he continued to wander among the tribes trying to get their support for another general attack against the British, it all fell through on April 20, 1769, when Pontiac was assassinated by an Illinois warrior. Full details of Pontiac's War, the Amherst policies and incidents that caused it and subsequent events are chronicled in the author's *The Conquerors* (Boston: Little, Brown, 1970; New York: Bantam, 1981).

101. The moment it was learned at Fort Pitt that Amherst had been recalled, the commander there, Capt. Simeon Ecuyer, wrote to his superior, Col. Henry Bouquet: *"What universal cries of joy and what bumpers of Madeira are drunk to his prompt departure!"*

102. The official list of prisoners liberated by Bouquet in this action, while incomplete, is as follows:

LIST OF CAPTIVES

. . . *taken by the Indians and delivered to Col. Bouquet by the Mingoes, Delawares, Shawanese, Wyandots, & Mohicans at Tuscarawas ye Muskingum Novem^r. 1764. Transmitted to Sir W^m. Johnson Bar^t. by Mr. Alex^r. McKee Agent for Ind^n. Affairs, Decr. 3^d. 1764*

Names of Males

No.	English & Indian	Where taken	When taken
1	Michael Patterson	*Virginia*	*1756*
2	John Bird	*ditto*	*1756*
3	George Yokeham	*ditto*	*1763*
4	Stephen Blankenship	*ditto*	*1758*
5	Thomas Harper	*ditto*	*1764*
6	Michael Lee	*ditto*	*1764*
7	George Lee	*ditto*	*1764*
8	John Huntman	*ditto*	*1764*
9	Adam Huntman	*ditto*	*1764*
10	Solomon Carpenter	*ditto*	-
11	John Gilmore	-	-
12	Jonas Wheat	-	-
13	John Freeling	*The above 13 with Col. McNed's volunteers*	
14	Frederick Myers	*ditto*	-
15	Leonard Hyard	*ditto*	*1764*
16	James Bell	*ditto*	*1764*
17	Thomas Collins	*ditto*	*1763*
18	James Price	*ditto*	*1757*
19	William Young	*ditto*	*1757*
20	Isaac Morris	*ditto*	-
21	Christopher Wirmshoud	*ditto*	-
22	Michael Cobble	*ditto*	-
23	Bridget's son	*ditto*	-
24	Cawacawache	*ditto*	-
25	Nicholas Petro	*ditto*	-
26	Philip Petro	*ditto*	-
27	Hance	*ditto*	-
28	John Williams	*ditto*	-
29	Daniel Rhoads	*ditto*	-
30	Henry Punnet	*ditto*	-
31	Mordecai Babson	*ditto*	-
32	Michael Rhoads	*ditto*	-
		The above 19 went with Major Fields to ??	

Females & Children

No.		Where taken	When taken
1	Barbara Rigar	*ditto*	*1758*
2	Dorothy Rigar	*ditto*	*1758*

3	Margaret Sivers	ditto	1758
4	Elizabeth Sivers	ditto	1758
5	Catherine Sivers	ditto	1758
6	Mary Lanciser	ditto	1755
7	her Child	ditto	1755
8	Elizabeth Nash [?]		-
9	?	?	?
10		ditto	-
11	Theo Chiloreu	Virginia	-
12	Elizabeth Mouse	ditto	1758
13	Eve Harper	ditto	-
14	Christina Howe	ditto	-
15	Margaret Yokeham	ditto	1763
16	Mary McCord	ditto	1763
17	Elizabeth Gilmore	ditto	-
18	Elizth Gilmore's dau^r	ditto	1763
19	Florence Hutchinson	ditto	1764
20	Mary Lee	ditto	1764
21	Catherine Lee	ditto	1764
22	Barbara Huntsman	ditto	1764
23	Susan Fishback	ditto	1755
24	Margaret Fishback	ditto	1755
25	Peggy Freeling	-	-
26	Peggy Cartmill	-	-
27	Molly Cartmill	ditto	-
28	Peggy Shepherd[?]	ditto	-
29	Elizabeth Stover	-	-
30	Elizth Stover's dau^r	-	-
31	Tamar	-	-
32	Elizabeth Snodgrass	-	-
33	Elizabeth Castle	The above 33 went with Col. McNich's[?] volunteers	
34	Eve Ice	-	-
35	William Ice	-	-
36	Lewis Ice	-	-
37	John Ice	-	-
38	Thomas Ice	-	-
39	Elizabeth Ice	-	-
40	Catherine Ice	-	-
41	Bryan, Rebecca	-	-
42	Anna Catherine	-	-
43	Sarah Price	-	-
44	Sally -	-	-
45	Caty Walbrook	-	-
46	Hannah Price	-	-
47	Polly	-	-

48	Hannah	-	-
49	Experience Wood	ditto	-
50	Mary Clouson	ditto	-
51	?		
52	?		
53	Mary Clover	Virginia	-
54	Pegy Colly	-	-
55	Conogomony	-	-
56	Alice Stedter	-	-
57	Molly Milch	-	-
58	Mary Craven	-	-
59	Pegy Pisenid	-	-

The above twenty-five went with Major Field's volunteers

PENNSYLVANIANS
  Males

1	John Jacob L. Roy	Pennsylvania	1755
2	Ephraim Walter	ditto	1757
3	John Walter	-	-
4	John Coatman	ditto	1758
5	David Johnson	ditto	1757
6	Marrill Devine	ditto	1763
7	Joseph Clemon	ditto	1755
8	Helty Clemon	ditto	1755
9	Horatio[?] Innes	ditto	1756
10	James Beaty	ditto	1763
11	Thomas Boyd	ditto	1757
12	James Campbell	ditto	1763
13	Andrew Sims	ditto	1764
14	Henry -	ditto	1756
15	Harry[?] Adams	ditto	-
16	Joseph Joriltzon[?]	ditto	-
17	Jacob Smither[?]	ditto	-
18	Joseph Studibaker	ditto	-
19	Christopher Tanner	ditto	-
20	Hans Adams	ditto	-
21	Simoni	ditto	-
22	Peters	ditto	-
23	Jammey	ditto	-
24	Pompadour	ditto	-
25	Tawaniona	ditto	-
26	?	ditto	-
27	?	-	-
28	?	-	-
29	Sowmouth	Pennsylvania	-
30	John Dunnahoe	ditto	-

31	William Lake	ditto	-
32	William Martin	ditto	-
33	James Martin	ditto	-
34	Robert Knox	ditto	-
35	John Fisher	ditto	-
36	John Biddle	ditto	-
37	John Diver	ditto	-
38	Stan Diver	ditto	-
39	John Palmer	ditto	-
40	[John]? McCulloch	ditto	-
41	John Gibson	ditto	-
42	Thomas Smallonson	ditto	-
43	Edward Henderson	ditto	-
44	Daniel Clomor	ditto	-
45	George Anderson	ditto	-
46	John Harvey	ditto	-
47	Jacob ?	ditto	-
48	? Hicks	ditto	-
49	? Hicks	ditto	-

	Females		
1	Sarah Boyd	ditto	-
2	Elizabeth Smith	ditto	-
3	Hannah Smith	ditto	-
4	her child	ditto	-
5	Elizabeth Henry	ditto	1756
6	Margaret Mallote	ditto	1755
7	Mary Villa	ditto	1756
8	Elizabeth Wilkins	ditto	1764
9	Mary Wilkins	ditto	1764
10	Elizabeth McLRoy	ditto	1755
11	her child	ditto	-
12	Mary McLRoy	ditto	1755
13	Catherine Heat	ditto	1756
14	Uley Strandman	ditto	1755
15	Catherine Strandman	ditto	-
16	Hanah Maria Gimback[?]	ditto	-
17	Kitty -	ditto	-
18	Beverly Miller	ditto	1756
19	Peggy -	ditto	-
20	Catherine Williams	ditto	-
21	Betty Young	ditto	-
22	?	?	?
23	Chrishana	Pennsylvania	-
24	Rachel Limmiger[?]	ditto	1755
25	Margaret Limmiger[?]	ditto	1756

26	Margaret Mansell	ditto	-
27	Dorothy Mansell	ditto	-
28	Elizabeth Franie	ditto	1755
29	Hannah Smith	ditto	-
30	Catherine Langesford	ditto	-
31	Peggy Baskin	ditto	1755
32	Ann Finley	ditto	1755
33	Mary Campbell	ditto	-
34	Mary Lowrey	ditto	1756
35	Jane Lowrey	ditto	1756
36	Susana Lowrey	ditto	-
37	Irena -	ditto	-
38	Phebe -	ditto	-
39	Christine Wampler	ditto	1756
40	Flatnose	ditto	-
41	Betty -	ditto	-
42	Agnus Davison	ditto	-
43	Molly Davison	ditto	-
44	Rachael-	ditto	-
45	Polly-	ditto	-
46	Catherine Bacon	ditto	-
47	Jean Crowe	ditto	-
48	Polly Crowe	ditto	-
49	Dorothy's son	ditto	-
50	David Bighead	ditto	-
51	Martha Martin	ditto	-
52	Luana Knox	ditto	-
53	Jean Knox	ditto	-
54	Mary Knox	ditto	-
55	Susana Knox	ditto	-
56	Eslhon[?] Flaherty	ditto	1756
57	Elizabeth Stimon	ditto	-
58	Mary Stewart	ditto	-
59	Jean M. Coon	ditto	-
60	Rachel Findres	ditto	-
61	Elizabeth Coon	ditto	-
62	And-	ditto	-
63	-two children	ditto	-
64	Catherine[?] Wampler	ditto	-
65	Rhoda Boyd	ditto	-
66	Elizabeth Studibaker	ditto	-
67	Dorothy's daughter	ditto	-

The above 67 women and children went under the care of Lieut. Colonel Clayton of the Pennsylvania Regiment

Virginians with Col. McNeil's Volunteers
Virginia 10th Major Field
Pennsylvanians with Col. Clayton

MEN	WOMEN & CHILDREN		
13	33	46	with Col. McNeal
19	26	45	with Major Field
49	67	116	with Lieut. Col. Clayton
Total		207	Men, Women & Children

[Source: Sir William Johnson Correspondence
Records of Superintendent's Office
RG 10 NAC, 1765 C. 1222 pp 313-314]

103.   Many colonial officials in America were becoming highly disgruntled at English home rule in the colonies, and this seemed to culminate with the Proclamation of 1763, which often stripped them of lands previously granted to them. George Washington, for example, was only one of those who lost vast tracts, he and others being stripped of the 2.5-million-acre grant he had received in the Ohio River Valley in 1760. In an angry letter to one of the other land speculators, he wrote: *"I can never look upon that proclamation in any other light (but I say this between ourselves) than as a temporary expedient to quiet the minds of the Indians."* Benjamin Franklin described the Proclamation as a yoke placed about the neck of the colonists to strangle them solely on the basis of economics, because of the value of the Indian trade. In his 1766 address to the British House of Commons, he said: *"The trade with the Indians, though carried on in America, is not an American interest. The people of America are chiefly farmers and planters; scarce anything that they raise or produce is an article of commerce with the Indians. The Indian trade is a British interest: it is carried on with British manufacturers, for the profit of British merchants and manufacturers."*

104.   This was the Cumberland River but, even though the stream had been renamed by the Walker party twenty years earlier at its upper reaches where it flowed through the Cumberland Gap, it was still referred to in its lower reaches by the name Shawanoe. The place where this incident occurred was just west of present Rockcastle, Trigg Co., Ky.

105.   The figure 20 M W^t signifies 2,000 pounds.

106.   Indenture was quite a prevalent means by which an individual or even whole families—usually very poor, often illiterate people—could sell themselves as servants to wealthy people who would pay their passage to the New World or, for those already in America, would provide (or promise) them the funds by which they could become settlers on their own following indenture. The terms of indenture might be from as short as six months or a year to upward of ten years. Most often a legal document was executed that bound both parties to the indenture agreement, such as the following: INDENTURE OF AN EMIGRANT SOLD TO PAY HIS PASSAGE MONEY Witnesseth, that John Peterson, of the county of Bedford and provence [sic] of Pennsylvania, yeoman, of his own free and voluntary will, for the consideration of the sum of £7.16.0

lawful Money of Pennsylvania, and for other good causes, he the said John Peterson hath bound and put himself, and by these Presents, doth bind and put himself servant to Richard Wells of the County afs'd, to serve him, his Executors, Administrators and assigns, from the Day of the Date hereof, for and during the full term of one years and six months, thence next ensuing. During all which Term the said Servant, said Richard Wells, his Executors, Administrators and assigns faithfully shall serve, and that honestly and obediently in all Things as a good and faithful Servant ought to do. And the said Richard Wells, his Executors, Administrators and assigns, during the said Term shall find and provide for the said Servant, sufficient Meat, Drink, Washing and Lodging. And for the Performance hereof both the said Parties bind themselves firmly to each other by these presents. IN WITNESS whereof they have hereunto interchangeably set their Hands and seals. Dated the thirteenth day of March, Anno Domini one thousand seven hundred and seventy-three. Done before me. George Woods, J.P. his Mark. John X Peterson

107.   This so-called National Road was the genesis of present U.S. Route 40.

108.   Fort Bedford was located 100 miles west of Carlisle on the site of the present city of Bedford, Bedford Co., Pa. Fort Ligonier was another 44 miles beyond that post, located on Loyalhannon Creek at Laurel Hill.

109.   This settlement was made on the site of the present town of Carmichaels, Greene Co., Pa.

110.   The Decker's Creek Settlement, first established in the fall of 1758, was situated at the mouth of the creek still bearing that name at the southern edge of the present city of Morgantown, Monongalia Co., W.Va.

111.   All these settlements were located in present Upshur Co., W.Va.

112.   Fort Stanwix, built by Gen. John Stanwix, was situated on the site of present Rome, Oneida Co., N.Y.

113.   The sum of £10,000 in goods was meant by the British to be distributed proportionately to the tribes on hand for the council who were giving up their lands and putting their marks to the treaty. The Iroquois, however, once the deal was made, imperiously demanded the full amount and it was given to them, thus making them culpable in large measure for consummating what was undoubtedly the greatest land fraud perpetrated against American Indian tribes.

114.   The Mohawk subchief, Abraham, who witnessed these proceedings, reported soon afterward to Sir William Johnson and related to him what had transpired. He then told Sir William, *"As to the pretensions of any inconsiderable people, behind our backs, we shall soon silence them, and we desire that you may assure the King that it was our property we justly disposed of, that we had full authority to do so."* The Iroquois, however, made no appearance in Ohio against the Shawnees or any other tribe. Having been the sole beneficiaries of the deal they had made, they were content to merely sit back and watch unfold the disaster they had instigated.

115.   This camp was situated in present Estill Co., Ky., at or near the site of the present village of Station Camp on Station Camp Creek.

116.   Findlay and Boone, along with Col. Knox and others who came along a little

later, were largely responsible for the genesis of the term *long hunters,* occasioned by their going out on hunts that lasted for months, sometimes even years, before their return.

117. This was the headwaters of Wheeling Creek, encountered by Zane's party most likely in the area where the stream passes beneath the present Pennsylvania Route 221, between present West Alexander and East Finley.

118. This is present Little Wheeling Creek.

119. Individuals were supposed to have no right to claim more than 400 acres, plus preemption rights to another 1,000 acres, but it is apparent that the Zane brothers claimed far more than this and evidently were never penalized for having done so.

120. This stream still bears the name of Buffalo Creek, which empties into the Ohio at the southern end of present Wellsburg, Brooke Co., W.Va. Williams's claim was located near the mouth of present Stotts Run, where it empties into present Buffalo Creek, just over two miles due north of present West Liberty, Ohio Co., and three creek miles downstream from present Bethany, Brooke Co., W.Va.

121. Isaac Williams did get back, eventually, after an odyssey lasting for ten years. He paddled down the Ohio all the way to the Mississippi, up that river to the Missouri and up the Missouri for about 200 miles. Before returning, he hired himself out as a hunter for various new settlements.

122. The hill from which Zane took his observation is the bluff that rises directly behind the present Lincoln School and through which present Interstate Route 70 passes in a tunnel.

123. This, of course, is the site of the present city of Wheeling, Ohio Co., W.Va.

124. Catherine Zane grew to maturity at Wheeling and eventually married Capt. Absalom Martin of the U.S. Army.

125. With the large number of claims being made in the Ohio Valley at this time, it was not surprising that there were overlappings of claims or multiple claims made for the same ground, especially when the parcel in question was choice. Just such a case occurred at Round Bottom, where the claims of Washington and George Rogers Clark conflicted with the claims of Cresap. The case was tied up in litigation for many years and was finally settled in favor of George Washington. Cresap did win a different judgment, however, in a land dispute with George Rogers Clark over a claim both men made near the mouth of Fish Creek at present Cresap's Bottom, Marshall Co., W.Va.

126. The present city of Parkersburg, W.Va., is located at the mouth of the Little Kanawha River. The Delaware village called Bulltown was then located three miles up the Little Kanawha from its mouth, on a bottom of the east bank where, at the mouth of present Dry Creek, stands the present village of Stewart, Wood Co., W.Va.

127. Included in Washington's claim here, though he didn't know it at the time, was the famous Burning Spring, discovered about eighteen months later by the Van Bibber party, for details of which see Note 133.

128. The Big Sandy River is the present boundary between West Virginia and Kentucky.

129. The Fry Claim of 2,084 acres, made by Washington, was located on the northwest bank of the present Louisa Fork of Big Sandy River, on the site of present Louisa, Lawrence Co., Ky.

130. This party surveyed in the area of the present Kentucky capital city of Frankfort, where they claimed 600 acres.

131. This party did quite a bit of surveying in the area that is now the city of Louisville, Ky.

132. In later years, due to his name being enshrined on it, this rocky shelf became known, as it remains today, as Van Bibber's Rock.

133. The burning surface of this spring was caused by subterranean natural gas leaking upward into the subsurface channel caused by the spring. Though sometimes it would be extinguished by heavy downpours, the site was noted for attracting lightning, which would again ignite it. It is still known today as Burning Spring and eventually became the site of the first natural gas well in America. It is located near the town of Coal Fork, Kanawha Co., W.Va.

134. Camp Union was established in 1770 on the site of present Lewisburg, Greenbrier Co., W.Va. Its official designation was Fort Savannah, but the name Camp Union was used while it was under construction and became so popular that the Fort Savannah designation more or less vanished.

135. These four men made their settlement on the site of present Frankford, Greenbrier Co., W.Va.

136. The nine others, besides Wetzel and Bonnett, were Conrod Stoup, Martin Stull, George Rhinehart, Jacob Reagen, Martin Kellar, John Pectoll, James Clark, Abraham Messer and Adam Grindstaff.

137. One story, unverified, states that the Wetzels and Bonnetts actually started out to claim on Wheeling Creek before the Zanes, but that Lewis Bonnett's saddle girth snapped, and while they were stopped to repair it, the Zane party passed them by and got claim to the lower Wheeling. While it is true that the Zane party may have passed them by, this occurred in 1770, during the second trip of the Zanes, when Ebenezer was bringing his wife to the cabin and claims made the preceding year. Thus, even had Bonnett not had the mishap, his party would still have found Wheeling Creek below the Forks all claimed by the Zane family.

138. John Wetzel's claim was located in the bottom on the west (left) side of Wheeling Creek, opposite the mouth of present Cricket Hollow, in what came to be known as the Sand Hills District of present Marshall Co., W.Va.

139. Whether it was Cricket Hollow Run that he followed upstream and where he encountered the bear cannot be authenticated.

140. The stream they followed up from Wheeling Creek is present Bruce Run, and the settlement was made on the site of the present unincorporated community of Sand Hill, Marshall Co., W.Va.

141. Boggs Settlement was established by William Boggs, Sr., about 1772, at the mouth of a ravine less than a half-mile north of the run, on the site of the old switching yards of the B&O Railroad just a few hundred feet south of the present Ohio-Marshall County line, in the southern edge of present Wheeling, W.Va.

142. The stream on which the McCullochs settled was present Short Creek. The McCulloch Settlement was situated at the Brooke-Ohio County line, a half-mile from the present village of Windsor, W.Va.

143. All these burial mounds, including the large one, were interconnected by low earthen entrenchments. They are situated on a second terrace 75 feet above river level. For many years it was believed that the second terrace was as natural as the first, but close studies in later years indicated that the second terrace, some 30 feet in thickness, was artificially constructed as a base for the mounds, which are themselves perfectly circular. Not unexpectedly, the large mound has received the most attention. Often described as one of the largest burial mounds discovered in the United States, the great Grave Creek Mound was described by an early archaeologist, S. D. Peet, as being comprised of cubic contents equal to the third pyramid of Mycerinus, but *"heaped up by a people destitute of the knowledge of iron, and who had no domestic animals or machinery to aid them."* No information has ever been uncovered that would explain who it might have been that made the curious markings in the giant beech tree at its summit, or who might have carved in the date 1734. Both the beech and oak at the summit were in a state of decay by 1818 and were finally cut down in 1828. The annular rings inside the oak indicated its age to be slightly more than 500 years, meaning the tree sprouted there sometime around the year 1300. No serious excavation was made at the mound until 1838, when an adit seven feet high by ten feet wide was excavated at the base, parallel to ground level, toward the center. At a distance of 111 feet diggers encountered the top of what turned out to be a vault lined with upright timbers side by side and covered over by similar timbers. The logged top was rectangular, eight feet wide by twelve feet long, and covered over with large flat stones common to the neighborhood, some of which had tumbled into the vault as the timbers rotted. When excavated, the vault was found to be seven feet deep. Inside were discovered two human skeletons, a male and a female, in what was described as a *"tolerable"* state of preservation. Articles of what appeared to have once been items of clothing and furnishings were positioned beside the skeletons, but decay had rendered them unidentifiable. There were also some worked stone implements and weapons that were in perfect condition. The two skeletons were of ordinary size; the female skeleton was unornamented. The male skeleton was surrounded by 650 ivory beads that had evidently been a necklace. They appeared to have been sawn from a single length of ivory, and then each piece was drilled through the center. With them, though whether a part of the necklace could not be determined, was an ivory ornament six inches in length. At that point another digging was begun at the summit of the cone, perpendicular to the tunnel at the base. At a depth of 36 feet—34 feet directly above the vault at the base—another burial vault was discovered approximately the size and description of the first. This one contained a single skeleton that had been ornamented around wrists and ankles with beaten copper rings three-eighths-inch thick, these ornaments having an aggregate weight of 17 ounces. Mummified skin and sinews were attached to the bones in the areas of encirclement by the rings. There were

also 200 mica discs and 17 large beads carved from bone, along with over 2,000 discs cut from shells. Most important, however, within the vault and just two feet from the skeleton, was found what has been named "the Inscribed Stone"—a smooth, oval-shaped stone inscribed with three lines of ancient characters sandwiched between parallel inscribed lines. The first line held seven characters, the second held nine, the third held seven. Beneath these was a larger hieroglyphic character. The stone, studied at the Royal Antiquarian Society in Copenhagen, was declared definitely not runic but possibly Celtiberic. Numerous other prehistoric earthen burial mounds have been found in this general area of the Ohio River in present Marshall County, W.Va. One was on the claim made by Michael Cresap at present Cresap's Bottom, three at Wells' Bottom, a few at Fish Creek and others elsewhere. On the Wetzel claims in the Sand Hills District of the county have been found mounds, oval in shape, constructed of rocks piled together to a height of three to four feet, and in that area the sand-rock base has been found to contain footprints of birds, hooved animals and humans, along with bored holes that were thought by the early settlers to have been hollowed out for molding lead, though no trace of lead has ever been found there. The Fish Creek rock mounds occur at intervals for a distance of some four miles. On upper Wheeling Creek, 4.5 stream miles below the town of Majorsville at the Pennsylvania border and a mile and a half above the tiny community of Viola, on the bottom directly across from the mouth of Wolf Run, are several of these curious stone mounds, ranging in size from ovals that are eight by ten feet to circular stone-pile structures as much as 75 feet in circumference. The largest of these was taken apart about 1835 and was found to contain from 500 to 600 skeletons, plus a large number of artifacts, including highly polished darts, arrowheads, spearheads, hatchets, skinning knives, pipes and pieces of pottery. In some areas the pottery shards are amazingly abundant and have been found layered to a depth of two feet or more. In all the mounds, earthen or stone, in this region that have thus far been opened, skeletal remains, ornaments, carved pipes, weapons and various implements have been found. Occasional finds are still made on the ground surfaces today. While all of the above mounds and remains were found in present Marshall Co., W.Va., some 35 miles above this, at present East Steubenville, Brooke Co., W.Va., a rather remarkable discovery of ancient remains was made in 1834. A stonemason, Samuel Cummings, crossed the Ohio from Steubenville, O., to inspect the rock ledges on the then Virginia (now West Virginia) side of the river to locate rock suitable for quarrying. Almost exactly opposite the foot of South Street in Steubenville, he found a huge rock that in some bygone age had tumbled from the overhang above. While inspecting it, he found, beneath accumulated debris and rubble, an ancient stone wall. He began pulling it apart and abruptly exposed a large vaultlike compartment in which there were an estimated 75 to 100 human skeletons *"packed together in perfect regularity."* Nathaniel Wells, who owned the land, lived several miles away and did not hear of the find for several days. In the meanwhile, word of the find spread, and hordes of people thronged to the site, mainly crossing over the river from Steubenville, and began carrying away skulls, bones, implements or whatever else could be found. Wells, who said he would have protected the find for scientific study had he known of it, did not arrive until virtually everything was gone.

144. The Tomlinson Settlement was located at the mouth of present Grave Creek, on the site of the present city of Moundsville, Marshall Co., W.Va.

145. Miss Harkness had an uncle, referred to only as Harkness, who was a trader and had been killed by the Shawnees at the same time as the husband of Elizabeth Tomlinson Martin, early in 1770.

146. Many of the uneducated settlers in this area, unable to handle French pronunciation of Chartier's, spoke or wrote the word in ill-conceived phonetics as Shirtee. The name of Chartier's Creek often appears this way in the early documents.

147. The name Catfish Camp continued to be used for quite a few years until the settlement became quite large and was renamed in honor of the first President of the United States. It was located on the site of present Washington, Washington Co., Pa.

148. Houston remained at his Catfish Camp only a year or so, by the end of which time so much settlement had occurred that he became disgusted, sold his claim there and descended Chartier's Creek about ten miles, where he established a new settlement at an unoccupied bottom on the west bank there. That settlement was made on the site of present Houston, Washington Co., Pa.

149. This new settlement by Andrew Van Swearingen was established in 1772 and was located within the present limits of the city of Wellsburg, Brooke Co., W.Va., at or near the site of the present Central Junior High School.

150. The name of the stream upon which Bane Settlement was established is present Bane Creek, and the settlement was on the site of present Banetown, Washington Co., Pa.

151. The stream is still called Booth's Creek, and the settlement was on the site of present Boothsville, Marion Co., W.Va.

152. Prickett's Settlement and Prickett's Fort were located at the mouth of present Prickett's Creek, five miles below present Fairmount and about a mile below the village of Baxter, Marion Co., W.Va.

153. Holliday's Cove was established in 1771 on the site of present Holliday's Cove, Hancock Co., W.Va. Present Harmon's Creek empties into the Ohio opposite the north edge of present Steubenville, Jefferson Co., O.

154. The mouth of the smaller creek where they camped was present Twomile Creek, just east of present Charleston, W.Va. The creek near the salt lick was present Campbell's Creek. Kenton was at this time using the alias of Simon Butler, as he believed he had killed a man in a fight and authorities were now searching for him. Later he learned he had not killed the man after all and was not a fugitive, so he resumed his true identity. To avoid confusion here, he will be referred to as Kenton, even during the alias period. Greater details of Simon Kenton's camp being attacked by Indians, of his continued search for

and eventual discovery of the Kentucky canelands and subsequent events of his remarkable life may be found in the author's *The Frontiersmen* (Boston: Little, Brown, 1967; New York: Bantam, 1968).

155.   The Wells claim was located on the site of the present community of Mechling Hill, which is (via Alt. State Route 27) five miles east of present Follansbee, Brooke Co., W.Va. The Wells preemption right extended eastward from his claim to the Pennsylvania border.

156.   The Kelly's Creek Settlement, established in 1773, was located 19 miles up the Kanawha River from the present capital city of Charleston, at the mouth of present Kelly's Creek, in the vicinity of the present village of Cedar Grove, Kanawha Co., W.Va.

157.   This cabin built by the surveyors Hedges and Young was located at the mouth of present Chalfant Creek, five miles downstream from present Augusta, a little over a mile above the present village of Wellsburg, Bracken Co., Ky., and about the same distance below the present village of Utopia, on the opposite side of the river in present Clermont Co., O. Some historians have claimed this to be the first cabin built in Kentucky, but that honor goes to the small trading post cabin built by John Findlay on Elkhorn Creek, in the vicinity of Lexington, 29 years earlier, in 1744. (See Note 34.)

158.   Gen. Gage, in correspondence to Sir William Johnson about the uselessness of Fort de Chartres, wrote: *"It has not the least command of the River, owing to an Island which lies exactly opposite to it, and the Channel is entirely on the other side for a great part of the year. This is impassible from a sand bar which runs across, even for small boats, and the French and Spaniards on the other side pass and repass at pleasure with contraband goods, forcing an illicit Trade, to our great disadvantage and a certain and very considerable loss to His Majesty's Revenue."*

159.   Stewart's name is spelled Stuart in some documents, but the former spelling seems to be the most accepted.

160.   The new village was situated at approximately the site of the present town Hazelton, Gibson Co., Ind. The number of Indian dead, given here as 20, is an estimate; all accounts agree that five families of Indians were slain, and since most Indian families had at least four or five members, the figure of *"about twenty"* seems reasonable.

161.   Kittanning had been reoccupied by the Indians after its destruction by Col. John Armstrong in 1756 and again after two subsequent attacks, but the village had never regained the size or strength it had previously known. A large number of the Delawares who emigrated at this time were of the Muncey subtribe, and they resettled, with permission of the Miami tribe, on the headwaters of the White River in the vicinity of present Muncie, Delaware Co., Ind.

162.   Chocolate was a very popular trade item among the northwestern tribes at this time, and many had developed an especial fondness for hot chocolate, which they made by boiling the chocolate lumps in water and adding heaping spoons of *melassa*—maple sugar—of their own manufacture.

163.   Gen. Thomas Gage wrote to Sir William Johnson on March 31, 1773, about

these attacks on traders, complaining bitterly: *"Scarce a year passes that the Pouteatamies are not guilty of killing Some of the Traders and of course plundering their Effects, which it becomes absolutely Necessary to put a Stop to."*

164. One of the youths captured on the Virginia frontier at this time was 17-year-old Marmaduke Van Swearingen, who was adopted into the Shawnee tribe, given the new name of Wehyehpihehrsehnwah—Blue Jacket—and so well adapted to the Indian way of life that he eventually became principal chief of the Maykujay sept of the tribe, founder of Blue Jacket's Town on the site of present Bellefontaine, Logan Co., O., and ultimately rose to become war chief of the entire tribe. A full account of his experiences and career as an Indian may be found in the author's historical narrative, *The Frontiersmen,* and in his young adult novel, *Blue Jacket: War Chief of the Shawnees* (Boston: Little, Brown, 1969; Dayton: Landfall Press, 1983).

165. The Pennsylvania/Virginia border in this region was a complex and confusing issue. James Hendricks, a Pennsylvania surveyor, admitted he could not say exactly where the colony's western boundary crossed the Monongahela, but he believed it was likely at the mouth of Chartier's Creek on the Ohio, four miles below (west) of Fort Pitt. Michael Cresap, from Maryland, asserted his opinion that Pennsylvania's domain did not extend beyond the Alleghenies and that the region in question was the King's land—an opinion eagerly accepted by those currently settling upon it. George Croghan, Pennsylvanian though he was, maintained that Pennsylvania's own actions in the past supported the view that it was Virginia's domain, pointing out that not many years before the Pennsylvania Assembly had refused to build a trading house or fort at the site of Fort Pitt, alleging it to be outside of William Penn's original grant, and adding that even afterward, when petitioned for funds to aid in ousting the French from Fort Pitt, the Pennsylvania Assembly had refused. William Crawford, Virginian, agreed with Croghan and declared that the region, including all of the Monongahela Valley, was Virginia land. Others who supported the Virginia viewpoint included Isaac Cox, George Vallandigham, William Gee, Thomas Smallman, Edward Ward, George McCormick, John Stephenson, Joseph Beckett, Dorsey Pentecost, John Connolly and John Gibson. This controversy involving the title to land lying on the Monongahela and Ohio rivers continued until the outbreak of the Revolutionary War and even then, though put in abeyance, was not fully settled until after that conflict ended. The claims were based on early, overlapping royal land grants; Virginia's claim based on the charter bestowed upon that colony by James I; Pennsylvania's claim based on the charter it had been granted by Charles II.

166. It is also known that at this time Lord Dunmore had secret meetings with Connolly, and while the full scope of these talks has never been definitely ascertained, later events seem to bear out the speculation that Connolly was ordered by Dunmore (1) to foment the Virginia-Pennsylvania border dispute in order to curtail cooperation between them in opposition to the British Crown, and (2) to foment warfare between the Indian tribes and the Americans in any way possible in order to thus prepare the way for achieving a

British alliance with the Indians, should an actual rupture occur between the Crown and the colonies. The fact that Pennsylvania abruptly agreed to make the Monongahela the boundary between itself and Virginia and that the offer was peremptorily rejected by Dunmore lends credence to the speculation, as do subsequent events.

167.   The village of Shamokin, at the time of the birth of Talgayeeta in 1731, was primarily a Cayuga village, but it also had a fair population of Senecas and Delawares. It was located just a short distance below the Forks of the Susquehanna, at the mouth of the present Shamokin River, on the site of the present city of Sunbury, Northumberland Co., Pa.

168.   The fame of Shikellimus for his hospitality reached so far that when Count Zinzindorf visited America in 1742, he made a special point of going far out of his way to visit Shikellimus at his village and spoke glowingly of it ever afterward.

169.   Talgayeeta's Town, better known to the whites as Logan's Spring, was located a few miles above present Lewiston and just below the present town of Reedsville in present Mifflin Co., Pa. The name Logan's Spring persists to this day. The author has previously written in both *The Frontiersmen* and *A Sorrow in Our Heart: The Life of Tecumseh* (New York: Bantam, 1992) that the father of Talgayeeta, Shikellimus, lived until 1774, but continued research has shown this to be an error and that Shikellimus died some years before that. The author apologizes for this earlier misinformation.

170.   On the Ohio two streams named Cross Creek have their mouths almost opposite one another, one on the Ohio side, one on the West Virginia side. The same holds true some twenty miles farther downstream, where there is a Wheeling Creek that empties into the Ohio from the Ohio side almost opposite the Wheeling Creek entering from the West Virginia side. To make it clear what stream they were talking about, the settlers referred to the streams entering from the Ohio side as Indian Cross Creek and Indian Wheeling Creek. To prevent confusion for the reader, the author will do the same in this work.

171.   As nearly as can be ascertained from descriptions that have been recorded, this spring is the one presently known as Lacock Spring, located 25 miles below Pittsburgh in the present town of East Rochester, Beaver Co., Pa.

172.   Briscoe's Settlement was established in early May 1773 by Dr. John Briscoe on a bottomland situated six miles upstream from the mouth of the Little Kanawha River (site of the present city of Parkersburg); located at the northernmost end of the present city of Vienna, on the present Briscoe oil field at the mouth of Briscoe Run, Wood Co., W.Va.

173.   The Taylor-McAfee party was still surveying up the Kentucky River when they learned of the attack on the Bullitt party. Fearing to descend the Kentucky back to the Ohio and risk encountering Indians, they had elected to return to Virginia overland, a journey they accomplished through the Cumberland Gap in safety but only after great hardships.

174.   John Floyd was the father of the John Floyd who later became Governor of

Virginia, and grandfather of John B. Floyd, who also subsequently became Virginia's governor. Hancock Taylor was the uncle of future U.S. President Zachary Taylor.

175. Baker's Bottom is a large level bottom located on the left (east) side of the Ohio River, 50 miles below Pittsburgh, where, in 1773, Joshua Baker claimed the land and erected a trading cabin just a few hundred yards downstream from the mouth of Yellow Creek on the right (west) side of the Ohio, two miles below present Wellsville, where the Ohio River makes a sharp bend and changes direction from a southwestern course to a southeastern course. Baker's cabin was located in the midst of Baker's Bottom at the mouth of Dry Run (still so called), a half-mile south of the present Waterford Park race and golf course, Hancock Co., W.Va.

176. Michael Cresap was the son of Col. Thomas Cresap, a Maryland officer prominent in the French and Indian War.

177. Site of present Brownsville, Fayette Co., Pa.

178. In his orders to John Floyd, Washington wrote that if difficulties prevented his claiming lands along the Scioto, then: *"I would go quite down to the Falls or even below; meaning thereby to get richer and wider bottoms, as it is my desire to have my lands run out on the banks of the Ohio."*

179. The Indian greeting of *"How"* is not, as many people believe, a creation of B-grade western movies. It stems from the greeting the English traders originally gave when meeting the Indians, *"How do you do?"* Unable to quite master the entire phrase, the Indians responded by parroting *"How'd'do."* This gradually evolved to *"Howdy,"* which the English themselves then picked up in turn from the Indians. The evolution became complete with simply the word *"How,"* usually accompanied either with a hand raised with palm facing forward in a peace sign, or with a simple handshake.

180. Though called Logan's Yellow Creek Camp or Logan's Hunting Camp, this village had been established by Talgayeeta as a new permanent home for his family and followers, estimated to number about 60 at this time. It was located just under a half-mile up Yellow Creek from its mouth, on a level bottom where there is now a rest area, 600 feet below the upper Conrail railroad bridge. The site, while in northeastern Jefferson County, is about two miles south and a little west of present Wellsville, Columbiana Co., O.

181. McMechen's Settlement was established late in 1773 or early in 1774 on what was for a time called McMechen's Bottom, just below the mouth of present McMechen's Run and in the northern portion of what is the present town of McMechen, Marshall Co., W.Va. Samuel Meason has very frequently been referred to in the early documents as Samuel Mason, and later in his life even he used the latter name. Early land claim documents and correspondence with Gen. Hand indicate, however, that the correct spelling of his name was Meason, as this was how he signed his own name at the time. That is how he will be referred to in this narrative.

182. Here, as earlier, the island is referred to as Wheeling Island to prevent confusion. Actually, the island had no known name when first discovered, but as

soon as Zane claimed land on it, the name Zane's Island was applied. Later, when Daniel Zane became owner, he attempted to establish a town there, to be named Columbia, and he also built and operated the Columbia Inn there. However, for whatever reason, Columbia was never incorporated, and the island eventually was annexed by the city of Wheeling and for a considerable period was called Wheeling Island. It is today a part of the city of Wheeling but is still referred to as Wheeling Island. A folk tale that Ebenezer Zane originally bought the island from Indians is wholly without foundation.

183.   Ann Zane, the first white child born at Wheeling (May 27, 1771), grew to maturity there but died unmarried. Sarah Zane also grew to maturity at Wheeling and eventually married Capt. John McIntire. Several years after his death she married the Rev. David Young of Zanesville, O.

184.   Cresap's Bottom was located at the site of present Cresap Bottom, Marshall Co., W.Va., a mile downstream and across the Ohio River from the present town of Powhatan Point, Belmont Co., O. George Rogers Clark later made a claim on Cresap's Bottom, which became a matter of litigation for a long period of time, and he eventually lost the land due to the prior claims made by Michael Cresap.

185.   This settlement was located at the site of the present community called Woodlands, just below the mouth of Fish Creek in Marshall Co., W.Va.

186.   George Washington and George Rogers Clark, though in communication for many years afterward, never met each other.

187.   Sandy Creek enters the Ohio River at the lower end of present Washington Bottom, less than a mile above present Newberry Island and three miles above present Mustapha Island.

188.   Horsehead Bottom was a Mingo village located in 1771 two miles up the Little Scioto River from the Ohio, then a mile and a half up Pine Creek (present Wards Run) at approximately the site of the present town of Slocum, Scioto Co., O.

189.   This whole story by Greathouse, though accepted by the men at the rendezvous, cannot be substantiated. It is stated that this Davis, assuming he ever existed at all, was never seen again after starting up the Kanawha and was believed killed by Indians. Only two traders named Davis were in operation in that area at this time. Unrelated, they were Robert Davis and Edward Davis, whose whereabouts were accounted for.

190.   One account, which cannot be substantiated, states that as the party started upriver, *"we met Killbuck, an Indian chief, with a small party. We had a long conference with him, but received little satisfaction as to the disposition of the Indians. It was observed that Cresap did not come to this conference, but kept on the opposite side of the river. He said that he was afraid to trust himself with the Indians. That Killbuck had frequently attempted to waylay his father to kill him. That if he crossed the river, perhaps his fortitude might fail him, and that he might put Killbuck to death."*

191.   The stretch of Ohio River called Long Reach begins at the upper end of present Paden Island, just at the northernmost point of Paden City, Wetzel Co., W.Va., and continues downstream to the westward bend that occurs six miles upstream from present Saint Marys, Pleasants Co., W.Va.

192. This place where they stopped is on the site of the present town of Hockingport, Athens Co., O.

193. This camp was located a few hundred yards upstream from the mouth of Pipe Creek at the Ohio River, two and a half miles below the mouth of Grave Creek on the opposite side of the Ohio (where Moundsville, W.Va., is presently located). Pipe Creek empties into the Ohio directly across from present Round Bottom, in present Belmont Co., O.

194. Existing evidence seems to indicate that these killings were done by Jacob Greathouse and his men, and that one of the men who came late on the scene and decried the killings was George Rogers Clark; the evidence also indicates that Michael Cresap was not present here.

195. The author has been unable to find an actual copy of either of John Connolly's circular letters, although the numerous accounts of their circulation and contents leave no doubt as to what they contained.

196. Since there is a Short Creek entering the Ohio on each side of the big river, the one entering from the Ohio country is designated, as the settlers did, Indian Short Creek to distinguish between them. The mouth of Short Creek entering the Ohio from the west is at the northern edge of the present town of Tiltonsville, Jefferson Co., O.

197. Some of the accounts of this incident state that Stevens was also killed, but this is an error that stems from a misinterpretation of the reports that he was shot. His wound was slight and he survived. He returned to the east shortly after this incident and disappears from historical mention.

198. Of the 32 whites who participated in this grisly affair, those who can be identified included the Greathouse brothers—Daniel and Jacob; the Mahon brothers—Raphael (Rafe) and John; Joseph Tomlinson (and according to some sources, his brother Samuel as well); Edward King, John Martin, George Cox, John Sappington, William Grills, Michael Myers, William Fitzgerald, Joseph Smith (a one-armed man), John Biggs and possibly Joshua Baker.

199. The only identified Indian victims were Taylaynee (also referred to by the name of John Petty, Talgayeeta's older brother), Mellana (Talgayeeta's wife, though it has been said by some that he had more than one wife at this time, and by others that he was unmarried); Molnah (Talgayeeta's nephew, son of Taylaynee); and Koonay (Talgayeeta's sister). Two accounts list Talgayeeta's mother, unnamed, as among the dead. There is a wide disparity among the reports in the number of Indians killed, with *"eight or ten"* being the lowest figure and 24 the highest. Most of the bodies of the second party to come over wound up in the water and were swept away by the current and, not being physically included among the on shore dead, have largely been overlooked. Of the ten who came over in the first group (seven warriors, two women and the two-year-old girl, but not including the close-to-birth fetus), all were killed except the little girl, who was subsequently carried to Catfish Camp (present Washington, Pa.) and from there to the Redstone area on the Monongahela, where she was turned over to William Crawford. He, in turn, subsequently placed her in the hands of her father, John Gibson, who saw to her upbringing, but apart from that bit of information, virtually nothing sub-

sequently appears about the daughter. In the second group to come over, there were 14 warriors, one woman and at least two, possibly three or four, boys approximately in their early teens; of whom all but two of the warriors were killed (two swimming to safety) and the woman survived (though it is not stated how this occurred). This means that at least 12 more were killed from among the second party, and so the death toll was probably 21. Most of the whites who took part later individually declared they had taken no part in the actual killing, but this is certainly an effort to absolve themselves of the atrocity and is not borne out by the facts that indicate that all, or virtually all, had to participate in order for what occurred to have taken place.

200.   At least three different elaborate lies were concocted by members of the Greathouse party to justify their attack on the Indians from Logan's Yellow Creek Camp. All differ considerably, yet all were depositions later given. The most accepted of these is that the Indians came over to Joshua Baker's store, drank his rum without paying for it, took clothing that did not belong to them and threatened Baker's life. Another widely accepted tale claims that the Greathouse party was innocently camping when attacked by the Mingoes and that all the shots fired by the Indians in their surprise attack missed, giving the whites opportunity to snatch up their weapons and fire back, killing most of the attackers.

201.   One account, largely fanciful, states that Talgayeeta's brother did not die in the burst of gunfire that broke out, that he was wounded and that, while he was in the agonies of death, Edward King leaped astraddle his breast and then stabbed him in the heart, saying aloud to his companions, *"Many a deer have I shived this way."* At least one account states that Talgayeeta's wife, Mellana, was a Shawnee woman, but this is almost certainly incorrect. One account also states that the Greathouse party hid the Indian bodies in dense brush, but this is believed erroneous.

202.   Some accounts have erroneously stated that Koonay was Talgayeeta's daughter. Some accounts also say there were two small children involved, but there was only one.

203.   Because he had been warned by Blue Jacket that such an attack was being planned against him and that the name Cresap had been overheard, Talgayeeta —Chief Logan—initially believed that it was Michael Cresap who had led the attack that wiped out his family. Many whites at this time thought the same, since Cresap was known to have led the previous attacks at Short Creek and Captina Creek and that he had also initially started leading this attack against Talgayeeta's people before reconsidering while en route and giving it up. It was not until much later in the year that Talgayeeta learned from his son-in-law, John Gibson, that Cresap had not led the murderous attack.

204.   Peter Jolly, later a respected judge, was 12 years old at this time and many years afterward wrote: *"I very well recollect my mother feeding and dressing the babe; chirruping to the little innocent and its smiling. However, they took it away and talked of sending it to its supposed father, Colonel George [actually John] Gibson, of Carlisle, Pa., who was then and had been for many years, a trader among the Indians."*

205. When most of the others continued their flight eastward, Edward King remained and lived with Houston for some time, but so far as can be determined, he and Chambers never spoke to each other again after this.

206. In some accounts the Greathouse boys are erroneously referred to as Gatewood and Tomlinson as Tumblestone, the latter an appellation locally applied to Tomlinson because of his habit of tumbling over the stones of prehistoric burial mounds in the area of his Grave Creek Settlement as he looked for ancient artifacts.

207. Twenty-six years later, still trying to absolve himself and Cresap of guilt in the Baker's Bottom affair, John Sappington, in a deposition given in Madison County and attested to by Samuel McKee, Jr., on February 13, 1800, made a sworn declaration in which he said, among other things regarding this atrocity: *"Logan's family (if it was his family) was not killed by Cresap, nor with his knowledge, nor by his consent, but by the Greathouses and their associates. . . . To the best of my knowledge, there were three Greathouses engaged in this business. . . . I know* that likewise that he (Cresap) was generally blamed for it, and believed by all who were *not acquainted by the circumstances, to have been the perpetrator of it. I know that he despised and hated the Greathouses ever afterwards on account of it. . . . I do not believe Logan had any relations killed, except his brother. Neither of the squaws who were killed was his wife. Two of them were old women, and the third, with her child which was saved, I have the best reason in the world to believe was the wife and child of General Gibson. I know he educated the child and took care of it, as if it had been his own. Whether Logan had a wife or not, I can't say, but it is probable that as he was a chief, he considered them all as his people."*

208. One account gives the location of this incident as occurring on the Kanawha River, but that is an error.

209. The mouth of George's Creek is the site of the present village of New Geneva, Friendship Co., Pa.

210. Site of the present community of Mount Sterling, about a mile and a half west of present Masontown, Fayette Co., Pa.

211. It was not until several years later that Rebecca Tomlinson Martin revealed to her brothers the adventure she had during their absence.

212. Samuel Meason was never further prosecuted for this crime. In fact, his leadership qualities were such that when Ohio County was formed, he was one of the men named to the rank of captain in the county militia. He served well in this capacity but later drifted into the role of an outlaw, formed a band of ruffians and became a notorious Ohio River pirate for a number of years before finally being killed by his own men.

213. Their Indian names are pronounced Out-HOW-wuh SHOCK-uh and SHESH-she-puck-WAH-wuh-luh. Their village of Chalahgawtha was located on the site of the present city of Chillicothe, Ross Co., O.—the name Chillicothe evolving from the phonetic pronunciation of Chalahgawtha.

214. Elinipsico is pronounced EL-len-NIP-sick-ko. Blue Jacket's Shawnee name was Wehyehpihehrsehnwah, pronounced Way-yeh-PEE-air-SANE-wah.

215. Among the several traders killed were one named Campbell, on the Tus-

carawas near present Newcomerstown, Tuscarawas Co.; another named Williams, near the mouth of the Hockhocking; and one named Proctor, on Indian Wheeling Creek, near present Bridgeport, Belmont Co., O.

216.   The intense hatred Connolly had built up for Alexander McKee is evident in the deposition later given by trader William Butler when an investigation was being made as to the causes of Dunmore's War. Butler stated: *"On the 27th day of May, Mr. McKee and I rode out about seven miles from town, and on our return were met on the road by a man from Mrs. McKee, who came to tell us that Connelly [sic] had sent a party of men to pull down Mr. McKee's house. When we came home, we found a guard of six armed men pulling down two out-houses, in Mr. McKee's back yard; he ordered them to desist, saying that he would defend his people at the risk of his life; upon which the men agreed to wait until we would talk to Mr. Connelly about the matter. We walked toward the fort with that intention, but were met by one Aston (a captain of Connelly's), at the head of about thirty armed men, followed by Connelly. Aston approached, and in a blasphemous manner accosted Mr. McKee, ordering the Virginia sheriff to seize him. Upon which the sheriff and Aston and several others seized him in a violent manner. Aston presented a rifle at Mr. McKee, threatened to shoot him down, which some of the by-standers prevented. Connelly came up at the same time, in a great rage, telling Mr. McKee that he would send him to Virginia in irons. He endeavored to expostulate with him, but all to no purpose, but told him he would tear down his dwelling house if he thought proper. He also accused Mr. McKee with being refractory on many occasions, and a fomenter of sedition, &c., &c., in opposition to the colony of Virginia, and that he had encouraged his servants to abuse one of his men, who was then present, calling the man to prove what he had asserted, but the man cleared Mr. McKee and his servants, saying that it was a man of Mr. Spear's who had struck him. Connelly being then confuted before upwards of sixty persons, said it was all as one of the magistrate's servants. Aston attempted to run the muzzle of his gun at Mr. McKee's face, but was prevented. In the meantime Connelly suffered a foresworn rascal (one Riely) to shake a stick at Mr. McKee, and abuse him in an outrageous manner, without bringing him to an account for so doing. In this manner Connelly enforces all his laws."*

217.   Despite the long and loud utterances of revulsion for what had taken place against the Indians, no charges were ever lodged or punishment levied against any of the white men who were involved in the instigation of this Indian war.

218.   Stoner and Boone set out on their respective missions on June 6, 1774.

219.   Greater details of the attack on the McKinzie family, the captivity of the girls and the long search by their father to locate and rescue them will be found in the author's *A Sorrow in Our Heart: The Life of Tecumseh.*

220.   On the site of present Harrodsburg, Mercer Co., Ky.

221.   This first Shepherd's Fort was built on the site of present Connellsville, Fayette Co., Pa.

222.   Fort Fincastle was built in the shape of a parallelogram, with a blockhouse at each corner and stout pickets eight feet high from one blockhouse to another. Within the enclosure of three-quarters of an acre were a storehouse, barracks room, garrison wells and a number of cabins for use of families. The principal entry was a gateway on the east side. The blockhouses were square, heavy,

double-storied buildings with the upper story projecting over the lower about two feet all around. They also projected slightly beyond the stockade, commanding all approaches so no lodgement could be made against the pickets to set them on fire or scale them. They were also pierced with loopholes for rifle fire. The roof sloped equally from each side upward and was surmounted at the peak by a quadrangular structure called the sentry box—an elevated post providing an extensive view on all sides. Usually the sentry box was occupied by two or three of the best riflemen during times of attack. The fort itself was situated a quarter-mile above the mouth of Wheeling Creek, on the site of present Wheeling, Ohio Co., W.Va.

223. Linn was two months recuperating from his wound; even then, when hunting, he would have to hold his ramrod under his wounded arm to support his rifle when aiming.

224. Wapatomica (meaning Capital Town and sometimes spelled Wapatomika) was being reestablished in present Logan Co., O., on the headwaters of the Mad River, 4.5 miles southeast of the French trading post of Bellefontaine. The new site was, for a long time earlier, a favored camping place and rendezvous of British traders, where, in 1751, a number who were trading there were taken prisoner by the French. This new Wapatomica's exact location was on the headwaters of the Mad River, on the west side of the stream, across a broad meadow to the first and second levels of the first ridge to the west of the base of the large hill presently called Mad River Mountain, 2 miles southwest of the present town of Zanesfield. The ridge upon which it was located runs from West Liberty to Zanesfield. The town was situated 3.5 to 4 miles north of Mackachack and about 2.5 miles south of the present town of Zanesfield (which was the site of Tarhe's Town, Tarhe—The Crane—being a renowned Wyandot chief), 4.5 miles southeast of the present Logan County seat of Bellefontaine. The town was largely on the second elevated bottom of the ridge. The land was later owned by a man named Hoague, with a lesser part of the tract owned by a man named Miller. Later, the entire tract was owned by Samuel and Solomon McCulloch, uncles of Judge Noah McCulloch of nearby Bellefontaine; and the property now [1994] is owned by the Westley and John Sidesinger families. Mackachack (also called Moluntha's Town) was located on the north side of present Mac-o-chee Creek, one mile east of the present town of West Liberty, Logan Co., O.

225. This group, perhaps numbering as many as 400, journeyed to the headwaters of the Suwannee River in the Okefenokee Swamp and reestablished themselves a few miles southeast of present Waycross, Ware Co., Ga.

226. The other Virginia delegates included Patrick Henry, Richard Henry Lee, Benjamin Harrison, Richard Bland and Edmund Pendleton.

227. Virtually all who wrote about this at the time, including Joseph Doddridge, John Burk and Alexander Scott Withers, agree that Lord Dunmore seriously tried to put the Lewis army in a position where it would be cut up by the Indians, yet this is all based on circumstantial evidence, and no documents are known to exist that confirm the inferences.

228. Andrew Lewis, in addition to having his brother, son and nephew as officers

in his army, had two other sons, Samuel and Thomas, as privates with the force.

229.   This canoe-making camp was situated on the site of the present capital city of Charleston, W.Va.

230.   The name of Dunmore County was, following the governor's precipitate departure for England, renamed to the present Shenandoah County.

231.   This delegation of Indians, never fully identified, is believed to have been sent by Hokolesqua of the Shawnees in a last bid for peace. Yet, there are historians who have implied that it was at this secret council, which involved some Iroquois—along with one that occurred with Shawnees and possibly some Delawares at the mouth of the Hockhocking River (present Hocking River) —that Dunmore entered into some sort of agreement that if the Indians did not attack his force, he would not merge his army with Lewis at Point Pleasant but would instead head overland to negotiate a peace with the Shawnees and other tribes; in the meanwhile, by doing so, leaving the Lewis force open to attack by the Indians assembling for that purpose. Various bits of evidence seem to indicate there may be some element of truth to the speculations.

232.   In his letter from Wheeling to George Washington, Crawford wrote: *"I this day am to set out with the first division for the mouth of the Hockhocking, and there to erect a post on your bottom, where the whole of the troops are to rendezvous."* A discrepancy of dates occurs at this time, since Crawford dated the letter to Washington as September 20 when, in actuality, the date was September 30.

233.   Some historians have speculated that while at Wheeling, Lord Dunmore received official dispatches from the British government that the probability of a revolutionary war breaking out had become very high and that he should proceed accordingly; and that this caused Dunmore to deviate from his original rendezvous plan so as to jeopardize the Lewis army and perhaps even cause its annihilation.

234.   After eighteen years of captivity, Joshua Snidow came back to Draper's Meadows with the view of resuming his life as a white man, but he soon found he could not adapt to the white life. He soon returned to the Indians and remained with them until his death at an old age.

235.   A story is prevalent in some accounts that Gen. Lewis beat Simon Girty with a cane at this time for some sort of impertinence on Girty's part, laying open Girty's scalp and causing profuse bleeding. Girty, it is said, swore vengeance for the attack. There does not seem to be either justification for such an act on the part of Gen. Lewis, nor acceptable verification that it ever really occurred.

236.   This creek is the present Campaign Creek which enters the Ohio a quarter-mile below the present town of Addison, Gallia Co., O.

237.   The Indians landed on the left side of the Ohio at the mouth of present Oldtown Creek.

238.   These two young hunters were James Robertson and a man identified only as Hickman (identified in one account, erroneous in other respects, as Valentine Sevier), the latter being the individual who was killed.

239.   Col. William Fleming, 45, who commanded the Botetourt Regiment, was an

intelligent Scotsman who had been born in Jedburgh and attended the University of Edinburgh and then emigrated to America in 1755. He had served as an ensign under Col. George Washington during the French and Indian War and until 1763, when he married Anne Christian. He recovered from the wounds he received at Point Pleasant, became county lieutenant of Botetourt in 1776, served in the Virginia Legislature 1777–79, was a member of the Virginia Council in 1780 and served 12 days as acting Virginia governor in June 1781. He died at age 66 on August 5, 1795.

240. Pucksinwah was also the father of Tecumseh who, at the time of this battle, was only six years old and in their village of Kispoko Town on the Scioto River, a few miles below present Circleville, Pickaway Co., O.

241. Chaquiweshe—The Mink—was married to Pucksinwah's daughter, Tecumapese. He was father of her son, Spemica Lawba, later to gain recognition as Johnny Logan. Some years afterward, Tecumapese married the warrior named Wasegoboah—Stand Firm—who was eventually killed beside Tecumseh at the Battle of the Thames near Chatham, Ont., October 5, 1813.

242. Lord Dunmore's force was at this moment moving up the Hockhocking River on its new route dictated by the governor. At this point Dunmore made an utterance that lends much credence to the long-existing belief that he colluded with the Indians in setting up the Lewis force for this battle. Dunmore suddenly paused in the march and then, apropos of nothing, spoke aloud a sentence that was overheard by at least a half-dozen of his aides and officers: *"I expect that right about now, General Lewis is having a very hot time of it."*

243. This approaching force was led by Col. William Christian—identified as Col. John Christie in some accounts—who was bringing his reinforcement of independent companies from Fincastle County.

244. Unfortunately, most historians have written that the Battle of Point Pleasant was a victory for the whites under Gen. Lewis, but the statistics certainly prove otherwise. The erroneous conclusion is reached because it was the Indians who finally withdrew from the field. The statistics are most revealing: Gen. Lewis had 75 men killed, including more than half his commissioned officers. An additional 140 were wounded, 88 of these beyond any further fighting in this campaign. Most accounts say the Indians had 300 killed, but this figure is based on a statement made by trader William McCulloch, who was not noted for his veracity in anything. In actuality, the Indians lost only 22 men, 14 of whom were killed on the battlefield and 8 who subsequently died of their wounds. Their total in nonmortally wounded was a mere 18. The final battle result: 215 casualties for the whites, 40 for the Indians—a ratio of over five to one. A considerably more detailed account of the Battle of Point Pleasant appears in the author's *A Sorrow in Our Heart: The Life of Tecumseh.*

245. Though often referred to as the Camp Charlotte Treaty, the agreement reached between the Indians and whites at Camp Charlotte was never formalized into a treaty. That treaty was to have been made the following spring at a general council to be held at Fort Pitt. Because of revolutionary war impending, however, that council was never held, the treaty was never made and the

agreement at Camp Charlotte was not binding on either side, though the Shawnees made a concerted effort to live up to it. The whites largely ignored it.

246.   Arbuckle, in Gen. Lewis's absence, had also auctioned off all the Indian para-phernalia picked up on the battlefield the day after the battle—23 guns, 27 tomahawks, a large number of war clubs, powderhorns and shot pouches, 80 blankets, numerous coats and some deer skins. The entire lot brought in £74.4s.6d. for the use of the army. Gen. Andrew Lewis served in command positions through the ensuing Revolutionary War until, just before the surren-der of Cornwallis at Yorktown, he became ill and set out for his home, a magnificent estate called Dropmore on the upper Roanoke River, but he died before reaching there while resting at the home of Col. William Buford. His body was transported to his estate and buried there, just outside the town limits of present Salem, Roanoke Co., Va.

247.   This camp, about four miles from Camp Charlotte, was located on the south bank of Congo Creek some 3.5 miles upstream from its mouth at Scippo Creek, which in turn flows into the Scioto River. Numerous accounts state that John Gibson was one of those who went on this mission to Talgayeeta, but existing evidence indicates Gibson never left Camp Charlotte during this period. Also, since Gibson was by this time aware that it was Greathouse, not Cresap, who had massacred Talgayeeta's family, he would certainly have passed that information along to Talgayeeta before the latter made his speech, but the content of Talgayeeta's speech makes it clear that he still considered Cresap responsible for the murder of his family. It was not until shortly later, accord-ing to Gibson's deposition, that Talgayeeta was finally informed by his son-in-law that Cresap had had no hand in killing Logan's family.

248.   Talgayeeta was at this time apparently still unaware that his sister's daughter, the child of Koonay and John Gibson, was still living.

249.   Most accounts entirely overlook the fact that Talgayeeta did, in fact, come near Camp Charlotte after dictating his speech, though continuing his refusal to meet or parley with Lord Dunmore. Gibson's deposition (made on April 4, 1800), however, indicates this is exactly what occurred.

250.   Seekonk was situated on the left (east) bank of the Olentangy River, at the northernmost limits of the present city of Worthington, Franklin Co., O.

251.   Crawford's mission, guided by Daniel Sullivan, who had once been a captive there but had escaped, was largely successful. Due to the presence of the detachment being discovered before dawn, the majority of the Mingoes made their escape in the darkness, but six were killed, several others wounded, plus 14 squaws and children taken prisoner.

252.   Benjamin Wilson, who was with the Dunmore army and who later rose to the rank of colonel, was enthralled by Hokolesqua at the talks and wrote of him: *"When he arose and spoke he was in no wise confused or daunted, but spoke in a bugle voice that could be distinctly heard all through the camp, without stammering or repeti-tion, and with peculiar emphasis. His appearance, while addressing Dunmore, made him the most dignified looking man I ever saw, truly grand and majestic, yet graceful*

and attractive. I have heard the finest orators in Virginia—Patrick Henry and Richard Henry Lee—but never have I heard one whose powers of delivery surpassed those of Cornstalk on this occasion.''

253. No written copy of the actual agreement exists, and some historians, in fact, claim that no such agreement regarding territorial adjustments was ever made; that the only true agreement made was that there was a declared truce and that white traders would hereafter be required to treat the Indians with greater respect and fairness in trade.

254. Some of these dozen or so captives were extremely reluctant to return to the whites and, in fact, after being turned over to them, several slipped away and returned to their adopted Indian way of life.

255. These four hostages were taken to Williamsburg and incarcerated there but, on the outbreak of the Revolutionary War, they escaped and returned to their people.

256. The preamble to that stirring and memorable utterance by Patrick Henry is as follows: *"The gentlemen may cry, Peace, Peace! but there is no peace. The war has actually begun! The next gale that sweeps from the north will bring to our ears the clash of resounding arms! Our brethren are already in the field! Why stand we here idle? What is it that the gentlemen wish? What would they have? Is life so dear or peace so sweet as to be purchased at the price of chains and slavery? Forbid it, Almighty God. I know not what course others may take, but as for me, give me liberty or give me death!''*

257. Involved with Henderson in this land scheme were William Johnston, John Williams, James Hogg, Leonard Hendly Bullock, John Lutterell and the Hart brothers—David, Nathaniel and Thomas.

258. McClelland's Station was established on the site of present Georgetown, Scott Co., and Patterson's Settlement was on the site of present Lexington, Fayette Co., Ky.

259. This Chalahgawtha was located at the site of the present little community of Oldtown, three miles north of present Xenia, Greene Co., O.

260. The larger watercraft that took settlers down the Ohio were known as keel-boats, broadhorns, barges and Kentucky boats. All were generally very roughly constructed and were very difficult to maneuver because of their bulkiness and great weight. They ranged in length from 50 to 100 feet and in width were usually 15 to 25 feet. The larger examples could carry 60 to 100 tons of cargo, livestock and people. Freight was usually stored in a rectangular construction called a cargo box at the front of the boat, while a flat-roofed cabin of sorts with slit-windows served as accommodation for the passengers. A tillerman normally took post on the roof of the cabin and generally kept the boat straight and tried to guide it through rough waters by use of a broad-bladed rudder about 20 to 30 feet in length, angled from the cabin roof to the water behind. Cattle, swine, horses and other livestock were usually confined in sectioned corrals rigged from the cargo box nearly back to the cabin house. Some of these boats were equipped with a mast and sail that could be used for greater speed when conditions permitted. These boats were most often constructed for a one-way passage only—downstream—relying for the most part

on the current to carry them to their destination. In by far the majority of cases, when the destination was reached, the boat would then be dismantled and the wood used in the construction of cabins, fences, outbuildings and the like.

261. It was not until June 29, 1776, however, that Virginia formally adopted its own constitutional government. On that same day the Virginians themselves elected Patrick Henry as governor.

262. Connolly, on reporting to the British Army, received a commission as a lieutenant colonel in the regular army and the following year was sent west to lead the British and Indian forces. While on the way he was captured by the Americans and imprisoned for four years. When released in 1780, he joined Gen. Lord Cornwallis at Yorktown, where he was again captured and again imprisoned, this time for two years. On his release he went to England but returned in 1788 as the British lieutenant governor of Detroit, where he failed to persuade leaders in Kentucky to change their allegiance to the Crown. During 1799 and 1800 he was British deputy superintendent of Indian affairs. He died January 30, 1813, at the age of 70.

263. Much greater details of these attacks by Chiungalla's force against the Kentucky settlements generally and the sieges lodged against Harrodsburg, St. Asaph's and Boonesboro may be found in the author's *The Frontiersmen* and *A Sorrow in Our Heart: The Life of Tecumseh.*

264. The George Baker cabin was located on the site where a large industrial complex is now located, at the mouth of Raccoon Creek, on the left bank of the Ohio River, four miles downstream from the mouth of Beaver River and the same distance below the present town of Monaca, Beaver Co., Pa.

265. All seven members of the Baker family survived and finally returned to the upper Ohio in 1782, after five years of captivity. The Indians had treated the captives reasonably well and headed toward Detroit with them. When they camped at the Mahoning River, however, the Indians had a discussion and decided to kill Mrs. Baker and the two youngest boys because the woman was too troublesome and the two smaller boys were slowing their progress. Baker, on learning of their plans, appealed to McCarty to prevent the executions or, if he could not, then to kill all in the family, as he would not care to survive. McCarty took pity on him and convinced the Chippewas to spare them, on the basis that they would be worth a little extra trouble for the reward they would get from Gen. Hamilton, which would be greater for living prisoners than for scalps. The eldest and youngest boys, George, Jr., and Michael, were sold to the Wyandots at Sandusky; the remainder were taken to Detroit and sold there to the British. Baker appealed to Gen. Hamilton to intercede with the Indians at Sandusky to get the two missing sons back. He did so, and the family was reunited in Detroit, where they remained captive for three years. Then they were moved to Chamblee, 12 miles from Montreal, where they remained another two years until finally exchanged and sent home via Lake Champlain, North River, Potomac and Pittsburgh.

266. Isaac Williams was born in 1737 and, as a young boy, moved with his parents and family to the frontier town of Winchester, site of the present city of

Winchester, Frederick Co., Va. Not long after that move, his father died and his mother subsequently married John Buckley. He remained with them until the outbreak of the French and Indian War, at which time he enlisted in Gen. Braddock's army. He never returned home after that, having entered the Indian trade for a while and then becoming involved in land speculation.

267. Jim Tomlinson apparently never returned to the Grave Creek Flats. Joe Tomlinson came back after an absence of eight years (in 1785) and abandoned it again in 1786.

268. One account states that the weather was *"frosty,"* but this is evidently a mistake.

269. One account states that they were working in a cornfield.

270. One account says that the Indians got five rifles from the cabin, but this is unlikely, since neither Lewis nor Jacob owned a gun at this time and Old John and George had brought along only their own guns.

271. The same account mentioned above states that the Indians got three horses near the creek and two others at the cabin, but this does not coincide with better-substantiated accounts from the Wetzel family.

272. One account states that Jacob violently threw the puppy away twice before finally consenting to carry it. Another says that he threw the puppy in Wheeling Creek, and there may possibly be some element of truth to this, in that the puppy is never again mentioned in any of the accounts.

273. Two different accounts state that Lewis was bleeding badly from the chest and that blood was spurting from his mouth as well; this is discounted since the wound was a deep graze and did not injure the lungs or any other internal organs. A third account states that the ball carried away a portion of Lewis's sternum.

274. Wetzel family tradition states that no pursuit of the raiding party was made, probably for the reasons stated by Capt. Meason. Also, following the trail would have meant returning the 14 miles to the Wetzel place, by which time the Indians would have had at least a 24-to-30-hour head start.

275. One account says it was Stillwater Creek, but the logistics do not seem to work out properly for this to have been true.

276. One account says Jacob refused to go back for the guns and so they left without them; this is not borne out, however, by the numerous other accounts that are explicit about the boys recovering the weapons and returning them to their father.

277. This little unnamed blockhouse at the head of Cresap's Bottom was situated on the left bank of the Ohio at the mouth of present Graveyard Run, one mile below and on the opposite side of the river from the mouth of Captina Creek and the present town of Powhatan Point, Belmont Co., O.

278. One account states that this incident occurred a year later, in 1778, but that is not possible, as Martin Wetzel was at that time a captive of the Indians. Following Baker's death, the Wetzels returned at once to Wheeling to report what had happened. A party returned the next day to the little blockhouse and solemnly buried the body on high ground a short distance from it. Those attending the funeral, in addition to the Wetzels, included Henry Baker and

family, George Baker, Samuel P. Baker, Reuben Roberts and family, Captain James Roberts, Aaron Hughes and the Raigor brothers, Thomas, William and Leonard. So distraught was Martin Wetzel at the death of his friend that he stated his wish for all to hear that when he died, wherever that happened, he wished to be brought here and buried beside John Baker. That wish was fulfilled when he died in 1830 at the age of 73.

279.   Unfortunately, the two men who were sent on this mission to Grave Creek have not been identified.

280.   The crossing occurred from just below the mouth of the Wheeling Creek on the Ohio side—at that time called Indian Wheeling Creek—at present Bridgeport, Belmont Co., O., directly across to the island and then almost due east across the island along the trail now essentially followed by Virginia Street, and landed about 200 yards below the old State Route 231 bridge in present Wheeling, Ohio Co., W.Va.

281.   In various accounts, McMahan's name is spelled McMahen, McMahon, Mahon and McMechen. McMahan is correct.

282.   Lt. Samuel Tomlinson was said, in one account, to have been a member of this party, but that is an error. Tomlinson, Capt. Meason's lieutenant, was with him when the detachment was ambushed. Andrew Zane, according to another account, was also in this party, but this is unconfirmed by any other report, all others saying there were just two whites, Greathouse and Boyd. In some of those accounts this Greathouse is named Daniel Greathouse, but that, too, is an error, since Daniel Greathouse had died of measles on October 26, 1775.

283.   There is no further information after this time about the slave named Ezra, but since his body was never found, it is assumed he was carried into captivity and was probably killed in a gauntlet run or tortured to death.

284.   Silas Zane had recently returned to Wheeling following a stint with the Continental Army, during which he was demoted for cowardice in action and sent home.

285.   Some accounts have confused this run of Betsy Wheat's after her baby with the later run of Elizabeth Zane to the fort for gunpowder and have stated that when she went for the baby, the Indians cried *"Squaw! Squaw!"* Actually, those calls were made during Elizabeth Zane's run. There were not yet any Indians in the Wheeling Settlement when Betsy Wheat's run was made.

286.   Accounts vary, some saying that Capt. Meason's company went out first and, when it was attacked, Capt. Ogle's company went out and fell into the same ambush. That seems unlikely, and the more generally accurate accounts state that all 26 men went out together and were ambushed at the same time.

287.   Abraham Rogers's name is spelled Abram Rodgers in some accounts.

288.   This is the figure given by Alexander Scott Withers in his valuable and generally very accurate *Chronicles of Border Warfare*. Other sources, including McKiernan, state that within the fort only 12 men and boys remained. Withers may have been including in his number the relief party under Col. Samuel McCulloch, which arrived later in the morning.

289. Nineteen of the 26 men of this party were killed on the spot, scalped and their weapons taken.
290. Sgt. Jacob Ogle was later found dead and scalped. He did not, as one account states, escape into the woods with two soldiers and die of his wounds there.
291. One account states that Meason's thigh bone was broken by the ball that struck him in the buttock, but that is not correct.
292. Francis Duke's body lay too close to the fort for the Indians to take his scalp immediately. After nightfall, his body was dragged to one of the cabins, where it was scalped and otherwise mutilated.
293. There has been much speculation as to the identity of this British officer and the white man with him, but no positive identification is known. Quite a few accounts say the man in frontier garb was Simon Girty, but that is not possible, since Girty was at this time still part of the garrison at Fort Pitt and did not defect to the British and Indians until the following March. Some say it was George Girty, but this too is incorrect, since he was presently in active service in the Continental Army and did not desert until the following April. There is a possibility, though very remote, that it was James Girty, who was at this time living with the Shawnees, but that too is unlikely, since the Shawnees took no part in this attack on Wheeling.
294. The point at which McCulloch reached the summit is where the Cumberland Road later was built.
295. At the site of present Woodsdale, Ohio Co., W.Va.
296. Because of its tremendous feat, Sam McCulloch's horse was kept and kindly favored until it finally died peacefully at the age of 34 years. The site where the plunge began is now commemorated with a tablet entitled McCulloch's Leap. Over the years that this incident had been told and retold, somehow the wild ride became attributed to John McCulloch instead of Samuel. The majority of accounts now existing give credit to John and, in an effort to settle it, historian Lyman Draper did extensive research into the subject and interviewed many people who were still alive that had been at Wheeling when the incident occurred. Among those who corroborated the fact that it was Samuel, not John, was Col. Archibald Woods, that interview being made in 1846. Samuel Zane was another of the many interviewed by Draper in 1846, and he, too, said the ride had been made by Samuel. Draper, in his notes (Draper-S-3/150) remarks, *"Major Samuel McCulloch, upon full reflection, made the leap."*
297. Ebenezer and Elizabeth Zane at this time had four surviving children—Catherine, 8, Ann, 5, Sarah, 4, and Rebecca, 1. A boy, Noah, who had been born on October 1, 1774, died in infancy.
298. Elizabeth Zane gained considerable renown as the heroine of this attack on Wheeling, until some years later when a Mrs. Lydia Cruger, daughter of Capt. John Boggs, made a statement saying the story of Mrs. Zane's dash for the gunpowder was not true, that the feat had been accomplished all right, but by her relative, Molly Scott. A certain amount of controversy has resulted ever since in regard to who made the effort, but enough solid documentation exists to affirm that it was, indeed, Elizabeth Zane who did it. What Mrs. Cruger's

motives were for coming out with her story is unknown, though the assumption is that she was jealous of the celebrity that had resulted to Mrs. Zane.

299.   Rachel Johnson, a slave belonging to Ebenezer Zane, had been with the Zane family for many years and had moved with the family to Wheeling. She was born October 20, 1736, and was interviewed by Dr. Lyman Draper in October 1845, when she was 109 years old. She had four children and was spoken of highly by all who ever knew her. She died in the summer of 1847 in her 111th year.

300.   It was about this time that documents referring to Andrew Van Swearingen began doing so without the prefix Van. It is not known whether Van Swearingen himself decided to drop it or if this was merely a matter of convenience by writers. There are some documents signed by him in subsequent years in which the name appears as Van Swearingen and, in light of such, that is how his name will be used throughout this narrative.

301.   One account states that Capt. Ogle *"lay in pain and terror for two or three days"* in the briar thicket, but that is a considerable exaggeration.

302.   Capt. Meason, at this time, lived on Buffalo Creek near Ramsey's Fort, that fort situated some six miles upstream on the Buffalo from its mouth on the Ohio, at the fording place of the Buffalo, three miles upstream from present McKinleyville, Brooke Co., W.Va.

303.   No accurate accounting of how many Indians were killed or wounded was ever made, although estimates ran from as few as 20 or 30 killed to as many as over 100.

304.   One account says Foreman had two sons and a nephew in the company, but the numbers have been switched. The two nephews were the sons of Foreman's older brother.

305.   One account states that the Foreman party, before reaching the upper end of The Narrows, paused and sat down and sang songs together, but this seems unlikely, not only in view of the fact that the marchers were still fresh and did not require a rest yet, but also because the idea of a possible ambush would have made them wish to get this rather treacherous portion of the trail behind them.

306.   No full list of the men of Foreman's company is known to exist, but the following list of known participants has been assembled from the various written accounts:

Brazier, Thomas	Private; killed.
Clark, James	Private; survived.
Cullen, John	Private; killed.
Cullen, William	Private; survived with broken leg.
Dickerson, Kinzie	Private; survived; rescued Cullen.
Engle, William	Private; survived.
Foreman, ____	Private; killed; nephew of commander.
Foreman, ____	Private; killed; nephew of commander.
Foreman, ____	Private; killed; son of commander.
Foreman, William	Captain, commanding.
Greathouse, Jacob	Private; survived.

Harkness, Robert   Private; survived.
Linn, William   Scout captain; survived.
McLane, Daniel   Private; survived.
Miller, John (15)   Private; survived.
Pugh, Jonathan   Private; captured.
Sheno, William   Private; half-breed; killed.
Shepherd, Moses (14)   Drummer; went back early.
Tomlinson, James   Private; survived.
Wilson, John   Private; survived with wounded arm.

Jonathan Pugh, long believed dead, remained a captive of the Indians for four and a half years before finally escaping from them.

307.　Daniel McLane later stated he could hear the tomahawk blows *"as if the Indians were cutting up beef."* That was probably a stretch of the imagination.

308.　In the various accounts, Cullen's name is also spelled Culler, Cullers, Cullens and Collins. Cullen appears to be correct. Some accounts say it was John Cullen, brother of William, who had his leg broken, but it was William. John Cullen was killed in the initial ambush.

309.　One account states that Cullen was taken to Shepherd's Fort, but that is an error. It was not until late the next day that a Dr. Frederick Puzee arrived from Fort Pitt, having been summoned to treat the wounded at Fort Henry. Immediately upon inspecting Cullen's wound, he announced the leg would have to be amputated. Cullen refused to let him do so and threatened to kill him if he tried. Much against his better judgment, Dr. Puzee cleansed the wound and set the bone as best he could under the circumstances. Cullen suffered great pain for a considerable while. His situation was not helped when, a short time later, he contracted smallpox. However, he survived both disease and injury and regained use of his leg. He lived to an old age, working as a shingle-maker at Wellsburg, Brooke Co., W.Va. After the war, Cullen was awarded the sum of £36 for his injury.

310.　Of the six who were taken captive, Jonathan Pugh was the only survivor, although his family thought he had been buried in the common grave along with the others. Pugh lived with the Wyandots for four and a half years before finally escaping and returning to his parents' home. His mother had since died. He showed up at his father's house on May 21, 1782, where he was at first thought to be a ghost. When he finally convinced them that he was flesh and blood, there was great rejoicing by his family and neighbors. His father was greatly overwhelmed to see again the son he had so long thought dead. In 1835 an inscribed stone monument was erected at the site of the ambush, at the extreme northern end of Washington Township at the Union Township line at the head of The Narrows, 4.5 miles upstream from present Moundsville, Marshall Co., W.Va.

311.　The Shepherd family remained in residence in Catfish Camp (later Washington, Pa.) for five years, although David Shepherd himself still spent much time in Wheeling operating his mill.

312.　Actually, in a queer twist of fate, Rachel Grist eventually did die of her wound. It appeared to heal well, and seven years later she married Capt.

Henry Jolly of Catfish Camp (later Washington, Pa.). They had five children
—four sons and a daughter—and then the old wound abruptly began giving
her severe pain. It quickly grew worse until she finally died at age forty in
dreadful agony.

313.   One account states that Hokolesqua came to Fort Randolph alone and was
incarcerated and that Elinipsico and Red Hawk came later to check on his
whereabouts and safety.

314.   Numerous disparate accounts of this incident exist, all of which are similar in
the main but vary widely in detail. As best the author can reconstruct the
matter, it appears that Capt. James Hall (whose title was evidently not military
but one bestowed by his followers) and several of his men had, some time
before (anywhere from a week prior to this incident to the day of it, but most
often reported as the day before), crossed the Ohio River (some say Kanawha
River) to hunt. Two of his hunters encountered two Shawnees (some accounts
say were ambushed by them), and in the resultant skirmish a white man named
Gilmore was killed. When the survivors returned to the Point Pleasant Settlement adjacent to Fort Randolph and learned of the three Shawnees being held
hostage, they raised a group of *"enraged soldiers"* and, resolved on revenge,
headed for the cabin where the trio of Shawnees were being held. The
murders were then committed as indicated. In Hokolesqua's body alone there
were nine (some say seven or eight, some eleven) bullet wounds, and the other
two were similarly riddled and also bludgeoned repeatedly after death. Red
Hawk, in some accounts, is described as a Delaware chief, but that is an error.
The bodies of the three Shawnees were buried near the present intersection of
Virginia and Kanawha streets in Point Pleasant. Sixty-three years later, in
1841, while excavations were being made at Point Pleasant for these streets,
the remains of the three were unearthed. The account states that *"the bones
were much broken and jammed as if by blows, & five or six balls also found among
them."* These bones were buried in the yard of the Mason County Courthouse, but no stone or marker of any kind was erected over them. Just before
the Civil War, Charles Dawson, at his own expense and labor, erected a rail
fence around the grave, and his sister, Susan Dawson, planted rose bushes atop
it. The fence and rose bushes were destroyed, however, by federal troops when
they occupied the town in 1863.

315.   Site of present Cleveland, Cuyahoga Co., O.

316.   This was the village called Kuskusskee, on the site of present New Castle,
Lawrence Co., Pa.

317.   Michikapeche and another squaw taken prisoner were released soon after the
army's return to Fort Pitt. There remains some question as to whether
Michikapeche was the wife or the mother of Pimoacan (Pipe). One account
states that Pimoacan's mother was wounded by Gen. Hand's men but escaped.

318.   One account states that Patrick Henry issued a formal apology to the Shawnee
nations, *"but the delivery of it was impossible."* Some months later the five men
named in the warrant were arrested in Rockbridge County and, according to
one report, *"went through the forms of a pretended trial, but there was scarcely a
family in that region that had not, at some time, suffered from Indian raids and*

murders, or had not lost friends or relatives in the Battle of the Point, or other Indian wars, and their prejudices were so strong against the Indians generally, that, although the facts were generally known, there was no one to prosecute, no one to testify; the trial was a farce, and the case was dismissed by default.''

319.   There is an account that states while Girty was jailed, he claimed he could escape and was challenged to do so; that he then did escape and was gone eight days before returning to surrender himself. That may have been on another of the three separate occasions when he was arrested and jailed, or it may simply be an exaggeration of the case described here.

320.   Several sources, without confirmation, suggest that the McKee family, originally from the Susquehanna Valley, was part Indian.

321.   The author is indebted to writer/historian Phillip W. Hoffman of Westlake Village, Calif., for his aid in clearing away much of the malevolent mythology that has accumulated around Simon Girty and for helping to bring into greater focus the actual causes for Girty's defection from the American cause to the British. Mr. Hoffman, after many years of intensive research, is currently preparing the most definitive and penetrating biography of Simon Girty ever written.

322.   Another of Simon Girty's younger brothers, George, was at this time a lieutenant in the Continental Army, stationed in the Kaskaskia area. As soon as he learned of Simon's defection to the British at Detroit, accompanied by their other brother, James, George Girty deserted his post, and he, too, defected. The three brothers were reunited at Detroit. For some reason not clearly understood, while McKee, Elliott and James Girty went westward to the Shawnee towns to speak with them, Simon Girty and his cousin, Robin Surphlet, took the more direct Indian trail northwestward to Detroit via Upper Sandusky. Because of Simon's defection, his land claims at Hannahstown were confiscated, but his Squirrel Hill Farm remained in the possession of his half-brother, John Turner. On his arrival at Detroit he was employed by Gen. Henry Hamilton in the Indian department.

323.   McKee's Town was where Alexander McKee paused en route to Detroit from Fort Pitt, during his defection, to establish a residence for himself and his Shawnee wife among the Shawnees. Very quickly other Indians moved close to him, and instead of just merely a residence, it became a small village named after him. Later, when the Kispokotha Shawnees moved their principal village of Kispoko Town away from the Scioto River, it was reestablished adjacent to McKee's Town and actually merged with it, with the two names—McKee's Town and Kispoko—used as variant names for the same place. It was located on a pleasant ridge on the south bank of an unnamed stream that was then named McKee's Creek, as it is at present. The precise location of the village was exactly 2.5 miles southeast of the present Logan County Courthouse in present Bellefontaine, O., and almost exactly the same distance northwest of the location at that time of the Shawnee capital village of Wapatomica. It was almost exactly at the point where present Township Road T-181 forms a T intersection with present Township Road T-179.

324.   Greater details of the capture of Daniel Boone and his saltmakers may be

found in the author's *The Frontiersmen* and *A Sorrow in Our Heart: The Life of Tecumseh.*

325. One source says that Martin Wetzel and John Wolf were captured near Ryerson's Station at the head of Wheeling Creek. Actually, while Ryerson's may have been the nearest station, it was not all that close, being distant about six miles from where the pair were captured.

326. Skootekitehi is pronounced Skoo-tey-keh-TEY-hee.

327. Some accounts contend that Lewis Wetzel tussled with the last Indian and finally killed him by stabbing him with his knife. The more reliable sources, however, agree that he reloaded while running, turned and shot his adversary dead.

328. Years later this incident was turned into a novel by Emerson Bennett, entitled *Forest Rose.* After returning to Dunkard Creek, Frazier and Rose Forrest remained there only a short time before selling their little place and moving on down the Ohio to Kentucky, where they eventually settled at Harrodsburg.

329. One source seems to exaggerate somewhat when it states that when John Wolf was being tortured, Martin saw him *"then sensibly with his bowels hanging out, & wished Wetzel, when he got in to tell his people of his fate."*

330. The four whites killed at Donnelly's Fort included William Pritchet, Alexander Ochiltree, James Burns and James Graham. There were reportedly seventeen Indians slain.

331. Gov. Patrick Henry's formal orders to George Rogers Clark were as follows: *"You are to proceed with all convenient speed to raise seven companies of soldiers, to consist of 50 men each, officered in the usual manner, and armed most properly for the enterprise, and with this force attack the British post at Kaskaskia. It is conjectured that there are many pieces of cannon, & military stores to considerable amount, at that place, the taking and preservation of which would be a valuable acquisition to the State. If you are so fortunate, therefore, as to succeed in your expedition, you will take every possible measure to secure the artillery & stores and whatever may advantage the State. For the transportation of the troops, provisions, &c. down the Ohio, you are to apply to the commanding officer at Fort Pitt for boats, and, during the whole transaction, you are to take especial care to keep the true destination secret. Its success depends upon this. Orders are therefore given to Captain Smith to secure the two men from Kaskasky. Similar conduct will be proper in similar cases. It is earnestly desired that you shew humanity to such British subjects & other prisoners as fall in your hands. If the white inhabitants at the post and the neighborhood will give undoubted evidence of their attachment to this State (for it is certain they live within its limits), by taking the test prescribed by law, & by every other way and means in their power, let them be treated as fellow citizens, and their persons and property duly secured. Assistance and protection against all enemies whatsoever shall be afforded them, & the Commonwealth of Virginia is pledged to accomplish it. But if these people will not accede to these reasonable demands, they must feel the miseries of war, under the direction of that humanity that has hitherto distinguished Americans, and which it is expected you will ever consider as the rule of your conduct, and from which you are in no instance to depart. The corps you are to command are to receive the pay and allowance of militia, and to act under the Laws and Regulations of this State now in force, as militia. The inhabitants at this post*

will be informed by you that in case they accede to the offers of becoming citizens of this Commonwealth, a proper garrison will be maintained among them, and every attention bestowed to render their commerce beneficial, the fairest prospects being opened to the dominions of both France & Spain. It is in contemplation to establish a post near the mouth of Ohio. Cannon will be wanted to fortify it; part of those at Kaskaskia will be easily brought thither, or otherwise secured, as circumstances will make necessary. You are to apply to General Hand for powder and lead necessary for this expedition. If he can't supply it, the person who has that which Captain Lynn brought from Orleans, can. Lead was sent to Hampshire by my orders, and that may be delivered to you. P. Henry.''

332. Fort McIntosh was built on the site of the present city of Beaver, Beaver Co., Pa. It was square in construction, its pickets enclosing some two acres and extending to the Ohio River, with no pickets on the river side and the main gate on the north.

333. Sam Brady's mother was the former Mary Quigley, daughter of an Irish immigrant who settled on Canandaguinnet Creek. She had bright blue, very intelligent eyes.

334. Samuel Brady's siblings were, in the order of their birth, James, John, Mary, William P., the twins, Hugh and Jane, Robert, Hannah and Liberty.

335. One account says he killed two before the other Indians reached him. If so, he must have snatched up one of the other guns stacked there.

336. According to a couple of the accounts, there was every likelihood that James Brady would have survived his wounds had he received prompt treatment. Brady's mother, it was said, was so heartbroken over James's death that she, also, soon died.

337. There is some contention over whether it was at this time of James's death that Samuel Brady made his vow of vengeance or when his father, John Brady, was killed by Indians. Most accounts agree on the former. Very little has been recorded of John Brady's death except that he was out with a man named Peter Smith when two Indians shot at them from ambush. Both balls hit John Brady, one of them through the heart, while Peter Smith was unscathed and escaped. John Brady's brother, Sam (for whom Capt. Sam Brady was named) said at the time, regarding John's death, *''I can't understand why the Almighty suffered so clever a man as John to be killed and permit so insignificant a man as Smith to escape.''*

338. Col. Crawford was made an acting brigadier general for the duration of this expedition.

339. This site is located three-quarters of a mile south of present downtown Bolivar, Tuscarawas Co., O.

340. The flour and beeves had been the responsibility of the commissaries Abram and Isaac Hite. They had been driven all the way from the east by a party under Capt. George Lockhart and were rangy and ailing. Lockhart said he had contemplated killing most of them en route and salting down the meat, but then discovered he did not have salt enough to do so and abandoned the idea.

341. At the time of its construction and ever afterward, some confusion has resulted from the name of Fort Laurens, as many people in their letters, journals and

reports misunderstood the name and reproduced it as Fort Lawrence. This even resulted, in later years, in the establishment of Lawrence Township in Tuscarawas County.

342. Simon Kenton endured a terrible ordeal among the Shawnees, running the gauntlet numerous times. At the Shawnee capital of Wapatomica he was condemned to be burned at the stake. He was saved through the intervention of Simon Girty, only to be recondemned a short time later. Girty and Chief Talgayeeta (Logan) then got the help of an Englishman they knew at Detroit, who managed to convince the Indians to bring him there for a reward. This was done, and Kenton was imprisoned there for half a year before finally escaping and making his way back through the Indiana country to Kentucky. Greater details of all this may be found in the author's *The Frontiersmen* and *A Sorrow in Our Heart: The Life of Tecumseh.*

343. Capt. Daniel Boone, on his return to Kentucky, was accused of collaborating with the Indians and was court-martialed on four separate counts. He defended himself and was ultimately exonerated on all charges and promoted to major. Fully reconstructed details of his trial may be found in the author's novel *The Court-Martial of Daniel Boone* (Boston: Little, Brown, 1973; New York: Bantam, 1987).

344. Simon Girty by this time had established his base of operations among the Wyandots at Half King's Town—the village of Chief Monakaduto—on the upper Sandusky River, three miles south and slightly east of the site of present Upper Sandusky, Wyandot Co., O.

345. Capt. Henry Bird (often referred to incorrectly as colonel, a rank he earned considerably later) was an officer of the British Eighth Regiment. His name has frequently been spelled Byrd.

346. Clark's force in the bateau, much to their mortification, did not arrive at Vincennes until two days after the surrender to Clark.

347. Lichtenau was located near the southern city limits of present Coshocton, Coshocton Co., O. Salem was located on the Tuscarawas about five miles north and a mile east of present West Lafayette in the same county. Gnadenhütten—meaning Tents of Grace—was located on the site of present Gnadenhutten, Tuscarawas Co., O., and Salem was located in that same county on the site of present New Philadelphia, some 18 miles downstream from Fort Laurens.

348. Greater details of this council held by the Shawnees, the speeches made, the arguments heard and other details may be found in the author's *The Frontiersmen* and *A Sorrow in Our Heart: The Life of Tecumseh.*

349. Gen. Henry Hamilton, whom Clark had captured at Vincennes, was not set at liberty as his men were. He was shackled and sent up the Ohio and Monongahela to Redstone, then taken overland from there to Williamsburg, where he was imprisoned and kept in irons, even in his cell.

350. Sometimes when an Indian was killed, the tribe to which the slain individual belonged would forgo declaring war or otherwise seeking retaliation against the perpetrators if a "present" of substantial significance were given to them as

an apology for the deed. This present, usually goods of one kind or another, normally went to the family of the dead man.

351.   Some accounts have suggested that Simon Girty was among the attackers, but this is discounted since Girty was at this time among the Wyandots of the Sandusky, deep in the Ohio interior. Fort Hand, deemed indefensible, was abandoned the succeeding fall and was shortly thereafter burned by the Indians.

352.   Christiana Sykes and all six of her children were surrendered by the Delawares 16 years later, on July 20, 1795.

353.   Potter's Fort was located just a short distance southwest of present Milesburg, Centre Co., Pa.

354.   This smaller stream, first named Redbank Creek, then called Brady's Bend Creek, is the present Sugar Creek, Armstrong Co., Pa., which enters the Allegheny directly opposite the north end of the present city of East Brady, Clarion Co., Pa.

355.   This Indian camp had been made on the site of what is now known as Brady's Bend in Brady's Bend Township, Armstrong Co., Pa.

356.   One account states that this party of Mingoes was led by a noted warrior whom the Americans referred to as Old Mate. It also states that Old Mate was wounded in the genitals but survived the wounding. Another account states that Old Mate, *"shot in the privates, was killed,"* and that ten other warriors were killed, but that is an error, since only one Indian was killed.

357.   In 1809, thirty years after this incident, Peter Henry, then a prosperous man, brought a fine horse to Peter Parchment as a reward and thanks for the long-ago rescue. Parchment was appreciative of the offer but declined to accept, saying he had only done his job.

358.   This may be the basis for one account that states there was a white renegade with this party of Indians, but since no other accounts mention this, it is believed to be erroneous.

359.   The name Brady's Bend stuck, and it has ever since been known by that name.

360.   The term *bark canoe* always seems to conjure up the picture of the picturesque birchbark canoe, but the Shawnees and early Ohio River frontiersmen rarely, if ever, used birch, which was not indigenous to the Ohio country. Several different types of trees were used for making the standard bark canoe, but the most favored was elm, since it was very flexible and easy to work. Two experienced Shawnee men could make a bark canoe suitable for crossing the Ohio River in about two hours. An elm with a good straight trunk would be chosen that was a foot and a half to two feet in diameter. Using tomahawks, a line would be cut through the bark all the way around the tree just above ground level. Another line would be cut straight up the trunk for ten to twelve feet, one of the Shawnees standing on the shoulders of the other when it became too high to work otherwise. Then the man on top would cut a line around the tree similar to the one at the base. Elm bark separates from the base wood quite easily, and they would pry it back, using the tomahawks as levers, until the bark came off in a single tube. One end of the tube would be flattened

together so the cut lines met exactly, and then, using sharpened wooden pegs, holes would be punched two or three inches apart about an inch or so inward from the ends of the tubular bark. The same thing would be done to the other end. Then long strands of tough wild grapevine would be used to lace each end very tightly. Finally, sections of sturdy branches would be cut just long enough to act as crossbars to prop the long cut apart to its fullest extent. Sometimes (not always) these crossbars would also be snugged in place with pieces of grapevine through peg-holes. The result was a square-ended canoe that was not much for looks and could not make much speed, but that could very nicely carry a couple of men and their gear across—or down—the broad river. Paddles were made from tough stiff sections of oak bark. Such bark canoes always leaked at the ends, but not as much as might be expected, and if the load weight, including the paddlers, were positioned close enough to the center, the canoe would bow downward in the middle, lifting the ends high enough that they would barely come in contact with the water. When finished using such a canoe, the Indians usually found a secluded backwater up a creek, filled the canoe with water and then put large rocks in it to sink it for possible use another time. The elm bark resisted rotting for a considerable time, and a canoe sunk in this manner in spring could be raised and used as late as the following fall, though it would almost never survive undamaged through a winter.

361. The author has been unable to find any identification of who this *"relative"* was who took charge of the Henry children. Nor was there any further record of their parents, who, the children reported, had been taken along with the other captives by the larger Indian group that had turned northward.

362. Col. John Bowman remained jealous of George Rogers Clark for many years and was said to "bad-mouth" Clark at any opportunity and, wherever possible, undermine Clark to his superiors.

363. More complete details of the Col. John Bowman campaign against Chalah-gawtha may be found in the author's *A Sorrow in Our Heart: The Life of Tecumseh.*

364. Full day-by-day details of Maj. Gen. John Sullivan's 1779 expedition against the Iroquois may be found in the author's *The Wilderness War* (Boston: Little Brown, 1978; New York: Bantam, 1979).

365. This ambush site was evidently somewhere in the vicinity of opposite the present town of West Monterey, Armstrong Co., Pa., about three miles upstream from present Bald Eagle Island.

366. One account, less reliable, claims there were 60 Indians in this war party, but that is believed to be an exaggeration.

367. Who this slain renegade actually was has never been ascertained, but as Nicholson averred, it was definitely not either George or James Girty, nor their half-brother, John Turner.

368. The militiaman killed when he dropped his own gun against a log was Pvt. William Hall of Pittsburgh. In at least one account, this incident is erroneously included as part of Brodhead's Coshocton Campaign in April 1781. Jacob

Fouts, of the Ramsey's Fort area on Buffalo Creek, was the brother of Andrew Fouts, who also lived here with his son, David.

369. The name of Dehguswaygahent—pronounced as Day-gus-WAY-guh-hent—in some accounts is spelled Dahgahswagaheh; it was, in addition to being translated as "the Fallen Board," also translated by some as "the Dropped Plank" or "the Rifle Stock Dropped." Dayoosta's name is pronounced Dah-YOU-stah.

370. Dahgahgahend's name is pronounced Day-GAH-guh-hend.

371. One account states, regarding Red Eye: *"And after he got over & was climbing up the bank or hill, a ball came so near him as to knock him down, yet without actually touching him."* Red Eye died at an advanced age at the Cold Spring Iroquois Reservation in 1830. Two other accounts state that the brief battle broke out before the canoes ever reached shore, but this is believed erroneous as it does not jibe too well with many of the minor details associated with the fight that have been better substantiated.

372. While there was a certain element of trophy-taking and revenge in the practice of taking Indian scalps, it was actually more economically based than anything else. Indian scalps had a definite commercial value—just as American scalps had commercial value for the Indians who turned them in at Detroit—since a rather high bounty was paid for them. Following the Allegheny Campaign, Brady turned in the scalps that had been taken and was paid accordingly. In the minutes of the Supreme Executive Council, Pennsylvania Colonial Records, it is noted: *"An order was drawn in favor of Col. Archibald Lochry, Lieutenant of the County of Westmoreland, for the sum of £12.10s state money, equal to 2,500 dollars continental money, to be by him paid to Captain Samuel Brady, as a reward for an Indian scalp, agreeable to a late proclamation of this board."*

373. Jonathan Zane's wound required surgery at Fort Pitt for the ball to be removed, but he responded well to treatment and was back on his feet within a month.

374. The Muncey Towns were situated about four miles downstream from the present town of Irvine, and 14 miles below the present city of Warren, county seat of Warren Co., Pa.

375. The Muncey Towns were never rebuilt after this destruction. Nor has there ever been any indication that any of the 30 brass kettles were recovered. In his later report to Gen. Washington, Col. Brodhead wrote: *"The troops remained on the ground three whole days destroying the towns and corn fields. I never saw finer corn, although it was planted much thicker than is common with our farmers. The quantity of corn and other vegetables destroyed at the several towns, from the best accounts I can recollect from the officers employed to destroy it, must certainly exceed five hundred acres, which is the lowest estimate, and the plunder taken is estimated at three thousand dollars."*

376. The Seneca village of Dunosahdahgah—The Burnt House—was situated at the site of the present community of Kinga, Warren Co., Pa.

377. This same young Seneca about two years later captured James Chambers, who

had been on Brodhead's Allegheny Campaign, and treated Chambers very roughly. Chambers was fortunate enough to escape before the execution that was planned for him.

378. Nantagoah—pronounced Nan-tuh-GO-uh—who was also known as Captain Crow, died at an advanced age in 1830 on the Iroquois Indian Reservation at Cold Spring.

379. One account states that Seneca Chief Gahgeote—known as Half Town to the Americans—having returned from opposing Gen. Sullivan on his campaign, learned of Brodhead's expedition and immediately raised 40 warriors and set out to engage him. Brodhead had, by that time, returned to Fort Pitt, but Gahgeote's party allegedly encountered four of Brodhead's men who had wandered off from the main party and became lost. Allegedly, the four fled upon seeing the Indians but were pursued and all four killed. This story, however, is generally discredited.

380. Beeler's Fort, established by the Beeler brothers, John and Samuel, in September 1778, was situated on a fairly broad bottom of Raccoon Creek about midway between present Murdocksville and Bavington, Washington Co., Pa.

381. David McMechen became a very successful attorney in Baltimore, where he finally died without ever having married.

382. James McMechen made his claims near the site of present Natrium, Wetzel Co., W.Va., and eventually became the owner of extensive tracts of land in that area and the sire of a large family there.

383. William McMechen, Jr., under the guidance of his eldest brother, David, also became a Baltimore attorney and subsequently a municipal judge there.

384. William McMechen lived up to his vow and remained at the rebuilt McMechen Settlement until his death in 1803. His son Benjamin inherited his father's place, and he, too, remained there, a successful and prosperous farmer owning 1,600 acres of McMechen's Bottom, until his death at age 78 in 1855. He and his wife, Mary, had fourteen children: Sidney, William, Hiram, David, James, Hanson, Mary, twins Elizabeth and Jane, Benson, Lydia, Ellen, Sheppard and Sallie.

385. The Shawnee graveyard at Chalahgawtha was located on present Shawnee Creek, 200 yards upstream from where it is crossed by present Hawkins Road, just northwest of Xenia, seat of Greene Co. The Baltimore & Ohio Railroad line was built over a portion of the graveyard.

386. *Kinnikinnick* (pronounced KIN-ny-kin-NICK) was a pungent blend of specially dried leaves—the blend often very individualistic—the principal ingredients being leaves of the red willow (osier) and sumac, and often dried bearberry and shredded dogwood bark. With the advent of greater white contact and Indian trade, ordinary smoking tobacco from the plant called *tabac* (tobacco), which grew abundantly in the wild from the Kan-tuck-kee region southward, was often mixed with the blend because of its constant and slow-burning attributes. The fragrance of *kinnikinnick* was strong but not unpleasant. Occasionally, for ritualistic purposes, especially among the tribal medicine men and seers, small amounts of crushed dried marijuana was added, but it

was not a constituent of the normal *kinnikinnick* mixture. Marijuana at this time was abundant as a wild plant throughout the present Midwest. So far as the author's research has determined, it had never been grown by the Indians as a crop, though tabac was, especially among the Cherokees, Creeks and Alabamas.

387. Capt. Henry Bird always wore full dress uniform when visiting the tribes, although other British officers often appeared among the tribes in mufti, or even in Indian garb; McKee was among the latter.

388. This was a party of 42 men under the general command of Maj. David Rogers, who had been sent downriver from Fort Pitt to the Spanish governor in New Orleans the previous spring to procure a loan of funds and as much ammunition and other supplies as possible; the money was needed for continuing the war against the British, and the supplies were much needed by the troops in the upper Ohio River forts. Rogers's second in command was Capt. George Gibson, brother of Col. John Gibson of Fort Pitt, and they were now on their return with the precious cargo of gunpowder, lead, new fusees (flintlock rifles), dry goods, rum and a chest of Spanish silver dollars. The boats reached Fort Nelson at the Falls of the Ohio (the settlement there soon to become Louisville) on August 29 and remained for about a month. When it left, it was augmented with a guard of 28 soldiers under Lt. Abraham Chaplin. The entire complement in the flotilla as it left the Falls of the Ohio was 70 men, which included hired polemen and guards, plus a few passengers from the Fort Nelson area, who were largely civilians and retired officers wanting to get to Fort Pitt and points east. Maj. Rogers also carried dispatches from George Rogers Clark and Col. John Todd to Gov. Thomas Jefferson, reporting on the weakness of Clark's command and that of the Kentucky settlements in general.

389. This attack occurred directly opposite the present Riverfront baseball stadium in Cincinnati, O.

390. Henry Applegate Jr. had arrived from his parents' claim on the site of the present town of Point Marion, Fayette Co., Pa., only about a mile from the present West Virginia border.

391. Mamatchtaga—Big Nose—except for one brief reference about him in October 1781, seems to disappear from history at this point until after the Revolutionary War. But his date with the executioner was only deferred, because he reappears as an unruly drunkard who eventually got into a fight while inebriated and shot and stabbed several people who later died of their wounds. He was tried for murder at Pittsburgh, found guilty and subsequently hanged. Pittsburgh merchant William Christy offered five gallons of whiskey to anyone who would skin out the executed Indian for him and tan the hide. Pvt. David Fitzgibbon, an Irishman who would do almost anything for liquor, took him up on it. When Christy received the tanned Indian skin from him, he had a pair of boot-legs made from it, and he cut the rest of it into wide strips that he gave to his friends for use as razor-strops. One of these strops is still part of the memorabilia collection of the Allegheny County Historical Society.

392.   This sugar camp was located approximately three miles south and slightly west of the present city of Aliquippa and a half mile northwest of the present community of Gringo, Beaver Co., Pa.

393.   The five young men killed were John Fulkes, Thomas Dillow, Lewis Tucker, and the Deavers brothers, Matthew and Richard.

394.   The war party had hidden their canoes in the mouth of present Peggs Run, 35 miles below Pittsburgh, where Cristoes Ferry was later established, four miles upstream from the mouth of Little Beaver River, and crossed the Ohio to the present city of Midland, Beaver Co., Pa. All the captives were adopted into the Wyandot tribe and spent quite a few years among them. When at last they were exchanged, one of the young women, who had married a Wyandot and had children with him, refused to return to the whites.

395.   This matter of snoring while sleeping in hostile Indian country was no joke. Many travelers had been killed in their sleep when their snores attracted the attention of Indians who might otherwise not have detected their presence. Some experienced frontiersmen would not camp with a party if even one of them snored loudly, but would make camp alone several hundred yards from the party.

396.   These prairie regions dotted with clumps of trees became known as the Sandusky Plains and, on the route taken by Brady, had their eastern edge between present North Robinson and Bucyrus in Crawford Co., O. The isolated groups of trees in these prairies were, in fact, called islands—a term that confused many of the early writers who had difficulty understanding its frequent use where there were no major bodies of water. Usually these islands of trees were circular or oval in general shape and ranged in size from a dozen to several hundred acres.

397.   This Half King's Town was located on the left (west) bank of the Sandusky River, about three miles upstream from the present city of Upper Sandusky, Wyandot Co., O., just opposite a brick house, still standing in 1993, that was built in 1840 by an Indian family. A little later, as will be seen, Monakaduto abandoned this village in view of the projected American expedition against the Sandusky Towns and established two other villages, farther down the Sandusky, that would be less vulnerable to attack by the whites. See Notes 497 and 498.

398.   Pimoacan's village was situated east of the present village of Crawford, Wyandot Co., O. The precise location was 1.3 miles east of Crawford on County Road 29 to Hurd Road, then north on Hurd Road for 500 feet, then on a level ground about 300 feet west of Hurd Road. Topographical coordinates are just north of the center of the southwest quarter of Section 25, T1S R13E, Crawford Township. On the northwestern edge of the village, the land dropped quickly a distance of 20 feet to the extensive bottomland of Tymochtee Creek.

399.   This is the site of the present southern edge of the town of Mingo Junction, three miles south of present Steubenville, Jefferson Co., O.

400.   A number of the accounts state that on his return from this first expedition to the Sandusky Towns, Brady encountered an Indian party that had kid-

napped a Mrs. Stoops and that he rescued her and brought her back to Fort Pitt with him, but those accounts confuse a similar mission when he did make this dramatic rescue of Mrs. Stoops twelve years later, as will be seen, in July 1792. They also state that on his return Brady took several squaws prisoner but they escaped; again, this was actually in his later expedition, not this one.

401. This cave was located in the bluffs less than a mile from the present town of Cave In Rock, Hardin Co., Ill.

402. Meason's two sons-in-law took part in his murder, but his son, John, escaped the attack and went to Canada, where he disappears from history.

403. It is recorded that 29 years later, when he was 50, Caleb Wells weighed 275 pounds, reportedly *"without an ounce of fat."* In 1860, shortly before his death at age 101, he still weighed 175 pounds.

404. Pryor's wife and daughter were never heard of again, and it was presumed at the time that they had been killed, since they could not travel as swiftly as the war party wished to travel.

405. This was near the site of the present town of Pocatalico, Putnam Co., W.Va.

406. So far as can be determined, Elizabeth Griffith was never seen again.

407. The Montour's Run settlement had been burned and the few inhabitants killed, so the recovered goods were subsequently sold at auction in Pittsburgh, with the proceeds used to procure supplies for Brady's company of Rangers. The body of one of the Indians who had been shot dead from the canoe resurfaced a few days later and drifted downstream, eventually becoming lodged on Brown's Island, 27 miles below where the action occurred and opposite Holliday's Cove Fort. Some weeks later Thomas Edgington's 12-year-old son, George, found the decayed remains of the body there and reported it. He was allowed to take the skull, which he cleaned. It was still a grisly memento in the George Edgington household when he was 92 years old in 1860, the bullet hole clearly evident. One of the other settlers who went to the island to view the remains took the finger bones home with him, intent upon making them into a set of knife and fork handles, but his wife vehemently objected, and he eventually discarded them.

408. When Brady's party returned to Fort McIntosh, they found that Pvt. Eldon Andrews had already placed himself under arrest and was in the guardhouse. Brady and his Rangers related what had occurred, and Andrews was cashiered and drummed out of the fort. He was last reported in Pittsburgh, where he joined with a party heading for Philadelphia. There seems to be no historical record of him subsequent to that.

409. Ira Marsh, interviewed by Lyman C. Draper in 1850, had as his neighbor some years earlier a man named Benjamin Williams of the Cold Springs Reservation who, though a white man, was a friend of Warhoytonehteh—Cornplanter—and who once possessed the Cornplanter Narrative. Marsh said that Williams corroborated this entire incident but related that there were more Indians killed and more prisoners rescued than was actually so. Williams also said he had it from Cornplanter's own lips that four of the Senecas escaped Brady's attack, Cornplanter by swimming the Allegheny and protect-

ing his head from bullets with a piece of wood; but that Cornplanter, who was always shy about confessing he had any part in barbarities, blamed *"some Wyandots who were with the party for wanting to burn the prisoners."*

410. Ruddell's Station, an outgrowth of the former Hinkson's Station and also known variously as The Cedars and Ruddell's Fort, was located on the north bank of the South Fork of the Licking River, three miles below present Ruddell's Mills, almost on the Nicholas-Harrison county line and about a half-mile in a straight course below the mouth of Townsend Creek, some twenty straight-line miles northeast of present Lexington, Ky. Martin's Station was located on Stoner Creek five miles from Ruddell's Station, three miles below present Paris, Bourbon Co., Ky.

411. Peckuwe—also known as Piqua Town—was located on a flat fertile bottom five miles west of present Springfield, Clark Co., O., between the present George Rogers Clark Memorial and the Mad River in George Rogers Clark State Park. The site is now bisected by Interstate Route 70.

412. This crossing by Girty and his Indians occurred just below the present site of the Warrenton Drive-In Theater, where the Ohio River begins a moderate curve to the west, forming a broad point of sorts—a place that has ever after been known as Girty's Point. It is directly across the river from the northern limits of the present village of Windsor Heights, Brooke Co., W.Va.

413. Dreams and "signs" before an expedition very often had great effect upon the Indians. Many expeditions that might have been very successful were aborted when a dream—especially one experienced by a sachem or wise man of the tribe—began coming true; very often other expeditions were aborted simply because an owl was seen flying in daylight or the shadow of a soaring vulture passed across the leader of the expedition.

414. This tributary was the East Fork of the Little Miami, with the hunting occurring in the vicinity of present Batavia, Clermont Co., O. One account states that the party was doing its hunting on the headwaters of the Sandusky River, but that is an error.

415. Bryan's Station (often erroneously written as Bryant's Station) was established by William Bryan, an uncle of Rebecca Boone, wife of Daniel. The settlement was located on North Elkhorn Creek, five miles northeast of present Lexington, Fayette Co., Ky., adjacent to where present Bryan Station Pike (State Route 57) crosses North Elkhorn Creek, near the site of the present village of Avon, at the Fayette-Bourbon county line. One account states that Wetzel made his escape to Grant's Station, but that is incorrect.

416. When Clark's letter was received by Congress, a notation was appended to it as follows: *"(Rhd. Peters of War Office, Apl. 13th 1781, Brig. Genl. Clark's letter before Congress—which was the first official intimation they had had of his expedition, except an application we had for 4 tons of powder on behalf of Va., wh. was furnished. The stores demanded may be furnished in a great degree.)"*

417. The John Vanmetre claim and cabin was located in a small bottomland along the west bank of Stott's Run about a mile and a half north of the present town of West Liberty, Ohio Co., W.Va., and the same distance southwest of the present town of Bethany, Brooke Co., W.Va.

418. Johnny Vanmetre was adopted into the Wyandot tribe and grew up with them. After the Indian wars he returned on several occasions to visit his father, but he always returned to the Wyandots. When the senior John Vanmetre eventually died, he left a bequest of part of his estate to Johnny, who came and got its value in cash and then returned to the Wyandots and was never heard of again.

419. The hostiles on the west side of the river, who escaped Brodhead's army, fled to the Indian towns on the upper Sandusky River and took up residence there.

420. Indayochee—spelled Indaochaie in Brodhead's report—was situated at about the location of the south end of the present Norfolk & Western Railroad bridge, two miles west and slightly north of the present town of West Lafayette, Coshocton Co., O.

421. Brodhead's camp was located at the site of the present town of Isleta, Coshocton Co., O. Salem, at the site of present Newcomerstown, was another four miles upstream, and Gnadenhütten some 12 miles above that, both on the sites of the present towns of the same name in Tuscarawas Co., O. The third Moravian missionary village, Schoenbrun, was located a dozen miles upstream on the Tuscarawas at the site of the present Schoenbrun Village State Memorial, two miles south of present New Philadelphia, Tuscarawas Co., O.

422. The Talgayeeta cabin was located on the southeast end of the small bridge presently crossing the Scioto River headwaters within the limits of the present city of Kenton, Hardin Co., O. Two years before, Kenton, who had been condemned to death by the Shawnees, had been rescued by his old friend Girty. However, a few weeks later, because of reverses the Indians had suffered in the war with the whites, Kenton was retaken by them and recondemned, at which time Talgayeeta had been instrumental in getting Kenton's death sentence waived so that he could be taken to Detroit for questioning by the British. Full details of Kenton's captivity, this incident and Kenton's ultimate escape from Detroit and return to Kentucky may be found in the author's *The Frontiersmen*.

423. During his captivity Billy Boggs remained greatly afraid that his part in Killbuck's murder would be discovered and that he would suffer a terrible death by torture. That did not happen, however. While being taken back to their villages by the Indians, he was tied to stakes, spread-eagled, at night without covering of any kind from the elements—and it rained often, causing him to contract a severe case of the ague. At the villages he was forced to run the gauntlet and nearly died under the beating he received. Along with young Presley Peek and several other captives, he was finally sold to the British at Detroit, where he was forced to undergo intensive questioning. Having been held captive for a year and a half, he was finally released as part of a prisoner exchange and returned to the upper Ohio Valley.

424. Shortly after the capture of his son and attack on his cabin, Capt. John Boggs temporarily abandoned his claim and moved his family to Wheeling.

425. Lower Sandusky was located about ten miles up the Sandusky River from its mouth at the western end of Sandusky Bay, on the site of the present city of

Fremont, Sandusky Co., O. The name of Chief Coon has sometimes been spelled Kuhn.

426.   Though all thought the wound Simon Girty suffered would prove mortal, he miraculously survived due to the treatment from the Indian healer. He was back on his feet in two weeks, though it was several months before he was fully functioning again. It is said that when Girty regained his health, he confronted Thayendanegea and placed two swords and two pistols on a table and told the Mohawk to take his pick and they would fight it out; but that Thayendanegea shed tears and begged forgiveness and Girty forgave him, but this is believed to be entirely spurious. In later years Girty went blind, it was believed perhaps justifiably, as the result of the injury he received from Thayendanegea's sword that night. One source, also believed unreliable, states that a trepanning operation was done on Girty and a silver plate was inserted in his head at that time. A deep dent remained in Girty's head ever after this injury. One account states that Girty's injury from Brant's sword did not occur until the war party was on its way back to Detroit with prisoners after the Ohio River attacks, but this does not fit with the facts presented in more verifiable accounts in other sources.

427.   Through one cause and another, the Moravians and the party of Delawares and Wyandots assigned to escort them, did not leave the Gnadenhütten area until September. Scotach, pronounced SKO-tash, is spelled Scotash in some of the accounts; Scotach is correct. Scoleh is pronounced SKO-leh. Dakadulah is pronounced Duh-KAH-ju-luh.

428.   This island later became famous as Blennerhasset Island, where Aaron Burr conceived and developed his conspiracy at the great mansion built there by Harmon Blennerhasset.

429.   One account states that Craycraft and Wallace were part of Lochry's force and were sent forward to overtake Clark and procure ammunition from him so Lochry and his men could hunt and defend themselves. This is unlikely, since Lochry and his men had plenty of ammunition when they left Wheeling.

430.   At least one account has placed Simon Girty, along with McKee, on the Kentucky side of the Ohio when this ambush was effected, but McKee was definitely on the Indiana side of the river for the ambush. If, in fact, a Girty was on the opposite side, it would have to be James Girty, who may have been part of the contingent of Indians that took post on that side. Gen. Irvine at Fort Pitt stated in his report that the Girty involved in the attack was George Girty, but this is an error; it was James.

431.   There is a frequently recurring story in the accounts of Thayendanegea— Joseph Brant—wherein he saved a number of prisoners when he discovered that they were members of the Masons, since he was alleged to be a Mason, too. In this case, it is reported in one account that after Lochry was tomahawked, *"a silver Masonic medal was found in Lochry's bosom & when Brant saw it he regretted his death & would have prevented the murder (by perhaps assigning some of his own Mohawks to guard him) had he known of Lochry being a Mason."* That story is very suspect.

432. In addition to Capt. Orr, other captains who survived capture included John Guthine (who later married Archibald Lochry's widow), Joseph Irvine, Thomas Shannon and Thomas Stokeley. The deserters, Lts. Paddy Hunter and Samuel Craig, also survived.

433. Capt. Thomas Shannon, of Ligonier Valley in Pennsylvania, was claimed by a Shawnee warrior and, after successfully running a gauntlet line at his village, was adopted by him. While other prisoners were sold to the British at Detroit, the Shawnees refused to surrender Shannon, who remained with them until the succeeding fall. At that time, after having previously shown his skill in shooting, he was permitted to accompany a hunting party of Shawnees to the Walhonding Valley in the vicinity of present Millwood, Knox Co., O. The Indians gave him a gun to hunt with and let him go out to hunt, but he felt sure they were watching him closely. He quickly killed a fine buck, brought it into camp and was patted on the shoulder and congratulated. The next day they gave him the gun again, and once more he set out. This time, not being watched so closely, he immediately struck out overland for Wheeling. He was close to his destination, still on the Ohio side of the river, when he unfortunately encountered a party of Wyandots returning from a raid against the settlements. He tried to flee but was overtaken and killed.

434. Of Lochry's entire force of 107 men (including himself), 41 were killed and about half that number wounded. Those who were tomahawked while captive were said to have been killed in direct retaliation for the prisoners executed by Col. Brodhead's men during the Coshocton Campaign the preceding spring. Most of the prisoners were required to run the gauntlet after reaching the Indian villages and a few died in the effort; the majority, however, were then taken to Detroit and sold to the British. Q.M. Richard Wallace was another of the captives adopted by the Indians; he was taken to Detroit to live among them there. He was hired out as a cooper by the Indians. Capt. Arent de Peyster, commanding Detroit, purchased the other prisoners and tried to purchase Wallace and a private named William Witherington, but the Indians would not sell. When, the following October, the Lochry detachment captives were being readied for transport to Montreal, Wallace was smuggled aboard the ship in a trunk on de Peyster's orders, and Witherington was rolled up in a blanket and carried aboard. The prisoners were quartered on Prison Island adjacent to Montreal for the winter and subsequently taken to Quebec. After a year as captives there, they were finally freed late in 1782 as part of a prisoner exchange. Most of these freed prisoners had reached their homes by May 1783.

435. Rebecca Hawkins was not heard of again. Presley Peek was kept in captivity for seventeen months before being returned in a prisoner exchange.

436. William Huston's body was buried on the spot where he was slain, and later the grave was marked and fenced.

437. It is believed the fire started when a gust of wind caused a shutter to swing and strike a lighted oil lamp on a sill in the stable within the fort. The smashed lamp landed in the hay, and within moments, with a strongly disadvantageous

wind blowing, the entire fort was afire. A few horses had been killed, but the garrison managed to escape with the majority of the animals and with their guns and powder, but the fort was soon entirely consumed.

438.   This was at the site of present Sand Island, just below the larger island presently called Shipping Port Island, in the Ohio River just off the northwestern end of present Louisville, Jefferson Co., Ky.

439.   Three of the crew members of this boat have been identified as James Powers, Peter Barr and James Lindley.

440.   Some accounts list Johnson's first name as Terry rather than Jerry.

441.   James Armstrong, who hailed from Carlisle, Pa., was something of a company comic, constantly telling jokes or relating improbable stories, such as his account of having single-handedly taken three or four Hessian soldiers prisoner, whom he said he had surrounded.

442.   Lt. Jerry Johnson's body was never recovered.

443.   Continuing with his downstream venture, Capt. Elliott stopped off at Natchez and then at Pointe Coupee. At the latter port he was offered $30 a barrel for his flour—$7,500 for his whole cargo—but refused to sell, believing he could get a better price at New Orleans. Arriving there, however, he found the market deflated and wound up having to sell his flour for only $12 per barrel. Entrepreneur that he was, Elliott took the $3,000 he got for the flour and bought good fur pelts at a cheap price. These he took to New York, where he made an exceptionally large profit of almost ten times what he paid for them. Elliott wound up being a contractor for Gen. Anthony Wayne, made a fortune in the process and was on the verge of calling it quits and going home when, just before the Battle of Fallen Timbers that ended the Indian war in 1794, he was attacked by a party of warriors and killed. Elliott's crewmen, James Lindley and Peter Barr, went from New Orleans to Pensacola, Florida, where they were hired by a trader in a small boat to help him transport a cargo of lime juice in kegs to New Orleans. They camped one night on the shore of a bayou between Mobile Bay and New Orleans, and all three were killed by attacking Choctaw Indians who had expected to find liquor in the kegs and destroyed the cargo when they discovered their error.

444.   Wells' Station was located at the site of the present village of Lynnview, a suburb of present Louisville, Jefferson Co., Ky.

445.   Samuel Wells, Sr., originally from the community of Opequon in Maryland, had served in Dunmore's army in 1774.

446.   Pvt. Daniel Whittaker, who hailed from Pittsburgh, was no relation to Pvt. Aquilla Whittaker, who was also with Floyd's party. Ravenscroft and King both spent a long time in captivity but were eventually freed in a prisoner exchange.

447.   It is reported that the cut Thayendanegea accidentally gave himself was so severe that he never entirely recovered from it.

448.   Eventually taken to Detroit as a prisoner, Samuel Murphy saw a large dry goods box half filled with scalps taken on the upper Ohio, for which the Indians had received bounty payment. While there he was treated by a British surgeon for the bullet wound in his hip, and he also received, as a gift from

Simon Girty, who was there, a new handkerchief with a pound of tea tied up in it and about six pounds of sugar. When Murphy was interviewed by Lyman Draper on September 1, 1846, he said, in this regard: *"Girty was good and kind to me; this is as true as you are sitting there."*

449.   This French swivel was part of the armament of Fort Duquesne. It had been spiked and cast into the river by the French themselves on November 24, 1758, when they evacuated and destroyed Fort Duquesne at the approach of the British.

450.   Andrew Poe was born September 30, 1742, in Frederick Co., Md. His father, George, a well-to-do landed Dutchman, was murdered by an Irishman in his employ when Andrew was 14 years old. A few years after that, Andrew came to the frontier, eventually taking up residence and working in the Pittsburgh area for some years. About 1773 he claimed land on Harmon's Creek, after which he returned to Maryland and convinced his brother, Adam, to return with him there to claim land for himself, which Adam did.

451.   Collier's Settlement was established in 1771 by Jacob(?) Collier on present Harmon's Creek, six miles upstream from the Ohio River at the mouth of Mechling Run, on the site of present Colliers, Brooke Co., W.Va.

452.   It seems probable that the camp Poe's party made for the night was located at or very near the site of the present community of Cherry Lake, 1.5 miles north of present New Cumberland, Hancock Co., W.Va.

453.   In some of the accounts, Dakadulah is misidentified as an Indian widely known on the frontier at that time as Big Foot, because of the great size of his footprints (13″ × 5¹/₂″), often found at scenes of Indian raids. However, the so-called Big Foot and Dakadulah were two entirely different Indians. The Wyandots are not known to ever have had an Indian named Big Foot, in their tongue or anyone else's, nor any warrior who matched Big Foot's description.

454.   One account states that Andrew Poe had momentarily gotten loose from Dakadulah's grasp, snatched up the Wyandot's cocked rifle and shot Scoleh dead, but both Adam and Andrew Poe themselves related that it was Adam who killed Scoleh.

455.   There are a number of considerably differing versions of the Andrew Poe fight, some of which have been elaborately exaggerated. The author has attempted to reconstruct this incident as accurately as possible, relying most heavily on the recollections of the members of Poe's party, especially Adam and Andrew Poe themselves, and interviews by Lyman Draper with descendants of the Poe family. Andrew Poe never recovered completely from his injuries; it was about a year before he could do anything, and his right hand, damaged beyond repair, became paralyzed and atrophied until it was about a third smaller than its original size. He lived for 41 years after this fight and died July 15, 1823, at the age of 80, at his home in Green Township, Beaver Co., Pa. Adam Poe lived to the age of 92 and died at his home in Massilon, O., in 1840.

456.   The place where Scotach came ashore with the bodies of his brother Scoleh and the three other Wyandot warriors was most likely on—or very close to—the site of the present village of Empire, Jefferson Co., O.

457. Captives' Town was established for the Moravian Indians who had been removed by force from their villages of Gnadenhütten, Schoenbrun and Salem
on the Tuscarawas River. They had been allowed to build a large number of
temporary wegiwas on a high flat ground upstream on the upper Sandusky
River from Half King's Town. There is nothing on the spot now where this
temporary Captives' Town was located in Pitt Township, Wyandot Co., O.,
east of present State Route 199 in a U-shaped bottom of the Sandusky River,
a mile downstream from the mouth of present Brokensword Creek. It was
across from present Township Road 60A, on the land presently (1993) owned
by Richard Coons and Agnes Miller.

458. It was this same young Indian woman who eventually was instrumental in
getting George Fulkes released so he could return to his own people on the
upper Ohio River.

459. This trail, sometimes called the Mahoning Trail, was a much-used trail that
connected the Cuyahoga Portage to the main trail leading to the Iroquois
nations. It was encountered by the Brady party at about the site of the present
village of Niles, Trumbull Co., O. Westward from this point, it more or less
followed the route of the present Baltimore & Ohio Railroad right-of-way to
present State Route 59 just south of Brady Lake, at which point it followed
what is now State Route 59 into the present city of Kent, Portage Co., O., to
the portage across the Cuyahoga River in the vicinity of the present location
of the Main Street bridge.

460. The stream, on the east side of which the Indians were camped, was present
Breakneck Creek, the camp itself located at the northeast end of the State
Route 59 bridge crossing the creek at this point. The lake to the north was the
present Brady Lake. The swamp in question has long since been drained.

461. This trail along the narrow ridge is the route followed by present Merrill
Road, which runs diagonally northeastward from State Route 59 for 1.1 miles
to Brady Lake Road.

462. It has never been accurately ascertained how many Indians were killed or
wounded in this very successful ambush, but from remarks made by the Indians themselves later and overheard by captives, there were probably a total—in
both the Indian camp and at the ambush scene—of 30 to 40 killed or
wounded.

463. This fording place was approximately where present Powder Mill Road crosses
Breakneck Creek.

464. Standing Rock, still known by that name, is 0.9 mile upstream from the Main
Street bridge at the northernmost edge of the city of Kent, along the western
bank of the Cuyahoga and at the southernmost corner of the present Standing
Rock Cemetery.

465. Between 1846 and 1858, historian Lyman C. Draper expended a great deal of
effort into discovering the truth about the so-called Brady's Leap. Many were
by this time claiming that it was a myth that had been concocted to aggrandize
the accomplishments of Samuel Brady, or that it had occurred at another
place, on another stream—such as Slippery Rock Creek, which Draper himself believed for a long time was the locale where the leap occurred. Scores of

documents were painstakingly studied, and in the end Draper, convinced of the Cuyahoga leap by the evidence presented to him by Dr. S. P. Hildreth, wrote a memo in which he stated, *"Hildreth . . . thinks there can be little or no doubt but Captain Brady made his leap over the Cuyahoga. I yield to this opinion, & discard the locale of Slippery Rock Creek."*

As part of his study, Draper had a practical surveyor, Gen. Samuel D. Davis of nearby Ravenna, O., measure the gap across the Cuyahoga at this point. It was precisely 22 feet, and the lower bench or ledge below the east bank extended for 30 to 40 feet. Wrote Draper in his memo: *"The ledge or bench was blasted off about 1840 when the canal was building."* The Baltimore & Ohio Railroad tracks now follow the east side of the river where Brady finally struggled to the top of the bank. In conclusion of his painstaking research into the matter, Dr. Draper wrote, *"I am now more than ever convinced of the Brady Leap legend, & have additional proof of the ambuscade at Brady's Lake. Both localities are admirably suited to the extraordinary feats which tradition says were performed at each; and they serve in my mind, since witnessing them, to go far to prove the correctness of the traditions."*

466. This fording place was approximately where the present Brady Lake Road bridge crosses Breakneck Creek.

467. This chestnut tree trunk angling into the water at the southern tip of Brady Lake remained there for a very long time and was still visible in 1813, 32 years after the Brady incident.

468. The full account of Kenton's life and amazing experiences may be found in the author's *The Frontiersmen*.

469. Simon Kenton and Martin Wetzel, though both lived for many years afterward, never met again.

470. Andrew Montour had claimed this island as his own in 1772, filed his claim and ultimately became sole owner of it. The elongated island begins five miles down the Ohio River from the Forks of the Ohio. It is five miles long and about a half-mile wide at its thickest area. It is presently known as Neville Island and is located in Allegheny Co., Pa.

471. Connoquenessing Creek enters Beaver River at the present line of Beaver and Lawrence counties, Pa., just below the city limits of Ellwood in the latter county.

472. The hunting camp had been made at just about the site of the present village of Greece City, Butler Co., Pa.

473. George Rousch and Neil Danagh made it back to Pittsburgh without mishap and informed authorities there. A party of 34 men was raised under Capt. Jacob Springer and, with Rousch and Danagh as guides, went back to the scene. They found the Indians gone and the body of Andrew Montour still there with broken pieces of the jug sticking in his mashed forehead. He had not been scalped.

474. Although no signature was appended to the letter written to Gov. Haldimand, the handwriting and other clues seem to indicate it was penned by Col. Guy Johnson, British superintendent of Indian affairs and nephew of the late Sir William Johnson. It also undermines the denials by the British, then and later,

that they were offering the Indians rewards for scalps and that those Indians were specifically ordered not to scalp women and children.

475.   David Williamson, always noted as a very popular individual, was born in 1752 near Carlisle, Pa., and first came to western Pennsylvania as a hunter when he was just a boy. Soon afterward he convinced his father to settle there. He became a member of the Washington County militia in 1777 with the rank of captain, and later became that unit's colonel.

476.   One account states that the Indians, after crossing the Ohio with their Wallace family prisoners, found Mrs. Wallace and her infant daughter slowing their progress too much and so tomahawked them. The two Wallace boys were kept alive and taken along to the Sandusky Towns where the elder one, ten-year-old James, died, though whether he died from natural causes or was killed is not stated. The younger Wallace boy, two-and-a-half-year-old Robert, apparently was returned to the Americans in a prisoner exchange some years later and was ultimately reunited with his father.

477.   Bilderback's name, in numerous documents, has been spelled as Builderback. It was this spelling that the author used when first referring to Capt. Bilderback in *The Frontiersmen*. A study of the pension rolls and army rolls indicates, however, that this individual signed his own name as Bilderback, which must be accepted as the correct spelling.

478.   Since there was no further mention of these boys escaping, it is assumed that they were subsequently found and imprisoned with the others.

479.   It has never been ascertained whether Col. David Williamson participated in the vote, though the assumption is that, as commander, he would have refrained from doing so unless there was a deadlock of equal votes on both sides. That he would probably have voted in favor of the execution is revealed in a comment he later made: *"For when they were killed the country would belong to whites, and the sooner this was done, the better."*

480.   This private, not identified, later boasted to Samuel Murphy and others of the manner in which he *"made good Injens"* of these two.

481.   Various accounts give different figures for the total number killed in the Moravian Massacre, as it would thenceforth be known. They range from as low as 90 to as high as 100. However, a close study of the existing documentation seems to indicate that a total of 96 deaths is the correct figure, which includes the four who were killed prior to the executions: Jacob, who was searching for his horse; the unidentified man in the canoe, evidently arriving from Schoenbrun; and the man and wife in the village who were tomahawked when the army first arrived. This means that the number actually killed in the two buildings—including the boy, Peter, who was burned to death while trying to escape—was 92. Only four escaped: Joseph Shabosh, Thomas, Esther, and Adam Stroud. These figures, of course, assume that the figures of 50 Moravians at each of the three towns were accurate, placing 100 in Gnadenhütten after the arrival of those from Salem. The addition of the man in the canoe, coming down from Schoenbrun, is offset by the escape of Joseph Shabosh in the cornfield. Finally, one account states in its entirety: *"One of Williamson's party saved a little boy of eight years old, took him home, and raised him to a man,*

when he left and returned to his tribe.'' Since this is not verified by any other account and the name of the boy or man is not provided, the incident is discounted. One account, repeated by some historians, claims that the Moravian Indians were deliberately set up by the British-allied Sandusky Indians to be killed by the Americans and that this *"was part of the British policy matured at Detroit, of having these peaceable Indians massacred by excited American border men, in order to bring over to the British side all the Indian tribes united against the colonists.''* There is no foundation in fact for such a statement.

482.   Adam Stroud grew to manhood among the Moravians and was eventually killed in a drunken brawl with some other Indians in the streets of Amherstburg, Ontario, just prior to the War of 1812. Esther also grew to maturity and married an Indian named Tripp. They lived close to Simon Girty, just south of Amherstburg, until the summer of 1813, when they disappeared from the pages of history.

483.   On arrival at Half King's Town, Edgington was forced to run the gauntlet, which he did bravely and well. Monakaduto liked what he saw and announced that he might adopt this white to take the place of his son Dakadulah, who had been killed six months earlier in the fight with Andrew Poe. Monakaduto's wife, however, whom Edgington referred to as *"the old queen,''* objected so strenuously and pouted so much about it that Monakaduto gave up on the idea. Edgington was held captive in the village for three months before finally being sold to the British at Detroit. From there he was shipped to Montreal and then to Kingston on the Hudson River, from which place he was released and returned to the upper Ohio in March 1793, his family having moved back to Chartier's Creek, not knowing whether he was still alive.

484.   John Heckewelder, in his account, is often flagrantly biased in his comments, yet there is some element of truth to the missionary's assertions of unnecessarily cruel treatment by Girty to himself, Zeisberger and the other missionaries and their families. Heckewelder said that Girty, before leaving Lower Sandusky to accompany raids on the upper Ohio—including the one in which he and Scotach captured Thomas Edgington—ordered Levallie not to give the missionaries the comfort of being transported to Detroit by boat but instead to drive them before him as if they were cattle, all the way around the western rim of Lake Erie, not allowing them to rest nor even to halt so the women could nurse their babies. Instead, as soon as Girty departed, Levallie requested boats from Detroit to come to Lower Sandusky and transport the missionaries there. While awaiting the boats, Levallie became very nervous for fear Girty would return before they could leave. As Heckewelder relates it: *"He did return and behaved like a madman on hearing that we were here, and that our conductor had disobeyed his orders, and had sent a letter to the commandant at Detroit respecting us. He flew at the Frenchman, who was in the room adjoining ours, most furiously, striking at him, and threatening to split his head in two for disobeying the orders he had given him. He swore the most horrid oaths respecting us, and continued in that way until after midnight. His oaths were all to the purport that he would never leave the house until he split our heads in two with this tomahawk and made our brains stick to the walls of the room in which we were! I omit the names he called us by, and the words*

he made use of while swearing, as also the place he would go to if he did not fulfill all which he had sworn he would do to us. He had somewhere procured liquor, and would, as we were told by those who were near him, at every drink renew his oaths, which he repeated until he fell asleep. Never before did any of us hear the like oaths, or know anyone to rave like him. He appeared like an host of evil spirits. He would sometimes come up to the bolted door between us and him, threatening to chop it to pieces to get at us. No Indian we ever saw drunk would have been a match for him. How we should escape the clutches of this white beast in human form no one could forsee.'' While Girty was dead drunk one night, the Frenchman got them into boats sent from Detroit and transported the missionaries there, where they arrived on May 19. They were first quartered in an old fort barracks near the waterfront, then were transferred to quarters outside town in Yankee Hall, so called because only prisoners brought in by Indians were quartered there.

485.   The new temporary village of the Moravians was established on the site of present Defiance, Defiance Co., O. The Moravians subsequently removed from here and established a permanent village on the Thames River in Ontario, near present Chatham.

486.   Interestingly enough, Col. James Marshall, county lieutenant of Westmoreland County, who was one of the principal movers in putting this project into motion, was not present at the meeting, nor was Col. John Evans, Monongalia County lieutenant, but both had written to Gen. Irvine that they would *"most heartily concur in any plan adopted for the good of the country."* Westmoreland County was instead represented at the meeting by its sublieutenant Col. Vallandigham. Also present were Col. Williamson, Col. Cook, Maj. Carmichael and Maj. Samuel McCulloch, as well as state legislature member James Edgar, among others.

487.   The Mingo Bottom rendezvous site was situated where the present Mingo Junction Filtration Plant is located.

488.   The actual crossing place was located some 400 yards short of a mile above the mouth of Cross Creek. While Mingo Island no longer exists, in 1782 it supported a heavy growth of large maples on good high ground. Most of that timber was washed away with the great flood of the Ohio in 1832, which reduced the size of the island to about ten acres. For many years afterward the remainder of the island was covered with scrub willow. It gradually eroded away and finally disappeared altogether about 1850.

489.   This bar, no longer in existence, was probably located in the vicinity of present Lock and Dam Number 16 opposite the present village of Ben's Run, Tyler Co., W.Va.

490.   The demand for the boatmen to surrender has been attributed to James Girty in one account. That he did so, or was even with this party, however, has not been confirmed.

491.   One account states that the ball that wounded Carr broke his thigh bone. This is evidently incorrect, since a few weeks later, as will be seen, he was out in a boat fishing with Thomas Carr when they were again attacked by Indians.

492.   That island was, for many years afterward, called Wetzel's Island. It washed away, however, during the especially strong flood of the Ohio in 1832.

493. In various accounts the number of Indians involved in this attack is given as 15, 20 or 30, and about 40. Since these were the same Indians that attacked the Parkinson boat, even the low figure of 15 is likely to be somewhat of an exaggeration. Had any of the larger reported numbers of Indians been attacking, chances are those in the canoe, as close to shore as it was, would all have been killed. The most plausible assumption is that the party of 15, who were off-loading the flour, saw the canoe approaching at a distance, and part of their number, probably no more than six or seven, ran up the shore to set up the ambush of the Wetzel party.

494. One account states that Mills, hearing the firing, crept up close, took one shot at the attacking Indians, killed one and then made his escape by land. That is highly implausible and unconfirmed by any other account. In any event, Mills did manage to get back to Wheeling safely.

495. Some days later Lewis Wetzel and his father, along with a strong party of men from Wheeling, returned to Captina Island, disinterred the body of George Wetzel and returned with it to the Wetzel farm on Wheeling Creek, where he was reburied.

496. Henry Baker was carried captive to the Wyandot villages, where he was condemned to death at the stake. Simon Girty, on hand at the time, bargained for Baker's life and saved him. Baker was then taken to Detroit, where he was closely questioned in regard to frontier defenses on the upper Ohio. Set at liberty, he hired himself out to a British trader in Detroit and worked for him for nearly a year.

497. This new village, called Monakaduto's Town, was established just north of the present village of Tymochtee in Section 17, R14E T1S, Wyandot Co.

498. The New Half King's Town was located five miles downstream (northeast) from the present city of Upper Sandusky and seven miles upstream on the Sandusky River on what is now State Route 67, its center at the location of Smithville church but the village itself on both sides of the Sandusky River. There were also several villages and clusters of wegiwas, mostly Delaware, in this area in conjunction with the Valentine McCormick Trading Post and the John Leith Trading Post.

499. Some of the militia bought cheaper horses, leaving the good ones at home, an act they would later learn to regret.

500. The term *army* in reference to the force of men who marched against the Sandusky Towns is not strictly correct but is used for convenience. It was not truly an army as strict military terminology defines such a body but rather, like other volunteer forces of the frontier, a collection of men mustered and formed into units, each unit usually from a specific geographical area, and whose officers were chosen at the site of rendezvous through popular election among the volunteers. The makeup of the Crawford Army, as it came to be known, is shown here as compiled from lists published in *Pennsylvania Archives,* 2nd Series (Harrisburg, 1888) and *Pennsylvania Archives,* 6th Series (Harrisburg, 1906). The most accurate accounting of this force may be found in the article by Parker B. Brown entitled "Reconstructing Crawford's Army of 1782" in *The Western Pennsylvania Historical Magazine,* vol. 65, no. 1 (January

1982). Brown states that by the evening of May 24 a total of 485 men had arrived at the rendezvous, but that by the time the army reached its destination, the whole force apparently amounted to 583 men.

501.   The rendezvous was 2.5 miles south of Steubenville, the area now covered by rail yards and steel furnaces.

502.   McCaddon died at age 98 in Newark, O., in 1846.

503.   Because Gen. Irvine and his regulars at Fort Pitt and Fort McIntosh did not participate in the campaign, some writers have stated that it was not a federally supported or even condoned operation. That is not true. Irvine simply had no instructions from Gen. Washington to participate in such a campaign; nor could he spare any of his regular force for that purpose. The fact that the army of volunteers was nevertheless under his control becomes evident, however, in his letter of November 10, 1799, from Carlisle, Pa., to John Lyon of Uniontown, in which he wrote: *"In looking over my instructions to the officer who should be appointed to command that* [Sandusky] *expedition, I find that he was enjoined to regulate rank of officers before he took up his line of march, and to impress on their minds that the whole must, from the moment they march, be, in all respects, subject to the rules and articles of war for the regular troops. All the troops, both regular and militia, were under my orders."* Although many writers then and since have implied (or even flatly stated, as did such Moravians as Loskiel, Zeisberger and Heckewelder) that the Sandusky Campaign was in reality a *"Second Moravian Campaign"* fashioned to wipe out the remainder of the Christian Indians, there is no element of truth in the allegation.

504.   The officer known in America as John Rose was actually a Russian nobleman of Baltic German extraction, born in the Province of Livonia in 1753. Preparing for a career in diplomacy and politics, he had attended two German universities, but he fled to America after dueling with, and killing, a nobleman. The American Revolution was just then breaking out, and assuming the alias of John Rose, he joined the Sixth Pennsylvania Battalion at Fort Ticonderoga as a hospital steward. It was there that he met and was befriended by William Irvine, then colonel in command. He participated in the march into Canada and the major defeat suffered at Three Rivers on June 6, 1776. He had, in the ensuing years, experienced a wide variety of adventures both on land and at sea, including even a period of incarceration in New York. Listed in Russian records as Gustav Heinrich Johann Wetter, Baron von Rosenthal, in American records he is usually listed as Gustavus Heinrich de Rosenthal. Rose (as he will hereafter be referred to) was a very literate and perceptive individual. Perhaps the most valuable account of the Sandusky Campaign has come from his pen, though his 20-day journal of this campaign was not even known to exist until 109 years after the expedition ended. Rose made astute and extensive daily entries in his journal during the campaign and afterward added endnotes that evaluated the expedition's officers and recommended changes that might, at some future time, improve a comparable volunteer frontier force. Rose took his journal with him when he returned to Russia two years after the expedition. When he died in 1829, his journals wound up in the Estonian State Archives at Tartu, where they would have lain forgotten

had not Rose's great-grandson in 1893 given a copy for publication to the Historical Society of Pennsylvania. It was published the following year under the title "Journal of a Volunteer Expedition to Sandusky" in the *Pennsylvania Magazine of History and Biography,* vol. 18, pp. 128–57, 293–328, and in 1969 by the Arno Press of New York.

505.   David Williamson, after the election, is reported to have said that he *"preferred Crawford should be chosen, as he is the oldest man."* Both men had the militia rank of colonel and, though Williamson was named as a major for this expedition, virtually everyone continued to refer to him as colonel. To avoid confusion, the rank of colonel will be used in reference to Williamson throughout this campaign.

506.   Daniel Leet had been Gen. Washington's brigade major at the time of the Cornwallis surrender and afterward had come west to help protect his father's family, who had settled in 1779 on Chartier's Creek a mile east of John Boggs' Station. Leet's name has been spelled Leets in various accounts about as often as Leet, though the latter appears to be correct.

507.   Thomas Nicholson, however, did not arrive at the rendezvous until the following day.

508.   The average age of the soldier in this army was 24. The eldest individual was Pvt. Michael Myers, who was 37, while the youngest was 16-year-old John Clark.

509.   John Crawford, son of Col. William Crawford, was not killed during the campaign as several accounts have suggested. Actually, he married, had seven children, applied for a federal pension in 1791, and died and was buried near Manchester, Adams Co., O.

510.   Though the records are incomplete, 19 company commanding captains have been identified, their 18 companies comprising a total of 485 men. (Some accounts say the total number at this point was 489 men, but that does not jibe with the official company count.) The 18 company commanders were: Joseph Bane (with 9 men), John Beeson (with John Biggs as co-commander) (32 men), Charles Bilderback (35 men), George Brown (32? men), Thomas Carr (34? men), John Dean (31? men), Timothy Downing (21 men), John Hardin, Sr. (12 men), John Hoagland (27 men), Andrew Hood (32 men), William Leet (26 men), John Miller (33 men), James Munn (33 men), Duncan McGeehon (20 men), Thomas Rankin (30 men), Craig Ritchie (21 men), Ezekiel Rose (21 men) and Eleazer Williamson (36 men). After being formed, the company of George Brown merged with that of John Hardin, Sr., but neither man was willing to give up command and serve under the other, so Hardin and Brown acted as co-captains of the same company. It is also likely that more companies showed up after the official tally was made and the army was on the march, raising the total number of the army to 583 men, the figure given by Maj. Thomas Gaddis.

511.   John Smith later became a U.S. senator from Ohio.

512.   A prevailing fiction exists that hardly had the last of Williamson's contingent left Mingo Bottom than some Wyandot warriors emerged from the woods. They had been watching the army from hiding since before dawn, and they

now rode over to a sign they had seen being tacked to a tree before the army began its march. The sign is alleged to have said: *"No quarter to be given to an Indian, whether man, woman or child."* This story originated when Moravian John Heckewelder wrote in his narrative (pp. 341–42) that he was told about it by an Indian who had heard it from another Indian, who had heard it from yet another. Later, in 1824, the triple hearsay was written down as historical fact by historian Joseph Doddridge, and since then most accounts of the campaign have included it as truth. No other source contemporary to Heckewelder's, however, makes any mention of such a sign or of such a sentiment being expressed in the army, and it is almost certain that it was invented by Heckewelder, who was noted for his extravagant prejudices against the American frontier people, especially following the massacre of his Moravian flock at Gnadenhütten.

513.   The Indians had been well aware of the army's presence long before Crawford came to the conclusion they were. Thomas Edgington, who had been taken prisoner well before the campaign and who was later exchanged, reported that shortly after the beginning of the Crawford Campaign, he overheard Indians saying that the army had been spied on while at the Mingo Bottom rendezvous, and the number of men had actually been counted twice before the army reached Schoenbrun on the Tuscarawas.

514.   This ravine is now part of the Dennis McWhorter farm, just north of State Route 103 near the present village of Tymochtee, Wyandot Co., O.

515.   Butler's British artillery consisted of a pair of three-pounder cannon of the type called the Grasshopper, plus a 4.4 caliber Royal mortar, commonly called a coehorn. The number of Rangers is not definitely known but was estimated at between 80 and 200, with 120 being the generally accepted figure. Some accounts have placed British Capt. William Caldwell in command of this Ranger party, but that is not possible since he was at that time rendezvousing near the mouth of the Cuyahoga—at present Cleveland—with a large force of Indians under Chief Joseph Brant—Thayendanegea—to march against the American settlements on the upper Ohio.

516.   This practice of referring to the isolated groves of trees in the prairie grasses as islands continues today and often confuses new visitors who, when they hear the names Long Island, Big Island, Green Island or Round Island, fully expect that they indicate actual islands in bodies of water. This is especially true in the case of landmark places, such as the large grove of trees where Crawford's army first engaged the Indians and that to this day is known as Battle Island.

517.   The private who died of exhaustion was not identified. This death occurred at approximately the point where present State Route 83 crosses the common border of Holmes and Wayne counties. A highway historical marker has been erected at this point.

518.   The route of the army was generally as follows: From the rendezvous place at present Mingo Junction, just below present Steubenville, Jefferson Co., O., on an almost due-west course that carried them across Jefferson and Harrison counties to the Tuscarawas and Schoenbrun at the site of the present city of New Philadelphia in present Tuscarawas County; then northwestward into

present Holmes County and then more on a due-west course practically along the present Holmes-Wayne county line; continuing to angle slightly north of west, their route took them through the lower portion of present Ashland County and through present Mansfield in Richland County, then present Ontario in the same county and entering present Crawford County (named in honor of Col. William Crawford) near the present town of Crestline; then continuing along the left bank of the Sandusky through the site of present Bucyrus and into present Wyandot County, near the present town of Wyandot. They spent the night of June 3–4 some 1,200 feet east of present Wyandot at the fine springs located along present U.S. Route 30, where Charles Dickens visited and drank in 1843. Here the river and their trail began angling northward to eventually come to the present city of Upper Sandusky.

519. The captive trader, John Leith, who was at this time camped at the site of present Tiffin, Seneca Co., O., while en route to his trading post near present Smithville, heard and noted the booming of the cannon, too, and thought the sound came from the New Half King's Town at McCormick's, but he was incorrect; in fact, he was only about ten miles from where the sound originated. That the reverberations of those cannon shots carried all the way to the army is rather remarkable, considering the usual muffling effect of fog and the considerable distance they traveled; at this time, though Matthew Elliott's Rangers were within a few miles of reaching and reinforcing the Delawares and Wyandots in their Sandusky Towns, Butler's artillery (a pair of three-pounder Grasshopper cannon and a 4.4 caliber Royal mortar or coehorn), traveling slower, were seven miles behind them, which would have placed them about in the vicinity of present McCutchenville or a little farther north on the trail from Detroit. This means the artillery was 20 miles or more distant from Crawford's army when the cannon shots were heard.

520. John Hoagland was a settler of the Pigeon Creek area.

521. These springs were located in the center of what is now the city of Upper Sandusky, county seat of Wyandot Co., O. The actual springs are now covered over, but they were located in front of the present Moose Lodge, at the intersection of Third and Wyandot streets.

522. Maj. Rose's movement carried his detachment due north from present downtown Upper Sandusky along the route of present State Routes 53 and 67 for 1-3/4 miles, at which point they angled in a more northeastward direction, following present State Route 67 another half-mile to the southeastern point of the grove of trees now known as Battle Island, where the present Battle Island Historical Marker is located, near the intersection of State Route 67 and County Road 47 (Temple Road). The grove at this point spread out to the northwest, north of County Road 47, stretching nearly to State Route 53, somewhat in the shape of a hot water bottle, with its neck pointing toward the southeast, the grove approximately a half-mile long and a quarter-mile wide. This *"vantage ground,"* as Maj. Rose referred to it, which soon became the site of the Battle of Sandusky, was atop a low hill that can be seen a half-mile northwest of the Battle Island Monument.

523. The ravine where the Indians were hidden was a half-mile west of the present

Parker covered bridge over the Sandusky River and about a mile north and west of the marker at the grave of Wyandot Chief Tarhe—The Crane. It runs into the Sandusky River and is located on the present U.S. Geological Survey topographical 7.5-minute Sycamore (Ohio) Quadrangle in Crane Township, Section 4, R14E T2S.

524.   Most of the accounts refer to Monakaduto by his English name, Half King, but some also use his alternative Wyandot name, Zhausshotoh.

525.   Capt. John Hoagland's brother, Pvt. Richard Hoagland, was captured by the Shawnees and tortured to death.

526.   James Munn was a settler from the Mingo Creek area.

527.   William Brady survived the retreat and returned home safely. Later he went west to settle in Scioto Co., O., where he worked as a blacksmith.

528.   The ambush, which Crawford feared might occur, appears to have been attempted by the Indians a short while later. Although the accounts of participants do not mention it specifically, the Draper Collection (DD-S-1/2) has an 1843 memorandum to Lyman Draper from Ohio Gov. Jeremiah Morrow stating that near the road by which they had arrived, *"a small party of warriors were observed, & were pursued a short distance, when it was suspected of being a decoy —the whites wheeled & then discovered themselves in the mouth of an ambuscade in the shape of a letter 'V'."* Evidently they were able to escape the trap that had nearly been sprung upon them.

529.   Jonas Sams was the son of an eastern Pennsylvania tailor who, following the death of his wife, had moved westward across the Alleghenies with his two sons. Jonas and his younger brother, Jonathan, had both become hunters, combing the mountains in their quest for deer, bear and turkeys. The two became successful Indian fighters after joining the Westmoreland County militia and participating in several expeditions against the Indians, as well as assisting in the regular border patrols.

530.   On the Pennsylvania rifle of the type Jonas Sams was shooting, the sights at both front and rear were fixed and could not be adjusted for different ranges. However, while the front sight was a blade sight, the rear was a V-notched sight. Thus, by saying *"I raised the hind sight,"* Jonas Sams actually meant that he changed the elevation of his eye as he lined up rear sight with front sight—a skill that came with experience. It should also be noted that an unresolved situation exists in regard to this remarkable shot made by Jonas Sams. The only British officer recorded as shot during the Battle of Sandusky was correctly identified as Capt. William Caldwell of the British Rangers, and Caldwell himself, in a letter to the Detroit commander shortly after the battle, remarks that he was forced to retire from the field early in the battle when a single ball passed completely through one of his legs and lodged in the other. What makes it peculiar is that Caldwell was mounted at the time on a fine white horse and it would seem that if the ball struck him in both legs, it would also have had to pass through the horse; yet Sams states that his ball fetched the officer to the ground *from* his horse and makes no mention whatever about the horse being hit as well, which he almost certainly would have done had the one-ounce lead ball he shot also passed through the horse. Whatever the

case, while the wounds Caldwell suffered were evidently severe enough to force that officer to leave the field of action, they must not have been too terrible, since Capt. Caldwell, within only a few weeks after this Battle of Sandusky, attended the Grand Council of tribes held at Chalahgawtha in early August, and subsequently joined in the invasion of Kentucky, which was a strenuous ride of some 200 miles.

531.   The term *on-briching,* to remove a fouled lead ball in the barrel, was in common usage at the time and meant this: The Pennsylvania or Kentucky rifle was equipped with a metal plug at the end of the breech facing the shooter. This plug could be removed and a small depression drilled or filed into the end of the plug that faced the firing chamber. With this done and the plug reseated, if and when a ball jammed, it was possible to dislodge it by forcing a small amount of very fine gunpowder through the touch hole and into the concavity in the plug. Then more powder was placed in the pan, and the gun was fired. The flint, as it was supposed to do, would spark and ignite the powder in the pan, and this ignition would continue through the touch hole to the powder in the concavity in the plug. The resultant burst usually had enough force to cause the jammed ball to exit out the muzzle of the gun. If, however, this maneuver failed, or the plug had not been drilled to allow the process, then the breech plug would have to be removed and the jammed lead ball pushed out with a ramrod.

532.   Among the volunteers was Francis Dunlavy, later a judge, who also reported seeing a number of cowards hiding among the baggage, horses and packsaddles, as well as behind logs, in the middle of the woods near the knoll. One of these was a man he identified as a Pvt. Saltzman.

533.   No official figure seems to exist for the number of enemies opposing the Americans at the Battle of Sandusky, but the most generally accepted estimate is slightly more than 600 warriors, before their number was increased by the arrival of the war party of 200 Shawnees to assist the Wyandots and Delawares.

534.   The soldier whose upper lip was shot away was not identified beyond the fact that he was a miller. He survived his wound.

535.   The British artillery never did arrive in time to be used against the Americans during this battle.

536.   These 15 deserters—not identified by name except for the Pvt. Saltzman, who had earlier hidden in cowardly fashion amid the baggage and horses in the center of the woods—managed to get back to Fort Pitt and quickly spread the story that Crawford's army *"was cut to pieces."*

537.   One account says the Shawnee reinforcement amounted to 1,100 warriors. A few other accounts say the Shawnee party amounted to 500 or 600 warriors, but these figures are clearly exaggerations, and 200 or thereabouts seems to be the correct figure. Contrary to popular belief, the Indians' practice of painting their faces and upper bodies in various designs—often geometrical—before battle or when going out on raids was not done to strike fear in their enemies but rather to look handsome in the event they were killed and were seen by the Great Spirit.

538.   Benjamin Newland was born in 1763 to Quakers William and Hannah (Ben-

son) Newland of York Co., Pa. A large, well-built youth who looked older than his years, he had joined the militia in 1779 at age 15 and, following the Battle of Yorktown, had helped guard British prisoners at Hagerstown, Md. He was ejected from the Society of Friends for taking up arms, and as soon as his term of enlistment was concluded, he settled in the west on his own. Within a year he was captured by the Shawnees, survived two severe gauntlet runs and was adopted into the tribe, living with them at Wapatomica. He had been taken to the Sandusky to *"prove himself as a new Shawnee warrior."* He eventually settled in Bedford, Ind., where the Newland (Newlon) family still lives.

539. The Oak Creek Trail to which Leet referred was the one that had been used the previous autumn by the Moravian Indians when they were forcibly removed from their Tuscarawas settlements to Sandusky by their nonproselytized brother Delawares and Wyandots.

540. Pvt. John Orr survived the retreat and finally reached his home on Maj. John McClelland's horse. His leg wound did not heal properly and left him with a pronounced limp for the rest of his life. He finally died in Preston County, Va., in 1840 at the age of 77.

541. The belief that Crawford, Slover and Knight had abandoned the army to their fate persisted for many years among some of the survivors, even though it later became widely known what had actually transpired.

542. It is believed that at least five of the sentries were killed at this time.

543. In his journal comments regarding the formation of the retreat and ensuing panic, Maj. John Rose wrote: *"under these circumstances to save the larger body could have been obtained only by sacrificing a part. But what part of our troops would have obeyed a commanding officer to plunge themselves in, between the Shawnoes and Delawares, whilst the main Body would make their escape by a circuitous march. Here let us ascribe to Providence and her marvelous imposition the execution of a plan, by which only, so large a Body could have been saved. She made use of a superlative Scoundrel for this end. A certain captain Hardin . . . , impelled by fear and rascality united, spoke largely against the measure adopted, concerning the roads chosen to retreat on. His fear fixed the enemy's number from 700 to 1000 . . . and he easily found a party among the younger Sort, to whom his age & experience were arguments of conviction. He actually moved from the ground W. towards the town* [a small Delaware village in that direction] *with a large gang, when Col. Crawford detained the main Body, just going to march off, and went to turn the Miller and the miller's followers. Hardin was fired on by the ennemy on leaving our camp; and this firing was supposed by every man an attack upon our encampment. Every man consequently run off, at the discharge of the very first gun, as if it had been a signal agreed upon, to disperse & shift as well as one could for himself. By a secret impulse the whole took pallmall to the south, collecting as they kick'd along, to some one officer or other; except some few* [that is, head of McClelland's division] *paraded in the front of the Line. These thinking the Rear was pushing after them and not willing to loose the chance of getting first through—cut & whipp'd at a horrid rate along the path, agreed to retire on. They mostly all, fell a sacrifice to the ennemy's fury, who narrowly watched the road.*

The small part also drew the ennemy's [sic] *attention, whilst the larger body got round* [the cranberry bog] *unmolested."*

544. No other mention is made of Jonathan Zane in the known accounts of the remainder of the expedition. He did, however, survive the Crawford Campaign and resumed his life at Wheeling, where he lived the rest of his life in his house located just a short distance above the present First Ward Public School. He had acquired much land, the majority of which was left to his nine children, Catherine, Eliza, Cynthia, Sally, Hannah, Nancy, Isaac, Asa and Benjamin.

545. Francis Dunlavy survived the campaign and later attended Dickinson College, where he studied for the ministry but soon gave up that aspiration when he decided he could not speak loudly enough to address large congregations. Still later he moved to Ohio and taught classical school near Cincinnati. During 1795 and 1796 he took an extensive tour of the Ohio River and Mississippi River by canoe, during which he recorded his impressions meticulously in Latin. He planned eventually to put these notes into a volume for publication, but one of his tenant farmers in 1825 came across the notes, which had faded with age, and, believing them to be trash, threw them away, to the everlasting regret of their owner. Dunlavy served as a congressman in the first Ohio legislature and then received an appointment as a circuit judge. He died in advanced years at his home in Lebanon, O.

546. Though no other account makes mention of it, years later during an interview, the Shawnee war chief, Shemeneto—Black Snake—said that during the retreat the Shawnees thought the British Rangers with them, in the darkness and confusion, were firing at them, and thereupon they retaliated by firing on their white allies.

547. One account says that these three, after great difficulty, finally made it back to the Virginia frontier and were rescued by a border patrol of Capt. Sam Brady's scouts. Actually, that is an error, as will be seen.

548. Pvt. William Nemins's surname is, in some accounts, spelled Nemons.

549. Pvt. William Collins and his unidentified companions made their way overland, traveling only at night and subsisting on anything they could find, from wild strawberries to grubs beneath the bark of rotting logs. In badly weakened condition, they finally reached Montour Bottom two weeks later, and there they remained a week until finally discovered by a man out claiming land. They were too weak to travel, so the unidentified man returned to the settlements, where horses were impressed to carry the four men home, where they recovered from their ordeal.

550. Myers rode the horse so hard that the animal gave out by morning, and Myers abandoned it and continued afoot. Eventually reaching the Schoenbrun ruins, he waded through chest-deep water to cross the Tuscarawas and, on the other side, connected with 50 of the volunteers, who were traveling as a group and cooking the meat of one of their horses that they had killed. The entire group got in safely four days later. Both Swigart and Myers managed to get home safely, too, though Myers lost his gun. Swigart, on foot all night, the following

day encountered the horse Myers had abandoned. The horse was reasonably rested by this time, and Swigart caught it, mounted and rode the rest of the way home at an easy pace. It is not known what became of him afterward.

551.   The five men who turned off on the lesser trail and headed eastward were never heard of again and apparently blundered back into the hands of the Indians. Jonas Sams and his four companions never did overtake the unit from which they had become separated, but about a fortnight later, famished and exhausted to the point that they could barely walk, they reached the Ohio River near the mouth of Yellow Creek. After resting there for a day, they followed the larger stream up to Fort McIntosh, where they found haven and were transported by boat to Fort Pitt.

552.   In these early returns of the Indians, it is believed they had with them about a dozen scalps and half again that many prisoners.

553.   The place where the horses of Col. Crawford and Dr. Knight gave out was approximately two miles northeast of the present town of Osceola in Crawford Co., O. They made camp in the same present county, on what is now Andrews Road, about at the boundary line of Holmes and Liberty townships.

554.   The Olentangy River is a major tributary of the Scioto River and empties into that latter stream some 35 miles downstream, within the limits of the present capital city of Columbus, Franklin Co., O.

555.   The group of 17 deserters was overtaken and killed on the west bank of the Olentangy River near the present (1993) Snyder Road bridge on the farms of John and Mary Ehmann and Alice and Gail Crall. The second group, 12 men, was pursued a mile farther to the southeast, where they, too, were slaughtered.

556.   The fight here was, many years later, dubbed the Battle of the Olentangy by historian Consul Wilshire Butterfield, and the designation stuck, though it was truly far more a skirmish than an actual battle. Later a monument commemorating the Battle of the Olentangy of June 6, 1782, was erected. It is located in Crawford Co., O., halfway between present Bucyrus and Galion on State Route 19 near the bridge crossing the Olentangy River. The actual fight, though, occurred not there but on a more elevated piece of ground just within sight to the northeast, five miles southeast of the present city of Bucyrus, in the northwest quadrant of Section 22, Jefferson Township, Crawford Co., O.

557.   Brigade Maj. Daniel Leet, as well as his brother, Capt. William Leet, survived the retreat. Maj. Leet subsequently resumed his work as a surveyor. He married within a year and settled with his wife on Chartier's Creek, three miles upstream from his father's place. He was employed in helping to lay out Western Pennsylvania's Depreciation Lands and later became a member of the justice court of the legislature. He also was prominent in assisting the poor with donations of clothing and food. He died in 1830 in Sewickley Valley, Allegheny Co., Pa.

558.   Capt. John Biggs was not burned at the stake, as some accounts have stated.

559.   In many of the accounts, Lt. Ashby is mistakenly identified as Lt. Ashley. He was a member of the Eighth Pennsylvania Regiment.

560.   Capt. Downing (and undoubtedly Capt. Munn as well) thought he had killed the Shawnee chief called Half Moon, but he was incorrect. The identity of the

subchief is not known, but the Shawnees themselves later admitted that their second Kispokotha war chief under their principal war chief, Shemeneto—Black Snake—,had been killed.

561. Pvts. John Clark and John Gunsaula were among those who survived the retreat. Later both men emigrated to Kentucky and then successively into Ohio, Indiana and Illinois, where they lived out the remainder of their lives.

562. Capt. Charles Bilderback, who had led off the massacre of the Moravians at Gnadenhütten three months earlier, survived the campaign and reached home safely.

563. Some of those wounded later said that had it not been for the attentiveness of Angus McCoy that night, they did not think they would have survived.

564. Crawford and his party crossed the Sandusky River two miles east of the present city of Bucyrus, close to a spring that later came to be known as McMichael's Spring but is today known as the Charles Weithman Spring.

565. The capture of Col. William Crawford and Dr. John Knight occurred in Sections 5 and 8 of, respectively, Jefferson and Jackson townships, Crawford Co., O.

566. Wingenund's Village—often referred to as Wingenund's Camp, to differentiate it from a second Wingenund's Village, somewhat larger, located more to the north and closer to the Sandusky River—was situated 9.5 miles east of present Bucyrus and a half-mile east-northeast of present Leesville, Crawford Co., O.

567. One account states that Biggs, traveling alone, got to within four or five miles of the Ohio River when he stumbled into a party of Wyandots returning from committing depredations on the upper Ohio. Biggs allegedly killed two of them before he was himself slain. Since Crawford and Knight saw the scalp of Biggs less than an hour after they had separated, however, the story is evidently incorrect.

568. The follow-up story of McQueen is rather interesting: Three of the Indians took the Frenchman off somewhere, and he was never heard of again. The lieutenant and Thomas McQueen were taken back to the Wyandot villages on the Sandusky and forced to run a brutal gauntlet, which both managed to survive, but the lieutenant was later burned at the stake. The fate of the Frenchman is unknown, but he was presumed killed. McQueen was compelled to run a number of different gauntlets after this as he was taken from village to village until, as he later put it, *"there wasn't a sound place in my head."* Those beatings were allegedly responsible for his later in life becoming blind and deaf. Finally, at one of the villages, a squaw bought him for a number of deer skins, and he was forced to do slave labor for her for a year. At the end of that time he was taken along when a party of warriors went to Detroit. There he watched for a chance to escape and finally did so, finding refuge at the fort. After the Indians were gone, he managed to get a job in the store of a British trader. Sometime later one of the Girty brothers (possibly James) was attacked at night by two men and severely beaten, and McQueen was blamed as having had a hand in it. He was imprisoned and kept in manacles for three months before finally being paroled, though restricted to the limits of Detroit. In

wandering about the town he fell in with four other men similarly paroled—one of them white and three blacks—and together they concocted a plan to escape. During the night they stole a boat and glided down the Detroit River to Lake Erie, planning to come ashore somewhere west of Sandusky Bay and then try to make their way south through Indian territory to Kentucky. When land loomed ahead of them, they made it to the shore and immediately thrust the boat back out into the water to drift away, so as not to draw attention to where they had made landfall. Too late they discovered they had landed on an island (probably one of the present Bass Islands, then known as the Sister Islands), and they were soon recaptured and taken back to Detroit. McQueen was again jailed in chains. A little later he was offered his freedom on condition that he enlist in the British Army, but he refused to do so. When peace was finally declared, he was given his freedom and returned home, only then learning that his brother, Benjamin, had been killed as the army retreated from the Battle of Sandusky. McQueen got married in 1801 and settled in Indiana, where he died shortly after the War of 1812. Three of his sons became Methodist ministers.

569.   This was the only act of cannibalism known to have occurred in the Crawford Campaign.

570.   James Paull made it back to the Ohio without further incident. He engaged in a few more Indian fights after that, though none of consequence. He was subsequently, in 1794, elected sheriff of Fayette Co., Pa. In that capacity, with the aid of a hooded executioner, he hanged the murderer of John Chadwick, who had been beaten to death with a club in his tavern. Chadwick, incidentally, was one of the survivors of the Sandusky Campaign.

571.   One account, apparently somewhat romanticized, states that the young Virginia private, Thomas Heady, actually escaped the ambush but accidentally blundered into a party of Wyandots a few hours later and engaged in a fierce hand-to-hand struggle with them, during which he suffered a tomahawk gash on his upper leg. He was then taken to the New Half King's Town at present Smithville, Wyandot Co., O.

572.   Joshua Collins, who had been brought to Monakaduto's Town the day before, had indeed been forced to run a gauntlet there, along with half a dozen other captives, one of whom had faltered in his run and was beaten to death. Collins was held at the town for three days and then taken 40 miles down the Sandusky to the British trading post at Lower Sandusky, on the site of the present city of Fremont, Sandusky Co., O. There he was sold to a party of British Rangers returning to Detroit. Held prisoner at Detroit for a time and questioned considerably about the recent campaign against the Sandusky Towns and the state of frontier defense on the Ohio, he was finally transported overland through Canada to New York, arriving there on December 4, 1782. There he was held for a short while longer before finally being turned over to the Americans at Dobbs Ferry on the Hudson River in a prisoner exchange. From there he continued home on foot and arrived there on January 23, 1783.

573.   Michael Walters and Christopher Coffman were awakened by their eight Chippewa captors before dawn the next morning and taken to Lower San-

dusky (present Fremont), but as they approached the town, they came to the gauntlet area, where a painted post stood at one end. At once fearful their prisoners would be taken from them and made to run the gauntlet here—and perhaps be killed—the Chippewas detoured away from the town, giving it a very wide berth, and returned to the river where it enters Sandusky Bay well below the town. They then camped until a bateau was brought to transport them all to Detroit. For some reason not disclosed to the captives, the Chippewas, as they neared Detroit, decided not to stop there but continued up the Detroit River, through Lake St. Clair, up the St. Clair River to the foot of Lake Huron and then along the Michigan coastline all the way up to the Mackinac Strait, where on June 18 they reached the British post called Michilimackinac. Here the Chippewas finally accepted a ransom from Lt. Gov. Patrick Sinclair and turned their prisoners over to him. Sinclair questioned the pair extensively and learned all the details of the American invasion against the Sandusky Towns—how and where the army had rendezvoused, the scope of its supplies and weapons, how and by whom it was officered and the details of the defeat by the Indians and British Rangers; all of which Sinclair wrote into a report which he sent to Gov.-Gen. Frederick Haldimand. The two men told him the expedition had been established by direction of Gen. Irvine of Fort Pitt, who commanded the Thirteenth Virginia Regiment, although that was not quite accurate since the Thirteenth Virginia no longer existed. In 1778 the Virginia Line was reduced, and the Thirteenth Regiment became the Ninth Regiment. Later, on February 12, 1781, a reorganization of Virginia Continental troops was made, and the Ninth Regiment received the new designation of Seventh Virginia Regiment. After being held three months at Michilimackinac, Walters and Coffman were taken to Montreal via Detroit, Fort Erie, Fort Niagara and Carleton Island, finally reaching their destination with other American prisoners from Detroit on October 28, where they were jailed. Both Walters and Coffman were eventually freed in a prisoner exchange two years later. Coffman got back first. Walters went home via Lake Champlain, Crown Point, Ticonderoga, Saratoga, Albany, Allentown and Harris Ferry (present Harrisburg, Pa.). He subsequently received the largest amount of back pay collected by any soldier of the Crawford Army, £102.

574. This fork in the trail was located some seven miles east of present Upper Sandusky, a quarter-mile east of the roadside rest area on U.S. Route 30.

575. John Leith, an American originally from Leith, Scotland, had been taken captive by the Indians many years before while engaged in the Indian trade. Though not adopted into a tribe, he was given the name of John Titt, and because of his trading abilities and the fairness with which he had always treated the Indians, he had been permitted to continue trading among them, with British goods, while still their prisoner. He eventually married an American woman—Sally Lowery—a widow, who had been taken captive with her son some years before and who then lived as a captive in a neighboring Delaware village. Since the couple were captives of different tribes, they were not permitted to live together, but they visited each other frequently. Over two hundred of their descendants still live in Wyandot and Crawford counties

in Ohio. Leith had small trading posts on the Sandusky River at Lower Sandusky (present Fremont) and at present Tiffin, but the store just east of the
gauntlet ground and just south of the Smithville Church, adjacent to the New
Half King's Town, was the principal post. Years before the Battle of Sandusky,
he had attempted to start another trading post on the Muskingum at Goschachgunk (present Coshocton) but was attacked by Mingo and Wyandot
marauders and lost 14 packhorse loads of furs to them. Leith eventually escaped his captivity and resumed his life on the American frontier.

576.   One account states that Crawford offered Girty $30,000 to save him; others,
probably more reliably, say the amount Crawford first offered was $1,000.

577.   No further details are known respecting the ultimate fate of Ens. William
Crawford, apart from the fact that the Shawnees there reported that several
captives taken from Col. Crawford's army were burned at the stake. Ens.
Crawford, never heard of again, is assumed to have been one of these.

578.   Contrary to the legend that has grown up around Simon Girty as the arch-
renegade who delighted in torturing prisoners, he strove far beyond what
might have been expected in his efforts to save Crawford's life; even, as will be
seen, to the point of ultimately putting his own life in jeopardy. His efforts to
save Crawford were extensive and fully corroborated by Mrs. Valentine Mc-
Cormick, wife of the proprietor of McCormick's Trading Post at the New
Half King's Town, who personally witnessed what he did. Most histories of
Crawford's campaign, his capture and execution have, unfortunately, been led
astray by what was long considered the foremost history of these events as
portrayed by Consul Wilshire Butterfield in his book, *An Historical Account of
the Expedition Against Sandusky Under William Crawford in 1782; with Biographical Sketches, Personal Reminiscences and Descriptions of Interesting Localities, including, also, Details of the Disastrous Retreat, the Barbarities of the Savages and the
Awful Death of Colonel Crawford by Torture* (Cincinnati, 1873). Sadly, Butterfield's history of the campaign must be largely discounted, since he was
himself strongly influenced by a highly prejudiced account of these events
attributed to Dr. John Knight and entitled *Dr. Knight's Narrative,* which was,
in fact, written and edited by Hugh H. Brackenridge, who interviewed Dr.
Knight at his bedside and grossly distorted what Knight told him. He was
equally prejudicial in respect to *John Slover's Narrative.* Brackenridge made no
secret of the fact that he positively detested the Indians and that he deliberately
set about to paint Simon Girty as the most villainously cruel and loathsome
renegade who ever lived. Anything Brackenridge encountered that showed
Girty capable of compassion was omitted or deliberately altered to Girty's
detriment. Prior to becoming involved with Dr. Knight, Brackenridge had for
some time published a Philadelphia political journal, in which his anti-Indian
leanings were clearly exposed. Indians were consistently referred to as savages
or monsters or worse in his writings, and in his editorial observations, included with both the John Slover and John Knight narratives, he refers to the
native people as those *"animals vulgarly called Indians."* He emphatically
claimed that white men could not deal with Indians in any respect because of
the cruelty and fierceness of the latter, that such Indians had no rights what-

ever to the land they occupied and that, in fact, all western lands belonged only to those who cultivated them in accordance to the dictates of God as they appeared in the Bible. Simon Girty's wife, Catherine, often stated emphatically in later years that Dr. Knight's narrative was *"either utterly untrue or greatly exaggerated."*

579.   The springs where they drank were the ones previously noted in present downtown Upper Sandusky, Wyandot Co., O. The path they followed northward was essentially that taken by present State Routes 57 and 63. The trail upon which they turned off to the northwest was encountered at approximately the site of the present Wyandot County Fairgrounds.

580.   Having left the area of the present Wyandot County Fairgrounds, the party traveled a little west of due northwest, and in a mile the trail angled more directly due west and followed the route presently taken by State Route 199. The unnamed Delaware village was located a short distance northeast of the site of the present village of Lovell, Wyandot Co., O.

581.   This trail from the east was the direct route from the New Half King's Town and McCormick's and Leith's trading posts on the Sandusky River at present Smithville to the principal Delaware village, Pimoacan's Town—also called Pipe's Town—on Tymochtee Creek. The place where this trail intersected the trail the Delawares and their captives was on was approximately a half-mile east of the present drive-in theater on State Route 199, nine-tenths of a mile northwest of present Lovell, Wyandot Co., O., the intersection itself the same distance due north of present Lovell.

582.   In his narrative, Knight is alleged to have said that at this time Girty berated him sharply and called him a *"damned rascal,"* but there is sufficient reason to believe that this remark was arbitrarily inserted by Hugh H. Brackenridge, Knight's extremely prejudiced editor. Brackenridge wrote down all of Knight's recollections at his bedside and later edited and published the popular and very widely circulated *Dr. Knight's Narrative,* which is replete with falsehoods and exaggerations and laid the foundation for Simon Girty being branded as the cruelest and most dastardly renegade of all time. In fact, Girty's attempt to save Crawford was not an isolated incident based on an old friendship; numerous well-documented accounts show that Girty consistently, where possible, helped American captives in a variety of ways, ranging from providing them with food, clothing and medical attention to saving them from execution.

583.   Tarhe's Town was located at the site of the present village of Zanesfield, Logan Co., O., on the upper reaches of the Mad River, four and a half miles upstream from the Shawnee principal village of Wapatomica. Buckangehela's Town was located at the mouth of present Buckangehela's Creek, where it enters the upper Great Miami River at the site of the present village of Degraff, also in Logan Co.

584.   The exact location of this site where Col. Crawford was burned was for many scores of years a matter of conjecture. In the early 1980s historian Parker B. Brown began an intensive investigation to locate definitively the exact site. Through an incredible feat of research extending over several years and

through a number of states, Brown little by little zeroed in on the location and finally established the site beyond any further doubt. The process of his remarkable historical detective work is fully laid out in an article he wrote that appeared in *The Western Pennsylvania Historical Magazine,* vol. 68, no. 1 (January 1985), under the title "The Search for the Colonel William Crawford Burn Site: An Investigative Report." Mr. Brown must be highly commended for his diligent and painstaking research into this matter. A monument was erected at a spot near the burn site (which was thought to be exactly on the burn site when erected) in 1877 and was dedicated on August 30 of that year. It is reached by going east on County Road 29 for one half-mile from the present village of Crawford, Wyandot Co., O. At this point a gravel drive goes due north 1,100 feet and terminates 200 feet south of the right bank of Tymochtee Creek at the Crawford Burn Site Monument. Upon this monument is the inscription: *"In memory of Colonel Crawford who was burnt by the Indians in this valley June 11, A.D. 1782."* The precise burn site, however, has been established by Mr. Brown's exhaustive research as being 600 feet south and just a little west of the monument, on the west side of the gravel road where, heading south, it makes a slight curve to the east. There is a structure on the site, as indicated on the U.S. Geological Survey 7.5-minute topographical McCutchenville Quadrangle, R13E, T1S, Section 26. The statements of five other captives who were on hand at the time of Crawford's death coincide very closely and go far to refute the account attributed to Dr. Knight by Hugh H. Brackenridge. Those statements are to be found in the Draper Papers as follows: Elizabeth Turner McCormick (DD-S-17/191-192, 204-205), Cornelius Quick (DD-E-10/146-147, 155-158), Stephen Chilton (DD-CC-11/264-268), Ambrose White (DD-CC-12/126-127) and Joseph Jackson (DD-C-11/62).

585.   Knight's account says in respect to this moment: *"Girty then came up to me and bade me prepare for death. He said, however, I was not to die at this place, but to be burnt at the Shawnese towns. He swore by gawd I need not expect to escape death, but should suffer it in all its extremities. He then observed, that some prisoners had given him to understand, that if our people had had him, they would not hurt him; for his part, he said, he did not believe it, but desired to know my opinion of the matter, but being at that time in great anguish and distress for the torments the Colonel was suffering before my eyes, as well as the expectation of undergoing the same fate in two days, I made little or no answer. He expressed a great deal of ill will for Colonel Gibson, and said he was one of his greatest enemies, and more to the same purpose, to all which I paid little attention."* No other account of the events at Crawford's execution mentions any such exchange, and it is suspected of being another editorial doctoring of the facts or, more likely, a fabrication inserted by Brackenridge as additional character assassination of Simon Girty.

586.   Because of the Knight account, which blames Simon Girty for this cruel and callous behavior, practically all subsequent accounts have continued to attribute the remark to him, when according to other witnesses, it was actually James Girty who said it and laughed.

587. One account, in considerable error throughout, claims that the burning of Col. Crawford began at nine P.M. and that he finally died at ten A.M., but that is in variance with all the other accounts, which maintain that the duration of the execution by torture was about two hours or a little more.

588. The same account that states the execution lasted for 13 hours (Note 587) states that the body was chopped to pieces and that these pieces were thrown into the fire and burned to ashes and that these ashes were scattered in Pimoacan's Town the next morning. That appears to be a distorted account, since Knight was led by his Shawnee captors to view the remains the following morning.

589. Tutelu, in some accounts, is shown as being a chief, but that is incorrect; he was merely a warrior of the Kispokotha sept of the Shawnee tribe.

590. Little more is heard of the Wyandot chief Pimoacan—Captain Pipe—for the next decade or more. He is known to have participated in and survived the Battle of Fallen Timbers in August 1794 and was subsequently a signer of the Treaty of Greenville in August 1795. In 1811 he attended a large Indian feast held at Greentown (in present Ashland Co., O.), after which he removed to Canada, where he died in his own house during the winter of 1813–14.

591. The winter following the Crawford Campaign, John Rose returned to Ohio with six scouts on a mission to confirm or repudiate reports that the British were building a fort at the mouth of the Cuyahoga River on the site of present Cleveland, O. Inclement weather plagued the party, making travel a great ordeal. Rose was not an agile man when on foot, and on this mission he was afoot a great deal. He seemed to have a special knack for stumbling over every exposed root and falling into every stream and body of water he encountered. The mission disclosed that the reports were false, and no such fortification was under construction. Rose somewhat miraculously returned in one piece, though he did lose his rifle along the way. In March 1783 he was ordered to Philadelphia to aid in expediting payment for the troops at Fort Pitt who were being mustered out of the service. A year later he took a ship home to Estonia, where he married the woman who had formerly been his mistress and, with her, had four children—two sons and two daughters. For his services, Congress gave him tracts of bounty land in both Pennsylvania and Ohio. Though he planned to return to settle in America, he was prevented from doing so by events and obligations in Estonia. One of his sons wound up being killed in a duel, and the other son drowned. His wife and both daughters predeceased him, and he was left without any family in his last years. He died in 1829 and was buried in the family vault built on his estate, but there is no monument or marker of any kind marking his grave.

592. Dr. John Donathy later received payment from the state of Pennsylvania for *"medicines and attendance upon wounded militia."* Pvt. John Walker recovered from his leg wound, but ten years later, in July 1792, while helping to defend Kirkwood's Blockhouse, he was shot in the stomach and died.

593. Pvt. Angus McCoy lived up to his promise. Pvt. John McDonald did manage to get home alive, more than 200 miles from where he was wounded, but he

lost consciousness shortly after arriving there and died a few days later. McCoy himself returned to his home on the upper Ohio, where for many years afterward he engaged in regular frontier patrols.

594.   David Williamson was later elected to three successive terms of one year each as sheriff of Washington Co., Pa. Later, however, he fell into debt and wound up losing his farm and his home. He died poverty-stricken and, according to unconfirmed reports, in the county jail.

595.   No official tally was ever made of the killed and missing in the Crawford Campaign—or Sandusky Campaign, as it was alternately called—but an unofficial tally of the various accounts of those who were killed, as reported in letters, journals, diaries and incidental reports, indicates that approximately 138 volunteers were killed in the battle or in the retreat that followed or later died of wounds received or were executed after being captured. Of these dead, 41 have been identified by name and rank by the author and include the following: Pvt. David Andrews, Pvt. Thomas Armstrong, Lt. Hankerson Ashby, Pvt. William Bays, Pvt. Robert Bell, Capt. John Biggs, Sgt. Jacob Bonham, Pvt. John Campbell, Col. William Crawford, Pvt. (Ens.) William Crawford, Lt. Joseph Eckley, Pvt. Thomas Ellis, Pvt. John Frazer, Pvt. James Guffee, Pvt. Conrad Harbaugh, Pvt. William Harrison, Pvt. John Hays, Pvt. Thomas Heady, Pvt. Philip Hill, Pvt. Henry Hoagland, Capt. John Hoagland, Pvt. Richard Hoagland, Pvt. John Hughes, Pvt. Robert Huston, Pvt. William Huston, Pvt. William Johnston, Pvt. James Little, Maj. John McClelland, Pvt. John McDonald, Pvt. John McKinley, Ens. ——— McMasters, Pvt. Benjamin McQueen, Pvt. Thomas Mills, Pvt. William Nemins, Pvt. Thomas Ogle, Pvt. Cornelius Peterson, Pvt. Lewis Phillips, Ens. Lewis Reno, Pvt. Sam ——— (Negro slave), Pvt. Walter Stevenson, Lt. Edward Stewart. Indian losses were not definitely known, but based on claims made by various individuals to have killed (or seen killed) Indians, the number appears to be about 17. How many were wounded is not determinable.

596.   One account suggests that Mills saw no Indians at all but merely elected to desert at this point, but there is no substance or corroboration to the allegation.

597.   The Indian Springs were located in present Belmont County, about two miles east of the present city of St. Clairsville. The first whites to settle there and claim the spring were the John McMahon family.

598.   One account states that Mills was shot in the heel.

599.   One exaggerated account says there were 40 Indians in the party, but that is incorrect; there were only 12.

600.   One account states that at this point Mills yelled out to Wetzel, *"For God's sake, Lewis, don't leave me!"* Whether Mills issued such a call is moot; whatever the circumstance, Wetzel and Davis had no option but to flee as swiftly as they could.

601.   One account states that Wetzel *"pulled the trigger & blew the Indian's head nearly to atoms."* Exaggeration is endemic in many of the initial accounts.

602.   Some of the more fanciful accounts attribute Long Pine with exclaiming, *"No catch him; gun loaded all the time."* This is hardly likely, since Long Pine knew

only a few individual words of English and Davis knew nothing of the Delaware tongue. Another larger-than-life account states that Wetzel stopped to scalp one of the Indians pursuing him and, having done so, started cutting his head off but had to give up and run on when the other pursuers approached. Though not opposed to taking scalps when he could, Wetzel, in such a perilous circumstance as this, simply would not have attempted something so foolhardy.

603.　Wetzel and Davis made it back to Wheeling without incident. Wetzel did not, as one account has it, have to run 12 miles to outrun his pursuers. A couple of days later a party of 20 men went out, guided by Davis and led, according to one account, by Samuel Brady. They found and buried the stripped and scalped body of Mills. One account says they found the bodies of three Indians and buried them hurriedly in a common grave, but this is unlikely since the Delaware party would not have left their dead behind to be scalped and otherwise mutilated unless their own lives were in jeopardy, which was not the case. That same account also says that in swimming back across the river on the return Wetzel caught a chill that lasted *"several years"* before it was allegedly cured by a French doctor named Pettee at Marietta; again a tall story without much foundation, especially since Marietta was not even founded until September 1786, more than four years later.

604.　The direct trail from the Delaware and Wyandot villages of the upper Sandusky River to the villages of the Shawnees on the upper Mad River took approximately the course presently followed southwestward by State Route 67 to present Kenton, Hardin Co., O., where it crosses the upper Scioto River, and then continued on present U.S. Route 68 to present Bellefontaine, Logan Co., O., then to Wapatomica, just southeast of Bellefontaine. Yet the place where Tutelu and Dr. Knight prepared to make this second camp was at the site of the present village of La Rue, Marion Co., O., about 13 miles down the Scioto from where the main Indian trail crosses it at present Kenton. Why Tutelu would have taken such a circuitous route to reach Wapatomica is a question to which the author has been unable to find a satisfactory answer.

605.　Tutelu bore the scar of the injury on the back of his head for the rest of his life. After the peace that came about as a result of the Greenville Treaty, he took up residence in the Zanesville area and called himself Col. George Washington. The story of how Dr. Knight escaped from him was common knowledge, and he took a good deal of ribbing about it from Indians and whites alike. Tutelu would grin and reply, *"Dr. Knight was a good man. He cured sick folks, and I did not want to hurt him."* Seven years after the peace, he became drunk at a tavern in Zanesville, O., and got into an argument with a white settler and threatened to kill him and take his scalp. When he finally staggered out of the tavern he was followed by some drinking companions of the settler who had been threatened. Tutelu was never again seen or heard of and was evidently killed and his body hidden.

606.　Slover finally reached Fort Henry at Wheeling in remarkably good condition on June 25, eleven days after his escape. He remained on the upper Ohio for a few years after that but eventually married and emigrated to the Red Banks in

Kentucky, where he and his wife raised seven children. He finally died in his own home at an advanced age.

607.   Hugh Henry Brackenridge did, in fact, take down and edit the detailed recollections of Dr. John Knight, which were then published under the title *Dr. Knight's Narrative*. It struck the American people, in its own way, with the same kind of impact that, half a century later, was produced by Harriet Beecher Stowe's *Uncle Tom's Cabin,* though with even greater distortion and manipulation of facts than utilized by Stowe. Both *Dr. Knight's Narrative* and *John Slover's Narrative* were published in Philadelphia the following year in April and in May, vol. 3 of *Freeman's Journal.* They made the anticipated enormous impact, painting the Indians, the British and Simon Girty with the bloodiest of brushes. Only in recent years have historians taken a closer look at the historical records, especially the accounts—of which there are many—that are at variance to the long-accepted "facts" as presented in *Dr. Knight's Narrative.* These investigations have caused many of them to blame Dr. Knight for presenting a grossly biased and even in some respects false presentation of what transpired. But an even closer investigation indicates that it was not Dr. Knight who distorted history but, rather, the man who edited what the surgeon dictated, Hugh Henry Brackenridge. Some critics have been outraged by this shift in interpretation and portray it as an attempt to whitewash America's most diabolical renegade, Simon Girty. That is not at all the case, and one of the more sterling examples of this detailed research and questioning of the assertions attributed to Knight is the excellent article by Parker B. Brown entitled "The Historical Accuracy of the Captivity Narrative of Doctor John Knight," which appeared on pages 53–67 of *The Western Pennsylvania Historical Magazine,* vol. 70, no. 1 (January 1987). Brown's research is extensive, penetrating and highly illuminating. He accepts as reasonably accurate the account of Knight's journey from Mingo Bottom to the Sandusky, the elements of the surgeon's escape from the Indians and the ordeal he overcame on his journey home through the wilderness. Where he takes great exception, however, is in regard to the capture of Knight and Crawford and the subsequent torture and death of Crawford. As Brown states in this respect: *"Here the editor* [Brackenridge] *had several objectives in mind when he polished his notes. He desired, first, to produce a popular, salable story. He also wanted to stir the western populace into such a rage that it would immediately rise up to turn back marauding war parties and revenge the tortured commander, Col. Crawford. In addition, he wished to shame eastern politicians so that they would release more government troops for frontier duty. To do this, Brackenridge accented every gruesome aspect of Crawford's ordeal. In so doing, he ignored important Indian motivations and circumstances, omitted significant recollections, and unjustly besmirched the character of Simon Girty, the British agent. . . . It is thus the editing that concerns us. Did Brackenridge, to guarantee the patriotic immortality and monetary success of the narrative, knowingly suppress pertinent facts and misrepresent significantly the behavior of participants in Crawford's captivity? The answer is yes."* Dr. John Knight served at Fort Pitt to the end of the Revolution and then married a niece of William Crawford. He served in Wayne's

campaign in the Northwest in 1793–95. After that, he and his wife moved to Shelby Co., Ky., where he became widely esteemed for his medical skill, and prior to 1820 he was performing successful cancer surgery.

608. An eighth child had been born to Ebenezer and Elizabeth Zane the preceding May 12. The child, a son, was named Samuel. His siblings were Catherine (13), Ann (10), Sarah (9), Rebecca (6), Noah (4), and John (2). Another brother, Noah, had died in infancy eight years earlier. Samuel, sickly since birth, also soon died.

609. Cane fishing poles were one of the first items of commerce to come out of Kentucky. They were harvested from the vast fabled wild canelands that occurred in a long swath of land running from near present Washington, Kentucky, almost to the Blue Licks of Licking River. Early hunters were attracted to the canelands because of the herds of buffalo that roamed through them and fed upon the tender young plants. The cane, long, limber and strong, had much the appearance of bamboo, growing to a height of 30 feet. The most favored for fishing were those from 10 to 15 feet in length.

610. One account, unsupported by confirming evidence from others, states that a fourth man, Briggs Steenrod, also accompanied the party.

611. Thomas Mills, Sr., survived his wounds and, though convalescent for two years following, suffered no lasting effects from any of them except the one that broke his leg, which left him with a permanently stiff knee. Henry Smith healed well and, until his death at age 80, bored all friends and relatives with repeated accounts of his great battle with a fair-size portion of the Wyandot tribe. Hamilton Carr suffered no wounds at all.

612. Some accounts say that these Indians were part of a war party of some 300 led by Simon Girty and that this portion had deliberately placed themselves to waylay the McCulloch brothers as they passed. The evidence, however, indicates that the Indians had been merely passing through the woods when they spotted the McCullochs and that they took advantage of the situation as best they could; had they known in advance of the approach of the McCulloch brothers and had time to better position themselves for ambush, almost certainly both Samuel and John McCulloch would have been killed. There are at least half a dozen accounts of the killing of Sam McCulloch, varying widely in respect to the circumstances of when and how the attack occurred. The version presented here seems the most accurate based on available evidence. Simon Girty could not possibly have been involved in this incident, since only a few days previous to this he had met and diverted an advancing force of several hundred Indians under British Indian agent Alexander McKee, Capt. William Caldwell and Chief Joseph Brant—Thayendanegea—marching toward the upper Ohio. This diverted force immediately went to a Grand Council of tribes that convened at the Shawnee village of Chalahgawtha on the Little Miami River where, three days after the death of McCulloch, Girty laid out his proposed plan of attack against Lexington and Bryan's Station in Kentucky.

613. Samuel McCulloch's widow, Mary, sister of frontiersman Alexander Mitchell,

subsequently married a settler named Andrew Woods. The small graveyard where McCulloch was buried has long since disappeared, and its exact location is not definitely known.

614.   The captive alluded to by Girty was Charles Beasley, brother of Capt. John Beasley, who was held by the Shawnees for a fortnight, during which time Girty had questioned him about the strength of Bryan's Station. Beasley finally managed to escape and made his way back to Bryan's, arriving there only two days before the attack.

615.   Greater details of the invasion and ambush will be found in the author's *A Sorrow in Our Heart: The Life of Tecumseh.*

616.   Hefler, his hand treated, returned to Wheeling on September 11, not knowing the place was then under siege. Two miles from Wheeling he stumbled into the Indians and tried to escape by running up Wheat's Run—present Wood's Run—but he was overtaken, tomahawked and scalped.

617.   Though Catfish Camp had been laid out by the Hoge brothers in 1781 as the new village of Washington, it did not officially become a borough until 1810 and finally acquired city status in 1923.

618.   Col. Ebenezer's fortified house was located at what is now the southeast corner of Eleventh and Main streets in present Wheeling, W.Va., Fort Henry itself was located to the rear of the stores that presently front on the west side of Main Street, half a block from the corner of Eleventh.

619.   A peculiar circumstance in respect to this period developed 67 years later. Lydia Boggs Cruger, daughter of Capt. William Boggs, on November 28, 1849, dictated a deposition stating—untruthfully, as it turns out—that her father was in command of Wheeling and Fort Henry at this time, when she was a girl of 18, the eldest of his daughters; and that while the fort was under siege, it was Molly Scott who ran through a hail of bullets to get ammunition from the fort and bring it to the fortified Zane house, an act that had heretofore been credited to Elizabeth Zane during the first Wheeling siege five years earlier. Some accounts, it should be noted, report that it was at this second siege of Wheeling, not the first, in which Elizabeth Zane made her famous dash for the gunpowder. It is not known what motivations may have prompted the 85-year-old Mrs. Cruger to make such false statements at a time when she was one of the last (if not the very last) living survivors of the second siege of Wheeling and could not be refuted. No other survivor, after this second siege, ever attributed the earlier powder run of Elizabeth Zane to Molly Scott, though the heroic act of Elizabeth Zane was well known by all. It did not seem to be a matter of self-aggrandizement by Mrs. Cruger, except for giving her father a more important role than he actually played, but rather an effort to attribute the earlier heroic act of Elizabeth Zane to Molly Scott, with whom she seemed to have no real connection. This curious act on Lydia Cruger's part has never been satisfactorily explained, although it may have stemmed from a misinterpretation of Molly's run from Zane's house to the fort on the morning of September 12, 1782, to get bacon to prepare for breakfast for the defenders in Zane's house—a passage she made to and fro without drawing any shots from the enemy.

620. George Greer's name has been spelled Green in some accounts; Greer is believed correct.

621. So far as can be determined, there were in all of Wheeling at the time of the attack 63 individuals, including 30 men, 17 wives, 12 girls and unmarried young women, and 4 young boys. In addition to the five men in Zane's house, the 23 men of fighting age in the fort included Silas, Jonathan and Andrew Zane; Matthew Carr and his grown sons Hamilton and Archibald; Tom Mills, Sr., still recovering from his wounds and unable to fight, and his only surviving son, Edward; Alexander McDowell, John Tate, Stephen Burkham and James Clark; George, Andrew and Jacob Reagan; Franklin and Henry Clark; Conrad Wheat, Edward Wright, James Salter, Conrad Stoup, Peter Neisinger; and James Smith, Sr., and his two grown sons, Thomas and Henry. There were also four boys in the fort who were less than 14 years old: Matthew Carr's other sons, George and Matthew, Jr., James Smith, Jr., and James Boggs. In addition to the four women in the Zane house, within the fort were 14 wives and 11 girls and young unmarried women, including 18-year-olds Lydia Boggs and Nancy Richards. Three men were added to the contingent in the fort after the battle began—boat Capt. Cobus (Cobe) Sullivan (identified as Daniel Sullivan in some accounts) and his two crewmen.

622. At least one account states that it was Abraham McCulloch whom he met. The more reliable accounts indicate it was Ebenezer McCulloch.

623. One account states that at this point, Francis Duke, son-in-law of Col. Shepherd, declared his intention to go in anyway and help them and was killed in the effort. That, of course, is incorrect and confuses this siege with the first siege in 1777, when, as already shown, Francis Duke, approaching from Vanmetre's Fort, not Shepherd's, unexpectedly ran into the attackers and was killed.

624. No surname has been discovered for the slave called Old Daddy Sam, who was 65 years old at this time. A native of Guinea on the African continent, he had been captured by slavers when just a young boy and shipped to America.

625. More than one historian has stated that the second siege of Wheeling can justifiably be called the last battle of the American Revolutionary War and that the last shot fired by a British soldier in that war was fired at Fort Henry in Wheeling.

626. Full details of Clark's second campaign against the Shawnees may be found in the author's *A Sorrow in Our Heart: The Life of Tecumseh*.

627. Haldimand, on direction from King George III, relayed instructions to Maj. de Peyster to tell the Indians that for the time being they should not *"push the War into the Enemies Country. . . . Nothing is more natural than this desire* [of the Indians to continue their attacks]. *Yet, under the express orders I have received it is impossible I can comply with their Request."*

628. Killbuck's Island, some four acres in extent, had often been used by whites and Indians alike on which to raise corn. It was not suitable for permanent habitation because it was inundated by spring flooding almost every year. The island finally washed away entirely about 1785.

629. Site of the present city of Parkersburg, Wood Co., W.Va.

630. The Chapman claim took in part of what is now the town of New Cumberland, Hancock Co., W.Va.

631. Skyles was never heard of again. Mr. and Mrs. Chapman built a bigger and better house and lived there until their deaths, naturally, in advanced years, never having once been bothered by Indians.

632. Soon after Brady's death, his partners, Capts. Lodge and Carnahan, also died —one by illness, the other by drowning—and the Kentucky land claims of the three were disputed by numerous counterclaims. The result was that the Brady heirs lost the land and never realized one dollar from it.

633. One of the principal emissaries sent out by the secretary of war for this delicate and dangerous mission of setting up a peace treaty with the Indians was an individual who had lived many years among them as a trader, spoke their language fluently and had established a reputation among them of being a fair and honest man—Maj. (later Gen.) Ephraim Douglas. He began his mission from Fort Pitt and, with horses and attendants, passed through the hostile wilderness to the Sandusky, then to British posts at Detroit, Niagara, Upper Canada and Oswego, in which effort he was aided by Alexander McKee, Matthew Elliott, Delaware Chief Pimoacan and, on behalf of the Iroquois, Mohawk Chief Thayendanegea.

634. This speech by Sagoyewatha is often stated in histories as having been given in 1822, but that is incorrect. It was made to Gen. Washington himself as soon as details of the Paris Treaty were made known and U.S. commissioners were authorized to purchase their lands.

635. In the land suits filed for possession of lands earlier claimed by Washington and his agents, the cases dragged on for many years before finally being settled in the favor of Washington, only because he had been very careful in keeping close records of the locations that had been claimed. Many others, who had been less careful in marking their lands, establishing their boundaries and carefully filing their claims, lost everything they had worked so hard to obtain.

636. Roughly, this border follows a line from present downtown Cleveland, O., south through Akron and Massilon to just below Navarre, then almost due west across the state to west of Indian Lake and then south through Sidney, Piqua, Troy, Dayton, Middletown and Hamilton to the point where the Great Miami joins the Ohio River at the Indiana line, eight miles west of present Cincinnati. The area encompassed by this boundary, to the south and east of the new line and north and west of the Ohio River, takes in approximately two-thirds of the entire present state of Ohio.

637. Weylendeweyhing is pronounced Way-lendy-WAY-hing.

638. It is uncertain exactly what location was meant by Kookhassing, a place name not repeated thereafter in documents.

639. The site of Fort Harmar, in the present Harmar suburb of Marietta, Washington Co., O., is now occupied by the Fort Harmar Monument.

640. Though the terminology Northwest Territory was coming into extensive usage at this period, it was not until sometime later that the designation became official and encompassed the area of the present states of Ohio, Michigan,

Indiana, Illinois, Wisconsin and that portion of Minnesota east of the Mississippi River.

641. The site where the Patrick party landed near the mouth of the Scioto was the site of present Portsmouth, Scioto Co., O. Up the Scioto he carved his initials, P.P., into beech trees; those initials, discovered later, resulted in the naming of present Pee Pee Creek and Pee Pee Township in Pike Co., O.

642. Neal's Station later was renamed Monroe, which itself, in time, was incorporated into present Parkersburg, W.Va.

643. Site of present Belleville, Wood Co., W.Va.

644. Whortem's Station was situated on the site of present Majorsville, Marshall Co., W.Va., almost on the Pennsylvania line.

645. Langfitt's claim was made on the site of present Hookstown, Beaver Co., Pa.

646. There were four basic reasons why Kentuckians were seeking statehood: They objected to Virginia's taxes, the Virginia government's inability to adapt its laws to the frontier, the state's refusal to permit pursuit of Indians north of the Ohio, and the fact that all cases appealed to a higher court had to be retried in Richmond.

647. Some accounts assume the body of Old John Wetzel was left where first buried by Lewis Wetzel near Baker's Station, but that is not true. A large stone was, indeed, crudely engraved with the letters J.W. and the year and remained at this site for many years, but the permanent burial was on the Wetzel farm above the forks of Wheeling Creek.

648. One account states that there were four Indians in this party, that the fourth escaped and ran off into the woods and that Wetzel, when he returned to Wheeling, was asked if he'd had any luck. The report says he replied, *"Not much. I treed four Injens, but one got away."* The other accounts, which agree on three Indians in the party, seem more accurate. Though Lewis Wetzel had killed quite a few Indians before this time, the death of his father seemed to trigger a remorseless vendetta within him against the Indians. There are dozens of accounts similar to this, in which he entered an Indian camp alone and killed the occupant(s)—so many, in fact, that they become repetitious. Thus, only a few that are representative or particularly significant will be dwelt upon here.

649. James Madison, of course, was elected fourth President of the United States in 1808.

650. This new fort, soon to be named Fort Finney, was constructed a short distance up from the river on the site of the present power plant, located just over a mile from the mouth of the Great Miami River, 20 miles downstream from present downtown Cincinnati, and a mile southwest of the community of Finney, at the base of the high bluffs upon which is located present Shawnee Lookout County Park, which the author had the honor to name when the park was first established.

651. Butler here refers to the present Maumee River. The portage from the upper waters of the Great Miami connects with the Auglaize River in the vicinity of present Wapakoneta, Auglaize Co., O., which in turn flows northward and

empties into the Maumee (also called Miami-of-the-Lake and Omee River), at the site of present Defiance in Defiance Co., O. The Maumee from that point flows northeast some 60 miles and empties into the southwestern end of Lake Erie at present Toledo, Lucas Co., O.

652. Kekewapilethy, pronounced KEK-ee-wop-pill-LETH-ee, has also been spelled Kekewepellethe in some accounts. He was a member of the Thawegila sept of the Shawnees and served for a brief period as third subchief of Wapatomica.

653. Monakaduto—Half King—had evidently fallen into ill health, which prevented his attendance.

654. The treaty was attested to by the treaty commissioners' clerk, Alexander Campbell, as well as by Maj. William Finlay, Capt. Thomas Doyle, Nathan M. Donnell, James Montgomery, Daniel Elliott, John Boyce, James Rinkings, Nathaniel Smith, Isaac Teans and James Sufferance. All the chiefs mentioned in the text signed the treaty with the exception of Blue Jacket, though some accounts (including *The Frontiersmen*) erroneously say that he did.

655. The Indian country, in this instance, meaning about three-quarters of the present state of Indiana.

656. This letter, before being dispatched, was also signed by two Maykujay subchiefs, Painted Pole and Shade.

657. Maj. Robert Finney, commander of the fort bearing his name, had ordered the fort evacuated as the river began rising precipitously following several days of heavy rainfall. Taking all their most essential gear with them, the garrison had moved to the top of the ridge on the west side of the Great Miami and camped there, expecting there would be some minor flooding and a major cleanup in store as soon as they could reoccupy the place. Within two days, however, the fort had been all but wholly inundated and, even as they had watched, was damaged severely by the juggernaut logs and trees propelled along by the irresistible current. Only three hours before the Shawnee war party under Blue Jacket showed up, Maj. Finney gave the order to move out, and the entire company headed west and south along the Ohio's north shore. When they reached the high ground opposite Louisville at the Falls of the Ohio, he ordered the construction of a new fort, this one, like the first, to be named Fort Finney.

658. Col. John Donelson, who had earlier been involved in surveying the Kentucky-Tennessee boundary, was the father-in-law of Andrew Jackson, later President of the United States.

659. The area chosen by Madison for land-claiming included the site of the present town of Burnaugh, Boyd Co., Ky.

660. Wetzel never received a penny of the payment that was due him, and neither restitution for his expenses nor the thousand acres of land that was promised.

661. Fred Earlywine's body was found the following day in the woods where the Delaware had tomahawked and scalped him. He was buried on the spot. Some accounts erroneously give his name as Abraham, but that was his father's name.

662. The run upon which they camped was the present Tom's Run, which they

encountered just west of the present community of Limestone, four miles upstream from its mouth at Middle Grave Creek.

663.   The canoe that was set adrift continued floating down the Ohio and finally wedged along the shore at Limestone, 300 miles downstream, the dead pig still in the bottom of the boat.

664.   Greater details of the establishment of Marietta and adjacent areas and the land fraud perpetrated in France to lure settlers from there to settle on the Ohio in this area—resulting in the French Grant—may be found in the author's *The Frontiersmen*.

665.   A tenth child had just been born to Ebenezer and Elizabeth Zane: a daughter named Hetty who, when grown, married Elijah Woods. The other living Zane children at this time were Catherine (17), Ann (14), Sarah (13), Rebecca (10), Noah (8), John (6), and Samuel (2). Two other sons had died in infancy, the first Noah (in 1774) and the first Samuel (in 1782).

666.   Full details of Logan's expedition against the Shawnee towns may be found in the author's *The Frontiersmen* (for the white perspective) and *A Sorrow in Our Heart: The Life of Tecumseh* (for the Indian perspective).

667.   Tarhe, at this time and afterward, evidently becomes the most important chief among the Wyandots. Monakaduto, who had long held this position of influence, had been ailing all this year of 1786 and had become very frail. Though present for this Grand Council, he did not speak for the Wyandots as did Tarhe. Monakaduto's health continued degenerating and seems to have resulted in his death shortly after the Grand Council. At any rate, while no account of his death seems to exist, he apparently disappears from the pages of history after this time.

668.   Pronunciations of the names of these chiefs are: Sindathon (SIN-duh-thon), Monakaduto (MON-uh-kuh-DUE-toe), Topenebe (Toe-PEN-uh-bee), Nanimisea (Nan-nuh-MISS-ee-yuh), Nescotnemeg (Nee-SCOT-nee-meg), Nichinesica (Nitch-ee-NESS-sik-kuh), Oulamy (OOOH-luh-mee), Wafrugahqualied (Wuh-FROO-guh-QUEE-uh-leed), Sekahos (See-KAH-hoes) and Wabacumaga (WAH-buh-koo-MAH-guh).

669.   Some accounts contend that Blue Jacket led an attack against the Americans at Vincennes on December 17. Undoubtedly Shawnee attacks were occurring there and in Kentucky, but they were not on this occasion led by Blue Jacket, who was indisputably at the Grand Council at the mouth of the Detroit River.

670.   The Weas and Piankeshaws later became recognized as full tribes in their own right. The Pepicokias, also called the Eel River Miamis, became absorbed into the Piankeshaws. The Kalatikas, the Mengakonias and the Ouiatenons ceased to exist as subtribes by the mid-nineteenth century through both attrition and absorption into the main body of Miamis. Smaller regional groupings such as those known as Mississinewas, Tippecanoes, Salamonies and Mishawakas never did receive the fullest recognition as subtribes and their designations were short-lived, though they remain as geographical names in present Indiana.

671.   The prisoner exchange occurred on the site of the present village of Aberdeen, Brown Co., O.

672.   These boundaries are basically the boundaries of the present states of Illinois, Indiana and Ohio.

673.   The Ohio Land Company purchase here was bounded by the Ohio River from the mouth of the Scioto to the intersection of the Seventh Range of Townships, then being surveyed; thence by said boundary to the northern boundary of the Tenth Range of Townships; thence by a due-west line to the Scioto and back down that stream to the point of beginning. Initially 1.5 million acres was petitioned for, but this was subsequently diminished to 964,285 acres.

674.   Campus Martius was located within the present city of Marietta, Washington Co., O. The site, at Second and Washington streets, is presently marked by the Campus Martius Museum.

675.   Site of present West Liberty, Ohio Co., W.Va.

676.   The dates of ratification of the U.S. Constitution for these six states this year were: Georgia on February 6, Maryland on April 28, South Carolina on May 23, New Hampshire on June 21, Virginia on June 25 and New York on July 26.

677.   Ginseng root is still highly prized, especially in the Orient, for medicinal purposes, and a cargo the size of Boone's would today be worth about half a million dollars.

678.   The island where Boone's boat sank was present Gallipolis Island, three miles below the mouth of the Kanawha River.

679.   A skeleton found some years later where a body had been stuffed into a hollow sycamore tree was believed to be that of John Filson, though never positively identified. Losantiville was founded at what is presently downtown Cincinnati, Hamilton Co., O. It was begun with the erection of four cabins, the first of which was built on present Front Street, near but east of Main Street. The lower table of land was at that time covered with sycamore and apple trees, the upper with beech and oak. Through this dense forest the streets were laid out, their corners marked upon the trees. This survey extended from Eastern Row (now Broadway) to Western Row (now Central Avenue) and from the river as far north as Northern Row (now Seventh Street).

680.   Fort Clendenin was established on the site of the present capital city of Charleston, W.Va. The unnamed fort a mile above was sometimes called the Ruffner Fort because it was built (probably by Clendenin) adjacent to the cabin of Silas Ruffner, one of his tenant farmers.

681.   This is the present Indian Run, which empties into the Muskingum River two miles above the Ohio River. The major encampment of the Indian delegates was directly across the Muskingum River from the present Washington County Fairgrounds.

682.   This small run flows into the Muskingum opposite of and just a little above present Sacra Via Park in Marietta.

683.   One account states that Wetzel was accompanied during this killing by Vachel Dickerson, but since both Dickerson brothers, Vachel and Kinzie, were out on

Ranger patrol duty with Capt. Samuel Brady at this time, that is evidently an error. Another account says the Indian, George Washington, was riding a horse and, after being shot, managed to ride his horse the rest of the way to Fort Harmar. That, however, is also erroneous, since not only was he scalped, he was carried to the fort for medical treatment by other Indians.

684. The friend of Wetzel who lived opposite the mouth of the Muskingum is identified in at least one account as Isaac Wiseman, but that is an error. Isaac Williams, brother-in-law of Joseph Tomlinson, is correct.

685. Prior to 1789, Abraham Covalt had purchased a tract of land from Judge Symmes on the Little Miami River for a settlement of seven families from Pennsylvania. It was being located above Columbia and was just now being established as a temporary camp while 17 cabins that would make up Covalt's Station were being erected. Later the station would be called Bethany Town.

686. Clements' Station was established by Forgerson and Elizabeth Clements and their nine children. The station has also been referred to in various accounts as Clement's, Clemen's, Clemmon's and Round Bottom Fort. Its precise location in present Cincinnati was at the south end of Miami Avenue at the south edge of Terrace Park, at the northeast boundary of Section 22, T5N, R2W, Madeira Quadrangle USGA 7.5-minute topographical map.

687. Ruhama (Mrs. Charles) Bilderback remained in captivity only a few months before being ransomed back from the Indians in March 1790, at which time she returned to her children who were still in Kentucky and, with them, left the frontier and returned east.

688. During the trek to the Indian villages, Mrs. Davidson gave birth to the baby, but when it became ill after a couple of days, it was thrown into the Tug River and drowned. On arrival at the first Indian town, the two daughters were tied to trees and shot to death for sport, and the two-year-old son was given to an Indian woman, who started away with him in a canoe, but the little boat capsized and the boy drowned. The two indentured children were taken away, and she never saw them again, though they were recovered in Canada three years later.

689. Matthias (Tice) Van Bibber was creased on the forehead by a ball and momentarily stunned, but he managed to regain his senses and escape. Jacob Van Bibber was held captive for two years before finally escaping and returning to Point Pleasant.

690. Shortly after this raid, Shemeneto—Black Snake—fell violently ill and quickly died, upon which Wehyehpihehrsehnwah—Blue Jacket—became war chief of the Shawnee tribe. Blue Jacket, who was originally a white youth captured and adopted into the tribe, became one of the most noteworthy chiefs in Shawnee history. For greater reconstructed details of his life, see the author's novel *Blue Jacket: War Chief of the Shawnees* as well as *The Frontiersmen* and *A Sorrow in Our Heart: The Life of Tecumseh*.

691. This installation—Fort Washington—was located at what is present downtown Cincinnati, O., a little east of Broadway, where Seventh Street crosses.

692. Kekionga at this time was also often called the Omee Town, Michikiniqua's

Town, Little Turtle's Town and the Miami Town. To avoid confusion, the proper name of Kekionga will be used except where, in quotation of letters or reports, one of the other names is used.

693. William Burnett's trading post, one of the most important in the Northwest, was located at the site of the present city of Niles, Berrien Co., Mich. Burnett was highly favored among the Potawatomies, especially because he had married Kawkeeme, sister of the tribe's powerful chief, Topenebe (Toe-PEN-uh-bee), whose name meant Sits Quietly. At least one account states that Burnett did not establish his post here until 1783, but that is incorrect; the post on the St. Joseph River was established in the spring of 1778. Another trading post of significant size was operated by trader John Kinzie of Detroit at the adjacent village of Miamitown, a mile or so down the Maumee. Burnett also had a smaller post, similarly named Burnett's, located at the mouth of the St. Joseph on Lake Michigan, usually operated by his agents.

694. Hamilton County, Ohio, as first established, had as its southern boundary the Ohio River. It extended northward up the Great Miami River to the place called the Standing Stone Forks; from there on a line due east to the Little Miami River and then down that stream to its mouth at the Ohio River.

695. The flatboats ascending the river usually stayed very close to the Kentucky shore, not only for protection from Indian attack from the Ohio side but also to minimize the amount of current they would have to buck. The crew of polemen would normally work on the shore side of each boat as they poled the craft upriver, each poleman starting at the front of the boat, jabbing his 20- or 30-foot-long pole into the bottom and then "walking" the boat past the pole until he reached the stern. At that point he would jerk his pole out of the water and rapidly return with it to the bow to start the whole process over again. Two to eight polemen were placed at intervals on the river side of each craft to continually push at the bottom, to keep the ungainly boat fairly close to shore. It was rugged work and progress was slow. Depending upon the weight of the cargo, each boat moved along at the rate of only a mile or two per hour.

696. Edmund Randolph was Governor of Virginia from 1786 to 1788; Beverley Randolph was Governor of Virginia from 1789 to 1791.

697. The Indian camp was located about a mile south of the present town of Ripley, Brown Co., O.

698. The Castleman and Martin children were bought from the Wyandots by British traders. The Martin youngsters were taken to Detroit where, the following fall, Moses and Sarah were redeemed and returned to their mother. Thomas remained in Detroit and eventually became a merchant there. The Castleman girls remained at Half King's Town with the trader who bought them, Angus McIntosh. Margaret was redeemed by her father in 1796, but it took another four years to get Mary back.

699. Both Purdy girls were later reunited with relatives in the Wheeling area following a prisoner exchange.

700. The spring branch where young Hale went for the water presently bears the name Hale's Branch.

701. That branch has ever since been known as Staten's Run.

702. Lewis Tackett and his mother remained captives of the Shawnees for two years before finally being ransomed and released. It is not known what happened to Sam Tackett, Betsy Tackett McElhany and the small boy who were also taken captive.

703. The wounded Indian managed to travel 20 miles before finally collapsing and dying from loss of blood. His remains were found several weeks later.

704. Charlestown managed to withstand any following Indian threats and thrived well, but the name itself did not last. Today that same village is the city of Wellsburg, seat of Brooke Co., W.Va.

705. The New French Store was the name given to a new trading post close to Kekionga that had been established by the trader John Kinzie. That initial name did not last long, and the post and little settlement that sprang up around it had become known as Miamitown. The open ground adjacent to the trading post had become a favored assembly place and staging ground for the Indians.

706. Some accounts say the Ottawa reinforcement amounted to 200 warriors, but that is incorrect. The entire Indian force amounted to 150 warriors and chiefs, almost evenly divided at 50 apiece for the Shawnees, Miamis and Ottawas, plus a few Potawatomies.

707. Gen. Harmar's contempt for the militia was evident in his report to Secretary of War Henry Knox, in which he wrote: *"My whole force was 1,453 (including two troops of cavalry) but from this number we may safely deduct 200 of the Militia as good for nothing."*

708. Almost all of the many accounts state that this detachment numbered around 200 men. One account, however, says it numbered 310 men, but it mistakes the Hardin detachment for one sent out by Harmar the previous day, numbering 300 men, under command of Lt. Col. James Trotter, consisting of 30 regulars, 40 light horse cavalry under militia Maj. Fontaine, and 230 riflemen. This detachment returned the same evening after having encountered, killed and scalped two Indians. Some accounts say Hardin was so disliked that many of the militia deserted from this detachment after traveling only two miles, but Harmar made no report of this, nor did any of the Indian accounts.

709. Various accounts claim the American loss in this skirmish ranged from a high of 181 men to as few as 22 (this latter number undoubtedly referring only to the regulars). The most frequently quoted number by the more reliable sources is 70, which jibes with Gen. Harmar's report, which also states that all but 7 of the 30 regulars were killed and bitterly berates the militia, who were at the rear, for fleeing in panic and abandoning the regulars to their fate. This ambush took place where the Indian trail leading toward the Elkhart River crosses the Eel River, six miles northwest of present Fort Wayne, at the place where present U.S. 33 crosses the Eel River, four miles southeast of present Churubusco, Allen Co., Ind. In one extraordinary incident a Maj. John Adams was struck by five different rifle balls and yet survived, carrying the balls within his body for the rest of his life.

710.   One account, usually reliable, states that the army did not stop its first retreat until it reached the remains of old Chalahgawtha on the Little Miami River, three miles north of present Xenia, Green Co., O., and that it was from that point that the second detachment was sent out, but this is entirely in error. The second ambush of the Americans took place only three days after the first —on October 22—and old Chalahgawtha was at least 160 miles distant from the scene of the first ambush. Even if the army troops had all been mounted, which they were not, the detachment could not have traveled such a great distance with the army and then returned the same distance, a total of at least 320 miles, in three days. The old Chalahgawtha mentioned must, in fact, have been the temporary town of that name established by the Shawnees just a mile upstream on the Maumee from the mouth of the Auglaize River, about 35 miles downstream from where the second ambush occurred, on the site of present Fort Wayne, Allen Co., Ind. After leaving the Chalahgawtha a mile upstream from the mouth of the Auglaize, the Shawnees established another Chalahgawtha on the Maumee River, this one on the north (left) bank, about three miles below Kekionga (in present Fort Wayne, Ind., just east of present Coliseum Blvd., which is U.S. Rt. 24). Over the years of their stay in Ohio, the Shawnees used a total of seven different locations for Chalahgawtha. These seven Ohio Chalahgawthas are identified and located in Amplification Note 3 of the author's *A Sorrow in Our Heart: The Life of Tecumseh*. The one located on the Maumee near the mouth of the Auglaize was the seventh and final one in Ohio. The one located on the Maumee in present Fort Wayne was the first and only Chalahgawtha the Shawnees established in Indiana.

711.   Sgt. Benjamin Whiteman of the Kentucky militia, who kept a daily detailed log of events of the expedition and who, following its termination, wrote one of the more accurate accounts of the entire campaign, wrote: *"Harmar was intemperate in his habits. He had never been accustomed to Indian fighting. His habits had disqualified him for the command and it was unquestionably the opinion of many of the officers and men of the army that General Harmar was panic stricken with the report made by spies that Girty was near the fort with a large party of Indians. Had he marched with two or three hundred men to the relief of Hardin on the morning of the 22nd, it is more than probable that the Indians would have been signally defeated."* Whiteman later rose to military renown as a general and was an important figure in the War of 1812.

712.   Gen. Harmar, in the first draft of his report, stated, *"Our loss is about 160 killed,"* but in this he erred and later corrected himself. His official return of killed and wounded, written on November 4, 1790, at Fort Washington, listed the following: total federal troops killed, 75, including Maj. Wyllys and Lt. Frothingham; total militia killed, 108, including Maj. Fontaine, Capts. Tharp, Scott and McMurtry, Lts. Clark and Rogers, and Enss. Sweet, Bridges, Higgens and Therlkeld. The Capt. Scott mentioned was Merritt Scott, son of Gen. Charles Scott.

713.   Gen. Harmar claimed in his report that *"the Indians killed is supposed to be 200."* Other accounts say about 100 Indians were killed and wounded. Since the Indians had only 150 warriors in their total force when they engaged the

Americans, these figures are obviously grossly inflated. Michikiniqua and Blue Jacket both later stated the same figures for the loss of the Indians in killed and wounded—a total of 30 dead and 15 who survived being wounded.

714. President George Washington, immediately upon learning the particulars of Harmar's abortive campaign, remarked to Secretary Knox, *"I expected little from it from the moment I heard he was a drunkard."*

715. The Big Bottom Settlement was established on a fine high bottom above the right bank of the Muskingum River, less than a mile south of present Stockport, Morgan Co., O. The place is now marked by the Big Bottom State Memorial.

716. One of those who surrendered was 41-year-old James Patton, who remained a captive of the Delawares for just over four years and was finally surrendered to the Americans on February 6, 1795.

717. Covalt's Station was located on the site of the Little Miami River, near present Miamitown, 15 miles northeast of present downtown Cincinnati, O.

718. Colerain (Dunlap's) Station was located 15 miles from present downtown Cincinnati, on the site of present Colerain.

719. This was at the mouth of present Snag Creek, just below the present town of Bradford, Bracken Co., Ky.

720. The Francis Riley claim and cabin were located at the east base of the ridge separating present Riddle's Run from Blockhouse Hollow, about 2,000 feet west of the Ohio River, approximately where the gravel pit is located, 1.2 miles southwest of the U.S. Post Office in present Brilliant, Jefferson Co., O.

721. This settlement was located on the site of present Wellsburg, Brooke Co., W.Va.

722. Carpenter's Station was located at the mouth of McKim's Run, at the northern edge of the present town of Brilliant, Jefferson Co., O.

723. Waxler's Station was located near the mouth of Short Creek at the site of present Warrenton, Jefferson Co., O.

724. One account says several other people were killed inside the cabin but does not identify them, and since no other account mentions this, it is believed to be in error.

725. Obviously killed, Abigail Riley was never heard of again, and there is no record that her remains were ever discovered. Ruth Schemmerhorn, who was to be executed, was saved by a French trader, who bought her from the Indians, and taken by him to his home in Canada, where the two were subsequently married.

726. Mrs. Riley was reunited with her husband, Francis, and the two subsequently returned to their cabin and lived their lives out there, Mrs. Riley finally dying just short of her hundredth birthday. Moses Riley eventually settled on Stillwater Creek, near the present town of Tippecanoe, Harrison Co., O., but his homestead is now beneath the waters of the impoundment known as Clendening Lake.

727. This camp made by the Brady party was located on or near the site of present Cadiz Junction, Harrison Co., O.

728. Most accounts state that Capt. Brady had 26 men with him. A close study of

the various details in each, however, indicates that they were 27 plus himself. The other members of Brady's party were Joseph Biggs, Peter Brown, James Campbell, Henry Darnell, Frank Dodd, James Downing, Joseph Edgington, William Griffith, Thomas Harper, William Harper, Solomon Hedges (who was only 16 years old), James Hoagland, William Huff, Thomas Madden, John McCormick, Francis McGuire, Thomas Patterson, William Sherrod, John Van Buskirk, Lawrence Van Buskirk (his name given as Lawson in some accounts), Caleb Wells, Charles Wells, Thomas Wells, Lewis Wetzel, James Williams, Joseph Williams and William Williams.

729.   The small stream they were following is now known by the name of Brady Run. The smoke they detected was coming from the site of present Fallston, Beaver Co., Pa.

730.   Beaver Blockhouse was located on the east bank of the Beaver River at the mouth of present Blockhouse Run, at the southern outskirts of present New Brighton, Beaver Co., Pa.

731.   This warrior's skeleton, his rusted gun beside him, was found several years later still in the hollow of the black oak.

732.   Most accounts place the number of Indians killed at four or five, a few as many as seven. The correct number of those dead at the scene of the attack was eight. Actually, if one includes the warrior shot by young Solomon Hedges, who took refuge in the hollow tree and died there of his wound, the final total of dead Indians in this attack was nine.

733.   One account states that Wilson hailed Brady from the far shore and berated him for the killing, and that Brady called back for Wilson to mind his own business or they would serve him in the same way. No other account mentions this, and the account is believed spurious and made in an effort to demean Brady.

734.   The Indian seen at this point was the Piankeshaw chief known as Captain Bull.

735.   This was Lt. Col. James Wilkinson, a regular army officer prominent on this frontier.

736.   The actual name of the village was Kithtippecanoe, and it was situated at the site of the present city of Logansport, Cass Co., Ind.

737.   Col. Wilkinson's report to Gen. Scott was as follows: "*Camp, Ouiattanan, June 3, 1791, One o'clock P.M. Sir:—The detachment under my command, destined to attack the village Kethlipecanunk, was put in motion at half after five o'clock last evening. Knowing that an enemy whose chief dependence is in his dexterity as a marksman and alertness in covering himself behind trees, stumps and other impediments to fair sight, would not hazard an action in the light, I determined to push my march until I approached the vicinity of the villages, where I knew the country to be cham-pagne* [actually, champaign, meaning level and open]. *I gained my point without a halt, twenty minutes before 11 o'clock and half an hour* [later] *assaulted the town at all quarters. The enemy was vigilant, gave way on my approach and in canoes crossed Eel Creek* [River] *which washed the north-east part of the town. That creek was not fordable. My corps dashed forward with the impetuosity becoming volunteers, and were*

saluted by the enemy with a brisk fire from the opposite side of the creek. Dauntless, they rushed on the water's edge, uncovered to the occasion, and finding it impassible [sic], returned a volley, which so galled and disconcerted their antagonists that they threw away their fire without effect. In five minutes the Indians were driven from the covering and fled with precipitation. I have three men slightly wounded. At half past 5 the town was in flames, and at 6 o'clock I commenced my retreat. I want language to do justice to the courage and good conduct of the gentlemen who composed my detachment; in neither could they be exceeded by veteran troops. I have the honor to be, Sir, Your most obedient servant, James Wilkinson."

738. The text of Gen. Scott's message to the Indians was as follows: *"TO THE VARIOUS TRIBES OF THE PIANKESHAWS AND ALL THE NATIONS OF RED PEOPLE LIVING ON THE WATERS OF THE WABASH RIVER—The sovereign Council of the Thirteen United States have long patiently borne your depredations against their settlements on this side of the great mountains, in hope that you would see your error and correct it by entering into bonds of amity and lasting peace. Moved by compassion and pitying your misguided councils, they have frequently addressed you on this subject, but without effect. At length their patience is exhausted and they have stretched forth the arm of power against you. Their mighty sons and chief warriors have at length taken up the hatchet; they have penetrated far into your country to meet your warriors and punish them for their transgressions. But you fled before them and declined the battle, leaving your wives and children to their mercy. They have destroyed your old town, Ouiattanon, and the neighboring villages and have taken many prisoners. Resting here two days to give you time to collect your strength, they have proceeded to your town of Kethlipecanunk; but you again fled before them, and that great town has been destroyed. After giving you this evidence of their power, they have stopped their hands because they are as merciful as strong, and they will indulge the hope that you will come to a sense of your true interest and determine to make a lasting peace with them and all their children forever. The United States have no desire to destroy the Red People, although they have the power; but should you decline this invitation and pursue your unprovoked hostilities, their strength will again be exerted against you. Your warriors will be slaughtered, your towns and villages ransacked and destroyed, your wives and children carried into captivity, and you may be assured that those who escape the fury of our mighty chiefs shall find no resting place on this side of the Great Lakes. The warriors of the United States wish not to distress or destroy women and children or old men, and although policy obliges them to retain some in captivity, yet compassion and humanity have induced them to set others at liberty, who will deliver you this talk. Those who are carried off will be left in the care of our great chief and warrior, General Saint Clair, near the mouth of the Miami and opposite to the Licking River, where they will be treated with humanity and tenderness. If you wish to recover them, repair to that place by the first of July next, determined with true hearts to bury the hatchet and smoke the pipe of peace. They will then be restored to you and you may again set down in security at your old towns and live in peace and happiness, unmolested by the people of the United States, who will become your friends and protectors and will be ready to furnish you with all the necessaries you may require. But should you foolishly persist in your warfare, the Sons of War will let loose against*

you and the hatchet will never be buried until your country is desolated and your people are humbled to the dust. Given under my hand and seal at Ouiatannon town, this fourth day of June, 1791. Charles Scott, B.G."

739. The term *pulse* is a collective for such vegetables as peas, beans and other legumes.

740. Fort Hamilton was built on the site of the present city of Hamilton, Butler Co., O.

741. Fort Jefferson was built at the junction of present Mud Creek and Prairie Outlet, on the site of the present village of Fort Jefferson, Darke Co., O.

742. This stopping place of St. Clair's army was on the site of the present village of Fort Recovery, Mercer Co., O.

743. This was the last known battle in which Simon Girty actually participated with the Indians against the Americans.

744. Included in this number are the estimated 200 wives, children, girlfriends and prostitutes who made up the camp-followers. Of the 52 officers in the battle, 39 had been killed and 7 wounded; of the 868 regular soldiers and militia in the battle, 593 were killed, 257 wounded. Discounting Maj. Hamtramck's detachment, which played no part in the battle, the final total was, out of 920 men in the army, 632 dead and 264 wounded. Of the whole force, only 24 men returned uninjured.

745. St. Clair's Defeat was then—and remains today—the greatest Indian victory over any American military force. No complete listing exists of all the Indians, or even all the chiefs, who took part in St. Clair's Defeat, but a listing of some of the more notable Indians known to have participated may be of value. They included: Apekonit (William Wells)—adopted Miami warrior; Berry—Shawnee warrior; Black Beard—Shawnee chief; Black Fish—Shawnee warrior; Black Partridge—Potawatomi chief; Buckangehela—Delaware principal chief; Carrymaunee (Walking Turtle)—Winnebago chief; Catahecassa (Black Hoof) —Shawnee principal chief; Chaubenee (Coal Burner)—Potawatomi chief; Chiuxca—Shawnee chief; Coonahaw—Shawnee warrior; Gomo—Potawatomi chief; Kasahda—Ottawa chief; Main Poche—Potawatomi chief; Michikiniqua (Little Turtle)—Miami principal chief; Mtamins—Potawatomi chief; Otussa—Ottawa chief; Pipe—Delaware chief; Siggenauk (Blackbird)— Wyandot chief; Stiahta (Roundhead)—Wyandot chief; Tarhe (the Crane)— Wyandot principal chief; Tecumseh—Shawnee warrior; Topenebe—Potawatomi chief; Wasegoboah (Stand Firm)—Shawnee warrior; Wehyehpihehrsehnwah (Blue Jacket)—Shawnee war chief; White Loon—Wyandot chief; Wingenund—Delaware chief.

746. Tobias Lear honored George Washington's directive and made no mention of this conversation or the President's reaction to the news until some time after Washington's death.

747. The bitter rivalry between George Rogers Clark and James Wilkinson lasted for many years. As a regular military officer of advanced education, Wilkinson detested the uncouth character of Clark, his lack of formal education and the fact that he was a militia officer, not a regular. Extremely jealous of Clark's achievements in taking Kaskaskia and Cahokia from the British, followed by

his remarkable capture of Vincennes and British Gen. Henry Hamilton, Wilkinson attacked Clark in the area where he was most vulnerable: in his insobriety. He denigrated Clark at every opportunity and was in part responsible for discrediting Clark among military and political leaders in the east and subsequently causing Clark to be stripped of his military standing and reputation. It was not until some 80 years after the death of James Wilkinson that it was discovered that, during all that time, Wilkinson had been accepting money from the Spanish government and acting as a spy for Spain and a traitor to his own country.

748. Fort St. Clair was erected on the site of the present city of Eaton, county seat of present Preble Co., O.

749. On June 4, 1792, three days after Kentucky officially became a state, the new state legislature met for the first time—that meeting held in Lexington at the large log building widely known as the Sheaf of Wheat Tavern, which was temporarily being used as the statehouse—and, by common consent, chose Isaac Shelby as the state's first governor.

750. Contrary to some persisting stories that Wayne received the sobriquet "Mad" because of his rash heroism in battle, especially at Stony Point, the nickname actually came about another way. When a deserter of the Revolutionary Army was caught, he told officials just to get in touch with Anthony Wayne, and he would set matters straight. The deserter was playing on the chance that Wayne, a long-ago neighbor in Pennsylvania, would help him. Wayne, who loathed deserters, utterly refused to help him and even failed to recognize him, whereupon the deserter angrily commented, *"He must be mad!"* The comment quickly went the rounds, and the nickname was there for keeps.

751. The James Stoops cabin was located within the present limits of the city of Pittsburgh, on the south side of the Ohio River in the present Corliss District, about 400 yards northeast of the present Fairywood School, between that institution and Wind Gap Road.

752. An interesting confusion develops in regard to the name of Mrs. Stoops, who in many historical documents is referred to as "Granny" Stoops. This is the name the author first encountered in reference to her, yet he found it peculiar that a woman who had a child only four years old and was evidently still relatively young should be referred to as "Granny," especially when none of her children were married and her eldest son was still less than 20 years old. This initiated a search of documents to learn more about her. It illuminates the sort of nightmare researchers frequently encounter in regard to names. It turned out that Jane Stoops was called "Janie" by her husband and close friends. One early historian used that name almost exclusively, and a subsequent historian—or his editor—misinterpreted his handwriting and inadvertently changed the name to "Jennie," which, in turn, was picked up by another historian who referred to her as "Jenny." The evolution of the name completed its course when another, more widely read historian mistook the handwritten "Jenny" for "Granny." Thus in the majority of accounts existing today, Jane Stoops is referred to as "Granny" Stoops.

753. Ebenezer and Elizabeth had their thirteenth (and last) child when Ebenezer

was 44 and Elizabeth 43. In addition to the newest infant, named Daniel (who lived to advanced years), their other eight living children at this time included Catherine, 23, Ann, 20, Sarah, 19, Rebecca, 16, Noah, 14, Samuel, 8, Hetty, 6, Mary, 4, and Jesse, 2. Three other sons died in infancy, the first Noah 18 years earlier, the first Samuel 10 years earlier and the first Daniel four years earlier.

754. Probably no incident in Brady's career has more confusing and improbable variations than this one, and a great many of the incidents that occurred on his first spying expedition against the Sandusky Towns in 1780 are attributed to this expedition 12 years later. The author has attempted to keep the story as straight as possible by accrediting only those incidents in which almost all accounts are in agreement.

755. Considerable confusion exists in the accounts about this occurrence; one says two squaws were taken prisoner while gathering strawberries and were led away with them.

756. One account states that only one of their two women prisoners escaped to the Indians at this time and that the other one was retained by them as they continued making their way back toward the settlements.

757. One of the many varied accounts says that Brady and his men constructed a raft and were floating down the Ohio with their squaw prisoner when the raft hit a snag and broke apart, dunking them all and losing all their supplies and gunpowder except for the load already in Brady's gun. Like so many of the accounts, it is far-fetched and most unlikely in view of the reliably known aspects of what occurred.

758. The account that states that the captive squaw remained with them through all of this is suspect, as they could hardly have effectively taken her along under such conditions, yet the story prevails. A couple of accounts also state that the war party had a dog with them that they put on the trail of the whites and that when it caught up to them, Brady silenced it by strangling the animal to death with his hands. Many aspects of this contradictory spying expedition of Brady's are reported in a very far-fetched manner, though some may have begun with an element of truth.

759. The Brady camp was made almost exactly on the Ohio–Pennsylvania line, about two miles down the Mahoning (southeast) of the present village of Lowellville in Mahoning Co., O.

760. One of the accounts says the warrior was mounted with the captive William in front of him and the captive Mrs. Stoops behind him, all on the same horse —a tale that is most unlikely.

761. It is not known what happened to the other two Wyandots who were with the party when they attacked the Stoops place.

762. Both John Wetzel and John Williamson had indeed heard the shots and Brady's initial shouts and, according to plan, they separated at once and raced away. Another account says they rushed to aid Brady, and then all three men escaped back to Fort McIntosh together with Mrs. Stoops. A further account relates that the squaw still being held captive by them escaped at this point and got to the Indians, where she prevented their killing little William

Stoops. The facts seem to indicate that although neither Wetzel nor William-son saw Brady or each other on the return, both arrived safely back at the settlements.

763.   One of the many accounts says that the Stoopses' dog had followed Jane Stoops when she was taken captive and was still following now, and that when Brady led her away the dog stayed to guard the child and the Indians had to kill it. Another account says he used her dog as a pillow when they rested at night, but that the continued following by the dog threatened to give away their presence to the Indians and so Brady finally was forced to strangle the animal. Yet another account states that Brady, while escaping with Mrs. Stoops, was all the while still herding along his two squaw captives and man-aged to get them back to Fort McIntosh. Finally, another account states that Brady led Mrs. Stoops away by holding her hand in his while carrying her three-year-old son under his other arm. All these tales are improbable and very unlikely to have occurred.

764.   There are a number of variations in regard to what happened to the Stoops boy, three-year-old William. Some say he was on the verge of being killed by the warriors when a squaw intervened and saved the boy after he had already been swatted alongside the head by the flat of a tomahawk; the squaw is stated by some to be one of the two held captive by Brady's party but managed to escape when the firing broke out; others say that she was part of the Wyandot party to begin with. Whatever the case, William was taken to Detroit, where he was sold to the British and held for three years. Finally, through the efforts of Alexander McKee, he was returned to his parents. Jane Stoops fainted dead away with joy when she finally recognized him. William remained a resident of the upper Ohio, married in 1801, had seven children and finally died on July 24, 1835.

765.   One of the accounts states that Brady, with a party of men, went back to the attack site to see if he could find the boy, William, which he did not, and to secure the scalp of the Indian he had killed, which he supposedly did, after discovering the body where the warrior's companions had hidden it about 100 yards distant from where he was killed, covering him with leaves and forest debris after first dressing him in ceremonial garb.

766.   Greater details of Hardin's mission and his ultimate death may be found in the author's *Gateway to Empire* (Boston: Little, Brown, 1983; New York: Bantam, 1984).

767.   Among the Indians in attendance at this farcical treaty were Le Gesse—The Quail—and Gomo, who had some degree of standing in the Potawatomi tribe but not enough to engage in such discussions, along with a common warrior named Wawiyezhi—Something Round—who claimed to be the son of the first king of his nation. Masemo—Resting Fish—was a Miami warrior with-out rank who also signed the treaty. They went so far with their hoax that two of them—Gomo and Le Gesse—even let themselves be taken east by military escorts to meet, with much pomp and ceremony, with President Washington as bona fide representatives of the Potawatomies. Not until they had been loaded with gifts and returned safely to their people was it discovered that the

whole thing was a trick and that none of the Indians who had signed the Putnam Treaty had had any right to treat for their nations. Le Gesse, unfortunately, died of natural causes during the trip home. The United States Congress, in the process of ratifying the treaty, was mortified when the truth came out, and the whole supposed treaty was trashed.

768. Col. Absalom Baird's letter to Gen. Wayne from Washington, Pa., dated July 21, 1792, said in part: *"On Wednesday last, a soldier belonging to Captain Paull's Company of six months' militia, was fired on by two Indians and wounded thro' the hand, but escaped. This happened on the road about half way between the two stations. The Inhabitants of the frontier have either fled into settlements, or have gathered together into block-houses, and are in great distress, having left their crops standing. In my opinion a few more spies would be necessary if they can be allowed, the present ones having too large a range."*

769. Lt. R. S. Howe's letter from Gallipolis, dated August 23, 1792, was addressed to Gen. James Wilkinson at Fort Washington, with a copy to Gen. Wayne. It stated, in part: *"On the 13th instant our scout of a Corporal and four men while returning from their daily custom of reconnoitering the fields and protecting the inhabitants while at work, were fired on, on their return at Six O'Clock Run, by a party of Indians within half a mile of the garrison. Adam Miller, of Captain Hughes' Company, was shot through the body, left arm, and scalped, notwithstanding which he came in by himself and is in a fair way to recover. Richd Stacey, of Captain Kirkwood's Company, was taken prisoner; the Corporal and the other two came in safe, with the loss of a gun and some clothing. The blockhouses were immediately put in order for action. The Indians continue around us constantly and we, together with the inhabitants, are constantly prepared to receive them, though it is with great difficulty Captain Rome* [the garrison commander] *can persuade them of the danger they have to apprehend."*

770. Wayne established Legionville on the site of the present city of Ambridge, at the western terminus of present Fourteenth Street. That same site, in 1824, gave rise to a German socialist community established by George Rapp and, after that, the site became the location of a town named Economy, which was later annexed into Ambridge. The site of Legionville and Economy is presently preserved as the Old Economy Historical Site.

771. The first regular streets that were laid out in Wheeling by Col. Ebenezer Zane were between present Eighth and Eleventh streets and extending from present Market Street to the Ohio River.

772. One account states that Brady and all seven of his men shot at the target, all but one hitting the black mark and the one that missed was only *"the thickness of a knife blade away from the black."* However, in view of Brady's remarks about two of his men, both before the contest and afterward, the account that states all eight men shot is apparently in error.

773. Samuel Ewalt remained sheriff for some years after this trial. He died in 1842 at the age of 90.

774. In view of the acquittal of Samuel Brady, the charges against Francis McGuire and *"other unidentified men of the party"* were dropped.

775. Kyashuta, also often appearing in the records as Guyashuta, Guyashutha and a

variety of other spellings, died peacefully in his camp on the Allegheny just below Conewango Creek in 1796.

776.   To the end of her life, Drusilla Van Swearingen Brady referred to her husband's return and the outpouring of support and joy at his return as one of the most heartfelt and affecting scenes she had ever witnessed.

777.   Benjamin Lincoln and Timothy Pickering were from Massachusetts, Beverley Randolph from Virginia.

778.   This council was being held within the limits of the present city of Toledo, Lucas Co., O.

779.   When he learned of the rejection by the Indians of the United States proposals, which he considered very just and fair, Thomas Jefferson stated that the summerlong negotiations were made *"to prove to all our citizens that peace was unattainable on terms which any of them would admit."* The United States was, according to his reasoning, justified in launching Wayne's army vigorously to smash the Indians for once and for all.

780.   The author is convinced that this unnamed spy was William Wells, also known as Apekonit (and later, Epiconyere), who had been captured by Indians as a boy and adopted by Michikiniqua—Little Turtle—principal chief of the Miamis, of which the Weas are a branch. The essential data about him, as given, in the main fit Wells except that he was three years older at this time than the spy Wayne describes, and he was born in Alexandria, Va., not Pennsylvania. These errors could simply have been a deliberate deception to keep his true identity and the fact of his being a spy secret.

781.   Both Peter Smith and William Fuller were surrendered by the Shawnees at Greenville, O., on December 6, 1795, and subsequently reunited with their families.

782.   This incident with the Indians has a special place in history, since this was the last recorded fight with Indians within Kentucky. At least one account states that the incident took place late in the winter, on March 8, 1794, but the December 2 skirmish appears to be the more reliable date.

783.   The Forty Foot Pitch where the attack occurred was on the site of present Ludlow's Springs, just east of present Eaton, Preble Co., O.

784.   The stonecutter who hastily made the marker neglected to carve Andrew Van Swearingen's given name on the stone, perhaps because many people at the time thought his surname was simply Swearingen and Van was his given name.

785.   Gen. Wayne named Fort Greenville after his friend and fellow officer of the Revolution, Gen. Nathanael Greene. It was located at the mouth of present Mud Creek, on the right (south) bank of present Greenville Creek, in the center of the present city of Greenville, Darke Co., O.

786.   Wayne's army reached the St. Clair Defeat site on Christmas Day.

787.   Site of the present village of Fort Recovery, Mercer Co., O.

788.   Thomas Mann was found shot twice through the chest and scalped; William Mann's body was recovered a few days later, wedged in some driftwood along the shoreline, shot through the head and stomach but unscalped.

789.   The stretch of ground covered by the fallen timbers extended along the northwest bank of the Maumee from present Turkeyfoot Rock, just over a mile

upstream from the present Interstate 475 bridge (this area presently called the Fallen Timbers State Memorial), to the narrow piece of ground between the head of present Silver Lake and the northern bulge of Blue Grass Island, 3,000 feet downstream from that same bridge; the lower (northeasternmost) portion of this Fallen Timbers area being exactly three miles upstream from the present Fort Miamis State Memorial.

790.   The military escort was under the command of Maj. Robert (William in some accounts) McMahon and consisted of 80 riflemen under Capt. Ara Hartshorn and 50 dragoons under Capt. Philip Taylor, plus ten drovers.

791.   The four officers killed at this time were Maj. Robert McMahon, Capts. Philip Taylor and Ara Hartshorn, and Lt. William Craig.

792.   Accounts of the number of casualties for both sides in this affair are greatly varied, ranging from as few as 14 whites killed to as many as 75; and equally ranging from as few as 17 Indians to as many as 80. The most accurate figures seem to be those given in the journal of William Clark, who states that the Indians had a total of 40 casualties, including 20 killed and 20 wounded, and that the total American casualties were 63, which included 23 killed and 40 wounded. It has been stated in several accounts, evidently generated by a claim made by Gen. William Henry Harrison in a speech to the U.S. House of Representatives in April 1819, that a small number of British took part in the Fort Recovery attack, including Simon Girty as well as a captain and six matrosses (gunner's mates) clad in Indian clothing, their faces blackened to avoid detection, but these accounts are open to question. In the *Western Star,* a newspaper published at Stockbridge, Mass., and not particularly noted for its accuracy, an item datelined Philadelphia, November 21, 1794, states: *"At Fort Recovery, a great number of British soldiers, with their faces blacked, assisted in the attack. Three British officers kept at a distance behind the assailants and directed the operations. Twenty-two Americans were killed, thirty wounded and three missing. If any circumstance could add to the atrocity of this behavior on the part of our grandam Mother Country, it is that these poor savages were led into the field with the greatest reluctance."*

793.   It has been reported that later it was discovered that the departing Ottawas and Chippewas had come across some Shawnee women working in the fields and robbed and raped them, but the author considers the allegations ill supported and unlikely.

794.   This camp was made on the site of the present village of Wilshire, Van Wert Co., O., on the Indiana border.

795.   Gen. Wayne initially believed this to be merely an accident, but he later became convinced, with ample justification, that it was a very nearly successful attempt on his life engineered by Gen. Wilkinson—an allegation he was never able to prove but that, in view of Wilkinson's other treacheries, was very probably correct.

796.   Most accounts state that Wayne, when he clashed with the Indians, had a total of 3,500 men (citing 2,000 regulars and 1,500 Kentucky militia), but this is incorrect. Wayne had 2,200 regulars and, initially, 1,600 volunteers, which

gave him 3,800 when he left Greenville, and the addition of Col. Barbee's contingent, which is mainly overlooked, gave him a total of 4,400 troops.

797. Roche de Boeuf was a collection point for cattle being moved past the 16-mile stretch of rapids on the old Maumee Rapids Trail (now called the Anthony Wayne Trail), located at the upstream edge of the present village of Waterville, Lucas Co., O.

798. It is from this Fort Defiance that the present city and county of Defiance, O., get their names. The fort was located on the site of the present Old Fort Defiance City Park.

799. All the sick and lame were left to garrison Fort Defiance under Maj. Hunt. Chief Snake was a minor Shawnee village chief whose village was located on approximately the site of the present village of Florida, Henry Co., O.

800. The camp on the night of August 16 was on the north bank of the river, at approximately the location where the present U.S. 6 bridge over the Maumee is located in Henry County.

801. The army encampment on the night of August 17 was at the site of the present town of Grand Rapids, in Lucas Co., O., probably where present Metropolitan Park is located.

802. As nearly as can be determined, the tribal breakdown of warriors taking part in this conflict are as follows: 100 Delawares, 100 Wyandots, 150 Miamis, 150 Ottawas, 200 Potawatomies, 500 Shawnees, 800 Chippewas; so reported Antoine Lanell, a Canadian trader captured by the Americans during the battle.

803. Some accounts say the Indian loss was in excess of 100. Col. Alexander McKee, in his official report, claimed only 19 Indians had been killed and about the same number wounded. Capt. William Clark, in his journal, said the Americans lost only 24 killed and that the *"loss of the enemy not precisely ascertained, but not more than thirty or forty were found dead, and a few Canadians."* Several accounts have the Americans suffering more than 100 killed. Wayne reported, most accurately it appears, that he had 44 men killed and 89 others wounded. He claimed that the Indian loss was about double his own. In actuality, the Indians' loss, while not certainly known, was very close to the same amount as Wayne's.

804. Later, when Chief Kinjoino of the Ottawas was asked to explain why the Indians had been beaten at Fallen Timbers, he replied with a remark that seemed to echo the belief of many of the Indians who participated in the battle: *"The Great Spirit was angry and She turned Her face away from Her red children."*

805. William Beckham survived, but his head wound subsequently caused him to lose his sight in one eye.

806. The little girl who had been dashed against the tree survived her injuries and years later married settler George Goodrich and subsequently lived out the remainder of her days with him on land he claimed in the area of present Shelbyville, Shelby Co., Ind.

807. This spot is now within the city limits of Charleston, Kanawha Co., W.Va.

808. David Spangler was captured on the site of the present city of Jeffersonville,

Clark Co., Ind. He was surrendered to Gen. Wayne at Greenville five months later, on May 15, 1795. Joseph Guy's captivity was shorter, and he was surrendered by the Delawares to Wayne at Greenville on February 11, 1795, nine weeks after being captured.

809.   George and Joe White Eyes were the sons of the Delaware Chief White Eyes who was murdered by Lewis Wetzel during Col. Brodhead's expedition against Goschachgunk (Coshocton) in April 1781, as he approached Brodhead under a flag of truce. As restitution for the murder, White Eyes' two sons, George and Joe, were given an education at Princeton by the government. Three years after the peace was established by the Greenville Treaty, George White Eyes visited Washington village on June 7, 1798, and drank too much. In his drunken state he encountered a 15-year-old boy and, for reasons not quite clear, attempted to kill the boy with his tomahawk. The boy was chased to his father's cabin, where he snatched up his father's rifle and killed George White Eyes with a single shot. In the hearing that followed, George White Eyes' own Delaware companions testified that he was at fault for the incident, and the boy, who had acted in self-defense, was exonerated.

810.   This incident occurred four miles upstream from the present village of Cochranton, Crawford Co., Pa. The Samuel Hulings settlement never developed into a town.

811.   James Thompson was held captive for three weeks and then released. He returned safely to the surveying party.

812.   Although the initial grant made in March 1795 was for 24,000 acres, this was increased the following month by 1,200 acres, when the initial grant was found to be not quite enough to supply the demand. Greater details of the fraudulent land sales in France and the formation of the French Grant may be found in the author's *The Frontiersmen.*

813.   This, of course, was at the site of present downtown Fort Wayne, Allen Co., Ind.

814.   A complete list of all the prisoners surrendered to Wayne is not known by the author to exist, but from an examination of the various reports that have been made, the following list of known information has been constructed by the author. Age, if given, was the individual's age at the time of capture: Altonton, Mary Ann, captured April 1, 1793, at Morgan's Station, Ky. Anthony, Elizabeth, captured March 26, 1793, on the Wilderness Road in Kentucky. Armstrong, John, capture date unknown; surrendered by Detroit River Wyandots. Ashby, David, 13, captured August 9, 1790, in Madison Co., Ky; surrendered September 14, 1795, by St. Joseph Potawatomies. Another Ashby, David, captured in May 1788 on Ohio River near mouth of Kentucky River. Ashby, Enoch, captured in May 1788 on Ohio River near mouth of Kentucky River. Ashby, John, captured in May 1788 on Ohio River near mouth of Kentucky River. Ashby, Polly, captured in May 1788 on Ohio River near mouth of Kentucky River. Ashby, Robert, captured in May 1788 on Ohio River near mouth of Kentucky River. Ashby, Susannah, captured in May 1788 on Ohio River near mouth of Kentucky River. Ashby, Thomas, captured in May 1788 on Ohio River near mouth of Kentucky River. Baldwin, Betsy, captured in

Kentucky. Barker, Susannah, captured April 1, 1793, at Morgan's Station, Ky.; surrendered on February 11, 1795, by Delawares. Beecroft, Benjamin, captured on April 1, 1793, at Morgan's Station, Ky. Beecroft, Rachael *[sic]*, 14, captured on April 1, 1793, at Morgan's Station, Ky.; surrendered on May 9, 1795, by Delawares. Bolling, Presley, captured in March 1789, on Brashear's Run, Brooke Co., Va. (W.Va.); surrendered in 1785 by Wyandots. Bozarth, Jenny, 40, captured on July 13, 1795, in Randolph Co., Va. (W.Va.); surrendered on September 9, 1795, by Shawnees. Bozarth, Valentine, 17, captured on July 13, 1795, in Randolph Co., Va. (W.Va.); surrendered on September 9, 1795, by Shawnees. Bozarth, Zedediah *[sic]*, 14, captured on July 13, 1795, in Randolph Co., Va. (W.Va.); surrendered on September 9, 1795, by Shawnees. Brice, James, captured on October 20, 1790, by Shawnees at Kekionga when left wounded on field of battle at Harmar's defeat. Brickell, John, 14, captured on March 9, 1791, at Pittsburgh, Pa.; surrendered on May 9, 1795, by Delawares. Brown, John, captured in 1791 on Ohio side of river near Falls of Ohio. Burge, James, captured in 1791, at Clarksville, Ind. Bush, Daniel, 16, captured in April 1791 on the Monongahela River; surrendered on June 10, 1795, by Delawares. Camp, John, captured in 1778 in Kentucky. Corder, Jenny, 28, captured on March 26, 1793, on the Wilderness Road in Kentucky; surrendered on July 10, 1795, by Wyandots. Cozad, Jacob, 13, captured in July 1794 in Harrison Co., Va.; surrendered on August 22, 1795, by Shawnees. Cozad, William, 14, captured in July 1795 in Harrison Co., Va.; surrendered on September 9, 1795, by Shawnees. Crumb, John, 16; surrendered by Shawnees. Davidson, David, 28, captured on June 3, 1791, in Wythe Co., Va.; surrendered September 6, 1795, by Wyandots. Dawson, Matthias, 17, captured in August 1792 on the Monongahela; surrendered February 6, 1795, by Delawares. Dillow, Rachael, surrendered in 1795 by Detroit River Wyandots. English, Betsey *[sic]*, surrendered in 1795 by Detroit River Wyandots. Everman, Jacob, captured October 20 on Maumee River at Harmar's defeat; surrendered in 1795 by Miamis. Flaim, Nancy, 16, captured in 1785 at Greenbrier, Va. (W.Va.); surrendered on September 6, 1795, by Wyandots. Ford, Polly, 8, captured in 1786 on the Wilderness Road in Kentucky; surrendered in 1795 by Shawnees. Frazier, Daniel, 15, captured in April 1790 in Powell's Valley, Ky.; surrendered on June 20, 1795, by British trader Ian McDougall. Fuller, William, 17, captured in September 1793 at North Bend, Ohio; surrendered December 6, 1795, by Shawnees. Gibson, David, 23, captured on December 5, 1790, at Dunlap's Station, Ky.; surrendered on August 7, 1795, by Wyandots. Glass, Robert, captured in 1779 in Kentucky; surrendered in 1795 by Shawnees. Glenn, David, captured in 1783 near Wheeling, Va. (W.Va.); surrendered in 1795 by Wyandots. Goodnight, Elizabeth; surrendered in 1795 by Shawnees at Fort Wayne. Grant, Alexander, 21, captured in 1781 on the Great Kanawha River; surrendered on July 30, 1795, by Wyandots. Green, Betsy, captured in 1790 in Kentucky; surrendered in 1795 by Shawnees. Green, Polly, captured in 1790 in Kentucky; surrendered in 1795 by Shawnees. Guy, Joseph, captured on December 17, 1794, near Fort Hamilton, Ohio; surrendered on February 11, 1795, by Delawares. Hart, Elizabeth,

29, captured on May 11, 1790, in Madison Co., Ky.; surrendered on September 14, 1795, by St. Joseph Potawatomies. Hart, Elizabeth and child, captured in 1789 on Salt River in Kentucky; surrendered in 1791 by Shawnees. Hart, Israel, captured in 1790 at Crab Orchard, Ky.; surrendered in 1795 by Shawnees. Hogling, Moses, captured in 1778 while fishing in Floyd's Fork, Ky.; surrendered in 1795 by Shawnees. Holbrook, Jenny, 14, captured in May 1789 in Madison Co., Ky.; surrendered on September 14, 1795, by St. Joseph Potawatomies. Holbruck, Jane, 10, captured on May 29, 1789, on Brashear's Run, Brooke Co., Va. (W.Va.); surrendered in 1785 by Wyandots. Holbruck, Sarah, captured on May 29, 1789, on Brashear's Run, Brooke Co., Va. (W.Va.); surrendered in 1785 by Wyandots. Horn, Kitty, captured in 1790 in Kentucky; surrendered in 1795 by Shawnees. Horn, Peggy, captured in 1790 in Kentucky; surrendered in 1795 by Shawnees. Horn, Polly, captured in 1790 in Kentucky; surrendered in 1795 by Shawnees. Johnson, James, captured on July 3, 1794, in Kentucky; surrendered on May 9, 1795, by Delawares. Johnson, John, captured in 1790 in Kentucky; surrendered in 1795 by Shawnees. Johnson, Joseph, captured in 1790 in Kentucky; surrendered in 1795 by Shawnees. Johnson, Patty, captured in 1790 in Kentucky; surrendered in 1795 by Shawnees. Johnson, Peggy, captured in 1790 in Kentucky; surrendered in 1795 by Shawnees. Keer, John, captured in 1790 in Kentucky; surrendered in 1795 by Shawnees. Kesine, Sarah, captured in September 1790 on Brashear's Run, Brooke Co., Va. (W.Va.); surrendered in 1785 by Wyandots. Love, Timothy, captured in May 1792, at head of Big Benson Creek in Kentucky; surrendered in 1795 by Shawnees. Lusk, Samuel, 18, captured in 1793 at head of Big Sandy; surrendered in 1795 by Shawnees. Martin, Thomas, captured in 1790 in Kentucky; surrendered in 1795 by Shawnees. McCarty, James, captured in 1790 on Ohio River above mouth of Green River; surrendered in 1795 by Shawnees. McKeever, Betsey *[sic]*, captured in 1783 in Kentucky; surrendered in 1795 by Detroit River Wyandots. McKensie, Betsy, captured in 1792 in Kentucky; surrendered in 1795 by Shawnees. McKensie, Nancy, captured in 1792 in Kentucky; surrendered in 1795 by Shawnees. Mitchell, Mary, captured in 1774 on the Wilderness Road in Kentucky; surrendered in 1795 by Ottawas. Mitchell, James Hughes, captured in 1787 on Ohio River near mouth of Great Miami River; surrendered in 1795 by Shawnees. Mitchell, Sally, 17, captured in October 1790 in Kentucky wilderness; surrendered on July 30, 1795, by Mingoes. Parsain, Sarah, 14, captured on August 9, 1790, in Madison Co., Ky.; surrendered on September 14, 1795, by St. Joseph Potawatomies. Patton, James, 41, captured on January 2, 1791, on the Muskingum River in Ohio; surrendered on February 6, 1795, by Delawares. Peek, Robert, captured in 1792 on Mill Creek near Cincinnati, O.; surrendered in 1795 by Shawnees. Peek, Thomas, captured in 1792 on Mill Creek near Cincinnati, O.; surrendered in 1795 by Shawnees. Porter, John, 28, captured on October 8, 1794, at Fort Defiance; surrendered on September 6, 1795, by Tuscaroras. Purdy, Ramona, captured in 1792 near Wheeling, Va. (W.Va.); surrendered in 1795 by Wyandots. Raughley, Victor, captured on April 1, 1793, at Morgan's Station, Ky.; surrendered in 1795 by

Shawnees. Rhea, Joseph, 20, captured in 1783 in Runell Co., Va.; surrendered on June 10, 1795, by Miamis. Rigil, Kissey, captured in 1792 in Kentucky; surrendered in 1795 by Shawnees. Riley, Margaret, captured in 1790 on shore of Ohio River just above Wheeling Creek; surrendered in 1795 by Mingoes. Riley, Peggy, captured in 1790 on shore of Ohio River just above Wheeling Creek; surrendered in 1795 by Mingoes. Riley, Ruth, captured in 1790 on shore of Ohio River just above Wheeling Creek; surrendered in 1795 by Mingoes. Romine, Isaac, captured in 1786, near Lee's Town, Ky.; surrendered in 1795 by Shawnees. Ruddell, Abram, captured on June 22, 1780, at Ruddell's Station, Ky.; surrendered in 1795 by Shawnees. Ruddell, Stephen, 10, captured on June 22, 1780, at Ruddell's Station, Ky.; surrendered in 1795 by Shawnees. Samuel, Robert, captured in April 1794 on Ohio River just below mouth of Salt River in Kentucky; surrendered in 1795 by Potawatomies. Scott, Merritt T., captured on October 20, 1790, at Kekionga, when left wounded on battlefield at Harmar's Defeat; surrendered in 1795 by Shawnees. Sharp, Mary, captured in 1786 near McAfee's Station in Kentucky; surrendered in 1795 by Shawnees. Shaw, John, captured in April 1792 near head of Beargrass Creek in Kentucky; surrendered in 1795 by Shawnees. Shaw, William, captured in April 1792 near head of Beargrass Creek in Kentucky; surrendered in 1795 by Shawnees. Sloane, John, 16, captured in February 1791 near Pittsburgh, Pa.; surrendered on July 20, 1794, by Delawares. Smith, Peter, captured in 1793 near Falls of Ohio; surrendered in 1795 by Potawatomies. Smock, John, captured in March 1794 on Brashear's Creek, Ky.; surrendered June 10, 1795, by Potawatomies. Smock, Peter, Jr., 14, captured in March 1794 on Brashear's Creek, Ky.; surrendered June 10, 1795, by Potawatomies. Spangler, David, 22, captured on December 9, 1774, at Falls of Ohio; surrendered on May 15, 1795, by Potawatomies. Stephenson, Jenny, 19, captured on August 11, 1792, in Madison Co., Ky.; surrendered on September 14, 1795, by Shawnees. Stephenson, Jane, captured in 1792 at Paint Lick, Ky.; surrendered in 1795 by Shawnees. Suddreth, Thomas, captured on October 20, 1790, at Kekionga when left wounded on field of battle at Harmar's Defeat; surrendered in 1795 by Miamis. Sykes, Christiana, 26, and six infant children, captured in 1779 on the Monongahela; surrendered July 20, 1795, by Delawares. Symmes, Sarah, 30, captured in 1785 near Wheeling, Va. (W.Va.); surrendered on December 2, 1795 by Miamis. Tackett, Elizabeth (Betsy), captured in October 1790 on Great Kanawha River; surrendered on July 20, 1795, by Shawnees. Tackett, Samuel, 16, captured in October 1790 on Great Kanawha River; surrendered on July 20, 1795, by Shawnees. Thorn, Samuel, Jr., 20, captured in March 1790 at Falls of Ohio; surrendered on June 5, 1795, by Potawatomies. Thorn, Samuel, Sr., captured in 1789 on Brashear's Creek, Ky.; surrendered in 1795 by Shawnees. Van Bibber, Joseph, captured in 1792 in Kentucky; surrendered in 1795 by Shawnees. Van Cleve, Samuel, captured in February 1794 on Brashear's Creek, Ky.; surrendered in 1795 by Potawatomies. Waggoner, Betsy, 16, captured in May 1793 on Monongahela; surrendered on October 20, 1795, by Shawnees. Waggoner, Mary, 14, captured in May 1793 on Monongahela; surrendered on October 20, 1795, by

Shawnees. Whelan, Michael, 30, captured November 4, 1791, at St. Clair's Defeat; surrendered on September 6, 1795, by Wyandots. Young, Elizabeth, and one child, captured on April 1, 1793, at Morgan's Station, Ky.; surrendered in 1795 by Shawnees.

815.   A good part of the reason why the British were finally willing to surrender these posts to the Americans had its basis in the fur trade. Due to various human conflicts and overharvesting of the fur animals in the Northwest Territory, less than one-fifth of the current British fur trade revenue in North America, of £200,000, was being generated from there, and the cost it was entailing to maintain these posts for that purpose and to maintain good relations with the tribes was really no longer worth the expense. New British trade routes to the far west, spearing far beyond the Mississippi and into the vast northwestern territory beyond, all the way to the Pacific, were opening far greater prospects for an unopposed continuation of the fur trade.

816.   Conner's Trading Post was situated at or near present Connersville, Fayette Co., Ind.

817.   Wampum strings (for minor points) and belts (for major issues) were always exchanged at such treaties as an important adjunct to record-keeping. Although such belts were valuable, they were not (as many easterners thought, and as many people still think) a form of currency. Rather, they were a form of record-keeping developed among the tribes through the centuries and used to impress indelibly the desired points embodied in the message of the speaker delivering them. Most often made from tubular shell beads strung into strings a foot and a half in length, the individual strands of the belt were skillfully woven together to form intricate variations of color and design, each significant in its own right and each imparting a special message. Even seasoned frontiersmen and traders who had been among the Indians for many years found it uncanny how an Indian could glance at such a belt and then recite verbatim the terms of a treaty or words of an agreement, as if he were reading from a printed page. Sometimes the strands woven together would form a belt as long as 10 or 12 feet, but most often they were only four or five inches wide and about three to four feet long. And though the belts were originally constructed from freshwater or ocean shell pieces drilled through in a laborious process with a slender flint drill rolled between the palms, a revolution in wampum belt construction had occurred when traders began stocking variously colored clear and opaque glass beads. Easterners became fond of snickering over the passion of the Indians for the beads, believing them to be for ornamentation purposes only. Such, in fact, was rarely the case. Those beads fulfilled as important a function in Indian record-keeping as did paper and pen for the whites; thus, beads became enormously profitable items in the Indian trade. In general terms (though there were variations), a black wampum belt signified war talk, while white was one of peace, prosperity and health. Violet signified tragedy, death, sorrow and disaster, sometimes even war. To make the message of the belts plainer, stick figures would be woven into the belts, or there would be geometric designs of various types—diamond shapes, stars, hexagons, parallel lines, wavy lines, intersecting line patterns, etc.—each with

its own significance. Metaphoric expressions transferred to beaded wampum belts required extreme care in preparation lest any wrong idea be relayed. Metaphors commonly used and transferred to wampum belts included a raised hatchet, signifying war, and a buried hatchet, signifying peace; kindling a fire, meaning deliberation and negotiations; covering the bones of the dead, meaning giving or receiving reparation and forgiveness for those killed; a black cloud, signifying a state of disaster or imminent war; brilliant sunshine or an unobstructed path between two nations signifying peace; a black bird, representing bad news; a white or yellow bird, good news. Indian speakers rarely spoke without lengths of wampum, either strings or belts or both, draped over their shoulders or arms, to which they referred frequently as they spoke and which were sporadically presented to dignitaries in attendance as points were made.

818. When the new secretary of war, Timothy Pickering, received a copy of the completed treaty on September 27, he expressed grave concern to both Gen. Wayne and President Washington that too few Potawatomi chiefs had been present to negotiate and sign the treaty, and that cessions of certain lands without the concurrence of all the chiefs might result in further strife on the far northwestern frontier. A listing of names of the 16 Potawatomi chiefs who signed the treaty, along with their alternative names and English translations of their names, appears in James A. Clifton's *The Prairie People* (Lawrence, Kan., 1977), pp. 152–55.

819. Gen. Wayne had been given sole power to negotiate for the United States in all matters, but with very specific instructions from President Washington, through Secretary of War Timothy Pickering, regarding what he should say and what his primary considerations should be—foremost of which being very large cessions of land.

820. Part of Wayne's specific instructions were to avoid making any such assertion, which would only serve to irritate and alienate those in attendance.

821. Although in the open council this is what Wayne told the chiefs that the treaty included, that treaty in its actual written form called for the Indians to turn over to white authorities any Indian guilty of killing a white person unjustly, but there is no mention whatever of whites turning over to the Indians any white person guilty of unjustly killing an Indian.

822. With those words, the Americans gained cession to more than half of the entire Ohio Territory without restriction. (See map, "The Partitioning of Ohio.") The final phrase did not limit the boundary to the Ohio country but instead, in drawing a line from Fort Recovery to opposite the mouth of the Kentucky River, the line did not go due south but angled in a south-south-westward direction, taking in a wedge-shaped piece of present southeastern Indiana. That line entered Indiana a thousand yards or so north of the southeastern corner of present Jay County and continued in the south-south-western line through the present counties of Randolph, Wayne, Union and Franklin, formed the western boundary of present Dearborn and Ohio counties and split the western end of present Switzerland County, terminating at the Ohio River close to the present village of Lamb.

823. Wayne was here doing a little improvising, since his instructions had authorized him to negotiate for only ten such tracts, but the attitude of the Indians in attendance made him feel he could push for the additional six and they would not question it, and in this he was quite correct and successful.

824. And, though Wayne did not say it, most importantly to cow the Indians and keep them in check in case of future unrest.

825. By the terms of the Greenville Treaty, the Indians ceded to the United States an area of territory comprising some 25,000 square miles, not even including those 16 separate tracts, which were each about six miles square. For this cession of such unbelievable value, economically, strategically and territorially, the United States agreed to pay in goods the value of $1,666 for each of the 12 tribes there represented, plus an additional annuity of $825 worth of goods to each of the tribes. When averaged out, it meant that the United States were paying one cent for every six acres acquired!

826. The completed Greenville Treaty was immediately dispatched special express by Wayne to Secretary of War Timothy Pickering, who in turn presented it to President George Washington. Heartily approving of it, the President presented it to the United States Senate on December 9, and on December 22, 1795, the Greenville Treaty, one of the most important treaties ever made between the Indians and the Americans, was ratified.

827. The headwaters of Deer Creek were located close to the headwaters of the Mad River but were in the Scioto River drainage, and the area where Tecumseh established his Deer Creek Village was northwest of present London, O., and close to the present boundary separating Champaign and Madison counties.

828. Sauganash (pronounced SAW-guh-nash) was the son of a Potawatomi woman, said to have been *"of remarkable beauty and keen intelligence"* but whose name is not known to be recorded, and a British officer of Detroit named Capt. William Caldwell, who was a sometimes trader and frequent liaison with the Indians in the company of McKee, Elliott and Girty. The name Sauganash was a nickname meaning The Englishman (which comes down in the Ottawa tongue as Sagonas). However, his real Potawatomi name was Tequitoh (teh-KWEE-toe) which, in English, means Straight Tree. One source, unverified by any other and discounted by the author, states that the mother of Sauganash was a Mohawk and the daughter of a chief named Rising Sun.

829. The exact number of Shawnees who threw in their lot with Tecumseh at that time is not known. Some sources have claimed more than 100, others as few as 16. From the size of the village ultimately established by Tecumseh at Deer Creek for himself and his followers, a reasonable guess would be that there were probably in the vicinity of 50 to 60.

830. Tecumseh did go on to put together the most comprehensive amalgamation of tribes ever produced in North America, forming this group over the period of the next 16 years until, in 1811, it was undermined by his megalomaniac younger brother, Lowawluwaysica, who by then had changed his name to Tengskwatawa and was known as The Prophet. Tecumseh then, with his remaining warriors, threw his lot in with the British to oppose the Americans in

the War of 1812, during which he was killed at the Battle of the Thames on October 5, 1813. Full details of all this may be found in the author's *A Sorrow in Our Heart: The Life of Tecumseh* (New York: Bantam, 1992).

831. David Bradford did not return to the Ohio with Wetzel. He remained in Louisiana and settled at Bayou Sara, where he drank himself to death.

832. It is generally assumed that Wetzel took his revenge on Pedro Hermoso by killing him, but Hermoso's body was never found, and Wetzel never admitted he had done so.

833. This place of Wetzel's was located opposite Fairfield Island in the present state of Mississippi, fairly close to where Interstate Route 20 crosses the Big Black River, 25 miles west of Jackson and 15 miles east of Vicksburg.

834. Lewis Wetzel was never apprehended for this murder. The remainder of his life is shrouded with bits and pieces of hearsay. In October 1829, when Lewis would have been 65, Capt. Ebenezer Clark, grandson of the Ebenezer Zane's second daughter, Elizabeth, met Lewis Wetzel in St. Louis. Wetzel was at that time living in the southern Missouri country among the Delawares in the area of Cape Girardeau. Sometime after that, when some Delawares and Absentee Shawnees turned up dead, Wetzel was suspected of the crimes, but he had already drifted away, and no one knew where he had gone. It is said that later he connected with a distant relative, Philip Sikes, with whom he journeyed to the Brazos River in Texas. There he built another cabin and remained there, hunting—and presumably shooting Comanche Indians—until he finally died in 1839 at the age of 75 and was buried near Austin, Texas. It is said that in his lifetime, he personally killed in excess of 70 Indians.

835. Martin Wetzel died almost exactly a year later, in the early fall of 1812 at the age of 55. He was, as he had wished, buried beside his old friend, John Baker, who had been killed when he and Martin were out Indian hunting together on August 22, 1777.

836. There was, by this time, however, relatively little game left to be found. Deer had dwindled to alarmingly low numbers. Despite the incredible numbers of woodland bison that had once roamed the Ohio River drainage, the last known buffalo killed was in 1815 by Archibald Price on the Little Sandy Creek tributary of the Elk River, itself a tributary of the Great Kanawha River, 12 miles from present downtown Charleston, W.Va. Elk had never been quite so abundant as buffalo, but they had been very numerous; nevertheless, the last known elk was killed on the Two Mile Creek tributary of Elk River in 1820 by a hunter named Billy Young, some five miles from present Charleston. Johnny Wetzel, hired as a hunter, worked at this trade for only a few years and then finally died in May 1815 at age 45.

837. Jacob Wetzel died at his place on the White River in Indiana, not far from present Indianapolis, in 1833 at the age of 67.

838. Daniel Boone, after a short illness, finally died at the home of his son, Col. Nathan Boone, on the Ferne-Osage River, a tributary of the Missouri, on September 26, 1820, at the age of 86.

839. Simon Kenton eventually moved even farther north in Ohio to the headwaters of the Mad River and lived with his daughter hardly a stone's throw from

where the village of Wyandot Chief Tarhe had been, on the site of the present town of Zanesfield, Logan Co., O., where he died on April 29, 1836, at the age of 81.

840.   Tecumseh's rise to power, his formation of the great amalgam of tribes—some 50,000 warriors—and the undermining by his ambitious brother of his great plan to drive the whites back east of the Alleghenies, may be found in the author's *A Sorrow in Our Heart: The Life of Tecumseh.*

841.   The steamboat *New Orleans* amazed and delighted settlers as she made her maiden voyage. At Wheeling she anchored for some time, and settlers from near and far came to see her, paying a quarter each for the privilege of wandering about on her and marveling at such a wonder. Her voyage all the way down to New Orleans was a distinct success, and for three years after that she made regular trips between New Orleans and Natchez. She was eventually lost in 1814 when she struck a snag near Baton Rouge, La., and sank.

Principal Sources

Prologue

AHC-I: 6–7, 409. ANM-59, 61, 64, 68, 173–75. ANNW- 1857: 261. ARAM-I: 39, 275, 545. BEAR-VI: 38, 53. BHUS-8–9. BOB-20–38, 59–68, 70–73. CG-82, 84. CHNY-VI: 532–33; VII: 267; IX: 1025, 1097; X: 480, 901. CP-I: 173, 186–87, 193, 196–99; II: 61–62, 201–203, 203_{fn}, 210–20, 229_{fn}, 249, 271–73, 360. CRNC-V: 78–79. CTM- April 6, 1882. DD-E-11: 133–38; DD-F-1: 20, 83; DD-G-2: 97, 109^{7-8}, DD-S-2: 164–65, 206, 208, 234; DD-S-3: 70, 137; DD-S-4: 113–15; DD-S-12: 105–106; DD-S-17: 195; DD-S-29: 44; DD-U-12: 45^2; DD-YY-1: 3, 115–16; DD-YY-2: 71–72, 85–88, 104–106, 141–42, 144–51, 178; DD-YY-3: 137, 140–41. DGW-I: 43, 45, 55–59, 65–67, 73_f, 74–77, 80, 84, 91, 93. EHWP-161, 173. EZP-3_{ff}, 35, 64_f, 78_f. GBIC-2–3, 5–6, 27–29, 79, 84, 103. GCWD-156–61, 163–65, 167–73, 176, 178, 180–81, 184–85, 189–90, 192–93, 196. GEO-I: 68–69, 82, 97, 102, 113–14, 172. GGU-1–3, 16–18, 27, 41–51, 53, 55–58, 61, 77–80, 82, 84, 193. GL-68–69, 123, 146. GMBP-27, 40–44, 86–87, 186–87, 254, 606–608, 615, 641, 654, 661–62, 665, 671–73. GW-4, 30–31, 38–43, 45–54, 61, 63–64, 66–71, 86–87, 90–92, 95, 97–100. HAWM-7–8. HC-I: 165. HCIN-164–67. HEAFD-45–46, 46_f. HFN-II: 86–87, 87_f, 106_{ff}–108. HG-7–16, 18–19, 19_{fl}. HH-I: 299, 310, 471, 909–10; II: 598–99, 682, 831. HISTA-59–68, 173–75. HOPH-19–21, 30–35, 35_f, 36–53, 60, 65, 87_f, 90–91, 133–34, 150, 153, 196. HPA-619. IUS-41, 56, 91. JCGW-5_f, 16, 17_f. JME-167–68. JRAD-LIX: 85–86, 161–63. KY-10, 31. LATT-15_f, LM-22, 25–26, 27_f, 28–30, 181, 185, 262, 293. LOFIC-126–28, 132–36. LSD-312. MAH-XV: No.3, March, 1886, 256–77. MAW-I: 53–58, 60, 60_f, 61–62, 62_f, 64, 64_f, 65, 77, 77_f, 78, 81–84, 86–89, 128–33, 133_f, 134–40, 142–51, 151_f, 152–55, 155_f, 156–61, 171–72, 181–83, 187, 191, 194–96, 199–201, 203–213, 210–11, 213–33, 337–38, 340, 342–47, 352, 368–69, 383, 392–93, 423–27; II: 132–44, 144_f, 145–51, 154–59, 159_f, 160–62, 246, 264, 320,

374, 407. **MB-**29–30, 51–52, 62, 94, 103, 106, 117–18, 121, 124–26, 134, 156, 162–64, 164$_f$, 166–70, 178, 180–81, 195–97, 200, 236–38, 273. **MGZ-**July 3, Aug. 29, 1754. **MPHC-XXXVI:** 25. **NC-**15. **NEV-**192–95, 207, 303. **NWR-XIX:** 262. **OC-**18, 37–41. **OSO-**3–4, 15–17, 26, 29–30, 34, 48, 90–91, 125, 128, 151–53, 188–89, 218, 252, 263–64, 285–86, 296–314, 316. **P-**32–33, 36–39, 41–51, 53–57, 65–68, 69, 76, 78, 88, 93, 97, 101–105, 113–17, 166–67, 216–17. **PECH-**166, 179. **PECOR-IX:** 212. **PEN-II:** 144 (O.S.), 770 (O.S.), 775 (O.S.); **IV:** 532 (O.S.); **VI:** 178–79; **VII:** 232, 405 (O.S.); **IX:** 228, 256. **RIB-I:** 414–15. **RRR-**81, 133, 141, 195. **SAT-**372. **SHAWT-**11–13. **SI-**3–5, 27–28. **TAC-**80–141. **TAP-**lxxiv, 1, 12–17, 19–30, 32–49, 51–63, 66–67, 69, 70–83, 85–102, 105–108, 115–20, 175–78, 211–12, 232–33, 243–46, 248–50, 251–58, 285, 328–29. **TC-**632–48, 664–60, 665–70. **TF-**50. **TFT-I:** 458–59. **TQUIL-**3–9, 11–12, 20. **TSST-**41. **VMHB-**Jan., 1894, 278–84. **VOD-**66$_f$, 185–87, 198$_f$, 199, 208–209, 211–20, 222–24, 226–30, 230$_f$, 231, 231$_f$, 232–36. **VSP-I:** 280. **WBD-**1561–62. **WE-**112–21, 125–34, 138–42. **WGW-I:** 31, 64, 73, 76, 79.

C h a p t e r   1

AHC-I: 11. **AHI-I:** 93–94. **AMAR-I:** 275, 545. **ANM-**59, 61, 64, 68–69, 173–75. **ARAM-I:** 273, 275. **ASIOH-**69–71, Note 88. **ASPPL-II:** 209. **BHW-**24. **BOB-**13$_{f1}$, 14, 19, 23–48, 58–61, 63–64, 66–71. **C-**298–303. **CDB-**11–12, 14. **CHNY-VII:** 650, 689–90, 716, 766, 786, 808, 816–17, 882–83, 892, 914, 982; **XI:** 836–41, 849–50. **CP-II:** 40$_{f1}$, 116$_{f1}$, 128$_{f1}$, 134, 134$_{f1}$, 136, 139–48, 148$_{f1}$, 149–50, 155–57, 162, 170–71, 176–78, 200, 200$_{f1}$, 201, 201$_{f1}$, 202–203, 203$_{f1}$, 204–205, 205$_{f1}$, 206–207, 207$_{f1}$, 208, 208$_{f1}$, 209–30, 230$_{f1}$, 231–33, 235, 235$_{f1}$, 236$_{f2}$, 237$_{f1}$, 238$_{f1}$, 240–42, 269, 276–80, 282–86, 286$_{f1}$, 287–89, 289$_{f1}$, 290–97, 297$_{f1}$, 298, 300, 302, 304–315, 342, 344–45, 347–53, 356–62, Apdx. E, F. **CQ-**42. **CWTJ-**34–35, apdx. 41. **DCN-**179. **DD-BB-1:** 2; **DD-C-1:** 347–49; **DD-E-11:** 83–138; **DD-F-2:** 31, 44; **DD-G-2:** 108^5, 181–82; **DD-S-2:** 9, 121, 145, 154, 183–84, 206–207, 212, 234, 238, 260–61, 274, 285, 295, 303–07, 334; **DD-S-3:**75–76, 137–38, 157; **DD-S-4:** 132–34; **DD-S-6:** 61–62; **DD-S-9:** 2–3, 40; **DD-S-12:** 108–109; **DD-S-15:** 82–83, 94–95; **DD-S-17:** 195–96; **DD-S-21:** 211–15; **DD-U-12:** 45$_2$; **DD-YY-1:** 3, 8; **DD-YY-2:** 15–16, 88, 142, 146–51, 158; **DD-YY-13:** 2$^{4-5}$. **DSD-**xx, 67, 67$_{163}$, 101, 115. **EHWP-**161, 173. **EWT-1:** 47–52, 126–66, 131, 139, 144–46, 154–66. **GBIC-**17, 20–21, 23, 35, 38–47, 51–52, 55–56, 58–64, 68–69, 73–75, 77–78, 82, 83, 87, 90–91, 93, 95–98, 100, 108–109, 109$_f$, 111$_f$, 115–21, 129–30, 134–35, 139$_f$, 140–41, 144–45, 149$_{f16}$, 155–57, 160, 181–84. **GCWD-**209–225, 231–36. **GGU-**6–7, 19–27, 48, 55–66, 73, 80–81, 193. **GMBP-**247, 249–55, 257–61, 671–72. **GTE-**18–23. **HC-I:** 34, 69–70, 639. **HG-**16, 19, 19$_{f1}$. **HH-I:** 471, 693, 910, 961; **II:** 593. **HIIL-**35. **HIMI-**Note No. 221. **HISTA:** 59, 61, 64, 68, 173–75. **HIT-IV:** 625. **HM-VIII:** 262. **HMUB-**31. **HOPH-**20, 22, 42, 49–72, 78–89, 92–93, 105, 116, 131–35, 150–53, 157–58, 162, 169–70, 174, 180–81, 191, 245–46, 256, 300, 306–307, 320, 332, 350, 358–59, 361–62, 365–66, 374–75, 405, 408, 411–12. **IHC-III:** 1–74, 254, 543; **XI:** 46, 475, 507, 529. **IHSP-II:** 11, 411, 415. **INT-**July 4, 1876. **IUS-**91. **JJS-**349$_f$, 350$_f$. **JRAD-LXX:** 211–301. **KY-**10, 31, 37–38, 91, 178. **LTSWJ-II:** 252. **MAH-XV:** No. 3, March 1886, 256–77. **MB-**265–66, 273–76, 280–83, 324–31. **MISSB-**456–57. **MPHC-X:** 216–17. **NAR-XXXIV:** No. 75,

434. **NCHA-VI:** 702, 704. **OSO-**36–37, 60–61, 64–65, 67, 70–72, 94, 114–15, 126–27, 141–42, 160–61, 218, 315–16. **P-**254–56, 262–64, 267, 269–83, 285–88, 298, 304, 308. **PEN-IV:** 532. **PG-**1, 912–13. **PHIL-**55. **PSWJ-VIII:** 224–25, 277–79, 672–73, 749; **PSWJ-XI:** Nos. 43, 50, 56, 97; **XII:** Nos. 42, 60, 127, 218; **XIII:** Nos. 30, 80; **XIV:** Nos. 28, 35, 44; **XV:** Nos. 109, 183; **XVII:** No. 189. **PWW-**156–57. **SI-**34–35. **SK-**32–34, 37–45, 128–30. **TAP-**15, 36, 41, 48–56, 62–67, 69–70, 100, 102–103, 105–106, 131, 178–80, 203–204, 232–33, 258–64, 267, 285–86. **TC-**632–48, 651, 654–60, 665–70. **TF-**19–21, 29–34, 56–63, 66–76, 78–88. **TGP-**1764: Dec. 7; 1765: April 28, May 18, 25, 26, July 12, August 3; 1766: April 7, 13; 1767: April 3; 1770: February 17. **TIAC-**476. **TP-**98. **TPP-**134. **TQIL-**9–11. **VOD-**236–37. **WO-**May 21, 1904.

Chapter 2

AHC-I-409. **ALREM/1776-III:** 205. **AMAR-I:** 275, 365, 395; **II:** 1193, 1542, 1671, 1747; **III:** 12, 18, 26, 485, 492–93; **V:** 416, 527, 767, 770–72, 818; **VI:** 763, 1046; **VII:** 395–96, 715. **ANM-**59, 61, 64, 68, 173–75. **ASIOH-**73. **ATC-**33–34, 50–52, 54–55, 63, 66, 69–70. **CDB-**15–17. **CHNY-VIII:** 323_2, 499, 507–508, 516, 519–20, 534, 621, 630, 688, 714, 718. **CISHS-I:** 39. **CISM-I:** 42. **CQ-**92, 94. **CTM-**April 6, 1882. **DD-BB-2:** 61; **DD-BB-3:** 118; **DD-E-11:** 83–138; **DD-F-1:** 98_f, 105^{15}, 115–16; **DD-F-2:** 52, 62, 67, 71, 81, 92, 102–104; **DD-F-5:** 23^1, 121. **DD-F-12:** 109; **DD-G-1:** 1^5, $3^{34-38,\ 40,\ 42}$, 15^{171-72}, 22^{69}, $24^{102-104}$; **DD-G-2:** 108^5, 109^{28}, 110^2, 111^1, 198; **DD-S-2:** 11, 56–63, 69, 121, 145, 182, 189, 212–15, 232, 238, 248, 256, 273–74, 278, 303–307, 309, 312, 323, 334, 340–41; **DD-S-3:** 6–18, 22–23, 76–79, 98–99, 112, 140–41, 158, 163–64, 305–311, 319–20, 339, 341–42; **DD-S-4:** 16, 132–34, 148–49, 196–97, 211; **DD-S-5:** 7; **DD-S-6:** 83, 286; **DD-S-7:** 123; **DD-S-8:** 45–46; **DD-S-9:** 61–64; **DD-S-12:** 105–106, 109–12; **DD-S-13:** 101, 104, 106–108, 110–11, 180, 184, 190–91, 202; **DD-S-14:** 16, 29, 124; **DD-S-15:** 15, 80–85, 89–93, 102–103, 229; **DD-S-17:** 80, 206; **DD-S-20:** 71–78, 186–91; **DD-S-21:** 217–20; **DD-S-22:** 110; **DD-S-24:** 42–43; **DD-S-31:** 399–401, 417; **DD-U-23:** 25–26; **DD-U-12:** 45^{2-3}; **DD-YY-1:** 1, 8, 115–16; **DD-YY-2:** 17–21, 73, 83, 91, 97, 146–51, 163, 165, 212; **DD-YY-3:** 146. **DSD-**109_{71}. **GBIC-**160–61. **GGU-**34–38, 65–72, 93–96, 144. **GJB-**124. **GTE-**32–35. **HC-I:** 34, 72–75. **HH-I:** 282, 391, 679, 875, 910, 961–63; **II:** 141, 270–71, 325, 346, 404–408, 410, 831. **HNAI-XV:** 662. **HNMM:** No. 326, July 1877. **HOPH-**15, 25, 35, 62–69, 71–73, 78–83, 85–88, 88_f, 89–91, 93–101, 105, 132–35, 147, 151, 153–56, 158–61, 168–70, 185, 191, 196, 255, 300, 350, 358–59, 363–64, 375–76, 414, 440, Appdx: A, B, C, D, E, F. **JJS-**237_f, 238–337, 337_f, 339_f, 341_f. **JNYPC-I:** 96; **II:** 31, 59, 300–301; **III:** 340. **KY-**33–36, 38–39. **LATT-**84, 98–100, 105–106, 114, 116. **LE-**52. **LM-**176–77. **LOJB-II:** 3_f. **LOSCH-II:** 107. **MAH-XV:** No. 3, March, 1886, 256–77. **MB-**347. **NAP-**384. **NAR/1832-XXXIV,** No. 75, 435. **NJT-**138. **NWR-XII:** 180. **NYGZ-**June 29, 1775. **OAHP-11R:** 167–96. **OAHQ-21:** 297. **OC-**49, 53, 90, 106, 114–15, 284, 288–90. **OSO-**12, 23, 36–37, 61, 102–103, 127–29, 148, 152, 159–60, 221. **PECH-**321–23. **PEJO-**Aug. 14, 1776. **PELG-**August 17, 1776. **PEN-IV:** 522, 632. **PFB-I:** 180. **PG-**Nov. 6, 1776. **PIOH-**127–28. **SHAWN:** 5. **SHAWT:** 1–11. **SI-**35, 38, 38_f, 40, 43_f, 44. **SK-**32–34, 45–54, 57–65, 68–72, 74–77, 79–90, 129–30. **T-**34–37, 41, 135. **TAP-**33–34, 55, 69, 103–104,

106–108, 179–201, 203–210, 212–13, 221–27, 264–67, 286. **TF**-88–126, 129–31, 137–41, 164–65. **TP**-99–100, 102. **TPP**-162. **TQIL**-1, 12–17, 20–21, 46–49, 217–18. **TRIB-I:** 50–51. **WCL**-95–96. **WHC-VII:** 123–87, 405–408; **VIII:** 209–223; **IX:** 97; **XII:** 7–13, 39–46. **WOTR-II:** 144, 480. **WWWAR**-447.

Chapter 3

AHC-I-409. **ANM**-208. **ATOU**-107–108, 160–61. **BRWN**-155–56. **CCNW**-1778–83. **CDB**-17–20. **CIV**-23–25. **CQ**-36, 63, 92–93. **DD-E-11:** 83–138, 202–216; **DD-F-1:** 98_g. **DD-F-4:** 1, 6, 178; **DD-F-5:** 33, 33^{1-3}, 35^2, 36, 122, 129; **DD-F-20:** 52; **DD-G-1:** 1^5, 4^4, 17^{125}, 18^{218}, 19^{247}, 27^{313}; **DD-G-2:** 108^7, $109^{27,\,29-30,\,63}$, 111^{30}, 114^{457}; **DD-G-3:** 9, 27, 33; **DD-S-2:** 6–7, 12, 29–30, 56, 59–63, 89, 91–92, 97, 112–13, 131, 134, 139, 147–50, 182–83, 185–86, 198, 206–211, 215–25, 232, 234, 236, 238–40, 254–55, 265, 271–72, 274–97, 308–309, 318, 321–23; **DD-S-3:** 23–34, 55–56, 59, 72, 79–80, 83, 113–34, 138–39, 142–43, 150–51, 153, 158–59, 162–67, 172, 213, 219–20, 257–58, 311, 320–23, 334, 350; **DD-S-4:** 184–85, 188, 191–93; **DD-S-5:** 10–16, 149–51; **DD-S-6:** 103–125, 129–40, 295, 302–303, 306; **DD-S-7:** 123–24; **DD-S-8:** 65–66; **DD-S-9:** 2–7, 13–14, 77, 90, 113–14, 118–19, 135, 138–39, 177, 185–86, 188–89; **DD-S-13:** 99–100, 102–103, 113–16, 120–21, 144, 146–47, 183; **DD-S-14:** 19, 129–30; **DD-S-15:** 13–16, 31–37, 114–15, 150–59, 165–68, 170–71, 174–80, 187–89, 200–216; **DD-S-17:** 53, 56–62, 80, 193–95, 197, 206–207; **DD-S-19:** 276–77; **DD-S-20:** 63–70, 85, 204–207, 244; **DD-S-21:** 158, 216–17, 253–54; **DD-S-22:** 93–98; **DD-S-24:** 43–45, 122–29; **DD-U-2:** 41–43, 49, 49^1, 50, 53, 55, 55^1, 56, 56^2; **DD-U-12:** 45^{4-6}; **DD-YY-1:** 4, 7; **DD-YY-2:** 70, 73, 86, 92–94; **DD-YY-3:** 120; **DD-YY-13:** 24. **DPEN**-227. **GGU**-82–86, 96–101. **GJB**-186, 195. **GTE**-35–48, 55–60. **GWAR-II:** 329. **HC-I:** 72–75. **HCBI**-240_{34}, 242_{36}, **HGRC**-57. **HH-I:** 378, 380–81, 467, 910–11; **II:** 270, 409–410, 693–94. **HHGC**-104, 112, 114–49, 156–57, 171–73, 177–88. **HOMAS-II:** 167–68. **HOPH**-27, 91–92, 101–106, 112, 114, 119, 132, 134, 140–42, 145, 147–48, 151, 154–56, 159, 161, 185–86, 247, 255–56, 258, 300, 359, 361, 363, 410, 413. **IHC-I:** 220, 232–33, 393; **II:** 610; **VIII:** 72, 252–55, 281–89, 295–97. **IMH-LIV:** March 1958, 55. **IOBL**-91–96. **JJS**-288, 339, 350_f. **JVEC**-1777, 1778. **KY**-34–39. **LATT**-131–32, 135–37, 141. **LM**-107. **LOJB-I:** 370; **II:** 245, 377. **LOSCH-II:** 397. **MAH-XV:** No. 3, March 1866, 256–77. **MLFL**-Dec. 12, 25, 1884. **MPHC-IX:** 368, 374–78, 442–52, 466, 479, 482–83; **X:** 275; **XIX:** 353, 375. **MWH**-Jan. 1886, 273. **NAR/1832-XXXIV:** No. 75, 433. **NWR-VI:** 112. **OC**-8, 12–14, 26, 41, 48, 56, 61–62, 114–15, 180–81, 217, 256, 258–63, 291. **OSO**-4, 63, 71, 115, 117, 153, 218–19, 315. **PFB-I:** 256. **SI**-49_f, 50, 50_f, 51–52. 52_f. **SK**-53–54, 58, 91–100, 102–144, 173, 203–204. **T**-71–82. **TAP**-221, 228–40, 258, 267–69. **TF**-167–72, 174–76, 178–229, 232–33, 245, 264. **TP**-101–105, 108, 156. **TPP**-163, 165–66, 168. **TQIL**-21, 23–25, 73. **TRINC**-11, 102. **WB**-272–73. **WHC-IX:** 482–83; **XI:** 125, 178–81; **XII:** 46–47. **WOTR**-633–34, 645. **WVHE-III:** 587–88.

Chapter 4

AHC-I: 11–12. **BRWN-**159–60. **C-**129–34. **CACDH-**1. **CISM-I:** 242. **CQ-**36–
37. **DD-BB-4:** 28; **DD-BB-5:** 115; **DD-F-7:** 66, 75–76; **DD-F-10:** 6; **DD-G-1:**
$4^{4,\,17}$; **DD-G-2:** 225; **DD-S-2:** 2–3, 93, 113–14, 122–23, 187, 207, 225, 238, 285–
86, 295–96, 306–307, 316, 319–21, 334–37; **DD-S-3:** 44, 53, 55, 57–62, 68–70,
81–84, 98–99, 108, 112–14, 116–18, 128–31, 135, 143–45, 153, 166–67, 209, 213,
217–20, 229, 237–38, 258–59, 300–301, 323–24, 335–36; **DD-S-4:** 3, 40–43, 99–
100, 122–26, 152, 159, 162–64, 179–83, 187–90, 193–94, 211; **DD-S-5:** 15–17, 21,
185–87; **DD-S-6:** 169–71, 289; **DD-S-9:** 120, 164–65, 188–89; **DD-S-14:** 130;
DD-S-15: 12–13, 77, 149, 159–63, 168–69, 181–82, 189–92, 217–23, 229–31;
DD-S-16: 5–8, 19, 23–24, 178–81, 206–209, 268; **DD-S-17:** 61, 197, 200, 215;
DD-S-19: 277–78; **DD-S-20:** 200; **DD-S-21:** 41–42; **DD-S-22:** 41–44; **DD-S-
24:** 169–72; **DD-S-28:** 23–25; **DD-U-2:** 56^{2-3}; **DD-YY-1:** 1, 3–4, 10; **DD-YY-
2:** 42–43; **DD-YY-8:** 36, 36^{1-3}, 38, 38^{1-2}; **DD-YY-12:** 12, 31. **EWT-2:** 181–84.
FCHQ-43-166–73. **GGU-**67, 73–74, 102–106. **GTE-**65–66, 92–106. **HA-II:** 475.
HC-I: 69–71, 72_f, 639. **HCBI-**209–210. **HH-I:** 88, 293, 387–89, 416, 467, 543,
603–604, 694, 746; **II:** 270–71, 693, 741–42. **HLW-**194. **HM-**May 1859. **HOO-**
551. **HOPH-**106–108, 133, 136, 145–46, 148, 161, 255–56, 300, 372–75, 411, 414.
IHC-I: 357, 433, 439, 456–57; **II: VIII:** 169–74, 300, 311–15, 359, 364–66. **JCC-**
Dec. 23, 1779. **KY-**38–39. **LATT-**68. **LM-**1–4, 102–108, 198, 293–94. **MARJ-**
April 18, 1780. **ME-**28–29. **MLJAH-**May 1, 1885. **MLJM-**Nov. 5, 1883.
MVHAP-II: 205–206. **MVHR-IX:** 379–80, 558; **X:** 367, 380–81; **XIX:** 415–16.
NFT-110–11. **NI-**Feb. 7, 1859. **NJT-**140. **OAHP-19:** 446–59. **OC-**14, 48–66,
68–70, 72–76, 78, 79_f, 122–29, 133, 204–206. **OSO-**178–79. **PEN-IV:** 219, 231.
PITTC-June, July 1779. **PKDS-**103. **SI-**51, 51_f, 52. **SIW-**29. **SK-**90, 94–95, 129,
140, 143, 145–49, 152–56, 180, 239–40. **TAP-**24, 240–42, 267, 269–70. **TF-**141,
165–67, 230, 232–50, 252–79. **TP-**105–109. **TPP-**163, 166. **TQIL-**22–24. **TRF-**
137. **WB-**267, 280–83. **WHC-IX:** 282; **XI:** 133, 210–11; **XVIII:** 375–76, 391–93,
398–99, 399_{98}, 400–401. **WVHE-III:** 590.

Chapter 5

ANM-61–72, 231–32, 284–89. **CFUO-**272–74. **DD-BB-5:** 113; **DD-E-11:** 83–
138; **DD-F-1:** 137; **DD-F-12:** 109; **DD-FF-1:**137; **DD-S-2:** 94–95, 152, 154–56,
164–65, 180–82, 187, 206, 208, 210–11, 215–25, 256–57, 265–68, 283, 287–95,
308–309; **DD-S-3:** 22, 24–28, 35–47, 49–50, 67–68, 84, 100–110, 171–72, 206,
325; **DD-S-4:** 158; **DD-S-5:** 18, 22–24, 226–32; **DD-S-8:** 115–27, 133–40; **DD-
S-9:** 133–34, 136–37, 162; **DD-S-10:** 3–4, 43–45, 47–48, 50–51, 140–43, 152–54,
157–58; **DD-S-11:** 37–40, 48–52; **DD-S-13:** 148–49; **DD-S-15:** 24–25; **DD-S-
16:** 33, 45, 47–60, 81–82, 178–81, 206–209, 268; **DD-S-20:** 196–99; **DD-S-21:**
107; **DD-S-22:** 22; **DD-S-24:** 45; **DD-U-12:** 45^7. **GGU-**106. **HH-I:** 436, 467,
480; **II:** 682; **XV:** No. 3, March 1886, 256–77. **OAHP-7:** 64–72. **PEN-**1779: 767;
1781: 250. **SI-**52, 70_f. **SK-**21, 42, 49, 55, 132, 156. **TF-**280–87. **TQIL-**24.
VERHC-II: 357. **WVHE-III:** 590–92.

Chapter 6

ACBHC-275–77. **ADOJM**-1823. **AHC-I:** 409. **AHFIA**-107. **AHOI**-110. **ALD-**B.171, F.1, Aug. 29, 1808; B.171, F.7. **AMDI**-Sep. 9, 1981; Jan. 29, 1982. **AMERH-7**-5–9, 103–107. **AMERL-XV:** May 1943, 169–80; **XIX:** Mar. 1947, 1–20. **AMP-I,** Nov. 1842, 377–78; **II:** 284; **XI:** 282–85. **ANM**-3–4, 120, 338, 341–42, 443–47. **ANNW**-795. **ANWEP**-10, 36–42. **ASBJL**-48. **ASSM**-1–15. **AWYCO**-15, 64. **BHW**-21. **BMWCO**-583–85. **BRADE**-x. **BTFO**-Sep. 11, 18, 25, Oct. 2, 9, 23, 30, Nov. 6, 13, 20, 27, Dec. 4, 11, 18, 25, 1992; Jan. 1, 8, 15, 22, 29, Feb. 5, 12, 19, 26, Mar. 5, 12, 17, 25, Apr. 2, 9, 16, 23, 30, May 7, 14, 21, 28, June 4, 11, 18, 25, July 2, 1993. **BUTBA**-MSS v.f/B. **BUTM2**-V-271. **BUTM5**-C-2/F-4. **BUTS:** Ser. 2, 546; Ser. 3, No. 8, 69–71, 97, 145, 146; Ser. 4, 69–70, 118. **CINC**-Dec. 24, 1836. **CJAOS** 21. **CQ**-37–38. **CVSP-III:** 235, 286. **DD-BB-5:** 112, 119; **DD-BB-11:** 20–21; **DD-C-11:** 62; **DD-C-12:** 123; **DD-CC-11:** 264–68; **DD-CC-12:** 126–27; **DD-CC-13:** 118–19, 123–24; **DD-E-8:** 78–79, 100–105; **DD-E-10:** 147, 155–56; **DD-E-11:** 2–5, 74, 83–138, 208–209; **DD-E-15:** 66; **DD-F-10:** 158–59; **DD-NN-1:** 11, 75–77, 84, 134; **DD-NN-7:** 13–14; **DD-S-1:** 2–3; **DD-S-2:** 1–8, 37, 40–41, 53–57, 60–68, 94–95, 97, 104–108, 156–60, 164–65, 184–85, 187–88, 206, 210–12, 215–19, 238–46, 248, 256, 293–95, 309–311, 337; **DD-S-3:** 6, 8, 16, 28, 46–47, 59, 62, 80, 103–107, 112, 132–34, 140, 150, 152, 157, 161–62; **DD-S-4:** 132–46, 185–86; **DD-S-5:** 3, 15–16, 29–31, 72; **DD-S-9:** 90–91, 103, 140–45, 184–87, 190; **DD-S-10:** 2–3, 16–20, 27–31, 58–60; **DD-S-11:** 9, 53–57, 61–65; **DD-S-12:** 12, 21; **DD-S-13:** 150, 155–57; **DD-S-16:** 178–81, 206–209, 268, 271; **DD-S-17:** 163, 191–93, 204–205, 212–13, 253; **DD-S-19:** 117–18, 186, 193–94; **DD-S-20:** 117–19, 200–201; **DD-S-25:** 167; **DD-U-2:** 86–93, 126, 136–37, 1203; **DD-U-11:** 12, 12^1, 31, 73, 102; **DD-U-12:** 45^{8-10}; **DD-YY-6:** 131–32; **DD-YY-11:** 12, 12^1; **DD-YY-13:** 2^{6-7}, 26–27; **DD-ZZ-8:** 30. **DIAH**-65, 484. **DJOKN**-1916. **DTEG**-Parts 1–18. **DTEI**-Parts 1–25. **DZMM**-88, 94. **EAI**-191. **EOWC**-iii, 7, 75–78, 132, 135, 142–43, 148, 152, 210, 212, 219, 225–27, 284–87, 290–91, 310, 328, 383–85$_{f10-11}$, 386–87. **EWPP**-13–15, 21–23, 32–33. **FAUO**-312. **FPLFF**-239–240. **FREEJ-III:** 106–109. **GENNO-CCLXXII:** 185. **GGU**-106–107. **HALD**-B/102/81. **HARHIS**-17–18. **HBJCO**-430–31. **HC-I:** 108–109. **HCBI**-205–207, 289–90. **HFN-HG**-49–50, 171–77. **HGOD**-213. **HH-I:** 483, 543, 882, 909; **II:** 169, 546, 682, 684–85, 885–92. **HHARD**-22–23. **HISRC-I:** 141–42, 144–45. **HISWCO**-120$_2$. **HIWW**-275, 328. **HOFCO-II:** 526. **HOPH**-26–27, 106, 111–25, 132–34, 142, 144, 148–49, 255, 300, 359, 362, 364, 414–15. **HRD**-474. **HWCP**-213, 288. **HWNUS**-225–26. **HWYCO**-22, 626–28, 747. **IMH-IX:** 104, 107–108; **INDAT**-2–4, 6–10, 12–21, 23–30, 47–48, 51–58. **IOBL**-130, 130$_6$, 166. **IONA**-27. **IPIUS**-5–6, 8. **IWM**-276. **IWPA**-171–77. **JMWAL**-t.89/v.14: 1, 11, 59, 180–81, 183. **JOSLO**-37–38. **JPP**-75–77. **JVES**-1–18, 137–39, 149–54, 156–57, 293, 303–304, 308–310, 312, 315–16, 327–28. **KATT-II:** 98. **KY**-369–70. **LOJB-I: II:** 228–31. **LOMJ**-190–97. **LTDZ**-237–38, 565, 576. **MAH-XV:** No. 3, March 1886, 256–77. **MOLI-V:** No. 4, 433–35. **MPHC-IX: X:** 595; **XIX:. MVHAP-II: III:** 188a. **MWH-II:** May 1885, 19–38; **III:** Sep. 1907, 121–36. **NAR/1832-XXXIV:** No. 75, 435–36. **NARWP**-MB-M/804; S.3590; S.4631; S.16730; S.17753; S.22390; S.33080; R.7270; W.2803; W.6646. **NCSJK**-14–15, 26. **NEWFAM**-9. **NNAIC**-lii–liii. **NOS**-130–31, 264–75, 278. **OAHJ-VI:** 1–34. **OAHP-6:** 153. **OAHP-8:** 474.

OAHQ-17: 582–84. **OAHQ-19:** 107. **OAHQ-43:** 275–77. **OC-**79, 131.
OHMAG-III: Sep. 1907, 121–36. **OLDWE-**28–30. **OMOO-**271. **OSO-**46, 67,
315, 317. **OTHW-**77. **PAPS-82-**151, 188–89, 201–225. **PAPS-96-**502. **PEJO-**
July 27, 1782. **PEN-**1st Ser., **V:** 253; **IX:** 547; 2nd Ser., **I:** 1; **XIV:** 2, 14; 3rd Ser.
XXIII: 199–201, 203–209, 217–19, 228–30, 321–23; 6th Ser., **II:** 220–21, 228, 256,
385–87, 390–92, 398. **PENRIF-**19, 74. **PENSA:** RG-4, Records . . . Militia,
1777–94. **PGNT-**195$_1$. **PHMB-XVIII:** 128–57, 293–328. **PIAFS-**104. **PPAC-**
Aug. 12, 1783. **PPOWC-I:** 1, 101, 112. **PSATC-**April 7, 1838. **REREM-**xi-xii,
309–15. **RESWV-**131–32. **REVAM-**1763–89. **RTV-**143–44. **SAF-**8, 15.
SAGAZ-Aug. 29, 1782. **SCIG-**Oct. 9, 1845. **SETWC-**21. **SFOS-**6, 11–13, 17.
SK-55, 204. **T-**55. **TAP-**213–14, 270. **TCHSJ-**105–06. **TF-**287–308. **TISAR-**4.
TITC-1–8. **TQIL-**24. **UAMS-**April 8, 1869. **USWC-**7. **VAHM-42-**Jan. 1934,
143–44. **VERHC-II:** 356. **VMHB-XIX:** Jan. 1911, 71; **IIXL:** 2, 143–44. **VOLF-**
314–15, 443–44. **WAYDEM-**Sep. 7, 1881. **WGW-VI:** 403. **WHC-XII:** 219–20.
WHIR-131, 134. **WICOR-**126–27, 129, 249–50, 289, 291, 304, 346, 363–65, 371,
375–76, 379. **WPHM-LXIV:** No. 4, Oct. 1981, 311–327; **LXV:** No. 1, Jan. 1982,
17–36; No. 2, April, 1982, 115–151; No. 4., Oct. 1982, 323–39; **LXVIII:** No. 1,
Jan. 1968, 43–66; **LXX:** No. 1, Jan. 1987, 53–67. **WHM-PB6** 311–312, 316.
WOON-vi–viii, xx. **WRMM-I:** 23.

Chapter 7

AHC-I: 13, 409–10. **BUTBA-**MSS v.f/B. **BUTM2-V-**271. **BUTM5-**C-2/F-4.
CFUO-297. **CQ-**50–51. **CTM-**April 6, 1882. **DD-BB-4:** 30; **DD-BB-6:** 110;
DD-BB-9: 60, 60$^{4-5}$; **DD-F-1:** 98$^{k-k1,\ l-m}$, 111^b, 138; **DD-F-10:** 160, 168–69;
DD-F-11: 3–4, 9–13; **DD-F-14:** 40; **DD-G-1:** 18^{219}; **DD-G-2:** 1^{10}, 5; **DD-S-2:**
7, 35–47, 54–55, 67–72, 95–103, 127–29, 131, 133, 152–54, 157–80, 188–89, 191,
194–95, 215–19, 232, 238, 246–47, 249–54, 257–58, 271, 274–78, 281–84, 294,
334–38; **DD-S-3:** 28, 51–52, 63, 83–84, 126–30, 151, 159, 169–71, 213–219, 238–
45, 249, 342, 347; **DD-S-4:** 144–45, 185–86; **DD-S-5:** 29, 87; **DD-S-6:** 152–59,
161–66, 297; **DD-S-7:** 131; **DD-S-9:** 78, 138, 177–78, 183–84, 188; **DD-S-10:**
53–67, 74–84, 90–91, 210–11; **DD-S-11:** 10–18, 58–65, 115–21, 160–68, 171–73,
203–206; 210–11, 213–14; **DD-S-12:** 1–9, 17–19, 21–22; **DD-S-13:** 149–51, 158–
76; **DD-S-15:** 27–28, 38–41; **DD-S-16:** 173–74; **DD-S-17:** 198, 236; **DD-S-18:**
200–202; **DD-S-21:** 171–72, 194, 204–206, 220–22, 229–32; **DD-S-22:** 44–47;
DD-S-24: 52, 63–78, 119–21, 212–15; **DD-U-11:** 11; **DD-U-12:** 45$^{11-15}$; **DD-U-**
23: 1–21; **DD-YY-1:** 10, 115–116; **DD-YY-2:** 119, 124–25; **DD-YY-3:** 120.
EAI-3–32. **EZP-**303–304. **GGU-**109–18. **GTE-**107–108, 114–16. **HC-I:** 34, 72,
639. **HH-I:** 308, 314, 411, 479, 732, 853, 907, 911; **II:** 144, 175, 244, 271, 593–94,
807. **HISTA-**162. **HOK-I: II:** 553, 562–63. **HOPH-**116, 121–30, 132–39, 144,
149, 151, 156, 161, 180$_f$, 181, 256, 359, 362, 375, 413–14, 442. **IC-**191. **JMWAL-**
t.89/v.14. **JOCC-XXV:** 680–95. **KY-**39–40, 369–370. **LE-**55. **LM-**111. **LOFIC-**
241. **LT-**184. **MAH-XV:** No. 3, March 1886, 256–77. **MBO-II:** 12–14. **ME-**42–
43. **MVHR-XX:** 138–39, 174–83. **MWH-II:** May 1885; Jan. 1886, 273. **NC-**23.
OC-49–52, 80–86, 89, 121, 130–31. **OSO-**23, 61, 159, 161. **PEN-**1st Ser. **X:** 83–
90; **XIV:** 3rd Ser., 554. **PPAC-**Nov. 18, 1783. **SI-**59–60, 65$_f$, 69. **SIW-**81. **SK-**12–
15, 49, 52, 57, 60, 75A, 79, 110, 128, 131, 137, 139, 141, 157–61, 163–70, 172–75,

183–85, 206, 208–209, 213, 217, 224. **T**-56. **TAP**-49, 131, 144, 212, 270–71. **TF**-308–336. **THOK**-205–215. **TISHS**-1904: 62, 62$_{f,\ 63-197}$, 63. **TP**-114–16. **TPP**-140–41, 182. **TQIL**-24–26. **VERHC-II:** 357. **XII:** 66–69. **WOD**-156$_{f54}$, **WVHE-III:** 596.

Chapter 8

AHC-I: 410. **ASPI-I:** 8–9. **BOI**-623. **CFUO**-289–97. **CINA**-Nov. 16, 1847. **CQ**-42, 98. **CTM**-April 6, 1882. **DD-BB-4:** 13^2; **DD-BB-8:** 56–58; **DD-BB-9:** 9–10; **DD-E-11:** 83–138; **DD-F-7:** 22, 55^6; **DD-F-10:** 162; **DD-F-11:** 27, 31–34; **DD-G-1:** 1^{10}; **DD-S-2:** 66–67, 93–94, 211, 220–22, 229–30, 232–33, 247–48, 282–83, 307–308, 312; **DD-S-3:** 79, 134, 153, 167–69, 234, 245–50, 252–54, 337; **DD-S-4:** 189; **DD-S-5:** 88–89, 192–93; **DD-S-6:** 159–61, 166–69, 172–75; **DD-S-7:** 114, 132; **DD-S-8:** 22–24, 48–49, 90; **DD-S-9:** 51–53, 104, 168–73; **DD-S-10:** 108–114; **DD-S-12:** 37, 39–54, 69–73, 116–27, 133–44, 147–51, 159–60, 167–72, 184–85; **DD-S-13:** 121–41; **DD-S-14:** 173–210, 212–14, 216–36; **DD-S-15:** 2–12, 26–31; **DD-S-16:** 96–113, 178–81, 206–209, 262–64, 266, 296–97; **DD-S-17:** 70–73; **DD-S-19:** 79–83, 87, 96–98; **DD-S-20:** 41; **DD-S-21:** 222–28, 235–36; **DD-S-24:** 46, 54–57, 61; **DD-U-4:** 158, 158^3; **DD-U-12:** 45^{14}; **DD-U-23:** 10–15, 22–24, 27–31, 33–51, 57–59, 61, 63–91; **DD-YY-1:** 5, 11; **DD-YY-2:** 22, 117, 143; **DD-YY-3:** 60, 120; **DD-YY-8:** 161; **DD-YY-12:** 35–36. **FWG**-85–97. **GGU**-10, 118–28, 132–35. **GL**-200. **GTE**-118–29, 131–33, 137–43. **GWHH**-148, 184. **HC-I:** 72–73, 73$_f$, 74–75. **HH-I:** 217, 245, 310, 325, 411, 502, 504, 746–48, 807, 853–54, 859, 876; **II:** 98–99, 172, 176, 271, 560–61, 685, 777–78, 780–81, 796, 807, 826. **HLW**-194. **HOPH**-69, 132–35, 138–41, 146, 151–52, 154–56, 300, 306, 323, 332, 350, 362, 364–65, 374–76, 405, 411–15. **IA**-71. **INBIO-II:** 184–85. **IUS**-91–92. **K**-39–40, 182–85. **KY**-40, 170. **LM**-208–210. **MAH-XV:** No. 3, Mar. 1886, 256–77. **MARJ**-Aug. 19, 1785. **ME**-56. **MIND**-77–125. **MVHR-II:** 264; **XXIV:** 24–25. **MWH**-Jan. 1886, 273. **NJT**-138$_f$, 139. **OC**-90–95, 114, 131–32, 210, 293–94, 294$_f$, 299. **OSO**-91–92, 130, 161–62, 179–80, 316–17. **PPAC**-July 4, 29, Sep. 4, 1786. **PWIW**-47–58, 92–116. **SAF**-4. **SI**-70$_f$, 73, 73$_f$, 81$_f$. **SIW**-45–52, 75, 105, 144. **SK**-15, 21, 26, 50–53, 55–56, 59–60, 74, 77–78, 83, 131, 137–38, 142, 169, 173–81, 185–92, 194–95, 201–202, 204–206, 209, 212–15, 223. **T**-53, 56. **TAP**-65, 131–33, 138–39, 168–69, 271–73, 286–90. **TF**-309, 336–68, 371–75, 377–81. **TISHS**-1902: 203–214. **TP**-116–19, 154. **TPP**-141–42, 167. **TPUS-II:** 31–35, 78–79, 158. **TQIL**-26–28. **TSR**-19–28. **WHC-XII:** 91. **WVHE-III:** 596.

Chapter 9

ACHW-96, 136, 147–49. **AHC-I:** 13, 410. **AHOT**-265–67, 279. **AHSO**-140. **ALA-II:** 121, 149. **ANOC**-15th Cong., 2nd Sess., I: 1015, 1016. **ASEYA**-21. **ASPI-I:** 36–38, 85, 92–94, 131–38, 197, 258, 308, 337, 354, 357, 434, 438–39, 446, 634; **II:** 134. **ATH**-31–32. **BOSG**-May 20, 1793. **BUTS:** Ser. 2; Ser. 3, No. 8; Ser. 4. **CFUO**-317. **CINA**-Sep. 2, 1846; 1847–48, 49; 1859, 92, 104. **CJGS-I:** 55, 369. **CLOE**-1. **CMHS**-3rd Ser., V: 159–63. **COLC**-Feb. 14, 22, Mar. 31, 1792. **CONW**-143. **CQ**-39, 52–54, 56, 68, 89, 91, 174. **CTM**-April 6, 1882. **DCN**-574.

DD-BB-4: 55, 57; **DD-BB-5:** 157–58; **DD-BB-8:** 73; **DD-E-11:** 83–138; **DD-F-1:** 118; **DD-FF-1:** 111[b]; **DD-G-1:** 20[363–364]; **DD-O-1:** 1086; **DD-S-2:** 72–78, 108–109, 111, 118–20, 124–25, 186–208, 222–23, 227–29, 232, 248, 296–302, 318, 339, 342; **DD-S-3:** 70, 118, 121, 131, 161–62, 209–210, 220–22, 231, 233, 250, 254–55, 259, 304–305, 341; **DD-S-4:** 77, 145–46, 150–51, 159–61, 185; **DD-S-5:** 30, 192–98, 213–14; **DD-S-6:** 19, 172–76, 179–83, 185–86, 195–96, 202–203; **DD-S-7:** 132–41; **DD-S-8:** 49–51, 69–70, 128–32, 145, 151; **DD-S-9:** 15–16, 35–39, 72, 74, 76–77, 95, 97, 99, 106–117, 122, 130, 139, 146–47, 161, 175–77; **DD-S-10:** 1–2, 26, 100–101, 115–18; **DD-S-12:** 73–74, 90, 94, 211–13; **DD-S-13:** 1–3, 6, 7, 9–15, 28, 33–34, 189; **DD-S-16:** 178–81, 206–209, 212–14, 217–18, 223, 246–49, 267; **DD-S-17:** 43–47, 68–69, 131, 206–208, 255; **DD-S-19:** 70, 86, 100–102, 104–107, 129–30, 137–41, 154–55, 182–83, 200–206, 223–34, 237, 288; **DD-S-20:** 41–47, 86–91, 98–101, 121–27; **DD-S-22:** 50–51, 53–55; **DD-S-31:** 303–304; **DD-U-4:** Letters of Harmar's Campaign, 1–199; **DD-U-11:** 66–67; **DD-U-12:** 45[14–15]; **DD-U-14:** 60–61, 147–49, 151–75, 201–203, 225–32; **DD-U-15:** 83–87, 112–18; **DD-W-2:** 343; **DD-YY-1:** 1, 11–12, 14–17, 24, 68, 83, 112, 115–16; **DD-YY-2:** 23, 127, 166; **DD-YY-3:** 37, 58; **DD-YY-7:** 98; **DD-YY-8:** 54. **EZP-**xx, 215$_f$. **FCHQ-46:** July 1972, 247–49. **FWG-**85–97. **GAZUS-**Jan. 15, 29, Feb. 15, Mar. 22, 1791; Jan. 21, 1792. **GGU-**29, 109, 123–24, 130–31, 135–52. **GL-**200. **GLIAP-**Fort Wayne Mss. **GTE-**144–53, 158–67, 176–82, 184–97. **HARPAP-**Letter 82, 86. **HC-I:** 34, 72, 73$_f$, 80, 82, 91–92, 639, 640. **HD-**34. **HG-**249–55, 261. **HH-I:** 144, 223–24, 232, 284, 300, 313–14, 342–44, 411, 426, 502, 529, 544, 558, 589, 669–71, 673, 679, 705, 742, 747–48, 750–51, 759, 778, 793, 854, 876, 907, 962; **II:** 141–44, 223–32, 420, 558–59, 685, 742. **HIWW-**312, 391–93. **HLW-**144, 194–95. **HOFW-**136–37, 145$_f$, 535. **HOPH-**25, 114, 131, 137–38, 140, 142, 144, 147, 149, 155, 315–17, 323, 332, 361–62, 365, 408, 410, 413–14. **HSOM-**139–140. **IA-II:** 18–23. **IC-**60, 191. **III-**124–25, 139–40. **INBIO-II:** 186. **JTUP-**195–96, 211, 215. **KY-**42–47. **KYGAZ-**70. **LATT-**68. **LCB-**389. **LE-**58–60. **LM-**316–17. **LT-**35, 40–45, 58, 68. **MAH-XV:** No. 3, March 1886, 256–77. **MARJ-**1791, 3; Jan. 13, 1792. **ME-**56, 66–67. **MIND-**77–125. **MPHC-IX: X: XIX: XXIV:** 261–62. **MVHR-XII:** 10–11; **XIV:** 187–97; **XXIV:** 101–102, 133–34, 220–22, 306–307, 329–30. **MWH-**Jan. 1886, 273–74. **NAP-**96. **NC-**72. **NESN-**83–91, 111–12, 268. **NJT-**32–54, 57, 123–25. **OAHP-11R:** 39. **OAHQ-33:** 238–52. **OAHQ-49:** 41–57. **OC-**43–44, 95–100, 121, 131. **OOTW-**159, 236–38. **OSO-**5, 100, 131, 162, 166–67, 179–81, 205–206, 286. **PEN-V:** 68–70, 106, 117–18. **PHIL-**175. **PIOH-**280, 301–304. **PPAC-**Oct. 18, 1786. **PWIW-**76–77, 126–28, 138, 145–200. **SCP-II:** 108–109. **SI-**80, 83, 83$_f$. **SIW-**39, 45, 53, 63, 65, 69, 81, 92, 105, 112, 115, 123, 129, 134, 139, 143. **SK-**15, 53, 55, 60–61, 63–65, 69–73, 75, 77–78, 80–82, 84–85, 87–90, 93, 96, 100, 137–38, 140, 146–47, 170, 176–78, 179, 181, 187–91, 194–212, 221. **SWA-**197–202. **T-**32, 57–62. **TAP-**34, 49, 57, 60, 66, 137–39, 170, 272–78, 288, 292, 293, 295–99. **TF-**384–441. **TP-**119–23, 125. **TPP-**142, 152–55, 163–64, 166. **TPUS-II: III:** 300–301, 311, 320–21. **TQIL-**31–34. **TRIB-I:** 22. **TRINC-I:** 194. **TSR-**21–22, 26–27. **USGB-**115–19. **VIEW-**104–105. **WHC-III:** 301–318; **VI:** 188; **XII:** 136. **WOD-**6–7, 7$_{f4}$. **WVHE-III:** 592–96.

Chapter 10 and Epilogue

ACHW-116, 147. **AHC-I:** 13, 410. **AHSO**-145. **AMP-II:** 185. **ASPI-I:** 227, 233, 241, 335, 338, 340–42, 349, 352–53, 357, 489, 559–60, 562–63, 575–78; **II: IV:** 578, 581–82; **V:** 489, 529. **ASPL-I:** 110. **ATH**-38–39. **BHW**-24. **BOI**-616. **CFUO**-321, 324, 325, 327. **CHOT**-365, 374. **CHSC-I:** 1934–35, 106. **CINA**-Sep. 2, 1846; Dec. 9, 14, 1847; April 11, 1848; 1859, 101–102. **CINC**-May 24, 1794; Feb. 7, 1795. **CJGS-II:** 18–36, 149–50, 262, 310–17; **III:** 281. **CLOE**-1. **COLC**-Sep. 8, 1792; March 16, 1793. **CQ**-56–60, 91–92, 123. **CTB**-34. **DD-BB-1:** 19; **DD-BB-4:** 55, 57–58, 63, 131; **DD-E-11:** 83–138; **DD-F-2:** 213–17; **DD-G-1:** 1^{10}; **DD-S-2:** 24–25, 57–59, 74–77, 92, 115–18, 120, 123–27, 132–33, 180, 213, 222–23, 229, 231, 234–37, 277, 284, 286–87, 302–303, 313–17, 323–24, 339–40, 350–51; **DD-S-3:** 60–62, 64, 68–69, 83, 112, 114–16, 118–19, 122, 127–28, 135–36, 148–49, 160–62, 165, 167, 169–73, 208–209, 224, 227–30, 233, 236, 301, 325–32, 341, 349–52; **DD-S-4:** 3, 6–7, 9–10, 152–54, 154^{1}, 155–57, 165–79, 184–86; **DD-S-5:** 18–20, 31, 217–18; **DD-S-6:** 175–76, 182–84, 187–96, 198–205; **DD-S-8:** 28–29, 31–33, 128–32, 141–43, 145, 147–51; **DD-S-9:** 25–26, 31–34, 40–41, 120–21, 124–31, 139–40, 144–45, 148–61, 165–68, 174–75, 183, 189; **DD-S-10:** 8–12, 101–102, 123; **DD-S-12:** 76–77, 90–94, 98–105; **DD-S-13:** 33–34, 41–47, 52–54, 57–59, 65, 80–82, 94, 120–21, 153–54; **DD-S-14:** 198–200; **DD-S-16:** 119^{5}, 164–74, 177–81, 206–209, 214, 216, 218, 221, 223, 227–28, 238–45, 248, 253–54, 265–66, 279; **DD-S-17:** 48–53, 62–63, 255; **DD-S-19:** 42–44, 52, 58, 60–62, 100–101, 104, 127, 172–73, 175–78, 187–92, 262–64, 281–85, 289; **DD-S-20:** 50–51, 90–97, 108–109, 113, 201–203, 244^{2}; **DD-S-21:** 190, 241; **DD-S-22:** 47–49, 58; **DD-S-24:** 59–60, 62; **DD-U-4:** 163^{3}, 166, 206, 221, 225, 225^{1}, **DD-U-5:** 24, 24^{1-2}, 25, 25^{1}, 26, 26^{1}, 30, 30^{1}, 43–44, 122, 122^{1-2}, 161, 161^{1}; **DD-U-11:** 66–67; **DD-U-12:** 45^{15-16}; **DD-U-15:** 79–81, 85, 88–90; **DD-U-16:** 117, 117^{1-3}, 118, 118^{7}, 119–20, 120^{6}, 120^{8}, 121, 121^{9-12}, 122, 122^{14-15}, 123, 123^{16}, 124, 124^{17-18}, 125, 125^{19}, 126–27, 127^{20-21}, 128, 128^{22-24}, 265–66; **DD-YY-1:** 1, 8, 11–17, 19–20, 35, 68, 162^{1}; **DD-YY-2:** 23, 33, 82, 127–31, 155–56, 167–69, 188; **DD-YY-3:** 36–37; **DD-YY-5:** 12; **DD-YY-6:** 24; **DD-YY-9:** 1; **DD-YY-12:** 22, 36–37; **DD-YY-13:** 2^{11}. **FMTC-XIII:** No. 76, April 1836, 500. **GGU**-147–48, 151, 153–79, 184–90, 193–94. **GLIAP**-"A Treaty of Peace and Friendship"; Simcoe to Dorchester, April 29, 1794. **GTE**-182–83, 187, 197–200, 207–210, 214–23, 231–36, 260. **GWHH**-36. **HC-I:** 34, 70. **HCBI**-213, 213_{13}, 214–15, 215_{14}, 216, 216_{15}, 313_{47}. **HG**-265. **HH-I:** 227, 284, 300–301, 307, 328, 342–44, 452–54, 502, 530, 543–45, 751, 754–55, 814, 850, 854, 876, 908, 953–54, 963–64; **II:** 137 139–43, 145, 172, 224, 232–34, 274, 291, 452, 492, 559, 685, 741, 780–81, 807. **HLW**-12–15. **HOK-I: II:** 574–75. **HOPH**-132–33, 140–41, 144–46, 149, 159, 171, 181, 197–98, 202, 300, 306, 316–19, 332, 361–63, 365–66, 376, 405, 412–14, 440. **HWY**-80, 140. **IA-I:** 85. **IC**-191–92. **IHC-I:** xvi. **IHSP-XXXVII:** Sep. 1944, 228–41. **IMH-IX: LIV: LVI:** Sep. 1960, 217–26. **INBIO-II:** 186. **IOBL**-358. **KY**-40, 46–48, 243. **KYGAZ**-29–30, 61. **LATT**-272–76. **LE**-60–62. **LEXGZ**-Nov. 11, 1791. **LOFIC**-246–48. **LOGB**-308. **LOJB-I: II:** 11. **LT**-65–66, 68, 71, 76. **LVMRW**-203. **MAH-XV:** No. 3, March 1886, 256–77. **MARJ**-Jan. 1, 1793. **MAYSV**-Jan. 1872. **ME**-80, 87–88, 93–97. **MOLI-V:** No. 4. **MVHR-XXIV:** 43–44, 108, 167, 394–96, 414–16, 470–72, 518–19, 551–54, 571–72, 587–93, 659–60; **XXXIV:** 734. **NAR/1832-XXXIV:** No. 75, 440. **NI**-April 20, 1819. **OAHQ-59:** July, 1950,

244. **OC-**41–42, 132–36, 217. **OHQ-70-**July 1961, 202–203. **OSO-**26, 165–66, 181, 286–88, 319. **PAC-IA-**438–39, 446. **PB-I:** 118, 173; **II:** 18, 184–85. **PECH-**366, 369. **PFB-I:** 50. **PG-**Aug. 8, 1792. **PGA-**Aug. 20, Sep. 13, 1792. **PHD-**Dec. 13, 1794. **PHIL-**280. **PMHB-XII,** No. 2 (1888), 173–84. **PIOH-**221–23. **PPAC-**Oct. 18, 1786. **PWIW-**225–31. **SAF-**17, 26. **SCP-II:** 274–75, 343–44, 344$_f$. **SI-**102, 102$_f$. **SIW-**29, 33, 36, 39, 41–42, 45, 53, 65, 75, 78–81, 88–90, 96, 100, 105, 111, 113, 118–19, 134, 136, 139, 141, 146, 148–50. **SK-**21, 55, 60, 70, 78–79, 85–86, 93, 95, 97, 99–104, 109, 128, 137, 148, 167, 172, 185–86, 193, 204, 213, 215–37, 239, 241–42. **SOTL-**341. **T-**64–65, 67–68, 85–86, 92, 135. **TAP-**49, 62, 138–39, 170, 172–73, 273, 276–80, 289, 291. **TF-**431–32, 441–57, 463–67, 474–81. **TISHS-**(1904) 88. **TP-**125–30, 132–35, 149–50, 153, 155. **TPP-**142–44, 146–48, 153–54, 167–68, 170, 180–81, 461. **TPUS-II:** 447–49, 454–55; **III:** 433–34. **TQIL-**34–39, 42, 74, 83. **TRINC-I:** 195. **TSR-**29–35. **USGB-**120–26. **VIEW-**105, 326. **WOD-**197, 197$_6$. **WHM-II:** (1918–1919) 65. **WS-**Dec. 9, 1794. **WVHE-III:** 588, 592–93.

Source Codes

Keyed to author or first word in Bibliography

ACBHC	Tobias	**ACHW**	Hatch	**ADOJM**	Holley
AHC	Pierce	**AHFIA**	Harbaugh	**AHI**	Dillon
AHOI	Ford	**AHOT**	Haywood	**AHSO**	Atwater
ALA	Pickett	**ALD**	Luckenbach	**ALREM**	Almon
AMAR	American	**AMDI**	Matthews	**AMERH-7**	La Farge
AMERL	Pearce	**AMP**	Hinde	**ANM**	Heckewelder
ANNW	Albach	**ANOC**	Annals	**ANWEP**	Paull
ARAM	Gallatin	**ASBJL**	Butterfield	**ASEYA**	Gallagher
ASIOH	Eckert	**ASPI**	American	**ASPL**	American
ASPPL	American	**ASSM**	Loudon	**ATC**	Campbell
ATH	Woehrmann	**ATOU**	Shirreff	**AWYCO**	Atlas
BEAR	Gipson	**BHUS**	Beard	**BHW**	Stevens
BMWCO	Bowen	**BOB**	Williams	**BOI**	Drake
BOSG	Boston	**BRADE**	Hamilton	**BRWN**	Kellogg
BTFO	Bucyrus	**BUTM2**	Butterfield	**BUTM5**	Butterfield
BUTBA	Butterfield	**BUTS**	Butterfield	**C**	Loeb
CACDH	Furer	**CBWV**	Withers	**CCNW**	Hayden
CDB	Eckert	**CFUO**	Downes	**CG**	Darlington
CHNY	O'Callaghan	**CHOT**	Haywood	**CHSC**	Chicago
CINA	Cincinnati	**CINC**	Cincinnati	**CISHS**	Collections
CISM	Cist	**CIV**	Alford	**CJAOS**	Hill
CJGS	Cruikshank	**CLOE**	Webb	**CMHS**	Massachusetts
CP	Parkman	**COLC**	Columbus	**CONW**	Quaife
CQ	Quaife	**CRNC**	North	**CTM**	Chicago
CVSP	Palmer	**CWTJ**	Washington	**CWTJ**	Washington
DCN	Blanchard	**DD-BB-**	Kenton	**DD-C-**	Boone
DD-CC-	Kentucky	**DD-E-**	Brady	**DD-F-**	Brant

DD-FF-	Mecklenburg	DD-G-	Brant	DD-NN-	Pittsburgh
DD-O-	Drake	DD-S-	Draper	DD-U-	Frontier
DD-W-	Harmar	DD-YY-	Tecumseh	DD-ZZ-	Virginia
DGW	Fitzpatrick	DIAH	Weslager	DJOKN	Ballard
DPEN	Day	DSD	Hough	DTEG	Croneis
DTEI	Croneis	DZMM	Bliss	EAI	Axtell
EHWP	Rupp	EOWC	Butterfield	EWPP	Ferguson
EWT-1	Thwaites	EZP	Coues	FAUO	Kellogg
FCHQ-43	Beckner	FCHQ-46	Edmunds	FMTC	Fraser
FPLFF	Darlington	FREEJ	Freeman	FWG	Griswold
GAZUS	Gazette	GBIC	Carter	GCWD	Wainwright
GENNO	Butterfield	GEO	Hughes	GGU	Gilbert
GJB	Hudleston	GL	Hatcher	GLIAP	Great
GMBP	Bouquet	GTE	Eckert	GW	Brooks
GWAR	Flexner	GWHH	Dawson	HA	Hodge
HALD	Haldimand	HARHIS	Cooprider	HARPAP	Harmar
HAWM	Jenkins	HBJCO	Caldwell	HC	Andreas
HCBI	Van der Beets	HCIN	Massachusetts	HD	Crew
HEAFD	Sargent	HFN	Colden	HG	Butterfield
HGOD	Parkins	HGRC	Thwaites	HH	Howe
HHARD	Hardin	HHGC	Barnhart	HIIL	Blanchard
HIMI	Claiborne	HISRC	Baughman	HISTA	Heckewelder
HISWCO	Crumrine	HIT	Schoolcraft	HIWW	De Hass
HLW	McAfee	HM	Historical	HMUB	Hoskiel
HNAI	Sturtevant	HNMM	Harper	HOFCO	Ellis
HOFW	Brice	HOK	Collins	HOMAS	Bradford
HOO	Taylor	HOPH	Newton	HPA	Gordon
HRD	Heitman	HSOM	Historical	HWCP	Forrest
HWNUS	Finley	HWY	Clarke	HWYCO	History
IA	Kappler	IC	Berton	IHC	Black
IHSP	Indiana	III	Beckwith	IMH	Indiana
INBIO	Thatcher	INDAT	Brackenridge	INT	Intelligencer
IOBL	Pritts	IONA	Driver	IPIUS	Prucha
IUS	Wissler	IWM	Washburn	IWPA	Sipe
JCC	Ford	JCGW	Toner	JJS	Cook
JME	Steck	JMWAL	MacLean	JNYPC	New York
JOCC	Hunt	JOSLO	Slover	JPP	Potts
JRAD	Thwaites	JVEC	Virginia	JVES	Rose
JTUP	Baily	KATT	Fredricksen	KY	Kentucky
KYGAZ	Kentucky	LATT	Drake	LCB	Brock
LE	Hatcher	LEXGZ	Lexington	LM	Quaife
LOFIC	Wood	LOGB	Glegg	LOJB	Stone
LOMJ	Seaver	LOSCH	Lossing	LSD	Parkman
LT	Drake	LTDZ	De Schweinitz	LTSWJ	Stone
LUMRW	McAllister	MAH	Magazine	MARJ	Maryland
MAW	Parkman	MAYSV	Maysville	MB	Flexner
MBO	Peyster	ME	Horsman	MGZ	Maryland
MIND	Anson	MISSB	Winsor	MLFL	LeSieur
MLJAH	Horrell	MLJM	Martin	MOLI	Monthly
MPHC	Michigan	MVHAP	Mississippi	MVHR	Mississippi
MWH	Magazine	NAP	Spencer	NAR/1832	National
NARWP	National	NC	Graham	NCHA	Winsor
NCSJK	Knight	NESN	Burnet	NEV	Tyler

NEWFAM	Newland	**NFT**	Stevens	**NI**	National
NJT	Schoolcraft	**NNAIC**	Vaughan	**NOS**	Doddridge
NWR	Niles	**NYGZ**	New York	**OAHJ**	Ohio
OAHP	Ohio	**OAHQ**	Ohio	**OC**	Galloway
OHMAG	Ohio	**OHQ/70**	Ohio	**OLDWE**	Hassler
OMOO	Metcalf	**OOTW**	Thornbrough	**OSO**	Thwaites
OTHW	Clarke	**P**	Peckham	**PAC-IA**	Canada
PAPS	American	**PB**	McBride	**PECH**	Trager
PECOR	Pennsylvania	**PEJO**	Pennsylvania	**PELG**	Pennsylvania
PEN	Pennsylvania	**PENRIF**	Dyke	**PENSA**	Pennsylvania
PFB	Lossing	**PG**	Pennsylvania	**PGA**	Philadelphia
PGNT	Connelly	**PHD**	Philadelphia	**PHIL**	Reynolds
PMHB	Pennsylvania	**PIAFS**	Paull	**PIOH**	Hildreth
PITTC	Pittsburgh	**PKDS**	Mastin	**PPAC**	Pennsylvania
PPOWC	Baughman	**PSATC**	Philadelphia	**PSWJ**	Flick
PWIW	Sword	**PWW**	Ellet	**REREM**	Dann
RESWV	Cox	**REVAM**	Gephart	**RIB**	Labaree
RRR	Cuneo	**RTV**	Slotkin	**SAF**	Hagan
SAGAZ	Salem	**SAT**	Drimmer	**SCIG**	Scioto
SCP	Smith	**SETWC**	Doddridge	**SFOS**	Sherrard
SHAWN	Howard	**SHAWT**	Trobridge	**SI**	Cotterill
SIW	Scamyhorn	**SK**	Kenton	**SOTL**	McKenney
SWA	McClung	**T**	Eggleston	**TAC**	Henry
TAP	Hale	**TC**	Eckert	**TCHSJ**	Doyle
TF	Eckert	**TFT**	Phillips	**TGP**	Gage
THOK	Smith	**TIAC**	Gordon	**TISAR**	Barnet
TISHS	Illinois	**TITC**	Levernier	**TP**	Edmunds
TPP	Clifton	**TPUS**	Carter	**TQIL**	Edmunds
TRF	Sosin	**TRIB**	McKenney	**TRINC**	Turner
TSR	Prucha	**TSST**	Gibson	**UAMS**	Uniontown
USGB	Burt	**USWC**	Gottfried	**VAHM**	Virginia
VERHC	Vermont	**VMHB**	Virginia	**VOD**	Andrews
VOLF	Vail	**VSP**	Virginia	**WAYDEM**	Wayne
WB	Kinzie	**WBD**	Neilson	**WCL**	Butterfield
WE	Eckert	**WGW**	Fitzpatrick	**WHC**	Wisconsin
WHIR	Heard	**WICOR**	Butterfield	**WO**	Washington
WOD	Quaife	**WOTR**	Ward	**WPHM**	Western
WHM	Wisconsin	**WOON**	Swiggett	**WRMM**	Western
WS	Western	**WVHE**	Cornstock	**WWWAR**	Kail
WYCOR	Wyandot				

Bibliography

NOTE: *Bold letters in parentheses following each entry represent the source code, which can be found in the listing on pages 766–768.*

Adams, R. G., ed. *The Journal of Major George Washington*. N.Y., 1940. (**JW**)

Albach, James R. *Annals of the West*. Pittsburgh, 1857. (**ANNW**)

Alford, Thomas Wildcat. *Civilization and the Story of the Absentee Shawnees*. As told to Florence Drake. Norman, Okla., 1936. (**CIV**)

———, and Clarence Edwin Carter, eds. *Collections of the Illinois State Historical Library*. Springfield. (**CISH**)

American Heritage Magazine. N.Y. (**AMERH**)

American Literature. N.Y. (**AMERL**)

American Philosophical Society Proceedings. N.Y., 1940. (**PAPS**)

American Pioneer. N.Y. (**AMP**)

American State Papers:
> *Indian Affairs*. 2 vols. Washington, 1832–34. (**ASPI**)
> *Land Claims*. Washington, 1836. (**ASPL**)
> *Public Lands*. 2 vols. Washington, 1832–61. (**ASPPL**)

Andreas, Alfred Theodore. *History of Chicago, from the Earliest to the Present Time*. 3 vols. N.Y., 1975. (**HC**)

Andrews, Matthew Page. *Virginia: The Old Dominion*. N.Y., 1937. (**VOD**)

Annals of Congress, 1st through 15th Congress. Washington. (**ANOC**)

Anson, Bert. *The Miami Indians*. Norman, Okla., 1970. (**MIND**)

Atlas of Wyandot County. Philadelphia, 1879. (**AWYCO**)

Atwater, Caleb. *A History of the State of Ohio, Natural and Civil*. Cincinnati, 1838. (**AHSO**)

Axtell, James. *The European and the Indian*. N.Y., 1981. (**EAI**)

Baily, Francis. *Journal of a Tour in the Unsettled Parts of North America in 1796 and 1797*. London, 1856. (**JTUP**)

Ballard, F. M. "Dr. John Knight." Typescript of 1916 in Filson Club Library, Louisville, Ky. (**DJOKN**)

Barnett, Louise K. *The Ignoble Savage: American Racism, 1790–1890.* Westport, Conn., 1975. (**TISAR**)

Barnhart, John D. *Henry Hamilton and George Rogers Clark in the American Revolution.* Crawfordsville, Ind., 1951. (**HHGC**)

Bartlett, J. R. "The Four Kings of Canada." *Magazine of American History,* March 1878. (**MAH**)

Baughman, A. J. *History of Richland County, Ohio.* Chicago, 1908. (**HISRC**)

———. *Past and Present of Wyandot County, Ohio.* Chicago, 1913. (**PPOWC**)

Beard, Charles A., and Mary R. Beard. *Basic History of the United States.* N.Y., 1944. (**BHUS**)

Beckner, Lucien. "John Findley: The First Pathfinder of Kentucky." (**FCHQ-43**)

Beckwith, Hiram W., ed. *Collections of the Illinois State Historical Library.* Springfield, 1903. (**CISHS**)

———. *The Illinois and Indiana Indians. Fergus Historical Series.* No. 27, Chicago, 1884. (**III**)

Berton, Pierre. *Flames Across the Border: 1813–1814.* Toronto, 1981. (**FLAB**)

———. *The Invasion of Canada: 1812–1813.* Boston, 1980. (**IC**)

Black Hawk War Papers. Part of the Illinois Historical Collections. Springfield. (**IHC**)

Blanchard, Rufus. *The Discovery and Conquests of the Northwest, including the Early History of Chicago, Detroit, Vincennes, St. Louis, Prairie Du Chien, Marietta, Cincinnati, Cleveland, Etc., Etc., and Incidents of Pioneer Life in the Region of the Great Lakes and Mississippi Valley.* Chicago, 1880. (**DCN**)

———. *History of Illinois.* Chicago, 1883. (**HIIL**)

Bliss, E. F., ed. *Diary of David Zeisberger, a Moravian Missionary among the Indians of Ohio . . .* Cincinnati, 1886. (**DZMM**)

Boone Papers. Part of the Draper Manuscript Collection in the archives of the State Historical Society of Wisconsin. 33 vols. Madison. (**DD-C**)

Boston Gazette. Boston, Mass. (**BOSG**)

Bouquet, Henry. *Colonel Henry Bouquet Papers.* Public Archives of Canada, Series A, IV. Ottawa, published in conjunction with the Gladwin Manuscripts, William L. Clements Library, Ann Arbor. Lansing, Mich., 1897. (**GMBP**)

Bowen, B. F. *Biographical Memoirs of Wyandot County, Ohio.* Logansport, Ind., 1902. (**BMWCO**)

Brackenridge, H. H. *Indian Atrocities: Narratives of the Perils and Sufferings of Dr. Knight and John Slover, Among the Indians During the Revolutionary War . . .* Cincinnati, 1867. (**INDAT**)

Bradford, Alden. *History of Massachusetts.* 2 vols. Boston. (**HOMAS**)

Brady and Wetzel Papers. 16 vols. Part of the Draper Manuscript Collection in the archives of the State Historical Society of Wisconsin. Madison. (**DD-E**)

Brant Miscellanies. Part of the Draper Manuscript Collection in the archives of the State Historical Society of Wisconsin. 3 vols. Madison. (**DD-G**)

Brant Papers. Part of the Draper Manuscript Collection in the archives of the State Historical Society of Wisconsin. 22 vols. Madison. (**DD-F**)

Brice, Wallace. *History of Fort Wayne, from the Earliest Known Accounts of this Point, to the Present Period.* Fort Wayne, Ind., 1868. (**HOFW**)

Brock, James. *Life and Correspondence of Major General Sir Isaac Brock.* London, 1847. (**LCB**)

Brooks, Edward Howard. *George Washington and the Fort Necessity Campaign, 1754.* Unpublished M.A. thesis in the Stanford Univ. Library Collection. 1947. (**GW**)

Bucyrus Telegraph-Forum. Bucyrus, O. (**BTFO**)

Burnet, Jacob. *Notes on the Early Settlement of the Northwestern Territory*. Cincinnati, 1847. (**NESN**)

Burt, Alfred L. *United States, Great Britain and British North America*. N.Y., 1961 (**USGB**)

Butterfield, Consul Willshire. *A Short Biography of John Leeth*. Cincinnati, 1883. (**ASBJL**)

————. *An Historical Account of the Expedition Against Sandusky Under William Crawford in 1782; with Biographical Sketches, Personal Reminiscences and Descriptions of Interesting Localities, including, also, Details of the Disastrous Retreat, the Barbarities of the Savages and the Awful Death of Colonel Crawford by Torture*. Cincinnati, 1873. (**EOWC**)

————. Brief Autobiography. Unpublished Mss., 1896. MSS. v.f./B, Western Reserve Historical Society, Cleveland. (**BUTBA**)

————. Butterfield Scrapbooks, unpublished. Western Reserve Historical Society, Cleveland. (**BUTS**)

————. Genealogical Notes. Unpublished Mss. Vol. 272. Ohio Historical Society, Columbus. (**GENNO**)

————. *History of the Girtys: Being a Concise Account of the Girty Brothers, Thomas, Simon, James and George, and of their Half-Brother, John Turner; also of the Part Taken by Them in Lord Dunmore's War, the Western War of the Revolution, and in the Indian War of 1790–95, with a Recital of the Principal Events in the West During these Wars, Drawn from Authentic Sources, Largely Original*. Columbus, 1950. (**HG**)

————. Unpublished Mss. Volume 55. Container 2, Folder 4, Western Reserve Historical Society, Cleveland. (**BUTM5**)

————. Unpublished Mss. Volume 271. Ohio Historical Center, Columbus. (**BUTM2**)

————, ed. *The Washington-Crawford Letters*. N.p., n.d. (**WCL**)

————. *Washington-Irvine Correspondence*. Madison, Wis., 1882. (**WICOR**)

Caldwell, J. A. *History of Belmont and Jefferson Counties, Ohio*. Wheeling, W.Va., 1880. (**HBJCO**)

Campbell, William W. *Annals of Tryon County: or, The Border Warfare of New York During the Revolution*. N.Y., 1831. (**ATC**)

Canada Papers Public *Archives of Canada*. Dominion Files. Ottawa. (**PAC**)
    Indian Affairs. Vol. II. RG/10 (**PAC-IA**)

Carter, Clarence Edwin. *Great Britain and the Illinois Country, 1763–1774*. Washington, 1910. (**GBIC**)

————, ed. *The Territorial Papers of the United States*. 26 vols. Washington, 1934–1962. (**TPUS**)

Chicago Historical Society Collections. Chicago. (**CHSC**)

Chicago Times. Chicago. (**CTM**)

Chicago Tribune. Chicago. (**CTB**)

Cincinnati Advertiser (also called *Cist's Advertiser*). Cincinnati. (**CINA**)

Cincinnati Chronicle. Cincinnati. (**CINC**)

Cist Miscellany. *Miscellany, I*. Cincinnati. (**CISM**)

Claiborne, J. F. *Historical Miscellanies*. N.Y., 1854. (**HIMI**)

Clarke, Peter Dooyentate. *History of the Wyandottes*. N.Y., 1917. (**HWY**)

————. *Origin and Traditional History of the Wyandot*. Toronto, 1870. (**OTHW**)

————. *The Prairie People: Continuity and Change in Potawatomi Indian Culture, 1665–1965*. Lawrence, Kan., 1977. (**TPP**)

Colden, Cadwallader. *The History of the Five Nations Depending on the Province of New York in America*. Ithaca, N.Y., 1964. (**HFN**)

Collins, Lewis and Richard Collins. *History of Kentucky*. 2 vols. Louisville, Ky., 1874. (**HOK**)

Columbus Centinel. Columbus. (**COLC**)

Comstock, Jim. *The West Virginia Heritage Encyclopedia.* Vol. 3. Richwood, W.Va., 1976. (**WVHE**)

Connelley, William Elcey, ed. *Provisional Government of Nebraska Territory and the Journals of William Walker.* Lincoln, 1899. (**PGNT**)

Cook, Frederick. *Journals of the Military Expedition of Major General John Sullivan against the Six Nations of Indians in 1779; with Records of Centennial Celebrations.* Auburn, N.Y., 1887 (**JJS**)

Cooprider, Cora Bell Harbaugh. *Harbaugh History.* Evansville, Ind., 1947. (**HARHIS**)

Cotterill, R. S. *The Southern Indians: The Story of the Civilized Tribes before Removal.* Part of *The Civilization of the American Indian* Series. Norman, Okla., 1954. (**SI**)

Coues, Elliott, ed. *The Expeditions of Zebulon Montgomery Pike to the Headwaters of the Mississippi River, through Louisiana Territory, and in New Spain in the Years 1805–'6– '7.* 3 vols. Minneapolis, 1965. (**EZP**)

Cox, Sandford C. *Recollections of the Early Settlement of the Wabash Valley.* Reprint ed. Freeport, N.Y., 1970. (**RESWV**)

Crew, Harvey W. *History of Dayton.* Dayton, O., 1889. (**HD**)

Croneis, Jim. "Down to Earth" column; "A Short History of the Indians of Crawford and Wyandot Conties," series of 25 parts in *Bucyrus Telegraph-Forum,* Sep. 11, 1992–Feb. 26, 1993. Bucyrus, O. (**DTEI**)

———. "Down to Earth" column; "Simon Girty: The Anomaly of the Old Northwest," series of 18 parts in *Bucyrus Telegraph-Forum,* March 5–July 2, 1993. Bucyrus, O. (**DTEG**)

Cruikshank, Ernest A., ed. *The Correspondence of Lt. Gov. John Graves Simcoe.* 5 vols., Toronto, 1923–31. (**CJGS**)

Crumrine, Boyd. *History of Washington County, Pennsylvania.* Philadelphia, 1882. (**HISWCO**)

Cuneo, John R. *Robert Rogers of the Rangers.* N.Y., 1959. (**RRR**)

Dann, John C. *The Revolution Remembered: Eyewitness Accounts of the War for Independence.* Chicago, 1980. (**REREM**)

Darlington, Mary C. *Fort Pitt and Letters From the Frontier.* Pittsburgh, 1892. (**FPLFF**)

Darlington, W. M. *Christopher Gist's Journals.* Pittsburgh, 1893. (**CG**)

Dawson, Moses. *A Historical Narrative of the Civil and Military Services of Major General William Henry Harrison and a Vindication of His Character and Conduct as a Statesman, a Citizen, and a Soldier.* Cincinnati, 1824. (**GWHH**)

Day, Sherman. *Historical Collections of the State of Pennsylvania.* Port Washington, N.Y., 1843. (**DPEN**)

De Hass, Wills. *History of the Early Settlement and Indian Wars of Western Virginia.* Wheeling, 1850. (**HIWW**)

De Schweinitz, Edmund A. *Life and Times of David Zeisberger, the Western Pioneer and Apostle of the Indians.* N.Y., 1870. (**LTDZ**)

Dillon, John B. *A History of Indiana from its Earliest Exploration to the Close of the Territorial Government in 1816 . . . and a General View of the Progress of Public Affairs in Indiana from 1816 to 1856.* Indianapolis, 1859. (**AHI**)

Doddridge, Joseph. *Notes on the Settlement and Indian Wars of the Western Parts of Virginia and Pennsylvania from the Year 1763 until the Year 1783, inclusive, Together with a View of the State of Society and Manners of the First Settlers of the Western Country.* Wellsburg, (West) Va., 1824. (**NOS**)

———. *Settlement of Western Country.* Bowling Green, O., 1923. (**SETWC**)

Downes, Randolph C. *Council Fires on the Upper Ohio.* Pittsburgh, 1940. (**CFUO**)

Doyle, Joseph B. *Twentieth Century History of Steubenville and Jefferson County, Ohio.* Chicago, 1910. (**TCHSJ**)

Drake, Benjamin. *Life of Tecumseh, and His Brother, the Prophet; with a Historical Sketch of the Shawanoe Indians*. Cincinnati, 1841. (**LT**)

Drake, Daniel. *Book of the Indians*. Cincinnati, 1840. (**BOI**)

————. *Indian Life and Times of Tecumseh*. Cincinnati, 1842. (**LATT**)

Drake Papers. Part of the Draper Manuscript Collection in the archives of the State Historical Society of Wisconsin. 2 vols. Madison. (**DD-O**)

Draper, Lyman Copeland. *Draper Notes: Notes of Border History taken on a Trip to the Western Part of Pennsylvania and the Adjoining Parts of New York and Ohio from January 30th to March 9th, 1850, Relating to the Lives and Adventures of Western Pioneers and the History of Warfare of the Six Nations*. Mss. narrative commencing on DD-S-4/1[1]. (**DD-S**)

Drimmer, Frederick. *Scalps and Tomahawks*. N.Y., 1957. (**SAT**)

Driver, Harold E. *Indians of North America*. Chicago, 1961. (**IONA**)

Dyke, Samuel E. *The Pennsylvania Rifle*. Lancaster, Pa., 1974. (**PENRIF**)

Eckert, Allan W. *A Sorrow in Our Heart: The Life of Tecumseh*. N.Y., 1992. (**ASIOH**)

————. *The Conquerors*. Boston, 1970. (**TC**)

————. *The Court-Martial of Daniel Boone*. Boston, 1973. (**CDB**)

————. *The Frontiersmen*. Boston, 1967. (**TF**)

————. *Gateway to Empire*. Boston, 1983. (**GTE**)

————. *Wilderness Empire*. Boston, 1969. (**WE**)

Edmunds, R. David. *The Potawatomis: Keepers of the Fire*. Norman, Okla., 1980. (**TP**)

————. *Tecumseh and the Quest for Indian Leadership*. Boston, 1984. (**TQIL**)

————. "Wea Participation in the Northwest Indian Wars, 1790–1795." *Filson Club Historical Quarterly,* vol. 46. (**FCHQ-46**)

Eggleston, Elizabeth E. *Tecumseh and the Shawnee Prophet*. N.Y., 1878. (**T**)

Ellet, Elizabeth E. *Pioneer Women of the West*. N.Y., 1852. (**PWW**)

Ellis, Franklin. *History of Fayette County, Pennsylvania*. Philadelphia, 1882. (**HOFCO**)

Ferguson, Russell J. *Early Western Pennsylvania Politics*. Pittsburgh, 1938. (**EWPP**)

Finley, James B. *History of the Wyandot Nation at Upper Sandusky*. Cincinnati, 1840. (**HWNUS**)

Fitzpatrick, John C., ed. *The Diaries of George Washington, 1748–1799*. 4 vols. N.Y., 1925. (**DGW**)

————. *The Writings of George Washington*. 39 vols. Washington, 1931–44. (**WGW**)

Flexner, James Thomas. *George Washington in the American Revolution*. 2 vols. Boston, 1967–68. (**GWAR**)

————. *Mohawk Baronet: Sir William Johnson of New York*. N.Y., 1959. (**MB**)

Flick, Alexander, ed. *The Papers of Sir William Johnson*. 13 vols. Albany, 1921–62. (**PSWJ**)

Ford, Governor Thomas. Edited by Milo Milton Quaife. *A History of Illinois from its Commencement as a State in 1818 to 1847*. 2 vols. Chicago, 1945. (**AHOI**)

Ford, Worthington Chauncey, ed. *Journals of the Continental Congress 1774–1789*. 18 vols. Original documents in LOC. Washington, 1904–1910. (**JCC**)

Forrest, Earle R. *History of Washington County, Pennsylvania*. N.p., n.d. (**HWCP**)

Fraser's Magazine for Town and Country. London, 1836. (**FMTC**)

Fredricksen, John C. "Kentucky at the Thames, 1813." *Register at the Kentucky Historical Society*. Spring 1985. (**KATT**)

Freeman's Journal. Philadelphia. (**FREEJ**)

Frontier Wars Papers. Part of the Draper Manuscript Collection in the archives of the State Historical Society of Wisconsin. 24 vols. Madison. (**DD-U**)

Gage, Thomas. *General Thomas Gage Papers*. William L. Clements Library Collection, University of Michigan. Ann Arbor. (**TGP**)

Gallagher, Richard, and Forrest Perrin. *A Surprising Election-Year Almanac*. N.Y., 1972. (**ASEYA**)

Gallatin, Albert. *Archives of America,* Vol. 2. Washington, 1922. (**ARAM**)

Galloway, William Albert. *Old Chillicothe: Shawnee and Pioneer History: Conflicts and Romances in the Northwest Territory.* Xenia, O., 1934. (**OC**)

Gazette of the United States. Philadelphia, 1791. (**GAZUS**)

Gephart, R. M. *Revolutionary America, 1763–1789.* Washington, 1892. (**REVAM**)

Gibson, Arrell M. *The Southern Slave Trade.* Norman, Okla., 1971. (**TSST**)

Gilbert, Bil. *God Gave Us this Country: Tekamthi and the First American Civil War.* N.Y., 1989. (**GGU**)

Gipson, Lawrence Harvey. *The British Empire before the American Revolution.* 6 vols. Caldwell, Ida., 1936–46. (**BEAR**)

Glegg, John. *Life of General Isaac Brock.* London, 1816. (**LOGB**)

Gordon, Harry. *Travels in the American Colonies.* Edited by Newton D. Mereness. N.Y., 1916. (**TIAC**)

Gordon, Thomas F. *History of Pennsylvania from Discovery to 1776.* Philadelphia, 1829. (**HPA**)

Gottfried, R. D. *Upper Sandusky Wyandot County Pictoral Memories.* Columbus, 1976. (**USWC**)

Graham, Lloyd. *Niagara Country.* N.Y., 1949. (**NC**)

Great Lakes Indian Archives Project. *Potawatomi Files, 1600–1900.* Bloomington, Ind. (**GLIAP**)

Griswold, Bert J., ed. *Fort Wayne, Gateway of the West, 1802–1813.* Indianapolis, 1927. (**FWG**)

Hagan, William T. *The Sac and Fox Indians.* Part of *The Civilization of the American Indian* Series. Norman, Okla., 1958. (**SAF**)

Haldimand Papers. (Frederic Haldimand). Part of the Burton Historical Collection at the Detroit Public Library. See also MPHC-19. (**HALD**)

Hale, John P. *Trans-Allegheny Pioneers.* 3rd ed. Radford, Va., 1971. (**TAP**)

Hamilton, Charles, ed. *Braddock's Defeat.* Norman, Okla., 1959. (**BRADE**)

Harbaugh, H. *Annals of the Harbaugh Family in America.* Chambersburg, Pa., 1856. (**AHFIA**)

Hardin, Jack, Jr. *History of the Hardins.* Kentucky Historical Society. Frankfort. (**HHARD**)

Harmar Papers. (Josiah Harmar). Part of the Draper Manuscript Collection in the archives of the State Historical Society of Wisconsin. 2 vols. Madison. (**DD-W**)

Harmar Papers. (Josiah Harmar). Letter Book E, William Clements Library, University of Michigan, Ann Arbor, Mich. (**HARPAP**)

Harper's New Monthly Magazine. Franklin Square, N.Y. (**HNMM**)

Hassler, Edgar W. *Old Westmoreland.* Pittsburgh, 1900. (**OLDWE**)

Hatch, Colonel William Stanley. *A Chapter of the History of the War of 1812 in the Northwest.* Cincinnati, 1872. (**ACHW**)

Hatcher, Harlan. *The Great Lakes.* Greenwood Press. Westport, CT, 1947. (**GL**)

———. *Lake Erie.* New York, 1945. (**LE**)

Hayden, William. *The Conquest of the Country North West of the River Ohio.* Indianapolis, 1896. (**CCNW**)

Haywood, John. *Civil and Political History of the State of Tennessee from its Earliest Settlement Up to the Year 1796, Including the Boundaries of the State.* N.Y., 1823. (**CHOT**)

———. *The Natural and Aboriginal History of the State of Tennessee up to the First Settlements.* N.Y., 1823. (**AHOT**)

Heard, J. Norman. *White Into Red: A Study of the Assimilation of White Persons Captured by the Indians.* Metuchen, N.J., 1973. (**WHIR**)

Heckewelder, Reverend John. *A Narrative of the Mission of the United Brethren Among the Delaware and Mohegan Indians.* N.Y., 1971. (**ANM**)

————. *An Account of the History, Manners, and Customs of the Indian Nations Who Once Inhabited Pennsylvania and the Neighboring States.* Philadelphia, 1876. (**HISTA**)

Heitman, Francis B. *Historical Register and Dictionary of the United States Army, from its Organization, September 29, 1789, to March 2, 1903.* 2 vols. Washington, 1903. (**HRD**)

Henry, Alexander. *Travels and Adventures in Canada Between the Years 1760 and 1776.* N.Y., 1809. (**TAC**)

Hildreth, S. P. *Pioneer History: Being an Account of the First Examinations of the Ohio Valley, and the Early Settlement of the Northwest Territory.* N.Y., 1971. (**PIOH**)

Historical Magazine. N.Y. (**HM**)

Historical Sketches of Michigan. Detroit, 1933. (**HSOM**)

History of Wyandot County, Ohio. Chicago, 1884. (**HWYCO**)

Hodge, Frederick Webb. *Handbook of American Indians North of Mexico.* 2 vols. BAE-30. Washington, 1907–10. (**HA**)

Holley, Horace. *A Discourse Occasioned by the Death of Colonel James Morrison.* Lexington, Ky., 1823. (**ADOJM**)

Horrell, J. A. Mss. letters of J. A. Horrell to Lyman Draper in DD. (**MLJAH**)

Horsman, Reginald. *Matthew Elliott, British Indian Agent.* Detroit, 1964. (**ME**)

Hoskiel, G. H. *History of the Mission of the United Brethren.* Part 2. (**HMUB**)

Hough, Franklin B., edited and with notes by. *Diary of the Siege of Detroit in the War with Pontiac.* Albany, N.Y., 1860. (**DSD**)

Howard, James H. *Shawnee: Ceremonialism of a Native Indian Tribe . . .* Athens, O., 1981. (**SHAWN**)

Howe, Henry. *Historical Collections of Ohio.* 2 vols. Cincinnati, 1902–1904. (**HH**)

Hudleston, F. J. *Gentleman Johnny Burgoyne: Misadventures of an English General in the Revolution.* Garden City, N.Y., 1927. (**GJB**)

Hughes, Rupert. *George Washington.* 4 vols. N.Y., 1927. (**GEO**)

Hunt, Gailland, ed. *Journals of the Continental Congress, 1774–1789.* Washington. (**JOCC**)

Illinois. *Transactions of the Illinois State Historical Society.* (**TISHS**)

Indiana Historical Society Publications. Bloomington. (**IHSP**)

Indiana Magazine of History. Indianapolis. (**IMH**)

Intelligencer. Vandalia, Ill. (**INT**)

Jenkins, Steuben. *Historical Address at the Wyoming Monument, 3rd July, 1878, on the 100th Anniversary of the Battle and Massacre of Wyoming.* Published in Wilkes-Barre, Pa. And DD-G-2/109. (**HAWM**)

Kail, Jerry (with editors of *Who's Who*). *Who Was Who During the American Revolution.* Barre, Mass., 1971. (**WWWAR**)

Kappler, Charles J., ed. *Indian Affairs, Laws and Treaties, 1778–1883.* 2 vols. N.Y, 1972. (**IA**)

Kellogg, Louise Phelps. *The British Regime in Wisconsin and the Northwest.* Madison, Wis., 1935. (**BRWN**)

————. *Frontier Advance on the Upper Ohio, 1778–1779.* Madison, Wis., 1916. (**FAUO**)

Kenton, Edna. *Simon Kenton: His Life and Period, 1755–1836.* Garden City, N.Y., 1930. (**SK**)

Kenton Papers. Part of the Draper Manuscript Collection in the archives of the State Historical Society of Wisconsin. 13 vols. Madison. (**DD-BB**)

Kentucky Papers. Part of the Draper Manuscript Collection in the archives of the State Historical Society of Wisconsin. 37 vols. Madison. (**DD-CC**)

Kentucky, University of. *Kentucky.* N.Y., 1938. (**KY**)

Kinzie, Juliette Augusta Magill (Mrs. John H.) *Wau-Bun: The "Early Day" in the North-West.* N.Y., 1856. (**WB**)

Knight, John. *Narrative of the Captivity and sufferings of Dr. John Knight.* See INDAT. (**NCSJK**)

Labaree, L. W. *Royal Instructions to British Colonial Gove, 1670–1776.* 2 vols. N.Y., 1935. (**RIB**)

LeSieur, F. V. Mss. letters of F. V. LeSieur, December 25, 1884, to Lyman Draper in DD. (**MLFL**)

Levernier, James, with Hennig Cohen. *The Indians and Their Captives.* Westport, Conn., 1977. (**TITC**)

Lexington Gazette. Lexington, Ky. (**LEXGZ**)

Loeb, Edwin Meyer. *Cannibalism.* Unpublished M.A. thesis in the Yale University Library Collection. (**C**)

Lossing, Benson J., ed. *Life of Schuyler.* (**LOSCH**)

———. *Pictorial Field Book of the War of 1812.* N.Y., 1869. (**PFB**)

Loudon, Archibald. *A Selection of Some of the Most Interesting Narratives of Outrages Committed by the Indians in their Wars with the White People,* N.Y., 1971. (**ASSM**)

Luckenbach, Abraham. Abraham Luckenbach Diary, 1808. Unpublished. F-1; Archives of the Moravian Church, Bethlehem, Pa. (**ALD**)

MacLean, J. P., ed. *The Journal of Michael Walters, A Member of the Expedition Against Sandusky in the Year 1782.* Tract 89, vol. 14 (1899). Western Reserve Historical Society, Cleveland. (**JMWAL**)

Magazine of Western History. New York. (**MWH**)

Martin, Joseph. Mss. letters of Joseph Martin to Benjamin Harrison. (**MLJM**)

Maryland. *Maryland Gazette.* (**MGZ**)

Maryland. *Maryland Journal.* (**MARJ**)

Massachusetts Historical Society. *Collections of the Massachusetts Historical Society.* Boston, Mass. (**CMHS**)

Massachusetts Historical Society Collections. *Historical Collections of the Indians of the Northeast.* Boston, Mass. Ser. I (1792). (**HCIN**)

Mastin, Bettye Lee. *Pioneer Kentucky as Described by Early Settlers.* Cincinnati, 1979. (**PKDS**)

Maysville Republican. Maysville, Ky. (**MAYSV**)

McAfee, Robert B. Edited by Van Tassel. *History of the Late War in the Western Country.* Part of the *Great American Historical Classics* Series. Bowling Green, O. 1919. (**HLW**)

McAllister, J. T. *List of the Virginia Militia in the Revolutionary War.* Hot Springs, Va., 1913. (**LVMRW**)

McBride, James. *Pioneer Biographies.* 2 vols. Cincinnati, 1869. (**PB**)

McClung, John A. *Sketches of Western Adventure.* Covington, Ky., 1832. (**SWA**)

McKenney, Thomas L. *Sketches of a Tour to the Lakes: Of the Character and Customs of the Chippeway Indians and of Incidents Connected with the Treaty of Fond du Lac.* Barre, Mass., 1972. (**SOTL**)

———, and James Hall. *The Indian Tribes of North America.* Totowa, N.J., 1972. (**TRIB**)

Mecklenburg Declaration. Part of the Draper Manuscript Collection in the archives of the State Historical Society of Wisconsin. 3 vols. Madison. (**DD-FF**)

Michigan Historical Society. *Michigan Pioneer and Historical Society Collections and Researches.* 40 vols. Lansing, Mich., 1877—1929. (**MPHC**)

Mississippi Valley Historical Association Proceedings. Vols. 1–4. Cedar Rapids, Ia., 1909–1912. (**MVHAP**)

Mississippi Valley Historical Review. St. Louis. (**MVHR**)

Monthly Literary Magazine. Boston. (**MOLI**)

Moorehead, Warren King. "The Indian Tribes of Ohio—Historically Considered."

Ohio Archeological and Historical Publications, Vol. VII, Columbus, 1927. (**OAHP-07**)

National Archives. *Revolutionary War Pension and Bounty-and-Warrant Application Files.* (**NARWP**)

National Intelligencer. Washington, D.C. (**NI**)

Neilson, William Allan, ed.-in-chief. *Webster's Biographical Dictionary.* Springfield, Mass., 1974. (**WBD**)

New York. *Journal of the New York Provincial Congress.* Albany. (**JNYPC**)

New York Gazette. N.Y. (**NYGZ**)

Newland, R. E., and L. L. *Newland (Newlon) Family.* Bedford, Ind., 1946. (**NEWFAM**)

Newton, J. H., with G. G. Nichols and A. G. Sprankle. *History of the Panhandle: Being Historical Collections of the Counties of Ohio, Brooke, Marshall and Hancock, West Virginia.* Wheeling, W.Va., 1879. (**HOPH**)

Niles Weekly Register. Baltimore. (**NWR**)

North American Review. Washington. (**NAR**)

North Carolina, State of. *The Colonial Records of North Carolina.* 10 vols. Raleigh, N.C., 1886–90. (**CRNC**)

O'Callaghan, Edmund B., ed. *Documents Relating to the Colonial History of the State of New York.* 15 vols. Albany, N.Y., 1853–87. (**CHNY**)

Ohio Archaeological and Historical Journal. Columbus. (**OAHJ**)

Ohio Archaeological and Historical Society Proceedings. Columbus. (**OAHP**)

Ohio Archaeological and Historical Society Quarterly. Columbus. (**OAHQ**)

Ohio Historical Quarterly. Columbus. (**OHQ**)

Ohio Magazine. Columbus. (**OHMAG**)

Palmer, William P. *Calendar of Virginia State Papers and Other Manuscripts.* Richmond, 1884. (**CVSP**)

Pargellis, S. McC. *Lord Loudon in North America.* New Haven, Conn., 1933. (**LLNA**)

Parkins, Almon E. *The Historical Geography of Detroit.* Port Washington, N.Y., 1918. (**HGOD**)

Parkman, Francis. *The Conspiracy of Pontiac in the Indian War After the Conquest of Canada.* 2 vols. Boston, 1894. (**CP**)

———. *Le Salle and the Discovery of the Great West.* Part 3 in the *France and England in North America* Series. Boston, 1894. (**LSD**)

———. *Montcalm and Wolfe.* 2 vols. Boston, 1894. (**MAW**)

Paull, Elisabeth M. *Paull-Irwin: A Family Sketch.* Privately printed, 1915, 1936. (**PIAFS**)

Paull, James. *A Narrative of the Wonderful Escape and Dreadful Sufferings of Colonel James Paul.* Cincinnati, 1869. (**ANWEP**)

Peckham, Howard A., ed. *Pontiac and the Indian Uprising.* Princeton, 1947. (**P**)

Pennsylvania Archives, 1st, 2nd, 6th Series. Philadelphia. (**PEN**)

Pennsylvania Colonial Records. Philadelphia. (**PECOR**)

Pennsylvania Gazette. Philadelphia. (**PG**)

Pennsylvania Journal and Weekly Advertiser. Philadelphia. (**PEJO**)

Pennsylvania Ledger. Philadelphia. (**PELG**)

Pennsylvania Magazine of History and Biography. Philadelphia. (**PMHB**)

Pennsylvania Packet. Pittsburgh. (**PPAC**)

Pennsylvania State Archives. RG-2, Records of the Comptroller General, Militia Loan Accounts, Militia 1777–94, Washington and Westmoreland County Operations. Harrisburg. (**PENSA**)

Peyster, Arent Schuyler de. Edited by J. Watts de Peyster. *Miscellanies by an Officer, 1774–1813.* N.Y., 1888 (**MBO**)

Philadelphia Diary. Philadelphia. (**PHD**)

Philadelphia General Advertiser. Philadelphia. (**PGA**)

Philadelphia Saturday Courier. Philadelphia. (**PSATC**)

Phillips, Paul Crisler. *The Fur Trade*. 2 vols. Norman, Okla., 1967. (**TFT**)

Pickett, Albert James. *History of Alabama*. 2 vols. Charleston, 1851. (**ALA**)

Pierce, Bessie Louise. *A History of Chicago*. 3 vols. Chicago, 1975. (**AHC**)

Pittsburgh and Northwestern Pennsylvania Papers. Part of the Draper Manuscript Collections in the archives of the State Historical Society of Wisconsin. Madison. (**DD-NN**)

Pittsburgh Casket. Pittsburgh. (**PITTC**)

Potts, Jonathan. *Jonathan Potts Papers*. Historical Society of Pennsylvania. (**JPP**)

Pritts, Joseph. *Incidents of Border Life*. Reprint ed. New York, 1977. (**IOBL**)

Prucha, Francis Paul. *Indian Policy in the United States*. Lincoln, 1981. (**IPIUS**)

———. *The Sword of the Republic*. Bloomington, Ind., 1969. (**TSR**)

Quaife, Milo Milton. *Checagou; From Indian Wigwam to Modern City: 1673–1835*. Chicago, 1933. (**CQ**)

———. *Chicago and the Old Northwest, 1673–1835*. Chicago, 1913. (**CONW**)

———. *Lake Michigan*. Indianapolis, 1944. (**LM**)

———. *War on the Detroit: Chronicles of Thomas Vecheres de Boucherville, and the Capitulation by an Ohio Volunteer*. Chicago, 1940. (**WOD**)

Randall, E. O. "The Dunmore War." *Ohio Archaeological and Historical Publications*. Vol. 11. Columbus, 1931. (**OAHP-11R**)

Reynolds, John. *The Pioneer History of Illinois*. Chicago, 1887. (**PHIL**)

Rose, John. *Journal of a Volunteer Expedition to Sandusky*. New York, 1969. (**JVES**)

Rupp, Israel Daniel. *Early History of Western Pennsylvania and of the West and of Western Expeditions and Campaigns from 1754 to 1833*. Pittsburgh, 1846. (**EHWP**)

Salem Gazette. Salem, Mass. (**SAGAZ**)

Sargent, Winthrop. *The History of an Expedition Against Fort Duquesne in 1755*. Philadelphia, 1855. (**HEAFD**)

Scamyhorn, Richard, and John Steille. *Stockades in the Wilderness*. Dayton, O., 1986. (**SIW**)

Schoolcraft, Henry Rowe. *History of the Indian Tribes*. 6 vols. Philadelphia, 1853. (**HIT**)

———. *Narrative Journal of Travels from Detroit Northwest through the Great Chain of American Lakes to the Source of the Mississippi River in the Year 1820*. Albany, N.Y., 1821. (**NJT**)

Scioto Gazette. Chillicothe, O. (**SCIG**)

Seaver, James E. *A Narrative of the Life of Mrs. Mary Jemison*. New York, 1956. (**LOMJ**)

Sherrard, R. A. *The Sherrard Family of Steubenville*. Philadelphia, 1890. (**SFOS**)

Sipe, C. Hale. *Indian Wars of Pennsylvania*. Harrisburg, Pa., 1929. (**IWPA**)

Slover, John. *John Slover's Narrative*. Cincinnati, 1869. (**JOSLO**)

Smith, William Henry. *The Saint Clair Papers; The Life and Public Services of Arthur St. Clair . . . with His Correspondence and Other Papers*. 2 vols. Cincinnati, 1881. (**SCP**)

Smith, Z. F. *The History of Kentucky*. Louisville, Ky., 1886. (**THOK**)

Slotkin, Richard. *Regeneration Through Violence: The Mythology of the American Frontier, 1600–1680*. Middletown, Conn., 1973. (**RTV**)

Sosin, Jack M. *The Revolutionary Frontier, 1763–1783*. N.Y., 1967. (**TRF**)

Spencer, Robert F. *The Native Americans: Prehistory and Ethnology of the North American Indians*. N.Y., 1965. (**NAP**)

Stevens, Frank E. *The Black Hawk War: Including a Review of Black Hawk's Life*. Chicago, 1903. (**BHW**)

Stevens, Wayne Edson. *The Northwest Fur Trade, 1763–1800.* Univ. of Illinois, *Studies in the Social Sciences,* vol. 14, no. 3 (Sep. 1926). Urbana, 1928. (**NFT**)

Stone, William L. *Life and Times of Sir William Johnson.* 2 vols. Albany, 1865. (**LTSWJ**)

————. *Life of Joseph Brant.* 2 vols. Albany, N.Y., 1865. (**LOJB**)

Sturtevant, William C., ed. *Handbook of North American Indians.* Vol. 15, Smithsonian Institution. Washington, 1978, (**HNAI**)

Swiggett, Howard. *War Out of Niagara.* New York, 1933. (**WOON**)

Sword, Wiley. *President Washington's Indian War.* Norman, Okla., 1985. (**PWIW**)

Taylor, James W. *History of Ohio, 1650–1787.* 2 vols. Sandusky, O., 1854. (**HOO**)

Tecumseh Papers. Part of the Draper Manuscript Collection in the archives of the State Historical Society of Wisconsin. 13 vols. Madison. (**DD-YY**)

Thatcher, B. B. *Indian Biographies.* N.Y., 1839. (**INBIO**)

Thornbrough Gayle, ed. *Outpost on the Wabash.* Indianapolis, 1964. (**OOTW**)

Thwaites, Reuben Gold, ed. *Account of an Expedition From Pittsburgh to the Rocky Mountains Performed in the Years 1819, 1820 by Order of the Honorable J. C. Calhoun, Secretary of War, Under the Command of Major S. H. Long, of the U.S. Topographical Engineers, Compiled from the Notes of Major Long, Mr. T. Say, and Other Gentlemen of the Party, by Edwin James, Botanist and Geologist to the Expedition.* Vols. 9, 15, 16 and 17 in the *Early Western Travels* Series. Cleveland, 1905. (**EWT**)

————. *How George Rogers Clark Won the Northwest: and Other Essays in Western History.* Chicago, 1904. (**HGRC**)

————. *The Jesuit Relations and Allied Documents; Travels and Explorations of the Jesuit Missionaries in New France, 1610–1791.* 73 vols. Cleveland, 1896–1901. (**JRAD**)

Tobias, James C., ed. *A Centennial Biographical History of Crawford County, Ohio.* Chicago, 1902. (**ACBHC**)

Toner, J. M. *Journal of Colonel George Washington.* Albany, N.Y., 1893. (**JCGW**)

Trager, James. *The People's Chronology: A Year-by-Year Record of Human Events from Prehistory to the Present.* N.Y., 1979. (**PECH**)

Trowbridge, Charles C. Edited by Vernon Kinietz and Erminie W. Voegelin. *Shawnese Traditions.* Ann Arbor, Mich., 1939. (**SHAWT**)

Turner, G. *Traits of Indian Character.* 2 vols. Philadelphia, 1846. (**TRINC**)

Tyler, Lyon Gardiner, ed. *Narratives of Early Virginia: 1606–1625.* N.Y., 1907. (**NEV**)

Uniontown American Standard. Uniontown, Pa. (**UAMS**)

Vail, R.W.G. *Voice of the Old Frontier.* New York, 1970. (**VOLF**)

Van Alstyne, Richard W. *The Indian on the New England Frontier, 1620–1675.* Unpublished M.A. thesis (1924) in University of Southern California Library. (**INEF**)

Van der Beets, Richard, ed. *Held Captive by Indians: Selected Narratives: 1642–1836.* Knoxville, Tenn., 1973. (**HCBI**)

Vaughan, Alden T. *Narratives of North American Indian Captivity: Selective Bibliography.* N.Y., 1983. (**NNAIC**)

Vermont Historical Collections. Montpelier, Vt. (**VERHC**)

Virginia. *Journal of the Virginia Executive Council, 1776–78.* Richmond. (**JVEC**)

Virginia Historical Magazine. Richmond. (**VAHM**)

Virginia Magazine of History and Biography. Richmond. (**VMHB**)

Virginia Papers. Part of the Draper Manuscript Collection in the archives of the State Historical Society of Wisconsin. 16 vols. Madison. (**DD-ZZ**)

Virginia State Papers. Vols. 1–4. Richmond, 1875–85. (**VSP**)

Wainwright, Nicholas B. *George Croghan: Wilderness Diplomat.* Chapel Hill, N.C., 1959. (**GCWD**)

Ward, Christopher. Edited by John Richard Alden. *The War of the Revolution.* 2 vols. N.Y., 1952. (**WOTR**)

Washburn, Wilcomb E. *The Indian and the White Man.* Garden City, N.Y., 1964 (**IWM**)

Washington, H. A., ed. *The Collected Writings of Thomas Jefferson.* 9 vols. N.Y., 1853–54. (**CWTJ**)

Washington Observer. Washington, Pa. (**WO**)

Wayne Democrat. Wooster, O. (**WAYDEM**)

Webb, George W. *Chronological List of Engagements between the Regular Army of the United States and Various Tribes of Hostile Indians which Occurred During the Years 1790 to 1898, Inclusive.* Chicago, 1939 (**CLOE**)

Western Pennsylvania Historical Magazine, The. Pittsburgh. (**WPHM**)

Western Review and Miscellaneous Magazine. Lexington, Ky., 1820. (**WRMM**)

Western Star. Stockbridge, Mass. (**WS**)

Williams, Edward G., ed. *The Orderly Book of Colonel Henry Bouquet's Expedition Against the Ohio Indians, 1764.* Pittsburgh, 1960. (**BOB**)

Winsor, Justin, ed. *The Mississippi Basin: The Struggle in America between England and France, 1697–1763.* Boston, 1895. (**MISSB**)

————. *Narrative and Critical History of America.* 8 vols. Boston, 1889. (**NCHA**)

Wisconsin. *Collections of the State Historical Society of Wisconsin.* Madison. (**WHC**)

Wisconsin Magazine of History. Madison. (**WHM**)

Wissler, Clark. Revised by Lucy Wales Kluckhohn. *Indians of the United States.* Garden City, N.Y., 1966. (**IUS**)

Withers, Alexander Scott. *Chronicles of Border Warfare: or, History of the Settlement by the Whites of North-Western Virginia and of the Indian Wars and Massacres in that Section of the State with Reflections, Anecdotes, etc.* Clarksburg, Va., 1831. (**CBWV**)

Woehrmann, Paul. *At the Headwaters of the Maumee: A History of the Forts of Fort Wayne.* Indianapolis, 1971. (**ATH**)

Wood, Norman B. *Lives of Famous Indian Chiefs.* Aurora, Ill., 1906. (**LOFIC**)

Wyandot County Republican. Upper Sandusky, O. (**WYCOR**)

Index

About the Author

A six-time Pulitzer Prize nominee, ALLAN W. ECKERT is an Emmy Award–winning scriptwriter and a Newbery Honor author of books for young readers. He is also the author of the popular six-volume historical series *Narratives of America* and the creator of *Tecumseh!,* an outdoor drama staged regularly in Chillicothe, Ohio, that has played to more than a million people over the past twenty years.